P9-BYX-541

Professional Java Server Programming
J2EE 1.3 Edition

Subrahmanyam Allamaraju
Cedric Beust
John Davies
Tyler Jewell
Rod Johnson
Andrew Longshaw
Ramesh Nagappan
Daniel O'Connor
Dr. P. G. Sarang
Alex Toussaint
Sameer Tyagi
Gary Watson
Marc Wilcox
Alan Williamson

Wrox Press Ltd. ®

Professional Java Server Programming
J2EE 1.3 Edition

First published September 2001

Published by Wrox Press Ltd,
Arden House, 1102 Warwick Road, Acocks Green,
Birmingham, B27 6BH, UK
Printed in the United States
ISBN 1-861005-37-7

Trademark Acknowledgements

Wrox has endeavored to provide trademark information about all the companies and products mentioned in this book by the appropriate use of capitals. However, Wrox cannot guarantee the accuracy of this information.

Credits

Authors
Subrahmanyam Allamaraju
Cedric Beust
John Davies
Tyler Jewell
Rod Johnson
Andrew Longshaw
Ramesh Nagappan
Daniel O'Connor
Dr. P. G. Sarang
Alex Toussaint
Sameer Tyagi
Gary Watson
Mark Wilcox
Alan Williamson

Additional Material
John Griffin
Richard Huss
Dan Malks

Technical Architect
Craig A. Berry

Technical Editors
Daniel Richardson
Steve Rycroft
Robert F.E. Shaw
Mark Waterhouse

Category Manager
Emma Batch

Author Agent
Velimir Ilic

Project Administrator
Simon Brand

Technical Reviewers
Rich Bonneau
Carl Burnham
Chris Crane
Jeremy Crosbie
Jacob Mathew
Vinay Menon
Ramesh Nagappan
Sumit Pal
Joel Peach
Phil Powers de George
Paramasivan Radha ganesan
Santosh Ramakrishnan
Don Reamey
Matt Staples
Andrew Watt

Production Project Co-ordinator
Emma Eato

Illustrations
Natalie O'Donnell

Cover
Chris Morris

Proof Reader
Chris Smith

Index
Andrew Criddle
Bill Johncocks

About the Authors

Subrahmanyam Allamaraju

Subrahmanyam Allamaraju is a Senior Engineer with BEA Systems Inc. He works in the areas of enterprise/distributed technologies, XML-based object models, and related areas. For more information about his activities, interests, and other works, check his web site at www.Subrahmanyam.com.

Subrahmanyam would like to thank Varaa for her hand in code samples (in the face of tight deadlines), and sharing his frustration as well as exhilaration.

Cedric Beust

Cedric Beust is a senior software engineer in the EJB team at BEA Systems Inc. He's been involved in implementing the EJB 2.0 version of the WebLogic EJB container and holds a PhD in computer science, from the University of Nice, France. Before that, he was working at Sun Microsystems where he focused mainly on CORBA. Over the years, Cedric has been involved in several committees such as EJB, CORBA, and C++. His interests range from everything that relates to distributed computing and software engineering in general, to hobbies such as golf, squash, tennis, and volleyball.

John Davies

John Davies is the CTO of Century 24 Solutions Ltd. (C24), www.C24Solutions.com, a London-based software house providing Java and J2EE based solutions for the financial market. C24's latest product, Elektra, designed to provide a single business view of complex financial transactions makes extensive use of all the J2EE technologies. John is currently engaged with BNP-Paribas leading the Technology Consulting Group recommending technologies for the current and future projects worldwide.

John started in IT in the late 70s in hardware, and then came assembler, C, C++ in '87, and finally Java in early '96. He spent over fourteen years as a consultant mainly in banking, ten of them outside the UK in a variety of countries including the US, Asia, and most of Europe where he learnt a few more languages (spoken). Between work and writing John teaches Java and XML for Learning Tree and is technical editor of their EJB 2.0 course. His hobbies include traveling, photography, classical guitar, piloting small planes, fine wines, good beer, spicy food, and socializing. He would like to thank fellow Astronomy graduate Steve Miller for proof reading, and say "Hi Mum, sorry about all the trouble I caused at school!".

Once again none of this would have been possible without the love and support from my fantastic wife Rachel, désole pour les longues nuits toute seule et merci pour Luc et James, je vous aime!

John can be reached at John.Davies@C24Solutions.com.

Tyler Jewell

Tyler Jewell is an evangelist for BEA Systems Inc. where he writes and speaks about enterprise technologies for developers. He is an expert trainer and mentor, specializing is large-scale e-business architectures.

Tyler has authored 19 training courses on e-business technologies and delivered over 200 technology seminars to clients and the public. He is co-author of "Mastering Enterprise JavaBeans 2.0" (O'Reilly 2001) and is working on "Java Web Services" (O'Reilly 2002). Tyler maintains a regular J2EE column at www.onjava.com, is a member of O'Reilly's Editorial Masthead, and is an advisor to www.theserverside.com, Your J2EE Community.

In his spare time, Tyler values his friends and family. His favorite hobby is Texas Hold 'Em poker where any two cards can win, but only if they are in his hand!

Rod Johnson

Rod Johnson is an enterprise Java architect specializing in scalable web applications. He spent the last twoS years designing a J2EE solution for FT.com, Europe's largest business portal, and is currently writing a book for Wrox Press on J2EE design and development.

After an arts degree majoring in music and computer science, Rod completed a Ph.D. in musicology before returning to software development. Rod has worked with Java on both client and server since its release, and has concentrated on Internet development since 1996. His main interests are J2EE architecture, EJB, and OO web development.

Rod divides his time between London and Sydney, and enjoys tennis, skiing, history, and playing the piano. He can be reached at rod.johnson@interface21.com.

Thanks to Kerry for her love and encouragement, as we begin our new adventure.

Andy Longshaw

Andy Longshaw is an independent consultant, writer, and educator specializing in J2EE, XML, Web-based technologies and components, particularly the design and architecture decisions required to use these technologies, successfully. Andy has been explaining technology for most of the last decade in his prior roles as a Principal Technologist with Content Master Ltd. and QA Training. Andy also gives conference sessions on J2EE, XML, and middle-tier component architectures. There is an unconfirmed rumor that some people stay awake during these sessions. He is pleased to receive any feedback, questions, and abuse about the design chapter he wrote for this book at www.blueskyline.com.

To Sarah, Adam, and Joshua who inspire everything that I do, and to my parents who ensured that I was educated enough to write this.

Ramesh Nagappan

Ramesh Nagappan is a Technology Architect specializing in Java and CORBA-based Distribution application architectures. He is a Java evangelist and also an active contributor for open source specifications and implementations. Before he hooked on to Java and CORBA, he worked as a Research engineer for developing CAD/CAM and Computational fluid dynamics solutions for aerospace applications. In the spare time he enjoys Water Sports and plying with his son Roger. He can be reached at nramesh@mediaone.net.

Dedicated to my wife Joyce and our son Roger for their love, support, and inspiration, and also to my beloved parents for brightening my life.

Dr. P. G. Sarang

A contractor to Sun Microsystems, Dr. Sarang trains Sun's corporate clients on various courses from Sun's official curriculum. He also conducts the "Train The Trainers" program and "Instructor Authorization Tests" on behalf of Sun.

As CEO of ABCOM Information Systems Pvt. Ltd., Dr. Sarang specializes in training and project development on the Java/CORBA platform. With almost 20 years of industry experience, Dr. Sarang has developed a number of products and successfully completed various industry projects. He is a regular speaker in many national and international conferences and regularly contributes technical articles to international journals and magazines. His current interests include .NET platform and C#.

"I would like to dedicate this writing to my mother for her continued support and patience."

Alex Toussaint

Alex Toussaint is Director of Engineering for Vignette Corporation in Austin, Texas. He has over 10 years of software development experience and has extensive experience with Java since 1996 and J2EE technologies since 1998. Alex has contributed articles on web applications and electronic commerce to online journals, such as Microsoft MSDN and he was a contributing author to the Professional Site Server book by Wrox. Alex has also been invited to lecture at the University of Texas at Austin Red McCombs School of Business on topics such as Electronic Commerce and Enterprise Software Development. Alex now lives in Austin, Texas with his wife Danielle and their little dog Sasha. Alex welcomes your e-mail at alex_toussaint@yahoo.com.

Sameer Tyagi

Sameer writes regularly for online and print publications. He has over four years of experience in software design and development and specializes in server-side Java-based distributed applications. (n-Tier architectures, JDBC, JNDI, EJB, JMS, RMI, JSP, Servlets, *et al.*) He has a Bachelors in Electronic Engineering and numerous other certifications.

He is a Java addict who gets his fix by jumping head-on into almost anything that compiles into bytecodes and is known to blame that newly discovered area of the brain called the Javasphere for such stimuli. When he's not going through another latte flavor, he can be found flying around at 15000 ft in a small Cessna.

Gary Watson

Gary Watson has been developing using Java for the past 4 years. He is a Freelance IT Consultant and currently a Technical Architect at the Financial Times, FT.com, working on a large J2EE solution. A graduate of the University of Teesside in 1993, Gary holds a first-class degree in Computer Science.

Whenever it's possible these days, Gary enjoys windsurfing, skiing, and flying model aircraft. He doesn't get to participate in these activities as often as he would like! He can be reached at Gary@com-contracts.demon.co.uk.

To my wife Angela for her love, support and encouragement as we strive through life together.

Marc Wilcox

Mark is in the professional services group at WebCT, Inc, the world's leading developer of Course Management Systems/Virtual Learning Environments. The next version of their product, code-named Cobalt, will be based on a J2EE application environment.

I would like to dedicate this book to Doug and Sammy, the world's greatest barbers.

Alan Williamson

Alan Williamson is as much of a veteran of the Java world than one can be, with a language that is still very much finding its feet in the world. Alan has over 15 years experience in the world of software development, graduating with full Honours in Computer Science from the University of Paisley. Alan has worked in mainly research and development roles until starting up the UK's first pure Java consultancy company 4 years ago, specializing in Java at the server side (http://www.n-ary.com/). Alan has also worked his way up to the dizzy heights of Editor-in-Chief of the worlds largest Java magazine; *Java Developers Journal*, and can be found talking at various conferences all over the place!

I would like to thank my dearest Ceri and my new son Cormac for holding the fort while I worked and researched this chapter. Great job well done. In addition to this I would like to thank Keith and Marion for doing their schoolteacher routines and reading over my chapter correcting my poor grammar. Finally I would like to thank all at Wrox for making this process of writing, not a painful one, but a joyous one.

Data

RDMS

JDBC

Application Logic

JavaMail

Mail Server

Java
Application

RMI

IIOP

CORBA
Server

JNDI

Directory Servic

JMS

Message Queue

Web Container

Servlets | JSPs | Tag Library

Client

HTTP(S)

(X)HTML/XML

Applet

Client Application

RMI/IIOP | JNDI | JTA | JDBC | JMS | JavaMail | JAAS | JCA | JAXP

J2EE
Application
Server

Session
Beans

JAF

Table of Contents

Table of Contents

Table of Contents

Table of Contents

Table of Contents

Data

RDMS

JDBC

Application Logic

JavaMail

Mail Server

Web Container

Client

Servlets JSPs Tag Library

(X)HTML/ XML

HTTP(S)

Java Application

RMI

RMI/IIOP JNDI JTA JDBC JMS JavaMail JAAS JCA JAXP

Applet

J2EE Application Server

IIOP

CORBA Server

Client Application

Session Beans

JNDI

JAF

Directory Service

JMS

Message Queue

Introduction

Welcome to the third time out for *Professional Java Server Programming*. Unlike the change from the first to second editions, the diffferences to the J2EE 1.3 version are relatively minor. The most basic changes is that all the chapters on servlets, JSP, and EJB have been updated to reflect the changes to the relevant specifactions, for example EJB 2.0. In addition, new chapters have been included for Features new to J2EE such as the Connector Architecture, and some chapters which were less relevant to core J2EE development have been removed.

The J2EE 1.3 Edition

The latest release of JSR-58, more commonly known as the **Java 2 Platform, Enterprise Edition (J2EE)**, represents the evolution of Sun Microsystem's server-side development platform into a more mature and sophisticated specification. Beyond the inclusion of some new sub-specifications such JAAS (the Java Authentication and Authorization Service) and the Connector Architecture, the actual container-centric nature of the J2EE specification has not changed significantly.

The more noticeable changes in this release relate to the modifications made to the sub-specifications, notably Servlet, JavaServer Pages (JSP) and Enterprise JavaBeans (EJB). Servlets gain events and filtering; JSP gain a new XML syntax and enhancements to the custom tag mechanisms; and EJB has some significant changes to its container-managed persistence model.

The current API versions in J2EE 1.3 stand at:

❑ Servlets 2.3

❑ JavaServer Pages 1.2

❑ Enterprise JavaBeans 2.0

❑ JDBC 2.0 Extension

❑ Java Message Service 1.0

- ❑ Java Transaction API 1.0
- ❑ JavaMail 1.2
- ❑ Java Activation Framework 1.0
- ❑ Java API for XML Processing 1.1
- ❑ Java Connector Architecture 1.0
- ❑ Java Authentication and Authorization Service 1.0

Over the course of this book we'll be looking at all of them.

What's Changed in this Edition of the Book?

You will find that a certain amount of the material in this J2EE 1.3 edition is very similar to that of its predecessor, the J2EE edition. This is because rather than significantly revamp what was essentially good, solid material, we've elected to simply update where relevant to remain consistent with the latest specs as identified by J2EE. In some cases, this has meant the inclusion of an additional chapter, but in others you'll find only small changes.

Having said that, there are some significant differences at the chapter level between this and the previous edition. The J2EE 1.3 edition contains chapters on the Java Connector Architecture, Web Services, Choosing an J2EE Implementation, and J2EE Packaging.

What's gone are the more extraneous chapters that were not core to learning about J2EE application development, such as Internationalization.

Who is this Book For?

This book is aimed at professional Java programmers who although they may not have much practical experience of, are at least familiar with, the fundamental concepts of network and web programming. It also assumes familiarity with the Java language and the core APIs – through reading Beginning Java 2, or some other tutorial book that covers similar ground. All the concepts that relate to server-side Java programming, however, will be covered assuming no prior knowledge.

Having said that, some familiarity with the basic server-side Java technologies is recommended as this book covers a large area of ground very quickly and does not claim to be exhaustive in all areas.

> In addition, owners of the previous J2EE edition of the book may not find that this edition adds much to their knowledge as a lot of the core material is very similar to the previous edition.

What's Covered in this Book

In this book, we discuss three things:

- ❑ The rules in the technology's specifications that developers must follow to write enterprise components
- ❑ The benefits and limits of the typical real-world vendor implementations of the J2EE specification
- ❑ The resulting practical aspects of real-word design using the J2EE technologies

The book has the following basic structure:

- ❑ We'll start with a look at the latest demands placed on a Java enterprise developer and how Java (more particularly J2EE) rises to meet these challenges. You'll also get your first real taste of the J2EE container architecture.

- ❑ After we're up to speed on the J2EE architecture we'll start by looking at some of the fundamental technologies in enterprise development: RMI, JDBC, and JNDI.

- ❑ Then we'll get back into J2EE more explicitly by looking at how to develop web components using Java servlets.

- ❑ Once we understand the servlet technology we'll look at how JavaServer Pages takes it and extends to provide a more felxible means of creating dynamic web content.

- ❑ We'll then take a step further into the enterprise by looking at the sophisticated component technology of Enterprise JavaBeans.

- ❑ Finally, we'll look at some larger J2EE issues such as design considerations and how to package your J2EE applications.

What You Need to Use this Book

Most of the code in this book was tested with the Java 2 Platform, Standard Edition SDK (JDK 1.3) and the Java 2 Platform, Enterprise Edition SDK 1.3 Reference Implementation. However, for some of the chapters, either the reference implementation is not sufficient or you need some additional software:

Web Container

In order to run the web components used in this book you will need a web container that supports the Servlet 2.3 and the JSP 1.2 specifications. We used the Reference Implementation, which uses the Jarkata Tomcat engine under the hood. You may need the latest build of Tomcat (available from http://jakarta.apache.org/tomcat) in order to run some of the JSP tag library examples.

EJB Container

For the EJB chapters you will also need an EJB container supporting version 2.0 of the EJB specification. We used BEA's WebLogic Server 6.1 – http://www.bea.com/.

Databases

Several of the chapters also require access to a database. For these chapters we used:

- ❑ Cloudscape (an in-process version comes with the J2EE RI), http://www.cloudscape.com/.

Additional Software

Finally, there are a few additional pieces of software that a couple of chapters also require:

- ❑ Sun's JNDI SDK, which is included with JDK 1.3
- ❑ Java Secure Sockets Extension (JSSE), 1.0.1, http://java.sun.com/products/jsse/
- ❑ LDAP server – Netscape's iPlanet Directory Server version 4.11, http://www.iplanet.com/

❑ SMTP and/or POP3 service

❑ The JSP Standard Tag Library, http://jakarta.apache.org/taglibs

❑ The IBM Web Services Toolkit, http://www.alphaworks.ibm.com/tech/webservicestoolkit

The code in the book will work on a single machine, provided it is networked (that is, it can see http://localhost through the local browser).

The complete source code from the book is available for download from:

http://www.wrox.com/

Conventions

To help you get the most from the text and keep track of what's happening, we've used a number of conventions throughout the book.

For instance:

> **These boxes hold important, not-to-be forgotten information which is directly relevant to the surrounding text.**

While the background style is used for asides to the current discussion.

As for styles in the text:

❑ When we introduce them, we **highlight** important words.

❑ We show keyboard strokes like this: *Ctrl-A*

❑ We show filenames and code within the text like so: doGet()

❑ Text on user interfaces and URLs are shown as: Menu

We present code in three different ways. Definitions of methods and properties are shown as follows:

```
protected void doGet(HttpServletRequest req, HttpServletResponse resp)
                    throws ServletException, IOException
```

Example code is shown:

```
In our code examples, the code foreground style shows new, important,
    pertinent code
while code background shows code that's less important in the present context,
    or has been seen before.
```

Customer Support

We always value hearing from our readers, and we want to know what you think about this book: what you liked, what you didn't like, and what you think we can do better next time. You can send us your comments, either by returning the reply card in the back of the book, or by e-mail to feedback@wrox.com. Please be sure to mention the book title in your message.

How to Download the Sample Code for the Book

When you visit the Wrox site, http://www.wrox.com/, simply locate the title through our Search facility or by using one of the title lists. Click on Download in the Code column, or on Download Code on the book's detail page.

The files that are available for download from our site have been archived using WinZip. When you have saved the attachments to a folder on your hard-drive, you need to extract the files using a de-compression program such as WinZip or PKUnzip. When you extract the files, the code is usually extracted into chapter folders. When you start the extraction process, ensure your software (WinZip, PKUnzip, etc.) is set to use folder names.

Errata

We've made every effort to make sure that there are no errors in the text or in the code. However, no one is perfect and mistakes do occur. If you find an error in one of our books, like a spelling mistake or a faulty piece of code, we would be very grateful for feedback. By sending in errata you may save another reader hours of frustration, and of course, you will be helping us provide even higher quality information. Simply e-mail the information to support@wrox.com; your information will be checked and if correct, posted to the errata page for that title, or used in subsequent editions of the book.

To find errata on the web site, go to http://www.wrox.com/, and simply locate the title through our Advanced Search or title list. Click on the Book Errata link, which is below the cover graphic on the book's detail page.

E-mail Support

If you wish to directly query a problem in the book with an expert who knows the book in detail then e-mail support@wrox.com, with the title of the book and the last four numbers of the ISBN in the subject field of the e-mail. A typical e-mail should include the following things:

- ❑ The **title of the book**, **last four digits of the ISBN**, and **page number** of the problem in the Subject field.
- ❑ Your **name**, **contact information**, and the **problem** in the body of the message.

We *won't* send you junk mail. We need the details to save your time and ours. When you send an e-mail message, it will go through the following chain of support:

- ❑ Customer Support – Your message is delivered to our customer support staff, who are the first people to read it. They have files on most frequently asked questions and will answer anything general about the book or the web site immediately.
- ❑ Editorial – Deeper queries are forwarded to the technical editor responsible for that book. They have experience with the programming language or particular product, and are able to answer detailed technical questions on the subject.
- ❑ The Authors – Finally, in the unlikely event that the editor cannot answer your problem, he or she will forward the request to the author. We do try to protect the author from any distractions to their writing; however, we are quite happy to forward specific requests to them. All Wrox authors help with the support on their books. They will e-mail the customer and the editor with their response, and again all readers should benefit.

The Wrox Support process can only offer support to issues that are directly pertinent to the content of our published title. Support for questions that fall outside the scope of normal book support, is provided via the community lists of our http://p2p.wrox.com/ forum.

p2p.wrox.com

For author and peer discussion join the P2P mailing lists. Our unique system provides **programmer-to-programmer™** contact on mailing lists, forums, and newsgroups, all in addition to our one-to-one e-mail support system. If you post a query to P2P, you can be confident that it is being examined by the many Wrox authors and other industry experts who are present on our mailing lists. At p2p.wrox.com you will find a number of different lists that will help you, not only while you read this book, but also as you develop your own applications. Particularly appropriate to this book are the **j2ee**, and **pro_java_server** lists.

To subscribe to a mailing list just follow these steps:

1. Go to http://p2p.wrox.com/

2. Choose the appropriate category from the left menu bar

3. Click on the mailing list you wish to join

4. Follow the instructions to subscribe and fill in your e-mail address and password

5. Reply to the confirmation e-mail you receive

6. Use the subscription manager to join more lists and set your e-mail preferences

Why this System Offers the Best Support

You can choose to join the mailing lists or you can receive them as a weekly digest. If you don't have the time, or facility, to receive the mailing list, then you can search our online archives. Junk and spam mails are deleted, and your own e-mail address is protected by the unique Lyris system. Queries about joining or leaving lists, and any other general queries about lists, should be sent to listsupport@p2p.wrox.com.

Data
RDMS
JDBC
Application Logic
Client
Web Container
Servlets
JSPs
Tag Library
HTTP(S)
(X)HTML/ XML
RMI/IIOP
JNDI
JTA
JDBC
JMS
JavaMail
JAAS
JCA
JAXP
J2EE Application Server
Applet
Client Application
Session Beans
JAF
JavaMail
Mail Server
RMI
Java Application
IIOP
CORBA Server
JNDI
Directory Service
JMS
Message Queue
ProfessionalJavaServerProgrammingJ2EE1.3Edition

1

The J2EE Platform

Today, Java is one of the most mature and commonly used programming languages for building enterprise software. The evolution of Java from a means of developing applets to be run in browsers, to a programming model capable of driving today's enterprise applications has been remarkable. Over the years, Java has evolved into three different platform editions, each addressing a distinct set of programming needs:

❑   **The Java 2 Platform, Standard Edition (J2SE):**
     This is the most commonly used of these Java platforms, consisting of a run-time environment and a set of APIs for building a wide variety of applications ranging from applets, through standalone applications that run on various platforms, to client applications for various enterprise applications.

❑   **The Java 2 Platform, Enterprise Edition (J2EE):**
     J2EE is a platform for building server-side applications. As you will see throughout this book, server-side applications have additional requirements during the development phase. J2EE provides the infrastructure for meeting these needs.

❑   **The Java 2 Platform, Micro Edition (J2ME):**
     The latest addition to the Java family, this edition enables the building of Java applications for "micro-devices" (devices with limited display and memory support, such as mobile phones, PDAs, etc.).

Of these three, J2SE is the most commonly used form of Java technology, and forms the basis for both J2EE and J2ME. J2SE is what is usually referred to as the **Java Development Kit (JDK)**. The current version of J2SE is 1.3, while the next version of J2SE, 1.4 is available as a beta.

This book is a journey through J2EE and in particular the 1.3 version of the specification. Since J2EE 1.3 requires J2SE 1.3, we will also be discussing some of the J2SE 1.3 features as appropriate.

In this book, we will start by introducing the programming needs for enterprise application development, the various technologies that are available for building such applications, and how to build such applications using those technologies. As we progress from chapter to chapter, we'll come across a wide variety of technologies, some of which are more complex than others, each fulfilling a specific set of technical needs.

This book will introduce you to almost the entire range of J2EE technologies. Despite the complexity of some of these areas, this book attempts to introduce each of these topics from fundamentals. In this way, you can study these topics in whichever order you prefer.

Programming for the Enterprise

J2EE has now been around for around four years. Over these years, it has replaced several proprietary and non-standard technologies as the preferred choice for building e-commerce and other web-based enterprise applications. Considering the multitude and complexity of technical infrastructure requirements for e-commerce applications, you will find out in this chapter how J2EE suits such requirements by providing a comprehensive infrastructure. Today, J2EE is the one of the two available alternatives for building e-commerce applications – the other alternative being Microsoft's Windows and .NET-based technologies.

From its inception, Java has triggered new programming models and technologies in different domains – ranging from devices, through telephony applications, to the enterprise. At the same time, Java has acted as a catalyst in making certain technology domains take more robust and secure shapes. Java's enterprise computing platform, the **Java 2 Platform, Enterprise Edition (J2EE),** is one such domain.

In the past, debates in the media, as well as in technical circles, used to question whether Java is a programming language or a platform upon to build and host applications. J2EE is in fact one of the most successful attempts by Sun and its associates in making Java credible as a *platform* for distributed enterprise computing.

But what is J2EE? Why is it relevant? Why should you choose this technology for building enterprise-level applications – from client-server to Internet to mobile? This chapter gives you a balanced view of J2EE, and assists you in answering these questions. The rest of this book takes a more in-depth look at the individual technologies and demonstrates how to successfully build and manage such enterprise applications.

In this introductory chapter, we'll focus on:

- ❑ The J2EE technical architecture
- ❑ What makes J2EE credible as a platform
- ❑ What are the challenges it addresses
- ❑ What technologies constitute the J2EE platform

First, however, let us start with the challenges of developing applications for today's enterprises.

The Enterprise Today

This book is about building enterprise applications, but what exactly do we mean by an enterprise?

An enterprise means a business organization, and enterprise applications are those software applications that facilitate various activities in an enterprise.

Enterprise applications can be those that cater to end-users via the Internet, partners via the Internet or private networks, various business units within the enterprise via various kinds of user interfaces, etc. In essence, enterprise applications are those that let an enterprise manage its business activities. Examples of such activities include resource planning, product inventories and catalogues, processing invoices, fulfillment of goods or services rendered, etc. Building applications for the enterprise has always been challenging. Some of the factors that contribute to this challenge and complexity are:

- **Diversity of information needs**
  In an enterprise, information is created and consumed by various users in a number of different forms, depending on specific needs. It is very common to find that each business activity may process the same information in a different form.

- **Complexity of business processes**
  Most of the enterprise business processes involve complex information capture, processing, and sharing. Very often, you will encounter complex logic to capture and process information. This leads to complex technical and architectural requirements for building enterprise applications.

- **Diversity of applications**
  Due to the complex nature of enterprise business processes, it is common to find that an enterprise consists of a large number of applications each built at various times to fulfill different needs of various business processes. This commonly leads to the presence of applications built using different architectures and technologies. One of the challenges that enterprises face today is a need to make such applications talk to each other so that business processes can be implemented seamlessly.

These factors are very common and enterprises incur a tremendous costs to build and manage applications that face these challenges.

Over the last few years, these challenges have taken more monstrous shapes. Through the Internet and the recent growth of e-commerce, an enterprise's information assets have now become more valuable. This shift to an information economy is forcing many businesses to re-think even their most basic business practices. In order to maintain a competitive edge, the adoption of new technologies to quickly meet the needs of the day has become a key factor in an enterprise's ability to best exploit its information assets. More importantly, adapting these new technologies to work in tandem with existing legacy systems has become one of the foremost requirements of the enterprise.

One place these shifts in business practices have been felt most keenly is at the *application development* level. Over the last few years, the funding and the time allocated to application development has been shrinking, while demands for building complex business processes have increased. However, these are both hurdles that developers can overcome, but there are also the following requirements to be met:

- **Programming Productivity**
  Direct adoption of new technologies is insufficient unless they are properly utilized to their full potential and appropriately integrated with other relevant technologies. Thus, the ability to develop and then deploy applications as effectively and as quickly as possible is important. Achieving this can be complicated by the sheer variety of technologies and standards that have been developed over the years, requiring highly developed skill sets, acquiring and keeping up with which is a problem in itself. Moreover, the rapid pace of change in standards themselves makes it harder to ensure efficient meshing of technologies.

❑ **Reliability and Availability**
In today's Internet economy, downtime can be fatal to a business. The ability to get your web-based operations up and running, and to keep them running, is critical to success. As if that wasn't enough, you must also be able to guarantee the reliability of your business transactions so that they will be processed completely and accurately.

❑ **Security**
The Internet has not only exponentially increased the number of potential users but also the value of a company's information, so the security of that information has become a prime concern. What's more, as technologies become more advanced, applications more sophisticated, and enterprises more complex, implementing an effective security model becomes increasingly difficult.

❑ **Scalability**
The ability for the application to grow to meet new demand, both in its operation and in its user base, is vital. This is especially true when we consider that an application's potential user base may be millions of individual users, via the Internet. To scale effectively requires not only the ability to handle a large increase in the number of clients but also effective use of system resources.

❑ **Integration**
Although information has grown to be a key business asset, much of this exists as data in old and outdated information systems. In order to maximize the usefulness of this information, applications need to be able to integrate with the existing information system – not necessarily an easy task as current technologies have often advanced far ahead of some of these legacy systems. The ability to combine old and new technologies is key to the success of developing for today's enterprises.

Are we looking for silver bullets to address these challenges? Despite the promises by evangelists and vendors alike, it is unwise to expect (or rely on) one solution to completely avoid or overcome these challenges. What enterprises seek is an enabling technology and infrastructure to simplify some of the complex technical issues. As you progress through this book, you will come across these issues.

None of these problem domains are especially new to enterprise developers. But solving them in a comprehensive and economical manner is still crucial. You may be aware that there have been several technologies to address one or more of the above demands. However, what has been missing is a comprehensive platform with a rich infrastructure and numerous architectural possibilities which also promotes a rapid development environment.

The purpose of J2EE is to simplify some of the technical complexities, and specify the following for building enterprise applications:

❑ A **programming model**, consisting of a set of application programming interfaces (APIs) and approaches to building applications

❑ An **application infrastructure**, to support enterprise applications built using the APIs

Is Java the Answer?

So far we have discussed our system architecture from an implementation-agnostic perspective. In fact, there exist many potential paths that you can take to actually implement your enterprise. There are essentially two major paths – one being driven by Microsoft, with its new .NET suite, and the second by Sun and other vendors such as BEA, IBM, Oracle, etc. Given these choices, why should Java make such a great choice? Let's take a look at some of its advantages.

Platform Independence

With an enterprise's information spread in disparate formats, across many different platforms and applications it is important to adopt a programming language that can work equally well throughout the enterprise without having to resort to awkward, inefficient translation mechanisms. A unifying programming model also reduces the difficulties encountered from integrating many of the different technologies that grow up specific to certain platforms and applications.

Managed Objects

J2EE provides a managed environment for components, and J2EE applications are **container-centric**. Both these notions are very critical to building server-side applications. By being managed, J2EE components utilize the infrastructure provided by J2EE servers without the programmer being aware of it. J2EE applications are also **declarative**, a mechanism using which you can modify and control the behavior of applications without changing code. At first glance, these features may appear cumbersome to implement. However, when you consider large-scale applications with several hundreds of components interacting to execute complex business processes, these features make both building and maintaining such applications less complex. Along with being platform-independent, this is one of the most important aspects of J2EE.

Reusability

Code reuse is the holy grail of all programming. Segregating an application's business requirements into component parts is one way to achieve reuse; using object-orientation to encapsulate shared functionality is another. Java uses both. Java is an object-oriented language and, as such, provides mechanisms for reuse. However, unlike objects, distributed components require a more complex infrastructure for their construction and management. Basic object-oriented concepts do not provide such a framework, but the Enterprise Edition of Java provides a significantly stringent architecture for the reuse of components. Business components (called Enterprise JavaBeans) developed in J2EE are coarse-grained (although the EJB 2.0 specification in J2EE 1.3 does allow a fine-grained approach), and reflective. By keeping these components coarsely-grained, it is possible to build complex business functionality in a loosely-coupled manner. Secondly, since the components are reflective, meaning that it is possible to identify certain meta data about the components, applications can be built by composing such components. Both these features encourage code reuse at a high granularity.

Modularity

When developing a complete server-side application, programs can get large and complex in a hurry. It is always best to break down an application into discreet modules that are each responsible for a specific task. This makes our applications much easier to maintain and understand. For example, Java servlets, JavaServer Pages, and Enterprise JavaBeans each provide a way to modularize our application, breaking our applications down into different tiers and individual tasks.

Despite the above features in its favor, it was not until early 2000 that Java introduced a unifying programming model for applications on the enterprise scale (not that it lacked the capabilities, but rather it was disorganized in the past). Sun recognized this shortcoming and released the **Java 2 Platform, Enterprise Edition (J2EE)**.

> **The idea behind the J2EE platform is to provide a simple, unified standard for distributed applications through a component-based application model.**

We will spend the rest of the chapter, and indeed the rest of the book, looking at what J2EE brings to server-side development with Java.

Enterprise Architecture Styles

Before we delve into the J2EE architecture, it is necessary to consider the architectural styles of contemporary distributed applications –2-tier, 3-tier, and n-tier architectures. The purpose of this section is mainly to enable the reader to recognize the scope of and place for these patterns. We should bear in mind, however, that in reality our applications may require more complex patterns – or sometimes a combination of them.

Although these architectural styles are quite common in today's enterprises, it is worth noting that these styles emerged due to the advent of cheaper hardware platforms for clients and servers, and networking technologies. Prior to this, what powered enterprises were mainframes with all the computing (from user-interface rendering to high-volume transaction processing) centralized. Subsequently, the client-server technology is what fuelled a widespread automation of enterprise.

Typical client-server systems are based on the 2-tiered architecture, whereby there is a clear separation between the data and the presentation/business logic. Such systems are generally data-driven with the server most of the times being a database server, and the client being a graphical user interface to operate on data. While this approach allows us to share data across the enterprise, it does have many drawbacks.

Two-Tier Architecture

In a traditional 2-tiered application, the processing load is given to the client PC while the server simply acts as a traffic controller between the application and the data. As a result, not only does the application performance suffer due to the limited resources of the PC, but the network traffic tends to increase as well. When the entire application is processed on a PC, the application is forced to make multiple requests for data before even presenting anything to the user. These multiple database requests can heavily tax the network:

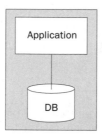

Another typical problem with a 2-tiered approach is that of maintenance. Even the smallest of changes to an application might involve a complete rollout to the entire user base. Even if it's possible to automate the process, you are still faced with updating every single client installation. What's more, some users may not be ready for a full rollout and may ignore the changes while another group may insist on making the changes immediately. This can result in different client installations using different versions of the application.

Three-Tier Architecture

To address these issues, the software community developed the notion of a 3-tier architecture. An application is broken up into three separate logical layers, each with a well-defined set of interfaces. The first tier is referred to as the **presentation layer** and typically consists of a graphical user interface of some kind. The middle tier, or **business layer**, consists of the application or business logic, and the third tier – the **data layer** – contains the data that is needed for the application.

The middle tier (application logic) is basically the code that the user calls upon (through the presentation layer) to retrieve the desired data. The presentation layer then receives the data and formats it for display. This separation of application logic from the user interface adds enormous flexibility to the design of the application. Multiple user interfaces can be built and deployed without ever changing the application logic, provided the application logic presents a clearly defined interface to the presentation layer. As you will see later in this chapter, and the rest of this book, J2EE provides several abstractions to meet the needs of each of these tiers. For instance, EJBs provide mechanisms to abstract both data access and business logic. Similarly, servlets and JavaServer Pages allow you abstract the presentation layer and its interaction with the business layer.

The third tier contains the data that is needed for the application. This data can consist of any source of information, including an enterprise database such as Oracle or Sybase, a set of XML documents, or even a directory service like an LDAP server. In addition to the traditional relational database storage mechanism, there are many different sources of enterprise data that your applications can access:

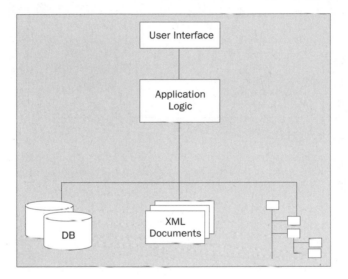

However, we're not quite finished with our subdivision of the application. We can take the segregation one step further to create an n-tier architecture.

n-Tier Architecture

As the title suggests, there is no hard-and-fast way to define the application layers for an n-tier system. In fact, this kind of system can support a number of different configurations. In an n-tier architecture the application logic is logically divided by function, rather than physically.

n-tier architecture breaks down like this:

- ❑ A **user interface** that handles the user's interaction with the application – this can be a web browser running through a firewall, a heavier desktop application, or even a wireless device.

- ❑ **Presentation logic** that defines what the user interface displays and how a user's requests are handled. Depending on what user interfaces are supported, you may need to have slightly different versions of the presentation logic to handle the client appropriately.

- **Business logic** that models the application's business rules, often through interaction with the application's data.
- **Infrastructure services** that provide additional functionality required by the application components, such as messaging, transactional support.
- The **data layer** where the enterprise's data resides.

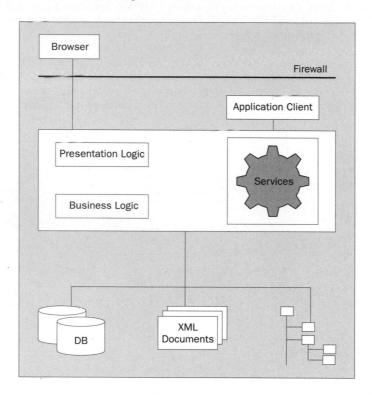

*Applications based on this architecture are essentially employing the **Model-View-Controller** (**MVC**) pattern. What this ultimately means is that the data (the model) is separated from how the information is presented (the view). In between this is the application/business logic (the controller) that controls the flow of the information. Thus, an application is designed based on these three functional components (model, view, and controller) interacting with each other.*

Enterprise Architecture

So far we have really been concentrating on a single application's architecture – we are in danger of considering these applications as "stovepipes". In other words, we might end up with many different applications – possibly even with different architectures – all of which don't communicate with one another. In an enterprise, we are looking to create a cohesive architecture incorporating different applications.

Rather than a change in architecture – enterprise architecture is basically just n-tier – we need a change in perception. To turn an n-tier system into an enterprise system, we simply extend the middle tier by allowing for multiple **application objects** rather than just a single application. These application objects must each have an interface that allows them to work together with each other.

An interface can be thought of as a contract. Each object states through its interface that it will accept certain parameters, perform certain operations, and return a specific set of results. Application objects communicate with each other using their interfaces, as shown in the following diagram:

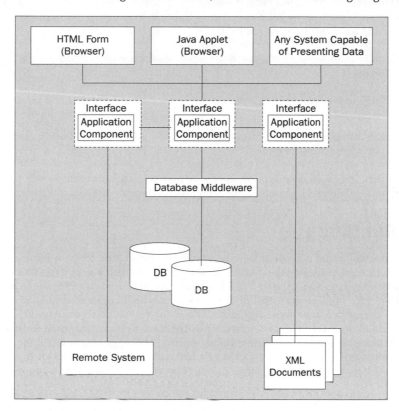

With enterprise architecture, we can have multiple applications using a common set of components across an organization. This promotes the standardization of business practices by creating a single set of business functions for the entire organization to access. If a business rule changes, then changes have to be made to the relevant "business object" and, if necessary, the associated interface and subsequently any object that accesses the interface. Note, however, that certain functionalities in existing legacy systems can't be removed and a "wrapper" (or interface) specific to this functionality has to be developed in the middle tier.

> It is important to note that when designing an object and its interface, it is a good idea to make the interface as generic as possible to avoid changes later on. Since other objects communicate with the interface and not the object itself, changes to the object, and not the interface, are relatively simple and quick.

In all these patterns, notice that user interfaces are what are shown at the top of each diagram. From these diagrams, you may get the impression that user interfaces are what always drive systems. Although this is the most commonly visible form of system interaction, as you consider intra- and inter-business application integration, and cross-enterprise business processes, you'll find applications interacting with other applications. Nonetheless, most of the technologies that we shall discuss, and the designs that you will find this book, apply to such systems as well.

The J2EE Platform

As you'll see in the rest of this book, J2EE is one of the best solutions that we've had so far for meeting the demands of today's enterprise. J2EE specifies both the infrastructure for managing your applications, and the service APIs for building your applications.

The J2EE platform is essentially a distributed application-server environment – a Java environment that provides the following:

❑   A set of Java extension APIs to build applications. These APIs define a programming model for J2EE applications.

❑   A run-time infrastructure for hosting and managing applications. This is the server runtime in which your applications reside.

The applications that you could develop with the above may be programs to drive web pages, or components to implement complex database transactions, or even Java applets, all distributed across the network.

The J2EE Runtime

While J2EE bundles together APIs that have been in existence in one form or another for quite some time, perhaps its most significant aspect is the abstraction of the **run-time infrastructure**. Note that the J2EE specification does not specify how a J2EE runtime should or could be built. Instead, J2EE specifies roles and interfaces for applications, and the runtime onto which applications could be deployed. This results in a clear demarcation between applications and the run-time infrastructure. This demarcation allows the runtime to abstract most of the infrastructure services that enterprise developers have traditionally attempted to build on their own. As a result, J2EE application developers could just focus on the application logic and related services, while leveraging the runtime for all infrastructure-related services. However, what are the infrastructure requirements of enterprise applications?

It is interesting to note that application development in a fast-paced environment, such as the Internet, typically leads to designs that are short-lived.

On the other hand, when considering the long-term design aspects, we may have difficulty finding a compromise between short-term and long-term demands. There are technologies that lend themselves to rapid development, and then there are technologies that let you build applications taking care of such long-term concerns as reusability, cost of maintenance, etc. Often the two do not mix, but J2EE is flexible enough to allow us to build applications that include both. This is because it lets you build each layer of your application loosely coupled to all other layers. Each layer can therefore evolve to meet respective evolutionary needs. Thus, by conforming to a system designed on interfaces, the implementation is highly extendable.

Apart from specifying a set of standard APIs, the J2EE architecture also provides a uniform means of accessing platform-level services via its run-time environment. Such services include distributed transactions, security, messaging, and so on. Before we see details of J2EE's approach, let's take a look at traditional distributed computing.

Until the advent of J2EE, distributed computing was, in general, considered as client-server programming. We would write a server application implementing an interface, a client application to connect to the server, and then start both the server and the client! Although this process seems so simple, in practice there are several critical stumbling blocks in this process, depending on the technology used.

For instance, consider a CORBA object request broker for building distributed applications. The typical procedure for building the server-side CORBA objects would start from specifying an interface, using the Interface Definition Language (IDL), for each object. Subsequent steps include compiling this IDL to generate "stubs" and "skeletons" for the language of your choice, implementing the object based on the skeleton, then writing the client application, preparing your environment, etc. Here the stub is the class that represents the CORBA object on the client side. The skeleton provides the method with which the server-side logic is implemented. This procedure in itself is not complicated and could easily be automated. As you will learn in this book, EJBs too require some of these steps and are conceptually similar to CORBA objects.

Now consider that our servers, as well as clients, require access to services such as distributed transactions, messaging, etc. To utilize such services, we'd be required to add a significant amount of plumbing code to our applications. More often than not, we'd be required to set up and configure different middleware solutions, and make API calls to the vendor-specific APIs to access the services. Apart from services such as relational database access, most of these services are either proprietary or non-standard. The result is that our applications will be more complex, time consuming, and expensive to develop, manage, and maintain.

Apart from having to manage all these different APIs, there is another critical demand on server-side applications. On the serverside, resources are scarce. For example, we cannot afford to create the same number of objects that we can typically afford to create in client-side applications. Other server-side resources that require special attention include threads, database connections, security, transactions, etc. Custom-building an infrastructure that deals with these resources has always been a challenge. This task is almost impossible in the Internet economy. Would you care to build a connection pool, or an object cache, or an "elegant" object layer for database access, when your development lifecycle is only three months?

Since these server-side requirements are common across a wide variety of applications, it is more appropriate to consider a platform that has built-in solutions. This lets us separate these infrastructure-level concerns from the more direct concern of translating your application requirements to software that works. The J2EE runtime addresses such concerns. Essentially, we leave it to the J2EE server vendor to implement the specific features for us in a standards-compliant manner.

As mentioned above, the J2EE does not specify the nature and structure of the runtime. Instead, it introduces what is called a **container**, and via the J2EE APIs, specifies a contract between containers and applications. You'll see more details of this contract at appropriate places later in this book.

Before looking into more details of J2EE containers, let's have a brief look at the J2EE APIs.

The J2EE APIs

Distributed applications require access to a set of enterprise services. Typical services include transaction processing, database access, messaging, multithreading, etc. The J2EE architecture unifies access to such services in its enterprise service APIs. However, instead of having to access these services through proprietary or non-standard interfaces, application programs in J2EE can access these APIs via the container.

A typical commercial J2EE platform (or J2EE application server) includes one or more containers, and access to the enterprise APIs is specified by the J2EE.

Note that J2EE application servers need not implement these services themselves; containers are only required to provide access to each service implementation via a J2EE API. For example, a J2EE implementation might delegate the Java Message Service API calls to a commercial message-oriented middleware solution. Yet another implementation might include a message-oriented middleware solution within a container.

19

The specification of the J2EE 1.3 platform includes a set of Java standard extensions that each J2EE platform must support:

❑ **JDBC 2.0**
More specifically, the JDBC 2.0 Optional Package. This API improves the standard JDBC 2.0 API by adding more efficient means of obtaining connections, connection pooling, distributed transactions, etc. Note that the next version of JDBC, the JDBC 3.0 API combines the extension API with the usual JDBC API. Future versions of J2EE may include JDBC 3.0.

❑ **Enterprise JavaBeans (EJB) 2.0**
This specifies a component framework for multi-tier distributed applications. This provides a standard means of defining server-side components, and specifies a rich run-time infrastructure for hosting components on the serverside.

❑ **Java Servlets 2.3**
The Java Servlet API provides object-oriented abstractions for building dynamic web applications.

❑ **JavaServer Pages (JSP) 1.2**
This extension further enhances J2EE web applications by providing for template-driven web application development.

❑ **Java Message Service (JMS) 1.0**
JMS provides a Java API for message queuing, and publish and subscribe types of message-oriented middleware services.

❑ **Java Transaction API (JTA) 1.0**
This API is for implementing distributed transactional applications.

❑ **JavaMail 1.2**
This API provides a platform-independent and protocol-independent framework to build Java-based e-mail applications.

❑ **JavaBeans Activation Framework (JAF) 1.0** This API is required for the JavaMail API. The JavaMail API uses JAF to determine the contents of a MIME (Multipurpose Internet Mail Extension) message and determine what appropriate operations can be done on different parts of a mail message.

❑ **Java API for XML Parsing (JAXP) 1.1**
This API provides abstractions for XML parsers and transformation APIs. JAXP helps to isolate specific XML parsers, or XML Document Object Model (DOM) implementations, or XSLT transformation APIs from J2EE application code.

❑ **The Java Connector Architecture (JCA) 1.0**
This API has recently been included in J2EE, and provides a means to integrate J2EE application components to legacy information systems.

❑ **Java Authentication and Authorization Service (JAAS) 1.0**
This API provides authentication and authorization mechanisms to J2EE applications.

Most of these API are specifications, independent of implementation. That is, one should be able to access services provided by these API's in a standard way, irrespective of how they are implemented.

The J2EE-specific APIs mentioned above are in addition to the following J2SE APIs:

❑ **Java Interface Definition Language (IDL) API**
This API allows J2EE application components to invoke CORBA objects via IIOP (see below).

❑ **JDBC Core API**
This API provides the basic database programming facilities.

❑ **RMI-IIOP API**
This provides an implementation of the usual **Java Remote Method Invocation (RMI)** API over the **Internet Inter-ORB Protocol (IIOP)**. This bridges the gap between RMI and CORBA applications. This is the standardized communication protocol to be used between J2EE containers.

❑ **JNDI API**
The **Java Naming and Directory Interface (JNDI)** API standardizes access to different types of naming and directory services available today. This API is designed to be independent of any specific naming or directory service implementation. J2SE also specifies a JNDI service provider interface (SPI), for naming and directory service providers to implement.

We will take a more detailed look at these APIs later in the chapter.

J2EE Architecture – Containers

As discussed in the previous section, a typical commercial J2EE platform includes one or more **containers**. But what exactly is a container?

> **A J2EE container is a runtime to manage application components developed according to the API specifications, and to provide access to the J2EE APIs.**

Beyond the identity associated with the runtime, J2EE does not specify any identity for containers. This gives a great amount of flexibility to achieve a variety of features within the container runtime.

The following figure shows the architecture of J2EE in terms of its containers and APIs:

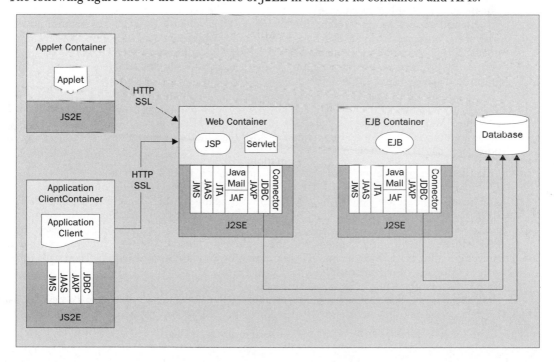

This architecture shows four containers:

- ❑ A **web container** for hosting Java servlets and JSP pages

- ❑ An **EJB container** for hosting Enterprise JavaBean components

- ❑ An **applet container** for hosting Java applets

- ❑ An **application client** container for hosting standard Java applications

In this book, our focus is limited to the web and EJB containers only.

Each of these containers provides a run-time environment for the respective components. J2EE components are also called managed objects, as these objects are created and managed within the container runtime.

In the above figure, the vertical blocks at the bottom of each container represent the J2EE APIs. Apart from access to these infrastructure-level APIs, each container also implements the respective container-specific API (Java Servlet API for the web container, and the EJB API for the EJB container).

The stacks of rectangles (servlets, JSP pages, and EJBs) in this figure are the programs that you develop and host in these containers. In the J2EE parlance, these programs are called **application components**.

Note that the above figure does not include the J2SE APIs listed above, that is, the Java IDL, JDBC core, RMI-IIOP, and JNDI.

In this architecture, there are primarily two types of clients:

- ❑ **Web clients** normally run in web browsers.
  For these clients, the user interface is generated on the serverside as HTML or XML, and is downloaded and then rendered by the browsers. These clients use HTTP to communicate with web containers. Application components in web containers include Java servlets and JSP pages. These components implement the functionality required for web clients. Web containers are responsible for accepting requests from web clients, and generating responses with the help of the application components.

  Other related types of clients include web-enabled mobile devices capable of rendering WML (Wireless Markup Language) or cHTML (Compact HTML). For such clients, content can be generated directly, or content generated as XML can be transformed into these markup languages using XML stylesheets.

- ❑ **EJB clients** are applications that access EJB components in EJB containers.
  There are three possible types of EJB clients. The first category is application clients. Application clients are standalone applications accessing the EJB components using the RMI-IIOP protocol. The second category of application clients are components in the web container. That is, Java servlets and JSP pages can also access the EJB components via the RMI-IIOP protocol in the same way as the application clients. The final category is other EJBs running within the EJB container. These communicate via standard Java method calls through a local interface (this is new in J2EE 1.3).

In either case, clients access application components via the respective container. Web clients access JSP pages and Java servlets via the web container, and EJB clients access the EJB components via the EJB container.

Container Architecture

Having seen the core constituents of J2EE, let's now return to our architecture discussion and study the architecture of a J2EE container:

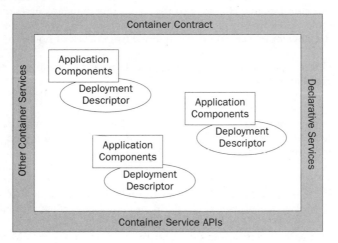

In this architecture, as developers we are required to provide the following:

❑ **Application components**
As discussed in the previous section, application components include servlets, JSP pages, EJBs, etc. In J2EE, application components can be packaged into archive files.

❑ **Deployment descriptors**
A deployment descriptor is an XML file that describes the application components. It also includes additional information required by containers for effectively managing application components.

The rest of this figure forms the container. The architecture of a container can be divided into four parts:

❑ **Component contract**
A set of APIs specified by the container, that your application components are required to extend or implement.

❑ **Container service APIs**
Additional services provided by the container, which are commonly required for all applications in the container.

❑ **Declarative services**
Services that the container interposes on your applications, based on the deployment description provided for each application component, such as security, transactions etc.

❑ **Other container services**
Other runtime services, related to component lifecycle, resource pooling, garbage collection, etc.

Let's now discuss each of the above in detail.

Component Contracts

As we mentioned earlier, the basic purpose of the container in the J2EE architecture is to provide a runtime for application components. That is, instances of the application components are created and invoked within the JVM of the container. This makes the container responsible for managing the lifecycle of application components. However, if they are to be manageable within the container runtime, they are required to abide by certain **contracts** specified by the container. In other words, applications should be developed according to a defined framework of operation.

To better understand this aspect, consider a Java applet. Typically, an applet is downloaded by the browser and instantiated and initialized in the browser's JVM. That is, the applet lives in the runtime provided by the JVM of the browser.

However, in order for the container to be able to create, initialize, and invoke methods on application components, the application components are required to implement or extend certain Java interfaces or classes. For example, considering the applet example again, a Java applet is required to extend the `java.applet.Applet` class specified by the JDK. The JVM of the browser expects your applets to extend this class. This enables the browser's JVM to call the `init()`, `start()`, `stop()`, and `destroy()` methods on your applets. These methods control the lifecycle of an applet – unless your applet extends the `java.applet.Applet` class, the browser JVM has no means of calling these methods to control its lifecycle.

In J2EE, all application components are instantiated and initialized in the JVM of the container. In addition, since J2EE application components are always remote to the client, clients cannot directly call methods on these components – in fact, clients make requests to the applications server and it is the container that actually invokes the methods. Since the container process is the only entry point into the application components, all application components are required to follow the contract specified by the container. In J2EE, this contract is in the form of interfaces and classes that your classes implement or extend, with additional rules that the component definition should follow.

There is one important implication of such a component contract. All J2EE application components are **managed**. The management includes location, instantiation, pooling, initialization, service invocation, and removal of components from service. These aspects of component lifecycle are the responsibility of the container, and the application has no direct control.

Let's now look at the various contracts specified by J2EE.

In the case of web containers, web application components are required to follow the Java Servlet and JSP APIs. In this model, all Java servlets are required to extend the `javax.servlet.http.HttpServlet` class, and to implement certain methods of this class such as `doGet()`, `doPost()`, and so on. Similarly, when compiled, classes corresponding to JSP pages extend the `javax.servlet.jsp.HttpJspPage` class.

In the case of EJB containers, session and entity enterprise beans are required to have `javax.ejb.EJBHome` and `javax.ejb.EJBObject` interfaces specified, while implementing either a `javax.ejb.SessionBean` or `javax.ejb.EntityBean` interface. Similarly, message-driven beans must implement both `javax.ejb.MessageDrivenBean` and `javax.jmx.MessageListener` interfaces. As you'll see in Chapter 14, the component specifications and implementations are also required to follow certain rules. Apart from the interfaces, all such rules form part of the component contract for EJB components.

Container Service APIs

As discussed earlier, the J2EE platform defines a set of Java standard extensions that each J2EE platform must support. J2EE containers provide a service-level abstraction of the APIs. As a result, you can access the service APIs such as JDBC, JTS, JNDI, JMS, etc., within the container, as though the underlying container is implementing them.

> **A container in the J2EE architecture provides a consolidated view of various enterprise APIs specified in the J2EE platform.**

In J2EE, application components can access these APIs via appropriate objects created and published in the JNDI service or implementation. For example, when we want to use JMS within our application components, we would configure our J2EE platform to create JMS connection factories, message queues and topics, and publish these objects in the JNDI service. Our applications can then look in the JNDI, obtain references to these objects, and invoke methods. In this process, it does not matter if the J2EE platform has a JMS implementation built in or if it is using a third-party messaging middleware solution.

Let's consider Java applets again. For example, if we want to play an audio file from an applet, we would call the `play()` method defined in the super-class (`java.applet.Applet`), with a URL pointing to the audio file. In this case, the functionality for playing audio files is implemented by the super-class. This is one of the approaches for code reuse. A better alternative to this approach is to delegate this functionality to a common component. Such a component need not be a part of the same inheritance hierarchy. All that is required is a reference to an object implementing this functionality. Once our application is able to get a reference to such an object, we can delegate the "play" functionality to that object. A significant advantage of this approach is that it allows other objects from more than one inheritance hierarchy to access the "play" functionality.

In the case of distributed applications this gets complicated, as the services are remote. Just as an analogy, consider the same audio component running as a separate server! How do we get hold of a reference to such a component? The solution is to let the J2EE platform create the audio component, and publish its name in a naming service (that is, JNDI) available to your application. This provides a simplified method of access to the service APIs. This also allows us to plug in different implementations of these services without disturbing the applications using the services. The following schematic illustrates this possibility:

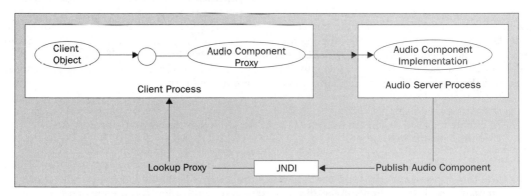

Notice the loose coupling between the implementation and the client. As long as the interface exposed by the proxy is unchanged, the implementation can be changed without affecting the client code. This is the most suitable form of abstraction on the serverside, as it not only uses delegation instead of inheritance, but also reduces coupling.

All J2EE service APIs use the above approach for providing services to applications.

The following are the key implications of this approach:

- ❑ As a single standard that can sit on top of a variety of existing database systems, transaction processing systems, naming and directory services, etc., the service APIs eliminate the inherent heterogeneity involved in bringing these technologies together in our applications.

- ❑ In J2EE, these services are also integrated tightly with the programming model. In later chapters, we'll see how to access these APIs seamlessly from our application components and clients.

- ❑ The J2EE platform also specifies a uniform mechanism for accessing these services.

Declarative Services

One of the important features of the J2EE architecture is its ability to dynamically interpose services for application components. This is based on declarations specified outside our application components. The J2EE architecture provides simple means of specifying such declarations. These are called **deployment descriptors**.

> **A deployment descriptor defines the contract between the container and component. As application developers, we are required to specify a deployment descriptor for each group of application components.**

For example, a set of EJB components can be described together in a single deployment descriptor file. Similarly, in the case of web containers, each web application is required to have a deployment descriptor specified.

Depending on the type of the component, certain types of services (such as transactions, security, etc.) can be specified in the deployment descriptor. The purpose of this approach is to minimize the application programming required in order to make use of such services.

The standard method of invoking services is via **explicit invocation**. For example, to implement transactions for database access, we can programmatically start a transaction before accessing the database, and commit or rollback the transaction once the business methods are completed. In the case of **declarative invocation**, our application components need not explicitly start and stop transactions. Instead, we can specify in the deployment descriptor that our business methods should be invoked within a new transaction. Based on this information, the container can automatically start a transaction whenever the business methods in your applications are invoked.

> **In simple terms, a declarative service is a service or action that is performed by the container on our behalf.**

How does this approach work? J2EE containers are, by nature, distributed and the application components are remote to clients. Accordingly, requests to application components and responses back from application components occur across process, platform, and network boundaries.

In addition, since application components are maintained in the container runtime, the container process is responsible for receiving the requests, and delegating them to appropriate application components. For instance, in the case of the EJB container, the container receives all client requests and delegates them to appropriate EJB objects deployed on the container. Similarly, in the case of web containers, the web container receives HTTP requests and delegates them to servlets and JSP pages. The following diagram depicts a simplified view of this invocation. In this figure, the remote interface is what the clients use to communicate with the EJB on the container. Note that the container process handles all requests and responses to and from the application components:

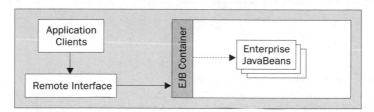

This approach gives the container an ability to **interpose** a new service before transferring a request to the application component. In the case of declarative transactions, the container can start the transaction before delegating the incoming request to the business method implication, and end the transaction as soon as the method returns.

What's the advantage of this approach? We can interpose new services without changing the application component. More specifically, this facility allows us to postpone decisions about such services to the run-time, instead of the design time. In other words, the container can selectively enhance our components based on the deployment descriptor.

For EJB containers, the declarative services include transactions and security. Both these can be specified in deployment descriptors. In the case of web containers, we can specify the required security roles for accessing components within web applications.

Other Container Services

The following are some of the runtime services that containers provide:

- **Lifecycle management of application components**
  This involves creating new instances of application components and pooling or destroying them when the instances are no longer required.

- **Resource pooling**
  Containers can optionally implement resource pooling such as object pooling and connection pooling.

- **Populating the JNDI namespace based on the deployment names associated with EJB components**
  This information is typically supplied at deployment time. We'll discuss more about deployment in the next section.

- **Populating the JNDI namespace with objects necessary for utilizing container service APIs**
  Some of the objects include data source objects for database access, queue and topic connection factories for obtaining connections to JMS, and user transaction objects for programmatically controlling transactions.

❑ **Clustering**
In J2EE, containers can be distributable. A distributable container consists of a number of JVMs running on one or more host machines. In this setup, application components can be deployed on a number of JVMs. Depending on the type of load-balancing strategy and the type of the component, the container can distribute the load of incoming requests to one of these JVMs. Clustering is essential for enhancing scalability and availability of applications.

Now that we have covered the architecture of J2EE applications, let's take a closer look at some of the various technologies included in the J2EE platform.

J2EE Technologies

Having discussed all the architecture of the J2EE platform, we now want to cover the collection of technologies that provide the mechanics we need to build large, distributed enterprise applications. This large collection, of quite disparate technologies, can be divided according to use:

❑ **The component technologies**
These technologies are used to hold the most important part of the application – the business logic. There are three types of components: JSP pages, servlets, and Enterprise JavaBeans; we will look at each of these in a moment.

❑ **The service technologies**
These technologies provide the application's components with supported services to function efficiently.

❑ **The communication technologies**
These technologies, which are mostly transparent to the application programmer, provide the mechanisms for communication among different parts of the application, whether they are local or remote.

Let's now examine how the J2EE APIs and associated technologies can be categorized.

Component Technologies

With any application, the most important element is modeling the necessary business logic through the use of components, or application level reusable units. Earlier in the chapter, we described a container as hosting the runtime for application components, so although the container may be able to supply many of the services and much of the communication infrastructure, it is ultimately the responsibility of the developer to create the application components. However, these components will be dependent upon their container for many services, such as lifecycle management, threading, and security. This allows us to concentrate on providing the requisite business functionality without getting into details of low-level (container-level) semantics.

The J2EE platform provides three technologies for developing components.

> One thing that should be made clear is that the J2EE platform does not specify that an application need make use of all three types of component technologies – in many cases using EJBs may well be overkill.

Web Components

These can be categorized as any component that responds to an HTTP request. A further distinction that can be drawn is based on the hosting container for the application components. As we saw earlier in the chapter, the two basic server-side containers are the web container and the EJB container.

Servlets

Servlets are server-side programs that allow application logic to be embedded in the HTTP request-response process. Servlets provide a means to extend the functionality of the web server to enable dynamic content in HTML, XML, or other web languages. With the release of J2EE 1.3, the Servlets specification has reached version 2.3.

We'll be working with servlets in Chapters 5 to 9.

JavaServer Pages

JavaServer Pages (JSP) provide a way to embed components in a page, and to have them do their work to generate the page that is eventually sent to the client. A JSP page can contain HTML, Java code, and JavaBean components. JSP pages are in fact an extension of the servlet programming model. When a user requests a JSP page, the web container compiles the JSP page into a servlet. The web container then invokes the servlet and returns the resulting content to the web browser. Once the servlet has been compiled from the JSP page, the web container can simply return the servlet without having to recompile each time. Thus, JSP pages provide a powerful and dynamic page assembly mechanism that benefits from the many advantages of the Java platform.

Compared to servlets, which are pure Java code, JSP pages are merely text-based documents until the web container compiles them into the corresponding servlets. This allows a clearer separation of application logic from presentation logic. This, in turn, allows application developers to concentrate on business matters and web designers to concentrate on presentation. With the current release of J2EE, the JSP specification reached version 1.2. Chapters 10 to 12 discuss JSP pages in detail.

A typical architecture for a web application involving JSP pages may look like this:

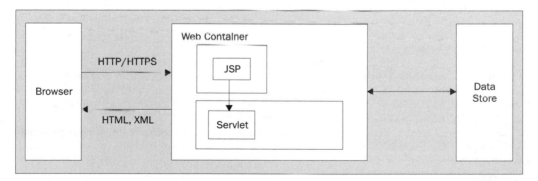

Enterprise JavaBean Components

Enterprise JavaBeans (EJB) 2.0 is a distributed component model for developing secure, scalable, transactional, and multi-user components. To put it simply, EJBs are (ideally) reusable software units containing business logic. Just as JSP pages allow the separation of application and presentation logic, EJBs allow separation of application logic from system-level services thus allowing the developer to concentrate on the business domain issues and not system programming. These enterprise bean business objects take three basic forms – again, it is not necessary to implement them all – **session beans**, **entity beans**, and **message-driven beans**. We'll see EJBs in action in Chapters 14 to 19.

Session Beans

Session beans themselves come in two types. A **stateful session bean** is a transient object used to represent a client's interaction with the system – it performs the client's requests in the application, accessing a database etc., and when the client's operations are complete it is destroyed (that is, it exists for the length of the client session) – one example of this is an application client sending a series of requests to an application to perform a business process. In such cases, a stateful session bean can track the state of the interaction between the client and the application. The alternative, a **stateless session bean**, maintains no state between client requests. Generally, this type of session bean is used to implement a specific service that does not require client state, for instance, a simple database update.

Entity Beans

An **entity bean** on the other hand is a persistent object that models the data held within the data store, that is, it is an object wrapper for the data. For instance, data about a purchase order can be modeled using a PurchaseOrder entity bean presenting an aggregated view of all purchase order related data. Compared to session beans that can be used by any client, entity beans can be accessed concurrently by many clients but must maintain a unique identity through a primary key. In fact, under the J2EE container architecture we can elect whether to have the persistent state of the entity bean managed for us by the container or whether to implement this "by hand" in the bean itself.

Message-Driven Beans

Message-driven beans are a special class of EJBs that are not meant for direct client invocation. The purpose of message-driven beans is to process messages received via JMS. Message-driven beans complement the asynchronous nature of JMS by providing a means of processing messages within the EJB container. When an application client or an application sends a message via JMS, the container invokes the appropriate message-driven bean to process the message.

XML

As mentioned in our overview earlier in the chapter, J2EE 1.3 includes the JAXP API. This serves to abstract XML parsing, and XML translation APIs. In addition, there are several other XML-related Java APIs are being developed currently. For a summary and further details, refer to http://java.sun.com/xml.

XML (Extensible Markup Language) influences how we view, process, transport, and manage data. XML is a self-describing language using which you can send data as well as its meta data. In today's enterprise systems, XML is used to represent business data both within and across applications.

One of the strengths of XML is the sharing of such "vocabularies", all of which use the same basic syntax, parsers, and other tools. Shared XML vocabularies provide more easily searchable documents and databases, and a way to exchange information between many different organizations and computer applications.

XML can be far more than just a description mechanism though:

❑   **Transforming XML**
Transformation allow a programmer to map an XML document in one form into another form based on a set of rules. XML transformations are used to translate between similar XML vocabularies as well as translating XML documents into other text-based file formats like comma-delimited values. This is the standard representation of data across an enterprise.

❑ **XML and Databases**

Although the XML data model is inherently hierarchical whereas databases are essentially relational – creating some mapping difficulties – it does provide a mechanism of integrating existing data into new systems. Many database vendors are now adding native support for XML into their engines in recognition that programmers need ways to interface XML and databases.

❑ **Server-to-Server Communication**

Complex enterprise applications often utilize differing server software running and distributed across many computing technologies. XML provides a layer of abstraction in order to integrate these dissimilar systems. XML can be obtained from one server, manipulated, and then passed to another server in such a way that it can understand the request.

Although we won't be explicitly covering XML in this book, we will encounter it when we create various J2EE deployment descriptors. For more information on using XML with Java, please refer to *Professional Java XML* and *Java XML Programmers Reference*, both by Wrox Publishing.

Service Technologies

As we have discussed, some of the J2EE services for application components are managed by the containers themselves, thus allowing the developer to concentrate on the business logic. However, there will be times when developers find it necessary to programmatically invoke some services themselves using some of the various service technologies.

JDBC

Although all data access should be accessible through the single standard API of the Connector architecture in the future, database connectivity is probably one of the key services that developers implement in their application component.

The **JDBC** API (un-officially standing for Java Database Connectivity) provides the developer with the ability to connect to relational database systems. As we will see in Chapter 4, it allows the transactional querying, retrieval, and manipulation of data from a JDBC-compliant database. For the moment, it is worth noting that J2EE adds an extension to the core JDBC API (which comes with J2SE) to give advanced features, such as connection pooling and distributed transactions.

Java Transaction API and Service

The **Java Transaction API (JTA)** is a means for working with transactions and especially distributed transactions independent of the transaction manger's implementation (the **Java Transaction Service (JTS)**). Under the J2EE platform, distributed transactions are generally considered to be container-controlled so we, as developers, shouldn't have to be too concerned with transactions across your components – having said that though, the J2EE transaction model is still somewhat limited, so at times it may be necessary to do the hard work yourself.

JNDI

The role of the **Java Naming and Directory Interface (JNDI)** API in the J2EE platform is twofold:

❑ Firstly, it provides the means to perform standard operations on a directory service resource such as LDAP, Novell Directory Services, or Netscape Directory Services

❑ Secondly, a J2EE application utilizes JNDI to look up interfaces used to create, among other things, EJBs, and JDBC connections

In the next chapter, we'll see how to use JNDI to access a directory service resource.

JMS

In the enterprise environment, the various distributed components may not always be in constant contact with each other. Therefore, there needs to be some mechanism of sending data asynchronously. The **Java Message Service (JMS)** provides just such functionality to send and receive messages through the use of message-oriented middleware (MOM).

JavaMail

JavaMail is an API that can be used to abstract facilities for sending and receiving e-mail. JavaMail supports the most widely used Internet mail protocols such as IMAP4, POP3, and SMTP, but compared to JMS it is slower and less reliable.

The Java Connector Architecture

The **Java Connector Architecture (JCA)**, introduced in version 1.3, is a standardized means by which J2EE applications can access a variety of legacy applications, typically Enterprise Resource Planning systems such as SAP R/3 and PeopleSoft. The Connector specification defines a simple architecture in which vendors of J2EE application servers and legacy systems collaborate to produce 'plug-and-play' components that allow you access the legacy system without having to know anything too specific about how to work with it.

JAAS

The **Java Authentication and Authorization Service** provides a means to grant permissions based on who is executing the code. JAAS utilizes a pluggable architecture of authentication modules so that you can drop in modules based on different authentication implementations, such as Kerberos or PKI (Public Key Infrastructure).

Communication Technologies

The final technology grouping is those technologies that provide the means for the various components and services within a J2EE application to communicate with each other – a distributed application would be pretty ineffectual if these technologies didn't provide the 'glue' to hold it all together.

Internet Protocols

As we are talking about n-tier applications in this book, our client will very often be a browser potentially situated anywhere in the world. A client's requests and the server's responses are communicated over three main protocols.

HTTP

HTTP or Hypertext Transfer Protocol is a generic, stateless, application-level protocol, which has many uses beyond simply hypertext capabilities. It works on a request/response basis. A client sends a request to the server in the form of a request method, URI (Uniform Resource Identifier), and protocol version, followed by a MIME-like message containing request modifiers, client information, and possible body content over a connection with a server. The server in turn responds with a status line followed by a MIME-like message containing server information, entity meta-information, and possible entity-body content.

TCP/IP

TCP (Transmission Control Protocol) over **IP (Internet Protocol)** is actually two separate protocols, which are typically combined into a single entity. IP is the protocol that takes care of making sure that data is received by both endpoints in communication over the Internet. When we type the address of a web site into our browser, IP is what ensures that our requests and the fulfillment of those requests make it to the proper destinations. For efficiency, the data being sent back and forth between a client and a web server is broken into several pieces, or packets. These packets do not all have to take the same route when they are sent between the client and the web server. TCP is the protocol that keeps track of the packets and makes sure they are assembled in the same order as they were dispatched and are error-free. Therefore, TCP and IP work together to move data around on the Internet. For this reason, we will almost always see these two protocols combined into TCP/IP.

SSL

Secure Sockets Layer (SSL) uses cryptography to encrypt the flow of information between the client and server. This also provides a means for both parties to authenticate each other. Secure HTTP (HTTPS) is usually distinguished from regular unencrypted HTTP by being served on a different port number (443, by default).

Remote Object Protocols

In applications where the components are often distributed across many tiers and servers, some mechanism for using the components remotely is required, preferably leaving the client unaware that the component is not local to itself.

RMI and RMI-IIOP

Remote Method Invocation (RMI) is one of the primary mechanisms in distributed object applications. It allows us to use interfaces to define remote objects. We can then call methods on these remote objects as if they were local. The exact wire-level transportation mechanism is implementation-specific. For example, Sun uses the Java Remote Method Protocol (JRMP) on top of TCP/IP, but other implementations, such as BEA WebLogic for instance, have their own protocol.

RMI-IIOP is an extension of RMI but over IIOP (Inter-ORB Protocol), which allows us to define a remote interface to any remote object that can be implemented in any language that supports OMG mapping and ORB. In Chapter 3, we'll take an in-depth look at how to write distributed applications with RMI.

JavaIDL

Through the use of **JavaIDL**, a Java client can invoke method calls on CORBA objects. These CORBA objects need not be written in Java but merely implement an IDL defined interface.

Developing J2EE Applications

The J2EE specification specifies the following steps in the application development and deployment process:

1. **Application component development**
During this step we model the business rules in the form of application components.

2. **Composition of application components into modules**
In this step, the application components are packaged into modules. This phase also involves providing deployment descriptors for each module.

3. **Composition of modules into applications**

This step integrates multiple modules into J2EE applications. This requires assembling one or more modules into a J2EE application, and supplying it with the descriptor files.

4. **Application deployment**

In the final step the packaged application is actually deployed and installed on the J2EE platform application server(s).

The J2EE platform specifies multiple levels for packaging, customization, and installation. Packaging is the process of composing applications out of application components. J2EE specifies a three-level packaging scheme for composing components into applications. These are: – application components, modules, and applications.

What is the purpose of these stages for application development and deployment? In J2EE, application architecture starts with decomposing the application into modules, and modules into application components. This is a top-down process towards building fine-grained building blocks. Once the development of these building blocks is achieved, we need to construct higher-level constructs from these fine-grained blocks. The notion of application packaging and deployment in multiple levels attempts to achieve this. In this process, we compose fine-grained application components into modules, and then modules into applications.

Application Development and Deployment Roles

Before we look at the development and deployment process in a bit more detail, let's take a brief sidetrack to examine who should be doing what. The J2EE specification, as well as defining a process, also defines a number of roles in development of J2EE applications:

❑ **J2EE Product Provider**

The J2EE Product Provider provides the base J2EE platform upon which we develop our applications. This will be our relevant server vendor who implements the container architecture and the J2EE APIs are defined by the J2EE specification.

❑ **Application Component Provider**

This is essentially the application developer who creates the application functionality, although it is possible to sub-divide the role into specific areas of expertise, for example, web developer, EJB developer, etc.

❑ **Application Assembler**

As we will see shortly, the application assembler takes the application components and packages them together through a series of modules and descriptor files so they can be deployed to the production servers.

❑ **Deployer**

The deployer takes the packaged application, installs, and configures it for the particular operating environment on which the application will be running.

❑ **System Administrator**

The System Administrator is responsible for maintaining and administering the application once it has been deployed.

❑ **Tool Provider:**

The Tool Provider provides tools that can be of use in the development and deployment of application components.

Note that this classification of roles may or may not suit your specific application, and this classification should only be considered as a typical set-up to provide some guidance.

Application Component Development

In J2EE, the development process starts with designing and developing application components. We'll be spending most of the book looking at this so there's no need to go any further here.

Composition of Application Components into Modules

A module is used to package one or more related application components of the same type. Apart from the application components, each module also includes a deployment descriptor describing the structure of the module. There are three types of modules in J2EE:

❑ **Web Modules**
A web module is a deployable unit consisting of Java Servlets, JSP pages, JSP tag libraries, library JAR files, HTML/XML documents, and other public resources such as images, applet class files, etc. A web module is packaged into a **Web ARchive file**, also called a **WAR** file. A WAR file is similar to a JAR file, except that a WAR file contains a WEB-INF directory with the deployment description contained in a web.xml file. We'll see more details of web modules and their packaging in later chapters.

❑ **EJB Modules**
An EJB module is a deployable unit consisting of EJBs, associated library JAR files, and resources. EJB modules are packaged into JAR files, with a deployment descriptor (ejb-jar.xml) in the META-INF directory of the JAR file.

❑ **Java Modules**
A Java module is a group of Java client classes packaged into JAR files. The deployment descriptor for a Java module is an application-client.xml file.

Composition of Modules into Applications

The highest level of packaging is in the form of applications. Each J2EE application is an independent unit of code within a virtual sandbox of its own. Typically, J2EE containers load each application using a different class loader such that each application is isolated from others. The purpose of such isolation is to allow multiple J2EE applications to coexist within a J2EE container.

A J2EE application consists of one or more modules composed into an **Enterprise Archive (EAR) file**. An EAR file is similar to a JAR file, except that it contains an application.xml file (located in the META-INF directory) describing the application:

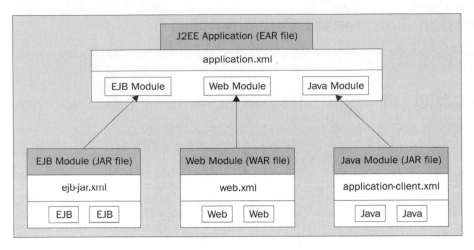

What is the role of the multiple descriptor files in the above figure? Fine-grained application components can be customized while integrating them into modules. This necessitates the use of a deployment descriptor in a module. However, not all information related to final deployment onto a J2EE platform will be available at the time of assembling modules. In addition, we need a means of specifying which modules make up the application. The `application.xml` file lets you achieve this.

The advantage of this structure is that it allows reuse at different levels. Application components can be reused across multiple web modules. For example, web components related to user login can be packaged into different web modules responsible for online ordering and customer service. Similarly, modules can be reused across multiple applications, so that an EJB module for shopping cart management need not be restricted to a single application, but can be packaged into multiple online commerce applications.

Without such a reusable means of packaging, the goal of component reuse will only be partially met. By defining the above structure, the J2EE allows more refined reuse of application components.

Application Deployment

Finally, application deployment is the process of installing and customizing packaged modules onto a J2EE platform. This process involves two steps:

❑ Preparing the application for installing onto a J2EE application server. This involves copying the EAR files onto the application server, generating additional implementation classes with the help of the container, and finally installing the application onto the server.

❑ Configuring the application with application server-specific information. An example is creating data sources and connection factories, as the actual creation of these objects is application server-specific.

Summary

You should now have a better idea of the topology of the J2EE landscape. In particular, we have seen how J2EE extends the traditional multi-tier architecture of distributed computing to include the concept of containers. We discussed the constituents of this container architecture, with relation to:

- ❑ The component contract
- ❑ Container services
- ❑ Declarative services
- ❑ Other run-time facilities

The following are the key points of this discussion:

- ❑ J2EE is a container-centric architecture. A container is more than a simple runtime: it provides several levels of abstraction. In later chapters, we will examine how these abstractions simplify application development.

- ❑ J2EE recognizes the need for composing components into modules, and modules into applications. This is an attempt to standardize reuse of application components and modules.

- ❑ J2EE represents a very intuitive approach to building applications. While the design process is top-down, the deployment process is bottom-up and is a composition process, composing modules from components and applications from components.

Having finished our introductory look at the J2EE perspective of server-side Java programming, we will start our more detailed journey with a closer look at service lookup using JNDI.

Data
JDBC
RDMS
Application Logic
Client
Web Container
Servlets
JSPs
Tag Library
HTTP(S)
(X)HTML/ XML
JavaMail
Mail Server
RMI/IIOP
JNDI
JTA
JDBC
JMS
JavaMail
JAAS
JCA
JAXP
J2EE Application Server
RMI
Java Application
Applet
IIOP
CORBA Server
Client Application
Session Beans
JAF
JNDI
Directory Servic
JMS
Message Queu

2

Directory Services and JNDI

The **Java Naming and Directory Interfaces (JNDI)** are designed to simplify access to the directory infrastructure used in the development of advanced network applications. **Directories** are a special type of databases that provide quick access to their data stores. Databases are usually thought of as the relational data storage model, as in Oracle, Microsoft SQL Server, etc. By contrast, a directory database stores information in a read-optimized, hierarchical form.

Traditionally, we have to use different APIs to access different directory services, such as Sun's Network Information Service (NIS) or the **Lightweight Directory Access Protocol (LDAP)**. However, JNDI supplies a standard API to access any type of directory. JNDI also allows us to store and retrieve Java objects on the network, such as from a J2EE-compliant application server, like BEA WebLogic.

In this chapter, we'll be answering the following questions:

❑   What is a directory service?

❑   What separates JNDI from a traditional directory API?

❑   What is LDAP, and how do we use it to work with a directory service?

Furthermore, by looking at some example programs, we'll demonstrate first hand the practical applications of using JNDI to manage directory information.

Naming and Directory Services

"The network is the computer" is a phrase that Sun Microsystems has used to sell a lot of hardware and software. It is also the central tenet of much successful Java programming. One of the reasons why Java has become so popular is because it has made network programming much easier than other languages, such as C. This is because Java is much more than just a language specification. Java has networking built into its core API, whereas languages such C require an external library to reproduce the same functionality. Built-in networking support helps make Java the success it is because the number of computers connected using the standard Internet protocols has grown at an exceptional rate.

Devices are often placed on a network to help make them easier to manage, which saves time, which in turn saves money. For example, in a multi-building complex a networked environmental system can report to a central server. This server can display the status of all of the air conditioners and thermostats in the various buildings to the environmental engineers. From this central source, the engineers can know when a unit is overheating, or when to schedule maintenance. If the environmental system were not networked, the members of the team would have to check each device individually, which would be a time-consuming task when dealing with dozens of buildings.

Of course, even if we have networked devices and a great development language like Java, it can be difficult to combine them effectively. Whenever a device is added to the network, configuration information must to be set. This configuration information includes properties like an IP address, a domain name, the abilities of each networked device, and user privileges for each device. This information is usually available to the device itself, but not always to the outside world.

For example, when we set up a new workstation on the network, we often need to configure it to use a specific network printer. Discovering the capabilities of the printers that are available is often not possible, because the printers do not make this information available. By using a directory service and Java, the printer's capabilities and configuration can be built into the network. Devices can then query the printer to discover if, for example, it can print in color.

The designers of the J2EE environment and its APIs understood these problems. This is why the Java Naming and Directory Interfaces (JNDI) API was made a fundamental part of J2EE. You will find that virtually all large J2EE applications use JNDI at some point.

To understand JNDI, we need a basic understanding of what a naming and a directory service are. We also need to understand why it is important that JNDI provides a standardized interface to these services.

Naming Services

> **A naming service is a service that enables the creation of a standard name for a given set of data.**

On the Internet, each host has a **Fully Qualified Domain Name (FQDN)** such as www.wrox.com or www.coe.unt.edu. An FQDN is constructed from a hostname, zero or more sub-domain names, and a domain name. For example:

FQDN	Hostname	Sub-Domain Name	Domain Name
www.coe.unt.edu	www	coe	unt.edu
www.wrox.com	www	–	wrox.com
www.p2p.wrox.com	www	p2p	wrox.com

Each FQDN is unique, so there is only one www.wrox.com and only one www.coe.unt.edu allowed. By using sub-domains and domain names, systems that share the same hostname are still considered separate entities. For example, www.p2p.wrox.com is different from www.wrox.com. In this case, the sub-domain p2p.wrox.com is actually below the root domain of wrox.com providing for its own unique namespace.

Directory Services

> A directory service is a special type of database that is optimized for read access by using various indexing, caching, and disk access techniques. The information in a directory service is described using a hierarchical information model.

The hierarchical information model that directory services employ is in contrast to the relational information model employed by databases, such as Oracle and Microsoft SQL Server, which are built to handle transactions; an operation only succeeds if a collection of smaller operations is successfully completed. A directory service is also usually designed so that it can be distributed and replicated.

A directory service will always have a naming service, but a naming service does not always have a directory service. A simple example of a directory service is a telephone book. A telephone book allows a user to look up the telephone number of a person quickly – provided the user knows the name of the person they are looking for.

Staying with this example for a moment, we can emphasize the benefit of networked directory services. Namely, a directory service is only as useful as the freshness of its information and the efficiency of performing a lookup. Static resources, such as physical copies of phone books, TV Guides, etc., become obsolete soon after being published, and they usually only offer one means of access (for example, via "surname" in the case of a phone book). An electronic directory service, on the other hand, is clearly more dynamic and enables much more flexible searching. The information that you receive is likely to be as fresh as when you queried it.

There are many directory (and 'pseudo-directory') services in use on networks today. One commonly used directory service is the **Domain Naming Service (DNS)** used on the Internet. DNS takes an FQDN and returns an IP address. This service is vital to the Internet as successful communication between two computers relies on each system knowing the IP address of the other.

IP addresses currently consist of 32 bit numbers, for example 198.137.240.92, while a hostname takes the form of www.wrox.com. Computers are happy dealing with numbers, but most humans are better at remembering names – it is a lot easier to remember www.wrox.com than it is to remember 198.137.240.92. The DNS system is an example of a highly specialized directory service. When we enter a hostname in a browser, the computer gets the server's IP address via DNS. We'll take a more direct look at the practical side of DNS with an example later in the chapter.

DNS actually provides us with a bit more information than just IP addresses. For example, the names of the machines that are responsible for routing mail, but it is still highly specialized in what it does.

Organizations often use one or more of the following general-purpose directory services:

- ❏   Novell Directory Services (NDS)
- ❏   Network Information Services (NIS/NIS+)
- ❏   Active Directory Services (ADS)
- ❏   Windows NT Domains

Although the NT Domains service is not a true directory service, many people try to use it as one.

Each of these directory services provides more information than the simple name-to-IP mapping we get from DNS. Each directory service also allows information to be stored about users (usernames and passwords), user groups (for access control), and computers (ethernet and IP addresses). NDS and ADS allow more functions – such as the location of network printers, and software – than either NIS or NT Domains.

As there are so many directory services (each with a proprietary protocol) and we have so many systems on our networks, some larger problems have arisen. Essentially, they boil down to two issues:

- ❑ Keeping track of users
- ❑ Keeping track of network resources such as computers and printers.

A particularly difficult scenario would be where users will need access to:

- ❑ A Novell system (which uses NDS) for file and print sharing
- ❑ An account on a Windows NT box for running Microsoft Office
- ❑ An account on an UNIX box (using NIS) to use e-mail and publish web pages

Unfortunately for network managers, none of these directory services can easily interact with each other, which makes it very difficult for the traditional application developer to interact with several different directory services. As a result users often end up with different usernames and passwords on each system. If a user leaves, it can be difficult to ensure that all their accounts are removed. Security holes occur in the form of 'orphan' accounts, which are accounts that belong to users who are no longer with an organization, yet still have open access to the systems.

A solution to these problems is to use JNDI, which provides a standard API to a variety of directory services. However, because not everyone uses Java, there needs to be another way to make it easier to communicate directory information between systems. The way to do this is to use LDAP.

LDAP

The **Lightweight Directory Access Protocol (LDAP)** was developed in the early 1990s as a standard directory protocol. LDAP is now probably the most popular directory protocol and, because JNDI can access LDAP, we'll spend some time learning how to harness LDAP to improve Java applications with JNDI.

> *LDAP can trace its roots back to the X.500 protocol (also known as the 'Heavy' Directory Access Protocol), which was originally based on the OSI networking protocols (an early 'competitor' to the Internet protocols.*

You will often interact with a server that has been specifically built for LDAP, such as the **iPlanet Directory Server**. However, LDAP can be a frontend to any type of data store. Because of this, most popular directory services now have an LDAP front-end of some type including NIS, NDS, Active Directory, and even Windows NT Domains.

> **LDAP defines how clients should access data on the server. It does not, however, specify how the data should be stored on the server.**

LDAP Data

Data in LDAP is organized in a hierarchical tree, called a **Directory Information Tree (DIT)**. Each 'leaf' in the DIT is called an entry and the first entry in a DIT is called the root entry.

An entry comprise a **Distinguished Name (DN)** and any number of attribute-value pairs. The DN is the name of an entry and must be unique, like the unique key of a relational database table. A DN shows how the entry is related to the rest of the DIT, just as the full path name of a file shows how it is related to the rest of the files on a system.

The path to a file on a system reads left to right when reading from root to file. A DN reads right to left when reading from root to entry, for example:

```
uid=scarter, ou=People, o=airius.com
```

The leftmost part of a DN is called a **Relative Distinguished Name (RDN)** and is made up of an attribute-value pair that is in the entry. The RDN in this example would be uid=scarter.

LDAP attributes often use mnemonics as their names. These are some of the more common LDAP attributes:

LDAP Attribute	Definition
cn	Common name
sn	Surname
givenname	First name
uid	User ID
dn	Distinguished Name
mail	E-mail address

Attributes can have one or more values. For example, a user can have more than one e-mail address so they would need more than one value for their mail attribute. Attribute values can be text or binary data and are referred to in name-value pairs.

There is also a special attribute called objectclass. The objectclass attribute of an entry specifies what attributes are required and what attributes are allowed in a particular entry. Like objects in Java, object classes in LDAP can be extended. When an object class is extended for a particular entry, the object class keeps the existing attributes, but new attributes can be specified.

Here is an example LDAP entry (which we'll see more of later in this chapter) represented in the **LDAP Data Interchange Format (LDIF)**, which is the most common way to show LDAP data in a human-readable format:

```
dn: uid=scarter, ou=People, o=fedup.com
cn: Sam Carter
sn: Carter
givenname: Sam
objectclass: top
objectclass: person
objectclass: organizationalPerson
objectclass: inetOrgPerson
```

```
ou: Accounting
ou: People
l: Sunnyvale
uid: scarter
mail: scarter@fedup.com
telephonenumber: +1 408 555 4798
facsimiletelephonenumber: +1 408 555 9751
roomnumber: 4612
```

Attributes also have matching rules. These rules tell the server how it should decide whether a particular entry is a 'match' or not for a given query. The possible matching rules are:

Matching Rule	Meaning
DN	Attribute is in the form of a Distinguished Name
Case-Insensitive String (CIS)	Attribute can match if the value of the query equals the attribute's value, regardless of case
Case-Sensitive String (CSS)	Attribute can match if the value of the query equals the attribute's value including the case
Telephone	Is the same as CIS except that characters like "–" and "()" are ignored when determining the match
Integer	Attribute match is determined using only numbers
Binary	Attribute matches if the value of the query and the value of the attribute are the same binary values (for example, searching a LDAP database for a particular photo)

The definition of attributes, attribute matching rules, and the relationship between object classes and attributes are defined in the server's schema. A server contains a pre-defined schema but, as long as the server supports the LDAP v3 protocol as defined in RFC 2251 (http://www.ietf.org/rfc/rfc2251.txt), the schema can be extended to include new attributes and object classes.

LDAP servers have other benefits. They support referrals – pointers to other LDAP directories where data resides – so a single LDAP server could search millions of entries from just one client request and LDAP data can be replicated to improve reliability and speed. LDAP also has a very strong security model using ACLs to protect data inside the server and supporting the **Secure Socket Layers (SSL)**, **Transport Layer Security (TLS)**, and **Simple Authentication and Security Layer (SASL)** protocols.

> *LDAP has growing momentum as a central directory service for network systems. For more information about LDAP you should see* Implementing LDAP *by Mark Wilcox, from Wrox Press, ISBN 1-861002-21-1.*

Introducing JNDI

While LDAP is growing in popularity and in usage, it is still a long way from being ubiquitous. Other directory services such as NIS are still in widespread use and are likely to remain so for some time yet. Another issue is that enterprise applications often need to support existing distributed computing standards such as the **Common Object Request Broker Architecture (CORBA)**, which is heavily used in many large organizations to allow different types of applications to interact with each other.

CORBA is a language- and platform-independent architecture that enables distributed application programming, where an application on one machine can access a function of a different application located on a different machine as if it was calling an internal function. CORBA uses the `COSNaming` (CORBA Object Service) service to define the location of available objects.

To overcome these difficulties, a standard Java API has been created to interact with naming and directory services. This API is analogous to how developers use JDBC to interact with all sorts of databases.

JNDI is very important for the long-term development of Java, particularly the Enterprise JavaBeans (EJB) initiative. The significance of EJBs to J2EE is reflected in the fact that a large proportion of this book is dedicated to them. Starting with Chapter 16, we'll see first-hand the importance of JNDI to the EJB functionality. A key component of the EJB technology is the ability to store and retrieve Java objects on the network. A directory service is going to be the primary data store for stable Java objects, which are retrieved from the network more often than they are stored. This is because when objects are loaded from the network, we want to be able to locate them quickly and a directory service enables very fast lookup and retrieval of data. This data can be anything, including a particular user's record or binary data like a serialized Java object.

The following diagrams will help to illustrate the relationship between directory services, JNDI, and LDAP. The first diagram shows the relationship between a client and a variety of directory services. Each directory service requires its own API, which adds complexity and "code bloat" to our client application:

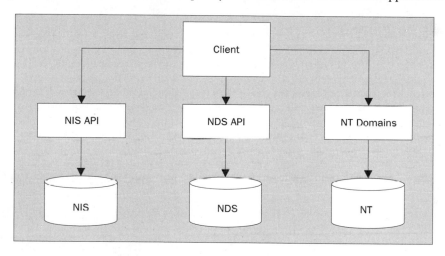

This can be simplified by using JNDI. There are still multiple servers and multiple APIs underneath, but to the application developer, it is appears to be a single API:

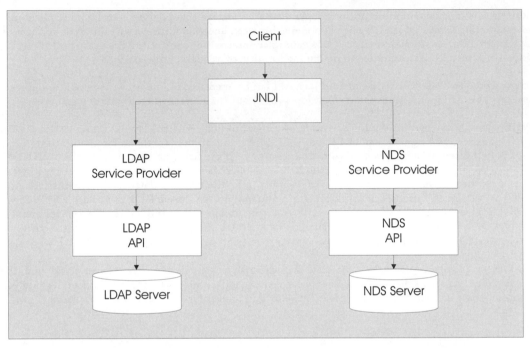

So, as application developers, we now have an easier time developing network applications because we can concentrate on a single API. However, we still face potential problems because not all JNDI service providers are created equal. **Service providers** in JNDI terminology are the drivers that allow interaction with different directory services. Each directory service is clearly different – they name their entries differently and have different capabilities – so developers still build applications that are larger and more prone to failure.

More importantly, it can be difficult to integrate with systems that can understand LDAP but are unable to use Java.

Finally, we show how JNDI and LDAP can work together, providing the most elegant solution:

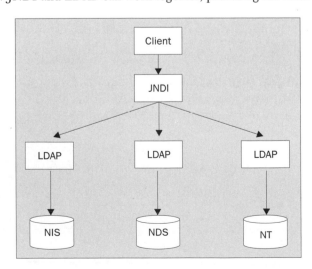

Here we use JNDI to communicate with various LDAP servers. The developer only has to worry about one particular protocol (LDAP) and one API (JNDI). Of course, we are relying on vendors to provide LDAP interfaces to their proprietary protocols. However, this is not a problem as for these popular directory services, there are additional products that allow us to communicate with them via LDAP.

The Tradeoffs

While JNDI provides a common API for programming to different directory services, there are tradeoffs that have to be made:

- ❑ One such tradeoff is that there is a lot of overhead. For example, every `DirContext` object (the objects that JNDI uses to interact with a directory service) must support a number of methods, most of which you will never use. When you implement a `DirContext` object, it is simple to leave them empty so that they do not cause problems with your application, but it does add extra weight in terms of memory and compiling time during program execution. We'll see an example of this later in this chapter.

- ❑ In addition, so that JNDI can keep a common interface, it does not always support all of the functions of the directory service. A good example of this is the LDAP `compare` command. This enables us to compare a particular value of an attribute in a single entry in the LDAP server. The LDAP server must return a result code instead of a full search result set, thus making the compare operation lightweight and quick. However, JNDI does not support a true LDAP compare, because LDAP is the only directory service that supports such an operation. Instead, JNDI performs a simple search that physically retrieves the entry into memory from the server and performs the compare operation in the application. The result appears the same to the application but we no longer have the benefits of a real LDAP compare.

- ❑ Finally, there is no way to gain direct access to the directory server connection, which means that it's very difficult to implement connection pooling or to check for connection timeouts in an application.

For most applications, these drawbacks do not present a serious problem. JNDI provides a common API to a variety of directory services, which is included as a standard part of Java, in the same way that JDBC provides a standard API to relational databases. In some cases, JNDI may be the only available API for a particular directory service like DNS or a Java application server like BEA WebLogic.

However, in some cases, applications do need low-level access to the directory service and if the application does not need any of the services that JNDI provides (like storage and retrieval of Java objects), we may want to turn to a low-level Java API. For example, in LDAP there is the Netscape Directory SDK for Java, which is actually more mature than the JNDI LDAP API. It is an open source SDK, available at http://www.mozilla.org/directory/.

JNDI may also not be the best solution when an application needs to manipulate files on the local file system. Unless Java objects like `DataSource` objects for JDBC programming are to be loaded, it is better in this case to use the standard classes available in the `java.io` package.

Why Use JNDI When We Have LDAP?

So, why do we need JNDI if we can communicate to systems via LDAP? Similarly, why do we need LDAP when we have JNDI? To answer these questions, let's look at how we could use JNDI or LDAP without the other.

LDAP Without JNDI

LDAP is great way to converge access to directory data through a single protocol. This is useful not just in Java programming but to other types of applications as well.

For example, LDAP is a great way to provide a standards-based network address book (most e-mail packages now have the ability to query an LDAP server for e-mail address lookups) or to easily keep track of devices on a network.

JNDI provides the ability to directly talk to different network directory services when we do not need LDAP. For example, you may need to determine if someone has access to a particular application based on their membership in a particular NIS group or you might need to retrieve an MX record in a DNS server. JNDI makes it easier for the developer in these cases by providing a consistent API instead of having to learn how to do the same thing using different sets of APIs.

JNDI Without LDAP

While you could provide a similar service to LDAP for your Java applications through JNDI, this would only be useful to your Java applications and you would likely have to repeat it in every Java application you write that needs this type of service.

LDAP is an open standard maintained by the Internet Engineering Task Force (IETF). This means that it is accessible from a variety of different clients and vendors. This is one of the great things about the Internet and why the Internet-based protocols have replaced proprietary protocols as the primary means of network based communications.

What About XML?

When XML was first unveiled there was some discussion as to whether it would replace all previous technologies including Java and LDAP. Of course, this didn't happen. Instead XML has become the de facto standard for persisting data, in particular when you need to exchange persistent data between applications written in different application languages (for example between Visual Basic and Java).

XML also has a role in LDAP and JNDI. There is a particular XML specification for LDAP called the **Directory Services Markup Language (DSML)** that is being developed primarily to distribute directory information via an XML-RPC-based protocol like SOAP. It consists of a markup language for representing directory services in XML. For more details, take a look at http://www.dsml.org/.

DSML is designed to replace the standard way of exchanging LDAP data outside of the LDAP protocol. The current standard is the LDAP Data Interchange Format (LDIF) and that's what we'll use to display our examples in this chapter.

Using JNDI

Now that we have a basic understanding of directory services, JNDI, and LDAP, it is time to get our hands dirty by doing some work.

To use JNDI as described in this chapter we'll need the following:

❑ JDK 1.3 from Sun, which includes JNDI as standard, or the JNDI Software Development Kit (SDK) 1.2.2 (available from http://java.sun.com/jndi/).

❑ An LDAP v3-compliant directory server. Netscape's Directory server, available from http://www.iplanet.com/downloads/download/index.html, is used in this chapter. All the examples you will see in this chapter are using the arius.com sample data that comes with this directory server.

While JNDI ships with JDK 1.3 and higher, you might still need to get the `ldap.jar` file from the JNDI 1.2.2 to get all of the functionality, including the ability to use LDAP controls and to store/retrieve RMI objects in an LDAP server.

Installing JNDI

Here are the general steps to follow to get things working on a typical system:

❑ Obtain connection information from your LDAP server administrator or install an LDAP v3-compliant server. I have used a variety of LDAP servers for various developments, including openLDAP (http://www.openldap.org) on Red Hat Linux 6.2, Eudora's free LDAP server for Windows (http://www.eudora.com), and The IPlanet 4 & 5 Directory servers (http://www.iplanet.com) on both Red Hat Linux 6.2 and Windows 2000.

❑ Install JDK 1.3, which contains JNDI and the basic LDAP provider. Unless you're using advanced LDAP features such as controls, you will not need to install anything else except the JDK 1.3. If you're exploring advanced LDAP features, read the JNDI page at http://java.sun.com/jndi/ for more information.

Now we are ready to use JNDI and LDAP.

JNDI Service Providers

You cannot use JNDI without using a service provider so we need understand what they are.

> A service provider is a set of Java classes that enable you to communicate with a directory service similar to the way in which a JDBC driver enables you to communicate to a database.

For a service provider to be available for use in JNDI it must implement the Context interface. Most of the service providers you will use will likely implement the DirectoryContext interface, which extends the Context interface to enable directory services.

What this means is that we only have to learn JNDI to know the API calls to connect to a naming or directory service, while the service provider worries about the ugly details like the actual network protocol and encoding/decoding values.

Unfortunately, service providers are not a panacea for using directory services. We must know something about the underlying directory service so that we can correctly name our entries and build the correct search queries. Unlike relational databases, directory services do not share a common query language such as SQL.

In JNDI 1.2, service providers can support a concept of **federation** where a service provider can pass an operation to another service provider if it does not understand the naming or operation scheme. For example if we wanted to find out the MX record (this contains the preferred destination e-mail server for a domain) for a particular domain from DNS, but our initial service provider was LDAP, it would not be able to answer the request. If federation was enabled it would be able to pass the request to the next service provider on the federation list, and, if it was a DNS service provider, it would be able to handle the request for us.

Ideally, this should be transparent to the application programmer. However, since this is a new feature, it has not been widely tested or implemented.

So to sum it up, a service provider enables our JNDI applications to communicate with a naming/directory service. The rest of the interfaces, classes, and exceptions all revolve around our interaction with a service provider.

How to Obtain JNDI Service Providers

If we download the JNDI SDK, we'll see that, along with the API and documentation, it comes with a number of existing service providers. These include providers for LDAP, NIS, COS, and the RMI registry and file system. Many different vendors also provide service providers for other directory services, or as replacements for the default providers that Sun ships. For example, Novell has a service provider for NDS, while both IBM and Netscape have written alternative service providers for LDAP.

It is easy to switch between service providers. For example to use the default Sun LDAP service provider we would make a call like this:

```
// Specify which class to use for our JNDI provider
env.put(Context.INITIAL_CONTEXT_FACTORY,
        "com.sun.jndi.ldap.LdapCtxFactory");
```

Now to switch to using IBM's LDAP service provider you would simply replace the com.sun.jndi.ldap.LdapCtxFactory with the full package name of the IBM LDAP service provider like this:

```
// Specify which class to use for our JNDI provider
env.put(Context.INITIAL_CONTEXT_FACTORY,
        "com.ibm.jndi.LDAPCtxFactory");
```

There is a list of existing service providers at http://java.sun.com/products/jndi/serviceproviders.html

Developing Your Own Service Provider

You may also need to implement your own service provider if you need to use a directory service (such as Windows NT domains or Banyan Vines) that does not already have an existing service provider.

In the JNDI SDK Sun provides an example of how to write a service provider. This JNDI tutorial is available at: http://java.sun.com/products/jndi/tutorial/index.html. Sun also provides a PDF document that describes the process of writing a service provider at ftp://ftp.javasoft.com/docs/jndi/jndispi.pdf. Netscape's LDAP service provider is available as an opensource project at http://www.mozilla.org/directory/.

Java and LDAP

Before we begin to actively look at how to use LDAP in Java, we should take a brief look at what LDAP is commonly used for in Java applications.

There are three basic applications of LDAP in Java today:

❑   Access Control

❑   White Pages Services

❑   Distributed Computing Directory

Let's take a look at these applications in greater detail.

Access Control

All applications dictate which users can access them. This can range from allowing anyone who can click on the application's icon to start it up to allowing only a user who matches a particular retinal scan to do so. Most applications lie in between these two extremes.

Access control can be broken into authentication and authorization.

Authentication

Authentication is determining who the person using a piece of software is. Because of the nature of computing we can never be 100% certain of who the user is, but various authentication mechanisms improve the odds that the user is who they claim to be.

Authentication requires the use of a shared secret, the most common form of which is a password. The user gives a username and a password. The username is used to look up the person's record in a database (this database can be a simple flat file like the UNIX `passwd` file or a sophisticated database like LDAP) and if the password given is the same as that stored in the database then we assume that the user is who they say they are.

Password-based authentication is the simplest but one of the least secure methods; because passwords are written down, they can be sniffed in transit over the networks, or they can be easily cracked when a nefarious person gains unauthorized access to the password database. In today's networked world, the biggest threat to passwords (outside of asking the user personally for their password) is to travel over the network in the clear. Thus, it is best to do things to protect passwords when they travel over the network. Two common mechanisms are **MD5** and **Secure Socket Layers (SSL)**.

Under MD5 the client first creates an MD5 hash of the password before passing it across the network. The server then compares this hash with the one it has stored in its database. While this does prevent someone from guessing the plaintext password and using it to login to other systems, this doesn't prevent someone from stealing the hashed password. This stolen hashed password could be used just like a stolen plaintext password to gain access to the system (known as the "man in the middle" attack). Another problem is that most systems do not store their passwords as MD5 (although certain BSD implementations do) so you might be forced to change everyone's passwords before you can implement this system.

Under SSL the entire network connection is encrypted. This protects not only the password, but also any data transferred between the client and the server. This is why SSL is often used to protect e-commerce applications. It is also useful in LDAP because LDAP servers often contain sensitive data like personal identification numbers, driver license numbers, etc. We do not want this data to travel over the network insecurely anymore than we want passwords to.

SSL also adds another form of authentication altogether and that is the **digital certificate**. Digital certificates use public key encryption to improve the authentication process. Under public key encryption the user has a private key, which only they have access to. All data encrypted by the private key can only be decrypted by the public key and vice versa. The server has access to their public key. Under SSL (which already encrypts all data transfer), the server sends the user some data to encrypt with their private key. The user encrypts the data and sends it back to the server. If the server can decrypt the data with the public key and the data matches, then it's assumed to be the user. The digital certificate standard (X.509) is an extension of the original directory services standard. Thus LDAP is one of the best ways of managing digital certificates. It is worth noting though that this user authentication actually happens *after* the SSL server has been authenticated.

LDAP has the capability to support a wide range of authentication services including passwords, digital certificates, and the Simple Authentication and Security Layer (SASL) protocol.

Authorization

After we have authenticated someone, we need to determine what they are actually allowed to do. For example, we might decide that only members of the Dwarves have the right to access the Snow White files. We might also add finer granularity than just simply saying someone has access or not. For example, we could say that members of the Jedi Council have full rights over items in the Force database, while members of the Jedi Knights have the ability to edit certain elements in the Force database, whereas padawan only have the ability to read the Force database.

We can use LDAP to develop sophisticated authorization policies.

White Pages Services

White pages services are services that enable someone to look up users based on attributes contained in their entries. For example, you can look up Mark Wilcox's e-mail address, and obtain the telephone number of the Engineering office, the building number of Human Resources, etc. They are called **white pages** because this type of information is similar to the type of information you find in the white pages of US telephone books.

These types of services are the most public of all LDAP operations and are what many, if not most, people use LDAP for. Under Java, we're putting it second because most white pages services are provided through an LDAP client found in an e-mail package like Netscape Messenger or Microsoft Outlook instead of through a Java application.

Java applications normally perform this function either as the back-end for a web page LDAP interface or to provide workflow services in an enterprise Java application. As an example, let's look at a simple situation in which John enters an electronic purchase order request for 100 widgets from Acme Widgets. The purchasing application has a business rule that says after a person enters a PO request it must be sent to the PO authorization person for their group. Therefore, the application looks up in LDAP to find out who the PO authorizer is for John's group in LDAP and sends them an e-mail notification using the authorizer's LDAP e-mail attribute.

Distributed Computing Directory

One of the fastest growing segments of server programming is distributed network programming, where an application uses code that actually resides separately from the running application. The code can be either in a separate JVM (or similar engine like a CORBA server) or on a different physical machine located on the other side of the world.

We often use this type of programming to make it easier to reuse existing legacy code or to improve application performance by offloading heavy processing onto a separate machine.

In Java, there are three distributed architectures available:

- ❑ Remote Method Invocation (RMI)
- ❑ Common Object Request Broker Architecture (CORBA)
- ❑ Enterprise JavaBeans (EJB)

All three provide a registry service that a client application uses to locate the distributed code. Because its specification was developed after JNDI, EJB utilizes JNDI for its registry services.

RMI and CORBA use their own independent registry services. One of the problems with these services is that they do not provide a mechanism to search their registry to discover what objects are available to use.

With JNDI and LDAP you can provide indirect references with the JNDI `Reference` object to these services. For example, you can have an entry with a name of `"Real Time Stock Quote Service"` that has an attribute that contains the actual network location to the RMI or CORBA object.

This type of service makes your code easier to understand and gives you more flexibility in your application. For example, if you need to move a particular distributed object to a new server, instead of having to change all of the applications that reference that object, you only have to change its location in LDAP and then all of the client applications will update their locations automatically the next time they reference the object.

LDAP can also store other descriptive attributes in an entry, so you could store better descriptions of your object in the directory to build white pages for objects. People who have actually been a part of projects for their companies to develop centralized code libraries often find that developing the code was the easy part; making the code easy to find is where the difficulties arise. Using LDAP as a class directory is a solution to these problems.

We could add other elements to the description of our stock quote object example. For instance, we could add things such as the development language used, a note about its purpose, and the name of the developer or development team.

Application Configuration

LDAP can also be used to store configuration information about an application. This is particularly helpful where the application is used by the same user but on different machines and it would be helpful to provide the same configuration information regardless of what machine the user used to access it.

Now we will move from talking in hypothetical terms and explaining the basic concepts, to actual practice. In the remainder of this chapter, we will see some real code and how to perform basic LDAP operations with JNDI.

LDAP Operations

Before we can perform any type of operation on an LDAP sever, we must first obtain a reference and a network connection to the LDAP server. We must also specify how we wish to be bound to the server – either anonymously or as an authenticated user. Many Internet-accessible LDAP servers allow some type of anonymous access (generally read-only abilities for attributes like e-mail addresses and telephone numbers), but LDAP also supports very advanced security features via ACLs that are dependent upon who the connection is authenticated as.

For example, an LDAP server may have several layers of rights for any given entry:

❑ Anonymous users can see an employee's e-mail address and telephone number.

❑ The employee can see their entire entry, but only modify certain attributes such as telephone number, password, and office room number.

❑ A user's manager can update an employee's telephone number and office room number, but nothing else. They can also see the employee's entire record.

❑ A small group, the Directory Administrators, have full rights to the entire server including the ability to add or remove any entry.

Standard LDAP Operations

There are a few standard operations in LDAP. These are:

❑ Connect to the LDAP server

❑ Bind to the LDAP server (you can think of this step as authenticating)

❑ Perform a series of LDAP operations:

   ❑ Search the server

   ❑ Add a new entry

   ❑ Modify an entry

   ❑ Delete an entry

❑ Disconnect from the LDAP server

We will step through each of these, demonstrating with examples where relevant.

Connecting to the LDAP Server with JNDI

We must first obtain a reference to an object that implements the `DirContext` interface. In most applications, we will use an `InitialDirContext` object that takes a hash table as a parameter. This hash table can contain a number of different references. It should contain a reference to a field with the key `Context.INITIAL_CONTEXT_FACTORY`, with a value of the fully qualified class name of the service provider, the hostname, and the port number to the LDAP server. These additional properties are set using the `Context.PROVIDER_URL` key. The value of this key should be the protocol, hostname, and port number to the LDAP server like this: `ldap://localhost:389`.

We first create a `Hashtable` to store our environmental variables that JNDI will use to connect to the directory service:

```
Hashtable env = new Hashtable();
```

Next, we specify the fully qualified package name of our JNDI provider. We are using the standard Sun LDAP service provider that comes with the JNDI SDK:

```
// Specify which class to use for our JNDI provider
env.put(Context.INITIAL_CONTEXT_FACTORY, " com.sun.jndi.ldap.LdapCtxFactory");
```

We must specify the hostname and port number to our LDAP server, for example:

```
// Specify host and port to use for directory service
env.put(Context.PROVIDER_URL, "ldap://localhost:389");
```

Finally, we get a reference to our initial directory context with a call to the `InitialDirContext` constructor, giving it our hash table as its only parameter. A directory context tells JNDI what service provider we will be using, what naming/directory server we will be connecting to, from what location we will we be accessing the directory from initially (for example, the search base), and any authentication information:

```
// Get a reference to a directory context
DirContext ctx = new InitialDirContext(env);
```

Binding

If you use the default values, the connection will be bound as anonymous. Many LDAP servers provide some type of read access to their directory data (for example, for address book applications). Specifically the type of access an application has to the LDAP server is dependent upon the **Access Control Lists (ACLs)** of the LDAP server. The ACLs that apply to an operation are determined by how the application is bound or authenticated.

LDAP allows for an extremely flexible security model. ACLs determine what particular access is available to an entry by an application. Because an entry can have several ACLs defined, it is possible that an entry will have several different views to an application simply by changing the binding (for example, who the application is authenticated as). LDAP also supports Transport Security Layer (TSL also still known as Secure Socket Layer (SSL)) for protecting content 'over the wire' or to improve authentication via client-certificates. Finally, LDAP supports the Simple Authentication and Security Layer (SASL) protocol that enables you to use other authentication/encryption mechanisms such as Kerberos without "breaking" the protocol.

You can specify authentication by specifying the `Context.SECURITY_AUTHENTICATION`, `Context.SECURITY_PRINCIPAL`, and `Context.SECURITY_CREDENTIALS` in the hash table passed to the `InitialDirContext` object.

To specifically bind to the server, we must provide the environment with the method for our authentication (for example, "simple", SSL, or SASL). Then we must specify the DN of the entry we wish to bind as and the entry's password:

```
Hashtable env = new Hashtable();

// This sends the id and password as plain text over the wire
env.put(Context.PROVIDER_URL, "myhost");
env.put(Context.SECURITY_AUTHENTICATION,"simple");
env.put(Context.SECURITY_PRINCIPAL, MGR_DN);
env.put(Context.SECURITY_CREDENTIALS, MGR_PW);

// Get a reference to a directory context
DirContext ctx = new InitialDirContext(env);
```

Simple, SSL/TLS, and SASL Security

The latest LDAP specification, LDAP v3, allows for three types of security:

- ❑ Simple
- ❑ SSL/TLS
- ❑ SASL

Let's look at each type, in turn.

Simple

Simple security means that you will only authenticate to the server using standard plain-text user IDs and passwords without any encryption on the network. This is by far the most common, and least secure of the various authentication methods. It is insecure for two reasons, one of which is that user IDs and passwords are transmitted to the server over a public network, where anyone can steal the user IDs and passwords off the network. Secondly, there is nothing to guarantee that the person who types in the user ID and password is the actual owner of that user ID and password.

SSL/TLS

The **Secure Socket Layer** protocol was developed by Netscape Communications to improve the security of web-based transactions. It has become an official standard called **Transport Layer Security (TLS)**, but is still often referred to as SSL.

SSL allows you to encrypt your entire transaction over the network, making it very hard for anyone to steal the information (such as your user IDs and passwords). Standard SSL does not verify the identity of the person who typed in the user ID and password (however, it does ensure that the machine you are issuing your ID and password to is "the real server"). Most servers that implement SSL also support client-certificates (certificates are text files that are used to vouch for the identity of the server and client) for user authentication. Instead of presenting a user ID and password to the system, you can present a certificate to the server. If the certificate you present matches an allowed certificate, you are granted access.

Certificates are considered more secure because they are hard to fake. However, certificates are typically stored as a file on a local user's machine, which means that if the client machine is compromised, then a certificate can be used just like a stolen user ID and password. When certificates are stored locally, a mechanism must be developed to recover them if the machine they are stored on crashes or is upgraded. Certificates can be stored on smart cards instead of files on a local machine for more security and reliability. The issuing and managing of client certificates is still in the early stages of development.

SASL

The **Simple Authentication and Security Layer (SASL)** is an Internet standard for implementing authentication mechanisms besides simple or SSL.

There are two popular SASL mechanisms. One is the **MD5** that we saw earlier, based on comparison of hashed-passwords. MD5 doesn't encrypt the transaction and it doesn't solve the problem of "who typed in the password". If the MD5-hashed password is stolen while on its way to the server, a hacker could use that to gain access to the system, just as if it was a plain-text password. It does however, make it harder to guess what the password originally was, so if a hacker does steal the hashed password, they won't be able to guess what the password was to try and use it to gain access to other systems.

The second popular SASL mechanism is called **Kerberos**. Kerberos encrypts the transaction, and in a Kerberos-aware network, it is very easy to implement a single-logon environment because of the way Kerberos works. However, managing a Kerberos network is very time- and resource-consuming, so many organizations are yet to implement Kerberos.

You can easily write your own SASL mechanisms, if your LDAP server supports them. Thus, it would be possible to enable biometric authentication, once it becomes available (or if your organization has access to the technology already). Biometric authentication uses part of a person's body such as their thumbprint or iris for their user ID and password. These systems are very secure.

LDAP v2 and LDAP v3 Authentication

In LDAP v2, all clients had to authenticate themselves before performing any operations. In LDAP v3, however, if a client does not authenticate itself before performing an operation, the connection is assumed to be an anonymous authenticated connection.

Searching an LDAP Server

The most used operation on any LDAP server is the search operation. Any advanced LDAP applications use searching as their core functionality. Essentially, all search functions take an LDAP connection handle, the base to start the search from, the scope of the search, and a search filter. A search filter is like a SQL query in that you tell the server the criteria to use to find matching entries. Searches always use an attribute name and a value to look for. Filters can use Boolean logic and wildcards. Some servers, such as the Netscape Directory server, support even more advanced query abilities such as "sounds like".

> *For the search examples in this section, we will be accessing the arius.com sample data that comes with the Netscape Directory Server.*

Example LDAP Filters

Some typical LDAP filters are shown in the following table:

Description	LDAP Filter
Find all users with the last name of Carter	`sn = Carter`
Find all users with last names that start with "Ca"	`sn = Ca*`
Find all object classes of the type `GroupofUniqueNames` that have "Managers" in their Common Name	`(&(cn = * Managers * ) (objectclass=groupofuniquenames))`

In JNDI, we use the search method of the `DirContext` interface. This will return back a `NamingEnumeration` object if the search is successful.

Later in this section, we will show you the various ways you can manipulate the values of this object to get back attributes and values of each returned entry.

Determining LDAP Scope

When you perform a search, you must specify the node (which we refer to as the **base**) of the tree you want to start at, as well as the scope of the search. The scope defines exactly how much of the tree you want to search. There are three levels of scope.

Scope	Description
`LDAP_SCOPE_SUBTREE`	This scope starts at the base entry and searches everything below it including the base entry.

Table continued on following page

Scope	Description
LDAP_SCOPE_ONELEVEL	This scope searches the entire tree starting one level below the base entry. It does not include the base entry.
LDAP_SCOPE_BASE	This scope searches just the base entry, useful if you want to just get the attributes/values of one entry.

Next we'll examine these three levels of scope with the aid of some diagrams.

LDAP_SCOPE_SUBTREE

The first figure, below, illustrates a search using LDAP_SCOPE_SUBTREE:

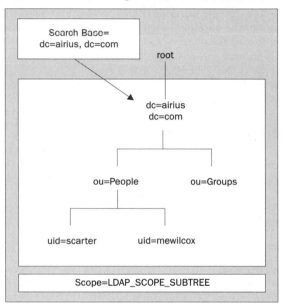

LDAP_SCOPE_ONELEVEL

Here we demonstrate an example of a search using LDAP_SCOPE_ONELEVEL:

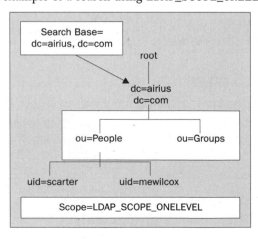

LDAP_SCOPE_BASE

Finally, we present a search using LDAP_SCOPE_BASE:

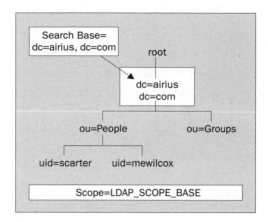

Performing a JNDI Search

We perform a search using the search() method of an object that implements the DirContext interface (such as the InitialDirContext class). The minimum requirement for this is the search base and a filter, although there are other parameters we can use to help manage the results.

We should note that in most LDAP APIs, we must specify the scope as a parameter in the LDAP search method. In JNDI, however, the scope is set in the SearchControls object, which is an optional parameter to the search() function of a DirContext interface (the InitialDirContext class provides an implementation of the search() function). By default, it is set to subtree. The search is actually performed with whatever object you have that implements the DirContext interface, such as the InitialDirContext class.

For our first example we'll show a very simple search example, where the search filter is "sn=Carter". This will return all entries that have a surname (the attribute specified by the mnemonic "sn") of Carter. This first example is an anonymous search.

The examples are non-GUI based to make it easier to understand what's going on, but there's nothing to prevent them from being included in a GUI. Remember, all of the source code for the examples described in this chapter can be downloaded from http://www.wrox.com. Here's what the code looks like:

```java
// Standard anonymous search
import java.util.Hashtable;
import java.util.Enumeration;

import javax.naming.*;
import javax.naming.directory.*;

public class JNDISearch {

    // Initial context implementation
    public static String INITCTX = "com.sun.jndi.ldap.LdapCtxFactory";
    public static String MY_HOST = "ldap://localhost:389";
    public static String MY_SEARCHBASE = "o=Airius.com";
    public static String MY_FILTER = "(sn=Carter)";
```

```java
public static void main(String args[]) {

    try {
        // Hashtable for environmental information
        Hashtable env = new Hashtable();

        // Specify which class to use for our JNDI provider
        env.put(Context.INITIAL_CONTEXT_FACTORY, INITCTX);

        // Specify host and port to use for directory service
        env.put(Context.PROVIDER_URL, MY_HOST);

        // Get a reference to a directory context
        DirContext ctx = new InitialDirContext(env);

        // Specify the scope of the search
        SearchControls constraints = new SearchControls();
        constraints.setSearchScope(SearchControls.SUBTREE_SCOPE);

        // Perform the actual search. We give it a searchbase, a filter,
        // and a the constraints containing the scope of the search.
        NamingEnumeration results = ctx.search(MY_SEARCHBASE,
                                               MY_FILTER, constraints);

        // Now step through the search results
        while (results != null && results.hasMore()) {
            SearchResult sr = (SearchResult) results.next();

            String dn = sr.getName();
            System.out.println("Distinguished Name is " + dn);

            Attributes attrs = sr.getAttributes();

            for (NamingEnumeration ne = attrs.getAll(); ne.hasMoreElements();) {
                Attribute attr = (Attribute) ne.next();
                String attrID = attr.getID();

                System.out.println(attrID + ":");
                for (Enumeration vals = attr.getAll(); vals.hasMoreElements();) {
                    System.out.println("\t" + vals.nextElement());
                }
            }
            System.out.println("\n");
        }
    } catch (Exception e) {
        e.printStackTrace();
        System.exit(1);
    }
}
}
```

After compiling and running this code, the output should look something like that shown in the screenshot below:

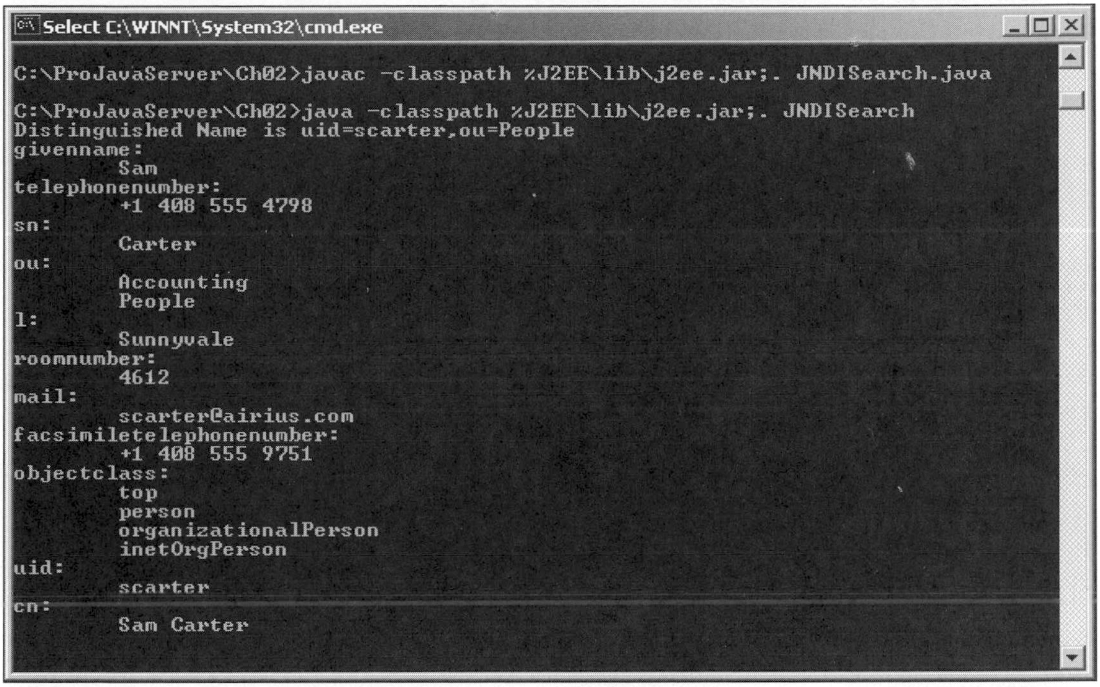

```
C:\ProJavaServer\Ch02>javac -classpath %J2EE\lib\j2ee.jar;. JNDISearch.java

C:\ProJavaServer\Ch02>java -classpath %J2EE\lib\j2ee.jar;. JNDISearch
Distinguished Name is uid=scarter,ou=People
givenname:
        Sam
telephonenumber:
        +1 408 555 4798
sn:
        Carter
ou:
        Accounting
        People
l:
        Sunnyvale
roomnumber:
        4612
mail:
        scarter@airius.com
facsimiletelephonenumber:
        +1 408 555 9751
objectclass:
        top
        person
        organizationalPerson
        inetOrgPerson
uid:
        scarter
cn:
        Sam Carter
```

How the Search Program Works

We perform a search using the search() method of an object that implements the DirContext interface (such as the InitialDirContext class). The minimum requirement for this is the search base and a filter. There are other parameters we can use to help manage the results. If the search is successful, a NamingEnumeration object will be returned.

After we get the initial context (which we set the variable ctx to), we next specify the scope of our search. If we do not specify a scope, JNDI will assume a scope of subtree, so this next line is actually redundant but is useful to show you how to specify the scope.

Let's now go through the process of how this code works. First, we set the scope to subtree:

```
// Specify the scope of the search
SearchControls constraints = new SearchControls();
constraints.setSearchScope(SearchControls.SUBTREE_SCOPE);
```

After we specify the scope, we can perform the actual search like this:

```
// Peform the actual search
NamingEnumeration results = ctx.search(MY_SEARCHBASE, MY_FILTER, constraints);
```

The NamingEnumeration class is equivalent to the SearchResults class in the Netscape Directory SDK for Java.

Each element in a NamingEnumeration object will contain a SearchResult object that we can retrieve:

```
SearchResult sr = (SearchResult) results.next();
```

Then we can get the DN of an entry:

```
String dn = sr.getName();
```

To get the attributes of an entry you use the getAttributes() method of the SearchResult class:

```
Attributes attrs = sr.getAttributes();
```

This will return a concrete object that implements the Attributes interface (the InitialDirContext class returns a BasicAttributes object).

After we have an Attributes object (remember this is a collection class), we can then step through the attributes using a NamingEnumeration object like this:

```
for (NamingEnumeration ne = attrs.getAll(); ne.hasMoreElements();) {
  Attribute attr = (Attribute)ne.next();
  String attrID = attr.getID();

  System.out.println(attrID + ":");
  for (Enumeration vals = attr.getAll();vals.hasMoreElements();) {
    System.out.println("\t" + vals.nextElement());
  }
}
```

The NamingEnumeration class gives us methods that we can use to step through each attribute that was returned in our search. Each element in the NamingEnumeration object will contain an Attribute object that represents an attribute and its values.

Each element in the Attribute object is an object that has implemented the Attribute interface (the InitialDirContext class uses BasicAttribute objects). The getID() method of the Attribute interface returns the name of the attribute. The getAll() method of the Attribute interface will return back a standard Java Enumeration object, which we can then access to get the values of the individual attribute.

In every LDAP server, there are certain attributes that are not going to be available to anonymous users because the access controls on the server. There are also certain attributes that may only be available to certain privileged users (pay scale, for example, may only be visible to Human Resources).

Authenticated Searching

The following shows how we can modify the example for an authenticated search:

```
import java.util.Hashtable;
import java.util.Enumeration;

import javax.naming.*;
import javax.naming.directory.*;
```

```
public class JNDISearchAuth {

  public static String INITCTX = "com.sun.jndi.ldap.LdapCtxFactory";
  public static String MY_HOST = "ldap://localhost:389";
  public static String MGR_DN = "uid=kvaughan, ou=People, o=airius.com";
  public static String MGR_PW = "bribery";
  public static String MY_SEARCHBASE = "o=Airius.com";

  public static String MY_FILTER = "(sn=Carter)";

  public static void main(String args[]) {
    try {
      // Hashtable for environmental information
      Hashtable env = new Hashtable();

      // Specify which class to use for our JNDI provider
      env.put(Context.INITIAL_CONTEXT_FACTORY, INITCTX);

      // Security Information
      // authenticates us to the server
      env.put(Context.PROVIDER_URL, MY_HOST);
      env.put(Context.SECURITY_AUTHENTICATION, "simple");
      env.put(Context.SECURITY_PRINCIPAL, MGR_DN);
      env.put(Context.SECURITY_CREDENTIALS, MGR_PW);

      // Rest of class is unchanged.
      DirContext ctx = new InitialDirContext(env);

      SearchControls constraints = new SearchControls();
      constraints.setSearchScope(SearchControls.SUBTREE_SCOPE);

      NamingEnumeration results = ctx.search(MY_SEARCHBASE,
                                             MY_FILTER, constraints);

      // Now step through the search results
      while (results != null && results.hasMore()) {
        SearchResult sr = (SearchResult) results.next();

        String dn = sr.getName();
        System.out.println("Distinguished Name is " + dn);

        Attributes attrs = sr.getAttributes();

        for (NamingEnumeration ne = attrs.getAll(); ne.hasMoreElements();) {
          Attribute attr = (Attribute) ne.next();
          String attrID = attr.getID();

          System.out.println(attrID + ":");
          for (Enumeration vals = attr.getAll(); vals.hasMoreElements();) {
            System.out.println("\t" + vals.nextElement());
          }
        }
        System.out.println("\n");
      }
    } catch (Exception e) {
      e.printStackTrace();
      System.exit(1);
    }
  }
}
```

This second search example is the same as the first, except that we have authenticated ourselves to the server.

So, if you try compiling and running this example, you'll see that it produces exactly the same output as before. Note that by default the LDAP server returns all of the attributes for a search. There may, however, be occasions when we don't want this, because we are only concerned with particular attributes.

Restricting the Attributes Displayed

In our third example, we ask to only be shown the common name (cn) and e-mail address (mail) attributes:

```java
import java.util.Hashtable;
import java.util.Enumeration;

import javax.naming.*;
import javax.naming.directory.*;

public class JNDISearchAttrs {

    // Initial context implementation
    public static String INITCTX = "com.sun.jndi.ldap.LdapCtxFactory";

    public static String MY_HOST = "ldap://localhost:389";
    public static String MY_SEARCHBASE = "o=Airius.com";

    public static String MY_FILTER = "(sn=Carter)";

    //Specify which attributes we are looking for
    public static String MY_ATTRS[] = {"cn","mail"};

    public static void main(String args[]) {
      try {
        //Hashtable for environmental information
        Hashtable env = new Hashtable();

        //Specify which class to use for our JNDI provider
        env.put(Context.INITIAL_CONTEXT_FACTORY, INITCTX);

        env.put(Context.PROVIDER_URL,MY_HOST);
        //Get a reference to a directory context
        DirContext ctx = new InitialDirContext(env);

        SearchControls constraints = new SearchControls();
        constraints.setSearchScope(SearchControls.SUBTREE_SCOPE);

        NamingEnumeration results =
        ctx.search(MY_SEARCHBASE,MY_FILTER,constraints);

        while (results != null && results.hasMore()) {
          SearchResult sr = (SearchResult) results.next();
          String dn = sr.getName() + ", " + MY_SEARCHBASE;

          System.out.println("Distinguished Name is " + dn);

          Attributes ar = ctx.getAttributes(dn, MY_ATTRS);

          if (ar == null) {
            System.out.println("Entry " + dn +
                               " has none of the specified attributes\n");
          } else {
```

```
                        for (int i =0;i<MY_ATTRS.length;i++) {
                          Attribute attr = ar.get(MY_ATTRS[i]);
                          if (attr != null) {
                            System.out.println(MY_ATTRS[i] + ":");
                            for (Enumeration vals = attr.getAll();vals.hasMoreElements();){
                              System.out.println("\t" + vals.nextElement());
                            }
                          }
                          System.out.println("\n");
                        }
                      }
                    }
                } catch(Exception e) {
                  e.printStackTrace();
                  System.exit(1);
                }
              }
            }
```

Since we have just specified the common name and mail attributes this time, the resulting restricted output should look like this:

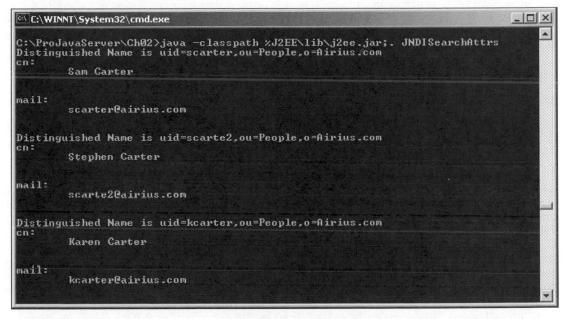

The difference between this code and our earlier example searches is that we now limit the number of attributes we want retrieved.

We created a String array that listed the attributes we wanted:

```
public static String MY_ATTRS[] = {"cn","mail"};
```

To retrieve this set of attributes we use the getAttributes() method of the DirContext interface, where we provide the DN of a specific entry and the array of attributes:

```
Attributes ar = ctx.getAttributes(dn, MY_ATTRS);
```

This will return an `Attributes` object.

We can then retrieve a particular `Attribute` object from an `Attributes` object:

```
Attribute attr = ar.get("cn");
```

At this point, we should emphasize that, although retrieving a specific set of attributes from an individual entry is very quick, it is not very practical for general searching. In a general LDAP search, the end user is not going to know the existing Distinguished Names of the entries they are looking for. So we will have to search the LDAP server and retrieve a set of entries.

In JNDI (as opposed to the Netscape Directory SDK for Java), this search will return all of the attributes associated with each individual entry. If we then make subsequent call to `getAttributes()` to retrieve a subset of attributes like in the previous example, this will require another call to the LDAP server and get back the subset of attributes. This is inefficient because it requires us to use extra memory for all of the attributes and extra bandwidth for the extra communication. The extra memory is required because our application must hold the data of the LDAP search results for us to process.

To improve performance in our Java applications, we want to reduce the amount of extraneous memory we use because the JVM's garbage collector can be slow to react, or slow your application to a crawl, as it reclaims memory. As garbage collection is improving and memory is cheap, we may be tempted to use this without a thought. However, there is another potential problem area and that is the fact that it does require us to use multiple network connections, where we might only have used one under a lower-level LDAP API.

This isn't to say that JNDI is bad to use, just that we should understand the implications of its use.

We can also use JNDI to add new entries to the server, delete entries, and modify existing entries. We'll take a look at these operations next.

Adding Entries

Using JNDI to add entries to an LDAP server is in fact more difficult than it is with other LDAP SDKs. This is because JNDI's primary goal is to read and write Java objects to the network. A consequence of this is that a programmer must jump through some extra hoops, such as creating a Java class for each type of entry they want to add to the LDAP server. Here we'll look at how to add and modify a simple entry in the LDAP server, but later in the chapter we'll learn how to use the LDAP server as an object store.

To store an entry in a LDAP server using JNDI, we must bind an object to a Distinguished Name (DN). This means that each object we store in the server (whether a simple person entry or a serialized Java class) must have a DN associated with it. Remember a DN is the unique name that each entry in a LDAP server must posses. If we switch to a different directory service (such as NDS) we will still be required to have a unique name for each object. Now if you are bit overwhelmed by this, just remember that it will become second nature over time and that we do this (provide an unique name) each time we save a file to hard disk. No file on the file system can share the same name. If we wish to have two files named `myfile.txt`, we must store them in separate directories in our file system otherwise one version will overwrite the other.

To store even a simple entry in the LDAP server, we must create a class that implements the `DirContext` interface. This interface defines how the object (be it a person or serialized Java class) should be stored into the directory server as well retrieved from the server. For instance, if you have a `Person` object, your class will specify how to build its DN, how to store the available attributes (for example, full name, e-mail address, telephone number, user ID, password, etc.) and provide various mechanisms to handle the retrieved data. The `DirContext` also provides for many more sophisticated data handling and is the basic interface for building a directory service provider.

As with any other LDAP SDK an add operation can only be performed by an authenticated user who has rights to add a new entry into the server. LDAP ACLs can be set up so that users can only add entries into particular parts of the directory tree.

Our next code sample shows a very simple `Person` class that implements the `DirContext` interface. Most of the methods in the interface are not actually implemented (except to throw exceptions) because we do not need them for our very simple example here. Note that this class is derived from the `Drink.java` example found in the JNDI tutorial (http://java.sun.com/products/jndi/tutorial/).

The methods that we implement here, `getAttributes()` and the constructor, enable us to store/retrieve the data in a `Person` class as traditional LDAP entries. The rest of the methods that we don't fully implement are primarily used to build full service providers. Instead, we simply throw exceptions stating that we don't support the particular service. New objects must also conform to the LDAP server's schema, or the entries will not be added.

It will be easier to explain how to add an entry with JNDI if we explain the code as we go along. Again, note that the complete source code for this example is available for download from the Wrox web site.

First is our class declaration. Note that we state that we will implement the methods for the `DirContext` interface:

```
import java.util.*;

import javax.naming.*;
import javax.naming.directory.*;

public class Person implements DirContext {
  String type;
  Attributes myAttrs;
```

Next we have our constructor. This constructor takes several strings that we will use to build an `inetOrgPerson` object class:

```
public Person(String uid, String givenname, String sn,
              String ou, String mail) {
    type = uid;
```

We will use the `BasicAttributes` class to store our attributes and their values. By specifying `true` in the `BasicAttributes` constructor we are telling it to ignore the case of attribute names when doing attribute name lookups:

```
    myAttrs = new BasicAttributes(true);
```

To add a multi-valued attribute we need to create a new `BasicAttribute` object, which requires the name of the attribute in its constructor. We then add the values of the attribute with the `add()` method:

```
    Attribute oc = new BasicAttribute("objectclass");
    oc.add("inetOrgPerson");
    oc.add("organizationalPerson");
    oc.add("person");
    oc.add("top");
```

```
Attribute ouSet = new BasicAttribute("ou");
ouSet.add("People");
ouSet.add(ou);

String cn = givenname + " " + sn;
```

Finally we add all of our attributes to the `BasicAttributes` object:

```
myAttrs.put(oc);
myAttrs.put(ouSet);
myAttrs.put("uid", uid);
myAttrs.put("cn", cn);
myAttrs.put("sn", sn);
myAttrs.put("givenname", givenname);
myAttrs.put("mail", mail);
}
```

When `getAttributes()` is called it will return our `BasicAttributes` object when requested by a name in the form of a String. It is designed to only return the attributes of a specific entry, but since this class will only hold one entry, it's not going to be called. We're showing one way to implement it if it was:

```
public Attributes getAttributes(String name) throws NamingException {
  if (! name.equals("")) {
    throw new NameNotFoundException();
  }
  return myAttrs;
}
```

This method does the same thing as the first `getAttributes()` but is only called when the name is passed a `Name` object:

```
public Attributes getAttributes(Name name) throws NamingException  {
  return getAttributes(name.toString());
}
```

The following method returns only the attributes listed in the String array `ids`. The String name should be a DN:

```
public Attributes getAttributes(String name, String[] ids)
                throws NamingException {
  if (! name.equals("")) {
    throw new NameNotFoundException();
  }

  Attributes answer = new BasicAttributes(true);
  Attribute target;
  for (int i = 0; i < ids.length; i++) {
    target = myAttrs.get(ids[i]);
    if (target != null) {
      answer.put(target);
    }
  }
  return answer;
}
```

This is a similar implementation to those of the other getAttributes() methods, except that it takes a Name object:

```
public Attributes getAttributes(Name name, String[] ids)
                throws NamingException {
  return getAttributes(name.toString(), ids);
}
```

The toString() method is used for serialization:

```
public String toString() {
  return type;
}
```

Finally, the following lines are used to implement methods that a JNDI service provider (such as the InitialDirContext class) would use to provide an application with services such as reading entries from the directory or for authenticating to the server:

```
// Not used for this example
public Object lookup(Name name) throws NamingException {
  throw new OperationNotSupportedException();
}

public Object lookup(String name) throws NamingException {
  throw new OperationNotSupportedException();
}

public void bind(Name name, Object obj) throws NamingException {
  throw new OperationNotSupportedException();
}
...
```

The full source code for this example and all of the examples in this book are available for download from http://www.wrox.com/

Next, we demonstrate the JNDIAdd.java class, which uses the Person class, developed above, to add an entry for Mark Wilcox to the LDAP server (we've seen most of this code already):

```
import java.util.Hashtable;
import java.util.Enumeration;

import javax.naming.*;
import javax.naming.directory.*;

public class JNDIAdd {

    // Initial context implementation
    public static String INITCTX = "com.sun.jndi.ldap.LdapCtxFactory";

    public static String MY_HOST = "ldap://localhost:389";
    public static String MGR_DN = "uid=kvaughan, ou=People, o=airius.com";
    public static String MGR_PW = "bribery";
    public static String MY_SEARCHBASE = "o=Airius.com";

    public static void main(String args[]) {
      try {
        // Hashtable for environmental information
        Hashtable env = new Hashtable();
```

```
        // Specify which class to use for our JNDI provider
        env.put(Context.INITIAL_CONTEXT_FACTORY, INITCTX);

        env.put(Context.PROVIDER_URL,MY_HOST);
        env.put(Context.SECURITY_AUTHENTICATION,"simple");
        env.put(Context.SECURITY_PRINCIPAL,MGR_DN);
        env.put(Context.SECURITY_CREDENTIALS,MGR_PW);

        // Get a reference to a directory context
        DirContext ctx = new InitialDirContext(env);

        Person p = new Person("mewilcox", "Mark",
                            "Wilcox", "ou=Accounting",
                            "mewilcox@airius.com");

        ctx.bind("uid=mewilcox,ou=People,o=airius.com", p);
    } catch(Exception e) {
        e.printStackTrace();
        System.exit(1);
    }
  }
}
```

First we must create a new Java object that implements the `DirContext` interface such as our `Person` class like this:

```
Person p = new Person("mewilcox", "Mark", "Wilcox",
                    "ou=Accounting", "mewilcox@airius.com");
```

Then we associate a name (specifically the DN of the entry) with this object in our current context with the `bind()` method of the `DirContext` interface like this:

```
ctx.bind("uid=mewilcox,ou=People,o=airius.com", p);
```

The `InitialDirContext` interface will actually perform an LDAP add operation. It will take all of the attributes we have placed into our Java class and then encode them for transfer into a LDAP server.

As we used the `BasicAttribute` class to build our attributes, they will be stored/retrieved as standard LDAP data and not as pure Java objects. This means that if you store your LDAP data this way any other LDAP client regardless if its written in C, Perl or Visual Basic will still be able to access it.

After successfully compiling and running our `Person.java` and `JNDIAdd.java` class files, we can see the result by looking in the airius.com directory of the Netscape Directory Server. Here we should see our new entry:

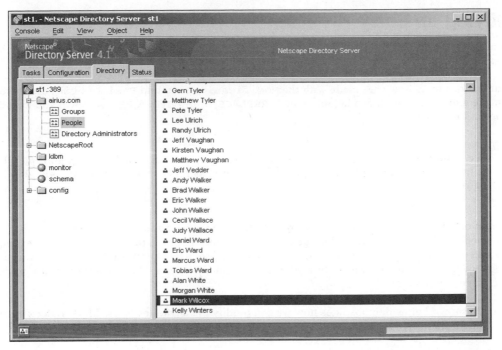

By double-clicking on the relevant name, we can check that all of our details have been added according to how we coded them:

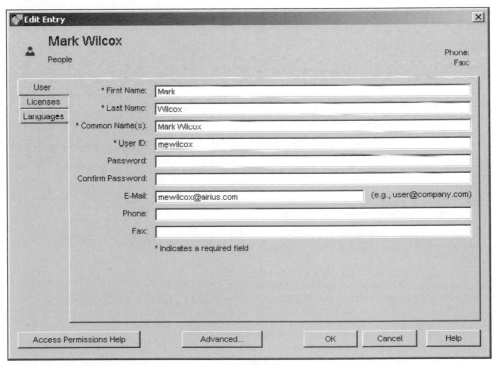

Modifying an Entry

Just as soon as you add an entry to an LDAP server, you'll need to modify it. This could be for a variety of reasons including changing a user's password, updating an application's configuration, etc.

Modifications to an entry are made with the `ModificationItem` and `BasicAttribute` classes. When we make a modification, it can be one of ADD, REPLACE, or DELETE. A REPLACE will add an attribute if it does not exist yet.

> **We should also be aware that if we perform a replace on an attribute that has multiple values without sending the extra values along with our replacement value, they will all be removed.**

Again, modifications must be performed by an authenticated user and those modifications that can be performed will be determined by the rights the bound entry has on a particular entry. For example, users can generally change their passwords but nothing else, while administrative assistants usually can change telephone numbers and mailing addresses. It usually takes a database administrator to do things like change a user's user ID.

The code shown below demonstrates how we can modify the attributes of the Mark Wilcox entry that we added in the previous example:

```java
import java.util.Hashtable;
import java.util.Enumeration;

import javax.naming.*;
import javax.naming.directory.*;

public class JNDIMod {

    // Initial context implementation
    public static String INITCTX = "com.sun.jndi.ldap.LdapCtxFactory";

    public static String MY_HOST = "ldap://localhost:389";
    public static String MGR_DN = "uid=kvaughan, ou=People, o=airius.com";
    public static String MGR_PW = "bribery";
    public static String MY_SEARCHBASE = "o=Airius.com";

    public static void main(String args[]) {

      try {
        // Hashtable for environmental information
        Hashtable env = new Hashtable();

        // Specify which class to use for our JNDI provider
        env.put(Context.INITIAL_CONTEXT_FACTORY, INITCTX);

        env.put(Context.PROVIDER_URL, MY_HOST);
        env.put(Context.SECURITY_AUTHENTICATION, "simple");
        env.put(Context.SECURITY_PRINCIPAL, MGR_DN);
        env.put(Context.SECURITY_CREDENTIALS, MGR_PW);

        // Get a reference to a directory context
        DirContext ctx = new InitialDirContext(env);
```

```
        ModificationItem[] mods = new ModificationItem[2];

        Attribute mod0 = new BasicAttribute("telephonenumber", "940-555-2555");
        Attribute mod1 = new BasicAttribute("l", "Waco");

        mods[0] = new ModificationItem(DirContext.REPLACE_ATTRIBUTE, mod0);
        mods[1] = new ModificationItem(DirContext.ADD_ATTRIBUTE, mod1);

        // DirContext.DELETE_ATTRIBUTE not shown here
        ctx.modifyAttributes("uid=mewilcox,ou=People,o=airius.com", mods);
    } catch(Exception e) {
        e.printStackTrace();
        System.exit(1);
    }
  }
}
```

To modify an entry we use the ModificationItem class. The ModificationItem takes a modification type (for example, ADD, REPLACE, or DELETE) and an Attribute object such as BasicAttribute. Here is a simple example that lets us add a new attribute, locality (the l attribute), with a new value of "Waco" to the entry:

```
Attribute mod1 = new BasicAttribute("l", "Waco");
        mods[1] = new ModificationItem(DirContext.ADD_ATTRIBUTE, mod1);
```

The actual modification is performed by the DirContext method, modifyAttributes(). Here is an example of this:

```
ctx.modifyAttributes("uid=mewilcox,ou=People,o=airius.com", mods);
```

Again this modifies the entry in the LDAP server using traditional LDAP and not as a Java object so that any other client can still access this data.

This time when we take a look at the Mark Wilcox's entry in the Directory Server, and click on Advanced... for a detailed view, we see that the phone number and locality have indeed been added to the directory:

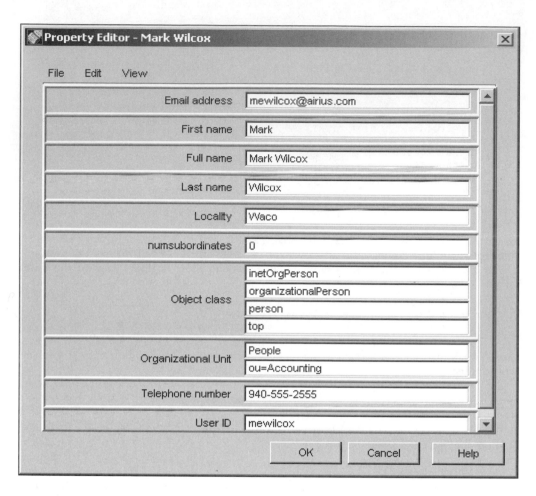

Delete an Entry

Eventually, you will need to remove entries from you LDAP server. This is easily accomplished by calling the `destroySubContext()` method of the `DirContext` interface, with the distinguished name of the entry that needs to be removed. Normally, delete operations are restricted to the LDAP database administrators.

Here is our example modified to delete an entry:

```java
import java.util.Hashtable;
import java.util.Enumeration;
import javax.naming.*;
import javax.naming.directory.*;

public class JNDIDel {
    // Initial context implementation
    public static String INITCTX = "com.sun.jndi.ldap.LdapCtxFactory";

    public static String MY_HOST = "ldap://localhost:389";
    public static String MGR_DN = "cn=Directory Manager";
    public static String MGR_PW = "jessica98";
```

```
    public static String MY_SEARCHBASE = "o=Airius.com";

    public static String MY_ENTRY = "uid=mewilcox, ou=People, o=airius.com";

    public static void main(String args[]) {
      try {
        // Hashtable for environmental information
        Hashtable env = new Hashtable();

        // Specify which class to use for our JNDI provider
        env.put(Context.INITIAL_CONTEXT_FACTORY, INITCTX);

        env.put(Context.PROVIDER_URL, MY_HOST);
        env.put(Context.SECURITY_AUTHENTICATION, "simple");
        env.put(Context.SECURITY_PRINCIPAL, MGR_DN);
        env.put(Context.SECURITY_CREDENTIALS, MGR_PW);

        // Get a reference to a directory context
        DirContext ctx = new InitialDirContext(env);

        ctx.destroySubcontext(MY_ENTRY);
      } catch(Exception e) {
        e.printStackTrace();
        System.exit(1);
      }
    }
  }
```

The only real difference in the code of this example is this line:

```
    ctx.destroySubcontext(MY_ENTRY);
```

So, after compiling and running this program, it will remove our entry from the LDAP server.

This was a whirlwind tour through LDAP. If you want more information, there are a number of resources. Wrox Press has a complete book on the subject, *Implementing LDAP* by Mark Wilcox, *ISBN 1-261002-21-1*, or you can check out the LDAP Guru web site at http://www.ldapguru.com/

Storing and Retrieving Java Objects in LDAP

One of JNDI's strongest attributes is its ability to use the network as an object store. What this means is that we can use the network to share Java objects either with distributed versions of an application or disparate applications. For example, we might create a class that calculates the sales tax of an item. This type of class could potentially be used in applications by our sales force to create purchase orders and by our accounting office to do their 'bean counting'.

We can use nearly any of the available JNDI providers to store our classes for us, but one of the most useful ways is by using an LDAP server to do this.

There are several reasons why you would like to use LDAP as your data store:

❑   Leverage an existing centralized resource

❑   Leverage existing open standards

- ❑ LDAP is available on the network "out of the box"

- ❑ LDAP is optimized for extremely quick read access

- ❑ LDAP has strong security built in

JNDI allows you to store several types of Java-related objects into the LDAP server:

- ❑ **Standard LDAP directory entries**
  This gives the ability to manipulate standard directory data (`inetOrgPerson`, `groupOfUniqueNames`, `objectclasses`, and so on). Standard directory data is smaller in size (and therefore quicker to access and modify) and you can share it between different languages. The ability to stay language-neutral with directory data is of utmost importance in a large enterprise, where several different languages (for example, Java, Perl, C/C++, Visual Basic, Cobol, etc.) maybe used for development.

- ❑ **Serialized Java objects**
  This gives the ability to store and retrieve Java objects that have been serialized (the current objects, and all related classes, are stored in a binary format) into the LDAP server. Probably the easiest format to use, but also requires the most bandwidth and storage space. This format is only understandable by Java in support for object persistence. The two most common uses of serialized Java objects are EJBs and JDBC `DataSource` objects.

- ❑ **References**
  As we discussed earlier, distributed computing platforms like CORBA and RMI use registries to keep track of the object classes they expose. However, these registries do not facilitate the ability to search on them and force you to hard-code the server location of the object in your application. A Java `Reference` object enables you to store data in the directory server as an indirect reference to the real object's location. For example, you could have a real time stock quote object on an RMI server. Instead of hard coding the location of the RMI registry in your application, you could connect to an LDAP server and locate the object "`cn=Real Time Stock Quote`", which contains the RMI URL to the stock quote object. This reduces the need to recompile your class every time you move the stock quote class to a different registry and it makes your code a bit easier to read.

The option you choose to use to store your objects will depend upon the application you are building and how you need to access the data. We'll look at these three objects in more detail in the next few sections.

Traditional LDAP

Organizations will often want to access the data in the directory service from a variety of clients using a number of different languages. A popular use of a directory service is for user authentication. Obviously storing user authentication data in a format that only Java can use reduces the number of applications that can use the directory for authentication. This in turn raises the cost of doing business because you then need another directory service for providing authentication services to applications that can't access Java objects.

A number of applications won't need authentication but could benefit from a directory service's address book features. For example, your e-mail program can use it to find the e-mail address of co-workers, your marketing department can use it to build mail-merged form letters, while your web developers can use it to make a custom portal for each customer. Each of these applications could be built using Java as the development language. Most importantly, your company can significantly reduce its overhead by maintaining consistent data about its people and clients in a central database.

One of the neat things about storing data in this fashion is that you can treat each entry like an object in Java, but other languages don't have to be object-oriented in order to access the data.

Serialized Java

If, however, we have a growing number of Java applications that need access to a central repository of pre-built Java objects, then we could use Java's serialization to store those objects into the LDAP server. Then when an application needs a particular object (for example a 3D rendering engine) it can retrieve it from the LDAP server, only when it's needed, then release it. Another nice feature of this is that when we update the rendering engine, all of the applications that are using the engine will have access to the update without having to patch the end-applications.

Java References

Finally, if we are in an all-Java environment we might wish to take advantage of Java references. References reduce the storage and bandwidth requirements of storing and retrieving entries because they don't store the entire object in the directory, instead only storing key components that are needed to rebuild the object in a factory class. Often the components stored are a URL that points to the real location of the object.

For example, if we create a standard printer object, we can build a `PrinterFactory` that might take the following parameters:

❑ Network location

❑ Color options – monochrome, color

❑ Specialties – postscript, graphic plotter

❑ Current status – out of paper, on-line

These parameters can be passed to `PrinterFactory` and will always return a `Printer` object that our application can use to print. It reduces bandwidth and storage because only the above parameters need to be stored. It's easier for an application programmer to deal with because part of the reference is the fully qualified package name of the actual factory, so we don't have to include it with our application, we just need to make sure the JVM can find the package.

> *If you want to read more about using JNDI and LDAP as a Java object store, you can see the official JNDI site at http://java.sun.com/jndi/.*

Returning to JNDI without LDAP

While LDAP is an important part of an Internet services network, and many people use JNDI so that they can use LDAP in their Java applications, LDAP is not the only option available. LDAP makes sense when you need to manage demographic information that doesn't change very often but needs to be accessed very quickly.

However, there are times when you need to access data that cannot be stored in LDAP, such as DNS entries or Enterprise JavaBeans.

While the rest of the chapter will concentrate on the **Domain Naming Service** (DNS), we should note that outside of LDAP, the most likely place we'll use JNDI is with EJBs and other J2EE services from an application server. We'll see some examples later in this book.

The reason why we focus on DNS here as opposed to a full J2EE example is that the examples in this chapter hope to demonstrate how flexible JNDI can be by using simpler examples than would be possible using EJBs.

Example DNS Application

To demonstrate how we might use the same basic JNDI classes but with different service providers, we will present a variation on the JNDISearch application that we used in our LDAP section.

> *This section requires the DNS JNDI Service provider that is available at the Java Developer's Connection and will be included in JDK 1.4 (it's currently there if you install the JDK 1.4 beta). The relevant files are* dns.jar *and* providerutils.jar, *which should both be placed into your classpath on running the program.*

LDAP and DNS both have entries. Each entry is access by a unique name (in LDAP it is the Distinguished Name and in DNS it is the canonical name). Both services are built in a hierarchy; remember that is one of the characteristics of a directory service.

DNS has a very well-defined way of building the tree (starting at top-level domains like .com, .us, .net, followed by second level domains like yahoo.com, followed by sub-domains and hosts). LDAP, on the other hand, has no set rules for building its tree structure (that's why you'll encounter DNs built like o=Acme Inc, c=US or o=acme.com or dc=acme, dc=com). Both services have entries that contain attributes with one or more values. LDAP has object classes that can define different types of entries. DNS only contains entries in regards to Internet hosts. LDAP has a strong authentication-based security model – DNS does not.

We have already seen the basics of this application earlier, so we will not spend much time explaining the details. We will focus on the DNS-specific parts.

```
import java.util.Hashtable;
import java.util.Enumeration;

import javax.naming.*;
import javax.naming.directory.*;

public class JNDISearchDNS {

  public static void main(String args[]) {
    try {
      // Hashtable for environmental information
      Hashtable env = new Hashtable();
```

Note that we're changing our provider factory from com.sun.jndi.dns.LDAPCtxFactory to com.sun.jndi.dns.DnsContextFactory. Since we're changing our factory, we need to change our provider URL as well from ldap:// to dns://. The 129.120.210.252 refers the IP address of the DNS server we will be communicating with:

```
// Specify which class to use for our JNDI provider
env.put("java.naming.factory.initial",
        "com.sun.jndi.dns.DnsContextFactory");
env.put("java.naming.provider.url", "dns://129.120.210.252/");
```

The instance variable, dns_attributes, contains the list of attributes we would like returned about a particular host, but there is no guarantee that all of these attributes will be available to us. For example, if the server is not a mail server, it won't have an MX record. Or the DNS administrator may not have the OS information in the HINFO field (below) because of security (if an attacker could determine the host OS for a particular machine, then they could focus their attack using tools to break that particular OS):

```
        String dns_attributes[] = {"MX", "A", "HINFO"};
```

Here we get the initial `DirContext` object and we attempt to retrieve the attributes for the host named `www.unt.edu`:

```
        // Get a reference to a directory context
        DirContext ctx = new InitialDirContext(env);
        Attributes attrs1 = ctx.getAttributes("www.unt.edu", dns_attributes);
```

Next we check to make sure that we got something back from DNS. The reason why we might not have any results is that there might not be any hosts that match our hostname in the DNS server:

```
        if (attrs1 == null) {
          System.out.println("host  has none of the specified attributes\n");
        } else {
```

Now we print out our results, using the same algorithm as earlier:

```
        for (int z = 0; z < dns_attributes.length; z++) {
          Attribute attr = attrs1.get(dns_attributes[z]);

          if (attr != null) {
            System.out.print(dns_attributes[z]+": ");
            for (Enumeration vals = attr.getAll();vals.hasMoreElements();) {
              System.out.println(vals.nextElement());
            }
          }

          System.out.println("\n");
        }
      }
    } catch(Exception e) {
      e.printStackTrace();
      System.exit(1);
    }
  }
}
```

The screenshot below shows what you might see returned from DNS:

In this example, there are two attributes for the DNS entry matching www.unt.edu. There's the `A` record which denotes the IP address of the host and there is an `HINFO` record, which says that the server is currently running UNIX.

As you can see, switching providers in JNDI is truly painless.

79

Summary

Directory services are an important part of a networked services environment. Directories provide the ability to associate human understandable (and memorable) names with the information computers need to operate (for example domain names to IP addresses, or common names to Java references). They also allow us to look up e-mail addresses and to associate permissions for secure environments.

LDAP provides us with a standard network protocol for communicating with directory services, while JNDI provides a standard API for Java to communicate with LDAP and specialized directory services that are not accessible via LDAP (such as DNS).

After this brief introduction to directory services, JNDI, and LDAP, you should understand the basics and will hopefully be able to venture on from here.

We will continue our journey through some of the fundamental elements of enterprise programming in the next chapter by taking an in-depth look at distributed computing enabled by RMI.

ProfessionalJavaServerProgrammingJ2EE1.3Edition
Data
RDMS
JDBC
Application Logic
Client
Web Container
Servlets
JSPs
Tag Library
HTTP(S)
(X)HTML/ XML
RMI/IIOP
JNDI
JTA
JDBC
JMS
JavaMail
JAAS
JCA
JAXP
J2EE Application Server
JavaMail
Mail Server
Java Application
RMI
Applet
IIOP
CORBA Server
Client Application
Session Beans
JNDI
JAF
Directory Servic
JMS
Message Queue

3

Distributed Computing Using RMI

Distributed computing has become a common term in today's programming vocabulary. It refers to the application design paradigm in which programs, the data they process, and the actual computations are spread over a network, either to leverage the processing power of multiple computers or due to the inherent nature of an application comprising different modules.

Remote Method Invocation (RMI) allows object-to-object communication between different Java Virtual Machines (JVM). JVMs can be distinct entities located on the same or separate computers – yet one JVM can invoke methods belonging to an object stored in another JVM. This enables applications to call object methods located remotely, sharing resources, and processing load across systems. Methods can even pass objects that a foreign virtual machine has never encountered before, allowing the dynamic loading of new classes as required. This really is quite a powerful feature.

If we want two Java applications executing within different virtual machines to communicate with each other there are a couple of other Java-based approaches that can be taken besides RMI:

- ❑   Sockets
- ❑   Java Message Service (JMS)

Basic network programming with sockets is flexible and sufficient for communication between programs. However, it requires all the involved parties to communicate via application-level protocols, the design of which is complex and can be error-prone. For example, consider a collaborative application, like a simple chat application for instance: for multiple clients to participate we would first need to design some sort of protocol, and then use sockets to communicate in that protocol with the server. RMI, on the other hand, is a distributed system that internally uses sockets over TCP/IP.

The difference between RMI and JMS is that in RMI the objects stay resident and are bound to the virtual machines (although method arguments and returns as well as stubs travel across the network), whereas in JMS the messages (objects) themselves travel asynchronously across the network from one JVM to another.

The RMI Architecture

Before we look at how the RMI mechanism works, let us define some frequently-used terms.

> To quote the specification, "In the Java distributed object model, a remote object is one whose methods can be invoked from another Java virtual machine, potentially on a different host. An object of this type is described by one or more remote interfaces, which are Java interfaces that declare the methods of the remote object. Remote method invocation (RMI) is the action of invoking a method of a remote interface on a remote object."

RMI's purpose is to make objects in separate JVMs look and act like local objects. The JVM that calls the remote object is usually referred to as a client and the JVM that contains the remote object is the server. One of the most important aspects of the RMI design is its intended transparency. Applications do not know whether an object is remote or local. A method invocation on a remote object has the same syntax as a method invocation on a local object, though under the hood there is a lot more going on than meets the eye.

> In RMI the term "server" does not refer to a physical server or application but to a single remote object having methods that can be remotely invoked. Similarly, the term "client" does not refer to a client machine but actually refers to the object invoking a remote method on a remote object. The same object can be both a client and a server.

Although obtaining a reference to a remote object is somewhat different from doing so for local objects, once we have the reference, we use the remote object as if it were local. The RMI infrastructure will automatically intercept the method call, find the remote object, and process the request remotely. This location transparency even includes garbage collection.

> A remote object is always accessed via its remote interface. In other words the client invokes methods on the object only after casting the reference to the remote interface.

The RMI implementation is essentially built from three abstraction layers:

❑ **The Stubs/Skeletons Layer**
   This layer intercepts method calls made by the client to the interface reference and redirects these calls to a remote object. It is worth remembering that stubs are specific to the client side, whereas skeletons are found on the server side.

❑ **The Remote Reference Layer**
   This layer handles the details relating to interpreting and managing references made by clients to the remote objects. It connects clients to remote objects that are running and exported on a server by a one-to-one connection link. In the Java 2 SDK, this layer was enhanced to support the activation framework (discussed later).

❑ **The Transport Layer**
   This layer is based on TCP/IP connections between machines in a network. It provides basic connectivity, as well as some firewall penetration strategies.

The following diagram shows these three layers, along with a breakdown of the transport layer. The descriptions on the right-hand side represent the OSI layers (OSI is concisely described at http://www.webopedia.com/TERM/O/OSI.html) :

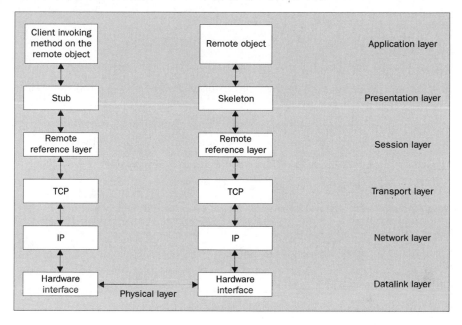

This layered architecture provides good implementation flexibility without affecting the application architecture. Each of the layers can be enhanced or replaced without affecting the rest of the system. For example, the transport layer implementation can be replaced by a vendor with the User Datagram Protocol (UDP) instead of TCP, without affecting the upper layers.

Next we'll look at some of these layers in more detail.

The Stub and Skeleton Layer

To achieve location transparency, RMI introduces two special kinds of objects known as stubs and skeletons that serve as an interface between an application and the rest of the RMI system. This layer's purpose is to transfer data to the Remote Reference Layer via marshaling and unmarshaling. Marshaling refers to the process of converting the data or object being transferred into a byte stream and unmarshaling is the reverse − converting the stream into an object or data. This conversion is achieved via object serialization.

The stub and skeleton layer of RMI lies just below the actual application and is based on the Proxy design pattern. In the RMI use of the Proxy pattern, the stub class plays the role of the proxy for the remote service implementation. The skeleton is a helper class that is generated by RMI to help the object communicate with the stub across the RMI link. The skeleton carries on a conversation with the stub; it reads the parameters for the method call from the link, makes the call to the remote service implementation object, accepts the return value, and then writes the return value back to the stub.

In short, the Proxy pattern forces method calls to occur through a proxy that acts as a surrogate, delegating all calls to the actual object in a manner transparent to the original caller.

Specific details about the proxy design pattern are beyond the scope of this book, but can be found in Design Patterns, Elements of Reusable Object-Oriented Software Erich Gamma, et al. (ISBN: 0-201-63361-2) or Patterns in Java: A Catalog of Reusable Design Patterns (ISBN: 0-471333-15-8.)

Let's now look at stubs and skeletons in a little more in detail.

Stubs

The stub is a client-side object that represents (or acts as a proxy for) the remote object. The stub has the same interface, or list of methods, as the remote object. However, when the client calls a stub method, the stub forwards the request via the RMI infrastructure to the remote object (via the skeleton), which actually executes it. The following lists the sequence of events performed by the stub in detail:

❑ Initiates a connection with the remote VM containing the remote object

❑ Marshals (writes and transmits) the parameters to the remote VM

❑ Waits for the result of the method invocation

❑ Unmarshals (reads) the return value or exception returned

❑ Returns the value to the caller

The stub hides the serialization of method parameters (parameters must be serializable; parameter passing is discussed in detail later) and the network-level communication in order to present a simple invocation mechanism to the caller.

In the remote VM, each remote object may have a corresponding skeleton.

Skeletons

On the server-side, the skeleton object takes care of all of the details of "remoteness" so that the actual remote object doesn't need to worry about them. In other words, we can pretty much code a remote object the same way as if it were local; the skeleton insulates the remote object from the RMI infrastructure. During remote method requests, the RMI infrastructure automatically invokes the skeleton object so it can work its magic. The following bullets list the sequence of events in detail:

❑ Unmarshals (reads) the parameters for the remote method (remember that these were marshaled by the stub on the client side)

❑ Invokes the method on the actual remote object implementation

❑ Marshals (writes and transmits) the result (return value or exception) to the caller (which is then unmarshaled by the stub)

The JDK contains the `rmic` *tool that creates the class files for the stubs and skeletons. Details about* `rmic` *can be found packaged with the JDK, or online at:*
http://java.sun.com/j2se/1.3/docs/tooldocs/tools.html

The Remote Reference Layer

The remote reference layer defines and supports the invocation semantics of the RMI connection. This layer provides a JRMP (Java Remote Method Protocol: see next section)-specific `java.rmi.server.RemoteRef` object that represents a handle to the remote object. A `RemoteStub` uses a remote reference to carry out a remote method invocation to a remote object.

In JDK 1.2 onwards stubs use a single method, `invoke(Remote, Method, Object[],` `long)` *on the remote reference to carry out parameter marshaling, remote method execution, and un-marshaling of the return value.*

The Java 2 SDK implementation of RMI adds a new semantic for the client-server connection: activatable remote objects (as we shall see later). Other types of connection semantics are possible. For example, with multicast, a single proxy could send a method request to multiple implementations simultaneously and accept the first reply (which would improve the response time and possibly improve availability). In the future, Sun is expected to add additional invocation semantics to RMI.

The Transport Layer

The transport layer makes the stream-based network connections over TCP/IP between the JVMs, and is responsible for setting and managing those connections. Even if two JVMs are running on the same physical computer, they connect through their host computer's TCP/IP network protocol stack. RMI uses a wire-level protocol called **Java Remote Method Protocol (JRMP)** on top of TCP/IP (an analogy is HTTP over TCP/IP).

JRMP is specified at http://java.sun.com/products/jdk/1.2/docs/guide/rmi/spec/rmi-protocol.doc.html. It is important to note that JRMP is specific to the Sun "implementation". Alternative implementations, such as BEA Weblogic, NinjaRMI, ObjectSpace's Voyager, and so on, do not use JRMP, but instead use their own wire-level protocol. Sun and IBM have jointly developed the next version of RMI, called RMI-IIOP, which is available with Java 2 SDK version 1.3 (or separately). Instead of using JRMP, RMI-IIOP uses the Object Management Group (OMG) Internet Inter-ORB Protocol (IIOP) to communicate between clients and server. IIOP also enables integration with CORBA objects.

From JDK 1.2 the JRMP protocol was modified to eliminate the need for skeletons and instead use **reflection** to make the connection to the remote service object. Thus, we only need to generate stub classes in system implementations compatible with JDK 1.2 and above. To generate stubs we use the − v1.2 option with rmic.

For a detailed description of how JRMP was modified to remove skeletons see the CallData, Operation, and Hash descriptions in the JRMP specification at http://java.sun.com/products/jdk/1.2/docs/guide/rmi/spec/rmi-protocol.doc3.html.

Reflection is an API in the `java.lang.reflect` *package in J2SE that enables Java code to discover information about the fields, methods, and constructors of loaded classes at runtime and operate on them.*

The RMI transport layer is designed to make a connection between clients and server, even in the face of networking obstacles. While the transport layer prefers to use multiple TCP/IP connections, some network configurations allow a single TCP/IP connection between a client and server (for example, some browsers restrict applets to a single network connection back to their hosting server). In this case, the transport layer multiplexes multiple virtual connections within a single TCP/IP connection.

The transport layer in the current RMI implementation is TCP-based, but again a UDP-based transport layer could be substituted in a different implementation.

Locating Remote Objects

There is still one crucial question that we haven't answered yet. How does a client find the object? Clients find remote services by using a naming or directory service. This may seem like circular logic. How can a client find the naming service? Simple: a naming or directory service is run on a host and port number that the client is already aware of (for example, a well known port on a public host). RMI can transparently look up these different directory services with the Java Naming and Directory Interface (JNDI), which was described in the previous chapter.

The RMI naming service, a registry, is a remote object that serves as a directory service for clients by keeping a Hashtable-like mapping of names to other remote objects. It is not necessary to have a single registry on a particular physical host. An object is free to start its own registry. The behavior of the registry is defined by the interface java.rmi.registry.Registry. RMI itself includes a simple implementation of this interface called the RMI Registry, (the rmiregistry tool with the JDK can also be started programmatically). The RMI Registry runs on each machine that "hosts" remote objects and accepts queries for services, by default on port 1099.

In simple terms, a remote object is associated with a name in this registry. Any time the clients want to invoke methods on this remote object; it obtains a reference to it by looking up the name. The lookup returns a remote reference, a stub, to the object. RMI also provides another class, the java.rmi.Naming class that serves as the client's interaction point with the object serving as the registry on the host for this lookup:

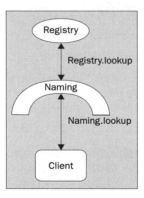

> It is important not to confuse the **java.rmi.Naming** with the JNDI context. Although they provide the same services, the **Naming** class specifically locates objects in the RMI registry. Sun provides a JNDI provider for RMI that allows clients to lookup RMI objects using a JNDI context. This JNDI-based RMI registry can be downloaded from **http://java.sun.com/products/jndi/**

The Naming class's methods take, as one of their arguments, a name that is a URL-formatted java.lang.String. Let's look at these methods and their descriptions:

Method	Description
`public static void bind( String name, Remote obj)`	Binds the remote object to a string name. The name itself is in the RMI URL format described below.
`public static String[]list( String name)`	Returns an array of the names bound in the registry.
`public static Remote lookup( String name)`	Returns a reference, a stub, for the remote object associated with the specified name.
`public static void rebind( String name, Remote obj)`	Rebinds (unbinds the name if it is already bound and binds it again) the specified name if it is already in use to a new remote object. This could be dangerous if different applications use the same name in the registry but is helpful in development.
`public static void unbind( String name)`	Removes the binding with specified name.

The methods in the `Naming` class and `Registry` interface have identical signatures and throw a variety of exceptions (discussed in the next section). There are a number of things that happen when a client invokes a lookup for a particular URL in the `Naming` class. First, a socket connection is opened to the host on the specified port (using a client socket factory if necessary). Next, since the registry implementation on the host itself is a remote object, a stub to that remote registry is returned from the host. This stub acts as the client proxy for the registry. Subsequently, the `Registry.lookup()` is performed on this stub and returns another stub, for the remote object that was registered with it on the server. Finally, once the client has a stub to the requested object, it interacts directly with the object on the port to which it was exported.

The URL takes the form:

```
rmi://<host_name>[:<name_service_port>]/<service_name>
```

Where:

❑   host_name is a name recognized on the local area network (LAN) or a DNS name on the Internet

❑   name_service_port needs to be specified only if the naming service is running on a port other than the default 1099

❑   service_name is the string name that the remote object is associated with in the registry

To facilitate this on the host machine, a server program exposes the remote object service by performing the following sequence of events:

1.   Creates a local object

2.   Exports that object to create a listening service, that waits for clients to connect and request the service

3. Registers the object in the RMI Registry under a public name

The code snippet below summarizes these steps:

```
// Create the object. Exporting happens in the constructor
HelloServer obj = new HelloServer();

// Bind the object to a name in the registry that has been
// started beforehand
Naming.rebind("/HelloServer", obj);
```

Similar to the `Naming` class there is another class, the `java.rmi.registry.LocateRegistry` that has various methods for directly getting a reference to the registry and for starting the registry. To reiterate, starting the registry (either by the tool or programmatically) is nothing but exporting the remote object that implements the `Registry` interface.

> The method **LocateRegistry.getRegistry(String host)** does not contact the registry on the host, but rather just looks up the host to make sure it exists. So, even though this method succeeded, this does not necessarily mean that a registry is running on the specified host. It just returns a stub that can then access the registry.

The JDK has a tool called `rmiregistry` that starts the registry on the host with the following command:

```
rmiregistry -J-Djava.security.policy=<policy file>
```

Alternatively, to start the registry with its default values:

```
start rmiregistry
```

Remember the registry is an object running in a JVM. The `-J` flag is used to pass parameters, such as the **policy file**, to the JVM.

You can also programmatically start the registry with the `LocateRegistry.createRegistry(int port)` *method or the more detailed* `LocateRegistry.createRegistry(int port, RMIClientSocketFactory csf,` `RMIServerSocketFactory ssf)`. *Both these methods return the stub, implementing the interface* `java.rmi.registry.Registry`.

Policy Files

Code is granted permissions in what is called a policy file. If we look in the `%JAVA_HOME%\jre\lib\security` directory, we will find the default policy file for our JVM named java.policy. This file can be edited either manually or by using the policytool program found in the `%JAVA_HOME%\bin directory`. For more information on policy files see *Professional Java Security, by Wrox Press, (ISBN 1-861004-25-7)*.

Before going through an example, we'll take a brief diversion and have a look at exceptions in RMI.

RMI Exceptions

As mentioned earlier, RMI is a distributed system that uses sockets over TCP/IP. In such a networked environment, many things could go wrong. It is important that the client is somehow notified about exceptions so that it can handle them in the appropriate manner, and thereby recover from problems as and when they occur. For example, you don't want a client to indefinitely wait for an input on the socket if the network goes down, or the host cannot be reached.

So that the client is aware of such conditions, every remote method must throw the `java.rmi.RemoteException` (or one of its super classes such as `java.io.IOException` or `java.lang.Exception`). The `RemoteException` is a generic exception and there are specialized subclasses that are thrown (and caught) for specific conditions. These are listed in the table below:

Exception	Description
AccessException	Thrown by certain methods of the `java.rmi.Naming` class (specifically – `bind()`, `rebind()`, and `unbind()`) and methods of the `ActivationSystem` interface (which we'll encounter shortly), to indicate that the caller does not have permission to perform the action requested by the method call.
AlreadyBound Exception	Thrown if an attempt is made to bind an object in the registry to a name that already has an associated binding. Note that this exception is not thrown (under the same conditions) if `rebind()` is used. However, use of `rebind()` may not be right under all scenarios.
ConnectException	Thrown if a connection is refused to the remote host for a remote method call.
ConnectIOException	Thrown if an `IOException` occurs while making a connection to the remote host for a remote method call.
MarshalException	Thrown if a `java.io.IOException` occurs while marshaling the remote call header, arguments, or return value for a remote method call.
NoSuchObject Exception	Thrown if an attempt is made to invoke a method on an object that no longer exists in the remote virtual machine. If this exception is thrown then it means that the object was garbage-collected or unexported. A common occurrence is if the "client or" clients repeatedly fail to renew their leases, and the leases expire. This could occur if, for example, the network is clogged with traffic or goes down. Also keep in mind that the stub with the client is valid only as long as the RMI server is alive. If you don't want the remote object to be garbage-collected then you should keep it alive in the server JVM by storing a reference to the implementation object in a static variable. As a locally reachable object, it won't be garbage-collected even in the event of extended unreachability of clients.

Table continued on following page

Exception	Description
NotBoundException	Thrown if an attempt is made to lookup() or unbind() in the registry a name that has no associated binding.
RemoteException	The common super class for a number of communication-related exceptions that may occur during the execution of a remote method call.
ServerError	Thrown as a result of a remote method call if the execution of the remote method on the server machine throws a java.lang.Error.
ServerException	Thrown as a result of a remote method call if the execution of the remote method on the server machine throws a RemoteException.
StubNotFound Exception	Thrown if a valid stub class could not be found for a remote object when it is exported.
Unexpected Exception	Thrown if the client of a remote method call receives, as a result of the call, a checked exception that is not among the checked exception types declared in the "throws" clause of the method in the remote interface.
UnknownHost Exception	Thrown if a java.net.UnknownHostException occurs while creating a connection to the remote host for a remote method call.
Unmarshal Exception	Can be thrown while unmarshaling the parameters or the results of a remote method call if: ❑ An exception occurs while unmarshaling the call header. ❑ If the protocol for the return value is invalid. ❑ If an IOException occurs while unmarshaling parameters (on the server side) or the return value (on the client side).

Developing Applications with RMI

Writing client-server applications using RMI involves six basic steps:

1. Defining a remote interface

2. Implementing the remote interface

3. Writing the client that uses the remote objects

4. Generating stubs (client proxies) and skeletons (server entities)

5. Starting the registry and registering the object

6. Running the server and client

Let's look at each step by developing a simple application as an example to gain some practical experience and aid our understanding of each step.

Defining the Remote Interface

An interface manifests the exposed operations and the client programmer need not be aware of the implementation (the interface in this case also serves as a marker to the JVM). A remote interface by definition is the set of methods that can be invoked remotely by a client:

❑ The remote interface must be declared public or the client will get an error when it tries to load a remote object that implements the remote interface, unless that client is in the same package as the remote interface

❑ The remote interface must extend the `java.rmi.Remote` interface.

❑ Each method must throw a `java.rmi.RemoteException` (or a superclass of `RemoteException`)

❑ If the remote methods have any remote objects as parameters or return types, they must be interface types not the implementation classes

Note that the `java.rmi.Remote` interface has no methods. It's just used as a marker by the JVM, in a similar fashion to how the `java.io.Serializable` interface is used to mark objects as being serializable.

For our example, we'll define our remote interface like this:

```
public interface HelloInterface extends java.rmi.Remote {

    // This method is called by remote clients and is implemented
    // by the remote object.
    public String sayHello() throws java.rmi.RemoteException;
}
```

> **If your object implements other interfaces, keep them distinct from the remote interface. You can also minimize the number of objects registered in the registry with a Factory design pattern or a single factory object.**

Implementing the Remote Interface

The implementation class is the actual class that provides the implementation for methods defined in the remote interface. The `java.rmi.server.RemoteObject` extends the functionality provided by the `java.lang.Object` class into the remote domain by overriding the `equals()`, `hashcode()`, and `toString()` methods.

Remember, the generic `java.rmi.server.RemoteObject` *is an abstract class and describes the behavior for remote objects.*

The abstract subclass `java.rmi.server.RemoteServer` describes the behavior associated with the server implementation and provides the basic semantics to support remote references (for example, create, export to a particular port, and so on).

`java.rmi.server.RemoteServer` has two subclasses:

- ❏   `java.rmi.server.UnicastRemoteObject` – defines a non-replicated remote object whose references are valid only while the server process is alive

- ❏   `java.rmi.activation.Activatable` – concrete class that defines behavior for on-demand instantiation of remote objects (see later section on activation)

The following diagram shows the two subclasses and their contained methods in relation to the `java.rmi.server.RemoteServer` class:

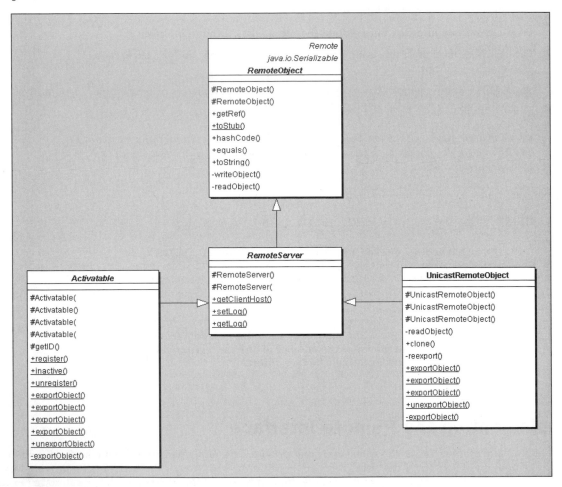

An object can exhibit remote behavior as a result of either of the following:

❑   The class extends `java.rmi.RemoteServer` or one of its subclasses (including other remote objects). The class must, however, invoke one of the superclass constructors so that it can be exported.

❑   The class explicitly exports itself by passing itself (`"this"`) to different forms of the `UnicastRemoteObject.exportObject()` methods.

The term "exporting" encapsulates the semantics that involve a remote object's ability to accept requests. This involves listening on a TCP (server) socket. Note that multiple objects can listen on the same port (see the section on Sockets for more information).

In addition to these, the class must implement one or more remote interfaces that define the remote methods.

A remote class can define any methods but only methods in the remote interface can be invoked remotely.

The `HelloServer` remote object implementation class for our example looks like this:

```java
import java.io.*;
import java.rmi.*;
import java.rmi.server.*;
import java.util.Date;

public class HelloServer extends UnicastRemoteObject
                         implements HelloInterface {

  public HelloServer() throws RemoteException {
    super();         // Call the superclass constructor to export this object
  }

  public String sayHello() throws RemoteException {
    return "Hello World, the current system time is " + new Date();
  }
}
```

Note that the source code for this example (and all of the examples in this book) is available for download from http://www.wrox.com/.

Writing the Client that Uses the Remote Objects

The client performs a lookup on the registry on the host and obtains a reference to the remote object. Note that casting to the remote interface is critical. In RMI, clients always interact with the interface, never with the object implementation:

```java
import java.rmi.*;

public class HelloClient {

  public static void main(String args[]) {
```

```
      if (System.getSecurityManager() == null) {
        System.setSecurityManager(new RMISecurityManager());
      }
      try {
        HelloInterface obj = (HelloInterface) Naming.lookup("/HelloServer");
        String message = obj.sayHello();
        System.out.println(message);
      } catch (Exception e) {
        System.out.println("HelloClient exception: " +e);
      }
    }
  }
}
```

Generating Stubs and Skeletons

Now that we have the remote interface and the implementation, we can generate the stubs and skeletons (or only stubs in Java 1.2) with the `rmic` tool *after* we have compiled the classes. Remember to set the directory that you are working from in your classpath; you can then use the following line in a command window:

```
rmic -v1.2 HelloServer
```

Note that the –v1.2 flag suppresses skeleton generation

Registering the Object

Now that we have the interface and the implementation, we need to make this object available to clients by binding it to a registry. This will allow clients to look the object up on the host by a `String` name. The stubs and skeletons (if any) are needed for registration. After all, it is the object stub that is going to be passed around from the registry to clients.

> **It is often mistakenly believed that the object must be bound to a registry for it to be used. In fact, this is not true. The object is available for use the moment it is successfully exported. It could behave as a client, invoke a method on another object, and pass itself to that object.**

The following code shows how we register our object:

```
import java.rmi.*;

public class RegisterIt {

  public static void main(String args[]) {
    try {
      // Instantiate the object
      HelloServer obj = new HelloServer();
      System.out.println("Object instantiated: "  + obj);
      Naming.rebind ("/HelloServer", obj);
```

```
            System.out.println("HelloServer bound in registry");
        } catch (Exception e) {
            System.out.println(e);
        }
    }
}
```

There are two methods in the `java.rmi.Naming` class that can bind an object in the registry:

❑   The `bind()` method binds an object to a string name and throws a
    `java.rmi.AlreadyBoundException` if the binding already exists

❑   The `rebind()` method, as used above, replaces any pre-existing binding with the new one

The registry must be running for the object to bind. It can be started by the tool, or programmatically as explained before. We start the executable with the following command line:

```
rmiregistry -J-Djava.security.policy=registerit.policy
```

The security policy is needed because of the Java 2 security model. The registry needs permissions to open sockets (a socket is an endpoint to a TCP connection), which are restricted to standard extensions in the default policy file.

Our policy file for this example, `registerit.policy`, grants all permissions:

```
grant {
  // Allow everything for now
  permission java.security.AllPermission;
};
```

Of course, we wouldn't use this policy in a production environment. By default there is a single system-wide policy file and a single user policy file. The system policy file is by default located at `%JAVA_HOME%\lib\security\java.policy` (use forward-slash with Solaris), while the user policy file is by default found at `%USER_HOME%\.java.policy`. Look at the tool documentation with your JDK for details about policies if you're not familiar with them. Also, it is worth keeping in mind that while starting the registry all classes and stubs must be available in the classpath, or the classpath should be not be set at all, to support dynamic loading.

Running the Client and Server

To run the client we should first compile and run the `RegisterIt.java` file. Then, we need to open yet another command window, so that we have a window running the RMI registry, one running the `RegisterIt` program, and the third to run the `HelloClient` class specifying our security policy file:

```
java -Djava.security.policy=registerit.policy HelloClient
```

The result of this simple example should look something like this:

```
C:\WINNT\System32\cmd.exe                                        _ □ ×

C:\ProJavaServer\Ch03>java -Djava.security.policy=registerit.policy HelloClient
Hello World, the current system time is Sat Mar 17 12:23:54 GMT 2001

C:\ProJavaServer\Ch03>
```

The RMISecurityManager

The java.rmi.RMISecurityManager extends the java.lang.SecurityManager class and provides the security context under which RMI applications execute. If no security manager has been set, stubs and classes can only be loaded from the local classpath and not from the host or code base (see the section later on *Dynamically Loading Classes*). This protects applications from downloading unsecure code via remote method invocations.

In JDK 1.3 there really is no need to subclass RMISecurityManager due to the policy-based access control. Furthermore, remember that the security manager in JDK 1.3 calls the AccessController.checkPermission(Permission) by default and refers to a policy file for permission checking.

There really is no reason to set the security manager to RMISecurityManager if an RMI program has a purely server role on all its communication links. RMISecurityManager (and user-defined security managers obtained by extending RMISecurityManager) are for subjecting the classes that are dynamically loaded by a client application to security control. If the client has access to the object definitions for the host there is no reason to use RMISecurityManager on the client side either.

Parameter Passing in RMI

The normal semantics for methods in a single JVM are governed by two rules:

> **If the type being passed is a primitive, then the parameter or result is passed by value. If, however, the type being passed is an object, then the object is passed by reference.**

When a primitive data type is passed as a parameter to a method the JVM simply copies the value and passes the copy to (or returns it from) the method. An object, on the other hand, resides in heap memory and is accessed by one (or more) references. When passed to a method, a copy of the reference variable is made (increasing the reference count to the object by one)and placed on the stack, and the copy is passed around.

Inside the method, code uses the copy of the reference to access the object. Invoking any method on the reference changes the state of the original object. Altering the reference itself does not affect the original object. However, altering the object that the reference points to alters the object that was initially created.

So when remote method invocation involves passing parameters or accepting a return value, what semantics are used? The answer depends on whether the parameters are primitive data types, objects, or remote objects. Let's look at these parameter types in more depth.

Primitive Parameters

When a primitive data type is passed as a parameter to, or returned from, a remote method, the RMI system passes it by value. A copy of the primitive data type is sent to the remote method and the method returns a copy of the primitive from its JVM. These values are passed between JVMs in a standard, machine-independent format allowing JVMs running on different platforms to communicate with each other reliably.

Object Parameters

A reference to an object doesn't make sense across multiple JVMs since the reference points to a value in the heap and different JVMs do not share heap memory. RMI sends the object itself, not its reference, between JVMs. It is actually the object that is passed by value, not the reference to the object. Similarly, when a remote method returns an object, a copy of the whole object is returned to the calling program.

A Java object can be simple, or it could refer to other Java objects in a complex graph-like structure. Since RMI must send the referenced object and all objects it references, it uses RMI Object Serialization to transform the object into a linear format that can then be sent over the network. Object serialization essentially flattens an object and any objects it references. Serialized objects can be de-serialized in the memory of the remote JVM and made ready for use by a Java program.

Passing large object graphs can use a lot of CPU time and network bandwidth. Try keeping object arguments to, and results from, remote methods simple for optimization. Objects being passed around must implement the `java.io.Serializable` or the `java.io.Externalizable` interface.

Remote Parameters

Passing remote objects as method arguments or return types is a little different from passing other objects. A client program can obtain a reference to a remote object through the RMI Registry program or it can be returned to the client from a method call (see the `HelloWorld` example in the next section). Passing remote objects is very important, especially for remote callbacks.

Consider the following code:

```
HelloInterface obj = (HelloInterface) Naming.lookup("/HelloServer");
MsgInterface msg = obj.getMsg();
```

What happens when the `MsgInterface` itself is a remote object that has been exported on the server?

RMI does not return a copy of the remote object. It substitutes the stub for the remote object, serializes it, and sends it to the client. Just as a note, if the client sends this remote object back to the server as another argument, the object is still treated as a remote object on the server and not local to the server (even though it is). Though this may seem like a performance overhead, it is crucial to preserve the integrity of the semantics.

Consider another case: what happens when the remote method returns a reference to `this`?

```
public class ThisServer extends UnicastRemoteObject
                    implements HelloInterface {

  public ThisServer()throws RemoteException{
    super();
  }
  public HelloInterface someMethod() throws RemoteException {
    return this;
  }
}
```

In the server code, this refers to the actual server implementation living in the server's JVM. However, clients have no direct contact with the other JVM. They deal with the proxy of the server's object, the stub. Behind the scenes, RMI always checks the input and output parameters from a remote method to see if they implement the Remote interface. If they do, they are transparently replaced with the corresponding stub. This gives clients the illusion that they are working with the local objects because even things like this can be exchanged between different JVMs.

> Remember, the class files themselves are never serialized, just the names of the classes. All classes should be capable of being loaded during de-serialization using the normal class loading mechanisms.

The Distributed Garbage Collector

One of the design objectives for the RMI specifications was to keep the client's perspective of remote objects the same as other objects within its own JVM. This implies that remote objects should also be subjected to garbage collection.

The RMI system provides a reference-counting distributed garbage collection algorithm based on Modula-3's Network Objects. Internally, the server keeps track of which clients have requested access to the remote object. When a reference is made, the server marks the object as dirty and when all clients have dropped the reference, it is marked as being clean. A clean object is marked for garbage collection and reclaimed when the garbage collector runs.

In addition to the reference-counting mechanism on the server, when a client obtains a reference, it actually has a lease to the object for a specified time. If the client does not refresh the connection by making additional dirty calls to the remote object before the lease term expires, the distributed garbage collector then assumes that the remote object is no longer referenced by that client (the reference is considered to be dead) and the remote object may be garbage collected.

A remote object can implement the java.rmi.server.Unreferenced interface. This has one method, unreferenced(), which is invoked by the RMI runtime when there are no longer any clients holding a live reference. This enables the distributed garbage collector (DGC) to check whether any remote references are still in use.

> The lease time is controlled by the system property java.rmi.dgc.leaseValue. (Its value is in milliseconds and defaults to 10 minutes.)

Of course all this dirty, clean, and leasing is never visible to users or clients. The DGC mechanism is completely transparent. The DGC mechanism is hidden in the stubs-skeleton layer and is abstracted in the java.rmi.dgc package.

It is important to remember that a remote object can be garbage collected, leaving it unavailable to clients (which typically results in a java.rmi.ConnectException). Due to these garbage collection semantics, a client must be prepared to deal with remote objects that have "disappeared". On the server, if you don't want your object to "disappear" you should always hold an explicit reference so that it is not garbage collected.

Remember, that the registry (itself a remote object) acts as a client to the server object and hence holds a lease to the object. So even if all the "actual" clients get disconnected from a server, the method `unreferenced()` may not be invoked on a server object while the registry holds a lease.

Consider the following modified version of the same `HelloWorld` example that demonstrates how distributed garbage collection works and how the `unreferenced()` method can be used. We discussed how a client could get a reference to a remote object as a result of a method invocation earlier in the section on parameter passing. This example uses that concept.

We modify the interface to return a remote object instead of a string:

```java
import java.rmi.*;

public interface HelloInterface extends java.rmi.Remote {
  public MsgInterface getMsg() throws RemoteException, Exception;
}
```

The remote object implementation of this interface is also quite simple:

```java
import java.io.*;
import java.rmi.*;
import java.rmi.server.*;
import java.util.Date;

public class HelloServer extends UnicastRemoteObject
                         implements HelloInterface {

  public HelloServer() throws RemoteException {
    super();
  }

  public MsgInterface getMsg() throws RemoteException, Exception {
    return (MsgInterface)new MsgServer();
  }
}
```

The `MsgInterface` has no methods and is just used to mark the object being passed around as remote:

```java
import java.io.Serializable;
import java.rmi.server.*;

public interface MsgInterface extends java.rmi.Remote {}
```

The simple implementation of this interface is designed to trap the events of the object by printing out information when the object is created, no longer referenced, finalized, and then deleted. This object also implements the `Unreferenced` interface and implements the `unreferenced()` method. The `unreferenced()` method will be called when there are no client references to the object; `finalize()` is called just before the object is garbage collected:

```java
import java.io.Serializable;
import java.rmi.server.*;
import java.rmi.*;
```

```
public class MsgServer extends UnicastRemoteObject
                       implements MsgInterface, Serializable, Unreferenced {

  // Set a counter for the number of instances of this class
  // that are created
  private static int counter;

  // Hold an id for the object instance
  private int id;

  public MsgServer() throws RemoteException {
    super();
    System.out.println("Created Msg:" + counter);
    counter++;
    setId(counter);
  }

  public void finalize() throws Throwable {
    super.finalize();
    System.out.println("Finalizer called for Msg: " + id);
  }

  public void unreferenced(){
    System.out.println("The unreferenced()method called for Msg: " + id);

    // If we need we can call unexportObject here since no one is using it
    // unexportObject(this, true);
  }

  private void setId(int id){
    this.id=id;
  }
}
```

The registration program remains the same as in the previous examples:

```
import java.rmi.*;

public class RegisterIt {

  public static void main(String args[]) {
    try {
      HelloServer obj = new HelloServer();
      Naming.rebind("/HelloServer", obj);
      System.out.println("HelloServer bound in registry");
    } catch (Exception e) {
      System.out.println(e);
    }
  }
}
```

We modify the client slightly to create multiple instances of the remote object MsgServer() on the server (we explicitly instantiate an object in the getMsg() method). We need to do this for our demonstration because the JVM runs the distributed garbage collector (like the usual garbage collector), only when it "feels like" there is a need to reclaim memory:

```
import java.rmi.*;

public class HelloClient {

  public static void main(String args[]) {
    if (System.getSecurityManager() == null) {
      System.setSecurityManager(new RMISecurityManager());
    }

    try {
      HelloInterface obj = (HelloInterface) Naming.lookup("/HelloServer");
      for(int i = 0; i < 100; i++) {
        MsgInterface msg = obj.getMsg();
      }
    } catch (Exception e) {
      System.out.println("HelloClient exception: " + e);
    }
  }
}
```

Start the server after compiling the classes and generating the stubs (and skeletons if necessary) for both
HelloServer and MsgServer with the following (changing the codebase path as appropriate, see the
next section for more on codebase):

```
javac *.java
rmic -v1.2 HelloServer
rmic -v1.2 MsgServer
rmiregistry -J-Djava.security.policy=registerit.policy
java -Djava.rmi.dgc.leaseValue=1000 -Djava.security.policy=registerit.policy
RegisterIt
```

Again you might want to experiment with the lease value property as well as the –ms and mx options
to set the heap memory for this example. Here's a snippet from the output when HelloClient is
executed with the default values:

```
java -Djava.security.policy=registerit.policy HelloClient
```

The leaseCheckInterval *in* sun.rmi.transport.DGCImpl *is read in from the*
sun.rmi.dgc.checkInterval *property without taking into account the current value of the*
leaseValue *variable. This causes a five-minute delay in removing unused objects, even if the*
leaseValue *is set to a lower value. To work around this problem set the*
sun.rmi.dgc.checkInterval *property to half of the setting of*
java.rmi.dgc.leaseValue.

Dynamically Loading Classes

We talked earlier about how references, stubs, parameters, and socket factories are sent to the client over the wire and how the class definitions are not. Dynamic class loading addresses the latter, making definitions available.

Dynamic class loading has been around for a long time in Java and this ability to dynamically load and instantiate classes is a very powerful concept. Applets, for example, are downloaded to the client browser from a web server and are executed in the client's JVM. This gives the client's runtime the ability to access applications that have never been installed in their system.

It is assumed that the reader is familiar with how applets work and how the codebase property is used for them. To summarize, codebase is the location from which the class loader loads classes into the JVM. This means that classes can be deployed in a central place, such as a web server, for a distributed system and all applications in the system can download the class files to operate.

There are two important system properties in RMI:

❑ java.rmi.server.codebase
This specifies the URL (a file://, ftp://, or http:// location) from where the classes can be accessed. If an object is passed around as a method argument or return type the client JVM needs to load the class files for that object. When RMI serializes the object it inserts the URL specified by this property alongside the object.

❑ java.rmi.server.useCodebaseOnly
This property is used to notify the client that it should load classes only from the codebase location.

Let us revisit the process of exporting and registering a remote object and put it under a magnifying glass:

❑ When instantiating the remote object and registering it with the registry (our RegisterIt program in the previous examples), the codebase is specified by the java.rmi.server.codebase property.

❑ When the bind() call is made, the registry uses this codebase to locate the stub for the object. Remember, the registry itself is a client to the object. Once this is successful the registry binds the object to a name and the codebase is saved along with the reference to the remote object in the registry.

❑ When a client requests a reference to the remote object, the registry returns the stub to the client. The client looks for the class definition of the stub in its local classpath (the classpath is always searched before the codebase), then the client loads the local class. If the stub class definition is not there in the classpath, the client will attempt to retrieve the class definition from the remote object's codebase which was stored in the registry.

❑ The class definition for the stub and any other classes that it needs, such as socket factories, are downloaded to the client JVM from the http or ftp codebase.

❑ When all the class definitions are available, the stub's proxy method calls to the object on the server.

Using the two properties and the downloading mechanism discussed, five potential configurations can be set up to distribute classes:

❑ **Closed**
There is no dynamic loading and all classes are located in the respective JVMs and loaded from the local classpath (`java.rmi.server.codebase` not set).

❑ **Dynamic client-side**
On the client, some classes are loaded from the local classpath and others from the codebase specified by the server.

❑ **Dynamic server-side**
This is similar to the dynamic client-side configuration. Some classes on the server are loaded locally and others from the codebase specified by the client (for example, in the case of callbacks from the server to client).

❑ **Bootstrapped client**
All of the client code is loaded from the codebase via a small program on the client ("bootstrap" loader).

❑ **Bootstrapped server**
Same as above, only on the server-side. The server uses a small program (bootstrap loader).

There are two classes, the `java.rmi.RMISecurityManager` and `java.rmi.server.RMIClassLoader` that check the security context before loading the class. The RMI system will only download classes from remote locations if a security manager has been set. The `RMIClassLoader` has one important method:

```
public static Class loadClass(String codebase, String name)
```

This method loads the class from the specified codebase. Other overloaded forms of this method take a URL for a codebase or a string list of multiple URL's

Let's take the `HelloWorld` example and set it up in the bootstrapped client and bootstrapped server configuration. This configuration is usually the most popular one due to its flexibility. We will download:

❑ All the classes on the client including the client class itself to the client from the web server

❑ All the server classes including the server class itself from a central web server

We will only need one simple bootstrap class for the client and one for the server.

First, let's tweak the `HelloClient` class a little so that it connects to the server when instantiated:

```java
import java.rmi.*;

public class HelloClient {

    public HelloClient() {
      try {
        HelloInterface obj = (HelloInterface) Naming.lookup(
          "rmi://localhost/HelloServer");
        String message  = obj.sayHello();
```

```
          System.out.println(message);
      } catch (Exception e) {
        System.out.println("HelloClient exception: " + e);
      }
    }
  }
```

That's it. We leave the remote implementation (`HelloServer.java`) and interface (`HelloInterface.java`) the same as our initial example.

Now let's write a bootstrap class (instead of the `RegisterIt.java` file we used earlier) that starts the server. It accesses the `codebase` property and loads the server class from the codebase using `RMIClassLoader`:

```java
import java.rmi.Naming;
import java.rmi.Remote;
import java.rmi.RMISecurityManager;
import java.rmi.server.RMIClassLoader;
import java.util.Properties;

public class DynamicServer {

  public static void main(String args[]) {

    // Create and install a security manager
    if (System.getSecurityManager() == null) {
      System.setSecurityManager(new RMISecurityManager());
    }

    try {
      Properties p = System.getProperties();
      String url = p.getProperty("java.rmi.server.codebase");
      Class serverclass = RMIClassLoader.loadClass(url, "HelloServer");
      Naming.rebind("/HelloServer",(Remote)serverclass.newInstance());
      System.out.println("HelloServer bound in registry");
    } catch (Exception e) {
      System.out.println(e);
    }
  }
}
```

When the downloaded class is instantiated with a `newInstance()`, the constructor for the class is invoked (our `HelloServer()` constructor) and the object is exported in the constructor and registered with the registry. Steps 1 to 5 that we mentioned earlier in the chapter (*Developing Applications with RMI*), occur in conjunction between the server and the registry.

There is a similar bootstrap program for the client that accesses the `codebase` property and loads the client class. When the downloaded client class is instantiated, it connects to the server and looks up the object. Again, steps 1 to 5 occur between the client and the registry:

```java
import java.rmi.RMISecurityManager;
import java.rmi.server.RMIClassLoader;
import java.util.Properties;
```

```
public class DynamicClient {

  public DynamicClient() throws Exception {
    Properties p = System.getProperties();
    String url = p.getProperty("java.rmi.server.codebase");
    Class clientClass = RMIClassLoader.loadClass(url, "HelloClient");

    // Start the client
    clientClass.newInstance();
  }

  public static void main (String args[]) {
    System.setSecurityManager(new RMISecurityManager());
    try {
      DynamicClient dc = new DynamicClient();
    } catch (Exception e) {
      System.out.println(e);
    }
  }
}
```

Compile all the classes and generate the stubs. Now we need to place the HelloWorld class files in a web server so that the DynamicServer can download them at runtime. For this example, we will use a small test HTTP server from Sun called ClassFileServer (also included in the source code).

Place the four class files for the HelloWorld example in a directory (\public_html) under the HTTP server.

First start the RMI registry using:

```
rmiregistry -J-Djava.security.policy=registerit.policy
```

then start the HTTP server. For ClassFileServer it would be something like this (assuming ClassFileServer is in the classpath):

```
java ClassFileServer 8080 %BOOK_HOME%\Ch03\Dynamic\webserver\public_html
```

The first parameter in this command line specifies the port that the server runs on, and the second parameter is the source for the files to be served. It will probably be a little quicker to set up a batch file to run these commands.

We then run the DynamicServer specifying the codebase as the web server:

```
java -Djava.security.policy=registerit.policy
     -Djava.rmi.server.codebase=http://localhost:8080/ DynamicServer
```

Finally run the DynamicClient, again providing the codebase:

```
java -Djava.security.policy=registerit.policy
     -Djava.rmi.server.codebase=http://localhost:8080/ DynamicClient
```

To summarize:

❑ When we start the DynamicServer it accesses the codebase, downloads the implementation class, and exports the object

❑ The registry uses the codebase to download the stub and bind the object, keeping track of the codebase used

❑ When you start the DynamicClient, it again contacts the codebase and downloads the client class and the stub, and invokes a method on the server object

To summarize the steps to execute the example:

Note: The downloadable source contains sample batch files to execute the code.

❑ Start the rmiregistry:

```
rmiregistry -J-Djava.security.policy=registerit.policy
```

❑ Start the class file server. Make sure the compiled classes from the first HelloWorld example as well as the stubs are available in the public_html folder:

```
java ClassFileServer 8080 %BOOK_HOME%\Ch03\Dynamic\webserver\public_html
```

❑ Start the DynamicServer:

```
java -Djava.security.policy=registerit.policy
    -Djava.rmi.server.codebase=http://localhost:8080/ DynamicServer
```

❑ Start the DynamicClient:

```
java -Djava.security.policy=registerit.policy
    -Djava.rmi.server.codebase=http://localhost:8080/ DynamicClient
```

Notice that all the HelloWorld client, server, and stub files are in one location. The only distribution for the server is one class and the only file needed for client distribution is one class:

```
C:\WINNT\System32\cmd.exe

C:\ProJavaServer\Ch03\Dynamic>java -Djava.security.policy=registerit.policy
-Djava.rmi.server.codebase=http://localhost:8080/ DynamicClient
Hello World, the current system time is Fri Aug 17 19:30:35 BST 2001

C:\ProJavaServer\Ch03\Dynamic>
```

Remote Callbacks

We discussed earlier how a client can get a reference to a remote object as a result of a method invocation. In fact, we actually saw how a remote object can be dynamically passed around in the DGC example earlier. Remember that we had initially emphasized that a client and server are terms used to describe a role, not physical locations or architectures. A client also can be a remote object. In many situations, a server may need to make a remote call to a client, for example, progress feedback or administrative notifications. A good example would be a chat application where all clients are remote objects.

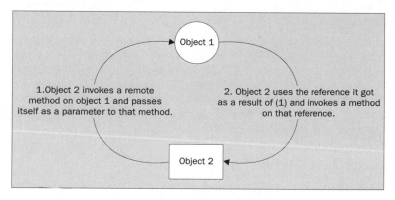

There is nothing really special about peer-to-peer communication or callbacks between remote objects. All that happens is a remote reference is passed around and methods are invoked on that reference.

Let us take the same HelloWorld example we looked at first and modify it to demonstrate callbacks.

The remote interface, HelloInterface, has one method that takes a ClientInterface as an argument:

```
public interface HelloInterface extends java.rmi.Remote {
  String sayHello(ClientInterface app) throws java.rmi.RemoteException;
}
```

For the client, the ClientInterface is also very simple, with only one method:

```
public interface ClientInterface extends java.rmi.Remote {
  void popup(String msg) throws java.rmi.RemoteException;
}
```

The HelloServer implements the HelloInterface and invokes the popup() method on the ClientInterface as shown below:

```
import java.io.*;
import java.rmi.*;
import java.rmi.server.*;
import java.util.Date;

public class HelloServer extends UnicastRemoteObject
                         implements HelloInterface {

  public HelloServer() throws RemoteException {
    super();
  }
  public String sayHello(ClientInterface ca) throws RemoteException {
    ca.popup("This is a message from the server!");
    return "Hello World, the current system time is " + new Date();
  }
}
```

The client that invokes methods on the server needs to be a remote object itself. Let us write a simple applet to demonstrate this. The applet exports itself and starts listening for incoming calls by explicitly invoking the UnicastRemoteObject.exportObject(this) method (an overloaded form of this method allows you to specify the port as well):

```java
import java.applet.*;
import java.awt.*;
import java.io.Serializable;
import java.rmi.*;
import java.rmi.server.*;

public class CallbackApplet extends Applet
                            implements ClientInterface, Serializable {

  String message = "-n/a-";
  Frame f =new Frame();
  Label l1= new Label("                    ");

  public void init() {
    f.add(l1);
    try {
      // Export the object
      UnicastRemoteObject.exportObject (this);
      String host = "rmi://" + getCodeBase().getHost()+ "/HelloServer";
      HelloInterface obj = (HelloInterface)Naming.lookup(host);
      message = obj.sayHello((ClientInterface)this);
    } catch (Exception e) {
      System.out.println("HelloApplet exception: " +e);
    }
  }

  // Display the message in the applet
  public void paint(Graphics g) {
    g.drawString(message, 25, 50);
  }

  // Implement the interface
  public void popup(String txt) throws RemoteException{
    l1.setText(txt);
    f.setSize(100,100);
    f.show();
  }
}
```

When the applet is loaded it locates the server object and invokes the remote method. It passes itself as an argument to that method. As a result of this, the stub is transported to the server and the server can now reverse roles. It acts as a client to this applet and can invoke the popup() method.

We need a simple HTML page for this applet (Applet.html):

```html
<html>
<applet codebase="http://localhost:8080/Callbacks" code="CallbackApplet.class"
        width=300 height=266>
</applet>
</html>
```

It's as simple as that! We generate the stubs for the client and server by executing rmic on CallbackApplet and HelloServer. Start the registry, and register the HelloServer with it using the same RegisterIt class as earlier.

The applet must be loaded from a web server on the host (remember unsigned applets can connect back to the host) and you can use either your own web server or the sample `ClassFileServer` used in the preceding example. All the classes needed by the client should be accessible on the web server. The stub class file definitions of the `CallbackApplet` should also either be available on the server objects classpath or should be dynamically loaded as we have seen earlier.

You can also test the application using `AppletViewer`. Set the preferences in **Applet Viewer** as "unrestricted".

Write an HTML file with the following code (`AppletViewer.html`):

```
<html>
  <applet codebase="." code="CallbackApplet.class" width=300 height=266>
  </applet>
</html>
```

Run the example after starting the registry and the server from the same directory as the HTML file and class files.

```
appletviewer -J-Djava.security.policy=registerit.policy AppletViewer.html
```

Finally, on running this example, we get something that looks like this:

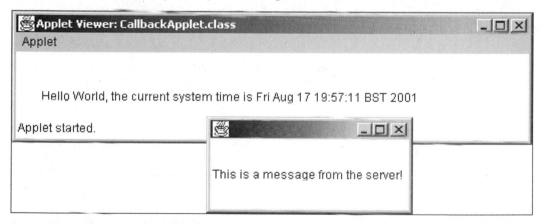

Object Activation

The remote objects discussed so far, are instances of a `java.rmi.UnicastRemoteObject` class, and have one main feature. They are accessible all the time, even when there are no clients executing. Consider the scenario when the number of remote objects, or the resources used by them on a server is high. This was identified as a major performance bottleneck in Java 2 so the concept of object activation was introduced.

> Object activation allows remote objects to be executed on an as-needed basis. That is, when an 'activatable' remote object is accessed (via a method invocation) if that remote object is not currently executing, the system initiates the object's execution inside an appropriate JVM. RMI uses lazy activation: this is where the activation of an object is deferred until a clients first use, the first method invocation.

So, what is the difference between an activatable object and the usual remote object from a client's perspective? None! To the client the entire activation mechanism is transparent and the client is never aware of what is happening behind the scenes.

The references to the remote object themselves can be thought of as lazy or faulting references. References to activatable objects contain persistent handle information that allows the activation subsystem to know that the object should be started if it is not already running. After an activatable reference is used the first time, the remote reference layer switches to a regular remote reference so that it doesn't have to go through the activation system subsequently.

Since the activation system can switch the lazy reference to a live remote reference, references to an activatable object are always available. However, references to a remote object don't survive a crash, or a restart.

To understand the actual semantics of using the activation model, let's take a moment to familiarize ourselves with a few useful terms:

❑ **Activator**
The activator is a major component on the server. It facilitates remote object activation by keeping track of all the information needed to activate an object and is responsible for starting instances of JVMs on the server if needed.

❑ **Activation Group**
An activation group creates instances of objects in its group, and informs its monitor about the various active and passive states. The closest analogy to an activation group is a thread group. An activation group is essentially a complete, separate instance of the JVM that exists solely to host groups of activated objects. This fresh JVM is started as needed by the activator. There can be multiple activation groups.

❑ **Activation Monitor**
Every activation group has an activation monitor that keeps track of an object's state in the group and the group's state as a whole. The activation monitor is created when the group is made active.

❑ **Activation System**
The activation system provides a means for registering groups and activatable objects to be activated within those groups. This works closely with the activator, which activates objects registered via the activation system, and the activation monitor, and obtains information about active and inactive objects, and inactive groups.

The activation model and its associated implementations is summarized in the following table:

Entity	Implementation	Implemented as
Activator	`java.rmi.activation.Activator`	Interface (notice that the activator is a remote object itself)
Activation Group	`java.rmi.activation.ActivationGroup`	Abstract class
Activation Monitor	`java.rmi.activation.ActivationMonitor`	Interface
Activation System	`java.rmi.activation.ActivationSystem`	Interface

The activation mechanism uses identifiers and descriptors. If this seems overwhelming at first , it is worth keeping these important points in mind:

❑ Every activatable object has an ID and a descriptor.

❑ Every activatable object belongs to an activation group. The group itself has an ID and a descriptor.

The Activation Group

An activation group, as mentioned before, is used to maintain a group of activatable objects. The activation group is associated with a group identifier (`java.rmi.activation.ActivationGroupID`) and a group descriptor (`java.rmi.activation.ActivationGroupDesc`) that identify and describe the activation group respectively.

An activation group is created explicitly as a result of invoking the `ActivationGroup.createGroup()` method:

```
public static ActivationGroup createGroup(ActivationGroupID id,
                                          ActivationGroupDesc desc,
                                          long incarnation)
```

Where:

❑ `id` is the activation group identifier

❑ `desc` is the activation group's descriptor

❑ `incarnation` is the activation group's incarnation number (zero on a group's initial creation)

The `ActivationGroupID`, besides identifying the group uniquely within the activation system, also contains a reference to the group's activation system. This allows the group to interact with the system as and when necessary. All objects with the same `ActivationGroupID` are activated in the same JVM.

An `ActivationGroupDesc` contains the information necessary to create or recreate the group in which to activate objects. It contains:

❑ The group's class name. Remember that `java.rmi.activation.ActivationGroup` is an abstract class and the activator (`rmid`) internally provides its concrete implementation (for example the class `sun.rmi.server.ActivationGroupImpl`).

❑ The location of the group's class.

❑ A marshaled object that can contain group specific initialization data.

`ActivationGroupDesc` contains an inner class `CommandEnvironment` that specifies the startup environment options for the `ActivationGroup` implementation classes. This allows exact control over the command options used to start the child JVM – a null `CommandEnvironment` refers to the `rmid` default values.

`ActivationGroupDesc` can be created using one of the two constructors specified below:

❑ Construct a group descriptor that uses system default for group implementation and code location:

```
ActivationGroupDesc(Properties overrides,
                ActivationGroupDesc.CommandEnvironment cmd)
```

❑ Specify an alternative group implementation and execution environment to be used for the group:

```
ActivationGroupDesc(String className, String location,
                MarshaledObject data, Properties overrides,
                ActivationGroupDesc.CommandEnvironment cmd)
```

We have taken a whirlwind tour of the activation groups here. Let us look at some code that summarizes the creation of activation groups:

```
// Create the group descriptor
Properties env = new Properties();
env.put("java.security.policy","file://%BOOK_HOME%/Ch03/Activatable/registerit.pol
icy");
ActivationGroupDesc mygroupdes = new ActivationGroupDesc(props, null);

// Get a reference to the activation system
ActivationSystem mysystem= ActivationGroup.getSystem();

// Register the group description with the activation system and get the group id
ActivationGroupID groupid = mysystem.registerGroup(mygroupdes);

// Now that we have the id and the descriptor we can explicitly create the group
ActivationGroup.createGroup(groupid, mygroupdes, 0);
```

ActivationID

Just as the `ActivationGroupID` is an ID for the group, the `ActivationID` is an ID for the object. Once the object is registered with the activation system, it is assigned an `ActivationID`. It contains two crucial pieces of information:

❑ A remote reference to the object's activator

❑ A unique identifier for the object

We will see how to register the object shortly.

Activation Descriptor

Every activatable object has a unique identifier containing a reference to the activator that the object is associated with (`ActivationGroupID`) and an ID that uniquely identifies the object (`ActivationID`). The activation descriptor contains all the information the system needs to activate an object:

❑   The activation group identifier for the object

❑   The name of the class being activated

❑   The location of the class for the object

❑   An optional marshaled object that contains initialization data

Remember all the descriptors and identifiers we talked about until now were associated with the group. Once the group is created we have an identifier for that group in the system. So all that is needed to recreate/activate the object at any time is the activation group identifier and the class detail.

The activation descriptor can be created by using one of four constructors:

❑   Constructs an activation descriptor for the object with the given `groupID` and `className` that can be loaded from the code location, with the optional initialization information data and restart specifics for if the object is activated on demand or restarted when the activator is restarted:

```
ActivationDesc(ActivationGroupID groupID, String className,
          String location, MarshaledObject data, boolean restart)
```

❑   Same as above but without the restart information:

```
ActivationDesc(ActivationGroupID groupID, String className,
          String location, MarshaledObject data)
```

❑   Again similar to the first, only that the activation group defaults to the current `ActivationGroupID` for the current instance of the JVM. It is worth noting that this constructor will throw an `ActivationException` if no current activation group has been explicitly created for this JVM:

```
ActivationDesc(String className, String location, MarshaledObject data,
          boolean restart)
```

❑   Simpler form of above, again without the restart information:

```
ActivationDesc(String className, String location, MarshaledObject data)
```

One of the useful things about activation is the restart flag in the constructors above. rmid remembers the remote objects that have registered with it and can recreate them when it (or the machine itself) restarts. This is possible because rmid keeps a log. By default this is in a log in the directory from which rmid was started and can be configured with the −log option. When rmid starts, it consults this log to gather information and restart any objects that were configured for restart.

Once the `ActivationDesc` has been created, it can be registered in one of the following ways:

❏ By invoking the static `Activatable.register(ActivationDesc desc)` method.

❏ By instantiating the object itself using the first or second constructor of the `Activatable` class (which take the `ActivationID` as a parameter). This registers and exports the object.

❏ By exporting the object explicitly via `Activatable`'s first or second `exportObject()` method that takes an `ActivationID`, the remote object implementation, and a port number as arguments. This registers and exports the object.

Behind the scenes, here is what happens:

❏ When a stub is generated for an activatable object, it contains special information about the object. This information includes the activation identifier and information about the remote reference type of the object.

❏ This stub for the object uses the activation identifier and calls the activator to activate the object associated with the identifier (the stub is the lazy/faulting reference).

❏ The activator locates the object's activation descriptor and activation group. If the activation group in which this object should be does not exist, the activator starts an instance of a JVM, creates an activation group, and then forwards the activation request to that group.

❏ The activation group loads the class for the object and instantiates the object (using special constructors that take several arguments, as we shall soon see).

When the object is activated, the activation group returns an object reference to the activator (this is a serialized or marshaled reference). The activator records the activation identifier and reference pairing and returns the live reference to the stub. The stub then forwards method invocations via this live reference directly to the remote object (the live reference is like any other remote reference).

Let us summarize everything we have covered until now by redoing the `HelloWorld` example we covered earlier to make it activatable.

Making Objects Activatable

As we have seen there are a few cooperating entities in the activation framework that make everything possible:

❏ The object itself.

❏ The wrapper program that registers the object. This is similar to the `RegiserIt` program we used earlier. It typically makes a few method calls to the activation system to provide details about how the object should be activated.

❏ The third entity is the activation daemon that records information like the registry, about when and what to do with the objects (this daemon is `rmid`).

Keeping these entities in mind, the steps to make an object activatable can be summarized as follows:

❏ The object should extend the `java.rmi.activation.Activatable` class instead of `UnicastRemoteObject` (there is an alternative to this as we shall see later).

❑ The object should include a special constructor that takes two arguments, its activation identifier of type `ActivationID`, and its optional activation data, a `java.rmi.MarshaledObject`. This is unlike non-activatable remote objects, which include a no argument constructor. This special constructor is called by the RMI system when it activates the object.

❑ An activation descriptor (`java.rmi.activation.ActivationDesc`) should be created and registered with the activator (`rmid`).

It is worth noting that the remote interface of the object does not need to be changed or modified in any way. This makes sense as we are only changing the implementation of the object's instance, not how the outside world sees the object.

Step 1: Create the Remote Interface

This is no different from what we had earlier:

```
import java.rmi.*;

public interface HelloInterface extends Remote {
  public String sayHello() throws RemoteException;
}
```

Step 2: Create the Object Implementation

This class extends `java.rmi.activation.Activatable` and implements the remote interface (since `Activatable` extends `RemoteObject`). Furthermore, it must contain a two-argument constructor that takes the `ActivationID` and `MarshaledObject` as arguments. This constructor should call the appropriate superclass constructors to ensure initialization:

```
import java.rmi.*;
import java.rmi.activation.*;
import java.util.Date;

public class HelloServer extends Activatable implements HelloInterface {

  public HelloServer(ActivationID id, MarshaledObject data)
        throws RemoteException {
    // Register the object with the activation system
    // then export it on an anonymous port
    super(id, 0);
  }

  public String sayHello() throws RemoteException{
    return "Hello World, the current system time is " + new Date();
  }
}
```

Step 3: Register the Object with the System

This class contains all the information necessary to register the object, without actually creating an instance of the object:

```
import java.rmi.*;
import java.rmi.activation.*;
```

```
import java.util.Properties;

public class RegisterIt {

  public static void main(String args[]) throws Exception {
    try {
      //Install a SecurityManager
      System.setSecurityManager(new RMISecurityManager());

      // Create the group
      Properties env = new Properties();
      env.put("java.security.policy",
              "file://%BOOK_HOME%/Ch03/Activatable/
               activation/registerit.policy");
      ActivationGroupDesc mygroupdes = new ActivationGroupDesc(env, null);
      ActivationGroupID mygroupid = ActivationGroup.getSystem().
                                registerGroup(mygroupdes);
      ActivationGroup.createGroup(mygroupid, mygroupdes, 0);

      // Create the details about the activatable object itself
      ActivationDesc objectdesc = new ActivationDesc("HelloServer",
                "file://%BOOK_HOME%/Ch03/Activatable", null);

      // Register the activation descriptor with the activator
      HelloInterface myobject = (HelloInterface)Activatable
                                            .register(objectdesc);

      // Bind the stub to a name in the rmiregistry
      Naming.rebind("helloObject", myobject);

      // Exit
      System.out.println("Done");

    } catch(Exception e) {
      System.out.println("Exception "+ e);
    }
  }
}
```

We're nearly finished. Now we can use the old client that we wrote for our initial example and execute it with the same policy and startup arguments:

```
import java.rmi.*;

public class HelloClient {

  public static void main(String args[]) {

    if (args.length < 1) {
      System.out.println ("Usage: java HelloClient <host>");
      System.exit(1);
    } else {

      try {
        HelloInterface server = (HelloInterface)Naming.lookup(
```

```
                                        "rmi://" + args[0] + "/helloObject");
            System.out.println(server.sayHello());
        } catch (Exception e) {
            e.printStackTrace();
        }
      }
   }
}
```

Compile the files then generate the stubs and skeletons for the remote object. Start the Activation system using the rmid utility and then start our program that registers our activatable objects:

```
rmid -J-Djava.security.policy=registerit.policy
```

Now we can execute the RegisterIt file:

```
java -Djava.security.policy=registerit.policy
    -Djava.rmi.server.codebase=file://%BOOK_HOME%/Ch03/Activatable/
    RegisterIt
```

Finally, we can use the client, as shown in the following output shot:

Note that you should have three or four command line windows open for this example:

❑   rmiregistry

❑   Rmid

❑   RegisterIt

❑   HelloClient

The last two could be done in one window.

Alternative to Extending the Activatable Class

Sometimes it may be not be possible to extend the Activatable class if the remote object needs to extend another class. For example, if we are writing an applet that we want to make activatable or a remote object, our applet would need to extend java.applet.Applet and in Java there is no such thing as multiple inheritance.

We saw earlier that it was possible to make an object remote by exporting the object directly using one of the export methods in the java.rmi.UnicastRemoteObject class rather than extending the UnicastRemoteObject class itself.

There is a similar alternative for activatable objects. While talking about activation descriptors we mentioned an `exportObject()` method. It is possible to register and export an object by invoking any of the export methods in the `java.activation.Activatable` class.

Let us rewrite our activatable `HelloServer` class to demonstrate this, keeping everything else the same:

```
import java.rmi.*;
import java.rmi.activation.*;
import java.util.Date;

public class HelloServer implements HelloInterface {

    public HelloServer(ActivationID id, MarshaledObject data)
            throws RemoteException {

        // Register and export it on an anonymous port
        Activatable.exportObject(this, id, 0);
        // OR
        /*
        Activatable.exportObject(this, id, 0,
                        new SomeRMIClientSocketFactory csf(),
                        new SomeRMIServerSocketFactory())
        //OR
        Activatable.exportObject(this, ".", data, false, 0);

        //OR
        Activatable.exportObject(this, ".", data, false, 0,
                        new SomeRMIClientSocketFactory(),
                        new SomeRMIServerSocketFactory());
        */
    }

    public String sayHello() throws RemoteException{
        return "Hello World, the current system time is" + new Date();
    }
}
```

In the above example, two of the constructors shown take socket factories as arguments. We will cover socket factories in a while. For now, just keep in mind that you can pass socket factories as arguments to your activatable objects

Starting Multiple JVMs other than with rmid

`rmid` or the activator itself is a remote object and executes in a JVM. Every object that is activated is activated in its activation group's JVM but sometimes it may be desirable to spawn a separate JVM for each activatable object (for example, in a large application you would want to eliminate the single point of failure by isolating objects in different JVMs). This is straightforward if you keep in mind what was mentioned when talking about the `ActivationGroupID`, that is, "All objects with the same `ActivationGroupID` are activated in the same JVM".

To start multiple JVMs, the object must have a different `ActivationGroupID` or in other words must be in a separate activation group. The following code shows how the same `HelloServer` object is registered differently so that each object has a different `ActivationGroupID` (and hence a different activation group).

Here's the class that registers our activatable objects:

```
import java.rmi.*;
import java.rmi.activation.*;
import java.util.Properties;

public class RegisterIt {
   public static void main(String[] args) {
      try {
         //Install a SecurityManager
         System.setSecurityManager(new RMISecurityManager());

         // create another one for a new VM
         Properties env = new Properties();
         env.put("java.security.policy",
                "file://%BOOK_HOME%/Ch03/Activatable/MultiVM/
                registerit.policy");

         ActivationGroupDesc mygroupdes = new ActivationGroupDesc(env, null);
         ActivationGroupID mygroupid = ActivationGroup.getSystem()
                                    .registerGroup(mygroupdes);
         ActivationGroup.createGroup(mygroupid, mygroupdes, 0);
         ActivationDesc objectdesc = new ActivationDesc("HelloServer",
                "file://%BOOK_HOME%/Ch03/Activatable/MultiVM/",
                 null);
         HelloInterface myobject = (HelloInterface)Activatable.register(
                                    objectdesc);
         Naming.rebind("helloObject", myobject);

         // Register another group's id
         ActivationGroupID mygroupid_2 = ActivationGroup.getSystem()
                                    .registerGroup(mygroupdes);
         ActivationDesc objectdesc_2 = new ActivationDesc("HelloServer",
                "file://%BOOK_HOME%/Ch03/Activatable/MultiVM/",
                 null);
         HelloInterface myobject_2 = (HelloInterface)Activatable.register(
                                    objectdesc_2);
         Naming.rebind("helloObject_2", myobject_2);

         System.exit(0);

      } catch (Exception e) {
         System.out.println(e);
         e.printStackTrace();
      }
   }
}
```

The client starts the new JVM on the server because of the lazy activation (activation the first time the method is invoked):

```
import java.rmi.*;

public class HelloClient {
```

```
public static void main(String args[]) {
  if (args.length < 1) {
    System.out.println ("Usage: java HelloClient <host>");
    System.exit(1);
  }
  try {
      HelloInterface obj = (HelloInterface)Naming.lookup(
                          "rmi://" + args[0] + "/helloObject");
      System.out.println(obj.sayHello());

      // Spawn the second VM on the server!
      HelloInterface obj_2 = (HelloInterface)Naming.lookup(
                          "rmi://" + args[0] + "/helloObject_2");
      System.out.println(obj_2.sayHello());

  } catch (Exception e) {
      System.out.println("HelloClient exception: " + e.getMessage());
      e.printStackTrace();
  }
 }
}
```

If we run this example, and look at the processes running when we run the client, we'll see that two Java VMs are used:

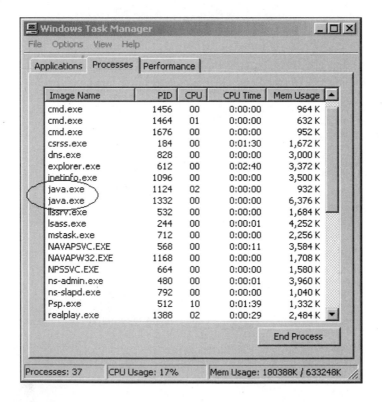

Deactivation

Activation allows an object to be started on demand, however it does not automatically deactivate an object. The decision to deactivate the object is left to the object itself. An activatable object can deactivate itself by invoking the `Activatable.inactive(ActivationID id)` method.

It is important to know the difference between un-registering and deactivating an object. Deactivation is a temporary state, allowing the activation system to restart the object later, whereas un-registering the object by `Activatable.unregister(ActivationID id)` permanently removes it from the activation system.

Another useful method is the `Activatable.unexportObject(Remote obj, boolean force)` method that can be used to unexport the object. The `boolean` is used to force the object to be unexported even if there are pending or in-progress calls.

> While activation can be a big improvement in performance when the number of objects in a system is large, by relieving the drain on the resources, you should take care while deciding on how and when to use it. The overhead required to create and reactivate an inactive object is large. It can involve creating a new JVM, loading, verifying classes, and deserializing a persistent object state. An object should typically decide on a safe time to stay alive. A good deactivation strategy could be based on the time since the last call was made.

Next we'll turn our attention to the Secure Sockets Layer. This section will assume that the reader is familiar with TCP/IP sockets and networking in Java.

Custom Sockets and SSL

A socket is an endpoint for communication. Two collaborating sockets, one on the local machine and the other on the remote machine, form a connection. This distinction between sockets and connections is very important.

There are two types of sockets, **connection sockets** and **listening sockets**, also referred to as client and server sockets, respectively. A connection socket exists on each end of an open TCP connection and is abstracted by the `java.net.ServerSocket` and `java.net.Socket` classes. A listening socket is not associated with any TCP connection, but only exists as an abstraction to allow the TCP kernel to decide which incoming connections are accepted, and who gets the newly accepted connection socket.

At any time, RMI has a small number of listening sockets, one for each listened-to port (usually just one because RMI exports all objects on the "default" port, unless a specific port is specified in the `export()` method discussed earlier). RMI also creates connection sockets for outgoing connections and incoming connections.

The number of outgoing connections only depends on the number of concurrent outgoing calls. The simple rule is:

❑ If a thread wants to make a remote call, and all the connections to the endpoint are in use, then RMI opens a new connection to carry the call

❑ If a connection is free (meaning there's no call in progress using that connection), then RMI will reuse it for the next remote call

RMI spawns one thread to listen to each listening socket (also usually one). When RMI accepts a new connection, it creates a new thread – one thread handles the new connection, and the other goes back to accept a new connection. When the connection closes, its associated thread also exits.

The connection-handling threads spawned by RMI are not serialized in any way. If the calls arrive at the same time they will be run in concurrent threads. The calls are still allowed to synchronize on Java objects but RMI does not do such synchronization automatically (the remote object is responsible for its own synchronization either by synchronized methods or by synchronized locking).

A common point of confusion is that if a remote stub is returned by a remote call, the client can sometimes be seen to make two connections to the server. This happens because the distributed garbage-collection subsystem needs to make a `DGC.dirty()` call to notify the server that a new entity holds a reference to the remote object.

> *You can use `netstat` to monitor listening sockets. The following screenshot shows the sockets just after the registry is started on 1099. `HelloServer` is exported to 2000 and is binding with the registry. The left column lists the open sockets on the machine. The first line is for the registry, the second for the object. The third shows that a socket has been opened by the object to the registry and the last line shows the socket opened by the registry to the object.*

A significant enhancement that was added to RMI from the Java 1.2 release was the ability to use custom socket factories based on the Factory design pattern. Instead of using the conventional sockets over TCP/IP, each object has the ability to use its own socket type. This allows the object to process data (rather than simply passing it), either before it is sent to, or after it has been received from, the socket.

In JDK 1.1.x, it was possible to create a custom `java.rmi.RMISocketFactory` subclass that produced a custom socket, other than the `java.net.Socket`, for use by the RMI transport layer. However, it was not possible for the installed socket factory to produce different types of sockets for different objects. For example in JDK 1.1, an RMI socket factory could not produce Secure Sockets Layer (SSL) sockets for one object and use the Java Remote Method Protocol (JRMP) directly over TCP for a different object in the same JVM. In addition, before 1.2, it was necessary for `rmiregistry` to use only your custom socket protocol.

The socket factory affected the whole system and not just a single object.

To see what this statement actually means, let us first see where in the RMI architecture sockets are involved, their types and purpose:

Location	Server socket	Client sockets
RMI registry	It opens a server socket (default port 1099) and waits for requests from: ❑ Servers to bind, re-bind and un-bind object implementations ❑ Clients who want to locate servers	It uses a client socket to establish a connection to a server object right after they have registered.
RMI servers (Remote implementation)	It opens a server socket on a user specified port via the `exportObject()` method or defaults to a random local port; it is used to accept connections from the client's (stub's) send responses.	A client socket is used while connecting to the registry, in particular to register the server implementation.
RMI Clients (objects invoking remote methods)	Not used	Client sockets are used for the communication with the RMI registry, to locate the server implementation and to make the actual RMI method call to the server

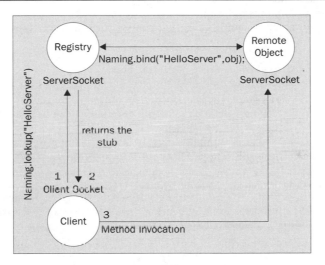

When a client performs a "lookup" operation, a connection is made to the server socket on the `rmiregistry`. In general, a new connection may or may not be created for a remote call. The RMI transport layer caches connections for future use. If there are any existing connections and at least one of them is free, then it is reused; otherwise the current implementation creates additional sockets on demand. For example, if an existing socket is in use by an existing call, then a new socket is created for the new call. Usually there are at least two sockets open since the distributed garbage collector needs to make remote calls when remote objects are returned from the server. A client has no explicit control over the connections to a server, since connections are managed at the RMI transport-layer level. Connections will time out if they are unused for a period.

As you can see, there are a number of communication points and sockets being used in this three-way communication among the client, the registry, and the object. It is also important to note that the registry is only needed to locate an object by its name. Once the object is located there is direct communication between the object and the client.

An object can specify what factory classes are needed for anyone to communicate with its socket type through the `java.rmi.server.UnicastRemoteObject` constructor (or `java.rmi.activation.Activatable` for that matter). Instances of these factories are used to create instances of the desired sockets types:

```
protected UnicastRemoteObject(int port, RMIClientSocketFactory csf,
                              RMIServerSocketFactory ssf)
```

As explained in the previous table, once the client has located an object, it uses a client socket to connect to the server socket that the object is listening on. The client socket factory must implement the `java.rmi.server.RMISocketFactory` interface. The client socket is created from this instance of the `RMIClientSocketFactory` by invoking the `createSocket()` method that returns an instance of the custom socket type to the specified server and port:

```
public Socket createSocket(String host, int port)
```

The server socket factory must implement the `java.rmi.server.RMIServerSocketFactory` interface and provide an implementation for the `createServerSocket()` method. The server socket is created (to start listening for incoming calls) by invoking the method implementation in the server socket factory class:

```
public ServerSocket createServerSocket(int port)
```

This is particularly useful when you want to encrypt the communication between the objects. For example, using SSL or TLS. Let us look at an example of how this can be done.

First we would need a couple of things, the foremost being a security provider that provides an implementation of the SSL protocol in Java. Many third party products available do this.

> **SSL and TLS both provide encryption and certification. Actually, Transport Layer Security (TLS) is the new Internet Engineering Task Force (IETF) standard and is based on SSL.**

SSL specifications can be found at http://home.netscape.com/eng/security/ and TLS specifications can be found in RFC 2246 at http://www.ietf.org/rfc/rfc2246.txt. Details about open source SSL implementations (SSLeay/OpenSSL) can be found at http://www.openssl.org/.

Sun provides the **Java Secure Sockets Extension (JSSE)** that implements a Java version of SSL and TLS protocols and includes functionality for data encryption, server authentication, message integrity, and optional client authentication.

The example discussed here uses JSSE. You would need to download it separately for J2SE (1.2 or 1.3) and it will be actually packaged with J2SE (1.4), see http://java.sun.com/products/jsse/ for more information.

There is going to be a performance overhead and the communication is going to be very slow due to the complexity of the handshake and the encryption involved. How the provider implements the algorithms would also affect performance. For example, a native implementation such the GoNative Provider (http://www.rtfm.com/puretls/gonative.html) is faster than its pure Java counterpart.

Let us first try to see what part of the communication we want/need to encrypt. The naming registry is implemented as a standard RMI service so attempts to register and lookup services will involve network connections being established. If you need the communication with the registry to take place over secure sockets then obviously the naming registry to would need to listen on secure server sockets.

A straightforward way to do this is to have your server start its own naming registry. This registry will then benefit from the server's SSL support. The server would need to invoke and set a socket factory explicitly and start the registry:

```
RMISocketFactory.setSocketFactory (some vendor provided factory);
LocateRegistry.createRegistry(someport);
```

The SSL socket factory can then be installed on the client before looking up the object and everything will be SSL-secured.

> Since the same socket cannot listen on two ports, it would be necessary to run two registries: a secure one and a normal one, if you needed to lookup on different protocols. Most vendors provide a secure registry with the Java-SSL implementation that can be used if you are not programmatically starting the registry.

In most cases, it is only the communication between the objects that is important and needs encryption, not the lookup, this is what we will look at in the following example. In order for communication to occur over SSL or TLS we need two things: keys and certificates. To see more information on these, see the links to the SSL and TLS documentation.

Before we do anything, we generate the keys and certificates using the JDK utility keytool. This is a certificate management tool used to manage public/private key pairs and associated certificates to be used in self-authentication and data integrity and authentication services, using digital signatures. In a commercial environment you would probably use keytool to generate a certificate request and use that request to obtain a certificate from a Certificate Authority (CA) like Verisign (http://www.verisign.com). For our purposes, we will generate a self-signed certificate (a certificate from the CA authenticating its own public key). In other words, we will use our own keys and certificates using the -genkey option in keytool.

Run the keytool utility with parameters something like this:

```
keytool -genkey -dname "cn=ProJavaServer, ou=Java, o=Wrox Press, c=US" -alias wrox
-keypass secret -storepass secret -validity 365 -keystore
%BOOK_HOME%\Ch03\SSL\.keystore
```

We can check the certificate by using keytool in a different way:

```
keytool -list -keystore %BOOK_HOME%\Ch03\SSL\.keystore -storepass secret
```

```
C:\WINNT\System32\cmd.exe                                                    _□×
C:\ProJavaServer\Ch03\SSL>keytool -genkey -dname "cn=ProJavaServer, ou=Java, o=Wrox Press, c=US" -alias
wrox -keypass secret -storepass secret -validity 365 -keystore C:\ProJavaServer\Ch03\SSL\.keystore

C:\ProJavaServer\Ch03\SSL>keytool -list -keystore C:\ProJavaServer\Ch03\SSL\.keystore -storepass secret

Keystore type: jks
Keystore provider: SUN

Your keystore contains 1 entry

wrox, 21-Mar-01, keyEntry,
Certificate fingerprint (MD5): 96:33:7D:6F:12:FF:FB:8F:A5:3C:A0:80:17:1F:67:44
```

This generates a keystore called "wrox" that contains the keys and the self-signed certificate and has the password "secret".

> *Please refer to the tool documentation packaged with JDK for details about how to use keytool, keys, and certificates in the Java 2 security architecture.*

Finally, we also export the generated certificate into a file `clientimport.cer` for use by clients using `keytool`:

```
keytool -export -keystore %BOOK_HOME%\Ch03\SSL\.keystore -storepass secret -file
clientimport.cer -alias wrox
```

> *Remember that we are not using browser-based SSL anywhere in these examples. If you want to do that then you need to generate certificates with the RSA algorithm (use the `-keyalg` option in `keytool`). For this you would need to install a provider that offers the RSA algorithm implementation since the JDK 1.2 keytool does not support it. For our purposes, the JSSE provider contains an implementation and RSA support is in-built in JDK 1.3. Also, the freeware JCE implementation available from http://www.openjce.org is a good security API provider.*

Let us now revisit and rewrite the `HelloWorld` example we used earlier, to secure the object-to-object communication.

Again, the remote interface remains unchanged:

```java
import java.rmi.Remote;
import java.rmi.RemoteException;

public interface HelloInterface extends Remote {
  public String sayHello() throws RemoteException;
}
```

We now rewrite the remote implementation of this interface:

```java
import java.rmi.*;
import java.rmi.server.UnicastRemoteObject;
import java.util.Date;

public class HelloServer extends UnicastRemoteObject
                         implements HelloInterface {
  public HelloServer() throws RemoteException {
    super(0, new MyClientSocketFactory(), new MyServerSocketFactory());
  }
```

```
      public String sayHello() {
        return "Hello World, the current system time is " + new Date();
      }
    }
```

Notice that the only difference is that we pass our own custom factories that will be used for this object instead of the default factories.

We now use the same program we used earlier to register this remote object:

```
    import java.rmi.*;

    public class RegisterIt {

      public static void main(String args[]) {
        try {
          // Instantiate the object
          HelloServer obj = new HelloServer();
          System.out.println("Object instantiated"  +obj);
          Naming.rebind ("/HelloServer", obj);
          System.out.println("HelloServer bound in registry");
        } catch (Exception e) {
          System.out.println(e);
        }
      }
    }
```

The pieces we passed so easily are the socket factories. Let us look at them in detail now. The `MyServerSocketFactory` class is used to create instances of the server socket on the port that the object was exported on. This class must implement the `java.rmi.server.RMIServerSocketFactory` interface and should be serializable (to facilitate possible transportation over the network). The secure interchange between the client and the server involves an exchange of keys and certificates and the socket created must first initialize communication with the client before exchanging any data. The JSSE implementation allows us to do this in a few lines of code. We open the keystore (that we generated) from the file using its password, initialize the SSL/TLS implementation, and return an instance of a secure socket:

```
    import java.io.*;
    import java.net.*;
    import java.rmi.server.*;
    import java.security.*;
    import javax.net.ssl.*;
    import javax.security.cert.*;
    import com.sun.net.ssl.*;

    public class MyServerSocketFactory implements RMIServerSocketFactory,
                                                  Serializable {
      // Implement the interface method
      public ServerSocket createServerSocket(int port)throws IOException {
        SSLServerSocketFactory ssf = null;
        try {
          // Set up key manager to do server authentication
```

```
            char[] passphrase = "secret".toCharArray();

            // Get a context for the protocol. We can use SSL or TLS as needed.
            SSLContext ctx = SSLContext.getInstance("TLS");
            KeyManagerFactory kmf = KeyManagerFactory.getInstance("SunX509");

            // Open the keystore with the password
            // and initialize the SSL context with this keystore.
            KeyStore ks = KeyStore.getInstance("JKS");
            ks.load(new FileInputStream (".keystore"), passphrase);
            kmf.init(ks, passphrase);
            ctx.init(kmf.getKeyManagers(), null, null);
            ssf = ctx.getServerSocketFactory();
        } catch (Exception e) {
          e.printStackTrace();
        }
        return ssf.createServerSocket(port);
    }
}
```

The client socket factory is used to create instances of the client sockets that connect to the instances of the server sockets generated from the above factory. It is assumed that the JSSE provider is also installed on the client machine:

```
import java.io.*;
import java.net.*;
import java.rmi.server.*;
import javax.net.ssl.*;

public class MyClientSocketFactory implements RMIClientSocketFactory,
                                              Serializable {

  public Socket createSocket(String host, int port) throws IOException {

    // We get the default SSL socket factory.
    SSLSocketFactory factory =
                    (SSLSocketFactory)SSLSocketFactory.getDefault();
    SSLSocket socket = (SSLSocket)factory.createSocket(host, port);
    return socket;
  }
}
```

The client remains unchanged:

```
import java.rmi.Naming;
import java.rmi.RemoteException;

public class HelloClient {

  public static void main(String args[]) {
    if (args.length < 1) {
      System.out.println("Usage: java HelloClient <host>");
      System.exit(1);
    }
```

```
    try{
      HelloInterface obj =(HelloInterface)Naming.lookup(
                                    "rmi://" + args[0] + "/HelloServer");
      System.out.println("Got a remote reference" + obj);
      System.out.println(obj.sayHello());
    } catch (Exception e) {
      System.out.println(e);
    }
  }
}
```

The `ssl.policy` file we use here is actually the same as that used in the previous examples:

```
grant {
  permission java.security.AllPermission;
};
```

We can now compile the classes and generate the stubs for the `HelloServer` using the `rmic` packaged with the JDK.

Two small configuration details need to be examined before executing the example. In order for the client to interact and exchange keys and certificates with the server, it must trust the provider of the digital certificate. In other words, since our certificate is self-generated the client VM should:

❑   Explicitly import the certificate into the keystore it is using and mark it as a trusted certificate

❑   Use the same keystore that we use on the server

For the second option, the JSSE provider must be installed on the client machine (if it is different from the server) in one of two possible ways:

❑   **Statically** in the `java.security` file

❑   **Dynamically** using `Security.addProvider(new com.sun.net.ssl.internal.ssl.Provider());`

For more specific details regarding these installation methods, the reader is referred to the JSSE documentation.

The client can import the certificate from the file we generated earlier, `clientimport.cer`, into the keystore it is using and mark it as trusted using `keytool` with the `-import` statement:

```
keytool -import -file clientimport.cer -alias wrox
```

Once this is done we first start the registry on the server (execute `rmiregistry`):

```
rmiregistry -J-Djava.security.policy=ssl.policy
```

then register the object with the registry:

```
java -classpath %CLASSPATH% -Djava.security.policy=ssl.policy -
Djava.rmi.server.codebase=file://%BOOK_HOME%/Ch03/SSL/ RegisterIt
```

> Remember to carefully install the JSSE. Put the **jar** files in your
> **<JAVA_HOME>\lib\ext** location and install the provider in your **java.security**
> file (see the file **INSTALL.txt** within the JSSE bundle for further details). If you have
> multiple runtime environments, be sure to edit the right security file. The easiest
> solution is to set the PATH to point only to whichever JDK you are using.

Now run the client and specify the keystore to use using the JSSE `javax.net.ssl.trustStore` property.
This is the keystore into which the certificate has been imported or the same keystore as the server:

```
>
java -Djava.security.policy=ssl.policy -Djavax.net.ssl.trustStore=.keystore
HelloClient localhost
```

```
C:\WINNT\System32\cmd.exe
C:\ProJavaServer\Ch03\SSL>java -Djava.security.policy=ssl.policy -Djavax.net.ssl.trustStore=
.keystore HelloClient localhost
Got a remote referenceHelloServer_Stub[RemoteStub [ref: [endpoint:[192.168.0.132:3436,MyClie
ntSocketFactory@471e30](remote),objID:[3a34f2:e5644237b5:-8000, 0]]]]
Hello World, the current system time is Thu Mar 22 03:15:15 GMT+00:00 2001
```

If we want the client to be an applet, a few configuration issues need to be resolved first:

❑ The client must have a J2SE 1.2 (or newer) JVM. At the time of writing Netscape 6 and 6.1
were the only browsers with J2SE 1.2 support. Hence, we would probably need to install the
Java plug-in software. (The Java plug-in is a one-time download that automatically upgrades
the browser's JVM to the latest version. It works with both IE and Netscape.)

❑ The client JVM must have the appropriate keystore and certificates installed.

❑ The client JVM should have the right policy, allowing sockets to be opened back to the server.

❑ The client JVM should have the security provider installed, or have the right security
permissions so that a security provider can be installed dynamically.

More information and downloads for the Java Plug-in can be accessed at
http://java.sun.com/products/plugin/.

Let us look at the applet below. It is simple, similar to the example we discussed earlier, except that it is an applet. It is important to realize that the applet has nothing to do with the browser's SSL configuration. The SSL connection happens at the RMI-socket level. The client socket-factory class is downloaded dynamically and the secure connection made to the server:

```java
import java.applet.*;
import java.awt.*;
import java.rmi.*;
import java.security.*;

public class SSLHelloApplet extends Applet{

  String message = "-n/a-";

  HelloInterface obj = null;

  // Get a reference to the object in applet initialization
  public void init() {
    try{
      Security.addProvider(new com.sun.net.ssl.internal.ssl.Provider());
      String host="rmi://" + getCodeBase().getHost() + "/HelloServer";
      HelloInterface obj = (HelloInterface)Naming.lookup(
                                    "rmi://localhost/HelloServer");
      message = obj.sayHello();
    } catch (Exception e){
      System.out.println(e);
    }
  }

  // Display the message in the applet
  public void paint(Graphics g){
    g.drawString(message, 25, 50);
  }
}
```

Below is the HTML page (index.html) for the above applet. This page is converted using the HTML converter tool packaged with the Java plug-in. When a client comes across this page, if a compatible version does not exist, the JRE 1.3 will be downloaded from the URL specified. (The Sun web site in this case):

```html
<html>
  <head>
  <title>Hello World</title>
  <head>

  <body>
    <center> <h1>Hello World</h1> </center>

The message from the HelloServer is:
<p>
<!--"CONVERTED_APPLET"-->
<!-- CONVERTER VERSION 1.3 -->
<object classid = "clsid:8AD9C840-044E-11D1-B3E9-00805F499D93"
        width = 500 height = 120 codebase =
"http://java.sun.com/products/plugin/1.3/jinstall-13-win32.cab#Version=1,3,0,0">
```

```
<param name = code value = "SSLHelloApplet" >
<param name = codebase value = "http://localhost:8080/hello/" >

<param name ="type" VALUE="application/x-java-applet;version=1.3">
<param name ="scriptable" VALUE="false">
<comment>
<embed type = "application/x-java-applet;version=1.3" code = "SSLHelloApplet"
codebase = "http://localhost:8080/hello/" width = 500 height = 120
scriptable=false pluginspage = "http://java.sun.com/products/plugin/1.3/plugin-
install.html"> <noembed></comment>

    </noembed></embed>
  </object>

<!--
<applet code = "SSLHelloApplet" codebase = "http://localhost:8080/hello/" width =
500 height = 120>
</applet>
-->
<!--"end_converted_applet"-->

  </body>
</html>
```

When the page above is accessed from the browser, the browser determines from the tags that a plug-in (JRE 1.3) is needed to load this component and prompts you to download it from the location that was specified in the `pluginspage` parameter (or `codebase` depending on the browser) – this is of course assuming that it isn't already installed:

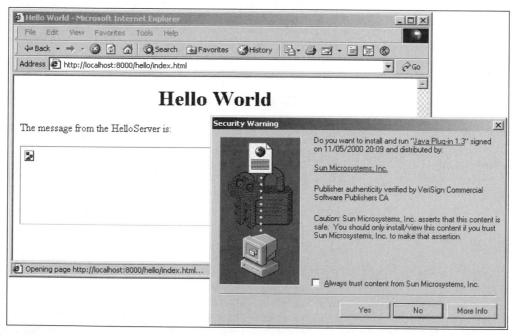

Once we download and install the plug-in and enable it from its console on our machine, we can access the same page. The browser will then load it in the new Java 1.3 JVM (rather than the browser's default JVM).

At this point, we need to make sure we add the necessary run-time parameters for the plug-in using the Java Plug-in applet in Control Panel. We need to add the `-Djava.security.policy` and `-Djavax.net.ssl.trustStore` parameters. In this example they will be:

```
-Djava.security.policy=%BOOK_HOME%\Ch03\SSL\ssl.policy
-Djavax.net.ssl.trustStore=%BOOK_HOME%\Ch03\SSL\.keystore
```

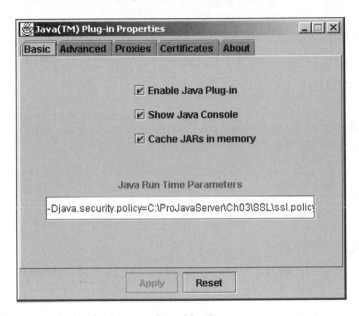

Finally, we should get a result that looks something like this:

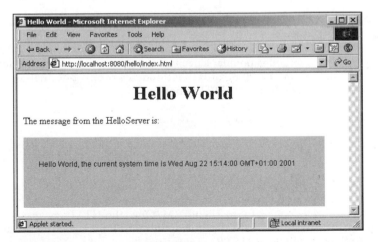

The same URL can be accessed using `appletviewer`:

```
appletviewer -J-Djava.security.policy=ssl.policy
             -J-Djavax.net.ssl.trustStore=.keystore
             http://localhost:8080/hello/index.html
```

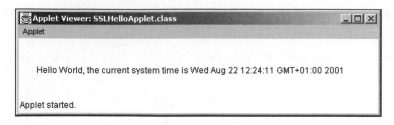

RMI, Firewalls, and HTTP

If you have worked in any networked enterprise, then you are probably familiar with how firewalls block all network traffic, with the exception of that intended for certain "well-known" ports. They are however necessary to protect the security of the network.

Since the RMI transport layer opens dynamic socket connections between the client and the server, the JRMP traffic is typically blocked by most firewall implementations. RMI provides a workaround to this.

There are three main methods to bypass firewalls:

❑ HTTP-tunneling

❑ SOCKS

❑ Downloaded socket factories

We'll examine each of these methods in turn.

HTTP Tunneling

To get across firewalls, RMI makes use of HTTP tunneling by encapsulating the RMI calls within an HTTP POST request. This method is popular since it requires almost no setup, and works quite well in firewall environments that permit handling of HTTP through a proxy, but disallow regular outbound TCP connections. There are two forms of HTTP-tunneling:

HTTP-to-Port

If a client is behind a firewall and RMI fails to make a normal connection to the server, the RMI transport layer automatically retries by encapsulating the JRMP call data within an HTTP POST request.

Since almost all firewalls recognize the HTTP protocol, the specified proxy server should be able to forward the call directly to the port on which the remote server is listening. It is important that the proxy server configuration be passed to the client JVM. Once the HTTP-encapsulated JRMP data is received at the server, RMI can automatically unwrap the HTTP tunneled request and decode it. The reply is then sent back to the client as HTTP-encapsulated data:

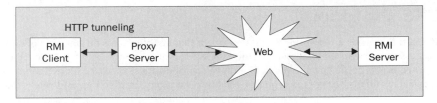

The proxy server configuration can be passed using properties, such as:

```
java -Dhttp.proxyHost=hostname -Dhttp.proxyPort=portnumber HelloClient
```

HTTP tunneling can be disabled by setting the property:

```
java.rmi.server.disableHttp=true
```

Http-to-CGI

If the server cannot be contacted from the client, even after tunneling, because it is also behind a firewall, the RMI Transport layer uses a similar mechanism on the server. The RMI Transport layer places JRMP calls in HTTP requests and sends those requests, just as above. However, instead of sending them to the server port it sends them to `http://hostname:80/cgi-bin/java-rmi?forward=<port>`. There must be an HTTP server listening on port 80 on the proxy, which has the `java-rmi.cgi` script. The `java-rmi.cgi` in turn invokes a local JVM, unwraps the HTTP packet, and forwards the call to the server process on the designated port. RMI JRMP-based replies from the server are sent back as HTTP packets to the originating client port where RMI again unwraps the information and sends it to the appropriate RMI stub.

> *The* `java-rmi.cgi` *script is packaged with the JDK and can be found in the* `bin` *directory. To avoid any DNS resolution problems at startup, the host's fully qualified domain name must be specified via a system property as:*
>
> ```
> java.rmi.server.hostname=www.host.domain
> ```
>
> *A servlet implementation of the CGI called a servlet handler is available from Sun at http://java.sun.com/j2se/1.3/docs/guide/rmi/archives/rmiservlethandler.zip.*

Another alternative to the `java-rmi.cgi` is using a port redirector (for example, DeleGate proxy) on port 80 that accepts connections and immediately redirects them to another port.

Although HTTP tunneling is an alternative, in general it should be avoided for the following reasons:

❑   There is significant performance degradation. While tunneling, the RMI application will not be able to multiplex JRMP calls on a single connection, due to the request-response HTTP paradigm.

❑   Using the `java-rmi.cgi` script (or servlet) is a big security loophole on the server. The script redirects any incoming request to any port, completely circumventing the firewall.

❑   RMI applications tunneling over HTTP cannot use callbacks.

The SOCKS Protocol

SOCKS (**SOCK**et **S**erver) is a networking proxy protocol that enables hosts on one side of a SOCKS server to gain full access to hosts on the other side of the SOCKS server without requiring direct IP reachability. The SOCKS server redirects connection requests from hosts on opposite sides of a SOCKS server (the SOCKS server authenticates and authorizes the requests, establishes a proxy connection, and relays data).

By default, JDK sockets use a SOCKS server if available and configured. Server sockets however do not support SOCKS so this approach is only useful for outgoing calls from the client to the server.

Downloaded Socket Factories

We have already discussed at length how custom sockets can be used. The factory classes can be coded to work around the firewall. Dynamically downloaded socket factories provide a good alternative to HTTP tunneling, but the code to bypass the firewall must be hard-coded in the factories. This is OK if you have a fixed network configuration and know how that particular firewall works. However, different clients can have different firewalls and there are questions regarding access rights to provide this tunneling and, of course, changing factory classes.

RMI Over IIOP

RMI over Internet Inter-Orb Protocol (IIOP) integrates Common Object Request Broker Architecture (CORBA)-compliant distributed computing directly into Java. RMI over IIOP, developed jointly by IBM and Sun, is a new version of RMI for IIOP that combines RMI's easy programming features with CORBA's interoperability.

RMI and CORBA have developed independently as distributed-objects programming models. RMI was introduced to provide a simple programming model for developing distributed objects whereas CORBA is a well-known distributed-object programming model that supports a number of languages. The IIOP protocol connects CORBA products from different vendors, ensuring interoperability among them.

> *The Object Management Group (OMG) – see* http://www.omg.org/ – *is the official keeper of information for CORBA and IIOP, including the CORBA 2.0 specifications available at* http://www.omg.org/technology/documents/specifications.htm. *Additionally, the IDL to Java mappings are available at* http://www.omg.org/technology/documents/formal/corba_language_mapping_specs.htm.

RMI-IIOP is, in a sense, a marriage of RMI and CORBA, since remote interfaces can be written in Java, and implemented using Java RMI APIs. These interfaces however can be implemented in any other language that is supported by an OMG mapping and a vendor-supplied ORB for that language. Similarly, clients can be written in other languages, using IDL derived from the Java remote interfaces.

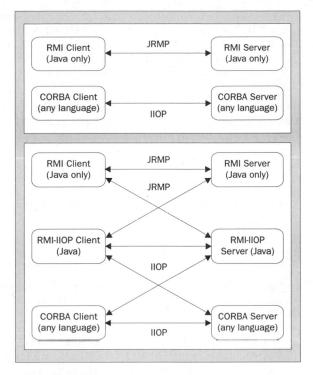

The figure above summarizes the RMI-IIOP marriage. It may seem that the arrows connecting the JRMP clients/servers to the RMI-IIOP client/servers are misplaced because they are different protocols. These arrows are actually in the right place because RMI-IIOP supports both JRMP and IIOP protocols.

One of the initial design objectives was to make migration to IIOP feasible, indeed easy, and to avoid the need for a third distributed model for developers to learn. The server object created using the RMI-IIOP API can be exported as either a JRMP or IIOP-supporting object by simply changing deployment-time properties (without changing or recompiling code).

RMI-IIOP also supports dual export, meaning that a single server object can be exported to support both JRMP and IIOP simultaneously.

Interoperability with CORBA

An RMI-IIOP client cannot necessarily access all existing CORBA objects. The semantics of CORBA objects defined in IDL are a superset of those supported by RMI-IIOP objects, which is why an existing CORBA object's IDL cannot always be mapped into an RMI-IIOP Java interface. It is only when a specific CORBA object's semantics happen to correspond with those of RMI-IIOP that an RMI-IIOP client can call a CORBA object. The connection between the RMI-IIOP client and CORBA server is sometimes (but not always) possible.

However, this issue should not be over emphasized because it only applies when dealing with existing CORBA objects. Looking at the lower half of the above figure, if we design a new object with an RMI-IIOP Java interface, we can make the following observations:

❑ The CORBA implementation: you can automatically generate its corresponding IDL with the `rmic` tool. From this IDL file you can implement it as a CORBA object in any acceptable language, like C++ for instance. This C++ object is a pure CORBA object that can be called by a CORBA client as well as an RMI-IIOP client without any limitations. To the RMI-IIOP client, this C++ CORBA object appears as a pure RMI-IIOP object because it is defined by an RMI-IIOP Java interface.

❑ The RMI-IIOP implementation: the object appears as a CORBA object to a CORBA client (because a CORBA client accesses it through its IDL) and as an RMI object to RMI clients (because they access it through its RMI-IIOP Java interface).

In short, the difference between a CORBA object and an RMI-IIOP object is only an implementation matter.

One of the reasons for the problems with existing objects mentioned above is that two significant enhancements to the CORBA 2.3 specifications were actually made to bring about the RMI-IIOP and CORBA interoperability. OMG accepted these specifications:

❑ **Objects by Value** specification: This is already defined in Java in the form of object Serialization and is intended to make other languages implement a similar protocol.

❑ **Java-to-IDL Mapping** specification: This is the mapping used to convert RMI Java interfaces into CORBA IDL definitions. It should not be confused with the IDL-to-Java mapping already defined in CORBA 2.2.

Both of these specifications are available at OMG, and they are also accessible at http://java.sun.com/products/rmi-iiop/index.html. OMG has officially accepted both specifications for CORBA 2.3 and JDK 1.3 to include both RMI-IIOP and an IDL-to-Java compiler.

Writing Programs with RMI-IIOP

There are some development differences in syntax though the overall model remains the same, significantly, RMI-IIOP uses the JNDI API to locate and register objects. Although the development procedure for RMI-IIOP is almost the same as that for RMI (JRMP), the runtime environment is significantly different in that communication is made through a CORBA 2.3-compliant ORB using IIOP for communication between servers and clients. Let's briefly look at these differences.

On the Server

There is no significant change in development procedure for RMI objects in RMI-IIOP. The basic steps and their order is still the same as outlined earlier in our `HelloWorld` example, with some changes that also reflect the use of JNDI to lookup and bind objects.

HelloServer.java

```
import java.rmi.*;
import java.util.Date;
import javax.rmi.PortableRemoteObject;
```

Implementation class of a remote object:

```
public class HelloServer extends PortableRemoteObject
                    implements HelloInterface {
```

The `PortableRemoteObject` is similar to the `UnicastRemoteObject` but provides the base functionality in the IIOP domain.

```
public HelloServer() throws RemoteException {
  super();      // Call the superclass constructor to export this object
}

public String sayHello() throws RemoteException {
  return "Hello World, the current system time is " + new Date();
}
}
```

❑ Generate a tie for IIOP with `rmic -iiop`:
   With the `-iiop` option the `rmic` compiler generates the stubs and tie classes that support the IIOP protocol. Without this `-iiop` option, `rmic` generates a stub and a skeleton for the JRMP protocol or only stubs if you also use the `-v1.2` option (remember skeletons are not needed in 1.2).

❑ Run `tnameserv.exe` as a name server:
   This server provides the IIOP `CosNaming` services to for clients to lookup objects.

❑ Generate IDL with `rmic -idl` for CORBA clients (if our object is also going to be accessed by CORBA clients).

❑ While starting the server the two important environment variables for the JNDI context must be set up.

   a. `java.naming.factory.initial`. This is the name of the class to use as the factory for creating the context.

   b. `java.naming.provider.url`. This is the URL to the naming service similar to the `rmi://` URL format described earlier. The `rmi://` is replaced by `iiop://` and the default port is 900 instead of the 1099 for the registry.

These properties can be specified either while starting the server as shown below or by hard-coding values into `java.util.Properties` and passing that to the `InitialContext` as we do in the next example:

```
java -Djava.naming.factory.initial=com.sun.jndi.cosnaming.CNCtxFactory
    -Djava.naming.provider.url=iiop://129.112.1.9:900 RegisterIt
```

In the Client

The client has the same import statement and uses the JNDI context to obtain a reference to the object, rather than using the registry. The JNDI `lookup()` method returns a `java.lang.Object`, which must then be cast using the `narrow()` method of `PortableRemoteObject`.

HelloClient.java

```
import java.rmi.*;
import javax.rmi.PortableRemoteObject;
import javax.naming.InitialContext;

public class HelloClient {

  public static void main(String args[]) {
    try {
```

Create the JNDI context and bind to it:

```
        InitialContext ctx = new InitialContext (); // Create the JNDI context
        Object obj = ctx.lookup("/EgServer");
```

This binds the object to the JNDI context just as the `Naming.bind()` method did.

```
        HelloInterface myobj = (HelloInterface) PortableRemoteObject
                                .narrow(obj, HelloInterface.class);

    String message = myobj.sayHello();
    System.out.println(message);
  } catch (Exception e) {
    System.out.println("HelloClient exception: " + e);
  }
  }
}
```

Again, the properties for the JNDI context (the context factory name and provider URL) *must* be passed to the client applications at runtime. That's basically it!

> *Sun provides a step-by-step guide packaged with the JDK on conversion of existing RMI programs and applets. This can also be accessed online at http://java.sun.com/j2se/1.3/docs/guide/rmi-iiop/rmi_iiop_pg.html.*

Note that we can also write a server that supports both IIOP and JRMP clients explicitly by:

- ❑ Exporting it to both protocols using the `exportObject()` method. Of course, in this case we do not need to extend either `PortableRemoteObject` or `UnicastRemoteObject`.

- ❑ Creating two `InitialContexts`, one to allow binding to the RMI registry and one to the `COSNaming` service, and binding the server in both.

- ❑ Not passing the naming service as a command line argument using the `-D` option.

For example if we wanted to make our initial `HelloServer` object accessible over both RMI (JRMP) and RMI-IIOP then it could be modified as shown below:

```
import java.rmi.RemoteException;
import java.rmi.server.UnicastRemoteObject;
import java.util.Date;
import javax.rmi.PortableRemoteObject;

public class HelloServer implements HelloInterface {

  public void HelloServer() throws RemoteException {
    PortableRemoteObject.exportObject(this); // Export for IIOP
    UnicastRemoteObject.exportObject(this);  // Export for JRMP
  }

  public String sayHello() throws RemoteException {
    return "Hello World, the current system time is " + new Date();
  }
}
```

The object can be registered with both contexts by modifying our `RegisterIt` file:

```java
import java.rmi.RMISecurityManager;
import java.util.Properties;
import javax.naming.InitialContext;

public class RegisterIt {

  public static void main (String[] args){
    try{
      if(System.getSecurityManager() == null) {
        System.setSecurityManager (new RMISecurityManager());
      }
      HelloServer obj = new HelloServer ();  // Create the object

      // Create a JNDIContext for JRMP and bind the object to the registry
      // Note we are using the RMI registry via JNDI and not the default
      // registry.
      Properties p_1 = new Properties();
      p_1.put("java.naming.factory.initial",
              "com.sun.jndi.rmi.registry.RegistryContextFactory");
      InitialContext ctx_1 = new InitialContext ();
      ctx_1.rebind ("HelloServer", obj);
      System.out.println ("HelloServer bound in JRMP registry");

      // Repeat the same step for the IIOP registry
      Properties p_2 = new Properties();
      p_2.put("java.naming.factory.initial",
              "com.sun.jndi.cosnaming.CNCtxFactory");
      InitialContext ctx_2 = new InitialContext (p_2);
      ctx_2.rebind ("RemoteHelloServer", obj);
      System.out.println ("HelloServer bound in IIOP registry");
    } catch(Exception e) {}
  }
}
```

We have swept through quite a lot in this section; so let's recap what we have just described. We have talked about what steps are involved in writing the RMI-IIOP server and client, the differences between them, and how the same server object can be written for both RMI-JRMP and RMI-IIOP clients. What we haven't mentioned, however, is how a CORBA client can request services of this object or how the RMI-IIOP client can access a CORBA object. Let's examine this a little more.

Once we have a Java interface (we are reusing the `HelloInterface` we wrote earlier), we can use the rmic with the `-idl` option to generate its IDL source.

In our case `rmic -idl HelloInterface` produces the following `HelloInterface.idl` file:

```
/**
 * HelloInterface.idl
 * Generated by rmic -idl. Do not edit
 * 20 August 2001 18:27:51  BST
 */

#include "orb.idl"
```

```
#ifndef __HelloInterface__
#define __HelloInterface__

  interface HelloInterface {

    ::CORBA::WStringValue sayHello();
  };
#pragma ID HelloInterface "RMI:HelloInterface:0000000000000000"

#endif
```

This `.idl` file can be used by any vendor-provided CORBA 2.3-compliant IDL compiler; we can generate a stub in our language of choice (we talk about C++ since it is a very common language for CORBA objects) to generate the stub classes for that language.

The same compiler can be used to generate skeleton/tie classes and the C++ server objects written to these classes, and IDL can be accessed with the RMI-IIOP clients that we wrote.

RMI-IIOP and Java IDL

Java IDL is an Object Request Broker provided with the JDK and can be used to define, implement, and access CORBA objects from Java. Java IDL is compliant with the CORBA/IIOP 2.0 Specification and the Mapping of OMG IDL to Java.

The first question relating to this topic that most developers ask is, "So is RMI being phased out in favor of RMI-IIOP?" The answer is an emphatic no! Another question that sometimes follows is, "Is RMI-IIOP a replacement for Java IDL?" Again, the answer is no. An RMI-IIOP client cannot necessarily access an existing CORBA object. If we want to use Java to access CORBA objects that have already been written, Java IDL is your best choice. With Java IDL, which is also a core part of the Java 2 platform, we can access any CORBA object from Java. The general recommendation for usage of RMI-IIOP and Java IDL is this: "If you want to use Java to access existing CORBA resources use Java IDL. If, conversely, you want to make Java RMI resources accessible to CORBA users you should use RMI-IIOP. If your application is going to be all Java, then use RMI-JRMP."

> The J2SE v1.3 includes a new version of the IDL-to-Java compiler **idlj** that takes an IDL file and generates the Java server and client bindings from it.

The IDL File

OK, remember the IDL we just generated above? Let's take that file (`HelloInterface.idl`) as a starting point for this example and see how we can write CORBA objects and use Java IDL:

```
#include "orb.idl"

#ifndef __HelloInterface__
#define __HelloInterface__

  interface HelloInterface {
```

```
      ::CORBA::WStringValue sayHello();
   };
#pragma ID HelloInterface "RMI:HelloInterface:0000000000000000"
#endif
```

There are two things that can happen with an IDL file. We can either write the server or we can write a client (as we just mentioned above in the RMI-IIOP example). We will do both in this example using the idlj compiler.

The Server Implementation

Let's examine the sequence of events associated with the server implementation:

❏   Generate the server-side bindings for the IDL file. This is done with the idlj compiler:

```
idlj -i %JAVA_HOME%\lib -fserver HelloInterface.idl
```

Where %JAVA_HOME% is the J2SE 1.3 installation directory. We include the orb.idl file with the -i option to the idlj compiler because it is referenced in the IDL file (remember that this IDL we started with was auto generated itself). The -fserver option tells the compiler to generate the server-side bindings.

❏   Write the implementation. In CORBA terminology, this is called a servant class.

The servant, HelloServant, is the implementation of the IDL interface and is a subclass of _HelloInterfaceImplBase, which is generated by the idlj compiler (for each XXX.idl file the compiler generates a _XXXImplBase.java file). The servant contains one method for each IDL operation. In this example, this is just the sayHello() method. Note that servant methods are just ordinary Java methods.

```
import java.util.Date;

public class HelloServant extends _HelloInterfaceImplBase {
   public String sayHello() {
      return "Hello World, the current system time is " + new Date();
   }
}
```

❏   Write the class that binds the implementation (the servant) to the naming service. This class is called the *server* in CORBA terminology.

So, the HelloServer class will look like this:

```
import org.omg.CosNaming.*;
import org.omg.CosNaming.NamingContextPackage.*;
import org.omg.CORBA.*;

public class HelloServer {
   public static void main(String args[]) {
      try {

         // create and initialize the ORB
         ORB orb = ORB.init(args, null);
```

```
        // create servant and connect it with the ORB
        HelloServant helloRef = new HelloServant();
        orb.connect(helloRef);

        // get the root naming context
        org.omg.CORBA.Object objRef =
          orb.resolve_initial_references("NameService");
        NamingContext ncRef = NamingContextHelper.narrow(objRef);

        // Bind the servant reference to the Naming Context
        NameComponent nc = new NameComponent("Hello", "");
        NameComponent path[] = {nc};
        ncRef.rebind(path, helloRef);

        // Wait for invocations from clients
        java.lang.Object sync = new java.lang.Object();
        synchronized (sync) {
          sync.wait();
        }
      } catch (Exception e) {
        System.out.println("Exception: " + e);
      }
    }
  }
}
```

Thus, it is clear from the code above that the server performs the following actions:

❑   Instantiates the ORB

❑   Instantiates the servant and connects it to the ORB

❑   Gets a CORBA object reference for a naming context in which to register the new CORBA object

❑   Binds the new object in the naming context under the name "Hello"

❑   Waits for invocations of the new object

The Client Implementation

Now let's follow the procedure associated with the client implementation. We will need to create a client subfolder before running this step:

❑   Generate the client-side bindings for the IDL file:

```
idlj -i %JAVA_HOME%\lib -td client -fclient HelloInterface.idl
```

❑   Write the client class. This can be an applet or a simple Java class.

```
import org.omg.CosNaming.*;
import org.omg.CORBA.*;

public class HelloClient{
  public static void main(String args[]){
    try{
```

```
        // create and initialize the ORB
        ORB orb = ORB.init(args, null);

        // get the root naming context
        org.omg.CORBA.Object objRef =
           orb.resolve_initial_references("NameService");
        NamingContext ncRef = NamingContextHelper.narrow(objRef);

        // resolve the Object Reference in Naming
        NameComponent nc = new NameComponent("Hello", "");
        NameComponent path[] = {nc};
        HelloInterface helloRef =
           HelloInterfaceHelper.narrow(ncRef.resolve(path));

        // call the Hello server object and print results
        String hello = helloRef.sayHello();
        System.out.println(hello);
    } catch (Exception e) {
        System.out.println("Exception : " + e) ;
    }
  }
}
```

Finally, we can run this example using the following sequence:

1. Compile all the java files:

```
javac *.java
```

2. Create the stubs for the server:

```
rmic -iiop HelloServer
```

3. Run the Naming service tnameserv:

```
tnameserv -ORBInitialPort 900
```

4. Start the server:

```
java -Djava.naming.factory.initial=com.sun.jndi.cosnaming.CNCtxFactory
     -Djava.naming.provider.url=iiop://localhost:900 HelloServer
```

5. Run the client HelloClient:

```
java -Djava.naming.factory.initial=com.sun.jndi.cosnaming.CNCtxFactory
     -Djava.naming.provider.url=iiop://localhost:900 HelloClient
```

With the previous two examples we have seen how to write an RMI-IIOP object and make it accessible to other CORBA clients. We have also seen how to take an IDL file and generate a CORBA object and access it with a Java-IDL client.

The idlj *supports both the inheritance and delegation models.*

This means given an interface XX in your IDL file, idlj *generates* _XXImplBase.java. *The implementation for XX that you write must extend from* _XXImplBase *class. This is known as the inheritance model.*

Sometimes this may not be useful if your implementation extends from another class. (Remember, a Java class can implement any number of interfaces but can extend only one class.)

In such a case you can tell the idlj *compiler to use the Tie model. In such a case for the interface XX in your IDL file,* idlj *will generate XX_Tie.java and the constructor to XX_Tie takes a XX as an argument.*

The implementation for XX that you provide is only required to implement the interface XX. To use it this implementation with the ORB, you must wrap your implementation within XX_Tie. For example:

```
XXImpl obj = new XXImpl ();
XX_Tie tie = new XX_Tie (obj);
orb.connect (tie);
```

As you can see the drawback of using the Tie model is that it adds an extra step and an extra method call.

The idlj *compiler's default server-side model is the inheritance model. To use the delegation model use:*

```
idlj -fserverTIE Hello.idl
```

or:

```
idlj -fallTIE Hello.idl
```

RMI-IIOP and J2EE

RMI-IIOP provides the following benefits to developers over RMI-JRMP:

❑ Interoperability with objects written in other languages via language-independent CORBA IDL

❑ Transaction and security contexts can be propagated implicitly because of the use of IIOP, which can implicitly propagate context information

❑ IIOP-based firewall support via IIOP proxies that can pass IIOP traffic in a controlled and manageable way

With IIOP as the transport protocol, Java RMI finds the support it needs to promote industrial-strength distributed application development, within a Java environment only. RMI-IIOP nevertheless has some weaknesses of its own compared to RMI-JRMP:

❑ No distributed garbage collection support is present. The RMI DGC interfaces do not represent object IDs as CORBA does, so those interfaces are not sufficient for CORBA/IIOP. You cannot rely on Java RMI/JRMP's features while using RMI-IIOP.

❑　Java's casting operator cannot be used in your clients directly after getting a remote object reference. Instead, you need to use a special method to get the right type.

❑　You are not allowed to inherit the same method name into your remote interface from different base remote interfaces.

❑　All constant definitions in remote interfaces must be of primitive types or Strings and evaluated at compile time.

So, what's the idea behind making RMI-IIOP the de facto protocol in J2EE instead of RMI-JRMP?

> **All J2EE containers are required to support JRMP and RMI-IIOP and the containers should also be able to expose all enterprise beans using RMI-IIOP via the remote interfaces of the beans.**

Enterprise JavaBeans (EJB) are a key constituent of J2EE; EJB components live within EJB containers, which provide the runtime environments for the components. EJB containers are developed by different vendors based on the EJB specifications (which use RMI semantics). Vendors are free to choose the implementation for their containers. To help interoperability for EJB environments that include systems from multiple vendors, Sun has defined a standard mapping of EJB to CORBA, based on the specification of Java-to-IDL mapping from OMG. That is, EJB interfaces are inherently RMI-IIOP interfaces.

Sun's EJB-to-CORBA mapping can be accessed at
http://java.sun.com/products/ejb/index.html.

As we'll see later in this book, EJBs present a model for creating distributed enterprise applications that can be deployed in a heterogeneous environment. Standard RMI with the JRMP fails to deliver on some aspects, such as:

❑　It's a Java only solution, and EJBs should also be accessible to other clients in an enterprise environment

❑　It does not support transaction and security context propagation across distributed JVMs (in fact, it does not support context propagation at all)

❑　It is not as scalable as IIOP

RMI-IIOP overcomes these limitations of RMI-JRMP. The EJB-to-CORBA mapping not only enables on-the-wire interoperability among multiple vendors' implementations of the EJB container, but also enables non-Java clients to access server-side applications written as EJBs through standard CORBA APIs. The EJB 2.0 specification enables inter-container operability using RMI-IIOP.

Tuning RMI Applications

The RMI API provides a lot of system properties that can be dynamically set at runtime with the −D option to the JVM. (For example, `java -Djava.rmi.dgc.leaseValue=30000 MyApp`). These are very useful for fine tuning performance and debugging applications. These properties are listed in the following tables, starting with a summary of all the properties that can be set in the client and server JVMs:

Property	First Introduced (version)	Description
`java.rmi.dgc.leaseValue`	1.1	The lease duration granted by the DGC to clients that access remote objects in this JVM. Clients usually renew a lease when it is 50% expired, so a very short value will increase network traffic and risk late renewals in exchange for reduced latency in calls to `Unreferenced.unreferenced`. The default value is 600000 milliseconds (10 minutes).
`java.rmi.server.codebase`	1.1	The locations from which classes that are published by this JVM may be downloaded. It can be a URL or space separated list of URLs (for 1.2) and can be set in both client and server JVMs.
`java.rmi.server.hostname`	1.1	The host name that should be associated with remote stubs for locally created remote objects, in order to allow clients to invoke methods on the remote object. The default value of this property is the IP address of the local host.
`java.rmi.server.logCalls`	1.1	Incoming method calls and exceptions will be logged to `System.err` if this is `true`.
`java.rmi.server.randomIDs`	1.1.8	If this value is `true`, object identifiers for remote objects exported by this JVM will be generated by using a cryptographically secure random number generator. The default value is `false`.
`java.rmi.server.useCodebaseOnly`	1.1	If this value is `true` the JVM cannot automatically load classes from anywhere other than the its local classpath and from the server's `java.rmi.server.codebase` property. This can be set in both client and server JVM's.
`java.rmi.server.useLocalHostName`	1.1.7	RMI now uses an IP address to identify the local host when the `java.rmi.server.hostname` property is not specified and a fully qualified domain name for the localhost cannot be obtained. If set to `true` RMI is forced to use the fully qualified domain name by default.
`java.rmi.server.disableHttp`	1.1	If this value is `true`, HTTP tunneling is disabled, even when `http.proxyHost` is set. The default value is `false` and this property is useful for client JVMs.

The next table lists the activation-specific properties:

Property	First Introduced (version)	Description
javsa.rmi.activation .port	1.2	The value of this property represents the TCP port on which the activation system daemon, rmid, will listen for incoming remote calls. The default value is 1098.
java.rmi.activation .activator.class	1.2	The class that implements the interface java.rmi.activation.Activator. This property is used internally to locate the resident implementation of the activator from which the stub class name can be found.

This final table provides a summary of properties that are specific to the SUN JDK implementation of RMI:

Property	First Introduced (version)	Description
sun.rmi.activation .execTimeout	1.2	The time that rmid will wait for a spawned activation group to start up. The default is 30,000 milliseconds.
sun.rmi.activation .snapshotInterval	1.2	The number of updates for which the activation system will wait before it serializes a snapshot of its state to the rmid log file on disk. An "update" refers to a persistent change in the state of the activation system (for example, the registration of an activatable object) since the last snapshot was taken. Changing the value of this property can be used to make rmid re-start more quickly (by taking snapshots of the log more often) or to make rmid more efficient (by taking snapshots of the log less often). The default value is 200.
sun.rmi.log.debug	1.2	If this value is true, details of rmid's logging activity are sent to System.err.

Table continued on following page

Property	First Introduced (version)	Description
sun.rmi.rmid.maxstartgroup	1.2	The maximum number of activation group JVMs that rmid will allow to be in the "spawning but not yet active" state simultaneously. If more VMs need to be started, they will queue up until one of the current spawn attempts either succeeds or times out. This property does not limit the maximum number of active VMs; it is intended to smooth out sudden spikes of activity to avoid reaching operating system limits. While setting the value of this property to a lower number may result in a longer startup time for rmid, and setting the value to a higher number could shorten the startup time, setting this value too high can crash rmid, because your system may run out of resources. The default value is 3.
sun.rmi.server.activation.debugExec	1.2	If this value is true, the activation system will print out debugging information to the command line that is used for spawning activation groups. By default, the value is false, so debugging information is not printed.
sun.rmi.dgc.checkInterval	1.1	How often the RMI runtime checks for expired DGC leases. The default value is 300,000 milliseconds.
sun.rmi.dgc.logLevel	1.1	Controls the logging of incoming and outgoing calls related to DGC lease granting, renewing, and expiration.
sun.rmi.dgc.server.gcInterval	1.2	When it is necessary to ensure that unreachable remote objects are un-exported and garbage-collected in a timely fashion, the value of this property represents the maximum interval that the RMI runtime will allow between garbage collections of the local heap. The default value is 60,000 milliseconds.
sun.rmi.loader.logLevel	1.2	Controls the logging of each class name and codebase, whenever the RMI runtime attempts to load a class as a result of unmarshaling either an argument or a return value. The codebase that is printed is the annotated codebase, but may not necessarily be the actual codebase from which the class gets loaded; the RMI class loader defers the class loading to the current thread's context class loader, which may load the class from the classpath, rather than the annotated codebase.

Property	First Introduced (version)	Description
`sun.rmi.server .exceptionTrace`	1.2	Controls the output of server-side stack traces from exceptions and errors that are thrown by dispatched, incoming remote calls. If this value is `true`, exception stack traces will be printed. By default (`false`), exception and error stack traces are not printed.
`sun.rmi.transport .logLevel`	1.1	Controls detailed logging throughout the transport layer.
`sun.rmi.transport .tcp.localHostName TimeOut`	1.1.7	Represents the time that the RMI runtime will wait to obtain a fully qualified domain name for the local host. The default value is 10,000 milliseconds.
`sun.rmi.transport .tcp.logLevel`	1.1	Controls detailed logging for the TCP-specific transport sub-layer.
`sun.rmi.transport .tcp.readTimeout`	1.2.2	Represents the time used as an idle timeout for incoming RMI-TCP connections. The value is passed to `Socket.setSoTimeout`. This property is used only for cases where a client has not dropped an unused connection as it should. The default value is 7,200,000 milliseconds (2 hrs).
`sun.rmi.dgc .cleanInterval`	1.1	Represents the maximum length of time that the RMI runtime will wait before retrying a failed DGC "clean" call. The default value is 180,000 milliseconds.
`sun.rmi.dgc .client.gcInterval`	1.2	When it is necessary to ensure that DGC clean calls for unreachable remote references are delivered in a timely fashion, the value of this property represents the maximum interval that the RMI runtime will allow between garbage collections of the local heap. The default value is 60,000 milliseconds.
`sun.rmi.loader .logLevel`	1.2	Controls the logging of each class name and codebase, whenever the RMI runtime attempts to load a class as a result of unmarshaling either an argument or return value. The codebase that is printed is the annotated codebase, but may not necessarily be the actual codebase from which the class gets loaded; the RMI class loader defers the class loading to the current thread's context class loader, which may load the class from the classpath, rather than the annotated codebase.
`sun.rmi.server .logLevel`	1.1	Controls the logging of information related to outgoing calls, including some connection-reuse information.

Table continued on following page

Property	First Introduced (version)	Description
sun.rmi.transport.connectionTimeout	1.1.6	Represents the period for which RMI socket connections may reside in an "unused" state, before the RMI runtime will allow those connections to be freed (closed). The default value is 15,000 milliseconds.
sun.rmi.transport.proxy.connectTimeout	1.1	Represents the maximum length of time that the RMI runtime will wait for a connection attempt (createSocket) to complete, before attempting to contact the server through HTTP. This property is only used when the http.proxyHost property is set and the value of java.rmi.server.disableHttp is false. The default value is 15,000 milliseconds.
sun.rmi.transport.proxy.logLevel	1.1	Controls the logging of events (createSocket and createServerSocket) when the default RMISocketFactory class is used. This type of logging is likely to be useful for applications that use RMI over HTTP. Events in custom socket factories are not logged by this property.

The Sun RMI properties described above are useful for debugging but it is important to remember – they are not officially supported and are subject to change. Properties that end ".logLevel" have output redirected to System.err with possible values of "SILENT", "BRIEF", and "VERBOSE".

Summary

We have covered a lot of ground in this chapter, ranging from the basic RMI architecture to HTTP-tunneling. If you're now feeling somewhat overwhelmed, take it a little slower. Go through the examples and write some test applications – that should get you on the move.

We have covered in the chapter:

- ❑ The RMI architecture.
- ❑ Developing RMI applications. The stages required for the creation of effective applications.
- ❑ Parameter passing in RMI, the types available, and their use.
- ❑ Object activation, the benefits of execution on an as-needed basis.
- ❑ RMI, firewalls, and HTTP. The different methods designed to allow JRMP traffic access through firewalls.
- ❑ The development of RMI over IIOP, and the integration of RMI with CORBA.

Keep in mind that even though RMI-IIOP is the model for J2EE, JRMP is still very much alive. If your application requires just Java-Java communication then RMI-JRMP is a feasible solution.

The inclusion of RMI-IIOP in the core JDK (from the J2SE 1.3 release), and its close association with EJB, establishes it as a foundation technology for enterprise middleware.

In hindsight, RMI has come a long way from its initial days when no distributed model existed in Java. Today it is the core of the Java distributed model in J2EE and is the base for future technologies, such as JINI, which are transforming the way in which devices and systems will be networked together. Though outside the scope of this chapter, Jini essentially takes the RMI model and architecture a quantum leap forward.

The following chapter will deal with database access using the Java Database Connectivity API (JDBC).

Data

RDMS

Application Logic

JDBC

Web Container

JavaMail

Mail Server

Client

Servlets   JSPs   Tag Library

HTTP(S)

(X)HTML/ XML

Java Application

RMI

RMI/IIOP   JNDI   JTA   JDBC   JMS   JavaMail   JCA   JAAS   JCA   JAXP

J2EE Application Server

Applet

IIOP

CORBA Server

Client Application

Session Beans

JNDI

JAF

Directory Service

JMS

Message Queue

Database Programming with JDBC

A relational database is usually the primary data resource in an enterprise application. The **JDBC** API provides developers with a way to connect to relational data from within Java code. Using the JDBC API, developers can create a client (which can be anything from an applet to an EJB) that can connect to a database, execute **Structured Query Language (SQL)** statements, and processes the result of those statements.

If you are familiar with SQL and relational databases, the structure of the JDBC API is simple to understand and use. The API provides connectivity and data access across the range of relational databases. It can do this because it provides a set of generic database access methods for SQL-compliant relational databases. JDBC generalizes the most common database access functions by abstracting the vendor-specific details of a particular database. This result is a set of classes and interfaces, placed in the java.sql package, which can be used with any database that has an appropriate **JDBC driver**. This allows JDBC connectivity to be provided in a consistent way for any database. It also means that with a little care to ensure the application conforms to the most commonly available database features, an application can be used with a different database simply by switching to a different JDBC driver.

However, there is more to database connectivity in an enterprise-level environment than simply connecting to databases and executing statements. There are additional concerns to be met including using connection pooling to optimize network resources and the implementation of distributed transactions. While some of the concepts behind these concerns are advanced we will find that addressing them is not itself complex.

We will discuss the **JDBC 3.0 API**, which, at the time of writing, is the latest version of the JDBC API. Version 2.0 of the JDBC API had two parts: the **JDBC 2.1 Core API** and the **JDBC 2.0 Optional Package API**, and although these two APIs have been combined into one in version 3.0, the JDBC classes and interfaces remain in two Java packages: java.sql, and javax.sql:

❏ `java.sql`
This package contains classes and interfaces designed with traditional client-server architecture in mind. Its functionality is focused primarily on basic database programming services such as creating connections, executing statements and prepared statements, and running batch queries. Advanced functions such as batch updates, scrollable resultsets, transaction isolation, and SQL data types are also available.

❏ `javax.sql`
This package introduces some major architectural changes to JDBC programming compared to `java.sql`, and provides better abstractions for connection management, distributed transactions, and legacy connectivity. This package also introduces container-managed connection pooling, distributed transactions, and rowsets.

We will not attempt to cover general database programming concepts in this chapter; basic knowledge of SQL and client-server application development is a prerequisite. There is not the space in a single chapter to cover database programming exhaustively so we will take a high-level approach to the JDBC API. Rather than attempting to discuss, build, and analyze large applications, we will study short snippets of code that illustrate the usage of various classes and interfaces from `java.sql` and `javax.sql`. In particular we will look at:

❏ Database connectivity using JDBC drivers

❏ How various SQL operations can be performed using the standard JDBC API including obtaining database connections, sending SQL statements to a database, and retrieving results from database queries

❏ How to map SQL types to Java

❏ Advanced features in the JDBC API, including scrollable resultsets and batch updates

❏ New features in the JDBC 3.0 API, including save points

We will then go on to consider macro-level issues including:

❏ Using the `javax.sql` package and JNDI to obtain database connections

❏ Connection pooling – including a discussion on traditional connection pooling versus data source based connection pooling

❏ Distributed transactions – how the `javax.sql` package, together with the Java Transaction API, enables distributed transactions

❏ The basic concepts of a rowset, and how they provide both a higher-level of abstraction for database access and the easy serialization of data

We will be mostly concerned with the `java.sql` package, apart from the creation of database connections, and the programmatic control of transactions.

We begin by understanding how Java applications can connect to, and communicate with, databases.

Database Drivers

It is important to understand that the JDBC abstracts database connectivity from Java applications. A database vendor typically provides a set of APIs for accessing the data managed by the database server. Popular database vendors such as Oracle, Sybase, and Informix provide proprietary APIs for client access. Client applications written in native languages such as C/C++ can use these APIs to gain direct access to the data. The JDBC API provides an alternative to using these vendor-specific APIs. Although this eliminates the need for the Java developer to access vendor-specific native APIs, the JDBC layer may still need ultimately to make these native calls. A **JDBC driver** is a middleware layer that translates the JDBC calls to the vendor-specific APIs.

Depending on whether the `java.sql` package or the `javax.sql` package is used, there are different approaches for connecting to a database via the driver. Irrespective of this, to access data you'll need a database driver, probably supplied by the database vendor or by a J2EE server provider. A driver is nothing but an implementation of various interfaces specified in `java.sql` and `javax.sql` packages.

There are four different approaches to connect an application to a database server via a database driver. The following classification is an industry standard and commercial driver products are categorized according to it.

Type 1 – JDBC-ODBC Bridge

Open Database Connectivity (ODBC) was originally created to provide an API standard for SQL on Microsoft Windows platforms and was later enhanced to provide SDKs for other platforms. ODBC is partly based on the X/Open Call-Level Interface (CLI) specification, which is a standard API for database access. This API provides bindings in the C and Cobol languages for database access. CLI is intended to be platform-and database-neutral, which is where ODBC diverges from the specification. Embedded SQL was one of the approaches considered for database access by the SQL Access Group. This involves embedding SQL statements in applications programmed in high-level languages, and preprocessing them to generate native function calls. ODBC defines a set of functions for direct access to data, without the need for embedded SQL in client applications.

The first category of JDBC drivers provides a bridge between the JDBC API and the ODBC API. The bridge translates the standard JDBC calls to corresponding ODBC calls, and sends them to the ODBC data source via ODBC libraries:

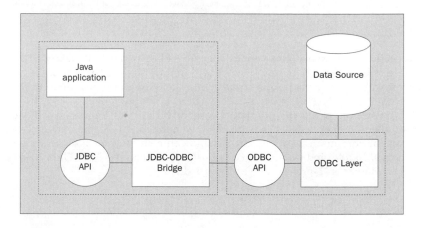

The process boundaries are marked with a broken line. The **JDBC-ODBC Bridge** translates the JDBC API calls into equivalent ODBC calls. The driver then delegates these calls to the data source. The Java classes for the JDBC API and the JDBC-ODBC Bridge are invoked within the client application process; the ODBC layer executes in another process. This configuration requires every client that will run the application to have the JDBC-ODBC Bridge API, the ODBC driver, and the native-language-level API, such as the OCI library for Oracle, installed.

This solution for data access is inefficient for high-performance database access requirements because of the multiple layers of indirection for each data access call. In addition this solution limits the functionality of the JDBC API to that of the ODBC driver. The use of a JDBC-ODBC should be considered for experimental purposes only.

J2SE includes classes for the JDBC-ODBC Bridge and so there is no need to install any additional packages to use it. However, you do have to configure the ODBC manager by creating **data source names (DSNs)**. DSNs are simply named configurations linking up a database, an appropriate driver, and some optional settings. The JDBC-ODBC bridge should work with most ODBC 2.0 drivers.

Type 2 – Part Java, Part Native Driver

Type 2 drivers use a mixture of Java implementation and vendor-specific native APIs to provide data access. There is one layer fewer to go through than for a Type 1 driver and so in general a Type 2 driver will be faster than a Type 1 driver:

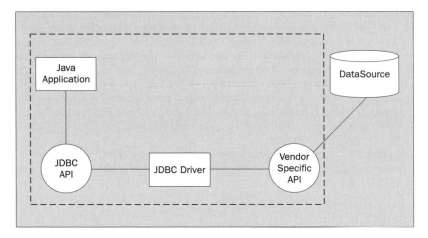

JDBC database calls are translated into vendor-specific API calls. The database will process the request and send the results back through the API, which will in turn forward them back to the JDBC driver. The JDBC driver will translate the results to the JDBC standard and return them to the Java application.

As with Type 1 drivers the part Java, part native code driver and the vendor-specific native language API must be installed on every client that runs the Java application. As the native code uses vendor-specific protocols for communicating with the database efficiently, Type 2 drivers are more efficient than Type 1 drivers. In addition we now have full use of the vendor's API. These two factors mean that Type 2 drivers are, in general, preferred over Type 1 drivers.

Type 3 – Intermediate Database Access Server

Type 3 drivers use an intermediate (middleware) database server that has the ability to connect multiple Java clients to multiple database servers:

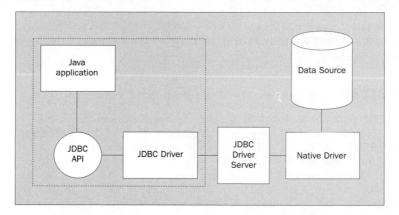

Clients connect to database servers via an intermediate server component (such as a listener) that acts as a gateway for multiple database servers. The Java client application sends a JDBC call through a JDBC driver to the intermediate data access server, which completes the request to the Data Source using another driver (for example, a Type 2 driver).

The protocol used to communicate between clients and the intermediate server depends on the middleware server vendor but the intermediate server can use different native protocols to connect to different databases.

BEA WebLogic includes a Type 3 driver. One of the benefits of using a Type 3 driver is that it allows flexibility on the architecture of the application, as the intermediate server can abstract details of connections to database servers.

Type 4 – Pure Java Drivers

Type 4 drivers are a pure Java alternative to Type 2 drivers:

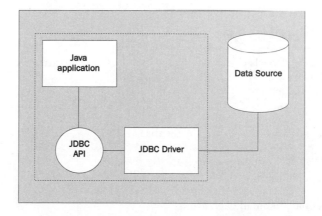

Type 4 drivers convert the JDBC API calls to direct network calls using vendor-specific networking protocols. They do this by making direct socket connections with the database. Type 4 drivers generally offer better performance than Type 1 and Type 2 drivers. Type 4 drivers are also the simplest drivers to deploy since there are no additional libraries or middleware to install. All the major database vendors provide Type 4 JDBC drivers for their databases and they are also available from third party vendors.

A list of available JDBC drivers, of all four types, is available at http://industry.java.sun.com/products/jdbc/drivers/. At the time of writing there were over 160 drivers available.

Getting Started

To start using JDBC with our applications, we need to install a driver. Of course, we also need a database server. For the sake of simplicity, in this chapter, we'll use the Cloudscape database for demonstrating the JDBC API as the J2EE Reference Implementation server from Sun includes a version of Cloudscape. Cloudscape is written using Java and can be found at `%J2EE_HOME%\lib\cloudscape\cloudscape.jar`.

You can also obtain an evaluation copy of Cloudscape at http://www.cloudscape.com. In order to use the JDBC API and the Cloudscape database, add the `cloudscape.jar` file to your `CLASSPATH`. Refer to the Cloudscape documentation for instructions on using CloudView, a GUI for accessing the Cloudscape database.

Cloudscape is a small-footprint database management system built in Java and can be used in either embedded or client-server mode. When used in embedded mode, Cloudscape executes within the client application process. This is the simplest mode for database management, as, apart from including the Cloudscape classes in your `CLASSPATH`, it does not involve any setup. Client-server mode lets you access Cloudscape in the traditional client-server manner.

As Cloudscape is implemented in Java, additional database drivers are not required since JDBC calls are mapped to Cloudscape Java API calls within the same process. In client-server mode, these calls are further mapped to RMI calls to the Cloudscape server process.

> *If you wish to use another database make sure that you follow the instructions given by the database vendor to set up the database, and install an appropriate database driver.*

The java.sql Package

The classes in the `java.sql` package can be divided into the following groups based on their functionality:

- ❑ Connection Management
- ❑ Database Access
- ❑ Data Types
- ❑ Database Metadata
- ❑ Exceptions and Warnings

Let's look at the classes available in each group.

Connection Management

The following classes/interfaces let you establish a connection to the database. In most cases, this involves a network connection:

Class	Description
java.sql.DriverManager	This class provides the functionality necessary for managing one or more database drivers. Each driver in turn lets you connect to a specific database.
java.sql.Driver	This is an interface that abstracts the vendor-specific connection protocol. You may find implementations of this interface from database vendors as well as third party database driver vendors.
java.sql.DriverPropertyInfo	Since each database may require a distinct set of properties to obtain a connection, you can use this class to discover the properties required to obtain the connection.
java.sql.Connection	This interface abstracts most of the interaction with the database. Using a connection, you can send SQL statements to the database, and read the results of execution.

Database Access

Once you obtain a connection, the following classes/interfaces let you send SQL statements to the database for execution, and read the results:

Class	Description
java.sql.Statement	This interface lets you execute SQL statements over the underlying connection and access the results.
java.sql.PreparedStatement	This is a variant of the java.sql.Statement interface allowing for parameterized SQL statements. Parameterized SQL statements include parameter markers (as "?"), which can be replaced with actual values later on.
java.sql.CallableStatement	This interface lets you execute stored procedures.
java.sql.ResultSet	This interface abstracts results of executing SQL SELECT statements. This interface provides methods to access the results row-by-row. You can use this interface to access various fields in each row.

The `java.sql.PreparedStatement` and `java.sql.CallableStatement` extend `java.sql.Statement`. All the three interfaces are conceptually similar, each offering a means of sending requests to execute SQL statements (stored procedures in the case of `java.sql.CallableStatement`), and obtaining the results of execution.

Data Types

The `java.sql` package also provides several Java data types that correspond to some of the SQL types. You can use one of the following types as appropriate depending on what a field in a result row corresponds to in the database:

Class	Description
java.sql.Array	This interface provides a Java language abstraction of ARRAY, a collection of SQL data types.
java.sql.Blob	This interface provides a Java language abstraction of the SQL type BLOB.
java.sql.Clob	This interface provides a Java language abstraction of the SQL type CLOB.
java.sql.Date	This class provides a Java language abstraction of the SQL type DATE. Although the java.util.Date provides a general-purpose representation of date, the java.sql.Date class is preferable for representing dates in database-centric applications, as this type maps directly to SQL DATE type. Note that the java.sql.Date class extends the java.util.Date class.
java.sql.Time	This class provides a Java language abstraction of the SQL type TIME, and extends java.util.Date class.
java.sql.Timestamp	This class provides a Java language abstraction of the SQL type TIME, and extends java.util.Date class.
java.sql.Ref	This class provides a Java language abstraction of the SQL type REF.
java.sql.Struct	This interface provides a Java language abstraction of SQL structured types.
java.sql.Types	This class holds a set of constant integers, each corresponding to a SQL type.

As we shall see later, in addition to the above, the JDBC API also specifies standard mappings between primitive types in Java and SQL.

The JDBC API also includes facilities for dealing with custom database types. These types can be represented as `java.sql.SQLData` objects, and data within these types can be accessed using `java.sql.SQLInput` and `java.sql.Output` interfaces that provide a stream-like interface to accessing data.

Database Metadata

The JDBC API also includes facilities to obtain metadata about the database, parameters to statements, and results:

Class	Description
java.sql.DatabaseMetadata	You can find out about database features using this interface. You can obtain an instance of this interface using the java.sql.Connection.
java.sql.ResultSetMetaData	This interface provides methods to access metadata of the ResultSet, such as the names of columns, their types, the corresponding table name, and other properties.
java.sql.ParameterMetadata	This interface allows you access the database types of parameters in prepared statements.

Exceptions and Warnings

The following classes encapsulate database access errors and warnings:

Class	Description
java.sql.SQLException	This exception represents all JDBC-related exception conditions. This exception also embeds all driver/database-level exceptions and error codes.
java.sql.SQLWarning	This exception represents database access warnings. Instead of having to catch this exception, you can use the appropriate methods on java.sql.Connection, java.sql.Statement, and java.sql.ResultSet to access warnings.
java.sql.BatchUpdateException	This is a special case of java.sql.SQLException meant for batch updates. We'll learn about batch updates later in this chapter.
java.sql.DataTruncation	This is a special case of java.sql.SQLWarning meant for data truncation errors. Note that data types do not always match between Java and SQL, and data transfer may involve data truncation.

Besides these features, the JDBC also provides facilities for logging, and associated security permissions to log.

In the following sections, we'll discuss some of the most commonly used classes and interfaces of this API. In particular, we will learn:

- ❏ How to load a database driver
- ❏ How to open a database connection
- ❏ How to send SQL statements to databases for execution
- ❏ How to extract results returned from a database query
- ❏ What prepared statements are
- ❏ The role of JDBC types
- ❏ Handling exceptions and warnings

Loading a Database Driver and Opening Connections

The `java.sql.Connection` interface represents a connection with a database. It is an interface because the implementation of a connection is network-protocol- and vendor-dependent. The JDBC API provides two different approaches for obtaining connections. The first uses `java.sql.DriverManager`, and is suitable for non-managed applications such as standalone Java database clients. The second approach is based on the `javax.sql` package that introduces the notion of data sources and is suitable for database access in J2EE applications.

Let's start by considering how connections are obtained using the `java.sql.DriverManager` class. In a single application, we can obtain one or more connections for one or more databases using different JDBC drivers. Each driver implements the `java.sql.Driver` interface. One of the methods that this interface defines is the `connect()` method that establishes a connection with the database, and returns a `Connection` object that encapsulates the database connection.

Instead of directly accessing classes that implement the `java.sql.Driver` interface, the standard approach for obtaining connections is to register each driver with the `java.sql.DriverManager`, and use the methods provided on this class to obtain connections. The `java.sql.DriverManager` can manage multiple drivers. Before going into the details of this approach, we need to understand how JDBC represents the location of a database.

JDBC URLs

The notion of a URL in JDBC is very similar to the way URLs are used otherwise. In order to see the rationale behind JDBC URLs, consider an application using several databases, each being accessed via a different database driver. In such a scenario, how do we uniquely identify a driver? Moreover, databases use different types of parameters for obtaining connections. How are parameters specified while making connections?

JDBC URLs provide a way of identifying a database driver. A JDBC URL represents a driver, and additional driver-specific information to locate a database and to connect to it. The syntax of the JDBC URL is as follows:

```
jdbc:<subprotocol>:<subname>
```

This has three parts separated by colons:

- ❑ Protocol: In the above syntax, `jdbc` is the protocol. This is the only allowed protocol in JDBC.

- ❑ Sub-protocol: The sub-protocol is used to identify a database driver, or the name of a database connectivity mechanism, chosen by the database driver providers.

- ❑ Subname: The syntax of the subname is driver-specific. A driver may choose any syntax appropriate for its implementation.

For example, for a Cloudscape database called "Movies", the URL to connect to it is:

```
jdbc:cloudscape:Movies
```

Alternatively, if we were using Oracle via the JDBC-ODBC bridge, our URL would be:

```
jdbc:odbc:Movies
```

where `Movies` is a DSN set up using our ODBC driver administrator.

As you see JDBC URLs are flexible enough to specify driver-specific information in the subname.

DriverManager

The purpose of the `java.sql.DriverManager` class in JDBC is to provide a common access layer on top of different database drivers used in an application. In this approach, instead of using individual `Driver` implementation classes directly, applications use the `DriverManager` class to obtain connections. This class provides three static methods to obtain connections.

The `DriverManager`, however, requires each driver needed by the application must be registered before use, so that the `DriverManager` is aware of it.

The JDBC approach for registering a database driver can seem obscure at first. In JDBC, you try to load the database driver using the current `java.lang.ClassLoader` object. Take a look at the following code snippet, which loads the Cloudscape's database driver:

```
try {
  Class.forName("COM.cloudscape.core.JDBCDriver");
} catch (ClassNotFoundException e) {
  // Driver not found.
  ...
}
```

At run time, the `ClassLoader` locates and loads the class `COM.cloudscape.core.JDBCDriver` from the `classpath` using the bootstrap class loader. While loading a class, the class loader executes any static initialization code for the class. In JDBC, each driver provider is required to register an instance of the driver with the `java.sql.DriverManager` class during this static initialization. This registration happens automatically when you load the driver class (using the `Class.forName()` call as above). The `java.sql.DriverManager` is a static class, and provides the following method for this purpose:

public static void registerDriver(java.sql.Driver)

Alternatively, we can specify a list of drivers using the Java properties mechanism. For example, the following snippet would allow the `java.sql.DriverManager` class to load the list of drivers when an attempt is made to establish a connection:

```
System.setProperty("jdbc.drivers", "COM.cloudscape.core.JDBCDriver");
```

> *You can specify multiple drivers as a list separated by colons (:).*

Once a driver has been registered with the `java.sql.DriverManager`, we can use its static methods to get connections. Later in this chapter, we shall discuss the `javax.sql.DataSource` interface that provides a better alternative to `java.sql.DriverManager` for J2EE applications. However, you may still be required to use the `java.sql.DriverManager` for direct database access outside J2EE applications.

The `java.sql.DriverManager` class specifies the following types of methods:

❑   Methods to manage drivers

❑   Methods to obtain connections

❑   Methods for logging

Let's look at each of these areas in turn.

Methods to Manage Drivers

The following methods manage drivers. Note that these methods are meant for driver implementation, and tools that manipulate drivers:

`public static void registerDriver(Driver driver)`

This method is used to register a driver with the `DriverManager`. A newly loaded driver class should call this method to make itself known to the `DriverManager`. Classes implementing the `Driver` interface call this method during the static initialization to register a class. Once registered, the driver manager holds a reference to the driver until it is deregistered. For security reasons, the driver manager associates the caller's class loader with each driver, so that classes loaded from a class loader will have access only to those drivers that are registered by classes loaded by the same class loader.

`public static void deregisterDriver(Driver driver)`

This method deregisters a driver from the driver manager.

`public static Driver getDriver(String url)`

Given a JDBC URL, this method returns a driver that can understand the URL.

`public static Enumeration getDrivers()`

This method returns an enumeration of all registered JDBC drivers registered by classes using the same class loader.

Methods to Obtain Connections

The driver manager has three variants of a static method `getConnection()` used to establish connections. The driver manager delegates these calls to the `connect()` method on the `java.sql.Driver` interface.

Depending on the type of the driver and the database server, a connection may involve a physical network connection to the database server, or a proxy to a connection. Embedded databases require no physical connection. Whether or not there is a physical connection involved, the connection object is the only object that an application uses to communicate with the database. All communication must happen within the context of one or more connections.

Let's now consider the different methods for getting a connection:

```
public static Connection getConnection(String url) throws SQLException
```

The `java.sql.DriverManager` retrieves an appropriate driver from the set of registered JDBC drivers. The database URL is specified in the form of `jdbc:subprotocol:subname`. Whether we get a connection with this method or not depends on whether the database accepts connection requests without authentication.

```
public static Connection getConnection(String url,
                                        java.util.Properties info)
        throws SQLException
```

This method requires a URL and a `java.util.Properties` object. The `Properties` object contains each required parameter for the specified database. The list of properties differs from database to database. Two commonly used properties for Cloudscape are `autocommit=true` and `create=false`. We can specify these properties along with the URL as `jdbc:cloudscape:Movies;autocommit=true;create=true`, or we can set these properties using the `Properties` object, and pass the `Properties` object in the above `getConnection()` method:

```
String url = "jdbc:cloudscape:Movies";
Properties p = new Properties();
p.put("autocommit", "true");
p.put("create","true");
Connection connection = DriverManager.getConnection(url, p);
```

The driver neglects nonexistent properties; if the property value is not valid, you may get an exception.

Note that these properties are driver-specific, and you should refer to your driver documentation for the list of required properties. To learn more about the available properties for Cloudscape 4.0, refer to http://www.cloudscape.com/docs/doc_40/doc/html/coredocs/attrib.htm.

```
public static Connection getConnection(String url, String user,
                                        String password)
        throws SQLException
```

The third variant takes user and password as the arguments in addition to the URL. Here is an example; the following code uses an ODBC driver, where `Movies` is a DSN set up in the ODBC configuration. This DSN corresponds to a database that requires a user name and password for getting a connection:

```
String url = "jdbc:odbc.Movies ";
String user = "catalog_admin";
String password = "catalog_admin";

Connection conn = DriverManager.getConnection(url, user, password);
```

Note that all these methods are synchronized, implying that more than one application thread cannot directly get hold of the same `java.sql.Connection` object. These methods throw a `SQLException` if the driver fails to obtain a connection.

Sometimes it is necessary to specify the maximum time that a driver should wait while attempting to connect to a database. The following two methods can be used to set/get the login timeout:

```
public static void setLoginTimeout(int seconds)
public static int getLoginTimeout()
```

The default value for the login timeout is driver/database-specific.

Methods for Logging

The following methods access or set a `PrintWriter` object for logging purposes:

```
public static void setLogWriter(PrintWriter out)
public static PrintWriter getLogWriter()
```

In addition, client applications can also log messages using the following method:

```
public static void println(String message)
```

This method is used in conjunction with the `PrintWriter` set by `setLogWriter()` method to print log messages.

Driver

In JDBC, each driver is identified using a JDBC URL, and each driver should implement the `java.sql.Driver` interface. For instance in Cloudscape, the `COM.cloudscape.core.JDBCDriver` class implements the `java.sql.Driver` interface, which specifies the following methods:

```
public boolean acceptsURL(String url)
public Connection connect(String url, Properties info)
public int getMajorVersion()
public int getMinorVersion()
public DriverPropertyInfo getPropertyInfo(String url, Properties info)
public boolean jdbcCompliant()
```

The `DriverManager` class uses these methods. In general, client applications need not access the driver classes directly.

Establishing a Connection

To communicate with a database using JDBC, we must first establish a connection to the database through the appropriate JDBC driver. The JDBC API specifies the connection in the `java.sql.Connection` interface. This interface has the following public methods:

Function	Methods
Creating statements	createStatement()
	prepareStatement()
	prepareCall()
Obtaining database information	getMetaData()
Transaction support	setAutoCommit()
	getAutoCommit()
	commit()
	rollback()
	setTransactionIsolation()
	getTransactionIsolation()
Connection status and closing	isClosed()
	close()
Setting various properties, clearing values and retrieving any warnings generated	setReadOnly()
	isReadOnly()
	clearWarnings()
	getWarnings()
Converting SQL strings into database-specific SQL and setting views and user defined types	nativeSQL()
	setCatalog()
	getCatalog()
	setTypeMap()
	getTypeMap()

The categories in the above table represent an attempt to break the methods into logical groups according to functionality. In the next few sections, we'll discuss most of these methods.

Here's an example of establishing a JDBC connection to the Cloudscape Movies database:

```
Connection connection;
String url = "jdbc:cloudscape:Movies;create=true"

try {

  connection = DriverManager.getConnection(url);

  // Data access using the connection object
  . . .
} catch (SQLException e) {
    // Deal with error here
} finally {
  try {
```

```
      connection.close();
    } catch(SQLException e) { // System error? }
}
```

In this example, the URL specifies the JDBC URL; create=true indicates that Cloudscape should create the Movies database if it does not exist. You should also always catch the SQLException, and try to close the connection after using the connection for data access.

In the JDBC API, there are several methods that throw a SQLException. In this example, the connection is closed in the finally block, so that the system resources can be freed up regardless of the success or otherwise of any database operations.

Let us now summarize what has been discussed so far using a simple example. This example registers the cloudscape driver and establishes a connection:

```java
// Import required packages
import java.sql.Driver;
import java.sql.DriverManager;
import java.sql.Connection;
import java.sql.DatabaseMetaData;
import java.sql.SQLException;
import java.sql.DriverPropertyInfo;
import java.util.Enumeration;
import java.util.Properties;

public class DriverTest {
  public static void main(String arg[]) {
    String protocol = "jdbc:cloudscape:c:/CloudscapeDB";
    String driverClass = "COM.cloudscape.core.JDBCDriver";

    // Register the Cloudscape driver
    try {
      Class.forName(driverClass);
    } catch (ClassNotFoundException cne) {
      cne.printStackTrace();
    }

    // Check the registered drivers
    Enumeration drivers = DriverManager.getDrivers();
    while (drivers.hasMoreElements()) {
      Driver driver = (Driver) drivers.nextElement();
      System.out.println("Registered driver: "
                         + driver.getClass().getName());
      try {

        // Does this driver accept the known URL
        if (driver.acceptsURL(protocol)) {
          System.out.println("Accepts URL: " + protocol);
        }
      } catch (SQLException sqle) {
        sqle.printStackTrace();
      }
    }

    // Get a connection from the DriverManger.
```

```
    try {
      Connection connection = DriverManager.getConnection(protocol);

      // Get the metadata
      DatabaseMetaData metaData = connection.getMetaData();
      System.out.println("Product name: "
                       + metaData.getDatabaseProductName());
      System.out.println("Driver name: " + metaData.getDriverName());
    } catch (SQLException sqle) {
      sqle.printStackTrace();
    }
  }
}
```

This example performs three tasks, the purpose of which is to familiarize you with the basics of JDBC programming:

❑ The first task is to register a driver. Since drivers perform this registration via static initialization, all you have to do is to load the class name for the specific drier you're using. In this example, we register the driver for Cloudscape. Note that you can register more than one driver from a given application.

❑ The second task is to find out what the registered drivers are. We use the `java.sql.DriverManager` to find out an enumeration of drivers currently registered. Since we've registered only one driver in the first step, the second step would find only one driver. The second step also determines if the driver found accepts the known URL. In this case, we determine if the driver accepts the URL "`jdbc:cloudscape:c:/CloudscapeDB`", where "`c:/CloudscapeDB`" is the name (and location) of the database for this application.

❑ The third step is to obtain a connection to the database using the `getConnection()` method on `java.sql.DriverManager`. After getting the connection, we also find out the some of the database metadata using the `java.sql.DatabaseMetaData` obtained by calling `getMetaData()` method on `java.sql.Connection`.

In order to test this example, you should add the Cloudscape libraries to your classpath. The main one we'll want for this example is `cloudscape.jar`, which you should find under `%J2EE_HOME%\lib\cloudscape` (or `%J2EE_HOME%\lib\system`).

After setting this classpath, compile and run this class. For Cloudscape 3.6.4, the output of this class will be as follows:

```
C:\WINDOWS\System32\cmd.exe
C:\ProJavaServer1.3\Ch04>java -classpath .;%JLIB%\cloudscape.jar DriverTest

Registered driver: c8e.cs.c
Accepts URL: jdbc:cloudscape:c:/CloudscapeDB
Product name: DBMS:cloudscape
Driver name: Cloudscape Embedded JDBC Driver

C:\ProJavaServer1.3\Ch04>_
```

This includes the driver class name, the accepted URL, the product name, and the driver name. Note that you will find that the driver name is somewhat cryptic. This is because Cloudscape libraries are obfuscated to prevent de-compiling.

Creating and Executing SQL Statements

We can use a `Connection` object to execute SQL statements by creating a `Statement`, a `PreparedStatement`, or a `CallableStatement`. These objects abstract regular SQL statements, prepared statements, and stored procedures respectively. Once we obtain one of these statement objects, we can execute the statement and read the results through a `ResultSet` object.

As shown the table above, the following methods create statement objects:

```
Statement createStatement() throws SQLException
```

This method creates a `Statement` object, which we can use to send SQL statements to the database. SQL statements without parameters are normally executed using `Statement` objects.

```
Statement createStatement(int resultSetType, int resultSetConcurrency)
           throws SQLException
```

This variant of `createStatement()` requires `resultSetType`, and `resultSetConcurrency` arguments. These arguments apply to `ResultSet` objects created by executing queries.

Of these two arguments, the first argument is used to specify the required `ResultSet` type. As we shall see later, there are three resultset types depending on the scrollability: forward only scrollable (`ResultSet.TYPE_FORWARD_ONLY`), scrollable but insensitive to changes made by other transactions (`ResultSet.TYPE_SCROLL_INSENSITIVE`), or scrollable and sensitive to changes made by other transactions (`ResultSet.TYPE_SCROLL_INSENSITIVE`). The `java.sql.ResultSet` interface specifies three constants as result types.

The second argument is used to specify if the `ResultSet` is read-only (`ResultSet.CONCUR_READ_ONLY`), or should be updateable (`ResultSet.CONCUR_READ_ONLY`).

The no-argument `createStatement()` method returns a `ResultSet` that is forward-only scrollable, and read-only.

The `createStatement()` method takes no arguments (except for type and concurrency where applicable) and returns a `Statement` object. The ultimate goal of a `Statement` object is to execute a SQL statement that may or may not return results. We will see an example soon.

```
public PreparedStatement prepareStatement(String sql) throws SQLException
```

We can get a `PreparedStatement` object by calling this method on a `Connection`. Later in this chapter, we shall walk through the usage of prepared statements for executing SQL statements.

```
public CallableStatement prepareCall(String sql) throws SQLException
```

This method is used to call a stored procedure.

The `Statement` interface has the following methods:

Function	Method
Executing statements	execute()
	executeQuery()
	executeUpdate()
Batch updates	addBatch()
	executeBatch()
	clearBatch()
Resultset fetch size	setFetchSize()
	getFetchSize()
	setFetchDirection()
	getFetchDirection()
Get current resultset	getResultSet()
Resultset concurrency and type	getResultSetConcurrency()
	getResultSetType()
Other	setQueryTimeout()
	getQueryTimeout()
	setMaxFieldSize()
	getMaxFieldSize()
	cancel()
	getConnection()

Statements also support the same methods for transaction support as the Connection object, together with the close() method.

There are two sub-interfaces PreparedStatement and CallableStatement, that are used for calling precompiled SQL statements and database stored procedures. These two interfaces specify additional methods for preparing statements and calling stored procedures.

An Example: Movie Catalog

In order to illustrate the JDBC API, let's consider a simple movie catalog. The database for this example consists of a table called CATALOG.

Let's consider a Java class CreateMovieTables that creates a CATALOG table, and inserts the data into the table. In this example, we retrieve the data from a text file, catalog.txt and insert into the CATALOG table.

Create the Movies Table

The initialize() method loads the driver, and obtains a connection. createTable() creates the table.

You can use the following method on the Statement object to insert data:

```
int executeUpdate(String sql) throws SQLException
```

executeUpdate() is used to execute SQL statements that do not return any results, for example INSERT, UPDATE, or DELETE statements. This method returns an integer that denotes the number of rows affected:

```
public class CreateMovieTables {
  static String driver = "COM.cloudscape.core.JDBCDriver";
  static String url = "jdbc:cloudscape:";
  Connection connection = null;
  Statement statement = null;
  // ...

  public void initialize() throws SQLException, ClassNotFoundException {
    Class.forName (driver);
    connection = DriverManager.getConnection(url + "Movies;create=true");
  }

  public void createTable() throws SQLException {
    statement = connection.createStatement();
    statement.executeUpdate("CREATE TABLE CATALOG" +
                            "(TITLE VARCHAR(256) PRIMARY KEY NOT NULL, " +
                            "LEAD_ACTOR VARCHAR(256) NOT NULL, " +
                            "LEAD_ACTRESS VARCHAR(256) NOT NULL, " +
                            "TYPE VARCHAR(20) NOT NULL, " +
                            "RELEASE_DATE DATE NOT NULL)");
  }
```

In this code, the variables connection and statement are instance variables of CreateMovieTables class. The createTable() method obtains a connection from the DriverManager. For Cloudscape, we specify the protocol as "jdbc:cloudscape:Movies;create=true".

When we create a table for the first time using this URL, the Cloudscape DBMS creates a subdirectory under the current working directory called "Movies" to store the data. Refer to Cloudscape documentation for specifying a different directory. In case you want to clean up your database, you may remove this directory, and recreate all the tables. You can access the Cloudscape documentation online at http://www.cloudscape.com/support/documentation.html.

In the above code, the executeUpdate() does not update any database records, and hence the method returns zero. In case of INSERT, UPDATE, or DELETE statements, you may be interested in the number of rows inserted, updated, or deleted.

Also note that the schema used in this example is for illustrative purposes only, and does not reflect realistic catalog data.

After getting a connection, the next step is to create a statement. We pass a SQL statement for creating the table using the executeUpdate() method on the statement. As you see from the SQL statement above, the CATALOG table has five columns.

Inserting Data

The insertData() method of the CreateMovieTables class reads movie records from a text file, and inserts them into the database:

```
public void insertData() throws SQLException, IOException {
  BufferedReader br = new BufferedReader(new FileReader("catalog.txt"));

  try {
    do {

      title = br.readLine();
      leadActor = br.readLine();
      leadActress = br.readLine();
      type = br.readLine();
      dateOfRelease = br.readLine();

      String sqlString = "INSERT INTO CATALOG " +
                  "(TITLE, LEAD_ACTOR, LEAD_ACTRESS, "+
                  "TYPE, RELEASE_DATE) " +
                  "VALUES('" + title +
                  "','" + leadActor + "','" + leadActress +
                  "','" + type + "','" + dateOfRelease + "')";

      statement.executeUpdate(sqlString);
      statement.close();
    } while(br.readLine() != null); // This reads the termination line

  } catch (IOException e) {
    e.printStackTrace()
  } finally {
    br.close();
  }
}
```

The format of the input file is title, leadActor, leadActress, type, and dateOfRelease entered in separate lines, followed by a separator line as shown below:

```
Austin Powers
Mike Myers
Liz Hurley
Comedy
1999-04-01
--------------
```

In the code above, the only statement that is relevant for our discussion is the statement.executeUpdate() method call to insert the data into the CATALOG table. Note that we did not catch the SQLException here. Instead we're letting the caller of this method catch the SQLException.

Methods for Exception Handling

As mentioned previously, most of the methods on JDBC interfaces and classes throw an instance of SQLException to indicate failure. However, depending on the drivers and databases that you're using, there could be several layers and sources of errors. In order to accommodate this, the SQLException can be nested, by embedding several exceptions in a linked list. We can use the getNextException() method on the SQLException class to retrieve all such exceptions. The following code snippet recursively traverses through the available exceptions. This approach could prove to be informative for handling exceptions in our JDBC applications:

```
  } catch(SQLException sqlException) {

    while(sqlException != null) {
      System.err.println(sqlException.toString());
      sqlException = sqlException.getNextException();
    }
  }
```

You can similarly retrieve warnings (including those that are vendor-specific) received or generated by the driver using the getWarnings() method on the connection:

```
SQLWarning warnings = connection.getWarnings();

while(warnings != null) {
  System.err.println(connection.getWarnings());
  warnings = warnings.getNextWarning();
}
```

Here is the complete source:

```
import java.sql.DriverManager;
import java.sql.Connection;
import java.sql.Statement;
import java.sql.PreparedStatement;
import java.sql.SQLException;
import java.sql.Date;
import java.io.BufferedReader;
import java.io.FileReader;
import java.io.IOException;
import java.io.EOFException;
import java.text.SimpleDateFormat;
import java.text.ParseException;

// This class requires a text file called catalog.txt containing the
// input data.

public class CreateMovieTables {

  static String driver = "COM.cloudscape.core.JDBCDriver";
  static String url = "jdbc:cloudscape:";

  String title, leadActor, leadActress, type, dateOfRelease;
  Connection connection;
  Statement statement;

  public void initialize() throws SQLException, ClassNotFoundException {
    Class.forName(driver);

    connection = DriverManager.getConnection(url + "Movies;create=true");
  }

  public void createTable() throws SQLException {
    statement = connection.createStatement();
    statement.executeUpdate("CREATE TABLE CATALOG" +
```

```
                              "(TITLE VARCHAR(256) PRIMARY KEY NOT NULL, " +
                              "LEAD_ACTOR VARCHAR(256) NOT NULL, " +
                              "LEAD_ACTRESS VARCHAR(256) NOT NULL, " +
                              "TYPE VARCHAR(20) NOT NULL, " +
                              "RELEASE_DATE DATE NOT NULL)");
  }

  public void insertData() throws SQLException, IOException {
    BufferedReader br = new BufferedReader(new FileReader("catalog.txt"));

    try {
      do {

        title = br.readLine();
        leadActor = br.readLine();
        leadActress = br.readLine();
        type = br.readLine();
        dateOfRelease = br.readLine();

        String sqlString = "INSERT INTO CATALOG " +
                           "(TITLE, LEAD_ACTOR, LEAD_ACTRESS, " +
                           "TYPE, RELEASE_DATE) " + "VALUES('" + title +
                           "','" + leadActor + "','" + leadActress +
                           "','" + type + "','" + dateOfRelease + "')";

        statement.executeUpdate(sqlString);
        statement.close();
      } while (br.readLine() != null); // This reads the termination line

    } catch (IOException e) {
      e.printStackTrace();
    }
    finally {
      br.close();
    }
  }

  public void close() throws SQLException {
    try {
      connection.close();
    } catch (SQLException e) {
      throw e;
    }
  }

  public static void main(String arg[]) {
    CreateMovieTables movies = new CreateMovieTables();

    try {
      movies.initialize();
      movies.createTable();
      movies.close();
    } catch (SQLException sqlException) {
      while (sqlException != null) {
        sqlException.printStackTrace();
        sqlException = sqlException.getNextException();
```

```
      }
    } catch (Exception e) {
      e.printStackTrace();
    }
  }
}
```

For the purpose of demonstration, this class is structured in terms of small methods, each of which performs specific JDBC functions. In this class, the `initialize()` method loads the driver, and creates a connection. The `createTable()` method creates a table using the `executeUpdate()` method on the `java.sql.Statement`. The `insertData()` method reads a number of records from a text file, and inserts them into the table. The `main()` method of this class is the controller that calls the other methods in sequence. Note that the `main()` method calls the `close()` method to close the statement and the connection.

Note that, of the fields inserted in the above code, although the RELEASE_DATE field is of type DATE, we used a `String` while creating the statement. This is valid as long as the `String` used can safely be coerced to a DATE field. In this example, the string used is of the form YYYY-MM-DD, which is coercible to a DATE field. However, in order to be type-safe, you should consider using prepared statements to execute SQL involving typed data such as dates, timestamps, numbers, etc.

For most of the remaining examples in this chapter, we follow the above class as a template. If you want to experiment with the JDBC API, you should add new methods in this class.

Querying the Database

The `Statement` object returns a `java.sql.ResultSet` object that encapsulates the results of execution. This is an interface that is implemented by driver vendors. You can scroll through the resultset using a cursor for reading the results in the `ResultSet`.

The following method, `executeQuery()`, in the `java.sql.Statement` interface allows you to execute SQL SELECT statements:

```
public ResultSet executeQuery (String sql) throws SQLException
```

There is also a generic `execute()` method that can return multiple results:

```
public boolean execute(String sql) throws SQLException
```

This `execute()` method can be used to execute stored procedures that are a known to give multiple results, or unknown SQL strings (for example, SQL statements read from another source at run time). This method returns a `Boolean` with value `true` when the execution results in one or more resultsets, or a value `false` when the execution results in one or more update counts. Using this return value, the application may call `getResultSet()` or `getUpdateCount()` methods to access the resultset or update count respectively.

The JDBC API 2.1 introduced two more types of `ResultSet` that allow scrolling in both forward and reverse directions but not all database vendors currently support this feature. We'll discuss scrolling later in this chapter.

Methods to Retrieve Data

The `java.sql.ResultSet` interface provides several methods for retrieving fields of different types. Depending on your schema, you should use appropriate methods to retrieve the data:

getArray()	getAsciiStream()	getBigDecimal()	getBinaryStream()
getBlob()	getBoolean()	getByte()	getBytes()
getCharacterStream()	getClob()	getDate()	getDouble()
getFloat()	getInt()	getLong()	getObject()
getRef()	getShort()	getString()	getTime()
getTimestamp ()	getURL()		

All these methods require either the column name (as a string) or the column index as the argument. The syntax for the two variants of `getString()` methods is shown below:

```
public String getString(int columnIndex) throws SQLException
public String getString(String columnName) throws SQLException
```

In cases where the column index is subjected to change due to changes in SQL or the database schema, it is preferable to use column names in these methods.

The return types of these methods vary from simple Java primitives such as `int`, `double`, `byte` etc., to special-purpose SQL types such as `java.sql.Blob`, and `java.sql.Clob`. The `getAsciiStream()`, `getBinaryStream()`, and `getCharacterStream()` methods allow access to arbitrarily long ASCII/character data by returning `java.io.InputStream` and `java.io.Reader` objects.

Let's get back to our movie catalog, and create another class, `QueryMovieTables`, to implement different types of queries. The following method, `queryAll()`, retrieves all the data from the CATALOG table:

```
public void queryAll() throws SQLException {
  System.out.println("Query All");
  Statement statement = connection.createStatement();

  String sqlString = "SELECT CATALOG.TITLE, CATALOG.LEAD_ACTOR, "+
                     "CATALOG.LEAD_ACCTRESS, CATALOG.TYPE, " +
                     "CATALOG.RELEASE_DATE FROM CATALOG";

  ResultSet rs = statement.executeQuery(sqlString);

  while(rs.next()) {
    System.out.println(rs.getString("TITLE") + ", " +
                       rs.getString("LEAD_ACTOR") + ", " +
                       rs.getString("LEAD_ACCTRESS") + ", " +
                       rs.getString("TYPE") + ", " +
                       rs.getDate("RELEASE_DATE"));
  }
}
```

This method first creates a `Statement` object, which it then uses to call `executeQuery()` with a SQL `SELECT` statement as an argument. The `java.sql.ResultSet` object returned contains all the rows of the `CATALOG` table matching the `SELECT` statement. Using the `next()` method of `ResultSet` object, we can iterate through all the rows contained in the resultset. At any given row, we can use one of the `getXXX` methods in the table above to retrieve the fields of a row.

What happens if the query (or any SQL being sent to the database via the driver for execution) is very expensive and takes a very long time to complete? This may happen, for instance, if the query is complex, or if the database is attempting to return a very large number of results. In order to control the time that the driver waits for the database to complete execution, the `java.sql.Statement` interface has two methods to get or set a maximum timeout.

For instance, we can modify the `queryAll()` method to set a maximum query timeout interval (in seconds) using the `setQueryTimeout()` method. You can use the `getQueryTimeout()` method to find the current query timeout interval in seconds (or the default, if not set explicitly). Once the database exceeds the query timeout interval, the driver aborts the execution and throws a `java.sql.SQLException`. For example, here we set the time out value to 1 second:

```
Statement statement = connection.createStatement();
statement.setQueryTimeout(1);
// Set SQL for statement
ResultSet rs = statement.executeQuery(sqlString);
```

ResultSetMetaData Interface

The `ResultSet` interface also allows us to find out the structure of the resultset. The `getMetaData()` method helps us to retrieve a `java.sql.ResultSetMetaData` object that has several methods to describe resultset cursors:

GetCatalogName()	getScale()
getTableName()	getPrecision()
GetSchemaName()	isNullable()
GetColumnCount()	isCurrency()
GetColumnName())	isSearchable()
GetColumnLabel()	isCaseSensitive()
GetColumnType()	isSigned()
GetColumnTypeName()	isAutoIncrement()
GetColumnClassName()	isReadOnly()
GetColumnDisplaySize()	isDefinitelyWritable()
isWritable()	

Given a resultset, we can use the `getColumnCount()` method to get the number of columns in the resultset. Using this column number, we can get the meta-information of each column.

For example, the following method in our example prints the structure of the resultset:

```
public void getMetaData() throws SQLException {
  System.out.println("MetaData of ResultSet");
  Statement statement = connection.createStatement();

  String sqlString = "SELECT * FROM CATALOG";

  ResultSet rs = statement.executeQuery(sqlString);

  ResultSetMetaData metaData = rs.getMetaData();

  int noColumns = metaData.getColumnCount();

  // Column numbers start from 1
  for(int i = 1; i < noColumns + 1; i++) {
    System.out.println(metaData.getColumnName(i) + " " +
                       metaData.getColumnType(i));
  }
}
```

The above method gets the number of columns in the resultset, and prints the name and type of each column. In this case, the column names are TITLE, LEAD_ACTOR, LEAD_ACTRESS, TYPE, and RELEASE_DATE. Note that the types of column are returned as integers. For example, all VARCHAR type columns will have the column type as 12, while DATE type is type 91. These types are constants defined in the java.sql.Types interface. Also note that the column numbers start from 1 instead of 0.

Such information may be used to decide how to treat such data. For instance, by knowing that the fifth column type is DATE, the application can determine that a java.sql.Date should be used to represent this data. Although such information can be derived by studying the database schema and the SQL used to extract data, database metadata may be used to reduce hard-coding such information.

Prepared Statements

JDBC prepared statements address the following requirements:

❏ Creating parameterized statements such that data for parameters can be substituted dynamically

❏ Creating statements involving data values that cannot always be represented as character strings

❏ Pre-compiling SQL statements to avoid repeated compiling of the same SQL statements

Let us briefly look at why these requirements are crucial.

In most cases, you may not have the complete information to construct a WHERE clause in SQL. For instance, to write a SQL SELECT statement to select the data of a user, while writing the JDBC code, you need to know the primary key value (such as a USER_ID) to construct the SQL. In most cases, such information is available only at runtime (say, from a user interface, or from some other application). Prepared statements address this problem by providing for parameters (expressed as question marks) in SQL.

Instead of using values, you may use "?" qualifiers in SQL. So, instead of creating a statement with the SQL string:

```
SELECT <select_fields> FROM <table_name> WHERE USER_ID = <value>
```

you can use a prepared statement with the SQL string:

```
SELECT <select_fields> FROM <table_name> WHERE USER_ID = ?
```

You can substitute actual values using methods on the `java.sql.PreparedStatement` interface.

The same applies to SQL involving complex data types such as long text data, binary data, or even timestamp data. Such data types (during inserts/updates, or in WHERE clauses of SQL) cannot be expressed as plain string. For instance, how would we create a SQL statement to update image data? Since prepared statements are parameterized, instead of expressing such data types in the SQL statement directly, you can set the data using various methods on the `java.sql.PreparedStatement` interface.

In addition, the same SQL statement can be executed many times with different parameters, and the database can compile such statements just once, thus improving performance. A `PreparedStatement` object can hold precompiled SQL statements. The following methods on the `java.sql.Connection` interface let us create `PreparedStatement` objects:

```
PreparedStatement prepareStatement(String sql) throws SQLException
PreparedStatement prepareStatement(String sql, int resultSetType,
                                   int resultSetConcurrency)
                                   throws SQLException
```

For example, in the `insertData()` method of the `CreateMovieTables` class, the SQL INSERT statement is executed a number of times. This statement must be compiled before it is executed. Compilation is a time-consuming process that typically involves parsing of the statement, binding with the tables and columns, any optimization, and code generation, so it may be better to use a `PreparedStatement` as an alternative. With prepared statements, this compilation is done only once.

To allow us to specify the data, prepared statements are parameterized, with each parameter represented as a question mark (?).

We can replace the `insertData()` method of the `CreateMovieTables` class with the following to make use of the `PreparedStatement` object:

```
public void insertPreparedData () throws SQLException, IOException {

  BufferedReader br = new BufferedReader(new FileReader("catalog.txt"));

  PreparedStatement preparedStatement =
      connection.prepareStatement("INSERT INTO" CATALOG" +
                                  "(title, lead_actor, lead_acctress, " +
                                  "type, release_date)" +
                                  "VALUES(?, ?, ?, ?, ?)");

  SimpleDateFormat dateFormat = new SimpleDateFormat("yyyy-MM-dd");

  try {
    do {
      preparedStatement.clearParameters();
      title = br.readLine();
      leadActor = br.readLine();
      leadActress = br.readLine();
      type = br.readLine();
```

```
            dateOfRelease = br.readLine();
            Date date = new Date(dateFormat.parse(dateOfRelease).getTime());

            preparedStatement.setString(1, title);
            preparedStatement.setString(2, leadActor);
            preparedStatement.setString(3, leadActress);
            preparedStatement.setString(4, type);
            preparedStatement.setDate(5, date);

            preparedStatement.executeUpdate();

        } while(br.readLine() != null);
    } catch (EOFException e) {
    } catch (java.text.ParseException pe) {
        pe.printStackTrace();
    } catch (IOException ioException) {
        ioException.printStackTrace();
    } finally {
        preparedStatement.close();
        br.close();
    }
}
```

Once the `PreparedStatement` is created, use the `setXXX` methods to set parameters for the `PreparedStatement`. For instance, we use the `setString()` method for setting `VARCHAR` parameters. Similarly, for setting SQL `DATE` type, we can use the `setDate()` method. These methods take the place-holder number as the first argument; so, `setString(1, title)` sets the value of the first ? to `title`.

Also note that the date object requires special treatment. There are four different objects that we can use for representing date and time. The `java.util.Date` class was the only date object available prior to the JDBC API. However, the `java.sql` package introduces three more classes:

public class Date extends java.util.Date

This `Date` class corresponds to the SQL `DATE` type. Therefore, we should use `java.sql.Date` in our JDBC programming to conform to the JDBC types:

public class Time extends java.util.Date

This class corresponds to the SQL `TIME DATE` type:

public class Timestamp extends java.util.Date

Neither of the `java.sql.Date` and `java.sql.Time` classes captures the precision of SQL `TIMESTAMP` type. The `java.sql.TimeStamp` class fills this gap. Time stamp objects can hold `TIMESTAMP`'s nanoseconds, in addition to the standard date and time fields. In general, if you're capturing specific instances of time, consider using `java.sql.TimeStamp`.

The JDBC API also provides facilities for invoking stored procedures. The `java.sql.CallableStatement` interface can be used for creating statements for executing stored procedures. The following methods on the `java.sql.Connection` interface create `CallableStatement` objects:

```
CallableStatement prepareCall(String sql) throws SQLException
CallableStatement prepareCall(String sql, int resultSetType,
                             int resultSetConcurrency)
                        throws SQLException
```

In practice, a stored procedure is not appropriate in a J2EE environment, as it couples the application very closely with a specific database.

Mapping SQL Types to Java

SQL data types and Java data types are not equivalent. While SQL types include types such as VARCHAR, NUMBER, and TIMESTAMP, data types in Java evolved from programming languages such as C and C++. This disparity between SQL types and Java data types has been addressed by the specification of generic SQL types, and their mapping to and from Java data types. The JDBC SQL types are specified in the java.sql.Types class, as constants.

There are two occasions where we require this mapping information: While setting input parameters for prepared statements (using setXXX() methods in the PreparedStatement interface), and while getting results from ResultSet objects (using getXXX() methods in the ResultSet interface). In both these cases, drivers map the types across JDBC and Java types.

The following table summarizes the JDBC types, and their mapping to Java types, and SQL data types:

JDBC Type	Purpose	SQL Type	Java Type
ARRAY	Represents SQL type ARRAY	ARRAY	java.sql.Array
BIGINT	64-bit signed integer	BIGINT	long
BINARY	Small, fixed length binary value	No correspondence. Check your driver documentation	byte[]
BIT	Single bit value (0 or 1)	BIT	boolean
BLOB	Represents SQL type BLOB for storing binary large objects	BLOB	java.sql.Blob
BOOLEAN	Represents SQL type BOOLEAN	BOOLEAN	java.lang.Boolean
CHAR	Small, fixed length character string	CHAR	String
CLOB	Represents SQL type CLOB for storing character large objects	CLOB	java.sql.Clob
DATALINK	Represents SQL type DATALINK	DATALINK	java.net.URL

JDBC Type	Purpose	SQL Type	Java Type
DATE	Date consisting of day, month, and year	DATE	java.sql.Date
DECIMAL	Fixed-precision decimal values	DECIMAL	java.math.BigDecimal
DISTINCT	For custom mapping of user-defined types	DISTINCT	User defined
DOUBLE	Double-precision floating-point numbers with 15 digit mantissa	DOUBLE PRECISION	double
FLOAT	Double-precision floating-point numbers with 15 digit mantissa	FLOAT	double
INTEGER	32-bit signed integer	INTEGER	int
JAVA_OBJECT	For storing Java objects	No correspondence	Object
LONGVARBINARY	Large, variable length binary value	No correspondence	byte[]
LONGVARCHAR	Large, variable length character string	No correspondence	String
NULL	To represent NULL values	NULL	null for Java objects, 0 for numeric primitives, and false for Boolean
NUMERIC	Fixed-precision decimal values	NUMERIC	java.math.BigDecimal
OTHER	For storing/retrieving database-specific types	No correspondence; meant for database/driver specific types	Object
REAL	Single-precision floating-point numbers with 7 digit mantissa	REAL	float
REF	NA	NA	NA
SMALLINT	16-bit signed integer	SMALLINT	short

Table continued on following page

JDBC Type	Purpose	SQL Type	Java Type
STRUCT	NA	NA	NA
TIME	Time consisting of hours, minutes, and seconds	TIME	java.sql.Time
TIMESTAMP	Time-stamp consisting of DATE, TIME, and a nanosecond field	TIMESTAMP	java.sql. TimeStamp
TINYINT	8-bit unsigned integer	TINYINT	short
VARBINARY	Small, variable length binary value	No correspondence.	byte[]
VARCHAR	Small, variable-length character string	VARCHAR	String

While this table summarizes all possible mappings between SQL and Java, in practice the support for these mappings varies from driver to driver. Moreover, since not all database vendors conform to all the SQL types, and there are also several vendor-specific SQL types in vogue, you should check your database and driver documentation for conformance to this mapping. If portability of your application is a concern, you should try to keep your SQL conformed to the most commonly used data types.

Transaction Support

In some applications, we might like to group together a series of statements that need either all to succeed or all to fail. In such cases, a group of SQL operations constitutes one unit of work. The notion of the transaction is important to preserve the integrity of business transactions that span multiple SQL operations. When multiple statements are executed in a single transaction, all operations can be committed (made permanent in the database) or rolled back (that is, changes to the database are undone).

The discussion in this section is limited to local transactions, that is, transactions performed with a single database from a single client. We shall discuss distributed transactions at length later in this chapter.

When a new Connection object is created, it is set to commit every transaction automatically. This means that every time a statement is executed, it is committed to the database and cannot be rolled back. The following methods in the Connection interface are used to demarcate transactions and either rollback or commit them to the database:

```
void setAutoCommit(boolean autoCommit) throws SQLException
void commit() throws SQLException
void rollback() throws SQLException
```

In order to begin a transaction, we call setAutoCommit(false). This will give us control over what is committed and when. A call to the commit() method will commit everything that was done since the last commit was issued. Conversely, a rollback() call will undo any changes since the last commit. However, once a commit is issued, those transactions cannot be undone with rollback.

Consider a business use case consisting of four steps, each involving executing a SQL statement, and additional logic implemented in the application: create an order, update the inventory, and create a shipping record. Business logic may require that all succeed together or else all should fail.

The failure of the creation of a shipping record may dictate that an order may not be created. In such cases, effects of SQL statements corresponding to the first two tasks (creating an order, and updating the inventory) should be undone – or rolled back.

The following code fragment illustrates this scenario:

```
Connection connection = null;

// Get a connection
...
try {
  // Begin a transaction
  connection.setAutoCommit(false);

  Statement statement = connection.createStatement();

  // Create an order
  statement.executeUpdate("INSET INTO ORDERS(ORDER_ID, PRODUCT_ID, ...) " +
                          "VALUES(...)");

  // Update inventory
  statement.executeUpdate("UPDATE TABLE INVENTORY " +
                          "SET QUANTITY = QUANTITY - 1 " +
                          "WHERE PRODUCT_ID = ...");

  // Create shipping record
  if(...) {
    // Business logic succeeded
    statement.execute("INSERT INTO SHIP_RECORD(...) VALUES (...)");
    connection.commit();
  } else {
    // Business logic failed. Can not proceed with this order
    connection.rollback();
  }
} catch (SQLException e) {
  // Handle exceptions here
} finally {
  // Close the statement and connection
}
```

In this snippet, once the rollback() method is called, the database restores the ORDERS and INVENTORY tables to their previous state. commit() makes the changes done by the INSERT and UPDATE statements permanent.

We'll discuss transactions in more detail later in this chapter.

Savepoints

The JDBC 3.0 API introduces save points. A **save point** is similar to a temporary marker set at a specific position during a set of database operations within a transaction. A savepoint allows you commit or rollback transactions partially. In order to understand the notion of a savepoint, consider using a word processor to edit a file. During the editing process, you can save the document several times. Each save operation is like setting a new save point. After a save operation, you can revert to the previously saved version by simply negating all the edits and reopening the same file. In a similar fashion, the `java.sql.Savepoint` mechanism lets you commit/abort at various save points.

Consider the following sequence of database operations:

```
Connection connection = null;

// Get a connection
...
try {
  // Begin a transaction
  connection.setAutoCommit(false);

  // Perform the first set of database operations
  ...

  // Perform the second set of database operations
  ...

  // Perform the third set of database operations
  ...
}  catch (SQLException e)  {
  // Handle exceptions here
}  finally {
  // Close the statement and connection
}
```

Suppose that the three sets of operations are logically related. For instance, if there is a failure while performing the second set of operations, there is no way to undo only the second set, and do some other set of corrective operations. The `commit()` and `rollback()` methods apply to the three sets of operations as a whole. You can overcome this limitation with save points.

Consider how the above can be implemented using save points:

```
Connection connection = null;

// Get a connection
...
try {
  // Begin a transaction
  connection.setAutoCommit(false);

  // Perform the first set of database operations
  ...

  Savepoint sp1 = connection.setSavepoint("First Batch");
```

```
    // Perform the second set of database operations
    ...

    // If there is a need to undo the second set of operations
    if(...) {
       connection.rollback(sp1);
       // Perform corrective operations if necessary
    } else {
       connection.releaseSavepoint(sp1);
    }

    // Perform the third set of database operations
    ...
} catch (SQLException e) {
// Handle exceptions here
} finally {
// Close the statement and connection
}
```

In this case, after performing the first batch of operations we set a save point with a given name (sp1). Note that the name is optional and is used by drivers to identify a save point. When the name is not set, drivers use an internally generated ID in place of the name. After setting this save point, at a later time, we can release the save point, or rollback all operations performed after setting the save point. In the above code, the call to rollback(sp1) rolls back the second set of database operations without affecting the first set of operations.

However, once you release a save point, any further rollback() call rolls back all the operations including those performed prior to setting up the save point.

You can set up more than one save point during a given transaction. However, any rollback performed on a save point invalidates all save points set afterwards. For instance, if you set three save points sp1, sp2, and sp3 (set in the same order), and you call rollback(sp2), the third save point, sp3, becomes invalid.

Once a save point is set, you can release it later using the releaseSavepoint() method on the java.sql.Connection object used to set the save point. Once a save point is released, you can use it to rollback. However, you cannot change the location of a save point once it is set during a transaction.

Note that the save point feature is relatively new in the JDBC API, and hence as of writing this chapter, not all JDBC drivers support this feature. You can determine if your database/driver supports this feature, using the following method on java.sql.DatabaseMetaData:

boolean supportsSavepoints() throws SQLException

Although the save point support is new in the JDBC API, databases such as Microsoft SQL Server, and Oracle support this feature.

Scrollable and Updateable Resultsets

Before JDBC 2.1, a ResultSet object created by executing a statement was, by default, forward-only scrollable. That is, we could traverse through the resultset using the next() method only. next() returns false when the last record is reached, and no more details can then be retrieved.

The JDBC 2.1 API (included in the J2SE 1.2 onwards) provides more flexible means of accessing results from `ResultSet` objects. These enhancements are categorized into the following:

❑   **Scrollable resultsets**
    The JDBC 2.1 `ResultSet` objects are scrollable. Scrollable resultsets have the ability to move the cursor backwards, and also support absolute positioning of the cursor at a particular row in the resultset.

❑   **Scroll sensitivity**
    The JDBC 2.1 API also specifies scroll-sensitive and scroll-insensitive resultsets. A scroll insensitive resultset represents a static snapshot of the results when the query was made. On the other hand, a scroll-sensitive resultset is sensitive to changes made to the data after the query has been executed, thus providing a dynamic view of the data as it changes.

❑   **Updatable resultsets**
    By default, resultsets are read-only. That is, contents of the resultset are read-only and cannot be changed. The JDBC 2.1 API also introduces updateable resultsets. When a resultset is updated, the update operation also updates the original data corresponding to the resultset.

The `java.sql.ResultSet` has additional methods to support these features. These are discussed in the following subsections.

Scrollable ResultSets

The `java.sql.ResultSet` interface specifies three types of resultsets:

❑   `TYPE_FORWARD_ONLY` – A resultset of this type supports forward-scrolling only.

❑   `TYPE_SCROLL_INSENSITIVE` – A resultset of this type supports scrolling in both directions.

❑   `TYPE_SCROLL_SENSITIVE` – A resultset of this type is sensitive to updates made to the data after the resultset has been populated. For instance, if your query returns 10 rows, and if another application removes two of the rows, your resultset will only have 8 rows. The same happens for inserts/updates too.

Before we use the methods of the `java.sql.ResultSet` interface for scrolling through the resultset, we should make sure that the JDBC driver supports these features. The `java.sql.DatabaseMetadata` interface provides several methods to discover the capabilities of the database driver.

To find out what resultset types are supported use `supportsResultSetType()`. For instance, the following code snippet should tell us the extent of the driver's support for these types:

```java
public void testScrollable() throws SQLException {
  boolean supports;

  DatabaseMetaData md = connection.getMetaData();

  supports = md.supportsResultSetType(ResultSet.TYPE_FORWARD_ONLY);

  if(supports) {
    System.out.println("TYPE_FORWARD_ONLY - Supports");
  } else {
    System.out.println("TYPE_FORWARD_ONLY - Does not support");
  }
```

```
      supports = md.supportsResultSetType(ResultSet.TYPE_SCROLL_INSENSITIVE);

      if(supports) {
        System.out.println("TYPE_SCROLL_INSENSITIVE - Supports");
      } else {
        System.out.println( "TYPE_SCROLL_INSENSITIVE - Does not support");
      }

      supports = md.supportsResultSetType(ResultSet.TYPE_SCROLL_SENSITIVE);

      if(supports) {
        System.out.println("TYPE_SCROLL_SENSITIVE - Supports");
      } else {
        System.out.println("TYPE_SCROLL_SENSITIVE - Does not support");
      }
  }
```

For scroll-sensitive resultsets, the following methods on `java.sql.DatabaseMetadata` return the level of sensitiveness:

> **public boolean othersUpdatesAreVisible(int type) throws SQLException**

This method returns `true` if changes made by other transactions will be visible for a scroll-sensitive resultset.

> **public boolean othersDeletesAreVisible(int type) throws SQLException**

`othersDeletesAreVisible()` returns `true` if deletions made by other transactions are visible in a scroll-sensitive resultset.

> **public boolean othersInsertsAreVisible(int type) throws SQLException**

`othersInsertsAreVisible()` returns `true` if insertions made by other transactions are visible in a scroll-sensitive resultset.

Similarly, the `java.sql.DatabaseMetadata` interface specifies `ownUpdatesAreVisible()`, `ownDeletesAreVisible()`, and `ownInsertsAreVisible()` methods to find out if changes made to the result are visible to this resultset.

The `java.sql.ResultSet` interface supports the following methods for scrolling through resultsets. These methods are grouped according to their usage.

Cursor Position Related Methods

> **public boolean isBeforeFirst() throws SQLException**
> **public boolean isAfterLast() throws SQLException**

`isBeforeFirst()` returns `true` if the cursor position is before the first row of the resultset. `isAfterLast()` returns `true` if the cursor position is after the last row of the resultset.

> **public boolean isFirst() throws SQLException**
> **public boolean isLast() throws SQLException**

isFirst() returns true if the cursor is at the first row of the resultset. isLast() returns true if the cursor is at the last row of the resultset.

```
public void beforeFirst() throws SQLException
public void afterLast() throws SQLException
```

These two methods returns true if the cursor position is before the first row or after the last row of the resultset respectively.

Methods for Scrolling

```
public boolean first() throws SQLException
public boolean last() throws SQLException
```

These methods move the cursor to the first row and last row of the resultset respectively.

```
public boolean absolute(int row) throws java.sql.SQLException
```

absolute() moves the cursor to the specified row in the resultset. The row argument can be positive or negative. A negative argument moves the cursor in the backward direction, while a positive argument moves the cursor in the forward direction.

```
public boolean relative(int rows) throws SQLException
```

This method moves the cursor by the specified number of rows relative to the current position of the cursor. If the argument is positive, this method moves the cursor forwards by the specified number of rows. If it is negative, this method moves the cursor backwards by the specified number of rows. If the specified number (positive or negative) is more than the available rows (forward or backward), this method positions the cursor at the first or the last row in the resultset. This method should not be called when the cursor position is invalid. For instance, after calling next() recursively till next() returns false (signifying the end of the resultset), we should not call relative(), as the current position is outside the resultset. Before calling relative(), we should bring the cursor to a valid potion using the absolute(), first(), or last() methods.

```
public boolean previous() throws SQLException
```

previous() moves the cursor to the previous row, relative to the current position. Unlike the relative() method, this method can be called even when there is no current row. For instance, after calling next() recursively until it returns false, we can call previous() to bring the cursor to the last row.

Fetch Direction and Size

```
public void setFetchDirection(int direction) throws SQLException
```

This method lets us set a fetch direction. The java.sql.ResultSet interface specifies three fetch direction constants – ResultSet.FETCH_UNKNOWN, ResultSet.FETCH_FORWARD, and ResultSet.FETCH_REVERSE. These types indicate the current fetch direction for the results.

The resultset may internally optimize the result structures for the specified type of scrolling.

```
public int getFetchDirection() throws SQLException
```

This method returns the current fetch direction.

```
public void setFetchSize(int rows) throws SQLException
```

This method gives a hint to the JDBC driver as to the number of rows that should be fetched from the database. Note that, when fetch size is set to 1, the resultset may fetch the data from the database whenever we call next(). By setting to a larger fetch size, we may be able to use better optimited fetches.

```
public int getFetchSize() throws SQLException
```

This method returns the current fetch size.

Note that inappropriate setting of fetch direction and size may affect performance. In setting these values we should consider the number of expected rows in the resultset, and its intended usage.

The following examples illustrate these methods. Note that the results of this code depend on driver support:

```
public void queryByScrollableResultSet() throws SQLException {
  connection.setAutoCommit(false);

  Statement statement =
          connection.createStatement(ResultSet.TYPE_SCROLL_INSENSITIVE,
                                     ResultSet.CONCUR_READ_ONLY);

  ResultSet scroller=
          statement.executeQuery("SELECT CATALOG.TITLE, " +
                                 "CATALOG.LEAD_ACTOR, " +
                                 "CATALOG.LEAD_ACTRESS, " +
                                 "CATALOG.TYPE, " +
                                 "CATALOG.RELEASE_DATE FROM CATALOG");
```

In order to test the methods for scrollable resultsets, first create a resultset. The above snippet populates a resultset object `scroller`:

```
  int type = scroller.getType();
  switch(type) {
    case ResultSet.TYPE_FORWARD_ONLY :
      System.out.println("Type = TYPE_FORWARD_ONLY");
      break;
    case ResultSet.TYPE_SCROLL_SENSITIVE :
      System.out.println("Type = TYPE_SCROLL_SENSITIVE");
      break;
    case ResultSet.TYPE_SCROLL_INSENSITIVE :
      System.out.println("Type = TYPE_SCROLL_INSENSITIVE");
      break;
  }

  System.out.println("Current fetch size: " + scroller.getFetchSize());
  scroller.setFetchSize(2);
  System.out.println("Fetch size reset to: " + scroller.getFetchSize());
```

The code above indicates the level of support for scrollable resultsets, and allows us to change the fetch size. In the same way we can find the level of support for concurrency.

The following code scrolls through the resultset in both backward and forward directions. As mentioned previously, the results of this code depend on driver support. As of writing, Cloudscape 3.6.4 supports read-only scrollable resultsets, but not updateable resultsets:

```
int count = 0;
System.out.println("Scrolling forward from the beginning ...");
while(scroller.next()) {
  System.out.println(count++ + ": " +
                     scroller.getString("TITLE") + ", " +
                     scroller.getString("TYPE"));
}

scroller.first();
System.out.println("Scroller moved to first.");

scroller.absolute(count/2);
System.out.println("Scroller moved to " + count/2);
System.out.println("Scrolling forward ...");
while(scroller.next()) {
  System.out.println("    " + scroller.getString("TITLE") + ", "
                     + scroller.getString("TYPE"));
}

scroller.first();
System.out.println("Scroller moved to first.");

int fetchDirection = scroller.getFetchDirection();
switch(fetchDirection) {
  case ResultSet.FETCH_UNKNOWN:
    System.out.println("Current fetch direction: FETCH_UNKNOWN");
    break;
  case ResultSet.FETCH_FORWARD:
    System.out.println("Current fetch direction: FETCH_FORWARD");
    break;
  case ResultSet.FETCH_REVERSE:
    System.out.println("Current fetch direction: FETCH_REVERSE");
    break;
}
scroller.setFetchDirection(ResultSet.FETCH_REVERSE);
System.out.println("Fetch direction set to FETCH_REVERSE");
scroller.absolute(-count/3);
System.out.println("Scroller moved to " + (-count/3));

System.out.println("Scrolling forward ...");
while(scroller.next()) {
  System.out.println("    " + scroller.getString("TITLE") + ", " +
                     scroller.getString("TYPE"));
}

scroller.previous();
scroller.relative(-2);
System.out.println("Scroller moved by -2 rows relative to the current" +
                   "position");

System.out.println("Scrolling forward ...");
while(scroller.next()) {
```

```
    System.out.println("      " + scroller.getString("TITLE") + ", " +
                        scroller.getString("TYPE"));
  }

  scroller.close();
}
```

Updateable Resultsets

By default, resultsets are read-only. That is, contents of the resultset are read-only and cannot be changed. The JDBC 2.1 API also introduces updateable resultsets. When a resultset is updated, the update operation also updates the original data corresponding to the resultset.

The `java.sql.ResultSet` interface specifies two constants to indicate whether the resultset is read-only or updateable:

❑ CONCUR_READ_ONLY – using this type of resultset, we cannot use any of the methods discussed below to insert, update, or delete rows

❑ CONCUR_UPDATABLE – with this constant, we can insert, update, or delete rows in the resultset

These types are called concurrency types. We can find out the concurrency type of a resultset by calling the `getConcurrency()` method on the resultset.

The `java.sql.ResultSet` interface specifies the following set of methods for updating results.

Updating a Row

The following set of `updateXXX()` methods are to update the elements of the current row in the resultset:

updateArray()	updateAsciiStream()	updateBigDecimal()
updateBinaryStream()	updateBlob()	updateBoolean()
updateByte()	updateBytes()	updateCharacterStream()
updateClob()	updateDate()	updateDouble()
updateFloat()	updateInt()	UpdateLong()
updateNull()	updateObject()	updateRef()
updateRow()	updateShort()	updateString()
updateTime()	updateTimestamp()	

These methods require the column name (as a string) or column index as the first argument, and an object of type XXX. For example, there are two variants of `updateTimestamp()` methods:

```
public void updateTimestamp(int columnIndex, Timestamp x)
public void updateTimestamp(String columnName, Timestamp x)
```

After calling these methods, we should call the `updateRow()` method to update the changes. Alternatively, we can call the `cancelRowUpdates()` method to cancel all the updates done so far.

The `rowsUpdated()` method lets we know whether the current row has been updated. The returned value depends on whether the resultset can detect updates or not.

Deleting a Row

We can use the `deleteRow()` method to delete the current row from the resultset as well as from the underlying database. The `rowDeleted()` method indicates whether a row has been deleted using the resultset. Note that a deleted row may leave a visible hole in a resultset. The `rowDeleted()` method can be used to detect such holes. While scrolling through a resultset that may have deleted rows, you can call this method to detect such deleted rows.

Inserting a Row

To insert a row in the resultset, and the underlying database, we should first use `moveToInsertRow()`, and then one or more of `updateXXX()` methods.

A call to the `moveToInsertRow()` method moves the cursor to the insert row. The insert row is a special buffer row associated with an updateable resultset. After moving the cursor to this row, we can use the usual `updateXXX()` methods to set the elements of this row. At the end of these calls, you should call `insertRow()` to finally insert the row in the database, and to clear the buffer row.

Batch Updates

Apart from scrollable resultsets, the JDBC API 2.1 also specifies support for batch updates. This feature allows multiple update statements (INSERT, UPDATE, or DELETE) in a single request to the database. Batching large numbers of statements can result in significant performance gains.

For example, we can re-modify the table for the `Movies` database but this time we can perform all INSERT statements in a single batch. We can also use prepared statements in a batch. When compared to the `insertData()` in the example, the only differences in this implementation are the calls to the `addBatch()` method, and `executeBatch()` method on the statement for batch update:

```java
public void insertBatchData() throws SQLException, IOException {
    BufferedReader br = new BufferedReader(new FileReader("catalog.txt"));
    statement = connection.createStatement();

    try {
      do {
        title = br.readLine();
        if(title == null) break;
        leadActor = br.readLine();
        leadActress = br.readLine();
        type = br.readLine();
        dateOfRelease = br.readLine();

        String sqlString = "INSERT INTO CATALOG VALUES('" + title + "','" +
                        leadActor + "','" + leadActress + "','" +
                        type + "','" + dateOfRelease + "')";

        statement.addBatch(sqlString);
      } while(br.readLine() != null);

      statement.executeBatch();

    } catch (EOFException e) {
    } finally {
```

```
        statement.close();
        br.close();
    }
}
```

Why does this result in better performance? Instead of executing a number of statements, we're performing all such updates in a single statement. This reduces the overhead on the database server, as it otherwise would have to allocate and maintain resources (cursors etc.) for each statement.

The javax.sql Package

The java.sql package is architecturally based on the client-server programming paradigm. As discussed in the previous sections, typical JDBC programming includes the following steps:

- ❑ Load the database driver (using the driver's class name)
- ❑ Obtain a connection (using the JDBC URL for the database)
- ❑ Create and execute statements
- ❑ Use resultsets to navigate through the results
- ❑ Close the connection

If you are familiar with it, you'll recognize this model as being exactly the same as ODBC. This programming model is well suited for desktop clients with long-held connections and localized database transactions. In such applications, one or more desktop clients (built using Visual Basic, PowerBuilder, etc.) connect to a central database, and make several round trips to the database for implementing various business use cases. This model is not, however, suitable for distributed Internet-based applications, mainly for the following reasons:

- ❑ **Connection management**
  There are two limitations with using java.sql.DriverManager for connection management. Every time a client requires a connection, this API tries to obtain a new connection. As we shall discuss later in this chapter, this style of connection management is not efficient for Internet-centric distributed applications. Secondly, java.sql.DriverManager does not isolate client applications from specific driver classes.

- ❑ **Transaction support**
  In addition, the java.sql package has no architectural support for distributed transactions. As we shall see later, distributed transaction support is essential to build scalable and fault-resilient enterprise applications.

The javax.sql package provides the following facilities to address the above:

- ❑ **JNDI-based lookup for accessing databases via logical names**
  Instead of each client trying to load the driver classes in their respective local virtual machines, using JNDI-based lookup allows us to access the database resources using logical names assigned to these resources.

- ❑ **Connection pooling**
  The javax.sql package specifies an additional intermediate layer for implementing connection pooling. That is, the responsibility for connection pooling is shifted from application developers to driver- and application server-vendors.

❑ **Distributed transactions**

The java.sql package specifies a framework for supporting distributed transactions transparently underneath the java.sql package. With this framework, distributed transaction support can be enabled in a J2EE environment with minimal configuration.

❑ **The Rowset**

A RowSet object is a JavaBeans-compliant object that encapsulates database resultsets and access information. A rowset may be connected or disconnected. Note that a resultset has to remain connected to the database. That is, the connection is open while the object exists. The rowset, however, allows us to encapsulate a set of rows, without necessarily maintaining a connection. The rowset also allows us to update the data, and propagate the changes back to the underlying database.

These facilities simplify JDBC programming in a distributed paradigm such as J2EE. Excepting the use of a rowset in place of a resultset, using JNDI, distributed transactions, and connection pooling services require only minimal changes to client applications. These services are now the responsibility of the JDBC driver and the J2EE application server. JDBC driver vendors and J2EE application server vendors can make use of the intermediate layers in this API to build these services.

Most of the classes and interfaces in this package are intended for application server and database driver vendors to implement in their products. The number of classes and interfaces that we will require to develop client applications is small. Therefore, in the rest of this chapter, our focus will be on gaining an insight into these services, and not on how to use these services for developing client applications. Wherever applicable, we'll provide code snippets that illustrate the programming aspects.

To test the concepts discussed in this chapter, you should either have the latest J2EE Reference Implementation from Sun Microsystems (available for download at http://java.sun.com/j2ee/) or a commercial J2EE application server. You will also need the drivers that support them. You should note, however, that not all driver and application server vendors currently support all the facilities in this API. Nonetheless, it is important to understand how these services could be designed. For an up-to-date list of vendors that support these features, please refer to the driver database at http://industry.java.sun.com/products/jdbc/drivers/.

In this section, we'll discuss the following:

❑ Data sources: how this mechanism works, and how it simplifies database access.

❑ Connection pooling: facilities for connection pooling in the javax.sql package.

❑ Distributed transactions: the background and concepts associated with distributed transactions. We'll see how the JDBC API, along with the Java Transaction API, manage distributed transactions.

❑ The rowset

JDBC Data Sources

The javax.sql package provides a replacement for the static java.sql.DriverManager class, although it is still included for backward compatibility. The replacement is the javax.sql.DataSource interface as the primary means of creating database connections. With respect to programming, the following are the noticeable factors:

- ❑ Instead of explicitly loading the driver manager classes in the runtime of the client application, we use a centralized JNDI service lookup to obtain a `java.sql.DataSource` object.

- ❑ Instead of using the `java.sql.DriverManager` class, we use a `javax.sql.DataSource` interface, which provides similar facilities for getting database connections.

This approach isolates client applications from the responsibility of database driver initialization. This means that client applications need not be aware of database driver classes and the database URL. These tasks now become the responsibility of the server administrator who configures data sources. As we'll see later in this chapter, this decoupling also allows additional services such as connection pooling and transaction support to be enabled without affecting client applications.

The javax.sql.DataSource Interface

The `javax.sql.DataSource` interface is a factory for creating database connections. A factory is a pattern used to create instances of classes without having to directly instantiate implementation classes.

The `javax.sql.DataSource` interface provides the following methods:

- ❑ `getConnection()`
- ❑ `getLoginTimeout()`
- ❑ `setLoginTimeout()`
- ❑ `getLogWriter()`
- ❑ `setLogWriter()`

Let's start with `getConnection()`.

The getConnection() Method

```
public Connection getConnection() throws SQLException
public Connection getConnection(String username,
                                  String password) throws SQLException
```

These methods return a connection to a data source. Note the return type of this method is a `Connection` object. This is the same as is returned by the `java.sql.DriverManager` interface. Note that when we retrieve a `Connection` object from the `java.sql.DriverManager` class, it is likely that the `Connection` object directly encapsulates a network connection. However, as we shall see later in this chapter, the `Connection` object need not directly encapsulate a physical database connection. Instead, the `Connection` object can delegate most of its operations to another layer that can implement connection pooling and distributed transactions.

The getLoginTimeout() Method

```
public int getLoginTimeout() throws SQLException
```

This method returns the time interval in seconds that the data source will wait while trying to get a database connection. The default login timeout is driver/database-specific.

The setLoginTimeout() Method

```
public void setLoginTimeout(int seconds) throws SQLException
```

This method specifies the time interval in seconds the data source should wait while trying to obtain a database connection.

Note that the JDBC driver will have a default timeout interval.

The getLogWriter() Method

```
public PrintWriter getLogWriter() throws SQLException
```

This method returns the current `java.io.PrintWriter` object to which the `DataSource` object writes the log messages. Note that by default, unless a `PrintWriter` object is set using the `setLogWriter()` method, logging is disabled and so the method will return `null`.

The setLogWriter() Method

```
public void setLogWriter(LogWriter out) throws SQLException
```

This method sets a `java.io.LogWriter` for logging purposes. For example, we can create a `PrinterWriter` object with `System.out` as the output stream, and set it for logging, as shown below:

```
PrintWriter logWriter = new PrintWriter(System.out);

// dataSource is the DataSource object
datasource.setLogWriter(logWriter);
```

Note that all these methods throw `java.sql.SQLException`.

As we see from the list of methods above, this interface is very simple, and its main responsibility is to create connections.

However, there are two questions concerning its usage: Who creates an object implementing this interface? How can application clients obtain this instance, so that applications can get connections? The next subsection answers these questions.

JNDI and Data Sources

A data source is considered as a network resource, retrieved from a JNDI service. In a JNDI service, applications can bind objects with names. Other applications can retrieve these objects using these names. Both the applications that *bind* objects to names in the JNDI service, and the applications that lookup for these names in the JNDI service can be remote. The JDBC API allows application server vendors and driver vendors to build database resources based on this approach.

The following diagram gives an overview of this approach:

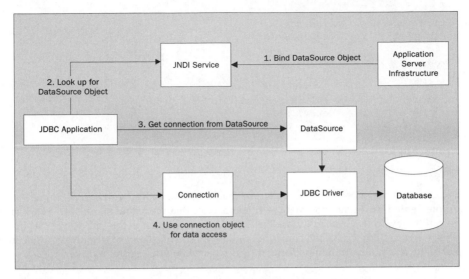

This diagram shows schematically how objects implementing the `javax.sql.DataSource` interface are made available in a JNDI service, and how JDBC application clients can lookup these objects, and create `Connection` objects.

Apart from JDBC application clients, and database resources, this figure shows two more components – a JNDI service, and an application (typically, a J2EE container) that binds the `javax.sql.DataSource` objects in the JNDI service. A JNDI service is a provider of the JNDI API. Typically, the application that binds the `javax.sql.DataSource` objects in the JNDI service is an application server (possibly implementing all J2EE services).

The following are the responsibilities of each of the blocks in the above figure:

❑   The driver or the application server ('infrastructure' in the figure above) implements the `javax.sql.DataSource` interface.

❑   The application server creates an instance of the object implementing the `javax.sql.DataSource` interface, and binds it with a logical name (specified by the application server administrator) in the JNDI service indicated by Step 1.

❑   The JDBC application (client) does a lookup in the JNDI service using this logical name, and retrieves the object implementing the `javax.sql.DataSource` interface. This is the second step in the above diagram.

❑   The JDBC application (client) uses the `DataSource` object and obtains database connections, as indicated by Step 3. The data source implementation may use the JDBC driver to retrieve a connection.

❑   The JDBC application (client) uses the `Connection` object for all its database access, using the standard JDBC API, the final step in the sequence.

Let's see the details of the first three steps.

Creating a Data Source

This is a simple process, and involves instantiating an object that implements the `javax.sql.DataSource` object, and binding it with a name. This is illustrated overleaf.

```
XDataSource x = new XDataSource(...);
// Set properties for the DataSource

// Create a context
try {

  Context context = new InitialContext();
  context.bind("jdbc/Orders", x);

} catch(NamingException ne) {
    // Failed to create the context or bind.
}
```

In the above code snippet, XDataSource is a class that implements the javax.sql.DataSource interface, implemented by driver and database vendors. Note that the actual name of this class is irrelevant for the application developer. Instead we use the logical name assigned to the DataSource. In the above example, this is jdbc/Orders. When compared to the java.sql.DriverManager-based approach, the above replaces the static initialization performed by drivers when you register a driver.

The InitialContext class is a class implementing the javax.naming.Context interface of the JNDI API. Depending on the environment (client-side or server-side) where we create the initial context, we may have to use the InitialContext constructor that takes a Hashtable object as an argument. This Hashtable should contain certain environment attributes that govern how the initial context is created.

Some of the most commonly used attributes include java.naming.provider.url, java.naming.security.principal, and java.naming.security.credentials. These attributes specify a provider (a URL pointing to a JNDI service) of the JNDI service, the identity (principal) of the application or the user on behalf of which this context is being created, and the credentials of the principal. While the first attribute specifies a location of the JNDI service, the second and third attributes specify the identity of the caller. These latter arguments may be used for implementing security and access control for the JNDI.

For a complete list of these attributes, refer the documentation of the javax.naming.Context interface (available online at http://java.sun.com/products/jndi/javadoc/javax/naming/Context.html).

Note that both the constructor of the javax.naming.InitialContext class and the bind method throw javax.naming.NamingException. This exception is the root class of all JNDI-related exceptions.

It is also worth mentioning that the above step is taken care of by the J2EE application server provider. That is, when we start a J2EE application server, the J2EE application server instantiates classes that implement the javax.sql.DataSource interface, and binds these objects with logical names in the JNDI service. Note that most of the J2EE application servers also include a JNDI service so it may not be necessary to set one up outside the application server.

While some of the J2EE application vendors implement the javax.sql.DataSource interface over existing JDBC drivers, there are javax.sql.DataSource implementations from different database vendors. At the time of configuring a J2EE application server, we'll be required to add the data source configuration for the database drivers that we plan to use. There are two different scenarios:

❑ Application server implementing the javax.sql package with third-party JDBC driver: In this case, we'll be required to specify the java.sql.Driver class while configuring the application server.

❑ JDBC driver vendor implementing the `javax.sql` package: In this case, we'll be required to specify the class that implements the `javax.sql.DataSource` interface. We can obtain this information from the driver vendor and the documentation.

In either case, note that there is additional layer between traditional database drivers and the API that we use for getting connections.

Retrieving a DataSource Object

Once the application server has bound a `DataSource` object into the JNDI service, any JDBC client application in the network can retrieve the `DataSource` object using the logical name associated with the data source. The following code snippet illustrates this:

```
// Create a context
try
{
    Context context = new InitialContext();
    DataSource dataSource = (DataSource) context.lookup("jdbc/x");
}
catch(NamingException ne)
{
    // Failed to create the context or lookup.
}
```

The process is very simple – we create an `InitialContext` object, and perform a lookup using the logical name assigned during the server configuration.

Since a JNDI service typically exists on a different VM and usually in a different machine, the `lookup()` operation will generally be a remote operation. From this, we may guess that `DataSource` implementation classes also implement the `java.io.Serializable` interface.

Key Features

Note the following key features of using a data source approach:

❑ There is no need for each client application to initialize JDBC drivers. As discussed previously, JDBC drivers require initialization in each client application. This will not be necessary with the `javax.sql` package. Instead the application server is required to make the data source objects available in the JNDI service.

❑ The client application need not be aware of the driver details. The only information required is a logical name. This makes the application code independent of drivers and JDBC URLs.

❑ Since this approach uses a JNDI service to locate data source objects using logical names, this approach provides a location-independent lookup of data sources. `DataSource` objects can be created, deployed, and managed in a JNDI service, independent of all application clients.

The Movie Catalog Revisited

Let's now modify the movie catalog application to use a data source. There are just two changes to be made to the `CreateMovieTables.java` and `QueryMovieTables.java` files. These are discussed below:

```
import java.sql.DriverManager;
import java.sql.Connection;
```

```
import java.sql.Statement;
import java.sql.ResultSet;
import java.sql.DatabaseMetaData;
import java.sql.ResultSetMetaData;
import java.sql.SQLException;

// import javax.sql classes
import javax.sql.DataSource;
// Import JNDI classes
import javax.naming.Context;
import javax.naming.NamingException;
```

Note the two additional import statements to import classes from `javax.sql`, and `javax.naming` packages.

The other change is in the `initialize()` method in which we originally loaded the driver, and created a connection. Instead of this, we should now obtain a `javax.sql.DataSource` object, and create a connection:

```
public void initialize() throws SQLException, NamingException {
    // Rather than registering the driver as below
    /*    Class.forName (driver);
    // lookup and obtain a DataSource object from JNDI
    Context initialContext = new InitialContext();
    dataSource = (DataSource) initialContext.lookup("jdbc/Cloudscape");

    // Replace
    //    connection = DriverManager.getConnection(url);
    // with using the DataSource object to obtain a connection.
    connection = dataSource.getConnection();
}
```

The first statement creates a `javax.naming.Context` object. The `InitialContext` class implements the `javax.naming.Context` interface and provides the starting point for resolution of names in the JNDI service.

In the above example, we use `initialContext` to lookup `jdbc/Cloudscape`. This is a name that we specify while configuring the application server, so that the application server can create an instance of `javax.sql.DataSource`, and bind it with the name `jdbc/Cloudscape` in the JNDI service. `jdbc` is the standard naming sub-context for all `DataSource` objects.

The `lookup()` method returns an object implementing the `javax.sql.DataSource` interface. Since the `lookup()` method actually returns a `java.lang.Object`, we need to cast it to `javax.sql.DataSource`.

The rest of the database operations are done as usual. In order to test this application, we require a J2EE application server that supports data sources for client applications.

Connection Pooling

A server application, by definition, performs a service for one or more clients. As the number of clients increases, so too does the importance of serving the clients as efficiently as possible.

One of the techniques used for efficiently serving clients requests is reusing resource-expensive objects as much as possible. There's always an overhead with creating an object – memory must be allocated, the object must be initialized, and the JVM must keep track of the object so that it can be garbage-collected when it's no longer needed. In general it's a good idea to minimize the number of objects we create in applications; more so in server-side applications (such as web applications), where the numbers of clients and client requests are not easily predictable.

In addition, objects that encapsulate network connections are more expensive to create than others. If we can reuse such an object the server's performance can be improved dramatically.

Object pooling is a technique for managing and reusing sets of objects. As creating `Connection` objects is one of the most expensive operations in terms of resources, the most frequent type of object pooling tends to be connection pooling. In JDBC, a `Connection` object represents a native database connection (except in in-memory databases – which are not very common in production systems). The database server must allocate communication and memory resources as well as authenticate the user and set up a security context for every connection. Although there are several parameters that dictate the time for obtaining a connection, it's not unusual to see connection times of one or two seconds (depending on connection, database load, etc.). By sharing a set of connections among clients, instead of trying to create them as and when required, we can improve the load on resources and therefore the responsiveness of the application.

A database connection pool benefits most of the server-side applications that access a database. Use a connection pool if the following characteristics describe your application:

❑ Users access the database through a small set of common database user accounts. The alternative is that each user uses a specific account. In Internet-centric applications, common user accounts are more common.

❑ A database connection is only used for the duration of a single request, as opposed to the combined duration of multiple requests from the same session.

If the first criterion is not true, it will not be possible to use a connection pool, although it may be possible to redesign the application to use a generic account. If the requirements of the application and any existing database allow us to move the user access control from the database to the application this would be preferred. This could be done with the addition of an Access Control List (ACL)

The second criterion is more interesting. A typical e-commerce application allows users to add items to a shopping cart at their leisure while they browse through the site. When the users finish the shopping they checkout and pay for the contents of the cart. We can design this application in at least two ways:

❑ The shopping cart is a database table. When the user enters the site we get a database connection and keep it until the user checks-out or leaves the site (or after session timeout). Each item added to the cart means adding a row to the table. If the user checks-out we commit the database transaction, and if the user leaves without buying we rollback the transaction. If the application follows this design, there is no need for a connection pool as each connection is associated with the data updates in the cart, and cannot be shared.

❑   The shopping cart content is kept in a regular in-memory object associated with the user. For example, in a servlet/JSP-based web application this object can be kept in the `HttpSession` object. Each item added to the cart means adding the item to the in-memory object. If the user checks out we get a database connection, add all items from the in-memory object as rows in a database table, and commit the transaction. If the user leaves without buying we simply drop the in-memory object. This model satisfies the criterion above so we can use a connection pool.

The `javax.sql` package provides a `DataSource` based connection pooling that is transparent to client applications. As we shall see shortly, in this approach, connection pooling can be enabled and configured by an administrator of a J2EE application server supporting this feature.

The traditional approach has long been programmatically adding connection pool support. Note that there are several variants of this traditional approach available – such as the `DBConnectionPool` discussed in the first edition of this book (also available in a short article form at http://www.webdevelopersjournal.com/columns/connection_pool.html), and the `DBConnectionBroker` (available at http://javaexchange.com/). Although such pools offer a range of services, in principle they are very similar. Before discussing the concepts behind the JDBC support for connection pooling, let's examine how traditional connection pooling is done.

Traditional Connection Pooling

In this approach, an application:

❑   Obtains a reference to the pool or an object managing several pools

❑   Gets a connection from a pool

❑   Uses the connection

❑   Returns the connection to the pool

The application is fully aware that it's using a pooled connection, so it should never close the connection. It should instead return the connection to the pool.

The implementation of the classic model typically consists of a class (say, `ConnectionPool`) managing a set of JDBC `Connection` objects. Such a class provides methods for initializing the pool (to set the number of connections to be opened at startup, JDBC URL, maximum number of connections, etc.), to get connections, and to return connections. Clients of this class first initialize the pool before getting connections. The following diagram illustrates this:

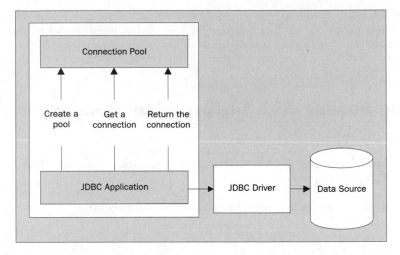

As we see from the figure above, connection pooling is treated as the client's responsibility. The client application creates the pool, retrieves connections, and frees the connections again. Apart from this, this approach requires a strict contract from the application client developer:

❑ The client application should not close the connection; it should only return it back to the pool. Such a contract, however, cannot be enforced strictly on client applications. If the client inadvertently closes the connection before returning it to the pool, the connection will be unusable; the pool will remove the reference to it and recreate it if necessary.

❑ When the client uses the Connection object within a transaction, and forgets to end (commit or rollback) the transaction, the connection pool cannot detect this. This leads to application transactions getting mixed up, and loss of consistency of data.

Although these points can be taken care of by careful coding practices, implementation of robust connection pooling is still a responsibility of the client application.

This classic connection pool is valid only for clients that share the same runtime. This is a client-side pool. Within the scope of this book, there are two possibilities under which multiple clients share the same environment:

❑ J2EE web applications deployed on a single container. In this case, multiple servlets and JSP objects will be invoked in different threads – but in the same runtime (provided the container is not distributed).

❑ A multi-threaded server application providing business methods for database access for the clients.

When connections are required from different client applications, the classic pool is not the right choice. For such cases, a server-side connection pool would be more appropriate. When each client maintains its own connection pool, it is likely that connection reuse may not happen optimally. A server-side connection pool avoids this. As we'll see in the next section, the JDBC API specifies connection pools that meet this requirement. Currently, most of the J2EE application servers provide this feature.

Leaving aside the details of which classes are used to hold connections, this approach is neither robust nor scalable. The fundamental flaw in classic connection pooling is that such a pool does not work with distributed transactions. It also plays havoc with container-managed environments such as web containers, since it forces you to have connections held in static variables, on which the container cannot enforce access control.

Connection Pooling with the javax.sql Package

The `javax.sql` package provides a transparent means of connection pooling. With this approach, the application server and/or the database driver handle connection pooling internally. As long as we use `DataSource` objects for getting connections, connection pooling will automatically be enabled once we configure the J2EE application server.

Before we go into details of this approach, here is a schematic view:

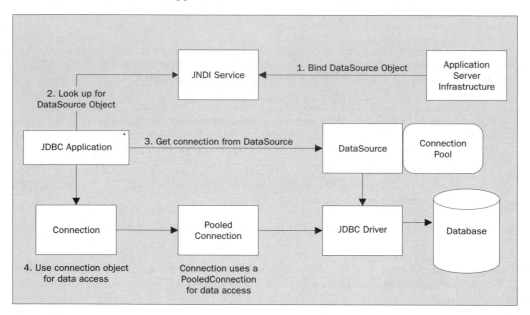

When compared to the first figure, the only change is the additional connection pool maintained by the application server in coordination with the JDBC driver. This means that there is no additional programming requirement for JDBC client applications. Instead, the administrator of the J2EE server will be required to configure a connection pool on the application server. The exact syntax and the names of classes are implementation-dependent. With a JDBC 2.0 compliant application server and database driver, however, the server administrator typically specifies the following:

❑ A class implementing the `javax.sql.ConnectionPoolDataSource` interface

❑ A class implementing the `java.sql.Driver` interface

❑ Size of the pool (minimum and maximum sizes)

❑ Connection time out

❑ Authentication parameters (login, password etc.)

In the rest of this section, we will discuss the interfaces related to connection pooling, and how connection pooling is implemented using these interfaces. The purpose of this section is to give you an insight into the JDBC 2.0 connection pooling. Apart from configuring the J2EE server to enable connection pooling, the client applications need not implement or access these interfaces directly.

The `javax.sql` package specifies three interfaces and one class for implementing connection pooling: `javax.sql.ConnectionPoolDataSource`, `javax.sql.PooledConnection`, `javax.sql.ConnectionEventListener`, and `javax.sql.ConnectionEvent`.

The javax.sql.ConnectionPoolDataSource Interface

This interface is similar to the `javax.sql.DataSource` interface. Instead of returning `java.sql.Connection` objects, this interface returns `javax.sql.PooledConnection` objects. That is, the connection pool data source is a factory for pooled connection objects. The following methods return `javax.sql.PooledConnection` objects:

```
public javax.sql.PooledConnection getPooledConnection()
       throws java.sql.SQLException

public javax.sql.PooledConnection
               getPooledConnection (String user, String password)
       throws java.sql.SQLException
```

The remaining methods in this interface are the same as those in the `javax.sql.DataSource` interface.

Even after we configure connection pooling, applications still use `javax.sql.DataSource` objects for getting connection objects as we've seen in the `initialize()` method of the movie catalog application. It is the `javax.sql.DataSource` object that uses the `javax.sql.ConnectionPoolDataSource` in order to create and maintain a connection pool. This is a part of the `DataSource` implementation (provided by the driver or server vendor). The connection pool remains transparent to the application code. Once the administrator sets up the connection pool, we'll automatically start to use pooled connections.

The javax.sql.PooledConnection Interface

When connection pooling is enabled, objects implementing the `javax.sql.PooledConnection` interface hold a physical database connection.

This interface is a factory of `javax.sql.Connection` objects. This interface specifies the following methods:

```
public java.sql.Connection getConnection() throws java.sql.SQLException
```

This method returns a `java.sql.Connection` object. However, the returned `Connection` object is actually a handle (or proxy) for the physical connection held by the `javax.sql. PooledConnection` object.

```
public void close() throws java.sql.SQLException
```

This method closes the connection to the database.

But what's the difference between a pooled connection and a connection?

❑ Firstly, the connection is a physical connection in JDBC client applications. With JDBC connection pooling, the Connection object does not hold a physical database connection. What the application gets is an abstraction of a regular Connection object. The Connection object uses the physical connection held by the pooled Connection object for all its data access.

❑ Secondly, when we call the close() method, the physical connection is not closed. The DataSource implementation merely removes the association between the connection object and the pooled Connection object. We can therefore close the connection after using it, after which the data source reuses the pooled connection.

❑ Thirdly, we need not return the Connection object to any pool. We merely close it, as we would do without connection pooling.

In other words, the Connection object is a wrapper over the PooledConnection. When the data source returns a connection, it maintains an association between the returned Connection object and the PooledConnection object, so that calls on the Connection object are delegated to the PooledConnection object.

The javax.sql.PooledConnection interface has two more methods for handling the association between the connection and the pooled connection. Remember that when the Connection object is closed, the connection pool should be notified, so that the pooled connection can be reused:

```
public void addConnectionEventListener(ConnectionEventListener listener)

public void removeConnectionEventListener(ConnectionEventListener listener)
```

These two methods are used by the connection pool implementation to add and remove connection event listeners.

The javax.sql.ConnectionEventListener Interface

The ConnectionEventListener interface has two methods:

```
public void connectionClosed(ConnectionEvent event)
```

This method is invoked when the application calls the close() method. The connection pool marks the connection for reuse.

```
public void connectionErrorOccured(ConnectionEvent event)
```

This method is invoked when fatal connection errors occur. The connection pool may close the Connection on this event and remove it from the pool.

The javax.sql.ConnectionEvent Class

This class represents connection-related events.

Note that this event handling mechanism is similar to AWT events. The connection pool adds connection event listeners to the pooled connection, and connection listeners are notified when connection events occur.

Connection Pooling Implementation

The JDBC API does not specify any specific algorithm for connection pooling. The interfaces that we discussed above are hooks for implementing a connection pool. In a typical implementation, the following steps occur when we call getConnection() on the data source:

❑   The data source first checks for a free PooledConnection object. If there is one, the connection pool returns a PooledConnection object to the data source. The data source then calls getConnection() on the PooledConnection object, which returns a Connection object.

❑   If there is no free PooledConnection object available in the connection pool, the data source uses a connection pool data source to get a new pooled connection.

As we can see, the javax.sql.ConnectionPoolDataSource interface is a factory for javax.sql.PooledConnection objects. Further, the javax.sql.PooledConnection interface is a factory for java.sql.Connection objects. The javax.sql.DataSource implements the connection pool, and coordinates pooled connections and regular connections with the help of the interfaces discussed above.

Since, a connection is purely a handle to a pooled connection (that holds the network connection), a connection may be created and closed a number of times using the same pooled connection. Moreover, the client API (the javax.sql.DataSource and java.sql.Connection interfaces) remains the same – this is because the connection pooling details are never exposed to the application.

To reiterate, the main advantage of this approach is its simplicity – for both client application developers, and system administrators. System administrators can enable/reconfigure the connection pool independently of all applications.

Distributed Transactions

While discussing the java.sql.Connection interface, we briefly discussed transactions. The java.sql.Connection interface has two methods – commit() and rollback(), to commit and recover from changes made, respectively. We control the transaction boundaries (that is beginning and ending) of transactions by calling setAutoCommit(false) at the beginning of a transaction, and by calling either the rollback() or the commit() method to end the transaction.

Such transactions are called **local transactions**. In a local transaction, client applications perform database read and write/update operations over a single Connection object.

In certain situations, however, we may have more than one client (for example two different servlets, or EJB components) participating in a transaction. Alternatively, the client may have to perform database operations across multiple databases in the same transaction. How would we implement such features?

This is where **distributed transactions** fit in. The javax.sql package, together with the **Java Transaction API (JTA)** can be used to implement distributed transactions.

In this section, we'll see an overview of distributed transactions, and see the relevant interfaces in JDBC and JTA.

What is a Transaction?

Enterprise applications often require concurrent access to distributed data shared among multiple components, to perform operations on data. Such applications should maintain integrity of data (as defined by the business rules of the application) under the following circumstances:

❑ **Distributed access to a single resource of data**
For example, we may have two application components implementing two parts of a business transaction – both using the same database, but different connections.

❑ **Access to distributed resources from a single application component**
For example, a component updating multiple databases in a single business transaction. This operation would require multiple `Connection` objects.

In both these cases, the methods provided by the core JDBC API are not adequate. This is because the methods provided on the `java.sql.Connection` for starting and ending transactions are associated with a single `Connection` object. In the above situations, however, this is not the case.

The concept of a transaction, and a transaction manager (or a transaction processing service) simplifies developing such applications to maintaining integrity of data in a unit of work as described by the **ACID** properties, guaranteeing that a transaction is never incomplete, the data is never inconsistent, concurrent transactions are independent, and the effects of a transaction are persistent. For more information on transactions refer to Chapter 17.

In the following section you will learn what ACID stands for, and how ACID properties are maintained by transaction processing systems.

Brief Background

In the distributed transaction-processing domain, the X/Open Distributed Transaction Processing (DTP) model is the most widely adopted model for building transactional applications. Almost all vendors developing products related to transaction processing, relational databases, and message queuing, support the interfaces defined in the DTP model.

This model defines three components:

❑ Application programs

❑ Resource managers

❑ Transaction manager

This model also specifies functional interfaces between application programs and the transaction manager (known as the **TX interface**), and between the transaction manager and the resource managers (the **XA interface**). Using TX-compliant transaction managers and XA-compliant resource managers (such as databases), we can implement transactions with the two-phase commit and recovery protocol to comply with the requirements for transactions.

Object Transaction Service (OTS) is another distributed transaction processing model specified by the Object Management Group (OMG). This model is based on the X/Open DTP model, and replaces the functional TX and XA interfaces with CORBA IDL interfaces (Common Object Request Broker Architecture Interface Definition Language). In this model, the various objects communicate via CORBA method calls over the Internet Inter ORB Protocol (IIOP). IIOP was specified by the OMG specifically to implement CORBA solutions over the Internet. The OTS model is interoperable with the X/Open DTP model. An application using transactional objects could use the TX interface with the transaction manager for transaction demarcation.

Within the J2EE architecture, the JDBC and the Java Transaction API provide interfaces for implementing distributed transactions. In addition, the Java Transaction Service (JTS) specifies a Java mapping of the OTS.

Transaction Processing – Concepts

Before we proceed to look into the relevant APIs in the JDBC and JTA, let's briefly discuss some of the concepts associated with distributed transactions:

❑   Transaction demarcation

❑   Transaction context and propagation

❑   Resource enlistment

❑   Two-phase commit

We'll start with transaction demarcation.

Transaction Demarcation

A transaction can be specified by what is known as transaction demarcation. **Transaction demarcation** enables work done by distributed components to be bound by a global transaction. For example, for local transactions as soon as we create a transaction and call `setAutoCommit(false)`, we start a transaction. Similarly, a call to `commit()` or `rollback()` ends the transaction.

This is not true for distributed transactions. The most common approach to demarcation is to take the thread executing the operations and mark it for transaction processing. This is called **programmatic demarcation**. The transaction so established can be suspended by unmarking the thread, and resumed later by marking the thread again. In order to mark and resume the transaction, the transaction context has to be explicitly propagated to the thread where the transaction is resumed. However, with component transaction processing systems such as EJB containers, this becomes the responsibility of the container.

The transaction demarcation ends after a commit or a rollback request to the transaction manager. The commit request directs all the participating resources managers to make the effects of the operations of the transaction permanent. The rollback request instructs the resource managers to undo the effects of all operations on the transaction.

An alternative to programmatic demarcation is **declarative demarcation**. In this technique, components are marked as transactional at the deployment time. This has two implications:

❑   Firstly, the responsibility of demarcation is shifted from the application to the container hosting the component. For this reason, this technique is also called **container-managed demarcation**.

❑   Secondly, the demarcation is postponed from application build time (static) to the component deployment time (dynamic).

Component-based transaction-processing systems such as application servers based on the Enterprise JavaBeans specification and Microsoft Transaction Server support declarative demarcation.

We'll learn about programmatic and container-managed transactions in Chapter 17.

Transaction Context and Propagation

Since multiple application components and resources participate in a transaction, it is necessary for the transaction manager to establish and maintain the state of the transaction as it occurs. This is usually done in the form of transaction context.

Transaction context is an association between the transactional operations on the resources, and the components invoking the operations. During the course of a transaction, all the threads participating in the transaction share the transaction context. Thus the transaction context logically envelopes all the operations performed on transactional resources during a transaction. The underlying transaction manager usually maintains the transaction context transparently. For instance, a Java client or an EJB component implementing transactions need not explicitly propagate the context. The underlying J2EE container handles this.

Resource Enlistment

Resource enlistment is the process by which resource managers inform the transaction manager of their participation in a transaction. This process enables the transaction manager to keep track of all the resources participating in a transaction. The transaction manager uses this information to coordinate transactional work performed by the resource managers and to drive two-phase commit and recovery protocol.

At the end of a transaction (after a commit or rollback) the transaction manager releases the resources. Thereafter, association between the transaction and the resources does not hold.

Two-Phase Commit

This protocol between the transaction manager and all the resources enlisted for a transaction ensures that either all the resource managers commit the transaction or they all abort. In this protocol, when the application requests that the transaction be committed, the transaction manager issues a **prepare** request to all the resource managers involved. Each of these resources will send a reply in turn indicating whether it is ready to commit its operations.

Only when all the resource managers are ready for a commit, does the transaction manager issue a **commit** request to all the resource managers. Otherwise, the transaction manager issues a rollback request and the transaction will be rolled back. The following diagram illustrates these phases:

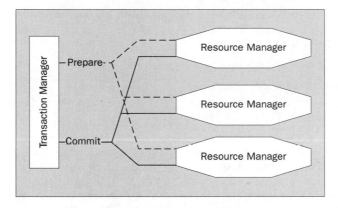

The dotted lines indicate the prepare process during which each resource manager indicates its willingness to commit. After all the resource managers indicate that they are ready for commit, the transaction manager issues the commit call shown using continuous lines.

How can the resource manager or transaction manager request for a rollback when the application has decided that the transaction should be committed? This could happen, say, for example when one of the resources that participated in the transaction is not reachable due to network or system failures. This might also happen if one of the resources holding locks on certain data can no longer hold the lock due to a timeout. The two-phase commit makes sure that each of the participating resources can actually commit the transaction.

The two-phase commit protocol does have its limitations. For instance, it cannot recover from cases where a resource manager indicated that it is ready to commit, but failed to commit (due to internal failures) upon a commit request. In this case, resources that committed prior to this failure cannot be rolled back. A similar situation arises when there is a network failure during the commit process.

Building Blocks of Transaction Processing Systems

Any typical transaction-processing architecture involves a transaction manager and a resource manager for each resource. These components abstract most of the transaction-specific issues from applications, and share the responsibility of implementation of transactions.

Application Components

Application components are clients for the transactional resources. These are the programs with which the application developer implements business transactions.

With the help of the transaction manager, these components create global transactions, propagate the transaction context if necessary, and operate on the transactional resources within the scope of these transactions. These components are not responsible for implementing semantics for preserving the ACID properties of transactions. As part of the application logic, these components generally make a decision whether to commit or rollback transactions. ACID, stands for Atomic, Consistent, Isolated, and Durable (which we discuss in more detail in Chapter 17).

The following are the typical responsibilities of an application component:

- ❏ Create and demarcate transactions
- ❏ Propagate transaction context
- ❏ Operate on data via resource managers

Resource Managers

A resource manager is a component that manages persistent and stable data storage systems, and participates in the two-phase commit and recovery protocols with the transaction manager. Examples are database systems, message queues, etc.

In addition, a resource manager is typically a driver or a wrapper over a storage system, with interfaces for operating on the data (for the application components). This component may also, directly or indirectly, register resources with the transaction manager so that the transaction manager can keep track of all the resources participating in a transaction. This process is called resource enlistment. The resource manager should also implement supplementary mechanisms (for example, logging) that make recovery possible.

Resource managers provide two sets of interfaces: one set for the application components to get connections and perform operations on the data, and the other set for the transaction manager to participate in the two-phase commit and recovery protocol.

The following are the typical responsibilities of resource managers:

- ❏ Enlist resources with the transaction manager
- ❏ Participate in two-phase commit and recovery protocol

Transaction Manager

The transaction manager is the core component of a transaction-processing environment. Its primary responsibilities are to create transactions when requested by application components, allow resource enlistment and de-listing, and to perform the commit/recovery protocol with the resource managers.

A typical transactional application begins by issuing a request to a transaction manager to initiate a transaction. In response, the transaction manager starts a transaction and associates it with the calling thread. The transaction manager also establishes a transaction context. All application components and threads participating in the transaction share the transaction context. The thread that initially issued the request for beginning the transaction, or, if the transaction manager allows, any other thread, may eventually terminate the transaction by issuing a commit or rollback request.

Before a transaction is terminated, any number of components and/or threads may perform transactional operations on any number of transactional resources known to the transaction manager. If allowable by the transaction manager, a transaction may be suspended and then resumed before finally being completed.

Once the application issues the commit request, the transaction manager prepares all the resources for a commit operation (by conducting a vote), and based on whether all resources are ready, issues a commit or rollback request.

The following are the typical responsibilities of a transaction manager:

❑ Establish and maintain transaction context

❑ Maintain association between a transaction and the participating resources

❑ Initiate and conduct two-phase commit and recovery protocol with the resource managers

❑ Make synchronization calls to the application components before the beginning and after the end of the two-phase commit and recovery process

JDBC Distributed Transactions

From the preceding section, it is clear that distributed transaction support is an absolute necessity for building distributed enterprise applications. Because J2EE is a technology for building such applications, JDBC includes distributed transaction support. The distributed transaction support in JDBC specifies the responsibilities of a database driver (equivalent to a resource manager in the above discussion).

The javax.sql package includes two interfaces – javax.sql.XADataSource and javax.sql.XAConnection. Note that, as per the convention followed by the X/Open DTP model, interfaces starting with letters "XA" stand for interfaces for resource managers – that is, database drivers, or application servers supporting distributed transactions.

The javax.sql.XADataSource Interface

This is a transactional DataSource. This interface is a factory for javax.sql.XAConnection objects, and is similar to the javax.sql.DataSource interface. However, instead of creating javax.sql.Connection objects, an implementation of this interface creates javax.sql.XAConnection objects. The javax.sql.XAConnection is a transactional Connection interface.

The following are the key methods in this interface:

```
public javax.sql.XAConnection getXAConnection()
                              throws java.sql.SQLException
public javax.sql.XAConnection getXAConnection (String user, String password)
                              throws java.sql.SQLException
```

The remaining methods in this interface are the same as those in the javax.sql.DataSource interface.

The javax.sql.XAConnection Interface

This interface provides support for distributed transactions. This interface extends the javax.sql.PooledConnection interface, and naturally enough supports all the methods specified in the javax.sql.PooledConnection interface. In addition to these methods, the javax.sql.XAConnection interface specifies the following additional method:

```
public javax.transaction.xa.XAResource getXAResource()
                                        throws java.sql.SQLException
```

What's the purpose of this method? To better understand the purpose of this method, let's consider the transaction processing concepts discussed in the previous section.

Application components in distributed transactions may access the data through multiple database connections. That is, a transaction consists of several connections, with each connection operating (reading, updating, or deleting) on a specified set of database resources. As discussed in the previous section, each resource must be enlisted, so that the transaction manager can keep track of all resources that may have been modified during the transaction. The JTA specifies the `javax.transaction.xa.XAResource` interface for this purpose. For each `Connection` object, the transaction manager obtains a `javax.transaction.xa.XAResource`, and enlists it under the current transaction.

The `javax.transaction.xa` package is a part of the Java Transaction API (JTA).

Before we go on to look at how we can implement distributed transactions, we must consider one additional interface.

The javax.transaction.UserTransaction Interface

Programmatic transaction demarcation is done with the use of the `UserTransaction` interface. This is unnecessary in container-managed environments such as EJB containers.

This interface is not a part of the JDBC, but of the Java Transaction API (JTA). We can access this API online at http://java.sun.com/products/jta/javadocs-1.0.1/index.html.

The `UserTransaction` interface encapsulates most of the functionality of a transaction manager, and is meant for application server (or transactional middleware) vendors to implement. The methods exposed by this interface provide the means to explicitly begin and end transactions:

```
public void begin() throws NotSupportedException, SystemException
```

With the help of this method, we can create a new transaction. The `NotSupportedException`, and `SystemException` are part of the `javax.transaction` package. The `NotSupportedException` is thrown when the transaction manager cannot start a transaction. As an example, this might happen if we're attempting to start a second transaction within the same thread. The `SystemException` is thrown in case of unexpected errors.

```
public void commit() throws RollbackException, HeuristicMixedException,
                            HeuristicRollbackException,
                            java.lang.SecurityException,
                            java.lang.IllegalStateException, SystemException
```

`commit()` explicitly commits all the database operations performed so far within the current transaction. The underlying transaction manager uses the two-phase commit and recovery process to complete the commit process.

```
public void rollback() throws java.lang.IllegalStateException,
                              java.lang.SecurityException,
                              SystemException
```

We can use this method to rollback the current transaction.

Of the above three methods, the first method marks the start of a transaction boundary, while the second and third methods explicitly end a transaction. These methods are used in explicit transaction demarcation.

```
public void setRollbackOnly() throws java.lang.IllegalStateException,
                                      SysemException
```

`setRollbackOnly()` allows an application to enforce roll back, and the transaction should not be committed from that point on. After calling this method, if we try to call the `commit()` method above the application will receive the `javax.transaction.RollbackException`.

```
public int getStatus() throws SystemException
```

This method returns the current status of the transaction. These status values are defined in the `javax.transaction.Status` interface.

```
public void setTransactionTimeout(int seconds) throws SystemException
```

We can specify the timeout interval for the transaction with `setTransactionTimeout()`. This allows the transaction manager to reclaim the pending transaction and rollback all changes in case the client remains inactive beyond this interval.

Steps for Implementing Distributed Transactions

The following steps are required for programmatic demarcation of transactions. In container-managed (declarative) transactions, the only step is the configuration.

Configuration

The first step is to configure the application server and the database driver, following the procedure outlined by your application server. Similar to `javax.sql.ConnectionPoolDataSource` and `javax.sql.PooledConnection` interface, the above two interfaces should be implemented by application server vendors and database driver vendors. Therefore, the application server environment should be configured to use the `javax.sql.XADataSource` interface. However, most of the J2EE application server vendors have their own implementations of this API, in which case we may not be required to do this configuration.

Beginning a Transaction

In order to begin a transaction, we should obtain an object implementing the `javax.transaction.UserTransaction` interface. The standard approach for retrieving this object is to perform a lookup in the JNDI service. The following code snippet illustrates this:

```
import javax.sql.*;          // Import the javax.sql package
import javax.naming.*;       // Import the JNDI API
import javax.transaction.*;  // Import the JTA

// ...

  try {
    Context initialContext = new InitialContext();
    UserTransaction ut = (UserTransaction)
              initialContext.lookup("javax.transaction.UserTransaction");

    ut.begin()
  }
```

Notice we import the `javax.transaction` package in addition to the `javax.sql`, and `javax.naming` packages.

In the above snippet, the JNDI lookup looks for `javax.transaction.UserTransaction`. This is the standard name associated with the `javax.transaction.UserTransaction` interface. The application server, which implements this interface, binds an object implementing this interface in the JNDI service.

Database Operations

Apart from certain constraints on calling specific methods on the `java.sql.Connection` object, the rest of the procedure for JNDI lookup for a data source object, creating connections, and executing SQL statements is the same. The following code snippet gives a snapshot:

```
DataSource dataSource = null;
UserTransaction ut = null;

 // Create a context
 ...

try {
  Context context = new InitialContext();
    dataSource = (DataSource) context.lookup("jdbc/x");
    ut = (UserTransaction)
          context.lookup("javax.transaction.UserTransaction");
} catch (NamingException ne) {
     // Failed to create the context or lookup.
}

Connection connection = dataSource.getConnection();

// ...

// Perform usual database operations

// ...

// Rollback the transaction in case of any failure of business condition
if(...){
  // Get the UserTransaction.
  ut.setRollbackOnly()
}

connection.close()

// Do something that uses another data source and another
// connection object
doSomeThing();

// ...
```

The above code is similar to what we would do in local database transactions. However, the implementation of the application logic can decide to raise a condition for rollback of the transaction.

Let's see what happens when we call the getConnection() method on the data source. With our application server configured for distributed transactions, the data source object uses the underlying implementation of the javax.sql.XADataSource interface for creating javax.sql.XAConnection objects. Note that an XAConnection is a special type of PooledConnection (javax.sql.XAConnection extends the javax.sql.PooledConnection interface). The DataSource, therefore, obtains a connection from this javax.sql.XAConnection object by calling the getConnection() method, and returns it to the application. Notice that this is exactly what happens with connection pooling.

There is one additional step: resource enlistment. Before returning a connection, the underlying transaction manager obtains the javax.transaction.XAResource object from the XAConnection, and enlists resources for the transaction. The javax.transaction and javax.transaction.xa packages have other packages that help in resource enlistment, and the two-phase commit and recovery process. As an application developer, however, we are only concerned with the javax.transaction.UserTransaction interface.

Ending a Transaction

The procedure for ending a transaction is similar to the way we start a transaction. We now call the commit() method on the UserTransaction object to end the transaction. We may need to perform an additional JNDI lookup to retrieve the UserTransaction object if the transaction is being closed from a different method or object to the one that started the transaction.

Special Precautions

Within a transaction, you cannot performing the following:

❑ We should not call the commit() and rollback() methods on Connection objects. This is because the user transaction object controls the transaction boundaries. These methods throw java.sql.SQLException when called within a transaction.

❑ We should not enable auto-commit on Connection objects. Note that auto-commit is contrary to the notion of transactions. When we retrieve a connection under a transaction, the connection will have auto-commit turned off by default, and an attempt to enable it by calling the setAutoCommit() method throws java.sql.SQLException.

RowSet Objects

The final feature of the javax.sql package we will examine is the rowset.

In simple terms a rowset is a JavaBean-compliant component that encapsulates database access including the result. The javax.sql.RowSet interface represents the basic functionality for a rowset. In order to see the benefits of using a rowset, let's consider a simple database access to fetch a set of rows. Let's first see how we would achieve this without using a rowset:

```
// Create a connection
connection = DriverManager.getConnection("jdbc:cloudscape:Movies");
connection.setAutoCommit(false);

// Create a statement
Statement statement = connection.createStatement();
```

```
// Execute a query
ResultSet rs = statement.executeQuery("SELECT * FROM CATALOG");

while(rs.next()) {
  // Scroll though and process the results
}
```

In this approach, there are at least three objects that represent different aspects of a query operation – a `java.sql.Connection` object for database connectivity, a `java.sql.Statement` object for executing a statement, and a `java.sql.ResultSet` object to hold the returned values.

Instead consider an approach where the same query operation is encapsulated by one single object:

```
JdbcRowSet rowSet = new JdbcRowSet();

rowSet.setCommand("SELECT * FROM CATALOG WHERE TYPE = 'ROMANCE'");
rowSet.setUrl("jdbc:clouscape:Movies");
rowSet.setUsername("sa");
rowSet.setPassword("");
rowSet.execute();

while(rowSet.next()) {
    // Scroll through and process the results.
}
```

The above code illustrates one possible application of `RowSet` objects. In this code, this `JdbcRowSet` class is part of the `sun.jdbc.rowset` package. This package is a reference implementation of the `RowSet` specification. You can download this along with examples from http://developer.java.sun.com/developer/earlyAccess/crs/.

Apart from this encapsulation, the main feature of a rowset is that a rowset object can be used as a JavaBean component. As a bean, a `RowSet` provides a set of mutators for setting properties, and a complementary set of accessors to get the values of those properties. In the above example, we programmatically call the setters to set the properties of the rowset. Instead, we could use a visual programming environment to create a `RowSet` object and set its properties.

`RowSet` objects also support JavaBean-style events. `RowSet` objects generate events when certain changes occur in the state of the rowset. Interested objects can register themselves as listeners for these events, and be notified as events occur.

> *In essence, a `RowSet` object is a JavaBeans component; having certain properties that can be manipulated by setters, and a set of events that interested objects can listen to. A `RowSet` object also encapsulates the results of executing a statement.*

The `javax.sql.RowSet` interface can be implemented as a separate layer on top of an existing JDBC layer. Sun's reference implementation is in fact such a layer, and we can use it on top of any JDBC 2.1-compliant JDBC driver.

The javax.sql.RowSet Interface

```
public interface RowSet extends java.sql.ResultSet
```

The `javax.sql.RowSet` interface extends the `java.sql.ResultSet`. This is because a rowset also encapsulates a set of rows (results) separately from the properties. As we have seen the `java.sql.ResultSet` interface offers a rich set of methods for accessing result rows. Therefore, all the methods that are applicable for a resultset are applicable for a rowset too.

Properties

The `javax.sql.RowSet` interface provides a set of JavaBeans properties that can be set at design time. With the help of these properties, the RowSet object can connect to a data source and retrieve a set of results at run time. The following are some of the commonly required parameters:

❑ URL: a JDBC URL.

❑ Data source name: Name of the data source. Depending on the implementation, the rowset may use either a URL or the data source name for obtaining a `Connection`.

❑ User name: User name for obtaining a connection.

❑ User password: Password for obtaining a connection.

❑ Transaction isolation: Transaction isolation level. This is a property of `java.sql.Connection`, which specifies a set of constants for isolation level.

❑ Command: The SQL statement. The command can also be a prepared statement string.

Events

RowSet objects can generate three types of events:

❑ Cursor movement events: These are generated when the cursor is moved. For example, calling a `previous()` method on the RowSet object would generate an event.

❑ Row change events: These events are generated when rows in a rowset are changed. For instance, deleting a row would generate an event.

❑ Rowset change events: These events are generated when the entire contents of the rowset changes. For instance, calling the `execute()` would change the entire contents of a rowset.

For application objects to be notified of these events, the JDBC API specifies the `javax.sql.RowSetListener` interface:

```
public interface RowSetListener extends java.util.EventListener
```

This interface specifies three methods:

```
public void cursorMoved(RowSetEvent event)
public void rowChanged(RowSetEvent event)
public void rowSetChanged(RowSetEvent event)
```

The RowSet object calls these methods when one of the listed events occurs.

Application objects implementing the `javax.sql.RowSetListener` interface can register and deregister for these events with the rowset, using the following methods on `javax.sql.RowSet`:

```
public void addRowSetListener(RowSetListener listener);
public void removeRowSetListener(RowSetListener listener);
```

These methods are similar to those that we find in AWT and Swing. We can dynamically add more than one listener. We can also remove these listeners dynamically.

When the `Listener` objects are notified, the `Listener` objects receive the `RowSet` object encapsulated in the `javax.sql.RowSetEvent`.

Command Execution and Results

After setting the properties, and the listeners, we can call the `execute()` method on the rowset to populate the results, and use any of the methods specified in the `java.sql.ResultSet` interface for scrolling and modifying the results. The `execute()` method internally obtains a database connection, prepares a statement, and creates a resultset.

Creating and using `RowSet` objects is very simple, and follows the JavaBeans model. In order to populate a resultset there are three tasks that we are required to do:

❑   Create a `RowSet` object

❑   Set its properties

❑   Execute it

Types of RowSet Objects

The JDBC API does not specify standard interfaces implementing the `javax.sql.RowSet` interface. The early access release from Sun, however, identifies three possible implementations. Although currently these are not part of the specification, in the future they could be added to the specification as part of a revised set of interfaces.

The following are three possible implementations of this interface:

❑   Cached rowsets (`sun.jdbc.rowset.CachedRowSet`)

❑   JDBC rowsets (`sun.jdbc.rowset.JdbcRowSet`)

❑   Web rowsets (`sun.jdbc.rowset.WebRowSet`)

These are specified in the `sun.jdbc.rowset` package, which is not part of the JDBC API. Currently, Sun provides a reference implementation of these `RowSet` objects in an Early Access release (currently release 4), which can be downloaded from Sun's Java Developer Connection web site (http://java.sun.com/jdc/). This early-access release includes implementations of these tree types of `RowSet` object.

All the above classes extend from the `sun.jdbc.rowset.BaseRowSet`, and implement the `javax.sql.RowSet` interface. The `BaseRowSet` class provides the common implementation for properties, events, and methods for setting parameters for `RowSet` objects (since rowset objects implement the `java.sql.ResultSet` interface).

Apart from the reference implementation, some of the JDBC driver vendors are beginning to support implementations for these types of RowSet. For a list of drivers supporting the rowset, see http://industry.java.sun.com/products/jdbc/drivers/.

In the following subsections, we'll briefly discuss each of these RowSet implementations.

The CachedRowSet Implementation

A JDBC resultset is a connected object. That is, as long as the resultset is open (and before we call the close() method on it), the resultset maintains a connection to the database. This is acceptable if we're holding the resultset for short intervals. However, when we intend to use resultset objects for significant periods of time, holding the connection would consume unacceptable levels of network resources. For instance, if a resultset has 1000 rows and the web application is displaying 10 results per page, we may be required to hold the Connection object for a significantly long time frame. This is not desirable. In order to address this, we would have to transfer the results to custom objects, so that we can release the statement and the connection immediately after executing the statement.

The **cached rowset** addresses this problem. Once a cached rowset has been created and the results populated, the statement and the Connection objects can be closed. The cached rowset maintains the result rows in a "disconnected" manner. When we update or modify the RowSet, the cached rowset connects to the database and performs the updates on the database and therefore limits the cost in resources.

The sun.jdbc.rowset.CachedRowSet class defines a cached RowSet.

```
public class CachedRowSet extends BaseRowSet
                    implements javax.sql.RowSet,
                               javax.sql.RowSetInternal,
                               java.io.Serializable,
                               java.lang.Cloneable
```

A cached rowset is a disconnected, serializable, cloneable, and scrollable container for rows of data. It extends sun.jdbc.rowset.CachedRowSet and implements the javax.sql.RowSet, RowSetInternal, java.io.Serializable, and java.lang.Cloneable interfaces. It is disconnected and therefore does not hold a Connection object. Since it is serializable and cloneable, we can create copies of our cached rowset and transfer them across the wire. For instance, an EJB component can create and return a cached rowset to a client across the network. The client can modify the RowSet, and send it back to the component, and the component can perform updates. In order for the applications to populate and access/modify the state of a cached rowset, the cached rowset also implements the javax.rowset.RowSetInternal interface.

The CachedRowSet object is suitable in at least two scenarios:

❑ The client application intends to hold the results for a significantly long time interval. This is true for web applications as well as client-server applications executing queries with possibly large number of rows in the result.

❑ The client has neither capacity nor the resources for connecting to a database. For instance, networked devices such as PDAs and other thin clients do not have resources to connect to databases. In such cases, a server-side application can create a cached rowset, and send it across the network to the thin client. The client can scroll through the rowset, and may also save it for later use. The client can send a copy of the results back to the server-side application whenever it updates it.

In effect, the cached rowset gives the ability to create a "downloadable" resultset.

The procedure for creating and using a cached rowset is similar to that seen at the beginning of this section:

```
CachedRowSet rowSet = new CachedRowSet();

rowSet.setCommand("SELECT * FROM CATALOG WHERE TYPE = 'ROMANCE'");
rowSet.setUrl("jdbc:cloudscape:Movies;create=true");
rowSet.setUrl("jdbc:cloudscape:Movies");
rowSet.setUsername("sa");
rowSet.setPassword("");
rowSet.execute();

while(rowSet.next()) {
   // Scroll through the results .
}
```

The cached rowset gets populated when the execute() method is called.

The updateXXX() methods are those specified in the java.sql.ResultSet interface, and are meant for updateable resultsets.

Since the cached rowset is disconnected, the database does not enforce any concurrency control on the data held by the cached rowset. In order to maintain optimum concurrency, the current implementation of a cached rowset caches the original value of the data. This copy represents the state of the cached rowset when the execute() was last called. We can access the original data by calling the getOriginal() and getOriginalRow() methods on the CachedRowSet object. These methods return ResultSet objects corresponding to cached rowset and the current row respectively.

Since the rowset is disconnected, we should call the acceptChanges() method to update the rowset:

```
rowSet.acceptChanges();
```

This method re-establishes a connection to the database, and makes the necessary updates to the database. If the original data held in the CachedRowSet does not match the data in the database, this method does not update the database with the changed values. Note that this method throws SQLException in case of failures while making the changes.

The JDBC Rowset Implementation

The **JDBC rowset** is a connected rowset. The purpose of the JDBC rowset is to provide a JavaBeans-type layer on top of java.sql.ResultSet. This is defined in the sun.jdbc.rowset.JdbcRowSet class:

```
public class JdbcRowSet extends BaseRowSet implements javax.sql.RowSet
```

In this class specification, unlike a cached rowset, a JDBC rowset is connected, is not serializable, and nor is it cloneable. It provides whatever features the underlying java.sql.ResultSet interface provides, with the added advantage of presenting itself like a JavaBean.

The Web Rowset Implementation

As of this writing, the rowset specification is not final and the implementation is being delivered as early access releases. The early access release implementation itself is not complete. In this section, let's therefore focus on the concepts behind the web rowset, without the programming detail.

The following represents the intended structure of this rowset type. The web rowset is intended for web-based applications. For this reason, the primary way in which it deviates from the cached rowset (which it extends) is that it communicates with other components by the use of XML over HTTP. The sun.jdbc.rowset.WebRowSet class represents a client-server implementation of the RowSet interface.

```
public class WebRowSet extends CachedRowSet
```

The web rowset implementation is expected to include the above class, a Java servlet, and a protocol for transmitting tabular data using XML as the data format.

The intended scenario for using a web rowset is as follows: A web client (possibly with Java or JavaScript support) retrieves a set of results using a sun.odbc.rowset.WebRowSet object. When the execute() method on the web rowset is called, it calls a servlet on the server side (which performs database access) to populate a resultset. Once the rowset is updated, the WebRowSet object sends the updated data to a server-side implementation of the rowset as XML data over the HTTP protocol. The server-side implementation then updates the database. WebRowSet objects use incremental caching of data, so that data can be retrieved in chunks from the server side. As the client browses through the web rowset, additional data is downloaded from the server-side.

Although specification as well as implementation of this class is currently incomplete, the goal of this WebRowSet class is as follows.

Over the Internet, it is not always possible to connect to a database server. Proxies and firewalls will often not allow this. Even if the proxy/firewall configurations allow this, opening up a database over the Internet posses a security threat. In order to avoid this, the server-side implementation of the web rowset would act as a proxy for the database. Therefore, the client-side implementation uses the server-side implementation to retrieve and update results. The main implication of this architecture is that it makes the database clients thin, and clients can use the HTTP protocol (instead of TCP/IP-based database protocols).

When the web client creates a web resultset and executes a command, the client-side implementation of the web rowset sends this request to the server-side implementation over HTTP. The server-side implementation would connect to the database, execute the command, and populate the RowSet. The server-side implementation would then write the data into an XML document, and send it back to the client-side implementation over HTTP.

This process is repeated when the client modifies the rowset, and calls acceptChanges(). The client-side implementation would send an XML copy of the web rowset to the server-side implementation over HTTP, and the server-side implementation would perform the actual updates.

This mechanism relies on HTTP and XML for exchanging commands and data between client- and server-side implementations. This eliminates the need for the client to connect to the database server over the Internet.

Based on this approach, we can expect more refined implementations for thin clients.

Summary

The purpose of this chapter has been to provide an overview of database programming using the JDBC API, and then introduce certain advanced concepts related to transactions and databases that are more relevant in an enterprise platform such as J2EE.

As mentioned at the beginning of this chapter, the goal of the first part of the chapter has been to discuss how to perform typical SQL operations using this API. The JDBC API is quite extensive and provides more facilities than can be covered in one chapter. Most of these features (such as batch updates, scrollable resultsets, etc.) are comparatively new, and most of the database vendors are only beginning to support these features. We're encouraged to check the documentation from the vendor before we plan to implement these features.

To summarize, in the first part of this chapter, we discussed the following:

- ❑ Database drivers, and how to load JDBC drivers
- ❑ Creating tables, and inserting data
- ❑ Prepared statements
- ❑ Mapping between SQL and Java types
- ❑ Batch updates
- ❑ Scrollable resultsets
- ❑ Save points

In the second part of this chapter, we discussed four advanced features of the JDBC API:

- ❑ The JDBC client applications need not be hard-wired to specific JDBC drivers, and to use vendor-specific JDBC URLs. Instead, the `DataSource` object, combined with the JNDI-based binding and lookup decouples vendor-specific database details from the client applications.

- ❑ The `javax.sql` package shifts the responsibility of connection pooling to J2EE application servers and JDBC drivers. With this approach, connection pooling is a matter of configuring the application server – there is no need to implement custom connection pools, as this mechanism offers a more reliable means of connection pooling.

- ❑ Distributed transaction processing has never been so simple. Using the `javax.transaction.UserTransaction` interface, we can explicitly demarcate transactions, while still using the standard JDBC API for database access.

- ❑ The `RowSet` interface and its implementations are an addition to the JDBC API. The goal of the `RowSet` is to provide for more flexible, bean-like data access. Sun is also working on Java Data Objects (JDO), presumably based on Microsoft's Active Data Objects. JDOs are expected to complement the JDBC API and provide database access at a higher level without using SQL. The JDO API is currently under development, and we could expect more advanced data access facilities in future. Look for announcements at http://java.sun.com/products/jdbc/.

In the next chapter we'll take a look at web applications, and the containers that manage them.

ProfessionalJavaServerProgrammingJ2EE1.3Edition
Data
Application Logic
Client
Web Container
Servlets
JSPs
Tag Library
HTTP(S)
(X)HTML/ XML
Applet
Client Application
RMI/IIOP
JNDI
JTA
JDBC
JMS
JavaMail
JAAS
JCA
JAXP
J2EE Application Server
Session Beans
JAF
JDBC
RDMS
JavaMail
Mail Server
RMI
Java Application
IIOP
CORBA Server
JNDI
Directory Servi
JMS
Message Queu

Introduction to Web Containers

As we discussed in Chapter 1, there are essentially two types of clients in the J2EE architecture – **web clients**, and **application clients**. Application clients date back to traditional client-server architecture in which application clients drive the user interaction (typically via a GUI) as well as the bulk of application logic (including database access). For this reason, application clients are called **fat clients**. Fat clients process the application logic locally. In a multi-tier architecture, application clients can delegate part of the application logic and database access to middle-tier components (such as Enterprise JavaBeans). Despite this distribution of application logic to middle-tier components, the stand alone application clients remain fat and require installation on each user's desktop.

With the advent of the Internet, web clients replaced many traditional stand alone application clients. The main driver of this change is the nature of web clients. In web-client based architectures, the user-interaction layer is separated from the traditional client layer. Web browsers manage the user interaction but leave the rest to applications on the server side, including the logic for driving the user interface, interacting with components in the middle-tier, and accessing databases. For an end user, the browser is the client for all web-based applications. Since such a general-purpose client does not impose any special requirements (apart from network access) on the client-desktop, web clients are also called **thin clients**.

The following features characterize typical web clients:

❑ A web browser or similar application manages user interaction; this is the client-layer.

❑ HTML (with JavaScript and/or DHTML) or XML (with XSLT) is used to create the user interface.

❑ HTTP(S) is the information exchange protocol used by the clients and applications. The application programs on the server side execute the application logic on behalf of browser clients.

The J2EE architecture offers a richly featured and flexible programming model for building dynamic web applications. As we discussed in Chapter 1, the J2EE architecture provides **web containers**, the Java Servlet API, and the JavaServer Pages API for the building and management of web applications. The web container provides the basic runtime environment and a framework for providing runtime support for web applications. The Java servlet and JSP technologies form the core material for the development of web applications.

This chapter introduces us to J2EE web containers, and the basics of web application development, in three distinct steps:

- ❑ We will discuss the basic anatomy of a web container. Starting with a brief introduction to HTTP, the emphasis will be on introducing the concepts of web containers, Java servlets, and JSP pages. We'll continue to learn more about these topics in subsequent chapters.

- ❑ We will walk through the creation of a simple but complete web application.

- ❑ We will discuss, in detail, the inner working of the example web application.

We begin by looking at how clients and servers in a web application communicate using the HTTP protocol.

The HTTP Protocol

In distributed application development, the communication protocol determines the nature of clients and servers and the relationship between them. This is also true in the case of web-based applications. The complexity of many of the features possible in our web browser and on the web server depends on the underlying protocol – that is, the **Hypertext Transfer Protocol (HTTP)**.

> **HTTP is an application-level protocol (generally implemented over TCP/IP connections). It is a stateless protocol based on requests and responses.**

Clients (such as web browsers) send requests to the server (such as the web server of an online store) to receive information (such as downloading a catalog), or to initiate specific processing on the server (such as placing an order).

HTTP Request Methods

As an application-level protocol, HTTP defines the types of request that clients can send to servers and the types of response that servers can send to clients. The protocol also specifies how these requests and responses are structured.

HTTP/1.0 specifies three types of request methods: **GET**, **POST**, and **HEAD**. HTTP/1.1 has five additional request methods: **OPTIONS**, **PUT**, **TRACE**, **DELETE**, and **CONNECT**. Of these, the GET and POST requests meet most common application-development requirements.

The GET Request Method

The GET request is the simplest and most frequently used request method. It is typically used to access static resources such as HTML documents and images. GET requests can be used to retrieve dynamic information, by including query parameters in the request URL. For instance, we can send a parameter name, with a value of Joe, appended to a URL as http://www.domain.com?name=Joe. The web server can use the value of this parameter to send specific content to a client.

The POST Request Method

The POST request method is commonly used for accessing dynamic resources. POST requests are typically used to transmit information that is request-dependent, or when a large amount of complex information must be sent to the server.

The POST request allows the encapsulation of multi-part messages into the request body. For example, we can use POST requests to upload text or binary files. Similarly, we can use POST requests in applets to send serializable Java objects, or even raw bytes to the web server. POST requests offer a wider choice than GET requests in terms of the contents of a request.

There are certain differences between GET and POST requests. With GET requests, the request parameters are transmitted as a query string appended to the request URL. In the case of POST requests, the request parameters are transmitted within the body of the request. This has two consequences. Firstly, since a GET request contains the complete request information appended to the URL itself, it allows browsers to bookmark the page and revisit later. Depending on the type and how sensitive the request parameters are, this may or may not be desirable. Secondly, some servers might impose restrictions on the length of a request URL. This limits the amount of information that can be appended to the request URL. Note that HTTP/1.1 does not impose any upper limit on the length. However, we cannot guarantee that HTTP servers/clients will support excessive lengths.

The HEAD Request Method

A client sends a HEAD request when it wants to see only the headers of a response, such as Content-Type or Content-Length.

GET and HEAD method requests should not be programmed to modify the information on the server. These requests can be reapplied many times without changing the data on the server and as such, are meant for information *retrieval* only.

Along with the type of the request, the client application also specifies the resource that it needs as part of the request header. For example, when we type http://java.sun.com/index.html in the address bar of our browser, the browser sends a GET request to the web server identified by java.sun.com for the resource index.html. In the HTTP lexicon, a **Uniform Resource Identifier (URI)** specifies a resource. The URI is the URL, excluding the domain name. In our example, the resource is the index.html file located on the document root of the web server serving the java.sun.com domain.

The HTTP Response

When a server receives an HTTP request, it responds with the status of the response, and some meta-information describing the response. All these are part of the **response header**. Except for the case of the HEAD request, the server also sends the content that corresponds to the resource specified in the request. If a browser sends a request to http://java.sun.com/index.html, it receives the content of the index.html file as part of the message.

The content header fields in the response contain useful information that clients may want to check in certain conditions. The typical header fields include: Date, Content-Type, and Expires. For example, the header field Expires of a page can be set to equal the same date in the Date header field to indicate that browsers should not cache the page. Web applications with time-sensitive content may need to set such fields.

Servers and clients that communicate using HTTP use **Multi-Purpose Internet Mail Extensions (MIME)** to indicate the type of content in request and response bodies. MIME types include text/html and image/gif. The first part of the header indicates the type of data (for example, text and image), while the second part indicates the standard extension (such as html for text, and gif for image). MIME is an extension of an e-mail protocol designed to allow the exchange of different kinds of data files. HTTP servers use MIME headers at the beginning of each transmission and browsers use this information to decide how to parse and render the content. Browsers also use MIME headers when transmitting data in the body of requests, to describe the type of data being sent. For example, the default MIME type encoding for POST requests is application/x-www-form-urlencoded.

The key features of HTTP you need to understand are:

❏ HTTP is a very simple and lightweight stateless protocol.

❏ The client always initiates the request. The server can never make a callback connection to the client.

❏ HTTP requires the client to establish connections prior to each request, and the server to close the connection after sending the response. This guarantees that a client cannot hold on to a connection after receiving the response. Either the client or the server can prematurely terminate a connection.

HTTP was originally meant for serving static information so we need to consider certain additional issues in order to be able to build dynamic applications that communicate with clients using HTTP. In this chapter, we'll see how to address some of these issues by using J2EE web containers.

Web Containers and Web Applications

Web applications are server-side applications. The most essential requirements for server-side application development are:

❏ **A programming model and an API**
A programming model for server-side applications specifies how to develop applications.

❏ **Server-side runtime support**
This includes support for applicable network services, and a runtime for executing the applications.

❏ **Deployment support**
Deployment is the process of installing the application on the server. This process also includes configuring application components, such as specifying initialization parameters and specifying any database.

To meet these requirements when building and running web applications, the J2EE specification provides the following:

❑ **Java Servlets and JavaServer Pages**
Java servlets and JavaServer Pages (JSP) are the building blocks for developing web applications in J2EE. In the J2EE lexicon, Java servlets and JSP pages are called the **web components**.

❑ **Web Applications**
A web application is a collection of Java servlets, JSP pages, helper classes and class libraries, static resources such as HTML, XHTML, or XML documents, and images.

❑ **A Web Container for Hosting Web Applications**
A web container is essentially a Java runtime that provides an implementation of the Java Servlet API, and facilities for JSP pages. The web container is responsible for initializing, invoking, and managing the lifecycle of Java servlets and JavaServer Pages.

❑ **A Packaging Structure and Deployment Descriptors**
The J2EE specification defines a packaging structure for web applications. The specification also defines a deployment descriptor for each web application. The deployment descriptor is an XML file that allows the customization of web applications at deployment time.

The diagram below shows the J2EE web container with two web applications deployed on the same container:

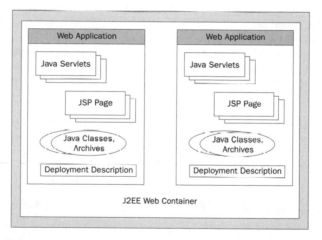

In this section, we will discuss some of the basic features of servlets, JSP pages, and deployment descriptors. The purpose of this discussion is to give an overview of what is involved in web application development. In the subsequent chapters, we'll learn about the process in more detail.

Java Servlets

Java servlets allow application logic to be embedded in the HTTP request-response process and are specified in the Java Servlet API Specification 2.3 available at http://java.sun.com/products/servlet/.

> **Java servlets are small, platform-independent server-side programs that programmatically extend the functionality of the web server. The Java Servlet API provides a simple framework for building applications on such web servers.**

To better understand the role of application logic in the request-response process, consider a web-based mail server. When we log in to our favorite web-based mail server, the server should be able to send a page with links to our mail, our mail folders, our address book, and so on. This information is dynamic, in the sense that each user expects to see their individual mailbox. To generate such content, the server must execute complex application logic to retrieve the mail and compose a page.

Clients can send client-specific or context information in the requests to the server, but how can the server decide how the content should be generated? HTTP does not define a standard means for embedding application logic during the response generation phase. There is no programming model specified for such tasks. HTTP defines how clients can request information, and how servers can respond, but it is not concerned with how the response could be generated.

This is where the benefits of server-side technologies such as Java servlets and JavaServer Pages become apparent. With these technologies, we can embed custom application logic during the request processing and response generation stages.

Java servlets are not user-invoked applications. Instead, the web container in which the web application containing the servlets is deployed invokes the servlets based on incoming HTTP requests. When a servlet has been invoked, the web container forwards the incoming request information to the servlet, so that the servlet can process it, and generate a dynamic response. The web container interfaces with the web server by accepting requests for servlets, and transmitting responses back to the web server.

When compared to CGI, and proprietary server extensions such as NSAPI or ISAPI, the servlet framework provides a better abstraction of the HTTP request-response paradigm by specifying a programming API for encapsulating requests and responses. In addition, servlets have all the advantages of the Java programming language, including platform-independence. Java servlet-based applications can be deployed on any web server with built-in (in-process) or connector-based (out-of-process) web containers, irrespective of the operating system and the hardware platform.

In order to understand how a servlet interacts with a web server via a web container, let's consider the basic invocation process with the web server receiving an HTTP request. As we've seen before, the HTTP protocol is based on a request-response model. A client connects to a web server and sends an HTTP request over the connection. Based on the request URL, the following sequence of events happens in a typical sequence (the rightward arrows indicate requests and leftward arrows indicate responses):

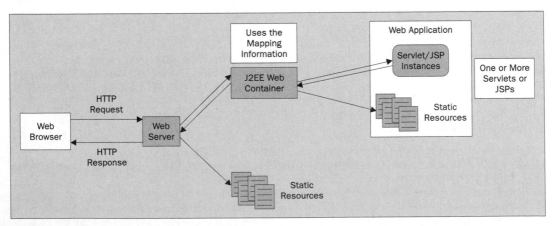

❑ The web server has to figure out if the incoming request corresponds to a web application in the web container. This requires an implicit understanding between the web server and the web container. Web containers use the notion of a **servlet context** to identify web applications. This context can be specified when the application is deployed onto the container.

❑ If the web container can handle the request, the web server delegates the request to it. We can think of this process as the web server invoking a method on the web container, passing it the request information.

❑ Once the web container receives the request, it decides which application should handle it. In a J2EE web application, an HTTP request can be mapped to a servlet, a JSP page, or any static resource. This mapping is based on URL patterns. Static resources include HTML/XML pages, images, and applet class files. All these resources are part of the web application. When we package and deploy a web application, we specify this mapping information. The web container uses this mapping information to map each incoming request to a servlet, a JSP page, or a static resource. If the resource is mapped to a static resource, the web container simply passes the resource as it is to the web server. This forms the body of the response that the web server sends to the browser.

❑ Based on the mapping information the web container determines if the request should be handled by a servlet. It the request is to be handled by a servlet the container creates or locates a servlet instance, and delegates the request. In later chapters, we'll see how the web container does this, and what factors govern this process.

❑ When the container delegates the request to a servlet, it also passes objects encapsulating the HTTP request and HTTP response to the servlet instance. To the servlet, these objects represent the request and response streams from the browser. The servlet can read the request information, and write a response to these streams. To write a response, the servlet can use the `println()` methods of the associated `java.io.PrintWriter` object. This is equivalent to writing content to the already opened connection from the web browser.

There are two steps to take in order to build and deploy a servlet-based application:

❑ Write the servlets with the required application logic. This is the development phase.

❑ Provide a context and optional URL pattern mapping information during the deployment phase. This mapping information is used to identify the appropriate servlet to handle a request.

JavaServer Pages

Dynamic content generation can be achieved by programmatic content generation, or template-based content generation. Java servlets fall into the first category, and JavaServer Pages (JSP) belong to the second. JSP pages are specified in the JavaServer Pages 1.2 specification, available at http://java.sun.com/products/jsp/

JavaServer Pages is an extension of the Java servlet technology. However, in contrast to servlets, which are pure Java programs, JSP pages are text-based documents. A JSP page contains two parts:

❑ HTML or XML for the static content

❑ JSP tags and scriptlets written in Java to encapsulate the logic that generates the dynamic content

Since a JSP page provides a general representation of content that can produce multiple views depending on the results of JSP tags and scriptlets, a JSP page acts like a template for producing content.

A template is a page of markup (such as HTML) with special placeholders (JSP tags and scriptlets) embedded. These placeholders contain processing information for the template processor (or content generator). In a JSP page, the usual markup allows us to define the static structure and content of a page. The additional JSP tags and scriptlets embedded in the page let us include programming logic to be executed during page generation.

The key advantage of this technology is that it helps to keep the content design and development activities loosely coupled with the design and development of the application logic. If we develop the content purely with Java servlets, the two activities will be strongly coupled. This is undesirable because such applications are more difficult to maintain.

In some template-driven technologies such as Active Server Pages (ASP), the templates are evaluated at runtime. That is, the template processor dynamically converts the special tags into normal content. This is a runtime process, and every time the page is requested, the template processor interprets the template again and again.

Unlike ASP, JSP technology is based on page-compilation. Instead of interpreting the JSP page, the web container converts it into a servlet class, and compiles it. This process typically happens when the web container invokes a JSP page for the first time in response to a request or at container startup. Web containers also allow us to precompile JSP pages into servlets. Most containers available today repeat this process whenever the JSP page is modified. This is called the page translation phase. The container invokes the generated/compiled servlet for subsequent requests to the JSP. This is the request-processing phase.

The different phases are show in the figure below (the unfilled arrow represent the page compilation process):

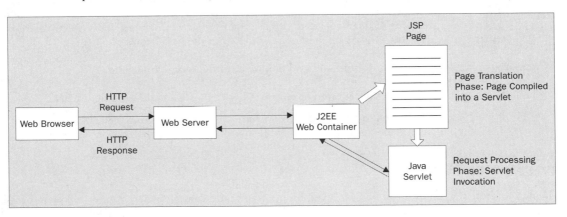

Once the JSP page is compiled into a servlet, the rest of the request processing and response generation is the same as described previously for servlets.

This architecture leads to very useful and flexible applications using JSP pages and servlets:

- ❑   We can use servlets alone for application logic and content generation

- ❑   We can also use JSP pages alone for application logic and content generation

- ❑   We can combine these, with the application logic handled by servlets, and content generation handled by JSP pages

Deployment Descriptors

Deployment descriptors are an integral part of J2EE web applications. They help to manage the configuration of web applications once they are deployed. For web containers, the deployment descriptor is an XML file called `web.xml` stored in the `/WEB-INF` directory of the web application. The Java Servlets specification provides a document type definition (DTD) for the deployment descriptor. This is available at http://java.sun.com/dtd/web-app_2_3.dtd.

A deployment descriptor has several purposes:

❑ **Initialization of parameters for servlets and web applications**
This allows us to minimize the amount of hard coding of initialization values within our web applications. For example, if our servlet requires access to a database, the best place to specify the details, such as the login and password, is the deployment descriptor. This allows us to configure our applications without having to recompile the servlets.

❑ **Servlet/JSP Definitions**
Each servlet or precompiled JSP page used in our web application should be defined in the deployment descriptor. This entry includes the name of the servlet or JSP, the class of the servlet or JSP, and an optional description.

❑ **Servlet/JSP Mappings**
Web containers use this information to map incoming requests to servlets and JSP pages. You will learn about these mappings in Chapter 9.

❑ **MIME Types**
Since each web application can contain several content types, we can specify the MIME types for each type in the deployment descriptor.

❑ **Security**
We can manage access control for our application using the deployment descriptor. For example, we can specify whether our web application requires a login and, if so, what the login page should be, and what role the user should have.

The deployment descriptor can also be used to customize other elements including welcome pages, error pages, and session configuration. We'll learn more about this in Chapter 9.

Structure of Web Applications

A web application has four parts:

❑ A public directory

❑ A `WEB-INF/web.xml` file

❑ A `WEB-INF/classes` directory

❑ A `WEB-INF/lib` directory

The public area is the root of the application, excluding the `WEB-INF` directory. If you're familiar with web servers such as Apache, this is equivalent to the `htdocs` directory where we would keep all our HTML files. The web container can serve any of the files under the public area.

The WEB-INF directory is a private area and the container will not serve contents of this directory to users. The files in this are meant for container use only. WEB-INF contains, among other things, the deployment descriptor, a classes directory, and a lib directory. The classes directory is used to store compiled servlets and other utility classes. If an application has packaged JAR files (for example, a third-party API packaged as a JAR file), they can be copied into the lib directory. The web container uses these two directories to locate servlets and other dependent classes.

Types of Web Containers

There are essentially three ways to configure web containers. Recall from Chapter 1 that a web container either implements the underlying HTTP services, or delegates such services to external web servers:

❑   **Web container in a J2EE application server**
    Most of the commercial J2EE application servers such as WebLogic, Inprise Application
    Server, iPlanet Application Server, and WebSphere Application Server now include web
    containers built in.

❑   **Web containers built into web servers**
    This is the case with pure Java web servers that contain integrated web containers. Jakarta
    Tomcat (from http://jakarta.apache.org), which is the web container reference
    implementation, also falls into this category. Tomcat includes a web server along with a web
    container.

❑   **Web container in a separate runtime**
    In the non-J2EE world, this is the most common scenario. Web servers such as Apache, or
    Microsoft IIS require a separate Java runtime to run servlets, and a web server plug-in to
    integrate the Java runtime with the web server. The plug-in handles communication between
    the web server and the web container. Commercially available servlet/JSP engines such as
    JRun from Allaire, and ServletExec from New Atlanta (now part of Unify's eWave product
    family) provide plug-ins to integrate with web servers.

The choice of a type of container depends entirely on the requirements of our application. For instance, if we were only interested in building a new Java-based web application, we would choose the second or the third configuration. However, with the unification of web and enterprise computing standards via the J2EE, the first configuration is becoming increasingly common.

A Simple Web Application

Now that we've seen the broad description of the J2EE web container architecture and web applications, let's build a web application so that we can walk through the basic aspects of developing web applications with J2EE.

Our web application will do two things:

❑   Prompt the user for a name and an e-mail address

❑   Print a welcome greeting based on the time of the day

Although there are many different combinations of servlets and JSP pages that could be used to develop this application, we'll use the following:

- ❑ An HTML page with a form to collect the name and e-mail address of the user
- ❑ A servlet to process the request and generate HTML to display a greeting message
- ❑ A deployment descriptor

Once we complete this exercise, you will realize how simple and intuitive the process of building a web application is.

Prepare the Web Container

To build, deploy, and run our web application we need a web container (formerly called a servlet/JSP engine) that complies with the Java Servlet specification 2.3, and JSP 1.2. There are several commercial products available in the market but in this and the following chapters, we recommend that you use the J2EE reference implementation from http://java.sun.com.

Create the HTML File

Create an HTML file with the following content, and save it as
`%BOOK_HOME%\Ch05\greeting\index.html`.

```html
<html>
  <head>
    <title>ProJava Registration</title>
  </head>
  <body>
    <h1>Welcome</h1>
    <form action="/greeting/servlet/GreetingServlet" method="POST">
      <p>Your Name <input type="text" size="40" name="name" /></p>
      <p>Your Email <input type="text" size="40" name="email" />
      <input type="submit" VALUE="Submit" /></p>
    </form>
  </body>
</html>
```

Note the content for the `<form>` tag. This tag has a POST request for a form collecting values for the parameters `name` and `email`.

Create a Servlet

The next step is to create a servlet. This servlet processes the HTTP POST request submitted from `index.html`. Create a Java class called `GreetingServlet` and save it as
`%BOOK_HOME%\Ch05\greeting\GreetingServlet.java`.

We don't need to worry about putting our servlet in the `classes` directory at this stage because the tool we will use to construct our web application will do this for us.

```
import javax.servlet.http.HttpServlet;
import javax.servlet.http.HttpServletRequest;
import javax.servlet.http.HttpServletResponse;
import javax.servlet.ServletException;

import java.io.IOException;
import java.io.PrintWriter;
import java.util.Calendar;
import java.util.GregorianCalendar;
public class GreetingServlet extends HttpServlet {

  protected void doPost (HttpServletRequest request, HttpServletResponse response)
                  throws ServletException, IOException {
    String name = request.getParameter("name");
    String email = request.getParameter("email");
    String message = null;
    GregorianCalendar calendar = new GregorianCalendar();
    if(calendar.get(Calendar.AM_PM) == Calendar.AM) {
      message = "Good Morning";
    } else {
      message = "Good Afternoon";
    }
    response.setContentType("text/html");
    PrintWriter out = response.getWriter();

    out.println("<html>");
    out.println("<body>");
    out.println("<p>" + message + ", " + name + "</p>");

    out.println("<p>  Thanks for registering your email (" + email +
                ") with us.</p>");
    out.println("<p> - The Pro Java Team. </p>");

    out.println("</body>");
    out.println("</html>");

    out.close();
  }
}
```

To be able to compile the servlet, you must have `j2ee.jar` (found in `%J2EE_HOME%\lib\`) in your CLASSPATH. Run the following command from `%BOOK_HOME%\Ch05\greeting\` to compile the servlet:

```
javac -classpath %J2EE_HOME%\lib\j2ee.jar;. GreetingServet.java
```

Constructing the Web Application

At this point, you should have the following files:

❑   `%BOOK_HOME%\Ch05\greeting\index.html`

❑   `%BOOK_HOME%\Ch05\greeting\GreetingServlet.java`

❑   `%BOOK_HOME%\Ch05\greeting\GreetingServlet.class`

Web components in J2EE are packaged in a **Web Application Archive (WAR)**, which is a JAR similar to the package used for Java class libraries. It is possible to create WAR files manually, however, we will use the `deploytool` that comes as part of the J2EE Reference Implementation. We will be using this tool to create applications in later chapters, and now is a good chance to learn some of its basic features.

Launch the J2EE deployment tool by executing the `deploytool.bat` file in the `%J2EE_HOME%\bin` directory. Create a new application by using either the New Application button or selecting New | Application from the File menu. Call the application `Greeting`:

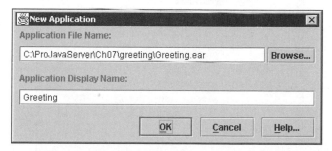

Our web application will be a part of this Enterprise application. Select the Greeting application in the left-hand tree pane and add a new Web Component using the File menu. Skip past the first screen of the New Web Component Wizard until you reach the WAR File screen:

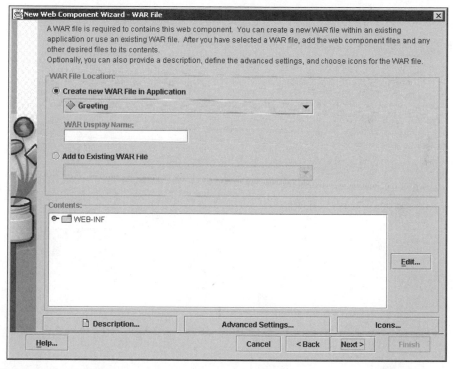

Hit the Edit button and add `GreetingServlet.class` and `index.html` to the web component:

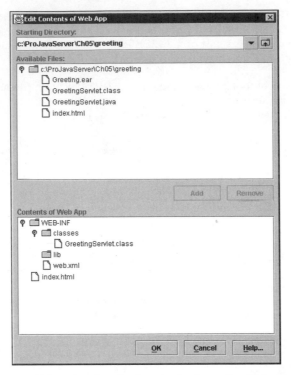

Move on to the next screen of the wizard and select to deploy a **Servlet** only:

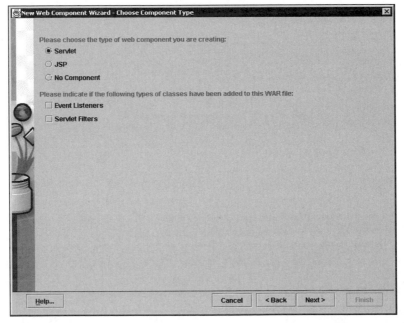

Go on to the next screen. Name the servlet **greeting** and choose our `GreetingServlet` class file:

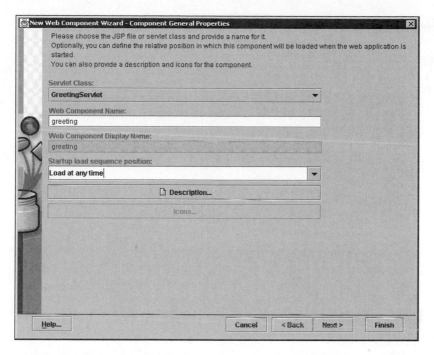

That's all we need to set in the wizard. You can either press the Finish button now, or keep going to the end of the wizard to see the deployment descriptor:

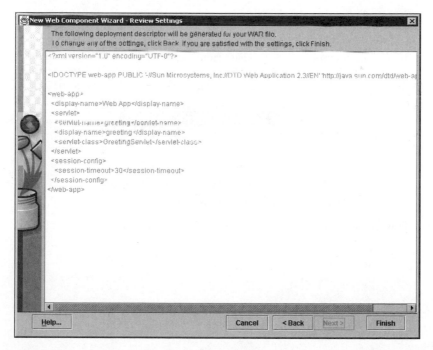

Once you exit the wizard, you'll see the newly created web component in the main window:

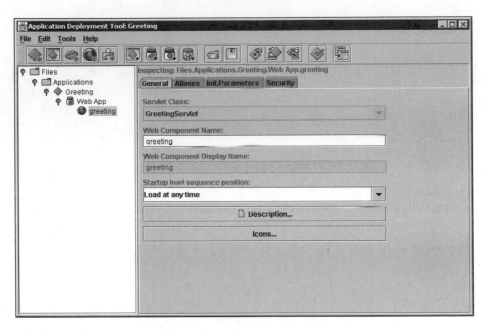

This completes the creation of our first web application.

Deploying the Web Application

The next step is to **deploy** our newly created web application onto a server so that it can be accessed by client browsers.

If the J2EE reference implementation server isn't running, you need to start it by running j2ee -verbose from within %J2EE_HOME%\bin. Then connect the deployment tool to the running server, by selecting Add Server from the File menu and adding a server called localhost:

Now we can deploy the web component. Select Deploy from the Tools menu to start the deployment wizard:

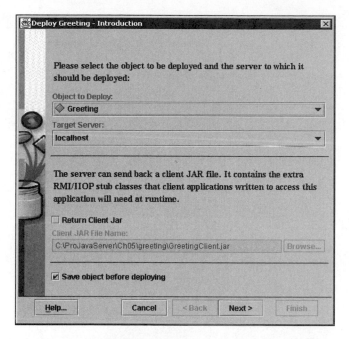

Make sure Greeting is selected as the object to deploy, and hit Next:

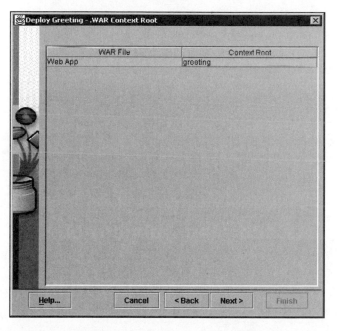

Set the Context Root to greeting; this sets the URL to access the application. Select Next and then Finish to start the deployment process:

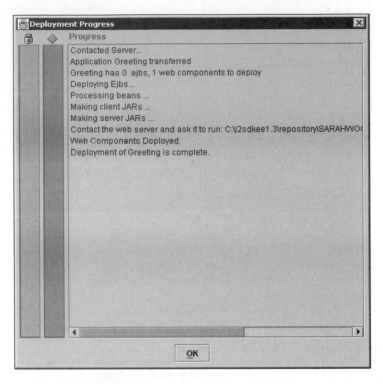

Now we're ready to try out our application.

Running the Web Application

The server should already be running, so open up your browser and navigate to http://localhost:8000/greeting/index.html, where you should see something like:

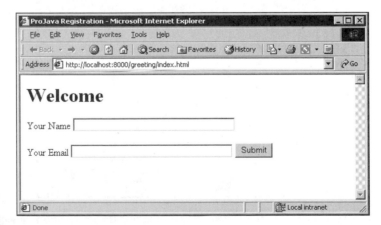

Enter your name, and e-mail address, and click on Submit. Your browser should display the following greeting from The Pro Java Server team. The actual greeting message depends on what time you run this application:

The next stage is to understand how this application works.

How the Application Works

The figure below shows what transpires between the web browser and the web application. The numbered arrows indicate the sequence in which requests and responses are processed:

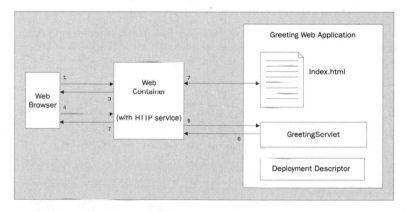

In response to the first request that the browser makes to the server (http://localhost:8000/greeting/index.html), the web container serves the index.html under \greeting\index.html.

In the current configuration, the URI path greeting maps to a web application located at \webapps\greeting. In general, web servers and containers consider index.html as the default welcome file in any directory under the URL path. The numbered arrows (1), (2), and (3) show this sequence.

The second request (http://localhost:8080/greeting/servlet/GreetingServlet) to the web container is the HTTP POST request with name and email parameters. Based on the path greeting/servlet, and the servlet definition in the deployment descriptor, the web container delegates this request to GreetingServlet. (We'll look at the deployment descriptor in a moment.)

The servlet then performs the following tasks:

❑ Extracts the request parameters: This involves extracting the "name" and "email" parameters from the request

❑ Executes application logic: In our example, this involves generating a greeting message

❑ Generates the response: After processing the request, the servlet generates an HTML document with the greeting message

The browser receives the response so generated by the servlet. This sequence is shown by numbered arrows (4), (5), (6), and (7). In brief, this is how web containers delegate requests to servlets in web applications. We'll learn more details of this process in Chapters 6 and 7.

The Greeting Servlet

Don't worry about understanding every line of code in GreetingServlet.java. Our aim here is simply to gain an overview of what the servlet does.

Import the Servlet Packages

The Java Servlet API consists of two packages: javax.servlet, and javax.servlet.http. Note that all javax packages are part of the of the Java 2 SDK, Enterprise Edition.

Of these two packages, the javax.servlet package contains servlet classes and interfaces that are independent of HTTP. The rest of the classes that are specific for HTTP are part of the javax.servlet.http package.

Apart from the above two, the GreetingServlet class also needs to import classes from the java.io and java.util packages:

```
import javax.servlet.ServletException;
import javax.servlet.http.HttpServlet;
import javax.servlet.http.HttpServletRequest;
import javax.servlet.http.HttpServletResponse;

import java.io.IOException;
import java.io.PrintWriter;
import java.util.Calendar;
import java.util.GregorianCalendar;
```

Class Declaration

All servlets are required to implement the javax.servlet.Servlet interface. However, for servlets in web applications, the javax.servlet.http.HttpServlet class provides an implementation of this interface. So, the GreetingServlet class extends the HttpServlet class:

```
public class GreetingServlet extends HttpServlet {
    ...
}
```

Service the HTTP POST Request

In the GreetingServlet servlet, the doPost() method handles the HTTP POST request. This method takes an HttpServletRequest object that encapsulates the information contained in the request, and an HttpServletResponse object encapsulating the HTTP response.

Our implementation of the doPost() method includes two tasks: to extract the FORM parameters from the HTTP request, and to generate the response.

Extract Parameters from HttpServletRequest

We can use the getParameter() method of the HttpServletRequest interface to extract parameters from the HTTP request:

```
String name = request.getParameter("name");
String email = request.getParameter("email");
```

The first call extracts the parameter named name in the <FORM> tag of the index.html file. Here is a recap:

```
<p>Your Name <input type="text" size="40" name="name"></p>
```

The getParameter() method looks into all the available parameters in the request, and extracts a parameter called name. Similarly, we can extract the email parameter. Note that these parameters need not be extracted in any particular order. For instance, we can first extract the email parameter and then extract the name parameter.

This ends the request-processing part. The next step is to prepare for the response.

Generate Response

The next step is to prepare the dynamic content to be sent to the user. In the response, we're interested in displaying a greeting message, such as:

Good Afternoon, Subrahmanyam Allamaraju

Thanks for registering your email (subrah@subrahmanyam.com) with us.

- The Pro Java Team.

In this example, the servlet uses the response stream associated with the response object to directly print the content. Note that JSP pages provide a better alternative for dynamic content generation. However, for the sake of simplicity, let's use servlets instead.

The following code snippet computes a greeting message depending on the current time of the day. Note that this is the only application logic performed in this application. As we'll see in Chapters 7 and 8, we can perform more complex application logic (such as database access) at this point:

```
String message = null;
GregorianCalendar calendar = new GregorianCalendar();
if(calendar.get(Calendar.AM_PM) == Calendar.AM) {
  message = "Good Morning";
} else {
  message = "Good Afternoon";
}
```

Note that this is a crude form of greeting message. The servlet uses a java.util.GregorianCalendar object to find out if the time of the day corresponds to AM or PM, and accordingly prepares the response with a message string.

After computing this message, the servlet is ready for generating the response. This involves the following steps:

❑ Setting a content type (MIME) for the response, in our example, this is `text/html`:

```
response.setContentType("text/html");
```

❑ Obtaining a `java.io.PrintWriter` object from the response object:

```
PrintWriter out = response.getWriter();
```

❑ Printing the response using the `PrintWriter` object:

```
out.println("<html>");
out.println("<body>");
out.println("<p>" + message + ", " + name + "</p>");

out.println("<p> Thanks for registering your email (" + email +
            ") with us.</p>");
out.println("<p> - The Pro Java Team. </p>");
out.println("</body>");
out.println("</html>");
```

❑ Closing the `PrintWriter` object:

```
out.close();
```

These steps result in the HTML document that is displayed in the browser in response to the POST request.

The Deployment Descriptor

In our example application, the deployment descriptor file (`web.xml`) is created by `deploytool` for us. If you look in `%J2EE_HOME%\public_html\greeting\` you will find a file named `original.war`. This is the WAR file for our `greeting` web application and because a WAR is a JAR, we can look at the contents of `original.war` using the standard `jar` tool. A zip tool, such as WinZip, is also capable of understanding WAR files. If you use one of these tools to examine `original.war` you will find the following structure:

```
\greeting
        \index.html
        \WEB-INF
                \web.xml
                \classes
                        \GreetingServlet.class
```

Note that the deployment tool has placed our servlet class in the correct directory. This demonstrates one of the advantages of using such a tool to create applications, rather than creating applications manually.

You can then open `web.xml` and examine its contents. Recall that this file includes the configuration information for our web application. The first line in the deployment descriptor is an XML declaration specifying the version of the XML and the encoding used:

```
<?xml version="1.0" encoding="ISO-8859-1"?>
```

This is followed by the document type declaration specifying the URI for the DTD used for this application:

```
<!DOCTYPE web-app PUBLIC '-//Sun Microsystems, Inc.//DTD Web Application 2.3//EN'
                     'http://java.sun.com/dtd/web-app_2_3.dtd'>
```

In the case of web applications, the DTD is part of the J2EE specification for web applications and is standard for all our web applications.

The actual definition of servlets is enclosed within <web-app> tags. Within the <servlet> tag, note the three entries for the name of the servlet, the display name of the servlet, and the fully qualified Java class. The <servlet> tag lets the web container know the name used to refer to a servlet:

```
<web-app>
  <display-name>Web App</display-name>
  <servlet>
    <servlet-name>greeting</servlet-name>
    <display-name>greeting</display-name>
    <servlet-class>GreetingServlet</servlet-class>
  </servlet>
  <session-config>
    <session-timeout>30</session-timeout>
  </session-config>
</web-app>
```

Recall that the FORM in index.html posts the request to a relative URL, /greeting/servlet/GreetingServlet. The value of <servlet-name> is an alias for the actual class name. This feature allows us to change the servlet class files without changing our HTML pages or other servlets. We can also deploy the same servlet more than once in the same web application. To do so, we just need to use different names.

Summary

This chapter provides an overview of web containers, without going into many of the details of the underlying APIs. The purpose of this chapter is to introduce you to web application development using Java servlets. Besides illustrating the Java servlet programming model with the help of a simple application, this chapter covered the following:

❑ The basics of HTTP: the different types of requests and details of the request-response paradigm of HTTP

❑ Java servlets, JSP pages, and deployment descriptors

❑ The steps involved in building a simple web application to collect data from users and generate a response using the J2EE reference implementation

While these areas illustrate the basic web application development model, there are several other features required to build useful production-quality web applications. The next several chapters will go deeper into the servlets and JSP technologies. Specifically, the next four chapters cover:

❑   In Chapter 6, we will discuss the Servlet API in detail. Besides this, this chapter will also discuss the lifecycle of servlets, and the request and response API.

❑   Chapter 7 will introduce you to the concepts of sessions and context, and their crucial role for web application development. This chapter will also discuss how you can use two or more servlets or JSP pages in collaboration.

❑   Chapter 8 will introduce you to filters. Filters let you intervene in the process of the container invoking servlets and JSP pages, or serving static content.

❑   Chapter 9 will discuss the deployment descriptor in detail and how to use it to provide security to applications.

These chapters will walk you through developing several web applications. These samples will focus on different aspects of the Servlet API, and will build on what you have learned in this chapter.

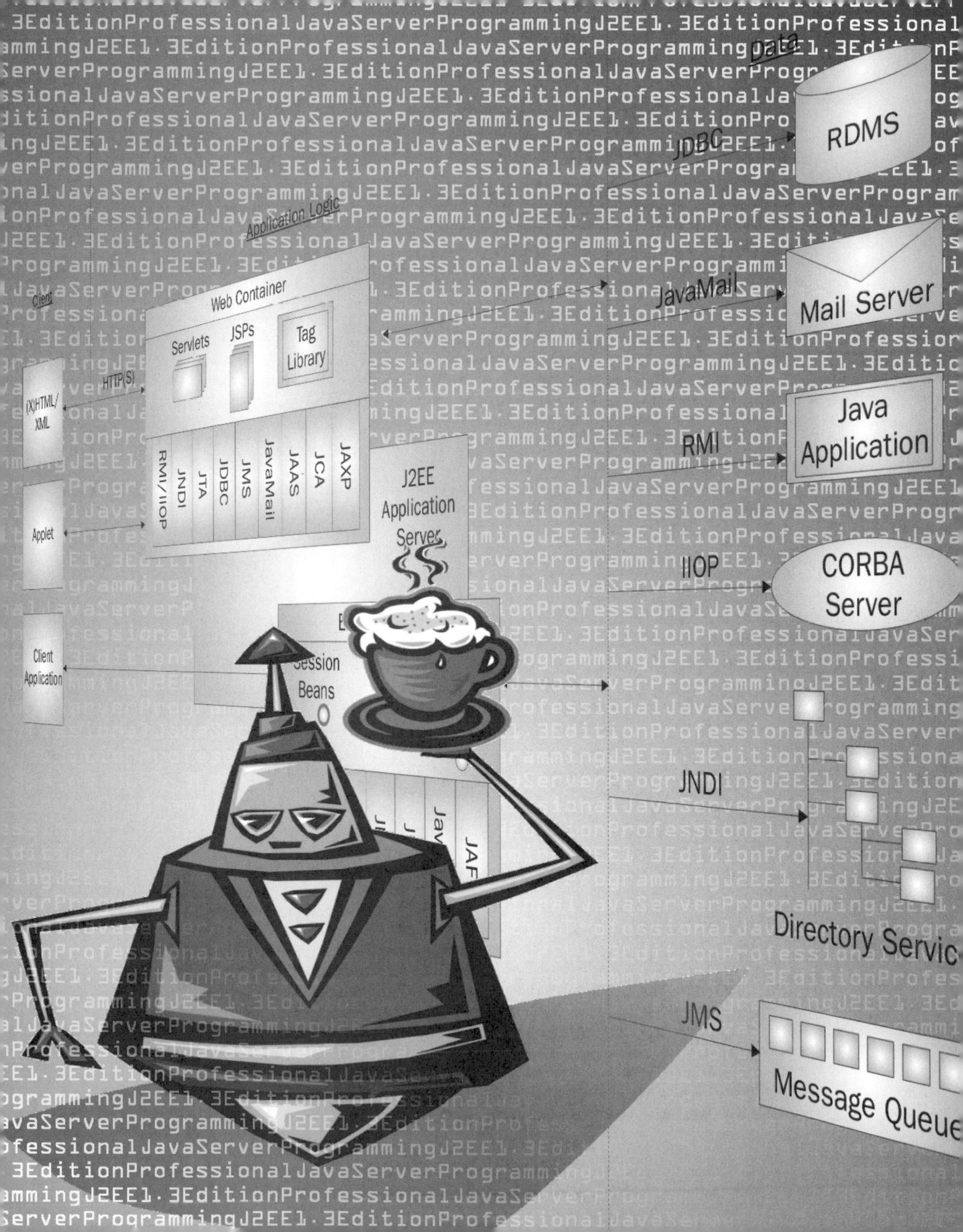

6

Servlet Programming

Servlets are the basic building blocks for building web-based interfaces to applications. The servlets technology provides a common programming model that is also the foundation for JavaServer Pages. In the previous chapter, we saw an overview of web applications and web containers, where we went into the programming requirements, and the basic structure of web applications. The focus then was to introduce the basic principles of web containers and web applications, and how web applications can be programmed to enhance the HTTP request-response process.

The goal of the next few chapters is to introduce you to the **Java Servlet API, version 2.3**, which can be downloaded from http://java.sun.com/products/servlet. This API includes two packages: `javax.servlet` and `javax.servlet.http`.

> *Note that the `javax.servlet` package has two sub-packages for JSP (`javax.servlet.jsp`), and JSP custom tags (`jsp.servlet.jsp.tagext`). These packages will be covered from Chapter 10 onwards.*

We'll cover the Java Servlet API in four steps:

- ❏ Servlet implementation
- ❏ Requests and responses
- ❏ Session, context, and servlet collaboration
- ❏ Filtering of requests and responses

> *In this chapter, our agenda is to discuss the first and second steps, while we'll discuss the third step in Chapter 7, and the fourth in Chapter 8. Additionally, we'll discuss the deployment aspects in Chapter 9.*

In this chapter, we'll examine the following:

- ❑ Classes and interfaces for servlet implementation, including servlet exceptions
- ❑ Servlet configuration
- ❑ The servlet lifecycle
- ❑ Requests and responses
- ❑ The servlet programming model

Note that this chapter is not meant to be a comprehensive reference to the `javax.servlet` and `javax.servlet.http` packages. Instead, we'll walk through these packages, and the concepts behind them, concentrating on how to use the API while developing applications. The Servlet API documentation should be kept handy while reading this chapter. You can access this documentation online at http://java.sun.com/products/servlet/2.3/javadoc/index.html.

Overview of the Java Servlet API

As we've already seen, the Servlet API is specified in two Java extension packages: `javax.servlet` and `javax.servlet.http`. The classes and interfaces in the `javax.servlet` package are protocol-independent, while the second package, `javax.servlet.http`, contains classes and interfaces that are specific to HTTP. Note that some of the classes/interfaces in the `javax.servlet.http` extend those specified in the `javax.servlet` package.

The figure below shows the class diagram for some of the core classes of the `javax.servlet` package, and some of their associations:

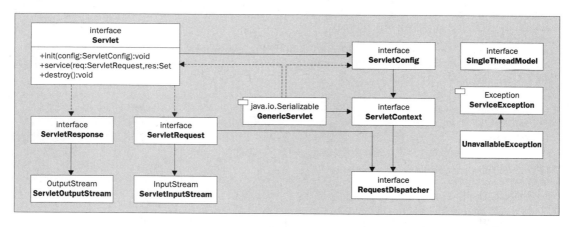

The continuous arrows depict associations, while broken arrows indicate dependencies. An association could be inheritance, composition, or even navigability. Dependency indicates some form of coupling between classes. For instance, the broken arrow from `javax.servlet.Servlet` interface to `javax.servlet.ServletRequest` indicates that the former depends on the latter, and any changes to the latter interface definition could lead to changes in the former.

The following figure shows some of the classes/interfaces from the `javax.servlet.http` package:

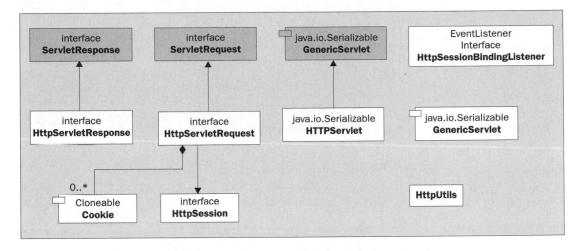

Note that the container maintains all these associations, as long as you're using the `javax.servlet.http` *package. However, if you're building specialized servlets extending the classes in the* `javax.servlet` *package, you'll have to maintain some of the associations yourself.*

These diagrams do not represent the complete Servlet API. For simplicity, these figures highlight only those classes/interfaces that are required to provide an overview of this API. We'll introduce the remaining part of the API over the course of the next few chapters.

What's the purpose of all these interfaces and classes? Consider the following questions:

❑ How does the web container manage the lifecycle of servlets? How can your servlets participate in this lifecycle?

❑ How do we implement application logic? Application logic in servlets is the programming logic to respond to HTTP requests. Depending on the architecture and complexity of applications, this could be database access, invoking the services of various EJBs and other middle-tier components, or using JMS to send messages to other enterprise applications, etc.

❑ How do we read HTTP requests and generate HTTP responses?

❑ How do we deal with exceptions in servlets?

❑ How can servlets interact with their environment?

We'll not attempt to answer these questions right now, but after reading this chapter, we should be able to answer them.

The table overleaf provides an overview of the Java Servlet API, which will be discussed in detail shortly. In this table, various interfaces/classes are grouped on their purpose and usage (which we'll discuss in a moment). Interfaces are shown in italic, while classes (whether abstract or not) and exceptions are shown in regular font. The additions to the Servlet API in version 2.3 are marked with an asterisk (*):

Purpose	Class/Interface
Servlet Implementation	*javax.servlet.Servlet*
	javax.servlet.SingleThreadModel
	javax.servlet.GenericServlet
	javax.servlet.http.HttpServlet
Servlet Configuration	*javax.servlet.ServletConfig*
Servlet Exceptions	javax.servlet.ServletException
	javax.servlet.UnavailableException
Requests and Responses	*javax.servlet.http.HttpServletRequest*
	javax.servlet.http.HttpServletRequestWrapper (*)
	javax.servlet.http.HttpServletResponse
	javax.servlet.http.HttpServletResponseWrapper
	javax.servlet.ServletInputStream (*)
	javax.servlet.ServletOutputStream
	javax.servlet.ServletRequest
	javax.servlet.ServletRequestWrapper (*)
	javax.servlet.ServletResponse
	javax.servlet.ServletResponseWrapper (*)
Session Tracking	*javax.servlet.http.HttpSession*
	javax.servlet.http.HttpSessionActivationListener (*)
	javax.servlet.http.HttpSessionAttributeListener (*)
	javax.servlet.http.HttpSessionBindingListener
	javax.servlet.http.HttpSessionBindingEvent
	javax.servlet.http.HttpSessionEvent (*)
	javax.servlet.http.HttpSessionListener (*)
Servlet Context	*javax.servlet.ServletContext*
	javax.servlet.ServletContextAttributeEvent (*)
	javax.servlet.ServletContextAttributeListener (*)
	javax.servlet.ServletContextEvent (*)
	javax.servlet.ServletContextListener (*)
Servlet Collaboration	*javax.servlet.RequestDispatcher*
Filtering	*javax.servlet.Filter* (*)
	javax.servlet.FilterChain (*)
	javax.servlet.FilterConfig (*)
Miscellaneous	javax.servlet.http.Cookie
	javax.servlet.http.HttpUtils

Web servers with Java Servlet implementations, such as Tomcat, WebLogic, Orion, iPlanet, JRun, and so on, use most of the interfaces and classes in the above table. In fact, apart from the various listener interfaces in the above table, there is only one abstract class (`javax.servlet.http.HttpServlet`) and one interface (`javax.servlet.Filter`) that are left for you to implement when building web applications. The container creates the rest of the runtime objects that are part of your application. Why is this so?

A web container is an application framework with a runtime environment. In the framework, application objects are created and invoked by the runtime. While invoking methods on the application objects, the container has to construct the objects for the arguments. For instance, consider the `GreetingServlet` of the previous chapter. In this servlet, the container creates and passes the `HttpServletRequest` and `HttpServletResponse` objects as arguments to the `doPost()` method:

```
proteced void doPost(HttpServletRequest request, HttpServletResponse response)
        throws ServletExceotion, IOException {
```

In the same fashion, the container creates all other objects (such as `ServletConfig`, `ServletContext`, `HttpSession`, and so on) that a servlet can access, directly or indirectly.

The table above categorized the classes/interfaces in the `javax.servlet` and `javax.servlet.http` packages, based on their role in web application development. So now let's look at this categorization in more detail:

❑ **Servlet Implementation**
The classes/interfaces in this category are meant for implementing servlets. For instance, the `GreetingServlet` class in the previous chapter extends the `HttpServlet` class. To develop our own servlets, we would implement one or more methods in these classes/interfaces. When we deploy servlets, the web container invokes these methods to control their lifecycle, and to execute application logic.

❑ **Servlet Configuration**
The `ServletConfig` interface belongs to this category. The Servlet API provides various means of accessing the `ServletConfig` object associated with a servlet. This object provides access to certain initialization parameters that can be configured while deploying a servlet. We'll demonstrate how this can be done later in the chapter.

❑ **Servlet Exceptions**
The Java Servlet API specifies two exceptions: `ServletException` and `UnavailableException`. Typically, servlets throw these exceptions, which the container then catches to perform appropriate error handling.

❑ **Requests and Responses**
There are four interfaces and two abstract classes in this category. These objects provide methods to access, and the underlying input and output streams associated with the, client connection. Using these objects, we can read data from the input, and write data back to the client.

In addition to the above, the Servlet 2.3 specification introduced wrapper classes for `ServletRequest`, `ServletResponse`, `http.HttpServletRequest`, and `http.HttpServletResponse` classes (as seen in the above table by classnames ending with "Wrapper"). Although all these classes are not abstract, they do not actually contain any functionality. We'll see the role of these wrapper classes later in this chapter.

❑ **Session Tracking**

Session tracking is one of the crucial parts of web application development. As we shall discuss in Chapter 7, HTTP, which is the basic protocol for web applications, is stateless. As a result, web applications cannot recognize multiple requests from the same HTTP client as originating from the same place. The notion of a **session** provides this abstraction. In simple terms, a session lets you group requests into a collected group. In addition, session management also involves associating data with each session. The Servlet API specifies the `javax.servlet.HttpSession` interface to provide this abstraction. We shall learn more about sessions in the next chapter.

❑ **Servlet Context**

The notion of servlet context is closely associated with the notion of a web application. The interface `javax.servlet.ServletContext` allows servlets in an application to share data. It also provides methods with which servlets can access the host web container. Using the `ServletContext` object, a servlet can log events, obtain URL references to resources, and set and store attributes that other servlets in the context can access. We shall cover servlet context in the next chapter.

❑ **Servlet Collaboration**

The Servlet API also provides an interface (`RequestDispatcher`) with which a servlet can invoke another servlet, a JSP, or even a static resource such as an HTML page. This mechanism helps you to control the flow of logic across multiple servlets and JSP pages programmatically, and is discussed in detail in Chapter 7.

❑ **Filtering**

The Servlet API has a mechanism with which we can introduce code (called a filter) to participate in the container's request/response process. Filters are a new feature of the Java Servlet API version 2.3. They do not generally create requests/responses; rather, they modify or adapt requests and responses to and from a web resource, which could have static or dynamic content. We shall discuss filters in detail in Chapter 8.

❑ **Other Miscellaneous API**

Under this category, you'll find two classes: `http.Cookie`, which you can use to create cookies, and `http.HttpUtils`, which provide miscellaneous helper methods. You'll find some examples of these classes in the next chapter.

In the following sections, we'll discuss the first four of these categories in detail.

Servlet Implementation

Let's start by taking a closer look at the classes and interfaces used for implementing servlets themselves.

The Servlet Interface

```
public interface Servlet
```

This interface specifies the contract between the web container and a servlet. In the object-oriented paradigm, an object can communicate with another object as long as the first object can reference the second object with a known interface – it need not know the name of the actual implementing class. In the case of the Servlet API, the `javax.servlet.Servlet` is the interface that containers use to reference servlets.

When you write a servlet, you must implement this interface directly or indirectly. You will most likely always implement the interface indirectly by extending either the `javax.servlet.GenericServlet` or `javax.servlet.http.HttpServlet` classes.

When implementing the `javax.servlet.Servlet` interface, the following five methods must be implemented:

```
public void init(ServletConfig config)
public void service(ServletRequest request, ServletResponse response)
public void destroy()
public ServletConfig getServletConfig()
public String getServletInfo()
```

The init() Method

```
public void init(ServletConfig config) throws ServletException
```

Once the servlet has been instantiated, the web container calls the `init()` method. The purpose of this method is to allow a servlet to perform any initialization required before being invoked against HTTP requests. The container passes an object of type `ServletConfig` to the `init()` method and, as we shall see later, a servlet can access its configuration data using the `ServletConfig` object. The `init()` method throws a `ServletException` in the event that it does not complete normally.

The Servlet specification guarantees that the `init()` method will be called exactly once on any given instance of the servlet, and the `init()` method will be allowed to complete (provided that it does not throw a `ServletException`) before any requests are passed to the servlet.

Some of the typical tasks that can be implemented in the `init()` method are:

❑   Read configuration data from persistent resources such as configuration files

❑   Read initialization parameters using the `ServletConfig` object

❑   Initializing one-time activities such as registering a database driver, a connection pool, or a logging service

The service() Method

```
public void service(ServletRequest request, ServletResponse response)
             throws ServletException, IOException
```

This is the entry point for executing application logic in a servlet. The container calls this method in response to incoming requests. Only after the servlet has been successfully initialized will the `service()` method be called. The `service()` method accepts two arguments, implementing the `javax.servlet.ServletRequest` and `javax.servlet.ServletResponse` interfaces respectively. The request object provides methods to access the original request data, and the response object provides methods with which the servlet can build a response.

The destroy() Method

```
public void destroy()
```

The container calls this method before removing a servlet instance out of service. This might occur if it needs to free some memory or if the web server is being shut down. Before the container calls this method, it will give the remaining `service()` threads time to finish executing (subject to some timeout period), so that the `destroy()` method is not called while a `service()` call is still underway. After the `destroy()` method is called, the container does not route requests to the servlet.

Activities that can be implemented in the `destroy()` method include:

❑ Performing cleanup tasks, such as closing any open resources, closing a connection pool, or even informing another application/system that the servlet will no longer be in service

❑ Persisting any state associated with a servlet

The getServletConfig() Method

```
public ServletConfig getServletConfig()
```

This method should be implemented to return the `ServletConfig` that was passed to the servlet during the `init()` method.

The getServletInfo() Method

```
public String getServletInfo()
```

This method should return a `String` object containing information about the servlet (for example, author, creation date, description, and so on). This is available to the web container, should it wish to display, for example, a list of servlets installed together with their descriptions.

The GenericServlet Class

```
public abstract class GenericServlet implements Servlet, ServletConfig,
                                                Serializable
```

The `GenericServlet` class provides a basic implementation of the `Servlet` interface. This is an abstract class, and all subclasses should implement the `service()` method. This abstract class has the following methods in addition to those declared in `javax.servlet.Servlet`, and `javax.servlet.ServletConfig`:

```
public init()
public void log(String message)
public void log(String message, Throwable t)
```

The `init(ServletConfig config)` method stores the `ServletConfig` object in a private transient instance variable (called `config`). You can use the `getServletConfig()` method to access this object. However, if you choose to override this method, you should include a call to `super.init(config)`. Alternatively, you can override the overloaded no-argument `init()` method in the `GenericServlet` class.

The `GenericServlet` class also implements the `ServletConfig` interface. This allows the servlet developer to call the `ServletConfig` methods directly without having to first obtain a `ServletConfig` object. These methods are `getInitParameter()`, `getInitParameterNames()`, `getServletContext()`, and `getServletName()`. Each of these methods delegates the calls to the respective methods in the stored `ServletConfig` object.

The `GenericServlet` class also includes two methods for writing to a servlet log, which call the corresponding methods on the `ServletContext`. The first method, `log(String msg)`, writes the name of the servlet and the `msg` argument to the web container's log. The other method, `log(String msg, Throwable cause)`, includes a stack trace for the given `Throwable` exception in addition to the servlet name and message. The actual implementation of the logging mechanism is container-specific, although most of the containers use text files for logging purposes.

The SingleThreadModel Interface

```
public interface SingleThreadModel
```

The Servlet API specifies a special **marker interface** called `javax.servlet.SingleThreadModel`.

During the lifetime of a servlet that does not implement this interface, the container may send multiple service requests in different threads to a single instance. This means that implementation of the `service()` method should be thread-safe. However, what's the alternative if the `service()` method of a servlet is not thread-safe?

The Java Servlet API specifies the `SingleThreadModel` interface for this purpose. Servlets can implement the `SingleThreadModel` interface (in addition to implementing the `javax.servlet.Servlet` interface or extending one of its implementation classes) in order to inform the container that it should make sure that only one thread is executing the servlet's `service()` method at any given moment.

For `SingleThreadModel` servlets, containers may follow one of the following approaches to ensure that each servlet instance is invoked in a separate thread:

❑ **Instance Pooling**
In this approach, the container maintains a pool of servlet instances. For each incoming request, the container allocates a servlet instance from the pool, and upon completion of the service, the container returns the instance to the pool.

❑ **Request Serialization**
In this approach, the container maintains a single instance of the servlet. However, since the container cannot send multiple requests to the instance at the same time, the container serializes the requests. This means that new requests will be kept waiting while the current request is being served.

In reality, a combination of these two approaches is more pragmatic, so that the container could maintain a reasonable number of instances in the pool, while still serializing requests if the number of requests exceeds the number of instances in the pool.

Note that the `SingleThreadModel` is resource-intensive, particularly if a large number of concurrent requests are expected for the servlet. The effect of the `SingleThreadModel` is that the container invokes the `service()` method in a synchronized block. This is equivalent to using the `synchronized` keyword for the servlet's `service()` method. Accordingly, when there are hundreds or even thousands of concurrent requests to the web container, the container may either serialize requests to the same instance of the servlet, or create that many instances. In the first case, the container's ability to process concurrent requests will be severely hampered due to serialization. In the later case, the container encounters more object allocation (which includes more object creation overhead and memory usage).

However, in cases where only a few statements of the `service()` method are not thread-safe, you should consider reducing the scope of synchronization, and explicitly synchronize such blocks using the `synchronized` keyword. Depending on how short such synchronization blocks are, this approach could improve performance.

> We should always consider redesigning our applications in order to avoid the **SingleThreadModel** or thread synchronization. If we cannot avoid them, it is important to be aware of the performance implications. With any thread-synchronization code, you're potentially blocking a web container thread.

The HttpServlet Class

```
public abstract class HttpServlet extends GenericServlet implements Serializable
```

The HttpServlet class extends GenericServlet, and provides an HTTP-specific implementation of the Servlet interface. This will most likely be the class that all of your servlets will extend. This class specifies the following methods:

```
public void service(ServletRequest request, ServletResponse response)
protected void service(HttpServletRequest request, HttpServletResponse response)
protected void doGet(HttpServletRequest request, HttpServletResponse response)
protected void doPost(HttpServletRequest request, HttpServletResponse response)
protected void doHead(HttpServletRequest request, HttpServletResponse response)
protected void doDelete(HttpServletRequest request, HttpServletResponse response)
protected void doOptions(HttpServletRequest request, HttpServletResponse response)
protected void doPut(HttpServletRequest request, HttpServletResponse response)
protected void doTrace(HttpServletRequest request, HttpServletResponse response)
protected long getLastModified(HttpServletRequest request)
```

The service() Methods

The HttpServlet has two variants of this method:

```
public void service(ServletRequest request, ServletResponse response)
        throws ServletException, IOException
```

This is an implementation of the service() method in the GenericServlet. This method casts the request and response objects to HttpServletRequest and HttpServletResponse, and calls the following overloaded service() method. Therefore, you should not override the above method.

```
protected void service(HttpServletRequest request, HttpServletResponse response)
        throws ServletException, IOException
```

This overloaded method takes HTTP-specific request and response objects, and is invoked by the first method above. HttpServlet implements this method to be a dispatcher of HTTP requests. As you'll see later in this chapter, the javax.servlet.ServletRequest interface provides a getMethod() method that returns the type of the HTTP method associated with the request. For instance, for GET requests, this method returns "GET" as a string. The service() method uses this string to delegate the request to one of the methods doXXX(). The javax.servlet.http.HttpServlet provides default implementations to all these methods.

In general, you should avoid overriding this method as it affects the default behavior of the service() method. The only situation that requires you to override it is when you want to change the default behavior, or when you want to include additional processing common to all doXXX() methods. Even in such cases, you should consider including a call to super.service() in your servlets.

The sequence of method calls when the container receives a request for a servlet is:

❑ The container calls the public service() method

❑ The public service() method calls the protected service() method after casting the arguments to HttpServletRequest and HttpServletResponse respectively

❑ The protected service() method calls one of the doXXX() methods, depending on the type of the HTTP request method

The doXXX() Methods

The `HttpServlet` class implements the following protected methods, one for each of the HTTP request methods:

```
protected void doGet(HttpServletRequest request, HttpServletResponse response)
    throws ServletException, IOException
protected void doPost(HttpServletRequest request, HttpServletResponse response)
    throws ServletException, IOException
protected void doHead(HttpServletRequest request, HttpServletResponse response)
    throws ServletException, IOException
protected void doDelete(HttpServletRequest request, HttpServletResponse response)
    throws ServletException, IOException
protected void doOptions(HttpServletRequest request, HttpServletResponse response)
    throws ServletException, IOException
protected void doPut(HttpServletRequest request, HttpServletResponse response)
    throws ServletException, IOException
protected void doTrace(HttpServletRequest request, HttpServletResponse response)
    throws ServletException, IOException
```

The signature of each of these doXXX() methods is the same as the protected service() method above – each takes HttpServletRequest and HttpServletResponse arguments, and throws ServletException and IOException.

The HttpServlet class provides proper implementations for the TRACE and OPTIONS methods, and there is no need for your servlets to override doTrace() and doOptions().

For the other five methods, the HttpServlet class provides implementations that return HTTP errors. For the case of HTTP 1.0 compliant containers, these methods return an HTTP error with status code 400, indicating that the request sent by the client is syntactically incorrect. For HTTP 1.1 compliant containers, these methods returns an HTTP error with status code 405, indicating that the requested HTTP method is not allowed for this servlet. This class uses the getProtocol() method of the javax.servlet.ServletRequest interface to determine the protocol.

Depending on your application, you should determine the HTTP methods to be supported by your servlet, and accordingly override the corresponding doXXX() methods (except those for TRACE and OPTIONS methods).

The getLastModified() Method

```
protected long getLastModified(HttpServletRequest req)
```

This method implements a conditional get operation. For instance, it should return the time that the servlet was last modified in milliseconds since January 1, 1970 00:00:00 GMT. The default implementation returns a negative number (-1) indicating that the time of modification is unknown.

HTTP 1.1 has the notion of conditional GET requests. The If-Modified-Since header is one of the headers that makes a request conditional. Clients conforming to the HTTP 1.1 can send this header with a date field (for example: If-Modified-Since: Sat, 01 Jan 2000 00:00:00 GMT). This header indicates to the server that if the requested resource has not been modified since the time indicated in the header, the server can serve a cached page without regenerating the page. In the case of servlets, the web container need not invoke the doGet() method, as all current versions of commonly used browsers such as the Internet Explorer 5.5, Netscape 6.0, and Opera 5.1 support HTTP 1.1 and take advantage of this header.

Your servlets can override this method to control caching of pages generated by the doGet() method.

Servlet Configuration

In the Java Servlet API, `javax.servlet.ServletConfig` objects represent the configuration of a servlet. The configuration information contains initialization parameters (a set of name/value pairs), the name of the servlet, and a `javax.servlet.ServletContext` object, which gives the servlet information about the container. The initialization parameters and the name of a servlet can be specified in the deployment descriptor (the `web.xml` file), for example:

```
<web-app>
   <servlet>
     <servlet-name>Admin</servlet-name>
     <servlet-class>com.wrox.admin.AdminServlet</servlet-class>
     <init-param>
        <param-name>email</param-name>
        <param-value>admin@admin.wrox.com</param-value>
     </init-param>
     <init-param>
        <param-name>helpURL</param-name>
        <param-value>/admin/help/index.html</param-value>
     </init-param>
   </servlet>
<web-app>
```

This example registers a servlet with name `Admin`, and specifies two initialization parameters, `email` and `helpURL`. The web container reads this information, and makes it available to the `com.wrox.admin.AdminServlet` via the associated `javax.servlet.ServletConfig` object. If we want to change these parameters, we can do so without having to recompile the servlet. We'll learn more about this approach in Chapter 9.

The deployment descriptor mechanism was introduced in the Servlet 2.2 specification. Web containers (then called servlet engines) complying with older versions of the specification provide vendor-specific means (such as properties files) to specify the initialization parameters.

The ServletConfig Interface

```
public interface ServletConfig
```

As we saw when we looked at the `GenericServlet` class, this interface specifies the following methods:

```
public String getInitParameter(String name)
public Enumeration getInitParameterNames()
public ServletContext getServletContext()
public String getServletName()
```

The getInitParameter() Method

```
public String getInitParameter(String name)
```

This method returns the value of a named initialization parameter, or `null` if the specified parameter does not exist. In the above example, calling the `getInitParameter()` method with `"email"` as an argument returns the value `"admin@admin.wrox.com"`.

The getInitParameterNames() Method

```
public Enumeration getInitParameterNames()
```

This method returns an enumeration of all the initialization parameters of a servlet. Using this enumeration, you can obtain the names of all enumeration parameters one after the other. If there are no initialization parameters specified, this method returns an empty enumeration. In the above example, calling getInitParameterNames() returns an enumeration containing two String objects: "email" and "helpURL".

The getServletContext() Method

```
public ServletContext getServletContext()
```

This method returns a reference to the ServletContext object associated with the web application. The javax.servlet.ServletContext is covered in more detail in the next chapter.

The getServletName() Method

```
public String getServletName()
```

This method returns the name assigned to a servlet in its deployment descriptor. If no name is specified, this returns the servlet class name instead.

Obtaining a Reference to ServletConfig

In the Java Servlet API, a servlet can obtain a reference to the javax.servlet.ServletConfig object in the following ways.

During Servlet Initialization

As discussed previously, the init() methods of the Servlet interface and the GenericServlet class have an argument of type javax.servlet.ServletConfig. During initialization of a servlet, the web container creates this argument, and passes it to the init() method. When you're overriding this init() method, you can access the javax.servlet.ServletConfig object.

However, when you're overriding the above init() method in the GenericServlet class, you should explicitly invoke super.init() as follows:

```
public init(ServletConfig config) {
    super.init(config);

    // Initialization here
}
```

The call to super.init(config) ensures that the GenericServlet class receives a reference to the ServletConfig object. The implementation of the GenericServlet class actually maintains a reference to the ServletConfig object (as a private transient instance variable), and requires that super.init(config) be called in subclasses.

Using the getServletConfig() Method

Servlets can also access the ServletConfig object by calling the getServletConfig() method. This method is specified in the javax.servlet.Servlet interface.

Alternatively, servlets extending the GenericServlet, or its subclass HttpServlet can also call the methods of the ServletConfig interface directly. This is because the GenericServlet also implements the ServletConfig interface.

Servlet Exceptions

The javax.servlet package specifies two exception classes: javax.servlet.ServletException, and javax.servlet.UnavailableException.

The ServletException Class

```
public class ServletException extends java.lang.Exception
```

This is a generic exception, which can be thrown by the init(), service(), doXXX(), and destroy() methods. The class provides the following constructors:

```
public ServletException()
public ServletException(String message)
```

While creating objects of type ServletException, you can embed any application-level exception (called the **root-cause**). The containers use the root-cause exception for logging purposes. For instance, you can embed a java.sql.SQLException in a javax.servlet.ServletException. There are two additional constructors to support root-cause exceptions:

```
public ServletException(Throwable cause)
public ServletException(String message, Throwable cause)
```

The getRootCause() method returns the root-cause exception:

```
public Throwable getRootCause()
```

The UnavailableException Class

```
public class UnavailableException extends ServletException
```

javax.servlet.UnavailableException is a special type of servlet exception. Since this servlet extends the javax.servlet.ServletException, all servlet methods that can throw a javax.servlet.Exception can also throw a javax.servlet.UnavailableException.

The purpose of this is to indicate to the web container that the servlet is either temporarily or permanently unavailable.

This class specifies the following constructors:

```
public UnavailableException(String message)
```

This constructs a new permanently unavailable exception with the given message:

```
public UnavailableException(String message, int seconds)
```

This constructs a new unavailable exception with the given message. The seconds argument indicates the duration in seconds for which the servlet is unavailable.

We shall discuss later the exact behavior of the container for temporary and permanent failures.

The Servlet Lifecycle

As discussed previously, the container is a runtime that manages the servlets. Of the various responsibilities of a container, lifecycle management is the most crucial. In the case of servlets, the lifecycle events are specified in the javax.servlet.Servlet interface of the Servlet API. Although the lifecycle management is a container's responsibility, as servlet developers, we should make sure that our servlets follow the lifecycle model, and that they are not implemented in a way that contradicts this.

The Servlet interface methods relevant to the servlet lifecycle are init(), service(), and destroy(). The lifecycle starts with the container calling the init() method, and ends with the container calling the destroy() method.

The lifecycle of a servlet consists of the following fundamental stages:

❏ **Instantiation**
The web container creates an instance of the servlet

❏ **Initialization**
The container calls the instance's init() method

❏ **Service**
If the container has a request for the servlet, it calls the servlets instance's service() method

❏ **Destroy**
Before destroying the instance, the container calls the servlet instance's destroy() method

❏ **Unavailable**
The instance is destroyed and marked for garbage collection

The UML state diagram below shows the possible transitions in the servlet lifecycle:

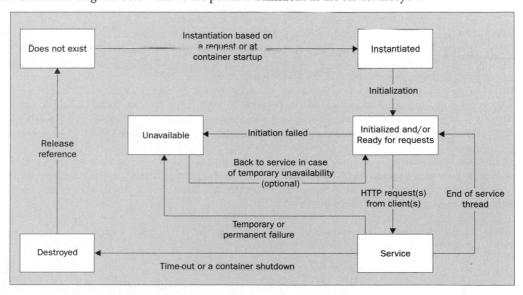

The container creates a servlet instance in response to an incoming HTTP request, or at container startup. After instantiation, the container initializes the instance by invoking its init() method. After initialization, the servlet instance is ready to serve incoming requests. The purpose of this initialization process is to load any initialization parameters required for the servlet. We'll see how this can be accomplished in the next section.

During the initialization process, a servlet instance can throw a ServletException, or an UnavailableException. The UnavailableException is a subclass of ServletException. While the ServletException can be used to indicate general initialization failures (such as failure to find initialization parameters), UnavailableException is for reporting non-availability of the instance for servicing requests. For example, if your servlet depends on an RMI server, and you're verifying if the server is reachable for service, your servlet instance can throw a UnavailableException to indicate that it is temporarily or permanently unavailabile. If your servlet instance determines that the unavailability should be temporary, it may indicate so while constructing the UnavailableException, by specifying the number of seconds of unavailability to the exception's constructor. When such a failure occurs, the container suspends all requests to your servlet for the specified period, and brings it back to an available state at the end of the period. If you don't specify an unavailability setting internally, the servlet will be unavailable when the container restarts. One of the applications of this exception is when one of your backend components or systems is not accessible temporarily. In general, if your application logic is such that certain failures can be resolved by retrying after a while, you can use this exception.

The container guarantees that before the service() method is called, the init() method will be allowed to complete, and also that before the servlet is destroyed, its destroy() method will be called.

The servlet may throw a ServletException or an UnavailableException during its service() method, in which case the container will suspend requests for that instance either temporarily or permanently. It is important for you to design your servlets considering temporary or permanent failures.

In theory, there is nothing to stop a web container from performing the entire servlet lifecycle each time a servlet is requested. In practice, web containers load and initialize servlets during the container startup, or when the servlet is first called, and keep that servlet instance in memory to service all the requests it receives. The container may decide at any time to release the servlet reference, thus ending the servlet's lifecycle. This could happen, for example, if the servlet has not been called for some time, or if the container is shutting down. When this happens, the container calls the destroy() method.

In the typical servlet lifecycle model, the web container creates a single instance of each servlet. But what happens if the servlet's service() method is still running when the web container receives another request? For servlets that do not implement the javax.servlet.SingleThreadModel interface, the container invokes the same servlet instance in each request thread. Therefore, it is always possible that the service() method is being executed in more than one service thread, requiring that the service() method be thread-safe. Apart from not accessing thread-safe resources (such as writing to files), we should also consider keeping our servlets stateless (that is, not define any attributes in your servlet classes). When defining instance variables in our servlets, we should make sure that such variables are manipulated in a thread-safe manner.

We've previously discussed the behavior of servlets implementing the javax.servlet.SingleThreadModel interface. Recall that, for such servlets, the container could either serialize requests, or maintain a pool of servlet instances and allocate each request to a different instance in the pool, or use a combination of these two.

The following diagram shows the sequence of events showing a servlet being loaded, servicing two requests in quick succession, and then being unloaded when the server is shut down:

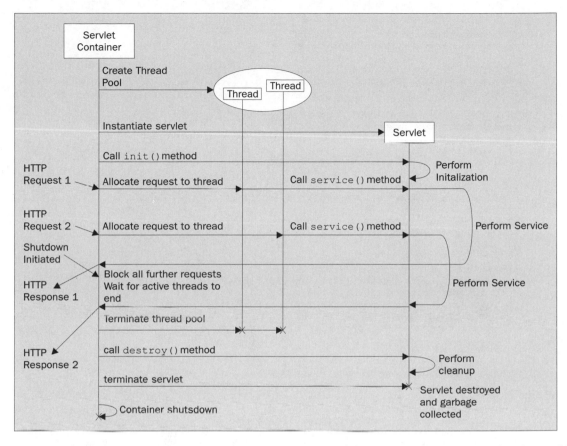

There is yet another situation where a container could create more than one instance of a servlet: this could be the case when a servlet class is added in the deployment descriptor more than once, possibly with different initialization parameters.

You might find the above instantiation approaches complex. In order to avoid problems, your servlets should make little or no assumption about instantiation. For example, we should not assume that the same servlet instance is used for all requests/clients, or that only one thread at a time is executing a service() method.

The Servlet Lifecycle – FreakServlet

Let's now consider an example, to better understand the servlet lifecycle. The example consists of a single servlet called FreakServlet, which demonstrates the various states in the lifecycle of a typical servlet, including unavailability. You'll shortly see why this is called a FreakServlet.

Enter the following source in %BOOK_HOME%\Ch06\freakServlet\src\FreakServlet.java, where BOOK_HOME is the root directory for your source code:

```
// Import servlet packages
import javax.servlet.http.HttpServlet;
import javax.servlet.http.HttpServletRequest;
```

```java
import javax.servlet.http.HttpServletResponse;
import javax.servlet.ServletException;
import javax.servlet.UnavailableException;

// Import other Java packages
import java.io.IOException;
import java.io.PrintWriter;

public class FreakServlet extends HttpServlet {
  java.util.Vector states;
  java.util.Random random;
  int waitInterval;
  public static final int DEFAULT_WAIT_INTERVAL = 10;

  public FreakServlet() {
    states = new java.util.Vector();
    random = new java.util.Random();
    waitInterval = DEFAULT_WAIT_INTERVAL;
    states.add(createState("Instantiation"));
  }

  public void init() throws ServletException {
    states.add(createState("Initialization"));
    String waitIntervalString =
      getServletConfig().getInitParameter("waitInterval");
    if (waitIntervalString != null) {
      waitInterval = new Integer(waitIntervalString).intValue();
    }
  }

  protected void doGet(HttpServletRequest request, HttpServletResponse response)
                throws ServletException, IOException {

    if (random.nextBoolean()) {
      // Not available for waitInterval seconds
      states.add(createState("Unavailable from doGet"));
      throw new UnavailableException("Unavailable from doGet", waitInterval);
    }

    states.add(createState("Service"));

    response.setContentType("text/html");
    PrintWriter out = response.getWriter();

    // Send acknowledgment to the browser
    out.println("<html>");
    out.println("<meta http-equiv=\"Pragma\" content=\"no-cache\">");
    out.println("<head><title>");

    out.println("FreakServlet: State History");
    out.println("</title></head>");
    out.println("<body>");
    out.println("<h1>FreakServlet: State History</h1>");

    out.println("<a href=\"/lifeCycle/servlet/freak\">Reload</a></p>");

    for (int i = 0; i < states.size(); i++) {
      out.println("<p> " + states.elementAt(i) + "</p>");
    }

    out.println("</body></html>");
    out.close();
```

```
  }

  public void destroy() {
    states.add(createState("Destroy"));
    system.out.println("Flushing state history of LifeCycleTest servlet.");
    for (int i = 0; i < states.size(); i++) {
      system.out.println(states.elementAt(i).toString());
    }
  }

  private String createState(String message) {
    return "[" + (new java.util.Date()).toString() + "] " + message;
  }
}
```

Create a web.xml file (deployment descriptor) in %BOOK_HOME%\Ch06\freakServlet\WEB-INF\ with the following <servlet> and <error-page> definitions:

```
<?xml version="1.0" encoding="ISO-8859-1"?>

<!DOCTYPE web-app
    PUBLIC "-//Sun Microsystems, Inc.//DTD Web Application 2.3//EN"
    "http://java.sun.com/j2ee/dtds/web-app_2_3.dtd">

<web-app>
  <servlet>
    <servlet-name>freak</servlet-name>
    <display-name>freak</display-name>
    <servlet-class>FreakServlet</servlet-class>
    <init-param>
      <param-name>waitInterval</param-name>
      <param-value>5</param-value>
    </init-param>
  </servlet>

  <error-page>
    <exception-type>javax.servlet.UnavailableException</exception-type>
    <location>/unavailable.html</location>
  </error-page>
</web-app>
```

Now, compile the servlet into the %BOOK_HOME%\Ch06\freakServlet\WEB-INF\classes directory. Refer to the previous chapter for instructions.

Also copy the following HTML into %BOOK_HOME%\Ch06\freakServlet\unavailable.html:

```
<html>
  <meta http-equiv="Pragma" content="no-cache">
  <head>
    <title>FreakServlet Unavailable</title>
  </head>

  <body>
    <h1>FreakServlet Unavailable</h1>

    <p>FreakServlet is temporarily unavailable. Please try
       <a href="/lifeCycle/servlet/freak">again</a>.</p>
  </body>
</html>
```

Now we need to create our WAR file for deployment in the J2EE Reference Implementation (we'll cover the web application wizard later in the chapter but for now we'll just get our servlet deployed as easily as possible).

Make sure you have the following files in following locations:

```
/unavailable.html
/WEB-INF/
          web.xml
          classes/
                    FreakServlet.class
```

Now create a WAR file using the jar command:

```
jar -cf FreakServlet.war unavailable.html WEB-INF
```

We're now ready to deploy the WAR file. Start the J2EE Reference Implementation server by running the `j2ee.bat` file in the `%J2EE_HOME%\bin` directory, then run the `deploytool.bat` file in the same directory, to start the deployment tool. When the deployment tool loads, create a new application called `freakServlet`:

Then add our WAR file to the new application by using the **Add to Application | Web WAR** option from the **File** menu:

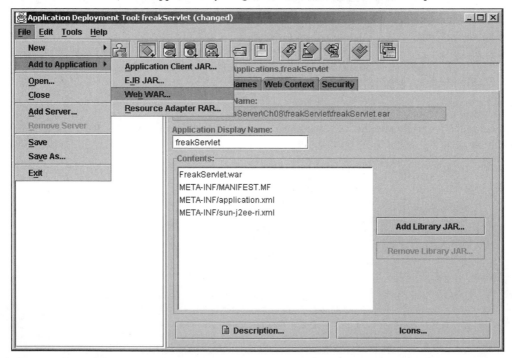

Select the WAR file in the open dialog to load the WAR file into the application. We can now simply deploy our application by choosing **Deploy** on the **Tools** menu:

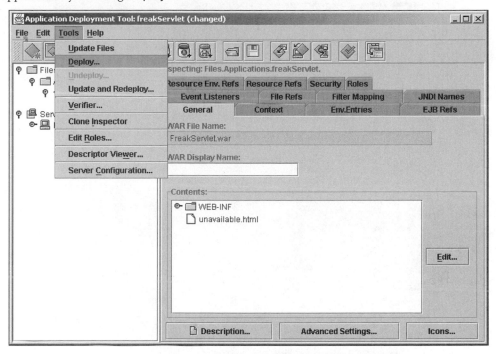

We don't need to do anything on the first screen besides double-check we're deploying the correct application:

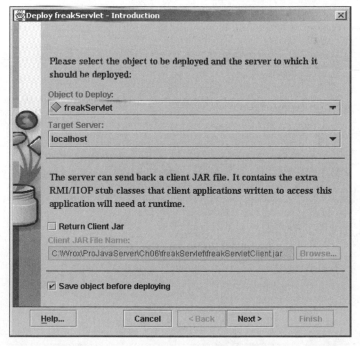

On the next screen, we need to provide the context that we will use to browse to our application. Set it to lifeCycle:

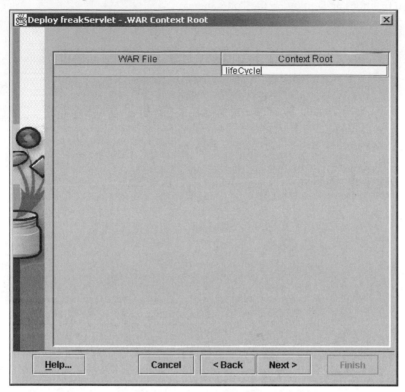

Proceed to the final screen and select Finish to deploy the application into the server:

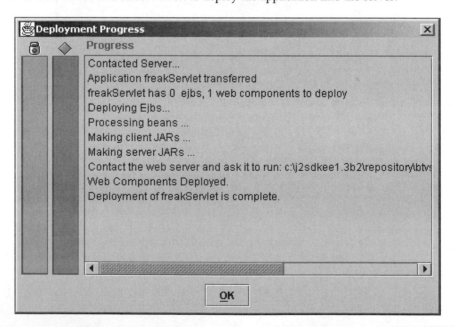

You're now ready to test this servlet. Browse to http://localhost:8000/lifeCycle/servlet/freak to load the servlet. Reload the URL a few times by using your browser's reload/refresh button. There are two types of responses that you could see in the browser. You will either see the list of states in the lifecycle of the FreakServlet, as follows:

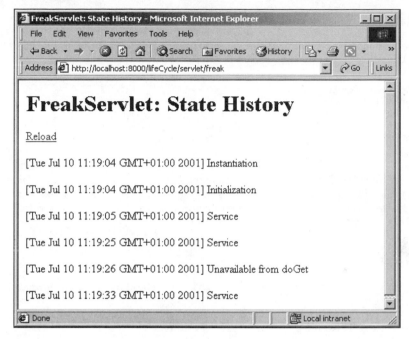

or you will see the response when the servlet enters the unavailable state:

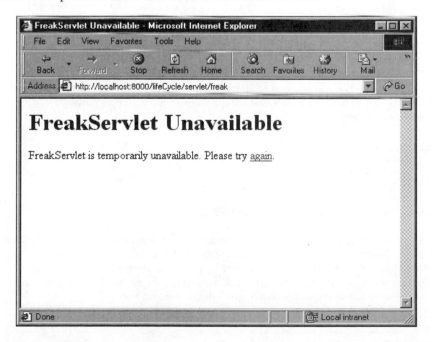

In either case, click on the Reload or again links in the browser to invoke this servlet a number of times.

Now let's see how these messages are generated.

Instantiation

This state corresponds to the construction of the servlet instance by the container. Refer to the constructor of FreakServlet:

```
public FreakServlet() {
    states = new java.util.Vector();
    random = new java.util.Random();
    waitInterval = DEFAULT_WAIT_INTERVAL;
    states.add(createState("Instantiation"));
}
```

This constructor initializes a vector and a random number generator. In this exercise, the vector states is used to store the states as they occur. Each state is represented as a string prepended by a date string. The random number generator is used to randomly throw UnavailableException from the doGet() method. A 'freak' servlet!

Initialization

This is the second state in any servlet. Refer to the init() method of the FreakServlet:

```
public void init() throws ServletException {
    states.add(createState("Initialization"));
    String waitIntervalString =
        getServletConfig().getInitParameter("waitInterval");
    if (waitIntervalString != null) {
        waitInterval = new Integer(waitIntervalString).intValue();
    }
}
```

This method adds another state called "Initialization" to the state history. It also extracts a parameter "waitInterval" from the servlet configuration. The FreakServlet uses this number while throwing UnavailableExceptions. Remember that we specified an initialization parameter (<init-param>) in the deployment descriptor:

```
<init-param>
    <param-name>waitInterval</param-name>
    <param-value>5</param-value>
</init-param>
```

This specifies an initialization parameter with name "waitInterval" with value "5".

When the web container loads a web application, it also loads the initialization parameters associated with the application. Upon loading the application, the container creates a ServletConfig object for each servlet in the application. You can obtain this ServletConfig object via the getServletConfig() method, and extract the initialization parameters. The getInitParameter() method may return a null value if the requested parameter is not found in the deployment descriptor.

Also note that only string parameters are allowed in the deployment descriptor. In the case of FreakServlet, since we're interested in an integer time interval, we should programmatically convert the extracted string "5" into an int.

Note that the above two states occur only once during the lifetime of a servlet instance.

Service

This is the third state in the servlet lifecycle. Refer to the implementation of the doGet() method. This method generates a random Boolean, and if the Boolean is true, throws an UnavailableException, indicating that this servlet will not be available for processing requests for the next waitInterval seconds:

```
if (random.nextBoolean()) {

  // Not available for waitInterval seconds
  states.add(createState("Unavailable from doGet"));
  throw new UnavailableException("Unavailable from doGet", waitInterval);
}
```

Before throwing the exception, the servlet adds a state called "Unavailable from doGet". In this case, you would see the browser output saying the servlet was unavailable. This page shows an error page indicating that the FreakServlet is unavailable. How is this page displayed?

Once the container receives the UnavailableException (or any exception mentioned in the throws clause of the service() method), the container verifies if an error page is specified in the deployment descriptor for that exception. In the case of FreakServlet, the deployment descriptor has the entry:

```
<error-page>
  <exception-type>javax.servlet.UnavailableException</exception-type>
  <location>/unavailable.html</location>
</error-page>
```

This specifies that the location of the error page for the UnavailableException. Upon finding this mapping information, the container displays the error page whenever this exception is thrown. You can extend this mechanism to display friendly messages in the case of other exceptions. If you do not specify error pages, and your servlet throws an exception, depending on the implementation of the container, you may get not-so-friendly messages. In the case of Tomcat (the servlet engine behind the J2EE Reference Implementation), you'll see a stack trace pointing to the source of the exception. Here is a sample stack trace:

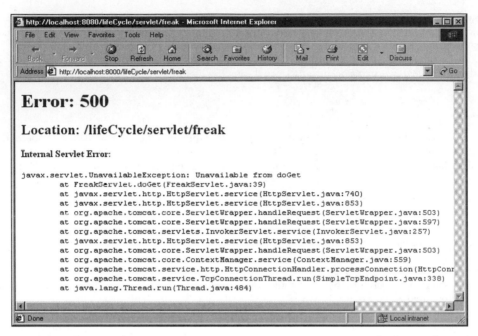

If the generated random number is `false`, `FreakServlet` generates a page displaying the states recorded so far. It uses methods in the `HttpServletRequest` interface to set the content type of the response, and generate the HTML:

```
        states.add(createState("Service"));

        response.setContentType("text/html");
        PrintWriter out = response.getWriter();

        // Send acknowledgment to the browser
        out.println("<html>");
        out.println("<meta http-equiv=\"Pragma\" content=\"no-cache\">");
        out.println("<head><title>");

        out.println("FreakServlet: State History");
        out.println("</title></head>");
        out.println("<body>");
        out.println("<h1>FreakServlet: State History</h1>");

        out.println("<a href=\"/lifeCycle/servlet/freak\">Reload</a></p>");

        for (int i = 0; i < states.size(); i++) {
          out.println("<p> " + states.elementAt(i) + "</p>");
        }

        out.println("</body></html>");
        out.close();
    }
```

There are four steps for generating the response:

❑   The first step is to set the content type for the response. The receiving application (the browser) uses this information to know how to treat the response data. In this case, since we're generating HTML output, the content type is being set to `"text/html"`.

❑ The second step is to get a `PrintWriter` object from the response. `PrintWriter` is a class from the `java.io` package that extends the `java.io.Writer` abstract class. In the case of servlets, the container constructs the `PrintWriter` object from the `java.io.OutputStream` object associated with the underlying network connection from the client. With TCP/IP based implementations, containers usually get a `java.io.OutputStream` object from the socket, use that object to create the `PrinterWriter` object, and associate it with the `HttpServletResponse` object. As a result, from within the servlet, you'll be able to write to the output stream associated with the network association.

❑ Note the `meta` tags in the HTML generated above. These tags indicates the browser that it should not cache this page. You'll find a similar tag in `unavailable.html`. Without these tags, you'll notice that your browser does not reload the page when you click on the **Reload** or **again** links.

❑ The `PrintWriter` class has several methods to print various data types to the associated stream. In this case, we use the `println()` method with a `java.lang.String` argument.

Finally, remember to close the `PrintWriter` object at the end.

Destroy

This is the final stage in the servlet lifecycle. In the case of `FreakServlet`, the `destroy()` method is called before shutting down the server, upon which the web container ensures that responses are properly flushed. The `FreakServlet` has a simple implementation for this state:

```
public void destroy() {
  states.add(createState("Destroy"));
  System.out.println("Flushing state history of LifeCycleTest servlet.");
  for (int i = 0; i < states.size(); i++) {
    System.out.println(states.elementAt(i).toString());
  }
}
```

This method adds a state called `"Destroy"` to the `states` vector, and outputs the complete state history to the server window

Finally, it is worth keeping in mind a couple of points on the usage of various Servlet API methods/objects during the lifecycle:

❑ Objects of classes such as `ServletConfig`, `ServletContext`, `HttpServletRequest`, and `HttpServletResponse` are valid only between the `init()` and `destroy()` method calls. That is, you should not use these objects before `init()` is called, or after `destroy()` is called. For example, your constructor should not use the `log()` method, because the `log()` method is implemented by the `ServletContext` object associated with your servlet. Your servlet instance will not have a valid reference to a `ServletContext` object before the call to `init()`.

❑ Also notice the vector that we're using as an instance variable in the `FreakServlet`. Since this is not a `SingleThreadModel` servlet, the container creates only one instance of this servlet, and routes all requests in concurrent execution threads to the `doGet()` method. Since this `states` vector is an instance variable, read and write operations on this object should be thread-safe. In the case of the `java.util.Vector` class, the `add()` and `size()` methods are `synchronized`. Because of this, multiple users of the `FreakServlet` can interact with its lifecycle, and still see the most up-to-date state history

This ends our discussion on the servlet lifecycle.

Requests and Responses

The `javax.servlet.HttpServletRequest` and `javax.servlet.HttpServletResponse` interfaces are the classes that servlets depend on for accessing HTTP requests and responses. As shown in the UML class diagram at the beginning of this chapter, here is the complete list of interfaces and classes for dealing with requests and responses:

- ❏ *javax.servlet.ServletRequest*
- ❏ javax.servlet.ServletRequestWrapper
- ❏ *javax.servlet.ServletResponse*
- ❏ javax.servlet.ServletResponseWrapper
- ❏ javax.servlet.ServletInputStream
- ❏ javax.servlet.ServletOutputStream
- ❏ *javax.servlet.http.HttpServletRequest*
- ❏ javax.servlet.http.HttpServletRequestWrapper
- ❏ *javax.servlet.http.HttpServletResponse*
- ❏ javax.servlet.http.HttpServletResponseWrapper

In this list, items in italics are interfaces, while the rest are abstract or concrete classes. The `HttpServletRequest` and `HttpServletResponse` interfaces are more specialized versions of `ServletRequest` and `ServletResponse` interfaces for the HTTP. The two classes can be used to read from and write to the input and output streams respectively. The classes with names ending with `Wrapper` are concrete classes of the corresponding interfaces.

The ServletRequest Interface

```
public interface ServletRequest
```

This interface specifies an abstraction of client requests for a servlet. The web container creates an instance of this object while calling the `service()` method of the `GenericServlet` or the `HttpServlet`. For reference, the complete list of methods in this interface is as follows:

```
public Object getAttribute(String name)
public void setAttribute(String name, Object attribute)
public Enumeration getAttributeNames()
public void removeAttribute(String name)
public Locale getLocale()
public Enumeration getLocales()
public String getCharacterEncoding()
public void setCharacterEncoding(String env)
public int getContentLength()
public String getContentType)
public ServletInputStream getInputStream()
public String getParameter(String name)
public Enumeration getParameterNames()
public String[] getParameterValues()
public Map getParameterMap()
public String getProtocol()
public String getScheme()
```

```
public String getServerName()
public int getServerPort()
public BufferedReader getReader()
public String getRemoteAddr()
public String getRemoteHost()
public boolean isSecure()
public RequestDispatcher getRequestDispatcher(String path)
```

Since this interface has quite a lot of methods, let's group them based on their usage, and discuss some of the most commonly required methods.

Methods for Request Parameters

The following methods can be used to access the request parameters. In the case of HTTP requests, these methods can be used for both GET and POST requests.

The getParameter() Method

```
public String getParameter(String name)
```

This will attempt to locate a parameter with the given key ,name, (case-sensitive) in the request and return its value. If there are multiple values for the given parameter, then this method returns the first value in the list. This method returns null if the key is not found in the request.

The getParameterValues() Method

```
public String[] getParameterValues(String key)
```

If a parameter can return multiple values, such as a set of check boxes, a multi-selection list, or even multiple controls with the same name, this method returns an array containing the parameter values.

The getParameterNames() Method

```
public Enumeration getParameterNames()
```

This method returns an enumeration of all of the parameter names for the request. If the request has no parameters, it returns an empty enumeration.

The getParameterMap() Method

```
public Map getParameterMap()
```

This method returns a java.util.Map containing all request parameters. In this map, the name of the parameter is the key while its value is the map value. Both keys and values are strings. Note that this map is immutable, and you can change the contents of this map.

Methods for Request Attributes

Apart from request parameters, web containers or servlets/JSPs can attach attributes to requests. The Servlet API specification specifies three different approaches for storing and retrieving attributes. One of them is attaching attributes to request objects. The other two approaches use the HttpSession, and ServletContext (to be discussed in the next chapter) for storing and retrieving attributes. As we shall see in Chapter 10, the JSP specification provides an additional mechanism using PageContext to store and retrieve attributes. Each of these approaches provides the notion of a scope for the attributes to exist. In the case of attributes attached to request objects, the lifetime of these attributes is that of the request itself.

In the servlet parlance, an attribute is a named Java language object. While setting an attribute, you assign a name to the attribute, and while retrieving the attribute, specify the same name. Names are String objects.

The purpose of attributes in the request scope is to allow the container or another servlet to send additional data to a servlet or a JSP. For the application developer, this is useful when using the RequestDispatcher object to forward requests from one servlet to another. We'll learn more about this approach in Chapter 7.

The following methods can be used to manage attributes in the request context.

The getAttribute() Method

```
public Object getAttribute(String name)
```

This method returns the value of the named attribute (or null if the named attribute does not exist).

The getAttributeNames() Method

```
public Enumeration getAttributeNames()
```

This method returns an enumeration of all the attributes contained in the request. It returns an empty enumeration if there are no attributes in the request.

The setAttribute() Method

```
public void setAttribute(String name, Object attribute)
```

This method sets a named attribute.

The removeAttribute() Method

```
public void removeAttribute(String name)
```

This method removes the named attribute from the request.

Methods for Input

As discussed previously, the ServletRequest holds a reference to the underlying client connection. Using the following methods, you can access the stream and writer objects associated with the request.

The getInputStream() Method

```
public ServletInputStream getInputStream() throws java.io.IOException
```

This method can be used to access the body of the request using a ServletInputStream object.

The getReader() Method

```
public java.io.BufferedReader getReader() throws java.io.IOException
```

This method can be used to access the body of the request using a buffered reader object.

The getCharacterEncoding() Method

```
public String getCharacterEncoding()
```

This method returns the name of the character encoding used in the body of this request.

The setCharacterEncoding() Method

```
public void setCharacterEncoding(String env)
```

This method can be used to override the name of the character encoding used in the body of the request. This method should be called before accessing parameters from the request, or before obtaining the `Reader` or `InputStream` from the request.

The ServletRequestWrapper Class

```
public class ServletRequestWrapper implements ServletRequest
```

This class provides a convenient implementation of the `javax.servlet.ServletRequest` interface. Except for a constructor, this class does not introduce any new methods. Discussion of the role of these wrapper classes is reserved for later in this chapter.

The HttpServletRequest Interface

```
public interface HttpServletRequest extends ServletRequest
```

The most commonly used methods in this interface are the methods for accessing request parameters. To understand how to use these methods, consider how HTTP allows data to be passed to the web server. As discussed in the previous chapter, HTTP allows you to submit parameters along with a request. In a GET request, these parameters are appended to the request URL in the form of a query string, whereas in a POST request the parameters are sent within the body of the request in `x-www-form-urlencoded` format. In any case, these parameters are represented as key-value pairs. HTTP does not require that the keys are unique, so for some keys, there can be a list of values. Examples include multiple selection listboxes or checkbox groups.

When you build an HTML form for GET or POST requests, you specify certain controls using `<input>` tags. Each control has a `type`, such as `checkbox`, `text`, or `submit`, and can also have a `name` and/or a `value`. The `name` attribute defines the key by which the value returned to the server will be known. The `value` attribute has different effects on different controls. Obviously, if we give more than one `<input>` tag the same name, we could have several key/value pairs with the same key as part of our request. The following table shows the values submitted to the server for different types of form controls:

Control Type	Description	Value Returned
text	Single line text input field, with `value` attribute as default content	Text entered by user, or the default
textarea	Multiple line text area, with `value` attribute as the default content.	Text entered by the user, or the default
password	Single line password entry field (shows * instead of character entered)	Text entered by user
checkbox	Standard checkbox	If checked: `value` attribute (or `"on"` if not specified) If *not* checked: no key-value pair returne;

Table continued on following page

289

Control Type	Description	Value Returned
radio	Standard radio button – all buttons with the same name form a button group, so only one can be selected	value attribute of selected radio button only
select	Used to create a list of items from which the user can select can be single-valued or multi-valued	User selected items or the default(s)
submit	Submit button, with value attribute as button caption	None, unless name attribute is supplied. Default for value is "Submit"
hidden	Form field that is not visible in the browser and thus cannot be modified by the user	value attribute

There are other controls, but these will do for now. The most common reason for having multiple controls with the same name is to be able to build sets of radio buttons and checkboxes, and multiple-selection select controls. The radio button set will return the single selected value, and checkboxes or multiple-selection select controls will return all of the selected values.

Any object that implements the HttpServletRequest interface (such as the HTTP request object passed in from the web container) will give the servlet access to all of the request data through its methods.

Note that since the HttpServletRequest interface is meant to encapsulate HTTP, this interface (in combination with the methods provided in the ServletRequest interface) provides numerous methods for accessing the HTTP request:

```
public String getAuthType()
public Cookie[] getCookies()
public long getDateHeader(String name)
public String getHeader(String name)
public Enumeration getHeaders(String name)
public Enumeration getHeaderNames()
public int getIntHeader(String name)
public String getMethod()
public String getContextPath()
public String getPathInfo()
public String getPathTranslated()
public String getQueryString()
public String getRemoteUser()
public boolean isUserInRole(String role)
public getUserPrincipal()
public String getRequestedSessionId()
public boolean isRequestedSessionIdValid()
public boolean isRequestedSessionIdFromCookie()
public boolean isRequestedSessionIdFromURL()
public String getRequestURI
public StringBuffer getRequestURL
public String getServletPath()
public HttpSession getSession()
public HttpSession getSession(boolean create)
```

The following are some of the most commonly used methods specified in the HttpServletRequest interface. You'll encounter some of the remaining methods in the next chapter.

Methods for Request Path and URL

The first group of methods allows a servlet to obtain the URL and request path with which it was invoked.

The getPathInfo() Method

```
public String getPathInfo()
```

This method returns any extra path information associated with the request URL. In general, you invoke a servlet using its alias or the class name. For instance, you can access a servlet `MyServlet` using the URL `http://host:port/myApp/MyServlet`, where `myApp` is the application context. However, you can send additional path information to the servlet, say, as `http://<HOST>:<PORT>/myApp/MyServlet/wrox`. In this case, `/wrox` is the additional path information. The servlet can use the `getPathInfo()` to obtain this path information.

This method returns `null` if there is no additional path in the request.

The getPathTranslated() Method

```
public String getPathTranslated()
```

This method translates the extra path information into a real path. For instance, in the above example, if the `MyServlet` class is located in the `c:\work\myApp\WEB-INF\classes` directory, this method returns `c:\work\myApp\wrox` as the translated path.

This method returns `null` if there is no additional path in the request.

The getQueryString() Method

```
public String getQueryString()
```

This method returns the query string associated with the request.

The getRequestURI() Method

```
public String getRequestURI()
```

This method returns the URI path associated with the request. In the above example, this method would return `/myApp/MyServlet/wrox`.

The getRequestURL() Method

```
public StringBuffer getRequestURL()
```

This method reconstructs the URL that the client used to make this request. The returned string includes the protocol, server name, port, and the server path for this request.

The getServletPath() Method

```
public String getServletPath()
```

This method returns the URI path associated with the servlet. This excludes any extra path information and query string. For instance, in the above example, this method would return `/myApp/MyServlet` as the servlet path.

Methods for HTTP Headers

The next group of methods allows servlets to read HTTP headers sent with the request.

The getHeader() Method

```
public String getHeader(String name)
```

This method returns the value of the named header from the HTTP request. This method returns `null` if the request does not include the specified header.

The getHeaders() Method

```
public Enumeration getHeaders(String name)
```

This method returns an enumeration of all request header values.

The getHeaderNames() Method

```
public Enumeration getHeaderNames()
```

This method returns an enumeration of names of request headers.

The getMethod() Method

```
public String getMethod()
```

This method returns the type of the HTTP request, such as GET, POST, and so on.

Apart from these methods, there are several methods specific to HTTP sessions. We shall discuss some of these methods in the next chapter.

The HttpServletRequestWrapper Class

```
public class HttpServletRequestWrapper implements HttpServletRequest
```

The class provides a convenient implementation of the `javax.servlet.http.HttpServletRequest` interface and, except for a constructor, it does not introduce any new methods. The role of these wrapper classes is discussed in detail later in this chapter.

The ServletResponse Interface

```
public interface ServletResponse
```

This is the response counterpart of the `ServletRequest` object, and abstracts most of the methods necessary for constructing responses from servlets. This interface specifies the following methods:

```
public String getCharacterEncoding()
public ServletOutputStream getOutputStream()
public PrintWriter getWriter()
public void setContentLength(int length)
```

```
public void setContentType(String type)
public void setBufferSize(int size)
public int getBufferSize()
public void reset()
public boolean isCommitted()
public void flushBuffer()
public void resetBuffer()
public void setLocale()
public Locale getLocale()
```

The following are some of the most commonly used methods of this interface.

Methods for Content Type and Length

These methods allow the servlet to set the response's MIME content type and the content length.

The setContentType() Method

```
public void setContentType(String type)
```

This method sets the content type of the response. If you're using the `PrintWriter` object (discussed shortly) to generate the response, before writing the response, you should call `setContentType()` to set the MIME type of the HTTP response. In the case of HTML, the MIME type should be set to `"text/HTML"`.

The setContentLength() Method

```
public void setContentLength(int size)
```

This method can be used to set the content-length header of the content.

Methods for Output

The following methods are useful for generating text or binary content in the response.

The getOutputStream() Method

```
public ServletOutputStream getOutputStream() throws java.io.IOException
```

This method returns a `ServletOutputStream` object that can be used for writing binary data in the response. This `ServletOutputStream` class is a subclass of `java.io.OutputStream`. On a given `HttpServletResponse` object, you should call this method only once. If you try to call this method more than once, you will encounter an `IllegalStateException`.

The getWriter() Method

```
public java.io.PrintWriter getWriter() throws java.io.IOException
```

This method returns a `PrintWriter` object that can be used to send character text in the response. The `PrintWriter` automatically translates Java's internal Unicode characters into the correct encoding so that they can be read on the client machine. With the `PrintWriter` object, you would typically write data to the response object using its `println(String string)` method. Similar to the `getOutputStream()` method, this method also should not be called more than once on a given `HttpServletResponse` object.

Moreover, only one of the above two methods should be called on any `HttpServletResponse` object.

293

Methods for Buffered Output

You can also send buffered response from your servlets. The following methods are useful for controlling the buffering.

If you're sending a large amount of data in the response, you should consider setting the buffer size to smaller values, so that the user can start receiving the data quickly.

Buffering also allows you to abort the content generated so far, and restart the generation.

The setBufferSize() Method

```
public void setBufferSize(int size)
```

This method sets the preferred buffer size for the body of the response. Note that the web container will use a buffer at least as large as the size requested.

The getBufferSize() Method

```
public int getBufferSize()
```

This method returns the actual buffer size used for the response.

The resetBuffer() Method

```
public void resetBuffer()
```

This method clears content of the underlying buffer without clearing the response headers or the status code. If the response has already been committed, this method throws an `IllegalStateException`.

The flushBuffer() Method

```
public void flushBuffer() throws java.io.IOException
```

This method forces any content in the buffer to be written to the client.

The isCommitted() Method

```
public boolean isCommitted()
```

This method returns a boolean indicating if the response in the buffer has been committed.

The reset() Method

```
public void reset()
```

This method is useful for resetting the buffer thereby discarding the content in the buffer.

The ServletResponseWrapper Class

```
public class ServletResponseWrapper implements ServletResponse
```

The class provides a convenient implementation of the `javax.servlet.ServletResponse` interface. Except for a constructor, this class does not introduce any new methods. We shall shortly see the role of these wrapper classes.

The HttpServletResponse Interface

```
public interface HttpServletResponse extends ServletResponse
```

The web container provides an object that implements this interface and passes it into the servlet through the `service()` method. The servlet can modify response headers and return results through the `HttpServletResponse` object. This interface includes the following methods:

```
public void addCookie (Cookie cookie)
public boolean containsHeader(String headerName)
public String encodeURL(String url)
public String encodeRedirecURL(String url)
public void sendError(int status)
public void sendError(int status, String message)
public void sendRedirect(String location)
public void setDateHeader(String headerName, long date)
public void setHeader(String headerName, String value)
public void addHeader(String headerName, String value)
public void addDateHeader(String headerName, long date)
public void addIntHeader(String headerName, int value)
public void setIntHeader(String headerName, int value)
public void setStatus(int status)
```

Apart from these methods, this interface also specifies a set of error codes that correspond to standard HTTP errors. Refer to the API documentation for this list.

The following are some of the basic methods for writing content in the response.

Methods for Error Handling

This group of methods allows a servlet to send an error message or to set the HTTP status code.

The sendError() Method

```
public void sendError(int status)
```

Servlets can use this method to indicate standard HTTP status codes. As seen in the case of `FreakServlet`, you can specify error pages for different HTTP errors and servlet exceptions. If there is a matching page for the specified status code, the container sends the specified page to the client. If there is no page specified, the container sends its default error page indicating the status code and a corresponding message.

The sendError() Method

```
public void sendError(int status, String message)
```

This message is similar to the `sendError(status)` method, except that it also accepts a status message. You can use this message to indicate specific failures.

The setStatus() Method

```
public void setStatus(int status)
```

This method can be used to send HTTP status codes that are not errors.

The sendRedirect() Method

```
public void sendRedirect(String location)
```

This method sends a redirect response to the client. The client receives the HTTP response code 302 indicating that temporarily the client is being redirected to the specified location. If the specified location is relative, this method converts it into an absolute URL before redirecting.

The HttpServletResponseWrapper Class

```
public class HttpServletResponseWrapper implements HttpServletResponse
```

The class provides a convenient implementation of the `javax.servlet.http.HttpServletResponse` interface. Except for a constructor, this class does not introduce any new methods. Next we'll take a detailed look at the role of these wrapper classes.

Role of Wrapper Classes

Four wrapper classes are introduced in the 2.3 version of the Servlet API, namely, `javax.servlet.ServletRequestWrapper`, `javax.servlet.ServletResponseWrapper`, `javax.servlet.http.HttpServletRequestWrapper`, and `javax.servlet.http.HttpServletResponseWrapper`.

All these classes add a constructor to the methods specified in the interfaces that they implement. The constructors are alike, and require an implementation of the interfaces they implement. For instance, to create an instance of `javax.servlet.http.HttpServletRequestWrapper`, you need to supply another implementation of the `javax.servlet.http.HttpServletRequest` interface.

Internally, all the methods of these classes delegate their job to the implementation class passed on via the constructor.

As you see, these classes do not add any extra functionality. So what exactly is their role? They simplify the job of creating concrete implementations of the request/response interfaces. For instance, consider a situation where we need to implement the `getParameter()` method of the `javax.servlet.http.HttpServletRequest` interface. Instead of implementing all the methods in this interface, we may use the wrapper class as shown in the following code snippet:

```
public class MyRequest extends HttpServletRequestWrapper {

  public MyRequest(HttpServletRequest request) {
    super(request);
    // Any other initialization
  }

  public String getParameter(String name) {
    // Your implementation here
  }
}
```

The remaining methods of this class simply delegate their implementation to the request object passed during construction. This way, we can modify the behavior of some or all of the methods of the request and response objects that the container provides.

However, where and how do we create instances of these classes? Note that, in order to instantiate these classes, we need a concrete implementation first. There are at least two scenarios where we get a chance to change the request and response objects:

❑ **The RequestDispatcher API**
From within servlets or JSP pages, you may invoke methods on the `javax.servlet.RequestDispatcher` interface. We'll learn more about this API in the next chapter. While invoking these methods, we need to explicitly pass on the request and response objects that are received via one of the `doXXX()` methods of our servlet. While doing so, we may create custom request and response objects and send them instead.

❑ **The Filter API**
There is a similar possibility with the filter API. As we'll see in Chapter 8, with the filter API we need to explicitly invoke the `doFilter()` method on the `FilterChain` object. This method requires request and response object. In this case too, we can send custom request and response objects instead of the request and response objects that the filter receives.

In both the cases, we can construct instances of custom request/response objects by passing the container-implemented instances as arguments.

In Chapter 9, we shall deal with a case where we need to modify the behavior of the container-supplied request object.

Servlet Programming – Tech Support Application

Having seen an overview of the Servlet API and the servlet lifecycle, let's now consider another application that involves:

❑ **Collecting a technical support request**
This part of the application illustrates obtaining parameters from HTTP requests

❑ **Storing the support request in a database**
This part of the application illustrates a thread-safe approach for generating sequence numbers, and storing data in the database

❑ **Generating a confirmation page**

This application requires a database for storing the technical support requests. In the current configuration, we are using the Cloudscape database.

> *Cloudscape is included within the J2EE SDK 1.3. You can also configure a different database by changing parameters in the deployment descriptor (described later).*

For this example, we will be creating a technical support request application for a fictitious company called XYZ Corporation. In order to develop this application, we will:

❑ Prepare an HTML page with a form to collect the technical support request

❑ Prepare the database tables, by creating the schema for the database tables

❑ Create the `TechSupportServlet` servlet to process the form, insert the request into the tables, and generate a confirmation page

Setting up the HTML Page

The purpose of this page is to provide a form for submitting technical support requests. You'll find that the controls used can be applied to numerous other forms. The following HTML contains the form for collecting technical support request data:

```html
<html>
<head>
  <title>XYZ Corporation, IT Department</title>
</head>
  <body>
    <h1>Technical Support Request</h1>
    <hr><br>
    <center>
      <form action="/techSupport/servlet/techSupport" method="POST">
      <table align="center" width="100%" cellspacing="2" cellpadding="2">
        <tr>
          <td align="right">First Name:</TD>
          <td><input type="Text" name="firstName" align="left" size="15"></td>
          <td align="right">Last Name:</TD>
          <td><input type="Text" name="lastName" align="left" size="15"></td>
        </tr>
        <tr>
          <td align="right">Email:</td>
          <td><input type="Text" name="email" align="left" size="25"></td>
          <td align="right">Phone:</td>
          <td><input type="Text" name="phone" align="left" size="15"></td>
        </tr>
        <tr>
          <td align="right">Software:</td>
          <td>
            <select name="software" size="1">
              <option value="Word">Microsoft Word</option>
              <option value="Excel">Microsoft Excel</option>
              <option value="Access">Microsoft Access</option>
              <option value="Outlook">Microsoft Outlook</option>
            </select>
          </td>
          <td align="right">Operating System:</td>
          <td>
            <select name="os" size="1">
              <option value="95">Windows 95</option>
              <option value="98">Windows 98</option>
              <option value="2KPro">Windows 2000 Pro</option>
              <option value="2KServer">Windows 2000 Server</option>
              <option value="XP">Windows XP</option>
            </select>
          </td>
        </tr>
      </table>

      <br>Problem Description
      <br>
      <textarea name="problem" cols="50" rows="4"></textarea>

      <hr><br>

      <input type="Submit" name="submit" value="Submit Request">
    </form>
  </center>
</body>
</html>
```

Here's what it looks like:

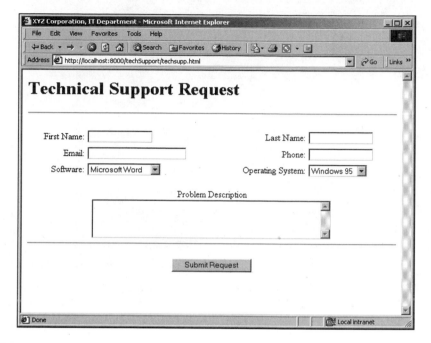

Prepare the Database

Before proceeding to write the servlet, we should prepare the database tables storing the technical support requests. Use your database vendor-provided tools (such as Cloudview for Cloudscape, or SQL Plus for Oracle) to create the database.

We'll use Cloudscape as it ships with the J2EE Reference Implementation. To work with Cloudscape we use a tool that is provided called Cloudview. To start Cloudview, from within the %J2EE_HOME%\lib\system directory run:

```
java -classpath tools.jar;cloudscape.jar COM.cloudscape.tools.cview
```

From the main window select File | New Database and create a new database under the default cloudscape folder (%J2EE_HOME%\cloudscape) called techSupport:

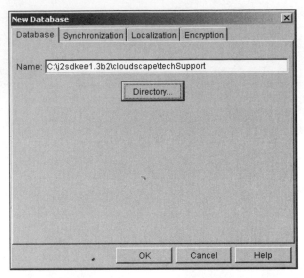

Then with the new database selected in the tree view, use the following SQL to create the table for this application:

```
CREATE TABLE SUPP_REQUESTS(REQUEST_ID        INT DEFAULT AUTOINCREMENT INITIAL 1
                                             INCREMENT 1 NOT NULL,
                           FIRST_NAME        VARCHAR(40),
                           LAST_NAME         VARCHAR(40),
                           EMAIL             VARCHAR(40),
                           PHONE             VARCHAR(15),
                           SOFTWARE          VARCHAR(40),
                           OS                VARCHAR(40),
                           PROBLEM           LONG VARCHAR);
```

The first column is set to an AUTOINCREMENT column, such that the database will automatically increment the REQUEST_ID column for us when a new request is being created.

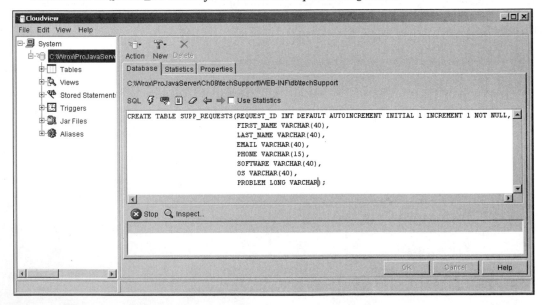

The schema for this application has one table, a SUPP_REQUESTS table for storing the technical support requests.

Writing the Servlet

Since the form in our HTML page has a POST request, we need to implement a servlet with the doPost() method overridden. In order to process the technical support request, there are several tasks that this method should perform:

❑ Extract form input from the HttpServletRequest, using the getParameter() methods

❑ Insert the data into a database table

❑ Read back from the new record the ID that the database has autoincremented for us

❑ Generate a confirmation page to the user with a reference number

The outline of the TechSupportServlet class is as follows:

```
// Import Servlet packages
import javax.servlet.ServletConfig;
import javax.servlet.ServletException;
import javax.servlet.UnavailableException;
import javax.servlet.http.HttpServlet;
import javax.servlet.http.HttpServletRequest;
import javax.servlet.http.HttpServletResponse;

// Import other Java packages
import java.io.PrintWriter;
import java.io.IOException;
import java.sql.Connection;
import java.sql.PreparedStatement;
import java.sql.ResultSet;
import java.sql.SQLException;
import javax.sql.DataSource;
import javax.naming.InitialContext;
import javax.naming.NamingException;

public class TechSupportServlet extends HttpServlet {

    // Methods will go here...

}
```

Extracting Form Data

To collect the data that the user entered into the form, we use the HttpServletRequest object's getParameter(String key) method. The only argument to this method is a String specifying the name of the parameter to be extracted. The following statements in the doPost() method of this servlet extracts the form parameters from the HttpServletRequest:

```
protected void doPost(HttpServletRequest req, HttpServletResponse res)
        throws ServletException, IOException {

    String firstName = req.getParameter("firstName");
    String lastName = req.getParameter("lastName");
    String email = req.getParameter("email");
    String phone = req.getParameter("phone");
    String software = req.getParameter("software");
    String os = req.getParameter("os");
    String problem = req.getParameter("problem");
```

Note that reading parameters from requests is simple. If the specified parameter is found in the request, the getParameter() method returns a valid String object. However, if the form does not contain the specified parameter at all, this method returns null. Note that JDBC drivers and databases expect legal field values (including non-null) in the SQL statements and prepared statements, and you may have to check for such conditions before executing JDBC statements.

Insert the Technical Support Request

After collecting the form parameters, the next step is to execute a SQL statement to insert this data:

```
int requestId = 0;
Connection connection = null;
String insertStatementStr =
  "INSERT INTO SUPP_REQUESTS (FIRST_NAME, LAST_NAME, EMAIL, PHONE, " +
  "SOFTWARE, OS, PROBLEM) VALUES(?, ?, ?, ?, ?, ?, ?)";
try {
  InitialContext initialContext = new InitialContext();
  DataSource dataSource =
            (DataSource)initialContext.lookup("jdbc/TechSupport");
  connection = dataSource.getConnection();

  PreparedStatement insertStatement =
    connection.prepareStatement(insertStatementStr);

  insertStatement.setString(1, firstName);
  insertStatement.setString(2, lastName);
  insertStatement.setString(3, email);
  insertStatement.setString(4, phone);
  insertStatement.setString(5, software);
  insertStatement.setString(6, os);
  insertStatement.setString(7, problem);
  insertStatement.executeUpdate();

  // Obtain the autoincremented requestId from the database
  String selectStatementStr = "SELECT MAX(REQUEST_ID) FROM SUPP_REQUESTS";

  PreparedStatement selectStatement =
                    connection.prepareStatement(selectStatementStr);
  ResultSet resultSet = selectStatement.executeQuery();

  resultSet.next(); // Move to the first row in the result set
  requestId = resultSet.getInt(1);

} catch (NamingException ne) {
  throw new ServletException("JNDI error", ne);
} catch (SQLException sqle) {
  throw new ServletException("Database error", sqle);
}
finally {
  if (connection != null) {
    try {
      connection.close();
    } catch (SQLException sqle) {}
  }
}
```

This method uses a java.sql.PreparedStatement for executing the INSERT statement. The steps for inserting the data into the SUPP_REQUESTS table are:

❑ Obtain a database connection using a JNDI lookup to a datasource

❑ Prepare a statement for the INSERT

❑ Set parameters for the prepared statement

❑ Execute the prepared statement

❑ Run another statement to get back the request_id

❑ Close the database connection in the finally block; this is to make sure that the connection is always closed

Generate the Response

The last step in the TechSupportServlet is to generate the response for the user:

```
    // Prepare the response
    PrintWriter out = res.getWriter();

    res.setContentType("text/html");

    out.println("<html><head><title>");
    out.println("Tech Support: Request Confirmation");
    out.println("</title></head>");
    out.println("<body>");
    out.println("<h1>Tech Support: Request Confirmation</h1>");
    out.println("<p>Thank you for your request. Your request with the " +
                "following reference number has been received.</p>");
    out.println("<p>Request Reference: " + requestId + "</p>");
    out.println("<p>Please note this number for future references.</p>");
    out.println("<p>Your request will be attended to within 24 hours.</p>");
    out.println("<p>Administrator <br>Techsupport team. </p>");
    out.println("</body></html>");

    out.close();
}
```

This completes the servlet.

Compile the Source

Compile the source files TechSupportServlet.java using the following command line:

```
javac -classpath %J2EE_HOME%\lib\j2ee.jar TechSupportServlet.java
```

Construct the Web Application

Launch the J2EE deployment tool by executing the deploytool.bat file in the %J2EE_HOME%\bin directory. Create a new application selecting New | Application from the File menu. Call the application TechSupport:

Then select the TechSupport application in the left-hand tree pane and add a new Web Component using the File menu. Skip past the first screen of the New Web Component Wizard until you reach the WAR File screen. Hit the Edit button so that we can add our servlet class file and html file to the web component:

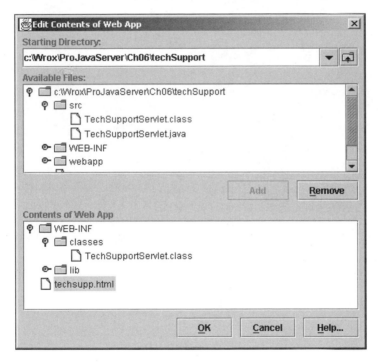

Move onto the next screen of the wizard and select to deploy a Servlet only:

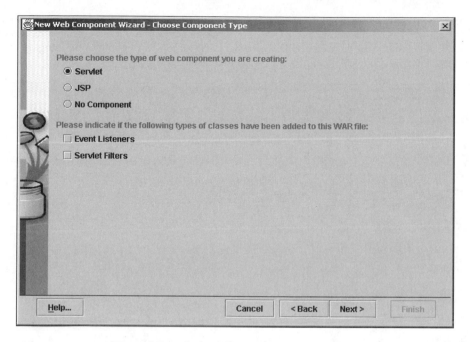

Then on to the next screen. Name the servlet techSupport and choose our TechSupportServlet class file:

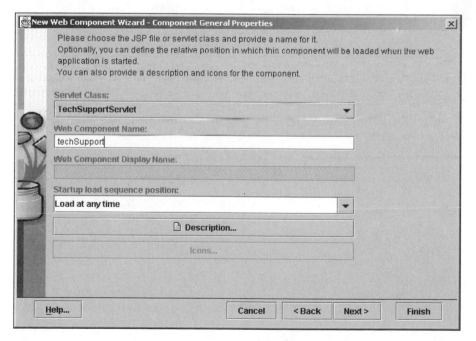

Skip through the next few screens of the wizard, accepting the default settings, until you reach the Resource References screen. Recall that in our servlet we gain a connection to the database using a datasource. Therefore, we need to inform the web application what datasource we are going to be using, in this case it was jdbc/TechSupport (we'll configure the datasource itself shortly):

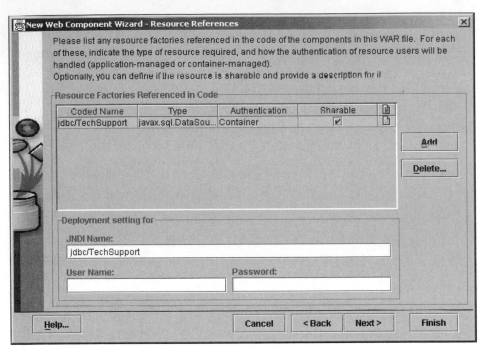

Keep going through the wizard until you reach the File references screen. Here we will set the techsupp.html file we created to be welcome screen for this web application. So, instead of entering the URL http://localhost:8000/techSupport/techSupp.html, you can just type http://localhost:8000/techSupport/ in your browser to load this file. We'll discuss more about welcome files in Chapter 9:

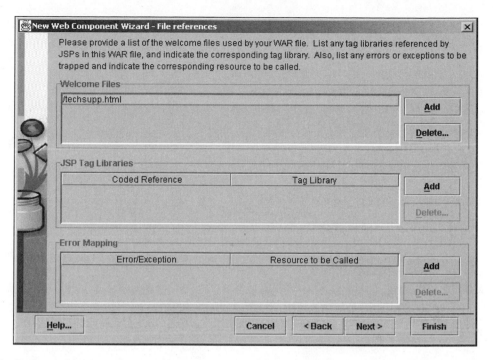

That's all we need to set in the wizard so you can either press the Finish button now, or keep going to the end of the wizard to see the deployment descriptor. Once you exit the wizard, you'll see the newly created web component in the main window:

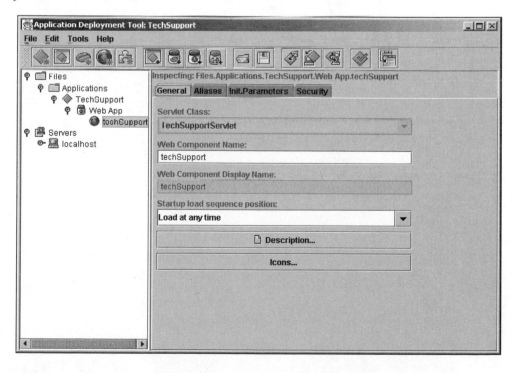

The Deployment Descriptor

Here's what the deployment descriptor for this web application looks like:

```xml
<?xml version="1.0" encoding="ISO-8859-1"?>

<!DOCTYPE web-app PUBLIC "-//Sun Microsystems, Inc.//DTD Web Application 2.3//EN"
    "http://java.sun.com/j2ee/dtds/web-app_2_3.dtd">

<web-app>

  <servlet>
    <servlet-name>techSupport</servlet-name>
    <servlet-class>TechSupportServlet</servlet-class>

  <welcome-file-list>
    <welcome-file>techsupp.html</welcome-file>
  </welcome-file-list>
</web-app>
```

Configuring the DataSource

Before we can deploy the application, we need to map the datasource reference we made in the wizard to the database we created earlier. To do this open the Server Configuration dialog from the Tools menu:

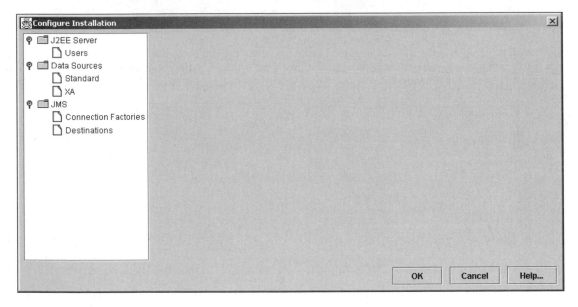

Select the Data Sources | Standard node, and create a new datasource called jdbc/TechSupport that points at the database we created:

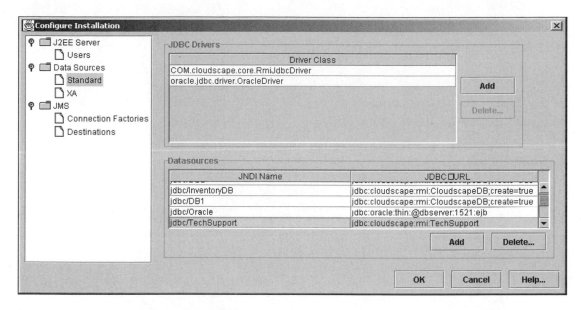

Deploying the Web Application

Having configured a new datasource we will need to restart the J2EE server if it running for the datasource to be created. If the server wasn't created then start the server now by running `j2ee -verbose` from within the `%J2EE_HOME%\bin` directory.

Now connect the deployment tool to the running server, by selecting Add Server from the File menu and adding a server called `localhost`:

Now we can deploy the web component. Select Deploy from the Tools menu to start the deployment wizard:

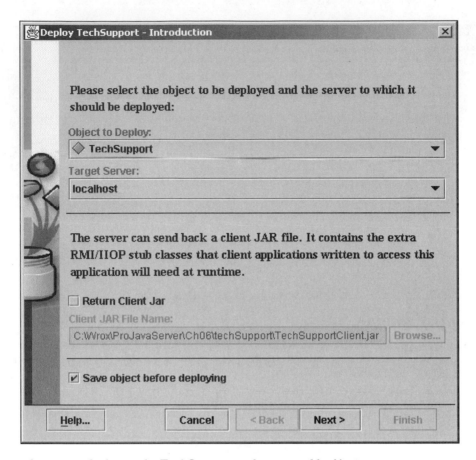

Make sure that we are deploying the TechSupport application and hit Next:

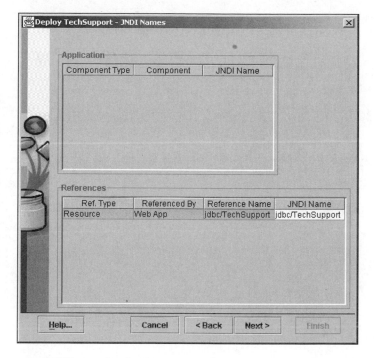

We should have set the JNDI name for the datasource when we created the application, but in case you didn't you can add it in here. Press Next to move to the next screen:

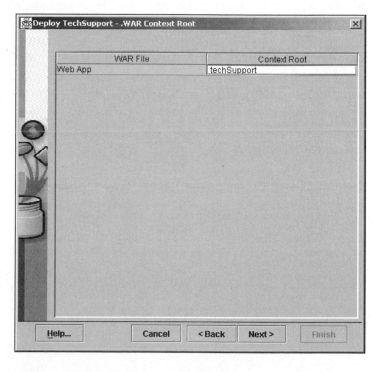

Set the Context Root of the application to be techSupport. This determines the URL to access the application. Select Next and then Finish to start the deployment process:

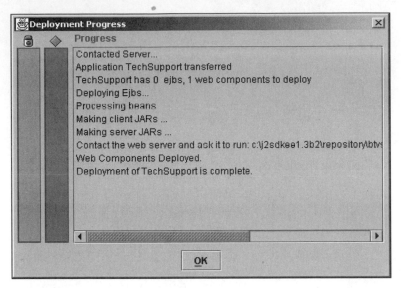

We are now almost ready to try out our application.

Tech Support in Action

There is one final step to perform before we can test this application. That is to start the Cloudscape database. This can be done by using the cloudscape.bat file in the %J2EE_HOME%\bin directory using a -start switch:

```
cloudscape -start
```

Open a browser and enter the URL http://localhost:8000/techSupport, and fill in the form:

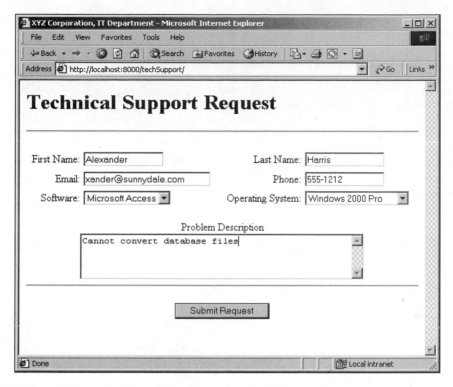

Upon submitting this form, the browser should generate the following response:

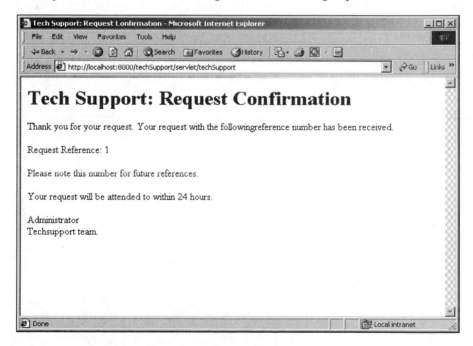

You may use your database vendor-provided tools to open the database tables to find that the data has successfully been added. In the case of Cloudscape, you can use the Cloudview application to open the database:

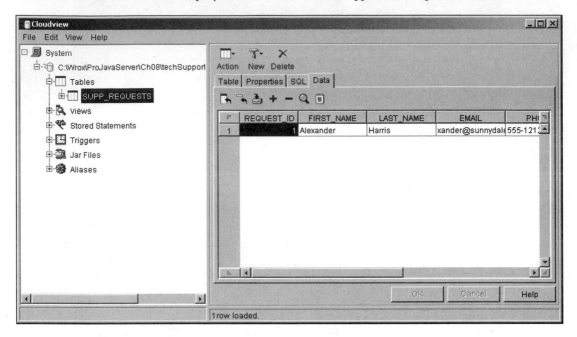

Make sure to shutdown the cloudscape database before launching Cloudview. This is because, in the default configuration, Cloudscape allows access to the database files from only one application at a time.

Summary

The Java Servlet API is both simple and powerful. It allows us to extend the functionality of any web server, with the help of a simple programming model.

The objective of this chapter has been to introduce the Servlet API and the lifecycle of servlets, and to demonstrate how to write servlet-based web applications. In this process, we've covered the following:

❑   When building a servlet, you need to implement the `Servlet` interface. You can do this by extending either `GenericServlet` or `HttpServlet`.

❑   The `HttpServlet` class extends `GenericServlet`, and provides additional HTTP-specific functionality.

❑   Servlets can implement the `SingleThreadModel` interface for enforcing synchronized access to the service methods. However, servlets that do not implement this interface should make sure that any servlet instance variables are accessed in a thread-safe manner. We've discussed the implications with the `FreakServlet` and the `TechSupportServlet`.

❑   The servlet lifecycle involves the `init()`, `service()`, and `destroy()` methods. The `FreakServlet` demonstrates the states associated with the lifecycle of a servlet instance.

❑   We use deployment descriptors to specify initialization parameters. This helps us avoid hard-coding such parameters within the servlets.

❑   You can use error pages to automatically send pre-designed HTML pages in response to HTTP errors and exceptions. This is a very flexible approach, and it is a good practice to do adequate error handling to prevent unfriendly container-generated messages from being sent to clients.

In the next chapter, we'll look at another part of the Servlet API, which deals with sessions, context and servlet collaborations.

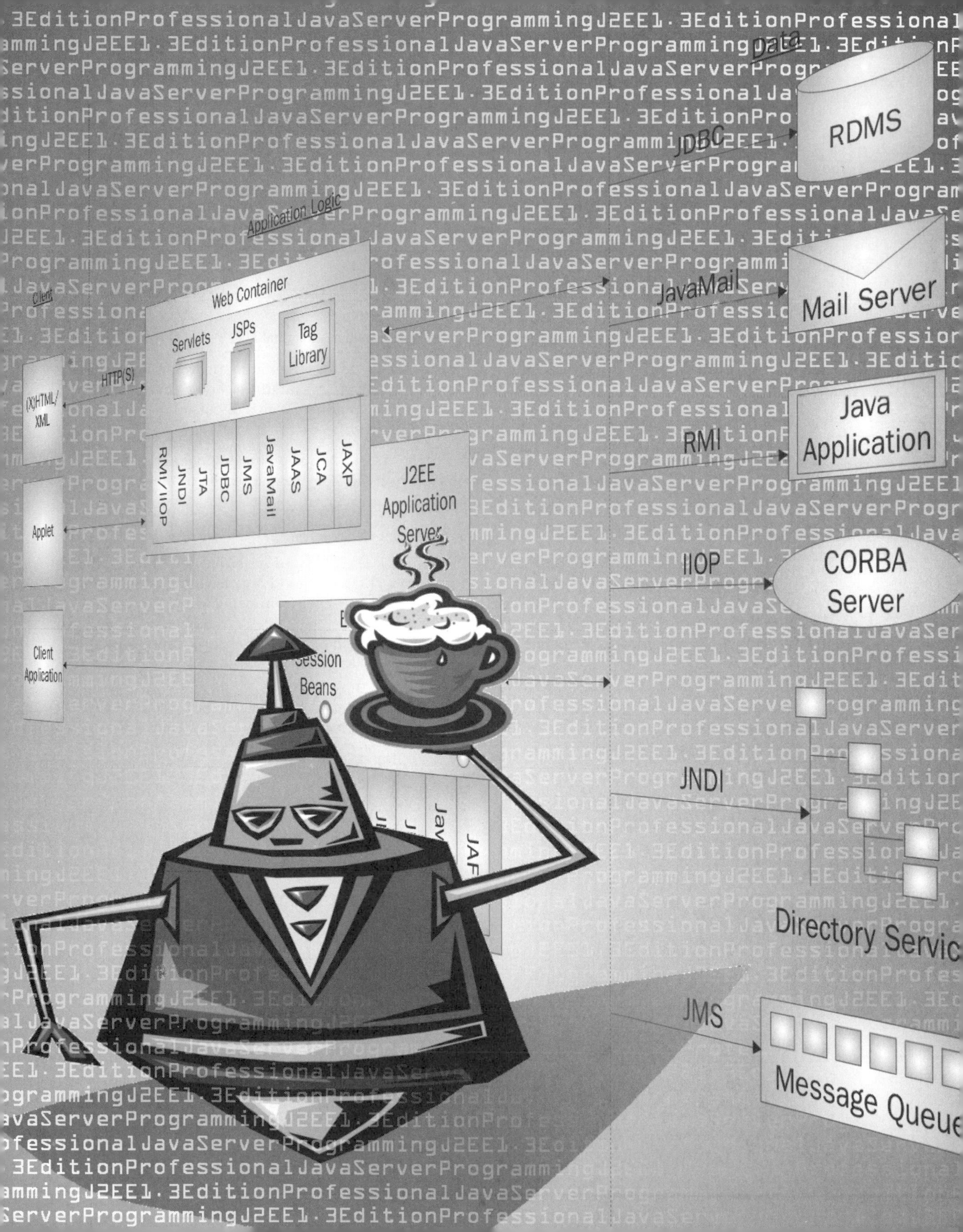

Servlet Sessions, Context, and Collaboration

In the previous two chapters we've covered the basic aspects of the Servlet API. In particular, we've discussed the lifecycle of servlets, and the APIs for reading requests and writing responses back to clients. These aspects of the Servlet API equip you to build servlets that generate dynamic web pages.

A servlet receives a request object, extracts parameters (if any) from it, processes any application logic (which may depend on the request parameters), and finally generates the response. Extending this model, you could build larger web applications by having several servlets, with each servlet performing a well-defined independent task.

This model is adequate so long as the application logic in each of these servlets is atomic – that is, so long as the application logic depends only on the parameters in the request (and, if applicable, any persistent data such as data stored in a relational database). For instance, in the Tech Support application the servlet gets all the support request data from the request, and as part of the application logic, writes the request data to a database, and sends a confirmation back. Now consider a familiar web application – an online store.

In a typical online store, the main application that drives the store is a shopping cart. An online store provides you with a browsable interface to a catalog. You can select items in the catalog, and add them to a shopping cart. Once you have added all the required items to the cart, you proceed to checkout, and place an order for the items in the cart.

However, such an application is not as simple as it appears. Where is the shopping cart maintained? Since the client is 'thin', it is the responsibility of the server to maintain the cart not only for you, but for all the other users that may simultaneously be browsing the catalog and adding items to their respective shopping carts. In order for this mechanism to work, the server should be able to individually distinguish each user and, accordingly, maintain each shopping cart. How do we build such a feature in a web application?

This is a typical requirement for web applications, where a 'user activity' happens across multiple requests and responses, and the server is required to associate some form of uniqueness to the each of the users. In the first part of this chapter, we'll discuss what is known as **session tracking** to address this requirement. We'll discuss some session-tracking approaches, particularly those used by the Java Servlet API.

As well as session tracking, we will consider another useful facility that the Servlet API provides. As we discussed in Chapter 6, servlets are part of web applications, and the notion of a web application is built on what is called **servlet context**. In simple terms, a context is a view of the web application and the web container. Servlets in an application can use this context to exchange information, or collaborate with other servlets, access resources, log events, etc. In the second part of this chapter, we'll discuss the Servlet APIs related to servlet context.

To demonstrate how session tracking and servlet context let you build complex web applications, we'll also study an online chat application – where multiple users can visit the site, create chat rooms, join a chat room, and exchange messages with other members in a chat room.

Finally, the Technical Support example from the last chapter will be revised to demonstrate a further useful servlet facility: **servlet collaboration**, which can be used to make a number of servlets work together to generate the response to a request.

> *Although the discussion in this chapter centers on servlets, the general ideas are also applicable to JSP-based web applications.*

Statelessness and Sessions

HTTP is a **stateless** protocol. A client opens a connection and requests some resource or information. The server responds with the requested resource (if available), or sends an HTTP error status. After closing the connection, the server does not remember any information about the client. So, the server considers the next request from the same client as a fresh request, with no relation to the previous request. This is what makes HTTP a stateless protocol.

A protocol is **stateful** if the response to a given request may depend not only on the current request, but also on the outcome of *previous* requests.

Typically, in a stateful protocol, multiple client requests and responses are sent across a single network connection between the client and server. Based on this connection, the server can identify such requests as forming a single session. For instance, consider the file transfer protocol (FTP). FTP is a stateful protocol, with multiple client requests and responses over a single connection in a given session. In this case, the connection is established with the first OPEN command, and is closed after the EXIT command (unless, of course, a network failure terminates the connection). Accordingly, the FTP server can associate all the client requests within a single session with the client. The server can also make decisions based on the state of the session. For example, an FTP server may limit the number of GET (for file download) requests within a session.

But why is it important to be stateful? A stateful protocol helps you develop complex application logic across multiple requests and responses. Let's consider an online bank. When you request a page containing balances of all your accounts, the server should be able to verify that you're a genuine account holder, and that you've established your credentials with the online bank. However, when the protocol is stateless, you'll be required to send your credentials with every request – in fact, each business transaction will be required to occur in a single request. This is not suitable for long business transactions that ought to happen across multiple requests, such as the online bank, or the shopping cart we discussed a moment ago.

For implementing flexible business transactions across multiple requests and responses, we need two facilities:

❑ **Session**
The server should be able to identify that a series of requests from a single client form a single working 'session'. By associating a specific request to belong to a specific working session, the shopping cart or the online banking application can distinguish one user from another.

❑ **State**
The server should be able to remember information related to previous requests and other business decisions that are made for requests. That is, the application should be able to associate state with each session. In the case of the shopping cart application, possible state could include the user's favorite item categories, user profile, or even the shopping cart itself.

However, in the case of HTTP, connections are closed at the end of each request, and hence HTTP servers cannot use the notion of connections to establish a session. HTTP is a stateless protocol, concerned with requests and responses, which are simple, isolated transactions. This is perfect for simple web browsing, where each request typically results in downloading static content. The server does not need to know whether a series of requests come from the same, or from different clients, or whether those requests are related or distinct. But this is not the case with web applications, where we need the ability to perform business transactions across multiple requests and responses.

With HTTP, in a transaction that spans multiple requests and responses, the web server cannot determine that all the requests are from the same client. A client, therefore, cannot establish a dialogue with the web server to perform a business transaction. However, the goal of HTTP has been to provide speedy and light information retrieval across the Internet, and a stateless protocol is the most suitable for such requirements.

Apart from being able to track users based on the notion of sessions, the server should also be able to remember any necessary information within a session. That is, the application programmer should be able to specify what data should be remembered within a given session, so that the application can use such information to make more informed decisions. This is very useful for transactions or processes spanning multiple requests and responses. With stateful protocols, the server associates a state with the connection: it remembers who the user is, and what it is that they're doing, with the help of the connection. However, this cannot be achieved with HTTP, as the lifetime of a connection is limited to a single request.

Over time, several strategies have evolved to address session tracking, and to manage state within a session. The Java Servlet API provides facilities for tracking sessions and maintaining state within a given session. With the help of these facilities, the server can associate all of the requests together and know that they all came from the same user. It can also associate a state with the connection: it remembers who the user is, and what it is that they're doing.

Note that HTTP 1.1 (http://www.w3.org/Protocols/rfc2068/rfc2068) provides for 'persistent connections', in which case clients and servers can use the same connection object for multiple requests/responses. When supported by both clients and servers, persistent connections reduce the latency associated with creating TCP/IP connections. Persistent connections are useful in cases where requests and responses occurring in a quick succession can be optimized using a single connection instead of one connection per request. However, persistent connections do not carry over session state. The discussion in this chapter remains the same with persistent connections.

Approaches to Session Tracking

There are essentially four approaches to session tracking:

- ❑ URL rewriting
- ❑ Hidden form fields
- ❑ Cookies
- ❑ Sessions using the Secure Sockets Layer (SSL)

Note that some books suggest user authentication as a means of session tracking. But user authentication is an application-level decision, and not all applications require user authentication for all resources in a web application.

Although the above four approaches differ in implementation details, all these are based on one simple trick – that is to exchange some form of a **token** between the client and the server.

Consider a client C and a server S. When C sends a request to S for the first time, S gives C a unique token. This token could be as simple or as complex as we wish it to be: a single number, a user name, or a session ID string. Whenever C visits S again, it also submits the token along with the request. S can now recognize C from this token.

This is the essence of session tracking:

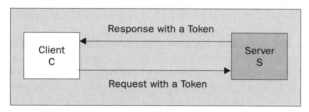

This simple technique for session tracking can be adapted in different ways, based on how such a token can be represented and exchanged. Let's now consider the above four approaches, and how these approaches represent the tokens, and how these tokens are exchanged in these approaches:

- ❑ **URL Rewriting**
  In this approach, the token is embedded in each URL. In each dynamically generated page, the server embeds an extra query parameter, or extra path information, in each URL in the page. When the client submits requests using such URLs, the token is retransmitted to the server. This approach is called URL rewriting, as it involves rewriting URLs in the response content to embed the extra token.

- ❑ **Hidden Form Fields**
  This approach is similar to URL rewriting. Instead of rewriting each URL, the server embeds hidden fields in each form. When the client submits a form, the additional fields will also be sent in the request. The server can use these parameters to establish and maintain a session.

- ❑ **Cookies**
  Cookie were invented by Netscape, and are one of the most refined forms of token that clients and servers can exchange. Unlike URL rewriting or using hidden form fields, cookies can be exchanged in request and response headers, and therefore do not involve manipulating the generated response to contain a token.

❑ **Secure Socket Layer (SSL) Sessions**

SSL is an encryption technology that runs on top of TCP/IP and below application-level protocols such as HTTP. SSL is the technology used in the HTTPS protocol. SSL-enabled servers can authenticate SSL-enabled clients, and use an encrypted connection between the client and server. In the process of establishing an encrypted connection, both the client and server generate what are called 'session keys', which are symmetric keys used for encrypting and decrypting messages. Servers based on the HTTPS protocol can use the client's symmetric key to establish a session.

But how can we choose between these approaches, and establish and maintain sessions in our web applications? The answer is that, with servlets, it is the *web container's* responsibility to provide the basic facilities for creating and maintaining sessions. The servlet specification allows web containers to use URL rewriting, cookies, or SSL sessions for session tracking. The actual technique used for establishing and tracking a given session depends on both the server's, and client's capabilities to participate in sessions. The Servlet API also provides you with an interface, objects of which let you manipulate session lifecycle, and associate state with sessions. There are certain guidelines that make sure that session tracking is functional irrespective of the technique used.

Before looking at the Servlet API's facilities for session tracking, let's discuss the first three approaches in more detail.

URL Rewriting

As we've discussed in the previous chapters, an HTTP request consists of the location of the server resource (URL), followed optionally by a query string containing pairs of parameters and values. An example of a URL is:

http://www.myserver.com/servlet/getSchedule;uid=joe?begPeriod=3&endPeriod=6

In this example, the server is `www.myserver.com`, the resource path is `/servlet/getSchedule;uid=joe`, and the query string is `begPeriod=3&end_period=6`.

Typically, browsers generate such requests while submitting forms with ACTION type GET. If you use POST requests in your forms, the two query parameters will be part of the body. As we've seen in the previous chapter, extra path information in the URL as well as the query parameters can be extracted from the `HttpServletRequest` object from within your servlet.

URL rewriting uses the same technique to embed client-specific unique tokens within each URL. For example, in the following, each URL path has an appended string `uid=joe`, where `uid` is a parameter unique for each user, with value `joe`:

```
<ul>
  <li><a href="http://www.myserver.com/servlet/usrmenu;uid=joe">
    User Prefs</a>
  </li>
  <li><a href="http://www.myserver.com/servlet/tsEntry;uid=joe">
    Time Sheets</a>
  </li>
  <li><A HREF="http://www.myserver.com/servlet/exEntry;uid=joe">
    Exp Form</a>
  </li>
</ul>
```

For the moment, let's assume that the servlet generated this dynamic content, postponing the question of how this can be done with the Servlet API. When the servlet generates the above snippet, it embeds the uid within each URL. When the user clicks on any of these hyperlinks, the uid is passed along with the request to the web container. The web container can now obtain the value of the uid from the request. As discussed in the previous section, the server sent the token as part of the URL, and the client sent it back along with the request, thus giving the container the ability to track the session of joe.

This approach is called URL rewriting since it involves rewriting all the URLs to include a unique token in the URL path. Although we used a parameter uid in the above example, the name of the parameter specified in the servlet specification is jsessionid. The actual generated URLs resemble the following:

http://www.myserver.com/servlet/usrmenu;jsessionid=123456789

URL rewriting requires that all pages in the application be dynamically generated. URL rewriting cannot be enforced for static HTML pages, because the unique URL path parameter (the jsessionid) is dynamic and differs from user to user. Also note that the jsessionid (or the uid in the above example) is a path parameter, and not a query parameter (like GET requests). Query parameters are &-separated name-value pairs, while the path parameter jsessionid=<...> is an encoded resource path.

Hidden Form Fields

In this approach, the unique token is embedded within each HTML form. For example, the following HTML specifies an input control of type Hidden:

```
<input type="Hidden" name="uid" value="joe">
```

When the request is submitted, the server receives the token as part of the request. Note that, similar to URL rewriting, the above content should be dynamically generated embedding the hidden parameter. In addition, each request should include a form submission, and hence may not be applicable to all types of pages.

The servlet specification does not use this approach.

Cookies

Cookies are the most commonly used means of tracking client sessions. Cookies were initially introduced by Netscape, and this technology was later standardized in RFC 2109 (http://www.faqs.org/rfcs/rfc2109.html). You can also read Netscape's preliminary specification at http://www.netscape.com/newsref/std/cookie_spec.html.

> **A cookie is a small piece of textual information sent by the server to the client, stored on the client, and returned by the client for all requests to the server.**

A cookie contains one or more **name-value** pairs with certain additional attributes, which are exchanged in the response and request headers.

Web servers send a cookie by sending the Set-Cookie response header in the following format:

```
Set-Cookie: Name=VALUE; Comment=COMMENT; Domain=DOMAINNAME; Max-age=SECONDS;
Path=PATH; secure; Version=1*DIGIT
```

Here Name is the name of the cookie, and VALUE is the value of Name, Max-age (optional) specifies the maximum life of the cookie in seconds, Domain (optional) and Path (optional) specify the URL path for which the cookie is valid, and secure (optional) specifies if the cookie can be exchanged over HTTP. For cookies implemented as per RFC 2109, the Version should be set to 1. The Version should be set to 0 for cookies implemented as per the original Netscape specification. Comment is an optional parameter that can be used to document the intent of the cookie.

Here is an example of a cookie:

```
Set-cookie: uid=joe; Max-age-3600; Domain=".myserver.com"; Path="/"
```

The above response header sends a cookie with name uid and value joe. The lifetime of this cookie is 3600 seconds, and is valid for the myserver.com domain (including all sub-domains) for the URL path /. The browser should discard this cookie after 3600 seconds. If the Max-age attribute is missing, the browser discards the cookie when you exit the browser.

Instead of specifying .myserver.com as the domain, you can also specify specific sub-domains such as www.myserver.com or some.myserver.com etc., in which case, the browser returns the cookie only to the specified sub-domains. For instance, information portals such as Yahoo specify entire the entire .yahoo.com domain for when setting cookies, so that Yahoo can identify/track you whether you're visiting http://my.yahoo.com, or shopping at http://shop.yahoo.com, or checking e-mail at http://mail.yahoo.com.

When a browser client receives the above response header, it can either reject it or accept it. For instance, you can configure your browser to accept or reject cookies. Let's consider that the browser accepts this cookie. When the browser sends a request to the http://www.myserver.com domain within the next one hour, it also sends a request header:

```
Cookie: uid=joe
```

The server can read this cookie from the request, and identify that the request corresponds to a client identified by uid=joe. This completes the token exchange necessary for tracking sessions.

A cookie is specific to a domain or a sub-domain, and can be set by the domain attribute in the cookie. Browsers use the domain and path attributes to determine if a cookie should be sent in the request header, and with what name-value attributes. Once accepted by a browser, the browser stores the cookie against the domain and the URL path.

If the client chooses to reject a cookie, the client does not send the cookie back to the server in the request header, and therefore the server fails to track the user session.

Note that the main advantage of this approach is that the cookies are not mixed with the HTML content and the HTTP request and response bodies. The container can transparently set cookies in the response headers, and extract cookies from request headers.

The Servlet API specification requires that web containers implement session tracking using the cookie mechanism. In this approach, the web container automatically sets a session tracking cookie with name jsessionid. When the container receives client requests, it checks for existence of this cookie, and accordingly track sessions.

However, since servers can transparently set cookies, which are stored in the user's computer and sent back to the server, cookies cause security concerns for many users. Refer to http://www.w3.org/Security/Faq/wwwsf7.html and http://www.ciac.org/ciac/bulletins/i-034.shtml for an overview of security concerns with cookies. In order to answer for such concerns, browsers allow you disable cookies. When cookies are disabled, servlet containers use URL rewriting to track sessions.

Although several sites require cookies and provide limited or no functionality when cookies are disabled, it is a good practice to design web applications to support URL rewriting.

Apart from session-tracking cookies, your web applications can explicitly set cookies in the response. Using the Servlet API, you can add several cookies in the response, and extract cookies from the request.

The Servlet API provides a class called `javax.servlet.http.Cookie` that represents a cookie from the perspective of the servlet. The servlet can create a new cookie, set its name and value, set max-age and so on, and then add the cookie to the `HttpServletResponse` object to be sent back to the browser. Cookies can also be retrieved from the `HttpServletRequest` object, and their values read. For the purpose of our present discussion, you can set the above cookie using the following code in your servlet :

```
// Create a new cookie with name and value arguments
Cookie c = new Cookie("uid", "joe");

// Set the life of the cookie
c.setMaxAge(60*60);  //Expires in 1 hour
c.setDomain(".myserver.com");
c.setPath("/");

// Send the cookie to the browser to be stored on the client machine
response.addCookie(c);
```

Similarly, you can retrieve cookies from requests using `getCookies()` method on the `HttpServletResponse` interface.

Possible applications for setting explicit cookies include targeted marketing, site personalization, usage tracking, etc.

Session Tracking with the Java Servlet API

In the Java Servlet API, the `javax.servlet.http.HttpSession` interface encapsulates the notion of a session. Web containers provide an implementation of this interface.

Since the notion of a session is associated with client requests, the `HttpServletRequest` interface provides the `getSession()` method, which you can use to access the `HttpSession` object associated with the client making the request. If you refer back to the class diagram for the `javax.servlet.http` package in Chapter 6, you'll notice an arrow between `HttpServletRequest` and the `HttpSession` interfaces. This means that, given an `HttpServletRequest` object, you can obtain the `HttpSession` object.

In order to associate state with sessions, the `HttpSession` interface provides methods with which we can set and get attributes from `HttpSession` objects. We'll cover these methods a little later in this chapter.

As we mentioned, web containers use either cookies or URL rewriting for establishing sessions. While most web containers rely on cookies alone for establishing sessions, some use cookies by default, and use URL rewriting when clients reject cookies. The actual creation of sessions is transparent to the application programmer. That is, you do not need explicitly to create, set, or get cookies, or rewrite URLs for session tracking. As you will see later, the only requirement is that you should encode all URLs in the response.

The Servlet API for session tracking consists of the following:

❑   Methods on the `javax.servlet.http.HttpServletRequest` interface for creating, and accessing `HttpSession` objects.

❑   A `javax.servlet.http.HttpSession` interface to represent sessions. This interface includes methods to associate state with sessions, and to configure and invalidate sessions.

❑   Methods on the `javax.servlet.http.HttpServletResponse` interface to encode URLs such that the web container can use URL rewriting when cookies are rejected by client browsers.

❑   The `javax.servlet.http.HttpSessionBindingListener` interface and the `javax.servlet.http.HttpSessionBindingEvent` class, to represent events associated with sessions.

We'll discuss each of these in the following sections.

Session Creation and Tracking

The methods from the `HttpServletRequest` interface for creating and tracking `HttpSession` objects are:

```
public HttpSession getSession(boolean create);
public HttpSession getSession();
```

Each of these methods returns the `HttpSession` object associated with the current request. If there is no session associated with the current request, the second method creates one. This could happen when the client refuses to join a session, for instance when the user disables cookies in their browser. The first method takes an additional Boolean argument, to indicate whether the container should attempt to create a new session if there is no session associated with the current request. If this argument is `false`, and if there is no session associated with the request, this method returns `null`.

From a servlet's perspective, session creation/tracking involves calling one of these two methods to obtain an `HttpSession` object. However, from the web container's perspective, there is more to it. As we discussed in the previous section, session creation involves establishing a token (based on a cookie, or the URL path parameter, or an SSL session key) that can be exchanged between the client and the server, and associating such a token with an `HttpSession` object. The web container receives the token as part of the request. When the `getSession()` method is called, the container retrieves the `HttpSession` object, based on this token.

In other words, session creation/tracking means that the web container is able to associate a request with a client, and the `HttpSession` object represents this association. The web container maintains this object for the duration of the client session, or a configurable timeout period. Since there can be several clients sending requests to the container, the container maintains separate `HttpSession` objects for each client. Consequently, you can associate state with each `HttpSession`, as you'll see shortly.

The HttpSession Interface

```
public interface HttpSession
```

This interface from the `javax.servlet.http` package encapsulates the notion of a session. An object of this type can be obtained using the `getSession()` method of the `HttpServletRequest` object. Note that, as with most of the other Servlet API interfaces discussed so far, web containers provide a suitable implementation internally, and what you see is an instance obtained via the `getSession()` method of the `HttpServletRequest` object.

The `HttpSession` interface has the following methods:

```
public Object getAttribute(String name)
public Enumeration getAttributeNames()
public long getCreationTime()
public String getId()
public long getLastAccessedTime()
public int getMaxInactiveInterval()
public void invalidate()
public boolean isNew()
public void removeAttribute(String name)
public void setAttribute(String name, Object attribute)
public void setMaxInactiveInterval(int interval)
```

These methods can be divided into two categories:

❑ **Methods for session lifetime:**
```
getCreationTime()
getId()
getLastAccessTime()
getMaxInactiveInterval()
invalidate()
isNew()
setMaxInactiveInterval()
```

❑ **Methods for associating attributes (state) with sessions:**
```
getAttribute()
getAttributeNames()
removeAttribute()
setAttribute()
```

Methods for Session Lifetime

Since sessions are maintained on the server side, and since HTTP is a stateless protocol, the web container cannot determine if the client intends to continue to use the web application. For example, consider a web-based mail application, such as Microsoft Hotmail. After reading the mails for a while, you may close the browser without actually logging out from the mail account.

> **Note that the server cannot detect this.**

As the number of users for a web application increases, the number of sessions increases too. Each session consumes memory on the server side, so it is unwise to keep sessions alive forever. As we shall see later, you should use the deployment descriptor element `<session-config>` to specify a reasonable interval based on how sensitive the data shared within a session is. For instance, most e-commerce sites limit this interval to under 30 minutes, while portals such as Yahoo use longer intervals.

In order to effectively manage session lifetime, the Servlet API provides several methods.

The getCreationTime() Method

```
public long getCreationTime()
```

This method returns the time that the session was created, in milliseconds since January 1, 1970 00:00:00 GMT.

The getId() Method

```
public String getId()
```

This method returns a `String` containing a unique identifier assigned to this session. This `String` is implementation-dependent.

The getLastAccessedTime() Method

```
public long getLastAccessedTime()
```

This method returns the time that the session was last accessed by the client, in milliseconds since January 1, 1970 00:00:00 GMT. This method can be used to determine the period of inactivity between two consecutive requests from a client.

The getMaxInactiveInterval() Method

```
public int getMaxInactiveInterval()
```

This returns the length of time in seconds that the session will remain active between requests before expiring.

The setMaxInactiveInterval() Method

```
public int setMaxInactiveInterval(int interval)
```

This method sets the length of time in seconds that the session will remain active between requests before expiring. You can use this method to programmatically set the session inactivity interval. The web container makes sure that the session is automatically invalidated after expiry of this interval.

Alternatively, you can use the `<session-timeout>` tag in the deployment descriptor to specify the maximum inactivity period:

```
<session-config>
  <session-timeout>
    300
  </session-timeout>
</session-config>
```

While the second approach allows you to specify the inactivity interval for the application, the first approach allows you to programmatically change this. Upon reaching this interval, the web container automatically invalidates the session.

The isNew() Method

```
public boolean isNew()
```

This method returns `true` if the session has been created on the server, but the client does not yet know about, or has not yet joined, the session. A client is considered to join a session when the client returns session tracking information previously sent by the server. When the client refuses to join the session, this method returns `true`, indicating that it is a new session. This can happen, for example, when the web container uses cookies alone for session tracking, and the client refuses to accept cookies.

The invalidate() Method

```
public void invalidate()
```

You can use this method to terminate sessions. For example, you can use explicit session invalidation for implementing a logout feature in your application. When the user chooses to log out, your server can invalidate the session, so that the user can no longer be associated with that session. Next time, when your servlet calls the `getSession()` method on the `HttpServletRequest`, you'll receive a new `HttpSession` object.

Demonstrating Session Lifecycle with Cookies

In order to become familiar with the lifecycle of `HttpSession` objects, let's now consider a simple servlet that lets us examine certain session attributes and invalidate existing sessions. We'll also examine the behavior of this servlet in the absence of cookies, and then discuss ways to generate web pages that work as desired, irrespective of whether the client browser accepts cookies or not.

We'll call this servlet `SessionLifeCycleServlet`. When invoked, this servlet generates a page showing the session status, session ID, creation time, last accessed time, and max inactive interval. The servlet uses the methods in the `HttpSession` interface to print the above information. Apart from this, this servlet also provides links to reload the page, and to invalidate the current session.

Here is a sample screenshot of this servlet's response:

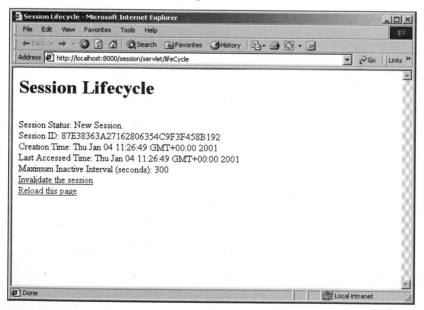

Notice that the session is new, since this is the first access. In order to see how the above response is generated, consider the following source code:

```java
// Import Servlet packages
import javax.servlet.ServletException;
import javax.servlet.http.HttpServlet;
import javax.servlet.http.HttpSession;
import javax.servlet.http.HttpServletRequest;
import javax.servlet.http.HttpServletResponse;

// Import Java packages
import java.io.PrintWriter;
import java.io.IOException;
import java.util.Date;

public class SessionLifeCycleServlet extends HttpServlet {
  protected void doGet (HttpServletRequest request,
                        HttpServletResponse response)
            throws ServletException, IOException {
    String action = request.getParameter("action");

    if (action != null && action.equals("invalidate")) {
      // Invalidate the session
      HttpSession session = request.getSession();
      session.invalidate();
      response.setContentType("text/html");
      PrintWriter out = response.getWriter();

      out.println("<html>");
      out.println("<head><title>Session Lifecycle</title></head>");
      out.println("<body>");
      out.println("<p>Your session has been invalidated.</p>");
      String lifeCycleURL = "/session/servlet/lifeCycle";
      out.println("<a href=\"" + lifeCycleURL + "?action=newSession\">");
      out.println("Create new session</a>");
      out.println("</body></html>");
    } else {
      HttpSession session = request.getSession();
      response.setContentType("text/html");
      PrintWriter out = response.getWriter();

      out.println("<html>");
      out.println("<meta http-equiv=\"Pragma\" content=\"no-cache\">");
      out.println("<head><title>Session Lifecycle</title></head>");
      out.println("<body bgcolor=\"#FFFFFF\">");
      out.println("<h1>Session Lifecycle</center></h1>");

      // Session information
      out.print("<br>Session Status: ");
      if (session.isNew()) {
        out.println("New Session.");
      } else {
        out.println("Old Session.");
      }
      out.println("<br>Session ID: ");

      out.println(session.getId());
      out.println("<br>Creation Time: ");
      out.println(new Date(session.getCreationTime()));
      out.println("<br>Last Accessed Time: ");
      out.println(new Date(session.getLastAccessedTime()));
      out.println("<br>Maximum Inactive Interval (seconds): ");
      out.println(session.getMaxInactiveInterval());
```

```
            String lifeCycleURL = "/session/servlet/lifeCycle";
            out.print("<br><a href=\"" + lifeCycleURL + "?action=invalidate\">");
            out.println("Invalidate the session</a></td></tr>");
            out.print("<br><a href=\"" + lifeCycleURL + "\">");
            out.println("Reload this page</a>");
            out.println("</body></html>");
            out.close();
        }
    }
}
```

Consider the highlighted parts of this source code. Let's look at the final `else` block first. This block is executed when servlet is invoked without any parameters, and performs the following steps:

- Calls `getSession()` on the `HttpSession`, with `boolean true` as an argument.

- Calls `getId()` to get the session ID.

- Calls `getCreationTime()` to get the creation time of the session. Since this method returns the creation as milliseconds since January 1, 1970 00:00:00 GMT, we need to convert this into a `Date` object using the new constructor.

- Calls `getLastAccessedTime()` to get the session's last accessed time.

- Calls `getMaxInactiveInterval()` to get the current max-inactive-interval setting.

After printing the above, the servlet also generates two links: one to reload the page, and the other to invalidate the session. The first link simply points to the same page. The `no-cache` meta-tag in the generated HTML lets you reload the page by clicking on this link.

Note that the second link has a query string `action=invalidate` appended. When you click on this link, the `if` block of the `doGet()` method will be executed. In order to see this servlet in action, compile this servlet and create the following deployment descriptor:

```
<?xml version="1.0" encoding="ISO-8859-1"?>
<!DOCTYPE web-app PUBLIC
   "-//Sun Microsystems, Inc.//DTD Web Application 2.3//EN"
   "http://java.sun.com/j2ee/dtds/web-app_2_3.dtd">

<web-app>
  <servlet>
    <servlet-name>lifeCycle</servlet-name>
    <display-name>lifeCycle</display-name>
    <servlet-class>SessionLifeCycleServlet</servlet-class>
  </servlet>

  <session-config>
    <session-timeout> <!-- In minutes -->
      5
    </session-timeout>
  </session-config>
</web-app>
```

> From now on I will assume that you know how to deploy a web component into the J2EE Reference Implementation server, and so I will only highlight those steps that are particular to each example. Refer back to the preceding chapters for more complete instructions on the process.

Once you have successfully deployed the servlet (using a context root of session), enter the URL http://localhost:8000/session/servlet/lifeCycle in your browser. Make sure that cookies are enabled in your browser configuration. The browser output should be similar to the one that was shown at the beginning of this example.

Now let's see what happens if the code in the else block is executed again. Click on the Reload this page link. Your browser output should be similar to the one shown below:

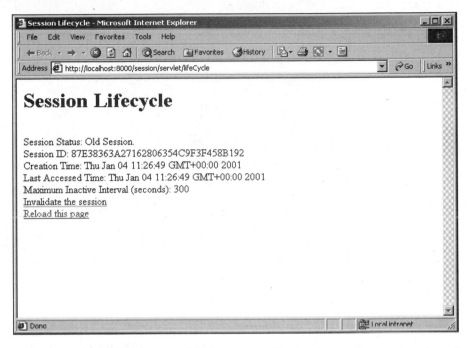

This time, you'll find that the session is old. The session ID and the session creation time also remain the same. Every time you click on the Reload this page link, what changes is the last accessed time.

This illustrates how simple it is to create and keep track of sessions. Let's now see what happens if you click on the Invalidate the session link. Since this URL has a query parameter action=invalidate, the if block of the doGet() method will be executed to generate the following output:

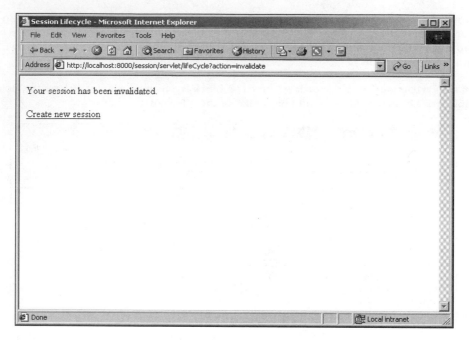

Now click on the Create new session link. The resulting page should be similar to the opening screen shot shown at the beginning of this example.

Now, examine the `if` block of the code. This part of the servlet gets the session from the request, calls the `invalidate()` method, and generates a new link back to the previous page.

Session Lifecycle without Cookies

In order to see the behavior of the `SessionLifeCycleServlet` without cookies, disable cookies in your browser, and invoke the URL http://localhost:8000/session/servlet/lifeCycle. This time, when you attempt to reload the page, you'll notice that the session is always new, implying that the web container is not able to track the session.

As discussed previously, in cases where clients refuse to accept cookies, web containers can use the URL rewriting mechanism to track sessions. However, in order for this mechanism to work, all URLs in the page should be encoded using the `encodeURL()` method in the `HttpServletResponse` interface. This method appends a path string of the form `";jsessionid=123456789"` to the input URL.

In the `SessionLifeCycleServlet`, replace both lines containing:

```
String lifeCycleURL = "/session/servlet/lifeCycle";
```

with:

```
String lifeCycleURL = response.encodeURL("/session/servlet/lifeCycle");
```

Recompile the servlet, and redeploy. This time you'll notice that the web container is able to track sessions. When you reload the servlet, you'll find that the session is old, and that the URL shown by your browser is something like:

http://localhost:8000/session/servlet/lifeCycle;jsessionid=To1010mC8978836221982393At

With the help of the container (that is, the `encodeURL()` method on the `HttpServletResponse` interface), we're now able to implement URL rewriting.

> **Whether or not users of your web applications enable cookies in their browsers, it is good practice to always encode the URLs as shown above so that browsers can participate in sessions.**

Methods for Managing State

As we discussed at the beginning of this chapter, another important requirement for building web applications, as well as identifying the client, is for the server to be able to remember information related to previous requests/decisions. In simple terms, this means that once a request is received, and a business decision is made, you should be able to store that information for later use.

For example, based on the login information, your online banking application might determine that you cannot transfer funds across your accounts. If the application is capable of storing that information, it need not re-execute the logic for that decision-making process every time you request a fund transfer during the session. Similarly, consider an online registration form. If the registration process involves collecting a large amount of data (say, filling in 4 or 5 forms), you might not wish to implement the entire process with a single HTML form. Instead, you should be able to implement this across multiple HTML pages (and requests). To do this, you should be able to validate and store information as soon as it is received from the client. One of the possibilities is to store such information in a persistent store such as a relational database. However, what if you prefer to perform the database update at the end of the process? Alternatively, consider cases where such information is temporary, but is required throughout the session.

The `HttpSession` interface has facilities that meet this requirement. The `setAttribute()` and `getAttribute()` methods of the `HttpSession` interface allow you to store unique attributes within the `HttpSession`, and retrieve them any time before the session expires. An attribute is essentially a Java language object identified by an attribute name.

The getAttribute() Method

```
public Object getAttribute(String name)
```

This method returns the attribute bound with the specified name in this session, or `null` if no object is bound under the name.

The getAttributeNames() Method

```
public Enumeration getAttributeNames(String name)
```

This method returns an enumeration of the names of all attributes bound to the current session. You can use these names with the `getAttribute()` method to retrieve the objects.

The setAttribute() Method

```
public setAttribute(String name, Object attribute)
```

This method binds (stores) an object in the session, with the given name. You can use the `getAttribute()` method to retrieve the object again. In the case of distributable containers (discussed below), this method may throw an `InvalidArgumentException`.

333

Since this method maintains only a reference to the attribute, you need to call this method whenever the object reference changes. For instance, when you add a Hashtable object as an attribute, the session holds only a reference to the Hashtable. Since adding elements to the Hashtable does not affect the reference to the Hashtable object, you need not call setAttribute() whenever you add/remove elements to the Hashtable. However, if you want to replace the Hashtable object with another Hashtable, you need to call the setAttribute() method again, passing the new Hashtable.

The removeAttribute() Method

```
public void removeAttribute(String name)
```

This method unbinds and removes an object with the given name from the session.

> Note that the above methods are not synchronized. However, it is quite possible that the same client access the same session in concurrent HTTP requests. For instance, this could happen if clients can span multiple browser windows (all participating in the same session). In order to avoid concurrent modifications of session variables, consider synchronizing access to these methods.

Multiple servlets executing requests can simultaneously access and modify the session attributes of a single session object at the same time. In case servlets in your application attempt to manipulate the same session attribute, you should make sure that such access is synchronized.

Also, as you'll see in Chapter 9, web applications can be marked as distributable, in which case all session attributes must implement the java.lang.Serializable interface. Most of the commercial web containers, such as those listed in Chapter 5, provide facilities for load distribution and fail-over across multiple JVMs. (This process is also known as clustering.) When the container is distributable, it runs in multiple JVMs (which can be on multiple machines), and your applications will be deployed on each of these JVMs. The purpose of such a setup is to allow the container to distribute the processing load across these JVMs. In such cases, the web container is free to move the session objects from one JVM to another JVM, and send all client requests for that session to this JVM. However, for the container to be able to swap the sessions, the objects contained in the HttpSession must also be serializable.

Finally, even non-distributable containers may provide session persistence. Consider the case of a web application with a large number of simultaneous users (and sessions). Only some of these sessions may be active, while the rest are not active, yet not inactive enough to be invalidated (based on session timeout). In such cases, the container can choose to **passivate** some of the least active sessions in a persistent storage such as the file system, so that the container can optimize the available memory. The container could later active such sessions based on user activity. In order to allow session passivation and activation, the attributes in the session should be serializable.

These constraints imply that you should avoid storing non-serializable attributes, such as database connections and input/output streams, in sessions.

Demonstrating State Management

Let's now build another simple servlet to demonstrate the methods for managing state in the HttpSession:

```
// Import Servlet packages
import javax.servlet.ServletException;
import javax.servlet.http.HttpServlet;
import javax.servlet.http.HttpSession;
import javax.servlet.http.HttpServletRequest;
```

```
import javax.servlet.http.HttpServletResponse;

// Import Java packages
import java.io.PrintWriter;
import java.io.IOException;
import java.util.Enumeration;

public class AttributeServlet extends HttpServlet {

  protected void doGet (HttpServletRequest request,
                        HttpServletResponse response)
             throws ServletException, IOException {

    HttpSession session = request.getSession();

    String name = request.getParameter("attrib_name");
    String value = request.getParameter("attrib_value");
    String remove = request.getParameter("attrib_remove");

    if (remove != null && remove.equals("on")) {
      session.removeAttribute(name);
    } else {
      if (name != null && name.length() > 0 && (value != null)
            && value.length() > 0) {
        session.setAttribute(name, value);
      }
    }

    response.setContentType("text/html");
    PrintWriter out = response.getWriter();

    out.println("<html>");
    out.println("<meta http-equiv=\"Pragma\" content=\"no-cache\">");
    out.println("<head><title>Session Attributes</title></head>");
    out.println("<body>");
    out.println("<h1>Session Attributes</h1>");

    out.println("Enter name and value of an attribute");

    String url = response.encodeURL("/session/servlet/attributes");
    out.println("<form action=\"" + url + "\" method=\"GET\">");

    out.println("Name: ");
    out.println("<input type=\"text\" SIZE=\"10\" name=\"attrib_name\">");

    out.println("Value: ");
    out.println("<input type=\"text\" size=\"10\" name=\"attrib_value\">");

    out.println("<br><input type=\"checkbox\"" +
                name=\"attrib_remove\">Remove");
    out.println("<input type=\"submit\" name=\"update\" value=\"Update\">");
    out.println("</form>");
    out.println("<hr>");
    out.println("Attributes in this Session");

    // Print all session attributes
    Enumeration e = session.getAttributeNames();
    while (e.hasMoreElements()) {
      String att_name = (String) e.nextElement();
```

```
        String att_value = (String) session.getAttribute(att_name);

        out.println("<br><b>Name:</b> ");
        out.println(att_name);
        out.println("<b>Value: </b>");
        out.println(att_value);
    }
    out.println("</body></html>");
    out.close();
  }
}
```

This servlet lets you enter name-value pairs in a HTML form, and add this data to the session. It also lets you remove attributes from session. Compile this servlet and add it to the web application we created earlier for the `SessionLifeCycleServlet`. Alternatively, here is the modification to the deployment descriptor that you would have to make:

```
...
<web-app>
  ...
  <servlet>
    <servlet-name>attributes</servlet-name>
    <display-name>attributes</display-name>
    <servlet-class>AttributeServlet</servlet-class>
  </servlet>
  ...
</web-app>
```

Enter the URL http://localhost:8000/session/servlet/attributes in your browser. The browser will display a form to enter a name and value of an attribute, and a checkbox to remove an attribute. Add any name-value pair and hit the **Update** button. You will find the list of current session attributes displayed below the form. Here is a typical output after entering a few attributes:

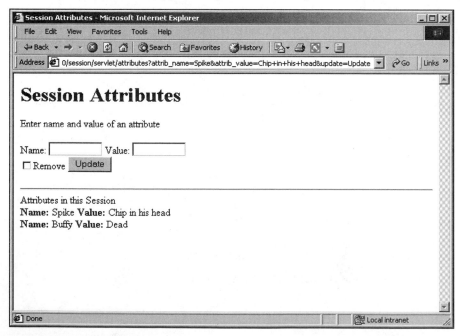

In order to remove any attributes from the session, enter the name of the attribute against the Name textbox, check the Remove checkbox, and hit the Update button.

This very simple application illustrates you how to store and retrieve attributes in the `HttpSession` object using the `setAttribute()`, `getAttribute()`, `getAttributeNames()`, and `removeAttribute()` methods.

Session Lifecycle Event Handling

In the previous section we've seen the lifecycle of sessions, which consists of the following:

❑ **Creation of a new session**
This happens when a client first makes an HTTP request to a web application.

❑ **Invalidation of a session**
This happens either when the session has timed-out due to inactivity, or when a servlet or JSP page explicitly invalidates a session

In addition, a container may passivate and activate sessions under the following conditions:

❑ When the session is inactive for a considerable amount of time (but not long enough for session invalidation), the container can conserve memory by writing the session to a persistent medium such as a file system. This process is called passivation. The container may reactivate the session when there is a request from the client. This is the process of activation.

❑ In a distributable container, the container may transfer the session from one JVM to another. This involves first passivating the session, then transferring it over wire to another JVM, and then activating it.

The Servlet API includes event-handling mechanisms whereby objects (either session attributes or others) can be notified of the above. The following are the event listeners:

❑ `HttpSessionListener`:
A listener interface for notifications when a new session is created, or when an existing session is destroyed (or invalidated)

❑ `HttpSessionActivationListener`:
A listener interface for notifications when a session is passivated or activated

In both these cases, the container encapsulates the associated event as an `HttpSessionEvent` object.

Let's us now discuss these listeners and the associated events in detail:

The HttpSessionListener Interface

```
public interface HttpSessionListener
```

This interface has the following methods:

```
public void sessionCreated(HttpSessionEvent event)
```

This method will be called when a new session is created in this web application.

```
public void sessionDestroyed(HttpSessionEvent event)
```

This method will be called when an existing session is destroyed (invalidated).

Any object may implement this interface to be notified of session creation/invalidation. However, you need to explicitly specify this object within the deployment descriptor.

For instance, consider a class `MySessionListener` implementing this interface. For an instance of this class to receive the above events, you would add the following to the deployment descriptor:

```
<listener>
    <listener-class>MySessionListener</listener-class>
</listener>
```

Based on this entry, whenever the container creates/invalidates a session, it will notify an instance of `MySessionListener`. The container creates instances of all listeners at the container startup or before creating any session.

What's the purpose of this listener? The main application of this listener is to perform any actions necessary before a session is created or destroyed. For instance, you may make calls to your backend systems to perform business actions when a new session is created.

The HttpSessionActivationListener Interface

```
public interface HttpSessionActivationListener
```

This interface can be used for notification of activation and passivation. This interface has the following methods:

The sessionDidActivate() Method

```
public void sessionDidActivate(HttpSessionEvent event)
```

The container calls this method after activating a session.

The sessionWillPassivate() Method

```
public void sessionWillPassivate(HttpSessionEvent event)
```

The container calls this method before passivating an existing session.

Attributes bound to sessions may implement this interface. When an attribute is bound to a session, the container invokes the above methods after passivating and before activating sessions.

Since this interface is meant for attributes to implement, there is no entry required in the deployment descriptor.

One of the situations in which this event helps is when an attribute holds references to remote objects such as EJBs or even non-serializable objects. In this case, the attribute can recreate those references when the `sessionDidActivate()` event is called.

The HttpSessionEvent Class

```
public class HttpSessionEvent extends java.util.EventObject
```

This is the event for both listeners discussed above. This class has a single method.

The getSession() Method

```
public HttpSession getSession()
```

With this method, the listener can access the HTTP session and its contents.

Session Attribute Event Handling

In addition to the above, there are two more listeners to monitor the state (attributes) of sessions. These listeners are based on the following activities:

❑   Adding an attribute to a session

❑   Replacing an attribute in a session with another object

❑   Removing an attribute from a session

Both the attribute participating in these actions and other objects can listen to these events. The following are the interfaces meant for handling these events:

The HttpSessionBindingListener Interface

```
public interface HttpSessionBindingListener extends java.util.EventListener
```

This interface can be used to notify an object when it is being placed into the session (using the `setAttribute()` method), or removed from the session (via the `removeAttribute()` method).

The valueBound() Method

```
public void valueBound(HttpSessionBindingEvent event)
```

The container calls this method on the object that is being bound to a session.

The valueUnbound() Method

```
public void valueUnbound(HttpSessionBindingEvent event)
```

The container calls this method on the object that is being unbound from a session. The unbinding can happen either by explicitly removing it from the session, or during session invalidation.

When the attribute implementing `HttpSessionBindingListener` is added to the `HttpSession`, the web container notifies the attribute that it is being bound to the session. Similarly, when the attribute is removed from the session, the web container notifies the attribute that it is being unbound from the session. The attribute can use the callback methods provided to initialize or clean up its state.

For instance, in a shopping cart application, consider the shopping cart attribute stored in the session. This object will be created when the customer first visits the site. Assume that the customer added items to the cart but, instead of proceeding to checkout, decided not to continue, and left the site. Later, when the user session expires, the container notifies the shopping cart attribute that it is being unbound from the session. The cart object can then save the shopping cart in a database.

When the same user revisits the site, the application binds the shopping cart attribute to the session again. This time, the shopping cart attribute can reload the saved shopping cart, and provide a seamless user experience for the customer.

> *Note that, in order for the shopping cart attribute to implement such tasks, it may need access to the* HttpSession *to which it is associated. As you'll see below, the* HttpSessionBindingEvent *provides access to the* HttpSession.

The HttpSessionAttributeListener Interface

```
public interface HttpSessionAttributeListener extends java.util.EventListener
```

This interface is similar to the HttpSessionBindingListener interface except that it is meant for any object to implement and be notified when the state of a session changes. This interface has the following methods:

The attributeAdded () Method

```
public void attributeAdded(HttpSessionBindingEvent event)
```

The container calls this method when an attribute is added to a session.

The attributeRemoved () Method

```
public void attributeRemoved(HttpSessionBindingEvent event)
```

The container calls this method when an attribute is removed from a session.

The attributeReplaced () Method

```
public void attributeReplaced(HttpSessionBindingEvent event)
```

The container calls this method when an attribute is replaced with another. This can happen, for instance, when you call the setAttribute() method on the session with the same name, but with a different value.

The HttpSessionBindingEvent Class

```
public class HttpSessionBindingListener extends HttpSessionEvent
```

This class represents session binding and unbinding events and has the following methods:

The getName() Method

```
public String getName()
```

This method returns the name of the attribute that was used while binding/unbinding the attribute in the session.

The getValue() Method

```
public Object getValue()
```

This method returns the value of the attribute that is being bound, unbound, or replaced.

The getSession() Method

```
public HttpSession getSession()
```

This method returns the `HttpSession` object from which the attribute is being bound/unbound or being replaced.

A Simple Shopping Cart using Sessions

In this section we will consider a simple shopping cart application, to illustrate various concepts associated with session tracking. Such applications typically allow a user to select items from a catalog and place them in a virtual shopping cart, before proceeding to the checkout and paying for the items.

This shopping cart application has two servlets: one for generating a catalog, and the other for adding items to a cart and displaying the contents of the cart. In this application, we'll use the same set of `HttpSession` methods that we used in the `AttributeServlet`. However, the purpose of the shopping cart is to demonstrate how these methods can be combined to build real-life applications.

Here we will consider a bare-bones implementation without most of the features that you would expect in a fully functional shopping cart. You are encouraged to add more functionality to this application while exploring the Java Servlet API.

The Catalog Servlet

The catalog consists of two parts. The first part is a statement showing the current number of books selected in the shopping cart, and the second is an HTML form, with the list of books displayed within a group of checkboxes.

The HTML form consists of a short list of items displayed in a table. Each item has a checkbox next to it for the user to select the item and add it to their shopping cart. In a typical shopping cart program, the catalog pages are generated from a database, but for our example, a static list is used for demonstration purposes:

```
// Import servlet packages
import javax.servlet.ServletException;
import javax.servlet.http.HttpServlet;
import javax.servlet.http.HttpSession;
import javax.servlet.http.HttpServletRequest;
import javax.servlet.http.HttpServletResponse;

// Import java packages
import java.io.PrintWriter;
import java.io.IOException;
import java.util.ArrayList;

public class Catalog extends HttpServlet {
  protected void doGet(HttpServletRequest req, HttpServletResponse res)
          throws ServletException, IOException {
    HttpSession session = req.getSession();
```

```
    int itemCount = 0;
    ArrayList cart = (ArrayList) session.getAttribute("cart");
    if (cart != null) {
      itemCount = cart.size();
    }

    res.setContentType("text/html");
    PrintWriter out = res.getWriter();

    out.println("<html><head><title>Simple Shopping Cart "
             + "Example</title></head>");
    out.println("<body><table border=\"0\" width=\"100%\"><tr>");
    out.println("<td valign=\"top\"><img "
             + "src=\"/cart/images/logo.gif\"></td>");
    out.println("<td align=\"left\" valign=\"bottom\">");
    out.println("<h1>WROX Book Store</h1></td></tr></table><hr>");
    out.println("<p>You've " + itemCount + " items in your cart.</p>");
    out.print("<form action=\"");
    out.println(res.encodeURL("/cart/servlet/cart"));
    out.println("\" method=\"post\">");
    out.println("<table cellspacing=\"5\" cellpadding=\"5\"><tr>");
    out.println("<td align=\"center\"><b>Add to Cart</b></td>");
    out.println("<td align=\"center\"></td></tr><tr>");
    out.println("<td align=\"center\">");
    out.println("<input type=\"Checkbox\" name=\"item\""
             + " value=\"Begining Java2 - JDK 1.4 Version\"></td>");
    out.println("<td align=\"left\">Item 1: "
             + " Begining Java2 - JDK 1.4 Version</td></tr><tr>");
    out.println("<td align=\"center\">");
    out.println("<input type=\"Checkbox\" name=\"item\""
             + " value=\"Professional Java XML\"></td>");
    out.println("<td align=\"left\">Item 2: "
             + " Professional Java XML</td></tr><tr>");
    out.println("<td align=\"center\">");
    out.println("<input type=\"Checkbox\" name=\"item\""
             + " value=\" Professional Java Server Programming\"></td>");
    out.println("<td align=\"left\">Item 3: Professional Java "
             + "Server Programming</td></tr>");
    out.println("</table><hr>");
    out.println("<input type=\"Submit\" name=\"btn_submit\" "
             + "value=\"Add to Cart\">");
    out.println("</form></body></html>");

    out.close();
  }
}
```

This servlet obtains the number of books from data stored in the `HttpSession`. It starts by using the `getSession()` method on the `HttpServletRequest` object to get the current session:

```
HttpSession session = req.getSession();
```

This is the first step required for creating and tracking HTTP sessions. You'll also find a similar `req.getSession()` call in the `ShoppingCart` servlet.

It then uses a `HttpSession` attribute `"cart"` to find and display the number of books in the cart. As we'll see in a moment, the `ShoppingCart` servlet stores and updates this attribute when items are added to the cart, using an `ArrayList` object to store the list of selected books.

```
ArrayList cart = (ArrayList) session.getAttribute("cart");
```

The rest of this servlet prepares the catalog. This generates a form with a POST action, which sends the list of selected books in the HTTP request.

The ShoppingCart Servlet

The ShoppingCart servlet is responsible for adding items to the cart. This servlet collects (from the POST request submitted by the Catalog servlet) the list of books selected, and updates the shopping cart. In this bare-bones implementation, the shopping cart is modeled as a java.util.ArrayList object holding the names of the items. This object is then stored as an attribute with the name "cart" in the HttpSession:

```
// Import servlet packages
import javax.servlet.ServletException;
import javax.servlet.http.HttpServlet;
import javax.servlet.http.HttpSession;
import javax.servlet.http.HttpServletRequest;
import javax.servlet.http.HttpServletResponse;

// Import java packages
import java.io.PrintWriter;
import java.io.IOException;
import java.util.ArrayList;
import java.util.Iterator;

public class ShoppingCart extends HttpServlet {

  public void doPost (HttpServletRequest req, HttpServletResponse res)
                     throws ServletException, IOException {
    HttpSession session = req.getSession(true);

    ArrayList cart = (ArrayList) session.getAttribute("cart");

    if (cart == null) {
      cart = new ArrayList();
      session.setAttribute("cart", cart);
    }

    PrintWriter out = res.getWriter();
    res.setContentType("text/html");

    String[] itemsSelected;
    String itemName;
    itemsSelected = req.getParameterValues("item");

    if (itemsSelected != null) {

      for (int i = 0; i < itemsSelected.length; i++) {
        itemName = itemsSelected[i];
        cart.add(itemName);
      }
    }

    // Print Current Contents of Cart
    out.println("<html><head><title>");
    out.println("Shopping Cart Contents");
    out.println("</title></head>");
    out.println("<body>");
    out.println("<h1>Items currently in your cart</h1>");
    out.println("<hr>");
```

```
      Iterator iterator = cart.iterator();
      while (iterator.hasNext()) {
        out.println("<p>" + iterator.next() + "</p>");
      }

      out.print("<hr><p><a href=\"");
      out.print(res.encodeURL("/cart/servlet/catalog"));
      out.println("\">Back to the shop</a></p>");

      out.close();
    }
  }
```

Remember that when a form contains multiple checkboxes with the same name, the parameter may have multiple values. Therefore, the getParameterValues() method is used to extract the selected books from the request.

Finally, we generate a page containing the current contents of the shopping cart, and a link back to the cart.

Compile these two Java files and create the following deployment descriptor:

```xml
<?xml version="1.0" encoding="ISO-8859-1"?>
<!DOCTYPE web-app PUBLIC
  "-//Sun Microsystems, Inc.//DTD Web Application 2.3//EN"
  "http://java.sun.com/j2ee/dtds/web-app_2_3.dtd">

<web-app>

  <servlet>
    <servlet-name>catalog</servlet-name>
    <display-name>catalog</display-name>
    <servlet-class>Catalog</servlet-class>
  </servlet>

  <servlet>
    <servlet-name>cart</servlet-name>
    <display-name>cart</display-name>
    <servlet-class>ShoppingCart</servlet-class>
  </servlet>

</web-app>
```

When you have deployed the application, using a context root of cart, open a browser at: http://localhost:8000/cart/servlet/catalog.

The screenshots opposite show the catalog and shopping cart. The catalog has only three entries, and is generated using the Catalog servlet:

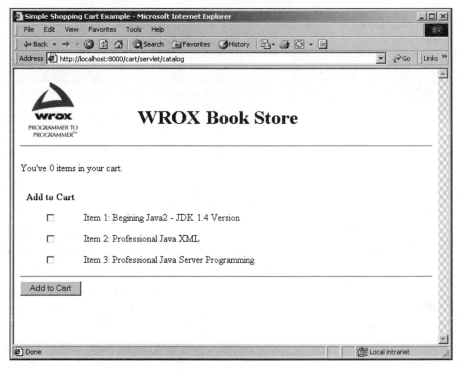

To add items to the cart, check the checkboxes against the item, and click the Add to Cart button. This will cause the `ShoppingCart` servlet to generate the shopping cart screen:

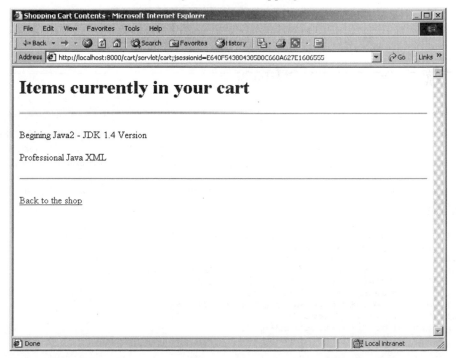

Servlet Context

In the Java Servlet API, the servlet context defines a servlet's view of the web application, and provides access to resources and facilities (such as logging) common to all servlets in the application. Unlike a session, which is specific to a client, the servlet context is specific to a particular web application running in a JVM. That is, each web application in a container will have a single servlet context associated with it.

Servlet context is yet another useful concept provided by the Servlet API. In the previous section, we saw how we could use HttpSession objects to maintain state relating to a single client on the server. The servlet context complements this facility by letting you maintain application-level state – that is, state information common to all servlets and clients in the application.

The Java Servlet API provides a ServletContext interface to represent a context: the resources shared by a group of servlets. In the 1.0 and 2.0 versions of the Servlet API the ServletContext interface only provided access to information about the servlet's environment, such as the name of the server, MIME type mappings, etc., and a log() method for writing log messages to the server's log file. Most implementations provided one servlet context for all servlets within a host, or per virtual host.

Since version 2.1 of the API, the role of the ServletContext interface has been revised to represent the environment for each web application, and to act as a shared repository of attributes for all servlets in the application. The interface allows servlets in the same context to share information through context attributes, in a similar manner to the session attributes we have already seen.

Each servlet context is rooted at a specific path in the web server. In the examples we've seen so far, we've had to specify a context root during the deployment process. For example, the TechSupport application of the previous chapter is associated with a context /techSupport. With the help of this notion, you can deploy multiple web applications under different context root names. All such applications can coexist as if they were deployed on different containers.

Let's take a look at the ServletContext interface.

The ServletContext Interface

```
public interface ServletContext
```

The ServletContext interface encapsulates the notion of a context for a web application. An object of this type can be obtained using the getServletContext() method of the HttpServlet object. HttpServlet in turn gets this object from the ServletConfig object that was passed to it during initialization.

The ServletContext interface specifies the following methods; web containers provide an implementation of the interface:

```
public String getMimeType(String fileName)
public URL getResource(String path)
public InputStream getResourceAsStream(String path)
public RequestDispatcher getRequestDispatcher(String path)
public RequestDispatcher getNamedDispatcher(String name)
public String getRealPath(String path)
public ServletContext getContext(String uriPath)
public String getServerInfo()
public String getServletContextName()
```

```
public Set getResourcePaths(String path)
public String getInitParameter(String name)
public Enumeration getInitParameterNames()
public Object getAttribute(String name)
public Enumeration getAttributeNames()
public void setAttribute(String name, Object attribute)
public void removeAttribute(String name)
public int getMajorVersion()
public int getMinorVersion()
public void log(String message)
public void log(String message, Throwable cause)
```

The getMimeType() Method

```
public String getMimeType(String fileName)
```

This method returns the MIME type of a file by its extension. As we shall see in Chapter 9, you can specify the MIME types that your application can handle in the deployment descriptor.

The getResource() Method

```
public URL getResource(String path)
```

This method returns the URL to a resource at the specified path, and can be used to construct URL objects for files in the local file system.

The getResourceAsStream() Method

```
public InputStream getResourceAsStream(String path)
```

This method is similar to getResource(), except that it returns an input stream associated with the URL.

The getRequestDispatcher() Method

```
public RequestDispatcher getRequestDispatcher(String path)
```

This method returns a RequestDispatcher object associated with the resource located at the current path. You can use the RequestDispatcher to delegate request/response processing to other resources within the application – we'll discuss RequestDispatcher in more detail later in this chapter.

The getNamedDispatcher() Method

```
public RequestDispatcher getNamedDispatcher(String path)
```

This method is similar to the getRequestDispatcher() method, except that this method accepts the alias names assigned to servlet classes in the deployment descriptor.

The getRealPath() Method

```
public String getRealPath(String path)
```

In a web application, resources are referred to by paths relative to the path pointing to the context, so this method lets you obtain the real path (on the server file system) from the path relative to the context.

The getContext() Method

```
public ServletContext getContext(String uriPath)
```

This method returns a `ServletContext` object associated with the specified URL on the server. However, due to possible security limitations imposed by the web container, this method might return `null`, as this method otherwise lets you gain access to context objects that belong to other web applications.

The getServerInfo() Method

```
public String getServerInfo()
```

This method returns the name and version of the servlet container on which the servlet is running. This information may be used for logging purposes.

The getServletContextName() Method

```
public String getServletContextName()
```

This method returns the display-name of the web application. Each application can be assigned a display name in the deployment descriptor by adding a `<display-name>` element. This method returns this name. This method returns `null` if this element is missing from the deployment descriptor.

The getResourcePaths() Method

```
public Set getResourcePaths(String path)
```

This method is functionally similar to executing a directory listing command. Given a path name relative to the root of the web application, this method returns all sub-paths.

The `ServletContext` interface provides two methods for logging purposes. Of these, the second method can be used to log exceptions, while the first method can be used for general-purpose logging.

The getInitParameter and getInitParameterNames() Methods

```
public String getInitParameter(String name)
public Enumeration getInitParameterNames()
```

As with servlets themselves, we can specify initialization parameters for servlet contexts. These can be specified in the deployment descriptor using `<context-param>` tags. With the help of the above two methods, you can access these parameters.

The getAttribute(), getAttributeNames(), setAttribute(), and removeAttribute() Methods

```
public Object getAttribute(String name)
public Enumeration getAttributeNames()
public void setAttribute(String name, Object attribute)
public void removeAttribute(String name)
```

The log() Methods

```
public void log(java.lang.String msg)
public void log(String message, Throwable throwable)
```

These four methods let you maintain the state of a web application. Any servlet can set an attribute, which can then be obtained by any other servlet within the same application, irrespective of whether these servlets are serving the same client or not. Using these methods, servlets can share information common to all servlets.

ServletContext Lifecycle Event Handling

The container creates the servlet context before attempting to serve any contents of a web application. Similarly, the container may delete the context before stopping to serve the contents of a web application. In order to handle these two events, the Servlet API specifies the following interface:

The ServletContextListener Interface

```
public interface ServletContextListener extends java.util.EventListener
```

An object of this interface receives events about the creation or destruction of a servlet context. This interface has the following methods:

```
public void contextInitialized(ServletContextEvent event)
```

This method will be called when a new context is created.

```
public void contextDestroyed(ServletContextEvent event)
```

This method will be called when an existing context is destroyed.

You can register a class implementing this interface using the <listener> element in the deployment descriptor:

```
<listener>
    <listener-class>MyContextListener</listener-class>
</listener>
```

Note that this is the same element that we can also use to specify classes implementing the HttpSessionListener interface.

ServletContextAttributeListener

```
public interface ServletContextAttributeListener extends java.util.EventListener
```

This interface is similar to the HttpSessionAttributeListener and gets notifies when there is change in the state of a context. This interface has the following methods:

```
public void attributeAdded(ServletContextAttributeEvent event)
```

The container invokes this method on the listener when a new attribute is added to the context.

```
public void attributeReplaced(ServletContextAttributeEvent event)
```

The container invokes this method on the listener when the value of an attribute is changed, but not the attribute itself. This happens when you call the setAttribute() method on the context with the name of a previously added attribute as the name.

```
public void attributeRemoved(ServletContextAttributeEvent event)
```

The container invokes this method on the listener when an attribute is removed from the context.

A Chat Application using Context and Sessions

In order to illustrate both the session and context in action, let us now consider a multi-room chat application for chatting over the web. Using this application, two or more users can enter a chat room and post messages. Other users participating in the same chat room receive those messages. In this scenario, any user may send a message any time, and once a user sends a message, all participating users of the chat room receive the message.

What does it take to build a chat application? For this exercise, let us consider browser-based chatting – that is all chat clients are browsers. In order to support such clients, we also need a web application. Each client can connect to this application for chatting as shown below:

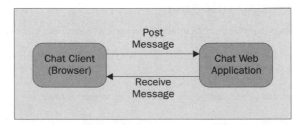

This setup is similar to any typical web application. From this, you can identify the following immediate requirements for this application:

- ❏ The server should provide some interface (an HTML form) for posting messages
- ❏ The client should periodically connect to the server and download any new messages

Although there is only one client shown in this picture, for a chat to take place you need two or more clients, interacting simultaneously with the server hosting the chat application. Since all users for a given chat room see the same messages, there should be a mechanism to share such data. We therefore have another requirement:

- ❏ The server should maintain messages posted to a chat room, and let all users download the messages

Besides these requirements, in order for multiple users chat on different topics, we also need a facility to maintain multiple chat rooms, leading to the following additional requirements:

- ❏ The server should facilitate managing multiple chat rooms. One should be able to create chat rooms as required, and delete a chat room when not required.
- ❏ The server should also provide a means to identify each user in a given chat room. That is, each client should be asked to provide a name before entering a chat room.

Of these, the need for multiple chat rooms, and simultaneous interaction between users sharing data, are what make this chat application challenging.

Let us now set to and build such an application. The purpose of this exercise is to illustrate how to use the Servlet API to build such an application.

Before proceeding to build such an application, let's first look at certain modeling requirements:

- ❏ The chat application consists of multiple chat rooms. Any user can leave a chat room and enter another chat room.
- ❏ In a given chat room, there will be more than one user exchanging messages.

In order to build such an application, we need to model certain classes:

❑ A ChatRoom class to represent a chat room.
Since a ChatRoom is shared across multiple users (and therefore multiple sessions), the ServletContext is the right place to store a ChatRoom. Since there can be more than one ChatRoom, we need to maintain a list of ChatRooms in the ServletContext.

❑ A ChatEntry to represent a chat message.
In a chat room, multiple messages are exchanged between users. A ChatEntry is part of a ChatRoom, and the ChatRoom class maintains a list of ChatEntry objects.

The diagram below gives an overview of relationships between these classes:

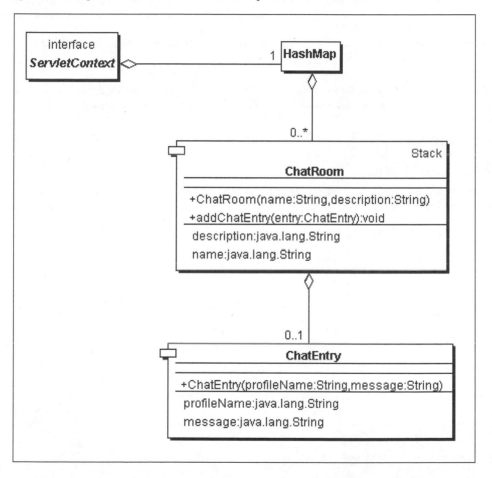

A java.util.HashMap class is used to hold a map of ChatRoom objects, and each ChatRoom contains a stack of ChatEntry objects. The HashMap object is the entry point to all the other objects, so a reference to the HashMap is stored as a ServletContext attribute under the name roomList.

The HashMap, ChatRoom, and ChatEntry objects together represent the state of the chat application. These classes represent the data model for this application.

Let us now look at the chat user's interaction with the server:

❑ **Room management**
We need a servlet to create and to delete chat rooms. Let's call the servlet `ChatAdminServlet`.

❑ **Joining a chat**
Once a set of chat rooms has been created, we need to provide a chat user with the available rooms, ask the user to identify themselves, and let them enter a chat room. Let us designate a servlet `ListRoomsServlet` to manage these tasks.

❑ **Chat**
The last step is the chat itself. For this task, we need to provide a means of posting a message, and another means of downloading chat messages. Let's designate a `ChatRoomServlet` for these tasks.

These three servlets are also responsible for providing any dynamic content (such as list of available chat rooms, chat messages, etc.).

Once you go through the chapter on JSP, and learn how to use JSP pages to provide dynamic content, you may revisit this application, and refactor it to use JSP pages in combination with the above servlets.

Let us now consider implementation of the above classes.

The ChatRoom Class

An instance of the `ChatRoom` class represents an individual chat room, and each instance maintains all the messages for a specific room:

```java
import java.util.Stack;

public class ChatRoom extends Stack {
  private String name;
  private String description;

  public ChatRoom(String name, String description) {
    this.name = name;
    this.description = description;
  }

  public void addChatEntry(ChatEntry entry) {
    push(entry);
  }

  public String getDescription() {
    return description;
  }

  public String getName() {
    return name;
  }
}
```

This class extends `java.util.Stack`. Each `ChatRoom` has a name, and a description. These values are passed to the constructor when the room is created. When a user enters a chat message, the `addChatEntry()` method is used to add the message to the room.

Though this class appears simple, there are certain reasons why we designed this class in the above manner. Firstly, multiple clients access a ChatRoom and add messages. In order to make sure that the ChatRoom is thread-safe, we need to synchronize access to methods that add/remove messages to the ChatRoom. However we're not doing so here, because the java.util.Stack class, which extends java.util.Vector, is synchronized. The methods that add and delete elements in a vector are implemented in a thread-safe manner.

The ChatEntry Class

A ChatEntry object represents a message in a chat room.:

```
public class ChatEntry {
    private String profileName;
    private String message;

    public ChatEntry(String profileName, String message)  {
        this.profileName = profileName;
        this.message = message;
    }

    public String getProfileName() {
        return profileName;
    }

    public String getMessage() {
        return message;
    }
}
```

A ChatEntry contains a chat message and the name of the user (profileName) that sent the message.

The Administration Servlet

ChatAdminServlet provides administration facilities for the chat application. This servlet implements both the doGet() and doPost() methods. The doGet() method will be invoked when you directly invoke the servlet, and the doPost() method when you delete or add chat rooms.

The response of this servlet when invoked for the first time is shown overleaf; with this user interface, you can add new chat rooms:

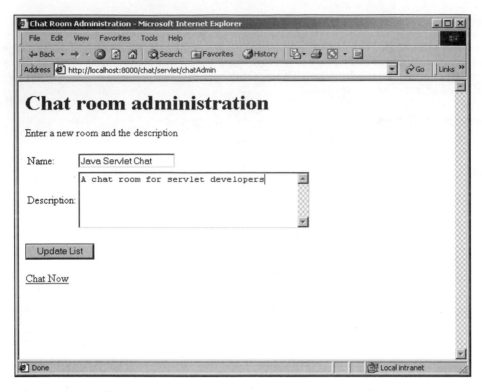

This servlet needs to implement:

- ❑ A doGet() method to generate a list of existing chat rooms (if any), followed by a form for creating a chat room.

- ❑ A doPost() method to process the response generated by the form submission. The processing involves creating a new chat room, or removing an existing room.

In all the servlets in this example, we use three context parameters specified in the deployment descriptor. These are: CHATROOM_PATH, LISTROOMS_PATH, and ADMIN_PATH. As you will see later in the deployment descriptor, these parameters point to the URIs of the ChatRoomServlet, ListRoomsServlet, and ChatAdminServlet respectively:

```
// Import servlet packages
import javax.servlet.ServletException;
import javax.servlet.UnavailableException;
import javax.servlet.ServletContext;
import javax.servlet.http.HttpServlet;
import javax.servlet.http.HttpServletRequest;
import javax.servlet.http.HttpServletResponse;

// Import java packages
import java.io.IOException;
import java.io.PrintWriter;
import java.util.HashMap;
import java.util.Iterator;

public class ChatAdminServlet extends HttpServlet {
```

```java
String chatRoomPath;
String listRoomsPath;
String chatAdminPath;

public void init() throws ServletException {
  ServletContext context = getServletContext();
  chatRoomPath = context.getInitParameter("CHATROOM_PATH");
  listRoomsPath = context.getInitParameter("LISTROOMS_PATH");
  chatAdminPath = context.getInitParameter("ADMIN_PATH");
  if(chatRoomPath == null || listRoomsPath == null ||
    chatAdminPath == null) {
    throw new UnavailableException("Application unavailable.");
  }
}

public void doGet (HttpServletRequest req, HttpServletResponse res)
        throws IOException, ServletException {
  res.setContentType("text/html");
  PrintWriter out = res.getWriter();
  out.println("<html>");
  out.println("<head><title>Chat Room Administration</title></head>");
  out.println("<body>");
  out.println("<h1>Chat room administration</h1>");
  out.println("<form method=\"POST\" action=\""
              + res.encodeURL(chatAdminPath) + "\">");

  // Check for existing chat rooms
  HashMap roomList =
    (HashMap) getServletContext().getAttribute("roomList");
  if (roomList != null) {
    Iterator rooms = roomList.keySet().iterator();

    if (!rooms.hasNext()) {
      out.println("<p>There are no rooms</p>");
    } else {
      out.println("<p>Check the rooms you would like to remove,"
                  + "and press Update List.</p>");

      while (rooms.hasNext()) {
        String roomName = (String) rooms.next();
        ChatRoom room = (ChatRoom) roomList.get(roomName);
        out.println("<input type=checkbox name=remove value='"
                    + room.getName() + "'>" + room.getName() + "<br>");
      }
    }
  }

  // Add fields for adding a room
  out.println("<p>Enter a new room and the description<p>");
  out.println("<table>");
  out.println("<tr><td>Name:</td><td><input name=roomname " +
              "size=50></td></tr>");
  out.println("<tr><td>Description:</td>");
  out.println("<td><textarea name=roomdescr cols=40 rows=5>");
  out.println("</textarea></td></tr>");
  out.println("</table>");

  // Add submit button
  out.println("<p><input type=submit value='Update List'>");
  out.println("<p><a href=\"" + listRoomsPath + "\">Chat Now</a>");
  out.println("</form>");
  out.println("</body></html>");
```

```
    out.close();
  }

  public void doPost(HttpServletRequest req, HttpServletResponse res)
          throws IOException, ServletException {
    HashMap roomList = null;

    // Check for existing chat rooms
    synchronized (getServletContext()) {
      roomList = (HashMap) getServletContext().getAttribute("roomList");
      if (roomList == null) {
        roomList = new HashMap();
        getServletContext().setAttribute("roomList", roomList);
      }
    }

    // Update the room list
    String[] removeList = req.getParameterValues("remove");
    synchronized (roomList) {
      if (removeList != null) {
        for (int i = 0; i < removeList.length; i++) {
          roomList.remove(removeList[i]);
        }
      }
    }

    String roomName = req.getParameter("roomname");
    String roomDescr = req.getParameter("roomdescr");

    if (roomName != null && roomName.length() > 0) {
      synchronized (roomList) {
        roomList.put(roomName, new ChatRoom(roomName, roomDescr));
      }
    }

    doGet (req, res);
  }

}
```

The key features of this class are:

❑   The init() method loads the paths to the three servlets from the context. The init() method throws an UnavailableException if these parameters have not been set in the deployment descriptor.

❑   The doGet() method checks for context attribute called roomList. If there is none, it creates a new HashMap object and stores it in the context.

❑   If the HashMap is not empty, the doGet() method then prints a list of rooms (name of each room and a checkbox) as part of the form to submit a POST request to the same servlet.

❑   The doPost() method processes the POST request; this method can simultaneously remove existing rooms and add a new room. This method retrieves the HashMap from the context, and depending on the type of request, either deletes existing rooms (specified by request parameter "remove"), and/or adds a new room (specified by request parameters roomname and roomdescr).

❑   After updating the HashMap, the doPost() method calls doGet(), to generate the list of rooms and the form.

Note that since the HashMap *is stored in the context as an attribute, all servlets participating in this application can access the list of rooms.*

We do not set the ServletContext roomList attribute after every update of the HashMap object. This attribute contains a reference to the HashMap object; we update the HashMap's data, but the *reference* is still the same, and we need not replace the HashMap object with another HashMap. Setting the attribute to the same object reference again would be redundant.

Servlets for Chatting

The ListRoomsServlet and ChatRoomServlet classes implement the end-user interface. They both access the context's state through the roomList attribute set by the ChatAdminServlet. Before we dive into the code, let's look at the overall design.

The ListRoomsServlet uses the HashMap object to get all ChatRoom objects, and sends a list of them to the client. The user can select the room to enter, causing the ChatRoomServlet to be invoked.

The ChatRoomServlet first uses the HashMap to get the ChatRoom selected by the user, and then gets all ChatEntry objects from the ChatRoom. It then sends a list of all the chat entries to the client. This servlet is also invoked when the user sends a new message to the room. In this case, it creates a new ChatEntry object and adds it to the selected ChatRoom.

The ListRoomsServlet Class

A chat user of this application first invokes the ListRoomsServlet, which lists all available rooms and allows the user to choose a name and enter a room. The screenshot below shows the response of the ListsRoomServlet after adding a couple of rooms:

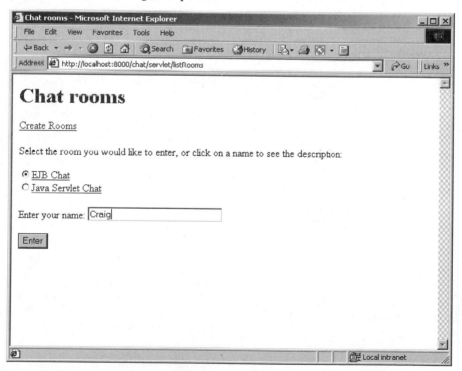

As shown above, the response of this servlet displays a list of chat rooms. When you click on a room, this servlet displays the description of the servlet. Alternatively, you can select a chat room (using the radio button next to the name of the room), enter a name (profile name), and click on Enter to enter into the chat room:

```java
// Import servlet packages
import javax.servlet.ServletException;
import javax.servlet.ServletContext;
import javax.servlet.http.HttpServlet;
import javax.servlet.http.HttpSession;
import javax.servlet.http.HttpServletRequest;
import javax.servlet.http.HttpServletResponse;

// Import java packages
import java.io.IOException;
import java.io.PrintWriter;
import java.util.HashMap;
import java.util.Iterator;
import java.net.URLEncoder;

public class ListRoomsServlet extends HttpServlet {

  String chatAdminPath;
  String listRoomsPath;
  String chatRoomPath;

  public void init() {
    ServletContext context = getServletContext();
    chatAdminPath = context.getInitParameter("ADMIN_PATH");
    listRoomsPath = context.getInitParameter("LISTROOMS_PATH");
    chatRoomPath = context.getInitParameter("CHATROOM_PATH");
    if(chatRoomPath == null || listRoomsPath == null ||
       chatAdminPath == null) {
      throw new UnavailableException("Application unavailable.");
    }
  }

  public void doGet(HttpServletRequest request,
                    HttpServletResponse response) throws IOException {
    response.setContentType("text/html");
    PrintWriter out = response.getWriter();

    String expand = request.getParameter("expand");
    HttpSession session = request.getSession();
    String profileName = (String) session.getAttribute("profileName");
    if (profileName == null) {
      profileName = "";
    }

    out.println("<html>");
    out.println("<head><title>Chat rooms</title></head>");
    out.println("<body>");
    out.println("<h1>Chat rooms</h1>");
    out.println("<form method=POST action=\"" + chatRoomPath + "\">");
    out.println("<p><a href=\"" + chatAdminPath
                + "\">Create Rooms</a></p>");

    // Get the list of rooms
    HashMap roomList =
      (HashMap) getServletContext().getAttribute("roomList");
    if (roomList == null) {
      out.println("<p>There are no rooms available right now.</p>");
    } else {
```

```
        // Add radio boxes for selecting a room
        out.println("Select the room you wouldlike to enter,"
                    + "or click on a name to see the description:<p>");

        Iterator rooms = roomList.keySet().iterator();
        boolean isFirst = true;
        while (rooms.hasNext()) {
          String roomName = (String) rooms.next();
          ChatRoom room = (ChatRoom) roomList.get(roomName);
          String listRoomsURL = listRoomsPath + "/?expand="
                                + URLEncoder.encode(roomName);
          listRoomsURL = response.encodeURL(listRoomsURL);

          out.println("<input type=radio name=roomName value=\"" + roomName
                      + "\"" + (isFirst ? " CHECKED" : "") + ">"
                      + "<a href=\"" + listRoomsURL + "\">" + roomName
                      + "</a><br>");
          isFirst = false;

          // Show description if requested
          if (expand != null && expand.equals(roomName)) {
            out.println("<blockquote>");
            if (room.getDescription().length() == 0) {
              out.println("No description available.");
            } else {
              out.println(room.getDescription());
            }
            out.println("</blockquote><br>");
          }
        }

        // Add a field for the profile name
        out.println("<p>Enter your name: ");
        out.println("<input name=profileName value='" + profileName
                    + "' size=30>");

        // Add submit button
        out.println("<p><input type=submit value='Enter'>");
        out.println("</form>");
      }

    out.println("</body></html>");
    out.close();
  }
}
```

The HTTP GET method is used to invoke the servlet, so we use the `doGet()` method to generate an HTML page with a form containing the list of rooms, the user name field, and an Enter button.

To generate the list of chat rooms, this method calls the `getAttribute()` method on the `ServletContext` to obtain the list of chat rooms. The servlet also creates a session for each user. Note that, as discussed in the previous example, all URLs are encoded to make use of URL rewriting in case cookies are not being accepted by chat users.

The ChatRoomServlet Class

As seen above, the `ListRoomsServlet` generates a page with a `<form>` tag with the action attribute set to the name of the `ChatRoomServlet`. The form contains a radio button control that holds the name of the selected room and a text field with the user's name, and uses the POST method to invoke the servlet again.

The `ChatRoomServlet` is given below:

```java
// Import servlet packages
import javax.servlet.ServletException;
import javax.servlet.UnavailableException;
import javax.servlet.ServletContext;
import javax.servlet.http.HttpServlet;
import javax.servlet.http.HttpSession;
import javax.servlet.http.HttpServletRequest;
import javax.servlet.http.HttpServletResponse;

// Import java packages
import java.io.IOException;
import java.io.PrintWriter;
import java.util.HashMap;
import java.util.Iterator;

public class ChatRoomServlet extends HttpServlet {
  String chatRoomPath;
  String listRoomsPath;

  public void init() throws ServletException {
    ServletContext context = getServletContext();
    chatRoomPath = context.getInitParameter("CHATROOM_PATH");
    listRoomsPath = context.getInitParameter("LISTROOMS_PATH");
    if(chatRoomPath == null || listRoomsPath == null) {
      throw new UnavailableException("Application unavailable.");
    }
  }

  public void doGet(HttpServletRequest req, HttpServletResponse res)
          throws IOException, ServletException {

    res.setContentType("text/html");
    PrintWriter out = res.getWriter();

    ChatRoom room = getRoom(req, res);
    if(room == null) {
      throw new ServletException("Room not found");
    }

    // Check if it's a request for a message list or a form
    String listPar = req.getParameter("list");
    if (listPar != null && listPar.equals("true")) {
      writeMessages(out, room, getProfileName(req));
    } else {
      out.println("<html>");
      out.println("<body>");
      out.println("<form method=\"post\" action=\""
                  + res.encodeURL(chatRoomPath) + "\" target=\"_top\">");

      out.println("<p>Enter your message:</p>");
      out.println("<input name=\"msg\" size=\"30\">");

      // Add a Submit button
      out.println("<p><input type=submit value='Send Message'>");

      // Add an Exit button
      out.println("</form>");
      out.println("<form action=\"" + res.encodeURL(listRoomsPath)
                  + "\" method=\"get\" target=\"_top\">");
      out.println("<input type=submit value=Exit>");
```

```
      out.println("</form>");

      out.println("</body></html>");
    }
    out.close();
  }

  public void doPost(HttpServletRequest req, HttpServletResponse res)
          throws IOException, ServletException {
    res.setContentType("text/html");

    ChatRoom room = getRoom(req, res);
    if(room == null) {
      throw new ServletException("Room not found");
    }

    String profileName = getProfileName(req);

    // Save message if any
    String msg = req.getParameter("msg");
    if (msg != null && msg.length() != 0) {
      room.addChatEntry(new ChatEntry(profileName, msg));
    }
    writeFrame(res, room);
  }

  private String getProfileName(HttpServletRequest req) {
    HttpSession session = req.getSession(true);
    String profileName = (String) session.getAttribute("profileName");
    if (profileName == null) {

      // Entered a room for the first time?
      profileName = req.getParameter("profileName");
      if (profileName == null || profileName.length() == 0) {
        profileName = "A spineless spy";
      }
      session.setAttribute("profileName", profileName);
    } else {

      // Entered a new room with a new name?
      String newName = req.getParameter("profileName");
      if (newName != null && newName.length() > 0
              && !newName.equals(profileName)) {
        profileName = newName;
        session.setAttribute("profileName", profileName);
      }
    }
    return profileName;
  }

  private ChatRoom getRoom(HttpServletRequest req,
                           HttpServletResponse res) throws IOException {
    HttpSession session = req.getSession(true);
    PrintWriter out = res.getWriter();

    String roomName = (String) session.getAttribute("roomName");
    if (roomName == null) {

      // Just entered?
      roomName = req.getParameter("roomName");
      if (roomName == null || roomName.length() == 0) {
        writeError(out, "Room not specified");
```

```
        return null;
      }
      session.setAttribute("roomName", roomName);
    } else {

      // Entered a new room?
      String newRoom = req.getParameter("roomName");
      if (newRoom != null && newRoom.length() > 0
              &&!newRoom.equals(roomName)) {
        roomName = newRoom;
        session.setAttribute("roomName", roomName);
      }
    }

    HashMap roomList =
      (HashMap) getServletContext().getAttribute("roomList");
    ChatRoom room = (ChatRoom) roomList.get(roomName);
    if (room == null) {
      writeError(out, "Room " + roomName + " not found");
      return null;
    }
    return room;
  }

  private void writeError(PrintWriter out, String msg) {
    out.println("<html>");
    out.println("<head><title>Error</title></head>");
    out.println("<body>");
    out.println("<h1>Error</h1>");
    out.println(msg);
    out.println("</body></html>");
  }

  private void writeFrame(HttpServletResponse res,
                          ChatRoom room) throws IOException {
    PrintWriter out = res.getWriter();

    out.println("<html>");
    out.println("<head><title>" + room.getName() + "</title></head>");
    out.println("<frameset rows='50%,50%' border=0 frameborder=no>");
    out.println("<frame src=\"" + res.encodeURL(chatRoomPath)
                + "?list=true\" name=\"list\" scrolling=\"auto\">");
    out.println("<frame src=\"" + res.encodeURL(chatRoomPath)
                + "?list=false\" name=\"form\" scrolling=\"auto\">");
    out.println("<noframes>");
    out.println("<body>");
    out.println("Viewing this page requires a browser capable of "
                + "displaying frames.");
    out.println("</body>");
    out.println("</noframes>");
    out.println("</frameset>");
    out.println("</html>");
    out.close();
  }

  private void writeMessages(PrintWriter out, ChatRoom room,
                             String profileName) {
    StringBuffer sb = new StringBuffer();

    out.println("<html>");
    out.println("<head><meta http-equiv=\"refresh\" content=\"5\"></head>");
    out.println("<body>");
```

```
        out.println("<b>Room: " + room.getName() + "</b><br>" + "<b>Identity: "
                  + profileName + "</b><br>");

      // List all messages in the room
      if (room.size() == 0) {
        out.println("<font color=red>There are no messages in this room " +
                    "yet</font>");
      } else {
        Iterator entries = room.iterator();
        while (entries.hasNext()) {
          ChatEntry entry = (ChatEntry) entries.next();

          String entryName = entry.getProfileName();
          if (entryName.equals(profileName)) {
            out.print("<font color=blue>");
          }
          out.println(entryName + " : " + entry.getMessage() + "<br>");
          if (entryName.equals(profileName)) {
            out.print("</font>");
          }
        }
      }
      out.println("</body></html>");
    }
}
```

When compared to the rest of the classes in this application, this servlet seems rather more complicated. The following screenshots shows you a chat session in progress:

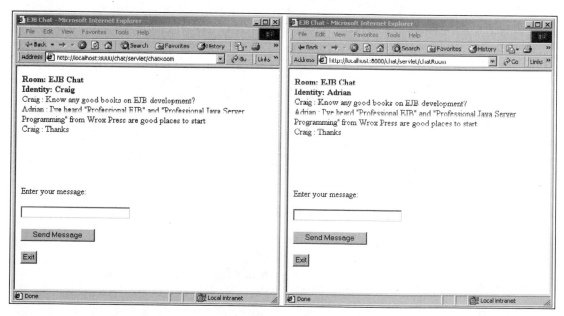

The following key points should help you navigate through this class:

❑   Each screenshot above has two HTML frames in it. Of these, the top frame is used to display the messages posted in the room, while the bottom frame is used for the user to enter new chat messages. The HTML frameset is generated in the `writeFrame()` method, invoked in `doPost()`.

❑ The doGet() method plays the dual role of generating both the frames. In order to decide whether it should generate a list of messages, or a form for entering a new message, it uses the request parameter list. If this parameter is true (when the GET request is generated by the top frame), doGet() generates the list of messages by calling the writeMessages() method. If this parameter is not present in the request (when the GET request is generated by the bottom frame), it simply generates the static form.

❑ The doPost() method is invoked when the user enters a new message. doPost() retrieves the current chat room using the getRoom() method, and the user name from the session. Using this data, it creates a new ChatEntry, and adds it to the chat room. It then calls writeFrame(), which forces two GET requests, one for each frame.

❑ Since new messages can be posted to the room almost continuously, we should refresh the top frame periodically. We use the refresh meta-tag to automatically reload this frame every 5 seconds. See the writeMessages() method for the implementation of this.

Chat Setup

In order to set up, build, and deploy the chat room, consider the following steps:

A Welcome Page

Create an index.html page:

```
<html>
  <head>
    <title>Chat Application</title>
    <body>
    <h1>Chat Application</h1>

    <p>Click <a href="/chat/servlet/chatAdmin">here</a> to
    administer chat rooms.</p>

    <p>Click <a href="/chat/servlet/listRooms">here</a> to view
    current chat rooms, and to join a chat room.</p>

    </body>
</html>
```

The purpose of this page is simply to provide links to the servlets in the application.

Deployment Descriptor

Here is the deployment descriptor:

```
<?xml version="1.0" encoding="ISO-8859-1"?>

<!DOCTYPE web-app
    PUBLIC "-//Sun Microsystems, Inc.//DTD Web Application 2.3//EN"
    "http://java.sun.com/j2ee/dtds/web-app_2_3.dtd">

<web-app>

  <context-param>
    <param-name>ADMIN_PATH</param-name>
    <param-value>/chat/servlet/chatAdmin</param-value>
  </context-param>
```

```xml
  <context-param>
    <param-name>LISTROOMS_PATH</param-name>
    <param-value>/chat/servlet/listRooms</param-value>
  </context-param>

  <context-param>
    <param-name>CHATROOM_PATH</param-name>
    <param-value>/chat/servlet/chatRoom</param-value>
  </context-param>

  <servlet>
    <servlet-name>chatAdmin</servlet-name>
    <display-name>chatAdmin</display-name>
    <servlet-class>ChatAdminServlet</servlet-class>
  </servlet>

  <servlet>
    <servlet-name>chatRoom</servlet-name>
    <display-name>chatRoom</display-name>
    <servlet-class>ChatRoomServlet</servlet-class>
  </servlet>

  <servlet>
    <servlet-name>listRooms</servlet-name>
    <display-name>listRooms</display-name>
    <servlet-class>ListRoomsServlet</servlet-class>
  </servlet>

  <servlet-mapping>
    <servlet-name>chatAdmin</servlet-name>
    <url-pattern>/admin</url-pattern>
  </servlet-mapping>

  <servlet-mapping>
    <servlet-name>chatRoom</servlet-name>
    <url-pattern>/chat</url-pattern>
  </servlet-mapping>

  <servlet-mapping>
    <servlet-name>listRooms</servlet-name>
    <url-pattern>/</url-pattern>
  </servlet-mapping>

</web-app>
```

As well as declaring the three servlet classes, this deployment descriptor also defines three additional context parameters. As we discussed previously, each of these parameters defines a string that points to a servlet. Why are these required?

In this application, servlets generate content that points to other servlets. For instance, the content generated by the `ListRoomsServlet` has links to `ChatRoomServlet` and `ChatAdminServlet`. Instead of hard-coding these values in each of the servlets, we have used these context parameters to get the actual URLs of the servlets.

Deploy and Test

When you deploy this application (context root as `chat`), you'll notice on the **Context** screen the context parameters we defined:

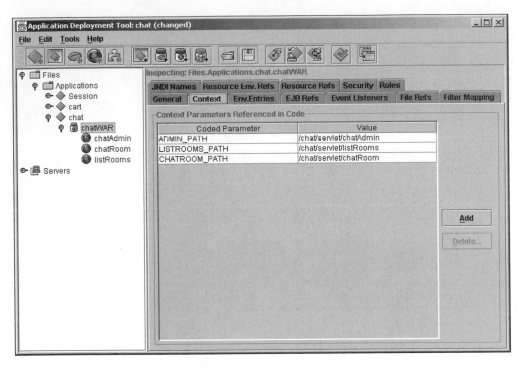

And for the ChatAdmin and ChatRoom servlets, you can also see the URL pattern that has been mapped as an Alias:

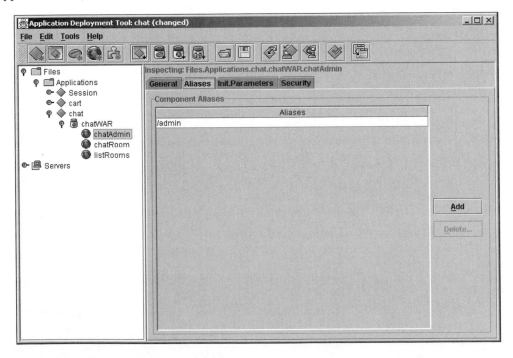

Enter http://localhost:8000/chat in your browser to access the welcome file created above. Use the administration link to create chat rooms.

To view the list of chat rooms and to join a chat room, you can use the Chat Now button on the admin page, or enter the URL http://localhost:8000/chat/servlet/listRooms directly. Use the radio buttons to select a chat room, enter your name, and click on Enter to enter the chat room.

In Chapter 9, we shall see how to protect the admin page, so that only a designated administrator can add/delete chat rooms.

Servlet Collaboration

In the typical servlet model, a servlet receives an HTTP request, executes some application logic, and prepares the response. This completes one request-response trip for the client. However, there are several scenarios in which this basic model is not adequate:

❑   A servlet receives an HTTP request from a client, processes application logic, and a JavaServer Page drives the response. In this case the servlet is not responsible for response generation. Instead, the JSP page is responsible for dynamic content.

❑   A servlet receives an HTTP request from a client, processes application logic partially, and hands over the request to another servlet. The second servlet completes the application logic, and either prepares the response, or requests a JSP page to drive the response.

In both the scenarios, the servlet is not completely responsible for processing a request. Instead, it delegates the processing to another servlet (or a JSP page, which is equivalent to a servlet at run time).

There are two types of solution for addressing the above requirements:

❑   **Servlet chaining**
This was once a very widely used approach, and supported by some of the servlet engine vendors. Although this is not supported by the Java Servlet API specification, for the sake of completeness, you'll find a short description below.

❑   **Request Dispatching**
Request dispatching allows one servlet to dispatch the request to another resource (a servlet, a JSP page, or any other resource). Prior to version 2.2 of the Servlet API, this approach used to be called 'inter-servlet communication'. The API used to provide a method to get an instance of another servlet using a name. See the documentation of the now deprecated getServlet() method of the javax.servlet.ServletContext interface. From version 2.2 of the API, request dispatchers replace this functionality.

Servlet Chaining

Servlet chaining predates J2EE and its component model. The idea of servlet chaining is very simple: you design a set of servlets, each of which does a single task. After developing these servlets, you configure your servlet engine to specify a chain of servlets for a given URL path alias. Once the servlet engine receives a request for this alias, it invokes the servlets in the specified order. This is similar to piping on Unix, where output of one program becomes input for another program in the pipe.

Suppose you've servlets A, B, and C executing three parts of a request-response process for a single customer service. Let's assume that /custService is the alias given to this chain (/custService=A,B,C). Consider a browser sending a request to the URL path pointing to this alias. The servlet engine sends all requests for this alias to servlet A. After executing servlet A's service method, the servlet engine invokes servlet B's service method, followed by servlet C's service method. The final response is then sent to the client. Briefly, this is servlet chaining. Refer to the figure below for an overview of this approach:

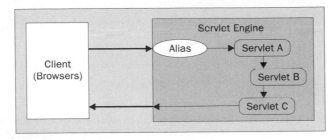

The key feature of servlet chaining is that you configure the servlet engine to do the chaining. During setup, you specify the order in which these servlets should be invoked.

Servlet chaining was initially introduced in the Java Web Server, but was never part of the Servlet API specification. You'll still find some books talking about servlet chaining, but be advised that this non-standard feature is not supported by most of the web containers today. Instead, you should consider using the request dispatching approach.

Request Dispatching

Request dispatching allows a servlet or a JSP page to dispatch a request to another servlet, (or a JSP page, or even a plain HTML page), which will then be responsible for any further processing and for generating the response.

When the web container receives a request, it constructs request and response objects and invokes one of the servlet's service methods with the request and response objects. This is a process of the web container dispatching a request to a servlet. What if this servlet wants to dispatch the same request to another servlet after some preliminary processing? For this purpose, the first servlet should be able to obtain a reference to the second servlet. Using this reference, the first servlet can dispatch a request to the second servlet. In simple terms, this is **request dispatching**.

The Java Servlet API has a special interface called javax.servlet.RequestDispatcher for this purpose.

RequestDispatcher Interface

```
public Interface RequestDispatcher
```

This interface encapsulates a reference to another web resource at a specified path within the scope of the same servlet context. A javax.servlet.RequestDispatcher object can be used to dispatch requests to other servlets and JSP pages.

This interface has two methods, which allow you to delegate the request-response processing to another resource, after the calling servlet has finished any preliminary processing.

The forward() Method

```
public void forward(ServletRequest request, ServletResponse response)
        throws ServletException, java.io.IOException
```

This method lets you forward the request to another servlet or a JSP page, or an HTML file on the server; this resource then takes over responsibility for producing the response.

The include() Method

```
public void include(ServletRequest request, ServletResponse response)
        throws ServletException, java.io.IOException
```

This method lets you include the content produced by another resource in the calling servlet's response.

Obtaining a RequestDispatcher Object

There are three ways in which you can obtain a `RequestDispatcher` object for a resource:

- ❑   `public RequestDispatcher getRequestDispatcher(String path)`
- ❑   `public RequestDispatcher getNamedDispatcher(String name)`
- ❑   `public RequestDispatcher getRequestDispatcher(String path)`

Although these methods serve the same purpose, the usage depends on what information is available to you.

The two `getRequestDispatcher()` methods accept a URL path referring to the target resource. However, the `getRequestDispatcher()` method on `javax.servlet.ServletContext` requires the absolute path (that is, the path name should be begin with a `/`). For example, if you have a servlet `/myWebApp/servlet/servlet1`, and want to get the `RequestDispatcher` object for `/myWebApp/servlet/servlet2`, you should specify the complete path relative to the root context. Here the root context is `/myWebApp`, and the absolute path is `/servlet/servlet2`.

The same method on `javax.servlet.ServletRequest` accepts both absolute and relative paths. In the above example, you could now also use `servlet2` as the path.

> *A `javax.servlet.ServletRequest` is associated with a URL path, and the web container can use this to resolve relative paths into absolute paths.*

The `getNamedDispatcher()` method is a convenience method that accepts a name associated with the servlet. This is the same name that you specify in the deployment descriptor in the `<servlet-name>` element.

Note that the target resource (except for static resources) should implement the same type of HTTP request that the original servlet receives.

Tech Support Revisited

Let's now revisit and enhance the Tech Support application from the last chapter. We'll consider the following additional features:

- ❑   Instead of collecting customer data (such as first name, last name, and telephone number) every time, let's introduce a customer registration page.
- ❑   Using the customer's e-mail address, determine if a customer is a revisiting customer or a new customer. If the customer is new, direct the customer to the registration page.

❑ After registration, direct the customer to a response servlet.

❑ If the customer is a revisiting customer, direct the customer to the response servlet.

❑ Maintain separate database tables for support requests and customer data.

As you'll see shortly, these enhancements require extensive use of `RequestDispatchers`. The figure below shows the overall flow in this application:

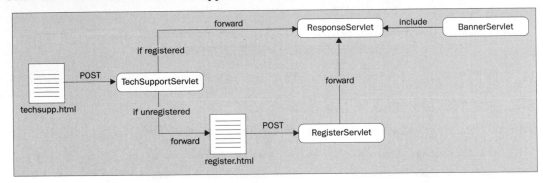

The flow shown above is very simple. The request from `techsupp.html` goes to the `TechSupportServlet`. If the customer is previously registered, `TechSupportServlet` forwards the request to the `ResponseServlet`. Otherwise, the flow proceeds to the `register.html` page, to collect customer information. On submitting the form in this page, the request goes to `RegisterServlet`, which inserts the customer data in the database. After registration, the flow then proceeds to the `ResponseServlet`.

The `ResponseServlet` generates a page with a response message, and includes the output of `BannerServlet`. `BannerServlet` simply writes an HTML 'banner' without the HTML headers and footers (`<html>`, `<body>`, etc.).

Let's now consider the implementation.

The techsupp.html Page

This is the same as the page you created in the original Tech Support application, except that the customer's first name, last name, and telephone number are no longer included in the form. The form sends the request to `TechSupportServlet`:

```
<html>

<head>
  <title>XYZ Corporation, IT Department</title>
</head>
  <body>
    <h1>Technical Support Request</h1>
    <hr><br>
    <center>
      <form action="/techSupport/servlet/techSupport" method="GET">
        <table align="center" width="100%" cellspacing="2" cellpadding="2">
          <tr>
            <td align="right">Email:</td>
            <td><input type="Text" name="email" align="left"
                       size="25"></td>
          </tr>
          <tr>
            <td align="right">Software:</TD>
```

```
        <td>
          <select name="software" SIZE="1">
            <option value="Word">Microsoft Word</option>
            <option value="Excel">Microsoft Excel</option>
            <option value="Access">Microsoft Access</option>
            <option value="Outlook">Microsoft Outlook</option>
          </select>
        </td>
        <td align="right">Operating System:</td>
        <td>
          <select name="os" size="1">
            <option value="95">Windows 95</option>
            <option value="98">Windows 98</option>
            <option value="NT">Windows NT</option>
            <option value="2KPro">Windows 2000 Pro</option>
            <option value="2KServer">Windows 2000 Server</option>
            <option value="XP">Windows XP</option>
          </select>
        </td>
      </tr>
    </table>

    <br>Problem Description
    <br>
    <textarea name="problem" cols="50" rows="4"></textarea>

    <hr><br>
    <input type="Submit" name="submit" value="Submit Request">
  </form>
</center>
</body>
</html>
```

This produces the form shown below:

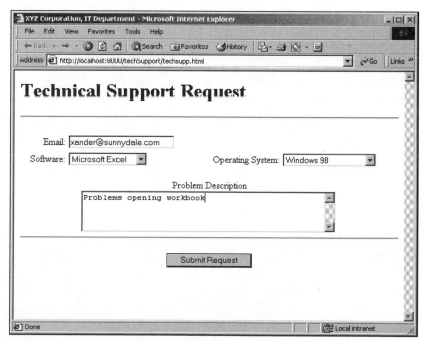

TechSupportServlet

This is a revised version of the original `TechSupportServlet` class discussed in Chapter 6, which first inserts the customer service request in the database, and then checks the customer database to see if a customer exists with the given e-mail address. If one does, it uses a request dispatcher to redirect the customer to `ResponseServlet`. If, however, the customer is unregistered, it forwards the request to `register.html`:

```java
// Import servlet packages
import javax.servlet.RequestDispatcher;
import javax.servlet.ServletException;
import javax.servlet.UnavailableException;
import javax.servlet.http.HttpServlet;
import javax.servlet.http.HttpSession;
import javax.servlet.http.HttpServletRequest;
import javax.servlet.http.HttpServletResponse;

// Import java packages
import java.io.PrintWriter;
import java.io.IOException;
import java.sql.Connection;
import java.sql.PreparedStatement;
import java.sql.ResultSet;
import java.sql.SQLException;
import javax.sql.DataSource;
import javax.naming.InitialContext;
import javax.naming.NamingException;

public class TechSupportServlet extends HttpServlet {

    protected void doGet(HttpServletRequest request,
                         HttpServletResponse response)
            throws ServletException, IOException {
        HttpSession session = request.getSession();

        // Extract customer information from the request
        String email = request.getParameter("email");
        String software = request.getParameter("software");
        String os = request.getParameter("os");
        String problem = request.getParameter("problem");

        int requestId = 0;
        Connection connection = null;
        String insertStatementStr =
            "INSERT INTO SUPP_REQUESTS (EMAIL, SOFTWARE, OS, PROBLEM) VALUES " +
            "(?, ?, ?, ?)";
        String selectCustomerStr =
            "SELECT CUSTOMERS.FNAME, CUSTOMERS.LNAME FROM CUSTOMERS WHERE "
            + "CUSTOMERS.EMAIL = ?";

        // Insert customer support request in the database
        try {

            InitialContext initial = new InitialContext();
            Datasource ds = (DataSource)initial.lookup("jdbc/TechSupport");
            connection = ds.getConnection();

            PreparedStatement insertStatement =
                connection.prepareStatement(insertStatementStr);
            insertStatement.setString(1, email);
            insertStatement.setString(2, software);
```

```
        insertStatement.setString(3, os);
        insertStatement.setString(4, problem);

        insertStatement.executeUpdate();

        // Now verify whether or not the customer is registered.
        PreparedStatement selectStatement =
          connection.prepareStatement(selectCustomerStr);
        selectStatement.setString(1, email);

        ResultSet rs = selectStatement.executeQuery();

        if (rs.next()) {
          // If found, attach first name and last name to the request.
          String firstName = rs.getString("FNAME");
          String lastName = rs.getString("LNAME");
          request.setAttribute("firstName", firstName);
          request.setAttribute("lastName", lastName);

          // Now invoke the Response servlet.
          RequestDispatcher rd =
            getServletContext().getNamedDispatcher("response");
          rd.forward(request, response);
        } else {

          // Customer is not registered. Need to register now.
          session.setAttribute("email", email);
          RequestDispatcher rd =
            request.getRequestDispatcher("/register.html");
          rd.forward(request, response);
        }
      } catch (NamingException ne) {
        throw new ServletException("JNDI error", ne);
      } catch (SQLException sqle) {
        throw new ServletException("Database error", sqle);
      }
      finally {
        if (connection != null) {
          try {
            connection.close();
          } catch (SQLException sqle) {}
        }
      }
    }
  }
}
```

Notice the changes we made to this servlet from its original version in the previous chapter.

This servlet inserts the customer support request in the database as usual. However, the INSERT statement does not include first name, last name, and phone number. As you will see shortly, the database schema now includes a customer table with this data.

Secondly, this servlet now uses request dispatchers to implement the desired flow. In order to decide whether the customer should be asked to register, this servlet checks for customer information in the Customer table. If there is no entry, this servlet forwards the user to the registration page. Otherwise, this servlet forwards the user to the response page. This process illustrates how you can implement the flow between servlets dynamically.

The register.html Page

This page contains a form that collects customer registration information: the customer's first name, last name, and phone number. The form sends the request to `RegisterCustomerServlet`:

```html
<html>
  <head>
    <title>Customer Registration</title>
  </head>
  <body>
    <center><h1>Customer Registration</h1></center>
    <hr>
      Please register.
      <form action="/techSupport/servlet/register" method="POST">
        <table>
          <tr>
            <td>First Name:</td>
            <td><input type="Text" name="txtFname" size="30"></td>
          </tr>
          <tr>
            <td>Last Name:</td>
            <td><input type="Text" name="txtLname" size="30"></td>
          </tr>
          <tr>
            <td>Phone Number:</td>
            <td><input type="Text" name="txtPhone" size="30"></td>
          </tr>
        </table>
        <br><input type="Submit" value="Submit Request">
      </form>
  </body>
</html>
```

This will produce the following form:

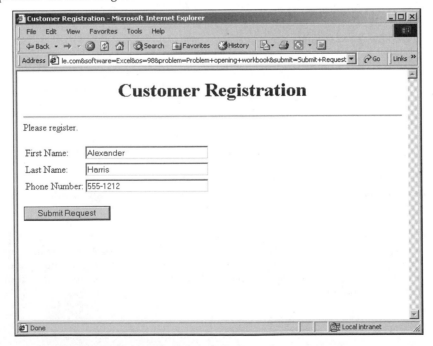

RegisterCustomerServlet

This servlet registers customer information. Upon registration, this servlet forwards the request to `ResponseServlet`:

```
// Import servlet packages
import javax.servlet.RequestDispatcher;
import javax.servlet.ServletException;
import javax.servlet.UnavailableException;
import javax.servlet.http.HttpServlet;
import javax.servlet.http.HttpSession;
import javax.servlet.http.HttpServletRequest;
import javax.servlet.http.HttpServletResponse;

// Import java packages
import java.io.PrintWriter;
import java.io.IOException;
import java.sql.Connection;
import java.sql.PreparedStatement;
import java.sql.SQLException;
import javax.sql.DataSource;
import javax.naming.InitialContext;
import javax.naming.NamingException;

public class RegisterCustomerServlet extends HttpServlet {

  public void doPost(HttpServletRequest request,
                     HttpServletResponse response)
          throws ServletException, IOException {

    HttpSession session = request.getSession();
    String fname = request.getParameter("txtFname");
    String lname = request.getParameter("txtLname");
    String email = (String) session.getAttribute("email");
    String phone = request.getParameter("txtPhone");

    Connection connection = null;
    String insertStatementStr = "INSERT INTO CUSTOMERS VALUES(?, ?, ?, ?)";
    try {
      InitialContext initial = new InitialContext();
      Datasource ds = (DataSource)initial.lookup("jdbc/TechSupport");
      connection = ds.getConnection();

      PreparedStatement insertStatement =
        connection.prepareStatement(insertStatementStr);
      insertStatement.setString(1, email);
      insertStatement.setString(2, fname);
      insertStatement.setString(3, lname);
      insertStatement.setString(4, phone);

      insertStatement.executeUpdate();

    } catch (NamingException ne) {
      throw new ServletException("JNDI error", ne);
    } catch (SQLException sqle) {
      throw new ServletException("Database error", sqle);
    }
    finally {
      if (connection != null) {
        try {
          connection.close();
        } catch (SQLException sqle) {}
```

```
      }
    }

    request.setAttribute("firstName", fname);
    request.setAttribute("lastName", lname);

    // Now invoke the Response servlet.
    RequestDispatcher rd =
      getServletContext().getNamedDispatcher("response");
    rd.forward(request, response);

  }
}
```

ResponseServlet

This servlet displays a confirmation message that the customer's request (and the profile, if entered) has been registered. This servlet 'includes' BannerServlet to include a banner in the content:

```
// Import servlet packages
import javax.servlet.RequestDispatcher;
import javax.servlet.ServletException;
import javax.servlet.http.HttpServlet;
import javax.servlet.http.HttpServletRequest;
import javax.servlet.http.HttpServletResponse;

// Import java packages
import java.io.PrintWriter;
import java.io.IOException;

public class ResponseServlet extends HttpServlet {

  protected void doPost(HttpServletRequest request,
                        HttpServletResponse response)
          throws ServletException, IOException {
    doGet(request, response);
  }

  protected void doGet(HttpServletRequest request,
                       HttpServletResponse response)
          throws ServletException, IOException {

    response.setContentType("text/html");
    PrintWriter out = response.getWriter();

    // Send acknowledgment to the customer
    out.println("<html>");
    out.println("<head><title>Customer Service Response</title></head>");
    out.println("<body>");
    out.println("<h1>Customer Service Request Received</h1>");
    out.println("<p>Thank you for your request.");
    out.println("<p>Your request has been recorded and will be "
                + "responded to within three business days.");

    // Include a banner
    RequestDispatcher rd = request.getRequestDispatcher("/servlet/banner");
    rd.include(request, response);

    out.println("</body></html>");
    out.close();
  }
}
```

BannerServlet

This servlet generates very simple banner with the current user's name, followed by a standard footer. Note that this servlet does not set the response type, because it is included in the response being generated by the `ResponseServlet`:

```
// Import servlet packages
import javax.servlet.ServletException;
import javax.servlet.http.HttpServlet;
import javax.servlet.http.HttpSession;
import javax.servlet.http.HttpServletRequest;
import javax.servlet.http.HttpServletResponse;

// Import java packages
import java.io.PrintWriter;
import java.io.IOException;

public class BannerServlet extends HttpServlet {

  protected void doPost(HttpServletRequest request,
                        HttpServletResponse response)
          throws ServletException, IOException {
    doGet(request, response);
  }

  protected void doGet(HttpServletRequest request,
                       HttpServletResponse response)
         throws ServletException, IOException {
    HttpSession session = request.getSession();

    String firstName = (String) request.getAttribute("firstName");
    String lastName = (String) request.getAttribute("lastName");

    PrintWriter out = response.getWriter();

    out.println("<hr>");
    out.println("Current User: " + firstName + " " + lastName);
    out.println("<hr>");
    out.println("XYZ Corporation, Customer Service.");
    out.println("<BR us at 1.800.xyz.corp.<br>");
  }
}
```

`ResponseServlet` and `BannerServlet` together produce this output:

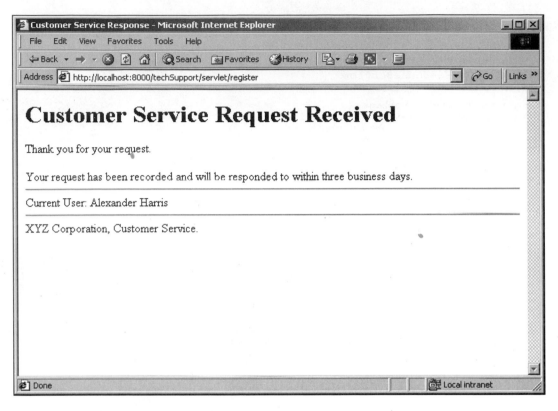

Tech Support Setup and Deployment

The deployment descriptor is similar to the previous chapter's version but with the addition of the new servlets:

```xml
<?xml version="1.0" encoding="ISO-8859-1"?>

<!DOCTYPE web-app
  PUBLIC "-//Sun Microsystems, Inc.//DTD Web Application 2.3//EN"
  "http://java.sun.com/j2ee/dtds/web-app_2_3.dtd">

<web-app>

  <servlet>
    <servlet-name>techSupport</servlet-name>
    <display-name>techSupport</display-name>
    <servlet-class>TechSupportServlet</servlet-class>
  </servlet>

  <servlet>
    <servlet-name>response</servlet-name>
    <display-name>response</display-name>
    <servlet-class>ResponseServlet</servlet-class>
  </servlet>

  <servlet>
    <servlet-name>banner</servlet-name>
    <display-name>banner</display-name>
    <servlet-class>BannerServlet</servlet-class>
```

```
    </servlet>

    <servlet>
      <servlet-name>register</servlet-name>
      <display-name>register</display-name>
      <servlet-class>RegisterCustomerServlet</servlet-class>
    </servlet>

    <welcome-file-list>
      <welcome-file>techsupp.html</welcome-file>
    </welcome-file-list>

    <resource-ref>
      <res-ref-name>jdbc/TechSupport</res-ref-name>
      <res-type>javax.sql.DataSource</res-type>
      <res-auth>Container</res-auth>
    </resource-ref>

  </web-app>
```

Of course we also need to modify the database. Delete the existing table and recreate it using the following SQL:

```
CREATE TABLE SUPP_REQUESTS(REQUEST_ID       INT DEFAULT AUTOINCREMENT INITIAL 1
                                            INCREMENT 1 NOT NULL,
                           EMAIL            VARCHAR(40),
                           SOFTWARE         VARCHAR(40),
                           OS               VARCHAR(40),
                           PROBLEM          VARCHAR(256));

CREATE TABLE CUSTOMERS(EMAIL               VARCHAR(40) PRIMARY KEY,
                       FNAME               VARCHAR(15),
                       LNAME               VARCHAR(15),
                       PHONE               VARCHAR(12));
```

If you still have the Tech Support application from the previous chapter deployed, undeploy it and replace it with this one. Remember to make sure the datasource resource is referenced in the deployment.

To test the application, enter the URL http://localhost:8000/techSupport. You should be able to navigate through the flow depicted at the beginning of this section. Don't forget that you need to have the database running!

Using RequestDispatchers for Collaboration

In this application, we used the RequestDispatcher for the following purposes:

Forwarding a Request to ResponseServlet

The TechSupportServlet checks in the customer database whether the customer is already registered. If so, the request is forwarded to the ResponseServlet:

```
if(rs.next()) {
    String firstName = rs.getString("FNAME");
    String lastName = rs.getString("LNAME");
    request.setAttribute("firstName", firstName);
    request.setAttribute("lastName", lastName);
```

```
                  // Now invoke the Response servlet.
                  RequestDispatcher rd =
                              getServletContext().getNamedDispatcher("response");
                  rd.forward(request, response);
             }
```

Since the ResponseServlet has an alias called response (specified in the deployment descriptor), we can use the getNamedDispatcher() method to get a RequestDispatcher object for the ResponseServlet. The same technique is used by the RegisterCustomerServlet to forward the request to the ResponseRequest.

Note that we're using the setAttribute() method on the request object to add the firstName and lastName attributes since the request is forwarded from either TechSupportServlet or RegisterServlet to the ResponseServlet, which then includes BannerServlet. BannerServlet can then get these attributes from the request object while generating the banner content. Refer to the source of BannerServlet to see how the banner is generated.

Forwarding Request to register.html

If the customer is not registered, the customer is directed to register.html:

```
             RequestDispatcher rd =
                request.getRequestDispatcher("/register.html");
             rd.forward(request, response);
```

We use the absolute path of register.html page to obtain a RequestDispatcher from the HttpServletRequest object, and call the forward() method to forward the request. Note that since register.html can only be invoked using a GET request, the form in techsupp.html had to use the GET method.

> Since the **forward()** method forwards the request to other resources, the calling servlet (**TechSupportServlet**) should not commit any output to the response. For example, you should not call **getWriter()** to get a **java.io.PrintWriter** object and write content to it. However, if any content is written to the response, you should call the **reset()** method on the response object.

For example, you should not call getWriter() to get a java.io.PrintWriter object and write content to it. However, if any content is written to the response, you should call the reset() method on the response object.

Including Banner in ResponseServlet

ResponseServlet includes in its response a banner generated by BannerServlet. The purpose of this banner is to print the name of the current customer, and a static banner message. The doGet() method in ResponsServlet includes the following code:

```
             RequestDispatcher rd = request.getRequestDispatcher("/servlet/banner");
             rd.include(request, response);
```

Notice the difference between the forward() and include(). Whereas forward() makes the new servlet wholly responsible for generating the response, include() merely includes the called servlet's response into the response from the calling servlet. Using this approach, you can compose responses from multiple servlets.

Summary

In this chapter, we've covered some of the important programming aspects of servlet-based application development:

❑ Session tracking and associating state (attributes) with sessions: In all the examples in this chapter, we used the session object to maintain the state of a session.

❑ Servlet contexts: In the chat application, we saw how the servlet context allows you to maintain application state. We've also used servlet context to access request dispatchers.

❑ Servlet collaboration: The revised Tech Support application illustrates how request dispatchers can be used to create conditional flow between servlets and static pages.

We have now covered the bulk of the Servlet API. In the next chapter, we will look at another feature called servlet filtering.

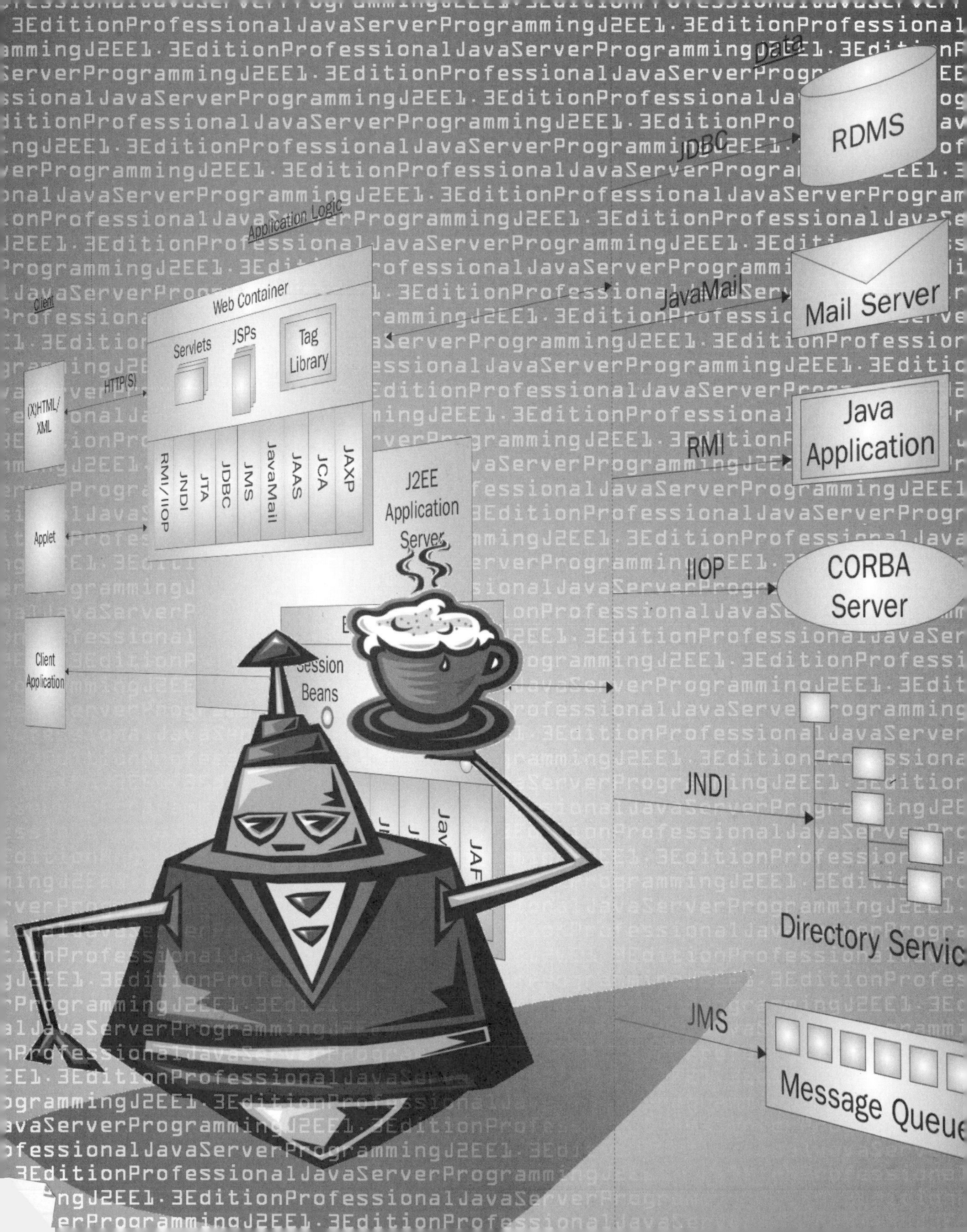

8

Filters for Web Applications

Filters are the most recent addition to the Java servlet technology. The Servlet specification version 2.3 introduces filters as a flexible means of interacting with HTTP requests and responses before and after the web container invokes web resources including servlets.

In the range of J2EE technologies, filters stand apart. As discussed in Chapter 1, J2EE application components are container-managed. Remember that when a client makes a request to a J2EE component, such as a servlet, JSP page, or EJB, the container receives the requests and then invokes the appropriate component instances managed in the container runtime. In the case of the web container, it receives HTTP requests and invokes various web application resources including servlets, JSP pages, HTML files, images, and so on. That is, the web container is the *interceptor* for HTTP requests to resources. The interception process includes various steps including identifying the web application, finding path mappings to resources, checking for authentication and authorization (more about these in the next chapter), and invoking resources. With the various servlet features, there is no facility to participate in this interception process. You cannot change, control, or peek into the way the container invokes resources.

For instance, consider the basic need to monitor requests to a specific kind of static file (such as certain types of images or documents) on the container, and log the requests to a specific database. In order to build this functionality, what you need is a facility to plug in some logic during the HTTP request handling process. That is, you need a facility to participate in the interception process. The purpose of a filter is to provide this facility.

Why are filters special? As of J2EE 1.3, filters provide the only mechanism by which we can plug in code to participate in the container interception process. Although filters are limited to the web container (that is, we can filter HTTP requests, but we can't filter requests to EJBs, and so on), we can perform several useful tasks with the help of filters in the web container.

With filters, we can configure the web container to invoke certain filter objects during the HTTP request-response process. In this manner, as web application developers, we can customize how HTTP requests are handled within a web container. Before discussing the possibilities, let us first look in detail at what a filter actually is.

This chapter presents an introduction to the filter API. To gain some practical knowledge, we'll enhance one of the web applications built in previous chapters to illustrate the power of filters in web containers.

What is a Filter?

> A filter is a servlet-like container-managed object that can be declaratively inserted within the HTTP request-response process.

Like a servlet, a filter object is instantiated and managed by the container and follows a lifecycle that is similar to that of a servlet. As we shall see later in this chapter, a filter has four stages: instantiate, initialize, filter, and destroy. These stages are similar to a servlet's instantiate, initialize, service, and destroy.

Filters also follow a deployment process close to that of servlets. In fact, the API of a filter is very similar to that of the servlet interface – a filter also operates on HTTP requests to produce and manipulate further HTTP requests and responses. So, how is a filter different from a servlet? In order to see the difference, let us consider how filters participate in the HTTP request-response process:

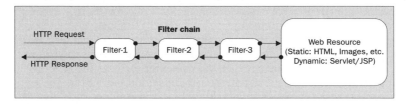

In this figure, there is a chain of three filters participating in the request-response process. Each filter (from left to right in this figure) can manipulate the request and response or implement some logic (including updating the HTTP session or the servlet context), and request the container to invoke the next filter (if any) in the filter chain. Ultimately, after invoking the last filter, the container processes the actual web resource. The process of resource handling is the same as discussed in the previous chapters. Alternatively, any filter in this chain can choose to abort the processing, and report an error in the HTTP response. The arrows between the filters, and between the third filter and the web resource are the `javax.servlet.ServletRequest` and `javax.servlet.ServletResponse` objects.

In this process, after each filter is processed, the control is transferred to the following filter in the chain. Similarly, after the web resource has been processed, the container returns the thread of execution back to the last filter. This step continues till the control is handed back to the first filter. In this manner, each filter gets an opportunity to participate both before and after invoking the web resource.

Let's now take a look at some of the possibilities that filters offer:

❑ **Validate HTTP requests**
Each filter has access to the HTTP request object and therefore can validate the contents of HTTP requests. If a request is invalid (that is, it contains invalid parameters, required parameters are missing, or values of the supplied parameters are invalid), the filter can abort processing and report HTTP errors to the container. In this way, we can avoid implementing any validation logic within servlets or JSP pages. We can also extend this idea to preprocess HTTP request parameters.

❑ **Log HTTP requests**
Based on the contents of HTTP requests, we can implement custom access logging for all web resources. Typically, logging is the prerogative of the web server, and there is usually no control over how logging is done. Filters give us a handle to implement our own logging (in addition to that of the server). With filters we can request application-specific logging. For instance, we can build logging based on specific business events – filters let us scan requests to determine the events.

❑ **Authorize HTTP requests**
Authorization is the process of checking if the client can access a given resource. Typically, web applications implement custom authorization code in every servlet and JSP page. Instead, we can implement custom authorization within a filter, and include the filter for all HTTP requests. As we'll see in the next chapter, we can also rely on web-container-managed declarative authorization.

❑ **Content Management**
A more sophisticated application might need to manage content dynamically. For instance, we can trigger processes to dynamically create content to which the actual HTTP request can map. Since the container invokes the filter before trying to locate the actual web resource, we can let the filter create the resource if necessary. For example, if the incoming HTTP request corresponds to an image for a topographical mapping system, we can invoke the respective logic to create the image, such that the web container would find it at the end of the filter chain.

❑ **Provide custom HTTP environment for servlets and JSP pages**
We can also use the filter mechanism to modify the request and response objects (and thereby the HTTP session as well). For instance, we can add additional data to the request object, or fill in missing/default parameters. We can also replace the request and response objects to provide additional behavior.

It should be noted that these tasks could all be performed within a servlet, albeit with some difficulty. There are, however, a couple of differences:

❑ A servlet is equivalent to a web resource except that it is dynamic. A filter, on the other hand, is not a resource that the container serves. Instead, the container invokes a filter while processing a request to "serve" a resource. In this way, filters give us an opportunity to participate in the process of serving any web resource. Note that in the previous figure, the web resource could be any standard resource – a **static resource** such as an HTML file, an image, a class file for an applet, and so on, or a **dynamic resource** such as a servlet or a JSP page.

❑ With the help of filters, we can effectively decouple the logic from servlets. We can declaratively introduce filters without changing our servlets.

❑ Filters can be used in any web application, including those containing completely static content.

The above list of scenarios is very typical, although we could implement more complex logic within filters.

It is tempting to compare filters with the request dispatcher mechanism that we discussed in the previous chapter. However, filters are different from the request dispatcher in several ways:

❑ The request dispatcher API is meant for servlets and JSP pages to forward the processing to another web resource, or include the contents of another web resource. However, forward and include can only happen from servlets or JSPs which themselves are first classed as web resources. We can't use this API to control what happens before the request reaches a servlet or JSP. On the other hand, a filter is invoked before the request reaches a servlet, a JSP, or, in fact, any other resource.

❑ We cannot use the request dispatcher API to intervene in the invocation of non-servlet or JSP resources, such as a static file. A filter, however, can be used to do so.

In the following sections, we'll study the filter API in more detail with the help of some examples.

A Sample Filter

In order to better illustrate the filter API, let's first implement a sample filter class for counting the number of requests to HTML pages deployed within a web application. The purpose of this sample is to illustrate the process of creating and deploying filters.

This example consists of the following:

❑ A filter to count the number of requests for HTML files. This filter stores the count in the current servlet context.

❑ A few HTML files. For the sake of illustration, we'll insert a simple HTML file at the root of this web application.

❑ A servlet to display the counter stored in the context.

Our focus with this example is on the filter class; the rest of the code is required only for demonstrating the filter in action, and we shall discuss the API in detail in the following section.

Let's first create the filter class called `CounterFilter`. As noted in previous chapters, the source code for the examples in this book is available for download from http://www.wrox.com:

```java
import javax.servlet.Filter;
import javax.servlet.FilterConfig;
import javax.servlet.FilterChain;
import javax.servlet.ServletContext;
import javax.servlet.ServletRequest;
import javax.servlet.ServletResponse;
import javax.servlet.ServletException;
import javax.servlet.http.HttpServletRequest;

import java.io.IOException;

public class CounterFilter implements Filter {
```

```
    FilterConfig config;

    public void init(FilterConfig config) {
      this.config = config;
    }

    public void doFilter(ServletRequest request,
                         ServletResponse response,
                         FilterChain chain)
              throws IOException, ServletException {

      ServletContext context = config.getServletContext();

      Integer count = (Integer) context.getAttribute("count");
      if(count == null) {
        count = new Integer(0);
      }

      count = new Integer(count.intValue() + 1);
      context.setAttribute("count", count);

      // Invoke the next filter (if any)
      chain.doFilter(request, response);
    }

    public void destroy() {}
  }
```

This class creates a filter by implementing the `javax.servlet.Filter` interface, an interface that is very similar to that of a servlet. It has the usual `init()` and `destroy()` methods. The only difference is that the filter has a `doFilter()` method that is invoked during the interception process. We'll shortly study these methods in more detail. For the time being, we only need consider the code in the body of this method. This code uses the `FilterConfig` object to access the servlet context. When invoked first time, this filter sets a context attribute "count". During subsequent invocations, the filter updates the count in the context. It then requests that the container processes subsequent filters by calling the `doFilter()` method on the chain object. Since we have only one filter in this example, the last call results in sending the contents of the `index.html` file over the response.

But how does the container invoke the filter in the first place? Let's come back to this question after creating the rest of application.

The next step is to create the servlet to display the counter:

```
import javax.servlet.ServletContext;
import javax.servlet.ServletException;
import javax.servlet.http.HttpServlet;
import javax.servlet.http.HttpServletRequest;
import javax.servlet.http.HttpServletResponse;

import java.io.IOException;
import java.io.PrintWriter;

public class DisplayCount extends HttpServlet {
```

```
    protected void doGet(HttpServletRequest request,
                         HttpServletResponse response)
                throws ServletException, IOException {

    ServletContext context = getServletContext();

    Integer count = (Integer) context.getAttribute("count");

    response.setContentType("text/html");
    PrintWriter out = response.getWriter();

    out.println("<html>");
    out.println("<meta http-equiv=\"Pragma\" content=\"no-cache\">");
    out.println("<body>");
    if(count != null) {
      out.println("The current count is " + count.intValue());
    } else {
      out.println("Count not available.");
    }
    out.println("</BODY>");
    out.println("</html>");
    out.close();
  }
}
```

This servlet reads the current count from the context, and prints it in the response.

Although we could create any HTML file, in this example we'll use the following HTML:

```
<html>
  <head>
    <title>Counter Filter</title>
  </head>

  <body>
    <h1>Counter Filter</h1>
    <p>Click <a href="/counter/servlet/display">here</a> to see the effect
       of the filter.</p>
  </body>
</html>
```

In order to deploy the above, create the following deployment descriptor (web.xml), also within the \WEB-INF\ directory:

```
<?xml version="1.0" encoding="ISO-8859-1"?>

<!DOCTYPE web-app
    PUBLIC "-//Sun Microsystems, Inc.//DTD Web Application 2.3//EN"
    "http://java.sun.com/j2ee/dtds/web-app_2_3.dtd">

<web-app>
  <display-name>counter</display-name>

  <filter>
```

```
          <filter-name>Counter</filter-name>
          <display-name>Counter</display-name>
          <filter-class>CounterFilter</filter-class>
      </filter>

      <filter-mapping>
          <filter-name>Counter</filter-name>
          <url-pattern>*.html</url-pattern>
      </filter-mapping>

      <servlet>
          <servlet-name>display</servlet-name>
          <display-name>display</display-name>
          <servlet-class>DisplayCount</servlet-class>
      </servlet>
  </web-app>
```

In this deployment descriptor, the two new elements, `<filter>` and `<filter-mapping>`, are highlighted. The first of these elements declares a filter in this web application; the order in which the filter elements appear in the deployment descriptor represents the order of the filter chain. In this example, the filter is named `Counter` and is implemented using the `CounterFilter` class we defined earlier. Observe that these two elements are similar to the `<servlet>` and `<servlet-mapping>` elements.

The second element, `<filter-mapping>`, is the one that indicates to the container what kind of requests should be filtered with a given filter. In the above deployment descriptor, the `<filter-mapping>` element declares that the filter `Counter` should be applied to all resources with extension `.html`. Whenever the container receives a request to an HTML file in this application, the container invokes this filter before serving the HTML file.

Deployment

In order to deploy this application, we must first create a web archive (WAR) file containing all the files required for the application.

Make sure you have the following files in the following locations:

```
counter/
        index.html
        WEB-INF/
                web.xml
                classes/
                        CounterFilter.class
                        DisplayCount.class
```

Now create the WAR file using the `jar` command:

```
jar -cvf counter.war index.html WEB-INF
```

We are now ready to deploy the WAR file. Start the J2EE Reference Implementation server by running the `j2ee.bat` file in the `%J2EE_HOME%\bin` directory. Once that has completed, run the `deploytool.bat` file in the same directory, to start the deployment tool. When the deployment tool loads, create a new application called `counter`.

We then add the `counter.war` to the new application using the **Add to Application** | **Web WAR** option from the **File** menu.

We are now ready to deploy the application on the server. Select the **Deploy** option from the **Tools** menu. We don't need to do anything on the first screen besides double-check we're deploying the correct application. On the next screen we need to provide the context that we will use to browse to our application. Set it to `counter`. Proceed to the final screen and select **Finish** to deploy the application into the server

In order to test the filter in action, launch our web browser and point it to http://localhost:8000/counter/index.html. This page displays a link to the `DisplayCount` servlet, and will look like this:

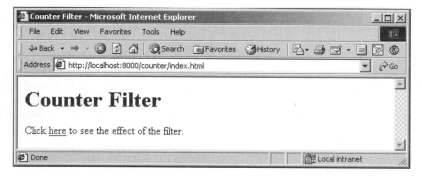

Before clicking on this link, reload the `index.html` page a few times. When we click on the link to the `DisplayCount` servlet, we'll notice that the counter is being incremented.

As we reload the `index.html` page, the filter is being invoked by the container behind the scenes. The filter is incrementing the count and storing it in the servlet context. In order to always get the latest count, we avoid browser caching by including a HTTP meta-tag "`no-cache`".

We can add a few more HTML files to this web application to find that the counter will be incremented whenever any HTML file is requested.

Besides illustrating how filters work, this example also illustrates the key point that the filter mechanism lets you intercept HTTP requests and responses irrespective of what the actual resources are.

In the next section we'll examine the finer details of the filter API.

The Filter API

The filter API consists of the following interfaces and classes:

❑ `javax.servlet.Filter`
The interface that all filters must implement.

❑ `javax.servlet.FilterConfig`
An interface that provides access to filter initialization parameters and the servlet context. This interface is created by the container and passed on to the filter instance during initialization.

❑ `javax.servlet.FilterChain`
An abstraction of a filter chain. This interface lets you invoke the next filter in the chain, or if the calling filter is the last filter in the chain, the resource at the end of the chain.

Let's now study these interfaces and classes individually in more detail.

The Filter Interface

```
public interface Filter
```

This interface from the `javax.servlet` package encapsulates the lifecycle methods of a filter. The lifecycle methods include `init()` and `destroy()`, which are invoked during initialization and destruction of the filter, and a `doFilter()` method, which is invoked whenever there is a request/response pair to be filtered.

The init() Method

```
public void init(FilterConfig config) throws ServletException
```

The container invokes this method before putting the filter into service. During the initialization, the container sends the configuration information (initialization parameters) to the filter via a `FilterConfig` object.

The doFilter() Method

```
public void doFilter(ServletRequest request, ServletResponse response,
                     FilterChain chain) throws IOException, ServletException
```

The container invokes this method while processing a filter. Using the `FilterChain` object, each filter may instruct the container to process the rest of the filter chain. We shall see this process in detail shortly. Notice that this method is similar to a servlet's `service()` method with the difference of the third parameter.

The destroy() Method

```
public void destroy()
```

The container invokes this method before taking the filter out of service. This could happen either at container shut down, or when the application is undeployed.

All these methods are container-invoked methods used during a filter lifecycle. The lifecycle of a filter consists of the following steps. Compare this with the lifecycle of a servlet.

❑ **Instantiate**
The container instantiates each filter class either at the container startup or sometime before a filter instance is required for invocation. For each web application, the container maintains one instance per filter. This is similar to servlets that do not implement the `SingleThreadedServlet` interface. In the case of distributed web containers, the container maintains one instance per application per virtual machine.

❑ **Initialize**
After instantiating a filter, the container calls the `init()` method. During this call, the container passes on initialization parameters to the filter instance.

❑ **Invoke**
For those requests that require a filter to process, the container invokes the `doFilter()` method that is required to implement the filter logic.

❑ **Destroy**:
The container calls this method before taking the filter out of service. In this method, the filter can implement any cleanup logic.

These stages are shown in the figure below. Of these stages, during the lifecycle of a filter, only the filtering phase occurs several times, while the remaining events typically occur once. In practice, the first two steps occur at container startup or when the application is deployed, while the last step occurs at container shutdown or when the application is undeployed (using container-provided tools, if there are any). The container always ensures that a filter is initialized before filtering can occur:

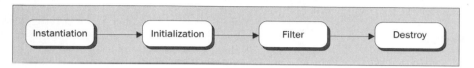

Both `init()` and `doFilter()` methods can throw `ServletException`, while the `doFilter()` method can also throw a `java.io.IOException`. When these methods throw a `ServletException`, the container cannot continue with the filter chain, which means that it cannot serve the web resource to which the request maps. Therefore, in cases where you want the container to serve the resource irrespective of any exceptions, it is important to make sure that the filters consume exceptions and log those cases appropriately.

The FilterConfig Interface

```
public interface FilterConfig
```

This interface is the `ServletConfig` equivalent for filters. The interface provides access to the filter environment, and has the following methods:

The getFilterName() Method

```
public void getFilterName()
```

This method returns the name of the filter as specified in the deployment descriptor. For instance, in the previous example, the name of the filter is `Counter`.

The getInitParameter() Method

```
public String getInitParameter(String name)
```

This method returns the value of the named initialization parameters or `null` if the parameter does not exist. We can specify initialization parameters in the deployment descriptor while declaring the filter.

The getInitParameterNames() Method

```
public Enumeration getInitParameterNames()
```

This method returns the names of the servlet's initialization parameters as an `Enumeration` of `String` objects, or an empty `Enumeration` if the servlet has no initialization parameters.

The getServletContext() Method

```
public ServletContext getServletContext()
```

This method returns a reference to the servlet context associated with the relevant web application.

The FilterChain Interface

```
public interface FilterChain
```

This interface provides the filter with a handle to invoke the rest of the filter chain. Each filter gets access to a `FilterChain` object when its `doFilter()` method is invoked. Using this object, the filter can let the container invoke the next filter in the chain.

The `FilterChain` interface has a single method:

The doFilter() Method

```
public void doFilter(ServletRequest request, ServletResponse response)
```

When a filter invokes this method, the container invokes the next filter in the filter chain. If the invoking filter is the last filter in the chain, the container invokes the requested web resource.

The following figure illustrates this process:

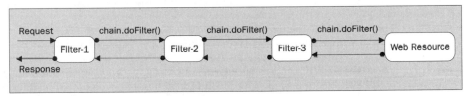

When a filter calls the `doFilter()` method on the `FilterChain` object, the container invokes the next filter in the chain. What if a filter does not want further processing? In this case, the filter can simply not call the `doFilter()` method on the `FilterChain` object. But why should a filter not want to continue with the chain? Consider, for instance, a filter that validates the incoming request. If the filter finds that the request is incomplete, invalid, or inappropriate, it may choose to abort the chain. In this case, the filter itself can write appropriate content back to the response.

Deployment Descriptor for Filters

As we have seen in our first example, in order to deploy filters in a web application, the following additional entries are required in the deployment descriptor:

❑ A `<filter>` element to declare each filter: This is similar to the servlet declaration in the deployment descriptor, and consists of a name, `<filter-name>`, the fully qualified class name of the filter, `<filter-class>`, and zero or more initialization parameters. For each parameter, we should specify a name, `<param-name>`, and a value, `<param-value>`. We can optionally specify a description, `<description>`, for each filter and for each initialization parameter.

❑ A `<filter-mapping>` element to specify URL patterns: The container uses URL pattern mappings to determine if one or more filters should be invoked before processing a web resource. The pattern corresponds to the URI associated with the web resource.

How does the container use these entries to invoke a filter chain? Let's consider a snippet of a deployment descriptor:

```
<filter-mapping>
  <filter-name>filter1</filter-name>
  <url-pattern>/product/catalog/</url-pattern>
</filter-mapping>

<filter-mapping>
  <filter-name>filter2</filter-name>
  <url-pattern>/product/catalog/</url-pattern>
</filter-mapping>

<filter-mapping>
  <filter-name>filter3</filter-name>
  <url-pattern>/product/catalog/</url-pattern>
</filter-mapping>
```

This declaration associates three filters for requests starting with `/product/catalog/`. Based on this configuration, the container forms a filter chain consisting of these three filters. If the URLs were different in these descriptors, the filter chain of calls would be altered, meaning that if there were a typo in the descriptor, and the second filter definition did not point to the same URL, the filter chain would then be of 1 and then 3. Whenever the container receives a request starting with `/product/catalog/`, it creates a `FilterChain` object abstracting these filters, and invokes the `doFilter()` method of the first filter. The order of filter invocations is determined solely by the organization of the descriptor file.

After required processing, the first filter may call the `doFilter()` method on the filter chain. This makes the container invoke the second filter. The second filter thus gets a chance to further process the request. Subsequently, it may call the `doFilter()` method on the filter chain object, which results in the invocation of the third filter. When the third filter calls the `doFilter()` method, the container starts processing the original. After this processing is done, control returns to the third filter. This process continues until control returns to the first filter, after which the filter process ends.

There are three key points to note here:

❑ The container relies on the order in which the mappings are declared in the descriptor to compose a filter chain.

❑ Each filter gets a chance to process before and after the actual resource is processed. This is due to the nesting of `doFilter()` calls.

❑ This process is completely declarative. You can enable or disable filters by including or removing filter mapping declarations in the deployment descriptor.

Here is a skeleton deployment descriptor showing the above elements:

```
<?xml version="1.0" encoding="UTF-8"?>

<!DOCTYPE web-app PUBLIC '-//Sun Microsystems, Inc.//DTD Web Application 2.3//EN'
'http://java.sun.com/dtd/web-app_2.3.dtd'>
```

```
<web-app>

   <!-- Declare filter definitions -->
   <filter>
     <filter-name> Name of the filter </filter-name>
     <filter-class> Class name for the filter </filter-class>
     <init-param>
       <param-name> Name of the parameter </param-name>
       <param-value> Value of the parameter </param-value>
     </init-param>
     <!-- More initialization parameters -->
   </filter>

   ...

   <!-- Map filters to requests -->
   <filter-mapping>
     <filter-name> Name of the filter </filter-name>
     <url-pattern> URL pattern </url-pattern>
   </filter-mapping>

   ...

   <!-- Declare servlets -->

</web-app>
```

The Chat Application with Filters

Let us now consider certain enhancements to the chat application that we developed in the previous chapter, and see how filters can be used to implement these enhancements:

❑ **Message Logging**
It is usual to log chat messages in a persistent data source for monitoring purposes. How do we implement such a logging for all chat messages?

❑ **Message Moderation**
How can we implement a message moderation system where messages containing objectionable or offensive words can be detected? When the application receives messages containing certain words, we may replace the actual message with a standard warning message.

One way to implement these features is to alter the ChatRoomServlet class:

❑ To log each message in a persistent data source such a database

❑ To scan each message for moderated words, and replace messages containing such words with a warning message

However, this involves modifying the ChatRoomServlet adding further complexity to it. In addition, such a mechanism will not be declarative. Instead, let's consider using filters to implement these features such that:

❑   We can implement these features without modifying existing code

❑   We can make these features declarative so that they can be deployed or removed without disturbing the actual chat application

In this section, we shall develop two filters, one for message logging, and the second for message moderation. These filters are shown below:

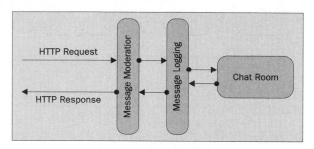

Message Logging

Let us consider a database table with columns PROFILE_NAME, ROOM_NAME, MESSAGE, and TIME_STAMP to log each chat message as they are being received by the chat application. Of these columns, the fourth column indicates the time at which the message was received by the container hosting the chat application. Create a new database to be used to hold the table for the chat application. Create the table MESSAGE_LOG with the following SQL CREATE statement:

```
CREATE TABLE MESSAGE_LOG (MESSAGE_ID          INT DEFAULT AUTOINCREMENT
                                              INITIAL 1 INCREMENT 1 NOT NULL,
                          PROFILE_NAME        VARCHAR(20),
                          ROOM_NAME           VARCHAR(20),
                          MESSAGE             VARCHAR(100),
                          TIME_STAMP          TIMESTAMP);
```

We can now write a filter to extract the name of the user profile, the name of the chat room, and the chat message from the request or the session. Enter the following filter:

```
import javax.servlet.ServletRequest;
import javax.servlet.ServletResponse;
import javax.servlet.ServletException;
import javax.servlet.Filter;
import javax.servlet.FilterChain;
import javax.servlet.FilterConfig;
import javax.servlet.http.HttpSession;
import javax.servlet.http.HttpServletRequest;

import java.io.IOException;

import java.sql.Connection;
import java.sql.DriverManager;
import java.sql.PreparedStatement;
import java.sql.SQLException;
import java.sql.Timestamp;
```

```java
import javax.sql.DataSource;
import javax.naming.InitialContext;
import javax.naming.NamingException;

public class MessageLogFilter implements Filter {

  public void doFilter(ServletRequest request,
                       ServletResponse response,
                       FilterChain chain)
            throws IOException, ServletException {

    // Invoke the next filter
    chain.doFilter(request, response);

    // Get the session
    HttpSession session = ((HttpServletRequest) request).getSession();

    // Get the chat message from the request
    String message = request.getParameter("msg");

    // Get the profile name from the session
    String profileName = (String) session.getAttribute("profileName");

    // Get the name of the room from the session
    String roomName = (String) session.getAttribute("roomName");

    // Create a timestamp
    Timestamp timeStamp = new Timestamp(System.currentTimeMillis());

    // Get a connection to the database
    Connection connection = null;
    String insertStatementStr = "INSERT INTO MESSAGE_LOG " +
      "(PROFILE_NAME, ROOM_NAME, MESSAGE, TIME_STAMP) VALUES (?, ?, ?, ?)";

    try {

      InitialContext initial = new InitialContext();
      DataSource ds = (DataSource)initial.lookup("jdbc/chat");
      connection = ds.getConnection();

      PreparedStatement insertStatement =
                          connection.prepareStatement(insertStatementStr);
      insertStatement.setString(1, profileName);
      insertStatement.setString(2, roomName);
      insertStatement.setString(3, message);
      insertStatement.setTimestamp(4, timeStamp);
      insertStatement.executeUpdate();

    } catch (NamingException ne) {
      throw new ServletException("JNDI error", ne);
    } catch (SQLException sqle) {
      throw new ServletException("Database error", sqle);
    }
    finally {
      if (connection != null) {
        try {
```

```
            connection.close();
        } catch (SQLException sqle) {}
      }
    }
  }
  public void destroy() {}
}
```

During initialization, this filter reads database details from the deployment descriptor. When the filter is invoked via the doFilter() method, it extracts the required information from the request and session, and inserts this data in the MESSAGE_LOG table.

Note that, in this filter, the first statement in the doFilter() method is a call to the doFilter() method on the filter chain. This is to let the ChatRoomServlet process the request first, meaning that the logging happens after the rest of the chain is processed. As we will see later, in the deployment descriptor the MessageLogFilter is the last filter, and is applied to all requests to the chat room. Accordingly, when a chat user posts a message to a chat room, the filter first lets the ChatRoomServlet do its job – which is to prepare the response. This is because, before logging the message, the MessageLogFilter invokes the next filter by calling the doFilter() method. This results in the container invoking the ChatRoomServlet. Once this is done, control returns to the MessageLogFilter, which then logs the message in the database.

The rest of this filter uses JDBC to make an INSERT into the message_log table of our database.

Message Moderation

Let us now consider message moderation that requires replacing messages containing offensive or objectionable words with a warning. Let's assume that words considered offensive or objectionable are supplied within a text file. In order to moderate messages, here are the steps required:

❑ Read the list of words from the text file.

❑ Scan each message entering each chat room. If a message contains one of the words listed in the text file, replace the message with a standard warning.

Both these steps should happen before the ChatRoomServlet is invoked so that by the time the messages are dispatched into the chat room and subsequently seen by chat members, the messages are already moderated. The same applies to the logging.

Consider the MessageModeratorFilter filter to implement these features. During the initialization, this filter can read the list of words, and during the doFilter() method, the filter can scan the chat message and modify it if required.

Before we see the completed code, we'll look at some of the important methods involved. Let's implement the init() method first:

```
public void init(FilterConfig config) throws ServletException {
  try {
    String fileName = config.getInitParameter("moderated_words_file");

    // Read the file containing words for moderation
    InputStream is = config.getServletContext()
```

```
                              .getResourceAsStream(fileName);
      BufferedReader reader = new BufferedReader(
                                 new InputStreamReader(is));
      wordList = new ArrayList();
      while(true) {
        String word = reader.readLine();
        if(word == null) {
          break;
        }
        wordList.add(word.toLowerCase());
      }
      reader.close();

      warningMessage = config.getInitParameter("warning_message");
      if(warningMessage == null) {
        warningMessage = "*** Message restricted";
      }
    } catch(IOException ie) {
      ie.printStackTrace();
      throw new ServletException("Error reading moderated_words.txt");
    } catch(Exception e) {
      e.printStackTrace();
    }
```

This method opens a file whose name is specified as an initialization parameter for this filter. The filter opens this file using the getServletContext() method of the FilterConfig object. Using this method, we can open files and other resources available within the web application. The init() method reads the words and stores them in a list. This method also reads a standard warning message via another initialization parameter.

Let us now consider the doFilter() method:

```
    public void doFilter(ServletRequest request,
                         ServletResponse response,
                         FilterChain chain)
              throws IOException, ServletException {
      String message = ((HttpServletRequest) request).getParameter("msg");
      if(message != null) {
        boolean setWarning = false;
        for(int i = 0; i < wordList.size(); i++) {
          if(message.toLowerCase().indexOf((String) wordList.get(i)) != -1) {
            setWarning = true;
            break;
          }
        }

        if(setWarning) {
          message = warningMessage;
          // How do we change the request parameter? We'll see shortly!
        }
      }

      // Invoke the next filter.
      chain.doFilter(request, response);
    }
```

This method extracts the message from the incoming request, and scans to see if any of the words from the previously created list occur within the message. If so, this method sets a `boolean setWarning` to `true`.

In the second part of this method, if `setWarning` is `true`, this method should change the message in the request to the warning message. However, there is no method such as `setParameter()` on the request object with which we can replace the original message with the warning message.

In order to cross this hurdle, consider two factors:

❏   We can use the `setAttribute()` method on the request object to set the modified message on the request. Although the `ChatRoomServlet` cannot extract this parameter via `getParameter()`, this is the only way we can add data to a request. Alternatively we can store the warning message within the session, but for the `ChatRoomServlet` to read it, we will be required to modify the `ChatRoomServlet`.

❏   The `doFilter()` call on the `FilterChain` object requires the request and response objects as arguments. Triggered by this call, the container invokes the `ChatRoomServlet` with the passed request and response objects.

Since the `ChatRoomServlet` servlet calls `getParameter()` to extract the message from the request, and since the filter sends the request and response objects to the servlet via the filter chain, we can substitute the original request object with a new request object. We can implement this new request class to return the modified message when the `getParameter()` method is called.

Let's consider such a request class now:

```
import javax.servlet.http.HttpServletRequest;
import javax.servlet.http.HttpServletRequestWrapper;
import java.util.List;

public class ModeratedRequest extends HttpServletRequestWrapper {

  List moderatedParameters;

  public ModeratedRequest(HttpServletRequest request,
                          List moderatedParameters) {
    super(request);
    this.moderatedParameters = moderatedParameters;
  }

  public String getParameter(String parameterName) {
    // If this parameter is one of the parameters being moderated,
    // it's an attribute. Else, it is a request parameter
    if(moderatedParameters.contains(parameterName)) {
      return (String) super.getAttribute(parameterName);
    } else {
      return super.getParameter(parameterName);
    }
  }
}
```

This class extends the `javax.servlet.http.HttpServletRequestWrapper` that provides an implementation of the `javax.servlet.http.HttpServletRequest` interface. The constructor of this class takes two parameters – an `HttpServletRequest` object, and a list containing request attributes that can be accessed as request parameters. As we discussed in Chapter 6, the `javax.servlet.http.HttpServletRequestWrapper` class implements the `javax.servlet.http.HttpServletRequest` interface. The implementation uses the `javax.servlet.http.HttpServletRequest` object supplied during construction for actual implementation. It essentially delegates all method calls to the supplied object.

The `getParameter()` method of this class delegates the call to the `getAttribute()` or `getParameter()` methods of the super class based on the name of the parameter. If the name of the parameter is contained in the list of parameters specified in the constructor, this method delegates the call to the `getAttribute()` method. For instance, if we include the name of the parameter "msg" in the list, a call to `getParameter("msg")` would result in a call to the `getAttribute("msg")` of the super class.

Using this technique, we can change the `doFilter()` method as follows:

```
if(setWarning) {
   message = warningMessage;
   request.setAttribute("msg", message);
   request = new ModeratedRequest((HttpServletRequest) request,
                                   moderatedParameters);
}
```

This code replaces the original request object with the custom request object providing all the same functionality except for the `getParameter()` method. In this code, the `moderatedParameters` is a list containing the word "msg" created in the `init()` method.

Here is the complete listing of the filter:

```
import javax.servlet.Filter;
import javax.servlet.FilterChain;
import javax.servlet.FilterConfig;
import javax.servlet.ServletException;
import javax.servlet.ServletRequest;
import javax.servlet.ServletResponse;
import javax.servlet.http.HttpServletRequest;

import java.io.InputStream;
import java.io.InputStreamReader;
import java.io.BufferedReader;
import java.io.IOException;
import java.util.ArrayList;

public class MessageModeratorFilter implements Filter {

   String protocol;
   ArrayList wordList;
   ArrayList moderatedParameters;
   String warningMessage;

   public void init(FilterConfig config) throws ServletException {
     try {
```

```
      String fileName = config.getInitParameter("moderated_words_file");
      // Read the file containing words for moderation
      InputStream is =
        config.getServletContext().getResourceAsStream(fileName);
      BufferedReader reader = new BufferedReader(new InputStreamReader(is));
      wordList = new ArrayList();
      while(true) {
        String word = reader.readLine();
        if(word == null) {
          break;
        }
        wordList.add(word.toLowerCase());
      }
      reader.close();

      // Get the warning message. If not found, use a default.
      warningMessage = config.getInitParameter("warning_message");
      if(warningMessage == null) {
        warningMessage = "*** Message restricted";
      }
      moderatedParameters = new ArrayList();
      moderatedParameters.add("msg");
    } catch(IOException ie) {
      ie.printStackTrace();
      throw new ServletException("Error reading moderate_words.txt");
    } catch(Exception e) {
      e.printStackTrace();
    }
  }

  public void doFilter(ServletRequest request,
                       ServletResponse response,
                       FilterChain chain)
           throws IOException, ServletException {
    // Get the message from the request.
    String message = ((HttpServletRequest) request).getParameter("msg");

    // Check if the message has objectionable words.
    if(message != null) {
      boolean setWarning = false;
      for(int i = 0; i < wordList.size(); i++) {
      if(message.toLowerCase().indexOf((String) wordList.get(i)) != -1) {
        setWarning = true;
        break;
      }
    }

      // If so, replace the message with the warning.
      if(setWarning) {
        message = warningMessage;
        request.setAttribute("msg", message);
        request = new ModeratedRequest((HttpServletRequest) request,
                                       moderatedParameters);
      }
    }
```

```
      // Invoke the next filter
      chain.doFilter(request, response);
   }

   public void destroy() {}
}
```

Deployment Descriptor

The next step is to modify the deployment descriptor to add the filter declarations and filter mappings. Here is the modified deployment descriptor:

```xml
<?xml version="1.0" encoding="ISO-8859-1"?>

<!DOCTYPE web-app
    PUBLIC "-//Sun Microsystems, Inc.//DTD Web Application 2.3//EN"
    "http://java.sun.com/j2ee/dtds/web-app_2_3.dtd">

<web-app>

  <display-name>chat</display-name>
  <context-param>
    <param-name>ADMIN_PATH</param-name>
    <param-value>/chat/servlet/chatAdmin</param-value>
  </context-param>

  <context-param>
    <param-name>LISTROOMS_PATH</param-name>
    <param-value>/chat/servlet/listRooms</param-value>
  </context-param>

  <context-param>
    <param-name>CHATROOM_PATH</param-name>
    <param-value>/chat/servlet/chatRoom</param-value>
  </context-param>

  <filter>
    <filter-name>MessageLogFilter</filter-name>
    <display-name>MessageLogFilter</display-name>
    <filter-class>MessageLogFilter</filter-class>
  </filter>

  <filter>
    <filter-name>MessageModeratorFilter</filter-name>
    <display-name>MessageModeratorFilter</display-name>
    <filter-class>MessageModeratorFilter</filter-class>
    <init-param>
        <param-name>moderated_words_file</param-name>
        <param-value>moderated_words.txt</param-value>
    </init-param>
    <init-param>
        <param-name>warning_message</param-name>
        <param-value>*** Message filtered by the moderator.</param-value>
    </init-param>
```

```
    </filter>

    <filter-mapping>
      <filter-name>MessageModeratorFilter</filter-name>
      <url-pattern>/servlet/chatRoom</url-pattern>
    </filter-mapping>

    <filter-mapping>
      <filter-name>MessageLogFilter</filter-name>
      <url-pattern>/servlet/chatRoom</url-pattern>
    </filter-mapping>

    <servlet>
      <servlet-name>chatAdmin</servlet-name>
      <display-name>chatAdmin</display-name>
      <servlet-class>ChatAdminServlet</servlet-class>
    </servlet>

    <servlet>
      <servlet-name>chatRoom</servlet-name>
      <display-name>chatRoom</display-name>
      <servlet-class>ChatRoomServlet</servlet-class>
    </servlet>

    <servlet>
      <servlet-name>listRooms</servlet-name>
      <display-name>listRooms</display-name>
      <servlet-class>ListRoomsServlet</servlet-class>
    </servlet>

  </web-app>
```

Also, create a text file named moderated_words.txt. Enter words in this file with each word in a new line. For demonstration purposes, enter the following in this file:

```
bad
pain
free
```

We also need the index.html file for the initial screen:

```
<html>
  <head>
    <title>Chat Application</title>
    <body>
    <h1>Chat Application</h1>

    <p>Click <a href="/chat/servlet/chatAdmin">here</a> to administer
        chat rooms.</p>

    <p>Click <a href="/chat/servlet/listRooms">here</a> to view current
        chat rooms, and to join a chat room.</p>

  </body>
</html>
```

Deployment

To deploy this application, we follow the same process as before. We start by creating the WAR file (`chat.war`).

Make sure you have the following files in the following locations:

```
chat/
      index.html
      moderated_words.txt
      WEB-INF/
                 web.xml
                 classes/
                            ChatAdminServlet.class
                            ChatEntry.class
                            ChatRoom.class
                            ChatRoomServlet.class
                            ListRoomsServlet.class
                            MessageLogFilter.class
                            MessageModeratorFilter.class
                            ModeratedRequest.class
```

To create the WAR file we will use the following `jar` command:

```
jar -cvf chat.war index.html moderated_words.txt WEB-INF
```

Again we start the J2EE server and the application deployment tool. This time create a new application called `chat.ear`. Add the `chat.war` to the application and we are again ready to deploy the application.

We don't need to do anything on the first screen besides double-check we're deploying the correct application. On the following screen we need to provide the context that we will use to browse to our application. Set it to `chat`. Proceed to the final screen and select Finish to deploy the application into the server.

Before you can run the application, we also need to create the datasource `jdbc/chat` that points to our newly created database. This can be done using the Server Configuration window. Refer to Chapter 6 for instructions on how to do it. Restart the server to load the new datasource and make sure the database is running.

To check the application browse to http://localhost:8000/chat/index.html. We should then see the following screen:

When a message is sent in the chat room that is moderated by the filter we will see the following:

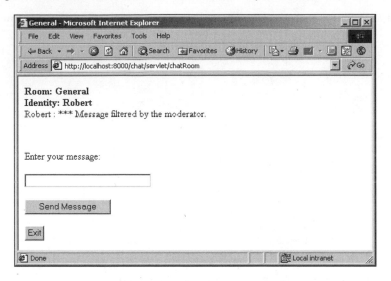

Chat with Logging and Moderation

When we start the application, and start sending chat messages, here is what happens:

1. The deployment descriptor specifies /chat as the mapping for both the filters. So, all requests mapping to http://localhost:8000/chat/servlet/chatAdmin cause the container to invoke these filters.

2. Since the MessageModeratorFilter is mapped first to the above path, the container invokes the MessageModeratorFilter first. This filter scans for objectionable/offensive words, and when such words are found, adds a request attribute called "msg" and creates a ModeratedRequest. This filter then calls the doFilter() on the FilterChain object.

3. The container then invokes the MessageLogFilter, since it is mapped next. However, before logging the message, the MessageLogFilter first calls the doFilter() method on the FilterChain object.

4. Since there are no more filters mapped for this request, the container invokes the ChatRoomServlet.

5. The ChatRoomServlet reads the request, creating a response as usual.

6. Control then returns to the MessageLogFilter. This filter proceeds to log the message, and then returns.

7. Control then returns to the MessageModeratorFilter. This filter has already moderated the message, and it returns.

The same events happen for each message posted to a chat room.

Let us now consider certain variations:

❑ In order to remove message moderation, simply remove the mapping for MessageModeratorFilter in the deployment descriptor.

❑ In order to remove message logging, simply remove the corresponding mapping from the deployment descriptor.

❑ With the above code, moderated messages will be logged instead of the original message. What if you instead want to log the original message before moderation? To do this, we can modify the MessageLogFilter to read the message using the getAttribute() call instead of the getParameter() call.

❑ We may also enhance this example to replace objectionable words with "***" instead of replacing the entire message.

You may try these variations on your own as an exercise.

Summary

Filters provide a powerful mechanism to programmatically alter how the container serves web resources. The filter mechanism is independent of the type of resource. It applies equally well to dynamic resources such as servlets or JSP pages, or static resources such as HTML files, images, and so on.

The examples in this chapter have illustrated two main points:

❑ We can introduce one or more filters within the request-response process.

❑ A filter can modify the environment for servlets and JSP pages. As illustrated by the MessageModeratorFilter, we can create new request, response, or even session objects for servlets or JSP pages. This feature opens up several possibilities for us to build more intelligent web applications.

When you plan to develop your own web applications, consider if some of the functionality qualifies for implementation in filters. You may also consider filters when you're adding new features to existing web applications. In general, if you find certain logic common to one or more servlets/JSP pages, or when you want to include dynamic behavior before invoking static content, consider using filters. Filters provide a declarative, and therefore loosely coupled, mechanism with which to add useful features.

In the next chapter, we will complete our exploration of the Servlet specification and look at some other topics involved with developing web applications.

Data
RDMS
JDBC
Application Logic
Client
Web Container
Servlets
JSPs
Tag Library
HTTP(S)
(X)HTML/ XML
RMI/IIOP
JNDI
JTA
JDBC
JMS
JavaMail
JAAS
JCA
JAXP
J2EE Application Server
Applet
Client Application
Session Beans
JavaMail
Mail Server
RMI
Java Application
IIOP
CORBA Server
JNDI
Directory Servic
JMS
Message Queue

Web Deployment, Authentication, and Packaging

The design and development processes in J2EE applications are clearly separated from those of deployment and packaging. The J2EE architecture achieves this by encouraging you to build loosely coupled, scalable, components. This allows the components to be reusable, which in turn allows the runtime configuration to be more flexible.

In this chapter, we will understand how to make use of the deployment and packaging facilities provided by the servlet container architecture. The techniques and strategies we learn will allow a greater degree of flexibility to be introduced into applications.

Specifically, we will cover:

❑   The rationale behind the structure of the web applications we have seen in earlier chapters

❑   How to map HTTP requests to different web application components

❑   How authentication models for web applications can be plugged into a web application without having to implement authentication at the application level

❑   The use of a deployment descriptor to configure various aspects of a web application, including servlet initialization and startup, session timeouts, MIME mappings, welcome files, and handling errors

Web Application Structure

A **web application** is a collection of many different types of files. A typical web application might include, among others:

- ❑ Servlets
- ❑ HTML pages
- ❑ Images
- ❑ JavaServer Pages (JSP pages)
- ❑ A deployment descriptor and other configuration files

The concept of a web application was introduced in version 2.2 of the Java Servlet specification. A web application is organized with a structured hierarchy of directories, with particular types of files stored in particular directories. These directories can then be packaged into a **web application archive (WAR)** file.

Directory Structure

The directory structure of a web application has two parts:

- ❑ A directory called WEB-INF that contains the resources that are not to be directly downloaded to a client; this directory is private – the client does not have direct access to the files in this directory. The WEB-INF directory typically contains dynamic resources such as servlets, as well as configuration files.

- ❑ A directory that contains those resources that are intended to be publicly available. This includes all the subdirectories of this directory, except of course for the private WEB-INF directory. This directory typically contains static resources such as HTML and image files.

For example, a web application could have this directory structure:

```
myWebApp\
          index.html
          login.jsp
          404NotFound.html
          images\
                  logo.gif
                  banner.gif
          literature\
                    summary.jsp
                    Y2001AnnualReport.pdf
                    Y2001PresidentAddress.pdf
          WEB-INF\
                  web.xml
                  classes\
                          ShoppingCart.class
                          Catalog.class
                          CheckOut.class
                  lib\
                      dbLibrary.jar
                      xmlTools.jar
```

In the above directory structure, myWebApp is the root directory of the web application. The public resources of this web application are the two HTML files, index.html and 404NotFound.html, and the one JSP file, login.jsp, and the files contained in the images and literature subdirectories, logo.gif, banner.gif, and Y2001AnnualReport.pdf. The other files, contained within the WEB-INF directory, are resources that are only accessible to the container.

A public resource is any file that is accessible to the client of the web application. Typical public resources include:

- ❑ HTML, XML, and JSP documents
- ❑ Image, audio, and video files
- ❑ Java applets – classes as well as JAR files containing applets
- ❑ Microsoft Office documents – Word, Excel, etc.

Client browsers can download these resources unchanged and render them as required. For example, when an HTML page includes an <APPLET> tag that refers to an applet in a JAR file, the web container delivers the JAR file to the client browser unchanged.

> *Although JSP pages are included as public resources in a web application, the container does not show them directly to clients. As we'll learn in Chapter 10, the container automatically converts JSP pages into servlets. The servlet is then compiled and invoked to generate the response for the client. However, since a JSP page is often considered more akin to an HTML document than to a Java class, JSP pages are also included under public resources.*

Typically, the container reads the static resource from the file system, and writes the contents directly to the network connection. The interpretation of the content of these resources is the responsibility of the client browser. In order to help the browser render the file correctly, the container sends the MIME type of the file. These MIME types can be set in the deployment descriptor of the web application.

Of course, there are certain resources that clients should not download directly. These may be files that the client should not view, such as configuration files, or they may be files that the container must perform some processing on before sending the response to the client, like servlets. These private resources are stored in the WEB-INF directory, or its subdirectories.

The types of resources that clients should not download directly include:

- ❑ Servlets – these components include application logic, and possibly access to other resources such as databases
- ❑ Any other files in the web application that servlets access directly
- ❑ Resources that are meant for execution or use on the server side, such as Java class files and JAR files for classes used by your servlets
- ❑ Temporary files created by your applications
- ❑ Deployment descriptors and any other configuration files

These resources are private and, as such, are accessible only to their own web application and the container. In order to accommodate private resources, the web container requires the WEB-INF directory to be present in your application. If your web application does not contain this directory it will not work. WEB-INF includes:

- ❑ A web.xml file. This is the deployment descriptor file.
- ❑ A subdirectory named classes. This directory is used to store server-side Java class files such as servlets and other helper classes, structured according to the usual Java packaging rules.
- ❑ A lib subdirectory to contain JAR files used by the web application.

411

This structure has several advantages. The most significant benefit is that several applications can coexist in the same web container without any conflict. Each application exists in a 'sand box'; the public and private resources of an application are independent of any other application that the container may be running. While this model seems very intuitive in standalone applications, it was not available on the server until web applications were introduced in J2EE.

Each web application should be managed independently of all other applications that may be running in the container, as we saw in the examples in earlier chapters. When a new application is added to the J2EE server, we can simply add the appropriate `context root` in the `deploytool` of the Reference Implementation (as described in the previous chapters), without disturbing any of the other applications.

In older versions of web containers (then called servlet 'engines'), we would have typically kept all our servlets under one /servlets directory, and kept all the public resources under the document root of the web server. This is equivalent to having one large application combining all the servlets. Grouping all the public resources under the web server's document root in this manner poses maintenance constraints as a change to a servlet can have unintended effects on other applications.

Another advantage to organizing resources in this way is that the container knows where to look for classes. The class loader of the container automatically checks the `classes` directory, as well as in the JAR files in the `lib` directory. This means that you don't need to explicitly add these classes and JAR files to the `CLASSPATH`. Remember that while deploying the sample applications in earlier chapters, we did not change the `CLASSPATH` settings because the container could locate and load the servlet classes automatically.

The public directory of a web application is similar to the document root directory of a conventional web server. When placing files in a conventional web server, public content is maintained in each web application under the application's root directory. The difference between a conventional web server and the web container is that each web application has its own document root.

There is another ramification of this organization. According to the servlet specification, a container should load classes/JAR files of each web application using a different class loader. It is for this reason that servlets, JSP pages, and other classes that are part of one web application cannot see classes in other applications, and therefore cannot share static variables or singleton classes, for example. Thus, even if you deploy the same web application twice (each mapping to a different URI), as far as the container is concerned they are two entirely different applications. Such applications cannot share information. As a result, web containers create a virtual partitioning of web applications within the container.

Web Archive Files

The various directories and files that make up a web application can be packaged into a **web application archive (WAR)** file. This process is similar to the packaging of Java class files into JAR files. The purpose of the packaging is the same; it is to provide a simplified way to distribute Java class files and their related resources. WAR files can be created using the same `jar` tool that is used to create JAR files. A web application can be deployed as a WAR file, rather than the unpackaged collection of directories and files.

Let's consider the chat application developed in Chapter 7. We'll package this application into a WAR file, and deploy the resulting WAR file in the container in place of the expanded directories and files.

The chat application was saved in `%BOOK_HOME%\CH07\chat\`. Open a command prompt, change the working directory to `this` directory, and execute the following command:

```
jar -cf chat.war *
```

This command packs all the contents under this directory, including subdirectories, into an archive file called `chat.war`. We used two command-line options:

❑ The -c option to create a new archive

❑ The -f option to specify the target archive file name

These two commands are used together as -cf. If the verbose option is specified, using -v, the names of the files and directories included in the archive will be output to the screen.

You can use the following command to view the contents of a WAR file:

```
jar -tvf chat.war
```

This command lists the contents of the WAR file:

```
Command Prompt                                                      _ □ X

C:\ProJavaServer\Ch07\chat>jar -cf chat.war *

C:\ProJavaServer\Ch07\chat>jar -tvf chat.war
      0 Tue Jul 31 17:43:26 BST 2001 META-INF/
     68 Tue Jul 31 17:43:26 BST 2001 META-INF/MANIFEST.MF
    335 Wed Jul 26 14:45:18 BST 2000 index.html
      0 Tue Jul 31 17:43:12 BST 2001 src/
   3820 Sat Jul 07 10:08:54 BST 2001 src/ChatAdminServlet.java
    444 Sun Jul 01 13:40:58 BST 2001 src/ChatEntry.java
    502 Sun Jul 01 13:41:20 BST 2001 src/ChatRoom.java
   6592 Sat Jul 07 10:10:56 BST 2001 src/ChatRoomServlet.java
   3480 Sat Jul 07 10:09:38 BST 2001 src/ListRoomsServlet.java
      0 Tue Jul 31 17:43:02 BST 2001 WEB-INF/
      0 Tue Jul 31 17:29:28 BST 2001 WEB-INF/classes/
   3676 Thu Jul 05 22:29:38 BST 2001 WEB-INF/classes/ChatAdminServlet.class
    565 Thu Jul 05 22:29:38 BST 2001 WEB-INF/classes/ChatEntry.class
    665 Thu Jul 05 22:29:38 BST 2001 WEB-INF/classes/ChatRoom.class
   5357 Thu Jul 05 22:29:40 BST 2001 WEB-INF/classes/ChatRoomServlet.class
   3348 Thu Jul 05 22:29:40 BST 2001 WEB-INF/classes/ListRoomsServlet.class
   1012 Sat Jul 07 10:50:46 BST 2001 WEB-INF/web.xml

C:\ProJavaServer\Ch07\chat>_
```

Instead of including all the contents, you may select individual files and subdirectories while creating WAR files. Refer to the JDK documentation for a full list of these command-line options for the `jar` tool. You can also use a standard ZIP file manipulation tools such as WinZip to create and manipulate WAR files. Note that the `jar` tool automatically creates the META-INF sub-directory and its contents.

Deploying a WAR File

Any JSP 1.1-compliant server will automatically deploy an application packaged as a WAR file, as long as the location of the WAR file is explicitly stated. We've been using the J2EE Reference Implementation for the examples in this book. As described in previous chapters, the server can be started by running the `j2ee.bat` file in the `%J2EE_HOME%\bin` directory. We can then deploy our WAR file by running the `deploytool.bat` file in the same directory, and following the instructions detailed previously in Chapters 5 and 6. After the application is successfully deployed and configured, you should be able to access the chat application through your web browser.

When should WAR Files be Used?

Although the format of a WAR file is the same as that of a JAR file, WAR files have significant differences from JAR files. The purpose of a JAR file is to package classes and their related resources into a compressed archive file; a WAR file represents a web application, not just a class archive.

So, when should we use WAR files? WAR files are not appropriate during the development stages, when the servlets in the web application are likely to be frequently recompiled. It would be time consuming to recreate a WAR file every time a servlet was recompiled. During the development stages, it is better to utilize the auto-reloading features of the web container. Many web containers provide auto-reloading facilities for compiled servlet class files and JSP files. This is a very useful feature when the components of an application are changing often. With an auto-reloading feature, the container does not need to be restarted when a change is made to a servlet or JSP page. Instead, the container will automatically reload the modified class.

The J2EE sever specifies the `reloadable="true"` attribute within a `<Context>` tag to enable auto-reloading:

```
<Context path="/chat"
    docBase="%BOOK_HOME%/Ch09/chat"
    reloadable="true">
</Context>
```

When this `<Context>` tag is added to `server.xml` under `%J2EE_HOME%\conf\`, the server automatically reloads Java class files and JAR files contained in `WEB-INF\classes` and `WEB-INF\lib` (if applicable). Auto-reloading requires the container to monitor the deployment directories periodically (the `docBase` directories in the case of Tomcat), which will lead to performance degradation. Because of the extra overhead incurred, automatic reloading is not recommended for use only in production-level web applications.

WAR files are more appropriate towards the end of application development phase, when the number of code changes decreases, and planning begins for the final production of the application.

With WAR files, we can package web applications using a logical structure and, when the WAR file is deployed, the container will have access to the resources within the web application. In the next section, we will address the question of how the container can locate resources that are requested, by either a client or another resource within the web application.

Mapping Requests to Applications and Servlets

In a web container, each web application is associated with a **context**, and all resources in a web application exist relative to that context. For example, in the greeting application in Chapter 5, the `index.html` file exists under the context `/greeting/`. You can access `index.html` at http://localhost:8080/greeting/index.html.

Each context also has a `ServletContext` object associated with it. To the web application, this `ServletContext` object represents a view of the web container and allows servlets to access the resources that are available to them. `ServletContext` is the virtual sandbox within which all information sharing for servlets and other web components occurs.

In earlier chapters, we've accessed servlets via the names specified for each servlet in the deployment descriptor. In this section, we will discuss how requests are mapped to servlets in a more generic and flexible fashion.

An HTTP request always contains a Uniform Resource Identifier (URI) identifying the requested resource. The terms Uniform Resource Locator (URL) and Uniform Resource Identifier (URI) are often used inconsistently in books, specifications, and other documents. This is partly because the URL is the one of the most commonly used subset of URIs for specific network protocols. We will use the terms as they are used in the Servlet API specification, which is largely the same as their use in the HTTP specification:

❑ A URI is any string used to identify an Internet resource, in a name space. Indeed, the address of any Internet resource can be encoded in the form of a URI.

❑ A URL is such a string, in a format for a specific protocol such as `http`, `ftp`, `telnet`, `news`, etc. This format includes a scheme (for example, `http`), the domain name of the server, a path, and possibly query string parameters.

❑ A URL path is the part of the URL that identifies the resource within a specific server; in other words, just the part that denotes the path.

For example, the URI http://www.wrox.com/Consumer is a URL for the scheme `http`, located at the server `www.wrox.com`, and the URL path of this resource is `/Consumer`.

From the above description, URLs and URIs seem very similar. However, the main difference is that a URI *may* or *may not* describe a physical resource, whereas a URL *must* describe a physical resource.

For instance, consider the `DOCTYPE` declaration of the web application deployment descriptor. The `DOCTYPE` declaration specifies a DTD for the deployment descriptor that the web container uses to validate the deployment descriptor. What this declaration contains is a URI, for example: http://java.sun.com/j2ee/dtds/web-app_2_3.dtd. The URI specified in this declaration may or may not exist physically. Although in the case of this particular example you will actually find a DTD at this location, this need not always be true. The XML parser that parses the deployment descriptor may instead map this URI to a DTD available in the local file system (using an entity resolver).

Web containers use the same concept to identify web applications, and the resources within them. With the help of the URL path, web containers can identify the application, the associated servlet context, and the resource within the application. For this to be possible, each web application must be mapped to a unique URL path prefix, for instance `/chat`. This path prefix specifies a unique namespace for all resources with the web application. The web container uses this prefix to map requests to resources within the web application.

In order to see how this mechanism works, consider a `help.html` file within the help subdirectory of an application, with its root deployed with a context path `/catalog` on a web container located at http://localhost:8000. This resource can thus be accessed as http://localhost:8000/catalog/help/help.html. This is similar to having a `help.html` file in the `/catalog/help` subdirectory under the document root of a web server located at http://localhost:8000. In this regard, the container behavior is similar to that of a web server, except that the container uses the context path name to identify the application.

The path name serves as the document root for locating resources within the application. For instance, consider two applications deployed on the same server: one with the context path `/techSupport` and the other with a context path `/chat`. When the web container receives an HTTP request with a path starting with `/chat` the container can determine that the request should be handled by the Chat application, and similarly it can determine that all requests starting with `/techSupport` will be handled by the Tech Support application.

This mechanism can be extended to servlets within applications. In the same way as the context path is used to map a request to a web application, URL path mappings can be used to map requests to servlets. There are two steps in this mapping process:

❑ **Defining alias names to servlets:**
Remember that, in the Chat application, we've defined three servlet classes in the deployment descriptor with alias names:

```
<servlet>
  <servlet name>chatAdmin</servlet-name>
  <servlet-class>ChatAdminServlet</servlet-class>
</servlet>

<servlet>
  <servlet-name>chatRoom</servlet-name>
  <servlet-class>ChatRoomServlet</servlet-class>
</servlet>

<servlet>
  <servlet-name>listRooms</servlet-name>
  <servlet-class>ListRoomsServlet</servlet-class>
</servlet>
```

This is just a mapping of short alias names to servlet class names. The alias names allow you to refer to servlets more easily, and to replace the implementation class for a servlet without having to modify the references to the servlet within the application. This naming is a part of the process of defining a servlet in the deployment descriptor.

❑ **Mapping URL paths to servlet alias names**
In previous examples, we've accessed servlets via a path such as
`/context_name/servlet/servlet_name`. For example, the `ChatAdminServlet` is accessed as http://localhost:8000/chat/servlet/chatAdmin. By mapping URL path requests to servlets instead, we will be able to provide our servlets with more logical names.

Let's study the second step (mapping URL paths to servlet alias names) in more detail. Consider the following rules for mapping URL paths to servlets:

URL path	Servlet Alias	URL
/admin	chatAdmin	http://localhost:8000/chat/admin
/listRooms	listRooms	http://localhost:8000/chat/listRooms
/chatRooms	chatRooms	http://localhost:8000/chat/chatRooms

The first two columns in this table list the URL path names that we intend to use for each servlet, while the third column shows the actual URLs that we can use to access these servlets.

In order to facilitate this mapping, we can use the `<servlet-mapping>` tags of the web application. For example, we could change the deployment descriptor of our chat application as shown below:

```
<?xml version="1.0" encoding="ISO-8859-1"?>

<!DOCTYPE web-app
    PUBLIC "-//Sun Microsystems, Inc.//DTD Web Application 2.3//EN"
    "http://java.sun.com/j2ee/dtds/web-app_2_3.dtd">

<web-app>
```

```
<context-param>
  <param-name>ADMIN_PATH</param-name>
  <param-value>/chat/admin</param-value>
</context-param>

<context-param>
  <param-name>LISTROOMS_PATH</param-name>
  <param-value>/chat/list</param-value>
</context-param>

<context-param>
  <param-name>CHATROOM_PATH</param-name>
  <param-value>/chat/chat</param-value>
</context-param>
...
<servlet>
  <servlet-name>chatAdmin</servlet-name>
  <servlet-class>ChatAdminServlet</servlet-class>
</servlet>

<servlet>
  <servlet-name>chatRoom</servlet-name>
  <servlet-class>ChatRoomServlet</servlet-class>
</servlet>

<servlet>
  <servlet-name>listRooms</servlet-name>
  <servlet-class>ListRoomsServlet</servlet-class>
</servlet>

<servlet-mapping>
  <servlet-name>chatAdmin</servlet-name>
  <url-pattern>/admin/*</url-pattern>
</servlet-mapping>

<servlet-mapping>
  <servlet-name>chatRoom</servlet-name>
  <url-pattern>/chat/*</url-pattern>
</servlet-mapping>

<servlet-mapping>
  <servlet-name>listRooms</servlet-name>
  <url-pattern>/list/*</url-pattern>
</servlet-mapping>
...
</web-app>
```

This modified deployment descriptor specifies that:

❑ Requests starting with /admin/* will be routed to the chatAdmin servlet. For example, when we input http://localhost:8000/chat/admin/, we will enter the administration page of the chat application.

❑ Requests starting with /chat/* will be routed to the chatRoomServlet servlet.

❑ Requests starting with /list/* will be routed to the listRoomsServlet servlet.

❑ Requests that do not match the above rules will be handled by the container in the usual manner.

We should also note the change in the values of ADMIN_PATH, LISTROOMS_PATH, and CHATROOM_PATH. In previous chapters these values pointed to paths starting with /servlet, but we can now use servlet mappings.

So what's the advantage in using servlet mappings instead of using paths pointing to servlets? When we use a mapping, various web pages (static, or dynamic) in a web application link to the mapping instead of a servlet. As a result, the pages that link to a servlet are loosely coupled to the servlet. You can change the mapping to point to an enhanced version of a servlet or a JSP, but the pages that link to the mapping are isolated from such changes.

Path mappings are relative to the context's URL path prefix. The container removes the context URI path prefix before evaluating the URL pattern mapping rules. This means that a request for /chat/admin is initially sent to the Chat application context. The Chat application context removes the URI path prefix, and compares the remainder of the path with the URL pattern mapping rules, in which it will discover that the request should be handled by the chatAdmin servlet.

A request with a URL that starts with something other than /chat is handed to a context with a matching URI path prefix, and the mapping rules specified for that web application are again applied to figure out how to handle the request.

In all the above mappings, we used names such as /chat, /admin, and /list to point to the three servlets. There is one consequence of this mapping. If you have content under subdirectories having similar names, the container will not be able to serve such content directly. For example, if you have an HTML page at %BOOK_HOME%/Ch9/chat/list/howto.html, the mapping /chat would prevent the container from serving this page. Instead, the servlet gets invoked when a user tries this URL. We should choose our mappings carefully to ensure that there are no such conflicts.

The figure below summarizes the path mapping for the chatAdmin servlet:

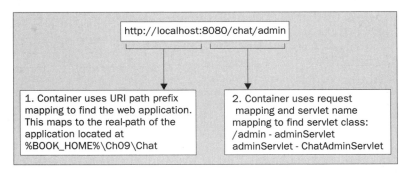

This diagram shows how the different parts of a URL map to:

❑   A server, with a web container

❑   A web application, and thereby a context

❑   A servlet to process the request

The server uses a URI path prefix map to locate the correct web application. The Chat application context uses the remainder of the URI path to find the name of the servlet to process the request, and finally a name-to-class map to locate the servlet class. We can construct a URL to access a web application from a client by using the following generalized pattern:

http://hoststring/ContextPath/servletPath/pathInfo

It is easy to move an application to a different place in the web container's name space as all URI paths within a context are relative to the context's root URI path. So if we introduce a new version of the Chat application, and we want to use the /chat prefix for the new version while still providing access to the old version at /oldchat, all we have to do is change the web container's context mappings. In this case we would map /chat to the new version and /oldchat to the old version.

Securing Web Applications

Controlled access to web applications, in order to guard valuable data and resources, is a very common requirement. The most commonly used approach for web application security is to use login forms, and authenticate users based on their login names and passwords. This approach is usually combined with Secure Sockets Layer (SSL) with server-side digital certificates obtained from certificate vendors such as VeriSign (http://www.verisign.com/).

SSL is a security protocol and specifies a process for web servers and browsers to establish a secure communication channel over HTTP. This protocol includes steps by which browsers and servers exchange certain private keys before exchanging application data. Browsers and servers use these private keys to encrypt and decrypt application data over HTTP. Since this protocol allows information to be exchanged in an encrypted form, it is more secure than sending information unencrypted.

Although more secure implementations are possible, and sometimes required, we will concentrate on how web containers and web applications can be configured to implement user authentication. Note that most web servers provide mechanisms to create realms, and access control lists to control access to various web resources. In this section, we're not concerned about such features, and instead we'll focus on the features possible with the servlet specification.

Before discussing details of how web containers can be set up to provide secure access, it is useful to understand the traditional approach that did not rely on the container. This was usually implemented as follows:

❑ Program the application to have one or more entry points with login forms. For example, in the Chat application, we can provide a login page, with a form to accept the login name and password of the Chat administrator.

❑ Authenticate the user when they submit the login form, preferably over HTTPS. For this purpose, you should verify against a previously created user database or a file that contains user login names and passwords. For example, in the case of the Chat admin servlet, we could maintain all users with administrative capabilities in a database. A new servlet would be required, called LoginServlet, to receive this request, connect to the database, and check if the user name and password match.

❑ Once the login is successful, the user would be forwarded to the admin servlet.

What safeguards can be introduced to prevent a user from directly accessing the admin servlet? There are two possibilities:

❑ The admin servlet should somehow be able to know that the user has already logged in. We can use a session attribute, username, which is set by the login servlet when the login is successful. The admin servlet can verify if this attribute exists in the session, and if not, can send some content explaining that the user cannot use the admin servlet.

❏ Alternatively, the admin servlet can redirect the user to a login servlet, and upon completion of login, instruct the login servlet to return the user back to the admin servlet. Consider the following pseudo-code to modify the admin servlet:

```
protected void doPost(HttpServletRequest req, HttpServletResponse res) {
  HttpSession session = req.getSession();
  String userName = session.getAttribute("username");
  if(username == null || username.length() == 0) {
    session.setAttribute("referrer", "/servlet/adminServlet");
    RequestDispatcher rd = request.getRequestDispatcher(
                       "/servlet/loginServlet");
    rd.forward(request, response);
  } else {
    // Authenticated user. Proceed with chat administration
    ...
  }
}
```

This code snippet tries to retrieve the username from the current user's session (note that the session exists whether or not the user has been authenticated). If the username is not found in the session, the servlet sets a new attribute referrer in the session, with the URL path of the admin servlet as its value. The admin servlet then directs the users to the login servlet via the RequestDispatcher.

Now, let's consider the loginServlet:

```
protected void doPost(HttpServletRequest req, HttpServletResponse res) {
  HttpSession session = req.getSession();
  String userName = req.getSession().getAttribute("username");
  if(username == null) {
    // Get the user name and password parameters from req.
    ...

    // Access the database and verify login and password
    ...
    // If successful
    if(...) {
      referrer = session.getAttribute("referrer");
      RequestDispatcher rd = request.getRequestDispatcher(referrer);
      rd.forward(request, response);
    } else {
      // Send content denoting login failure.
      ...
    }
  }
}
```

This servlet checks whether the user is valid, and if so, redirects the user back to the referrer; in our case, this is the admin servlet.

The above code snippets give one possible generic approach for implementing authentication. Note that you should include the first code snippet (shown for ChatAdminServlet) in all servers that require authenticated access.

This approach is called **programmatic security**. That is, the developer implements security by programming for it. If you want to implement security for a servlet, or for that matter a JSP page, you would have to explicitly modify the servlet or JSP page to verify whether the session belongs to an authenticated user and, if not, direct the user to the loginServlet. This approach is often satisfactory for small applications for which the security requirements and users rarely change.

There is another approach, called **declarative security**. In this approach, you do not program for security; instead, you declare that particular resources require authenticated access and that the user should have a specific role.

Declarative security allows the web container to effectively implement the pseudo-code we wrote for the admin servlet, and to completely implement the login servlet. If the container detects that there is no authenticated user associated with the session, it can direct the user to a login page and verify the login name and password. If the username and password are valid, the user is redirected to the admin servlet. We simply need to instruct the container as to which servlets require authenticated access by making appropriate additions to the deployment descriptor.

In J2EE, the authentication mechanism is based on **roles**. A role designates responsibilities and privileges of the user. For example, if two users Jack and Jill are designated as the administrators for the Chat application, we can assign a particular role, chatAdministrator, to both Jack and Jill. Although Jack and Jill are two different users, they can both play the same role in the application. Similarly, a single user can play multiple roles in a given web application.

The servlet API specification specifies four possible types of authentication:

- ❑ HTTP basic authentication
- ❑ HTTP digest authentication
- ❑ HTTPS client authentication
- ❑ Form-based authentication

Of these, conventional web servers such as Apache implement both basic and digest authentication approaches. Let's look at these authentication types in a little more detail:

- ❑ **Basic authentication** is based on a simple username and password. When a web page or a resource is designated with basic authentication, the web server requests that the browser send a user name and password. Based on this, the browser displays a dialog box to capture the username and password, and sends these values to the web server. This approach can also be combined with SSL.

- ❑ **Digest authentication** is similar to basic authentication, except that the passwords are transmitted in hashed form. In this approach, the browser sends a hashed version of the password (and a random string sent by the server, called a nonce) entered by the user. Hashing algorithms, such as MD5, generate one-way hash (a code) for a given clear-text. The browser performs the same operation on the stored password, and checks if the hash values are the same. Since hashed passwords are exchanged (instead of plain-text passwords), this approach is considered more secure than basic authentication over HTTP. However, this mechanism is not as widely used as basic authentication or HTTPS client authentication. For more information on this approach, see RFC-2069 (http://www.ietf.org/rfc/rfc2069.txt).

- ❑ **HTTPS client authentication** requires the use of public key certificates and HTTPS (HTTP over SSL). This is a more secure approach, in that it requires a digital certificate that can be used to verify if the user is who they claim to be.

❑ **Form-based authentication** is the final form of authentication specified by the servlet specification. Using this approach, you can also define custom login and error pages for authentication.

Let's now look at the facilities provided by the Servlet specification for programmatic and declarative security. We will limit ourselves to the API for accessing user credentials with form-based login, and see how form-based authentication can actually be implemented.

Programmatic Security

The `HttpServletRequest` interface provides the following methods to retrieve user/role information from the request:

The getAuthType() Method

```
public String getAuthType()
```

This method returns the authentication type used to protect the servlet. Possible return values are `BASIC` to indicate basic authentication, `SSL` to indicate SSL-based authentication, or `null` otherwise.

The getRemoteUser() Method

```
public String getRemoteUser()
```

Returns the login of the user making this request; the return value depends on the implementation of the container.

The getUserPrincipal() Method

```
public java.security.Principal getUserPrincipal()
```

Returns the `Principal` object associated with the current user session. A `Principal` object is used to represent an identity, such as the login or even a digital certificate, belonging to the requesting user.

The isUserInRole() Method

```
public boolean isUserInRole(String role)
```

Returns `true` if the current user has the role specified in the argument.

It is worth noting that these methods may or may not have been implemented in your web container. Their purpose is to allow a more sophisticated implementation of authentication. These methods merely provide access to information that may have been gathered by the underlying web container implementation.

Form-Based Authentication

The form-based authentication approach is based on the web container invoking a login page automatically, based on the security constraints set on a page or resource in the web application. Let's consider implementing a form-based login feature for the chat application.

First, we'll define a role called `chatAdministrator` with capabilities such as "add to", "delete from", and "modify the list of chat rooms". Since all these activities can be performed by the `ChatAdminServlet`, a role called `chatAdministrator` is required to invoke this servlet.

Let's designate Joe as the user holding the `chatAdministrator` role. Joe can also have other roles such as `sysAdministrator`. The objective is to allow only those users that have a role called `chatAdministrator` access to invoke the chat admin servlet.

We begin with the deployment descriptor and would add the following to the `web.xml` file of our Chat application:

```
<web-app>
  <!-- Insert servlet and context definitions -->

  <security-constraint>
    <web-resource-collection>
      <web-resource-name>Chat Administration</web-resource-name>
      <description>Chat Administration</description>
      <url-pattern>/admin/*</url-pattern>
      <url-pattern>/servlet/chatAdmin</url-pattern>
      <http-method>GET</http-method>
    </web-resource-collection>
    <auth-constraint>
      <description>Chat Administrator</description>
      <role-name>chatAdministrator</role-name>
    </auth-constraint>
    <user-data-constraint>
      <transport-guarantee>NONE</transport-guarantee>
    </user-data-constraint>
  </security-constraint>

  <login-config>
    <auth-method>FORM</auth-method>
    <realm-name>
    Form-Based Authentication for Chat Administration.
    </realm-name>
    <form-login-config>
      <form-login-page>/login.html</form-login-page>
      <form-error-page>/error.html</form-error-page>
    </form-login-config>
  </login-config>
</web-app>
```

The above deployment description specifies the security constraint and the authentication scheme. More specifically, the `<security-constraint>` tag includes definition of a resource collection, and the authorization requirement. The resource collection in the above includes all GET and POST requests with the URL-pattern `/admin/*`. The `<user-data-constraint>` tag specifies how data should be transmitted across the wire. The possible values are NONE, INTEGRAL, and CONFIDENTIAL. The value NONE used here means that there is no transport requirement; a value of INTEGRAL would indicate the underlying data transmission should guarantee integrity of data, and a value of CONFIDENTIAL would require that the underlying transmission should prevent other entities from observing the data. Support for these values depends on both the clients and servers. For instance, SSL-enabled client browsers and web containers can participate in CONFIDENTIAL transmission.

The `<security-constraint>` element also includes an `<auth-constraint>` tag for the resource collection. In the example above, this element includes the `<role-name>` element with value `chatAdministrator`. Hence, only users with role `chatAdministrator` are allowed to access the resources.

The next step is to define a login configuration. The `<login-config>` tag specifies how authentication should be performed. In our example, we are using a form-based authentication, which requires us to specify a login-page and an error-page. Whenever login is required, the web container automatically sends the login page. Whenever a login fails, the web container automatically sends the error page. In our example, we are using `login.html` and `error.html` pages respectively to achieve this.

Here is the login.html page:

```html
<html>
  <head>
   <title>Login Authentication</title>
  </head>

  <body>
   <h1>Please Login</h1>
   <form action="j_security_check" method="POST">
    <table border-"0" width="30%" cellspacing="3" cellpadding="2">
      <tr>
       <td><b>Login</b></td>
       <td><input type="text" size="20" name="j_username"></td>
      </tr>
      <tr>
       <td><b>Password</b></td>
       <td><input type="password" size="10" name="j_password"></td>
      </tr>
      <tr>
       <td><p><input type="submit" value="Sign in"></td>
      </tr>
    </table>
   </form>
  </body>
</html>
```

The servlet specification requires that the form action parameter be j_security_check, the login input name j_username, and the password input name be j_password. The j_security_check is a resource within the container that implements the authentication. There are no such constraints on the error.html page. Here is a sample error.html file:

```html
<html>
  <head>
   <title>Login Authentication</title>
  </head>
  <body bgcolor="#e0d0c0">
   <h1>Login now to create chat rooms</h1>
   <h3>Sorry, incorrect username/password. Try again</h3>
   <form action="j_security_check" method="post">
    <table border="0" width="30%" cellspacing="3" cellpadding="2">
      <tr>
       <td><b>Login</b></td>
       <td><input type="text" size="20" name="j_username"></td>
      </tr>
      <tr>
       <td><b>Password</b></td>
       <td><input type="password" size="10" name="j_password"></td>
      </tr>
      <tr>
       <td><input type="submit" value="Sign in"></td>
      </tr>
    </table>
   </form>
  </body>
</html>
```

This page includes the login form again with a message requesting another attempt, although you could have any other content here.

The next step is to add our user Joe. The exact procedure depends on the implementation of security realms provided by the container. With the J2EE Reference Implementation, which runs with Tomcat, new users and roles can be added in the `%J2EE_HOME%\conf\tomcat-users.xml` file:

```
<tomcat-users>
  ...
    <user name="joe" password="joe" roles="chatAdmin" />
</tomcat-users>
```

After adding the new user and role, when we enter http://localhost:8000/chat/admin in our browser, we should see the `login.html` page in which we could input the required login and password. The server verifies these values, and then invokes the admin servlet. Note that once we login, the login is valid only for the current session. Also, if we enter an incorrect login name or password, the container will send the `error.html` page.

This authentication mechanism is very simple to implement, and requires no changes to your existing source code. You simply have to decide what roles each resource requires, and specify them in the deployment descriptor.

There is, however, a limitation with this approach. At present, the Servlet specification does not address support for custom login-password verification. It is up to the container implementer to decide how and where to store login and password data, and verify the data. J2EE application servers like Tomcat, Orion, and WebLogic provide APIs that can be used to implement custom authentication. The container invokes these APIs during the authentication phase. All a developer has to do is implement certain interfaces specified in the proprietary APIs. These APIs can also be used to build interfaces to create and manage users and user roles. You should check with your server documentation before planning any security solution.

In our simple chat example, deployed with the Reference Implementation, login names and passwords would be stored using plain text in the `%J2EE_HOME%\conf\tomcat-users.xml` file. There are two limitations with this approach:

❑ Passwords are stored in plain text, which as a format is not acceptable for any secure online application.

❑ There is little or no infrastructure support to manage user accounts. Changes require modifying the XML file.

The current Servlet specification does not address these limitations. In order to implement effective security, we would need to use vendor-specific APIs.

Deployment Configuration

You can customize many important web application configurations via the deployment descriptor. These configurations include:

❑ **Context initialization parameters** – specify and access context initialization parameters

❑ **Servlet initialization parameters** – specify and access servlet initialization parameters

❑ **Servlet loading** – specify the startup properties of servlets and the order in which to load them

❑ **Session configuration** – specify the session timeout interval

❑ **MIME mappings** – specify MIME types for documents in the web application

❑ **Welcome pages** – the page that the container invokes when the request URL maps to the root of the application

❑ **Error pages** – can be used to send meaningful documents for standard HTTP errors and custom exceptions

❑ **Distributable applications** – finally, we'll take a brief look at distributable applications, and how we can enable distribution

The Java Servlet specification version 2.3 specifies the deployment descriptor in a DTD with the DOCTYPE declaration:

```
<!DOCTYPE web-app
    PUBLIC "-//Sun Microsystems, Inc.//DTD Web Application 2.3//EN"
    "http://java.sun.com/j2ee/dtds/web-app_2_3.dtd">
```

All web application deployment descriptors should include this DOCTYPE declaration.

The DTD of the deployment descriptor for web applications is available in Chapter 13 of the Servlet specification. You can read this online at http://java.sun.com/j2ee/dtds/web-app_2_3.dtd. You should keep the DTD handy as you proceed with this section.

Context Initialization Parameters

Context parameters are attributes that are part of a servlet context. All servlets and JSP pages within a web application can get and set these attributes. The getInitParameter() and getInitParameterNames() methods discussed in Chapter 8 can be used to retrieve the context initialization parameters. In the examples in Chapter 8, we used these context initialization parameters to specify database driver and protocol settings, and the URL paths of various servlets.

You can set context initialization parameters by using <context-param> elements in the deployment descriptor. The following deployment descriptor adds an attribute called name:

```
<web-app>
  ...
  <context-param>
   <param-name>name</param-name>
   <param-value>Jack</param-value>
   <description>Name of Jack. Jack is Jill's brother.</description>
  </context-param>
  ...
</web-app>
```

The <param-name> element refers to the name of the context parameter; this is the name used to retrieve the parameter from the ServletContext using the getInitParameter() method. The <param-value> corresponds to the String value returned by getInitParameter().

Optionally, a <description> element can be added for each context parameter, to make the deployment descriptor more descriptive. Context initialization parameters are applicable to all servlets sharing the same context.

Servlet Initialization Parameters

Just as parameters can be set for the context, initialization parameters can be specified for each servlet. This is done using the <init-param> element. The following deployment descriptor snippet sets two initialization parameters:

```
<web-app>
...
  <servlet>
   <servlet-name>Jack</servlet-name>
   <servlet-class>mypackage.Jack</servlet-class>
   <init-param>
    <param-name>name</param-name>
    <param-value>Jill</param-value>
    <description>Name of Jill. Jill is Jack's brother.</description>
   </init-param>
  </servlet>
</web-app>
```

An initialization parameter called name is set for the mypackage.Jack servlet. Use the getInitParameter() method on the ServletConfig object to retrieve this initialization parameter.

Unlike context initialization parameters, servlet initialization parameters are specific for each servlet. Initialization parameters can be used to specify startup information for a servlet. You may recall that our FreakServlet example of Chapter 6 had an initialization parameter to specify an interval for servlet unavailability. The FreakServlet would use the following code in its init() method to read the value of this parameter:

```
public void init() throws ServletException {
    states.add(createState("Initialization"));
    String waitIntervalString =
        getServletConfig().getInitParameter("waitInterval");
    if(waitIntervalString != null) {
        waitInterval = new Integer(waitIntervalString).intValue();
    }
}
```

The same initialization procedure applies to filters also. As we saw in the last chapter, you can add <init-param> elements for each filter to specify initialization parameters and their values. Refer to the relevant deployment descriptor for the filters introduced in the previous chapter.

Loading Servlets on Startup

Loading a servlet involves loading the servlet class from the deployment archive, instantiation of the servlet, and servlet initialization. By default, the container does not guarantee any order in which servlets are loaded. The container may wait until a request is received before loading a servlet.

Depending on your application design, you may want to specify that one or more servlets be loaded during the startup of the web application. Furthermore, these servlets may need to be loaded in a particular order. The optional <load-on-startup> element lets you specify just such a requirement:

```
<web-app>
 ...
  <servlet>
   <servlet-name>Jack</servlet-name>
```

```
      <servlet-class>mypackage/Jack</servlet-class>
      <load-on-startup>10</load-on-startup>
    </servlet>
    <servlet>
     <servlet-name>Jill</servlet-name>
     <servlet class>mypackage/Jill</servlet-class>
      <load-on-startup>20</load-on-startup>
    </servlet>
    ...
  </web-app>
```

When the `<load-on-startup>` element is present for a servlet, the container loads it at the container startup. In order to enforce an order in which servlets are loaded, you should specify a positive integer for each servlet; the container loads servlets in the order specified by these integers. When this element is not specified, the load order is left to the container. If you specify the same value to two or more servlets, the container may use any order to load such servlets.

Session Timeout

`HttpSession` objects consume memory on the serverside and so should not live long after a period of client inactivity. Each client, as identified using the `HttpServletRequest` object, that accesses the web application will have a unique `HttpSession` object associated. If an application has 10,000 active users, the container will have 10,000 `HttpSession` objects, each of which may contain several attributes. In order to limit the drain on resources that this would cause, a session timeout should be specified.

A timeout can be specified in two ways:

❑   Programmatically by calling the `setMaxInactiveInterval()` method on the `HttpSession` object

❑   Using the `<session-timeout>` element in the deployment descriptor

The following snippet from a deployment descriptor illustrates the second approach:

```
<web-app>
  <!-- Servlet definitions -->

  <session-config>
   <session-timeout>120</session-timeout>
  </session-config>
</web-app>
```

The timeout interval is specified in minutes. The container will automatically invalidate the session if the elapsed time between consecutive requests from a client is greater than the specified timeout interval. The `getMaxInactiveInterval()` method on the `HttpSession` object returns the interval in seconds.

MIME Mappings

The HTTP protocol uses **Multipurpose Internet Mail Extensions (MIME)** to describe content. Both web servers and clients use MIME types to indicate the type of content being exchanged. A MIME type is a string of the form `type/sub-type`. Examples of some of the common MIME types include `text/html`, `text/txt`, and `image/gif`.

When a web server sends a document to a client, the server should include a section in the response to indicate the type of the document. Web browsers use this information to render the document correctly. For example, if the web server sends a PostScript document without specifying the correct content type, the browser may not be able to identify that the request body contains a PostScript document and will most likely render it incorrectly. Most modern browsers (and indeed many web containers) will try to identify the content type based on the extension specified in the request. However, it is still good practice to specify MIME types for all types of content that the web server is likely to send.

For dynamic content, the servlet generating the content should explicitly specify the MIME type by using the `setContentType()` method on the `HttpServletResponse` object. But how should we specify the content types of the documents in the public area of a web application? As we discussed at the beginning of this chapter, the web container serves such documents directly to the requesting clients. So that the container can correctly specify the MIME types for these documents, the possible MIME types should be included in the deployment descriptor of the application. For example, if our web application contains Microsoft Word documents, we would specify the following MIME type in the deployment descriptor:

```
<web-app>
  <!-- Servlet definitions -->

  <mime-mapping>
   <extension>doc</extension>
   <mime-type>application/msword</mime-type>
  </mime-mapping>
</web-app>
```

The container uses this information to correctly set the content type in the response header. Using this MIME type, browsers will then be able to correctly identify how the content should be rendered.

When a standard MIME type for a document cannot be found, both web containers and browsers will use a default type. The default type is usually `text/plain`.

Welcome Files

The default welcome file for a web site is usually either an `index.html` or `index.htm` file. The same applies for a web application. When you type the URL path pointing to a web application (for example, http://www.myserver.com/chat), the container displays the welcome file associated with the `chat` application. The container also serves a welcome file when a request URL points to a directory that cannot be resolved to a servlet.

You are not limited to using `index.html` and `index.htm` as the welcome files for your web applications. Any public resource, such an HTML or JSP document, can be specified as a welcome file by using the `<welcome-file-list>` element in the deployment descriptor. For example, the following snippet specifies a list of files as welcome files:

```
<web-app>
  <!-- Servlet definitions -->

  <welcome-file-list>
   <welcome-file>index.html</welcome-file>
   <welcome-file>summary.jsp</welcome-file>
  </welcome-file-list>
</web-app>
```

The web container uses the first available file as the welcome file. Consider the example web application structure that we looked at earlier in the chapter:

```
myWebApp\
        index.html
        login.jsp
        404NotFound.html
        images\
                logo.gif
                banner.gif
        literature\
                summary.jsp
                Y2001AnnualReport.pdf
                Y2001PresidentAddress.pdf
        WEB-INF\
                web.xml
                classes\
                        ShoppingCart.class
                        Catalog.class
                        CheckOut.class
                lib\
                        dbLibrary.jar
                        xmlTools.jar
```

Here is the effect of the above welcome file specification in the deployment descriptor:

URL	Result
http://<HOST:PORT>/myWebApp	myWebApp/index.html
http://<HOST:PORT>/myWebApp/literature	myWebApp/literature/summary.jsp
http://<HOST:PORT>/myWebApp/images	Shows directory listing of myWebApp/images/

In the first case, the container serves the index.html file while in the second case the container serves the summary.jsp as index.html is not available. The images/ directory has no welcome file set, therefore this would simply display a list of the directory contents.

Error Pages

We briefly discussed error pages in Chapter 6. The deployment descriptor provides developers with a flexible mechanism for providing error pages based on various exceptions and HTTP error messages. Before we go into more details of this mechanism, it's useful to briefly discuss how standard HTTP errors are relevant in servlet programming.

There are two ways a servlet can indicate a failure. In both cases, the actual logic for detecting an error is the responsibility of the servlet. The difference is the procedure for indicating an error to the web container.

Sending Errors

The first approach is to use these methods of HttpServletResponse:

```
public void sendError(int statusCode) throws IOException
public void sendError(int statusCode, String message) throws IOException
```

Both of these methods will set the HTTP response status code and commit the response. The first of these methods accepts a status code, while the second one also accepts a user-defined message to further clarify the error.

No further output should be written after executing the sendError() method because after sendError() is called, the web container sends an HTTP status code and HTTP status message in the response headers. If configured correctly, the web container may send a particular document explaining the error. The container may also log the error. The client can extract the status code and status message from the response headers.

The following table describes the most common HTTP error codes. All these error codes are defined as constants in the HttpServletResponse interface:

HTTP Code	Error Code	Description
400	SC_BAD_REQUEST	The request was syntactically incorrect
401	SC_UNAUTHORIZED	Indicates that the request requires HTTP authentication
403	SC_FORBIDDEN	The server understood the request but refused to fulfill it
404	SC_NOT_FOUND	The requested resource is unavailable
500	SC_INTERNAL_SERVER_ERROR	An error within the HTTP server caused the request to fail
501	SC_NOT_IMPLEMENTED	The HTTP server does not support the functionality needed to fulfill this request
503	SC_SERVER_UNAVAILABLE	The HTTP server is overloaded and cannot service the request

Throwing ServletException

The second approach to indicate a failure is to throw a javax.servlet.ServletException or one of its subclasses. You could design a set of classes that extend ServletException, and throw these from within your servlets as appropriate.

Consider, for example, a servlet that performs database access using the JDBC API. A common exception that the servlet might encounter is java.sql.SQLException. Since the container cannot gracefully handle non-servlet exceptions such as this, the exception cannot be re-thrown to the container. Your servlet must therefore throw a subclass of javax.servlet.ServletException whenever it receives a java.sql.SQLException. For example, consider the following snippet of code from the servlet:

```
try {
  // Database access fails due to a lack of a connection
} catch(SQLException e) {
  throw new TryAgainException(e.getMessage(), e);
}
```

The `TryAgainException` could be specified as follows:

```
public class TryAgainException extends ServletException {
  public TryAgainException(String message, Throwable cause) {
    super(message, cause);
  }
}
```

With this code, the container will receive a `TryAgainException` whenever the servlet encounters a `java.sql.SQLException`.

The next step is to understand how to make the container handle these exceptions.

Handling HTTP Errors and Exceptions

By using `<error-page>` elements in the deployment descriptor, you can specify how a web application should handle HTTP errors and runtime exceptions. For each HTTP error or exception, the URL of a resource can be specified so that whenever the container receives a matching HTTP error or exception, the container will send the specified resource to the client.

This deployment descriptor extract ensures that the container will send the `/errors/TryAgain.html` file if either a `TryAgainException` exception is received or the `HttpServletResponse.SC_SERVER_UNAVAILABLE` error code occurs:

```
<web-app>
  <!-- Servlet definitions -->

  <error-page>
   <exception-type>javax.servlet.TryAgainException</exception-type>
   <location>/errors/TryAgain.html</location>
  </error-page>

  <error-page>
   <exception-type>503</exception-type>
   <location>/errors/TryAgain.html</location>
  </error-page>
</web-app>
```

So how should we choose whether to throw exceptions or generate HTTP error codes? HTTP error codes can be used to specify common HTTP errors. However, to do this you will have to map your application errors to appropriate HTTP error codes and this is not always easy. HTTP error codes have a well-defined meaning, and inappropriate error codes may change the meaning of the error. It is more flexible to use subclasses of `javax.sql.ServletException` to indicate application errors.

The value of the `<location>` tag can point to a servlet, a JSP page, or a static file. In cases where the location is a servlet or a JSP page, the servlet throwing the exception can set the following details regarding the error using the `setAttribute()` method in the `HttpServletRequest` interface:

- ❑   Status code for `javax.servlet.error.status_code`
- ❑   Exception type for `javax.servlet.error.exception_type`
- ❑   Message for `javax.servlet.error.message`

The error-handling servlet or JSP page can access these attributes from the request object.

For instance, let's assume that the location is a servlet – `ShowErrorServlet`. This servlet could find more about how the error occurred by using the following code in its `doGet()` method, like this:

```
protected void doGet(HttpServletRequest request,
                     HttpServletResponse response) {
  // Get the status code
  String statusCode = (String)
                 request.getAttribute("javax.servlet.error.status_code");
  Throwable exeption = (Throwable)
                 request.getAttribute("javax.servlet.error.exception_type");
  String message = (String)
                 request.getAttribute("javax.servlet.error.message");

  // Take appropriate action here

}
```

Thus, this servlet has access to what caused the exception. This approach is similar to a catch block of exception handling, except that it happens over the HTTP request. The above servlet handling the error has access to not only the message and error code, but also the exception object thrown by the servlet throwing the exception.

Distributable Applications

Version 2.2 of the J2EE specification introduced the notion of **distributable applications** and **distributable containers**. The purpose of these features is to address scalability, availability, and performance. A distributable web container consists of a number of Java Virtual Machines (JVMs), running on one or more host machines.

Before we discuss distributable applications in detail, let us look at how web containers are typically set up. The following diagram shows a simple (hardware) installation of a web container:

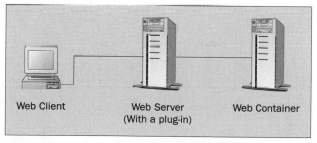

Web Client   Web Server   Web Container
               (With a plug-in)

Most commercial web containers provide an out-of-process connection mechanism such that a web container can be deployed behind an existing web server. There are several advantages to this approach, the most critical of which is the ability to integrate with an existing web server. Secondly, the web server can serve all the static content, leaving the web container to process dynamic content.

On what basis does the web server send requests to the web container? Web servers typically specify a plug-in API whereby HTTP requests of certain types can be delegated to implementations of this API. Depending on certain attributes of an incoming HTTP request, the web server invokes a specified plug-in which in turn can send the request to the web container. Let's see how.

For instance, the Apache web server has an API for building modules. A module is a plug-in that can be deployed on the Apache web server, and can process HTTP requests. Web servers such as the iPlanet Web Server and Microsoft IIS have similar APIs.

Most commercial web containers include such plug-in implementations for the more commonly used web servers. Depending on the web server in use, you can easily install one of these plug-ins. The installed plug-in will have the capability to invoke the web container. For this mechanism to work, you need specify what kind of requests should be delegated to the plug-in. Examples of this configuration include specifying a prefix in the path, such as all requests beginning with "chat" as in the case of our example, or all requests to files with extension such as "jsp", etc. Whenever the web server receives a HTTP request matching these criteria, it invokes the installed plug-in, which then sends the request to the web container.

Let us now return to the discussion of distributable web containers and web applications. First, let's answer an important question: what is the purpose of distribution? Consider a web application deployed on a web container with a single instance of a JVM running. Typically, this will be the JVM processing all HTTP requests, processing database logic (if implemented via servlets/JSP pages, and not delegated to EJBs), and other business logic. As the number of users accessing the web application increases, the same JVM (and hence the same server hosting it) has to process the increased load. Due to the increased load, the server's ability to process all the requests within satisfactory time limits will be hampered. In addition, as each request takes longer to finish, the server's ability to accept more requests will also decline. Overall, the responsiveness of the container deteriorates with increased load.

Now consider a situation where there are two more JVMs hosting the same web application with a mechanism to direct each request to one of the JVMs running on each different server. With such a mechanism, the processing could be distributed across multiple JVMs and servers. This increases the overall processing capability of the container. The following schematic shows such a cluster with three nodes:

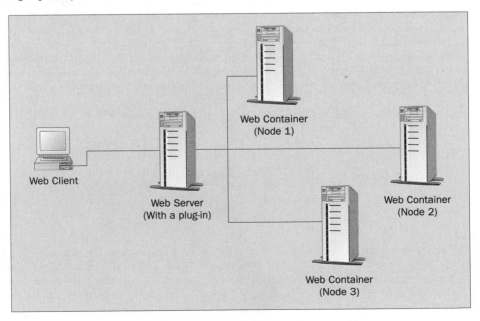

Typically, the plug-in deployed on the web server acts as a load-balancer. Alternatively, there could be another node deployed between the web server and the other nodes, to act as a load balancer. The load balancer is the one that coordinates request handling across the nodes in the cluster. By having more multiple instances to share the load, you can increase the container's ability to process heavier loads.

In theory, distribution is a simple approach to distribute load across multiple processes running on multiple servers. However, in practice setting up distribution is not as simple as it sounds, and requires advanced vendor-specific configurations. Besides configuring the cluster in a network, which could be the hardest for a novice, one of the configuration steps is to choose a **load-distribution strategy**. This strategy is the method by which the container is instructed to distribute load across nodes in a cluster. One of the most commonly used strategies is called "round-robin", which involves sending each request to the next node in the cluster. Containers also provide strategies that are more advanced. Such strategies take into consideration the processing capacity of each machine, and their current process loads, priorities, etc. Refer to your container's documentation for more specific details.

Another consequence of clustering is to provide **failure-recovery**. Failure-recovery is to do with how to allow seamless processing of requests in spite of a server crash. Load distribution mechanisms usually have the capability to detect a server crash (by polling or some other form of communication) and send requests to one of the functional nodes so that new requests can be processed without failure.

Perhaps one of the most obvious effects of clustering is that, in a cluster, a request from a client can be processed by any node. There is one exception to this, as we shall see shortly.

Once a cluster is set up, the process of enabling distribution for web applications is quite simple. Add the element <distributable> at the beginning of the deployment descriptor (before specifying any context parameters):

```
<web-app>
   ...
   <distributable />
   ...
</web-app>
```

This element indicates to the container that this application may be distributed in a cluster.

Although this process of specifying that an application is distributable is simple, both load distribution and failure recovery get complex when it comes to web applications maintaining session and context. As we saw in the previous chapters, we can store information in session and context objects. So what happens to these objects in a cluster where any node can process a request?

When a web container receives an HTTP request to a web application, as we discussed previously, the container creates and manages a session for the sender of the request. Servlets and JSP pages handling the request can store information (state) in the session. Since session itself is an object, it is maintained within the JVM of this node. What happens when the next request from the same user is sent to a different node in the cluster? For the other node to process this request seamlessly, it should have the same session available. Otherwise, all session/state information will be lost. In order to allow this, web containers replicate the session information into other nodes too. Whether the container replicates the session information to all nodes in the cluster or not depends on the container implementation. Some containers designate a secondary node to each node, and limit replication only to the secondary node. Others may replicate the state to all nodes in the cluster.

In order for the session information to be replicable, the data stored in the session must be serializable. When you attempt to store non-serializable objects within the session of a distributable web application, the container may throw an IllegalArgumentException.

Session replication also helps in failure recovery. Consider a situation where the node crashes between two consecutive requests. Since the session is replicated, the container could establish the session on another node, and send the request to that node. This allows seamless processing. However, what happens if the server crashes while processing a request? This is implementation-specific, but a container should be able to resend the same request to another node.

There is one exception to session replication. Some containers allow **session pinning**. This refers to an approach whereby all requests during a session are sent to the same node (they are "session pinned" to a node). In such cases, you may disable session replication. Note that session pinning is a double-edged sword. If you decide to use session pinning and disable session replication, you would gain performance improvements, as there is no replication overhead. However, at the same time, such a cluster cannot recover from failures.

Finally, what happens to the servlet context? The servlet specification does not require context information to be replicated in a cluster. Therefore, a web application on each node maintains its own context. For this reason, we should carefully analyze if various servlets/JSP pages write information to the context. As the context is not shared, there is a chance of inconsistencies. We should consider storing any shared context information in a persistent store such as a database.

The same applies to static variables and singleton classes too. Since such variables are local to the JVM, make sure that they do not hold read-write information.

To conclude, clustering is a very useful feature to enable both load balancing and failure recovery. As a developer, you need take only two steps to make use of this feature: make the application distributable (via the deployment descriptor) and make sure all session variables are serializable.

Summary

In this chapter, we've seen how to package and securely authenticate web applications, and how to use the deployment descriptor to configure web applications at deployment time. The important deployment configuration parameters that we've studied are:

- ❑ Context initialization
- ❑ Servlet initialization
- ❑ Servlet loading
- ❑ Session configuration
- ❑ MIME mappings
- ❑ Welcome and error pages

In the J2EE architecture, we will be using this mechanism throughout, from servlets, to messaging, to transactions, to enterprise beans. As we cover these topics in the rest of this book and start building production-quality applications, we will see how powerful and flexible this mechanism is.

This chapter concludes our coverage of Java servlets. Before we move on to look at JavaServer Pages and other aspects of the Java 2 Platform, Enterprise Edition, it's worth noting that J2EE has changed the way we do server-side programming. It's true that we still follow the basic Java programming tenets for building our applications, but as the technology becomes increasingly sophisticated, the containers tend to pose more and more restrictions on exactly what can and cannot be done. If, as developers, we recognize this and stick to these restrictions in both letter and spirit, our applications will be far more robust for the extra effort.

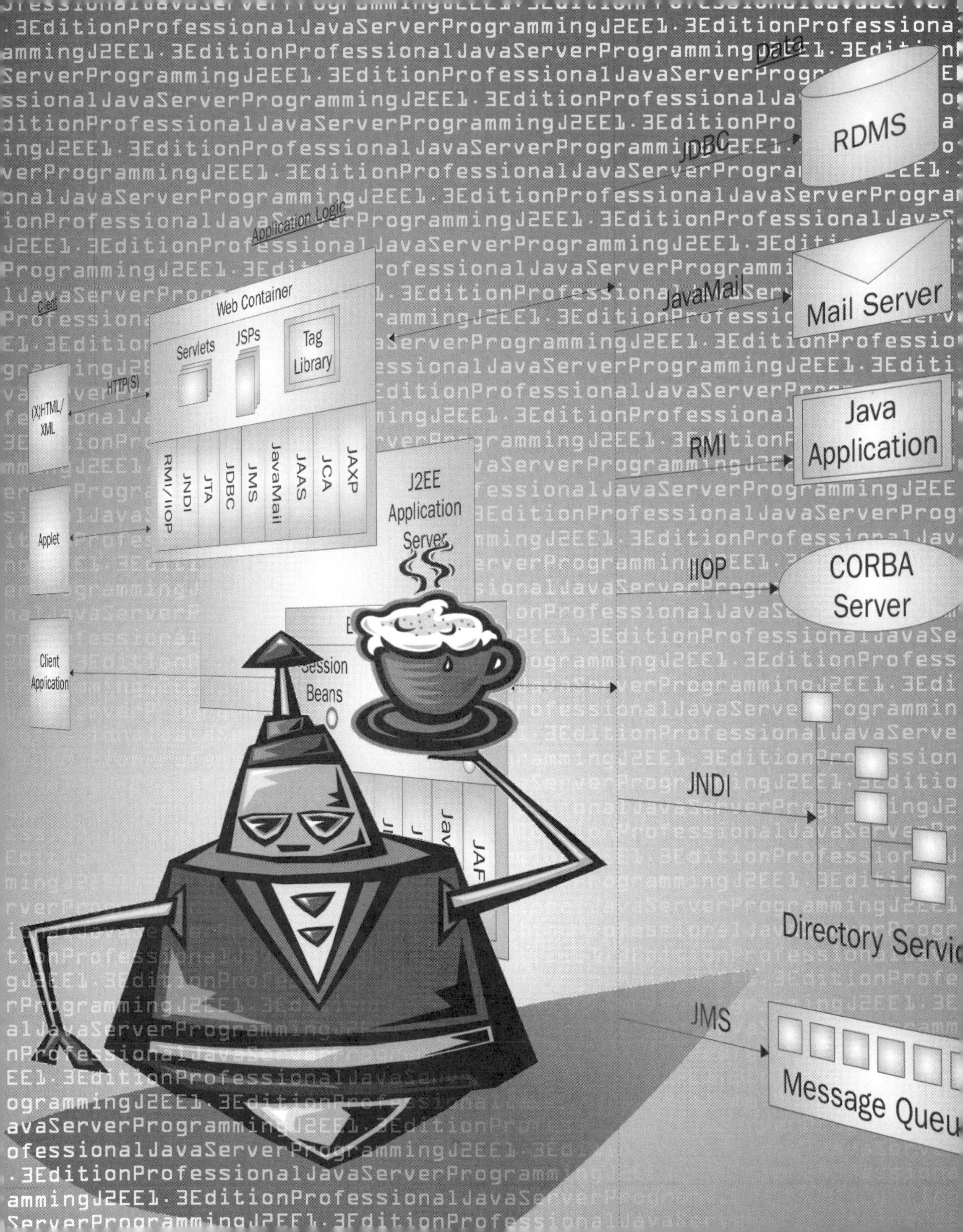

10

JSP Basics and Architecture

The goal of the **JavaServer Pages (JSP)** specification is to simplify the creation and management of dynamic web pages by providing a more convenient authoring framework than servlets. JSP pages combine static markup, like HTML and XML, with special scripting tags. JSP pages resemble markup documents, but each JSP page is translated into a servlet the first time it is invoked. The resulting servlet is a combination of the markup from the JSP file and embedded dynamic content specified by the scripting tags.

In this chapter we will look at:

❑ The building blocks of JSP pages: directives, scripting elements, and the standard actions

❑ The implicit objects provided to allow JSP pages to access their environment, and the concept of object scope

❑ The enhancements introduced in the new JSP 1.2 specification, and their implications for JSP developers

❑ An example application illustrating the core JSP syntax and access to helper Java classes from JSP pages

❑ How to use JSP pages as part of well-designed Java web applications

The JSP 1.2 Specification

Since the release of the JSP 1.0 specification in September 1999 and its rapid support by server vendors, JSP has been a mature and widely adopted approach to the generation of web content. The JSP 1.1 specification (December 1999) added important new capabilities: most significantly, the ability to write custom tag extensions (discussed in the next chapter).

If you've already worked with JSP pages, you might wonder how JSP 1.2 differs from JSP 1.1, and how much the differences matter. The following is a quick summary of the most important enhancements and changes. If you haven't worked with JSP 1.1, you should skip to the next section.

❏ JSP 1.2 assumes the Java 2 platform, whereas JSP 1.1 could be run under Java 1.1.

❏ JSP 1.2 requires the 2.3 release of the Servlet API. (The JSP 1.2 and Servlet 2.3 specifications have been developed in parallel under JSR-053. Little JSP 1.2 functionality actually calls on Servlet 2.3 enhancements. The support for Servlet 2.3 "web application events" in JSP 1.2 tag extensions is one example.)

❏ The <jsp:include> standard action no longer flushes the buffer prior to the include. This is a welcome change, as this flushing behavior proved a major limitation in JSP 1.1.

❏ There are major enhancements to tag extension support. These will be discussed further in Chapter 11. They make it easier to work with the tag extension API, and add the option of more sophisticated translation-time validation.

❏ The XML representation of JSP pages is further developed, and JSP engines are required to accept the XML representation of JSP pages as well as JSP pages in the regular syntax. This makes it easier to automate the authoring of JSP pages, and provides the basis for a new validation mechanism for usage of custom tag libraries (see Chapter 11).

❏ A new constructor has been added to the class `JspException` enabling the creation of an exception holding a message and a `Throwable` root cause (rather than merely a message). This means that stack traces can be preserved, making it easier to debug applications using the new constructor.

The good news is that JSP 1.2 is entirely backward-compatible. With every revision of the J2EE specifications, the body of production J2EE solutions grows, and Sun has taken this on board. For example, while there are new DTDs for tag library descriptors, containers are required to support the JSP 1.1 DTD. The API changes are also backward-compatible, although there have been some deprecations.

Overall, the changes are evolutionary rather than revolutionary but certainly significant and welcome. JSP 1.2 isn't markedly more powerful than JSP 1.1, but it is easier to work with.

Introducing JSP

JSP, like other Java APIs, is a specification provided by Sun for vendors to implement. The JSP specification builds on the functionality provided by the servlet specification. So how are JSP pages different from servlets?

Servlets are Java's answer to CGI scripts. They are more elegant and perform better than CGI scripts. They execute on the server and intercept browser requests, acting as a sort of middle layer between clients and lower-level applications. Servlets are well suited to deciding how to handle client requests and invoking other server-side objects, but are not so well suited for generating content. Experience has shown that markup generation from Java code is hard to implement and maintain. Servlets have to be written by developers familiar with Java.

JSP pages, on the other hand, can be designed and developed less like programs and more like web pages. JSP pages are ideal when we need to display markup with embedded dynamic content. However, although generating HTML is much easier than with a servlet, JSP pages are less suited to handling processing logic.

JSP pages can use JavaBeans with a specified **scope** or **tag extensions** (which are covered in Chapters 11 and 12) to achieve a clean separation of static content and the Java code that produces dynamic web applications. This allows JSP pages to be created and maintained by designers with presentation skills, they do not need to know Java.

While there is an overlap between their capabilities, think of servlets as controller objects, and JSP pages as view objects. Don't think that you need to make a choice between using servlets and JSP pages in a web application; they are complementary technologies, and a complex web application will use both.

A simple JSP page that includes the current date in an HTML page would look like this:

```
<%@page import="java.util.Date"%>

<html>
  <body>
    The current time is <%= (new Date()).toString() %>
  </body>
</html>
```

To run the examples in this chapter we will need to create a new application. Create the directory `%J2EE_HOME%\public_html\JSPExamples\`. Save the example code as `simpleJSP.jsp` in our source directory, `%BOOK_HOME%\Ch10\JSPExamples`.

To deploy this web application using the J2EE Reference Implementation (RI) we must first start the J2EE server. Then copy the `simple.jsp` file from the source directory to the `\public_html\JSPExamples\` directory.

All we have to do now is navigate to http://localhost:8000/JSPExamples/simpleJSP.jsp and we should see something similar to:

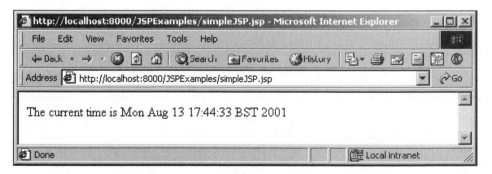

The JSP page and dependent files are together known as a **translation unit**. The first time the JSP engine intercepts a request for a JSP, it compiles the translation unit into a servlet. This is a two-stage process. The JSP source code is converted into a servlet and this servlet is then compiled.

The Reference Implementation stores both the servlet source and compiled code in the `%J2EE_HOME%\repository\<server_name>\web\JSPExamples` directory (the `<server_name>` part will vary with the name of your computer). Here we will find a `.java` and a `.class` file. The `.java` file contains the source code for the servlet created from `simpleJSP.jsp`.

The first time a JSP is loaded by the **JSP container** (also called the **JSP engine**), the servlet code necessary to implement the JSP tags is automatically generated, compiled, and loaded into the servlet container. This occurs at **translation time**. It is important to note that this occurs only the first time a JSP page is requested. There will be a slow response the first time a JSP page is accessed, but on subsequent requests the previously compiled servlet simply processes the requests. This occurs at **run time**.

If we modify the source code for the JSP, it is automatically recompiled and reloaded the next time that page is requested. A lot of work is happening behind the scenes, and you, the developer, are receiving the payoff, in the form of authoring convenience. (The servlet engine will usually manage this by making the generated servlet class expose a timestamp. Before each request, this timestamp can be compared with the file system's modification timestamp on the JSP file. Recompilation will be necessary only if the JSP file's timestamp is later than the class's timestamp.)

> *Note that for JSP compilation to succeed, a JSP compiler must be available to the servlet engine at translation time. Please refer to the documentation of your servlet engine to see if any additional steps are required to set this up. For example, in the Orion server, the* `tools.jar` *file must be copied from the JDK distribution to the server's root directory. Many servers (such as JRun and WebLogic) ship with a compiler as part of the distribution.*

The distinction between translation time and run time is very important in understanding how JSP pages work as this terminology will be used in later chapters. This figure summarizes the process:

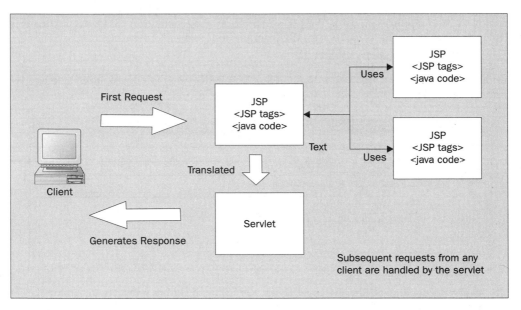

This also shows how a JSP page can dynamically invoke other JSP pages. To the client this is transparent; it appears that the original JSP page performs all the processing. A JSP page can call another JSP page (or any resource in the current web application) because the generated servlet has access to the `RequestDispatcher` mechanism we were introduced to in Chapter 7.

The servlet class generated at the end of the translation process represents the well-defined relationship between a container and a JSP. According to the JSP specification, which the containers implement, the servlet class must extend a superclass that is either:

❑ A JSP container specific implementation class that implements the `javax.servlet.jsp.JspPage` interface and provides some basic page-specific behavior. (Since most JSP pages use HTTP, their implementation classes must actually implement the `javax.servlet.jsp.HttpJspPage` interface, which itself extends `javax.servlet.jsp.JspPage`).

❑ Specified by the JSP author via an `extends` attribute in the page directive.

The `javax.servlet.jsp.JspPage` interface contains two methods:

```
public void jspInit()
```

This is invoked when the JSP is initialized, and is analogous to the `init()` method in servlets. Page authors may provide initialization of the JSP by implementing this method in their JSP pages.

```
public void jspDestroy()
```

This is invoked when the JSP is about to be destroyed by the container, and is analogous to the `destroy()` method in servlets. Page authors may provide cleanup of the JSP by implementing this method in their JSP pages.

The `javax.servlet.jsp.HttpJspPage` interface contains a single method:

```
public void _jspService(HttpServletRequest request,
                        HttpServletResponse response)
         throws ServletException, IOException
```

This method corresponds to the body of the JSP page and is used for threaded request processing, just like the `service()` method in servlets.

> **The implementation of this method is generated by the container and should never be provided by page authors.**

These three major life event methods work together in a JSP, as seen below:

❑ The page is first initialized by invoking the `jspInit()` method, which may be defined by the page author. This initializes the JSP in much in the same way as servlets are initialized, when the first request is intercepted and just after translation.

❑ Every time a request is made to the JSP, the container-generated `_JSP pageservice()` method is invoked, the request is processed, and the JSP generates the appropriate response. This response is taken by the container and passed back to the client.

❑ When the JSP is destroyed by the server (for example at shut down), the `jspDestroy()` method, which may be defined by the page author, is invoked to perform any cleanup.

Note that in most cases the `jspInit()` and `jspDestroy()` methods don't need to be provided by the JSP author, and can be omitted.

The Nuts and Bolts

Let's look at what makes up a JSP page. The structure of a JSP page is a cross between a servlet and a static web page, with Java code enclosed between the constructs <% and %> and other XML-like tags interspersed.

There are three categories of JSP tags:

❑ **Directives**
These affect the overall structure of the servlet that results from translation, but produce no output themselves.

❑ **Scripting Elements**
These let us insert Java code into the JSP page (and hence into the resulting servlet).

❑ **Actions**
These are special tags available to affect the runtime behavior of the JSP page. JSP supplies some **standard actions**, such as <jsp:useBean>, which we'll cover later in this chapter and we can write our own tags, as we shall see in Chapter 11. These **custom actions** are usually referred to as **tag extensions** or **custom tags**.

There are some general rules that apply to JSP pages:

❑ JSP tags, like XML tags, are case-sensitive.

❑ Directives and scripting elements have a syntax that is not based on XML, but an alternative XML-based syntax is also available. This is not, however, intended for manual authoring but rather for JSP pages created by specialized software.

❑ Tags based on XML syntax have either a start tag with optional attributes, an optional body, and a matching end tag; or they have an empty tag, possibly with attributes:

```
<mylibrary:somejsptag attributename="attribute value">
  body
</mylibrary:somejsptag>
```

or:

```
<mylibrary:somejsptag attributename="attribute value" />
```

❑ In template text, a literal <%, which would otherwise start a scripting element, is quoted as <\%; a literal %>, which would otherwise terminate the scripting element, is quoted as %\>.

❑ Attribute values in tags always appear quoted, as in XML. Either single or double quotes can be used. The special strings ' and " can be used (just as in HTML) if quotes are contained in the attribute value.

❑ Any whitespace within the body text of a document is not significant, but is preserved during translation into a servlet.

❑ URLs used by JSP pages follow servlet conventions, and a URL starting with a /, called a context-relative path, is interpreted with reference to the web application to which the JSP page belongs. (The ServletContext is available as an implicit object within JSP pages, as we will see later.)

❑ If the URL does *not* start with a / it is interpreted relative to the current JSP.

The conventions for relative URLs are the same because both JSP pages and servlets can be deployed in web applications.

> *Don't be tempted to deploy applications as a set of JSP pages on the file system under your server's document root; a web application is a standard deployment unit supported by all compliant servers, and resolves such otherwise tricky issues as the application classpath and mappings from public virtual URLs to application resources.*

JSP Directives

JSP directives configure the code generation that the container will perform in creating a servlet. They are used to set global values such as class declarations, methods to be implemented, output content type, and so on, and do not produce any output to the client. Directives have scope for the entire JSP page; in other words, a directive affects the whole JSP page, but only that page. Directives begin with <%@ and end with %>, and the general syntax is:

```
<%@ directivename attribute="value" attribute="value" %>
```

There are three main directives that can be used in a JSP:

- ❑   The page directive
- ❑   The include directive
- ❑   The taglib directive

The page Directive

The page directive is used to define and manipulate a number of important attributes that affect the whole JSP page. A page can contain any number of page directives, in any order, anywhere in the JSP page. They are all assimilated during translation and applied together to the page. However, there can be only one occurrence of any attribute-value pair defined by the page directives in a given JSP. An exception to this rule is the import attribute; there can be multiple imports. By convention, page directives appear at the start of a JSP page.

The general syntax of the page directive is:

```
<%@ page ATTRIBUTES %>
```

Where the valid attributes are the following name value pairs:

Attribute	Description	Default value
language	Defines the scripting language to be used. This attribute exists in case future JSP containers support multiple languages.	Java
extends	The value is a fully qualified class name of the superclass that the generated class, into which this JSP page is translated, must extend.	Omitted by default
	This attribute should normally be avoided, and only used with extreme caution, because JSP engines usually provide specialized superclasses with a lot of functionality to be extended by the generated servlet classes. Use of the extends attribute restricts some of the decisions that a JSP container can make.	

Table continued on following page

Attribute	Description	Default value
import	Comma separated list of packages or classes, with the same meaning as import statements in Java classes.	Omitted by default.
session	Specifies whether the page participates in an HTTP session. When true the implicit object named session, which refers to the javax.servlet.http.HttpSession, is available and can be used to access the current/new session for the page.	true
	If false, the page does not participate in a session and the implicit session object is unavailable.	
buffer	Specifies the buffering model for the output stream to the client.	Implementation-dependent; at least 8kb
	If the value is none, no buffering occurs and all output is written directly through to the ServletResponse by a PrintWriter.	
	If a buffer size is specified (for example, 24kb), output is buffered with a buffer size not less than that value.	
auto Flush	If true, the output buffer to the client is flushed automatically when it is full.	true
	If false, a runtime exception is raised to indicate a buffer overflow.	
isThread Safe	Defines the level of thread safety implemented in the page.	true
	If the value is true the JSP engine may send multiple client requests to the page at the same time.	
	If the value is false then the JSP container queues up client requests sent to the page for processing, and processes them one at a time, in the order in which they were received. This is the same as implementing the javax.servlet.SingleThreadModel interface in a servlet.	
info	Defines an informative string that can subsequently be obtained from the page's implementation of the Servlet.getServletInfo() method.	Omitted by default
error Page	Defines a URL to another JSP page within the current web application, which is invoked if a checked or unchecked exception is thrown. The page implementation catches the instance of the Throwable object and passes it to the error page processing. The error page mechanism is very useful, and avoids the need for developers to write code to catch unrecoverable exceptions in their JSP pages. See the isErrorPage attribute below.	Omitted by default
isError Page	Indicates if the current JSP page is intended to be another JSP page's error page.	false
	If true, then the implicit variable exception is available, and refers to the instance of the java.lang.Throwable thrown at runtime by the JSP that caused the error.	

Attribute	Description	Default value
content Type	Defines the character encoding for the JSP and the MIME type for the response of the JSP page. This can have either of the form "MIMETYPE or MIMETYPE; charset=CHARSET with an optional white space after the ";". CHARSET, or character encoding if specified, must be the IANA value for a character encoding.	The default value for the MIMETYPE is text/html; the default value for the CHARSET is ISO-8859-1.

Unrecognized attributes result in fatal translation errors.

Example

The following JSP, pageDirective.jsp, contains an attribute-rich page directive:

```
<%@ page language="Java" import="java.rmi.*,java.util.*"
    session="true" buffer="12kb" autoFlush="true"
    info="my page directive jsp" errorPage="error.jsp"
    isErrorPage="false" isThreadSafe="true" %>

<html>
  <head>
    <title>Page directive test page</title>
  </head>
  <body>
    <h1>Page directive test page</h1>
    This is a JSP to test the page directive.
  </body>
</html>
```

The include Directive

The include directive instructs the container to include the content of a resource in the current JSP, inserting it inline, in the JSP page, in place of the directive. The specified file must be accessible and available to the JSP container. The syntax of the include directive is:

```
<%@ include file="Filename" %>
```

The only available attribute, file, specifies the filename of the file to include. This is a relative path within the current WAR, beginning with a forward slash. Note that it is *not* necessarily a public URL within the WAR, as the include directive has access to all files within a WAR, even those not publicly visible. The included content need not always be a JSP; HTML fragments, or indeed any other text resource, may be included.

The following are examples of valid filenames:

❑ /debug.jsp
  This will include the contents of the debug.jsp file in the WAR's root directory.

❑ /WEB-INF/templates/standardFooter.html
  This will include the standardFooter.html file in the WAR's /WEB-INF/templates directory. This file cannot be requested directly, as anything under the WEB-INF directory is not published by the servlet engine.

The content of the included file is parsed by the JSP only at *translation time*, that is, when the JSP page is compiled into a servlet.

> *The include **action** is used to include resources at run time, as we will see later.*

Most JSP containers will keep track of the included file and recompile the JSP page if it changes. The container may, however, choose not to do this.

Since compilation of the included file will not occur until it has been included in the context of another, complete JSP, the included file does not need to be a valid JSP. It may, for example, rely on imports or beans that it does not declare. In such cases, we should follow these conventions:

- ❑ Use an extension other than JSP for the included file. The JSP specification recommends that we use `.jspf` or `.jsf`.

- ❑ Place incomplete page fragments in a directory of our web application that is not publicly visible, to prevent system users requesting them directly. Anywhere under the `WEB-INF` directory (as shown in the second example above) will do: our servlet engine will not publish content under this directory, yet files placed under it will still be visible to the `include` directive.

- ❑ Document any context requirements of your page fragment (such as variable and import assumptions) in a JSP header comment.

Example

The included file can be either a static file (such as an HTML file) or another JSP page. In either case, the result will be the same as if the entire contents of the file had been typed into the including JSP page instead of the `include` directive.

The example below, `includeDirective1.jsp`, requests the inclusion, during compilation, of a copyright file containing a legal disclaimer written in HTML:

```html
<html>
  <head>
    <title>Include directive test page 1</title>
  </head>
  <body>
    <h1>Include directive test page 1</h1>

    <%@ include file="/JSPExamples/copyright.html" %>
  </body>
</html>
```

`copyright.html` contains the following:

```html
<p>&copy; 2001 Wrox Press</p>
```

Copy both of these files into the `%J2EE_HOME%\public_html\JSPExamples` directory. Then navigate to http://localhost:8000/JSPExamples/includeDirective1.jsp; we should see something similar to:

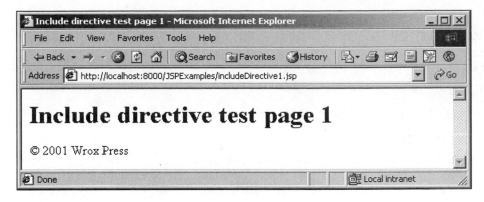

This next example shows how a JSP page can be included. Consider the file `includeDirective2.jsp`:

```
<html>
  <head>
    <title>Include directive test page 2</title>
  </head>
  <body>
    <h1>Include directive test page 2</h1>

    <%@ include file="/JSPExamples/included.jsp" %>
  </body>
</html>
```

The code for the included JSP `included.jsp` is:

```
<%@ page import="java.util.Date" %>
<%= "Current date is " + new Date() %>
```

Save both these files to the JSPExamples directory. Once copied navigate to http://localhost:8000/JSPExamples/includeDirective2.jsp; should see something similar to:

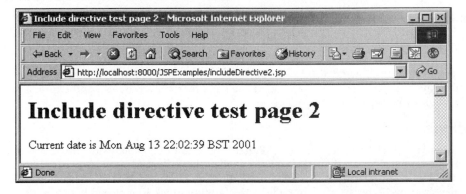

When `includeDirective2.jsp` is translated, the included part of the servlet code, stripped of comments, looks like this:

```
out.write("<html>\r\n   <head>\r\n     <title>Include directive test page
2</title>\r\n   </head>\r\n   <body>\r\n     <h1>Include directive test page
2</h1>\r\n\r\n     ");
out.write("\r\n");
out.print("Current date is " + new Date());
out.write("\r\n");
out.write("\r\n   </body>\r\n</html>\r\n");
```

We can see that the code from the included file has been included inline into the servlet code.

The taglib Directive

The taglib directive allows the page to use **tag extensions (custom tags)** – see Chapter 11 and 12. It names the **tag library** that contains compiled Java code defining the tags to be used. The engine uses this tag library to find out what to do when it comes across the custom tags in the JSP. The syntax of the taglib directive is:

```
<%@ taglib uri="tagLibraryURI" prefix="tagPrefix" %>
```

and the available attributes are:

Attribute	Description	Default value
uri	A URI (Uniform Resource Identifier) that identifies the tag library descriptor. A tag library descriptor is used to uniquely name the set of custom tags and tells the container what to do with the specified tags.	No Default Not specifying a value causes a compilation error
tagPrefix	Defines the prefix string in prefix:tagname that is used to define the custom tag. The prefixes jsp, jspx, java, javax, servlet, sun, and sunw are reserved. If this value is mytag then when the container comes across any element that starts like <mytag:tagname ... /> in the JSP, it references the tag library descriptor specified in the URI.	No Default Not specifying a value causes a compilation error

Tag libraries are a very powerful feature of JSP, and will be covered in detail in Chapters 11 and 12.

Scripting Elements

JSP scripting elements allow Java code – variable or method declarations, scriptlets (blocks of Java code evaluated in the order in which they appear as the page receives a request), and expressions – to be inserted into our JSP page.

Declarations

A **declaration** is a block of Java code in a JSP that is used to define class-wide variables and methods in the generated servlet. Declarations are initialized when the JSP page is initialized, and have instance scope in the generated servlet, so that anything defined in a declaration is available throughout the JSP to other declarations, expressions, and code. A declaration block is enclosed between <%! and %> and does not write anything to the output stream. The syntax is:

```
<%! Java variable and method declarations %>
```

Example

Consider the simple JSP below, `declaration.jsp`:

```
<%!
  int numTimes = 3;

  public String sayHello(String name) {
    return "Hello, " + name + "!";
  }
%>

<html>
  <head>
    <title>Declaration test page</title>
  </head>
  <body>
    <h1>Declaration test page</h1>

    <p>The value of numTimes is <%= numTimes %>.</p>
    <p>Saying hello to reader: "<%= sayHello("reader") %>".</p>
  </body>
</html>
```

This declares an `int` variable called `numTimes`, and a `sayHello()` method that greets the requested person. Further down the page, expression elements (to be covered shortly) are used to return the value of `numTimes` to the browser and to invoke the `sayHello()` method.

Save `declaration.jsp` to the `JSPExamples` directory, and view
http://localhost:8000/JSPExamples/declaration.jsp; will then see the following:

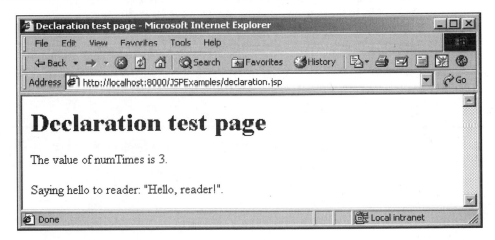

The generated servlet contains the declaration code:

```
import javax.servlet.*;
// ... more import statements

public class _0002fdeclaration_jsp extends HttpJspBase {

  int numTimes = 3;
```

```
public String sayHello(String name) {
  return "Hello, " + name + "!";
}

// ... More generated code
```

Note that the code from the declaration in the JSP is not placed in the `_jspService()` method of the generated servlet, but is directly inserted into the class itself, to define static or instance variables and methods.

Scriptlets

A **scriptlet** is a block of Java code that is executed during the request-processing time, and is enclosed between `<%` and `%>` tags. What the scriptlet actually does depends on the code itself, and can include producing output for the client. Multiple scriptlets are combined in the generated servlet class in the order they appear in the JSP. Scriptlets, like any other Java code block or method, can modify objects inside them as a result of method invocations.

In the Reference Implementation, all the code appearing between the `<%` and `%>` tags in the JSP gets put into the `service()` method of the servlet, as is, in the order in which it appears. It is therefore processed for every request that the servlet receives. The syntax for scriptlets is:

```
<% Valid Java code statements %>
```

Example

In `scriptlet.jsp` below, a scriptlet executes a loop ten times. It includes a message each time in the HTML sent to the browser, using the implicit object `out`. It also sends each message to the `System.out` stream, that is, to the console window in which the RI is running:

```
<html>
  <head>
    <title>Scriptlet test page</title>
  </head>
  <body>
    <h1>Scriptlet test page</h1>

    <%
      for(int i=0;i< 10;i++) {
        out.println("<b>Hello World. This is a scriptlet test " + i +
                "</b><br>");
        System.out.println("This goes to the System.out stream " + i);
      }
    %>

  </body>
</html>
```

Save `scriptlet.jsp` to the `JSPExamples` directory, add the file to the `%J2EE_HOME%\public_html\JSPExamples` directory, and request
`http://localhost:8000/JSPExamples/scriptlet.jsp`. The output to the browser window should be:

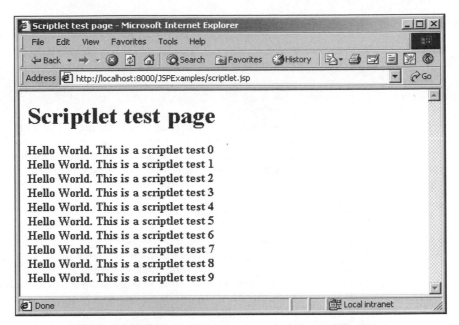

and the following should appear in the console window where the J2EE server is running:

Scriptlets can be broken up by static content, so long as compound statements are used in them and the structure of the curly braces is logical. For example, the following code fragment (based on an example later in this chapter) shows the use of a scriptlet to handle control flow, while JSP syntax is used within the scriptlet to output content. The developer can use the <% and %> tags to move between Java scriptlet and normal JSP content at will. There are no restrictions on the JSP code that may appear within scriptlets (other scriptlets, actions, directives, expressions, and template data may be used).

```
<%
  if ("Richard".equals(request.getParameter("userName"))) {
%>

Hello Richard. You're logged in.

<% } else { %>

You're not Richard.
Your user name is <%= request.getParameter("userName")%>

<% } %>
```

Note that code like the following example of incorrect scriptlet usage won't work as expected:

```
<%
  if ("Richard".equals(request.getParameter("userName")))
%>

Hello Richard. You're logged in.
```

Because the `if` statement doesn't use a compound statement (that is, there is no {), the statement executed if the `if` condition is true will probably be the generated servlet's `out.println()` statement to preserve the whitespace after the scriptlet, and the scriptlet line is useless for handling control flow. We will always see "Hello Richard. You're logged in." (By the way, Sun's Java coding conventions recommend the use of compound statements, wherever possible, to avoid this kind of error in Java code.)

This use of scriptlets and JSP content is frequently found in JSPs.

Developers often confuse declarations and scriptlets. A declaration uses the `<%!` syntax and defines variables and methods of instance scope. A scriptlet defines variables and code local to the `_jspService()` method. This means that static variables and methods can only be defined in declarations. It also means that variables defined in declarations may be accessed from multiple threads. As in the case of servlet instance variables, thread safety will be a real issue. Scriptlets pose no thread safety issues. So don't use declarations without good reason. Declarations are often used for efficiency. For example, if a read-only variable is expensive to initialize, it makes sense to do it once in the lifetime of the JSP page, rather than once per request.

Expressions

An **expression** is a shorthand notation for a scriptlet that sends the value of a Java expression back to the client. The expression is evaluated at HTTP request processing time, and the result is converted to a `String` and displayed.

An expression is enclosed in the `<%=` and `%>` tags. If the result of the expression is an object, the conversion is done by using the object's `toString()` method. The syntax is:

```
<%= Java expression to be evaluated %>
```

Example

Consider the example JSP below; save it as `expression.jsp` in the `JSPExamples` directory. This JSP page sets up a simple counter and demonstrates declarations, scriptlets, and expressions working together:

```
<html>
  <head>
    <title>Expression test page</title>
  </head>
  <body>
    <h1>Expression test page</h1>

    <%! int i=0 ; %>

    <%
      i++;
    %>
```

```
      Hello World!
      <%= "This JSP has been accessed " + i + " times" %>

   </body>
</html>
```

An int variable i is declared, and initially has the value 0. Each time this instance of the generated servlet is called, for instance when the browser requests http://localhost:8000/JSPExamples/expression.jsp, the variable is incremented by the scriptlet. Finally, an expression is used to print out the value of i, together with some surrounding text.

After this JSP has been requested seven times, the browser will display:

Note that while code in scriptlets follows normal Java grammar, ending statements with a semicolon, a JSP expression, however complicated it may be, does not end with a semicolon.

Comments

JSP supports hidden comments. Any content between the delimiters <%-- and --%> will be ignored by the container at translation time. JSP comments don't nest so any content except a terminating --%> is legal within JSP comments.

If we want to see comments in the generated output, we can always use HTML or XML comments with the <!- and -> delimiters; these will simply be treated as normal template data by the container.

We can use JSP comments to document details of our implementation as we do in Java code. However, we could choose to use just JSP comments rather than HTML comments to document our markup structure as well. This means that we can be as verbose as we like without bloating the generated content.

We are also free to use the standard Java comment syntax within JSP scriptlet elements.

Standard Actions

Standard actions are well-known tags that affect the runtime behavior of the JSP and the response sent back to the client. They must be implemented to behave the same way by all containers. Unlike custom tags these actions are available by default and do not require taglib declarations in order to use them.

When the container comes across a standard action tag during the conversion of a JSP page into a servlet, it generates the Java code that corresponds to the required predefined task.

For example when it comes across the standard include action:

```
<jsp:include page="myjsp.jsp" flush="true" />
```

It includes the output produced by a request with the same parameters to myjsp.jsp in the response, in place of the action tag.

The standard actions serve to provide page authors with basic functionality to exploit for common tasks. The standard action types are:

- ❑ <jsp:useBean>
- ❑ <jsp:setProperty>
- ❑ <jsp:getProperty>
- ❑ <jsp:param>
- ❑ <jsp:include>
- ❑ <jsp:forward>
- ❑ <jsp:plugin>

<jsp:useBean>

To separate code from presentation, it is often a good idea to encapsulate logic in a Java object (a JavaBean), and then instantiate and use this object within our JSP. The <jsp:useBean>, <jsp:setProperty>, and <jsp:getProperty> tags assist with this task.

The <jsp:useBean> action is used to instantiate a JavaBean, or to locate an existing bean instance, and assign it to a variable name (or id). We can also specify the lifetime of the object by giving it a specific **scope**. <jsp:useBean> ensures that the object is available, with the specified id, in the appropriate scope as specified by the tag. The object can then be referenced using its associated id from within the JSP page, or even from within other JSP pages, depending on the scope of the JavaBean.

There are two forms of syntax for the <jsp:useBean> action tag. The first contains no body, and simply makes the object available to the remainder of the JSP page:

```
<jsp:useBean id="name" scope="scopeName" bean_details />
```

The second form contains a body that will be evaluated if the bean is instantiated. The body may contain any JSP content, but it usually consists of scriptlets and <jsp:setProperty> actions, which configure the new bean:

```
<jsp:useBean id="name" scope="scopeName" bean_details>
  Body
</jsp:useBean>
```

Where bean_details is one of:

- ❑ class="className"
- ❑ class="className" type="typeName"
- ❑ beanName="beanName" type="typeName"
- ❑ type="typeName"

The possible attributes are:

Attribute	Description	Default value
id	The case-sensitive name used to identify the object instance. If the bean was created by a servlet and made available to the JSP page using the setAttribute() method, the id of the <jsp:useBean> action must match the name given to the attribute.	No default value
scope	The scope within which the reference is available. Possible values are "page", "request", "session", or "application".	page
class	The fully qualified class name.	No default value
bean Name	The name of a bean, as we would supply to the instantiate() method in the java.beans.Beans class. This attribute can also be a request-time expression. It is permissible to supply a type and a beanName, and omit the class attribute. The beanName follows the standard bean specification and can be of the form a.b.c, where a.b.c is either a class, or the name of a serialized resource in which case it is resolved as "a/b/c.ser". (See the JavaBeans specification for more details.)	No default value
type	This optional attribute specifies the type of the scripting variable to be created, and follows standard Java casting rules. The type must be a superclass of the bean's class, an interface implemented by it, or the bean's class itself. Just like any casting operation, if the object is not of this type then java.lang.ClassCastException can be thrown at request time.	The value of the class attribute

The underlying processes that occur are:

❑ The container tries to locate an object that has the specified id, within the specified scope.

❑ If the object is found, and a type has been specified in the tag, the container tries to cast the found object to the specified type. A ClassCastException is thrown if the cast fails. If the object is not found in the specified scope, and no class or beanName is specified in the tag, an InstantiationException is thrown.

❑ If the object is not found in the specified scope, and the class can be instantiated, then this is done, and a reference to the object is associated with the given id, in the specified scope. If this fails then an InstantiationException is thrown.

❑ If the object is not found in the specified scope and a beanName is specified, then the instantiate() method of java.beans.Beans is invoked, with the beanName as an argument. If this method succeeds, the new object reference is associated with the given id, in the specified scope.

❑ If a new bean instance has been instantiated and the `<jsp:useBean>` element has a non-empty body, the body is processed; during this processing the new variable is initialized and available. Scriptlets or the `<jsp:setProperty>` standard action can be used to initialize the bean instance, if necessary.

The meanings of the possible values of the scope attribute are:

❑ `page` scope means that the object is associated with this particular request to this page.

❑ `request` scope means that the object is associated with this particular client request. If the request is forwarded to another JSP using the `<jsp:forward>` action, or if another JSP is included using the `<jsp:include>` action, the object will be available.

❑ `session` scope means that the object will be available during any requests made by the same client within the current session.

❑ `application` scope means that the object will be available in any JSP page within the same web application.

Note that the last three scope values are the same as those available to servlets when accessing `request`, `session`, and `application` attributes using the Servlet API.

The container looks for the Java class we specified in the classpath for that web application. If we are creating a bean of a class we have written ourselves, we place the compiled class file either under the `WEB-INF\classes` directory in our web application, or in a JAR file in the `WEB-INF\lib` directory.

Once we have looked at `<jsp:setProperty>` and `<jsp:getProperty>` we will be in a position to see an example of how to use the `<jsp:useBean>` action.

<jsp:setProperty>

The `<jsp:setProperty>` standard tag is used in conjunction with the `<jsp:useBean>` action described in the preceding section, to set bean properties. Bean properties can be either simple or indexed. The property names follow JavaBean conventions.
The properties in a bean can be set either:

❑ At request time from parameters in the request object

❑ At request time from an evaluated expression

❑ From a specified string, or hard coded in the page

When setting bean properties from the `request` object, the JSP can choose to set all properties in the JavaBean via the standard action:

```
<jsp:setProperty name="help" property="*"/>
```

or a single property can be set explicitly by an action such as:

```
<jsp:setProperty name="help" property="word"/>
```

The `<jsp:setProperty>` action uses the Java bean's introspection mechanism to discover what properties are present, their names, whether they are simple or indexed, their type, and their accessor and mutator methods.

The syntax of the `<jsp:setProperty>` action is:

```
<jsp:setProperty name="beanName" propertydetails />
```

where `propertydetails` is one of:

- ❑ `property="*"`
- ❑ `property="propertyName"`
- ❑ `property="propertyName" param="parameterName"`
- ❑ `property="propertyName" value="propertyValue"`

Note that `propertyValue` is a string or a scriptlet. The attributes are:

Attribute	Description
name	The name of a bean instance, which must already have been defined by a `<jsp:useBean>` tag. The value of this attribute in `<jsp:setProperty>` must be the same as the value of the `id` attribute in `<jsp:useBean>`.
property	The name of the bean property whose value is being set.
	If this attribute has the value `"*"`, the tag looks through all the parameters in the `request` object and tries to match the request parameter names and types to property names and types in the bean. The values in the request are assigned to each matching bean property unless a request parameter has the value `""`, in which case the bean property is left unaltered.
param	When setting bean properties from request parameters, it is not necessary for the bean have the same property names as the request parameters.
	This attribute is used to specify the name of the request parameter whose value we want to assign to a bean property. If the `param` value is not specified, it is assumed that the request parameter and the bean property have the same name.
	If there is no request parameter with this name, or if it has the value `""`, the action has no effect on the bean.
value	The value to assign to the bean property. This can be a request-time attribute, or it can accept an expression as its value.
	A tag cannot have both `param` and `value` attributes.

When properties are assigned from string constants or request parameter values, conversion is applied using the standard Java conversion methods; for example, if a bean property is of type `double` or `Double` the `java.lang.Double.valueOf(String)` method is used. However, request-time expressions can be assigned to properties of any type, and the container performs no conversion. For indexed properties, the value must be an array.

<jsp:getProperty>

The `<jsp:getProperty>` action is complementary to the `<jsp:setProperty>` action, and is used to access the properties of a bean. It accesses the value of a property, converts it to a string, and prints it to the output stream to the client.

To convert the property to a string, the action:

❑ Invokes the `toString()` method on the property, if it is an object

❑ Converts the value directly to a string, if it is a primitive, using the `valueOf()` method of the corresponding wrapper class for the primitive type

This is just like the behavior of the `System.out.println()` method.

The syntax is:

```
<jsp:getProperty name="name" property="propertyName" />
```

and the available attributes are:

Attribute	Description
name	The id of the bean instance from which the property is obtained.
property	The name of the property to get; this is the instance variable in the bean. Of course, we must create a bean before using `<jsp:getProperty>`.

Having seen the `<jsp:useBean>`, `<jsp:setProperty>`, and `<jsp:getProperty>` actions, let's build a simple example using all three. Our example will ask the user for their name and their favorite programming language, and then issue a verdict on their choice. The initial HTML page, `beans.html`, is very simple:

```html
<html>
  <head>
    <title>useBean action test page</title>
  </head>
  <body>
    <h1>useBean action test page</h1>

    <form method="post" action="beans.jsp">
      <p>Please enter your username:
      <input type="text" name="name">
      <br>What is your favorite programming language?
      <select name="language">
        <option value="Java">Java
        <option value="C++">C++
        <option value="Perl">Perl
      </select>
      </p>

      <p><input type="submit" value="Submit information">
    </form>

  </body>
</html>
```

This sends a POST request to beans.jsp with two parameters: name and language. This JSP page, beans.jsp, is also quite simple:

```
<jsp:useBean id="languageBean" scope="page" class="com.wrox.beans.LanguageBean">
  <jsp:setProperty name="languageBean" property="*"/>
</jsp:useBean>

<html>
  <head>
    <title>useBean action test result</title>
  </head>
  <body>
    <h1>useBean action test result</h1>

    <p>Hello, <jsp:getProperty name="languageBean" property="name"/>.</p>

    <p>Your favorite language is
        <jsp:getProperty name="languageBean" property="language"/>.</p>

    <p>My comments on your language:</p>
    <p><jsp:getProperty name="languageBean" property="languageComments"/>
    </p>
  </body>
</html>
```

All the Java code has been removed to the LanguageBean class. beans.jsp creates an instance of LanguageBean with page scope, and uses the property="*" form of the <jsp:setProperty> action to set the bean's name and language properties. It can then use the <jsp:getProperty> action to retrieve the values of these properties, and also the languageComments property.

Finally, the source of LanguageBean is as follows:

```
package com.wrox.beans;

public class LanguageBean {

    private String name;
    private String language;

    public LanguageBean() {
    }

    public void setName(String name) {
        this.name = name;
    }

    public String getName() {
        return name;
    }

    public void setLanguage(String language) {
        this.language = language;
    }

    public String getLanguage() {
        return language;
    }
```

```
public String getLanguageComments() {
  if (language.equals("Java")) {
    return "The king of OO languages.";
  } else if (language.equals("C++")) {
    return "Rather too complex for some folks' liking.";
  } else if (language.equals("Perl")) {
    return "OK if you like incomprehensible code.";
  } else {
    return "Sorry, I've never heard of " + language + ".";
  }
}
}
```

This is a simple Java bean class with a no-argument constructor, set and get methods for the `name` and `language` properties, and also a `getLanguageComments()` method. This last method uses the value of the language property to issue some comments on the user's chosen language – this is invoked by the `<jsp:getProperty name="languageBean" property="languageComments"/>` action in `beans.jsp`.

Save `beans.html` and `beans.jsp` to the JSPExamples directory, and `LanguageBean.java` to `JSPExamples\src\com\wrox\beans\`. Compile the bean into `%J2EE_HOME%\public_html\JSPExamples/WEB-INF/classes` by running the following command from the `src` directory:

```
javac -d ../WEB-INF/classes com/wrox/beans/LanguageBean.java
```

We now need to create a web application. Start the J2EE server and the deployment tool. Create a new application and call it JSPExamples; we now need to add a web component to the application. Do this by going to the File | New | Web Component... We now need to select the application the WAR is to be added to, select JSPExamples. For the WAR Display Name enter JSPExamples. We then need to add the beans.html, beans.jsp, and the LanguageBean.class files. In the following screen choose JSP as the component type. On the next screen select the JSP Filename, beans.jsp, and the Web Component Name as beans. Select Finish, we are now ready to deploy the web component. Go to the Tools menu and click Deploy... For the Context Root enter JSPExamples and then Finish.

Navigate to http://localhost:8000/JSPExamples/beans.html, and you will see:

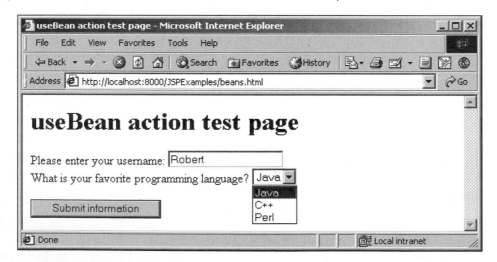

Enter your name and choose your favored language, then click the Submit information button:

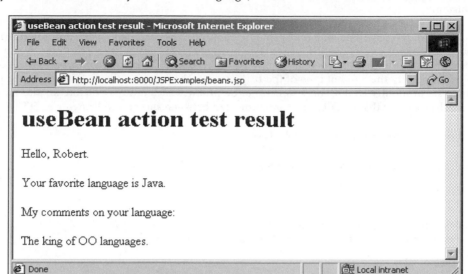

The advantage of this approach over that used in previous examples, in which Java code and HTML were we freely mixed, should be clear. By removing the logic to the LanguageBean class the JSP page is much more readable, and therefore easily edited by someone who is a skilled web designer but does not necessarily understand the details of Java programming.

Using JavaBeans is just one way to avoid having excessive amounts of Java code in JSP pages. Other strategies include using servlet controllers and JSP tag extensions.

<jsp:param>

The <jsp:param> action is used to provide other, enclosing, tags with additional information in the form of name-value pairs. It is used in conjunction with the <jsp:include>, <jsp:forward>, and <jsp:plugin> actions, and its use is described in the relevant sections that follow. The syntax is:

```
<jsp:param name="paramname" value="paramvalue" />
```

The available attributes are:

Attribute	Description
Name	The key associated with the attribute. (Attributes are key-value pairs.)
Value	The value of the attribute.

<jsp:include>

This action allows a static or dynamic resource, specified by a URL, to be included in the current JSP at request-processing time. An included page has access only to the JspWriter object, and it cannot set headers or cookies. A request-time exception is thrown if this is attempted. This constraint is equivalent to that imposed on the include() method of javax.servlet.RequestDispatcher used by servlets for this type of inclusion.

If the page output is buffered, the developer can choose whether the buffer should be flushed prior to the inclusion.

The include action pays a small penalty in efficiency, and the included page cannot perform all operations permitted in top-level JSP pages. The included page cannot attempt to modify the response's headers: this forbids operations such as modifying the response's content type or setting cookies. While attempting to modify the content type of the response clearly makes no sense in an included page, the inability to set or modify cookies may sometimes be problematic, and may dictate an alternative approach. (Remember that cookies are communicated between server and browser in HTTP headers.)

The syntax of the <jsp:include> action is:

```
<jsp:include page="URL" flush="true" />
```

or:

```
<jsp:include page="URL" flush="true">
  <jsp:param name="paramname" value="paramvalue" />
  ...
</jsp:include>
```

The attributes of the <jsp:include> action are:

Attribute	Description
page	The resource to include. The URL format is the same as described earlier for the include directive.
flush	This attribute is optional, with the default value of false. If the value is true, the buffer in the output stream is flushed before the inclusion is performed.

There is an important enhancement to the JSP 1.2 specification with respect to flushing. In JSP 1.1 the only legal value of the flush attribute was true. Allowing includes without flushing the buffer is a major advance for JSP 1.2, as once the buffer has been flushed it is impossible to forward to another resource within the web application or use an error page.

A <jsp:include> action may have one or more <jsp:param> tags in its body, providing additional name-value pairs. The included page can access the original request object, which will contain both the original parameters, and the new parameters specified using the <jsp:param> tag. If the parameter names are the same, the old values are kept intact, but the new values take precedence over the existing values.

For example, if the request has a parameter param1=myvalue1, and a parameter param1=myvalue2 is specified in the <jsp:param> tag, the request received on the second JSP will have param1=myvalue2, myvalue1. The augmented attributes can be extracted from the request using the getParameter(String paramname) method in the javax.servlet.ServletRequest interface.

It is important to understand the difference between the include *directive* and this include *action*:

Include Type	Syntax	Takes Place	Included Content	Parsing
directive	`<%@ include file="filename" %>`	Compilation time	Static	Parsed by container.
action	`<jsp:include page="URL" />`	Request-processing time	Static or Dynamic	Not parsed but included in place. The specified URL is specified at run time as a separate resource. The included URL may map to a servlet, rather than a JSP.

The `include` directive lets us include resources into multiple pages but requires the including pages to be retranslated if any included resources change. This means that unless our JSP container is smart enough to store and check dependency information at request-processing time, we may need to update the modification date on all pages statically, including a modified page fragment, to ensure that they are updated. The `include` action includes files at request-processing time.

❑   Use the `include` directive if your resource is not going to change frequently

❑   Use the `include` action when the resource changes frequently or is dynamic

Let's look at an example. The JSP below, `includeAction.jsp`, shows both the include types, for both a static and a dynamic resource:

```
<html>
  <head>
    <title>Include Action test page</title>
  </head>
  <body>
    <h1>Include Action test page</h1>

      <h2>Using the include directive</h2>

      <%@ include file="included2.html" %>
      <%@ include file="included2.jsp" %>

      <h2>Using the include action</h2>

      <jsp:include page="included2.html" flush="true" />
      <jsp:include page="included2.jsp" flush="true" />

  </body>
</html>
```

The two included files are `included2.html`:

```
<p>This is some static text in the html file</p>
```

and `included2.jsp`:

```
<%@ page import="java.util.Date" %>
<%= "Current date is " + new Date() %>
```

Save these files in the `%J2EE_HOME%\public_html\JSPExamples` directory, start the J2EE server, then request http://localhost:8000/JSPExamples/includeAction.jsp; you will then get something similar to:

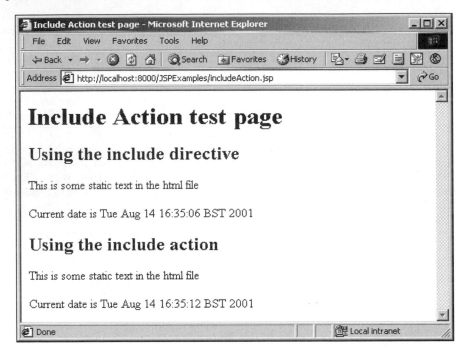

There is a subtle difference between the outputs from the two types of include. Let us look at an excerpt from the generated servlet class, tidied up a little:

```
// ...

public void _JSP pageservice(HttpServletRequest request,
                            HttpServletResponse response)
                throws IOException, ServletException {
    // ...

    out.write("<html>\r\n  <head>\r\n    <title>Include Action test
page</title>\r\n  </head>\r\n  <body>\r\n    <h1>Include Action test
page</h1>\r\n\r\n    <h2>Using the include directive</h2>\r\n\r\n    ");
    out.write("<h3>This is some static text in the html file</h3>");
    out.write("\r\n    ");
    out.write("\r\n");
    out.print( "Current date is " + new Date() );
    out.write("\r\n\r\n    <h2>Using the include action</h2>\r\n\r\n    ");
    {
      String _jspx_qStr = "";
      out.flush();
      pageContext.include("included2.html" + _jspx_qStr);
```

```
          }
          out.write("\r\n        ");
          {
            String _jspx_qStr = "";
            out.flush();
            pageContext.include("included2.jsp" + _jspx_qStr);
          }
          out.write("\r\n\r\n   </body>\r\n</html>\r\n");

      // ...
      }
```

The highlighted lines in the above code show how the container in-lines the resources for the include *directive*, and invokes them dynamically for the include *action*. To reiterate the difference, see what happens when the included resources are changed, without changing the parent JSP that includes them. Change included2.html so that it contains:

```
   <p>This is some new text in the html file</p>
```

and change included2.jsp so that its contents are now:

```
   <p>This is the new JSP</p>
```

When the page is requested again, the output will look like this:

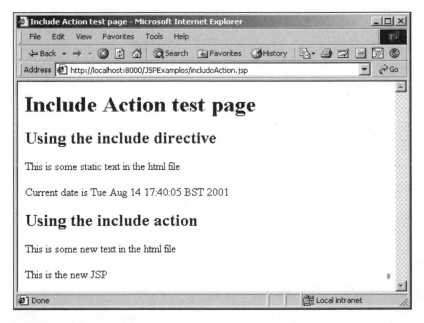

The parts included using the include *directive* are not altered, because the parent JSP (includeAction.jsp) has not changed and hence is not recompiled; however, the parts included using the include *action* are changed, because the include action performs the inclusion afresh each time the parent JSP is requested.

As compilation strategies for static includes are not mandated in the JSP specification, the behavior of this example may differ between different JSP containers. Some will track dependencies and automatically recompile the parent JSP; JRun 3.0 does this, for example. Most containers will not detect the change, and behave as in the screenshots above. So running this example will tell you whether or not your JSP container requires you to remember to update the date on top-level files when included files change.

<jsp:forward>

The `<jsp:forward>` action allows the request to be forwarded to another JSP, a servlet, or a static resource. This is particularly useful when we want to separate the application into different views, depending on the intercepted request. We saw this design approach applied to servlets in Chapter 7, and will see more of it later in this chapter. The syntax is:

```
<jsp:forward page="URL" />
```

or:

```
<jsp:forward page="URL">
  <jsp:param name="paramname" value="paramvalue" />
  ...
</jsp:forward>
```

The resource to which the request is being forwarded must be in the same web application as the JSP dispatching the request. Execution in the current JSP stops when it encounters a `<jsp:forward>` tag. The buffer is cleared (this is a server-side redirect and the response buffer is cleared when it is processed) and the request is modified to assimilate any additionally specified parameters. These parameters are assimilated in the same way as described for the `<jsp:include>` action.

If the output stream was not buffered, and some output has been written to it, a `<jsp:forward>` action will throw a `java.lang.IllegalStateException`. The behavior of this action is exactly the same as the `forward()` method of the `javax.servlet.RequestDispatcher`.

Let's see a simple example of the `<jsp:forward>` action in use: a simple login form. The login form itself, in `forward.html`, is straightforward, sending a POST request to `forward.jsp`:

```html
<html>
  <head>
    <title>Forward action test page</title>
  </head>
  <body>
    <h1>Forward action test page</h1>

    <form method="post" action="forward.jsp">
      <p>Please enter your username:
      <input type="text" name="userName">
      <br>and password:
      <input type="password" name="password">
      </p>

      <p><input type="submit" value="Log in">
    </form>

  </body>
</html>
```

`forward.jsp` is the first JSP page we have seen which contains no HTML code:

```
<%
  if ((request.getParameter("userName").equals("Richard")) &&
      (request.getParameter("password").equals("xyzzy"))) {
%>

<jsp:forward page="forward2.jsp" />

<% } else { %>

<%@ include file="forward.html" %>

<% } %>
```

This checks whether the username and password are acceptable to the system, and if so forwards the request to `forward2.jsp`; if the login attempt fails, it uses the `include` directive to present the login form to the user again.

Finally, `forward2.jsp` presents the successfully logged-in user with a welcome page. Since the original request, including the form parameters, has been forwarded to this JSP, we can use the request object to display the user's name:

```
<html>
  <head>
    <title>Forward action test: Login successful!</title>
  </head>
  <body>
    <h1>Forward action test: Login successful</h1>

    <p>Welcome, <%= request.getParameter("userName") %>

  </body>
</html>
```

Save all these files in the JSPExamples directory in the server, and request
http://localhost:8000/JSPExamples/forward.html:

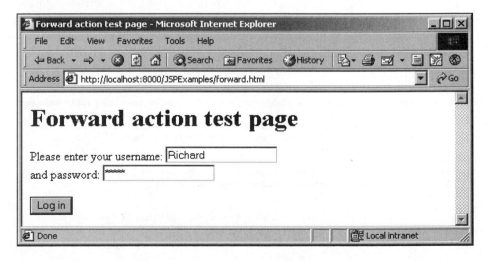

Entering the username Richard and the password xyzzy, we get to this page:

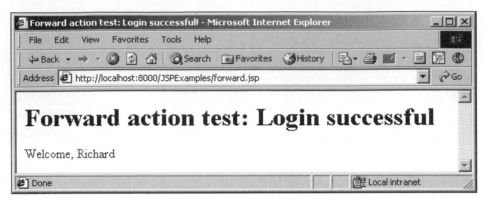

If any other username or password is entered, the login form is displayed again.

Using a controller servlet to forward an incoming request to the appropriate view is usually preferable to using a JSP controller. Remember that JSP pages are good at generating content, and not so good at handling processing logic.

<jsp:plugin>

The <jsp:plugin> action provides easy support for including Java applets in JSP-generated pages. It is used to generate browser-specific HTML tags (<object> or <embed>) that result in the download of the Java Plug-in software, if required, followed by the execution of the applet or JavaBean component that is specified in the tag. (This relies on JSP detecting our browser by parsing its user agent string.)

The reasons for using the <jsp:plugin> action to reference applets, rather than doing it by hand in JSP template data, are that <jsp:plugin> lets us forget about browser differences for once, and the resulting code references the Java Plug-in – a standard, recent implementation of Java, rather than whatever possibly slow or non-compliant Java VM our browser was shipped with (if it has Java support at all). The <jsp:plugin> tag has two optional support tags:

❑   <jsp:params> – to pass additional parameters to the applet or JavaBeans component

❑   <jsp:fallback> – to specify the content to be displayed in the client browser if the plug-in cannot be started because the generated tags are not supported. The <jsp:fallback> tag works like the <noframes> tag.

The syntax of this action is:

```
<jsp:plugin type="bean|applet" code="objectCode" codebase="objectCodebase"
            align="alignment" archive="archiveList" height="height"
            hspace="hspace" jreversion="jreversion" name="componentName"
            vspace="vspace" width="width" nspluginurl="url"
            iepluginurl="url" >
  <jsp:params>
    <jsp:param name=" paramName" value=" paramValue" />
    <jsp:param name=" paramName" value=" paramValue" />
    ...
  </jsp:params>
  <jsp:fallback> Alternate text to display </jsp:fallback>
</jsp:plugin>
```

The available attributes for the `<jsp:plugin>` tag are:

Attribute	Details	Required
type	Identifies the type of the component: a JavaBean, or an Applet.	Yes
code	Same as HTML syntax.	Yes
codebase	Same as HTML syntax.	No
align	Same as HTML syntax.	No
archive	Same as HTML syntax.	No
height	Same as HTML syntax.	No, but some browsers do not allow an object of zero height due to security issues
hspace	Same as HTML syntax	No
jreversion	The Java runtime environment version needed to execute this object. Default is "1.1".	No
name	Same as HTML syntax.	No
vspace	Same as HTML syntax.	No
title	Same as HTML syntax.	No
width	Same as HTML syntax.	No, but some browsers do not allow an object of zero width due to security issues
nspluginurl	URL where the Java plugin can be downloaded for Netscape Navigator. Default is implementation defined.	No
iepluginurl	URL where the Java plugin can be downloaded for Internet Explorer. Default is implementation defined.	No

The following example shows the `<jsp:plugin>` standard action in use, and the HTML generated by the RI for an Internet Explorer 5.5 client running on Windows 2000. We took the applet from the examples shipped with the JDK version 1.3.0. To run it, take the whole `MoleculeViewer` sample tree from the JDK, place it in a WAR, and place the following JSP (`applet.jsp`) in the root of the `MoleculeViewer` directory.

```
<p>This is the molecule viewer example from the
JDK 1.3.
<p/>

<jsp:plugin type="applet"
  code="XYZApp.class"
  codebase="./"
  width="300" height="300">
  <jsp:params>
  <jsp:param
    name="model"
    value="./models/HyaluronicAcid.xyz" />
```

```
    </jsp:params>
    <jsp:fallback>
      <p> unable to start plugin </p>
    </jsp:fallback>
  </jsp:plugin>
```

When this JSP is requested, the RI will generate the following HTML. Note that the generated HTML takes care of operating-system specific details such as the Windows CLASSID:

```
<object classid="clsid:8AD9C840-044E-11D1-B3E9-00805F499D93" width="300"
height="300"  codebase="http://java.sun.com/products/plugin/1.2.2/jinstall-1_2_2-
win.cab#Version=1,2,2,0">
<param name="java_code" value="XYZApp.class">
<param name="java_codebase" value="./">
<param name="type" value="application/x-java-applet;">
<param name="model" value="./models/HyaluronicAcid.xyz">
<comment>
<embed type="application/x-java-applet;"  width="300"  height="300"
pluginspage="http://java.sun.com/products/plugin/" java_code="XYZApp.class"
java_codebase="./" model=./models/HyaluronicAcid.xyz
>
<noembed>
</comment>
<p> unable to start plugin </p>

</noembed></embed>
</object>
```

When we request `applet.jsp`, we should see the following in our browser. (We used IE 5.5, but the point is that the same JSP will work identically in other browsers).

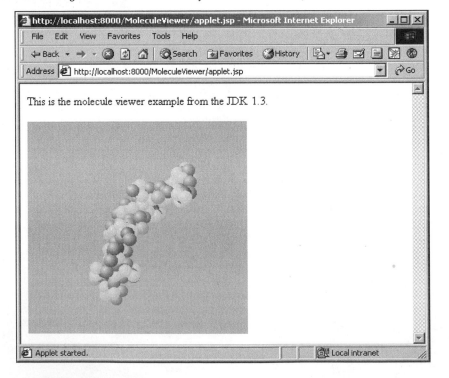

472

Implicit Objects

The Servlet API includes interfaces that provide convenient abstractions to the developer, such as `HttpServletRequest`, `HttpServletResponse`, and `HttpSession`. These abstractions encapsulate the object's implementation; for example, the `HttpServletRequest` interface represents the HTTP data sent from the client along with headers, form parameters, and so on, and provides convenient methods like `getParameter()` and `getHeader()` that extract relevant data from the request.

JSP provides certain implicit objects, based on the Servlet API. These objects are accessed using standard variables, and are automatically available for use in our JSP without writing any extra code. The implicit objects available in a JSP page are:

❑ request

❑ response

❑ pageContext

❑ session

❑ application

❑ out

❑ config

❑ page

The Request Object

The `request` object represents the request that triggered the `service()` invocation. The `HttpServletRequest` provides access to the incoming HTTP headers, request type, and request parameters, among other things. Strictly speaking, the object itself will be a protocol- and implementation-specific subclass of `javax.servlet.ServletRequest`, but few (if any) JSP containers currently support non-HTTP servlets. It has `request` scope.

The Response Object

The `response` object is the `HttpServletResponse` instance that represents the server's response to the request. It is legal to set HTTP status codes and headers in the JSP page once output has been sent to the client (even though it is not permitted in servlets), as JSP output streams are buffered by default). Again, the object itself will, strictly speaking, be a protocol- and implementation-specific subclass of `javax.servlet.ServletResponse`. It has `page` scope.

The PageContext Object

The `pageContext` provides a single point of access to many of the page attributes and is a convenient place to put shared data within the page. It is of type `javax.servlet.jsp.PageContext`, and has `page` scope.

The Session Object

The `session` object represents the session created for the requesting client. Sessions are created automatically, and a new session is available even when there is no in-coming session (unless, of course, you have used a `session="false"` attribute in the `page` directive, in which case this variable will not be available). The `session` object is of type `javax.servlet.http.HttpSession`, and has `session` scope.

Often it is worth marking our pages as not requiring a session. For simple or stateless applications this will maximize scalability by ensuring that our application can run on a cluster of servers without the overhead of session-state replication between machines in the cluster. However, an application that requires a lot of session state without using an `HttpSession` will be difficult to maintain.

The Application Object

The `application` object represents the servlet context, obtained from the servlet configuration object. It is of type `javax.servlet.ServletContext` and has `application` scope.

The Out Object

The `out` object is the object that writes into the output stream to the client. To make the `response` object useful, this is a buffered version of the `java.io.PrintWriter` class, and is of type `javax.servlet.jsp.JspWriter`. The buffer size can be adjusted via the `buffer` attribute of the page directive.

The Config Object

The `config` object is the `ServletConfig` for this JSP page, and has `page` scope. It is of type `javax.servlet.ServletConfig`.

The Page Object

The `page` object is the instance of the page's implementation servlet class that is processing the current request. It is of type `java.lang.Object`, and has `page` scope. The `page` object can be thought of as a synonym to `this` within the page.

Scope

The scope of JSP objects – JavaBeans and implicit objects – is critical, as it defines the how long, and from which JSP pages, the object will be available. For example, the `session` object has a scope that exceeds a single page, as it may span several client requests and pages. The `application` object can provide services to a group of JSP pages that together represent a web application.

JSP scopes internally rely on contexts. A context provides an invisible container for resources, and an interface for them to communicate with the environment; for example, a servlet executes in a context (an instance of `ServletContext`, in fact). Everything that the servlet needs to know about its server can be extracted from this context, and everything the server wants to communicate to the servlet goes through the context.

A good rule of thumb is that everything in JSP is associated with a context, and every context has a scope.

What happens when a bean tag is compiled for the different values of `scope` can be seen below.

Page Scope

An object with page scope is bound to the `javax.servlet.jsp.PageContext`.

This is relatively simple – it means that the object is placed in the `PageContext` object, for as long as this page is responding to the current request. An object with this scope can be accessed by invoking the `getAttribute()` methods on the implicit `pageContext` object.

The object reference is discarded upon completion of the current `Servlet.service()` invocation (in other words, when the page is fully processed by the servlets generated from the JSP). When generating the servlet, the servlet engine creates an object in the `service()` method, which follows the usual object scope convection in Java. This object is created and destroyed for each client request to the page.

This is the default scope for objects used with the `<jsp:useBean>` action.

Request Scope

Request scope means that the object is bound to the `javax.servlet.ServletRequest`, and can be accessed by invoking the `getAttribute()` methods on the implicit `request` object.

The object reference is available as long as the `HttpRequest` object exists, even if the request is forwarded to different pages, or if the `<jsp:include>` action is used. The underlying, generated servlet relies on binding the object to the `HttpServletRequest` using the `setAttribute(String key, Object value)` method in the `HttpServletRequest`; this is transparent to the JSP author. The object is distinct for every client request (in other words it is created afresh and destroyed for each new request).

Session Scope

An object with session scope is bound to the `javax.servlet.jsp.PageContext`, and can be accessed by invoking the `getValue()` methods on the implicit `session` object.

The generated `servlet` relies on binding the object to the `HttpSession` using the `setAttribute(String key, Object value)` method. This too is transparent to the JSP author. The object is distinct for every client, and is available as long as the client's session is valid.

Application Scope

Application scope means that the object is bound to the `javax.servlet.ServletContext`. An object with this scope can be accessed by invoking the `getAttribute()` methods on the implicit `application` object.

This is the most persistent scope. The generated servlet relies on binding the object to the `ServletContext` using the `setAttribute(String key, Object value)` method in the `ServletContext`. This is not unique to individual clients and, consequently, all clients access the same object, as they all access the same `ServletContext`.

When accessing application variables, take care your code is thread-safe. Application variables are often populated on application startup, and read-only thereafter.

JSP Pages as XML Documents

The JSP 1.1 specification introduced an alternative, XML-based syntax for JSP pages, replacing directives and scripting elements with XML-compliant alternatives. The JSP 1.2 specification takes this a step further by requiring JSP engines to accept JSP pages as XML documents, and basing the new tag library validation mechanism (discussed in Chapter 11) on the XML representation of JSP pages.

The XML syntax is not intended for hand authoring of JSP pages, and so will never replace the JSP syntax we have discussed so far. However, an XML-based syntax may be preferable when JSP pages are machine-authored, and makes it easy to manipulate JSP pages.

One reason that representing JSP pages as XML documents facilitates machine-authoring and page manipulation is the power and convenience of XSLT, the stylesheet language for XML transformations. XSLT stylesheets can easily be used to transform XML JSP documents into almost any required form. Note also that it is difficult to generate documents in the normal JSP syntax using XSLT. An XSLT stylesheet is itself an XML document, and JSP constructs such as <% are not allowed in XML documents. See *XSLT Programmer's Reference 2nd Edition* (Wrox Press, 2001, ISBN 1-861005-06-7) for more information on XSLT.

JSP pages in XML form can be validated using either the DTD or XML Schema definition supplied in the JSP 1.2 specification. The DTD is more readable, but the schema definition is favored as the validation standard.

The following examples illustrate the syntax of the XML equivalents of the JSP constructs we have seen so far.

Directives

For a JSP directive of the form:

```
<%@ directiveName ATTRIBUTES %>
```

the equivalent XML-based syntax is:

```
<jsp:directive.directiveName ATTRIBUTES />
```

The exception is the `taglib` directive, which is represented by an `xmlns:` attribute within the JSP page's root element. The natural match between tag library prefixes and XML namespaces illustrates Sun's efforts to make JSP more XML-aware, even if the regular syntax can never be XML-compliant.

Scripting Elements

A JSP declaration of the form:

```
<%! declaration code %>
```

is represented in XML as:

```
<jsp:declaration> declaration code </jsp:declaration>
```

A scriptlet of the form:

```
<% scriptlet code %>
```

is represented by:

```
<jsp:scriptlet> scriptlet code </jsp:scriptlet>
```

Finally, an expression of the form:

```
<%= expression code %>
```

is represented by:

```
<jsp:expression> expression code </jsp:expression>
```

Actions

The JSP action syntax is already based on XML. The only changes necessary are due to quoting conventions, and to the syntax of any request-time attribute values.

Example Page

The following example of a simple JSP page in normal and XML form is taken from the JSP 1.2 specification. Note that the XML form is more verbose, and not easily hand-authored, given the need to escape scriptlet content in CDATA elements. (This is necessary because some characters used in the Java language such as < are not legal in XML without escaping.)

JSP Syntax

```
<html>
  <head>
    <title>positiveTagLib</title>
  </head>
  <body>
    <%@ taglib uri="http://java.apache.org/tomcat/examples-taglib"
       prefix="eg" %>
    <%@ taglib uri="/tomcat/taglib" prefix="test" %>
    <%@ taglib uri="WEB-INF/tlds/my.tld" prefix="temp" %>
    <eg:test toBrowser="true" att1="Working">
    Positive Test taglib directive </eg:test>
  </body>
</html>
```

XML Syntax

```
<jsp:root xmlns:jsp="http://java.sun.com/jsp_1_2"
          xmlns:eg="http://java.apache.org/tomcat/examples-taglib"
          xmlns:test="urn:jsptld:/tomcat/taglib"
          xmlns:temp="urn:jsptld:/WEB-INF/tlds/my.tld">
  <jsp:cdata><![CDATA[<html>
    <head>
      <title>positiveTagLig</title>
    </head>
    <body>
  ]]></jsp:cdata>
  <eg:test toBrowser="true" att1="Working">
    <jsp:cdata>Positive test taglib directive</jsp:cdata>
  </eg:test>
  <jsp:cdata><![CDATA[
    </body>
  </html>
  ]]></jsp:cdata>
</jsp:root>
```

JSP Technical Support

Now that we're familiar with core JSP functionality, let's return to our Technical Support application from Chapter 7, and convert it to a JSP-based application. The modified application will illustrate the use of directives, standard actions, scriptlets, and session JavaBeans.

The application will work in the same way as before. The user goes to the welcome page, then enters an e-mail address and details of the technical problem:

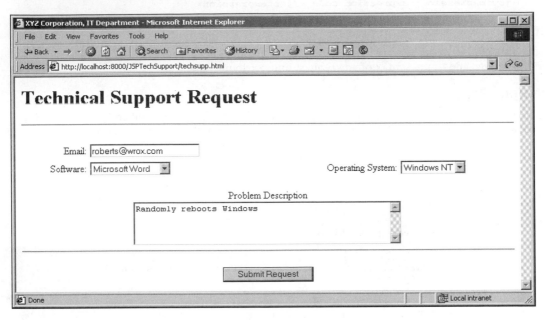

On clicking Submit Request, the application checks whether the user is known to the system (based on their e-mail address), and if not forwards the request to the customer registration page:

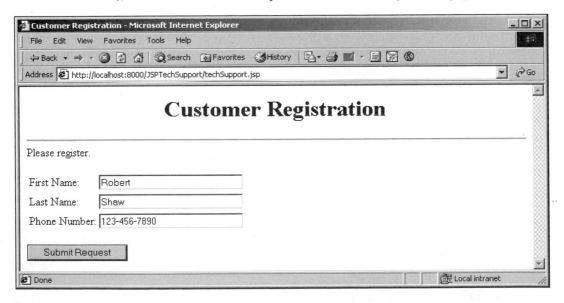

Once these details have been entered, the confirmation page is displayed:

(If the user's e-mail address is already registered, the user will be taken straight to this page rather than to the registration form.)

Application Design

The broad structure of the application is roughly the same as before, except that JSP pages replace the servlets and the logic is removed to a `JavaBean`:

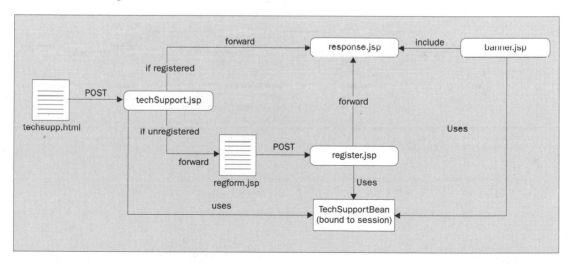

`TechSupportServlet` has been replaced by `techSupport.jsp`, `register.html` by `regform.jsp`, `RegisterCustomerServlet` by `register.jsp`, `ResponseServlet` by `response.jsp`, and `BannerServlet` by `banner.jsp`.

The TechSupportBean provides our 'model' of the application logic, and is used throughout the process of dealing with a support query: an instance is created in techSupport.jsp and bound to the session, and it is then reused in other JSP pages in the application. The file JDBCHelper.java encapsulates the code necessary for the database access. As information is gathered (from the forms and the database) it is stored in the bean's properties. By the time our user reaches response.jsp, the bean contains all the data about the support request, together with the user's details obtained either from an existing database entry or from the details supplied in the registration form. It can then be used in formulating the response to the user.

The Welcome Page

techsupp.html is the entry form to the system, and is virtually unchanged from the version in Chapter 7. The only difference is that we now use the POST method and send the request from the form to techSupport.jsp:

```
<html>
<!-- techsupp.html -->
  <head>
    <title>XYZ Corporation, IT Department</title>
  </head>
  <body>
    <h1>Technical Support Request</h1>
    <hr><br>
    <center>
      <form action="/JSPTechSupport/techSupport.jsp" method="POST">
        <table align="center" width="100%" cellspacing="2" cellpadding="2">
          <tr><td align="right">Email:</td>
            <td><input type="text" name="email" align="left"
                    size="25"></td></tr>
          <tr><td align="right">Software:</td>
            <td><select name="software" size="1">
                  <option value="Word">Microsoft Word</option>
                  <option value="Excel">Microsoft Excel</option>
                  <option value="Access">Microsoft Access</option>
                </select></td>
            <td align="right">Operating System:</td>
            <td><select name="os" size="1">
                  <option value="95">Windows 95</option>
                  <option value="98">Windows 98</option>
                  <option value="NT">Windows NT</option>
                </select></td></tr>
        </table>

        <br>Problem Description<br>
        <textarea name="problem" cols="50" rows="4"></textarea>
        <hr><br>
        <input type="submit" name="submit" value="Submit Request">
      </form>
    </center>
  </body>
</html>
```

This page is designated as the application's welcome file in web.xml:

```
<?xml version="1.0" encoding="ISO-8859-1"?>

<!DOCTYPE web-app
```

```
    PUBLIC "-//Sun Microsystems, Inc.//DTD Web Application 2.3//EN"
    "http://java.sun.com/dtd/web-app_2.3.dtd">

<web-app>

<display-name>JSPTechSupport</display-name>
  <welcome-file-list>
    <welcome-file>techsupp.html</welcome-file>
  </welcome-file-list>
  <resource-ref>
    <res-ref-name>jdbc/techSupportDB</res-ref-name>
    <res-type>javax.sql.DataSource</res-type>
    <res-auth>Container</res-auth>
  </resource-ref>
</web-app>
```

The Request-Processing JSP

When the user submits a technical support request, the information from their browser is sent to techSupport.jsp. This page contains no presentation details; it creates an instance of TechSupportBean bound to the session (if one does not already exist), and uses the <jsp:setProperty> action to set the bean's e-mail, software, operating system, and problem properties to the values submitted by the user. Note the specification of an error page in a page directive; if this page encounters any exception, error.jsp will be invoked, and will have access to the offending exception:

```
<%-- techSupport.jsp --%>

<%@ page errorPage="/error.jsp" %>

<jsp:useBean id="techSupportBean" scope="session"
class="com.wrox.techsupport.TechSupportBean" />
<jsp:setProperty name="techSupportBean" property="*"/>
```

It then uses a scriptlet to call the bean's registerSupportRequest() method, which stores the support request details in the database's SUPP_REQUESTS table and checks in the CUSTOMERS table to see whether this e-mail address is already registered:

```
<% techSupportBean.registerSupportRequest(); %>
```

Finally, we use the bean's isRegistered() method to retrieve details of whether or not the customer was recognized, and forward the request either directly to response.jsp if they were, or to regform.jsp otherwise:

```
<% if (techSupportBean.isRegistered()) { %>
    <jsp:forward page="response.jsp"/>
<% } else { %>
    <jsp:forward page="regform.jsp"/>
<% } %>
```

The JDBCHelper class

This is a package-visible class used to obtain a connection and cleanup after JDBC access.

```
package com.wrox.techsupport;

import java.sql.*;
```

```
import javax.sql.*;
import javax.naming.*;

class JDBCHelper {

  //jndiName is the JNDI name of the data source to use to get a connection.
  private String jndiName = "techSupportDB";

  // Creates new JDBCHelper
  public JDBCHelper(String jndiName) {
    this.jndiName - jndiName;
  }

  // @param jndiName JNDI name of the data source to use to
  //   get a connection
  Connection getConnection() throws NamingException, SQLException {
    Context initCtx = null;
    try {
      // Obtain the initial JNDI context
      initCtx = new InitialContext();

      // Perform JNDI lookup to obtain resource manager connection factory
      DataSource ds = (javax.sql.DataSource)
        initCtx.lookup("java:comp/env/jdbc/" + jndiName);

      // Invoke factory to obtain a connection.
      return ds.getConnection();
    }
    finally {
      // Don't forget to close the naming context
      if (initCtx != null) {
        initCtx.close();
      }
    }
  }

  // Always cleans up, even if it encounters a SQL exception
  void cleanup(Connection databaseConnection,
               Statement statement1,
               Statement statement2) throws SQLException {
    try {
      // Close the database connection and statement
      if (statement1 != null) {
        statement1.close();
      }
      if (statement2 != null) {
        statement2.close();
      }
    }
    finally {
      // Make sure we always try to close the connection, even
      // if something went wrong trying to close a statement
      if (databaseConnection != null) {
        databaseConnection.close();
      }
    }
  }
}
```

The TechSupportBean

So, how does `TechSupportBean` do all this work for `techSupport.jsp`? Let's start with the easy bit – the class declaration, member variables, and the property getter and setter methods:

```java
// TechSupportBean

package com.wrox.techsupport;

import java.sql.*;

public class TechSupportBean {

    // JNDI name of the data source this class requires
    private static final String DATA_SOURCE_NAME = "techSupportDB";

    private String email;
    private String software;
    private String os;
    private String problem;
    private String firstName;
    private String lastName;
    private String phoneNumber;

    private boolean registered;

    private JDBCHelper jdbcHelper;

    public TechSupportBean() {
        jdbcHelper = new JDBCHelper(DATA_SOURCE_NAME);
    }

    public void setEmail(String email) {
        this.email = email;
    }

    // ... and similarly for the software, os problem, firstName, lastName,
    // and phoneNumber properties

    public String getEmail() {
        return email;
    }

    // ... and similarly for the software, os problem, firstName, lastName,
    // and phoneNumber properties

    // ... more properties and methods ...
}
```

In a production-quality application, the driver class name and the JDBC URL might be read from context parameters in the deployment descriptor. (Better still, we could use a database connection pool managed by the servlet engine, or access the database only through a layer of EJBs.)

We have also provided setter and getter methods for several properties we haven't dealt with yet: `firstName`, `lastName`, and `phoneNumber`. These details will either be retrieved from the database (if the user is already registered), or obtained in a moment from the registration form. Remember that this bean will be used throughout the user's session, not just from `techSupport.jsp`.

The real work happens in the `registerSupport()` method, and the actual code is very similar to that in Chapter 7. We reuse the `Sequencer` class with a few changes, as we will see soon. (This generates the unique support request numbers from the `SEQ_NO` table.) The main difference is that the `registerSupportRequest()` method does not actually forward the request itself – it simply sets a `boolean` property, `registered`, which is `true` if the user is registered, and which can be accessed from the controlling JSP. If the customer was registered, we additionally set the bean's `firstName`, `lastName`, and `phoneNumber` properties so they can subsequently be accessed from other JSP pages:

```java
public void registerSupportRequest() throws SQLException,
                                     javax.naming.NamingException {

  int requestId = 0;
  Connection connection = null;
  String insertStatementStr =
    "INSERT INTO SUPP_REQUESTS VALUES(?, ?, ?, ?, ?)";
  String selectCustomerStr =
    "SELECT CUSTOMERS.FNAME, CUSTOMERS.LNAME FROM CUSTOMERS " +
    "WHERE CUSTOMERS.EMAIL = ?";

  PreparedStatement insertStatement = null;
  PreparedStatement selectStatement = null;

  try {
    connection = jdbcHelper.getConnection();

    insertStatement = connection.prepareStatement(insertStatementStr);
    requestId = Sequencer.getNextNumber(jdbcHelper);

    insertStatement.setInt(1, requestId);
    insertStatement.setString(2, email);
    insertStatement.setString(3, software);
    insertStatement.setString(4, os);
    insertStatement.setString(5, problem);

    insertStatement.executeUpdate();

    // Now verify if the customer is registered or not.
    selectStatement = connection.prepareStatement(selectCustomerStr);
    selectStatement.setString(1, email);

    ResultSet rs = selectStatement.executeQuery();

    if (rs.next()) {
      setFirstName(rs.getString("FNAME"));
      setLastName(rs.getString("LNAME"));
      setPhoneNumber(rs.getString("PHONE"));

      // The customer was registered - we can go straight to the
      // response page
      registered = true;
    } else {
      registered = false;
    }
    rs.close();
  }
  finally {
    jdbcHelper.cleanup(connection, selectStatement, insertStatement);
  }
}
```

That's it for the moment in `TechSupportBean`, but we will need to come back and add one more method shortly.

The Registration Form

If the user was not registered, the request is forwarded to `regform.jsp`, where a registration form is displayed. In this version of the application, this page is a JSP simply so that a POST request can be forwarded to it, though we could of course add further personalization to the form using the details entered so far.

The code is very simple, and again is very similar to the corresponding page in the servlet version of the application:

```html
<html>
<!-- regform.jsp -->
  <head>
    <title>Customer Registration</title>
  </head>
  <body>
    <center><h1>Customer Registration</h1></center>
    <hr>
      Please register.
      <form action="/JSPTechSupport/register.jsp" method="POST">
        <table>
          <tr><td>First Name:</td>
              <td><input type="text" name="firstName" size="30"></td></tr>
          <tr><td>Last Name:</td>
              <td><input type="text" name="lastName" size="30"></td></tr>
          <tr><td>Phone Number:</td>
              <td><input type="text" name="phoneNumber" size="30"></td></tr>
        </table>
        <br><input type="submit" value="Submit Request">
      </form>
  </body>
</html>
```

With the details entered, the user can submit their registration to `register.jsp`.

The Registration JSP

```jsp
<%-- register.jsp --%>

<%@ page errorPage="/error.jsp" %>

<jsp:useBean id="techSupportBean" scope="session"
class="com.wrox.techsupport.TechSupportBean" />
<jsp:setProperty name="techSupportBean" property="*"/>

<% techSupportBean.registerCustomer(); %>

<jsp:forward page="response.jsp"/>
```

This is very reminiscent of `techSupport.jsp`, but if anything even simpler. We need to set the bean's `firstName`, `lastName`, and `phoneNumber` properties from the details supplied in the form, and call the bean's `registerCustomer()` method to enter these details in the database. Add the following code to the end of `TechSupportBean.java`:

```
// In TechSupportBean.java

public void registerCustomer() throws SQLException,
                                javax.naming.NamingException {
  Connection connection = null;
  PreparedStatement insertStatement = null;
  String insertStatementStr = "INSERT INTO CUSTOMERS VALUES(?, ?, ?, ?)";
  try {
    connection = jdbcHelper.getConnection();

    insertStatement = connection.prepareStatement(insertStatementStr);
    insertStatement.setString(1, email);
    insertStatement.setString(2, firstName);
    insertStatement.setString(3, lastName);
    insertStatement.setString(4, phoneNumber);

    insertStatement.executeUpdate();
  }
  finally {
    jdbcHelper.cleanup(connection, insertStatement, null);
  }
}
}
```

Finally, the request is forwarded to `response.jsp`.

The Response and Banner JSP pages

By now, whether the user was registered or not, the request will have been forwarded to `response.jsp` and the TechSupportBean's properties will be fully populated with details of the user and their support request. `response.jsp` prints out a simple message, using a static `include` to incorporate the banner page footer, `banner.jsp`:

```
<%-- response.jsp --%>

<%@ page errorPage="/error.jsp" %>
<html>
<head><title>Customer Service Response</title></head>
<body>
<h1>Customer Service Request Received</h1>

<p>Thank you for your request, which has been recorded and will be
responded to within three business days.</p>

<%@ include file="/banner.jsp" %>

</body></html>
```

`banner.jsp` itself simply accesses the bean once more to extract and print the user's name:

```
<%-- banner.jsp --%>

<jsp:useBean id="techSupportBean" scope="session"
class="com.wrox.techsupport.TechSupportBean" />

<hr>
Current User:
<jsp:getProperty name="techSupportBean" property="firstName" />
```

```
<jsp:getProperty name="techSupportBean" property="lastName" />
<hr>
XYZ Corporation, Customer Service at 1.800.xyz.corp.<br>
```

Note how much more convenient it is to generate the banners using JSP than servlets (as in Chapter 7).

The Error Page

Finally, we provide a simple error page, error.jsp, which is referenced by all the JSP pages that might fail during processing:

```
<%-- error.jsp --%>

<%@ page isErrorPage="true" %>

<html>
<head>
  <title>XYZ Corporation, IT Department</title>
</head>
  <body>
    <h1>Technical Support</h1>

    <p>We're sorry, an error occurred processing your request.</p>

    <p>You got a <%= exception %>

  </body>
</html>
```

Deploying the Application

All that remains is to ensure that the necessary files are in the correct directories, and that the Java classes are compiled:

❑   The JSP and HTML pages are placed in the JSPTechSupport directory.

❑   Place web.xml, as usual, in the JSPTechSupport/WEB-INF directory. This ensures we have a valid web application that can be deployed in any container.

❑   The Java source file TechSupportBean.java goes in JSPTechSupport/src.

❑   Compile the Java source file into the JSPTechSupport/WEB-INF/classes directory by running the command:

```
javac -d ../WEB-INF/classes *.java
```

from the src directory.

❑   Now we need to create the WAR file for the application. Enter the following command in the JSPTechSupport folder:

```
jar -cvf JSPtechSupport.war *.*
```

We now need to start the J2EE server and the application deployment tool.

❑ Create a new application `JSPTechSupport.ear` and add the `JSPTechSupport.war` file as a new web archive.

❑ Now select the application and click on the Resource Refs tab. We now need to add a new resource reference. Enter the following values for the reference:

Coded Name: `jdbc/techSupportDB`
Type: `javax.sql.DataSource`
Authentication: `Container`
Sharable: Leave ticked (as default)
JNDI Name: `jdbc/TechSupport`

❑ Now deploy the application, entering `JSPTechSupport` for the context.

❑ Start the Cloudscape database and restart the J2EE server.

❑ Finally, we can navigate to http://localhost:8000/JSPTechSupport.

So, how have we fared in converting the Technical Support application to JSP? The use of a JavaBean to encapsulate the database access and application logic has avoided a lot of the pitfalls into which we might otherwise have fallen. The JSP pages divide cleanly into two groups:

❑ Those providing flow control and updating the application model, `techSupport.jsp` and `register.jsp`, which contain no HTML markup and do not create the response themselves.

❑ Pages made up largely of HTML, with only occasional action and expression tags: `regform.jsp`, `response.jsp`, `banner.jsp`, and `error.jsp`.

This clean architecture will provide a good basis for any future enhancements to the application.

JSP Design Strategies

So far we have talked about how JSP pages execute within a container, and the nuts and bolts of JSP tags and directives. Let's now look some of the design paradigms that can be used with JSP pages to ensure we develop clean and maintainable applications.

JSP pages are a great way of presenting dynamic content, but they don't solve all the problems of developing maintainable web applications. Experience has shown that using JSP pages to handle an application's entire web interface can create as many problems as it solves.

There is a real danger in using JSP pages inappropriately. Many JSP pages in production systems are hard to read and maintain. They often consist of Java code in scriptlets and HTML markup, with transitions between levels of abstraction that no experienced developer would tolerate in a Java application. While the Java language itself does a good job of helping developers to write maintainable code, JSP provides little help and much temptation to write messy code that does not support even procedural reuse.

The key issue is maintainability; it costs a lot more to maintain the average piece of software than to write it in the first place. It's important that JSP pages don't contain an excessive amount of Java content. If they contain a lot of scriptlets, they will pose a maintenance problem to both Java developers, who may not be expert in complex markup, and page designers, who may be confused by the Java and may inadvertently break it when tweaking the page's look and feel. Typically, this problem indicates that the underlying architecture is poorly designed.

Remember that JSP pages complement servlets: they do not replace them. Complex web applications will employ servlets and JSP pages in those tasks that they perform best.

Now that we are familiar with both servlets and JSP pages, let's review the strengths and weaknesses of each.

Servlets are the only choice for generating binary content. They are also better at performing control logic. Often we don't know exactly what should be displayed, or how it should be formatted, until we have performed processing that may involve access to enterprise data. For example, if we try and fail to access a database, we might want to display an entirely different view from that displayed on successful retrieval of data. To handle such situations, using a servlet **controller** to perform the processing, then forward to the appropriate JSP view is an elegant solution. (We'll discuss this terminology a little later.)

When we need to do some processing, before we know what we want to display and possibly how we should format it, a servlet is a better choice than a JSP. It can perform the processing before choosing a JSP view to forward the request to for the final display.

JSP pages are much better than servlets at displaying markup. This is because the generation of markup from Java code is awkward to program and hard to maintain. On the other hand, a JSP that consists largely of HTML or XML with a limited amount of embedded dynamic content is easy to read and maintain. In other words, JSP pages are best suited to use as **view** components. A view is a screen presentation of the state of a data **model**. Typically, the model will be a Java bean, accessed by a view JSP using the `<useBean>` standard action we've discussed.

When we know what we want to display and how we want to display it, and have all the data we need to display in the form of JavaBeans, a JSP view is the correct choice.

Application requirements vary in complexity, and there is no single correct solution for all problems. Having considered some of the issues, let's look at some of the major choices in JSP design, starting with simple, easy-to-program approaches.

There are two main approaches to JSP design:

- ❑ **Page-centric** designs. In these designs, requests are made directly to the JSP page that produces the response. These are sometimes referred to as **JSP Model 1** designs.

- ❑ **Controller** or dispatcher designs, in which the request is initially made to a JSP or a servlet that acts as a mediator or controller, dispatching requests to JSP pages and JavaBeans as appropriate. These are sometimes referred to as **JSP Model 2** designs.

Page-Centric or Client-Server Designs

In this approach, JSP pages or servlets access the enterprise resources (a database, for example) directly, or through a JavaBean, and generate the response themselves:

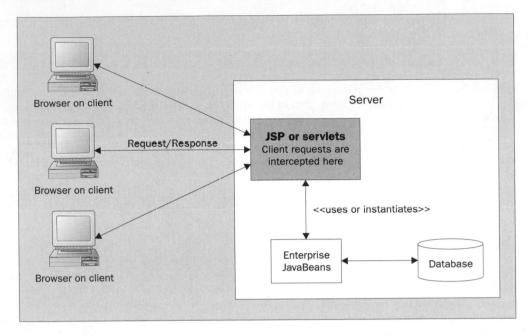

The advantage of such an approach is that it is simple to program and allows the page author to generate dynamic content easily, based upon the request and the state of the resources.

However this architecture does not cope well as application complexity increases, and indiscriminate use of it usually leads to excessive Java code embedded within the JSP pages.

There are two main variants here: the **Page-View** and **Page-View with Bean** architectures.

Page-View

This basic architecture involves direct request invocations to a JSP page made up of embedded Java code (scriptlets) and markup tags that dynamically generate output for substitution within the HTML.

It is very easy to get started, and is a low-overhead approach from a development standpoint. All of the Java code may be embedded within the HTML, so changes are confined to a limited area, reducing complexity. The figure below shows the architecture:

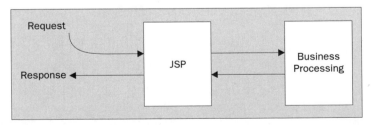

The big tradeoff here is in the level of sophistication. As the scale of the system grows, the limitations of this approach, such as including too much business logic in the page, surface. As we shall see, utilizing a mediating JSP or servlet and JavaBeans components allows us to separate developer roles more cleanly, and improves the potential for code reuse.

The Page-View architecture is handy for prototyping, as it is easy to get quick results. It is the approach most developers use when first learning JSP. However, it is too unsophisticated to be used in any but trivial real-world applications.

Page-View with Bean

This architecture is a refinement of the same basic approach when the Page-View architecture becomes too cluttered with business-related code and data access code. The architecture now evolves into a more sophisticated design, as shown in the figure below:

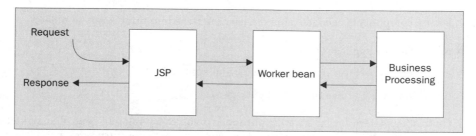

The Java code representing the business logic and simple data storage implementation has migrated from the JSP to the JavaBean worker. This refactoring leaves a much cleaner JSP with limited Java code, which can be comfortably owned by an individual in a web-production role, since it encapsulates mostly markup tags.

Additionally, a less technical individual could be provided with property sheets for the JavaBean workers, providing a listing of properties that are made available to the JSP page by the particular worker bean, and the desired property may simply be plugged into the JSP `<jsp:getProperty>` action to obtain the attribute value.

Moreover, we now have created a bean that a software developer can own, so that its functionality may be refined and modified without the need for changes to the HTML or markup within the JSP source page. We have created cleaner abstractions in our system by replacing implementation with intent.

The JSP Technical Support sample application we have just discussed used a form of the Page-View with Bean architecture.

The Front Controller Pattern

The Page-View with Bean approach is a significant improvement on the basic Page-View architecture. However, it still leaves JSP pages needing both to perform (or, at least, to initiate) request processing and to present content. These tasks are quite distinct for many pages, and request processing may be complicated.

If a JSP is a view, the idea that it should handle incoming requests to the application it belongs to is clearly flawed. How do we know that this JSP is the correct view in all cases? How should it react to recoverable errors? (Presenting an error page may be an over-reaction.) Some JSP pages may need to manipulate session, application-wide resources, or state before the response can be generated. Others may need to examine request values to check whether to redirect the request. Simply mapping request properties onto a bean (see the discussion of JSP beans below) is not a universal solution, especially if redirection may be required.

If you encounter these problems while creating a JSP web application, it is a clear indication that the design needs to be revisited. Fortunately, there is a well-known and elegant solution, often called the JSP Model 2 Architecture. More recently, when included in the catalog of Sun Java Center J2EE Patterns, it has been called the **Front Controller pattern**.

This is an attempt to apply the **Model-View-Controller (MVC)** architecture to web applications. The MVC architecture was first documented for Smalltalk user interfaces and has proven one of the most successful OO architectural patterns. (It is also the basis of Java's Swing interface packages.) MVC is discussed in Chapter 1 of the classic OO text *Design Patterns: Elements of Reusable Object-Oriented Software* (Gamma, Helm, Johnson and Vlissides, Addison-Wesley 1995, ISBN 0-201-63361-2).

MVC divides the components needed to build a user interface into three kinds of object:

❑ A model data or application object

❑ View objects to perform screen presentation of application

❑ A controller object to react to user input

The Front Controller pattern for Java web applications involves having one controller servlet or JSP as a single point of entry into a whole application or group of pages. This entry point produces no output itself but processes the request, optionally manipulates session and application state, and redirects requests to the appropriate JSP view or a sub-controller that knows how to handle a subset of all requests to the application. Models are provided by Java beans created or managed by the controller and made available to JSP views.

Front Controller implementations often include an action or similarly named parameter in each request. The value of this parameter is examined by the controller, which uses it to decide how to process the request. Alternatively, the controller JSP or servlet can intercept all incoming requests, and determine the appropriate processing strategy based on the request URL.

The Front Controller architecture is one of the most valuable approaches to building maintainable JSP systems. It is a true design pattern for JSP pages. Systems built using it tend to be more flexible and extensible than those using a page-centric approach, and achieve a much better separation of presentation and content.

Implementing a Front Controller Architecture

The request controller pattern can be implemented in one JSP consisting of a long scriptlet and no HTML generation, but this is inelegant. Java classes, not JSP pages, are the correct place for control logic. Compare, for example, the definition of methods in JSP pages and Java classes. JSP declaration syntax is inelegant, and allows no opportunity to use Javadoc, or to expose methods to other objects. A better alternative is to use a Servlet controller, or make a JSP controller delegate control logic to a controller class.

Let's consider a simple implementation of request controller architecture using a controller servlet. The minimal requirements will be:

❑ One controller servlet to handle all incoming requests and delegate processing to "request handler" helper classes. Note that the controller shouldn't do the processing itself, as this would make the application hard to extend.

❑   One request handler helper class to do the processing for each type of request. (A "type of request" will be defined by its URL within the application, or the value of a particular parameter.) The `RequestHandler` interface will define a single method, `handleRequest()`, that will do any necessary processing in response to a request and return the URL of the JSP view that should render the response. This will enable the controller to delegate request processing to this sub-controller, without knowing how the processing is implemented.

❑   A number of page or model beans to provide model data for JSP views.

❑   Some view JSP pages.

In more complex applications, a session object might be required. This would be created and accessed by request handler classes, and would not be manipulated by JSP pages. (Remember that a view shouldn't change the state of a system.)

There will be more view JSP pages than request handlers (one request handler may forward the response to different views, depending on the result of logic processing). There will be at most the same number of page beans as views.

At first sight this may look unnecessarily complex in comparison with a Page-Centric JSP Model 1 approach. There *are* more individual components; the virtue is that each component has clearly defined responsibilities, and Java classes and JSP pages are used where they are most appropriate. The greater conceptual complexity will prove far more manageable than the JSP code complexity that tends to result from adopting a less sophisticated approach.

Let's see how this might fit together by examining each component in turn.

Controller Servlet

There will be one instance of the application's controller servlet, which will handle all incoming requests. We can map all application URLs onto the controller servlet in a WAR's `web.xml` file, meaning that the application's public URLs will not correspond to physical JSP pages, but will be virtual.

The controller servlet won't know how to handle each individual request. Its main responsibility will be to decide which request handler helper class should handle each request, and to delegate request processing to it. If we put all our application logic in the controller, we'd end up with a monolithic, procedural class, and most likely, difficult-to-maintain chains of if/else statements. It would be hard to add new functionality. By using delegation, we can add new functionality very easily: new types of requests can be handled by additional request handlers. Request handlers are effectively sub-controllers.

The controller will choose a request handler for each request based on a set of mappings from request type to the request handler instances it maintains. These mappings might be based on request URL or the value of a special `"action"` parameter. Although we won't try to implement this in the simple example code here, these mappings should be defined outside Java code. A `.properties` file or XML configuration document would be ideal.

Delegating request processing to helper classes and using mappings will mean that the controller servlet will be generic; it won't need to be modified or recompiled as the functionality of a particular application changes. With different mappings, the same controller servlet could be used for many applications.

Request Handlers

Unlike the controller servlet, implementations of the `RequestHandler` interface (which we'll look at shortly) will be application-specific. Each request handler will perform the following steps:

- ❑ Examine the parameters of incoming requests

- ❑ Update application state if necessary

- ❑ Obtain any necessary data to display and make it available to views in the form of session or request attributes. (JSP pages will access these using `<jsp:useBean>` actions.)

- ❑ Choose a JSP view to which the controller will forward the response

Since `RequestHandler` implementations are Java classes, they can take full advantage of Java's object orientation. For example, an application might include an abstract `RequestHandler` implementation that retrieves the user's session state and calls a protected abstract method to be defined by subclasses to handle the request given the session state.

Like the controller servlet, `RequestHandler` implementations must be thread-safe, as they will be shared between many users.

Page Beans

These will be simple Java objects, constructed by request handlers and set as attributes in the request to make them accessible to view JSP pages using the `<jsp:useBean>` tag. Page beans won't do markup generation or execute any logic. They will be treated as read-only objects by JSP views and will provide the model data the views require.

JSP Views

The JSP views in this architecture will contain no workflow logic. The views will be given beans containing the data they need, and will simply display it, possibly using custom tags if the data is complex. They will have no need to examine request parameters; all choices will have been made before the JSP is called. They will not change the state of the system.

Yet JSP pages play a vital role in this architecture. They are ultimately responsible for all content generation.

Note that we'll need two sets of names in the cases where a request URL matches the natural view name. For example, let's suppose we have a login form, and the view for the form is `login.jsp`. If we map the URL `login.jsp` onto the controller servlets, we'll never be able to display the JSP view. Our preferred solution to this problem is to use `<pagename>.html` as the public URL, mapped onto the controller, and leave the `.jsp` URL as a view. There is no need to expose `.jsp` URLs publicly: if a resource generates HTML, it's best to make that clear in the URL.

Implementation

Now let's look at one possible implementation of this approach. First, let's consider the complete listing of the `RequestHandler` interface. This contains a single method, `handleRequest()`, which will be called by the controller:

```
package com.wrox.proj2ee.ch10;

import java.io.*;
import javax.servlet.*;
import javax.servlet.http.*;

public interface RequestHandler {

  /**
```

```
     * @return the URL of the view that should render the response
     * (probably a JSP), or null to indicate that the response has been
     * generated already and processing is complete.
     */
    String handleRequest(HttpServletRequest request,
                         HttpServletResponse response)
          throws ServletException, IOException;
}
```

The interface will be implemented by application-specific helper classes to which a controller servlet will delegate request processing.

The implementations of this interface will be the core of the web tier of our application and enable the controller to delegate application-specific logic. The return value of the `handleRequest()` method will probably be the URL within our application of a view JSP; in some cases it could be the URL of a static HTML page, or a servlet within the same web application. A return value of `null` will have a special meaning, indicating to the controller that the `RequestHandler` implementation built the response itself. This is necessary to support those cases when a JSP view *isn't* appropriate: for example, if we need to generate binary data.

The controller servlet will examine incoming requests, and call one of its registered request handlers for each. Let's choose the request handler to use based on the request's URL within the web application, as returned by calling the `HttpServletRequest.getServletPath()` method. The controller's `init()` method will build a hash table of `RequestHandler` instances, keyed by the request URL. If the controller doesn't find a handler for a particular request, it will send an HTTP response code 404 ("Not Found"). (Of course, in real applications we might want to be more helpful to the user in this situation. For example, a more sophisticated controller with access to the user's session state might call a non application-specific method asking the session state for the most appropriate view to prompt the user to continue their session.)

The `ControllerServlet` listing follows. Note that for the sake of simplicity we've hard-coded the initialization of the handler hash table in the `init()` method: this wouldn't happen in a real implementation, which would use an external configuration file and therefore avoid dependencies on application-specific classes. We've also used a `System.out.println` statement in the `doGet()` method to show the servlet path of incoming requests. A production application would use a logging package such as Apache log4J instead of relying on console output:

```java
package com.wrox.proj2ee.ch10;

import java.io.*;
import java.util.*;

import javax.servlet.*;
import javax.servlet.http.*;

/**
 * Simple fragment of a controller Servlet using
 * mappings from application URL to a number of
 * RequestHandler helper classes.
 */
public class ControllerServlet extends HttpServlet {

  // Hash table of RequestHandler instances, keyed by request URL
  private Map handlerHash = new HashMap();

  // Initialize mappings: not implemented here
  public void init() throws ServletException {
```

```
        // This will read mapping definitions and populate handlerHash
        handlerHash.put("/login.html", new
                        com.wrox.proj2ee.ch10.app.ShowRecordRequestHandler());
        handlerHash.put("/showInfo.html", new
                        com.wrox.proj2ee.ch10.app.ShowRecordRequestHandler());
    }


    /**
     * Based on the URL within our application, choose a RequestHandler
     * to handle the request and delegating processing to it.
     * Return an HTTP error code 404 (not found) if there's no RequestHandler
     * mapped to this URL.
     */
    public void doGet(HttpServletRequest request,
                      HttpServletResponse response)
                throws ServletException, IOException {

        System.out.println("Controller: servlet path is [" +
                            request.getServletPath() + "]");

        RequestHandler rh = (RequestHandler)
            handlerHash.get(request.getServletPath());
        if (rh == null) {
            response.sendError(HttpServletResponse.SC_NOT_FOUND);
        } else {
            // If we get to here, we have a handler for this request
            String viewURL = rh.handleRequest(request, response);
            if (viewURL == null) {

                // The RequestHandler has finished output: do nothing
            } else {

                // The RequestHandler told us the view to use
                // Forward the response to it
                request.getRequestDispatcher(viewURL).forward(request, response);
            }
        }
    }
}
```

Note that nothing in this class (besides the mapping initializations hard coded to simplify the example) is specific to a particular application.

The Java code for our application will reside in its request handler implementations. To illustrate what it might look like, imagine we're building a simple application that displays the data we hold about users in our data store (probably a relational database, but we won't make our JSP pages dependent on such a low-level detail).

The entry point to our application will be showInfo.html, which will prompt the user to enter their name if it isn't known to the system, and display their record if it is. There will be a page allowing the user to correct their name if no data is found for the submitted name.

The URL showInfo.html will be handled by one RequestHandler implementation. Each of these cases (username not submitted, data found for username, and username not found) will require a separate view. This is a good example of a crucial aspect of the request-controller architecture: one URL (and hence one request handler) may produce different views under different circumstances.

Let's call the required `RequestHandler` implementation `ShowRecordRequestHandler`. As data retrieval isn't web-specific, `ShowRecordRequestHandler` will use a helper class outside the web tier to perform the data lookup. A listing of the `ShowRecordRequestHandler` will look like this. To emphasize the distinction between generic controller functionality and application-specific code, this request handler and its support classes live in a separate package, `com.wrox.proj2ee.ch12.app`, from the controller class and `RequestHandler` interface:

```java
package com.wrox.proj2ee.ch10.app;

import java.io.*;
import javax.servlet.*;
import javax.servlet.http.*;

import com.wrox.proj2ee.ch12.*;

/**
 * Will show the data we hold about the user,
 * or force the user to enter their name so that we can
 * look them up
 */
public class ShowRecordRequestHandler implements RequestHandler {

  private DataStore dataStore;

  public ShowRecordRequestHandler() {
    dataStore = new DataStore();
  }

  /**
   * @return the the URL of the view that should render the response
   * (probably a JSP), or null to indicate that the response has been
   * output already and processing is complete.
   */
  public String handleRequest(HttpServletRequest request,
                              HttpServletResponse response)
              throws ServletException, IOException {
    String name = request.getParameter("name");
    if (name == null) {
      return "enterName.jsp";
    } else {
      // Do database lookup for the user
      DataBean dataBean = dataStore.getInfo(name);
      if (dataBean == null) {
        return "sorryNotFound.jsp";
      } else {
        // We have data for this user
        // Create model object based on retrieved data
        // DataModelBean dataBean = retrieve data and create object
        request.setAttribute("dataBean", dataBean);
        return "showInfo.jsp";
      }
    }
  }
}
```

The first task of this class is to examine the request and look for a name parameter. If no name parameter is found, `ShowRecordRequestHandler` will send the user to the "enter name" view. If a name parameter is present, `ShowRecordRequestHandler` will use a helper class to look up the data. If no data is found, it will send the user to the "not found" view.

The most interesting case is when data is retrieved for a user. In this case, we need to make this data available to the view JSP before returning its URL. We do this by creating a page bean to hold the data, and adding it to the request as an attribute. This will enable a JSP view to retrieve it using the `<jsp:useBean>` tag.

The implementation of the page bean is very simple: it's a Java bean exposing the necessary properties, and providing a convenience constructor taking all the required arguments:

```java
package com.wrox.proj2ee.ch10.app;

public class DataModelBean {

  // Holds value of property forename
  private String forename;

  // Holds value of property surname
  private String surname;

  // Holds value of property email
  private String email;

  // Creates new DataBean
  public DataModelBean() {
  }

  public DataModelBean(String forename,String surname,String email) {
    this.forename = forename;
    this.surname = surname;
    this.email = email;
  }

  /** Getter for property forename
   *  @return Value of property forename.
   */
  public String getForename() {
    return forename;
  }

  /** Setter for property forename
   *  @param forename New value of property forename.
   */
  public void setForename(String forename) {
    this.forename = forename;
  }

  /** Getter for property surname.
   * @return Value of property surname.
   */
  public String getSurname() {
    return surname;
  }

  /** Setter for property surname.
   * @param surname New value of property surname.
   */
  public void setSurname(String surname) {
    this.surname = surname;
  }
```

```
    /** Getter for property email.
     * @return Value of property email.
     */
    public String getEmail() {
      return email;
    }

    /** Setter for property email.
     * @param email New value of property email.
     */
    public void setEmail(String email) {
      this.email = email;
    }
  }
```

Since the data lookup process is not web-specific, we provide a helper class to implement it. Note that a real implementation of DataStore would look up an enterprise data source such as a database, or perhaps connect to an EJB server. In this case, we've simply populated the data values inline:

```
package com.wrox.proj2ee.ch10.app;

import java.util.*;

public class DataStore {

  // HashMap of DataModelBean objects keyed by user name
  private static Map dataMap = new HashMap();

  static {
    dataMap.put("rod", new DataModelBean("Rod", "Johnson",
                              "rod.johnson@interface21.com"));
    dataMap.put("detective", new DataModelBean("Sherlock", "Holmes",
                              "supersleuth@221b.co.uk"));
    dataMap.put("watson", new DataModelBean("John", "Watson",
                              "sidekick@221b.co.uk"));
  }

  // Creates new DataStore
  public DataStore() {
  }

  public DataModelBean getInfo(String username) {
    return (DataModelBean) dataMap.get(username);
  }
}
```

Don't feel that you need to use the <jsp:useBean> tag to instantiate JSP beans. Remember there is a very useful form of this tag that does not specify an implementing class, which throws an exception if no such object is defined in the HTTP session or request. Simply omit the class attribute of the <jsp:useBean> tag, and specify only the type, like this:

```
<jsp:useBean id="dataBean" scope="request" type="DataModelBean"/>
```

Beans used in such pages can be instantiated through a complete <jsp:useBean> tag in another JSP, or can be placed in the session or request by a controller.

As we are using a distinct layer of data objects as models, the same data objects could also be used to provide data for a Swing interface. Note that is advisable to retrieve all data before invoking any JSP views; a view shouldn't access data that is lazily loaded, as this might cause unexpected failures that cannot be handled by the controller. It is also important for views to avoid being dependent on data-source specific code.

The JSP page views will contain no logic. As each JSP view represents a particular outcome of the processing of a request, request controller architectures will typically require more JSP pages than Page-Centric JSP Model 1 designs.

Here are listings showing how the three JSP views might look. Of course, the HTML would be much more complex in a real application. But because these JSP pages contain no logic, a page designer could update them without altering application functionality.

showInfo.jsp is a dynamic page, taking information from the model bean created by the RequestHandler for the public URL showInfo.html:

```jsp
<%@page contentType="text/html"%>

<%-- Access bean placed in the request by ShowInfoRequestHandler --%>
<jsp:useBean id="dataModelBean"
  scope="request"
  type="com.wrox.proj2ee.ch10.app.DataModelBean" />

<html>
<head><title>Hello <%=dataModelBean.getForename()%></title></head>
<body>

Welcome <b><%=dataModelBean.getForename()%> <%=dataModelBean.getSurname()%></b>!

<p/>The email address we hold for you is
<i><%=dataModelBean.getEmail()%></i>

<p/>A real application would need to show more complex information...
Custom tags (see Chapter 11) can help to display more complex
data.

</body>
</html>
```

enterName.jsp is static. However, it's a good idea to make it a JSP in case we want to add dynamic content later:

```jsp
<%@page contentType="text/html"%>
<html>
<head><title>Log in</title></head>
<body>

<%-- Doesn't need a bean: in fact could be a static page --%>

<form method="GET" action="showInfo.html">
    Please enter your name:
    <input type="text" name="name" value="" />
</form>

</body>
</html>
```

Likewise, `sorryNotFound.jsp` is a static page:

```jsp
<%@page contentType="text/html"%>
<html>
<head><title>Sorry</title></head>
<body>

<%-- We could also use a bean here to hold the name the user submitted,
        which we couldn't look up --%>

Sorry, we couldn't find you in our database.
Maybe you entered your name incorrectly.
Please <a href="login.html">try again</a>.

</body>
</html>
```

The following simple `web.xml` file will register the controller servlet with the servlet engine, and map the public URLs (`login.html` and `showInfo.html`) to the controller:

```xml
<?xml version="1.0" encoding="UTF-8"?>

<!DOCTYPE web-app PUBLIC '-//Sun Microsystems, Inc.//DTD Web Application 2.3//EN'
'http://java.sun.com/dtd/web-app_2.3.dtd'>

<web-app>
  <display-name>MVC demo</display-name>
  <description>mvc-demo</description>

  <servlet>
    <servlet-name>controller</servlet-name>
    <servlet-class>com.wrox.proj2ee.ch10.ControllerServlet</servlet-class>
  </servlet>

  <servlet-mapping>
    <servlet-name>controller</servlet-name>
    <url-pattern>*.html</url-pattern>
  </servlet-mapping>

</web-app>
```

Now create a WAR file (`MVC.war`) containing all the files in the following directory structure:

```
MVC/
     enterName.jsp
     showInfo.jsp
     sorryNotFound.jsp
     WEB-INF/
             web.xml
             classes/
                     com/
                         wrox/
                             proj2ee/
                                     ch10/
                                          ControllerServlet.class
                                          requestHandler.class
                                          app/
                                              DataModelBean.class
                                              DataStore.class
                                              ShowRecordRequestHandler.class
```

Start up the J2EE server and then the deployment tool. Create a new application and add the WAR file to it. Now deploy the application giving the **Context Name** as MVC.

All requests to registered URLs will go to the ShowRecordRequestHandler. Requesting showInfo.html without providing a name parameter will cause ShowRecordRequestHandler to forward the response to enterName.jsp:

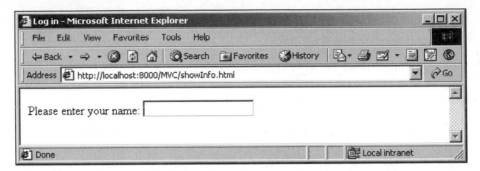

If an unrecognized name, such as daniel, is entered, ShowRecordRequestHandler will forward the response to sorryNotFound.jsp:

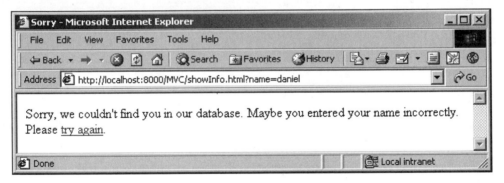

If a recognized name, such as detective, is entered, the user will see the details associated with that name. The ShowRecordRequestHandler will have looked up the data store, created a DataStoreBean object and made it available as a request attribute, before forwarding the request to showInfo.jsp:

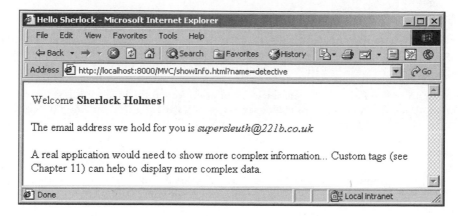

This example ignores the complexity of real application data and data access, but it implements the MVC architecture cleanly, making it easy to see how it could be enhanced to meet real-world requirements. It's clear where the additional code required would go: most likely, JDBC code in the `DataStore` class, additional properties on the `DataModelBean` class, and the exposure of additional properties (but without the introduction of control logic) in the JSP views. If any exception were encountered accessing data, it could be handled by the `DataStore` and `ShowRecordRequestHandler` Java classes. This means that we can code our JSPs without worrying about the need to handle low-level errors. (We could add another JSP, invoked in the event of a system error.)

Benefits

JSP pages produced using a front controller architecture will have the right level of responsibility, and scriptlets will only be necessary if they are genuinely concerned with presentation.

There are further benefits in running all application URLs through a single point of entry. For example, it is easy to implement consistent performance monitoring, logging, error reporting, and security.

I have led a team implementing a front controller architecture at a complex, high-volume web site. Our proprietary controller framework offers much richer functionality than that we've just seen, but the basic concepts are the same. A library of custom tags handles the presentation of complex data in JSP views. A hierarchy of request handlers abstracts common functionality, while the framework offers sophisticated management of session state. (Following the principle that views shouldn't manipulate application state, session objects are not accessible to JSP pages.) Through careful J2EE design, only web-specific application logic is included in the web tier.

The benefits have been substantial. All our applications use the same controller framework and basic structure:

- ❏ Almost all JSP pages can be maintained by the design team
- ❏ Security is handled by the controller and is transparent to JSP views
- ❏ Detailed performance and usage statistics are available for all applications without the need to write application-specific code
- ❏ The controller servlet handles error reporting transparently in a consistent manner

As you may have noticed, our simple example above does not attempt to handle errors. A realistic controller servlet will offer error logging and an analogous mechanism to JSP error pages.

Using a Generic Controller Framework

While it is important to understand the design involved and how to go about implementing it, a good option may be to use a generic request controller framework. Struts, from the Apache Project, is such a product, in open source. See http://jakarta.apache.org/struts/index.html for more details.

Struts aims to provide a flexible model-view-controller approach for Java web development. The most important component is a generic controller servlet, which is configured outside Java code, and which dispatches requests to `Action` classes provided by the application developer. (This approach is very similar to that we've just discussed.) Struts also provides handy custom tags, and support for data binding using Java reflection.

Struts is only just beginning to be widely used, but if it gains the interest (and contribution!) it deserves from Java web developers, it may deliver substantial benefits in productivity and maintainability.

Summary

We've talked about JSP syntax, constructs, and semantics, and have seen a complete application illustrating core JSP functionality. We've also discussed design paradigms for JSP applications.

There is still a lot to cover, but with what has been covered in this chapter, and your own knowledge of HTML, you can start to develop JSP-based dynamic web applications. JSP syntax isn't very complicated, so if you understand what was presented in this chapter you're ready to be productive with JSP pages. You should now understand:

- ❑ How a JSP is compiled into a servlet by the container
- ❑ The distinction between translation time and request time
- ❑ JSP directives and actions, and how to embed Java code and expressions in JSP pages
- ❑ How to use Java beans from JSP pages
- ❑ The implicit objects available to JSP pages, and the concept of object scope
- ❑ Issues and strategies for designing maintainable and extensible web applications that make best use of JSP

It is also worth keeping mind that writing JSP pages can sometimes be painful, especially without an IDE. This is mainly because debugging a JSP page is not as easy as debugging a Java program with `jdb` or your favorite debugger. You need to debug the generated servlet and relate it back to the JSP source; there are quite a few products now that allow you do this (such as Enhydra and JBuilder). Refer to the documentation with your servlet engine for information about its support for integrated debugging using popular IDEs.

In the next chapter, we will move on to look at a major feature of the JSP specification: **tag extensions**. Tag extensions, like JavaBeans, help us to avoid having excessive Java code content in JSP pages. They not only add rich functionality to the standard JSP syntax, but also promote application maintainability.

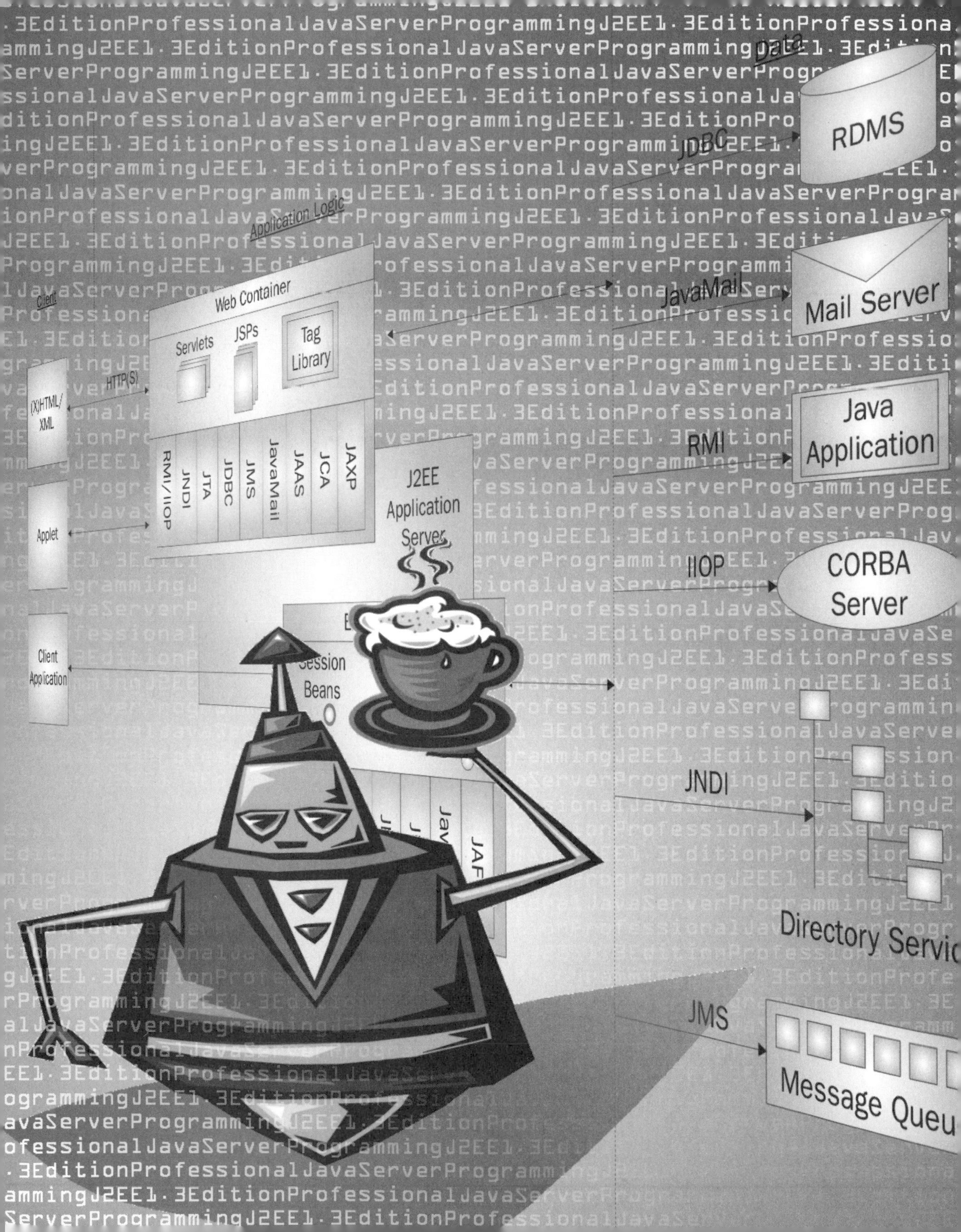

11

JSP Tag Extensions

Probably the most important addition to the JSP 1.1 specification was support for **tag extensions** (or **custom tags**). This support is further enhanced in the JSP 1.2 specification, confirming tag extensions as one of the most important features of JSP.

Tag extensions look a lot like standard HTML or XML tags embedded in a JSP page, but they have a special meaning to the JSP engine at translation time, and allow custom functionality to be invoked without having to write Java code within scriptlets. This allows a JSP developer to invoke application functionality without having to know any of the details of the underlying Java code. Tag libraries also offer portable runtime support, authoring/modification support, and validation.

In this chapter, we'll look at the basics of writing our own tags, including:

- ❑ The basic ideas of tag extensions
- ❑ The anatomy of a tag extension
- ❑ How to deploy a tag library
- ❑ How to create custom tag extensions
- ❑ The enhancements to tag extension support in the JSP 1.2 specification

We'll begin by looking at what we can accomplish with tag extensions.

Tag Extensions

Let's consider the `<jsp:forward>` standard action that is provided by the JSP specification. This tag dispatches the current request to another JSP page within the current web application. It can be invoked with the following syntax:

```
<jsp:forward page="next.jsp" />
```

We can also add additional parameters to the request before forwarding it, by using a version of `<jsp:forward>` that has one or more `<jsp:param>` tags nested within it:

```
<jsp:forward page="next.jsp" >
  <jsp:param name="image" value="house.gif" />
  //...
</jsp:forward>
```

Tag extensions allow a vast range of new functionality to be added to JSP pages and they can be invoked in an intuitive way, similar to that of standard actions. For example, we could create a tag named `<wrox:forward>`, specify what attributes and sub-tags (if any) it requires, and implement it so that it performs a custom action before forwarding the current request to a new JSP page. Not only can such tags be added simply into a JSP page, they encourage the separation of code and presentation, because the call is decoupled from the class that implements the functionality associated with the tag.

The key concepts of tag extensions are:

❑ **Tag name**
A JSP tag is uniquely identified in a page by a combination of a **prefix** (in this case `jsp`), and **suffix** (in this case `forward`), separated by a colon. The prefix identifies a **tag library** (analogous to an XML namespace) and the suffix identifies a particular tag in that library.

❑ **Attributes**
Tags may have **attributes** (which use XML attribute syntax). Our `<jsp:forward>` tag has one attribute (`page`), while the `<jsp:param>` tag has two (`name` and `value`). Attributes can be required or optional.

❑ **Nesting**
Tag extensions can detect nesting at run time and cooperate. A tag directly enclosing another tag is the **parent** of the tag it encloses. In our example, the `<jsp:forward>` tag is the parent of the `<jsp:param>` tag. Any tag enclosing another tag, directly or more distantly, is an **ancestor** of the enclosed tag.

❑ **Body content**
The body content is anything between the start and end elements in a JSP tag, excluding sub-tags. A tag extension can access and manipulate its body content.

❑ **Scripting variables**
Tags can define variables that can be used within the JSP page in tag body content or (depending on the scope of the variables) after the tag has been closed. The `<jsp:useBean>` standard action is an example of a tag that defines a scripting variable available throughout the remainder of the JSP.

> One or more Java classes implement the functionality of a tag. The tag handler (the class that implements the tag itself) is a JavaBean, with properties matching the tag's attributes. A Tag Library Descriptor (TLD) file is an XML document that describes a tag library, which can contain one or more tag extensions. The JSP **taglib** directive must be used to import the tag library's tags in each JSP page that wishes to use any of them.

Why, besides a clever syntax, might we choose to use tag extensions rather than JavaBeans in our JSP pages? How are tag extensions more than just another way of allowing JSP pages to parcel out work to Java classes?

Due to the rich interaction between the host JSP page and tag extensions, we can use tag extensions to achieve what beans can only achieve in conjunction with scriptlets. Tag extensions can access the implicit `pageContext` object, write to the output writer, redirect the response, and define scripting variables. As an indication of their power, all the standard JSP actions provided via tags of form `<jsp:XXXX>` could be implemented using tag extensions if we wished.

Tag extensions can be used to deliver a range of functionality that is limited only by developers' imaginations (and of course, sensible programming practice). Some of the typical uses of tag extensions are to:

❑ Conceal the complexity of access to a data source or enterprise object from the page author, who may not be experienced with enterprise data

❑ Introduce new scripting variables into the page

❑ Filter or transform tag content, or even interpret it as another language

❑ Handle iteration without the need for scriptlets

Tag extensions differ from JavaBeans in that they are common building blocks, rather than tailored resources for a particular page or group of pages. Tags receive the attributes that control their behavior from the JSP page using them, not from the request to a particular JSP page (as in the case of request-bean property mappings). Consequently, a well-designed tag extension may be used in many JSP pages.

This reusability is particularly important. Since the implementation and interaction between tag extensions and the JSP engine is well defined in the JSP specification, libraries of tag extensions can be developed and distributed. Generic tags can be developed for particular industries or application types. Many vendors currently offer such tag libraries, often as part of a larger product such as an application server.

Tag extensions, although introduced only in JSP 1.1, are an established concept in dynamic page generation. Products such as ColdFusion and Apple's WebObjects have delivered rich functionality through custom tags for many years (albeit in a proprietary context) and this experience in the use of custom tags can be valuable resource to JSP developers.

Tag extensions are a particularly welcome addition to the JSP developer's armory because they are easy to implement. The API surrounding them is relatively simple, and it's possible to use them to achieve results quickly and easily. This is a reflection of the elegance of the design of the tag extension mechanism – in true Java spirit it delivers rich functionality without excessive complexity

The examples and most of the discussion in this chapter and the next assume that tag extensions will be used to generate HTML or XHTML markup. While this is currently their most likely use, tag extensions can be used to generate any content type supported by JSP. However, this doesn't include binary content types: servlets should be used to generate non-text output.

JSP 1.2 Tag Extension Enhancements

Before we look in detail at the tag extension infrastructure, let's quickly review the changes between JSP 1.1 and JSP 1.2.

If you haven't worked with tag extensions in JSP 1.1, you might want to skip this section for now. However, as JSP 1.2 containers must support JSP 1.1 tag libraries, you'll find this summary relevant in the future if you're called upon to maintain existing code.

The significant changes are:

❑ The authors of the specification have tried to make the tag extension API more powerful, and easier to use. There are two new tag handler interfaces: `IterationTag`, which makes it easier to develop simple tag handlers that repeatedly evaluate their body content; and `TryCatchFinally`, which helps handle errors.

❑ It is now possible to declare scripting variables in a tag library descriptor, rather than by using a `TagExtraInfo` class.

❑ It is now possible to perform sophisticated validation at translation time of the use of tags in a library, based on the entire structure of each JSP page attempting to use one or more tags from the library. This is done using the new `TagLibraryValidator` class.

❑ New elements have been added to the TLD to accommodate these changes. In a non-functional change, the names of many elements have changed to include hyphens: for example, `tlibversion` becomes `tlib-version`.

❑ Support has been added in the TLD for the **application lifecycle events** introduced in the Servlet 2.3 specification. Tag libraries can include application-event listeners, which will be notified of events such as a change in servlet context attributes.

The good news is that all the changes are backward compatible as the new API is a superset of the JSP 1.1 tag extension API and JSP 1.2-compliant servlet engines are required to accept tag libraries using the old API and the JSP 1.1 TLD DTD. However, this doesn't mean that the 1.1 and 1.2 versions of TLD DTDs are compatible. The DTDs differ slightly in structure and significantly in element names. So, when maintaining a JSP 1.1 tag library, we have two choices: we can leave the TLD in the 1.1 DTD and make the required changes as if we were running JSP 1.1; or we can choose to upgrade the DTD to the JSP 1.2 DTD before making the changes. The deciding factors will probably be whether or not we would like to use any of the new JSP 1.2 features, and whether any JSP 1.1 installations will still require the tag library.

Note that although we can use those elements of the JSP 1.2 API accessible from the 1.1 DTD (such as the `IterationTag` interface) in a tag library declared with a JSP 1.1 DTD. This may prove confusing to users of your tag library and should be avoided.

A Simple Tag

Before we look at the tag extension API and the supporting infrastructure in detail, let's implement a simple tag. The simplest case is a tag without attributes or body content, which outputs some HTML. We'll also add some dynamic content to prove that the tag is working and doing something. Our aim is to create a tag that creates the following output (the angle brackets enclose dynamic information supplied at run time):

Hello world.
My name is <tag handler implementation class> and it's <date and time>

We'll call our simple tag `hello`, and here's how we might use it in a JSP page. The first line is a declaration used to import the tag library, which we will discuss in detail later:

```
<%@ taglib uri="/hello" prefix="examples" %>

<html>
  <head>
```

```
       <title>First custom tag</title>
    </head>

    <body>

      <p>This is static output. Tag output is shown in italics.</p>
      <p><i>
        <examples:hello>
        </examples:hello>
      </i></p>

      <p>Closing the tag without a body will have the same effect:</p>
      <p><i>
        <examples:hello />
      </i></p>

      <p>This is static template data again.</p>

    </body>
</html>
```

To implement the tag we need to define a tag handler (a Java class implementing the tag's functionality), and provide a tag library descriptor. We can then import the tag library into any JSP page that requires it.

The tag handler class must react to callbacks from the JSP engine when it encounters tags in JSP pages at run time. The most important of these callbacks are doStartTag(), which is called when the opening of the tag is encountered, and doEndTag(), which is called when the closing tag is encountered. The implementation of HelloTag is very simple, as most of the work of implementing the custom tag is done by the TagSupport superclass provided by the JSP API. Don't worry if some of the details are puzzling: we'll look at this class, as well as the API it uses, in more detail in a moment.

```
package tagext;

import java.io.IOException;
import java.util.Date;
import javax.servlet.jsp.*;
import javax.servlet.jsp.tagext.TagSupport;
```

The TagSupport superclass is a convenience class provided in the tag extension API. It already implements the javax.servlet.jsp.tagext.Tag interface:

```
public class HelloTag extends TagSupport {

  public int doStartTag() throws JspTagException {
    return EVAL_BODY_INCLUDE;
  }
```

The doStartTag() method will be called when the JSP engine encounters the start of a tag implemented by this class:

```
public int doEndTag() throws JspTagException {
  String dateString = new Date().toString();
  try {
```

We obtain the current `JspWriter` from the tag's context and write to it:

```
        pageContext.getOut().write("Hello world.<br/>");
        pageContext.getOut().write("My name is " + getClass().getName() +
                            " and it's " + dateString + "<p/>");
    } catch (IOException ex) {
    throw new JspTagException(
            "Fatal error: hello tag could not write to JSP out");
    }
```

The `doStartTag()` method returns a value indicating whether or not to evaluate any body content this tag may have. The legal return values are `EVAL_BODY_INCLUDE` (meaning to evaluate the tag's body content and any sub-tags) and `SKIP_BODY` (meaning tag contents will be ignored):

```
    return EVAL_PAGE;
    }
}
```

The `doEndTag()` method will be called when the JSP engine encounters the end of a tag implemented by this class. It returns a value indicating whether or not the engine should evaluate the remainder of the JSP page. The legal return values are `EVAL_PAGE` (the usual case), and `SKIP_PAGE`.

The tag library descriptor, which we'll name `hello.tld`, maps the tag to the tag handler class and defines the way JSP pages may interact with the `HelloTag` class:

```
<?xml version="1.0" encoding="ISO-8859-1" ?>

<!DOCTYPE taglib
        PUBLIC "-//Sun Microsystems, Inc.//DTD JSP Tag Library 1.2//EN"
        "http://java.sun.com/dtd/web-jsptaglibrary_1_2.dtd">

<taglib>
  <tlib-version>1.0</tlib-version>
  <jsp-version>1.2</jsp-version>
  <short-name>examples</short-name>
  <description>Simple example library. Author: Rod Johnson</description>

  <tag>
    <name>hello</name>
    <tag-class>tagext.HelloTag</tag-class>
    <body-content>JSP</body-content>
    <description>
      Simple hello world example.
      Takes no attributes, and simply generates HTML
    </description>
  </tag>
</taglib>
```

The tag's suffix when used in any JSP must be `hello`, and its prefix is `examples` when imported into this JSP page. So, to use the tag in a JSP we should use `<examples:hello>`.

As a tag library can include any number of tags, we'll simply add extra `<tag>` elements to this tag library descriptor for the remaining examples in this chapter.

We'll discuss deployment options for tag libraries in more detail later, but in the meantime, let's look at how we can get this example running in the J2EE Reference Implementation. We need to package the tag library descriptor, the Java classes that implement the tags in the library, and the JSP pages that use the tags in a WAR. This is the structure of the WAR file for this simple example is:

```
hello.jsp
WEB-INF/
        web.xml
        classes/
                tagext/
                        HelloTag.class
        tlds/
            hello.tld
```

There are a few WAR conventions specific to using tag libraries. We should place our tag library descriptor files in the WEB-INF/tlds directory and the web.xml file includes a map to let the server know where to find the URIs and the TLD resource path. The map is described using the <taglib> tag.

This is the web.xml file for our simple example:

```xml
<?xml version="1.0" encoding="UTF-8"?>

<!DOCTYPE web-app PUBLIC '-//Sun Microsystems, Inc.//DTD Web Application 2.2//EN'
'http://java.sun.com/j2ee/dtds/web-app_2.2.dtd'>

<web-app>
  <display-name>tagext</display-name>
  <description>Tag extensions examples</description>

  <session-config>
    <session-timeout>0</session-timeout>
  </session-config>

  <taglib>
    <taglib-uri>/hello</taglib-uri>
    <taglib-location>/WEB-INF/tlds/hello.tld</taglib-location>
  </taglib>

</web-app>
```

To package our WAR, run the following command from within %BOOK_HOME%\Ch11\ Note that we exclude the .java source files as they would unnecessarily inflate our WAR and can cause problems at deployment time:

```
jar -cvf hello.war WEB-INF/classes/tagext/*.class WEB-INF/tlds/hello.tld
    WEB-INF/web.xml *.jsp
```

Start up the J2EE server, and the deployment tool. Then follow these steps to deploy our WAR to the server:

- ❑ Create a new application, call it something descriptive – we used JSPTags
- ❑ Select File | Add to Application | Web WAR, and select hello.war
- ❑ Set the context root of our application to /tagext
- ❑ Deploy the application to the server

> **As we create new JSP pages and tag extensions you will have to rerun these steps and re-deploy the application to the J2EE server.**

If you navigate to http://localhost:8000/tagext/hello.jsp, you should see something like:

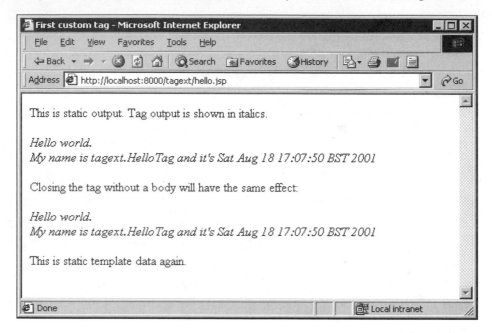

If we fail to close the tags in our JSP page, or try to access tags that are not found in the imported tag library, an error will occur. The resulting error messages are not specified in the JSP specification, but most implementations should be reasonably informative and helpful. If a server simply returns a page reporting an HTTP response code 500 (Internal Server Error), it is usually instructive to look in the server's log files for more information.

WARs are portable, so even though other JSP engines will use different deployment conventions to those of the RI, the WAR itself will not need to change.

Anatomy of a Tag Extension

The minimal requirement to implement a tag extension is a tag handler class and a tag library descriptor.

❑   A **tag handler** is a JavaBean that implements one of three interfaces defined in the `javax.servlet.jsp.tagext` package: `Tag`, `IterationTag`, or `BodyTag`. These interfaces define the lifecycle events relevant to a tag and most importantly, the calls that the class implementing the tag will receive when the JSP engine encounters the opening and closing tags.

❑   A **tag library descriptor** or **TLD**, which is an XML document that contains information about one or more tag extensions.

An additional class may also be specified in the TLD that performs custom validation of tag attributes. Of course, the classes implementing a tag may use any number of helper classes, which will also need to be packaged with the tag so that it is a complete deployable unit.

Before tags can be used in a JSP, the `taglib` directive must be used to import a tag library and associate the tags it contains with a prefix.

Let's look at each of these requirements in turn.

Tag Handlers

When the JSP engine encounters a tag extension in a JSP page at translation time, it parses the tag library descriptor to find the required tag handler class, and generates code to obtain, and interact with, the tag handler. The interface implemented by the tag handler defines callbacks that the servlet (created from the JSP page) will make to the tag handler instance at run time.

For performance reasons, JSP engines will not necessarily instantiate a new tag handler every time a tag is encountered in a JSP page. Instead, they may maintain a pool of tag instances, which can be reused where possible. When a tag is encountered in a JSP page, the JSP engine will try to find a `Tag` instance that is not being used, initialize it, use it, and finally free it (but not destroy it), leaving it available for further use. The programmer has no control over any pooling that may occur.

While the repeated use model is similar to a servlet lifecycle, note one very important difference: tag handler implementations don't need to concern themselves with thread safety. The JSP engine will not use an instance of a tag handler to handle a tag unless it is free. This is good news: as with JSP authoring in general, developers need to worry about threading issues less often than when developing servlets. After all invocations of the tag handler are completed, the container will invoke the tag handler's release() method. This will free any remaining resources and prepare the tag handler for garbage collection. Many tags do not need to implement the release() method, and can simply rely on the empty default implementation inherited from the abstract superclasses provided by the tag extension API.

The javax.servlet.Jsp.tagext.Tag Interface

The `Tag` interface defines a simple interaction between the JSP engine and the tag handler, which is sufficient for tags that don't need to manipulate their body content or evaluate it repeatedly. Its core methods are the calls received when the JSP engine encounters the tag's opening and closing tags: `doStartTag()` and `doEndTag()`. Before we look at the method contracts in more detail, a sequence diagram helps to visualize the calls made to the tag handler by the compiled servlet. Assume that the container already has a tag handler instance available, and is in the default state:

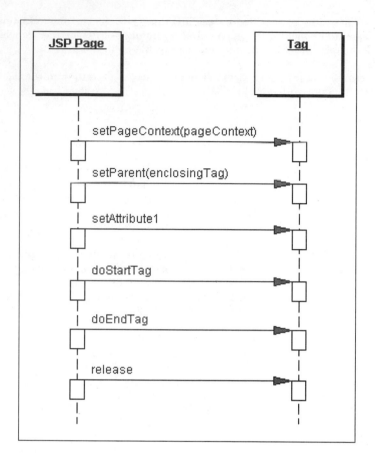

Let's look at the messages in more detail:

- ❑ The container initializes the tag handler by setting the tag handler's pageContext property, which the tag handler can use to access information available to the JSP page using it.

- ❑ The container sets the tag handler's parent property. (The parent will be set to null if the tag is not enclosed in another tag.)

- ❑ Any tag attributes defined by the developer will be set. This is a mapping from the XML attributes of the tag to the corresponding properties of the tag handler bean. For example, in the case of a tag invoked like this: <mytags:test name="John" age="43" />, the container will attempt to call the setName() and setAge() methods on the tag handler. The container will attempt to convert each attribute to the type of the corresponding bean property: for example, the string "43" would be converted to an int in this case. If the type conversion fails, an exception will be thrown and must be handled by the calling JSP page. (From the JSP page's point of view, there is no difference between an exception thrown by a tag handler and one thrown by an expression of a scriptlet in the page.)

- ❑ The container calls the tag handler's doStartTag() method and then the doEndTag() method.

❑ This message may not occur after all tag invocations. The container calls the `release()` method. Tag handlers differ from page beans in that their lifecycle is entirely independent of that of the JSP pages that use them. Tag handlers must support repeated use before destruction, possibly in a number of JSP pages. The implementation of the `release()` method must ensure that any resources required during the tag's execution are freed. The JSP specification states that `release()` is guaranteed to be called before the tag handler is eligible for garbage collection. The specification also states that there may be multiple calls to `doStartTag()` and `doEndTag()` before release is called. Whether a tag handler instance will ever be invoked again after `release()` has been called is not entirely clear from the specification, but it appears to imply that it will not be.

Lets look at the `doStartTag()` and `doEndTag()` methods:

`int doStartTag() throws JspException`

This is called after the tag has been initialized, when the JSP engine encounters the opening of a tag at run time. Its return value should be one of two constants defined in the `Tag` interface: `EVAL_BODY_INCLUDE`, which instructs the JSP engine to evaluate both the tag's body and any child tags it has, or `SKIP_BODY`, which instructs the JSP engine to ignore the body. This method can throw a `JspException`, (as will most of the methods in the tag handler API when an error condition is encountered) but how it will be handled will depend on the JSP page using the tag. Most JSP pages will use an error page, so an exception thrown in a tag will typically abort the rendering of the page.

`int doEndTag() throws JspException`

`doEndTag()` is called when the JSP engine encounters the closing tag of an element at run time. Its return value can be `EVAL_PAGE` or `SKIP_PAGE`. `EVAL_PAGE` will cause the JSP engine to evaluate the rest of the page, `SKIP_PAGE` to terminate evaluation of the page. The `SKIP_PAGE` return value should be used only with very good reason as using tag handlers to terminate page evaluation can be confusing, and there will usually be a better way to implement the required functionality. One legitimate use might be to terminate page output if it is established that the user has insufficient privileges to view the whole of the page.

There are also a number of methods that relate to tag nesting, initialization, and reuse:

`Tag getParent()`
`void setParent()`

The specification also requires methods to expose the `parent` property. A tag's parent is the tag that directly encloses it in a JSP. Tag implementations can query their parent at run time, in order to obtain context information:

`void setPageContext (PageContext pc)`

`setPageContext()` is an initialization method that makes the `PageContext` of the JSP available to the tag.

`void release()`

`release()` is a call to the tag handler to release any resources, perhaps to close a JDBC connection or open a socket that the handler requires for its function. The implementation of the `release()` method must not assume anything about the state of the tag handler's properties; the specification states that when `release()` is invoked, all properties will have been reset to an unspecified value. The API also provides a class `TagSupport` that implements the `Tag` interface and provides default empty methods for the methods defined.

The javax.servlet.jsp.tagext.IterationTag Interface

The `IterationTag` interface has been added in JSP 1.2, and extends the `Tag` interface. It provides a single new method that allows the tag to repeat the evaluation of the tag body content:

```
int doAfterBody() throws JspException
```

`doAfterBody()` is called each time the tag's body has been processed (where `doEndTag()` would have been called in the case of an implementation of the `Tag` interface). The valid return values of `doAfterBody()` are `EVAL_BODY_AGAIN` and `SKIP_BODY`. A return value of `EVAL_BODY_AGAIN` directs the JSP engine to evaluate the tag's body and any child tags again, resulting in at least one more call to this method. A return value of `SKIP_BODY` causes the processing of body content to terminate, which can be used to conditionally loop through the tag content.

In JSP 1.1, it was necessary to use the `BodyTag` interface to perform iteration. The introduction of the much simpler `IterationTag` interface is good news, as the `BodyTag` interface introduces unnecessary complexity in the case of simple looping constructs.

The javax.servlet.jsp.tagext.BodyTag Interface

`BodyTag` extends `IterationTag`, adding extra callbacks and other methods and allowing the developer to work with the tag's body content.

In JSP 1.1, BodyTag extended Tag. However the change is backward compatible, as the doAfterBody() method has merely been moved from BodyTag into the new IterationTag interface.

A sequence diagram that displays the interaction between calling JSP and tag handler in the case of a body tag is much more complex than that of the `Tag` interface:

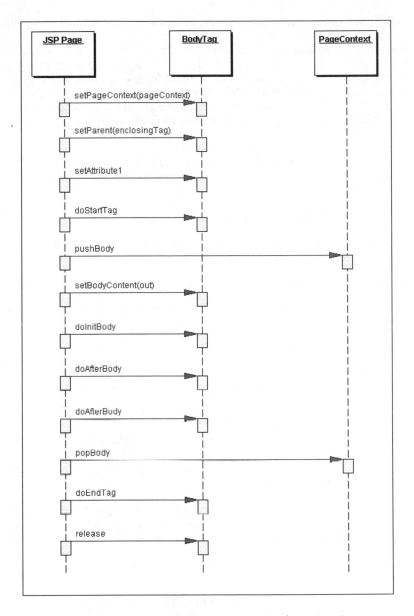

The extra steps (compared to the invocation of the Tag interface) involve the preservation of the JSP page's JSPWriter (messages 5 and 10), and the possibility of repeated calls to the doAfterBody() method, which enables the BodyTag implementation to take control of the tag's execution at run time.

Some of the inherited methods of the BodyTag interface use different return values to support the richer functionality. The following is a discussion of the most important methods, both those that are new and those with enhanced functionality:

```
int doStartTag() throws JspException
```

This is called when the opening tag is encountered, as for the simpler tag interfaces. However, the meaning of the return values differs. Three return values are supported in JSP 1.2: SKIP_BODY, in which case the body content will be ignored; EVAL_BODY_INCLUDE, which has the same meaning as in an IterationTag; and EVAL_BODY_BUFFERED. Returning EVAL_BODY_BUFFERED causes a BodyContent object to be created to buffer the results of body evaluation and support later manipulation by the tag handler. If EVAL_BODY_BUFFERED is returned, the developer is responsible for actually outputting the body content, probably in the doEndTag() method. It is the possibility of BodyContent buffering that allows a BodyTag to transform or suppress its body content.

> *In JSP 1.1, the only way to evaluate the body content was by returning the now deprecated constant EVAL_BODY_TAG. This had the same effect as the new EVAL_BODY_BUFFERED constant. In JSP 1.1 it was not possible for a BodyTag to work like an IterationTag: the developer always had to output the body content in the doEndTag() method.*

void setBodyContent(BodyContent bodyContent)

This initialization method is used to set the object used to manipulate body content. It is only invoked if doStartTag() returned EVAL_BODY_BUFFERED.

int doInitBody() throws JspException

Like setBodyContent(), this method is invoked by the JSP engine only if doStartTag() returned EVAL_BODY_BUFFERED. In this case, it is invoked after setBodyContent().

int doAfterBody() throws JspException

This method is inherited from the IterationTag interface and works in the same way. As for IterationTags, valid return values are EVAL_BODY_AGAIN and SKIP_BODY.

The javax.servlet.jsp.tagext.BodyContent Class

The BodyContent class is the key to the buffered BodyTag functionality. BodyContent is a subclass of JspWriter that can be used to manipulate the body content of BodyTag implementations and store it for later retrieval. The getBodyContent() method of BodyTagSupport returns the BodyContent instance associated with a particular tag.

To understand how the BodyContent class works, consider how JspWriter objects are handled in JSP pages using BodyTags (messages 5 and 10 from the previous sequence diagram). Before the BodyTag begins to evaluate its body content, the generated JSP implementation class includes the following line:

```
out = pageContext.pushBody();
```

After the BodyTag's methods have been called, it includes a matching call:

```
out = pageContext.popBody();
```

What this means is that each BodyTag is able to manipulate its BodyContent without automatically affecting the JspWriter of the enclosing JSP page (or tag). To generate output, the BodyTag needs to write the contents of its BodyContent into its enclosing writer explicitly (see below). This is the key difference between BodyTag and Tag implementations. Tag implementations have no such flexibility, and so cannot modify or suppress their body content. They can, however, prevent it from being evaluated altogether by returning SKIP_BODY in the implementation of doStartTag().

The most interesting methods in the `BodyContent` class are:

`void clearBody()`

This clears the body content, which is useful if we want to manipulate the body content before writing it out.

`JspWriter getEnclosingWriter()`

This returns the enclosing `JspWriter`, which may be the writer of an enclosing tag, or the writer of a JSP page itself. We normally use this method to get a `JSPWriter` to which we can write the body content stored in a body tag when we have finished manipulating it. For example, we might use the following lines of code in the `doEndTag()` method of a `BodyTag` subclass to obtain the tag's body content and output it (in this case, unchanged):

```
BodyContent bodyContent = getBodyContent();
if (bodyContent != null) {
  bodyContent.getEnclosingWriter().write(sbOut.toString());
}
```

This ensures that if there is any body content held in the tag, it will be written to the enclosing JSP writer.

`String getString()`

This method returns the content already held in the `BodyContent` object, as a `String`. We can call this in any callback method to find out the cumulative results of evaluation. Calling `getString()` followed by `clearBody()` in the `doAfterBody()` callback of `BodyTag` allows us to examine, in turn, the result of each evaluation of the tag's body content.

Convenience Classes

Some of the methods from the `Tag`, `IterationTag`, and `BodyTag` interfaces will be implemented the same way in most tags, so the `javax.servlet.jsp.tagext` package includes two convenience implementations for `Tag` and `BodyTag`: `TagSupport` and its subclass `BodyTagSupport`. Classes that implement tag extensions will normally be derived from one of these. The class diagram below shows the relationship between these classes and the `Tag` and `BodyTag` interfaces:

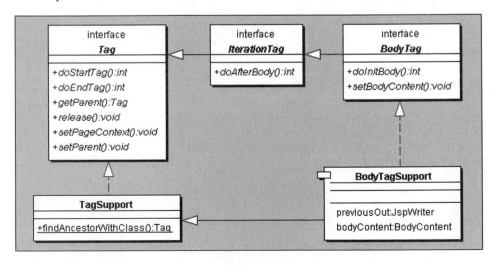

TagSupport and BodyTagSupport are concrete, rather than abstract classes. As such they provide complete implementations of the corresponding interfaces. These implementations do nothing except return the appropriate values that allow the JSP engine to continue rendering the page. Therefore developers can safely omit methods that they are not interested in. For instance, developers don't usually concern themselves with handling the parent property and setPageContext(). The release() method can also be omitted if it is not necessary to free resources. The methods that a developer will normally want to override are doStartTag() and doEndTag() for all tags; doAfterBody() for IterationTags and BodyTags; and doInitBody() for BodyTags.

TagSupport also makes an important convenience variable available to subclasses: pageContext (the saved PageContext that was set by the JSP engine when the tag was first used in a page). The doStartTag() method of BodySupportTag returns EVAL_BODY_BUFFERED and produces the same behavior as BodyTagSupport offered in JSP 1.1, automatically capturing the output in a BodyContent object. BodyTagSupport provides a getBodyContent() method, making it possible to obtain the buffered content and manipulate it.

There is no convenience implementation of the IterationTag interface, as it adds only one new method to Tag, doAfterBody(), which always needs to be implemented by the tag developer. However, the TagSupport class can be used as the superclass of an IterationTag.

Objects Available to Tag Handlers

All tag handlers have automatic access to more context information than that available to JavaBeans used in JSP pages. This is available through the PageContext object tag handlers that are passed on initialization. As you'll recall, javax.servlet.jsp.PageContext is a convenient holder for information about the runtime of a JSP page, including the request and response objects, and references to objects such as beans used by the JSP page.

This amount of access equals power. Note, though, that it is poor style to modify the request and response objects directly from a tag handler. Custom tags should be thought of as generic building blocks intended for use in a wide variety of contexts and should not be concerned with the parameters passed to the JSP page. Although a tag handler *can* access request parameters, relying on doing so will greatly reduce its reusability.

The Simple Example Revisited

To catch our breath after all this theory, let's look again at the Java implementation of the simple example we introduced earlier. We see that the tag handler extends TagSupport, and so gets most of its functionality already implemented. It has no state and accesses no file or other resources, so there is no need to override the release() method. We simply use doEndTag() to access the PageContext, obtain a JspWriter, and generate output:

```
package tagext;

import java.io.IOException;
import java.util.Date;
import javax.servlet.jsp.*;
import javax.servlet.jsp.tagext.TagSupport;

public class HelloTag extends TagSupport {
```

This method will be called when the JSP engine encounters the start of a tag implemented by this class. It returns a value indicating whether to evaluate any body content this tag may have. The legal return values are EVAL_BODY_INCLUDE (meaning to evaluate the tag's body content and any sub-tags) and SKIP_BODY (meaning tag contents will be ignored).

```
public int doStartTag() throws JspTagException {
   return EVAL_BODY_INCLUDE;
}
```

This method will be called when the JSP engine encounters the end of a tag implemented by this class. It returns a value indicating whether or not to evaluate the remainder of the JSP. The legal return values are EVAL_PAGE (the normal case), and SKIP_PAGE.

```
public int doEndTag() throws JspTagException {
   String dateString = new Date().toString();
   try {
      // Obtain the current JspWriter from the tag's context
      // and write to it
      pageContext.getOut().write("Hello world.<br/>");
      pageContext.getOut().write("My name is " + getClass().getName() +
                              " and it's " + dateString + "<p/>");
   } catch (IOException ex) {
      throw new JspTagException(
              "Fatal error: hello tag could not write to JSP out");
   }
   return EVAL_PAGE;
}
}
```

Note that we need to check for IOExceptions when generating output. Any exception encountered while processing the tag must be wrapped as a JspException if it is to be re-thrown. It is good practice to use the javax.servlet.jsp.JspTagException subclass of JspException. (Note that, confusingly, this *isn't* in the same package as the other classes specific to tag handlers.)

We could actually have omitted the doStartTag() method. We include it for completeness, but in fact it does exactly what its superclass TagSupport's doStartTag() method does; it instructs the JSP engine to evaluate the tag's content and any sub-tags, and could be used to set up any resources that the tag will need, such as opening a connection to a database.

Tag Library Descriptors

A **Tag Library Descriptor (TLD)** is an XML document with a .tld extension that describes one or more tag extensions.

> *There are many advantages in the use of XML notation for TLDs, as well as for other J2EE deployment descriptors. XML documents are easy for tools to author and easy to validate. Yet because XML is text-based, they are also easy to edit manually. It's also easy to extract information from an XML document, because it's so well structured. For example, an XSLT stylesheet could easily be used to produce human-readable documentation for a TLD.*

A tag library allows us to group tags with similar functionality by providing tag extensions and relating them with Java classes. TLDs must conform to one of two Document Type Definitions (DTDs) included in the JSP 1.2 specification. Many of the tag library elements are intended mainly to provide support for JSP authoring tools, so we'll only look at the ones vital to developers. Before trying out these tags you should make sure your JSP container supports them.

This section refers to the tag library DTD included in the JSP 1.2 specification, available at http://java.sun.com/dtd/web-jsptaglibrary_1_2.dtd. This differs from that included in the JSP 1.1 specification. (Most of the differences are minor, such as the addition of a hyphen in many element names, although JSP 1.2 also adds some new elements.) JSP 1.2-compliant containers must accept tag libraries conforming to the JSP 1.1 DTD, to ensure backward compatibility. The JSP 1.1 DTD is available at http://java.sun.com/j2ee/dtds/web-jsptaglibrary_1_1.dtd. You can refer to the comments in that document when maintaining JSP 1.1 tag libraries.

The root element is `<taglib>`, defined in the DTD by:

```
<!ELEMENT taglib (tlib-version, jsp-version?, short-name, uri?,
   display-name?, small-icon?, large-icon?, description?,
   validator?, listener*, tag+) >
```

❏ `tlib-version` is the version of the tag library implementation and is defined by the author of the tag library. The version should be specified in decimal form. Examples of valid versions are 0.7 and 1.12.

❏ `jsp-version` is the version of the JSP specification the tag library depends on. Currently the value to use is 1.2 (the default), unless you are working with a JSP container that supports only JSP 1.1, in which case you will need to specify 1.1. This element is optional.

❏ `short-name` is a simple default name that could be used by a JSP authoring tool. The best value to use is the preferred prefix value: that is, a suggestion as to a prefix to use when importing the tag library. Although there is no way of enforcing this, hopefully developers using the library will follow this suggestion, and consistency will be achieved between all users of the tag library. The `shortname` must not contain whitespace, or start with a digit or underscore.

❏ `description` is an arbitrary text string describing the tag library. Think of it as the equivalent of a Javadoc comment relating to an entire class or package; the authoring tool may display it when the tag library is imported in.

❏ `validator` is a sub-element introduced in JSP 1.2. It can be used to specify a Java class that can be used at translation time to validate use of the tags in the tag library. Validation is performed on the XML form of JSP pages in the tag library.

❏ `listener` is a sub-element introduced in JSP 1.2. This integrates tag libraries with the support for application-level events introduced in the Servlet 2.3 API. We'll cover this element later in this chapter.

The `<tag>` element is the most important. It's defined in the DTD as:

```
<!ELEMENT tag (name, tag-class, tei-class?, body-content?, display-name?,
small-icon?, large-icon?, description?, variable*, attribute*, example?) >
```

❏ `name` is the name that will identify this tag (after the tag library prefix).

❏ `tag-class` is the fully qualified name of the tag handler class that implements this tag. This class must implement the `javax.servlet.jsp.tagext.Tag` interface – of course it may implement one of the subclasses `IterationTag` or `BodyTag`.

❏ `tei-class` defines a subclass of `javax.servlet.jsp.tagext.TagExtraInfo` that will provide extra information about this tag at run time to the JSP page. Not all tags require a `TagExtraInfo` class.

- ❑ body-content is an optional attribute that specifies the type of body content the tag should have. Three values are legal: tagdependent, JSP, and empty. The default (and most useful) is JSP, which means that the tag's body content will be evaluated at run time like any other JSP content. tagdependent signifies that the JSP engine should *not* attempt to evaluate the content, but accept that while it may not understand it, it means something to the tag handler, and should therefore be passed unchanged. empty is useful when a tag should not have any body content. If this value is used, and the tag is not empty, the JSP translation will fail.

- ❑ variable sub-tags are used to indicate that a tag declares scripting variables available to JSP pages using it. This is an important function, which we'll look at in more detail later.

- ❑ The optional <example> sub-element of the <tag> element is an addition to JSP 1.2 and provides an informal description of the use of the tag. When using this element, remember to escape the < and > characters to ensure that the TLD remains a well-formed XML document. The contents of the example element could be displayed by an authoring tool to provide useful information to help JSP developers using it.

<attribute> sub-tags of a <tag> element describe each attribute accepted (or required) by the tag. The DTD definition is:

```
<!ELEMENT attribute
    (name, required?, rtexprvalue?) >
```

- ❑ name is the name of this attribute, as it will appear in JSP pages using the tag.

- ❑ required specifies whether or not this attribute is mandatory. The valid values are true (the attribute is required), and false (the default, signifying an optional attribute). The attribute may have a default value.

- ❑ rtexprvalue specifies whether the attribute value can be the result of a JSP expression, or whether it has a fixed value at translation time when the tag is used in a JSP page. Valid values are true and false. The default is false, which means that expressions are forbidden. If the value of rtexprvalue is true, the following JSP code would be legal:

```
<examples:mytag attrib="<%=myObject.getValue()%>">
```

Allowing attributes to take expression values can be very useful as it allows their behavior to be determined at run time. For example, tag attributes will very often be set to the value of properties of JSP beans. This relies on the use of a JSP expression. The only advantage to using a value of false is that it ensures that *all* information about a tag's usage (including attribute values) can be made available to a validation class at translation time.

Our example's TLD was very straightforward. As our tag takes no attributes and has no associated TagExtraInfo class, only a minimum of elements were required:

```
<?xml version="1.0" encoding="ISO-8859-1" ?>
<!DOCTYPE taglib
        PUBLIC "-//Sun Microsystems, Inc.//DTD JSP Tag Library 1.2//EN"
        "http://java.sun.com/dtd/web-jsptaglibrary_1_2.dtd">

<taglib>
  <tlib-version>1.0</tlib-version>
  <jsp-version>1.2</jsp-version>
  <short-name>examples</short-name>
  <description>Simple example library</description>
  <tag>
```

```
        <name>hello</name>
        <tag-class>tagext.HelloTag</tag-class>
        <body-content>JSP</body-content>
        <description>
           Simple hello world example.
           Takes no attributes, and simply
           generates HTML/
        </description>
     </tag>
  </taglib>
```

Using Tag Extensions in JSP Pages

Unlike the standard actions such as `<jsp:forward>`, custom tags must be explicitly imported into JSP pages before they can be used, using a `taglib` directive. The syntax of this is shown below:

```
<%@ taglib uri="<uri>" prefix="examples" %>
```

The `uri` attribute tells the JSP engine where to find the TLD for the tag library and the `prefix` attribute tells the JSP engine what prefix will be given to tags from this library in the remainder of the JSP page.

A JSP page may import any number of tag libraries. The `taglib` directive will cause an exception at translation time if the tag library cannot be located, while the first attempt to access any tag defined in the TLD will cause a `ServletException` at run time if not all the classes required to support the tag implementation can be loaded.

Once the tag library has been imported into the page, tags in a library can be called as follows:

```
<examples:someTag name="Rod">
  //...
</examples:someTag>
```

The way in which custom tags are used in JSP pages is an example of the effort to introduce XML conventions into JSP syntax. Note that, unlike HTML attributes, the attributes of custom tags *must* be enclosed in double or single quotes, in accordance with the XML specification. Tag prefixes use the same syntax as XML namespaces.

When a tag requires no body content, it is best to use the XML shorthand to make this explicit:

```
<examples:hello name="Rod" />
```

> **Tag prefixes are chosen in JSP pages, not, as one might expect, in tag libraries. The choice of prefix is a matter for developers, but consistency among JSP pages importing the same tag library is desirable. It is best to adopt the value of the `shortname` element in the tag library. The prefixes `jsp:`, `jspx:`, `java:`, `javax:`, `servlet:`, `sun:`, and `sunw:` are reserved. It's perhaps unfortunate that Sun has not defined a unique naming system such as the Java package naming system for tag library prefixes. Choosing a prefix unique to a company or organization is advisable: for example, instead of using the potentially clashing short name `tables`, it might be advisable to use `myCompany_tables`.**

Deploying and Packaging Tag Libraries

There are three main ways of deploying and using tag libraries with a JSP engine, and we should be familiar with all of them. The mechanisms reflect three different ways of mapping `uri` attributes used in the `taglib` directive onto TLD locations, and they are:

- ❑ Referencing the tag library descriptor using a mapping element in the web application deployment descriptor, `web.xml`.

- ❑ Packaging the tag libraries as JARs. This provides convenient support for third-party tag libraries that are distributed as a black box.

- ❑ Treating the `uri` attribute as an actual URL, relative or absolute, pointing to a publicly accessible TLD.

Let's discuss each of these in turn;

Mapping in web.xml

In this approach to deployment, the tag library descriptor, the Java classes required to implement the tags, and the JSP pages that use the tag library are shipped together in a WAR. This is the approach we've taken in this chapter. The `taglib` directive will look like this:

```
<%@ taglib uri="/hello" prefix="examples" %>
```

We don't specify the actual filename of the TLD, so there is no need to use the TLD extension. The server knows where to look in the current web application's WAR for a `.tld` file matching this URI because the mapping from URI to file location is specified in the `web.xml` file in a `<taglib>` element. The complete `web.xml` file for our simple example looked like this:

```xml
<?xml version="1.0" encoding="UTF-8"?>

<!DOCTYPE web-app PUBLIC '-//Sun Microsystems, Inc.//DTD Web Application 2.2//EN'
'http://java.sun.com/j2ee/dtds/web-app_2.2.dtd'>

<web-app>
  <display-name>tagext</display-name>
  <description>Tag extensions examples</description>

  <session-config>
    <session-timeout>0</session-timeout>
  </session-config>

  <taglib>
    <taglib-uri>/hello</taglib-uri>
    <taglib-location>/WEB-INF/tlds/hello.tld</taglib-location>
  </taglib>

</web-app>
```

The `<taglib>` element contains two sub-tags: `<taglib-uri>` specifies the URI that should be used in JSP pages wishing to use the tag library and `<taglib-location>` specifies the path to the tag library descriptor within the WAR. This path does not need to be publicly available to users of the web server, as the server will not publish anything that is in the `WEB-INF` directory.

To understand how this works we should remember the important directories in the WAR:

❑ WEB-INF
  This contains the web.xml file, in which the TLD URI-location mapping must be specified.

❑ WEB-INF/classes
  This contains Java classes required to implement tag libraries or otherwise support the functionality of the web application.

❑ WEB-INF/lib
  This contains JAR files containing additional classes required to support the functionality of the web application.

❑ WEB-INF/tlds
  By convention (although not mandated in any specification) this contains the tag library descriptors (but not tag handler classes) that will be made available to JSP pages in the web.xml file. The TLDs could actually be placed anywhere in the WAR (so long as a mapping is included in the web.xml file), but adhering to this convention makes it easier to understand the WAR's structure.

Use this mechanism for tag libraries that are part of a particular application, rather than standard deployment units that will be reused elsewhere.

Packaged Tag Library JAR

A tag library may be distributed in a JAR file in which the /META-INF subdirectory contains the tag library descriptor, named taglib.tld. The JAR file should also contain the classes required to implement the tags defined in the tag library, but will not contain any JSP pages that use the tag library. In this case, the taglib directive in JSP pages should refer to this JAR, which will probably be within a WAR. This enables custom tags to be supplied in self-contained units – a vital precondition for the successful distribution of third-party custom tags.

The taglib directive will look like this:

```
<%@ taglib uri="/WEB-INF/lib/hellotags.jar" prefix="examples" %>
```

When including such a tag library JAR in a web application, we place it under the /WEB-INF/lib directory, to ensure that the classes it contains will be on the application classpath.

Default Mapping

The simplest means of deployment is to simply place the tag library descriptor under the server's document root (or to make it available to the application as an external URL), and ensure that the Java classes required to implement the tags are on the application's classpath. There is no attempt to package a tag library or an application. In this case, the taglib directive will look like this:

```
<%@ taglib uri="./hello.tld" prefix="examples" %>
```

The URI is simply a path on the host server, which may be relative (as in this example) or absolute. In this approach, the tag library descriptor (although not the classes implementing the tag handler) is always publicly available; anyone could view it by simply typing in its URL. It's also easy to forget to make the supporting classes available to the application. For these reasons this approach isn't recommended, although it's easy to get started by using it.

Mapping Combinations

We don't need to obtain all the tag libraries an application uses in the same way. It is common to combine the first and second methods by looking in the web.xml file for mappings of application-specific tag libraries, and looking inside packaged JARs for more generic tag libraries, but all these approaches can be combined in a single application.

Writing Tag Extensions

Once the initial concepts are grasped, implementing tag extensions is surprisingly easy, so let's put some of this theory into practice.

Processing Attributes

Our simple example is all very well, but it doesn't take advantage of the dynamic potential of custom tags. We *could* interrogate the PageContext to implement context-specific behavior, but there are more flexible alternatives. (Interrogating the PageContext would narrow the set of JSP pages in which we could use the tag.)

> **The easiest way to parameterize tags is to pass in XML attributes.**

How do we make our tags handle attributes? The answer, not surprisingly, is that attributes in a TLD tag element map onto bean properties of the corresponding tag handlers. The mapping of attributes onto tag handler properties is, as we might expect, handled by the JSP engine through reflection. Not only does it work with primitive types; we can pass *any* type to a tag handler. (Draft versions of the JSP 1.1 specification included a type sub-element of the attribute TLD element but the type is now detected using reflection.)

Whether an attribute is required or optional is specified in the TLD, as is whether attributes can take the value of a JSP expression at run time.

Let's suppose we decide to pass a name as an attribute. We can change our simple example so that it can display any name we pass to the page as a parameter.

First, we need to write a tag handler with a name property. With this minor change, it's pretty much like HelloTag. The new or changed lines are highlighted:

```
package tagext;

import java.io.IOException;
import java.util.Date;
import javax.servlet.jsp.*;
import javax.servlet.jsp.tagext.*;

public class AttribHelloTag extends TagSupport {

  private String name;

  public String getName() {
    return name;
  }
```

```
public void setName(String name) {
  this.name = name;
}

public int doStartTag() throws JspTagException {
  return EVAL_BODY_INCLUDE;
}

public int doEndTag() throws JspTagException {
  String dateString = new Date().toString();
  try {
    pageContext.getOut().write("Hello <b>" + getName() + "</b>.<br/>");
    pageContext.getOut().write("My name is " + getClass().getName() +
                               " and it's " + dateString + "<p/>");
  } catch (IOException ex) {
    throw new JspTagException("Hello tag could not write to JSP out");
  }
  return EVAL_PAGE;
}
}
```

Save this class file in `WEB-INF/classes/tagext`. Don't be tempted to omit the property getter method `getName()`, which at first sight may seem unnecessary, as we could simply access the name instance variable after the `setName()` has been called. Some JSP engines may rely on the presence of both methods at translation time, and such bean properties should normally be readable as well as writable as a matter of style.

Now we must add a tag entry to our TLD describing the new tag, and to specify that it requires an attribute, `name`:

```
<tag>
  <name>helloAttrib</name>
  <tag-class>tagext.AttribHelloTag</tag-class>
  <body-content>JSP</body-content>
  <description>Simple example with attributes</description>
  <attribute>
    <name>name</name>
    <required>true</required>
    <rtexprvalue>true</rtexprvalue>
  </attribute>
</tag>
```

The JSP container will throw an exception if the required `name` attribute is not specified, and the attribute can be set with the run time value of an expression, as well as with a static string (the value of `rtexprvalue` being `true`).

Now we can get slightly more ambitious in the calling JSP, `helloAttribute.jsp`. We invoke the tag twice, to demonstrate using both static and runtime attribute values. We also offer the user help in working out how to call the page:

```
<%@ taglib uri="/hello" prefix="examples" %>

<html>
  <head>
    <title>Simple tag with an attribute</title>
  </head>
```

```
    <body>
      <p>This is static output.</p>
      <p><i><examples:helloAttrib name="Rod" /></i></p>
```

Now provide an attribute value at run time:

```
      <% String readerName = request.getParameter("reader"); %>
      <p>
      <% if (readerName != null) { %>
```

If we have a value we can work with:

```
          Thank you. You told me your name<br />
          <i><examples:helloAttrib name="<%=readerName%>" /></i>
      <% } else { %>
```

If we don't have a value to work with we encourage the user to supply their name:

```
          You're too shy to tell me your name.
          Try again, using the <b>reader</b> parameter:
          <br />remember I trusted you with my fully-qualified class name!!
      <% } %>
      </p>
      <p>This is static output again.</p>

    </body>
  </html>
```

The tag can now display any name we please. The structure of its output varies depending on whether we pass in the reader parameter used for the runtime attribute value. Repeat the steps we outlined earlier to create and deploy the WAR, then navigate to http://localhost:8000/tagext/helloAttribute.jsp. The following screenshots illustrate the two cases (note the URLs). In the first case, no parameters are supplied to the page:

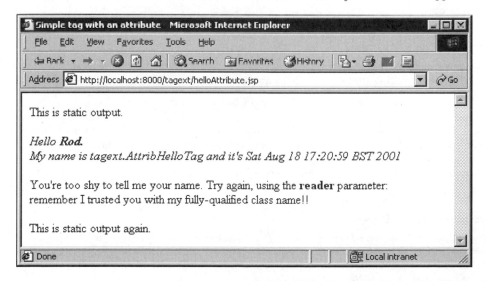

When we specify a reader parameter we see a runtime attribute value. To see this in action, navigate to http://localhost:8000/tagext/helloAttribute?reader=yourName:

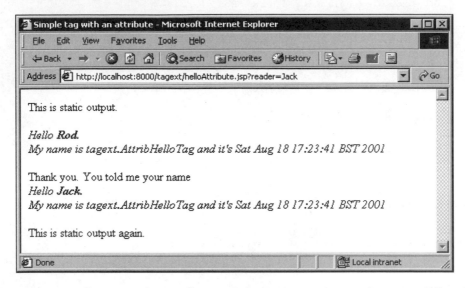

Attributes are an excellent way of controlling tag behavior at run time, and are especially valuable in ensuring that tags are generic and reusable.

As elegant as the attribute/property mechanism is, there is one annoying problem with passing string attributes to tags. Specifying certain characters in attributes is messy. The double quote character, for example, is illegal in an attribute, and we must use the entity reference " if we want to include it. This rapidly becomes unreadable if the data includes multiple quotation marks. Attributes are also unsuited to handling lengthy values, as they soon become unreadable.

So there are limits to what can sensibly be achieved with attributes. Where complicated markup is concerned, consider the alternatives:

❑   Processing markup and expressions in the body of the tag, possibly repeatedly

❑   Defining a subtag that configures its ancestor

❑   Implementing the tag to read its markup from a template file or URL

The most elegant of these solutions (although not always the most feasible) is to manipulate the tag body. This will only be useful if the tag defines scripting variables that the tag body can use.

There is a curious and confusing inconsistency in JSP syntax when non-`String` *tag attributes are the results of JSP expressions. Let's suppose we want to pass an object of class* `examples.Values` *(a kind of list) to a tag extension. The syntax:*

```
<wrox:list values="<%=values%>"
```

is problematic, because we know from the JSP specification that an expression "is evaluated and the result is coerced to a string which is subsequently emitted into the current out `JspWriter` *object." In the case of the custom tag above, however, the value of the expression is* not *coerced to a string, but passed to the tag handler as its original type.*

Body Content

So far we have used tags only to generate markup. We haven't considered what custom tags may do to their body content (that is, anything found between their start and end tags).

Let's suppose we modify `hello.jsp`, our first example, to add some code inside one of the tags, like this:

```
<examples:hello>
    This is tag content!
</examples:hello>
```

We also delete the `<examples:hello />` tag. The result, saved in the file `helloTagContent.jsp`, is that the content we have added is output in addition to any output generated by the tag. Whether the content appears before or after the tag's output depends on whether we chose to do tag output in the `doStartTag()` or `doEndTag()` methods. In the case of the `HelloTag`, the output will appear *before* the tag's own output:

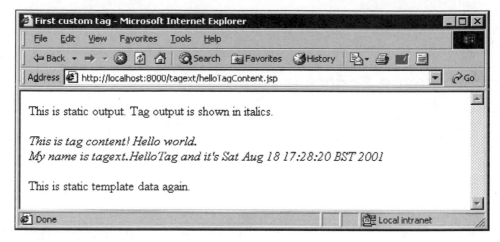

Tag content will be treated at run time like any other JSP content (so long as the body content type is set in the TLD to be JSP), so it may include expressions. (JSP is the default content type.) Try modifying the last example like this:

```
<examples:hello>
This is tag content containing an expression: 37 * 16 = <%= 37 * 16 %>
</examples:hello>
```

Scriptlets are also legal, as is any other valid JSP content. The following will produce the same result:

```
<examples:hello>
<% int a = 37; %>
<% int b = 16; %>
This tag contains expressions and scriptlets:
  <%=a%> * <%=b%> = <%= a * b %>
</examples:hello>
```

The output of the second of these examples is shown in `helloDynamicTagContent.jsp`:

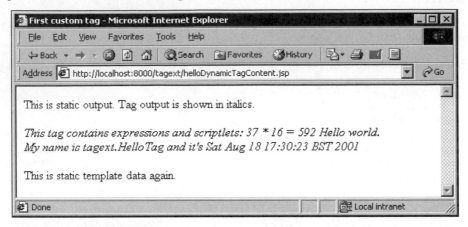

To do anything really useful with body content, however, we need to make our tags define scripting variables, or manipulate their body content.

Tags Introducing Scripting Variables

We don't always want tags to produce output themselves. It can be very useful for custom tags to introduce new scripting variables into the page, leaving the calling JSP pages to control the presentation without performing the processing involved in determining the content.

JSP 1.1 offered one way of introducing scripting variables; JSP 1.2 offers two. This section will look at the JSP 1.2 method, which should be used in most new tag libraries because it is simpler and more intuitive, before discussing the JSP 1.1 method (which is still supported and which offers more power for complex tags).

Two steps are required to introduce scripting variables in a custom tag in JSP 1.2:

❑ Add one or more `<variable>` sub-tags to the relevant `<tag>` element in the TLD

❑ Write code to add the variables to the `PageContext` in the tag handler itself

The variable element is declared in the tag library DTD as follows:

```
<!ELEMENT variable
((name-given | name-from-attribute), variable-class?,
declare?, scope?) >
```

Let us examine each sub-element in turn:

❑ `name-given`
The name by which the scripting variable will be accessed in the JSP. It must be a legal Java identifier.

❑ `name-from-attribute`
An alternative to name-given, specifying an attribute whose *translation time* value will be given to the variable. For example, if the name-from-attribute has the value "sport," and the tag is invoked like this: `<mylib:game sport="tennis"/>` the tag handler may create a variable named "tennis". Two cautions apply here: it will be the responsibility of the tag handler to check the value of the relevant attribute to decide what name to give the new variable (see below for examples of variable creation in tag handlers); and runtime values are not permitted. It would be illegal to try to use this hypothetical tag like this: `<mylib:game sport="<%=sportsBean.getPreferredSport()%>" />`.

❑ `variable-class`
Should be the fully qualified name of the variable's type. In practice, it will not be tested by the JSP engine at translation time, but used directly in code generation. For example, if `java.lang.Integer` is specified for variable name, the JSP engine will generate a declaration such as `java.lang.Integer count;` in the Java class representation of the JSP page. This element is optional, the default being string.

Note that the Reference Implementation (which uses Tomcat 4.0 beta 4) handles this element incorrectly. If the element is omitted for a variable of type `java.lang.String`, *the JSP page cannot be compiled. To work around this the optional element must always be included, which we do in the examples in this chapter.*

❑ `declare`
Is a `boolean` parameter that controls whether a new variable is to be created, or whether the tag will simply update the value of a variable already in the calling JSP page's `PageContext`. Valid values are `true`, `false`, `yes`, and `no`. It is generally good practice to create new variables, although this may cause a translation-time error if the JSP page has already used the variable name. Name conflicts can also arise if the same tag is nested, and descendants try to create new variables with the same name while an earlier one is still in scope. If the value of the `declare` parameter is `true`, and a new variable is to be created, the JSP engine can generate Java code to declare a variable in the same way as a scriptlet may declare a variable – in the `_JSP pageservice()` method. In either case, the JSP will obtain the value for the variable set by the tag handler by looking in the `PageContext`. This element is optional with a default value of `true`.

❑ `scope`
Three types of scope are defined for variables introduced within custom tags: NESTED, AT_BEGIN, and AT_END. If NESTED scope is specified, the variables are available to the calling JSP only within the body of the defining tag. (They will remain visible even if other tags are invoked within the defining tag.) If AT_BEGIN scope is specified, the variables will be available to the remainder of the calling JSP after the start of the defining tag. If AT_END scope is specified, the variables will be available to the remainder of the calling JSP after the end of the defining tag. Unless there is a strong reason for using the variables after the tag has been closed, the preferred scope is NESTED. In JSP pages, as in programming generally, additional variables introduce complexity.

Changes to the Tag Handler

We must not forget to modify the tag handler itself. Before they will be available to JSP pages using the tag, variables must be added to the `PageContext` like this:

```
pageContext.setAttribute("variableName", myObject);
```

Scripting Variables Example

Suppose we've decided that we'd like our `Hello` tag to be more configurable. Having `"Hello"` and other English text hard coded makes it of little use in other language environments. Suppose we decide to use the tag to provide all the dynamic values we've seen it output (name, class name, and date), but control the presentation entirely in the JSP page.

First, we create a tag entry in our TLD that declares the new tag, with a variable sub-element for each scripting variable it creates:

```
<tag>
  <name>helloVars</name>
  <tag-class>tagext.VarHelloTag</tag-class>
```

```
  <body-content>JSP</body-content>
  <description>Simple example with scripting variables</description>
  <variable>
    <name-given>name</name-given>
```

java.lang.String is the default, and so the following element should really be optional, but as we discussed the Reference Implementation generates incorrect JSP servlets without it:

```
    <variable-class>java.lang.String</variable-class>
  </variable>
  <variable>
    <name-given>className</name-given>
  <variable-class>java.lang.String</variable-class>
  </variable>
  <variable>
    <name-given>date</name-given>
    <variable-class>java.util.Date</variable-class>
  </variable>
  <attribute>
    <name>name</name>
    <required>true</required>
    <rtexprvalue>true</rtexprvalue>
  </attribute>
</tag>
```

Because most of the sub-tags of `<variable>` are optional and have sensible default values, these variables can be declared concisely. The `name` variable is of the default type (`java.lang.String`), and both require default scope (NESTED).

The tag handler itself is very simple, but differs from those we've seen so far in that it generates no markup. All it does is add values for the variables we've just declared in the TLD to the `PageContext` in its `doStartTag()` method. (Any object can be made available to a JSP page by adding it to the `request`, `session`, or `application` object as an attribute. The `javax.servlet.jsp.PageContext` object associated with each JSP page provides an easy access to all namespaces associated with the JSP page.)

As these variables are only available within the tag, it would be useless to add them in the `doEndTag()` method. However, if the scope was specified to be AT_END, they could be added in the `doEndTag()` method.

```java
package tagext;

import java.io.IOException;
import java.util.Date;
import javax.servlet.jsp.*;
import javax.servlet.jsp.tagext.*;

public class VarHelloTag extends TagSupport {

  private String name;

  public String getName() {
    return name;
  }

  public void setName(String name) {
    this.name = name;
  }

  public int doStartTag() throws JspTagException {
```

We make the variables available to calling JSP pages:

```
        pageContext.setAttribute("name", name);
        pageContext.setAttribute("className", getClass().getName());
        pageContext.setAttribute("date", new Date());
        return EVAL_BODY_INCLUDE;
    }

    public int doEndTag() throws JspTagException {
```

We don't need to generate any markup here as we've provided variables enabling calling JSP pages to generate it themselves:

```
        return EVAL_PAGE;
    }
}
```

The calling JSP page, `helloWithVariables.jsp`, can now do all the work of rendering the output:

```
<%@ taglib uri="/hello" prefix="examples" %>

<html>
  <head>
    <title>Bonjour: Tag with scripting variables</title>
  </head>

  <body>
    <p>HTML</p>
    <p><i>
      <examples:helloVars name="Isabelle">
        Bonjour <%=name%>. Je m'appelle <%=className%>.<br/>
        C'est <%=date%>
      </examples:helloVars>
    </i></p>
    <p>Plus de HTML.</p>
  </body>
</html>
```

The screen output will be something like:

537

Note that we don't *need* to use the scripting variables we've created. The contents of the <examples:helloVars> tag could be static, in which case it would output the HTML unchanged, or the tag could be empty, in which case it would produce no HTML output at all.

As the scripting variables introduced by tags must be placed in the PageContext by the JSP engine, only object variables can be created. This is a minor annoyance when we would really like a primitive type. Also remember that even if they are never accessed, the values of all the scripting variables must still be computed and placed in the PageContext.

Programmatic Definition of Scripting Variables

There was only one way of defining scripting variables in JSP 1.1. Instead of being defined in the TLD using the <variable> element, variables were defined in Java code, in the value of a method return. The new method, which we've just discussed, is simpler and should be preferred in most new tag libraries. It is also more in keeping with the J2EE philosophy of preferring declarative to programmatic configuration.

However, the method introduced in JSP 1.1 is important not only because it is used in most existing tag libraries, but because it is slightly more powerful than the declarative method. This is because it makes it possible for complex choices to be made at translation about which variables to expose, and what names to give them. Such choices could be based on the attribute values supplied at translation time.

Three steps were required in JSP 1.1 to define scripting variables:

❑ Specify a TagExtraInfo class in the tag's entry in the TLD. This is a class that provides additional information about a tag's implementation at translation time.

❑ Implement the TagExtraInfo class to define the names, types, and scopes of the variables.

❑ Define the scripting variables in the tag handler class itself. This step is identical to that required in the JSP 1.2 method.

Note that the code in the tag handler itself is identical to the JSP 1.2 version.

To illustrate this, let's take our VarHelloTag and make it define the same variables using a TagExtraInfo class. (Incidentally, this demonstrates that it is possible, and sometimes useful, to have multiple TLD entries for the same tag handler class.) Let's look at the first two steps in turn. (We can skip the third, as we will use the same tag handler class as in the previous example.) First, we specify in the TLD that the TagExtraInfo class we're about to write will be associated with this tag. The necessary tag element looks like this:

```
<tag>
  <name>helloTEIVars</name>
  <tag-class>tagext.VarHelloTag</tag-class>
  <tei-class>tagext.VarHelloTagExtraInfo</tei-class>
  <body-content>JSP</body-content>
  <description>Simple example with scripting variables</description>
  <attribute>
    <name>name</name>
    <required>true</required>
    <rtexprvalue>true</rtexprvalue>
  </attribute>
</tag>
```

Note that we don't use any <variable> elements. Next, we write the TagExtraInfo class. This must be derived from the JSP API class javax.servlet.jsp.tagext.TagExtraInfo. TagExtraInfo is an abstract class, containing four methods. Three are concerned with tag library validation, which we'll discuss later. The only method we're interested in right now has the following signature:

```
VariableInfo[] getVariableInfo(TagData td)
```

The data held in the `VariableInfo` class should look very familiar, as it's the same as is specified in the `<variable>` TLD element we've just explored. There is a single constructor, which allows us to specify all the fields:

```
VariableInfo(String varName, String className, boolean declare, int scope)
```

These parameters correspond to the TLD elements:

- **Variable Name** (`varName`)
  The name by which the scripting variable will be accessed in the JSP. It must be a legal Java identifier.

- **Class Name** (`className`)
  Should be the fully qualified name of the variable's type.

- **Declare** (`declare`)
  Is a Boolean parameter with the same meaning as the `variable` element's `declare` sub-element.

- **Variable Scope** (`scope`)
  Three constants defined in the `VariableInfo` class (NESTED, AT_BEGIN, and AT_END) correspond to the scopes we've already discussed.

The following listing shows the complete `TagExtraInfo` implementation. Save it as `VarHelloTagExtraInfo.java` in the usual directory:

```
package tagext;

import javax.servlet.jsp.tagext.*;

public class VarHelloTagExtraInfo extends TagExtraInfo {
```

We're not interested in the other methods of this class as the no operation (NOP) implementations of the superclass will do:

```
public VariableInfo[] getVariableInfo(TagData data) {
    return new VariableInfo[] {
```

The use of NESTED scope means that these scripting variables will only be available inside the `VarHelloTag`:

```
    new VariableInfo("name", "java.lang.String", true,
                     VariableInfo.NESTED),
    new VariableInfo("className", "java.lang.String", true,
                     VariableInfo.NESTED),
    new VariableInfo("date", "java.util.Date", true, VariableInfo.NESTED)
    };
  }
}
```

The `VarHelloTagExtraInfo` class will now be interrogated by the JSP container at translation time, as it creates a servlet from each JSP using the `VarHelloTag`. The `VarHelloTagExtraInfo` class supplies the same variable information that the `<variable>` TLD elements did in the previous example. When we use the new `helloTEIVars` tag the results will be identical to the results of using the `helloVars` tag.

> It is an error to mix the two methods of defining scripting variables. If a tag entry in a TLD has `<variable>` sub-tags, it is an error for any **TagExtraInfo** class associated with it to return anything but **null** in its **getVariableInfo()** method.

Iteration and Manipulation of Body Content

What we've done so far with body content and scripting variables, using the Tag interface, is all very fine, but it still doesn't help us to do anything really exciting with a tag's body content. What if we want to repeat the body content a number of times, or suppress it under some circumstances, or filter it?

To do this, we need a richer API. Remember the IterationTag and BodyTag interfaces? IterationTag extends Tag to support repeated evaluation of body content without transformation or suppression and BodyTag extends IterationTag to allow manipulation of body content in addition to iteration.

Repeated Evaluation with the IterationTag Interface

One of the most common uses of custom tags is to handle iteration. Control flow is handled much more cleanly in Java classes (such as tag handlers) than in JSP pages, so placing iteration in custom tags can improve the maintainability of JSP pages dramatically.

Let's modify our VarHelloTag so that it can say hello to several people, using the name variable, and make the other scripting variables we've already used, className and date, available only after the looping of the tag has been completed.

We'll need to change the property that is passed in from a single String (name) to an indexed type, for this example we'll use java.util.List. We'll also need an instance variable to control our iteration over the list and so we add an index variable to do this.

To handle the iteration, we'll make our tag class implement IterationTag. Remember that IterationTag adds a single method to tag:

int doAfterBody()

This method enables us to decide after each time the tag's body content has been processed whether to continue processing it, or move on to the end tag.

In our new VarHelloIterationTag class, the doAfterBody() method will return EVAL_BODY_AGAIN until the list has been exhausted. With each iteration, the value in the name variable is reset. At run time, the body content of this tag will be evaluated for each element in the list, with the variable's value always up to date:

```
package tagext;

import java.io.IOException;
import java.util.*;
import javax.servlet.jsp.*;
import javax.servlet.jsp.tagext.*;
```

```
public class VarHelloIterationTag extends TagSupport
                               implements IterationTag {
```

We start with a list of names passed in:

```
    private List names;
    private int index;
```

We then output what we're building up while iterating over the body content:

```
private StringBuffer output = new StringBuffer();
```

Getter and setter for the names property/attribute:

```
public List getNames() {
    return names;
}

public void setNames(List names) {
    this.names = names;
}

public int doStartTag() throws JspTagException {
    setLoopVariables();
```

The return value is the same as for a normal, non-iterating, tag:

```
    return EVAL_BODY_INCLUDE;
}
```

The JSP engine will call this method each time the body content of this tag has been processed. If it returns SKIP_BODY, the body content will have been processed for the last time. If it returns EVAL_BODY_AGAIN, the body will be processed and this method called at least once more:

```
public int doAfterBody() throws JspTagException {
```

If we still haven't got to the end of the list we continue processing:

```
    if (++index < names.size()) {
        setLoopVariables();
        return EVAL_BODY_AGAIN;
    }
```

If we get to here, then we've finished processing the list:

```
    return SKIP_BODY;
}
```

This method is implemented to direct the JSP engine to evaluate the rest of the calling JSP page, and to expose the two variables defined with scope AT_END:

```
public int doEndTag() {
    pageContext.setAttribute("className", getClass().getName());
    pageContext.setAttribute("date", new Date());
    return EVAL_PAGE;
}
```

Make the variables available for each iteration:

```
private void setLoopVariables() {
  pageContext.setAttribute("name", names.get(index).toString());
  pageContext.setAttribute("index", new Integer(index));
}
}
```

The `<tag>` element in the TLD must declare the four scripting variables. Note the two scopes used (the default NESTED, and AT_END) to distinguish between the loop variables and the variables to be made available after the tag has been processed:

```
<tag>
  <name>helloIterator</name>
  <tag-class>tagext.VarHelloIterationTag</tag-class>
  <body-content>JSP</body-content>
  <description>Simple iterative example</description>
  <variable>
    <name-given>name</name-given>
    <variable-class>java.lang.String</variable-class>
  </variable>
  <variable>
    <name-given>index</name-given>
    <variable-class>java.lang.Integer</variable-class>
  </variable>
  <variable>
    <name-given>className</name-given>
    <variable-class>java.lang.String</variable-class>
    <scope>AT_END</scope>
  </variable>
  <variable>
    <name-given>date</name-given>
    <variable-class>java.util.Date</variable-class>
    <scope>AT_END</scope>
  </variable>
  <attribute>
    <name>names</name>
    <required>true</required>
    <rtexprvalue>true</rtexprvalue>
  </attribute>
</tag>
```

In the calling JSP, `helloIterator.jsp`, we define a `List` and add a few elements to give the tag something to display:

```
<%@ taglib uri="/hello" prefix="examples" %>

<%!
```

Normally we don't declare variables in JSP pages (or implement methods) but this example should be self-contained:

```
java.util.List names = new java.util.LinkedList();
```

A JSP can override this method to perform initialization. It's analogous to the `GenericServlet` `init()` method. This code will run only when the JSP page is loaded:

```
    public void jspInit() {
        names.add("Rod");
        names.add("Isabelle");
        names.add("Bob");
    }
%>

<html>
  <head>
    <title>Iterator tag</title>
  </head>

  <body>
    <p>HTML. Output generated using tags is italicized.</p>
    <p><i>
      <examples:helloIterator names="<%=names%>">
        Hello <b><%=name%></b>. You're entry <%=index%> in my list.<br/>
      </examples:helloIterator>
    </i></p>
    <p><i>
    We've finished looping, but I can now access the tag's
    </i>className<i> (<%=className%>)
    and </i>date<i> (<%=date%>) scripting variables.
    </i>
    <p>More HTML.</p>
  </body>
</html>
```

The output will look like this:

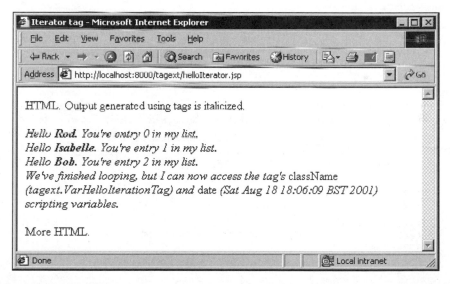

Although we developed it from our previous examples, this is almost a generic solution for list iteration. It conceals the looping from the JSP and makes the successive list values and positions available. With minor changes, this class could take a `Collection`, or a Swing `ListModel`, and make it available to any JSP page.

The main reason that this tag is so generic is that it doesn't generate markup. The more a tag extension allows a calling JSP page to control its own output, the more useful it is.

Body Tags that Filter their Content

Some tags need to perform filtering or other processing on their body content. This could be a simple text transformation, or could even interpret the tag's content as a custom language. The following simple example takes the tag's body content and writes it, reversed, into the calling JSP page.

To do this, we need to use the most powerful of the three tag extension interfaces, BodyTag. This adds a new doInitBody() method in addition to those inherited from the IterationTag interface.

Unlike Tags and IterationTags, BodyTags don't need to output all their body content as it was evaluated by the JSP engine. The BodyContent class enables them to access the body content as it is built up (possibly by repeated evaluation, controlled in the same way as by a normal IterationTag). To use this more powerful functionality, the developer of the tag handler must write code to output this body content – possibly in its original form, but perhaps in a filtered or suppressed form. Usually this output code is found in the doEndTag() method.

Remember that a body tag has a nested JSPWriter object to itself. (This is how it is possible for the body content to be suppressed or manipulated – it has not yet been written to the enclosing JSPWriter.) This means that when we want to write output in doEndTag(), we need to obtain the enclosing JSPWriter object.

Implementing the reversal is trivial; all we need to do is obtain the body content as a String, use it to initialize a StringBuffer, and call the StringBuffer's reverse() method before writing out the resulting String:

```
package tagext;

import java.io.IOException;
import javax.servlet.jsp.*;
import javax.servlet.jsp.tagext.*;

public class ReverseTag extends BodyTagSupport {
```

We're happy to inherit the remaining methods from the BodyTagSupport superclass. Called after processing of body content is complete, we use to obtain the tag's body content and write it out reversed:

```
public int doEndTag() throws JspTagException {
  BodyContent bodyContent = getBodyContent();
```

Do nothing if there was no body content:

```
if (bodyContent != null) {
  StringBuffer output = new StringBuffer(bodyContent.getString());
  output.reverse();
  try {
    bodyContent.getEnclosingWriter().write(output.toString());
  }
  catch (IOException ex) {
    throw new JspTagException("Fatal IO error");
  }
}
```

Process the rest of the page:

```
    return EVAL_PAGE;
  }
}
```

The tag library entry is also very simple. There are no variables and no attributes, so we don't need any sub-elements. The TLD doesn't care which of the three Tag interfaces the tag supports: the container will establish this at translation time using reflection.

```
<tag>
  <name>reverse</name>
  <tag-class>tagext.ReverseTag</tag-class>
  <body-content>JSP</body-content>
  <description>Simple example</description>
</tag>
```

A simple JSP page, reverse.jsp, shows the tag in action:

```
<%@ taglib uri="/hello" prefix="examples" %>

<html>
  <head>
    <title>Reverse tag</title>
  </head>

  <body>
    <i><p>
      <examples:reverse>
        Don't try to put HTML markup in here:
        the results will be very interesting
        Hello world
      </examples:reverse></p>
      <p><examples:reverse>
        Able was I ere I saw Elba
      </examples:reverse>
    </p></i>
  </body>
</html>
```

This will produce the following output:

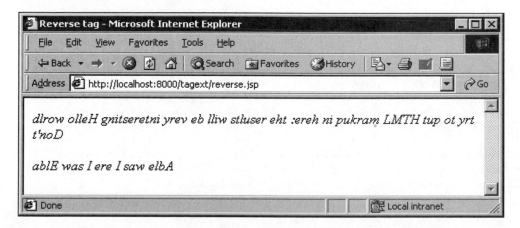

The result of placing HTML markup in the tag body will be unpredictable; so the tag is used twice in order that some formatting markup can be introduced between the tag instances.

There are many useful applications for filtering body tags. For example we could perform an XSLT transform on some XML content.

Tag Nesting

We might expect that the specification of tag nesting within our custom tags would be done in the TLD. However, TLDs don't allow for this, and nesting must be implemented by cooperating tag handler classes. Fortunately, the API helps us in this respect by providing methods with tag handlers we can use to obtain information about their parents and other ancestors. Although programmers of tag handlers must ensure that they enforce their desired tag nesting, the dynamic discovery of tag nesting at run time allows greater flexibility than would be possible if nesting were mandated in a static file. However, the absence of a formal grammar like a DTD or XML schema does place a responsibility on developers to ensure that any cooperation between tags is well documented.

Why might we use tag nesting? A common reason is to handle more complex iteration, for example nested tags can simulate nested loops. Another use is to let nested tags benefit from the context of the enclosing tag or tags.

Suppose we have additional information that we want to display for the people named in our list, but that because this information is expensive to retrieve from a database or legacy system we don't want the tag to retrieve these fields on every iteration of the loop. (This need to retrieve regardless of usage is perhaps the only disadvantage of using scripting variables.)

One solution is to use a descendant tag that draws its context from the enclosing tag and performs the additional lookups only when required (that is, only when the descendant tag is used). Let's implement a `NameTag` that requires no attributes, but retrieves additional information for the user its parent is currently processing. This information, `nationality` and `city`, will be exposed through scripting variables. Note that the child tag, like any body content, will be evaluated each time the parent iterates over its body content.

The JSP code invoking this functionality might look like this (we use a scriptlet to define and display the extra information only when desired):

```
<examples:hellos names="<%=names%>" >
  Hello <%=name%>. You're entry <%=index%> in my list.
  <% if (condition) { %>
    <examples:nameInfo>
      <b>Nationality:</b> <%=nationality%> <b>City:</b> <%=city%>
    </examples:nameInfo>
  <% } %>
  <br/>
</examples:hellos>
```

To implement this, we'll first need to add a method to `VarHelloIterationTag` that exposes the necessary context, `String getName()`.

While we're at it, we'll create an interface `NameContext` that contains this new method. This way, we can make `VarHelloIterationTag`, which already defines a `getName()` method, implement the interface and provide the necessary context for our new sub-tags.

The NameContext interface is trivial:

```
package tagext;

public interface NameContext {
```

Return the name currently exposed by this object (probably an enclosing tag, but making this an interface ensures it's a general solution):

```
    String getName();
}
```

The modification to VarHelloIterationTag (beyond making it implement NameContext) is also trivial as we simply the implement a new method:

```
        public String getName() {
           return names.get(index).toString();
        }
```

Now let's look at the new NameInfoTag tag handler. Its main tasks are to obtain the context from an enclosing tag, and to retrieve the additional information. Note how it enforces correct nesting. There is a getParent() method in the Tag interface, but it is usually preferable to use findAncestorWithClass(). We don't want to limit the context in which we can use our tags, as we can't guarantee that another tag might not stand in the hierarchy between the two cooperating tags. If one or more tags are present, and we have hard coded reliance on a particular parent tag class or interface, the nested tag will fail to find the ancestor it requires to provide its context.

For simplicity, we've hard coded the additional data in the class, in a hash table. For the sake of the example we'll imagine that this data is actually very expensive to retrieve. The extra information about people in the list will be their nationality, and the city they currently live in:

```
package tagext;

import java.io.IOException;
import java.util.*;
import javax.servlet.jsp.*;
import javax.servlet.jsp.tagext.*;

public class NameInfoTag extends TagSupport {
```

Create the data store:

```
    private HashMap  infoHash = new HashMap();
```

Populate the data store. In a real application, this data would be sourced from a real data store such as a database:

```
    public NameInfoTag() {
       infoHash.put("Rod", new PersonalInfo("Australian", "London"));
       infoHash.put("Isabelle", new PersonalInfo("French", "Gabon"));
       infoHash.put("Bob", new PersonalInfo("Australian", "Sydney"));
    }

    public int doStartTag() throws JspTagException {
       String nationality = "Unknown";
       String city = "Unknown";
```

Test whether this tag has an ancestor of the required type, which we can use to obtain a name to look up. Note that using the findAncestorWithClass() static method is more flexible than using getParent(). getParent() will fail if one or more tags separate this tag from the desired tag in the runtime hierarchy of tag handlers:

```
NameContext nameContextAncestor =
             (NameContext) TagSupport.findAncestorWithClass(
                                                  this,
                                          NameContext.class);
```

The exception thrown here will be handled by the JSP engine like any exception thrown in a scriptlet/expression, or an exception thrown by a bean. (Redirection to an error page would be the likely outcome):

```
if (nameContextAncestor == null) {
  throw new JspTagException("NameTag must only be used within " +
                            "a NameContext tag");
}
```

If we get to this point, we have a valid ancestor from which we can obtain a context:

```
String name = nameContextAncestor.getName();
PersonalInfo pi = (PersonalInfo) infoHash.get(name);
if (pi != null) {
  nationality = pi.getNationality();
  city = pi.getCity();
}
pageContext.setAttribute("nationality", nationality);
pageContext.setAttribute("city", city);
return EVAL_BODY_INCLUDE;
}
```

This inner class containing additional data retrieved for each name is used internally to enable the two required fields for each person to be stored as a single object in a hash table:

```
private class PersonalInfo {
private String nationality;
private String city;

public PersonalInfo(String nationality, String city) {
  this.nationality = nationality;
  this.city = city;
}

public String getNationality() {
  return nationality;
}

public String getCity() {
  return city;
}
}
```

We'll also need a new entry in our TLD file, remembering to use variable sub-tags to declare the scripting variables the new tag creates:

```
<tag>
  <name>nameInfo</name>
  <tag-class>tagext.NameInfoTag</tag-class>
  <body-content>JSP</body-content>
```

```
      <description>
      Tag to be nested within a tag implementing the NameContext interface
      </description>
      <variable>
        <name-given>nationality</name-given>
        <variable-class>java.lang.String</variable-class>
      </variable>
      <variable>
        <name-given>city</name-given>
        <variable-class>java.lang.String</variable-class>
      </variable>
    </tag>
```

Let's now create a JSP page to use the new tag, so that the additional lookup is performed only some of the time. Of course application logic would normally determine this, but for the sake of this example we will simply decide this randomly. The JSP page, `helloIteratorWithNesting.jsp`, is very similar to the previous example:

```
<%@ taglib uri="/hello" prefix="examples" %>

<%!
  java.util.List names = new java.util.LinkedList();

  public void jspInit() {
    names.add("Rod");
    names.add("Isabelle");
    names.add("Bob");
    names.add("Jens");
  }
%>

<html>
  <head>
    <title>Nested tags</title>
  </head>

  <body>
    <p>HTML.</p>
    <i>
      <% java.util.Random rand = new java.util.Random(); %>
      <examples:helloIterator names="<%=names%>" >
        Hello <%=name%>. You're entry <%=index%> in my list.
        <% if (rand.nextInt(3) != 0) { %>
            <examples:nameInfo>
              <b>Nationality:</b> <%=nationality%> <b>City:</b> <%=city%>
            </examples:nameInfo>
        <% } %>
        <br />
      </examples:helloIterator>
    </i>
    <p>More HTML</p>
  </body>
</html>
```

We've also added a new entry, `Jens`, to the list of names, to show what happens when no extra information is available. We handle this situation gracefully, as it doesn't justify throwing an exception that would abort the rendering of any JSP using the tag. Instead, the placeholder value `"Unknown"` is placed in the `PageContext`. Note the use of a scriptlet inside the `<examples:hellos>` tag to perform the necessary conditional logic. This doesn't produce any output, and is evaluated each time the `<example:hellos>` tag processes its body content. Only if the condition is true (this is quasi-random in this example) will the subtag be evaluated, its variables calculated and added to the `PageContext`, and, finally, its body content evaluated.

The output should look something like this:

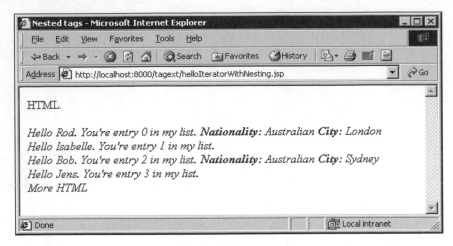

Try changing the example to move the `<examples:nameInfo>` tag outside the scope of a `<examples:hellos>` tag. Your JSP engine should provide a helpful error message, including the wording of the exception we made the `NameTag` throw in this case. As usual, some servers will display this error message to the client; others, like WebLogic 6.1, will show a generic "Internal Error" page but log the error.

Once again we have seen the power of the ability to define scripting variables. Since the implementations of the tags don't contain any markup, we could easily use these tags to generate a content type other than HTML.

Validating the Use of Tag Extensions in JSP Pages

As we've seen, tag library descriptors allow us some control over how a tag extension is used in JSP pages. For example, we can specify which attributes are permitted and even which are required. We can declare the scripting variables that the tag makes available to JSP pages that use it. However, there are times when more sophisticated validation might be required.

Imagine a `userDetails` tag that exposes the details of registered users as scripting variables. To identify the user in question, the tag has three attributes: `username`, `password`, and `userid`. As a user can be identified to the system by either a unique username/password combination or a numeric `userid` primary key, the tag could be used in two ways: by specifying both username and password attributes, or by specifying only the `userid` attribute. Supplying all three attributes, or any combination other than these two doesn't make sense. Ideally, we'd like to be able to flag invalid use at translation time, rather than at run time. Unfortunately, we can't do that using the attribute definitions in the TLD. All we can do is to mark all three attributes as optional, which would allow the authoring of nonsensical JSP pages that provided *none* of the three.

JSP 1.2 provides two ways of performing such sophisticated validation. Either a `TagExtraInfo` class can be provided that performs the required validation, or a `TagLibraryValidator` object can be associated with the whole tag library by using the `<validator>` sub-element of the top-level `<taglib>` element. The first method has been available since JSP 1.1; the second was introduced with JSP 1.2.

The implementation of such sophisticated validation is beyond the scope of an introductory chapter on tag extensions, but the following is a brief discussion of each of these approaches in turn.

We've previously seen the use of a `TagExtraInfo` class as one way of declaring the scripting variables exposed by a tag. If a `TagExtraInfo` class is used, the JSP engine will invoke its Boolean method `isValid(TagData data)` at translation time. The `javax.servlet.jsp.tagext.TagData` class will have been populated by the JSP engine with data about the attribute values given to the tag by the JSP. Both the names and values of static attributes will be available, but only the names of attributes with run time values will be available. This functionality is easy to use, and powerful enough to solve the problem we identified with the `userDetails` tag discussed above. We could check that the attributes present were a legal combination. As it is so easy to use, validation using a `TagExtraInfo` class is the best option in many cases.

The second approach, introduced in JSP 1.2, involves specifying in the TLD an object extending the `javax.servlet.jsp.tagext.TagLibraryValidator` abstract class that can validate the use of tags in the entire tag library. `TagLibraryValidator` contains a method with the signature:

```
String validate(String prefix, String uri, PageData page)
```

This method returns `null` if the tag's usage is valid, and an error message if the usage is invalid. If a `TagLibraryValidator` class is specified in the TLD for a tag library, the JSP engine must invoke its `validate()` method at translation time every time a tag from the library is encountered in a JSP. The prefix argument will identify the particular tag used, while the `PageData` argument will expose the XML document view of the JSP page.

Using a `TagLibraryValidator` is more complex than performing validation using a `TagExtroInfo` class. However, it is much more powerful. Not only can the attributes passed to the tag be taken into account; the entire page structure can be considered. All elements of the page – declarations, scriptlets, and template data – will be available via navigation of the XML document. It is also possible to return a helpful error message for the JSP developer about what went wrong.

If extremely sophisticated tag usage validation is required, a `TagLibraryValidator` class can solve just about any problem. However, for simpler validation requirements, using a `TagExtraInfo` class will be equally as effective and much easier to implement.

Handling Errors

Some errors can be avoided through the use of strict translation-time validation, but there remains the question of what tag handlers should do if they encounter an error condition at run time. The answer depends on whether the error is serious enough to invalidate the work of the calling JSP page, and whether the tag is likely to be important enough to the page's structure to justify causing the calling page to redirect to an error page.

If the error is minor, the best solution is to output suitable error markup, or nothing at all – depending on the tag's purpose. An HTML comment could be added that explains the error in more detail. If the error is a major one, the best approach is to make the tag handler method that detects the problem throw a `JspTagException`. This will, in most cases, cause the calling page to redirect to an error page.

JSP 1.2 adds a new interface, `javax.servlet.jsp.tagext.TryCatchFinally`, that offers an alternative approach to error handling. Callbacks in the `TryCatchFinally` interface can be used to intercept exceptions thrown by any tag handler method invoked by the container at run time. This means that if a tag handler throws an exception, it won't necessarily break the calling JSP page and result in the display of an error page. Instead the tag handler implementation has a chance to react to the exception.

Any tag handler can implement the `TryCatchFinally` interface. It contains two methods, the purposes of which are apparent from their names:

`public void doCatch(Throwable t) throws Throwable`

This method will be invoked if the tag handler's `doStartTag()`, `doEndTag()`, or (if applicable) `doInitBody()` or `doAfterBody()` method throws any exception, checked or unchecked. It can either take the appropriate action and suppress the `Throwable`, or rethrow it to be handled by the JSP using the tag. Even if this method is able to clean up whatever problem occurred, no subsequent callbacks will be invoked on the tag handler by the container for this use of the tag. (That is, if `doStartTag()` throws an exception, even if `doCatch()` successfully applies a workaround, `doEndTag()` will not be invoked by the container.)

`public void doFinally()`

This will be invoked in all cases, whether or not a `Throwable` was encountered during the work of the tag, and can be used to perform cleanup after each tag handler invocation.

Note that `doCatch()` will not be invoked if an exception results from the invocation by the container of a property setter on the tag handler.

Our next example shows how the `TryCatchFinally` interface could be used. It creates a dummy `Object` named `thisMustBeNullAfterInvocation` to simulate a resource that must be freed to avoid resource leaks. In this case, if this object isn't null after a (possibly incomplete) invocation of the tag handler's methods, imagine we have a resource leak that might affect the stability of our server. (In a real-world application, the resource could be a socket or database connection.)

Our example uses `System.out` statements to illustrate the behavior of the container and so we will need to refer to our server's log to review the output:

```
package tagext;

import java.io.IOException;
import java.util.*;
import javax.servlet.jsp.*;
import javax.servlet.jsp.tagext.*;

public class TryCatchFinallyIterationTag extends TagSupport
                                 implements IterationTag,
                                            TryCatchFinally {

  private List names;
  private int index;
  private StringBuffer output = new StringBuffer();
```

We'll use this object to decide whether or not to throw an exception:

```
  private Random rand = new Random();
```

The `thisMustBeNullAfterInvocation` variable is used to simulate an expensive resource. If this isn't `null`, imagine that this tag has left a DB connection or socket open:

```
  private Object thisMustBeNullAfterInvocation;

  public List getNames() {
    return names;
  }
```

```
    public void setNames(List names) {
      this.names = names;
    }

    public int doStartTag() throws JspTagException {
```

Display this object's hash code, to show the pooling strategy of the container:

```
      System.out.print("----------------\ndoStartTag on tag with hashCode= " +
                       hashCode() + ": ");
```

Check resource usage: no resources should be consumed before we start doing our work:

```
      checkResourceUsage();
```

Pretend to allocate expensive resource:

```
      thisMustBeNullAfterInvocation = new Object();
      setLoopVariables();
```

The return value is the same as for a normal, non-iterating, tag:

```
      return EVAL_BODY_INCLUDE;
    }
```

The JSP engine will call this method each time the body content of this tag has been processed. If it returns SKIP_BODY, the body content will have been processed for the last time. If it returns EVAL_BODY_TAG, the body will be processed and this method called at least once more. We store content in a StringBuffer, rather than write output directly:

```
    public int doAfterBody() throws JspTagException {
```

If we still haven't got to the end of the list, continue processing:

```
      if (++index < names.size()) {
```

We throw an exception every so often, to demonstrate TryCatchFinally behavior:

```
        if (rand.nextInt(3) % 5 == 0)
          throw new JspTagException("Random error");
        setLoopVariables();
        return EVAL_BODY_AGAIN;
      }
```

If we get to here, we've finished processing the list:

```
      return SKIP_BODY;
    }

    public int doEndTag() {
      System.out.println("doEndTag: ");
      return EVAL_PAGE;
    }
```

Make the variable available for each iteration:

```
private void setLoopVariables() {
  pageContext.setAttribute("name", names.get(index).toString());
  pageContext.setAttribute("index", new Integer(index));
}

public void release() {
```

You can uncomment this line to see how a JSP engine handles tag pooling:

```
  // System.out.println("release");
}
```

`doEndTag()` may not have been called if this method is called. Alternatively, the error might have occurred in `doEndTag()` itself:

```
public void doCatch(Throwable t) throws Throwable {
  System.out.println("doCatch: " + t);
  pageContext.getOut().println("<font color=\"red\">" +
                    "Invoked <b>doCatch</b> because of (" +
                    t + ")</font>");
}
```

This will be called after `doEndTag()` – if `doEndTag()` is called:

```
public void doFinally() {
  System.out.println("doFinally: cleaning up");
  // Cleanup
  thisMustBeNullAfterInvocation = null;
}
```

This method checks that our pretend resource has been safely released:

```
private void checkResourceUsage() {
  if (thisMustBeNullAfterInvocation != null) {
    System.out.println("************ RESOURCE LEAK: resource non-null");
  } else {
    System.out.println("Resource usage OK");
  }
}
}
```

The TLD entry is simple. It doesn't need to specify that this tag handler implements the `TryCatchFinally` interface:

```
<tag>
  <name>tcfIterator</name>
  <tag-class>tagext.TryCatchFinallyIterationTag</tag-class>
    <body-content>JSP</body-content>
    <description>
      Simple illustration of TryCatchFinally interface
    </description>
    <variable>
      <name-given>name</name-given>
```

```
              <variable-class>java.lang.String</variable-class>
          </variable>
          <variable>
            <name-given>index</name-given>
            <variable-class>java.lang.Integer</variable-class>
          </variable>
        <attribute>
          <name>names</name>
          <required>true</required>
          <rtexprvalue>true</rtexprvalue>
        </attribute>
      </tag>
```

The calling JSP, tryCatchFinally.jsp, is pretty similar to our earlier Iterator example, but its output will vary because the doAfterBody() method of the TryCatchFinallyIterationTag sometimes throws exceptions at run time:

```
<%@ taglib uri="/hello" prefix="examples" %>

<%!
  java.util.List names = new java.util.LinkedList();

  public void jspInit() {
    names.add("Rod");
    names.add("Isabelle");
    names.add("Bob");
  }
%>

<html>
  <head>
    <title>TryCatchFinally example</title>
  </head>

  <body>
    <p>HTML. Output generated using tags is italicized.</p>
    <i>
      <p>
        <examples:tcfIterator names="<%=names%>">
          Hello <b><%=name%></b>. You're entry <%=index%> in my list.<br/>
        </examples:tcfIterator>
      </p>
    </i>
    <p>More HTML.</p>
  </body>
</html>
```

The output will vary with the quasi-random choice of whether the tag handler should throw an exception in its doAfterBody() method, but it will look something like this:

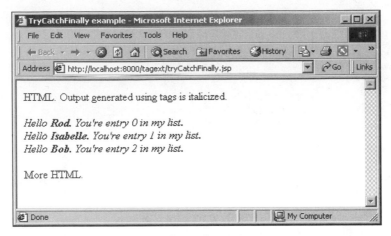

Or if an error occurs, something like this:

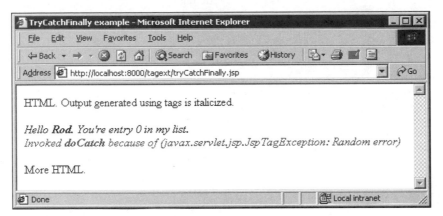

The JSP engine will log the callbacks the tag received. In the case of the Reference Implementation, the following output appeared in the server console window:

Because we've included the hash code of the tag instance on each invocation, this output will also reveal the pooling strategy our container uses for tag handlers. (This screenshot illustrates that the Reference Implementation isn't reusing tags most of the time.)

Try removing `TryCatchFinally` from this tag handler's `implements` clause. Now, the tag handler won't have the ability to suppress exceptions and output appropriate HTML, and the calling page will simply break.

TryCatchFinally – A Danger to Good Design?

While there are situations in which the `TryCatchFinally` interface may be useful, some developers have serious misgivings about its use in principle (and even the wisdom of adding it to the API):

❑ Using an API to simulate a perfectly good language feature (Java exception handling) suggests there's something wrong with what the API is trying to do.

❑ The `TryCatchFinally` option might encourage the undertaking of error-prone tasks such as data retrieval in tag handlers. This poses two problems: JSP pages should really be used as views, concerned with displaying rather than retrieving data and it may be too late to do anything appropriate about the error once the tag has been invoked. For example: What if we have lost connectivity to our database? By choosing to access it only in a tag invoked after lots of page generation has been completed, we can't be sure that the buffer hasn't been flushed, and content sent back to the client. If it has, we might have generated irrelevant formatting information when we really needed to tell the client that we couldn't offer a normal service.

One welcome addition to the JSP API in JSP 1.2 for handling runtime errors is the new constructor to `JspException` that takes both a string message and a `Throwable` root cause. Like the `ServletException` constructor taking the same arguments, this makes it easy to add useful context information when a problem is encountered, while still preserving the stack trace of the problem itself. Unfortunately, (as of the JSP 1.2 Proposed Final Draft 2) the `JspTagException` still has no constructor with these arguments, and not even a constructor taking a root cause. This is an oversight in the specification that makes it more difficult to write maintainable applications. The solution, until the API is made more consistent, is to create a subclass of `JspTagException` for your organization, provide it with a constructor taking a `String` message and `Throwable` root cause, and throw it in place of `JspTagException`.

Application Lifecycle Events

The Servlet 2.3 specification (which is of course closely linked to the JSP 1.2 specification) introduces the concept of **application lifecycle events**, and the ability to register any number of listener beans that receive notifications as they occur. There are two kinds of application events: **servlet context events**, and **HTTP session events**.

Servlet context events are fired when a servlet context has been created and is available to service requests, when a servlet context is about to be shut down, or when attributes on the servlet context have been added, removed, or replaced. Servlet context event listeners can be used to manage resources or state held for an entire application (or tag library) at virtual machine level. They must implement either the `javax.servlet.ServletContextListener` or the `javax.servlet.ServletContext AttributesListener` interface.

HTTP session events are fired when a user's `HttpSession` object has been created, invalidated, or timed out or when attributes have been added, removed; or replaced on an existing `HttpSession` object. HTTP session-event listeners can be used to manage resources or state maintained on behalf of a particular user, or to maintain information about the usage of an entire application. They must implement either the `javax.servlet.http.HttpSessionContextListener` or the `javax.servlet.http.HttpSesessionAttributesListener` interface

The JSP 1.2 specification builds on this new Servlet API feature, allowing tag libraries, as well as web applications, to register application-event listeners. Before we look at a simple example showing how to use this new tag library functionality, let's consider why it has been introduced, and what need it addresses.

A key feature of the tag extension mechanism is the ability to distribute self-contained tag libraries that can be reused in many web applications. It's important that a tag library can be used without modifications to the application's web.xml deployment descriptor (besides the necessary <taglib> element to tell the application where the tag deployment can be found). The ability to register web application listeners in tag libraries means that tag libraries can react as necessary to web application events to co-ordinate the behavior of all the tags they contain – without the need to modify web applications that use them.

Let's consider a realistic scenario. What if the tag handler classes in a tag library need to maintain shared resources with a lifecycle linked to the entire library, rather than run-time invocations of individual tags? Multiple tags might need to access an EJB server, and require a reference to a session bean home object. Clearly it would be inefficient for each tag handler to connect to this resource every time it is invoked from a JSP page. The management of the resource connection belongs to the entire library, not each individual tag. We could address this problem by using a singleton object accessible from all tags, but where would it be initialized? It would be possible to initialize it the first time a tag needs the resource at run time, but this would be an inelegant and error-prone solution.

A better solution is to use a servlet context listener to acquire the resource and make it available to all tags in the library when an application using the tag library starts up, and to free the resource when the application shuts down. While a listener could be registered in the web.xml deployment descriptor of each web application using the tag library to do this, this would complicate use of the tag library; developers using it shouldn't need to worry about its internal plumbing. If, however, the listener is registered in the tag library descriptor itself, the workings of the tag library will remain private, and it is guaranteed to work the same way in every web application in which it is used.

Let's look at an implementation of a simplified version of the above scenario. Imagine that we need to make a shared object available to all tags in our examples tag library. We will register a servlet context listener in the tag library descriptor to initialize the shared object and make it available to the other tags, and free it when the application shuts down.

To register a servlet context listener, we need to add a <listener> element to our TLD. The <listener> element comes immediately before the first <tag> element (but after the <description> and <validator> elements if these are present). The <listener> element contains a single sub-element, <listener-class>, which contains the fully qualified class name of the servlet context listener bean. It's possible to register any number of listeners in a TLD by using multiple <listener> elements, but we will need only one:

```
<listener>
  <listener-class>
    tagext.listeners.ExamplesTLDServletContextListener
  </listener-class>
</listener>
```

Now we need to implement the tagext.listeners.ExamplesTLDServletContextListener listener bean we have registered as a listener. Note that we must supply a no-argument constructor, following standard JavaBeans conventions. There are only two methods in the javax.servlet.ServletContextListener interface:

- ❑ void contextInitialized(ServletContextEvent sce)
  This will be invoked when the web application is started up. We can use it to initialize our shared object.

- ❑ void contextDestroyed(ServletContextEvent sce)
  This will be invoked before the application shuts down. We can use it to free any state maintained by our tag library.

There is a single method, getServletContext(), in the javax.servlet.ServletContextEvent class, which enables us to access the servlet context of the current application. We use the setAttribute() method of this ServletContext object to make the shared object available to the tag handlers in the application. (They can access it using the getAttribute() method of the PageContext object available to them at run time, making the servlet context object a useful means of resource sharing at run time.)

The implementation of the listener is very simple:

```
package tagext.listeners;

import javax.servlet.*;

public class ExamplesTLDServletContextListener
            implements ServletContextListener {

  public static final String SHARED_OBJECT_NAME = "sharedObject";

  public ExamplesTLDServletContextListener () { }

  public void contextInitialized(ServletContextEvent sce)  {
    DummySharedObject dso = new DummySharedObject(
                                        System.currentTimeMillis()
                                    );
    System.out.println("Putting shared object " + dso +
                       " in ServletContext for examples tag library");
    sce.getServletContext().setAttribute(SHARED_OBJECT_NAME, dso);
  }

  public void contextDestroyed(ServletContextEvent sce) {
    System.out.println("ServletContext destroyed event: would " +
                       "free any resources held");
  }
}
```

For the sake of this example, the shared object is very simple, merely maintaining the time it was created, and exposing it in a getCreationDate() method. A shared object in a production tag library would be likely to acquire and expose resources required by tags in the library:

```
package tagext.listeners;

import java.util.Date;

public class DummySharedObject {

  private long timeCreated;

  public DummySharedObject(long timeCreated) {
    this.timeCreated = timeCreated;
  }
```

```
   public Date getCreationDate() {
     return new Date(timeCreated);
   }
 }
```

Since the `ExamplesTLDServletContextListener` class has been registered as a servlet context listener, all tags in the examples library can assume that the shared object will be available through the `PageContext` object available to them at run time. The following simple tag obtains a reference to the shared object, and prints out its creation date to JSP pages that use it:

```
package tagext.listeners;

import java.io.IOException;
import java.util.Date;
import javax.servlet.jsp.*;
import javax.servlet.jsp.tagext.TagSupport;

public class SharedObjectAccessTag extends TagSupport {

  public int doEndTag() throws JspTagException {
    String dateString = new Date().toString();
    try {
```

Get hold of the shared object:

```
      DummySharedObject dso =
                 (DummySharedObject) pageContext.getAttribute(
                      ExamplesTLDServletContextListener.SHARED_OBJECT_NAME,
                      PageContext.APPLICATION_SCOPE);
      if (dso == null) {
        throw new JspTagException(
                 "Error: shared object not found in servlet context. " +
                 " It should have been made available by the " +
                 "ExampleTLDServletContextListener");
      }
      pageContext.getOut().write("I got hold of the shared object, " +
                             "and it was created at " +
                             dso.getCreationDate());
    } catch (IOException ex) {
      throw new JspTagException("Fatal error: " +
                             "hello tag could not write to JSP out");
    }
```

This return value means that the JSP engine should continue to evaluate the rest of this page:

```
    return EVAL_PAGE;
  }
 }
```

Before we can access the tag from JSP pages, we will need to add the following `<tag>` element to our TLD, `hello.tld`. It uses exactly the same syntax as the `<tag>` elements we've seen before, as the new tag handler's access to the shared object is a Java implementation detail that doesn't impact its use from JSP pages:

```
    <tag>
      <name>listenerTest</name>
      <tag-class>tagext.listeners.SharedObjectAccessTag</tag-class>
      <body-content>JSP</body-content>
```

```
      <description>
        Simple example of JSP 1.2 TLD listener functionality.
        Takes no attributes, and simply generates HTML
      </description>
    </tag>
```

The following simple JSP, `tld-listener.jsp`, calls the new `listenerTest` tag:

```
<%@ taglib uri="/hello" prefix="examples" %>

<html>
  <head>
    <title>Example of JSP 1.2 TLD listener functionality</title>
  </head>

  <body>
    <p>This is static output.</p>
    <i><p><examples:listenerTest /></p></i>
    <p>This is static output again.</p>
  </body>
</html>
```

The following screenshot illustrates the output we should see when we request this JSP page. It shows that the shared object was initialized by the `ExamplesTLDServletContextListener` object registered in the TLD and successfully accessed by the `SharedObjectAccessTag` tag handler at run time. If we re-request this page, the output won't change, as we continue to access the same shared-object instance:

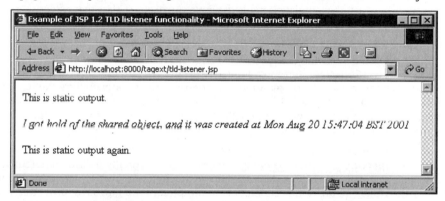

Such registration of a servlet context listener in a TLD is likely to become commonplace in JSP 1.2 applications and offers a welcome new way to integrate the implementation of the tags in a library.

> *Since a "shared object" added to the `ServletContext` has application scope, it can be accessed concurrently by multiple threads, and must be threadsafe. The issues are the same as for any object with application scope in a web application.*

HTTP session listeners can also be registered in TLDs. The registration of an HTTP session listener does not address the same pressing need as the registration of servlet context listeners, but will be useful for some tag libraries. As a hypothetical example, consider a tag library to be shipped as a demonstration, which permits no more than three concurrent users. The tag library could register an HTTP session listener that maintained a count of the active sessions. The `javax.servlet.http.HttpSessionListener` interface contains two methods:

```
void sessionCreated(HttpSessionEvent e)
void sessionDestroyed(HttpSessionEvent e)
```

The implementation of the `sessionCreated()` method could increment a session counter, while the `sessionDestroyed()` method could decrement the session counter. Each tag in the library could check the session count exposed by the session listener (which could add itself as an attribute of the application's `ServletContext`), and throw a `JspTagException` if the session count exceeded the maximum.

Tag Extension Idioms

In order to stress the mechanics of tag handlers themselves, we have deliberately used simple examples to this point. However, the range of functionality that can be delivered with tag extensions is very wide.

Some of the most important possibilities are:

❑ **Generating HTML output**
This is the simplest use of custom tags. It has some merit in that a standard building block is available, and can be changed simultaneously everywhere it occurs if necessary. However, in general, using Java code to generate HTML is clumsy and inflexible. Using JSP static includes (via the include directive) may be a superior alternative.

❑ **Using template content to generate HTML output**
This is a more sophisticated variant of the above, avoiding having messy markup generation in Java code and allowing modification of the generated markup without recompilation. Usually a mechanism will need to be designed and documented for controlling variable substitution and any other ways in which the template is made dynamic. An abstract class that extends `TagSupport` or `BodyTagSupport` could provide standard template lookup and variable interpolation for use across a system. This is a common idiom, and can be very useful in real-world systems.

❑ **Defining scripting variables**
This is usually a superior alternative to using tags to generate markup directly, especially when iteration is concerned. All computation and control flow is controlled by the tag handler classes, rather than the calling JSP page, but the scripting variables are used within the JSP page to allow markup generation to be changed easily. As a general rule, tags that define variables should not generate markup.

❑ **Transforming or interpreting tag body content**
This is an especially powerful use of tag extensions, with virtually unlimited potential. For example, a tag could establish a database connection and execute SQL contained in its body to display the results. A tag could implement an interpreter for a language, providing entirely new syntax and functionality within JSP pages. (For example, it would be conceivable to design an `asp` tag that would interpret a subset of ASP for running legacy code.) In some of these cases, the `tagdependent` value should be used to describe the body content in the TLD.

Some of the possibilities of this idiom are not compatible with writing maintainable code. JSP is a standard, understood by a whole development community, whereas your tag content may not be, unless you choose some other standard such as SQL. It is also possible to create nested tags that interact in surprising ways; this also reduces readability.

❑ **A gatekeeper role**
A custom tag can check for login or some other condition, and redirect the response if the result is unsatisfactory. Alternative approaches worth considering are using Servlet 2.3 Filters or a controller servlet, in the **front controller** design pattern.

❏ **Concealing access to enterprise objects or APIs that should not be visible**
This is an easy way of providing a JSP interface to enterprise data. However, note that it is not consistent with good J2EE design to write tags that access databases via JDBC. Consider the alternative of a true n-tier architecture, in which the tag handlers access business objects such as session EJBs implementing the J2EE Session Façade design pattern.

❏ **Exposing complex data**
Custom tags can be used to expose data (for example, in a list or table) that might otherwise require complicated JSP logic to display. This is one of the best applications of custom tags, and usually the best way of displaying such data in JSP pages.

❏ **Handling iteration**
This is a simple and practical way of avoiding a profusion of scriptlets in JSP pages. In this case it is especially important to make tags as generic as possible.

Remember that custom tags are building blocks, and will be most useful when they can be reused easily. The following principles help to make tag extensions reusable:

❏ Make tags as configurable as possible. This can be achieved through tag attributes and using nesting to provide context. Optional attributes can be used where default values can be supplied.

❏ Avoid generating HTML in tag handlers unless absolutely necessary.

❏ When tags handlers must generate HTML we should ensure that the generated HTML can be used in a wide variety of contexts. Try to avoid generating <html>, <form>, and other structural tags; instead consider reading the HTML from a template file.

❏ Avoid making custom tags do unexpected things to the request and response objects. Just because tag handlers can access these objects through the PageContext doesn't mean that it's a good idea. For example, how obvious will it be to a reader of a JSP page using a custom tag that the tag may redirect the response? Unless the tag's documentation is scrupulous, figuring this out might require plunging into the source code of the tag. Consider another example: if a tag were to flush the JSP page's output buffer, the JSP engine would be unable to redirect to an error page if anything went wrong during the rendering of the rest of the JSP page. This would limit the usefulness of the tag and, again, the behavior would be a challenge for a JSP developer to figure out.

When and how to use tag extensions is further discussed in the next chapter. The key point to remember, however, is that some caution is called for in using custom tags. Using too many tag extensions can make JSP pages unreadable: the end result will be your own language, which may be the most efficient approach to solving a particular problem, but won't be intelligible to an outside observer, especially if your tags cooperate in complex ways.

Summary

Tag extensions, or custom tags, are a powerful extension to the JSP model. Their use is limited only by the ingenuity of developers, and they are an essential building block of well-engineered JSP interfaces. The enhancements in JSP 1.2 make them even more powerful and easier to develop.

Tag extensions can access the JSP PageContext and their behavior can respond dynamically to the XML attributes they are invoked with, as well as their body content. They are implemented using:

❏ Java classes implementing tag behavior

❏ XML Tag Library Descriptor (TLD) files describing one or more tags, and the attributes they require

❏ Optional extra classes defining validation behavior and scripting variables introduced by the tags

Tag extensions are a valuable way of separating presentation from content in JSP interfaces. Since they are a standard part of JSP, there are a growing number of third-party tag libraries, which are becoming increasingly valuable building blocks in JSP development.

Importantly, once the initial concepts are grasped, tag extensions are remarkably easy to develop. The tag extension mechanism allows us to build, portable, simple, and expressive extensions to our JSP pages – all built upon existing concepts and machinery.

In the next chapter we will go on to look at some more complex examples of tag extensions.

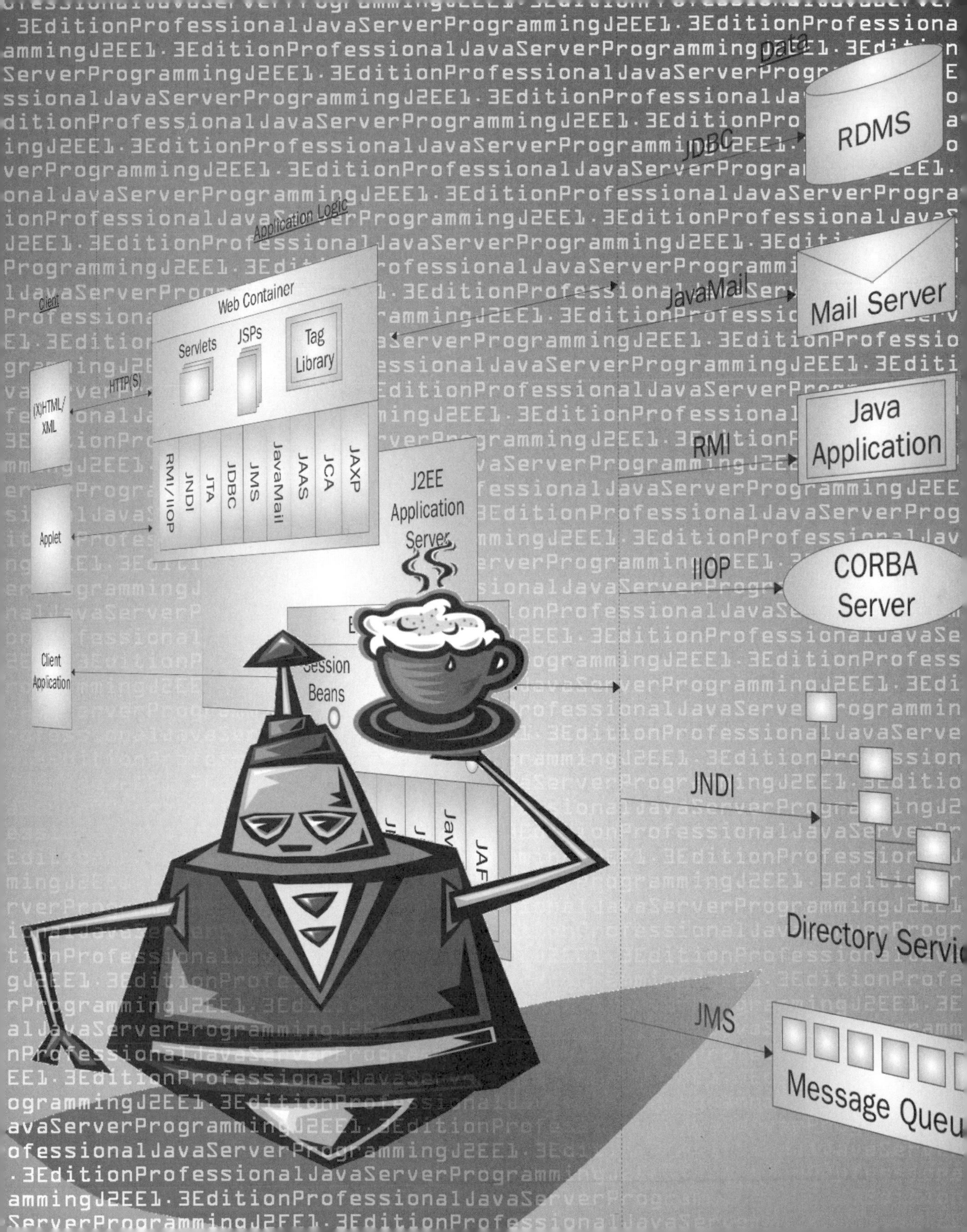

12

Writing JSP Applications with Tag Libraries

The JSP specification version 1.0 introduced us to the notion of **standard actions** or built-in JSP tags that must be implemented by every server vendor. As JSP application authors, we can now firmly rely on and use standard actions irrespective of the version of the JSP container or application server we use.

The overhaul of the JSP syntax and the provision of standard actions seemed a luxury for those of us using JSP containers that loosely adhered to version 0.9x of the specification. That all seems so long ago now, but in reality, it has just fallen in with the explosion and popularity of Internet-related technologies over the last couple of years.

The specification stated that future versions would provide a tag extension mechanism to allow **custom actions** to be defined and used by application developers and application-server vendors alike. Version 1.1 of the JSP specification provided us with the mechanism for defining custom actions packaged as **tag libraries**. This was met with great enthusiasm from the Java and web communities, and had direct implications for a number of different groups:

- ❑ **JSP application authors** could define and use their own tags scoped at the application, project, or organization level

- ❑ **Application-server vendors** could provide extensions to their implementation of the specification

- ❑ **Third-party organizations** could provide commercially viable tag libraries, specific to their line of business

Providing a mechanism for defining our own tags is great but, until now, no provision had been made for standard tags that tie into one of the most powerful development products on the market today: Java itself. The Java API provides us with facilities for accessing files, network resources, databases, and an extensive range of enterprise technologies.

Much time and effort is being spent at Sun Microsystems and open source organizations to bring together some common concepts and design patterns to facilitate access to Java APIs and create a **JSP Standard Tag Library (JSPTL)**. The JSPTL is being defined and developed through the Java Community Process (JCP) under Java Specification Request (JSR) 052 and can be found at http://www.jcp.org/jsr/detail/52.jsp.

In this chapter we're going to identify and focus on many common features of JSP-based web applications. As JSP application authors, we've all used standard Java concepts such as iteration and conditional statements, and are experimenting with newer concepts like internationalization, XML, and XSLT. We'll look at how the implementation of these features can be unified and made much easier using tag libraries. In particular, we'll initially:

❑ Review the benefits of custom tags and custom libraries

❑ Take a brief look at some examples of the existing vendor and open-source tags libraries available today

❑ Introduce the JSP Standard Tag Library (JSPTL), and show how to get it and what it currently covers

We'll then move on to demonstrate the use of the tags that compose the JSPTL. Other common concepts, not currently covered by the JSPTL (but shortly to be defined as part of the JSPTL), such as internationalization, HTML form handling within JSP pages, and XML and XSL Transformations (XSLT) will also be covered in detail, using some tags put together specifically for the purpose of this chapter.

Having covered the JSPTL and other commonly used features of JSP applications we'll then move on to a practical and realistic registration application as our main example.

Finally, we'll conclude by looking at what lies ahead for the JSPTL.

Benefits of Using Custom Tag Libraries

The Java 2 Platform, Enterprise Edition (J2EE) specification defines a number of key roles such as J2EE product provider, application-component provider, application assembler, deployer, system administrator, and J2EE tool provider. In particular, the role of application-component provider is responsible for producing the various components that make up a J2EE application. In actual fact, this role usually encompasses a number of roles, such as HTML document designers, document programmers (those that produce the dynamic application web components such as JSP pages, and servlets) and Enterprise JavaBean (EJB) developers.

Many commercial organizations have totally separate application development and web authoring teams. Developers aren't (and in many cases don't want to be) concerned with the intricacies of HTML and JavaScript for creating great-looking web pages. In the same respect, web page authors don't want to concern themselves with the specifics of practical OO modeling and application development. They just want to take the content provided and transform it into a web interface, through which the user interacts with the application.

With the separation of page author and application developer roles, JSP pages are a step in the right direction in helping to divide the presentation (the static HTML template data) from the content (often dynamically produced data in the form of JavaBeans). This is in contrast to, say, servlets, where the content and presentation are more tightly coupled. Custom tags further aid in the process of separation of presentation from content within JSP pages.

Introducing customs tags within our JSP applications has the following advantages:

- ❑ Separation of presentation from content:
  - ❑ Developers create custom tags
  - ❑ Page authors design web pages
- ❑ Encapsulate behavior and promote reuse. Customs tags written by application developers can wrap up creation of and access to dynamically produced data from a variety of sources: databases, EJBs, JavaSpaces, Java Data Objects (JDO), and file systems and expose data to web page authors. Moreover, incorporation of customs tags standardizes web page layout and construction.
- ❑ Enable sophisticated authoring tools and IDEs. Many J2EE providers offer sophisticated JSP authoring tools, which simplify use of custom tags within JSP pages or go as far as to offer complete personalization solutions that generate content specific to each user or type of user. An example of this is BEA's WebLogic Personalization Server.

Some examples of customs tag libraries are discussed in the next section.

Examples of Existing Tag Libraries

The fast pace of commercial web development has led to many different vendor and open source tag libraries emerging. This is great for JSP application authors, having a variety of tags to choose from. The use of one or a few really large and well-documented tag libraries would lead to short learning curves for JSP developers. Imagine being able to move from one project to another and reuse the same tag libraries.

There are many examples of tag libraries out there today:

- ❑ BEA's WebLogic Server 5.1 and 6.0; Commerce and Personalization Server standard with customizable JSP based templates – see http://commerce.beasys.com for more details.
- ❑ Allaire's JRun 3.x Enterprise Server; JRun provides some simple and useful tags for enterprise applications, which greatly simplify JSP application development – see http://www.allaire.com/products/jrun.
- ❑ The Jakarta Taglibs Project; an ongoing open source repository for JSP custom tag libraries and associated tools. This Jakarta project, part of the Apache Software Foundation effort, is helping to define the JSPTL and many of the contributors are actively participating in the formation of the JSPTL itself.

  The JSPTL is released through the Jakarta Taglibs Project and the reader is encouraged to find out more about this project at http://jakarta.apache.org/taglibs/index.html.

With the advent of the JSPTL, I look forward to the day when we can all work with a unified tag library, covering much of the common functionality currently offered by the variety of tag libraries available today.

Introducing the JSP Standard Tag Library (JSPTL)

The JSPTL is a standard JavaServer Pages Tag Library. It encapsulates core functionality, common to many JSP applications. For example, rather than use scriptlets or vendor-specific tags for basic concepts like iteration over lists, the JSPTL defines a standard `forEach` tag that achieves this.

569

Shortly after the release of the JSP 1.1 specification, it was noted that the widespread use of custom tags could lead to duplication of effort in defining tags to access our well-known Java APIs. With increasing acceptance of the specification it soon became apparent this might happen all too soon and JSR-052 was raised to address the issue. The JSR and further discussion by the industry gave birth to the JSPTL.

The obvious benefits of the introduction of a standard library of tags are:

❑ Consistent interface for common tags between application-server vendors. Like standard actions, developers can rely on these tags to be present and implemented in a consistent manner. All developers need do is package the JSPTL with the application.

❑ Brings together common ideas for useful tags that provide through access to the Standard Edition and Enterprise Edition APIs.

❑ Simplifies JSP and web application development.

❑ Reduces the amount of scriptlet code in JSP pages, in a unified manner.

❑ Allows futher integration of JSP authoring tools into web application development.

At time of writing, the JSPTL was released as Early Access EA1.1. It's still early days, but getting to know it now will probably influence the way you write JSP pages from this moment on. The next sections describe how to get it and what the JSPTL covers.

Obtaining the JSPTL

The JSPTL is hosted and released through the Jakarta Taglibs project. It can be downloaded from http://jakarta.apache.org/taglibs/doc/jsptl-doc/intro.html.

Download the JSPTL release and release documentation from the link above. You'll need it to run the examples that follow in this chapter.

What does the JSPTL Cover?

The JSPTL EA1.1 covers the following areas:

❑ Control flow

    ❑ Iteration

    ❑ Conditional logic

❑ Expression languages

❑ Expression-language tags

The key focus during the early phases of the JSPTL is to design and build the foundations for the variety of tags that will ultimately be included. Getting it right and coming up with a useable and popular library will largely depend on the work carried out over the coming months. At the moment both iterative and conditional forms of control flow are covered.

Promised later, are tags for internationalization, JDBC, JSP-templates, XML/XSLT and I/O. Further still, the JSPTL promises tags that tie into J2EE, such as JavaMail, JNDI, JMS, and many of the up-and-coming JAX APIs such as JAXM, JAXB, and JAX-RPC.

Getting Started with the JSPTL

The JSPTL EA1.1 uses features of the JSP 1.2 specification and so requires a JSP 1.2- and Servlet 2.3-compliant container. For the purpose of this chapter, we'll be using the Sun J2EE Reference Implementation server – but any other suitable container such as BEA's WebLogic Server 6.x should be fine. Remember; generally we write web applications to the specification, not the server!

The JSPTL actually comprises two tag libraries. While the two tag libraries contain virtually the same tags, they differ in how the values of attributes are specified at request time to tags in each library. The first tag library, JSPTL request-time expression values (jr), contains tags that accept attribute values as string literals or request time expression values (rtexprvalues) using scriptlet expressions like "<= scriptlet_expr %>". There were plenty of examples of rtexprvalues introduced in Chapter 11. The following JSP fragment shows an example of the use of the forEach tag in the jr library:

```
<%@ taglib uri="http://java.sun.com/jsptl/ea/jr" prefix="jr" %>

<jsp:useBean id="companyPageBean" type="..." />

<jr:forEach var="employee" items="<%= companyPageBean.getEmployees() %>" >

<!-- Processing -->

</jr:forEach>
```

The first line is the taglib directive that brings the jr tag library into the JSP page. All tags from the library will be prefixed with jr within the scope of the page. The third line brings in a company page bean, after which, the fifth line onwards iterates over a list of employees in the company.

The second tag library (jx), JSPTL with eXpression-language support, contains tags that only accept attribute values as string literals that can represent expression-language expression values (elexprvalues) and do not accept rtexprvalues. The values of attributes supplied to tags from this library represent expressions that are interpreted and evaluated by the configured expression-language:

```
<%@ taglib uri="http://java.sun.com/jsptl/ea/jx" prefix="jx" %>

<jx:forEach var="employee" items="$companyPageBean.employees" >

<!-- Processing -->

</jx:forEach>
```

In the example above, the use of the dollar ($) meta-character in $companyPageBean.employees is defined by the expression-language in order to discriminate expressions from string literals.

In comparing the two tag libraries, using the examples shown above, we can instantly see the differences. The jr library is very similar in its use to the tag libraries we have seen to date. Attribute values are supplied explicitly through JSP rtexprvalue expressions. On the other hand, the jx library introduces a very powerful concept indeed – expression-language expressions. These expressions add meaning to the string literal values specified as attributes to tags.

> In the first example, we had to locate a bean and then call the getter methods for the properties of the bean we were interested in, namely **employees**. In the second example however, we simply named the bean and the nested property on the bean we were interested in. As we specified this using the expression, **$companyPageBean.employees**, the expression-language evaluator evaluates this for us by locating the bean in scope and inspecting the **employees** property.

In the next section we'll look at the tags that make up the JSPTL in depth, with some examples.

Integrating the JSPTL into Your JSP Pages

Right, we've discussed benefits of tag libraries, looked at some of the libraries available, and been introduced to the JSPTL. Before we look at the tags that make up the JSPTL let's build our first example.

An Iteration Example

As a simple example to demonstrate the power of the JSPTL, we'll look at a JSP page that iterates through a list of colors. We've named this simple example forEachColor.jsp, accordingly. Lets take a look at the JSP first, and then discuss how the example was put together later:

```
<%@ taglib uri="http://java.sun.com/jsptl/ea/jx" prefix="jx"%>

<html>
<head>
  <title>An example JSPTL forEach Tag with Colors!</title>
</head>
<body bgcolor="#FFFFFF">

How does one remember colors of the rainbow?<BR>
<br>
<br>
<table width="300" border="1">
  <tr>
    <td width="67%"><b><i>Name</i></b></td><td><b><i>RGB Value</i></b></td>
  </tr>
<jx:forEach var="color" items="$colors" >
  <tr bgcolor="#<jx:expr value='$color.RGBValue'/>">
    <td><jx:expr value="$color.name"/></td>
    <td><jx:expr value="$color.RGBValue"/></td>
  </TR>
</jx:forEach>
</body>
</html>
```

The first line imports the JSPTL tag library with expression-language support (jx). Following that is a small amount of HTML to create a table to hold our list of colors. The shaded area of the code shows what's interesting. A forEachTag iterates through a list of colors, creating a row for each color, with the row background set to the color RGB value.

With forEachColor.jsp in the right place (see *Getting it Running* below) the output below will be shown in your browser.

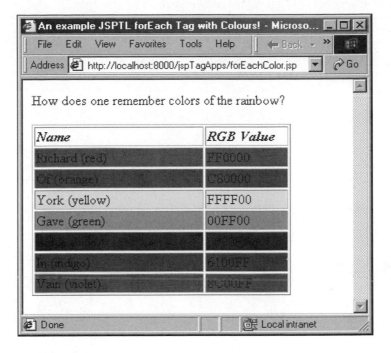

Getting it Running

We'll look at the tags that compose the JSPSTL in more detail later. In the meantime, let's get this example running.

The forEachColor.jsp JSP refers to the list of colors via the "$colors" expression. In order to create some colors to show, we use a ServletContextListener implementing class to create a list of sample colors at startup. The class, JSPTLExamplesInit, is shown below:

```
package jsptl.examples.startup;

import java.util.*;

import javax.servlet.*;
import writingjsps.jsptl.examples.beans.*;

public class JSPTLExamplesInit implements ServletContextListener {

  public void contextInitialized(ServletContextEvent scEv) {
    createData(scEv);
  }

  public void contextDestroyed(ServletContextEvent scEv) {}

  //Creates JSP scoped attributes for use in the JSPTL examples.
  private void createData(ServletContextEvent scEv) {
```

```
      // Create some colors
      ColorBean colors[] = new ColorBean[] {
        new ColorBean(" Richard (red)", "FF0000"),
        new ColorBean(" Of      (orange)", "C80000"),
        new ColorBean(" York    (yellow)", "FFFF00"),
        new ColorBean(" Gave    (green)", "00FF00"),
        new ColorBean(" Battle  (blue)", "0000FF"),
        new ColorBean(" In      (indigo)", "6100FF"),
        new ColorBean(" Vain    (violet)", "8C00FF")
      };
      scEv.getServletContext().setAttribute("colors", colors);
    }
  }
```

The servlet container calls the JSPTLExamplesInit class when the application is started and initialized. In our example, the container calls the contextInitialized() method, which simply calls the createData() method to create a list of colors and pop them into the servlet context.

The ColorBean class, used to create the colors[] array, is listed below:

```
package jsptl.examples.beans;

public class ColorBean {
  private String name;
  private String rgb;

  public ColorBean() {}

  public ColorBean(String name, String rgb) {
    setName(name);
    setRGBValue(rgb);
  }

  public String getName() {
    return name;
  }

  public void setName(String name) {
    this.name = name;
  }

  public String getRGBValue() {
    return rgb;
  }

  public void setRGBValue(String rgb) {
    this.rgb = rgb;
  }

  public String toString() {
    return getName() + "=" + getRGBValue();
  }
}
```

Let's create a Web ARchive (WAR) for the web application that will house the examples we put together in this chapter. As mentioned previously, we'll be using features of the JSP 1.2 and Servlet 2.3 specifications so we'll run the examples using the Sun Reference Implementation server that conforms to these specifications.

The only thing left to do now is define the web application descriptor, web.xml. The following is the web.xml file for our example:

```xml
<?xml version="1.0" encoding="ISO-8859-1"?>

<!DOCTYPE web-app
    PUBLIC "-//Sun Microsystems, Inc.//DTD Web Application 2.3//EN"
           "http://java.sun.com/j2ee/dtds/web-app_2_3.dtd">

<web-app>
  <description>
    Writing JSP Applications with Tag Libraries example web application.
  </description>
   <display-name>JSPtaqWAR</display-name>

  <!--
       A context parameter that specifies
       the default expression language for the application.
   -->
  <context-param>
     <param-name>javax.servlet.jsptl.ExpressionEvaluatorClass</param-name>
     <param-value>org.apache.taglibs.jsptl.lang.spel.Evaluator</param-value>
  </context-param>

  <listener>
    <listener-class>
      jsptl.examples.startup.JSPTLExamplesInit
    </listener-class>
  </listener>

  <taglib>
    <taglib-uri>http://java.sun.com/jsptl/ea/jx</taglib-uri>
    <taglib-location>/WEB-INF/tlds/jx.tld</taglib-location>
  </taglib>

  <taglib>
    <taglib-uri>http://java.sun.com/jsptl/ea/jr</taglib-uri>
    <taglib-location>/WEB-INF/tlds/jr.tld</taglib-location>
  </taglib>
</web-app>
```

Now we're ready to deploy the example. Create a directory for the WAR, called jspTagApps.

Having created the WAR root directory, now create the following structure underneath, including our forEachColor.jsp, the JSPTL tag library JAR (see *Obtaining the JSPTL*), the JSPTL tag library descriptors (refer to Chapter 11, *JSP Tag Extensions*, for tag library descriptors), the JAXP jaxp.jar and crimson.jar JARs bundled with the JSPTL, and, of course, the JSPTLExamplesInit class in the right package under WEB-INF/classes:

```
jspTagApps/
          forEachColor.jsp
          WEB-INF/
                  web.xml
                  classes/
                          jsptl/
                                examples/
                                         startup/
                                                 JSPTLExamplesInit.class
                                         beans/
```

```
                                        ColorBean.class
            lib/
                crimson.jar
                jaxp.jar
                jsptl.jar
            tlds/
                jr.tld
                jx.tld
```

The structure above can reside anywhere on your file system, but keep hold of it for the other examples in this chapter. Finally, you could also deploy as a WAR file by JARing up the whole directory structure:

```
jar  cvf jspTagApps.war *
```

Now we have to add this WAR file to an application EAR file, for which we will use the RI Deployment Tool utility. The only thing we need to specify (other than the name of the EAR file, and the WAR file we want) is the context root for our web application:

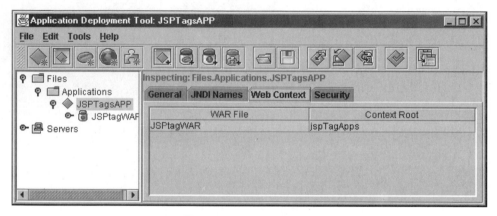

Let's now look at what tags are in the JSPTL EA1.1 and put together some examples.

The JSPTL Tags

We'll start by discussing some of the design issues considered by the JSPTL team in putting together the JSPTL. We'll then look at some basic tags that are used in conjunction with the more complex tags in the library, and then define the more complex iteration and conditional tags themselves.

Some JSPTL Design Considerations

The JSPTL has been put together as part of a Java Community Process (JCP). As a result, in-depth analysis of the needs of the Java community has been carried out and a focused design phase undertaken. In particular, the following main issues were considered:

❑   **Keep tags' interfaces small**. The number of attributes of tags has been kept to a minimum in order to not 'clutter' tag interfaces and provide tags that can achieve just about anything through their extensive numbers of attributes.

❏ **How a tag collaborates with its environment**. Tags usually collaborate with their environment implicitly or explicitly. Tags collaborate implicitly with their environment by implementing a well-defined interface that can be exposed by the ancestor tag hierarchy (through the `TagSupport.findAncestorWithClass(...)` method). Tags collaborate explicitly by exposing information to the environment in which they operate. Traditionally, within a JSP scripting environment, this has been achieved by exposing one or more scripting variables.

The JSPTL design team has elected not to expose information using scripting variables as a general case. Rather, explicit collaboration is achieved by exposing information via scoped attributes, set using the `ServletContext` class.

With these design considerations in mind, the next section introduces the most basic tags that make up the JSPTL.

Some Basic Tags

The following table shows the JSPTL tags that are used in conjunction with the other tags in the JSPTL. These tags are concerned with returning the value of an expression-language expression value, either directly onto the JSP page, or through a scoped attribute. As a knock-on effect of the decision of the JSPTL team to make the JSPTL tags create scoped attributes on demand, through the `ServletContext`, these tags are concerned with making scoped attributes available to the JSP page or the traditional JSP scripting environment.

Tag	Attribute	Description

expr		Evaluates an expression-language expression and outputs the result to the JSP page. Similar in behavior to JSP scriptlet expressions, `<%= ... %>`.
		
		Example:
		
		`<jx:expr value="$employee.address.postcode"/>`
		`<jx:forEach var="color" items="$colors">`
		`  <TR bgcolor="#<jx:expr value='$color.RGBValue'/>">`
		`    <TD> <jx:expr value="$color.name"/> </TD>`
		`    <TD><jx:expr value="$color.RGBValue"/></TD>`
		`  </TR>`
		`</jx:forEach>`

	value	An expression-language expression, as expected by the configured expression–language.
	default	A default expression to evaluate and return the value of, if the expression fails to evaluate. The body of the `expr` tag can also be used to contain a default or fallback value if the expression did not evaluate.

set		Sets the result of an expression into a named, scoped attribute.
		Example:
		
		`<jx:set var="postCode"`
		`        value="$employee.address.postCode"/>`
		`<jx:set var="userName" value="$user.userName"`
		`        scope="request"/>`

Table continued on following page

Tag	Attribute	Description
	var	The name to assign the scoped attribute.
	value	An expression-language expression, as expected by the configured expression-language.
	scope	The scope of the attribute whose value is to be set: page, request, session, or application. Defaults to page.
declare		Declares a scripting variable with the specified name and whose value corresponds to the value of a scoped attribute with the same name.
		This tag provides a bridge, from the explicit form of collaboration of JSPTL tags with their environment (through scoped attributes), to the JSP scripting environment.
		This tag is available in both the jr and jx tag libraries.
		Example:
		`<jx:expr id="postcode" type="java.lang.String"/>`
	id	As suggested by the JSP 1.1/1.2 Specification, this attribute signifies the name of a scripting variable that will be created by the tag and will be available after the tag within the JSP page.
	type	The declared type of the scripting variable.

We won't go into any more detail about these tags here. We've already seen some examples of their use and will be seeing plenty more throughout this chapter. Let's move on and look at the iteration and conditional control flow tags.

Control Flow Tags

Control flow tags provide the mechanism for conditional inclusion, execution, and iteration within JSP pages. While such mechanisms can be implemented using the corresponding Java programming language statements within JSP scriptlets, this can be cumbersome and (depending on the size and complexity of the JSP pages) can lead to a large amount of Java code within the JSP pages. Moreover, imagine having to match up a number of compound statement bracket pairs ({}) in a lengthy JSP.

The problems of Java code and bracket-matching are themselves compounded when conditional and iterative statements are nested. Having these constructs implemented as custom tags simplifies JSP development in a most natural way. Consider the following JSP fragment using scriptlets:

```
<html>
<head>
...
</head>
<body>
...
...
<% if (expression1) { %>
  <!-- other HTML markup produced when expression1 == true -->
    <% for (Iterator iter= myList.iterator(); iter.hasNext();) {
```

```
                  com.acme.MyItem myItem = (com.acme.MyItem) iter.next();
          %>
      <!-- other HTML markup to be looped over for each item in myList -->
          <% if (expression2) { %>
           <!--  other HTML markup produced when expression2 == true -->
             <%
               }
           %>
         <%
           }
         %>
   <%
     }
   %>
   ...
   ...
   <body>
   </head>
   </html>
```

Let's now take a look at the same JSP fragment with the scriptlets replaced with their corresponding tag implementations:

```
<html>
<head>
...
</head>
<body>
...
...
<jr:if test="<%= expression1 %>">
   <!--  other HTML markup produced when expression1 == true -->
   <jr:forEach var="myItem" items="<%= myList %>" >
     <!-- other HTML markup to be looped over for each item in myList -->
     <fnd:if test="<%= expression2 %>">
     <!--  other HTML markup produced when expression2 == true -->
     </fnd:if>
   </jr:forEach>
</jr:if>
...

<body>
</head>
</html>
```

We can see quite a difference between the two code samples above. Using custom tags for conditional and iterative constructs introduces the following benefits:

❑ Minimizes the amount of Java code in JSP pages, thus reducing their size

❑ Reduces the risk of mismatched brackets and other compile-time errors introduced with the use of Java scriptlets

❑ Allows inexperienced or non-JSP authors to use familiar concepts without the need for implementation in Java

❑ Tends more toward the representation of JSP pages as XML documents, introduced by the JSP 1.1 specification

❏ Conditional and iterative constructs are abstracted above the Java programming language

❏ Makes reading JSP pages easier, which in turn makes debugging them easier

Lets take a look at the iteration and conditional tags that come with the JSPTL.

Iteration Tags

The number of iteration tags in the JSPTL, so far, is small. In fact, the following table shows the two tags that facilitate iteration in JSP pages. It can be argued that this is a good thing. Not only is the number of tags small, but the tags and their interfaces are simple too. The iteration tags in the library are shown below:

Tag	Attribute	Description
forEach		The main tag for iteration. This tag supports iteration in two main modes: over a list of objects or over a range of values.
		For iteration over a list of objects, a vast number of the standard Java indexed data types are supported, including: arrays and all implementations of `java.util.Collection`, `java.util.Iterator`, `java.util.Enumeration`, `java.util.Map`, `java.sql.ResultSet` and `java.util.Hashtable`. Also supported is a `java.lang.String` of comma separated values ("red","green","blue"). We saw the `forEach` tag in action in the introduction to the JSPTL section, *Integrating the JSPTL into Your JSP pages*:
		<pre>\<jx:forEach var="color" items="$colors" \>\n \<TR bgcolor="#\<jx:expr value='$color.RGBValue'/\>"\>\n \<TD\>\<jx:expr value="$color.name"/\>\</TD\>\n \<TD\>\<jx:expr value="$color.RGBValue"/\>\</TD\>\n \</TR\>\n\</jx:forEach\></pre>
		For iteration over a range, the body of the `forEach` tag is iterated over that number of times. For example, to iterate between 10 and 100, inclusive:
		<pre>\<jx:forEach var="n" begin="10" end="100"\>\n The value is \<jx:expr value="$n"/\>\</TD\>\n\</jx:forEach\></pre>
		It is important to note that the two modes can be combined to iterate over a range of the items in a collection.
	var	The name to assign the scoped attribute that represents the current item of the collection being iterated over. In the case where the Iteration object is a `java.util.Map`, the current item exposed will be a `java.util.Map.Entry` object. In the case where the Iteration object is a `java.sql.ResultSet` the current item exposed will be the `java.sql.ResultSet` itself, positioned at the next row.

Tag	Attribute	Description
	items	The indexed data type or collection of items to be iterated over.
	status	A status object that represents the current status of the iteration cycle. This is a JSPTL defined type, `javax.servlet.jsptl.IteratorTagStatus`. This interface is discussed in the next section.
	begin	A range starting value.
	end	A range end value.
	step	Iteration over a range of values will only process values in the range at every 'step' item in the range or collection being iterated over.
forTokens		The forTokens tag is an extension of the forEach tag. It provides the same behavior, only it iterates over a string of delimited values. `<jx:forTokens var="color" items="red|green|blue" delims="|"> The color is <jx:expr value="$color"/> </jx:forTokens>`
	var	Same behavior as the var attribute of the forEachTag.
	items	A string or an expression-language expression that evaluates to a `java.lang.String` containing the delimited values to iterate over.
	status	Same behavior as the status attribute of the forEachTag.
	begin	Same behavior as the begin attribute of the forEachTag.
	end	Same behavior as the end attribute of the forEachTag.
	step	Same behavior as the step attribute of the forEachTag.

Let's take a look at the examples that come with the JSPTL in order to learn more about the iteration tags. When you downloaded the JSPTL, there was included an example web application, `jsptl-examples.war`, that is great for looking at all the possible combinations of use of the iteration and conditional tags.

The examples WAR file for the JSPTL requires the latest version of Tomcat to run (available from http://jakarta.apache.org/tomcat/index.html). To get the examples running, simply drop the `jsptl-examples.war` into the `webapps` directory of Tomcat and restart the server. The following screen shows the welcome page of the JSPTL examples application:

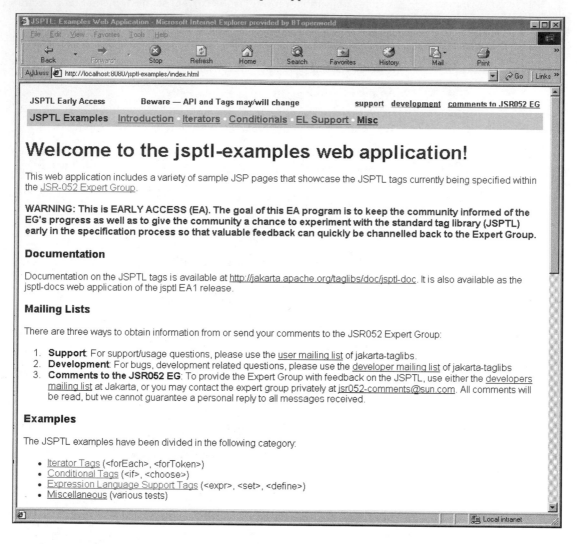

With Tomcat running, you can get to this page via http://localhost:8080/jsptl-examples. Click the Iterator Tags link and you arrive at the page for exploring and testing the iteration tags:

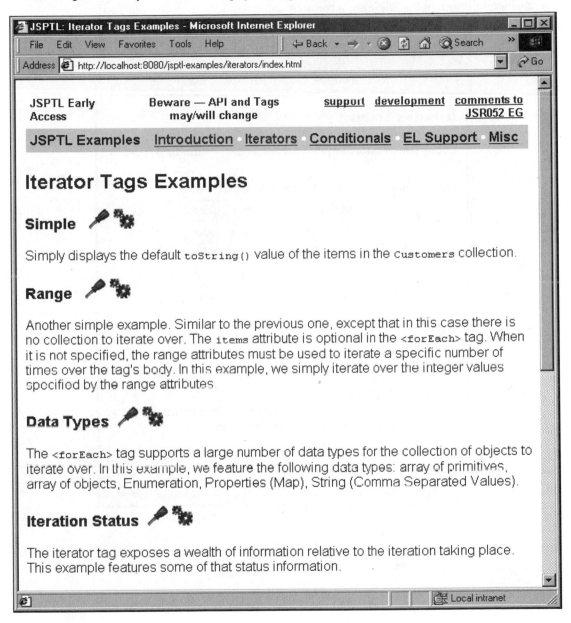

Through this page, you can explore each tag by running each example and then looking at the code for the example through the two icon links. For example, if we run the Iteration Status Tag example, we get the output shown in the following screenshot:

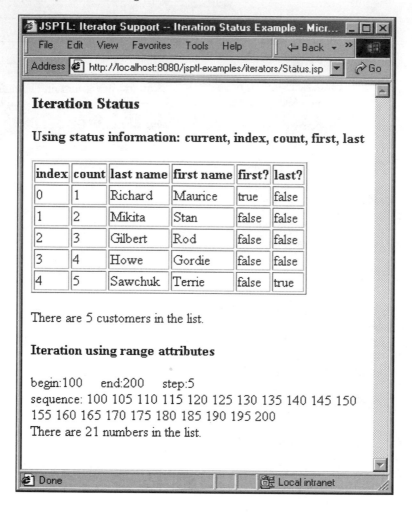

Then we can look at how the example was written:

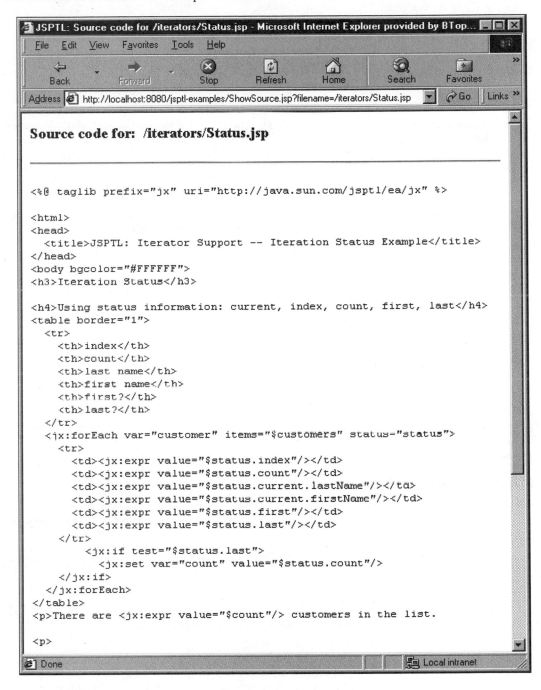

```
<%@ taglib prefix="jx" uri="http://java.sun.com/jsptl/ea/jx" %>

<html>
<head>
  <title>JSPTL: Iterator Support -- Iteration Status Example</title>
</head>
<body bgcolor="#FFFFFF">
<h3>Iteration Status</h3>

<h4>Using status information: current, index, count, first, last</h4>
<table border="1">
  <tr>
    <th>index</th>
    <th>count</th>
    <th>last name</th>
    <th>first name</th>
    <th>first?</th>
    <th>last?</th>
  </tr>
  <jx:forEach var="customer" items="$customers" status="status">
    <tr>
      <td><jx:expr value="$status.index"/></td>
      <td><jx:expr value="$status.count"/></td>
      <td><jx:expr value="$status.current.lastName"/></td>
      <td><jx:expr value="$status.current.firstName"/></td>
      <td><jx:expr value="$status.first"/></td>
      <td><jx:expr value="$status.last"/></td>
    </tr>
      <jx:if test="$status.last">
        <jx:set var="count" value="$status.count"/>
      </jx:if>
  </jx:forEach>
</table>
<p>There are <jx:expr value="$count"/> customers in the list.

<p>
```

To round off the discussion about the JSPTL iteration tags let's discuss the following issues:

❑ Within the iteration cycle, obtaining information about the current status of that cycle

❑ Extending the iteration tags to provide custom forms of iteration

These two issues are discussed in the next sections.

Iteration Status

The `forEach` and `forTokens` tags each provide an object that can be used to establish the status of the iteration process. The name of the scoped attribute created can be specified via the `status` attribute. The type of the object is `javax.servlet.jsptl.IteratorTagStatus`. The following table shows the main properties of the `IteratorTagStatus` object created:

Property	Type	Description
current	Object	The current item of the list of items iterated over.
index	int	The zero-based index of the current item in the list of items iterated over.
count	int	The one-based position of the current item in the set of items eligible to be iterated over. This value increases by one for each item, regardless of the begin, end, or step attributes of the iteration tag.
		For example, if begin=1, end=10 and step=2 then the set of items eligible for iteration over is 1, 3, 5, 7, and 9. These have position counts of 1, 2, 3, 4, and 5 respectively.
first	boolean	Indicates whether the current item is the first item in the iteration cycle.
last	boolean	Indicates whether the current item is the last item in the iteration cycle.

The iteration tag status example, run and inspected in the last section, showed how the status information was put to good use.

Iteration Tag Extensibility

Most iterative tasks can easily be achieved with the JSPTL iteration tags. However, failing that, the iteration tag mechanism is extensible. If you can't achieve what you need with the JSPTL tags, you can extend the standard tags and define your own.

The following table shows the three types the JSPTL provides to developers to aid in the creation of custom iteration tags:

Type	Description
interface IteratorTag	The main interface for writing custom iteration tags.
interface IteratorTagStatus	The JSPTL iteration tags provide the status of the iteration cycle within the scope of the tag. Custom iteration tags that conform to the IteratorTag interface must also provide this information through the IteratorTagStatus object, as discussed in the previous section, *Iteration Status*.

Type	Description
abstract class IteratorTagSupport	Abstract base class for building custom iteration tags. Custom iteration tags just implement the hasNext() and next() methods, providing the stop mechanism of the iteration cycle and the items iterated over in sequence.

Conditional Tags

Again, as with the iteration tags, the number of conditional tags so far in the JSPTL is small. As one would expect, there is an if tag and an if-then-elseif-else or switch equivalent tag, called choose.

The following table shows the four tags that facilitate conditional control flow in JSP pages:

Tag	Attribute	Description
if		A simple conditional tag, which only evaluates its body if the supplied condition is true. The tag also, optionally, exposes a scoped attribute representing the value of the condition.
		Example:
		<pre><jx:if var="isMale" test="$employee.sex == 'M'"> The test for a employee is a male. </jx:if> <jx:if var="isMale" test="$employee.sex == 'M'" /> The employee is male was <jx:expr value="$isMale"/></pre>
	var	The name to assign the scoped attribute that represents the value of the evaluated condition as a Boolean.
	test	An expression-language expression, if used with the jx tag library or a request-time expression, if used with the jr tag library. The expression must evaluate to a boolean primitive or primitive wrapper Boolean object.
choose		The tag equivalent to the Java switch statement. The following example shows its usage:
		<pre><jx:choose> <jx:when test="$employee.age >= 65"> The employee is a pensioner. </jx:when> <jx:when test="$employee.age >= 40"> The employee is middle-aged. </jx:when> <jx:otherwise> The employee is not middle-aged or a pensioner. </jx:othewise> </jx:choose></pre>
		Only the body of the first when tag whose condition evaluates to true is evaluated. If none of the when conditions is true, the body of an otherwise tag is evaluated, if there is one.

Table continued on following page

Tag	Attribute	Description
when		The when tag, only used in context of a parent choose tag.
otherwise		The otherwise tag, only used in context of a parent choose tag.

To see the conditional tag examples that came with the JSPTL download, click the Conditional Tags link on the examples home page, http://localhost:8080/jsptl-examples/index.html. You'll arrive at the Condition Tags Examples page, shown in the following screenshot:

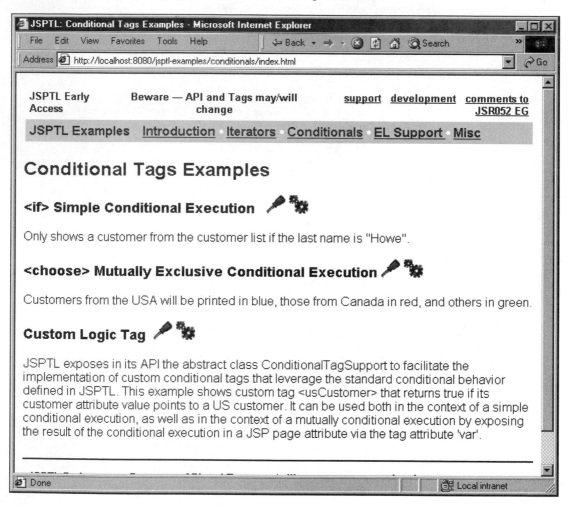

If we run the <choose> Mutually Exclusive Conditional Execution example, we should see output as shown in the following screenshot:

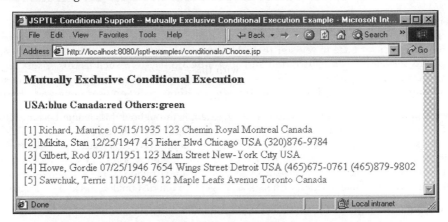

If we then inspect the code for the example, we should see in the following:

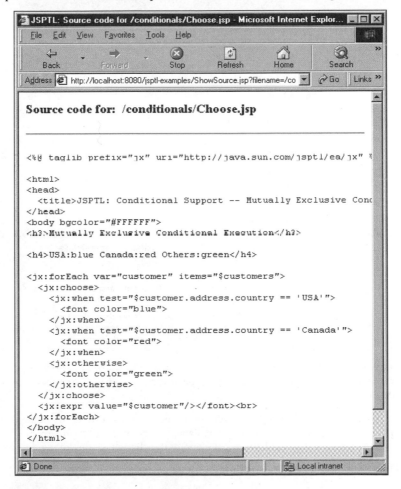

A Registration and Authentication Application

In this section, we'll define a generic registration and authentication application that will be built and used extensively throughout the rest of this chapter to demonstrate the JSP tags we'll be using. Any web site that requires its user base to register their details, for reasons such as online purchases or subscription to services, has a registration and authentication system such as this. Users register their details on the site in order to use the site's services. Users who subsequently return to the site are required to authenticate themselves, usually by entering their assigned username and chosen password.

We'll be working with a registration and authentication example throughout this chapter because it's a very common (and useful) web application. It seems one cannot escape having to enter credentials on the Internet these days – so who are we to argue? While the application defined here is very simplistic, it provides us with an ideal opportunity to demonstrate how to manage the complexity and minimize some of the messiness in our JSP pages, particularly with iteration and conditional logic. Also, given that registration systems hosted on the web are exposed to a population of different nationalities, we'll look at the goals of internationalization and web page simplification.

The following diagram shows the main web components of our registration application:

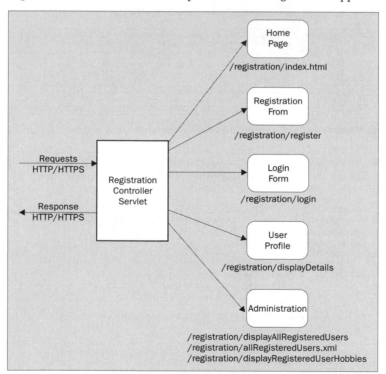

As you might expect from any web site registration application, there are forms for initial registration and subsequent login. Also provided are a display page for reviewing your registration details and pages for the administration of users.

We shall proceed by building the registration application, step by step, from the welcome page through to the administration pages of the application. As we move through the construction process, we'll explore the tags that are used on each page with the final goal, toward the end of the chapter, of deploying the whole application.

Let's start right at the beginning then, with the home page.

The Welcome Page

The welcome page of acts as a main entry point to all the facilities provided by the application. In reality, most sites on the web don't have a page dedicated to registration. Instead, registration and authentication tends to be hidden behind links or parts of the site that require it.

The welcome page is provided here to act as the initial focal point for the application. The page is simple HTML with links to the other parts of the application. The code for the welcome page, index.html, is shown below:

```
<font face="arial, helvetica" size="4" color="#996600">
Welcome to the Registration Home Page
</font><br>

<p>From here you can run all the components of the registration application.<br>
Just click on the links below:

<ol>
<li>Register as a new user, <a href="register">Click Here!</a>
<li>Login in as an existing user, <a href="login">Click Here!</a><br>
   <b>Note:</b>You must have registered first, within the same session.
<li>View your user profile, <a href="displayDetails">Click Here!</a><br>
   <b>Note:</b>You must have registered first, within the same session.
<li><b>Administration</b> - view all registered users,
   <a href="displayAllRegisteredUsers">Click Here!</a>
<li><b>Administration</b> - view all registered users as XML,
   <a href="allRegisteredUsers.xml">Click Here!</a>
<li><b>Administration</b> - view all registered users and their hobbies,
   <a href="displayRegisteredUserHobbies">Click Here!</a>
</ol>
```

We'll discuss how to get the application running later. For the time being, we'll look at the code, explore the principles employed on each page of the application, and show relevant screenshots of the expected output. The welcome page will be located at http://localhost:8000/jspTagApps/registration/index.html and is shown in the following screenshot:

As previously mentioned, and for future reference, this page can be used to access any part of the registration application.

The Registration Controller Servlet

The Registration Controller Servlet provides the mechanism for mapping requests to JSP pages. Consider the Model-View-Controller (MVC) architecture shown below:

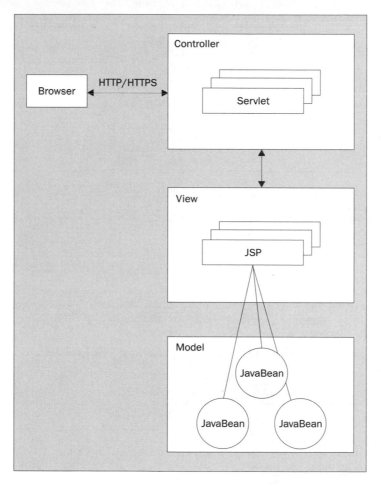

When a JSP page gets executed, it renders its view content from the JavaBeans by a controller servlet at runt ime. This simple approach to JSP development, and the way it separates control and business logic from JSP pages, has been publicized as part of J2EE Blueprints of Sun Microsystems. It has proven to be the best approach to date for producing reliable and scalable web-based applications. Whether the providing mechanism is simply a controlling servlet or a more elaborate request-handling framework, such as the Jakarta Struts framework, the model remains the same. You can find out about the Apache Jakarta Struts Project at http://jakarta.apache.org/struts/index.html.

When a request is made to the application, the controller servlet performs any work up-front, then decides what JSP page or pages to invoke. In our example application, the decision process or 'rules' that decide what JSP is invoked for a request are in the code itself. In more elaborate frameworks, like Struts, the mapping rules may be configurable through Java property or XML files.

The code for the controller servlet, `RegistrationControllerServlet`, is shown below:

```java
package writingjsps.registration;

import java.util.*;

import java.io.IOException;
import java.sql.SQLException;
import javax.servlet.*;
import javax.servlet.http.*;
import java.text.*;

public class RegistrationControllerServlet extends HttpServlet {
  private static final String USER_COOKIE_NAME = "writingJSPAppsUserCookie";
  private static String regions[] = new String[] {
              "UK & Ireland", "Western Europe", "Eastern Europe",
              "North America", "South America", "Middle East & Africa",
              "Asia", "Australasia"
  };

  private static String roles[] = new String[] {
              "Java Developer", "Director/CEO", "Manager",
              "Sales Person", "Office Worker",
              "Industrial/Manufacturing Worker"
  };

   private UserManager userManager;

  public RegistrationControllerServlet() {}

  public void init() {

    // Create the UserManager, used to store/retrieve user information
    // to/from the database.
    userManager = new UserManager();
  }

  public void doGet(HttpServletRequest request,
                    HttpServletResponse response) throws ServletException {
    handleRequest(request, response);
  }

  public void doPost(HttpServletRequest request,
                    HttpServletResponse response) throws ServletException {
    handleRequest(request, response);
  }

  // Handles all requests to the registration subsystem.
  public void handleRequest(HttpServletRequest request,
                            HttpServletResponse response)
                            throws ServletException {
    String requestURI = request.getRequestURI();

    try {
      if (requestURI.indexOf("register") >= 0) {
        registerNewUser(request, response);
```

```
        } else if (requestURI.indexOf("regFormSubmit") >= 0) {
          doNewRegistration(request, response);
        } else if (requestURI.endsWith("login")) {
          loginExistingUser(request, response);
        } else if (requestURI.indexOf("loginFormSubmit") >= 0) {
          doLoginUser(request, response);
        } else if (requestURI.indexOf("displayDetails") >= 0) {
          displayExistingUserDetails(request, response);
        } else if (requestURI.indexOf("displayAllRegisteredUsers") >= 0) {
          displayAllRegisteredUsers(request, response);
        } else if (requestURI.indexOf("allRegisteredUsers.xml") >= 0) {
          createAllRegisteredUsersXMLDocument(request, response);
        } else if (requestURI.indexOf("displayRegisteredUserHobbies") >= 0) {
          displayRegisteredUserHobbies(request, response);
        } else {
          response.sendError(HttpServletResponse.SC_NOT_FOUND);
        }
      } catch (Exception ex) {
        ex.printStackTrace();
        throw new ServletException("An error occurred handling request:", ex);
      }
    }

    // Registers a new user entry point.
    public void registerNewUser(HttpServletRequest request,
                                HttpServletResponse response)
                             throws ServletException, IOException {
      request.setAttribute("user", new User());
      request.setAttribute("regions", regions);
      request.setAttribute("roles", roles);
      RequestDispatcher rd =
        getServletContext().getRequestDispatcher("/registration/regForm.jsp");
      rd.forward(request, response);
    }

    // Registers a new user using the details in the request.
    public void doNewRegistration(HttpServletRequest request,
                                  HttpServletResponse response)
                             throws ServletException, IOException,
                                                      SQLException {
      User user = new User(request.getParameter("username"));
      user.setForename(request.getParameter("forename"));
      user.setSurname(request.getParameter("surname"));
      user.setEmailAddress(request.getParameter("emailAddress"));
      user.setCompanyName(request.getParameter("companyName"));
      user.setMainHobby(request.getParameter("mainHobby"));
      user.setPassword(request.getParameter("password"));
      user.setRegion(request.getParameter("region"));
      user.setRole(request.getParameter("role"));
      user.setFavoriteWebSiteURL(request.getParameter("favoriteWebSiteURL"));

      try {
        SimpleDateFormat df = new SimpleDateFormat("dd-MMM-yyyy");
        user.setDateOfBirth(request.getParameter("dateOfBirth") != null
                            ? df.parse(request.getParameter("dateOfBirth"))
                            : null);
      } catch (ParseException ex) {
        user.setDateOfBirth(null);
      }

      try {
        userManager.registerNewUser(user);
```

```
        request.setAttribute("user", user);
        serveUserCookie(user, response);
        getServletContext().getRequestDispatcher("/registration/thankyou.jsp")
          .include(request, response);
    } catch (UsernameAlreadyChosenException ex) {
      RequestDispatcher rd =
        getServletContext()
          .getRequestDispatcher("/registration/tryAnotherUsername.jsp");
      rd.forward(request, response);
    }
  }

  // Serves the user cookie for users that have registered or logged in.
  private void serveUserCookie(User user, HttpServletResponse response) {
    response.addCookie(new Cookie(USER_COOKIE_NAME,
                                  user.serializeToString()));
  }

  // Log in an existing user entry point.
  public void loginExistingUser(HttpServletRequest request,
                                HttpServletResponse response)
                                throws ServletException, IOException {
    RequestDispatcher rd =
        getServletContext()
                .getRequestDispatcher("/registration/loginForm.jsp");
    rd.forward(request, response);
  }

  // Logs a user into the registration system.
  public void doLoginUser(HttpServletRequest request,
                          HttpServletResponse response)
                          throws ServletException, IOException,
                                                   SQLException {
    try {
      User user = userManager.login(request.getParameter("username"),
                                    request.getParameter("password"));
      serveUserCookie(user, response);
      response
              .sendRedirect("/jspTagApps/registration/displayDetails");
    } catch (NoSuchUserException ex) {
      RequestDispatcher rd =
          getServletContext()
                  .getRequestDispatcher("/registration/noSuchUser.jsp");
      rd.forward(request, response);
    }
  }

  // More methods for handling requests:
  // displayExistingUserDetails, displayAllRegisteredUsers etc. etc.

}
```

Don't worry if you don't fully understand what the controlling servlet is doing at this stage. We'll discuss the code and deploy the application later. The constructor creates an instance of a UserManager class. The UserManager class is used for storing and retrieving registered user information to and from a database. Again, this will be discussed in the deployment section.

The `handleRequest()` method is what's interesting here. It contains the 'rules' we discussed, for mapping requests to the JSP pages invoked. We can see how the URLs shown in the diagram above are mapped to their corresponding JSP. For example, how `/registration/register` is mapped to the `registerNewUser` method that sets up some data (user, roles, and regions) and then forwards on to `/registration/regForm.jsp`, which shows the registration form.

Let's now take a look at the other JSP pages of the application.

The Registration Form Page

As a new user, the first step within a registration system is to record some information about you. In our application you can achieve this through option one of the welcome page, or directly via http://localhost:8000/jspTagApps/registration/register.

The controller servlet maps the request to a form for entering new registration details, `regForm.jsp`, shown below:

```
<%@page import="java.util.*" %>
<%@page import="java.text.SimpleDateFormat" %>

<%-- Bring in the HTML Helper tag library --%>
<%@taglib uri="/html" prefix="html" %>

<jsp:useBean id="user" type="writingjsps.registration.User"
             scope="request" />

<html>
<head>
<title>Registration</title>
</head>
<body>
<font face="arial, helvetica" size="4" color="#996600">Registration</font>

<html:form method="post" actionURI="./regFormSubmit">
  <table border="0">
  <tr>
    <td>User Name:</td>
    <td>
      <html:textInput name="username"
                      value="<%= user.getUsername() %>"
                      numberOfColumns="20" />
    </td>
  </tr>
  <tr>
    <td>First Name:</td>
    <td>
      <html:textInput name="forename"
                      value="<%= user.getForename() %>"
                      numberOfColumns="20" />
    </td>
  </tr>
  <tr>
    <td>Last Name:</td>
    <td>
      <html:textInput name="surname"
                      value="<%= user.getSurname() %>"
                      numberOfColumns="20" />
    </td>
```

```
    </tr>
    <tr>
     <td>Email:</td>
     <td>
       <html:textInput name="emailAddress"
                       value="<%= user.getEmailAddress() %>"
                       numberOfColumns="30" />
     </td>
    </tr>
    <tr>
     <td>Date Of Birth: <br>
        (e.g 01-Jan-1965)
     </td>
     <td>
       <html:textInput name="dateOfBirth"
                       value='<%= new
                            SimpleDateFormat("dd-MMM-yyyy")
                                        .format(user.getDateOfBirth()) %>'
                       numberOfColumns="20" />
     </td>
    </tr>
    <tr>
     <td>Region of Origin: <br>
          (Please choose one)
     </td>
     <td>
       <html:list name="region" id="aRegion"
                 items='<%= (Object[])request.getAttribute("regions") %>'
                 itemType="java.lang.String">
          <option value="<%= aRegion %>"><%= aRegion %></option>
       </html:list>
     </td>
    </tr>
    <tr>
     <td>Company Name:</td>
     <td>
       <html:textInput name="companyName"
                       value="<%= user.getCompanyName() %>"
                       numberOfColumns="20"/>
       <br>
     </td>
    </tr>
    <tr>
     <td>Your Role:</td>
     <td>
       <html:list name="role" id="aRole"
                 items='<%= (Object[])request.getAttribute("roles") %>'
                 itemType="java.lang.String">
          <option value="<%= aRole %>"><%= aRole %></option>
       </html:list>
     </td>
    </tr>
    <tr>
     <td>Main Hobby:</td>
     <td>
       <html:textInput name="mainHobby"
                       value="<%= user.getMainHobby() %>"
                       numberOfColumns="30"/>
     </td>
    </tr>
    <tr>
     <td>Favorite Web Site URL:</td>
```

```
          <td>
            <html:textInput name="favoriteWebSiteURL"
                            value="<%= user.getFavoriteWebSiteURL() %>"
                            numberOfColumns="30" />
          </td>
        </tr>
        <tr>
          <td>Password:</td>
          <td>
            <html:passwordInput name="password" numberOfColumns="20" /><br>
          </td>
        </tr>
        <tr>
          <td>Confirm Password:</td>
          <td>
            <html:passwordInput name="password" numberOfColumns="20" /><br>
          </td>
        </tr>
        </table>

        <input type="submit" value="Register!">
      </html:form>
    </body>
  </html>
```

The form served collects some useful information about the user. The JSP page initially brings in an HTML helper tag library:

```
<%-- Bring in the HTML Helper tag library --%>
<%@taglib uri="/html" prefix="html" %>
```

It then finds the registration user bean, created by the registration controller servlet before this page was called:

```
<jsp:useBean id="user" type="writingjsps.registration.User"
             scope="request" />
```

The properties of the user bean are bound to the registration form using tags from the HTML tag library imported. The reasons for this, and the benefits of using tags for HTML form binding are discussed fully in the next section. The following screenshot shows the registration form served:

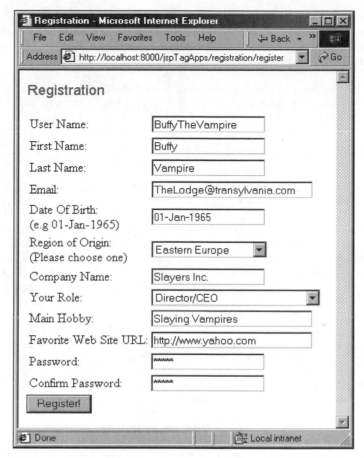

Let's take a short detour and look at the benefits of using JSP tags for HTML form handling and the tags used in this example.

Tags for HTML Form Handling

Employing user input within HTML web pages is achieved with the `<form>`, `<input>`, `<select>`, and `<option>` HTML tags. If your web pages are entirely HTML-based, these are just about the only option you have for data input through a browser. Alternatives might include the use of Applets or Java WebStart within your application. In cases where the client needs to remain fairly lightweight and load times are an issue, these alternatives may not be the best option.

The HTML `<input>` tag is pretty much a catch-all, where the exact type of input component required is specified using a `type` attribute, such as `type="text|password|checkbox|image|button..."`. Use of the `<input>` tag requires the correct use of the attributes for the type of input being deployed. It's often difficult to remember which attributes can be used with a specific type and their intended meaning. For example, `size` represents the number of visible characters for a text input, but the number of pixels for an image input.

There is no attribute that specifies that an input field requires entry, and there is no validation or enforcement of the type of data entered; the user can miss out or decide not to complete a field or enter character data in a field that is really for entry of numeric values. In such cases, form `<input>` fields with potentially invalid values are submitted back to the server for processing.

Some of the initial validation the application on the server performs is checking for mandatory field completion and correct typing of all entered fields. These checks are performed up-front, before any application-specific or cross-field validation can be performed. Invalid or missing values mean the original input form will get sent back to the client for further attention.

Our design guides tell us that business logic belongs in the business model tier on the server. But should this include basic forms of validation, such as mandatory field requirement and type safety?

There is now at least minimal scripting capability in most forms of web client. With the advent of JavaScript and its newer regular expression capabilities, clients capable of doing so can easily perform such trivial validation. The use of JSP tags for the binding of bean properties to HTML form fields can bring in some of the benefits of client-side validation by generating client side code within the JSP page itself. This removes such *trivial* validation from the application, frees cycles on the server, and the application can proceed with application-specific validation and business rule checking.

At the time of writing, there is no defined HTML tag library within the JSPTL. However, there is rather a lot of activity in this area generally and in open source repositories on the web. Once again, one must be careful how much goes into a tag library consisting of HTML helper tags. Too little, and we arrive at a situation with duplication of effort to achieve trivial concepts like enforcing mandatory field entry on the client or type formatting. Too much, and we see a "theft" of business type logic from the application model tier onto the client views. Striking the right balance is always the key.

One other point to mention, while we're looking at the "right and wrong" guidelines of JSP pages is the matter of HTML markup generation within JSP tags. As a general rule of thumb, having tags generate HTML probably isn't a good idea – Java's string manipulation, concatenation, and handling capabilities are rather limited and expensive, and generating HTML ties those tags to JSP that generate HTML only. However, when considering what we're setting out to achieve with an HTML helper tag library, generating simple HTML form markup is the aim.

The HTML tag library, written for and used within our registration application, is very simple. Its goal is to replace HTML `<form>` and `<input>` elements directly. However, implementing methods of form validation using JavaScript on the client is beyond the scope of this chapter.

The table below lists the tags that compose the HTML tag library. As there are so many, the detail and usage of attributes is not given.

Tag	Attributes	Description
form		Equivalent to an HTML `<form>` element.
textInput	name, value, required, disabled, readOnly, numberOfColumns, description, tabIndex, accessKey, onFocus, onLoseFocus, onSelect, onChange	Equivalent to an HTML `<InPUT type="text" ...>` element. Note that this tag has a `required` attribute. If validation was supported, JavaScript could be employed on the client to ensure entry of the generated input field. Validation can be achieved by client-side scripts called by the `onFocus()`, `onLoseFocus()`, `onSelect()`, or `onChange()` methods.

Tag	Attributes	Description
passwordInput	name, value, required, disabled, readOnly, numberOfColumns, description, tabIndex, accessKey, onFocus, onLoseFocus, onSelect, onChange	Equivalent to an HTML `<input type="password" ...>` element. Note that this tag has a `required` attribute. If validation was supported, JavaScript could be employed on the client to ensure entry of the generated input field.
integerInput	name, value, required, disabled, readOnly, numberOfColumns, description, tabIndex, accessKey, onFocus, onLoseFocus, onSelect, onChange	Equivalent to an HTML `<input type="text" ...>` element. Note that this tag has a `required` attribute. If validation was supported, JavaScript could be employed on the client to ensure entry of the generated input field. If JavaScript and regular expressions were employed on the client, entry of this field could be restricted to an integer pattern.
realInput	name, value, required, disabled, readOnly, numberOfColumns, description, tabIndex, accessKey, onFocus, onLoseFocus, onSelect, onChange	Equivalent to an HTML `<input type="text" ...>` element. Note that this tag has a `required` attribute. If validation was supported, JavaScript could be employed on the client to ensure entry of the generated input field. If JavaScript and regular expressions were employed on the client, entry of this field could be restricted to a real number pattern.
booleanInput	name, showBothValues, value, required, disabled, readOnly, numberOfColumns, description, tabIndex, accessKey, onFocus, onLoseFocus, onSelect, onChange	There is no direct equivalent HTML element for entering Boolean values. This tag generates a `<select>` and `<option>` tags to create the input component. Note that this tag has a `required` attribute. If validation was supported, JavaScript could be employed on the client to ensure entry of the generated input field. If JavaScript and regular expressions were employed on the client, entry of this field could be restricted to a real number pattern.
list	id, items, itemType, name, allowsMultipleSelections, disabled, tabIndex, onFocus, onLoseFocus, onChange, visibleRows	A list tag that facilitates generation of HTML `<select>` with specified and embedded `<option>` tags. Iterates over `items` of type `itemType`, allowing a list of `<option>` HTML elements to be created.

Table continued on following page

601

Tag	Attributes	Description
radioButton	name, value, label, valueAndLabel, required, checked, disabled, tabIndex, onFocus, onLoseFocus, onChange	Equivalent to an HTML `<input type="radio" ...>` element. Note that the value and label of the generated radio button can be specified separately as value and label, or together as valueAndLabel.
checkbox	name, value, label, valueAndLabel, required, checked, disabled, tabIndex, onFocus, onLoseFocus, onChange	Equivalent to an HTML `<input type="checkbox" ...>` element. Note that the value and label of the generated radio button can be specified separately as value and label, or together as valueAndLabel.

There are many tags shown in the previous table. To show the usage of all of them would be beyond this chapter. As these tags mostly wrap their HTML counterparts, the simplest and best way to demonstrate their usage and impact within a JSP application would be to show how they were used within our registration example application, regForm.jsp:

```jsp
<%@page import="java.util.*" %>
<%@page import="java.text.SimpleDateFormat" %>

<%-- Bring in the HTML Helper tag library --%>
<%@taglib uri="/html" prefix="html" %>

<jsp:useBean id="user" type="writingjsps.registration.User"
             scope="request" />

<font face="arial, helvetica" size="4" color="#996600">Registration</font>

<html:form method="post" actionURI="./regFormSubmit">
    <table border="0">
    <tr>
        <td>User Name:</td>
        <td>
            <html:textInput name="username"
                            value="<%= user.getUsername() %>"
                            numberOfColumns="20" />
        </td>
    </tr>
...
...
    <tr>
        <td>Your Role:</td>
        <td>
            <html:list name="role" id="aRole"
                       items='<%= (Object[])request.getAttribute("roles") %>'
                       itemType="java.lang.String">
                <option value="<%= aRole %>"><%= aRole %></option>
            </html:list>
        </td>
    </tr>
...
```

```
...
   <tr>
     <td>Password:</td>
     <td>
        <html:passwordInput name="password" numberOfColumns="20" /><br>
     </td>
   </tr>
   <tr>
     <td>Confirm Password:</td>
     <td>
        <html:passwordInput name="password" numberOfColumns-"20" /><br>
     </td>
   </tr>
   </table>

   <input type="submit" value="Register!">
</html:form>
```

The registration form, regForm.jsp, uses the form, textInput, passwordInput, and list tags of the library. When the form is submitted, the registration controller servlet processes the form and performs a check with the chosen username. If a user with the chosen username does not already exist, it stores the user's details in the user database and forwards the new registrant to a "thank you" page. If the chosen username is already taken, the registration controller forwards to a registration error page, accordingly.

Both the thank you page and the registration error page are discussed in the next two sections.

Thanks for Registering!

Once registered, a thank you page is displayed. As one might expect, the thankyou.jsp page is really quite small, and yet it will introduce a very powerful concept in JSP pages. It's a concept not seen too often in web pages – not often enough, really. Lets start by taking a look at the JSP code:

```
<%@page import="writingjsps.registration.*" %>

<%@taglib uri="/internationalisation" prefix="i18n" %>

<jsp:useBean id="user" type="writingjsps.registration.User" scope="request" />

<%-- Load the resource bundle for the page --%>
<i18n:resourceBundle name="writingjsps.registration.RegistrationResources">

<%-- Display the greeting message, inserting the user properties --%>
<i18n:message name="greetingMessage" arg0="<%= user.getForename() %>"
              arg1="<%= user.getUsername()%>" /><br>

<html>
<head>
<title>Thank You</title>
</head>

<body>
<p>Thanks for registering!<br>

<p>Be sure to check out your user profile by<br>
clicking <a href="displayDetails">here</a>.

<p>In the meantime, have fun working with JSP tag library applications.
```

```
<p>Many thanks,<br>
<br>
Everyone at Wrox Press Ltd.<br>
<a href="http://www.wrox.com">www.wrox.com</a><br>
<hr>

<%-- Show the disclaimer notice from the bundle --%>
<i18n:string name="appDisclaimer">
&copy; Wrox Press Ltd, 2001
</i18n:string>

</i18n:resourceBundle>
</body>
</html>
```

At first glance the page seems harmless enough. But the focus area, shown highlighted, has been internationalized. The page imports a basic tag library, written to demonstrate the concept in this chapter, for internationalization. Incidentally, while we're on the subject of internationalization, the very commonly used abbreviation in the IT world is **i18n** (internationalization – i with 18 characters afterward, followed by n).

Having registered a random TV personality, the `thankyou.jsp` page was displayed, as shown in the following screenshot:

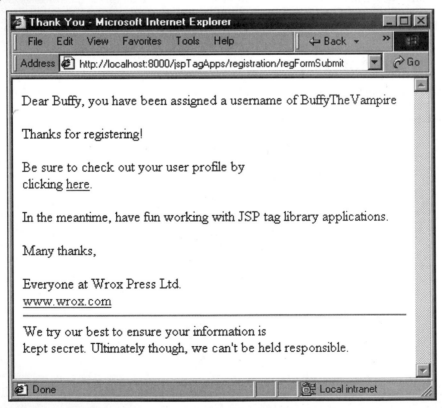

Internationalization was achieved in this JSP using Java resource bundles. As many readers of this book may not know very much about resource bundles, we'll go over the basic concepts next. We'll then round off this example by looking at how the tags work in this page.

Internationalizing our JSP Code

The internationalization of our applications has been made much more apparent because of the Internet. With anyone able to access our applications over the web, from anywhere in the world, the need to push information to the user in their own language, or tailored in some way to their tastes or cultural preferences, becomes very important.

Once again, though, Java comes to the rescue on this subject. Suddenly, with the use of resource bundles (`java.util.ResourceBundle`) within our application, the subject of internationalization doesn't seem so tricky. With Java's close attention to locale-sensitive detail, and its application within resource bundles, the ability to tailor applications to specific clienteles is obtained effortlessly and almost for free. Let's take a quick refresher to see how resource bundles work and then look at how they can be effectively utilized within a JSP application.

What is a Resource Bundle?

A resource bundle is simply a repository for a number of resources. In actual fact, a resource bundle can be thought of as a number of name-value pairs.

A resource bundle is given a name – termed a **base name**. For example, if all the resources for an application were contained within just one bundle (not likely in a large application), it might be called `MyAppResources`. However, specific locale names can be appended onto the base bundle name to create more bundles, specific to each locale. For example, we might create bundles called:

- `MyAppResources`
- `MyAppResources_fr`
- `MyAppResources_fr_CH`
- `MyAppResources_en`
- `MyAppResources_en_US`
- `MyAppResources_en_GB`

Generally, locale names are of the form, `<language>_<country>`, with a language and optional region where the language is used. So, for example, `MyAppResources_fr_CH`, specifies resources under `MyAppResources` in French, spoken in Switzerland, and `MyAppResources_fr` just specifies resources in French generally, without regard to where it is used.

Resource bundles are implemented either as Java classes or as `.properties` files, with names like the examples shown above. Refer to the Java 2, Standard Edition API reference for specific details regarding the `ResourceBundle` class.

How Resource Bundles are Located

In this section we'll look at how resource bundles are located and used with an application.

Resource bundle lookups are performed on the basis of:

- The client's desired locale.
- The current, default locale as returned by `Locale.getDefault()`. In the case of a web application, this would be the locale of the server.
- The root resource bundle – whose name is the chosen base name.

Let's look at an example. Considering our resources, identified by the base name MyAppResources, if the user's desired locale is determined as _fr_CH (French – Switzerland) and the default locale on the server is _en_GB (English – United Kingdom) then the search order for resources within the bundles would be as shown in the following diagram:

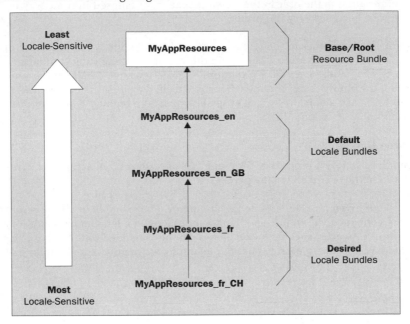

In other words, the user's desired locale is French-speaking Switzerland so look for French resources, preferably as spoken or used in Switzerland. But, if specified resources within the desired French bundles don't exist then try the default locale bundles. Again, if the resources within the default locale bundles could not be found then fall back to the root resource bundle, whose name is the chosen base name. The search is performed hierarchically.

Applying Resource Bundles to JSP Applications

Now we'll examine how the concept of resource bundles can be applied effectively within JSP applications. Initially we'll look at some tags for abstracting resource bundles, and then we'll go back to the thank you page of the registration application and see how they were employed.

We've created an internationalization tag library to demonstrate just how easy internationalizing applications can be. As mentioned previously, it's made pretty easy in Java. However, as yet, little has surfaced in the definition of the JSPTL regarding an internationalization tag library. When it is included, it'll be based on principles very similar to those outlined here.

The tags in the internationalization library are shown in the table below:

Tag	Attribute	Description
resourceBundle		Loads a ResourceBundle and makes it available within the scope of its tag body.
	name	The fully qualified base name of the resource bundle to employ. For example, com.wrox.writingjsps.i18n.MyAppResources.

Tag	Attribute	Description
	locale	The locale to employ for lookups of resources in the resource bundle. If not specified, depending on the value of the useClientLocale attribute, either the locale of the requesting client or the default locale will be used.
	useClientLocale	Determines whether or not to employ the client's locale, if successfully detected, for lookups within the loaded resource bundle. Defaults to true.
string		Returns the value of a specified property in the resource bundle in context.
	name	The name of the property in the resource bundle whose value is to be returned.
	alt	An alternative value to be used if the specified property could not be found in the resource bundle. Specifying a value for this attribute will implement a fallback, preventing exceptions from being thrown in the event that resources could not be found. Supplying a body to the tag as the alternative value can also use the same fallback mechanism.
message		Returns the value of a specified property in the resource bundle in context as a message, formatted by the java.text.MessageFormat class. The arguments to the message format are specified using the args or arg<n> attributes or by immediate child messageArg tags.
	name	The name of the property in the resource bundle, whose value is to be returned.
	alt	An alternative value to be used if the specified property could not be found in the resource bundle. Specifying a value for this attribute will implement a fallback, preventing exceptions from being thrown in the event that resources could not be found. Supplying a body to the tag as the alternative value can also use the same fallback mechanism.
	args	An array containing the arguments.

Table continued on following page

Tag	Attribute	Description

messageArg		A message argument tag. Must be used as an immediate child of the message tag. Arguments will be substituted into the message in the order of appearance of <messageArg> tags under the parent message tag. So the following message
		
		 `<i18n:message name="greetingMessage"`
		`        arg0="<%= user.getForename() %>"`
		`        arg1="<%= user.getUsername()%>"`
		`/>`
		
		 Could be rewritten, using the <messageArg> tag:
		
		 `<i18n:message name="greetingMessage">`
		`  <i18n:messageArg`
		`      value="<%= user.getForename()`
		`%>"`
		`  <i18n:messageArg`
		`      value="<%= user.getUsername ()`
		`%>"`
		`</i18n:message>`

	value	The argument value.

Now let's take a look at how internationalization was introduced to the registration example and the thankyou.jsp page. As a registration application sits up-front of any website, it's actually quite fitting that such an application should be internationalized, so as to reach the widest audience possible.

After users register, they are forwarded to the thank you page, as we saw earlier. The page simply takes some of the user information from a User bean, uses it to thank the user for registering, and provides a couple of links to forward them on to some other interesting areas. The code for the JSP was shown earlier.

The page uses the resourceBundle tag to load the named resource bundle, writingjsps.registration.RegistrationResources, into scope. What this means is that any of the other internationalization tags can then be used within the scope of this tag and its loaded bundle(s). We can see there is a message tag that loads a resource, greetingMessage, and supplies both the user's first name and chosen username as parameters to the message. Further down, we can see how the string tag has been used to load and display a disclaimer notice that could, quite rightly, be specific to the region where the user is based.

It's up to the application designer to specify how many specific international regions will be catered for and to provide bundles for those locales under the specified base name. For our purposes, we will create the following resource bundles:

1. writingjsps.registration.RegistrationResources.properties, which contains the following information:

```
greetingMessage=Hi {0}, you''re username is {1}!
appDisclaimer=We try our best to ensure your information is<br> \
kept secret. Ultimately though, we can't be held responsible.
```

2. `writingjsps.registration.RegistrationResources_en.properties`; this file has nothing to add to the base bundle.

3. `writingjsps.registration.RegistrationResources_en_GB.properties`, which contains the following information:

```
greetingMessage=Dear {0}, you have been assigned a username of {1}
```

4. `writingjsps.registration.RegistrationResources_en_US.properties`, which contains the following information:

```
greetingMessage=Hey {0}, you're now known as {1}!
appDisclaimer=Subject to US export and Data Protection policies.
```

5. `writingjsps.registration.RegistrationResources_fr.properties`, which contains the following information:

```
greetingMessage=Bonjour {0}!
```

Starting from the top, the listing shows the default (base) bundle (1), followed by bundles for English (2), English/UK (3), English/US (4), and French (5) resource bundles. The content of each bundle is listed after each.

All that's left now is to demonstrate the effect of different locales on the requesting client and server. The locale of the Operating System and, hence, the server, can be changed in Windows 98/NT/2000 through the **Control Panel | Regional Settings** icon. If you're using Microsoft Internet Explorer (IE) 5.x, you can alter the client accepted languages via **Tools | Internet Options| Languages...** For Netscape users, go to **Preferences**, select the **Navigator** section, click on the **Languages** option, and select the language you want.

The following screenshot shows the results when we have our Tomcat server running in the English/GB locale, and then configure IE with French as the preferred language:

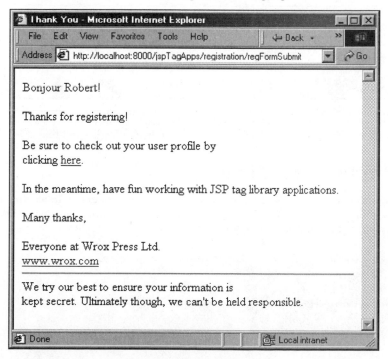

The French resource bundle was picked up automatically and loaded because the browser reflected the user's desire (actually, via the HTTP accept-languages header) for French content. As the French bundle had overridden the greetingMessage property, this was picked up and used from that bundle. However, the French bundle didn't provide a specific disclaimer property and neither did the server's default locale English or English/GB bundles. This means this property must reside in the base bundle otherwise an error would occur. The property was present in that bundle and was loaded from it.

As a final example, if we now change our browser's preferred locale to English/US, the following screen shots illustrate what happens:

The results above clearly reflect the fact the English/US locale bundle overrides both the greetingMessage and appDisclaimer message, specifically for United States regional clients.

The Registration Error Page

If, during registration, a username is chosen that matches the username of an existing user, the registration controller servlet forwards the registrant to the registration error page. The code for the tryAnotherUsername.jsp page is really very simple and is listed below:

```
<%@page import="writingjsps.registration.*" %>

<html>
<head>
<title>Registration Errors</title>
</head>
<body>
```

```
<p>Sorry, that username was already taken. Please go back in your browser and
<a href="#" onclick="window.history.go(-1)">choose another username</a>.
</body>
</html>
```

The results of attempting to register as an existing member is shown in the following screenshot:

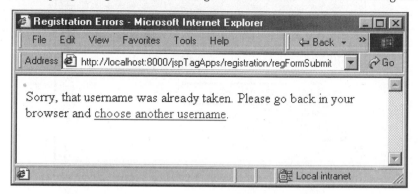

At this point, another username could be chosen by going back to the registration form.

That's the registration pages taken care of. Lets now look at logging back into the site.

The Login Form Page

When users register on any web site, they are usually expected to choose a username and password. This information is used to authenticate users whenever they return to the web site.

We've already seen the form that collects this and other information in our registration application. Registered users log into the system using option two of the welcome page, or directly via http://localhost:8000/jspTagApps/registration/login.

The controller servlet maps the login request to the login form JSP, loginForm.jsp, shown below:

```
<%@page import="java.util.*" %>
<%@page import="writingjsps.registration.*" %>

<%@taglib uri="/html" prefix="html" %>

<font face="arial, helvetica" size="4" color="#996600">Login</font>

<html:form method="post" actionURI="./loginFormSubmit">
  <table border="0">
  <tr>
    <td>User Name:</TD>
    <td><html:textInput name="username" numberOfColumns="20" /></td>
  </tr>
  <tr>
    <td>Password:</td>
    <td><html:passwordInput name="password" numberOfColumns="20" /></TD>
  </tr>
  </table>

  <input type="submit" value="Login">
</html:form>
```

Just like the registration form, this login form JSP imports and uses the HTML helper tag library to create the login form and input fields. In this example, the number of visible characters for each field has been set to 20. The following screenshot shows the login form served:

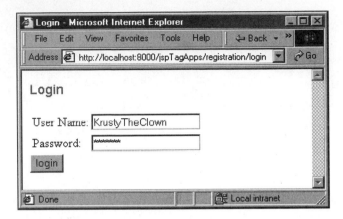

The login form, `loginForm.jsp`, uses the `form`, `textInput,` and `passwordInput` tags of the HTML tag library. We discussed these tags in the last section. When the form is submitted, the registration controller servlet processes the form elements and ensures the user's credentials are valid, and a user with the specified username and password exists in the registration database.

If the user's credentials check out, the controller servlet serves a user cookie. The cookie persists between requests to the registration application and authenticates the user to the application upon each subsequent request. After the cookie is served, the controller forwards the user on to the page that displays the user profile.

If the details entered do not correspond to those of a registered user, the controller servlet forwards on to a login error page.

The user profile and login error pages are discussed in the next sections.

Viewing your User Profile

Web site registration applications allow registered users to view and, potentially, edit their registration details. Although, within the scope of this book, the registration application in this chapter does not allow changes to registration information, it does provide for viewing existing registration details.

Users that have logged in, as discussed in the last section, can view their user profile through option three of the home page, or directly via http://localhost:8000/jspTagApps/registration/displayDetails.

The controller servlet maps the request for the user profile to `displayDetails.jsp`. This JSP displays the authenticated user information. The code for the JSP is listed below:

```
<%@page import="java.util.*" %>
<%@page import="writingjsps.registration.*" %>

<%@taglib uri="/foundation" prefix="fnd" %>
<%@taglib uri="http://java.sun.com/jsptl/ea/jx" prefix="jx"%>

<fnd:number id="pageStartTime" value="<%= System.currentTimeMillis()%>" />
<jsp:useBean id="user" type="writingjsps.registration.User"
```

```
                    scope="request" />

<html>
<head>
<title>User Profile</title>
</head>

<body>
<font face="arial, helvetica" size="4" color="#996600">User Profile</font>

<table border="0">
<tr>
  <td>User Name:</td><td><%= user.getUsername() %></td>
</tr>
<tr>
  <TD>First Name:</td><td><%= user.getForename() %></td>
</tr>
<tr>
  <td>Last Name:</td><td><%= user.getSurname() %></td>
</tr>
<tr>
  <td>Email:</td><td><%= user.getEmailAddress() %></td>
</tr>
<tr>
  <td>D.O.B.:</td><td><fnd:dateFormat date="<%= user.getDateOfBirth() %>"
                                    format ="dd MMMM, yyyy" />
  </td>
</tr>

<fnd:number id="ageThisYear"
    value="<%= new Date().getYear()-user.getDateOfBirth().getYear() %>" />
<tr>
  <td>Age This Year:</td><td><%= ageThisYear %></td>
</tr>
<tr>
  <td>Actual Age:</td><td><%= user.getAge() %></td>
</tr>
<fnd:boolean id="isPensioner"
            value="<%= ageThisYear.intValue() >= 65 %>" scope="REQUEST" />
<tr>
  <td>Pensioner This Year:</td><td><%= isPensioner %></td>
</tr>
<tr>
  <td>Region of Origin:</td><td><%= user.getRegion() %></td>
</tr>
<tr>
  <td>Company Name:</td><td><%= user.getCompanyName() %></td>
</tr>
<tr>
  <td>Your Role:</td>
  <td><%= user.getRole() %>
    <jx:if test="$user.role == 'Java Developer'" >
      <img src="images/duke_30x29.jpg" alt="Duke of Java" align="middle">
    </jx:if>
  </td>
</tr>
<tr>
  <td>Main Hobby:</td><td><%= user.getMainHobby() %></td>
</tr>
<tr>
  <td>Favourite Web Site:</td>
  <td><%= user.getFavoriteWebSiteURL() %> 
```

```
        <a href='serverSideIncludePeek.jsp?url=
            <fnd:encode><%= user.getFavoriteWebSiteURL() %></fnd:encode>'
            target="inANewWindowPlease">Click Here to Peek!</a>
   </td>
 </tr>
 <tr>
   <td>Last Accessed Account:</td>
   <td><fnd:dateFormat date="<%= user.getLastAccessed() %>"
                     format="dd-MMM-yyyy HH:mm:ss z" /></td>
 </tr>
 </table>

 <fnd:number id="pageEndTime" value="<%= System.currentTimeMillis()%>" />
 <% String message = "Page took " +
                 (pageEndTime.longValue()-pageStartTime.longValue()) +
                 "ms to generate!"; %>
 <fnd:log message="<%= message %>" />

 </body>
```

This JSP code generated the sample user profile page seen in the following screenshot:

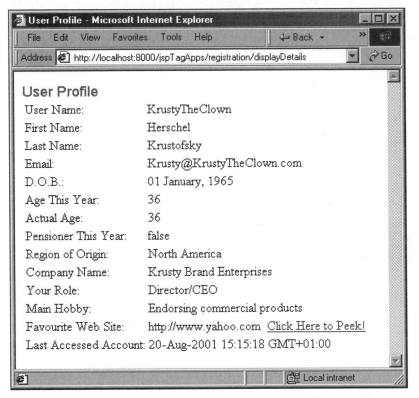

At first glance, this page appears to do a lot. When a request to this page is made, the controller servlet authenticates the user, creates a `User` bean for holding properties of the user, and makes this bean available to the JSP page in the request. This page locates and uses the `User` bean:

```
<jsp:useBean id="user" type="writingjsps.registration.User"
            scope="request" />
```

There are then a number of scriptlets for extracting the user properties for display by the JSP:

```
...
<tr>
  <td>User Name:</td><td><%= user.getUsername() %></td>
</tr>
<tr>
  <td>First Name:</td><td><%= user.getForename() %></td>
</tr>
<tr>
  <td>Last Name:</td><td><%= user.getSurname() %></td>
</tr>
...
```

Let's take a look at the tags used within the page. The page imports the jx tag library, from the JSPTL, and uses the if tag from that library to test whether the role of the user is "**Java Developer**". If it is, an image of Duke (of Java) is inserted into the page, beside the displayed role. This was achieved by the code snippet shown below:

```
<%@ taglib uri="http://java.sun.com/jsptl/ea/jx" prefix="jx"%>
...
...
<tr>
  <td>Your Role:</td>
  <td><%= user.getRole() %>
    <jx:if test="$user.role == 'Java Developer'" >
      <img src="images/duke_30x29.jpg" alt="Duke of Java" align="middle">
    </jx:if>
  </td>
</tr>
...
```

As Krusty is not a Java Developer, the image wasn't added to the page.

A number of other tags are used within the displayDetails.jsp page. These are described in the next section.

Some Fundamental Tag Ideas In JSP

The user profile view page, displayDetails.jsp, used the JSPTL if conditional tag. But it also used a number of other tags, written for this application, to demonstrate some common concepts within JSPs. I call these tags fundamental or foundation tags. Such a library would sport tags that would be used in many JSP based web applications.

The JSP imported the foundation tags library with the taglib directive:

```
<%@taglib uri="/foundation" prefix="fnd" %>
```

Looking back at the parts of the JSP page we've highlighted, we can see that the number, boolean, dateFormat, and log tags were all used from this library (they were all prefixed by the tag library prefix in the page). The following table presents a brief description of the tags from this library:

Tag	Attribute	Description
number		Declares a numeric script variable and optionally assigns a value to it.
	id	Specifies the name of a scripting variable to be created to represent the number. The id attribute has special meaning when used with tags that create script variables. Refer to the JSP specification for further details.

Table continued on following page

Tag	Attribute	Description
	Value	The initial value of the numeric. This can be a numeric constant, primitive or wrapper type of type `short`, `integer`, `long`, `float`, or `double`. Defaults to zero.
	scope	The scope of the variable: page, request, session, or application. Defaults to page scope.
Boolean		Declares a boolean script variable and optionally assigns a value to it.
	id	The name of the scripting variable to be created.
	Value	The initial value of the boolean variable: `true` or `false`. Defaults to `false`.
	scope	The scope of the variable: page, request, session, or application. Defaults to page scope.
dateFormat		Outputs a string representation of a date, formatted according to the specified `format` parameter for the specified locale and time zone.
	date	The `java.util.Date` to be formatted.
	format	The format that the string representation of the date is to take. This is based entirely on the patterns provided by the `java.text.Simple DateFormat` class in the Java 2 Standard Edition.
		For example, "yyyy.MM.dd hh:mm:ss" would produce output of the form "1997.10.02 15:10:25" and "EEE, MMM d, yyyy" would produce output of the form "Wed, August 19, 1998".
	timeZone	The name of a known time zone. Specified to offset the time to a specific time zone and cater for daylight saving time.
	locale	A `locale` is used to sensitize formatting of the date to a particular locale. If not specified, the clients preferred locale is used, if possible, otherwise the default locale of the server is used.
log		Logs its body or specified message using the Servlet Logging API.
	message	Specifies the message to be logged.
	throwable	Specifies a `java.lang.Throwable` to be logged.
encode		A tag that URL-encodes its body. Refer to the `java.net.URLEncoder` class for further information.

The declaration tags, `number` and `boolean`, provide an easy way for JSP authors to declare and use scripting variables within their JSP pages. This is particularly useful, over declaration of variables in JSP scriptlets, when the page author is not necessarily an expert in Java or for creating scripting variables whose scope is beyond that of the JSP page on which they are declared.

The `number` tag creates a numeric scripting variable without paying too much attention to the explicit numerical type. In fact, because the tag is based on the `java.lang.Number` type, it can represent the values of any numeric primitive or primitive wrapper type. Here's the example taken from the user profile display page:

```
<%@page import="java.util.*" %>
<%@page import="writingjsps.registration.*" %>

<%@taglib uri="/foundation" prefix="fnd" %>
<%@taglib uri="http://java.sun.com/jsptl/ea/jx" prefix="jx"%>

<fnd:number id="pageStartTime" value="<%= System.currentTimeMillis()%>" />
<jsp:useBean id="user" type="writingjsps.registration.User"
             scope="request" />

<html>
<head>
<title>User Profile</title>
</head>

<body><font face="arial, helvetica" size="4" color="#996600">User Profile</font>

<table border="0">
<tr>
  <td>User Name:</td><td><%= user.getUsername() %></td>
</tr>
...
...
<fnd:number id="ageThisYear"
     value="<%= new Date().getYear()-user.getDateOfBirth().getYear() %>" />
<tr>
  <td>Age This Year:</td><td><%= ageThisYear %></td>
</tr>
<tr>
  <td>Actual Age:</td><td><%= user.getAge() %></td>
</tr>
<fnd:boolean id="isPensioner" value="<%= ageThisYear.intValue() >= 65 %>"
             scope="REQUEST" />
<tr>
  <td>Pensioner This Year:</td><td><%= isPensioner %></td>
</tr>
...
...
</table>
...
...
</body>
</html>
```

We can see, from the highlighted section above, that a scripting variable, `ageThisYear`, is created and initialized to the age, this year, of the user whose details are being displayed.
The `boolean` tag creates a Boolean-type scripting variable and assigns it an initial value. The example shown above creates the Boolean variable, `isPensioner`, and this value is output as part of the user information. These declaration tags, and what they achieve, are pretty much self-explanatory.

The ability to format a date quickly and effectively, without having to create `DateFormat` objects in JSP scriptlets, can be achieved using the `dateFormat` tag. The JSP used the tag to format the date and time the user last accessed their account. This was achieved with comparative ease, when compared to the amount of code needed in a JSP scriptlet to achieve the same result and is reiterated below:

```
<td><fnd:dateFormat date="<%= user.getLastAccessed() %>"
                    format="dd-MMM-yyyy HH:mm:ss z" /></td>
```

617

The two other tags used in the user profile JSP are `log` and `encode`. The `log` tag was used to output the page generation time, in milliseconds, to the server log. Until the Java SDK 1.4 release, log handling will not come as standard within the Java APIs. The `log` tag simply logs its message through the `ServletContext.log` method. Where the logged messages go is entirely server-specific. They generally go into the standard `out` or `err` logs of the web server. In the case of the Reference Implementation, they go to `%J2EE_HOME%\logs\<server>\web\catalina.<date>.log`.

How often do we need to URL-encode URLs in our JSP pages? In fact, any text that contains reserved characters, whether in URLs or the body of the HTML document, should be encoded. The encode tag was used to achieve this with ease, when compared to, say, using the `java.net.URLEncoder` each and every time. The tag was used to encode the user's favorite URL:

```
<td>Favourite Web Site:</td>
<td><%= user.getFavoriteWebSiteURL() %> 
  <a href='serverSideIncludePeek.jsp?url=
            <fnd:encode><%= user.getFavoriteWebSiteURL() %></fnd:encode>'
      target="inANewWindowPlease">Click Here to Peek!</a>
</td>
```

The user profile page is served to users who successfully log in. Let's now take a look what happens in our registration application if login is unsuccessful.

The Login Error Page

If an invalid username or password was entered at login, the registration controller forwards to the login error page. The code for the `noSuchUser.jsp` page is quite short and is listed below:

```
<%@page import="writingjsps.registration.*" %>

<html>
<head>
<title>Login Errors</title>
</head>
<body>
<p>Sorry, you have entered an invalid User Name or Password.<br>
Please <a href="/jspTagApps/registration/login">try again</a>.<br>
</body>
</html>
```

The results of an attempt to log in as a non-registered user are shown in the following screenshot:

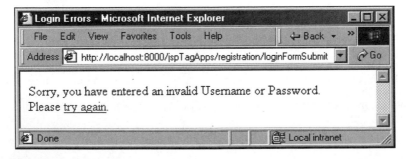

At this point, you could try again or give up trying to guess the usernames and passwords of registered users!

Viewing the User's Favorite Web Site

The user profile page, introduced in the last section, provided a link with which to peek at a registered user's favorite web site. We say peek, because it doesn't provide a direct link to the web site. Instead, the link provided is to another page within the registration application. The JSP page, called `serverSideIncludePeek.jsp`, includes the content of the site directly on the server-side and relays it back to the client, in the response.

To achieve this, the page uses a **server-side include tag (SSI)**, `ssi`. The JSP page is listed below:

```
<%@taglib uri="/foundation" prefix="fnd" %>

<fnd:ssi uri='<%= request.getParameter("url") %>'>
Oops, we were unable to find the web site you requested:
  <%= request.getParameter("url") %>
</fnd:ssi>
```

The Click Here to Peek link on the User Profile page runs the `serverSideIncludePeek.jsp` page. The page itself, the server-side include concept, and the `ssi` tag are discussed in the next section.

Server-Side Includes (SSI)

The JSP specification provides us with a number of convenient and useful mechanisms for including content within JSP pages. For static content, incorporated at translation time, we can use the **include directive** as follows:

```
<%@ include file="notes/disclaimer.html" %>
```

Files included with this directive are incorporated at compile or translation time. Once included, they form an integral part of the JSP that contains the `include` directive. The JSP container also parses content included in this way.

For inclusion of dynamic content – that is, content to be incorporated at request time – we can use the include **standard action**:

```
<jsp:include page="<%= notesBean.getDisclaimerURI() %>" />
```

Content included in this way is incorporated in the same manner as the `include()` method of the `RequestDispatcher` class, obtained via a call to `ServletContext.getRequestDispatcher()`. However, in both of the include methods shown above, the URI specified in the included `file` or `page` must be relative to the web application performing the include.

There are times when it may be more convenient to include content within JSP pages at request time, from outside of the scope of the current web application. In fact, there are some cases when this is the only option. For example, if the content to be included has been generated outside of the application by another process.

> There is currently no mechanism provided in the JSP specification to perform inclusion of content not originating from within the document hierarchy of the JSP application.

However, the server-side include concept allows for inclusion of content on the serverside from within the document hierarchy of the web application, or from outside of it. Content included from outside of the document hierarchy of the web application has to be included dynamically.

So, the idea of SSIs may sound interesting, but like most paradigms in IT development, it comes with some limitations and tradeoffs. We'll outline these drawbacks in the following section.

Some Issues with Server-Side Includes

Including content on the serverside could degrade performance on the web server. But, if we cache the data, then performance should improve, right? If we cache data on the server, how often should we refresh it? There are design and implementation issues concerned with server-side includes, which include the following points:

❑ **Performance on the server** – too much included at the server end, dynamically, could ultimately degrade performance on the server.

❑ **Caching data for too long could lead to stale content** – caching content that changes frequently runs the risk of potentially serving stale data to clients. This raises the concern, "Do we cache dynamic data at all and, if so, for how long?"

❑ **Purge cached data when update requests fail** – if periodic requests are made to update content in a cache and some or all of those requests fail, do we purge the potentially stale content and throw an application error, or should the application be given the data from the cache? Generally, the application should continue normally and, perhaps, subsequent requests to update the cache might succeed, but not always.

❑ **Provide an alternative or fallback** – for content that may need to be included regularly or may not always be retrievable, an alternative message should be available to display to the client.

All of these issues should be addressed when considering using SSIs within JSP pages. Finding the right balance can mean the difference between a responsive server, which appears to serve the latest content, or a sluggish server that tends to serve stale content or fail regularly if content could not be found.

In the next section we'll demonstrate how server-side includes can be incorporated into a JSP using a custom tag.

A Server-Side Include Tag

The server-side include tag (`ssi`) shown below can be considered an alternative to the standard `include` action, differing only in that it allows the URI to identify a resource that can reside within the document hierarchy of the web application (the standard behavior within JSP pages), or outside of it. No effort is made here, however, to implement server-side caching of included content.

The `ssi` tag and its attributes are described in the table below:

Tag	Attribute	Description
Ssi		An include tag that can include static or dynamic content, within or outside of the JSP application performing the include.
	uri	The URI, relative or absolute, of the resource to be included. The resource must have a content type that is text based, such as `text/html`.
	throws Errors	A Boolean that determines whether any exceptions thrown attempting to include the resource should be thrown out of the JSP page where the resource was included.

Tag	Attribute	Description
	throws Errors (continued)	If throwsErrors is true and an exception is thrown processing the include, an errorPage specified using the page directive will be invoked.
		If throwsErrors is false and the ssi tag has a body, the body of this tag is evaluated and outputted as content to the JSP page performing the include. In effect, this fallback mechanism is similar to the alternative attribute (alt) used in HTML elements.
		Defaults to false.

Getting back to out user profile, the Click Here to Peek link references the serverSideIncludePeek.jsp page. Clicking the link to peek at the web site, the link opens another window that displays the results of the serverSideIncludePeek.jsp, as shown in the following screenshot:

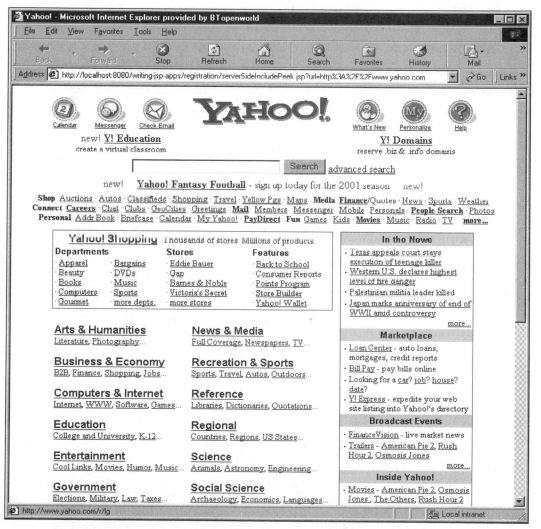

Behold, our registration application has the ability to include content from anywhere in the world! In fact, using yahoo.com is a good example of a site whose content and behavior can be included by third parties. In order to achieve this portlet or sub-window approach, all links within the home page need to be absolute. We can even perform searches on yahoo.com from the peek view window.

The code snippet for serverSideIncludePeek.jsp that performs the actual include is shown below:

```
<fnd:ssi uri='<%= request.getParameter("url") %>'>
Oops, we were unable to find the web site you requested:
  <%= request.getParameter("url") %>
</fnd:ssi>
```

Note that the body of the tag houses some alternative text. This text will be displayed if, for any reason, the content at the specified URI could not be included. It's a good idea to always include something descriptive to clients in the event of failure, like the following:

If, however, the content of the specified URI could not be loaded and we had used an abbreviated form of this code:

```
<fnd:ssi uri='<%= request.getParameter("url") %>' />
```

We would get the following kind of error, which is not very pleasant for the user requesting the page:

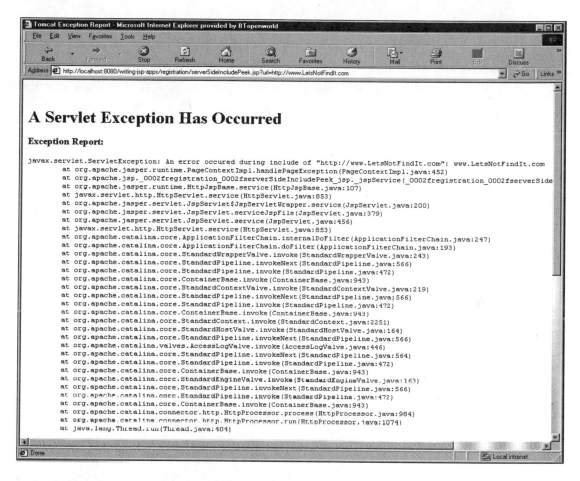

Administration: The Display-All-Users Page

The registration application provides some useful administration features. One of those features is a summary display of all registered users. The All Registered Users page is selected as option four on the home page, or directly as http://localhost:8000/jspTagApps/registration/displayAllRegisteredUsers.

Once again, the controller servlet intercepts the request, then interrogates the database to find all users and constructs an administration page bean containing a list of the users for rendering in the JSP page. The controller maps the URL /registration/displayAllRegisteredUsers to the display JSP, displayAllRegisteredUsers.jsp.

The code for the displayAllRegisteredUsers.jsp page is listed below:

```
<%@page import="java.util.*" %>
<%@page import="writingjsps.registration.*" %>

<%@taglib uri="/foundation" prefix="fnd" %>
<%@taglib uri="http://java.sun.com/jsptl/ea/jx" prefix="jx"%>
<%@taglib uri="http://java.sun.com/jsptl/ea/jr" prefix="jr"%>
```

623

```
<jsp:useBean id="adminPageBean"
             type="writingjsps.registration.RegistrationAdminPageBean"
             scope="request" />

<html>
<head>
<title>All Registered Users</title>
</head>
<body>
<font face="arial, helvetica" size="4" color="#996600">All Registered
Users</FONT><br>
on
<fnd:dateFormat format="dd-MMM-yyyy 'at' HH:mm:ss z">
  <fnd:currentSystemTimeMillis/>
</fnd:dateFormat><br>
<br>

<jr:choose>
  <jr:when test="<%= adminPageBean.getRegisteredUsers().length == 0 %>">
      Currently there are no registered users!
  </jr:when>
  <jr:otherwise>
    <table border="1">
      <tr bgcolor="black">
        <td><font color="white">User Name</font></td>
        <td><font color="white">Email Address</font></td>
        <td><font color="white">Last Accessed Account</font></td>
      </tr>
      <jx:forEach var="aUser" items="$adminPageBean.registeredUsers"
                  status="status">
        <jx:declare id="aUser" type="writingjsps.registration.User" />
        <tr>
          <td><jx:expr value="$aUser.username" /></td>
          <td><jx:expr value="$aUser.emailAddress" /></td>
          <td><fnd:dateFormat date="<%= aUser.getLastAccessed() %>"
                              format ="dd-MMM-yyyy HH:mm:ss z" /></td>
        </tr>
      </jx:forEach>
    </TABLE>
  </jr:otherwise>
</jr:choose>
</body>
</html>
```

The following screenshot shows an example of the expected results from this page:

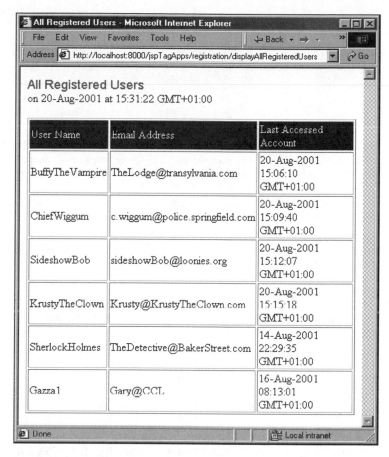

Let's take a look at the tags used within the page. The page imports both the jr and the jx tag library, from the JSPTL, and uses a variety of tags from those libraries: choose, when, otherwise, forEach, declare, and expr tags. The choose tags, and subsequently the when and otherwise tags, are used to test whether there are any users to display or not. As mentioned in the sections that discussed the JSPTL tags, the choose tag is the equivalent to the Java switch statement or if-then-elseif-else block. Here we use it to test if there aren't any users to display or if there are:

```
<choose>
  <when ...no users...>
    // Currently there are no registered users!
  </when>
  <otherwise ...we must have some users...>
    // Iterate through and display a summary of registered users
  </otherwise>
</choose>
```

We've already seen examples that use the forEach tag. However, this page uses the declare tag to bridge between the scoped attribute environment, used by the JSPTL tags, and the JSP scripting environment:

```
<jx:forEach var="aUser" items="$adminPageBean.registeredUsers"
            status="status">
```

```
            <jx:declare id="aUser" type="writingjsps.registration.User" />
        <tr>
          <td><jx:expr value="$aUser.username" /></td>
          <td><jx:expr value="$aUser.emailAddress" /></td>
          <td><fnd:dateFormat date="<%= aUser.getLastAccessed() %>"
                              format ="dd-MMM-yyyy HH:mm:ss z" /></td>
        </tr>
      </jx:forEach>
```

As the page iterates through the list of users, a JSP scripting variable, aUser, is created for each user within the loop. We've already come across the dateFormat tag in the section on the user profile display page, *Viewing your User Profile*. The dateFormat tag uses the lastAccessed property of the user bean, referred to by the scripting variable, to format the date and time the user last accessed the site.

One final point to note is the use of a new tag, currentSystemTimeMillis, used in conjunction with the dateFormat tag:

```
on
<fnd:dateFormat format="dd-MMM-yyyy 'at' HH:mm:ss z">
  <fnd:currentSystemTimeMillis/>
</fnd:dateFormat><br>
```

This tag originates from the foundation library, introduced in previous examples. The tag is described in the following table for clarity:

Tag	Description
currentSystemTimeMillis	Outputs the parsed date in milliseconds since January 1, 1970, 00:00:00 GMT. Used in conjunction with the dateFormat tag.

The concept and use of the currentSystemTimeMillis tag is simple. When used as the body of the dateFormat tag, it supplies the current date and time for formatting. It does exactly that in our example above.

Administration: An XML-based Web Service

Another of the administration pages provides a list of the registered users as an XML document. In the last section, we looked at an administration page to view summary information about all registered users. The page discussed in this section performs a similar function, but rather than generating an HTML page, listing the users, it generates an XML document containing the user information.

As this generates content information only, without regard as to how the information is to be presented, it can be used by other parts of the registration application or even by external parties that make calls to it. In real life, if the registration application were to front a real web site, the external parties could be third-party clients who need to know who has accessed the site. Although our registration application has been kept simplistic in functionality, these kinds of XML interface are loosely referred to as **web services**.

While there is a lot of discussion these days about ways to register these services (perhaps using WSDL and UDDI) and call them (perhaps using Simple Object Access Protocol – SOAP), plain and simple *XML* services are, nonetheless, web services. We'll look at web services in more detail in Chapter 22 *J2EE and Web Services*.

We'll look at another part of the application that makes use of the service, in the next section.

The XML document created is not generated by a JSP. The document is created by the registration controller servlet and returned to the caller directly. The controller receives the request for the document, as shown by the sample of controller servlet code below:

```
public void
        createAllRegisteredUsersXMLDocument(HttpServletRequest request,
                                            HttpServletResponse response)
                                        throws ServletException,
                                            IOException {
    try {
      User allUsers[] = userManager.findAll();

      UsersToXMLConverter usersToXMLConverter =
        new UsersToXMLConverter(allUsers);
      response.setContentType("text/xml");
      response.getWriter().write(usersToXMLConverter.getXMLDocument());
    } catch (Exception ex) {
      throw new ServletException("An unexpected error occurred when " +
                                 "converting user information to XML",
                                 ex);
    }
}
```

The controller servlet processes the request by finding all registered users and supplying an array of users to a helper class, `UsersToXMLConverter`, which converts the list to XML document form. For completeness, the code for the `UsersToXMLConverter` class is shown below:

```
package writingjsps.registration;

import java.io.*;

import javax.xml.parsers.DocumentBuilderFactory;
import javax.xml.parsers.DocumentBuilder;
import javax.xml.parsers.ParserConfigurationException;
import org.xml.sax.SAXException;
import org.w3c.dom.*;

public class UsersToXMLConverter {
  private String xmlDoc;

  public UsersToXMLConverter(User users[]) throws Exception {
    convertUserListToXML(users);
  }

  public String getXMLDocument() {
    return xmlDoc;
  }

  private void convertUserListToXML(User users[]) throws Exception {
    DocumentBuilderFactory dbf = DocumentBuilderFactory.newInstance();
    DocumentBuilder db = dbf.newDocumentBuilder();
    Document doc = db.newDocument();
    Element rootNode = doc.createElement("USERS");
    rootNode.setAttribute("number", Integer.toString(users.length));

    for (int n = 0; n < users.length; n++) {
      Element userNode = doc.createElement("USER");
```

```
        userNode.setAttribute("username", users[n].getUsername());
        userNode.setAttribute("forename", users[n].getForename());
        userNode.setAttribute("surname", users[n].getSurname());
        userNode.setAttribute("emailAddress", users[n].getEmailAddress());
        userNode.setAttribute("mainHobby", users[n].getMainHobby());

        rootNode.appendChild(userNode);
    }

    doc.appendChild(rootNode);
    XMLDocumentStringifier xmlStringifier =
                new XMLDocumentStringifier("ISO-8859-1", false, true);
    xmlDoc = xmlStringifier.toString(doc);
  }
}
```

The UsersToXMLConverter class uses the JAXP 1.1 API (the default, if running under Tomcat 4) and the DOM 2.0 API, to construct the document and return it as a string to the caller.

This service is requested as option five from the home page, or directly as http://localhost:8000/jspTagApps/registration/allRegisteredUsers.xml. The following screenshot shows an example of the expected results from this page, using IE:

Deploying the Registration Application

Well, having been through the construction process of the registration application, let's deploy the application in your environment.

The registration application and sourcecode is available for download from the Wrox web site, at http://www.wrox.com/. If you didn't already do so for the early sections on the JSPTL, download all the files for this chapter and follow the steps below to get the application up and running:

❑   With the Reference Implementation server running, take the `jspTagApps.war` file, and add it to an application EAR file using the deployment tool:

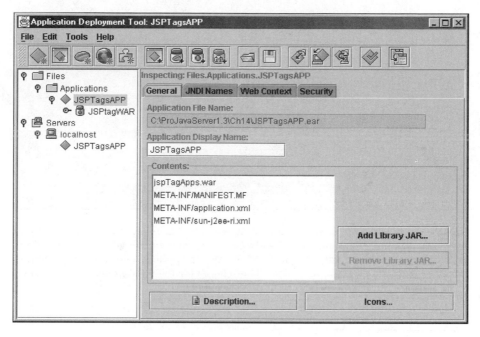

❑   Select the WAR file, click on the **Resource Refs** tab, and add a resource factory of type `javax.sql.Datasource`:

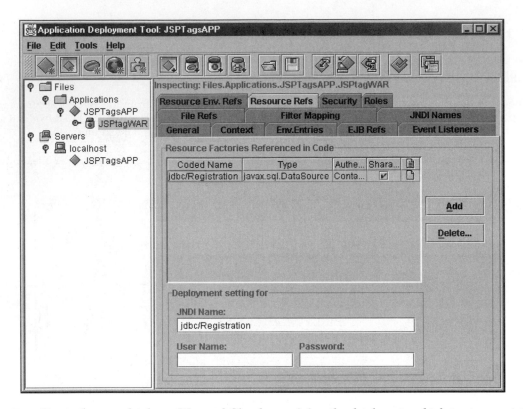

❑ Create the user database. We used Cloudscape 3.6 as the database in which to store registered user information. If you haven't already got it, you can download the database from http://www.cloudscape.com/. The database for the application is already present in the WAR as `WEB-INF/db/registrationDB`. The schema for the database is shown below:

```
CREATE TABLE USERS (
    USERNAME VARCHAR(30) NOT NULL ,
    FORENAME VARCHAR(30) NOT NULL ,
    SURNAME VARCHAR(30) NOT NULL ,
    EMAILADDRESS VARCHAR(80) NOT NULL ,
    DATEOFBIRTH TIMESTAMP NOT NULL ,
    COMPANYNAME VARCHAR(100) NOT NULL ,
    MAINHOBBY VARCHAR(100) NOT NULL ,
    PASSWORD VARCHAR(30) NOT NULL ,
    ROLE VARCHAR(50) NOT NULL ,
    FAVORITEWEBSITEURL VARCHAR(200) NOT NULL ,
    LASTACCESSED TIMESTAMP NOT NULL ,
    REGION VARCHAR(50) NOT NULL ,
    AGE INT NOT NULL
)
```

You'll want to put this database somewhere on your hard drive, and reference it when you set up the `DataSource` using the Deployment Tool. The `DataSource` should have the JNDI name `jdbc/Registration` since that is what the application will be looking for (one of the classes we didn't look at, `UserManager`). Select Tools ||Server Configuration… from the Deployment Tool main window, and in the Configure Installation dialog set up a standard data source to point to the database:

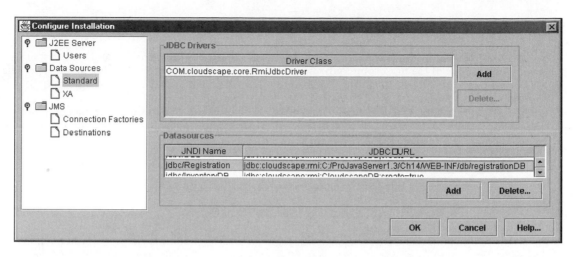

❑ Start the Cloudscape `RmiJdbc` database using the following command:

```
cloudscape -start
```

❑ Finally, request the home page URL of the application,
http://localhost:8000/jspTagApps/registration/index.html.

This chapter was concerned with writing JSP applications with tag libraries and, as a result, the construction of the registration application was largely focused on the JSP pages and the tags they employed. The reader is encouraged to explore the `jspTagApps.war` application, its structure, and the classes contained within.

What Lies Ahead: The Standard Tag Library

With the release of the JSP Standard Tag Library (JSPTL), the boundary between **generic** and **application-specific** custom tags is going to be much more defined. Very generic concepts like control flow, date and time handling, internationalization, and XML/XSLT processing will be taken care of by the JSPTL.

This leaves the JSP application developer free to focus more on application development with application-centric tag libraries. As well as a standardized library of JSP tags, the JSPTL promises to deliver the following:

❑ **A definition of how the tags interact with the environment** – for nested tags, or tags that must be nested within other tags, how these tags interact with their parents.

❑ **Extensibility** – a method for extending tags in the JSPTL.

❑ **Expression Language Support** – additional meanings of attribute values. We saw plenty of these in the examples presented in this chapter.

Look out for the release of the JSPTL, and get the releases at http://jakarta.apache.org/taglibs/.

Summary

We've covered a lot in this chapter, looking at the benefits to developers, vendors, and businesses of standardizing some of the most commonly-used tags today. There's a lot of work going into this process at the moment, and the introduction of the JSPTL promises to be exciting and beneficial all round.

After reading this chapter, you've hopefully gained a firm understanding of some of the common patterns and usage of the Java 2, Standard and Enterprise Edition APIs that can be exploited through a set of common and consistent tags. We looked at:

- ❏ The benefits of using custom tag libraries
- ❏ Some of the current vendor-specific tag libraries out there today
- ❏ The proposed introduction of the JSP Standard Tag Library

We then took a glimpse at a registration application, used throughout this chapter, as the main example. The registration application was built to use and exploit to the fullest the sample JSPTL-like tags outlined in the sections that followed.

Having introduced the main example, we looked at several aspects of day-to-day JSP development, covering tag libraries for:

- ❏ Fundamental tags, such as those for declaration, control flow, data and time handling, server-side includes, and other miscellaneous tags
- ❏ Internationalization
- ❏ Wrapping HTML forms
- ❏ Creating XML views of data contained in a relational database

With these concepts in mind, we're now ready to start using common JSP tags within our applications. Look out for the JSPTL; it's going to exploit all of these concepts and, in doing so, create a storm on the Java and web technology fronts.

In the next chapter, we move on to look at the JavaMail API, and how we can use it.

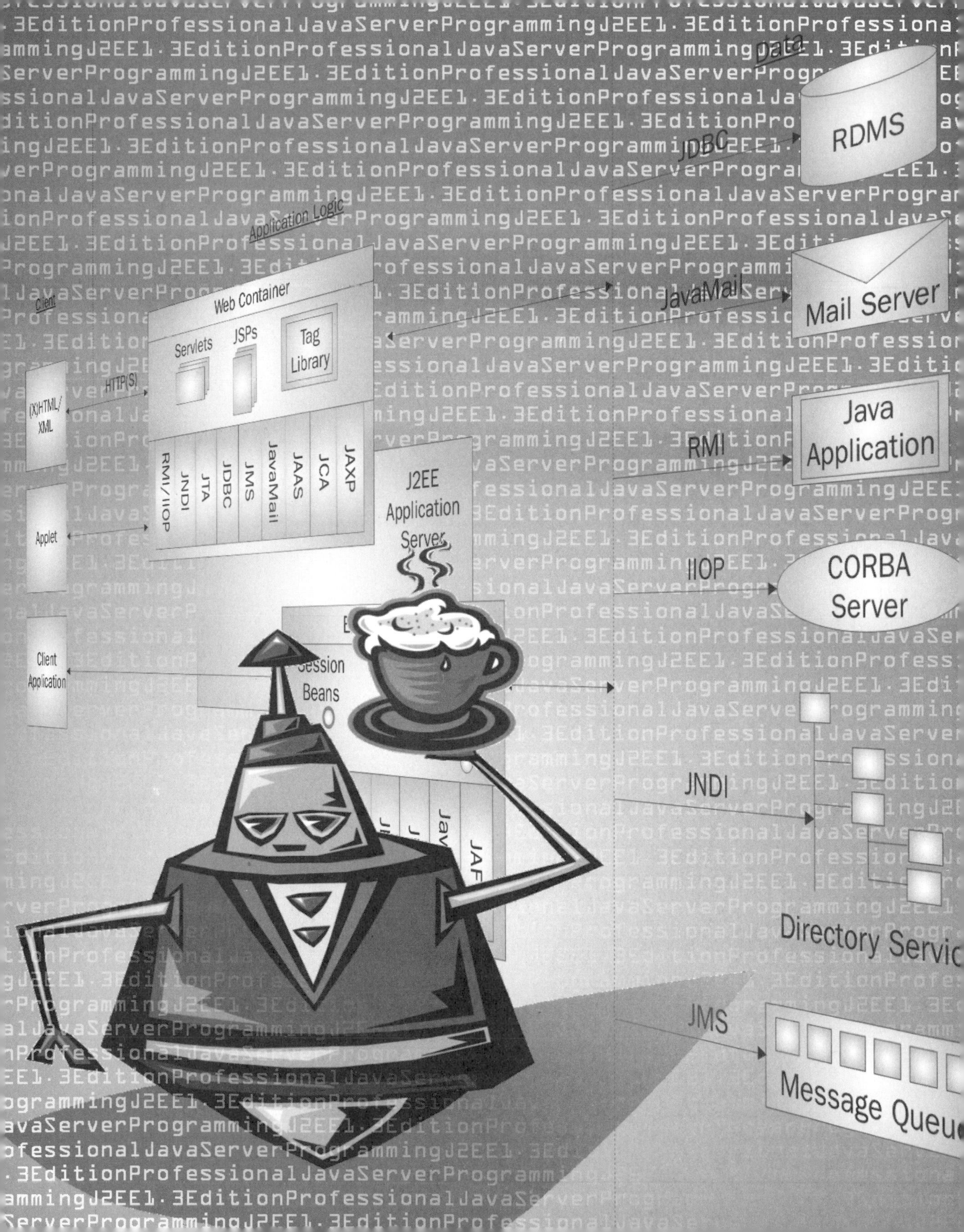

13

JavaMail

E-mail is one of the oldest networked-computer technologies still in use today, predating the World Wide Web by some 20 years or so. People live and breathe e-mail: businesses thrive on their use of e-mail, families are brought closer together with e-mail, nearly everyone has an e-mail address. However, it may surprise you to learn that, for a tool that is so heavily relied on, the underlying technology is relatively simple.

The sending and receiving of Internet e-mail has never been a complicated task. It is a simple matter of opening up a connection (or "socket") for communication, transferring data, and then closing down the socket, all with a very small set of commands. This has made the technology tremendously robust.

Ironically, the actual transfer of e-mail messages has never presented too much of a problem, it's the interpretation of the content of the e-mail body that has caused much confusion. It is this aspect of the e-mail story that the **Multipurpose Internet Mail Extensions (MIME)** protocol has played a large part in solving. For example, using a purely ASCII based system, how would one transfer a binary file such as an image or executable in such a way that the receiving end knows how to deal with it? This is the sort of exchange that the MIME standard can achieve.

> **The JavaMail API is an abstract suite of classes that enable the implementation of message-based systems.**

The JavaMail API has done to the message world what JDBC did for the database world – it provides an abstract method of interacting with a large range of message stores. JavaMail makes it easy to incorporate complete e-mail connectivity within any Java program, servlet, bean, or applet. The complexities associated with packaging up an e-mail for successful receipt and delivery have been abstracted away to be just a set of method calls.

The JavaMail API was first introduced as a standalone package but now ships as part of the core J2EE API. That said, it can still be downloaded as a separate package to be used with applications outside of the J2EE space (as discussed later).

In this chapter we'll go through the logistics of using the JavaMail API to handle e-mail without having to worry too much about the underlying protocols. By the end of this chapter you will:

❑ Appreciate and understand the POP, SMTP, and IMAP protocols

❑ Discover the use and power of MIME within message makeup

❑ Understand the overall structure of the JavaMail API

❑ Install and configure the JavaMail API for non-J2EE applications

❑ Send an e-mail with and without attachments

❑ Receive an e-mail dealing with attachments where necessary

❑ Navigate and use remote folders

Mail Protocols

The protocols that underpin the workings of electronic mail are well established and very mature in this arena. Although not completely necessary, it is never a bad idea to get a feeling of what the JavaMail API is attempting to abstract for you. In this section we'll take a quick a look at the core protocol implementations that are bundled as part of the JavaMail distribution:

❑ Simple Mail Transport Protocol (SMTP)

❑ Post Office Protocol version 3 (POP3)

❑ Internet Message Access Protocol (IMAP)

Additionally, although it's not strictly a transport protocol, we'll also take a look at the protocol used for packaging up mail content:

❑ Multipurpose Internet Mail Extensions (MIME)

Earlier releases of the JavaMail API did not include a POP3 implementation. To access POP3 servers, one had to use a third-party implementation. As you can imagine, some felt that failing to deliver one of the most common protocols was a significant oversight on Sun's part. The latest release of JavaMail (1.2), which is specified as part of J2EE 1.3, has rectified this.

SMTP

The **Simple Mail Transport Protocol (SMTP)**, first proposed way back in 1982, is a protocol designed for the delivery of mail messages to servers. Its staying power can be attributed to its extreme simplicity in moving, or relaying messages around servers. SMTP is merely a delivery agent and is not used by users for reading e-mail.

Due to the fact that SMTP can act as a relay server (that is, it can deliver e-mail on behalf of another server) it has been open to abuse by spammers who are known to send large volumes of unsolicited mails to users all over the world. For this reason, many system administrators have blocked, or restricted, their SMTP server's capability, and will only accept e-mail that is specifically addressed to that server's user base.

Mention the word "spam" to any one and the chances are they know exactly what you are talking about, and I don't mean the great Monty Python song. Spam is unsolicited e-mail, and spammers are people (or organizations) that generate these large mailings. In order to give themselves a little more creditability, they may even pretend to be originating from a respected domain other than their own. For example, using SMTP it is very easy to send an e-mail and make it look as if it came from billgates@microsoft.com. This is known as relaying. Most SMTP servers will check for this, but many do not. So beware!

It's important to take note of these restrictions to the SMTP server's capability, as it can appear that our JavaMail application isn't sending e-mail properly and we may be looking at the code for reasons why. If we have a problem, the chances are that the server we are attempting to send e-mail to is not the host for that e-mail and has had its relaying capabilities significantly restricted.

Just like any protocol, SMTP has its restrictions. For example, when you're composing the header fields for an SMTP transaction, these must not exceed 512 characters. Moreover, the data part of the message mustn't have any lines greater than 1000 characters. However, we needn't worry too much about these restrictions as the JavaMail API takes care of all these for us.

You can read more about the specifics of SMTP by referring to the original RFC#821 document, available from http://www.rfc-editor.org/rfc/rfc821.txt.

POP3

The **Post Office Protocol (POP)** is the mechanism by which the majority of people collect their e-mail. Operating much like a mailbox at a real post office, POP3 enables a user to collect, or download, their e-mail, store it locally, and (optionally) remove it from the server. It is then the responsibility of the user to take care of the e-mail from there on in, by filing it in some logical storage. The POP server does not offer any storage facilities beyond the single mailbox that new mail will be delivered to. In fact, it can be a little confusing to new users since many modern day e-mail clients, such as Microsoft Outlook for instance, give the illusion that the server is doing far more than it actually is.

POP has been in its present state, version 3.0, since late 1988, but its roots go back as far as 1984. Again, it is a very well established protocol and its staying power can also be attributed to the simplicity of the protocol's instruction set.

For further details of POP3, have a look at the RFC#1939 document at http://www.rfc-editor.org/rfc/rfc1939.txt.

IMAP

The **Internet Message Access Protocol**, or **IMAP**, is a protocol that many enterprise e-mail servers employ; it offers a far richer set of functions than POP or even SMTP. With POP the premise is that the user is responsible for the storage of e-mail, whereas with IMAP the server is. IMAP offers a folder structure for the user to interact with and all messages are stored on the server with technically no need to download e-mail to the user's local machine.

This has the major advantage, for the user, of keeping all their e-mails in one central place, irrespective of the client they are using to log in with. IMAP offers far more functionality than just advance storage options, but the ability to deliver and search e-mails is also offered within this protocol.

Conversely, storing everyone's messages there places a large burden on the server, with huge amounts of disk space being required. This is one of the main disadvantages of the IMAP protocol, which is why it is not employed by organizations with poorly developed server infrastructure. If the server goes down, we lose everyone's e-mail, as opposed to just a single client computer falling over and losing just one user's mail.

JavaMail supports this protocol through the use of its API. However, it is fair to note at this point, that many of the features of IMAP are dependent purely on the mail server. JavaMail merely passes the request on through to the backend server and collates any results. It is occasions like this that JavaMail resembles the functionality offered by JDBC (JDBC merely passes the processing through to the backend database and doesn't actually do any major processing itself).

Although a far superior protocol to the likes of SMTP and POP, IMAP is not in as common use as the others, so make sure your server supports IMAP before attempting any communication using this protocol. It's worth noting that the majority of the commercially available mail servers include IMAP as part of the standard build (for example, Microsoft Exchange, Lotus cc:Mail, and Eudora WorldMail to name but a few).

You can read more about IMAP by referring to the RFC#2060 document at http://www.rfc-editor.org/rfc/rfc2060.txt. Additionally, to learn more about the various implementations of IMAP, and which e-mail servers support it, refer to http://www.imap.org/.

MIME

Internet mail is fundamentally based on pure ASCII text and on the whole, does not permit non-ASCII data to be used. At first this may seem a little restrictive, but after consideration of the wide variety of machine types over which e-mail messages are exchanged with one another, it is clear that, for practical purposes, choosing the lowest common denominator would ensure that data arrived safely and securely. However, the need to start attaching non-ASCII files to mail messages soon became apparent and a standard was required to deal with the encoding of binary files into ASCII in such a way that they could be transported and, when received, decoded back into their native binary representation.

The Multipurpose Internet Mail Extension (MIME) defines this translation and all the rules that are associated with the transmission. It sounds a lot more complicated than actually is and, although it can be quite cumbersome to develop, it's really nothing to worry about. The JavaMail API takes care of a lot of the tedious work for us and ensures all the necessary protocols and translations are handled correctly. For more information on MIME visit http://www.oac.uci.edu/indiv/ehood/MIME/MIME.html.

JavaMail Overview

The JavaMail API is quite a large collection of classes and interfaces, totalling somewhere near 100. This makes it sound tremendously complicated, but we shouldn't feel intimidated by numbers. In fact, we don't need to worry about understanding every single detail to be able to utilize the API. This is the power of an object-oriented system: the ability to abstract the implementation away and present a clear and concise interface to the functionality.

In this section we'll take a look at the major components that make up the JavaMail API. Later in this chapter we'll delve deeper into some of the more commonly used classes to give some feeling of just how flexible this API really is.

There are four major areas:

- ❑ **Session Management**
  The session aspect of the API defines the interaction the mail client has with the network. It handles all aspects associated with the overall communication, including which protocol to use for transfer and any default values that may be required.

- ❑ **Message Manipulation**
  Since the whole premise of the JavaMail API is to send and receive mail messages, it shouldn't come as any great surprise to learn of the rich API that exists for creating and manipulating mail messages.

- ❑ **Mail Storage and Retrieval**
  If a message isn't being sent or received, it's in storage. Messages are stored in hierarchies that are not unlike those of files and directories. The JavaMail API has a suite of classes for managing this storage, including adding, deleting, and moving messages.

- ❑ **Transportation**
  Last, but not least, is the delivery of the message. The JavaMail API provides easy mechanisms for this.

Installation and Configuration

JavaMail is included as part of the J2EE distribution, although we can also easily use the JavaMail API with any other edition by simply downloading the latest release from the following website: http://java.sun.com/products/javamail.

At the time of writing, the latest release, JavaMail 1.2 (released December 2000), shipped with implementations for SMTP, IMAP, and POP3. The inclusion of the POP3 implementation is a new addition to the distribution of the API and completes the collection of the most common protocols people use to access mail. Before using the JavaMail API, it is necessary to download and include the JAR file that makes up the **JavaBeans Activation Framework (JAF)**. This is a single JAR file, `activation.jar` that needs to be placed in your classpath. The JAF can be accessed at the Sun site using the following link: http://java.sun.com/beans/glasgow/jaf.html, and we will see later on in the chapter why JAF is so important to the JavaMail API.

The JavaMail API ships with a variety of different JAR files that allow us to customize your installation and distribution. The simplest JAR file is the `mail.jar` that contains the entire API and all three protocol implementations.

The second configuration allows us to include only the implementations that your application deals with. To that end, we require the `mailapi.jar`, with the `imap.jar`, `smtp.jar` and `pop3.jar` being completely optional.

> *We will compile the examples in this chapter by simply using the `j2ee.jar` file in our classpath. This will ensure we have all the protocols to hand.*

Quick, Send Me an e-Mail!

Before we take a detailed tour of the JavaMail API, let's take a quick look at one of the most common tasks associated with e-mail: sending a single mail message via SMTP. An example of a situation in which we could employ this routine would be to provide a feedback form on a web page, or to report some state your application was in. So without further ado, let us have a look at some code:

```
import javax.mail.*;
import javax.activation.*;
import javax.mail.internet.*;
import java.util.*;

public class SendSMTP extends Object {
  public static void main(String args[]) {
    try {

      // Set up the default parameters
      Properties props = new Properties();
      props.put("mail.transport.protocol", "smtp");
      props.put("mail.smtp.host", "yourmail.yourserver.com");
      props.put("mail.smtp.port", "25");

      // Create the session and create a new mail message
      Session mailSession = Session.getInstance(props);
      Message msg = new MimeMessage(mailSession);

      // Set the FROM, TO, DATE and SUBJECT fields
      msg.setFrom(new InternetAddress("me@mine.com"));
      msg.setRecipients(Message.RecipientType.TO,
                        InternetAddress.parse("info@cormac.com"));
      msg.setSentDate(new Date());
      msg.setSubject("this is a subject");

      // Create the body of the mail
      msg.setText("Hello from my first e-mail with JavaMail");

      // Ask the Transport class to send our mail message
      Transport.send(msg);

    }catch(Exception e) {
      System.out.println(e);
    }
  }
}
```

This small program, although not very practical since all the values are hard-coded, illustrates just how little we actually need to know about the underlying protocols to successfully send an e-mail.

> *This program assumes that the server which we are attempting to deliver the message via has relaying authorised for your client IP address, or the e-mail address we are sending to/from is valid for that server. So don't panic if your e-mail isn't coming through; it may well be due to the forwarding SMTP server. Check with the administrator of that machine to find out whether or not you are authorised.*

We won't go into too much detail here on the actual steps associated with sending the e-mail, as we will be taking a much closer look at the JavaMail API in subsequent sections. For the moment, it's fair to note that, in this instance, the majority of the work is involved with creating the actual mail message: setting its various properties such as the FROM, TO, and SUBJECT fields.

The JavaMail API helps the developer at each step of the process. There are classes to aid in the production and validation of the majority of the aspects associated with constructing this mail. For example, later on in this chapter we'll discover utilities to help us handle the complexities associated with working with Internet e-mail addresses.

JavaMail API

This section will take a look at some of the core classes that make up the JavaMail API. We will take a look at the overall responsibility of the class, as well as some of the more common methods that are worthy of special note. In the next section, we'll take a look at putting all these classes to work and illustrating some of their common uses.

javax.mail.Session

The `javax.mail.Session` class defines the mail session used for communicating with remote mail systems. For those familiar with servlet sessions, note that this interpretation of sessions shares no common functionality. A session, in the JavaMail context, is merely used for storing information about the logistics of establishing a connection session with the server. Thus, it is not uncommon for sessions to be shared among users if, for example, they are all using the same SMTP server. Note that the `Session` does not handle any authorization, per se. As we shall discover, this is performed later on. The `Session` can, however, hold login information. So we should be careful when making the decision about whether or not to share the `Session` with every other class running in the JVM at the time.

The `Session` class has no public constructors with which to create a new instance. Instead, we obtain one by calling one of the static methods of the class. The first method returns an unshared, private `Session` instance with the `Properties` passed in:

        static Session getInstance(Properties prop)

If, however, we wish to have a `Session` that can be shared among other users within the JVM, we would use the following call to obtain a new instance:

        static Session getDefaultInstance(Properties prop)

The difference in the two calls is that when we make subsequent calls to the latter method, it will return the same instance that was returned on the first call. All parameters within the `Properties` class will be ignored. If we need a new instance each time, we can use any of the `getInstance()` methods instead. If, however, we were going to be using the same set of parameters each time, for example providing a front-end to your company mail server, then it would be more efficient to use the same `Session` each time.

The `Session` object uses the `java.util.Properties` class to allow for the different parameters that can be passed in. We can obtain an instance of this class by either creating a new one and filling in the necessary parameters, or by using the one returned from the call to `System.getProperties()`. The JavaMail API defines a set of parameters that are used by the core protocols. A brief description and the default values of these JavaMail environment properties are given in the table below. Note that this list is by no means exhaustive; it is feasible that other protocol implementations, for example Network News Transfer Protocol (discussed later), may require additional information. Such information – what settings are available, etc. – should be provided with the protocol documentation.

> The **Session** object is the key to the JavaMail experience. It is through this object that we can access the other major areas of the API.

Note that some concepts introduced in the following table may seem unfamiliar at present, but will be addressed in much greater detail later on in the chapter.

Property	Description	Default Value
`mail.transport.protocol`	This is the default transport protocol thatis returned when `getTransport()` is called	The first available one from the configured protocols.
`mail.store.protocol`	This is the default store protocol that will be returned when `getStore()` is called	The first available one from the configured protocols.
`mail.host`	This is the default host both the transport and store protocols will use, should their own host not be specified	Local Machine
`mail.user`	This is the default user both the transport and store protocols will use, should their own users not be specified	`user.name`
`mail.from`	This is the return address of the current user.	`username@host`
`mail.protocol.host`	This overrides the `mail.host` for the protocol specified	`mail.host`
`mail.protocol.user`	This overrides the `mail.user` for the protocol specified	`mail.user`
`mail.debug`	This is the debug setting for the session.	`false`

Returning to our quick SMTP send-mail example, we see the process that we used to obtain a Session variable isn't steeped in as much mystery now. Here we are creating a new instance of the Properties and populating the key properties with information specifying that when we use all the default transport mechanisms, we wish to use SMTP as our delivery agent:

```
Properties props = new Properties();
props.put("mail.transport.protocol", "smtp");
props.put("mail.smtp.host", "yourmail.yourserver.com");
props.put("mail.smtp.port", "25");
Session mailSession = Session.getInstance(props);
```

The Session that we have obtained is private to us, meaning that, should we make some changes to the parameters and re-obtain a Session variable, the Session returned will not reflect the updates that we have just made through the Properties.put(...) method.

The Session object gives us the functionality to now access folders and stores on a remote system through the use of simple method calls. We will see this in action later on in the chapter.

javax.mail.Authenticator

In the majority of cases where we are reading mail (or even sending it) we will need to supply information to authenticate the connection. This usually takes the form of a username and password of some description. The JavaMail API provides for this eventuality very cleanly by means of the Authenticator class. When a Session comes to the point where it requires the necessary authentication details it makes a call to this class for the required information. For this to happen, there are two variations on the static methods we used to obtain a Session in the previous section:

```
static Session getInstance(Properties prop, Authenticator auth)
static Session getDefaultInstance(Properties prop, Authenticator auth)
```

As you can see, the only difference is the additional reference to the Authenticator object. If we pass in null as the Authenticator reference, we will effectively be making the same call as shown before.

But what's the point of passing in a null? By passing in a null object for the Authenticator we are stating that we do not wish the Session object to worry about the authentication process, we will do this ourselves, should the need arise.

Building an authentication module is relatively straightforward as long as we implement the necessary interfaces and adhere to the simple rules. When the Session needs the password, it will make a call to the method:

```
javax.mail.PasswordAuthentication getPasswordAuthentication()
```

This method is from the Authenticator abstract class. The PasswordAuthentication class is merely a wrapper that allows the username and password to be conveniently passed back to the calling method.

Let's work through a simple example to demonstrate this overall process. We'll assume that when asked we simply look up the default user within a text file of passwords. OK, granted it's not the most secure way of handling this, but for our purposes it illustrates the point without getting bogged down in the complexities of connecting to a database, for instance, which would be a far more sensible choice. Let us call our text file of usernames and passwords passwd.silly and insert the following lines into it:

```
# passwd.silly
# The username is on the left hand side with the password on the right

user_one=silly
user_two=password
user_three=12345
```

To begin with, we simply subclass the Authenticator class, providing an implementation for the getPasswordAuthentication() method, as shown in the code next:

```java
import javax.mail.*;
import java.io.*;
import java.util.*;

public class StupidAuthenticator extends Authenticator{
  Properties passwordList;

  public StupidAuthenticator() {
    super();
    try {
      // Load in the password key file
      passwordList  = new Properties();
      passwordList.load(new FileInputStream("passwd.silly"));
    } catch(Exception e) {
      System.out.println(e);
    }
  }

  public PasswordAuthentication getPasswordAuthentication() {
    if (passwordList.containsKey(getDefaultUserName())) {
      return new PasswordAuthentication(getDefaultUserName(),
```

```
                            (String)passwordList.get(getDefaultUserName()));
      } else {
        return null;
      }
    }
  }
}
```

When this class is first created, it attempts to load a key-data text file of usernames and passwords using the standard `java.utils.Properties` mechanism. After that, the class sits dormant until a `Session` object calls upon it using the `getPasswordAutentication()` method, which subsequently performs a lookup in the `Properties` object and creates a new instance of `PasswordAuthentication` and returns it. Otherwise `null` is returned.

To integrate this class into the `Session`'s authentication procedure, we would modify our original code to include the `StupidAuthenticator` class:

```
Properties props = new Properties();
props.put("mail.transport.protocol", "smtp");
props.put("mail.smtp.host", "yourmail.yourserver.com");
props.put("mail.smtp.port", "25");
StupidAuthenticator sA = new StupidAuthenticator();
Session mailSession = Session.getInstance(props, sA);
```

This would then have the desirable effect of handing off all responsibility for gathering passwords to the `StupidAuthenticator` object.

javax.mail.Message

One of the core features of JavaMail, as we might expect, is the ability to work with messages. As we have seen, the actual procedure to send an e-mail isn't that complicated. However, the area that does cause a lot of confusion and head-scratching is the generation of the actual message to be sent. Adhering to all the MIME standards to ensure safe and coherent transmission can indeed be a tricky beast to master.

Fear not. JavaMail comes to the rescue. The API offers a rich library of classes to make the construction and deconstruction of mail messages a relatively painless process, and it all starts with the `javax.mail.Message`. This abstract class provides the basic container for the representation of a mail message, as illustrated schematically in the following diagram:

A mail message is made up of two major components: the header and the content. The header contains all the information that describes the message's characteristics, for example, the subject field, the recipients of the message, who the message came from, date it was sent, etc. All these fields and more are part of the header. The actual message data itself is found in the content section. The `Message` class defines this composition by implementing the `javax.mail.Part` interface, which deals with the functionality associated with constructing the content.

Now, this is where the JavaMail API appears to get complicated, when dealing with message contents. The reason is that the MIME specification allows for multi-parts, each with its own encoding and attributes, to be sent in one message. This is what makes MIME so powerful and, at times, such a pain to work with. We'll take a look at this array of classes and interfaces and hopefully shine some light on this web of interconnecting classes.

Although we are going to be using the most common message format, MIME, the JavaMail API has been designed to utilize any type of message, allowing for other implementations to exist. For the purposes of this chapter, we'll concentrate on the standard that we are most likely to use within an Internet environment.

javax.mail.internet.MimeMessage

The `Message` class is an abstract class and therefore to actually use a mail message must use a sub-classed implementation. The one implementation that is part of the JavaMail API is the `javax.mail.internet.MimeMessage`. There are a number of ways in which we can obtain a new instance of this class. The first method is to actually call one of its public constructors:

```
public MimeMessage(Session session)
public MimeMessage(MimeMessage msg)
```

The first method creates an empty `MimeMessage` based on the `Session` properties passed in. This is the most common way. An alternative to that is to use the copy-constructor, which creates a new message instance with all the same properties and content as the one passed in. This can be a very inefficient way of creating a new `MimeMessage` and ought to be avoided if possible. One of the reasons that we may think of using this derivative is when creating a message that is a reply to an existing e-mail. Fortunately, the creators of the JavaMail API were a step ahead on that front and conveniently offer the method:

```
public Message reply(boolean replyToAll)
```

which can be used to easily create a new `Message` with all the necessary headers set, including modifying the subject to include the `"RE:"` prefix, should it not be already set.

Since this class is used to work with Internet mail messages, we'll take a quick look at some of the methods available to access the common header fields that exist as part of the message specification (as detailed in RFC#822 – see http://www.rfc-editor.org/rfc/rfc822.txt). Here is a header plucked straight from a message received from the popular hotmail.com service (note that a number of fields have been removed for clarity):

```
Message-ID: <001e01c0feab$0366b7e0$8c74f5d1@computer>
From: "Cormac Williamson" <cormacwilliamson@hotmail.com>
To: alan@n-ary.com
Subject: Re: thanks
Date: Tue, 26 Jun 2001 21:46:39 -0400
MIME-Version: 1.0
Content-Type: text/plain; charset=us-ascii
X-Priority: 3
X-MSMail-Priority: Normal
X-Mailer: Microsoft Outlook Express 5.00.2615.200
```

Let's take a more detailed look at some of the most common fields that might be found in a typical header.

From

The mail message must have originated from at least one person and this is detailed in the `From` header in the mail message. This field must be a valid formatted Internet Mail address and the `Message` class provides a set of methods for setting and retrieving this data. To read the field, use the method:

```
Address[] getFrom()
```

This will return an array of `javax.mail.Address` objects that represent the e-mail addresses. Don't worry too much about the makeup of this class just yet; we'll be taking a closer look at its functionality later on in this chapter. For the moment, consider it as a wrapper class for representing a valid Internet e-mail address.

Conversely, setting the field can be achieved through a number of simple access methods:

```
void setFrom()
void setFrom(javax.mail.Address fromAddress)
```

The first version may confuse you a little. How do we set the `From` field without actually passing it anything? Well, if you remember back to the `Session` discussion, we discussed the various default properties that we could associate with a given mail session. This method merely uses the default property from the `Session` for the `From` field for the message. The second method simply allows us to specify an alternative address to be used for the `From` field.

In addition to this, should we wish to set multiple addresses for the `From` field, we can use the method:

```
void addFrom(Address[] moreAddresses)
```

This will add the array of addresses to the existing `From` field.

To, CC, and BCC

There are three broad classifications for addressing mail messages: `To`, `CC`, and `BCC`. The `To` field is generally intended for the recipients that the message is directly addressed to. The `CC` field stands for "Carbon Copy" (for historical reasons), and is for recipients that are receiving a copy of the message, where they are publicly acknowledged. The `BCC` field stands for "Blind Carbon Copy", and this is for the recipients that receive a copy of the message which the other recipients do not see.

Essentially all three categories operate in the exact same way and, to that end, the `Message` class makes it easy to set and retrieve the various headers:

```
void setRecipient(Message.RecipientType type, Address[] addresses)
void setRecipient(Message.RecipientType type, Address address)
Address[] getRecipients(Message.RecipientType type)
Address[] getAllRecipients()
```

In addition to the `setRecipient(...)` methods, there exist `addRecipients(...)` method derivatives for easily appending new addresses to existing address fields. The `Message.RecipientType` defines the following constants:

```
Message.RecipientType.TO
Message.RecipientType.CC
Message.RecipientType.BCC
```

Furthermore, the `MimeMessage` defines an additional type for use with protocols that are servicing newsgroups via the Network News Transfer Protocol (NNTP) protocol:

MimeMessage.RecipientType.NEWSGROUPS

Using these methods we can set the various fields, as shown in the following sample code extract:

```
Session mailSession = Session.getInstance(props);
Message msg = new MimeMessage(mailSession);

msg.setRecipients(Message.RecipientType.TO,
                  InternetAddress.parse("info@cormac.com"));
msg.setRecipients(Message.RecipientType.CC,
                  InternetAddress.parse("info@wrox.com"));
msg.setRecipients(Message.RecipientType.BCC,
                  InternetAddress.parse("secret@wrox.com"));
```

Reply-To

There are instances where we may wish a mail message to come from a specific person, but the reply to go to somewhere else. For example, say your company CEO announced a major product, he could originate the e-mail, but if anyone replies for more information, he may wish his sales team to follow it up. The mail standard allows for this through the special `Reply-To` header field.

The API provides two methods for working with this header field. To set the field, use the method:

void setReplyTo(Address[] addresses)

If we do not make a call to this method, it is assumed to be `null` and the Reply-To header will not be included in the resulting message header. To retrieve the Reply-To header, simply make a call to:

Address[] getReplyTo()

If the header wasn't present, this method will return the same information as if we were calling `getFrom()`.

Subject

As we might expect, methods exist for setting the `Subject` header of a mail message:

void setSubject(String subject)
String getSubject()

Date

The `Date` field of the mail message is accessed using the following methods:

void setSentDate(Date date)
Date getSentDate()

Message ID

Each mail message traveling around the Internet is meant to have a unique identifier. So in theory, if all the e-mails make it to one large data store, we'll be able to index them. The JavaMail API generates the message ID for us when the message is saved. We can read the `Message-ID` field in the messages:

String getMessageID()

647

Other...

The message header was designed to be flexible enough to allow any number of headers to appear. We can use this feature to communicate extra data between mail messages. For example, Microsoft uses this feature a lot when messages are being transferred between Microsoft mail clients. When two Outlook clients are exchanging data, for instance, the application puts additional information in the header to allow simple things such return receipts or scheduling information.

To add a new header use:

```
void setHeader(String name, String value)
```

And conversely to read a specific header we can use:

```
String getHeader(String name, String delimiter)
```

The default delimiter used in e-mail headers is the comma (,), but this isn't a hard and fast rule and we can actually specify our own delimiter. In addition to these methods, there is a whole range of methods that allow greater access to the information within the message header.

javax.mail.Part

The JavaMail API offers a rich interface for putting together a rather complex set of message parts, which is all controlled through the use of the javax.mail.Part interface and its derivatives. It's fair to comment that many programmers initially get a little anxious wondering just how the relationships all fit together. With that in mind, let's take a step back for a moment and have a look at the overall structure.

We can think of the construction of mail messages as happening in logical blocks, or parts, where each block is in actual fact a unit of data. For example, a file attachment would be considered a block, as would the main body text for the message, which would be another block. Now, consider the fact that, in its initial form, a message can only have one block of data. How can we attach multiple data blocks to a single message?

This problem is what the MIME standard solves with its variety of MIME types. But let's stay with the JavaMail world for the moment before looking at specific implementations.

A message can either contain either a single block or a special block that itself can hold a list of blocks. Furthermore, a block can either hold a single block or a special block to indicate a list. And so forth, and so forth.

In JavaMail, a message can only hold a single piece of data or a javax.mail.Multipart as its content. The Multipart class is a placeholder for multiple Parts to exist. However, there is a special relationship with a Part that is contained within a Multipart content, rather than being part of the core top-level message content. A special class called javax.mail.BodyPart is used within a Multipart content list to denote the blocks of data that make up the overall block of content.

So, a Multipart class can only hold BodyPart classes, and a BodyPart, itself much like the Message class, can either hold a single block of content or a single Multipart class. This is demonstrated in the following diagram, which illustrates the content composition of a typical message:

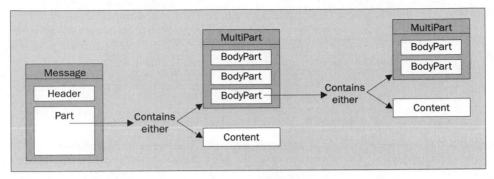

JavaMail provides an implementation of this structure using MIME. The MIME implementation follows this model and the actual classes use the same names as their abstract counterparts, except for the word `Mime` placed in front of each. Before we go deeper into the classes, we'll take a look at just how the content is stored. To do this we need to have a quick look at the JavaBeans Activation Framework.

JavaBean Activation Framework

If the world contained only the core data types of Java, then the place would be an easier environment to work in. Obviously, this isn't the case. The MIME standard, however, permits a wide range of data types to be sent as content in any part as long as it's properly labeled using the 'xxx/yyy' convention. For example, we have already seen at least one MIME data type, `text/plain`, which is easily handled with a `java.lang.String` object.

This is probably the easiest form of content and is therefore not really representative of the bigger picture. To cope with this, the JavaMail API employs the services of the JavaBean Activation Framework (JAF) to give a clean and consistent interface to the wide range of data types that may exist.

You can learn more about the JAF by visiting the web site address at Sun:
http://java.sun.com/beans/glasgow/jaf.html

The JAF provides the `javax.activation.DataHandler` class for handling the necessary operations that can be performed on the data. When the `Part` class is handling content, all operations are performed through the `DataHandler` class, although the `Part` class does expose some shortcut methods, which we'll see later.

To give a feel for the functionality on offer from the `DataHandler` the next table shows some of the more common methods:

Method	Description
`String getContentType()`	Returns the MIME type of the object, including any parameters associated with it.
`Object getContent()`	Returns the data. If the `DataHandler` was created with an object, then this method returns it. If the data was created using a `DataSource` then this will attempt to find the content `Object` and return that. Otherwise, an `InputStream` is returned.
`InputStream getInputStream()`	Returns an input stream to the object that is holding/representing the data.
`OutputStream getOutputStream()`	Returns an output stream to the object that is holding/representing the data so the content may be overwritten.
`void writeTo OutputStream OutputS)`	This is a convenience method that will write the data content to the output stream passed in.

649

The JavaMail API provides default `DataHandlers` for the most common MIME types:

- ❏ `text/plain` – for messages that are just pure ASCII text
- ❏ `text/html` – for messages that are constructed using HTML text
- ❏ `multipart/mixed` – for messages that are made up of different types, for example, containing an attachment
- ❏ `message/rfc822` – defines the Internet standard for text messages

Although you may not have realized it, in our simple and crude example of sending an e-mail, the `MimePart` class was actually handling the `DataHandler` for us. Remember how we set the content for the text mail?

```
msg.setText("Hello from my first e-mail with JavaMail");
```

The `MimeMessage` class has provided some convenience methods that allow us to quickly set the data for simple content types. We could have achieved the same effect by calling all the components ourselves:

```
String messageBody = "Hello from my first e-mail with JavaMail";
DataHandler dh = new DataHandler(messageBody, "text/plain");
msg.setDataHandler(dh);
```

In this example we created a new instance of the `String` class and set it with our message body's text. Next we created a new `DataHandler` instance, passing in a `String` object, and labeling this data with the type `text/plain`. Finally we set the message content to this new `DataHandler` instance. Note that these components are wrapped up for us in a single call to `MimeMessage.setText(…)`.

Getting at the information utilizes the `DataHandler` class and the `Part` interface defines some shortcut methods for us, for example the `Part.getContent()` method called on a part that was of type `text/plain` would return a `String` object. But for illustration purposes and to reinforce the notion that a specific `DataHandler` class handles the message content, we'll go the long way round:

```
DataHandler dh = msg.getDataHandler();
if (dh.getContentType().equals("text/plain")) {
  String messageBody = (String)dh.getContent();
}
```

We first retrieve an instance of the `DataHandler` that is holding the data for us. We then check the content type of the data. This allows us to determine how to use the `Object` that is returned to us from the call to `DataHandler.getContent()`. Remember, we created this instance of `DataHandler` by passing in a `String` reference to its constructor, therefore, as per the JAF API documentation, a call to `getContent()` will return the original object we used to create the content, which in this instance is the `String` reference. So we forward cast the `Object` reference returned from `getContent()` to a `String` object.

We will see later on in the chapter how to use the `getInputStream()` feature of the `DataHandler` class to handle data types that don't have a `DataHandler` implementation, for example the MIME type `image/jpeg` that is used to represent images.

javax.mail.Multipart

As we discussed in the previous section, a multipart is designed to manage multiple parts as a single unit. The most common scenario in which we might find this is when attaching a file to an e-mail. The message body would be one part and the file attachment would be another. Therefore we would have to use a multipart MIME message to package this up for successful transmission. Take a quick look at the following code snippet that illustrates the construction of the two parts of the mail message:

```
MimeMessage msg = new MimeMessage(session);
Multipart mailBody = new MimeMultipart();

// Create the first part
MimeBodyPart mainBody = new MimeBodyPart();
mainBody.setText("Here is the file I promised you.");
mailBody.addBodyPart(mainBody);

// Create the second part with the attachment
FileDataSource fds = new FileDataSource("c:\\temp\\photo.jpg");
MimeBodyPart mimeAttach = new MimeBodyPart();
mimeAttach.setDataHandler(new DataHandler(fds));
mimeAttach.setFileName(fds.getName());

mailBody.addBodyPart(mimeAttach);

msg.setContent(mailBody);
```

As you can see, first of all we create a new instance of `MimeMultipart`, the implementation for the `Multipart` abstract class. This will serve as a placeholder that will allow us to insert as many parts as we require. In this example we only need two: one for the message text and another for the file.

We then create an instance of `MimeBodyPart` that will hold the content for our message text and, as can be seen, since we know the message text is of type `text/plain`, we are using the shortcut method `setText(...)` to set the text. After this, we take the instance and attach it to the `MimeMultipart` by making a call to `addBodyPart(...)` passing in our `MimeBodyPart` reference.

We repeat this for the file attachment, ending with a call to the method `addBodyPart(...)`. Finally, once we have finished creating all the necessary parts that make up the multipart message, we set the content of our original `MimeMessage` to that of the `MimeMultipart`. Don't worry too much about the logistics of attaching a file; we'll take a much greater look at this in the example that deals directly with attachments, later on in the chapter.

Internally the `Multipart` stores the various parts in a `java.util.Vector` and, to that end, the majority of the public methods of this class are merely wrappers, allowing us to manage the list of `BodyParts`. The more common methods of `Multipart` are shown in the following table:

Method	Description
Void addBodyPart BodyPart bp)	Adds the `BodyPart` bp to the end of the list of currently held `BodyParts`.
Void addBodyPart BodyPart bp, int index)	Adds the `BodyPart` bp to the list at the specified index.
BodyPart getBodyPart int index)	Returns the `BodyPart` that is at the position passed in.
String getContentType()	Returns the MIME type for this `Multipart`.
int getCount()	Returns the number of `BodyParts` in the list.
Part getParent()	Returns the parent that is presently holding this `Multipart`. Returns `null` if not associated yet.
boolean removeBodyPart BodyPart bp)	Removes the `BodyPary` bp instance from the list. Returns `true` if successful, or `false` if not found.

Table continued on following page

Method	Description
`boolean removeBodyPart (int index)`	Removes the `BodyPart` instance from the list at the specified position. Returns `true` if successful, or `false` if not found.
`void setParent(Part parent)`	Associates the parent for this `Multipartget`.

As you can see there isn't much complexity associated with the `Multipart` class. Its main purpose is to simply manage the list of `BodyParts` it has been asked to hold. Speaking of `BodyParts`, let us take a closer look at the properties associated with holding data.

javax.mail.BodyPart

Following on from the previous section, a `BodyPart` is the abstract class that is used to denote the part that makes up a `Multipart`. The `BodyPart` class is identical to the `Part` class except for the addition of one extra method to obtain the `Multipart` this part is included in:

`Multipart getParent()`

Again, nothing too complicated here.

Message Content

The `Message` has a variety of methods that allow us to determine how to handle message content and data makeup. As we've discovered, a message can be made up using a number of different `Parts` and, to this end, all the methods described in this section are found in the `Part` interface as opposed to the `Message` abstract class.

The MIME specification defines that all content type descriptions be in the xxx/yyy format, where xxx is the major type, and the yyy is the sub-type. Each `Part` can have its own MIME format and to determine the format we can use the method:

`String getContentType()`

This could return, for example, the type of `"text/plain; charset=us-ascii"` as seen in the Internet mail message earlier. You may think that this is invalid since it seems to have extra information after the xxx/yyy format, but this data is parameter data. The MIME standard allows for extra information to be transferred in this attribute that will aid in the decoding and encoding stage.

Since we make a lot of decisions based on just the xxx/yyy format, we have a helper method that assists us in determining whether a given MIME type is present. The method:

`boolean isMimeType(String mimeType)`

makes it easy for us to determine a given type. We can pass in `"text/plain"` to see if the content type is of that type. We can even pass in `"text/*"` to see if the MIME type is of at least `"text/"` type. This is particularly useful when determining if the content is of a `multipart/*` or not. For example:

```
if (msg.isMimeType("multipart/*") {
    System.out.println("This message has multiple parts");
}
```

In addition to this, the MIME specification allows for further description through the optional attributes: description, disposition, and filename. There are specifics on how this information should be packaged up, but since we are working through the JavaMail API, we don't really need to worry about the underlying format; our lives are made easier through the method calls. Let's take a closer look at these optional attributes.

The description field allows us to set some descriptive notes about this particular MIME part. Naturally, there are methods to accomplish this:

```
String getDescription()
void setDescription(String desc)
```

The disposition field is particularly useful, especially in the scenario where HTML formatted e-mails are being used. It describes whether a part should be saved as an attachment or used internally to display the message. The JavaMail API defines two String constants for this status:

```
static public String ATTACHMENT
static public String INLINE
```

Using this we can either set or check the disposition of the part by calling the methods accordingly:

```
String getDisposition()
void setDisposition(String disp)
```

So, for example, if we were to check to see that a particular Part, containing an attachment, should be used internally or saved out to disk, we could use the following call:

```
String dispos = msg.getDisposition();
if (dispos == null || dispos.equalsIgnoreCase(Part.ATTACHMENT)) {
  System.out.println("This part should be treated as an attachment");
}
```

Lastly the MIME specification states that if it's a file attachment, then we can offer a possible name to use when saving the attachment. The filename passed will not contain any directory information and will be simply the name of the file, including any extension should the file have one. Methods for operating with this field are as we would expect:

```
String getFileName()
void setFileName(String fname)
```

In addition to these parameters, we can determine the message size and line count by calling the following methods:

```
int getSize()
int getLineCount()
```

This is particular useful information for clients to allow them to determine whether or not they should bother downloading the message over a slow connection, for example on a wireless device. However, please note that it is not always possible to retrieve the dimensions of a mail message. If the values cannot be determined then −1 is returned. If that's not enough to put you off using these methods, also consider the fact that, due to message encoding algorithms, the values they return may not be a true reflection of the actual size and line count of a particular message part.

Message Flags

As we've seen already, a message has a wide range of attributes associated with it to describe its contents and addressing properties. However, none of the attributes we've looked at thus far go anyway towards giving a message a "state". For example, at present, we have no real way of telling whether a message is new, or whether it's a reply to an existing mail, or even if it has been read or answered. The JavaMail API aids the developer by providing a mechanism to easily store this type of information within each message.

It has to be noted at this point that these status flags should not be relied on. Their implementation is down to the individual provider and whether or not it is possible to determine a message's status. Here, the provider is responsible for the implementation of the underlying protocol. For example, determining the status of SEEN may not be possible in a newsgroup (NNTP) implementation, since the NNTP protocol does not have a state to represent whether a news group post has been read, as this is usually left to the client program to keep track of.

In addition to the standard flags, JavaMail API allows the addition and manipulation of user-defined status flags.

The management of the flags is performed using the wrapper class `javax.mail.Flags`. This class manages all the status flags including the system and user-defined statuses.

The core system flags offer a broad range of characteristics and are as follows:

❑ `Flags.Flag.ANSWERED`
   If the message has been answered by another e-mail, then this flag is set.

❑ `Flags.Flag.DELETED`
   If the message has been flagged for deletion, the flag is set. As we will see later on in the chapter, after a call to expunge the folder, all the messages with this flag set will be deleted.

❑ `Flags.Flag.DRAFT`
   If the message has not been sent this flag is set.

❑ `Flags.Flag.FLAGGED`
   If this has been set, then the client has flagged the message for some reason.

❑ `Flags.Flag.RECENT`
   If set the message has been received since the last time the client opened the folder.

❑ `Flags.Flag.SEEN`
   If the flag has been read this flag is set. The client may change the state of this flag should they desire.

❑ `Flags.Flag.USER`
   This flag determines whether or not the folder can support user-defined flags. Note this isn't the actual user-defined flag, merely an indication of the possible existence of such flags.

The support of these flags is entirely up to the provider. For example, the POP protocol only has support for the `Flags.Flag.DELETED` flag. None of the others are supported. At first this may seem a little hit-and-miss with respect to what supports what. Fortunately it is not as bad as it sounds, and we can determine which flags are supported by making a call to the method:

```
public Flags getPermanentFlags()
```

This is called from the `javax.mail.Folder` class (we will be taking a close look at the `Folder` class later on in the chapter). Flags are used to track the statuses of messages and allow us to perform operations on just certain messages that satisfy a particular status. For example, as we will discover later on, we can easily list all the messages in a folder that have the SEEN flag set.

The `javax.mail.Message` class has a suite of methods that allow us to check and set the status of the flags. For example, to check whether a message has been read or not, we could use:

```
if (msg.isSet(Flags.Flag.SEEN))
   System.out.println("This message has been read");
}
```

Message flags are a wonderful addition to the tracking of messages, but be careful when using them: they can't be relied on across all implementations of the underlying protocol and, we'll need to check whether or not the mail server actually supports them. The main flag handling methods from `javax.mail.Message` are summarized in the following table:

Method	Description
`boolean isExpunged()`	This checks whether or not the message has been expunged after being marked for deletion. To clarify this term, in this context "expunged" indicates whether or not the message has been removed from the folder.
`boolean isSet(Flags.Flag flag)`	This method checks for the status of the specified flag.
`Flags getFlags()`	This returns a copy of the Flags object. Note that should we modify any of the flags within this object, it will have no effect on the flags in the message class.
`void setFlags(Flags flag, boolean set)`	This method sets or clears all the flags in the message that are in this flag object. Any flags that are in the message flags that are not in this one, are unaffected.
`void setFlags(Flags.Flag flag, boolean set)`	This method sets the given flag to a given state.

javax.mail.Address

Anyone who has written classes that have had to deal with Internet e-mail addresses will know the hassles associated with all the different formats an address can take. It can be a parsing nightmare at times. Each message has at least one address associated with it. The `javax.mail.Address` is the class that is used to denote this address.

However, as you may appreciate, with the JavaMail API attempting to be everything to every message-based system, addresses can differ greatly between systems. For example, the address for a message destined for a newsgroup is not the same as one destined for an Internet e-mail account. For this reason, the base class `javax.mail.Address` has very little functionality with only a minimal number of methods exposed.

Instead the subclasses provide all the real functionality. The JavaMail API ships with two implementations:

- ❏ `javax.mail.internet.InternetAddress`
- ❏ `javax.mail.internet.NewsAddress`

javax.mail.internet.InternetAddress

An e-mail address must contain an address, optionally with an name associated with it. For example the following two e-mail addresses are valid Internet e-mail addresses:

```
"Alan Williamson" <alan@n-ary.com>
<alan@n-ary.com>
```

When we have more than one e-mail address to express, for example in the `To` field of a message header, we would concatenate the addresses using the comma as a separator. So we do not have to continually parse and concatenate e-mail addresses, the JavaMail API provides a helper class:

`javax.mail.internet.InternetAddress`

This takes all of the hard work away from this task. Methods exist to make the creation and handling of e-mail addresses a trivial task:

```
InternetAddress MyAddress = new InternetAddress();
MyAddress.setAddress("alan@n-ary.com");
MyAddress.setPersonal("Alan Williamson");
System.out.println("MyAddress=" + MyAddress.toString());
```

As you probably noticed in the previous sections, it's very rare for us to work with a single individual address; more often than not we'll be using lists or arrays of addresses. To this end, the `InternetAddress` has a couple of static methods to make the parsing of textual forms of these lists a very easy task:

```
InternetAddress toField[] = InternetAddress.parse(
                            "alan@n-ary.com,ceri@n-ary.com"
                    );
for (int x=0; x < toField.length; x++) {
  System.out.println("toField["+x+"].Address="+toField[x].getAddress());
  System.out.println("toField["+x+"].Personal="+toField[x].getPersonal());
}
```

There is a derivative of `InternetAddress.parse(…)` that takes in a `boolean` value to force the tolerance of the parsing algorithm:

`public InternetAddress[] InternetAddress.parse(String a, boolean strict)`

If `strict` is set to `false`, then the list of addresses can be separated by spaces in addition to commas. If `strict` is set to `true`, then the majority of the rules laid out in RFC#822 are adhered to. We would use this method if we were allowing a user to enter a list of names when creating e-mail messages.

javax.mail.internet.NewsAddress

The newsgroup addressing differs from that for e-mails. A newsgroup message has at least a newsgroup name, with an optional host name. The JavaMail API provides an implementation for this with the `javax.mail.internet.NewsAddress` class.

This class operates in the same manner as the `InternetAddress` class discussed in the previous section, providing methods for easily handling both individual addresses and lists of addresses:

```
NewsAddress myNews = new NewsAddress("comp.lang.java.programmer");
MyNews.setHost("news.sun.com");
System.out.println("myNews.newsgroup=" + myNews.getNewsgroup());
System.out.println("myNews.host=" + myNews.getHost());
```

javax.mail.Store

So far we have seen how the JavaMail API deals with the individual message and the properties and actions associated with that. Next, we'll look at the management of messages and how JavaMail provides for the handling of groups of messages.

Messages are organized into folders and these folders are held within a single store. By default, a store must have at least one folder in which messages can reside. This requirement allows the JavaMail API to provide a uniform access method across all the different protocols. For example the POP protocol has no notion of folders and simply stores its messages as one list. But for the sake of abstraction any implementations of the POP protocol must provide the `INBOX` folder.

Before we can access folders, we must first obtain a `javax.mail.Store` object instance, typically from the `javax.mail.Session` object discussed previously in the chapter. The `Store` class provides the access methods to the folders hierarchy and authenticates the connection should the underlying protocol require it.

A `Store` object instance can be retrieved from the `Session` instance in any of the following ways:

```
public Store getStore()
public Store getStore(Provider provider)
public Store getStore(String protocol)
public Store getStore(URLName urlname)
```

The first version of `getStore()` uses the default protocol, specified in the system property `mail.store.protocol`, to create the `Store` object. The second version uses the supplied `Provider` instance to create and return an instance. The third version allows us to use another protocol other than the default one specified in the `Properties` object that was used to create the `Session`, while the fourth version uses a special object, `URLName`, to create the `Store` object.

Once we have obtained the `Store` object, we need to connect to the mail storage before we start to retrieve and work folders. This is performed with a single call to the `connect(...)` method, passing in the necessary authentication details should the underlying storage require it.

The following code extract illustrates a typical scenario for retrieving the `Store` object for connecting to a POP server:

```
// Set up the default parameters
Properties props = new Properties();
props.put("mail.transport.protocol", "pop");

// Create the session and create a new mail message
Session mailSession = Session.getInstance(props);

// Get the Store and connect to the server
Store mailStore = mailSession.getStore();
mailStore.connect("yourpop.server.com",110,"yourname","yourpassword");

// Proceed to manipulate folders
```

The `connect(…)` method comes in a number of flavors dependent on the authentication required. Should the connection to the underlying message store fails, the `connect(…)` methods throws the `javax.mail.AuthenticationFailedException`.

At this point, the `Store` instance is ready for usage, giving access to the folder database.

Accessing Folders

It is through the `Store` object that we retrieve references to its folders. A folder is represented with the `javax.mail.Folder` class and will be discussed in the next section. By default, the `Store` object must provide at least one folder. This is due to the fact that some mail services don't support the notion of folders at all and this maintains a layer of abstraction for the JavaMail API. This ensures that no special cases exist, irrespective of the mail protocol. Folder access methods are summarized in the following table:

Method	Description
`Folder getDefaultFolder()`	Retrieves the top-level or root folder for the store. In the instance of the POP protocol, this is the `INBOX` folder.
`Folder getFolder(String name)`	Returns the folder within the store, irrespective of whether or not it exists. We can then in turn call the `Folder.exists()` method to determine its state. This is useful when we wish to create new folders.
`Folder getFolder(URLName name)`	Similar in usage to the method above, except the folder is addressed using the `URLName` object.
`Folder[] getPersonalNamespaces()`	Returns an array of folders that are considered to be accessible by the current user.
`Folder[] getUserNamespaces(String user)`	Returns an array of folders that are considered to be accessible by the current user and the given user passed in. This method supports the notion that a manager may have granted different access privileges to, say, their secretary and other team members.
`Folder[] getSharedNamespaces()`	This method returns an array of folders that are considered to be accessible by all.

Therefore code for accessing the one and only folder within a POP box for a given user would be:

```
// Get the Store and connect to the server
URLName urlname = new URLName("pop3://alan:ceri@www.hotmail.com");
Store mailStore = mailSession.getStore(urlname);
mailStore.connect();

// Proceed to manipulate folders
Folder inbox = mailStore.getDefaultFolder();

// or Folder inbox = mailStore.getFolder("INBOX");
```

Note the special use of the keyword `INBOX`. This keyword is reserved and is a special name to denote the folder in which the user will receive their messages. Note, not all protocols offer the `INBOX` folder. Indeed, the NNTP newsgroup protocol has no concept of inboxes.

Using the methods shown, in order to access the folders, we generally have to know the name of the folder beforehand. In addition to this, a folder can contain both messages and folders. The `Folder` object lends us a hand in this discovery by giving us some access methods that allow us to easily list all the folders contained within. We can do this using the method:

```
Folder[] javax.mail.Folder.list()
```

This method can be run on a closed folder and will return an array of all the folders that are contained under the present folder. This will only list the folder's top-level folders and not drill down any deeper. However, on some message servers, certain folders cannot contain sub-folders, and only have messages within them. NNTP groups, for example, can only have posts within them and not other newsgroups. Therefore, before we do any listing it is advisable we check that such a list can be produced, like this:

```
Folder listOfFolders[] = null;
if ((thisFolder.getType() & Folder.HOLDS_FOLDERS)) {
  listOfFolders = thisFolder.list();
}
```

As seen from this code extract, the `getType()` method from the `Folder` class returns the status field for this folder, which is an integer bit-field with each bit representing a given state. The static `Folder.HOLDS_FOLDERS` is just one of the statuses that we can perform a check on by using the logical AND function. Other statuses that we can check on for a given folder include whether or not the folder is "read-only" (`Folder.READ_ONLY`), whether the folder can contain messages itself (`Folder.HOLDS_MESSAGES`), or if the contents of the folder can be changed (`Folder.READ_WRITE`).

The `Folder` object doesn't stop there. We can use a specialised version of the `list(...)` method that allows us to pass in a search string to either narrow or broaden the set of results returned. For example consider the following:

```
Folder listOfFolders[] = thisFolder.list("Clients%");
```

This would return all the folders within the current folder, `thisFolder`, that began with the string 'Clients'. The `%` is a special wildcard that allows us to scope the current folder. Now consider the following example:

```
Folder listOfFolders[] = thisFolder.list("C*");
```

This would return all the folders, including any sub-folders, that started with the letter `C`. The wildcard `*` is similar to the `%` character except it also searches all the sub-folders and, when used on its own, can list all the folders in a complete hierarchy, as shown in the following code sample:

```
// Set up the default parameters
Properties props = new Properties();

// Create the session and create a new mail message
Session mailSession = Session.getInstance(props);

// Get the Store and connect to the server
URLName urlname = new URLName("imap://alan:ceri@mail.microsoft.com");
Store mailStore = mailSession.getStore(urlname);
mailStore.connect();
```

```
// Proceed to list all the folders
Folder thisFolder = mailStore.getDefaultFolder();

if (thisFolder != null) {
  if ((thisFolder.getType() & Folder.HOLDS_FOLDERS) != 0) {
    Folder[] listOfFolders = thisFolder.list("*");
    for (int x=0; x < listOfFolders.length; x++) {
      System.out.println("FolderName=" + listOfFolders[x].getName());
    }
  }
}
```

In addition to the `list(...)` methods, there are a couple of extra methods that limit the search to just the folders that the user has subscribed to. Depending on whether or not the message server we are connected to can support it, we can subscribe to a folder. At this point we will be given notifications of any changes of state in that folder:

```
Folder[] listSubscribed()
Folder[] listSubscribed(String search)
```

Remember that many of these `listXXX(...)` methods are rendered useless in some protocol implementations since the underlying storage doesn't support them (like POP3, for example).

javax.mail.URLName

JavaMail has introduced a very clean and uniform addressing scheme to be used when accessing mail storage systems, based on the URL syntax. The format, as we can see, is not unlike a standard URL and encapsulates all the information required to access a given resource inside a mail service:

```
<protocol>:://<username>:<password>@<server>[:<port>][/<foldername>]
```

The class, `javax.mail.URLName`, encapsulates all the functionality for working with these addresses, providing the necessary methods to build and extract given information. The JavaMail API encourages the use of this as an addressing scheme and we will see that many of the methods use this as the address as opposed to carrying around up to five individual pieces of information.

The example below shows how to connect to a remote server using the `URLName` object:

```
// Set up the default parameters
Properties props = new Properties();
props.put("mail.transport.protocol", "pop");

// Create the session and create a new mail message
Session mailSession = Session.getInstance(props);

// Get the Store and connect to the server
URLName urlname = new URLName("pop3://alan:ceri@www.hotmail.com");
Store mailStore = mailSession.getStore(urlname);
mailStore.connect();

// Proceed to manipulate folders
```

We will see extensive use of the `URLName` class in the subsequent sections as we take a closer look at how to interact with individual messages inside a given folder. The `Store` class exposes a method to obtain the `URLName` for a session: `getURLName()`. As you can probably imagine, this could present a security problem since the password would be in clear view. For this reason, the password information is not available when getting the `URLName` back out.

Note that this class, URLName, has absolutely no relationship to the `java.net.URL` *class. Although the functionality offered by* URLName *is very similar to that available from the URL class, it is important not confuse the two.*

javax.mail.Folder

A folder is used as a container for a list of messages. Folders themselves can contain additional folders thus providing a directory-like structure to the message archive. The purpose of the `Folder` object is to facilitate the communication and management of messages. Folders are by default initially retrieved in a closed state and, before any operations that basically change the contents of the folder are executed, the folder must first be opened.

Not all operations require the folder to be opened. For example, listing folders, renaming the folder, and monitoring for new messages can all happily be performed while the folder is closed. Once the folder is opened, however, we can also retrieve messages, change notifications, and perform any other function that the folder object offers.

Messages within a folder are numerically addressed from 1 to the total number of messages in the folder. This is very analogous to the way the POP protocol treats its messages, with the numbering being in the order they are received, with the lowest number being the oldest message. However this ordering cannot always be relied on and it's best to order the messages beforehand, should your application call for it.

The message number is usually fixed between a folder being opened and then subsequently closed. When deleting a message, the numbering of the messages does not get recalculated until the call to the `expunge()` on the `Folder` object occurs. When we expunge a folder, all the messages that have been marked for deletion will be finally removed from the folder and deleted. After this call, the message will not be retrievable, from this folder at least. So we should be aware that this will permanently delete the marked messages and then cause a renumbering of the messages in the folder to occur. Tracking messages through this numbering scheme can be problematic and lead to undesired results. If possible, we should refer to the message using the `Message` reference.

Opening and Closing Folders

Before we can list any messages we must first put the folder into an open state. This is performed by calling:

```
void open(int mode)
```

The `open(...)` method will place the folder into either a READ_ONLY or READ_WRITE state depending on the `mode` passed in. The underlying implementation is responsible for determining whether or not a particular mode is valid. For example, some implementations, such as IMAP, will permit multiple users to read a given folder and in some cases, even multiple users to write to the folder. But some POP implementations will probably not allow concurrent readers.

We can check to see the state the folder was opened in by calling the `getType()` method, for example:

```
if (thisFolder.getType() == Folder.READ_ONLY) {
  System.out.println("This folder was opened with READ_ONLY access");
} else {
  System.out.println("This folder was opened with READ_WRITE access");
}
```

Once a folder is opened we can begin using the majority of the access methods. After we've finished with a folder, it's best to perform an explicit `close(...)` to allow the underlying protocol to clean up any resources there and then as opposed to leaving it for the garbage collector to come along at a later date.

The `close(...)` method takes in an additional `boolean` parameter, which indicates whether or not an expunge operation should be performed. If this is `true`, then a call to `expunge()` occurs, permanently deleting any messages marked with the `Flag.DELETED` flag.

There may be instances were we are passed a `Folder` object and we're not too sure what state it's in. We can easily determine whether or not it's open by calling:

```
boolean isOpen()
```

Listing Messages

The `Folder` object is designed to hold messages and, to that end, it provides a rich method list for retrieving messages held within the folder. Messages are returned as lists, using arrays. The objects returned are meant to be lightweight in the sense that not all the information about a message is available immediately. For example, if we were to retrieve the contents of a folder that held 10 messages, with each having a 10MB file attachment, that wouldn't equate to a 100MB memory usage. Instead the message attributes and contents are retrieved when calls to the specific access methods are made. Note that this is purely down to the implementation of the underlying protocol, but in the majority of instances it is adhered to since non-adherence would cause problems with bandwidth and general memory management. A brief description of each message retrieval method available from `javax.mail.Folder` is given in the following table:

Method	Description
`int getMessageCount()`	Returns the total number of messages held in this folder, or `-1` if the total cannot be determined for some reason.
`boolean hasNewMessages()`	Returns `true` if any of the messages held within the folder has the flag `Flag.RECENT` set. The exact definition of a new message is purely down the underlying implementation.
`int getNewMessageCount()`	Similar to the method above, except returns the number of messages that have the flag `Flag.RECENT` set, or `-1`, if it cannot be determined for some reason.
`int getUnreadMessageCount()`	Returns `true` if any of the messages held within the folder has not got the flag `Flag.SEEN` set.
`Message getMessage(int index)`	Returns a lightweight version of the message at the given index.
`Message[] getMessages()`	Returns an array of all the messages contained within this folder.
`Message[] getMessages(int start, int end)`	Returns an array of all the messages contained within this folder, that are in the range specified by `start` and `end`.
`Message[] getMessages(int index[])`	Retrieves all the message that are referenced by the array of indexes passed in.

The following code, demonstrates the listing of all the messages within a POP folder and displaying the subject field for each:

```
// Set up the default parameters
Properties props = new Properties();
Props.put("mail.transport.protocol", "pop");

// Create the session and create a new mail message
Session mailSession = Session.getInstance(props);

// Get the Store and connect to the server
URLName urlname = new URLName("pop3://alan:ceri@www.hotmail.com");
Store mailStore = mailSession.getStore(urlname);
mailStore.connect();

// Proceed to get the folder
Folder rootFolder = mailStore.getDefaultFolder();
Folder inbox = rootFolder.getFolder("INBOX");
inbox.open(Folder.READ_ONLY);

Message [] allTheMessages = inbox.getMessages();
for (int x=0; x < allTheMessages.length; x++) {
  System.out.println("ID:" + x
                        + " Subject:" + allTheMessages[x].getSubject());
}

inbox.close(false);
mailStore.close();
```

Although JavaMail provides the necessary methods to determine various totals regarding a folder's status, this is not always done in the most efficient manner. For example, let us assume we wanted a count of all the messages that have recently been delivered, as per the getNewMessageCount() method. Depending on whether the underlying protocol can provide this functionality or not, this could result in a call to retrieve all the messages and then checking the individual message flag statuses.

What was first an innocent enough call for some numerical statistics has turned out to be quite an expensive operation. To that end, it is sometimes best just to retrieve the messages yourself and run through them once, calculating all the necessary totals in one pass.

Advanced Message Fetching

As we discussed previously, when we ask for a message list, we get lightweight references to the actual message data, with the data being retrieved as and when it is called upon through its access methods. Therefore, although we have a reference to a Message, the underlying data for that message may not actually be loaded in memory but may still reside at the remote server. Although, on the whole, it is a very efficient system, there are instances where we may wish to explicitly request that certain parts of the message are pre-filled with data when they are retrieved from the server.

The JavaMail API supports this through the use of the javax.mail.FetchProfile, which lists the data that is required. The Folder class provides the following method:

void fetch(Message[] messageList, FetchProfile fProfile)

So, for a given list of messages, this method fetches the given data for each message:

```
FetchProfile fProfile = new FetchProfile();
fProfile.add("To");
fProfile.add("From");
fProfile.add("Subject");
thisFolder.fetch(thisFolder.getMessages(), fProfile);
```

This example creates a new instance of the FetchProfile and adds the given mail header fields it would like to be fetched from the server for all the messages in the call from getMessages(). In our example we looked for the header fields, To, From, and Subject. However, the FetchProfile class knows that the majority of people want groups of data to be retrieved, and to this end, a group can be asked for instead of specifying the individual fields.

The three groups of fields that are defined for use with the FetchProfile are:

- ❑ FetchProfile.Item.ENVELOPE
  This includes the common header fields: From, To, CC, BCC, ReplyTo, Subject, and Date.

- ❑ FetchProfile.Item.CONTENT_INFO
  This includes the information regarding the content, but not the content itself. Therefore information such as the content type, disposition, description, size, and line count are fetched.

- ❑ FetchProfile.Item.FLAGS
  This is all the status flags for the message.

Modifying our example before, we could instead write:

```
FetchProfile fProfile = new FetchProfile();
fProfile.add(FetchProfile.Item.ENVELOPE);
thisFolder.fetch(thisFolder.getMessages(), fProfile);
```

Copying and Moving Messages

Chances are that, if a store can support the notion of multiple folders, it will permit the feature of copying and moving messages among different folders. To copy a list of messages we simply call the method from the Folder class:

```
void copyMessages(Message [] messageList, Folder toFolder)
```

This method runs through the list of messages and copies the given messages, which must be part of the present folder, to the folder specified. The reason the messages must be part of the present folder is to allow the server side to hopefully optimize the transfer by not having to move all the data via the client.

Moving messages is a simple matter of copying first and then marking each message with the delete flag. But do remember to copy the messages before deleting, even though the deletion isn't performed until the folder is expunged.

Searching Messages

It is important to push as much processing to the server side as possible and for this reason, a frequent operation that client-side applications do is to search their message stores. The JavaMail API provides a very flexible search interface to build searches that can be very complex in nature. It is hoped the underlying implementation will pass this search to the server to perform.

The Folder object provides two methods for searching out messages.

```
Message[] search(SearchTerm term)
Message[] search(SearchTerm term, Message[] messageList)
```

These methods return a list of Messages that match the criteria, or an empty array if not. Consider the following example that lists all the messages that came from alan@n-ary.com or cormac@n-ary.com.

```
SearchTerm st = new OrTerm(new FromStringTerm("alan@n-ary.com"),
                           new FromStringTerm ("cormac@n-ary.com"));
Message[] messageList = thisFolder.search(st);
```

The `javax.mail.search` package provides a rich suite of classes that allow us to build up very complex search expressions. By building on the `SearchTerm` class, the JavaMail API offers the following logical operators:

- ❑ `AndTerm(SearchTerm LHS, SearchTerm RHS)`
  `AndTerm(SearchTerm items[])`

- ❑ `OrTerm(SearchTerm LHS, SearchTerm RHS)`
  `OrTerm(SearchTerm items[])`

- ❑ `NotTerm(SearchTerm LHS)`

In addition to these, the `ComparisonTerm` object offers the following constants for building up numerical comparisons:

- ❑ `ComparisonTerm.EQ`
  Equal to

- ❑ `ComparisonTerm.GE`
  Greater than or Equal to

- ❑ `ComparisonTerm.GT`
  Greater than

- ❑ `ComparisonTerm.LE`
  Less than or Equal to

- ❑ `ComparisonTerm.LT`
  Less than

- ❑ `ComparisonTerm.NE`
  Not Equal to

The message fields that can be searched include:

- ❑ `BodyTerm(String pattern)`
- ❑ `FlagTerm(Flags flags, boolean set)`
- ❑ `FromStringTerm(String pattern)`
- ❑ `FromTerm(Address add)`
- ❑ `MessageIDTerm(String messageID)`
- ❑ `MessageNumberTerm(int messageNumber)`
- ❑ `ReceivedDateTerm(int comparison, Date date)`
- ❑ `RecipientStringTerm(Message.RecipientType type, String pattern)`
- ❑ `RecipientTerm(Message.RecipientType type, Address add)`
- ❑ `SentDateTerm(int comparison, Date date)`
- ❑ `SizeTerm(int comparison, int size)`
- ❑ `SubjectTerm(String pattern)`

To see some of these details in action, let's look at a quick example that, on the surface, looks complicated but, as we will see, is actually very easy to implement. Let us assume that we wanted to search for all messages from alan@n-ary.com or javamailhelp@wrox.com that have the phrase JavaMail somewhere in the subject header:

```
SearchTerm st1 = new OrTerm(new FromStringTerm("alan@n-ary.com"),
                            new FromStringTerm ("javamailhelp@wrox.com"));

SearchTerm st2 = new AndTerm(st1, new SubjectTerm("JavaMail"));
Message[] messageList= thisFolder.search(st2);
```

As we can see, it is a simple matter of building up the logical comparison using the various classes available through the javax.mail.search package.

javax.mail.Transport

The final class in our exploratory look at the JavaMail API is the class that is responsible for the delivery of messages, javax.mail.Transport. Most of the time we will be using the SMTP protocol for delivery and, as a convenience, the Transport class offers a static method for the sending of messages, as we have seen earlier in the chapter.

```
Transport.send(msg)
```

However, if we wish to have a little more control over the delivery of the message, consider the example below that implicitly gets the specific Transport object instance, manually connects, and then performs a send on the message.

```
try {

    Transport myTransport = session.getTransport("smtp");
    myTransport.connect();
    myTransport.sendMessage(msg, msg.getAllRecipients());
    myTransport.close();

} catch (SendFailedException sfe){

    Address[] list = sfe.getInvalidAddresses();
    for (int x=0; x < list.length; x++) {
      System.out.println("Invalid Address: " + list[x]);
    }

    list = sfe.getUnsentAddresses();
    for (int x=0; x < list.length; x++) {
      System.out.println("Unsent Address: " + list[x]);
    }

    list = sfe.getValidSentAddresses();
    for (int x=0; x < list.length; x++) {
      System.out.println("Sent Address: " + list[x]);
    }
  }
}
```

The advantage of this mechanism, as opposed to the static call, is that if we are sending large numbers of messages, the underlying protocol doesn't have to keep connecting to the server for each message. Instead the same connection is used. The important feature to notice here is the try ... catch block.

Should something go wrong, the send(...) methods throw a SendFailedException with a whole host of diagnostic information that gives us a clue as to which addresses got an unsuccessful delivery notification. Three lists of addresses are available to us in the event of an error:

❑ Address[] getInvalidAddresses()
    Returns the addresses that didn't get the message delivered because of the fact the addresses couldn't be resolved due to, say, incorrect formatting.

❑ Address[] getUnsentAddresses()
    Returns the addresses that didn't get accepted for delivery. For example, if the server doesn't support relaying it will not send a message to a user outside their domain.

❑ Address[] getValidSentAddresses()
    These are the addresses that were accepted for delivery.

It is important to note that, although a message is accepted for delivery, there is no guarantee that it will make it to its final destination. The only thing that can be assured is the transmission from our application to the server that the transport layer is communicating with. This does not necessarily indicate a successful delivery to the end user.

Working with Mail

Now that we have gone through all the core classes and their relationship with respect to the manipulation of messages and folders, let us put them to the use in some examples that will demonstrate their usage.

The purpose of this section is not to provide us with a complete, all-singing, all-dancing mail client (that's your job!), but to give some practical experience, through working with examples that show us clearly what is going on without cluttering up the rest of the program with distractions.

> *All the examples in this chapter are small command-line applications. They are compiled and run with minimal fuss. If you are using the J2EE libraries then simply compile from the command line using the j2ee.jar file that will be part of your J2EE installation. In this way, you do not need to explicitly specify the mail.jar and activation.jar files. Alternatively, if you are not using the J2EE libraries, you will need to add both of these files to your classpath in order to compile and run the examples.*

Sending Mail

Probably the first thing you want to do is to send some e-mail. We have already seen, earlier in the chapter, how to send a basic plain-text e-mail using the SMTP protocol. Now let's have a look at an application that is a little more functional.

The class shown, javamail_send, takes in four parameters: smtpServer, toE-mail, fromE-mail, and the e-mail body. As can be seen, we parse out the command-line parameters and proceed to set up the session to the server:

```
import java.util.*;
import java.io.*;
import javax.mail.*;
import javax.mail.internet.*;
import javax.activation.*;
```

```
public class javamail_send extends Object {

  public static void main(String args[]) {

    String smtpServer = null;
    String toEmail    = null;
    String fromEmail  = null;
    String body       = null;

    // Parse the Command line parameters
    for (int x=0; x < args.length-1; x++) {
      if (args[x].equalsIgnoreCase("-S")) {
        smtpServer = args[x+1];
      } else if (args[x].equalsIgnoreCase("-T")) {
        toEmail = args[x+1];
      } else if (args[x].equalsIgnoreCase("-F")) {
        fromEmail = args[x+1];
      } else if (args[x].equalsIgnoreCase("-B")) {
        body = args[x+1];
      }
    }

    if (smtpServer == null || toEmail == null ||
        fromEmail == null || body == null) {
        System.out.println("Usage: javamail_send -S <server>
                           -T <toemail> -F <from> -B <body>");
        System.exit(1);
    }

    try {
      // Set up the default parameters
      Properties props = new Properties();
      props.put("mail.transport.protocol", "smtp");
      props.put("mail.smtp.host", smtpServer);
      props.put("mail.smtp.port", "25");

      // Create the session and create a new mail message
      Session mailSession = Session.getInstance(props);
      Message msg = new MimeMessage(mailSession);

      // Set the FROM, TO, DATE and SUBJECT fields
      msg.setFrom(new InternetAddress(fromEmail));
      msg.setRecipients(Message.RecipientType.TO,
                        InternetAddress.parse(toEmail));
      msg.setSentDate(new Date());
      msg.setSubject("Test Mail");

      // Create the body of the mail
      msg.setText(body);

      Transport.send(msg);

      msg.writeTo(System.out);

    } catch (Exception e) {
      System.out.println(e);
    }
  }
}
```

We create the e-mail message in the usual way using the `MimeMessage` class with as little information as is necessary. After all the necessary properties of the message are set, we use the static method `Transport.send(...)` to the deliver the message. It's as simple as that!

After compiling our Java code, making sure to include the appropriate JAR file(s) in the classpath, we can run our program. Here's what the command-prompt window showing the output of our simple `javamail_send` program should look like:

```
C:\ProJavaServer\Ch13>java -classpath %J2EE_HOME%\lib\j2ee.jar;. javamail_send -
S localhost -T steve@st1 -F jiminy@cricket.com -B 'Hello world! This is a test...
'
Message-ID: <1242644.997441877033.JavaMail.stephenr@st1>
Date: Fri, 10 Aug 2001 12:11:16 +0100 (GMT+01:00)
From: jiminy@cricket.com
To: steve@st1
Subject: Test Mail
Mime-Version: 1.0
Content-Type: text/plain; charset=us-ascii
Content-Transfer-Encoding: 7bit

Hello world! This is a test...
C:\ProJavaServer\Ch13>
```

At the end of our program, we do a simple dump of the core message by making a call to `Message.writeTo(...)`, which should produce an e-mail with a message similar to the one shown below:

```
Message-ID: <1242644.995371833448.JavaMail.stephenr@st1>
Date: Tue, 17 Jul 2001 13:10:33 +0100 (GMT+01:00)
From: jiminy@cricket.com
To: steve@st1
Subject: Test Mail
Mime-Version: 1.0
Content-Type: text/plain; charset=us-ascii
Content-Transfer-Encoding: 7bit
Return-Path: jiminy@cricket.com

Hello world! This is a test...
```

Note the presence of the headers and the composition of the e-mail, as discussed earlier in this chapter.

Sending Attachments

Having seen how easy it is to send basic e-mail, let's have a look at sending something a little more complicated – file attachments. We touched on this a little earlier and noted that we must build up the system using a series of different MIME bodies, one representing the message text, and the other holding the necessary information for the file we wish to send.

Taking the example from the previous section, we'll need to add an extra parameter to indicate the attached file and replace the previous `try...catch`, as shown in the code extract overleaf. The complete source code for this example can be found in the file `javamail_send_attachment.java`, available, along with all the source code of this book, from www.wrox.com:

```java
//Import statements, as before.

public class javamail_send_attachment extends Object {

  public static void main(String args[]) {

    String smtpServer = null;
    String toEmail    = null;
    String fromEmail  = null;
    String body       = null;
    String file       = null;

    // Parse the Command line parameters
    for (int x=0; x < args.length-1; x++) {
      if (args[x].equalsIgnoreCase("-S")) {
        smtpServer  = args[x+1];
      } else if (args[x].equalsIgnoreCase("-T")) {
        toEmail     = args[x+1];
      } else if (args[x].equalsIgnoreCase("-F")) {
        fromEmail   = args[x+1];
      } else if (args[x].equalsIgnoreCase("-B")) {
        body    = args[x+1];
      } else if (args[x].equalsIgnoreCase("-A")) {
        file    = args[x+1];
      }
    }

        if (smtpServer == null || toEmail == null ||
          fromEmail == null || body == null || file == null) {
        System.out.println("Usage: javamail_send_attachment -S <server>
                        -T <toemail> -F <from> -B <body> -A <file>");
        System.exit(1);
        }

    try {
      // Set up the default parameters
      Properties props = new Properties();
      props.put("mail.transport.protocol", "smtp");
      props.put("mail.smtp.host", smtpServer);
      props.put("mail.smtp.port", "25");

      // Create the session and create a new mail message
      Session mailSession = Session.getInstance(props);
      Message msg = new MimeMessage(mailSession);

      // Set the FROM, TO, DATE and SUBJECT fields
      msg.setFrom(new InternetAddress(fromEmail));
      msg.setRecipients(Message.RecipientType.TO,
                    InternetAddress.parse(toEmail));
      msg.setSentDate(new Date());
      msg.setSubject("Test Mail with attachment");

      // Create the first part
      Multipart mailBody = new MimeMultipart();

      MimeBodyPart mainBody = new MimeBodyPart();
      mainBody.setText(body);
      mailBody.addBodyPart(mainBody);

      // Create the second part with the attachment
      FileDataSource fds = new FileDataSource(file);
```

```
        MimeBodyPart mimeAttach = new MimeBodyPart();
        mimeAttach.setDataHandler(new DataHandler(fds));
        mimeAttach.setFileName(fds.getName());
        mailBody.addBodyPart(mimeAttach);

        // Create the body of the mail
        msg.setContent(mailBody);

        Transport.send(msg);

        System.out.println("The e-mail below was sent successfully");
        msg.writeTo(System.out);

    } catch(Exception e) {
        System.out.println(e);
    }
}
```

Since this message has two different parts, we need to create the body of the core message with a `MimeMultipart` class. This allows us to put together the various parts of the e-mail, which we'll do one at a time. The first one is the message body and with this we use a `MimeBodyPart` class to hold the message text, which we then add to the `MimeMultipart` instance by calling the `addBodyPart(...)`.

The file attachment is the next phase of the problem we must tackle. We use this by creating another instance of `MimeBodyPart`, which will be used to hold our file attachment. The class from the JavaBean Activation Framework, `FileDataSource`, is used to handle the attachment for the file. We then use this to create our `DataHandler` instance, which is then be used to set the data handler in the `MimeBodyPart`. We can set the file name of the attachment with a call from the `FileDataSource` class. As before, we take this `MimeBodyPart` instance and add it to the list of the parts being handled by the `MimeMultipart` instance.

Finally we take the `MimeMultipart` instance and set the main body of the message to this object with the call to `msg.setContent(...)`.

For sheer curiosity value, let's have a quick look at the resulting e-mail message that is generated this time. Looking at the mail message below, we can see that the mail header is pretty much the same, except the `Content-Type` has been changed to reflect that this is a multipart message, where each part of the message is separated using a uniquely generated string, such as:

```
----=_Part_0_1472506.994107400236
```

If you seek out this string, you will see another set of `Content` headers. These describe the data makeup of that particular section. Notice the part that handles the file attachment. This describes all the information that was used to encode the binary data for the file attached, which in this instance is `base64`.

The JavaMail API handles all this mail creation for us. As we can see, the overall format of the file is relatively straightforward. Ironically, one of the trickier parts is choosing a boundary string for the MIME parts. It mustn't appear as part of the data for each section; otherwise the parsing algorithm used for decoding the message will be confused.

We can compile and run the program in the usual way; here's a sample of the output below:

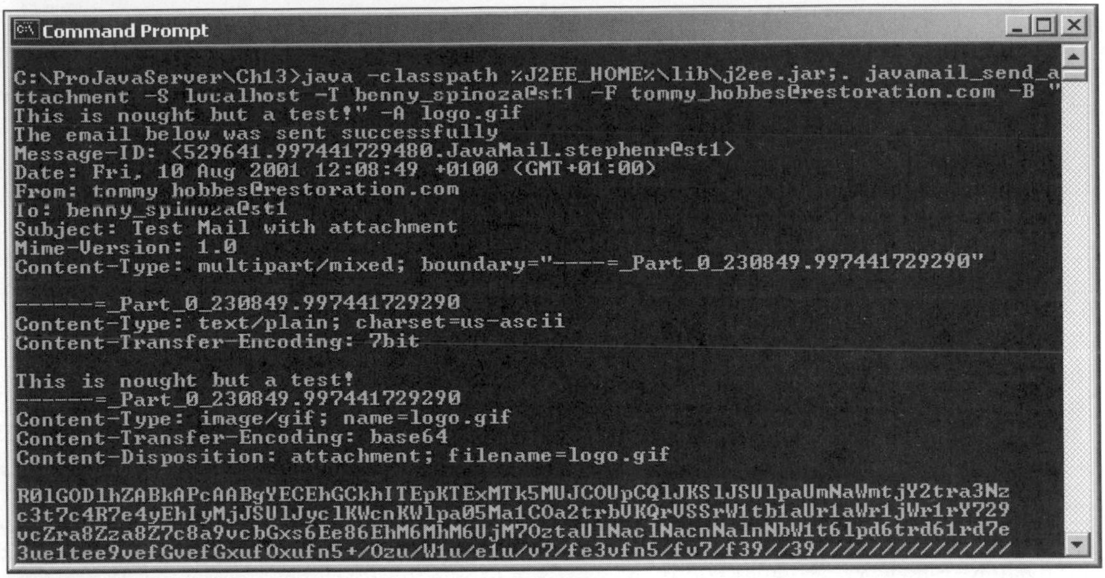

Now that we've seen how easy it is to send messages and attachments, let's take a look at another aspect of mail management – reading mail.

Reading Mail

Receiving e-mail is as simple as sending it, as long as we follow the proper steps. With this in mind, there are a number of things we can demonstrate. With the following example, we'll illustrate the major concepts of dealing with mail, by building a simple command-line access tool for POP3 mail.

This will be a very simple tool: nothing too fancy and it most certainly will not replace our Outlook or Eudora clients! So don't expect too much.

Essentially it will list all the messages held on a POP server and allow the user to interact with this list. But first of all let's build the framework for this application.

```
import java.util.*;
import java.io.*;
import javax.mail.*;
import javax.mail.internet.*;
import javax.activation.*;

public class javamail_pop extends Object {

  public static void main(String args[]) {

    if (args.length != 1) {
      System.out.println("Usage: javamail_pop <urlname>");
      System.exit(1);
    }
```

```java
    URLName urlname = new URLName(args[0]);

    try {
      // Set up the default parameters
      Properties props = new Properties();
      props.put("mail.transport.protocol", "pop");
      props.put("mail.pop.port", "110");

      // Open up the session
      Session session = Session.getInstance(props);
      Store store = session.getStore(urlname);
      store.connect();

      // Open up the folder
      Folder folder = store.getDefaultFolder();
      if (folder == null) {
        System.out.println("Problem occurred");
        System.exit(1);
      }

      Folder popFolder = folder.getFolder("INBOX");
      popFolder.open(Folder.READ_ONLY);

      System.out.println("Opened with: " + popFolder.getMessageCount());

      BufferedReader cmdPrompt = new BufferedReader(
                                    new InputStreamReader(System.in));
      displayMessages(popFolder);

      for(;;) {
        System.out.println("Enter command (exit to end)");
        System.out.print("% ");
        String cmd = cmdPrompt.readLine().toLowerCase();
        if (cmd.equalsIgnoreCase("exit")) {
          break;
        } else {
          displayMessages(popFolder);
        }
      }

      popFolder.close(false);
      store.close();

    } catch (Exception e){
      System.out.println(e);
    }
}

// Displays the list of messages from the given folder.
// Display only the message id, from and subject fields
private static void displayMessages(Folder folder) throws Exception {

  Message[] listOfMessages = folder.getMessages();
  FetchProfile fProfile = new FetchProfile();
  fProfile.add(FetchProfile.Item.ENVELOPE);
  folder.fetch(listOfMessages, fProfile);

  System.out.println("Message List:");

  for (int x=0; x < listOfMessages.length; x++) {
```

```
      StringBuffer sb = new StringBuffer(32);

      // Message ID starts from 1
      sb.append("# " + (x+1));

      Address[] addList = listOfMessages[x].getFrom();
      if (addList.length > 0) {
        sb.append("\t" + ((InternetAddress)addList[0]).getAddress());
      }
      sb.append("\t\t" + listOfMessages[x].getSubject());

      System.out.println(sb.toString());
    }

    System.out.println("End of message list\r\n");
  }
}
```

We run this application from the command line passing in the URLName string which describes all the necessary information to connect to the POP3 server. For example:

```
% <javaruntime> javamail_pop pop3://mypopname:mypoppassword@www.hotmail.com
```

The first thing this small application does is to create an instance of the URLName class and use this to obtain access to the Store that holds the folder hierarchy. Once we have this, we can then obtain the top-level folder, which will allow us to access the special folder INBOX (the only valid folder for the POP protocol). Here's an example screen output from the author's own POP3 test server:

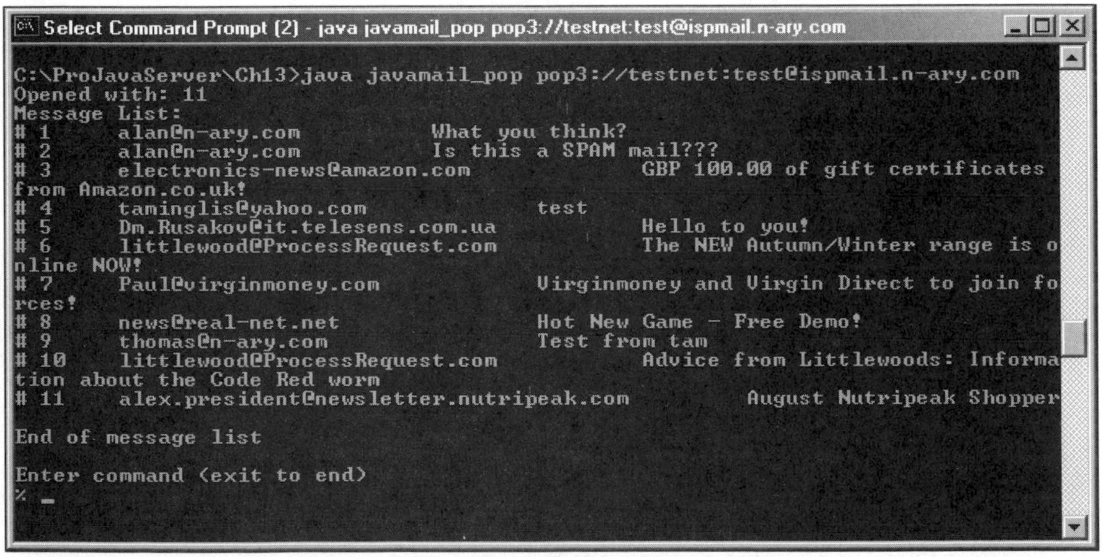

We will use a simple command-line type interface using the InputStream from System.in. By creating a BufferedReader object instance we can easily look for complete commands by simply calling the readLine() method. By putting this inside a continuous loop, we can easily have multiple commands and let the user exit the session by typing in exit.

One of the most fundamental methods in this application is the `displayMessage(…)`. This takes the given folder and lists all the messages contained within it, displaying the message ID, From field, and subject for each message.

Another point worth mentioning is the use of the `FetchProfile` class. Remember what this was for? This is used to fill in the lightweight message references with all the necessary information regarding the message header. After the call to fill in the information, we simply run round the message loop extracting the necessary information.

The next stage is to add to our command-line application the functionality to display a particular message ID's content. The first thing that we need to do is to add in the facility for processing the `display <id>` command. We make the necessary addition to make the core `for` loop look like the following code:

```
for(;;) {
  System.out.println("Enter command (exit to end)");
  System.out.print("% ");
  String cmd = cmdPrompt.readLine().toLowerCase();
  if (cmd.equalsIgnoreCase("exit")) {
    break;
  } else if (cmd.indexOf("display") == 0) {
    displaySingleMessage(popFolder, cmd);
  } else {
    displayMessages(popFolder);
  }
}
```

This simply looks for the `display` keyword and, when found, calls the `displaySingleMessage(…)` method as detailed next. This method then parses out the message ID and attempts to retrieve the message at that given index by call the `getMessage(…)` method. After that, the message is written to the output stream by simply calling the `writeTo(…)` method:

```
private static void displaySingleMessage(Folder folder, String cmd)
                                                    throws Exception {
  int c1 = cmd.indexOf(" ");
  if (c1 == -1) {
    System.out.println("display <id>");
    return;
  }

  int messageID = Integer.parseInt(cmd.substring(c1+1));
  Message mess  = folder.getMessage(messageID);

  mess.writeTo(System.out);
  System.out.println("End of message\r\n");
}
```

It doesn't take a Java genius to work out that this application is fraught with pitfalls. There is very little functionality going on with respect to checking that the ID of the desired message is indeed in the range listed by the folder. In addition to this, by simply allowing the exception to be thrown and caught by one `try`/`catch` block, the error handling is a little crude. Here we see the `display` keyword in action:

Remember, the purpose of this application isn't to build a fully robust POP client, but instead to illustrate some basic JavaMail principals.

Deleting Mail

Let us extend our pop-client to include the ability to delete a message in the folder. We can simply add in the ability to the message loop to handle the `delete <id>` command, which in turn calls the `deleteSingleMethod(…)`, like this:

```
for(;;) {
  System.out.println("Enter command (exit to end)");
  System.out.print("% ");
  String cmd = cmdPrompt.readLine().toLowerCase();
  if (cmd.equalsIgnoreCase("exit")) {
    break;
  } else if (cmd.indexOf("display") == 0) {
    displaySingleMessage(popFolder, cmd);
  } else if ( cmd.indexOf("delete") == 0 ) {
    deleteSingleMessage( popFolder, cmd );
  } else {
    displayMessages(popFolder);
  }
}
```

This method parses out the message ID and retrieves that message. We wish to delete this message and, as we know from the previous sections, there is no explicit delete method for it. Instead we have to set the DELETED flag to true and then when the folder is closed the messages with this flag will be removed. Here's what our new method looks like:

```
private static void deleteSingleMessage(Folder folder, String cmd)
                                                  throws Exception {
  int c1 = cmd.indexOf(" ");
  if (c1 == -1) {
    System.out.println("delete <id>");
```

```
    return;
}

int messageID = Integer.parseInt(cmd.substring(c1+1));
Message mess  = folder.getMessage(messageID);

mess.setFlag(Flags.Flag.DELETED, true);

System.out.println("Deleted message\r\n");
}
```

If we run this code as it is now, we will discover one small implementation problem; it doesn't work! The message doesn't get deleted. Why not? Well it's quite subtle really and it's small problems like this that we have to look for when working with folders.

Initially we opened the folder in the mode READ_ONLY. This effectively locked out all modifications to the folder and all messages contained within. By changing the opening mode, as shown below, we can make our application burst into life with the power to delete messages:

```
popFolder.open(Folder.READ_WRITE);
```

Receiving Attachments

There is one final piece of functionality we really ought to add, and that's the ability to save attachments out to disk. We'll add in the command save <id> that will look up a given message, see if there are any attachments associated with it, and then save them one at a time, out to disk (into the current directory). As before we modify the main command processing loop to look for the save command and call the new method:

```
} else if ( cmd.indexOf("save") == 0 ) {
    saveAttachment( popFolder, cmd );
```

Here's the saveAttachment(...) method in full:

```
private static void saveAttachment(Folder folder, String cmd)
                                                throws Exception {
  int c1 = cmd.indexOf(" ");
  if (c1 == -1) {
    System.out.println("save <id>");
    return;
  }

  int messageID = Integer.parseInt(cmd.substring(c1+1));
  Message mess  = folder.getMessage(messageID);

  if (mess.isMimeType("multipart/*")) {

    Multipart multipart = (Multipart)mess.getContent();

    for (int i=0, n=multipart.getCount(); i<n; i++) {
      Part part = multipart.getBodyPart(i);

      String disposition = part.getDisposition();
      if (disposition != null &&
            (disposition.equals(Part.ATTACHMENT) ||
                    disposition.equals(Part.INLINE))) {
```

```
        FileOutputStream outFile = new
                            FileOutputStream(part.getFileName());
        BufferedInputStream in = new
                            BufferedInputStream(part.getInputStream());
        int c;
        while ((c-in.read()) != -1) {
          outFile.write(c);
        }
        outFile.close();
        System.out.println("Attachment: "+part.getFileName()+" written");
      }
    }
  }
}
```

As with our other methods, we parse out the given ID and retrieve that message from the folder. Next we make the assumption that our message attachments will be part of a multipart/* message as opposed to appearing on their own. This may not always be the case, since we can send a message with just the file and no accompanying text.

Having discovered that the MIME type is indeed of a multipart/* of some kind, we cast our message content to a Multipart and run through the list of parts. We look at the disposition of the message, and if that's marked as either an ATTACHMENT or an INLINE then it is saved to disk.

Saving a file is a simple matter of reading a byte from the InputStream and writing it out to an appropriate FileWriter class.

Remember, the full source code for this example, and all of the other examples in this chapter, is available for download from www.wrox.com.

Saving and Loading Mail

We can use the JavaMail API for a whole host of applications involving e-mail and one of the things we may want to do is to save a given e-mail in either a database or a file for use later on. Say, for example, we were writing an application to send e-mails to a relay server. What if the relay server wasn't available? How could we cache the e-mails locally until the mail server came back online again?

Once we have our e-mail represented in a MimeMessage instance we would think we could simply serialize it using Java's object serialization methods. However, we would be wrong! The JavaMail API doesn't support serialization on many of its objects, with the MimeMessage being one of them. The reason for this lies in the number of external references that the underlying Message class holds, for example Store and Session. So if the object had been restored again, it would have invalid references. Do not fear – help is at hand.

The technique we use to save and restore mail messages may seem a little long-winded and not very efficient but, as we will discover, is the simplest to understand.

As we have already discussed, a mail message is just plain ASCII text, laid out in a known manner comprising a header followed by the data or contents of the message. To save a message we simply save the ASCII representation of the finally constructed e-mail and put it into a file or database. To load the message back in again, we simply read the text file and ask the JavaMail API to decode the message again, as if it were coming from the mail server.

Let's have a look at this in action with a modification of the example we used before. Instead of sending the e-mail out immediately we will save it to disk for e-mailing later.

```java
import java.util.*;
import java.io.*;
import javax.mail.*;
import javax.mail.internet.*;
import javax.activation.*;

public class javamail_save extends Object {

  public static void main(String args[]) {

    String smtpServer = null;
    String toEmail    = null;
    String fromEmail  = null;
    String body       = null;

    // Parse the Command line parameters
    for (int x=0; x < args.length-1; x++) {
      if (args[x].equalsIgnoreCase("-S"))
        smtpServer = args[x+1];
      } else if (args[x].equalsIgnoreCase("-T")) {
        toEmail = args[x+1];
      } else if (args[x].equalsIgnoreCase("-F")) {
        fromEmail = args[x+1];
      } else if (args[x].equalsIgnoreCase("-B")) {
        body = args[x+1];
      }
    }

    if (smtpServer == null || toEmail == null ||
        fromEmail == null || body == null) {
        System.out.println("Usage: javamail_save -S <server>
                            -T <toemail> -F <from> -B <body>");
        System.exit(1);
    }

    try {
      // Set up the default parameters
      Properties props = new Properties();
      props.put("mail.transport.protocol", "smtp");
      props.put("mail.smtp.host", smtpServer);
      props.put("mail.smtp.port", "25");

      // Create the session and create a new mail message
      Session mailSession = Session.getInstance(props);
      Message msg = new MimeMessage(mailSession);

      // Set the FROM, TO, DATE and SUBJECT fields
      msg.setFrom(new InternetAddress(fromEmail));
      msg.setRecipients(Message.RecipientType.TO,
                        InternetAddress.parse(toEmail));
      msg.setSentDate(new Date());
      msg.setSubject("Test Mail");

      // Save the SERVER that we wish to send this e-mail to
      msg.setHeader("X-Server", smtpServer);

      // Create the body of the mail
      msg.setText(body);
```

```
        //-[ Save the e-mail out to a file
        String filename = System.currentTimeMillis() + ".e-mail";
        FileOutputStream outFile = new FileOutputStream(filename);
        msg.writeTo(outFile);
        outFile.close();

        System.out.println("E-mail has been saved:" + filename);

    } catch (Exception e){
        System.out.println(e);
    }
  }
}
```

Reading through it, there is nothing too unfamiliar with this example. But notice how are we are using the fact we can place additional information into the header to store the SMTP server that the user wishes to use to send the file. Since we aren't going to be sending it in this instance, we have to keep the name of the server somewhere, and the easiest place for this in the header of the mail message with the X-Server field. After that we simply create the message as normal, but instead of handing it off to the Transport class for delivery, we write the contents to a file using the writeTo(…) method. We are creating a relatively unique filename by using the system clock. However, in a multithreaded environment this wouldn't be guaranteed to produced a unique number as it is feasible for two or more threads to be calling the System.currentTimeMillis() method at the same time.

The resulting file is a simple text file that can be viewed in any text editor. Satisfy your curiosity and open it up, and get a feel for what the JavaMail API has done. Looking at the header you will see the inclusion of our special X-Server field:

So, having written the message to disk, the flipside of the operation is to load it and to then send it back out. This is done very easily through the MimeMessage class constructor that allows us to pass in an InputStream to the message source. We can utilise this and take the InputStream from the file.

The following example will take all the files ending with the extension ".e-mail", and attempt to send them to the Transport class for delivery. This example takes a directory as an argument (use "." for the current directory), and for each file with the ".e-mail" extension it will call the sendMail(…) method:

```java
import java.util.*;
import java.io.*;
import javax.mail.*;
import javax.mail.internet.*;
import javax.activation.*;

public class javamail_sendAll extends Object {

  public static void main(String args[]){
    if (args.length == 0) {
      System.out.println("Usage: javamail_sendAll <directory>");
    } else {
      new javamail_sendAll(args[0]);
    }
  }

  public javamail_sendAll(String spoolDirectory){
    processMailList(spoolDirectory);
  }

  private void processMailList(String spoolDirectory) {
    File rootDir = new File(spoolDirectory);
    String listOfFile[] = rootDir.list(new fileFilter());

    for (int x=0; x < listOfFile.length; x++) {
      File thisFile = new File(rootDir, listOfFile[x]);

      sendMail(thisFile);

      thisFile.delete();
    }
  }

  private void sendMail(File filename) {
    String To = filename.getName(), From = "", Subject="";
    String mailServer = "";

    try {
      // Load in the file
      BufferedInputStream in = new BufferedInputStream(
                                    new FileInputStream(filename));

      // Set the Session and Server properties
      Session mailSession = Session.getInstance(new Properties());

      MimeMessage msg = new MimeMessage(mailSession, in);
      in.close();

      // Message is now in, deal with the custom header
      mailServer = msg.getHeader("X-Server", ",");
      msg.removeHeader("X-Server");

      // Now we need to deliver it
      Properties props  = mailSession.getProperties();
      props.put("mail.smtp.host", mailServer);

      // Set the To, From
      To      = msg.getHeader("To", ",");
      From    = msg.getHeader("From", ",");
      Subject = msg.getSubject();
```

```
      // Send the message
      Transport.send(msg);

      System.out.println("MailOut: To=" + To + "; From=" + From
                      + "; Subject=" + Subject + "; Server="
                      + mailServer + "; Size=" + filename.length()
                      + " bytes");

   } catch(Exception ) {
      System.out.println("MailOutFail: To=" + To + "; From=" + From
                      + "; Subject=" | Subject | "; Server="
                      + mailServer  + "; Size=" + filename.length()
                      + " bytes:" + e);
   }
}

class fileFilter implements FilenameFilter {
  public fileFilter(){}
  public boolean accept(File dir, String name) {
    if(name.indexOf(".e-mail") != -1) {
      return true;
    } else {
      return false;
    }
  }
}
}
}
```

The sendMail(...) method is where all the magic happens, taking in a File object to the file we wish to open up and send. Having created a BufferedInputStream to the file, we are now in a position to create the MimeMessage for eventual delivery. Passing in the InputStream into the constructor is all we have to do. If something goes wrong, an Exception will be thrown. Otherwise it will be business as usual.

Remember that we put the SMTP server details into the header? Well, we'd better take that back out again (unless we want to keep it in there, of course). There is no real reason for it to stay there as it serves no purpose except for this class. We then take the SMTP server and set the property in the session with it. Once we have done that, we can send it to the Transport class for delivery.

The output of this class can be seen below where a message will be printed for all successful messages sent:

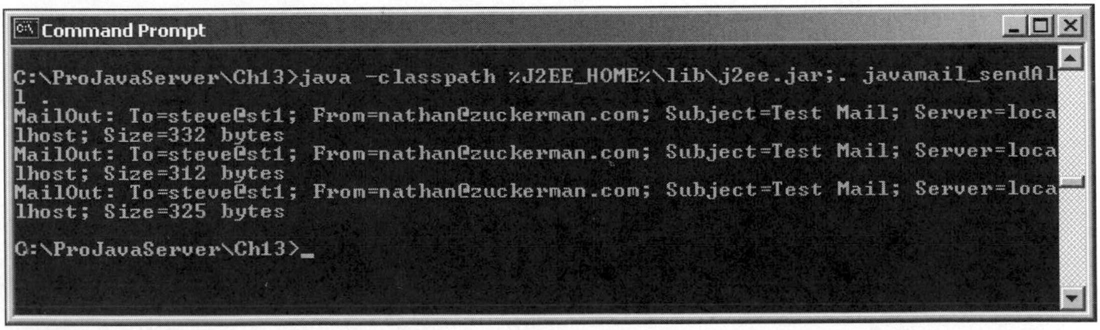

JavaMail Resources

There are plenty of resources that provide more information on the JavaMail API – just do a search for JavaMail in any search engine and you will discover many people working with it. Below are a couple of the well-known resources that can be very useful:

❑ Official JavaMail API – http://java.sun.com/products/javamail/
This is the URL where you will find the official documentation and downloads.

❑ jGuru: JavaMail – http://www.jguru.com/faq/home.jsp?topic=JavaMail
This is an excellent resource, moderated by John Zukowski who does an excellent job of answering all JavaMail related questions (mine included!).

Summary

We've now reached the end of our journey through the wonders of the JavaMail API. As you can now hopefully appreciate, it's very impressive and extremely flexible in the art of accessing and interacting with messages. The API completely abstracts away the actual implementation details of the underlying protocols to give us complete and unobstructed access to the mail messages.

Back in 1971, a computer engineer, by the name of Ray Tomlinson started the whole ball rolling by sending the first ever-recorded e-mail, "I sent a number of test messages to myself from one machine to the other" he recalls. He also adds, "The test messages were entirely forgettable...".

> *You can read more on the history of e-mail from the site,*
> *http://www.pretext.com/mar98/features/story2.htm (thanks to Rachael Milligan for finding this excellent resource).*

That's over 30 years of maturing, and it's now one of the most widely used applications on the Internet. Its staying power can be attributed to the fact that we, as human beings, love to communicate and exchange messages, and that want hasn't died, even after 3 decades. However, we can't take all the credit for the popularity of e-mails; many systems use this well trodden route for communicating between themselves, sending control and status information to other systems as an integral part of their day-to-day operation.

The next wave of applications for this technology is about to arrive with the J2ME platform beginning to take hold in the world of the mobile phone and PDA. It won't be long before our mobile users are asking for access to their "legacy" e-mail system through their browser on the move. We now have the power to deliver this solution, quickly and reliably, through the use of the JavaMail API.

In the next chapter, we will look at one of the most significant changes to the J2EE specification – the update of the Enterprise JavaBeans specification to version 2.0.

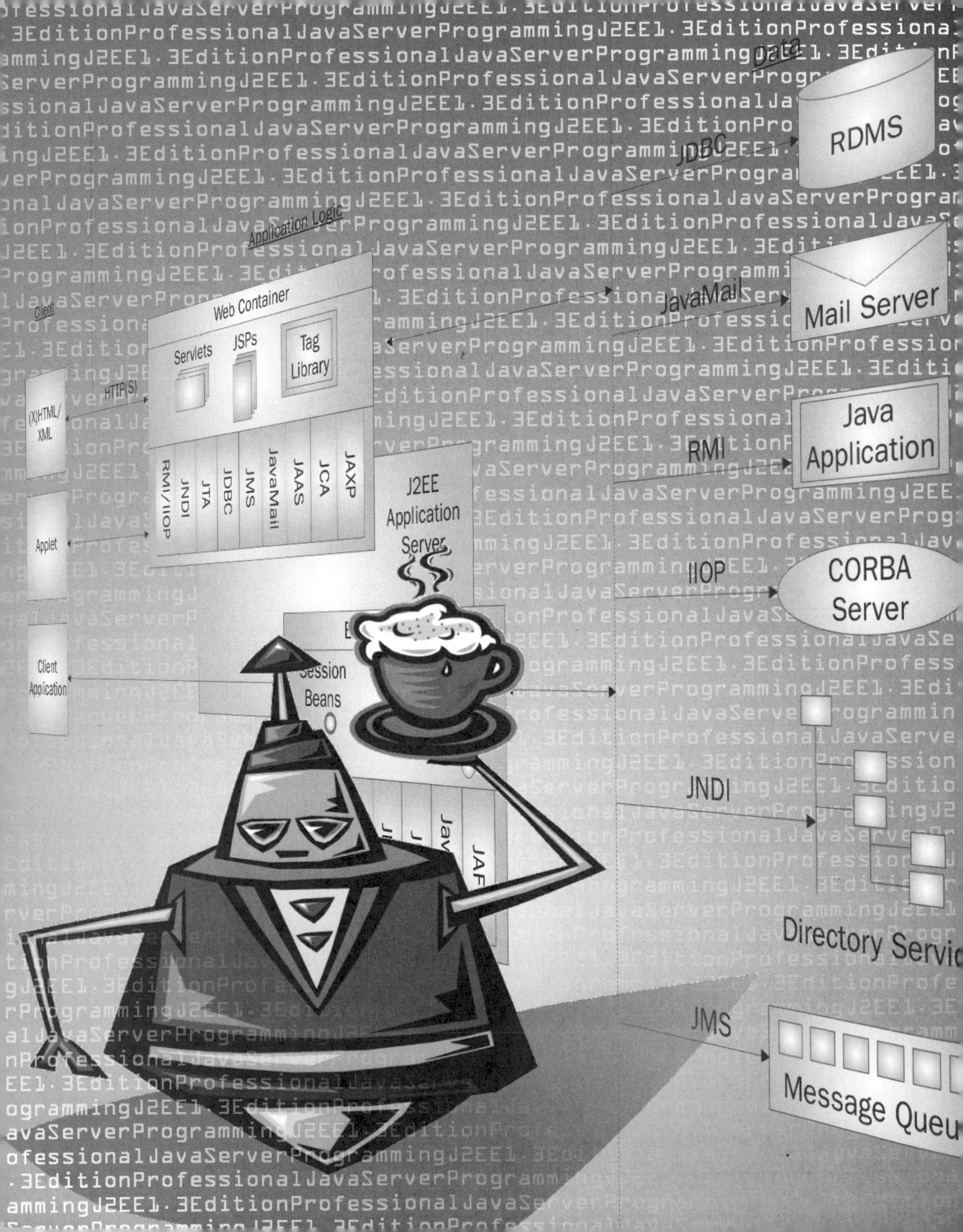

14

EJB Architecture and Design

In previous chapters, we've talked about Java APIs that can be used to build server-side applications. Some of these APIs, such as JDBC and JNDI, provide access to low-level services that any application can use. Other APIs, such as servlets and JSP, allow the creation of components that execute in a structured environment (the container) that provides higher-level services. This chapter introduces an API for a new type of J2EE component – **Enterprise JavaBeans (EJB)**.

EJB components are designed to encapsulate business logic, and to protect the application developer from having to worry about many system level issues, including transactions, security, scalability, concurrency, communication, resource management, persistence, error handling, and operating-environment independence.

The main changes in the EJB 2.0 specification from version 1.1 are:

❑ A new type of EJB has been introduced, the **message-driven bean**. This is an EJB that can perform asynchronous operations via the Java Messaging Service (JMS).

❑ The container now tracks changes made to entity beans very precisely, and can therefore issue extremely optimized queries and updates to the database.

❑ The specification defines a standard query language called **EJB QL**. This language allows specific requests to be made on the database, without regard to the nature of the underlying persistence store.

❑ The container will maintain relationships between entity beans, so developers no longer need to maintain them.

❑ A new interface, the **local interface**, has been introduced on top of the home and remote interfaces. EJBs that expose local interfaces can be invoked without the overhead of copying the parameters, unlike remote interfaces.

All these additions will be discussed in depth in the following five chapters that are concerned specifically with EJB technology. In this chapter, we will take a general look at why we would develop EJB components in applications and we'll see how to create our own simple EJB. In particular, we'll look at the following issues:

❑   The services that an EJB container provides and the mechanisms by which they are provided

❑   The circumstances in which it makes sense to use EJB components in an application

❑   What an EJB component looks like

❑   How a client programmer (who might be developing server-side web components) views and accesses an EJB

❑   How an EJB developer views an EJB component and the rules that they must follow when creating EJB components

❑   How to use EJBs successfully in a web architecture

After we have covered this background information, we'll talk about the design process for an architecture that uses EJB components, which will allow us to create a practical example that can be carried forward to subsequent chapters:

❑   Chapters 15, 16, and 19 will discuss in detail the three main types of EJB components: session beans, entity beans, and message-driven beans. Session and entity beans have two main sub-types. Session beans can be stateful or stateless; and entity beans can have bean-managed or container-managed persistence. We'll look at the tradeoffs and design uses for each type and sub-type of bean by developing alternative versions of simple EJB components. In addition, we'll further implement the example we explore in this chapter.

❑   Chapter 17 examines in detail four of the services that an EJB container will provide: transactions, security, exception handling, and remote communication. Some of this material is a little complicated, but we'll need to understand it to use EJB components in a real-world high-volume environment.

❑   Chapter 18 looks at EJB components from the perspective of the development process. We'll examine the roles that are explicitly defined in the EJB specification, and the activities that are necessary for each role. Also, we'll extend the sample application from Chapters 15 through 17 to include a web interface. This allows us to consider how we should set up our environment for an application with both web and EJB components.

We'll begin by defining exactly what EJBs are – and aren't. We'll also take a brief look at some of things EJBs can be used for.

What are EJBs?

> **An EJB is just a collection of Java classes and an XML file, bundled into a single unit. The Java classes follow certain rules and provide specific callback methods, as defined by the J2EE container environment and EJB specifications.**

An EJB runs in an EJB container. The EJB container runs within an application server and takes responsibility for system-level issues. This division of labor between the EJB developer and the container, which allows the developer to concentrate on the business logic rather than system-level programming, is an important part of the thinking behind the Enterprise JavaBeans technology.

EJBs are a Java technology so it should come as no surprise that they are not tied to any particular operating system. For example, we can write an EJB on Windows 2000 and deploy it on Linux, Solaris, or even the AS/400. The significance of this really becomes apparent when you consider that the only comparable technology (available today) to the EJB model, Microsoft's .NET (COM), runs exclusively on Microsoft platforms. (A comparison of COM and EJB can be found at http://java.sun.com/products/ejb/ejbvscom.html.)

> *The CORBA Component Model is essentially a multi-language superset of the Enterprise JavaBeans specification. In time, these language-neutral components may play an important role in many application architectures. There are several implementations of the CORBA Component Model and some of them are opensource. Pointers to such implementations can be found at http://ditec.um.es/~dsevilla/ccm/.*

The intent of the EJB specification is to provide a definition of how server-side components should interact, so that developers can choose between several vendors and switch between them easily. In many ways, the specification achieves this goal but there are still certain points that we as developers need to be aware of so that the EJBs we create remain as vendor-neutral as possible.

EJBs are just a *specification* for a server-side component architecture (within the J2EE environment) that any company can implement. If an EJB doesn't take advantage of any proprietary extensions of a particular implementation, it can be moved from one implementation to another as the requirements of the application change. The EJB might be developed on a cheap, opensource, server, but deployed on a high-end container that has features (such as load balancing and fail-over) that provide a high degree of reliability.

EJBs are reusable components. Component-based development has proved its worth in developing client applications (for example, no one would consider building a GUI without using pre-built components). An EJB is intended to be a reusable bundle of business logic. Even if EJBs are not sold for reuse outside a single company, it will be possible to reuse the business logic in different contexts within one company.

EJBs can work with any type of client. This is a by no means exhaustive list of where EJBs can be employed:

- ❑ EJBs can be used in conjunction with servlets and JSP pages to provide access for web clients.
- ❑ EJBs can be accessed directly from Java clients using RMI.
- ❑ CORBA can be used to access EJBs on a server that supports RMI/IIOP.
- ❑ XML can be used through a servlet to provide access for any type of client that supports XML. This idea has recently been submitted to the World Wide Web Consortium and has become a specification of its own under the name **Simple Object Access Protocol (SOAP)**. You can find more information on SOAP at http://www.w3.org/TR/SOAP/.

EJBs have many benefits. They can boost developer productivity; they can help structure the model behind your company's interactive web site; and they can even be made to scale to the largest e-commerce application.

Before we go any further, it's important to clear up a common source of confusion to developers new to EJBs – how they are related to JavaBeans.

Enterprise JavaBeans vs. JavaBeans

Enterprise JavaBeans was perhaps an unfortunate choice of name because the EJB API – also known as component architecture – has little in common with the similarly named JavaBeans component architecture. JavaBeans and Enterprise JavaBeans have very different goals, implementation, and use.

> The JavaBeans architecture is designed to provide a format for general-purpose
> components, whereas the Enterprise JavaBeans architecture provides a format for
> highly specialized business-logic components deployed in a J2EE environment.

EJB components, servlet components, and JSP components have more in common with each other, than
any of them has with JavaBeans. The following chart will help you to understand how EJB technology is
related to other Java component technologies.

Component	Purpose of component	Tier of execution	Typical services provided by the runtime execution environment
JavaBeans	General-purpose component architecture	Any	Java libraries. Other services vary greatly with the container (for example, Microsoft Word document, Java application).
Servlets	Implements a request-response paradigm, especially for web protocols	Server (specifically the web tier)	Lifecycle services, network services, request decoding, response formatting.
JavaServer Pages	Provides for the generation of dynamic content, especially for web environments	Server (specifically the web tier)	All servlet services, scripting, tag extensions, response buffering.
Enterprise JavaBeans	Provides for the encapsulation and management of business logic	Server (specifically the business-logic tier)	Persistence, declarative transactions and security, connection pooling, lifecycle services, support for messaging services.

Varieties of Beans

The primary goal of EJB technology is to provide standard component architecture for the creation and use of
distributed object-oriented business systems. This ambitious goal could not be met with only one model for a
component, so the EJB 2.0 specification provides three models for callback methods and run-time lifecycles. The
three types of EJB that implement these models are **entity beans**, **session beans**, and **message-driven beans**.

The differences between these three types of EJB are quite complex, and so each is covered in a chapter
that explains the callback methods of the EJB as well as where and when they should be used. (Chapter
15 covers session beans; Chapter 16 entity beans, and message-driven beans are discussed in Chapter
19.) However, as this distinction is so fundamental, we'll review the key differences here.

A session bean is intended for use by a single client at a time, so we can think of it almost as an
extension of the client on the server. It may provide business logic, such as calculating the rate of return
for an investment, or it may save state, such as a shopping cart for a web client. A session bean's lifespan
is no longer than that of its client. When the client leaves the web site, or the application is shut down,
the session bean is free to disappear. It is no longer available for access by other clients.

Think of an entity bean as an object-oriented representation of data in a database. Like a database, it can be
accessed simultaneously by multiple clients. An entity bean might represent a customer, a product, or an
account. The lifespan of an entity EJB is as long as that of the data it represents in the database.

Each of these types of EJB has two important sub-types. A session-bean can be either **stateful** or **stateless**. A stateful bean can keep information on behalf of its client across method calls (like a shopping-cart bean would). A stateless bean cannot (nor would it need to, for example a calculator bean). This is an important distinction and, in practice, stateful and stateless session EJBs are used for very different purposes.

An entity bean can have its relationship to the data in the database managed by the programmer (**bean-managed persistence**) or by the container (**container-managed persistence**). This distinction will often be important from the perspectives of productivity or performance. However, you can use both types of bean interchangeably in your design.

A message-driven EJB is invoked asynchronously and can receive and act upon JMS messages via the Java Messaging Service (JMS) provider. Typically, a client will post a message to a specific JMS Queue or Destination and all the message-driven EJBs that are subscribed to this destination will receive this message.

How many different types of beans must we decide between? The answer to this question depends upon the standpoint from which it's asked:

- ❑ From the standpoint of callback methods and the base interfaces that the EJBs must implement, there are three: session beans, entity beans, and message-driven beans.

- ❑ From the standpoint of your architecture, there are four: stateful session beans, stateless session beans, entity beans, and message-driven beans.

- ❑ From the standpoint of your implementation, there are five: stateful session beans, stateless session beans, entity beans with container-managed persistence, entity beans with bean-managed persistence, and message-driven beans.

By the time we have worked through the chapters on EJB, we will fully understand the issues and tradeoffs involved in each type of EBJ.

Why use EJBs?

The design of a server-side Java application must takes into account how servlets, JSP pages, and Enterprise JavaBeans work together, and which are appropriate in different circumstances. Large numbers of web sites have demonstrated that it is possible to provide dynamic content using servlets or JSP pages alone, so it might seem that this new API adds unnecessary complexity to the development process.

The EJB specification is intended to provide enterprise-level services. That is, to provide functionality that is fundamental to an organization's purpose, regardless of the scale. Accordingly, the EJB specification has some complexity in its administration and programming model. Just as a simple web site with no dynamic requirements should be written in plain HTML, an application with only modest business-logic requirements is best served by avoiding the complexity of EJBs. It should use a servlet and JSP implementation (using JavaBeans for the business logic and data access).

The EJB API allows developers to avoid programming systems-level services, leaving them free to concentrate on the business logic. A web site that only needs to provide dynamic content to its users probably doesn't require those systems-level services in the first place but many applications do require those services, and EJB technology fulfils this need.

Sun's documentation for the Java 2 Enterprise Edition platform includes a publication discussing how the various J2EE technologies fit together. This document, *Designing Enterprise Applications with the Java 2 Platform, Enterprise Edition* (also known as *J2EE Blueprints*) is available from http://java.sun.com/j2ee/blueprints/ and lists four architectures for web applications:

❏ Basic HTML

❏ HTML with JSP pages and servlets

❏ Servlets and JSP pages that access modular JavaBeans components

❏ Servlets, JSP pages, JavaBeans components, and Enterprise JavaBeans

These architectures are increasingly complex, but also increasingly robust. As we have seen, it's simple to write a JSP page or servlet that provides dynamic content. It's also possible to embed scripting and dynamic data access right in the presentation logic to enable rapid application development. However, the resulting code will be difficult to extend and maintain. Additionally, the roles of web designer and business logic developer will be difficult to separate.

Any complex application will benefit from a modular approach. We have seen how JavaBeans can be used with JSP pages to separate the data processing from the presentation logic, providing greater ease of maintenance and code reuse. Although additional work may be required up front, all but the simplest web applications will be better for the investment.

In one sense, adding EJB technology simply extends this modularity to a further level. As the requirements of an application increase in complexity, access to the business logic and persistent data is moved to EJB components. However, the decision to use EJBs should not be based on application complexity alone. EJB technology is also appropriate when the services provided by an EJB container are required. The typical advantages provided by an EJB container, and often referred to as system level services, include, but are not limited to transactions, scalability, persistence, security, future growth possibilities, remote access, pooling, tightly controlled resources and access from other types of clients. Keep in mind that EJBs come with certain tradeoffs, and you don't get the above advantages without cost. An application has a certain amount of overhead depending on the frequency and size of network calls it makes, and more memory will be consumed when the application server is present.

The best way to decide if EJBs are appropriate is to think of them as the *business objects* of an application. They are object-orientated representations of business rules – what an organization owns, what it owes, how it operates, who works there, who can get credit, what's for sale, how much to charge, and so on. If an application needs access to these rules, it should do it through the business-object representation. However, if the application needs to capture the complexity of a process; if it needs to read, validate, transform, and write data in consistent units; if it needs to be kept secure; or if it needs to be reused in different contexts then it makes sense to take advantage of the services that an EJB container can provide.

The EJB specification is designed to represent business objects without making the business-logic programmer provide system-level services. Therefore, EJB technology is not suited to be used as a reporting system, for analytical processing, or to serve files to the web. But if an application needs to access business logic of any complexity, writing the business logic as EJB components will open up new possibilities in developer productivity, application deployment, performance, reliability, and code reusability.

The EJB Container and its Services

A container is an execution environment for a component. The component lives in the container and the container provides services for the component. Similarly, a container often lives in an application server, which provides an execution environment for it and for other containers:

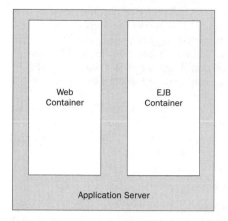

Technically, a component interacts only with its container and the resources the container provides. However, as the interface between the container and an application server isn't well defined, a single vendor will usually provide both and so the distinction will often be meaningless. If an API between a container and an application server is ever standardized, the distinction will become more important.

An EJB component is usually written is to take advantage of the services that the container (that is, the execution environment) provides. Understanding what these services are will help us to understand when it is appropriate to use EJB components in application design, and what role they should play. Let's look at some of the services an EJB container should provide.

Persistence

We can, if we choose to, read and write to a database using the JDBC API directly. This may be appropriate if we simply need to read some data to generate a dynamic web page, or update some simple information. If we have complex needs, EJBs provide **persistence** services. These services range from simple connection pooling to managing the persistence automatically, and keeping the application developer from ever having to write SQL code.

Writing data-access code is error prone and time consuming unless a tool (such as an object/relational mapping framework) is used. The EJB specification recognizes this fact, when it says of EJBs that do not take advantage of automatic persistence:

> *"We expect that most enterprise beans will be created by application development tools which will encapsulate data access in components".*

Consider some of the issues involved if we create the data access code for an application:

❑ How do we generate updates to the database optimized for the data that has changed?

❑ How do we sufficiently test these dynamically generated updates?

❑ How do we handle the situation where complicated graphs of objects must be synchronized with the database?

❑ How do we handle mappings of data types to different databases?

❑ How do we map relationships between Java objects to relationships between database tables?

❑   How do we maintain the consistency of the persistent representation, when the updates can come not only from other J2EE servers in a cluster but also from non-J2EE servers accessing the database and even from non-Java processes? (For the curious, this is typically handled through a technique called two-phase commit and implemented by a protocol called XA. While discussing this technology is beyond the scope of this book, you will find a detailed description of how transactions are handled by EJBs in the next chapters.)

None of these tasks are impossible, or even difficult for a qualified programmer; but they may add no value to your product, and simply be an unnecessary cost. The persistence services provided by an EJB execution environment can make the difference between success and failure in a real-world project that has time, budget, and personnel constraints.

Declarative Transactions

It's true that the JDBC API provides functionality to manage a transaction, so this could conceivably be done from a servlet or JSP. However, transaction management can be complex, particularly if multiple data-access components or multiple data sources are involved. On the other hand, complex transactions with EJBs can be managed without any coding.

The Java API related to transaction management, **Java Transaction API (JTA)** provides a standard interface between a transaction manager, an application server, a resource manager, and an application or application component, but almost none of this API is intended for use by application programmers.

A second API related to transaction management, **Java Transaction Service (JTS)** is even less likely to be directly useful to an application programmer. This specification is intended for vendors who need to map a JTA implementation to the CORBA Object Transaction Service 1.1 specification. Now that we're aware of these APIs, we can safely forget about them.

Declarative Security

In a real-world application, access to data and business logic functionality must be secure. It is possible for the developer to provide security using servlets or JSP pages, but this is a complex and error-prone task. If multiple servlets or JSP pages use classes with common business logic, a custom security framework would need to be provided by the application. Fortunately, access to EJB components can be regulated without any coding.

> *The EJB security model has been criticized for its simplicity. For example, it is unable to specify security based on instances of EJBs (only classes). For this reason, EJB developers tend to rely on security provided at the web level, which is a mature and proven approach.*

Error Handling

Few applications of any size will be successful without a clear and consistent error-handling framework. The EJB specification clearly defines how errors affect transactions, client results, server logging, and component recovery.

Component Framework for Business Logic

Developing software that represents complex business logic requires a large investment in an enterprise's resources. Realizing this, software developers have for decades been pursuing the goal of software reuse. EJBs are server-side components that can be used simultaneously by many different clients. If the business logic embodied in your application requires a large development investment, this is an ideal way to enable maximum returns.

Scalability

The EJB specification requires the application developer to follow certain rules in coding business-logic components. These rules are designed to allow application servers to manage large numbers of simultaneous clients, all of which are making significant demands on business-logic components and data-access components. Components are also designed to run on multiple Java Virtual Machines and the application server is enabled to work in a cluster (across multiple machines) and to recover from the failure of any clustered node.

Although web servers can be made to scale, web containers are not designed specifically to scale components with business logic and data-access code, unlike EJB containers. Chapter 15 discusses how many users can share instances of a service session EJB (known as pooling), conserving system resources. The equivalent service component on the web tier, a JavaBean, will not be pooled without custom programming. Furthermore, Chapter 16 discusses how an EJB container can use various strategies to cache entity data. There is no equivalent mechanism available for servlets or JSP pages.

Portability

Although the application developer can provide some of the same services as an EJB container, each of those services must be developed and integrated separately. If a changing business environment imposes new requirements on an application, those new requirements must be met with custom code (or purchased technology that must be integrated by hand). Since EJBs are written to an industry-standard API, they can often be run unmodified in a new J2EE-compliant application server.

Manageability

The basic problem with managing web components that contain business logic and perform data access is that they are not visible to management tools. For instance, consider the problem of controlling who can change a customer's credit line. To secure this functionality with EJBs, you simply use the declarative access control that the EJB container provides to manage access, add, or remove users from the appropriate role. To secure the equivalent application developed exclusively with web components, you must secure access to every user interface (that is, web view) that provides this functionality.

How the Container Provides Services

It helps to have some idea of the mechanisms by which the EJB container provides its various services to EJB components:

❑ There are clearly defined responsibilities between the various parts of an application using Enterprise JavaBeans components – the client, the EJB container, the EJB component and the persistence manager. The definition of these responsibilities is formally known as a **contract**.

❑ The services that the container provides are defined in such a way that they are **orthogonal** to the component. In other words, security, persistence, transactions, and other services are separate from the Java files that implement the business logic of the component.

❑ The container **interposes** on every call to an EJB component so that it can provide its services. In other words, the container puts itself between the client and the component on every single business-method call.

Contracts

A contract is simply a statement of responsibilities between different layers of the software. If each layer of the software follows the rules of its respective contract, it can work effectively with the layer above and the layer below, without knowing anything else about those layers.

This means that we can mix and match layers without rewriting our code, as long as we stick to the contract, and nothing but the contract. There are three well-defined layers in the EJB 2.0 specification: client, bean, and container. Because of the contracts between these layers, our bean can run in different containers, unmodified. Provided there is strict adherence to the contract on all sides, our client can access different beans, unmodified:

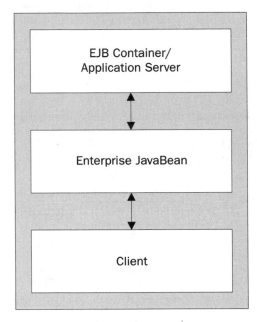

Of course, the contracts are written with more than portability in mind. The rules are carefully crafted to make it possible for server vendors to build their servers on many different technologies, with many different capabilities. We can follow these relatively simple rules and patterns to take advantage of the services and capabilities of any of these application servers.

What kinds of rules are there? We'll cover them in detail in later chapters, but the main ones are:

❑   The developer of an EJB component (also known as the 'bean provider') must implement the business methods (any method that provides access to the logic of the application) in the implementation class.

❑   For entity beans using Container-Managed Persistence (CMP), the bean provider must provide definitions for abstract methods that represent the CMP fields of the beans: (getName()/setName(), etc.).

❑   The bean provider must define the enterprise bean's home and remote (or local) interfaces for session and entity beans (this is not needed for message-driven beans).

- For session beans, the bean provider must implement the container callbacks defined in the `javax.ejb.SessionBean` interface.

- For entity beans, the bean provider must implement the container callbacks defined in the `javax.ejb.EntityBean` interface.

- For a message-driven bean, the bean provider must implement the `onMessage()` method.

- The bean provider must not use programming practices that would interfere with the container's runtime management of the enterprise bean instances. For example, the specification explicitly prohibits creating threads in an EJB or accessing the file system. These limitations make the EJBs more portable as they must use the services provided by the EJB container to create such functionality.

Services

The EJB container provides the bean programmer with services. For the most part, the bean programmer just needs to follow the rules to take advantage of these services. The developer can simply tell the container the details of what should be provided. This is known as **declarative semantics**, and is one of EJBs most useful features. Declarative information is specified in an XML file known as the **deployment descriptor**. For many features, even this declarative information is not necessary, and the container will provide the feature without any work by the bean programmer.

One of the services available in every application server with an EJB container is transaction management. Transactions keep data consistent in the face of data conflict or failure. The container will let an application developer indicate – without any programming – how changes to the enterprise's data by the client must be treated to ensure consistency. Another important service provided by EJB containers is automatic persistence. This is an optional feature for the bean developer, but it offers many projects a valuable alternative to writing thousands of lines of data access code.

Containers provide many other services, including:

- Declarative security, which protects EJB resources from unauthorized access

- Resource management (such as connection pooling) and concurrency control, which make access from multiple users and data transfer to multiple sources easier

- Error handling, which makes it easier for the application developer to be productive

- Communication services, which make remote access easier

> The container developer, not the business-logic programmer, implements all these services. This is possible because the business logic components – the Enterprise JavaBeans – follow the contract defined in the specification.

Containers may provide optional services. An important option for large projects is clustering for fail-over and scalability. Management tools are not part of the EJB specification, but are provided as an optional component by server vendors, and can be important to the success or failure of any project. The possible optional services are limited only by a vendor's imagination. As the Java APIs expand to envelop the world, some of these additional services will likely become standardized. One example is the Java Management Extensions API (JMX), which provides a lowest common denominator for management implementations.

Interposition

An application developer follows the rules of the bean-development contract, and the container is then able to provide system-level services, but how is this possible? There is a lot to it. Writing a quality EJB container is a difficult task but there is one central concept that makes it easier for the bean developer to understand what is happening, **interposition**.

Think back to Chapter 3, where we covered RMI. In RMI the stub interposes between the client interface and the remote object to provide marshaling and network transport. In the same way, the EJB container interposes between the client business interface and the EJB business logic to provide services such as transactions, security, error handling, and persistence management.

A typical method call from a remote client to an EJB goes like this:

- ❑ The client makes a call on an RMI stub
- ❑ The RMI stub interposes on the method call in order to marshal parameters and send the information across the network
- ❑ A skeleton on the server side un-marshals the parameters and delivers them to the EJB container

The method call hasn't reached the business logic yet as there is a second interposition. Some of the following steps may be optimized away, but the logical structure is:

- ❑ The container will examine the security credentials of the caller of that method
- ❑ It will start or join with any required transactions
- ❑ It will make any necessary calls to persistence functions
- ❑ It will trigger various callbacks to allow the EJB component to acquire resources
- ❑ It will call the actual business method
- ❑ Once the business method is called, the container will do some more work with transactions, persistence, callbacks, and so on
- ❑ Finally, the results of the business method, be it returned data or an exception, will be sent back to the remote client

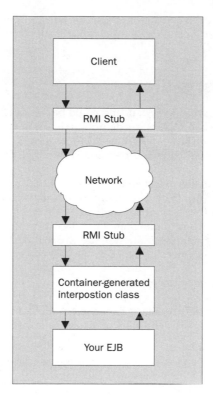

This explains the reason behind one of the less intuitive parts of EJB technology. Application developers can write an interface that declares business logic functions (represented by the RMI Stub in the figure above), and write a class that implements those functions. To get a clear picture of the difference between the Remote and the Home interface, think of the Home interface as a factory; it is the entry point to the EJB, and is the only entity that can be reached from the outside.

Once we get an instance of the Home interface, we ask it to create or locate EJBs. These EJBs are then accessible through their Remote interface. However, the class isn't required to implement the interface. In fact, the programmer is strongly discouraged from implementing that interface in their business logic class in order to avoid situations where you could directly access the EJB instance instead of going through the proxy generated by the container.

> *The new local interface in the 2.0 specification works in the same manner as the remote interface described above except without the need to use RMI stubs and skeletons as the call is in the same VM.*

Working with EJBs

The Enterprise JavaBeans specification is written for a number of different audiences, but we are concerned with only three of them:

- ❑ The client developer
- ❑ The EJB developer (also referred to as 'bean provider')
- ❑ The EJB container developer

We will not address the technical requirements of the specification from the container developer's point of view but we will take a closer look at those aspects of EJB development that are directly relevant to the server-side programmer.

The Client Developer's VIew

A client is any user of an Enterprise JavaBean, and could be a Java client-side application, a CORBA app, a servlet, or even another EJB. A server-side programmer designing a web application, or using a servlet to mediate communication with an EJB, needs to understand how EJBs are accessed and used. In large projects, it is quite likely that the web programmer and the EJB programmer are different people.

The client programmer has a smaller set of concerns than a bean developer with regard to using EJBs. They need to know how to find or create the bean, how to use its methods, and how to release its resources. A client always uses the same procedure for object creation, lookup, method invocation, and removal, regardless of how an EJB is implemented or what function it provides to the client. The client doesn't need to worry about the implementation of the EJB, callbacks that the EJB container will make on the EJB, or the nature of the services provided to the EJB.

Session and entity beans have the following interfaces:

❑ A **home interface,** primarily for lifecycle operations such as creating, finding, and removing EJBs. The home interface isn't associated with a particular bean instance, just with a type of bean.

❑ A **remote interface** is for business methods. Logically, it represents the client's view of a particular bean instance on the server. The remote interface also provides some infrastructure methods associated with a bean instance, rather than a bean type. Alternatively, the bean may use a **local interface**, which is similar to the remote interface, but is only accessible by EJBs in the same deployment unit.

It is important to understand that session and entity beans must have a home interface, but it's optional whether they have either a remote interface or a local interface (or both).

A client programmer will acquire a home interface through JNDI (which is explained in Chapter 2). This home interface can then be used to:

❑ Create or find an instance of a bean, which will be represented to the client as a remote interface

❑ Execute business methods on that instance of the bean

❑ Get a serializable reference to the bean, known as a **handle**

❑ Remove the bean

The removal of a bean can mean radically different things depending on the type of bean and it's important to be clear on these differences. In the case of a stateful session bean, it means the developer has finished using it. The server can then release the resources associated with that bean. In the case of a stateless session bean, it means the same thing – although the server probably wasn't consuming any resources for the bean because it lacked state to begin with. Since stateless bean instances are pooled, it could also mean that the instance that's in use is returned to the pool of available session beans. In the case of an entity bean, removing the bean means removing its object view representation in the persistent data store – in other words, deleting it from the database.

Let's work through the process step-by-step. We will use an example of a client application that wants to call a `placeOrder()` method on an `OrderManagement` stateless session bean. This example is meant only to give an idea of the types of classes we will be writing and, as such, its functionality is rather limited. Even so, in order to gain some practical experience we will deploy the bean in an application server and run the client.

Start by creating a directory `%BOOK_HOME%\Ch14\OrderManagement\` in which we will create the application. Let's now take a look at the procedures involved with developing the client code. Our EJB classes will be in a package `orderMgmt`, so we need to import it, as well as the other classes our client uses:

```
import orderMgmt.*;
import java.util.Properties;
import javax.naming.Context;
import javax.naming.InitialContext;
```

Next, we begin the actual `Client` class:

```
public class Client {
  public static void main(String[] args) {
    try {
```

First, the client will need to be authenticated in some server-specific way. If the client is a web application, for example, the authentication may use SSL. Second, the client will need to get a properly initialized `InitialContext` as the starting point for the JNDI lookup. If the client is an EJB executing in a container, and the EJB it would like to reference is declared as a resource in the XML deployment descriptor, the `InitialContext` will be ready to use as soon as it is instantiated.

If the client is executing outside of a container, the `InitialContext` will require certain server-dependent properties. These can be provided in code or using a resource file. The initialization of the context will be specific to your application server or JNDI provider. For our example, we'll do it programmatically using values appropriate for WebLogic Server 6.1:

```
        Properties prop = new Properties();
        prop.put(Context.INITIAL_CONTEXT_FACTORY,
                 "weblogic.jndi.WLInitialContextFactory");
        prop.put(Context.PROVIDER_URL, "t3://localhost:7001");
        Context ctx = new InitialContext(prop);
```

Now, let's find the home interface for the `OrderManagement` bean. The first step is to look it up using the initial context we have just set up. The name we use to look up the bean depends on the type of client. If the client is an EJB executing in a container, and the EJB it would like to reference is declared as a resource in the XML deployment descriptor, then the name will be a sub-context of the name `java:comp/env/`. Furthermore the specification recommends, but does not require, that names of EJBs be bound in the subcontext `ejb`. Therefore, we might look up the home interface like this:

```
    Object objref = ctx.lookup("java:comp/env/ejb/OrderManagement");
```

From the perspective of a client executing outside of a container, the bean can be bound to any name in the JNDI namespace. For our client we look the home interface up like this:

```
        Object objref = ctx.lookup("OrderManagement");
```

The client JNDI namespace may include the home interfaces of EJBs from multiple application servers located anywhere on a network. In general, the client doesn't need to know the location of the EJB or the identity of its server; it doesn't need to know anything but the name to which the bean's home interface is bound.

Next, we need to cast this home interface reference to the `OrderManagementHome` class. This isn't quite as simple as an ordinary Java language cast. To ensure that the client works with any underlying communication protocol, the specification recommends that the client use RMI-IIOP via the `narrow()` method of `javax.rmi.PortableRemoteObject`. IIOP in particular does not support simple casting:

```
OrderManagementHome home =
        (OrderManagementHome)javax.rmi.PortableRemoteObject.narrow(
                            objref, OrderManagementHome.class);
```

We use the home interface to create an instance of the `OrderManagement` class. It's important to understand that this instance is created on the server. All we have on the client is a remote reference to it (in other words, the client has a stub). The code looks like this:

```
OrderManagement orderManagement = home.create();
```

Now, we can use the business methods defined in the `OrderManagement` bean. In this case, we want to call the `placeOrder()` method. Let's assume that it takes three parameters: customer name, product name, and quantity. The code might look like this:

```
orderManagement.placeOrder("Cedric",
                    "J2EE Server Programming", 1000);
```

Finally, we can signal to the server that we are done using this instance of the `OrderManagement` bean. We could do this using the lifecycle home interface, but it is actually more convenient to call a utility `remove()` method defined in every EJB remote interface, like this:

```
        orderManagement.remove();
    } catch (Exception e) {
        e.printStackTrace();
    }
  }
}
```

Using Enterprise JavaBeans technology from the client can really be this simple and writing a client that uses distributed functionality with EJBs is only moderately more difficult than writing a local client. Save the code for the `Client` class in `%BOOK_HOME%\OrderManagement\Client.java`. We can't compile this class yet because we haven't created the `orderMgmt` package that contains the EJB classes. The bean provider creates these classes, and we look at their view of the EJB now.

The Bean Provider's View

The main responsibility of the bean programmer is to write business logic. As much as possible, the Enterprise JavaBeans specification tries to relieve bean programmers of any system-level tasks. In exchange, the bean programmer must structure their code in a particular way.

No matter what type of EJB the programmer is writing – stateless session, stateful session, message-driven or entity – there are typically three primary Java class files and one XML file that must be created. Two of these Java files are the interfaces discussed in the previous section: the home interface and the remote or local interface. The third file is the class that contains the actual business logic, as well as some required callback methods. Finally, the XML file, called the **deployment descriptor** and named `ejb-jar.xml`, contains structural information about the bean. It declares the bean's external dependencies and specifies certain information about how services such as transactions and security should work.

There may also be additional Java classes that support the operation of the bean; helper classes that implement business logic, or, in the case of an entity bean with a compound primary key, a class that represents that key.

All these files are packaged up into a JAR – the standard Java deployment unit that is essentially a zip file. There can be many beans in a single JAR file, but each JAR file will contain only one `ejb-jar.xml` file. The XML deployment descriptor must go into a specific directory (so the EJB container will know where to look for it). That directory is META-INF, which must be in all capital letters.

> *A common source of frustration for beginning EJB component developers is to put their deployment descriptor in* `Meta-inf` *or* `meta-inf`.

The rest of the files go in directories appropriate to their packages. For the `OrderManagement` example bean on which we are currently working, the structure of our JAR file will be as follows:

```
META-INF\
          ejb-jar.xml

orderMgmt\
          OrderManagement.class
          OrderManagementHome.class
          OrderManagementBean.class
```

There are many ways to create this JAR file, ranging from specialized tools, to zip-file utilities, to the standard JAR tool in the JDK. Use whatever method you prefer; the result will be the same. We will create the JAR file using the JDK tool.

There will also be server-dependent information that needs to be specified when the bean is deployed. For instance, logical resource names and security roles will need to be mapped to actual entities in a specific operating environment. Fields in entity beans using container-managed persistence may need to be mapped to specific database table columns. Exactly what additional information needs to be specified will vary, but the specification is written so that EJBs can be developed without considering this.

Most likely, an EJB developer will be working from a design that includes the business-logic interface they should provide. This interface is a good starting point from which to build an Enterprise JavaBean. The methods in that interface will probably correspond to the methods in the EJB remote interface, with one difference: because EJBs can be accessed remotely, every method in the remote interface (and the home interface) must be declared to throw `java.rmi.RemoteException`. Since `RemoteException` is a checked exception, this ensures that the client will be aware of issues such as the potential for network failure.

The remote interface of an EJB must extend `javax.ejb.EJBObject`, which extends `java.rmi.Remote`. `EJBObject` declares some common methods that relate to any instance of an EJB:

```
package javax.ejb;

public interface javax.ejb.EJBObject extends java.rmi.Remote {
```

```
EJBHome getEJBHome()
        throws java.rmi.RemoteException;

Handle getHandle()
        throws java.rmi.RemoteException;

Object getPrimaryKey
        throws java.rmi.RemoteException;

boolean isIdentical(EJBObject obj)
        throws java.rmi.RemoteException;

void remove()
        throws java.rmi.RemoteException, javax.ejb.RemoveException;

}
```

For a local interface, the only difference is that the methods do not throw RemoteException *in their signature and that they extend* EJBLocalObject *instead of* EJBObject.

The EJB developer, in general, doesn't need to write code to support these methods: they are available to the client developer in every bean that they use. Some won't make sense in certain contexts, in which case calling them results in an exception.

Here is a class diagram of the relationship between the three classes, using our OrderManagement interface for the business interface. Note that java.rmi.Remote is a tagging interface with no methods:

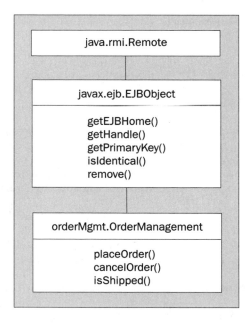

Let's continue with our example order management bean. We already know that there is a `placeOrder()` method and we'll also develop `cancelOrder()` and `isShipped()` methods. We'll make the unrealistic (but simple to implement) assumption that a customer could identify an order by indicating the product ordered. The EJB's remote interface would look like this:

```
package orderMgmt;

public interface OrderManagement extends javax.ejb.EJBObject {
    void placeOrder(String custName, String prodName, int quantity)
      throws java.rmi.RemoteException;

    void cancelOrder(String custName, String prodName)
      throws java.rmi.RemoteException;

    boolean isShipped(String custName, String prodName)
      throws java.rmi.RemoteException;
}
```

Create a directory `orderMgmt` to hold the classes in our `orderMgmt` package and save this code as `%BOOK_HOME%\Ch14\OrderManagement\orderMgmt\OrderManagement.java`.

Notice that the application developer *never implements this interface.* You may wonder who does implement it; the answer is that the EJB container does. There are several ways that a container may implement this interface, but think of it generating and compiling Java code in the background when you deploy your bean. The code that it generates is where the container provides services such as transaction management and security. This code is where the interposition we discussed earlier actually happens.

Of course, the application developer implements the interface in the sense that they must provide the business logic in an implementation class. However, they need not ever write:

```
OrderManagementBean implements OrderManagement
```

Moreover, developers are strongly discouraged from doing so. This is the container's privilege.

The next task in writing the order management bean is to write the home interface, which must extend `javax.ejb.EJBHome`. `EJBHome` looks like this:

```
package javax.ejb;

public interface EJBHome extends java.rmi.Remote {

  EJBMetaData getEJBMetaData()
        throws java.rmi.RemoteException;

  HomeHandle getHomeHandle()
        throws java.rmi.RemoteException;

  void remove(Handle handle)
        throws java.rmi.RemoteException, javax.ejb.RemoveException;

  void remove(Object primaryKey)
        throws java.rmi.RemoteException, javax.ejb.RemoveException;
}
```

These methods are available to the client programmer, without any additional work by the EJB developer. The bean programmer will write a home interface, derived from this interface, which adds one or more methods depending on the type of bean. A stateful session bean will add one or more `create()` methods. An entity bean will add zero or more `create()` methods, and one or more `finder()` methods (these are explained in the chapter on entity beans). A stateless session bean, such as our order management bean, must define exactly one (parameterless) `create()` method.

Our `OrderManagement` EJB's home interface, which should be saved as `%BOOK_HOME%\Ch14\OrderManagement\orderMgmt\OrderManagementHome.java`, looks like this:

```
package orderMgmt;

public interface OrderManagementHome extends javax.ejb.EJBHome {
   OrderManagement create()
      throws java.rmi.RemoteException, javax.ejb.CreateException;
}
```

Most of the work in writing an EJB will be in developing the actual business logic. One class, often called the 'bean' class or 'implementation' class, is the central point for development of this business logic. Of course, like any Java class, this bean class may defer processing to other helper classes.

The specific structure of the bean class is dependent on the type of EJB. An entity bean must be derived from `javax.ejb.EntityBean`, a session bean must be derived from `javax.ejb.SessionBean`, and a message-driven bean will extend `javax.ejb.MessageDrivenBean`. The bean class must implement the callbacks defined in its respective interface – although those callback methods may often be left blank.

The bean class must have a `public` method named `ejbCreate()` (with matching arguments) corresponding to every `create()` method declared in the home interface. You can create as many overloaded versions of `ejbCreate()` as you need, just make sure you match them with `ejbPostCreate()` methods (which will be empty most of the time.) For a session bean, the return type will be `void`. For an entity bean, the return type will be the class of the primary key (we'll see more about this later). An entity bean must also implement a corresponding `ejbPostCreate()` method. For an entity bean with bean-managed persistence, methods must be implemented that correspond to the finder methods declared in the bean's home interface. Again, we'll discuss all these callbacks later. For the moment, as we are implementing a session bean here, we will use the session bean callbacks.

Finally, the bean class must have business logic methods corresponding to those that were declared in the bean's remote interface. The logic in these methods is the reason we create an EJB in the first place.

The structure of our order management bean class might look like this:

```
package orderMgmt;

import javax.ejb.SessionContext;

public class OrderManagementBean implements javax.ejb.SessionBean {

   public void placeOrder(String custName, String prodName, int quantity) {
      System.out.println("Order placed for " + quantity + " copies of " +
                         prodName + " to be shipped to " + custName);
   }

   public void cancelOrder(String custName, String prodName) {
      System.out.println("Order cancelled");
   }
```

```
   public boolean isShipped(String custName, String prodName) {
     System.out.println("Order shipped");
     return true;
   }

   public void ejbCreate() {
     System.out.println("ejbCreate() called");
   }

   public void ejbRemove() {
     System.out.println("ejbRemove() called");
   }

   public void ejbActivate() {
     System.out.println("ejbActivate() called");
   }

   public void ejbPassivate() {
     System.out.println("ejbPassivate() called");
   }

   public void setSessionContext(SessionContext ctx){
     System.out.println("setSessionContext() called");
   }
}
```

Note that, for this sample EJB, none of the methods contain any business logic. The methods do, however, output messages to the user. This is so that we can follow what methods are called, and when. Save the code as
`%BOOK_HOME%\Ch14\OrderManagement\orderMgmt\OrderManagementBean.java`.

The only part of our EJB that we haven't yet discussed is the deployment descriptor. As this is written in an XML format, it can easily be read and edited by programmers. In general, however, you will probably produce this file using a tool, perhaps one that comes with your chosen application server or IDE. As the deployment descriptor for this example is simple, we will create it by hand.

The various elements of the deployment descriptor are discussed in detail in the following chapters. Here, without further explanation, we present the XML deployment descriptor, `ejb-jar.xml`, for our simple `OrderManagement` example:

```
<!DOCTYPE ejb-jar PUBLIC '-//Sun Microsystems, Inc.//DTD Enterprise JavaBeans
2.0//EN' 'http://java.sun.com/j2ee/dtds/ejb-jar_2_0.dtd'>

<ejb-jar>
 <enterprise-beans>
   <session>
      <ejb-name>OrderManagement</ejb-name>
      <home>orderMgmt.OrderManagementHome</home>
      <remote>orderMgmt.OrderManagement</remote>
      <ejb-class>orderMgmt.OrderManagementBean</ejb-class>
      <session-type>Stateless</session-type>
      <transaction-type>Container</transaction-type>
   </session>
 </enterprise-beans>

 <assembly-descriptor>
```

```
    <container-transaction>
      <method>
        <ejb-name>OrderManagement</ejb-name>
        <method-name>*</method-name>
      </method>
      <trans-attribute>Required</trans-attribute>
    </container-transaction>
  </assembly-descriptor>
</ejb-jar>
```

We can develop and test this simple bean on the WebLogic application server for which there is a 30-day evaluation copy available for download at
http://commerce.bea.com/downloads/weblogic_server.jsp.

During installation, you will be presented with a number of options, but you can just accept the default values. You will also be prompted for a password to run the server, and a user name and password to start the Console (used to manage WebLogic). Make sure you make a note of these values, as you will need them later.

Once you have installed WebLogic, you should check that it is working. Start the WebLogic Server (if you are using Windows 2000 the command will have been added to the Start menu). Enter your password when prompted and, when the server has started, open your browser and navigate to http://localhost:7001/. If the installation of WebLogic was successful you will see something like:

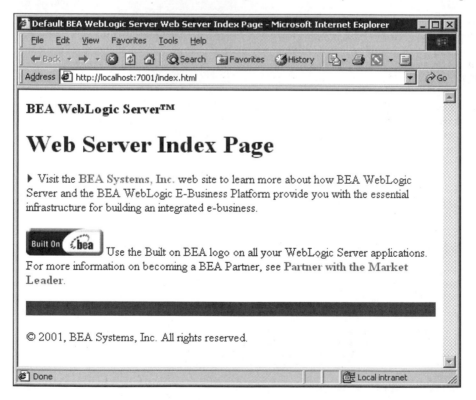

If you are using a server other than WebLogic, you will also need to make changes to the code for this example. You will need to refer to your application's documentation for instructions of how to do this.

At this stage, we have the following directory and file structure:

```
OrderManagement\
                Client.java
                orderMgmt\
                        OrderManagement.java
                        OrderManagementBean.java
                        OrderManagementHome.java
                META-INF\
                        ejb-jar.xml
```

We'll also need an additional deployment descriptor before we can deploy our bean to WebLogic. The `weblogic-ejb-jar.xml` file contains any references to external resources, clustering details, etc., relevant to the bean and is specific to WebLogic. For the case of our simple example, however, all this descriptor contains is the information specifying the JNDI name of the home class:

```
<!DOCTYPE weblogic-ejb-jar PUBLIC
        '-//BEA Systems, Inc.//DTD WebLogic 6.0.0 EJB//EN'
        'http://www.bea.com/servers/wls600/dtd/weblogic-ejb-jar.dtd'>

<weblogic-ejb-jar>
  <weblogic-enterprise-bean>
    <ejb-name>OrderManagement</ejb-name>
    <jndi-name>OrderManagement</jndi-name>
  </weblogic-enterprise-bean>
</weblogic-ejb-jar>
```

We are now ready to compile our classes. To compile the EJB classes we need to ensure that we include the `javax.ejb` package in our classpath. We can do this by including `%J2EE_HOME%\lib\j2ee.jar` in the classpath.

Run the following command from the `%BOOK_HOME%\Ch14\OrderManagement\` directory to create the classes for our EJB:

```
javac -classpath .;%J2EE_HOME%\lib\j2ee.jar orderMgmt\*.java
```

We now have the following files and directories that we will package into a JAR file:

```
OrderManagement\
                orderMgmt\
                        OrderManagement.class
                        OrderManagementHome.class
                        OrderManagementBean.class
                META-INF\
                        ejb-jar.xml
                        weblogic-ejb-jar.xml
```

To create the JAR file run the following command from the `%BOOK_HOME%\Ch14\OrderManagement\` directory:

```
jar cvf OrderManagement.jar META-INF/ orderMgmt/*.class
```

After we have developed a component, the next step to deploy it on the application server. We will walk through the process of deployment on WebLogic 6.1, which as our EJB is so simple, will be quite a quick process.

707

Start up the WebLogic Server, and then start the WebLogic console; you will be prompted for the user name and password you entered during installation:

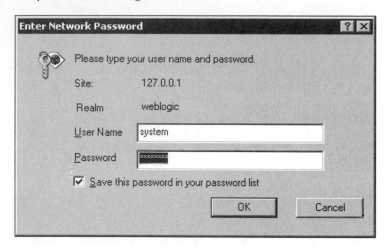

Once you've entered these you will be presented with the console home page:

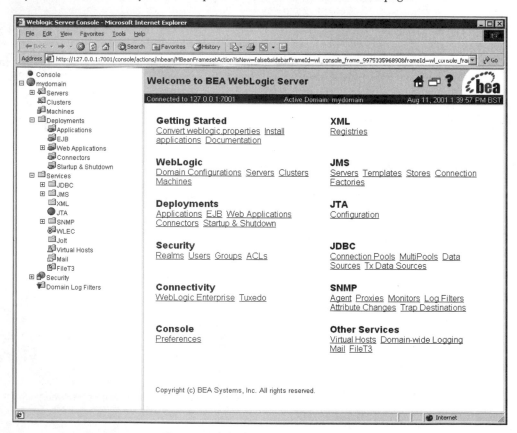

Click on EJB under the Deployments section, and then click Install a new EJB. Then click the Browse button and select the OrderManagement.jar that we created:

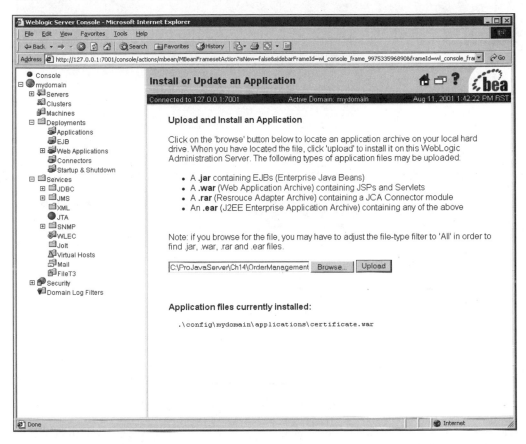

Then click Upload to deploy the JAR file on WebLogic; you will see a screen confirming the successful upload and installation of the application:

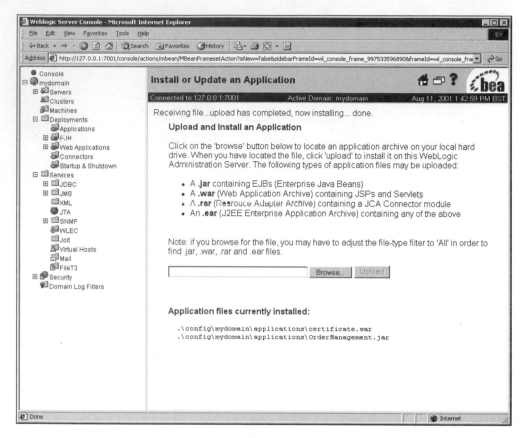

You can see at the bottom of this page that `OrderManagement.jar` is now listed as an installed application.

We're now ready to compile and run our client program. To compile the client, run the following command from `%BOOK_HOME%\Ch14\OrderManagement`:

```
javac -classpath
.;%J2EE_HOME%\lib\j2ee.jar;%BEA_HOME%\lib\weblogic.jar;OrderManagement.jar;
Client.java
```

We also need to have these classes in our classpath when we run the client. To run the client execute the following command:

```
java -classpath
;%J2EE_HOME%\lib\j2ee.jar;%BEA_HOME%\lib\weblogic.jar;OrderManagement.jar; Client
```

Ideally, you will want to have a separate client JAR file that contains only the needed classes: the home and the remote interfaces. For now, we'll simply add the `.jar` file of the EJB we just deployed to the classpath.

You should see something like:

```
Command Prompt                                                              _ □ ✕
Microsoft Windows 2000 [Version 5.00.2195]
(C) Copyright 1985-2000 Microsoft Corp.

C:\projavaserver\ch14\OrderManagement>jar cvf OrderManagement.jar META-INF/ orderMgmt/*.class
added manifest
ignoring entry META-INF/
adding: META-INF/ejb-jar.xml(in = 809) (out= 343)(deflated 57%)
adding: META-INF/weblogic-ejb-jar.xml(in = 362) (out= 200)(deflated 44%)
adding: orderMgmt/OrderManagement.class(in = 411) (out= 231)(deflated 43%)
adding: orderMgmt/OrderManagementBean.class(in = 1517) (out= 692)(deflated 54%)
adding: orderMgmt/OrderManagementHome.class(in = 289) (out= 200)(deflated 30%)

C:\projavaserver\ch14\OrderManagement>
```

The client program has run successfully, but hasn't output anything to screen. At first this might seem strange, after all we called the `placeOrder()` method, which includes the command:

```
System.out.println("Order placed for " + quantity + " copies of " +
                    prodName + " to be shipped to " + custName);
```

So we might expect to see output to the screen detailing the order that the client placed. However, the method is called on the EJB, which runs on the server, not the client. So, the `placeOrder()` method has been executed on the server. If we look at the command prompt that is running the WebLogic server we see that `placeOrder()` was indeed successfully executed:

```
Start Default Server                                                        _ □ ✕
er "myserver" for domain "mydomain">
<11-Aug-01 14:08:51 BST> <Notice> <Management> <Starting discovery of Managed Se
rver... This feature is on by default, you may turn this off by passing -Dweblog
ic.management.discover=false>
<11-Aug-01 14:09:07 BST> <Notice> <Management> <Application Poller not started f
or production server.>
<11-Aug-01 14:09:07 BST> <Notice> <WebLogicServer> <SSLListenThread listening on
 port 7002>
<11-Aug-01 14:09:07 BST> <Notice> <WebLogicServer> <ListenThread listening on po
rt 7001>
<11-Aug-01 14:09:08 BST> <Notice> <WebLogicServer> <Started WebLogic Admin Serve
r "myserver" for domain "mydomain" running in Production Mode>
setSessionContext() called
ejbCreate() called
Order placed for 1000 copies of J2EE Server Programming to be shipped to Cedric
```

We can also see that `setSessonContext()` and `ejbCreate()` are called by the EJB container. However, `ejbRemove()` does not appear to have been called despite the fact that we call `remove()` on the instance of the EJB in the client program. This is because it is up to the EJB container when it calls this method.

What an EJB Cannot Do

We've talked at length about the benefits of programming to the EJB specification if you are developing a transactional system. As application developers, we are relieved of system-level programming tasks. This is a great advantage for programmer productivity, application capability, and system reliability. Nevertheless, to really benefit, we must agree to work within the framework of EJB technology, and this means there are certain things we cannot do without losing some degree of portability. Specifically, the EJB 2.0 specification prohibits EJBs from doing the following:

❑   Using the synchronized keyword and synchronization primitives in general

❑   Using AWT or other graphic primitives

❑   Asking for input from the keyboard

❑   Usinghe java.io package

❑   Performing network operations such as accepting or listening on a socket

❑   Creating a ClassLoader

❑   Loading a native library

It is, however, unlikely that the typical application developer will run into these restrictions.

Some other, more common, programming techniques are also restricted. A typical application developer may well run into these restrictions, and will want to know the reason for the restrictions, and how their goal can be otherwise accomplished. As such, in the next few sections we'll examine some of these restrictions.

Threads or the Threading API

We can't use the synchronized keyword in any of your bean class methods. Synchronizing the accesses of multiple beans could lead to deadlock. (We can still use utility classes with synchronized methods, such as Vector.) We can't start, stop, suspend, or resume a thread.

According to the specification, allowing the bean to manage threads would decrease the EJB container's ability to properly manage the runtime environment. Some implementations associate transaction or security contexts with the thread; if the bean were to create additional threads, this mechanism might not work. Alternatively, consider the case where an application service provider wants to host beans from multiple customers on a few big Unix boxes. This ASP needs to monitor and control resource usage of each application, so that it can meet its quality of service guarantees. One such resource is thread usage. If a bean were allowed to create additional threads, this would be harder to manage and control.

The truth is that it should be possible, perhaps in some future version of the specification, to provide a special threading API. This API could allow the EJB component to retrieve threads from a container-managed pool of threads, subject to whatever limitations and management the container and the system administrator desired. There are no fundamental technical problems with this approach, but the specific API does not exist today in the EJB 2.0 specification.

In general, the application developer can trust the container to manage threads efficiently for them. Typically, there will be a pool of threads that are managed by the server. When a client request arrives, one of those pooled threads would be assigned to process that particular request. Explicit thread management shouldn't be necessary in most cases, and is unlikely to be possible in any case.

What about when the business logic for a single request requires parallel processing of several independent paths for efficient operation? For example, let's say that before we return an answer from our business method, we need to get information from an ERP system, a legacy sales management system, and a Lotus Notes server. Each of these systems takes ten seconds to process a request, and none of them depends on data from any of the others. Calling them in parallel might take around ten seconds. Calling them in series will require at least thirty. Unfortunately, there is no good answer for this situation in the current version of the specification.

AWT

EJBs cannot use the AWT to display information or to input information from a keyboard.

It's very unlikely that an application server would allow direct interaction between your EJB and the keyboard or monitor. An application developer who wanted to do this should reconsider their understanding of the separation between the GUI and the business logic layers.

Act as a Network Server

This means we can't listen, accept, or multicast on a socket. It doesn't mean we can't use sockets at all (a common misconception) – we *can* use a socket as a client. If the EJB were to act as a network server, it would interfere with the container's ability to use it as a business logic component. If we need to serve files, we use an appropriate environment, such as a servlet container.

Write to Static Fields

This is a hard one for many programmers to let go of. There are at least two problems with writing to static fields. First, we would need to protect them against concurrent accesses, which would violate the rule about thread synchronization. Second, static fields are only visible in one Java JVM. But many EJB containers will utilize multiple virtual machines for reasons of performance or reliability, and sometimes those virtual machines will be on multiple physical machines. There is no mechanism to propagate the update of a static field. This doesn't mean we can't use static fields at all: they just need to be read-only. We should probably declare any static field as `final` to enforce this requirement. Instead of writable static fields, we should use an appropriate shared resource, like a database.

The java.io Package

The specification states the following:

> *"The file system APIs are not well-suited for business components to access data. Business components should use a resource manager API, such as JDBC API, to store data."*

This is certainly true. File systems do not provide support for transactions, for instance. Another problem is that we cannot portably depend on a specific file-system structure – or even the existence of a file system at all (What if the EJB container is embedded in a database?). If we want to load a resource, we should use the Java API method `java.lang.Class.getResourceAsStream()`. If we want to load or store data, we use a database or the equivalent.

Load a Native Library

According to the specification, this is for security reasons. Any time we load a native library, we have portability concerns as well.

What if we absolutely need native code for some reason? Actually, how to develop any type of resource for your EJBs to access is currently under-specified. Look for a solution to this problem in form of the Client Connectivity Interface API, which is currently part of the Java Community Process (see http://jcp.org/ for more details).

Use 'this' as an Argument or Return Value

This restriction certainly needs some clarification. We can't return a `this` reference of our bean class to the client, or pass it as a parameter to a method call to another bean. The reason is that all interactions with the bean must pass through the interposition class that we discussed earlier. This doesn't mean that we can't pass the reference to the bean instance reference to a helper class; we can and probably will. The helper class is considered part of the bean class, and doesn't need to go through the interposition class.

By the way, this is one of two reasons that we shouldn't implement the remote interface in our bean class. If it doesn't implement the interface, it can't be accidentally passed as a parameter or return value for a method expecting that remote interface. (The other reason not to implement the remote interface is that it's bad form to have to provide useless, empty implementations of the methods in `javax.ejb.EJBObject`.)

Instead of passing the `this` reference, pass the result of `SessionContext.getEJBObject()` or `EntityContext.getEJBObject()`.

Loopback Calls

We can't, in the case of session beans, and we probably shouldn't, in the case of entity beans, use loopback calls. Loopback calls are situations where EJB A calls EJB B, and EJB B then calls EJB A. Session beans are designed to be non-reentrant. Any time a call comes to them while they are processing another call, an exception is thrown. If you think about it, this isn't such a serious limitation on session beans. A stateless session bean will never be involved in a loopback, because a new instance will be used for every method call. A stateful session bean shouldn't be referred to by any other EJB, but only by the client. A re-entrant call means that the client called it simultaneously from two different threads in the same transaction. Entity beans should not be designed to use loopback calls if possible, because:

❑ The entity bean programmer must design the entity bean with this possibility in mind

❑ The container cannot distinguish a legal loopback from an illegal concurrent call in the same transaction context

We can probably get whatever effect we're looking for without requiring loopback calls.

EJB Components on the Web

The decision to use EJB technology in a web application may be made based on the requirements of the application for transactions, persistence, security, scalability, and so on. However, deciding on technology is only the first step. How should such a web application be structured? A web application can maximize its flexibility and modularity by using EJBs as part of a classic **model-view-controller (MVC)** design. This pattern for building user interfaces originated in the Smalltalk world, and has found widespread applicability in the design of countless projects.

> **A design pattern is an arrangement of classes, their responsibilities, and their relationships that serves as a reusable solution to a particular design problem.**

For more information see:

❑ Sun's own J2EE site at
http://developer.java.sun.com/developer/technicalArticles/J2EE/patterns/PatternsIntroduction.html

❑ The Server Side at http://www.theserverside.com/patterns/index.jsp

There are three classes of objects in the MVC design pattern:

❑ **The model:**
This is the data and business-logic component (sometimes known as the application object or business object, depending on the context). A model can serve multiple views.

❑ **The view:**
This is the presentation component, also known as the user-interface component. There might be many views providing different presentations of a single model.

❑ **The controller:**
This is the component that responds to user input. The controller translates user-interface events into changes to the model, and then defines the way the user-interface reacts to those events. In some versions of MVC, the view and the controller are collapsed into a single entity.

These three classes of objects are not components in the sense that EJBs are components: they are **logical divisions of functionality**. The aim of using these divisions to design a web application is to decouple the business logic, the presentation logic, and the web site design. There are at least four advantages to this:

❑ The application will be more resilient in the face of change. A web page's design can be changed without knowledge of either business logic or site structure. Business logic or the data model can be changed without knowledge of web page design or site structure. Site structure can change without affecting business logic or the data model. A new type of interface, such as a wireless application, can be added simply by replacing the view.

❑ Business logic programmers, web site designers, and graphic artists can work independently. A likely point of failure in any large programming project is miscommunication among team members. If the elements of the project are decoupled, less communication is necessary and the project's people can work on what they do best.

❑ The separation of business logic, presentation logic, and web site design encourages the development of specifications and clear documentation of the code.

❑ The most expensive resources, such as experienced technical developers, are free to concentrate on the most complex part of the application.

In this architecture, the model component should often be implemented using EJB components. The motivation for this is that EJBs execute in a container that provides system-level services to the application developer. These services are not available outside the container, so model functionality – data access and business logic – that occurs in a servlet, JSP page, or JavaBean component would not be able to take advantage of these services.

The view component can be implemented using JSP pages. The technique of using JSP pages to separate business logic and presentation logic (with JavaBeans and tag libraries) was discussed earlier in this book. In a highly structured application, these JSP pages will relate only to the display of model data.

The controller component is implemented using a combination of a servlet or JSP page, possibly an EJB, and some helper classes. Using a controller in web application design is a valuable concept that overcomes many of the problems inherent in developing web applications. The controller component's servlet or JSP page receives all requests for application URLs. This first part of the controller, sometimes called a 'front component', can ensure that security is uniformly applied, application state is initialized, and important workflow isn't bypassed. Using this application design means that it's easy to prevent someone reaching a page out of sequence.

The next phase of the controller component translates the web request into generic application 'events'. This is important to remove from other application components any dependency on the specifics of web protocols (such as HTTP). It would be possible to skip this step, but this would prevent subsequent components from being reused in different contexts.

The final phase of the controller component is a JavaBean proxy (not an EJB), which may forward the generic application events to the Enterprise JavaBean controller. This controller is responsible for any update to the application's transactional data, accessed through EJB components. This EJB controller returns a notification of any changes in the model to the JavaBean proxy. This proxy can then notify the relevant JSP views that the model has been updated.

Since the view component is decoupled from the model and the controller components, it can be replaced for different clients. For instance, one client may require an HTML document be returned to it, while another client may require an XML document. JSP pages that generate HTML or XML may be chosen dynamically in this architecture.

The following diagram describes a basic implementation of a model-view-controller implementation for a web site:

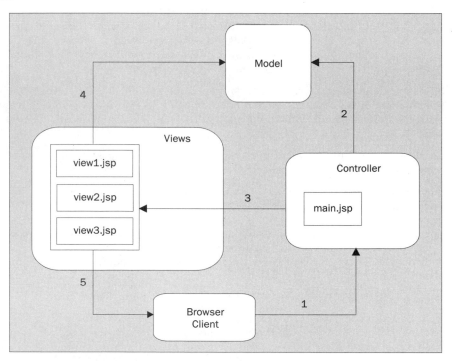

The browser client makes an HTTP request (GET or POST) [1]. All such requests go to the 'front component,' which in this case is a JSP page called main. The controller implementation (which can be a JavaBean, an EJB, or a combination) updates the model if necessary by forwarding the user-interface event, possibly in a transformed or normalized form [2]. The controller selects a view for display [3], which then updates itself against the model [4]. The view's output is returned to the client [5].

We'll look at an example of this model-view-controller architecture in Chapter 18, where a web interface is provided for the manufacturing example that we begin to develop in the next chapter.

> *Sun also provides an example of this architecture in its J2EE Blueprints document, in the form of an e-commerce site that sells pets on the web. Sun's version adds two additional layers of abstraction, by introducing a layer that translates web events into application events, and by providing event notification architecture between the model and the views (which cache some model data). If you are interested in exploring this topic beyond what is presented in this book, you can download the Blueprints document from Sun's web site at http://java.sun.com/j2ee/blueprints.*

Client-Tier Access to EJBs

Sometimes the presentation logic and workflow are handled on the client tier, as in the case of a Visual Basic application. Such an application might still implement the model-view-controller pattern on the client side, but there would not necessarily be a need to provide this level of structure on the server. There might still be a need to take advantage of services that an EJB container can provide. In the cases where web services are not needed, a client application will probably access EJBs directly.

In the simplest case, a client can access an Enterprise JavaBean remotely using RMI. This is certainly the case for Java GUI clients. A client written in a language other than Java can also access an EJB directly using IIOP (or Internet Inter-ORB Protocol, which is a standard protocol that allows CORBA Object Request Brokers (ORBs) to interoperate).

> *For this to happen the application server must also function as a CORBA ORB. IIOP communication transport is made mandatory in the EJB 2.0 draft specification, and all compliant application servers will have ORB functionality.*

Another possibility that provides maximum flexibility in terms of client access is a model EJB whose data is transformed by a 'view' servlet. The Servlet API provides for servlets that are capable of sending and receiving arbitrary data in a 'request/response' format. A client that requires that a particular format be used to communicate with the server can use such a servlet to mediate communications with the EJBs it needs:

So when would this direct access architecture be appropriate (with or without a mediating 'view' object)? This is the design that would be used to implement a client-server application. Choosing between direct access to EJBs and web access to EJBs is often the same as choosing between a 'thin-client' web app and a 'fat-client' (but still three-tier) client-server app. Many factors will influence this decision, such as client-interface requirements and application-distribution issues.

One rule of thumb is that Internet access (or any distributed access) by a large group of users will typically indicate that a web application is required, and access to enterprise data should be mediated by a view component and a controller component on the web tier. Another rule of thumb is that users on a local network will frequently expect a level of client services that may require a stand-alone GUI client, rather than a web browser; this stand alone GUI can access the Enterprise JavaBeans tier directly. Java applets are the wildcard, combining the distribution advantages of a web application with the presentation abilities of a stand alone GUI. Rather than call a method on an EJB directly using RMI, they will sometimes access EJBs through a servlet, using HTTP to bypass corporate firewalls.

Of course, there's nothing to stop us from directly accessing an EJB from a servlet to provide a simple web page, rather than using the model-view-controller architecture discussed above. If we have a web application of limited scope, and an existing EJB that we want to reuse, this approach can be appropriate. In addition, if we have a web application with limited presentation and navigation needs, but heavy business logic and data access requirements, we might find ourselves directly accessing an EJB from a servlet or a JSP page's helper class. Before we take this approach in a web application, we should consider carefully if there is any chance for the scope of the project to increase – now or in the future.

Design of the EJB Tier

Up until this point, the discussion about design of applications using Enterprise JavaBeans has essentially ignored the design of the EJB tier itself. In developing the EJB components for an application, we are essentially implementing a model of our enterprise. The design of this tier should be largely independent of the design of the web tier or the client tier. This independence promotes reusability of the business logic and data access components, which in many systems are the most difficult and expensive to develop. It also allows presentation logic to change independently of the business logic. This is an important design goal for most systems, because presentation logic tends to be more volatile than business logic.

UML Use Cases

Unified Modelling Language (UML) is the standard language for expressing the model of software systems. **Use cases** are a subset of UML that express the functionality the software should deliver, as perceived by external **actors** (something outside the software, such as a person or another software system). A single use case specifies one complete function, such as 'place an order' or 'submit an employee evaluation'. Use cases describe what to do, but not how to do it. How they are actually implemented by the software is unimportant at this stage of the design process.

> *Currently, there is no direct support for Enterprise JavaBeans components in the UML. However, a UML "profile" for Enterprise JavaBeans is currently being developed under the Java Community Process (JCP). This profile is a set of extensions that would allow UML to directly express (in a standard way) the structure and semantics specific to EJBs. This would ensure that these models were portable across tools from different vendors. For more details, readers are referred to the specification request document at* http://www.jcp.org/aboutJava/communityprocess/review/jsr026/. *(It is worth noting that UML tools like 'Rational Rose' and 'Together J' have recently provided features that include modeling an EJB.)*

An EJB developer must be able to translate a use case into a functional implementation. The functionality of a use case begins when an **actor** makes a request of the system. It doesn't end until the software has accomplished the purpose embodied by that request. As a great deal of code might be needed to implement each use case, the correspondence between use cases and EJBs is not one-to-one. In fact, multiple EJBs will be used to implement most use cases, and both session beans and entity beans are used in many scenarios.

Analysis Objects

In UML, a use case model is realized by modeling classes that implement that use case, along with their relationships and interactions. The exact procedure for modeling a use case – the process, the diagrams – is unimportant to understanding how to represent a use case by EJBs. What is helpful is to consider three types of **analysis objects** that the inventor of use cases, Ivar Jacobson, described from his experiences in building large, maintainable software systems (see *Object-Oriented Software Engineering, A Use Case Driven Approach* from Addison-Wesley Publishing *ISBN 0-201-45535-0*) – and how these types of objects can be expressed using EJBs.

Interface Objects

The interface object (also known as a **boundary object**) is responsible for controlling access to the EJB tier from any client. This includes other server-side components, such as servlets and JSP pages. An excellent example of an interface object is the controller servlet for the web application's model-view-controller architecture. (Note that we are using the word 'interface' generically, and not in the sense of the Java language `interface` keyword.)

> **An interface object should always be represented by a session bean in the implementation.**

The capabilities of the client and requirements of the specific application will determine whether the session bean should be stateful or stateless.

Control Objects

Control objects provide services to the application. They model functionality that is not naturally associated with a particular entity or interface. Often, this is because more than one entity needs to be operated on at one time; an example might be determining if there is sufficient inventory to manufacture a product. Other times, it may be because a relevant entity was not identified in the model; an example might be charging to a credit card.

> **Control objects should be represented by session beans in the implementation (home interface business methods can also be used to implement control objects).**

Because they can be called from other EJBs, control objects should always be stateless. Conversational state in the EJB tier, if it exists at all, should always be maintained in an interface object, to avoid complexity and improve scalability.

Entity Objects

Entity objects model those business objects that should maintain their state after the use case completes. Typically, this means that they represent data from the database. Some examples are a customer, a product, an order, a personnel evaluation, a network event, or a deadline for a project.

> **Entity objects are often, but not always, represented by entity beans in the implementation model. Sometimes they are represented by dependent objects inside an entity bean, and sometimes they are implemented without any object representation at all (for example, by JDBC code in a session bean).**

Of course, there are endless classification schemes by which you can organize your object model. Jacobson chose these three classifications because he believed the most stable systems were designed so that changes to that system could be kept as isolated as possible. Notice that this is also a motivation for the more general principle of separating design logic from business logic.

How do these three types of objects help to ensure that changes to the system remain local to a small portion of the implementation? There are two primary differences between this, and a simple object model that only represents entities such as products, customers, employees, or contracts:

❑ Interface objects protect the other object types from the volatility of other tiers of the architecture. As a general rule, the further you travel from the data model to the client, the more it is that likely the implementation will need to change. Business logic in the EJB tier will change gradually as the policies it represents change. The design of a web application may undergo continuous revision as the users discover new opportunities to improve productivity and convenience. Changes to the interface should only affect the interface object.

❑ Control objects preserve the locality of functions that cut across multiple real-life entities. It is, of course, possible to break this functionality apart and assign it to the entities that are affected, since entities model behavior as well as representing data. However, when the time comes that this functionality needs to be modified, it's easiest if it can be changed in one place.

Analysis models of use cases are not developed in isolation. The appropriate analysis objects are often determined in an iterative process that involves consideration of multiple use cases. As a rule of thumb, an interface object will represent access to a set of related use cases for a particular class of users via a particular method (which could be via a web application, a GUI client, a business-to-business XML protocol such as SOAP or XML-RPC, an ERP system, or almost anything else). A control object will often represent the activities associated with a single use case.

Analysis vs. Implementation

Just as there is not a one-to-one correspondence between use cases and EJBs, there is also no one-to-one correspondence between analysis objects (interface, control, and entity) and EJB components. Analysis objects are logical creations that must then be mapped to actual implementation classes. We've already seen one example of this lack of one-to-one correspondence in the model-view-controller web application design, where the interface object spans two tiers: the controller session bean (EJB tier) and the proxy JavaBean (web tier).

Why should we perform an analysis that does not result in an object model that we can directly implement using Enterprise JavaBeans? The goals of the analysis phase are to provide a resilient structure for our application and to understand how the functionality should be divided between component roles (interface, entity, or control). Once this structure has been established, we can then consider the effects of the implementation tools and component architecture on our design. In this particular case, of course, we must consider the capabilities and limitations of the EJB implementation environment.

Sometimes a design model, whose purpose it is to refine and formalize the analysis model, will come before the implementation environment is taken into account. The exact process is unimportant to understanding the effects of using EJB technology in the design of your application.

The most important limitation, and the one that drives an implementation model from an architectural standpoint, is that EJBs are **heavyweight components**. This means that there is a cost to implementing an object as an EJB, which must be taken into account. This cost exists for two reasons:

❑ EJBs are intended to be accessible by remote clients. Any communication across a network has associated costs.

❑ The services provided by the EJB container have setup costs. The container must take action to provide each access of a component's business logic with protection from unauthorized access, support for transactional use, and controlled transfer of enterprise data, so access to an EJB component can be thought of as relatively expensive.

As a consequence of being heavyweight components, EJBs are often used to represent an aggregation of objects that exist in the analysis model. Those other objects may have a correspondence in the implementation, but they may be simple lightweight Java objects (such as JavaBeans components), rather than EJBs. Furthermore, functionality that might be represented by multiple operations on the analysis objects should be transformed into a single operation on an object in the implementation.

Let's consider how this aggregation of objects or functionality would apply to the three types of objects in the analysis model:

❑ **Interface objects** will typically be represented by a single object for each outside user in the analysis model, and a single session bean in the design. However, operations available to the user interface will probably need to be aggregated in the implementation. A good example is model attribute access. Getter and setter methods are usually not appropriate on remote objects, because each call to get or set data means another round-trip across the network. Therefore, the interface object will need to accept and return some sort of collection in response to data updates and retrieval. Depending on the situation and the capabilities of the client, it may be possible to reference a control object directly. If no interface-specific functionality is required, no interface session bean should be developed.

❑ **Control objects** often correspond to a single use case in the analysis model. This analysis-model object contains the business logic necessary to perform a sequence of operations, modify and retrieve data from the relevant entity objects, and validate the results. In the implementation, a use case will typically have a representation in a single method of the interface session EJB. For example, the 'place an order' use case might have a corresponding method in the interface session EJB `placeOrder(CustomerInfo, ShoppingCart)`. Control functionality specific to the type of user will probably be implemented right in that interface object, either directly or as a helper object, depending on its complexity. However, in many cases control object functionality will be common to multiple use cases. For instance, multiple use cases may require order-placement functionality. Control functionality that is common to multiple use cases should be moved into a session bean or multiple session beans that provide reusable services. In this common case, the role of the implementation's interface session bean will be to translate the request into a generic form, to ensure that workflow rules aren't violated, and to call the appropriate service-layer beans. Service-layer beans will be implemented as stateless session beans. The combination of interface session bean plus service-layer session beans will compose the control object.

❑ **Entity objects** have the greatest variation in their deviation from the analysis model. Even while doing analysis, it is sometimes difficult to identify what should be modeled as an attribute (that is, a 'member variable') and what should be a domain object (that is, a 'class'). This is made even more difficult in the implementation, because entity objects are often the most heavyweight of all the Enterprise JavaBean types. This is because they are accessed in greater numbers. In a particular use case, there may be one interface session bean, three or four session beans providing control functionality, and potentially hundreds (or even thousands) of participating entity beans. Also, entity beans need to load their state from the database, which is a relatively expensive operation in most environments. It's not unusual for first-class entities in the analysis model to be represented by attributes in the implementation or modeled as JavaBeans. It is even possible to implement entity objects as data-access classes used by session beans, and to exclude entity beans from your implementation altogether. (Since entity beans provide important persistent services, this is not usually recommended. See Chapters 15 and 16 on session and entity beans for more detail about their use and design.)

Our choice of technology also has an affect on the final design. One of the most important factors will be the object/relational mapping capabilities of the products we choose. Some application servers with EJB support, even some of the more popular ones, have only limited support for automatically persisting complex entity objects to underlying relational tables. If this is the case with your application server, you have several choices. Sometimes we can purchase add-on products that will provide container-managed persistence in cooperation with the application server. We may choose an object/relational-mapping tool that is not directly supported by our container. In this case, we have the option of using entity objects with bean-managed persistence, or session beans that update the database directly.

An important rule to remember is that session beans are not designed to represent transactional data. A session bean may update the database, but it must not model data directly. This is because it does not have the container callbacks and management that entity beans do, to allow them to intelligently participate in transactions, synchronize concurrent accesses, respond to errors, and so on. We will cover this in more detail at the beginning of Chapter 16, in the section about trying to construct an entity-equivalent out of a session bean. Finally, we might choose to model dependent objects as entity beans. This is not an ideal situation, but support for the correct database mappings with this approach is practically guaranteed with any EJB container.

Scalability requirements may affect our choice of component type when implementing an interface object. It is more expensive to maintain conversational state on the server than on the client. The choice of stateful or stateless session bean for the interface component will often be made based on the volume of use planned for the application. Obviously, storing state in different tiers can result in significantly different implementations.

The Role of State in the Interface Object

The EJB specification provides for two types of session beans: stateful and stateless. Stateless session beans are always used for the services layer. Choosing a type of session bean for the interface object is more difficult. Allowing the interface object to have state may simplify application design. For instance, a client such as a web browser may not be able to manage state as effectively. However, in reality, it is almost always possible to keep state in a tier closer to the client.

One of the main advantages to keeping conversational state in an interface object session bean is to enforce the workflow of a use case or set of use cases. Consider the not-uncommon situation where, prior to making a purchase, a web visitor must either sign in and allow the application to retrieve the relevant customer information, or create a customer record with shipping information, contact information, optional e-mail, and site preferences. A stateful session bean interface object could enforce this requirement. A stateless session bean would need to depend on the user interface to do so, because it could not remember the customer's actions between method calls.

An Example of EJB Design

Over the course of the next five chapters, we will be building a small sample application. By now, most programmers know that we can build an e-commerce application using EJB technology. It's understandable that this application space is referenced so often – many of the people who are interested in server-side Java programming want to write an application to support commerce on the web. However, the basic techniques are broadly applicable to almost any Java server-side solution, so for a change, we'll use an example that includes some manufacturing. In this chapter, we'll consider its design.

Consider the case of a company that develops products, takes orders for those products, and then manufactures them and ships them. Some simple initial requirements might be as follows:

❑ The engineering department needs to be able to define a product as a series of steps that the manufacturing facility will follow to build it.

❑ We need to be able to take orders over the web, and by phone using operators who are recording orders from our salespeople. We need to be able to notify the manufacturing department that an order for a particular product, to be delivered on a particular date, has been placed. The identifier for this order is unique within a particular sales division, but each sales division has its own numbering scheme for orders and duplicate order numbers may exist between sales divisions.

- We need to be able to cancel an order on which manufacturing has not yet started. We need to be able to prevent the cancellation of an order on which work has already started.

- The manufacturing department needs to be able to select an appropriate order for manufacture, based on the time required to build a product and the maximum time that the company will hold a product in inventory.

- Management must be able to retrieve a list of overdue orders.

- The manufacturing department must be able to notify the shipping department that a product is ready for shipment. It must be able to indicate the carrier that is appropriate for the size and weight of the product manufactured, and the loading dock to which the product has been sent. It must be able to identity itself, in case there is a quality problem with the product, and must be able to record the date completed, in order to respond to customer inquiries.

For this hypothetical company, we can identify six actors:

- An engineer
- A web customer
- A phone operator who takes orders from a catalog
- A floor manager who manages the manufacturing process
- A crew member that actually builds the product ordered
- A manager who tracks overdue orders

There will also be seven use cases:

- Create a Product
- Place an Order
- Cancel an Order
- Select an Order for Manufacture
- Build a Product
- Ship an Order
- List Overdue Orders

Here is a use case diagram that might result from our analysis:

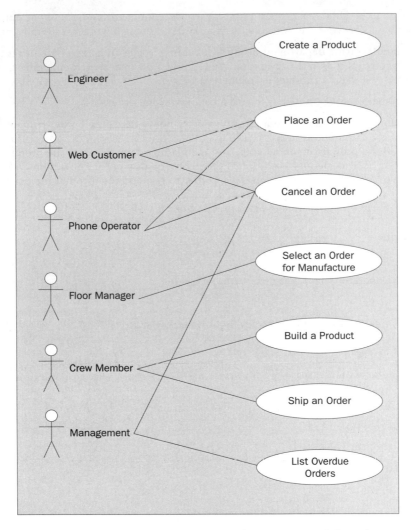

Now we'll consider the fine details about what must be done to accomplish each use case. The steps of each use case that we will actually implement in our example are emphasized in bold.

Create a Product

❑ **Select a product identification tag and a descriptive product name**

❑ **Add the routing steps to be followed during the manufacture of the product**

❑ Create the inventory records necessary managing the manufacturing process of this product

❑ Set the price

Place an Order

❑ Calculate the total price of the order

❑ Validate the payment method

- ❑ **Record the order**
- ❑ Return order-tracking information to the customer
- ❑ E-mail confirmation of the order

Cancel an Order

- ❑ **Make sure that the order is not already being manufactured**
- ❑ **Change the order status to cancelled**
- ❑ Credit the customer account or credit card
- ❑ E-mail confirmation of the cancellation

Select an Order for Manufacture

- ❑ **List the eligible orders, defined as those where the status is open, and today's date is greater than the due date of the order minus the time it takes to build it, minus the time that we're willing to have it sit in inventory**
- ❑ **Choose one of them to build the corresponding product**
- ❑ Ensure that sufficient inventory exists
- ❑ Decrement the inventory
- ❑ Check minimum inventory levels; contact supplier if necessary

Build a Product

- ❑ **Iterate through the routing steps defined for that product, following the instructions**

Ship an Order

- ❑ **Indicate the carrier chosen and the loading dock to which the finished product will be moved**

List Overdue Orders

- ❑ **List the overdue orders, defined as those where the status is open and today's date plus the lead-time required for manufacture is greater than the due date, or those where the status is in-process, and today's date is greater than the due date**

We'll implement two sets of interfaces to this application: a set of stand alone Java clients and a web application. For the purposes of this analysis, let's use our imaginations and envisage that there are several other clients: a Swing GUI that the phone operator uses; a Visual Basic application that the guys in engineering use; and a Palm Pilot interface that the manufacturing crews use (the rest of the clients will use web interfaces). For each client application, there is an interface object in our analysis model.

UML has an extension method, called a **stereotype**, which 'specializes' an element defined in the modeling language. A stereotype can be represented by text surrounded by brackets (<<interface>>) or by an icon. Interface objects, control objects, and entity objects have standard stereotypes, with icon representations. The stereotype icon for an interface object in UML looks like this:

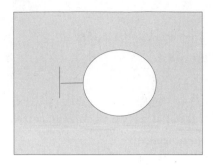

By inspecting the use cases, we can identify the following entity objects in the analysis model (the ones we actually use in our simplified implementation are in bold):

- **Product**
- **Order**
- **Routing step**
- **Shipment**
- Account
- Supplier
- **Shipping company**
- Customer

The stereotype for an entity object in UML looks like this:

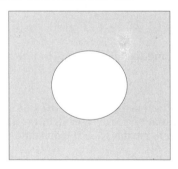

Typically, there is a one-to-one correspondence between use cases and control objects. The control objects here would be:

- Create a Product
- Place an Order
- Cancel an Order
- Select an Order for Manufacture
- Build a Product
- Ship an Order
- List Overdue Orders

The stereotype for a control object in UML looks like this:

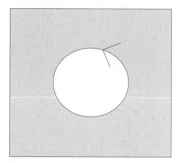

Let's look at three different views of a possible analysis model. The first view shows the use case actors and their respective interface objects:

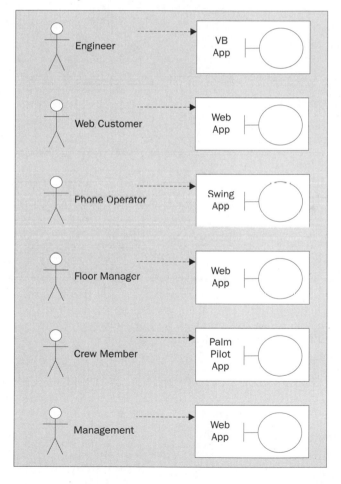

The second view shows the interface objects and the control objects with which they interact:

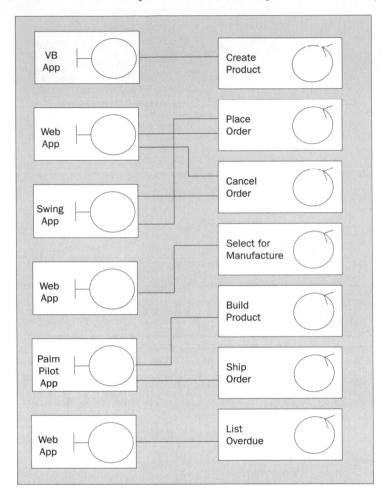

Finally, the third view shows how the control objects interact with entity objects. Notice how the object model, even for what amounts to a 'toy' problem, is sufficiently complicated that it is probably better viewed in segments with a modeling tool, than drawn all at once:

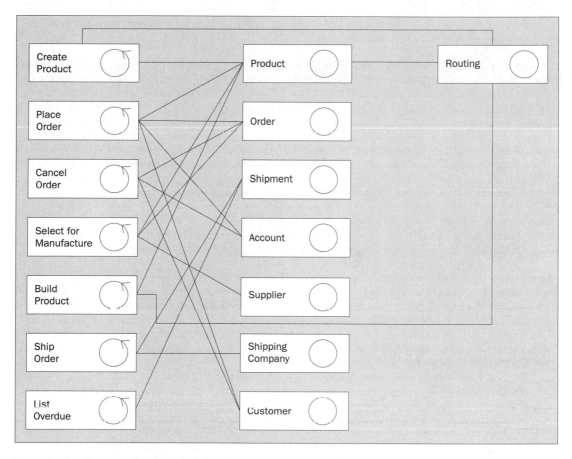

Fortunately, this complexity is hidden from any user interface by the interface objects. Notice also that functionality such as 'place order' could have been located across the order, product, account, and customer objects. However, this would have increased the surface area of our design.

The analysis model now needs to be translated into an implementation appropriate for our environment. As noted before, this will not be a simple one-to-one translation from analysis object to EJB component. Let's start by considering the interface objects:

Actor	User Interface Type	Interface Object Implementation
Engineer	Visual Basic	Session Bean (RMI-IIOP)
Web customer	Web Application / JSP pages	JavaBean proxy / Session Bean
Phone operator	Swing GUI	Session Bean
Floor manager	Web Application / JSP pages	JavaBean proxy / Session Bean
Crew member	Palm Pilot XHTML	Servlet to Session Bean
Management	Web Application / JSP pages	JavaBean proxy / Session Bean

Notice that in four of the six cases, the interface object from the analysis model could translate into multiple components on multiple tiers.

One detail that isn't evident from this table is that there aren't necessarily six different session beans. The phone operator, web customer, and business-to-business customer may be able to share a single session bean interface. You may recall the earlier discussion about the model-view-controller architecture. There was a class in the controller component responsible for translating web requests into generic application events. This translation makes it possible to consider reusing the interface session bean for more than one interface. Of course, it may also be that the requirements of the different applications necessitate the provision of custom functionality. In this case, different interface objects would be used. For instance, in the real world web customers and our salespeople's customers may get different pricing, different credit approval processes, different limits on orders, drop-ship orders rather than deliveries from inventory, etc., depending on the profile of the customer.

Let's consider the entity objects next. Assume that we have an application server with adequate object-relational mapping capabilities. Furthermore, assume that we are going to use entity beans where appropriate, so that we can take advantage of our container's persistence services.

There are at least two changes that we are going to make from the analysis model to the implementation. First, we are going to demote routing steps from a first class business object (that is, a component) to an attribute of the product (that is, a member variable). This is done in recognition of the fact that entity beans are heavyweight objects, and we don't want to have every use of a line item to have to pass through the container's services layer. A common rule of thumb is that objects whose lifecycle (creation and destruction) is completely controlled by another object should be attributes of that EJB entity, even if they were first-class objects in the analysis.

An EJB container has many opportunities for to optimize 'heavyweight' calls between components that are executing in the same Java Virtual Machine. The extent to which a container will do this varies greatly between vendors.

Secondly, we are going to model the shipments as a session bean service, rather than an entity. The reason for this approach is to simplify development. The manufacturing application doesn't need to access the shipment information once it is added to the database. Having a single business method that uses SQL might be marginally better than writing an entity bean whose only purpose was to be created, in terms of development cost.

Finally, let's consider the control objects. In the analysis model there were seven: Create a Product, Place an Order, Cancel an Order, Select an Order for Manufacture, Build a Product, Ship an Order, and List Overdue Orders. We could make seven session beans to represent these control objects. But besides being heavyweight objects at execution time, EJBs have a certain amount of weight in the development process too. Each EJB must have at least three Java files and some configuration information. All other things being equal, one EJB is better than three. Placing, canceling, and listing orders seem cohesive enough to put into a single service bean ("Manage Orders"). Likewise, selecting an order for manufacture, building the product, and shipping the order all take place on the factory floor ("Manufacture"). The "Create a Product" control object should probably have a session bean of its own.

One issue we will have to consider is whether we can combine any control objects and interface objects into a single session bean. The answer will depend on the complexity of our system and the requirements we will have for component reuse. We can reuse a session bean implementation of a control object more easily than a session bean implementing both interface and control logic. Those reasons are the same as those we had earlier for differentiating between interface and control logic in the analysis model – localization of changes. Additionally, if your interface object has state, it cannot be reused by other EJB components at all, because that state must belong to a single client.

We have to consider one last issue: to what extent should we factor additional functionality into its own stateless session service EJBs? If this were a description of our enterprise's entire software implementation, we could probably stop at this point. Certain aspects of the control objects' functionality would probably be implemented as JavaBean helper classes, but this would be an implementation detail irrelevant to the EJB framework. However, it is more likely that we would need to consider which services might be used by other control objects in parts of the software that haven't been described here. For example, it is quite likely that checking inventory levels will be done by accounting or management software. So, the functionality to check inventory levels should be promoted to a stateless session bean that provides methods related to inventory. Another example is the e-mail that we sent in several of the use cases. It is quite likely that there will be enterprise-wide policies on the form that e-mails to customers should take. So there should be a session bean with the responsibility to send these e-mails to customers.

It's sometimes difficult to determine what should be implemented as a stateless session bean and what should be a helper class or function. There is a basic trade off between implementation efficiency and ease of coding on the one hand (for helper classes), and reusability and manageability on the other hand (for stateless session bean services). One thing that favors stateless session beans is that, even though there are still costs associated with calling them compared to generic Java code, they are the least costly of the three types of beans. They can be pooled and reused efficiently, unlike stateful session beans, and do not have persistence requirements, unlike entity beans. In general, if some piece of functionality would be useful on its own to multiple clients, it should at least be considered for promotion to a reusable service. However, the largest grouping of functionality possible should be chosen for promotion.

Summary

This chapter introduced Enterprise JavaBeans, which are designed to encapsulate business logic, and to protect the application developer from having to worry about system-level issues.

We learned the following about EJBs:

- ❑ They are intended for transactional systems

- ❑ They are portable, reusable, server-side components that execute in a container

- ❑ They assist developer productivity, extend application capability, and improve system stability

- ❑ They are accessible from many different types of clients

- ❑ There are four types of beans: stateful session, stateless session, entity, and message-driven

- ❑ There are four major parts to entity and session beans: the home interface, the remote and/or local interface, the implementation class, and the XML deployment descriptor; message-driven beans only have one Java class: the bean class

- ❑ The enterprise bean developer must follow certain rules to get the benefits of EJB technology

- ❑ The role of different EJBs can be understood by analyzing a model of an enterprise in terms of interface objects, control objects, and entity objects

In the next chapter, we'll look at session beans more closely and begin to implement a version of the application that we've analyzed in this chapter.

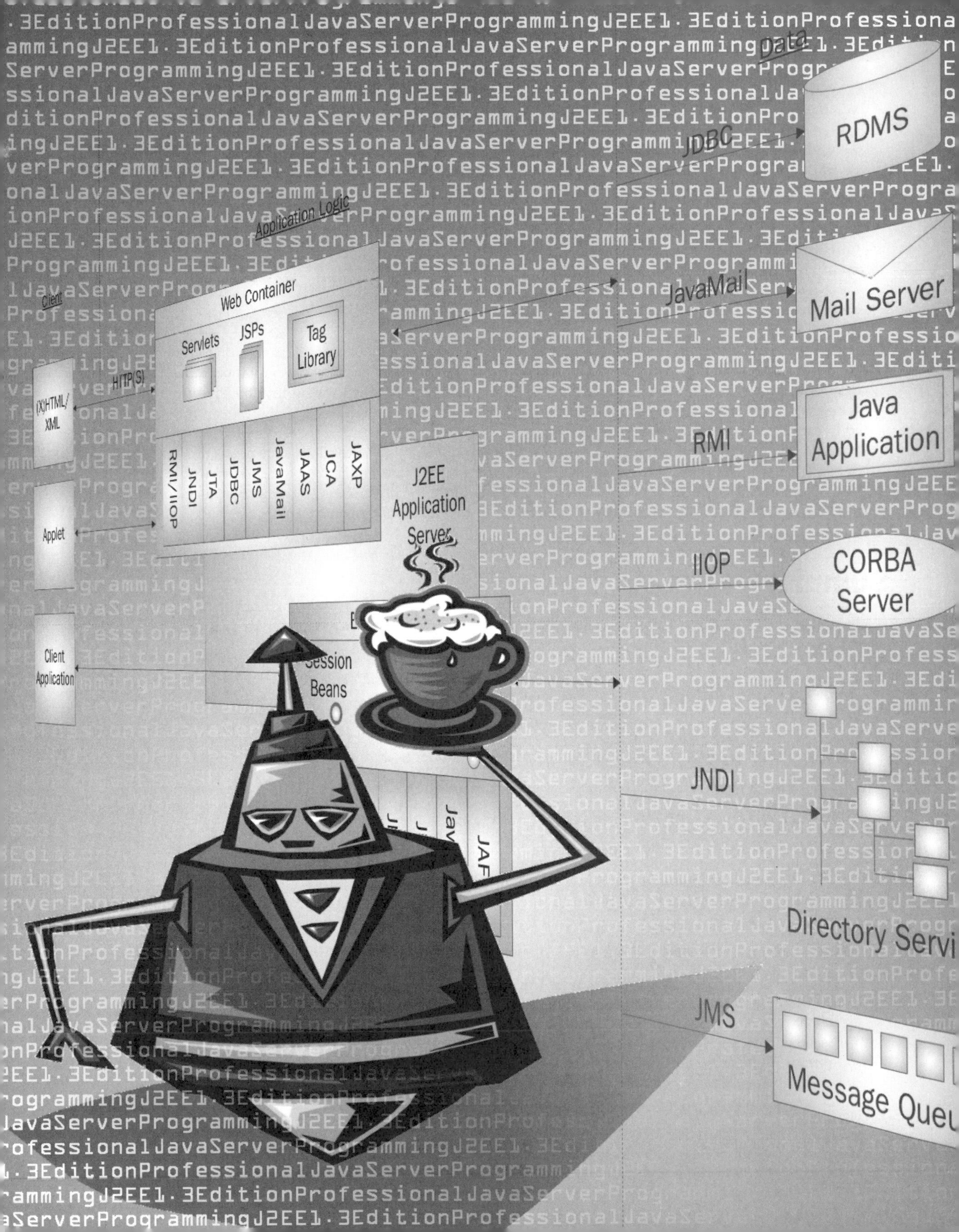

Session Beans and Business Logic

The Enterprise JavaBeans 2.0 specification provides three different models for Enterprise JavaBeans, entity beans, session beans, and message-driven beans. In this chapter we will discuss **session beans**. (The following chapter discusses entity beans, with message-driven beans being described in Chapter 19.) The session bean is used to represent workflow, business logic, and application state.

The following topics are covered in detail:

- ❏ The differences between stateful and stateless session beans
- ❏ The role of session beans in implementing business logic
- ❏ The use of session beans as a façade
- ❏ The tradeoffs to consider for storing state on various tiers of your design
- ❏ The use of session beans to access persistent storage
- ❏ The callbacks and lifecycle of a session bean
- ❏ How to use a JDBC connection in your code
- ❏ How to access environment variables

As we discuss the callbacks and lifecycle of a session bean, we'll develop two simple beans: a stateless session bean and a stateful session bean. In addition, we'll continue developing the manufacturing example for which we did some design in the last chapter. In the context of this application, we'll talk about some basic implementation techniques, such as returning view objects to the client. However, this application makes use of several entity beans, so we'll have to wait until Chapter 16 before we can actually compile, deploy, and run these beans.

Session Beans and State

There are two types of session beans: **stateful** and **stateless**. Those two types have much in common:

❑ Both implement the `javax.ejb.SessionBean` interface, and therefore have the same container callbacks

❑ Both represent a private resource for the client that created them

❑ Both are intended to model a process or a task

❑ Both can update shared data, but do not represent that shared data in the way that an entity bean does

In fact, the only way that an EJB container can distinguish a stateless session bean from a stateful session bean is to look in the XML descriptor file to find the session-type the programmer intended.

The primary difference between the two types of beans – as is obvious from their names – is how they treat **client state** (in other words, their variables).

> **A stateful session bean can keep data between client accesses. A stateless session bean cannot.**

This simple but important difference has complex ramifications for the design of your system. We'll talk about this later in the chapter, but a basic rule to keep in mind is that stateful session beans should only be used at the *boundary* of the object model.

Recall the simple division of functionality for objects in the analysis model that we described in the last chapter. There are three basic types: **interface objects**, **control objects**, and **entity objects**. An EJB component that represents an interface object may be implemented as a stateless or stateful session bean. An EJB component representing a control object that is called from an EJB component representing an interface object must be a stateless session bean. Entity objects in the analysis model do not always have a corresponding component in the implementation. When they do, that component must be an entity bean. Although a session bean can update shared data, it cannot represent that data in the way that an entity bean can. (You can read more about this in Chapter 16 on entity beans.)

Representing Business Logic

An entity bean is a complete data entity while a session bean controls how these entites interact and the overall process.

A good architecture for many purposes is to arrange these session beans into two layers. The lower layer provides generic, reusable services, such as 'release work-order' or 'validate credit card' (we'll refer to this as the **services layer**). This is where the control objects in the analysis model are implemented. The higher layer provides controlled access to these services from clients such as an MRP system (manufacturing resource planning) or a shopping-cart servlet (we'll refer to this as the **access control layer**). This is where the interface objects in the analysis model are implemented.

In the previous chapter, we discussed the reason for differences between the analysis model and the actual implementation of the application. We might combine control-related activities, such as notifying a manager that a customer is approaching their credit limit, with interface-related activities, such as providing an interface to e-commerce functionality for JSP pages. Obviously the division of labor between these two layers will not be clear-cut. In general, it's better to err on the side of caution by separating reusable components out of your initial design.

For this architecture to work, a certain category of information known as **conversational state** must be maintained. Conversational state represents information that is created during an exchange of requests and replies. As the dialogue between both tiers progresses, conversational state will accumulate meaningful information on the history of the exchange, allowing subsequent requests to refer to this history.

There is one thing of which you will want to be aware, if you do use this architecture. Conversational state should *never* be maintained in the services layer. It must *always* be kept in the access-control layer, if it is saved in an EJB at all. In other words, a control object should never depend on keeping state between business method calls. A control-object implementation can be part of a stateful session bean if the programmer has combined a control object with an interface object to simplify things, but the control object should not depend on this state. One reason why not is that it reduces the reusability of the control object in different contexts. There is, however, a more general formulation of this rule prohibiting service-layer state, based on EJB-specific criteria.

> If you are using stateful session beans, *they should never be chained together* through mutual business method calls.

The EJB container has the option of discarding state after a configurable time-out period. In other words, it can destroy your stateful session bean and throw an exception the next time you try to call it. Managing state with multiple expirations introduces unnecessary complication into your design.

Session Beans as a Façade

Perhaps the most important design pattern to emerge so far in systems using Enterprise JavaBeans technology is to use the session bean to provide a **façade** to a client.

> A façade is a higher-level interface to a set of interfaces in a subsystem, and can be considered a more general case of the analysis-model interface object discussed earlier.

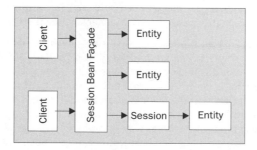

As you can see from the diagram, using a session bean to provide a façade means that there is only one point of entry to our system. From the clients' point of view, there is only the one session bean to interact with, since all their interaction is with that one bean, which in turn passes their requests on to other parts of the system. Thus, we can see why this pattern is known as the façade pattern, because it provides a front (façade) to our system.

There are several generally applicable reasons to use the façade pattern, such as reducing complexity and minimizing dependencies between subsystems. These reasons were discussed in the previous chapter, and all these reasons apply to the case of EJBs. But there are several additional reasons to provide a client a façade that are specific to distributed systems and Enterprise JavaBeans technology.

A typical client will need to access the business logic in multiple session beans and the validation logic in multiple entity beans. Consider the following four advantages to using a façade, rather than accessing those session and entity beans directly from the client:

❑ **Decreased network traffic**
Network traffic has always been a limitation on the performance of distributed object systems. Object-oriented programming typically involves numerous calls to methods that implement discrete and limited functionality. The classic examples are get and set methods. If these method calls are occurring remotely, all the parameters and return values must be sent across the network.

For instance, assume that a client wants to sum the results of calling getPrice() on a collection of 100 entity beans. If the client called the entity beans directly, every single invocation and every single response would travel across the network. If the client called a session bean façade that did the addition for it, only one invocation and one response need travel across the network. By invoking the entity beans locally, the session bean façade in our example reduced network traffic by two orders of magnitude. (Of course, this assumes that the façade is on the same machine – or on an isolated network link – with the other beans that it accesses.)

❑ **Declarative transactional control**
In a typical business system, the results of multiple operations must be applied as a single unit. Take the example of an account transfer in a banking system. The transfer involves two operations: deleting money from one account and adding money to the other. If one operation should fail and the other succeed, either the bank or the customer would loose some money. If a session bean façade makes both calls, the EJB container can manage the process automatically based on declarative information provided by the developer. If the client makes both calls, the client is responsible for ensuring that the operations are atomic – both must succeed or both must fail.

❑ **Fewer unnecessary interpositions**
To provide its services to EJBs, the container adds a layer of indirection between the client and the bean. This layer will inevitably consume some resources on the server, such as processor time and memory space. If an EJB is calling another EJB in the same container, some of this work can be optimized away (for example, by using local component interfaces, which allow direct Java calls to be made between EJB's; local component interfaces will be explained in the next chapter), and server resources can be saved for business logic. For instance, the server may avoid some security checks after the first one has succeeded.

❑ **Business logic on the correct tier**
If multiple calls to multiple beans are necessary to provide a business function, there will usually be some order and relationship to these calls. Along with tightly coupling the client layer to the business logic layer's implementation, making these calls from the client means that a certain amount of workflow is located on the client tier. By using a session bean as a façade, the client is no longer tightly coupled to the business logic, and more of the workflow is preserved on the server. The typical way to organize your application is to limit entity beans to represent strictly rows in your database while a single business method on a session bean will group several calls to one or several entity beans.

In general, all our accesses to EJBs from client applications should be through a small number of session bean façades. Obviously this rule does not apply to EJBs themselves, which can have non-façade session or entity beans as clients; otherwise the façade would need a façade, and so on ad infinitum. There will be circumstances that create additional exceptions to this or any design rule. Consider the disadvantages carefully before deciding that you have one of those exceptions.

The Difficult Problem of Conversational State

State can be divided into two types: **transactional** and **conversational**.

❑ Roughly speaking, transactional state is the data you store in the persistent store. Multiple clients can read and modify this data without conflict. If the application server crashes or is restarted, the data is still available in the data store. An example would be an order that a customer has placed.

❑ Conversational state is the data cached in application variables, either on the client, the EJB container or the application server. This is private data that isn't accessible by other clients. An example of this is the ubiquitous web site shopping cart. If the conversational state isn't turned into transactional state, it can disappear when a component of the application (on the client or server) disappears.

This section refers exclusively to conversational state. Conversational state does not include implementation artifacts such as a connection to a database or a socket that is maintained throughout the life of the component, regardless of the actions of the client.

> *Keeping transactional data consistent is a difficult problem. Fortunately, it is one that the computer industry has a lot of experience at solving. Relational databases are a mature technology and the techniques for using them effectively are well known. Meanwhile the problem of where to store conversational state, while perhaps objectively easier, is also a newer problem (at least in terms of modern multi-tiered designs) and more likely to provoke a lively discussion among experienced application designers.*

Any non-trivial application will have conversational state. Depending on the client, this state can be stored in different ways. A Swing GUI can obviously store state in Java objects. A web browser can store state on the client (cookies, hidden fields, URL rewriting, and so on) or on the server (HTTP session). State that is logically conversational may actually be stored in a transactional database, or it may simply be stored in memory.

Session beans offer another place in which state can be stored. Under certain circumstances, this can make application development easier. State can be stored in a unified way for multiple types of clients: a web client, a Swing GUI client, and a Palm Pilot, for instance. The alternative would be maintaining state by three different methods, which may not allow the same capabilities present with your application server.

However, the potential advantages in application development must be balanced against the cost in application scalability and performance. To understand the tradeoff, it helps to understand a little about what is happening behind the scenes with the EJB container.

Logically, all session beans are mapped one-to-one with a particular client reference, as shown in the following diagram. The EJB is created when the client calls create() and destroyed when the client calls remove():

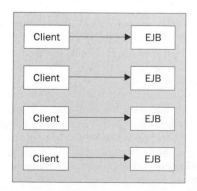

If there are five thousand web clients using your application, there will be five thousand session beans on the server. With a stateless session bean, however, the container has the opportunity for a tremendous optimization by pooling beans. Since they don't have state, there is no effect on the bean from any client's call – so one bean can be reused for multiple clients:

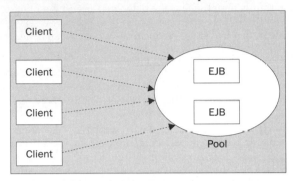

This has a great effect on the available resources. Rather than five thousand stateless session beans, a container might have a pool of just fifty. Of course, the pool could be dynamically adjusted to meet an arbitrary number of concurrent requests for service.

> *A "pool" is simply a collection of instances that are available to service requests. A particular server might pool components, threads, database connections, socket connections, and many other resources. This pooling is invisible to the component developer, although the administrator of the server may be able to change its behavior.*

If stateless session beans don't have state, why would they have variables? Stateless session beans can have permanent state that is not associated with a particular client. For instance, a bean might have an open socket to a resource used by every client. Why can't they be multi-threaded? This is by design, to simplify the development model for EJB components. As EJBs are never accessed by more than one thread at a time, the bean programmer doesn't need to worry about synchronizing access to this permanent state. Also, stateless session beans can have temporary state associated with a client within a particular method call. They just can't maintain this state across method calls.

For instance, imagine that the client has called the EJB method `calculateDemand(Product product)`. This method calls ten helper methods. As a convenience, the programmer might set a `product` variable, rather than passing the `product` to all ten helper methods. However, the next time the session bean is called, nothing can be assumed about the value of that `product` variable.

> *Personally, I don't think you can do this and have well-structured code. Those state variables seem too much like global variables to me, which by consensus the software development industry has been against since the 1970s.*

To help the EJB container manage a large number of stateful session beans, callbacks and rules were included in the specification to give the container the ability to move a stateful session bean to temporary storage, and restore it from that storage, between transactions. The algorithm the container uses to decide when to store a bean is specific to the EJB container. Storing a bean is called **passivation**, and reactivating it is called **activation**.

Activation and passivation are effective methods to deal with the problem of limited server resources. Still, if it's important for your application to scale, the best practice is to keep state on the client and pass it back to the server with each invocation. In the case of a Java client, this may actually be easier than using a stateful session bean. In the case of a thin web client, state storage on the client can be difficult, largely because of the variations of environments and permissions in which your client application may be run. You will have to carefully analyze the tradeoffs of performance, security, and development productivity.

Session Beans and Persistent Storage

The end result of business logic is often the modification of data in or addition of data to our enterprise's persistent store. The Enterprise JavaBeans specification provides for entity beans to represent this data and to provide persistence services.

However, it is possible to bypass entity beans and access a persistent store (such as a database) directly from our session beans. In other words, our session beans will become responsible for the functionality represented by entity objects in our analysis model. As we are bypassing many of the container's persistence services, this will usually introduce additional complexity into our development effort. If we are using an object database or an object-relational mapping tool, this does not apply and a pure session-bean approach may be the way to go. Under certain circumstances, we can also increase our performance by coding direct data access via JDBC and session beans instead of using entity beans.

Under other circumstances, a pure session-bean approach will have a detrimental effect on performance because we will end up implementing a lot of complex services that application-server developers have already optimized for us, such as thread and connection pooling, pre-activation of beans, and so on. Determining which is the case in our situation will involve consideration of database locking strategies, data-access patterns in our application, our EJB container's implementation, and isolation-level requirements. Before you go profiling different architectures, ask yourself how much you really need to scale. Most of us don't work for an airline or the IRS. The most common situations will call for using entity beans with container-managed persistence for operations on single entities and small groups. Session beans will be an appropriate vehicle for operations on a set of data (a count, sum, or list).

If we build our system using nothing but stateless session beans, we will be using one of the oldest architectures for large systems. The biggest systems were once built using Transaction Processing monitors. These TP monitors played the same role that an EJB container does today. Rather than a bean method, the application programmer would write a program that could take startup parameters. The client program would make a call to the TP monitor, which would run the program with the client's parameters. All state would be maintained in the database. This architecture can be made to work for very large transactional systems that don't have caching requirements beyond that provided by the database.

The Enterprise JavaBeans 1.0 specification made container support for entity beans optional; the expectation was that developers using a container without support for entity beans would code direct access to the database in session beans, probably through a tool of some sort. Even though version 1.1 made support for Entity beans from the container mandatory, it still remains a valid choice to depend on session beans exclusively. The EJB 2.0 specification introduces radical improvements to entity beans, so that not using them should be a very carefully made decision.

The Financial Aid Calculator Bean

EJB components have callback methods by which the container provides them with notifications about their lifecycle (when they are about to be created, destroyed, saved to a persistent store, or retrieved from a persistent store). These callback methods are defined for each type of bean (session, entity, and message-driven) in interfaces in the `javax.ejb` package. Both stateful and stateless session beans have the same callback methods, because they must both implement `javax.ejb.SessionBean`. However, these callback methods are used in different ways, because stateful and stateless session beans have different lifecycles within the container.

We're going to look at the use and lifecycle differences of stateful session beans and stateless session beans by implementing the same functionality twice. Then we'll implement it a third time, showing how stateful and stateless session beans can cooperate (one in the access control layer and one in the services layer.)

The application we're going to write will calculate the financial aid that a student will require to attend a university, by applying a formula that takes into account university costs and family resources.

> *If you happen to be a university administrator rather than a Java programmer, you should know that I made this formula up and you should not subject your students to it.*

First, let me describe the formula we'll be using. Our final calculation will be that the student's need equals the cost of university minus the sum of their parent's contribution and their summer earnings. Our client application will print this out, along with the applicant's name (so that they don't feel quite as unhappy with a bad result).

The formula has several intermediate steps. The cost of university is calculated as the sum of three numbers: tuition and fees; room and board; and books and supplies. The parent's contribution is calculated as the sum of three numbers: a percentage of parent 1's income; a percentage of parent 2's income; and a percentage of their assets. The percentage of assets available is also calculated using three numbers: the value of their liquid assets; the value of their primary home; and the value of their other assets. Of course someone who was good at math could roll all these steps into one formula but for the sake of simplicity, we will implement this formula in three distinct steps in our session bean.

The Stateless Financial Need Calculator Bean

Let's begin with the stateless session bean version. Remember, there are four basic parts to an EJB component: its remote interface, its home interface, its implementation class, and its deployment descriptor. First, we'll define our remote interface.

The Financial Need Calculator Remote Interface

This provides the client access to the EJB's business functionality. Like every remote interface in Java, every method must declare that it throws `java.rmi.RemoteException`. As described in the previous chapter, this interface must extend `EJBObject`:

```
package finCalc.stateless;

import javax.ejb.EJBObject;

public interface FinancialNeedCalculator extends EJBObject {

  public double calculateNeed(double attendanceCost,
                             double parentsContribution,
                             double studentSummerWork)
              throws java.rmi.RemoteException;

  public double calculateAttendanceCost(double tuitionAndFees,
                                        double booksAndSupplies,
                                        double roomAndBoard)
              throws java.rmi.RemoteException;

  public double calculateParentsContribution(double parent1Contribution,
                                             double parent2Contribution,
                                             double groupContribution)
              throws java.rmi.RemoteException;

  public double calculateParentContribution(double income)
              throws java.rmi.RemoteException;
```

```
        public double calculateGroupContribution(double liquidAssets,
                                                 double primaryHomeValue,
                                                 double otherAssets)
                    throws java.rmi.RemoteException;

    public String getMessage(String applicant, double need)
                    throws java.rmi.RemoteException;
}
```

Since our session bean is stateless, we must pass application state data back and forth between the client and the server.

The Financial Need Client

The result of every intermediate calculation must be returned to the client from the server, and then handed back to the server from the client when it's needed for a later step. To illustrate this point, here's the client we will use:

```
package finCalc.stateless;

import java.util.Properties;
import javax.naming.Context;
import javax.naming.InitialContext;

public class TestClient {

  // Test data

  public static void main(String[] args) {

    try {
      Properties prop = new Properties();
      prop.put(Context.INITIAL_CONTEXT_FACTORY,
               "weblogic.jndi.WLInitialContextFactory");
      prop.put(Context.PROVIDER_URL, "t3://localhost:7001");

      Context ctx = new InitialContext(prop);

      Object objref = ctx.lookup("StatelessFinancialNeedCalculator");

      FinancialNeedCalculatorHome home =
        (FinancialNeedCalculatorHome) javax.rmi.PortableRemoteObject
          .narrow(objref, FinancialNeedCalculatorHome.class);

      FinancialNeedCalculator calculator = home.create();

      double attendanceCost =
        calculator.calculateAttendanceCost(30000.0, 500.0, 2000.0);

      double parent1 =
        calculator.calculateParentContribution(55000.0);

      double parent2 =
        calculator.calculateParentContribution(35000.0);

      double group = calculator.calculateGroupContribution(10000.0,
                                                           150000.0,
                                                           6000.0);

      double parentsContribution =
```

```
            calculator.calculateParentsContribution(parent1, parent2, group);

        double need = calculator.calculateNeed(attendanceCost,
                                               parentsContribution,
                                               2500.0);

        System.out.println(calculator.getMessage("Daniel", need));

        calculator.remove();

    } catch (Exception e) {
        e.printStackTrace();
    }
  }
}
```

We can see that the client must save the results of intermediate steps like
`calculateParentContribution()` for use in later steps such as
`calculateParentsContribution()`. Let's move on to the rest of the bean before discussing the code.

The Financial Need Calculator Home Interface

The home interface is the second basic part to an EJB component. This interface gives the programmer
access to lifecycle functionality such as the creation and destruction of the component. We can see its
use in the sample client, above. The programmer creating a session bean need only worry about
declaring "create" methods in the home interface. For the writer of a stateless session bean, there can
only be one `create()` method with no parameters. The reason for this should be obvious – if the EJB
doesn't have state, what will it matter if you give it a parameter when you create it? It will have
"forgotten" it by the first business method call.

The home interface for a stateless session bean is the most boring piece of code in the world, because it
will always take this form (just change the package name, the interface name, and the return value from
the `create()` method):

```
package finCalc.stateless;

import javax.ejb.EJBHome;

public interface FinancialNeedCalculatorHome extends EJBHome {
    FinancialNeedCalculator create() throws java.rmi.RemoteException,
                                             javax.ejb.CreateException;
}
```

The Financial Need Calculator Implementation Class

The implementation class is the third basic part to an EJB component. It has both container callback
methods and business-logic implementation methods. For a session bean, it must implement the
`javax.ejb.SessionBean` interface, which provides it with a template of callback methods that the
container requires. In addition, the EJB developer must add an `ejbCreate()` method for each
`create()` method in the home interface, with matching parameters and a return type of `void`. Of
course, for a stateless session bean there will be one of these with no parameters. Here is the class for
our financial need calculator bean:

```
    package finCalc.stateless;

    import javax.ejb.SessionBean;
    import javax.ejb.SessionContext;

    public class FinancialNeedCalculatorEJB implements SessionBean {

      // Lifecycle methods
      public void ejbActivate() {}

      public void ejbPassivate() {}

      public void ejbRemove() {}

      public void ejbCreate() {}

      public void setSessionContext(SessionContext ctx) {}

      // Business methods
      public double calculateNeed(double attendanceCost,
                                  double parentsContribution,
                                  double studentSummerWork) {
        double need = attendanceCost - (parentsContribution
                                      + studentSummerWork);
        return (need < 0.0) ? 0.0 : need;
      }

      public double calculateAttendanceCost(double tuitionAndFees,
                                             double booksAndSupplies,
                                             double roomAndBoard) {
        return tuitionAndFees + booksAndSupplies + roomAndBoard;
      }

      public double calculateParentsContribution(double parent1Contribution,
                                                 double parent2Contribution,
                                                 double groupContribution) {
        return parent1Contribution + parent2Contribution + groupContribution;
      }

      public double calculateParentContribution(double income) {
        return (income * 0.2);
      }

      public double calculateGroupContribution(double liquidAssets,
                                               double primaryHomeValue,
                                               double otherAssets) {
        return (liquidAssets * 0.3) + (primaryHomeValue * 0.05)
                                    + (otherAssets * 0.075);
      }

      public String getMessage(String applicant, double need) {
        return "Dear " + applicant + ", your need has been
              calculated at " + need + ".";
      }
    }
```

The first thing you'll notice about the lifecycle and framework methods is that they're all empty. The business logic programmer, in the default case, doesn't need to do anything. The container will do all the heavy lifting. Let's look at them individually.

public void ejbCreate()

In a stateless session bean, the `ejbCreate()` method will not necessarily be called in correspondence with a call to the bean's home interface `create()` method by the client. You should think of `ejbCreate()` as a constructor, to initialize the bean with resources that can be used by any client. (Client-specific resources aren't relevant to a stateless session bean.)

We can define a no-argument `ejbCreate()` method of our own, if we want. In such a constructor, however, we can't access any of the following:

❑   `SessionContext` methods: `getEJBHome()`, `getCallerPrincipal()`, `isCallerInRole()`, and `getEJBObject()`

❑   The environment (which would normally be available in the JNDI tree under `"java:comp/env"`)

❑   Resource managers (such as a JDBC connection)

❑   Other EJBs (the `ejbCreate()` method runs with an unspecified transaction context)

> *You shouldn't define a constructor with arguments; if you do, it will never get called. Your EJB's lifecycle is controlled by the container and it will always use the no-arguments constructor. If you, out of sheer obstinacy, do define a constructor with arguments, you must also define one without arguments. Otherwise, the container won't be able to instantiate your bean. The specification mandates this behavior, because initialization should be done in one of the lifecycle methods and so there's no reason to add complexity to the configuration process to allow a different constructor to be called.*

public void ejbActivate()
public void ejbPassivate()

The container never passivates (and therefore never activates) a stateless session bean, and these two callback methods will therefore never be called. They need to be implemented because they are used for stateful session beans, and so are declared in the `SessionBean` interface.

public void ejbRemove()

The `ejbRemove()` method is called by the container before it removes its references to the component and allows its memory to be reclaimed. Any resources that were allocated in `ejbCreate()` should be deallocated here.

> *Note that the EJB programmer must not define a `finalize()` method to deallocate any resources. In addition to being a bad programming practice in general (there are no guarantees about when, or if, `finalize()` will be called), it is also specifically prohibited by the Enterprise JavaBeans specification. Most of these resources are typically either released by the JVM or by the operating system after a certain time. For persistent data, one way to clean up these allocated resources would to periodically scan for any stale information.*

public void setSessionContext(SessionContext ctx)

If the programmer wants to use the `SessionContext` in any business method, they must save a reference to it when the container calls `setSessionContext()`. The container will call this method right before `ejbCreate()`, so the programmer can access it in the `ejbCreate()` method if desired.

The session context provides the following to the bean programmer:

❑   The `getEJBObject()` method returns the session bean's remote interface.

❑   The `getEJBHome()` method returns the session bean's home interface.

- ❏ The `getCallerPrincipal()` method returns the `java.security.Principal` that identifies the invoker of the bean instance's EJB object.

- ❏ The `isCallerInRole()` method tests if the session bean instance's caller has a particular role. For example, certain operations might need the user identity to be changed to someone else's. This method will tell you who exactly is calling your method so you can act accordingly.

- ❏ The `setRollbackOnly()` method allows the instance to mark the current transaction such that the outcome of the transaction must be a rollback. Only instances of a session bean with container-managed transaction demarcation can use this method. (This is the normal case.)

- ❏ The `getRollbackOnly()` method allows the instance to test if the current transaction has been marked for rollback. Only instances of a session bean with container-managed transaction demarcation can use this method. (This is the normal case.)

- ❏ The `getUserTransaction()` method returns the `javax.transaction.UserTransaction` interface. The instance can use this interface to demarcate transactions and to obtain transaction status. Only instances of a session bean with bean-managed transaction demarcation can use this method. In general, you should let the container manage your transactions.

If the programmer wanted access to any of this functionality, they would write code that looked something like the following:

```
if (ctx.isCallerInRole("administrator") {
  // do something useful
}
// else do nothing
```

Note that the session context must not be stored in a transient variable. This is so that the reference won't be lost during passivation. (The rule should probably be followed with stateless session beans, even though they won't be passivated.)

These callback methods are used by the container at well-defined points in the session bean's lifecycle. The following diagram may help you to conceptualize the process:

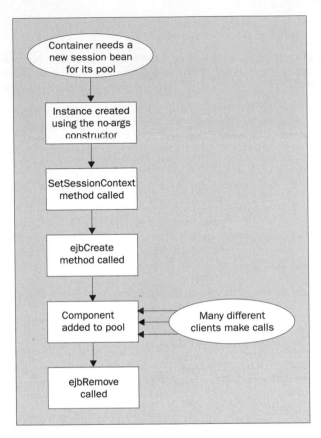

Note that the `ejbCreate()` and `setSessionContext()` methods are not correlated with any particular client's use of the component. The container decides when it needs a new instance. This may or may not be prompted by a client's business method call. If the container wants to decrease the size of the pool, it will call `ejbRemove()` on one of the instances and then remove it from the active pool. Formally, this is called **transitioning** from the *method-ready* state to the *does-not-exist* state.

The Deployment Descriptor

The last basic part of an EJB component is its deployment descriptor. You will typically create this with a tool (although modifying it by hand isn't difficult). Here is the deployment descriptor for our financial need calculator (this is pretty much its minimal form):

```
<!DOCTYPE ejb-jar
    PUBLIC "-//Sun Microsystems, Inc.//DTD Enterprise JavaBeans 2.0//EN"
          "http://java.sun.com/dtd/ejb-jar_2_0.dtd">

<ejb-jar>
  <enterprise-beans>
    <session>
      <ejb-name>StatelessFinancialNeedCalculator</ejb-name>
      <home>finCalc.stateless.FinancialNeedCalculatorHome</home>
      <remote>finCalc.stateless.FinancialNeedCalculator</remote>
      <ejb-class>finCalc.stateless.FinancialNeedCalculatorEJB</ejb-class>
```

```
      <session-type>Stateless</session-type>
      <transaction-type>Container</transaction-type>
    </session>
  </enterprise-beans>

  <assembly-descriptor>
    <container-transaction>
      <method>
        <ejb-name>StatelessFinancialNeedCalculator</ejb-name>
        <method-name>*</method-name>
      </method>
      <trans-attribute>Supports</trans-attribute>
    </container-transaction>
  </assembly-descriptor>
</ejb-jar>
```

Finally, we need to give a JNDI name to the bean's home, and this is achieved by the using the following `weblogic-ejb-jar.xml`:

```
<!DOCTYPE weblogic-ejb-jar
    PUBLIC '-//BEA Systems, Inc.//DTD WebLogic 6.0.0 EJB//EN'
            'http://www.bea.com/servers/wls600/dtd/weblogic-ejb-jar.dtd'>

<weblogic-ejb-jar>
  <weblogic-enterprise-bean>
    <ejb-name>StatelessFinancialNeedCalculator</ejb-name>
    <jndi-name>StatelessFinancialNeedCalculator</jndi-name>
  </weblogic-enterprise-bean>
</weblogic-ejb-jar>
```

We can now run this example. Create a JAR file with your class files and deployment descriptor in the following directories:

```
META-INF/
          weblogic-ejb-jar.xml
          ejb-jar.xml
finCalc/
        stateless/
                FinancialNeedCalculator.class
                FinancialNeedCalculatorHome.class
                FinancialNeedCalculatorEJB.class
```

Deploy this JAR in your application server. If you're using WebLogic Server 6.0 and above, simply drop it in the `%WEBLOGIC_HOME%/config/mydomain/applications/` directory. Set up your client's classpath according to your application server's requirements. For this example, we've used WebLogic 6.1; we've also copied the `weblogic.jar` file from the WebLogic `/bin` directory to the directory from where we invoke the `TestClient`:

```
java -classpath .;weblogic.jar finCalc.stateless.TestClient
```

You should get this result:

```
Dear Daniel, your need has been calculated at 1050.0.
```

The Stateful Financial Need Calculator Bean

Now let's develop another version of this EJB component, as a **stateful** session bean. The main difference between stateful and stateless session beans is that a stateful session bean can store application state between method calls, whereas a stateless bean cannot. In our new version of the bean, we'll take advantage of this capability by storing all the input parameters between method calls, and then calculating the result all at once.

The Stateful Financial Need Remote Interface

Here is the new remote interface:

```
package finCalc.stateful;

import javax.ejb.EJBObject;

public interface FinancialNeedCalculator extends EJBObject {

  public void setStudentSummerWork(double studentSummerWork)
           throws java.rmi.RemoteException;

  public void setAttendanceCosts(double tuitionAndFees,
                                 double booksAndSupplies,
                                 double roomAndBoard)
           throws java.rmi.RemoteException;

  public void setParentIncome(double income)
           throws java.rmi.RemoteException, TooManyParentsException;

  public void setGroupAssets(double liquidAssets,
                             double primaryHomeValue,
                             double otherAssets)
           throws java.rmi.RemoteException;

  public String getMessage() throws java.rmi.RemoteException;
}
```

The setParentIncome() method can be called twice. I've introduced a new class to this example – TooManyParentsException – to be used in the event that the setParentIncome() method is called a third time:

```
package finCalc.stateful;

public class TooManyParentsException extends Exception {
  public TooManyParentsException() {}
}
```

The Stateful Financial Need Calculator Home Interface

A stateful session bean's home interface can be slightly more interesting than a stateless session bean's home interface, because there can be multiple create() methods with various signatures. It makes sense to be able to pass information to a stateful session bean's create() methods, because that stateful session bean can "remember" what the client told it during subsequent business method calls. Here is the calculator's home interface, which takes the applicant's name as a parameter (which will be used in formatting the message):

```
package finCalc.stateful;

import javax.ejb.EJBHome;

public interface FinancialNeedCalculatorHome extends EJBHome {

  FinancialNeedCalculator create(String applicant)
          throws java.rmi.RemoteException, javax.ejb.CreateException;
}
```

The Stateful Financial Next Calculator Implementation Class

Notice how the stateful session bean's implementation class has taken on the "workflow" that was located in the client in the stateless session bean example. The getMessage() method looks almost identical to the client:

```
package finCalc.stateful;

import javax.ejb.SessionBean;
import javax.ejb.SessionContext;

public class FinancialNeedCalculatorEJB implements SessionBean {

  String applicant;
  double studentSummerWork;
  double tuitionAndFees;
  double booksAndSupplies;
  double roomAndBoard;

  double parent1Income;
  boolean parent1Set;

  double parent2Income;
  boolean parent2Set;

  double liquidAssets;
  double primaryHomeValue;
  double otherAssets;

  public void ejbActivate() {}

  public void ejbPassivate() {}

  public void ejbRemove() {}

  public void ejbCreate(String applicant) {
    this.applicant = applicant;
    parent1Set = false;
    parent2Set = false;
  }

  public void setStudentSummerWork(double studentSummerWork) {
    this.studentSummerWork = studentSummerWork;
  }

  public void setAttendanceCosts(double tuitionAndFees,
                                 double booksAndSupplies,
                                 double roomAndBoard) {
    this.tuitionAndFees = tuitionAndFees;
    this.booksAndSupplies = booksAndSupplies;
```

```
      this.roomAndBoard = roomAndBoard;
    }

    public void setParentIncome(double income)
                throws TooManyParentsException {
      if (parent2Set) {
        throw new TooManyParentsException();
      } else if (parent1Set) {
        this.parent2Income = income;
        this.parent2Set = true;
      } else {
        this.parent1Income = income;
        this.parent1Set = true;
      }
    }

    public void setGroupAssets(double liquidAssets,
                              double primaryHomeValue,
                              double otherAssets) {
      this.liquidAssets = liquidAssets;
      this.primaryHomeValue = primaryHomeValue;
      this.otherAssets = otherAssets;
    }

    public String getMessage() {
      double attendanceCost = this.calculateAttendanceCost(tuitionAndFees,
                                                          booksAndSupplies,
                                                          roomAndBoard);

      double parent1 = this.calculateParentContribution(parent1Income);

      double parent2 = this.calculateParentContribution(parent2Income);

      double group = this.caculateGroupContribution(liquidAssets,
                                                    primaryHomeValue,
                                                    otherAssets);

      double parentsContribution =
                  this.calculateParentsContribution(parent1, parent2, group);

      double need = this.calculateNeed(attendanceCost,
                                      parentsContribution,
                                      studentSummerWork);

      return this.getMessage(applicant, need);
    }

    public void setSessionContext(SessionContext ctx)
                throws javax.ejb.EJBException, java.rmi.RemoteException {}

    private double calculateNeed(double attendanceCost,
                                double parentsContribution,
                                double studentSummerWork) {
      double need = attendanceCost - (parentsContribution
                                    + studentSummerWork);
      return (need < 0.0) ? 0.0 : need;
    }

    private double calculateAttendanceCost(double tuitionAndFees,
                                          double booksAndSupplies,
                                          double roomAndBoard) {
      return tuitionAndFees + booksAndSupplies + roomAndBoard;
```

```
    }

    private double calculateParentsContribution(double parent1Contribution,
                                                double parent2Contribution,
                                                double groupContribution) {
      return parent1Contribution + parent2Contribution + groupContribution;
    }

    private double calculateParentContribution(double income) {
      return (income * 0.2);
    }

    private double caculateGroupContribution(double liquidAssets,
                                             double primaryHomeValue,
                                             double otherAssets) {
      return (liquidAssets * 0.3) + (primaryHomeValue * 0.05)
                              + (otherAssets * 0.075);
    }

    private String getMessage(String applicant, double need) {
      return "Dear " + applicant +
             ", your need has been calculated at " + need + ".";
    }
  }
}
```

Except for the `create()` method discussed earlier, the lifecycle methods (`ejbActivate()`, `ejbPassivate()`, `ejbRemove()`, and `setSessionContext()`) in this bean are empty, as like they were for the stateless session bean. The main difference is that `ejbActivate()` and `ejbPassivate()` may actually be called, depending on the container configuration and resource utilization. Before a bean is swapped out to temporary storage the container will call `ejbPassivate()`. Before the bean is recreated from that storage, the container will call `ejbActivate()`.

Why are these callback methods important? If the bean programmer had acquired and saved a resource that couldn't be passivated (a database or socket connection), they would need to release it in `ejbPassivate()` and reacquire it in `ejbActivate()`. More formally, the bean developer must ensure two things are true after `ejbPassivate()` returns:

❑   The objects that are assigned to the bean's non-transient fields must be ready for serialization. They must be null, a serializable object, or an EJB-related object that the container will handle. These special EJB-related objects include remote interfaces, home interfaces, `SessionContext` objects, a reference to the environment naming context or any of its subcontexts, or a reference to a `UserTransaction` object. Often, this will be true without any action in `ejbPassivate()`.

❑   The bean developer must close any open resources, such as open sockets and open database cursors. Typically, a bean will not maintain open resources; rather, it will acquire them from the container as needed. The bottom line? Typically, `ejbPassivate()` will be left empty and the container will handle the details.

The same is true of the `ejbActivate()` callback. It exists to give the developer a chance to reacquire any resources that it closed during `ejbPassivate()`. Typically, this method will be left empty. One word of warning: if we have state that the container can't manage during passivation and activation (such as a non-serializable object stored in a non-transient variable), the container is free to ignore this part of your EJB when it passivates it.

Compare this diagram to the earlier one for a stateless session bean:

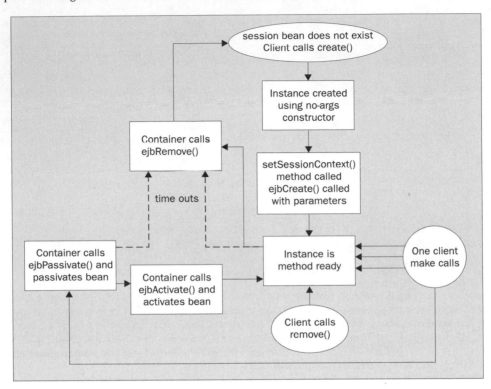

The additional complexity is from the container's need to effectively manage per-client state: ejbActivate(), ejbPassivate(), time outs, and the client's requirement to control the creation and destruction of instances.

The Client for the Stateful Financial Need Calculator

Here is the new client. Unlike the previous version, there is no dependency in the order in which the methods are called. The stateful session bean has taken responsibility to perform the calculations in the correct order at the end of the workflow. Alternatively, it could process the information as it is received, and enforce the workflow by throwing an exception if one of its methods were called out of the correct order:

```
package finCalc.stateful;

import java.util.Properties;
import javax.naming.Context;
import javax.naming.InitialContext;

public class TestClient {

  // Test data

  public static void main(String[] args) {
    try {
      Properties prop = new Properties();
      prop.put(Context.INITIAL_CONTEXT_FACTORY,
```

```
                    "weblogic.jndi.WLInitialContextFactory");
        prop.put(Context.PROVIDER_URL, "t3://localhost:7001");

        Context ctx = new InitialContext(prop);

        Object objref = ctx.lookup("StatefulFinancialNeedCalculator");

        FinancialNeedCalculatorHome home =
          (FinancialNeedCalculatorHome) javax.rmi.PortableRemoteObject
            .narrow(objref, FinancialNeedCalculatorHome.class);

        FinancialNeedCalculator calculator = home.create("Daniel");

        calculator.setParentIncome(55000.0);
        calculator.setParentIncome(35000.0);
        calculator.setGroupAssets(10000.0, 150000.0, 6000.0);
        calculator.setAttendanceCosts(30000.0, 500.0, 2000.0);
        calculator.setStudentSummerWork(2500.0);

        System.out.println(calculator.getMessage());

        calculator.remove();

      } catch (Exception e) {
        e.printStackTrace();
      }
    }
  }
```

The Deployment Descriptors

Here is the new deployment descriptor, indicating that this is a stateful session bean:

```
<!DOCTYPE ejb-jar
    PUBLIC "-//Sun Microsystems, Inc.//DTD Enterprise JavaBeans 2.0//EN"
            "http://java.sun.com/dtd/ejb-jar_2_0.dtd">
<ejb-jar>
  <enterprise-beans>
    <session>
        <ejb-name>StatefulFinancialNeedCalculator</ejb-name>
        <home>finCalc.stateful.FinancialNeedCalculatorHome</home>
        <remote>finCalc.stateful.FinancialNeedCalculator</remote>
        <ejb-class>finCalc.stateful.FinancialNeedCalculatorEJB</ejb-class>
        <session-type>Stateful</session-type>
        <transaction-type>Container</transaction-type>
    </session>
  </enterprise-beans>

  <assembly-descriptor>
    <container-transaction>
      <method>
         <ejb-name>StatefulFinancialNeedCalculator</ejb-name>
         <method-name>*</method-name>
      </method>
      <trans-attribute>Supports</trans-attribute>
    </container-transaction>
  </assembly-descriptor>
</ejb-jar>
```

The `weblogic-ejb-jar.xml` is very similar to the previous one, we simply changed the home class name and its JNDI name:

```
<!DOCTYPE weblogic-ejb-jar
    PUBLIC '-//BEA Systems, Inc.//DTD WebLogic 6.0.0 EJB//EN'
            'http://www.bea.com/servers/wls600/dtd/weblogic-ejb-jar.dtd'>

<weblogic-ejb-jar>
  <weblogic-enterprise-bean>
    <ejb-name>StatefulFinancialNeedCalculator</ejb-name>
    <jndi-name>StatefulFinancialNeedCalculator</jndi-name>
  </weblogic-enterprise-bean>
</weblogic-ejb-jar>
```

We can now run this example. We should create a JAR file with our class files and deployment descriptor in the following directories:

```
META-INF/
            ejb-jar.xml
            weblogic-ejb-jar.xml
finCalc/
        stateful/
                    FinancialNeedCalculator.class
                    FinancialNeedCalculatorHome.class
                    FinancialNeedCalculatorEJB.class
                    TooManyParentsException.class
```

Now, to deploy the bean to WebLogic we again place a copy of the JAR file into the `applications/` directory of our server instance. Then we run the test client again:

```
java -classpath .;weblogic.jar finCalc.stateful.TestClient
```

and get the same results:

```
Dear Daniel, your need has been calculated at 1050.0.
```

We can create a second client that demonstrates how three parents are unacceptable to our somewhat conservative EJB component and will throw an exception:

```
package finCalc.stateful;

import java.util.Properties;
import javax.naming.Context;
import javax.naming.InitialContext;

public class TestClient2 {
  public static void main(String[] args) {
    try {
      Properties prop = new Properties();
      prop.put(Context.INITIAL_CONTEXT_FACTORY,
                "weblogic.jndi.WLInitialContextFactory");
      prop.put(Context.PROVIDER_URL, "t3://localhost:7001");

      Context ctx = new InitialContext(prop);

      Object objref = ctx.lookup("StatefulFinancialNeedCalculator");
```

```
FinancialNeedCalculatorHome home =
   (FinancialNeedCalculatorHome) javax.rmi.PortableRemoteObject
     .narrow(objref, FinancialNeedCalculatorHome.class);

FinancialNeedCalculator calculator = home.create("Daniel");

calculator.setParentIncome(55000.0);
calculator.setParentIncome(35000.0);
calculator.setParentIncome(65000.0);
calculator.setGroupAssets(10000.0, 150000.0, 6000.0);
calculator.setAttendanceCosts(30000.0, 500.0, 2000.0);
calculator.setStudentSummerWork(2500.0);

System.out.println(calculator.getMessage());

calculator.remove();

      } catch (Exception e) {
      e.printStackTrace();
      }
   }
}
```

When we run this client, we should get a stack trace that looks something like this (results will vary with operating system, Java virtual machine, and so on):

```
finCalc.stateful.TooManyParentsException
     at weblogic.rmi.internal.BasicOutboundRequest.sendReceive(
       BasicOutboundRequest.java:85)
     at weblogic.rmi.internal.BasicRemoteRef.invoke(BasicRemoteRef.java:133)
     at weblogic.rmi.internal.ProxyStub.invoke(ProxyStub.java:35)
     at $Proxy2.setParentIncome(Unknown Source)
     at finCalc.stateful.TestClient2.main(TestClient2.java:26)
```

Of course, a more sophisticated client would have caught the exception and handled it gracefully.

Combining Stateful and Stateless Beans

Let's develop one final version of this application, where we have two EJB components: one in the **access control layer** and one in the **services layer**. This will make some of the design principles that we've been talking about more explicit. We already have our services layer EJB component done – it's just the stateless version that we've already looked at.

The next step is to gut the stateful session bean of all its calculations and have it call that session bean instead.

The New Stateful Need Calculator Interfaces and Client

We start with the same home and remote interfaces and the same exception class as our stateful session bean example (apart for the packages; we're using finCalc.both).

The client is also in a different package, and has one other slight difference, because it's looking up a different component:

```
Object objref = ctx.lookup("FinancialNeedCalculatorInterface");
```

Apart from changing the lookup, the client is the same as in the stateful example.

The New Stateful Need Calculator Implementation Class

The implementation class is quite different, because rather than having a bunch of private implementation methods (like our last example), it calls on the stateless session bean to provide it with results. The Enterprise JavaBeans specification allows EJB components in a single application to reference each other by a logical name, typically (as per the spec's recommendation) in the format `java:comp/env/ejb/bean-name`. This link must be declared in the deployment descriptor. At application deployment time, the deployer binds the references of the actual referenced beans into the namespace of the referring bean using application-server specific tools.

The "namespace" of an EJB is just the arrangement of objects that are accessible to it through JNDI.

The developer of the EJB component can indicate the specific deployed bean to which they would like the reference to refer, by adding an `<ejb-link>` element in the deployment descriptor.

The code with which we do this lookup bears examination:

```
InitialContext initial = new InitialContext();
finCalc.stateless.FinancialNeedCalculatorHome home =
  (finCalc.stateless.FinancialNeedCalculatorHome)
    javax.rmi.PortableRemoteObject.narrow(
      initial.lookup("java:comp/env/ejb/CalculatorService"),
                     finCalc.stateless.FinancialNeedCalculatorHome.class);
```

Unlike a standalone client, an EJB does not need to configure the `InitialContext` properties before accessing other application objects through JNDI. The container will handle the configuration. Otherwise, this is the same code we've been seeing in our clients all along. (We're using the fully qualified name of the service bean class, including the package, because otherwise it has exactly the same name as our access control bean.)

Here is the entire class:

```
package finCalc.both;

import javax.ejb.SessionBean;
import javax.ejb.SessionContext;
import javax.naming.InitialContext;

public class FinancialNeedCalculatorEJB implements SessionBean {

    String applicant;
    double studentSummerWork;
    double tuitionAndFees;
    double booksAndSupplies;
    double roomAndBoard;

    double parent1Income;
    boolean parent1Set;

    double parent2Income;
    boolean parent2Set;

    double liquidAssets;
    double primaryHomeValue;
    double otherAssets;
```

```
public void ejbActivate() {}

public void ejbPassivate() {}

public void ejbRemove() {}

public void ejbCreate(String applicant) {
  this.applicant = applicant;
  parent1Set = false;
  parent2Set = false;
}

public void setStudentSummerWork(double studentSummerWork) {
  this.studentSummerWork = studentSummerWork;
}

public void setAttendanceCosts(double tuitionAndFees,
                               double booksAndSupplies,
                               double roomAndBoard) {
  this.tuitionAndFees = tuitionAndFees;
  this.booksAndSupplies = booksAndSupplies;
  this.roomAndBoard = roomAndBoard;
}

public void setParentIncome(double income)
        throws TooManyParentsException {
  if (parent2Set) {
    throw new TooManyParentsException();
  } else if (parent1Set) {
    this.parent2Income = income;
    this.parent2Set = true;
  } else {
    this.parent1Income = income;
    this.parent1Set = true;
  }
}

public void setGroupAssets(double liquidAssets,
                           double primaryHomeValue,
                           double otherAssets) {
  this.liquidAssets = liquidAssets;
  this.primaryHomeValue = primaryHomeValue;
  this.otherAssets = otherAssets;
}

public String getMessage() {
  try {
    InitialContext initial = new InitialContext();
    finCalc.stateless.FinancialNeedCalculatorHome home =
      (finCalc.stateless.FinancialNeedCalculatorHome) javax.rmi
        .PortableRemoteObject.narrow(initial
          .lookup("java:comp/env/ejb/CalculatorService"),
                  finCalc.stateless.FinancialNeedCalculatorHome.class);

    finCalc.stateless.FinancialNeedCalculator calculator = home.create();

    double attendanceCost =
      calculator.calculateAttendanceCost(tuitionAndFees,
                                         booksAndSupplies,
                                         roomAndBoard);
```

```
        double parent1 =
          calculator.calculateParentContribution(parent1Income);

        double parent2 =
          calculator.calculateParentContribution(parent2Income);

        double group =
          calculator.calculateGroupContribution(liquidAssets,
                                                primaryHomeValue,
                                                otherAssets);

        double parentsContribution =
          calculator.calculateParentsContribution(parent1, parent2,
                                                  group);

        double need = calculator.calculateNeed(attendanceCost,
                                               parentsContribution,
                                               studentSummerWork);

        return calculator.getMessage(applicant, need);
    } catch (javax.ejb.CreateException ce) {
      throw new javax.ejb.EJBException(ce);
    } catch (javax.naming.NamingException ne) {
      throw new javax.ejb.EJBException(ne);
    } catch (java.rmi.RemoteException re) {
      throw new javax.ejb.EJBException(re);
    }
  }

  public void setSessionContext(SessionContext ctx)
            throws javax.ejb.EJBException, java.rmi.RemoteException {}
}
```

The Deployment Descriptors

The deployment descriptor provides information to the container about both beans. It also sets up the reference from our stateful session bean to the stateless one:

```
<!DOCTYPE ejb-jar
    PUBLIC "-//Sun Microsystems, Inc.//DTD Enterprise JavaBeans 2.0//EN"
            "http://java.sun.com/dtd/ejb-jar_2_0.dtd">

<ejb-jar>
  <enterprise-beans>
    <session>
      <ejb-name>FinancialNeedCalculatorInterface</ejb-name>
      <home>finCalc.both.FinancialNeedCalculatorHome</home>
      <remote>finCalc.both.FinancialNeedCalculator</remote>
      <ejb-class>finCalc.both.FinancialNeedCalculatorEJB</ejb-class>
      <session-type>Stateful</session-type>
      <transaction-type>Container</transaction-type>
      <ejb-ref>
        <ejb-ref-name>ejb/CalculatorService</ejb-ref-name>
        <ejb-ref-type>Session</ejb-ref-type>
        <home>finCalc.stateless.FinancialNeedCalculatorHome</home>
        <remote>finCalc.stateless.FinancialNeedCalculator</remote>
        <ejb-link>FinancialNeedCalculatorService</ejb-link>
      </ejb-ref>
    </session>
    <session>
      <ejb-name>FinancialNeedCalculatorService</ejb-name>
```

```
      <home>finCalc.stateless.FinancialNeedCalculatorHome</home>
      <remote>finCalc.stateless.FinancialNeedCalculator</remote>
      <ejb-class>finCalc.stateless.FinancialNeedCalculatorEJB</ejb-class>
      <session-type>Stateless</session-type>
      <transaction-type>Container</transaction-type>
    </session>
  </enterprise-beans>

  <assembly-descriptor>
    <container-transaction>
      <method>
        <ejb-name>FinancialNeedCalculatorInterface</ejb-name>
        <method-name>*</method-name>
      </method>
      <trans-attribute>Supports</trans-attribute>
    </container-transaction>
    <container-transaction>
      <method>
        <ejb-name>FinancialNeedCalculatorService</ejb-name>
        <method-name>*</method-name>
      </method>
      <trans-attribute>Supports</trans-attribute>
    </container-transaction>
  </assembly-descriptor>
</ejb-jar>
```

`weblogic-ejb-jar.xml` now contains definitions for both homes:

```
<!DOCTYPE weblogic-ejb-jar
    PUBLIC '-//BEA Systems, Inc.//DTD WebLogic 6.0.0 EJB//EN'
            'http://www.bea.com/servers/wls600/dtd/weblogic-ejb-jar.dtd'>

<weblogic-ejb-jar>
  <weblogic-enterprise-bean>
    <ejb-name>FinancialNeedCalculatorInterface</ejb-name>
    <jndi-name>FinancialNeedCalculatorInterface</jndi-name>
  </weblogic-enterprise-bean>
  <weblogic-enterprise-bean>
    <ejb-name>FinancialNeedCalculatorService</ejb-name>
    <jndi-name>FinancialNeedCalculatorService</jndi-name>
  </weblogic-enterprise-bean>
</weblogic-ejb-jar>
```

You should create a JAR file with your class files and deployment descriptor in the following directories:

```
META-INF/
          ejb-jar.xml
          weblogic-ejb-jar.xml
finCalc/
        both/
              FinancialNeedCalculator.class
              FinancialNeedCalculatorHome.class
              FinancialNeedCalculatorEJB.class
              TooManyParentsException.class
        stateless/
                    FinancialNeedCalculator.class
                    FinancialNeedCalculatorHome.class
                    FinancialNeedCalculatorEJB.class
```

Deploy this JAR in your application server and run the client, to get the same result as before.

Implementing Our Manufacturing Application

It's time to begin implementing the sample application for which we performed some analysis in the previous chapter. Now, how do we translate this analysis into an actual implementation? Any software implementation will be influenced by a variety of factors, including development costs, performance and scalability requirements, user expectations, personnel, and so on. In this case, we will assume that these factors motivate us to keep the implementation simple, largely because that's best for the academic purpose of explaining how EJBs are used.

The slice of the analysis model that we've chosen to implement has four entity objects: product, routing instructions, orders, and shipments.

- ❑ A product will consist of an identifier, a human-readable name, and an ordered list of routing instruction entities to control the manufacturing process

- ❑ An order will consist of the product ordered, a due date, an identifying key (order number plus sales division), and a status (open, canceled, manufacture in-process, and completed)

- ❑ The shipment information will consist of an order key, a loading dock, a manufactured-by field, and a date completed

- ❑ A routing instruction has a sequence (an integer) and an instruction (a `String`)

The entity objects in the analysis model will usually translate into entity beans, or attributes of entity beans, in the implementation. In this case, we will have two entity beans:

- ❑ An order

- ❑ A product, with routing instructions as a simple attribute

  Note that in other circumstances, routing instructions might need to be a first class entity. I once worked on an Enterprise Resource Planing system where this would have been the case, because routing instructions were shared by multiple products. Here their lifecycle depends completely on their parent product, which always makes an entity a strong candidate for being implemented as an attribute.

As mentioned in the last chapter, it might make sense to update shipment information directly from a session bean. Note that this session bean can manipulate the database directly, but does not represent a 'shipment entity'. The reason for this approach is development simplicity. Also, by updating the database directly, we are demonstrating a valid alternative choice of which you should be aware.

The code is quite simple, so we're only having two session beans that are responsible for implementing all the control and interface objects:

- ❑ A stateless session bean used to manage orders, which also has a utility function to create sample products

- ❑ A stateful session bean used to control the manufacturing process

Even with the simplicity of the requirements, we're cheating a little; it doesn't make sense to have the product creation mixed in with order management. Once we start modeling the complexity of a real-world organization, we will want to start dividing our functionality into more cohesive access-control and service-level components.

Let's consider the roles that these two session beans play. First, each serves as an interface object to some of the clients in this application. The EJB that controls the manufacturing process manages the conversational state for its manufacturing clients. It can use this state directly to ensure that the rules of the workflow (such as a product must be selected before its routing can be displayed) are followed. However, we should keep in mind that two distinct roles are involved in this: interface object implementation and control object implementation. An application's state must be contained in the client or an 'interface' object. Actually, using this state is really the job of a service object, if we were to match EJB components up to their analysis roles perfectly.

The stateless session EJB that manages orders acts as an interface object for some clients, but it also acts as a pure control object for the manufacturing EJB. As the business methods in EJBs tend to have coarse-grained functionality, it's not unusual that a client with a similar 'theme' to a particular service-layer session bean can use that bean directly as its interface. However, if reusability and maintainability are important concerns, we should avoid specializing this session bean for particular clients. Instead, introduce a component that separately implements the interface functionality if necessary.

Note that creating lists of entities is a function of control objects in the analysis model, but the situation is more complicated in an implementation using Enterprise JavaBeans technology. Collections of entities can be produced using a factory method on an entity bean's home interface; these factory methods are known as **finder methods**. These finder methods will be explained in Chapter 16, but basically they return an EJB remote interface or collection of remote interfaces that meet application-defined criteria. However, returning a collection of entities to the client violates the guideline that the implementation of the analysis model should be hidden behind a façade, and can also have negative consequences for performance. Therefore, it is recommended to use the session bean façade again: this EJB will invoke a finder on an entity bean and will perform some additional transformations (such as restricting the returned values or re-packaging them in Java objects) before returning them to the clients. As we will see in the next chapter, this is usually achieved with local interfaces

The clients are complete abstractions. In the real world, they probably would be web applications or Swing GUI clients, and the functionality would be more clearly divided and flexible. (In Chapter 18, we actually develop a simple web front-end to this application.) Here they exist only to test the server-side code and demonstrate how EJBs can be used. There are four clients, although one of those clients is spread out over two executable classes. Note that all client access is to one of the session beans. In keeping with the façade pattern, no non-bean client accesses an entity bean:

- ❏ The CreateProducts class calls a utility function to create sample products for use in the other examples. We won't discuss it further here.

- ❏ The PlaceSampleOrders class places six orders that are due for delivery at various times. Two of the orders are needed so far in the future that they shouldn't yet be scheduled for manufacture; two orders are ready to be manufactured, and can be finished on time; and two are overdue if lead time is taken into account.

- ❏ ManageSampleOrders prints out the overdue orders to System.out. It then cancels the first overdue order.

- ❏ The final client has two classes, BeginManufacture and CompleteManufacture; these are two different executable classes. The BeginManufacture class creates a stateful session bean, which it uses to print out the orders that are eligible for manufacture. It then selects the first order available, serializes a handle to that EJB for use by the next application, and exits. The CompleteManufacture class prints out the product routings in order, ships the product, and calls remove() on the session bean.

This sample application is much simpler than a real-world application would ever be. However, the techniques demonstrated here could be valuable to your development efforts using Enterprise JavaBeans technology. The complete code for these examples can be downloaded from the Wrox web site at http://www.wrox.com/.

Clients and the Business Logic Interfaces

In this section, we'll look at the implementation of the home and remote interfaces of the session beans, and the clients that use them. In the development process, the business interfaces provide a contract to the clients, which should not need to know about the details of the implementation. We won't actually look at the implementation classes until the next section – and we won't see the deployment descriptor until the next chapter, because it describes the entity beans as well as the session beans. If you're very curious you can peek ahead a few pages.

Here is a quick rundown on the classes we'll look at in this section. First, in the factory.manage_orders package:

- ❑ ManageOrders (remote interface)
- ❑ ManageOrdersHome (home interface)
- ❑ DuplicateOrderException
- ❑ NoSuchOrderException
- ❑ NoSuchProductException
- ❑ OpenOrderView
- ❑ OverdueOrderView

In the factory.manufacture package:

- ❑ Manufacture (remote interface)
- ❑ ManufactureHome (home interface)

Finally, in the factory.client package:

- ❑ ContextPropertiesFactory
- ❑ BeginManufacture
- ❑ CompleteManufacture
- ❑ PlaceSampleOrders
- ❑ ManageSampleOrders
- ❑ CreateProdcuts

Mixed in with this code, there are two new discussions of EJB technique. The first is **handle serialization**, and the second is how to handle **listing behavior**.

The remote interfaces of the two session beans, factory.manage_orders.ManageOrders and factory.manufacture.Manufacture, represent all the business logic available to the four clients.

The ManageOrders EJB

ManageOrders is the stateless session bean. Its remote interface looks like this:

```
package factory.manage_orders;

import javax.ejb.*;
import java.util.Date;
import java.rmi.RemoteException;
import factory.order.OrderNotCancelableException;

public interface ManageOrders extends EJBObject {
  void placeOrder(int salesDivision, int orderNumber,
                  String product, Date dateDue)
      throws RemoteException,
             NoSuchProductException,
             DuplicateOrderException;

  void cancelOrder(int salesDivision, int orderNumber)
      throws RemoteException,
             NoSuchOrderException,
             OrderNotCancelableException;

  OverdueOrderView[] getOverdueOrders() throws RemoteException;

  OpenOrderView[] getSchedulableOrders() throws RemoteException;

  void createSampleProducts() throws RemoteException;

  void createProduct(String id, String name) throws RemoteException;

  void addRoutingInstruction(String id, int sequence, String instruction)
      throws RemoteException;
}
```

An order has a key consisting of a sales division plus an order number. The method to place an order provides a unique combination of division and order number. The method to cancel an order must reference an existing division and order number combination. The product to be manufactured is identified by an existing string key. If any of these expectations are violated, an exception (NoSuchProductException, DuplicateOrderException, or OrderNotCancelableException) is thrown. Here are those classes:

```
package factory.manage_orders;

public class DuplicateOrderException extends Exception {

  public DuplicateOrderException() {}
}
```

```
package factory.manage_orders;

public class NoSuchOrderException extends Exception {

  public NoSuchOrderException() {}
}
```

```
package factory.manage_orders;

public class NoSuchProductException extends Exception {
```

```
      public NoSuchProductException() {}
}
```

Here is the home interface. As is the case with all stateless session beans, it is unremarkable:

```
package factory.manage_orders;

import java.rmi.RemoteException;
import javax.ejb.*;

public interface ManageOrdersHome extends EJBHome {
  ManageOrders create() throws RemoteException,
                               CreateException;
}
```

The two methods to retrieve lists of orders (getOverdueOrders() and getSchedulableOrders()) return arrays of 'view objects'. This is one strategy of several to provide lists of information. Another possible strategy is to return a class that implements the java.sql.ResultSet interface or the new javax.sql.Rowset interface (see Chapter 4), with the information provided in rows and columns.

The reader with experience in building business systems will notice that, in terms of listing behavior, we've given ourselves an easy task here. We can assume there will be a manageable number of open or overdue orders to return from these methods. However, it's easy to think of cases where the result set will not be manageable.

For instance, consider a "search" or "open" interface in a client application where the user can set arbitrary criteria on the search. If the client doesn't set useful criteria on their search, some applications could try to return millions of rows of data.

The correct solution to this problem will depend on the specifics of our application. Perhaps we can return a chunk of rows, tell the user there is more data, and make them refine the search. We could have the client pass a marker to the server with each request, so that all the data can be returned in discrete chunks).

Another closely related issue not demonstrated by this sample application is how to transfer data about a single entity from the server to a client application. This is a common requirement. Many applications will present screens designed to edit the data associated with an entity such as a customer, a product, or a company. The same issues that motivate the use of the façade pattern prevent individual calls to the server to retrieve or set data. This means we shouldn't use a sequence of calls like getFirstName(), getMiddleName(), getLastName(), getAddr1(), getAddr2(), and so on. The data needs to be transferred in a collection of some kind (our method might be getSimpleCustomerData()).

What should this collection look like? The two basic strategies mirror those for returning simple lists of information. The first is to return a **view object**, which should be a simple serializable collection of data, like OverdueOrderView or OpenOrderView. Here is the code for OpenOrderView; notice it is just structured data with no functionality:

```
package factory.manage_orders;

import java.io.Serializable;
import java.util.Date;

public class OpenOrderView implements Serializable {
  public final int salesDivision;
```

```
   public final int orderNumber;
   public final String product;
   public final Date dateDue;

   public OpenOrderView(int salesDivision, int orderNumber,
                        String product, Date dateDue) {
     this.salesDivision = salesDivision;
     this.orderNumber = orderNumber;
     this.product = product;
     this.dateDue = dateDue;
   }
}
```

And here is the code for OverdueOrderView:

```
package factory.manage_orders;

import java.io.Serializable;
import java.util.Date;

public class OverdueOrderView implements Serializable {
   public final int salesDivision;
   public final int orderNumber;
   public final String product;
   public final String status;
   public final Date dateDue;

   public OverdueOrderView(int salesDivision, int orderNumber,
                           String product, String status,
                           Date dateDue) {
     this.salesDivision = salesDivision;
     this.orderNumber = orderNumber;
     this.product = product;
     this.status = status;
     this.dateDue = dateDue;
   }
}
```

The benefit of this approach is that it is simple to program and understand the code; the disadvantage is that the view object is specific to a particular client or type of client, introducing coupling between the client and server

The second strategy is to use a generic class with self-describing data. When talking about listing behavior, we mentioned implementing java.sql.ResultSet. As we are sending information about a single entity, and because that information might have non-tabular data (tree data or subordinate grid data), ResultSet isn't the ideal interface in this case since this type maps very specifically rows in a database and not a more complex structure. A good alternative is to return a java.util.Map, with key-value pairs representing a description of the data (perhaps an identifying Integer) and the data itself. The client could request just the data it needed, and the server could send this data with no foreknowledge of the request.

The Manufacture EJB

Manufacture is the stateful session bean; its remote interface looks like this:

```
package factory.manufacture;

import javax.ejb.*;
import java.rmi.RemoteException;
```

```
import factory.manage_orders.OpenOrderView;
import factory.manage_orders.NoSuchOrderException;

public interface Manufacture extends EJBObject {
  OpenOrderView[] getOpenOrders() throws RemoteException;

  void selectForManufacture(int salesDivision, int order_number)
         throws RemoteException, NoSuchOrderException,
                BadStatusException;

  boolean hasNextRouting() throws RemoteException, NoSelectionException;

  String getNextRouting() throws RemoteException, NoSelectionException;

  void ship(String carrier, int loading_dock) throws RemoteException,
                                                     NoSelectionException;
}
```

Note that, unlike with the ManageOrders bean, there is an implied order to these method calls. You must first select an order for manufacture. You then work through the routings (presumably building the product as you go). Finally, you ship the product. If you neglect to select the order before trying to read the routings for it, or before shipping it, a NoSelectionException will be thrown. This is easy to program with a stateful session bean. If we had made this a stateless session bean, we would have needed to pass the selected order as a parameter to every method call. We would also have needed to pass a cursor of some sort to the hasNextRouting() and getNextRouting() methods, because the bean, having no state, couldn't track this for us.

Also unlike the ManageOrders bean, there is something interesting in the home interface: a create() method with a parameter. This parameter identifies the 'cell' that is manufacturing the product. When the product is shipped, this information will automatically be added to the shipments table. Here is that home interface:

```
package factory.manufacture;

import javax.ejb.*;
import java.rmi.RemoteException;

public interface ManufactureHome extends EJBHome {
  Manufacture create(String manufactureCellID)
            throws RemoteException, CreateException;
}
```

> *As a reminder, a stateless session bean can't have any parameters in its create() method, nor is there any reason to want it to have any. Since a stateless session bean doesn't save information on behalf of a client, any information you provided in a create() method would be gone by the time you made the first business method call. Bottom line: if you've seen one home interface for a stateless session bean, you've seen them all.*

The Application Clients

The clients reference the server entirely through the two session bean interfaces. To keep things simple, all the clients are classes with only a static main() function. (To see web clients for these EJB components, look in Chapter 18.) They all follow a simple two-step pattern:

❑   Acquire a reference to a session bean

❑   Use that reference to accomplish some business purpose

Acquiring a reference to a session bean is done in these examples in one of two ways. First, there is the "get the home interface from JNDI/create a session bean" route. That code looks like this, for the stateless session bean:

```
ContextPropertiesFactory factory = new ContextPropertiesFactory();
Properties prop = factory.getInitialContextProperties();
InitialContext initial = new InitialContext(prop);

Object homeObject = initial.lookup("ManageOrders");

ManageOrdersHome home = (ManageOrdersHome)
        PortableRemoteObject.narrow(homeObject, ManageOrdersHome.class);

ManageOrders manageOrders = home.create();
```

Or this, for the stateful session bean (the only real difference being the parameter to the `create()` method):

```
ContextPropertiesFactory factory = new ContextPropertiesFactory();
Properties prop = factory.getInitialContextProperties();
InitialContext initial = new InitialContext(prop);

Object homeObject = initial.lookup("Manufacture");

ManufactureHome home = (ManufactureHome)
        PortableRemoteObject.narrow(homeObject, ManufactureHome.class);

Manufacture manufacture = home.create(MANUFACTURE_CELL);
```

`ContextPropertiesFactory` is a class we'll write ourselves. There are many ways to set up the properties for `InitialContext`; the best two are probably to put a `jndi.properties` file on the classpath, or to load an application-specific properties resource file using `getResourceAsStream()`. To make it clearer what is happening, we have removed this level of indirection from the sample clients. Here is `ContextPropertiesFactory` for WebLogic:

```
package factory.clients;

import javax.naming.Context;
import java.util.Properties;

public class ContextPropertiesFactory {

  public Properties getInitialContextProperties() {
    Properties prop = new Properties();
    prop.setProperty(Context.INITIAL_CONTEXT_FACTORY,
                     "weblogic.jndi.WLInitialContextFactory");
    prop.setProperty(Context.PROVIDER_URL, "t3://localhost:7001");
    return prop;
  }

  public void makePropertiesDefault() {
    System.setProperties(getInitialContextProperties());
  }
}
```

In general, we can pass these properties to the `InitialContext` in its constructor. If our EJB container's vendor requires these properties to be set when we are restoring an EJB reference from a handle, we will need to set the system properties with these values, like we do in `makePropertiesDefault()`.

The second way that we acquire a reference to a session bean in these examples is to get it from a `Handle` that has been serialized to disk. At the end of the 'begin manufacture' client, the `Handle` is serialized as follows:

```
Handle handle = manufacture.getHandle();
FileOutputStream file_out = new FileOutputStream(FILE_NAME);
ObjectOutputStream out = new ObjectOutputStream(file_out);
out.writeObject(handle);
System.out.println("Written object for next stage.");
```

At the beginning of the 'complete manufacture' client, the reference to the stateless session bean is restored as follows:

```
FileInputStream inStream = new FileInputStream(FILE_NAME);
ObjectInputStream in = new ObjectInputStream(inStream);
Handle handle = (Handle)in.readObject();
Manufacture manufacture = (Manufacture)
    PortableRemoteObject.narrow(handle.getEJBObject(), Manufacture.class);
```

Both home references and remote references have `Handles` that can be serialized, and also transferred between programs using such methods as files, sockets, or RMI. They can be saved in a servlet's session, and can even be e-mailed (or more practically, moved around with messaging middleware). Remember, though, that references to remote objects in EJB are single-threaded. Simultaneous access from multiple clients or multiple threads is an error and will result in an exception being thrown. For example, a client is not allowed to look up a stateful session bean and then spawn threads to call its business methods concurrently.

Let's now look at those two clients in their entirety. We'll start with `BeginManufacture`.

The BeginManufacture Client

This client reads the pending orders and initiates manufacturing of the involved goods. It stops halfway, stores the handle to the `ManufactureEJB` in a serialized file and exits. This file will then be read by the next client to complete the order (in a real application, we would need a more rigorous way to pass this information along than a file, such as a database):

```
package factory.clients;

import java.rmi.RemoteException;
import javax.ejb.*;
import javax.naming.*;
import javax.rmi.PortableRemoteObject;
import java.util.Properties;
import java.io.*;

import factory.manufacture.Manufacture;
import factory.manufacture.ManufactureHome;
import factory.manage_orders.OpenOrderView;

public class BeginManufacture {

    private static final String MANUFACTURE_CELL = "Station1";
    private static final String FILE_NAME = "C:/current_product.ser";

    public static void main(String[] args) {

        try {
            ContextPropertiesFactory factory =
                new ContextPropertiesFactory();
            Properties prop = factory.getInitialContextProperties();
```

```
      InitialContext initial = new InitialContext(prop);

      Object homeObject = initial.lookup("Manufacture");

      ManufactureHome home =
        (ManufactureHome) PortableRemoteObject.narrow(homeObject,
            ManufactureHome.class);

      Manufacture manufacture = home.create(MANUFACTURE_CELL);
      OpenOrderView[] openOrders = manufacture.getOpenOrders();

      if (openOrders.length == 0) {
        System.out.println("Nothing to make; go home.");
        return;
      }

      System.out.println("Selecting from the following open orders:");
      for (int iter = 0; iter < openOrders.length; iter++) {
        OpenOrderView openOrder = openOrders[iter];

        System.out.println("Sales Division: " +
                            openOrder.salesDivision + "; Order #: " +
                            openOrder.orderNumber + "; Product: " +
                            openOrder.product + "Date due: " +
                            openOrder.dateDue);
      }

      // Get the first open order
      for (int iterFind = 0; iterFind < openOrders.length;
          iterFind++) {
        try {
          OpenOrderView openOrder = openOrders[iterFind];
          manufacture.selectForManufacture(openOrder.salesDivision,
                                     openOrder.orderNumber);
          Handle handle = manufacture.getHandle();
          FileOutputStream file_out = new FileOutputStream(FILE_NAME);
          ObjectOutputStream out = new ObjectOutputStream(file_out);
          out.writeObject(handle);
          System.out.println("Written object for next stage.");
          break;
        } catch (factory.manufacture.BadStatusException bse) {

          // Someone grabbed it before we did
          bse.printStackTrace();
        }
      }

    } catch (FileNotFoundException fnfe) {
      fnfe.printStackTrace();
    } catch (RemoteException re) {
      re.printStackTrace();
    } catch (IOException ioe) {
      ioe.printStackTrace();
    } catch (factory.manage_orders.NoSuchOrderException nsoe) {
      nsoe.printStackTrace();
    } catch (NamingException ne) {
      ne.printStackTrace();
    } catch (CreateException ce) {
      ce.printStackTrace();
    }
  }
}
```

The 'begin manufacture' client prints out a list of the open orders that are eligible for manufacture. The client doesn't need to worry about these eligibility requirements; this is a business rule that is implemented on the server. Next the client selects one of these items for manufacture:

This code is slightly more complicated than any of the other client-side code we will encounter. We have a list of open orders; why do we need to catch an exception that would only be thrown if we tried to manufacture an order that wasn't open?

Between the time when we got the list of open orders and the time we tried to select one of those orders for manufacture, some other manufacturing cell could have already started work on that same order. The problem is that we could be working with stale data. Within a single transaction (and depending on isolation levels), we could be sure that our list of open orders would remain open until we selected one for manufacture. But we cached data on the client (in the form of the openOrders array), and now we must deal with the possibility that our cached data is stale, hence the loop.

Note that our loop, although it has the virtue of simplicity, is not a perfect solution to this problem. We could go through the entire original list of open orders without finding one that was still opened, in which case we would exit the program without doing any more work. But in the meantime, new orders could have been placed. With the current solution, we need to run the program again if that happens. This is a special case of a more general problem that will be discussed in Chapter 17 on transactions.

The CompleteManufacture Client

This client resumes where the previous client left off. It reads the serialized file that contains the partial ManufactureEJB and completes the manufacturing:

```
package factory.clients;

import java.rmi.RemoteException;
import javax.ejb.*;
import javax.naming.*;
import javax.rmi.PortableRemoteObject;
import java.util.Properties;
import java.io.*;

import factory.manufacture.Manufacture;
import factory.manufacture.ManufactureHome;
import factory.manage_orders.OpenOrderView;

public class CompleteManufacture {
```

The file for the FILE_NAME variable below might need to be changed to match our system. In addition, in a "real-world" situation paths would never be hard-wired but configurable:

```
  private static final String FILE_NAME = "C:/current_product.ser";
  private static final String CARRIER = "State Express";
  private static final int LOADING_DOCK = 1;

  public static void main(String[] args) {

    try {
      ContextPropertiesFactory factory =
        new ContextPropertiesFactory();
      factory.makePropertiesDefault();
```

```
        FileInputStream inStream = new FileInputStream(FILE_NAME);
        ObjectInputStream in = new ObjectInputStream(inStream);
        Handle handle = (Handle) in.readObject();
        Manufacture manufacture =
          (Manufacture) PortableRemoteObject
            .narrow(handle.getEJBObject(), Manufacture.class);
        System.out.println("Product routings:");

        while (manufacture.hasNextRouting()) {
          String routing = manufacture.getNextRouting();
          System.out.println(routing);
        }

        System.out.println("Product finished; shipping...");
        manufacture.ship(CARRIER, LOADING_DOCK);
        manufacture.remove();

      } catch (Exception e) {
        e.printStackTrace();
      } catch (Throwable t) {
        t.printStackTrace();
      }
    }
  }
```

This 'complete manufacture' client picks up where the 'begin manufacture' client left off.

Notice that we take care to remove the stateful session bean from the server. This isn't important with stateless session beans because they aren't consuming any resources on the server to begin with; remove() is typically a no-op. But if we fail to remove a stateful session bean when we're finished with it, it will live on, clogging up the memory (or at least the passivation store) of the server until it times out.

The PlaceSampleOrders Client

The 'place sample orders' client creates six orders. We have chosen due dates for the orders so that two orders will be overdue, two orders will be schedulable and not overdue, and two orders will be due far enough in the future that they should not be scheduled. This will exercise all of our business logic. Here is the code:

```
package factory.clients;

import java.rmi.RemoteException;
import javax.ejb.*;
import javax.naming.*;
import javax.rmi.PortableRemoteObject;
import java.util.Properties;
import java.util.Calendar;
import java.util.Date;

import factory.manage_orders.ManageOrders;
import factory.manage_orders.ManageOrdersHome;

public class PlaceSampleOrders {

// Note that in a production environment,
// these would be set in a properties file
  private static final int SALES_DIVISION_1 = 1;
  private static final int SALES_DIVISION_2 = 2;
  private static final int SALES_DIVISION_3 = 3;
```

```
      private static final int ORDER_1 = 1;
      private static final int ORDER_2 = 2;
      private static final int ORDER_3 = 3;
      private static final int ORDER_4 = 4;
      private static final int ORDER_5 = 5;

      private static final String PRODUCT_1 = "DESK01";
      private static final String PRODUCT_2 = "CHAIR01";
      private static final String PRODUCT_3 = "LAMP01";

      public static void main(String[] args) {

        try {
          ContextPropertiesFactory factory = new ContextPropertiesFactory();
          Properties prop = factory.getInitialContextProperties();
          InitialContext initial = new InitialContext(prop);

          Object homeObject = initial.lookup("ManageOrders");

          ManageOrdersHome home = (ManageOrdersHome)
                      PortableRemoteObject.narrow(homeObject,
                                                  ManageOrdersHome.class);

          ManageOrders manageOrders = home.create();

          Calendar calendarNotSchedulable = Calendar.getInstance();
          calendarNotSchedulable.add(Calendar.DAY_OF_YEAR, 14);

          Calendar calendarSchedulable = Calendar.getInstance();
          calendarSchedulable.add(Calendar.DAY_OF_YEAR, 5);

          Calendar calendarOverdue = Calendar.getInstance();

          manageOrders.placeOrder(SALES_DIVISION_1, ORDER_1, PRODUCT_1,
                              calendarNotSchedulable.getTime());

          manageOrders.placeOrder(SALES_DIVISION_2, ORDER_1, PRODUCT_2,
                              calendarNotSchedulable.getTime());

          manageOrders.placeOrder(SALES_DIVISION_1, ORDER_2, PRODUCT_3,
                              calendarSchedulable.getTime());

          manageOrders.placeOrder(SALES_DIVISION_2, ORDER_2, PRODUCT_1,
                              calendarSchedulable.getTime());

          manageOrders.placeOrder(SALES_DIVISION_1, ORDER_3, PRODUCT_2,
                              calendarOverdue.getTime());

          manageOrders.placeOrder(SALES_DIVISION_2, ORDER_3, PRODUCT_3,
                              calendarOverdue.getTime());

        } catch (Exception e) {
          e.printStackTrace();
        }
      }
    }
```

This client simply gets a reference to the ManageOrders EJB, and uses it to place six orders. Each order has the sales division, order number, the actual product being ordered, and the due date.

The ManagerSampleOrders Client

The 'manage orders' client lists the orders that are overdue, and then cancels the first overdue order:

```java
package factory.clients;

import java.rmi.RemoteException;
import javax.ejb.*;
import javax.naming.*;
import javax.rmi.PortableRemoteObject;
import java.util.Properties;

import factory.manage_orders.ManageOrders;
import factory.manage_orders.ManageOrdersHome;
import factory.manage_orders.OverdueOrderView;
import factory.manage_orders.OpenOrderView;

public class ManageSampleOrders {

  public static void main(String[] args) {

    try {
      ContextPropertiesFactory factory = new ContextPropertiesFactory();
      Properties prop = factory.getInitialContextProperties();
      InitialContext initial = new InitialContext(prop);

      Object homeObject = initial.lookup("ManageOrders");

      ManageOrdersHome home = (ManageOrdersHome)
                  PortableRemoteObject.narrow(homeObject,
                                            ManageOrdersHome.class);

      ManageOrders manageOrders = home.create();

      // List overdue orders
      OverdueOrderView[] overdueOrders = manageOrders.getOverdueOrders();

      for (int iter = 0; iter < overdueOrders.length; iter++) {
        OverdueOrderView overdueOrder = overdueOrders[iter];
        System.out.println("Product " + overdueOrder.product +
                        " is due on " + overdueOrder.dateDue +
                        ".  It's status is " +
                        overdueOrder.status + ".");
      }

      // Cancel first overdue order
      if (overdueOrders.length > 0) {
        OverdueOrderView overdueOrder = overdueOrders[0];
        System.out.println("About to cancel an order...");
        try {
          manageOrders.cancelOrder(overdueOrder.salesDivision,
                              overdueOrder.orderNumber);
          System.out.println("Canceled order for " +
                          overdueOrder.product.trim() + ".");
        } catch (factory.manage_orders.NoSuchOrderException nsoe) {
          System.out.println("Failed to find order.");
        } catch (factory.order.OrderNotCancelableException once) {
          System.out.println("Cannot cancel an order in production.");
        }
      }
    } catch (RemoteException re) {
      re.printStackTrace();
```

```
      } catch (NamingException ne) {
      ne.printStackTrace();
      } catch (CreateException ce) {
      ce.printStackTrace();
      }
  }
}
```

This code is quite simple to understand. Notice the `OrderNotCancelableException`. This is the client-side expression of a business rule on the server that does not allow orders to be cancelled once production has started. The exception that you throw in your business logic is automatically forwarded to the client, unless it is a `RuntimeException` or error. For more information about exception handling in EJBs, see Chapter 17.

Ideally, our client should indicate whether an operation would succeed before it is attempted. For instance, the button or menu-item could be grayed-out. Obviously, a more creative approach will be required for a web browser or mobile clients (WAP-enabled phones, PDAs, and so on). In any case, this exception will indicate which business rule was violated and allow feedback to the client.

The CreateProducts Client

Finally, the client that creates some sample products:

```
package factory.clients;

import java.rmi.RemoteException;
import javax.ejb.*;
import javax.naming.*;
import javax.rmi.PortableRemoteObject;
import java.util.Properties;

import factory.manage_orders.ManageOrders;
import factory.manage_orders.ManageOrdersHome;

public class CreateProducts {

  public static void main(String[] args) {

    try {
      ContextPropertiesFactory factory = new ContextPropertiesFactory();
      Properties prop = factory.getInitialContextProperties();
      InitialContext initial = new InitialContext(prop);

      Object homeObject = initial.lookup("ManageOrders");

      ManageOrdersHome home = (ManageOrdersHome)
                    PortableRemoteObject.narrow(homeObject,
                                              ManageOrdersHome.class);

      ManageOrders manageOrders = home.create();

      manageOrders.createSampleProducts();

    } catch (RemoteException re) {
      re.printStackTrace();
    } catch (NamingException ne) {
      ne.printStackTrace();
    } catch (CreateException ce) {
      ce.printStackTrace();
    }
  }
}
```

The `CreateProducts` client is another simple bit of code; we obtain a reference to the `ManageOrders` EJB and tell it to create some sample products.

Stateless Session Bean Implementation

Our sample application's stateless session bean, `ManageOrders`, has the main implementation class `factory.manage_orders.ManageOrdersEJB`. We have divided this class into sections:

- ❏ Business methods
- ❏ Implementation helper methods
- ❏ Lifecycle and framework methods

In addition, we will see the code for another class in this section: `ProductCreationHelper`. This regular Java class assists us with our implementation.

Business Methods

The business methods implemented in this class correspond to the business methods declared in the bean's remote interface. They match up based on a convention: they have the same name and method signature.

Note that we don't throw `java.rmi.RemoteException` from any implementation method. Throwing it is allowed, but is deprecated behavior. In general, the bean developer should throw an application exception to indicate a business logic error, and an `EJBException` to indicate a system error of some sort.

Let's look first at the business methods:

```
package factory.manage_orders;

import javax.ejb.*;
import javax.naming.*;
import javax.rmi.PortableRemoteObject;
import java.rmi.RemoteException;
import java.util.Date;
import java.util.Collection;
import java.util.Iterator;
import java.util.LinkedList;

import factory.order.OrderHome;
import factory.order.Order;
import factory.order.OrderPK;
import factory.order.StatusStrings;
import factory.product.Product;
import factory.product.ProductHome;
import factory.product.RoutingInstruction;
import factory.order.OrderNotCancelableException;

public class ManageOrdersEJB implements SessionBean {

    private static final int MILLIS_IN_DAYS = 86400000;
```

The `placeOrder()` method makes use of both our sample's entity beans, `Order` and `Product`, which will be covered in more detail in Chapter 16. This method calls two helper methods, `getProductHome()` and `getOrderHome()`. These encapsulate JNDI access to the home interfaces, and will be looked at briefly in the next section:

```
    // Business methods
    public void placeOrder(int salesDivision, int orderNumber,
                           String productName, Date dateDue)
              throws NoSuchProductException, DuplicateOrderException {

      try {

        // Find the product
        ProductHome productHome = getProductHome();
        Product product = productHome.findByPrimaryKey(productName);

        // create the order
        OrderHome orderHome = getOrderHome();
        orderHome.create(salesDivision, orderNumber, product, dateDue);

      } catch (NamingException ne) {
        throw new EJBException(ne);
      } catch (RemoteException re) {
        throw new EJBException(re);
      } catch (FinderException fe) {
        if (fe instanceof ObjectNotFoundException) {
          throw new NoSuchProductException();
        } else {
          throw new EJBException(fe);
        }
      } catch (CreateException ce) {
        if (orderExists(salesDivision, orderNumber)) {
          throw new DuplicateOrderException();
        } else {
          throw new EJBException(ce);
        }
      }
    }
```

It's worth considering how business logic concerns dictate responses to the handling of `FinderException` and the `CreateException`. If the finder exception is a result of the product not being found in the database, a checked exception, `NoSuchProductException`, is sent to the client. If the finder exception is because of some other, indeterminate cause, the unchecked `EJBException` is thrown instead (the client will receive a `RemoteException`). A similar pattern exists with the `CreateException`, although we need to use the `orderExists()` helper function to determine the cause of the `CreateException`.

The business method `cancelOrder()` doesn't introduce anything new. The `OrderNotCancelable Exception` is thrown by the order's corresponding business method `cancelOrder()`:

```
    public void cancelOrder(int salesDivision, int orderNumber)
            throws NoSuchOrderException, OrderNotCancelableException {

      try {

        // Find the order
        OrderHome orderHome = getOrderHome();
        OrderPK orderPK = new OrderPK(salesDivision, orderNumber);

        // Cancel it
        Order order = orderHome.findByPrimaryKey(orderPK);
        order.cancelOrder();

      } catch (NamingException ne) {
        throw new EJBException(ne);
```

```
      } catch (RemoteException re) {
        throw new EJBException(re);
      } catch (FinderException fe) {
        if (fe instanceof ObjectNotFoundException) {
          throw new NoSuchOrderException();
        } else {
          throw new EJBException(fe);
        }
      }
    }
  }
```

The business methods getOverdueOrders() and getSchedulableOrders() build on the
functionality offered by the Order entity bean's home methods, findUncompletedOrders() and
findOpenOrders(). The business methods then apply additional business rules to screen the
collections returned from the finder methods. Several parameters (lead time and maximum inventory
time) come from helper methods that will be explained in the next section:

```
  public OverdueOrderView[] getOverdueOrders() {

    try {
      LinkedList overdueOrders = new LinkedList();
      Date today = new Date();
      long todayMillis = today.getTime();
      long leadTimeMillis = getLeadTimeDays() * MILLIS_IN_DAYS;
      OrderHome orderHome = getOrderHome();
      Collection uncompletedOrders =
        orderHome.findUncompletedOrders();
      Iterator iterUncompletedOrders = uncompletedOrders.iterator();

      while (iterUncompletedOrders.hasNext()) {
        Order uncompletedOrder =
          (Order) PortableRemoteObject
            .narrow(iterUncompletedOrders.next(), Order.class);
        Date dateDue = uncompletedOrder.getDateDue();
        String status = uncompletedOrder.getStatus();
        long dueDateMillis = dateDue.getTime();
        if ((status.equals(StatusStrings.OPEN)
                  && (todayMillis + leadTimeMillis > dueDateMillis))
             || (status.equals(StatusStrings.IN_PROCESS)
                  && (todayMillis > dueDateMillis))) {
          OverdueOrderView view =
            new OverdueOrderView(uncompletedOrder
              .getSalesDivision(), uncompletedOrder
              .getOrderNumber(), uncompletedOrder
                .getProductOrdered().getName(), status, dateDue);
          overdueOrders.add(view);
        }
      }

      OverdueOrderView[] overdue =
        new OverdueOrderView[overdueOrders.size()];
      return (OverdueOrderView[]) overdueOrders.toArray(overdue);

    } catch (NamingException ne) {
      throw new EJBException(ne);
    } catch (RemoteException re) {
      throw new EJBException(re);
    } catch (FinderException fe) {
      throw new EJBException(fe);
    }
  }
```

```
public OpenOrderView[] getSchedulableOrders() {

  try {
    LinkedList schedulableOrders = new LinkedList();
    Date today = new Date();
    long todayMillis = today.getTime();
    long maxInventoryTimeMillis = getMaxInventoryTimeDays()
                                  * MILLIS_IN_DAYS;
    long leadTimeMillis = getLeadTimeDays() * MILLIS_IN_DAYS;
    OrderHome orderHome = getOrderHome();
    Collection openOrders = orderHome.findOpenOrders();
    Iterator iterOpenOrders = openOrders.iterator();

    while (iterOpenOrders.hasNext()) {
      Order openOrder =
        (Order) PortableRemoteObject.narrow(iterOpenOrders.next(),
                                            Order.class);
      Date dateDue = openOrder.getDateDue();
      long dueDateMillis = dateDue.getTime();
      if (todayMillis >= dueDateMillis - leadTimeMillis
                          - maxInventoryTimeMillis) {
        OpenOrderView view =
          new OpenOrderView(openOrder.getSalesDivision(),
                            openOrder.getOrderNumber(),
                            openOrder.getProductOrdered().getName(),
                            dateDue);
        schedulableOrders.add(view);
      }
    }

    OpenOrderView[] schedulable =
      new OpenOrderView[schedulableOrders.size()];
    return (OpenOrderView[]) schedulableOrders.toArray(schedulable);

  } catch (NamingException ne) {
    throw new EJBException(ne);
  } catch (RemoteException re) {
    throw new EJBException(re);
  } catch (FinderException fe) {
    throw new EJBException(fe);
  }
}
```

The business methods createProduct() and addRoutingInstruction() are for use by the web interface we will develop in Chapter 18. They both make use of entity beans, which we will be examining more closely in the next chapter. The createProduct() method takes the ID and name of the product as parameters, using these to create a product entity bean with an empty routing instruction list. The product entity bean will insert a corresponding record in the database. After the product has been created, the addRoutingInstruction() method can be used to add corresponding routing instructions, one at a time:

```
public void createProduct(String id, String name) {

  try {
    ProductHome productHome = getProductHome();
    productHome.create(id, name, new RoutingInstruction[]{});

  } catch (NamingException ne) {
    throw new EJBException(ne);
  } catch (CreateException ce) {
```

```
        throw new EJBException(ce);
      } catch (RemoteException re) {
        throw new EJBException(re);
      }
    }

    public void addRoutingInstruction(String id, int sequence,
                                      String instruction) {

      try {
        ProductHome productHome = getProductHome();
        Product product = productHome.findByPrimaryKey(id);
        product.addRoutingInstruction(sequence, instruction);

      } catch (FinderException fe) {
        throw new EJBException(fe);
      } catch (NamingException ne) {
        throw new EJBException(ne);
      } catch (RemoteException re) {
        throw new EJBException(re);
      }
    }
```

The `createSampleProducts()` business method exists only to kick-start the sample application, but one feature is worth discussing: its implementation is in a helper class:

```
    public void createSampleProducts() {

      try {
        ProductHome productHome = getProductHome();

        // Create three sample products
        ProductCreationHelper pch = new ProductCreationHelper(productHome);
        pch.createAll();

      } catch (NamingException ne) {
        throw new EJBException(ne);
      }
    }
```

In general, this helper class is identical to the main implementation class from the specification's point of view, as far as the limitations and privileges of EJBs go. We still can't create threads, access the file system, and so on. That's the case with `ProductCreationHelper`, which takes actions that could just as easily have been in-line:

```
package factory.manage_orders;

import javax.ejb.EJBException;
import factory.product.Product;
import factory.product.ProductHome;
import factory.product.RoutingInstruction;
import factory.product.NoSuchRoutingInstruction;

public class ProductCreationHelper {

  ProductHome productHome;

  public ProductCreationHelper(ProductHome productHome) {
    this.productHome = productHome;
  }
```

```java
public void createAll() {

  try {
    createDesk();
    createChair();
    createLamp();

  } catch (Exception e) {
    e.printStackTrace();
    throw new EJBException(e);
  }
}

public void createDesk() throws Exception {

  RoutingInstruction compress = new RoutingInstruction(5,
                          "Compress the wood.");
  RoutingInstruction stain = new RoutingInstruction(10,
                          "Stain the wood.");
  RoutingInstruction assemble = new RoutingInstruction(15,
                          "Assemble the desk.");
  RoutingInstruction[] routings = new RoutingInstruction[] {
    compress, stain, assemble
  };

  productHome.create("DESK01", "Compressed Wood Desk", routings);
}

public void createChair() throws Exception {

  RoutingInstruction extrude = new RoutingInstruction(5,
                          "Extrude plastic.");
  RoutingInstruction glue = new RoutingInstruction(10,
                          "Glue together.");
  RoutingInstruction paint = new RoutingInstruction(15,
                          "Spraypaint.");
  RoutingInstruction[] routings = new RoutingInstruction[] {
    extrude, glue, paint
  };

  productHome.create("CHAIR01", "Quality Plastic Chair", routings);
}

public void createLamp() throws Exception {

  RoutingInstruction getBulb = new RoutingInstruction(5,
                          "Get bulb from inventory.");
  RoutingInstruction getLamp = new RoutingInstruction(10,
                          "Get lamp from inventory.");
  RoutingInstruction screwTogether = new RoutingInstruction(15,
                          "Screw together.");
  RoutingInstruction frayCord = new RoutingInstruction(20,
                          "Pre-fray the cord");
  RoutingInstruction[] routings = new RoutingInstruction[] {
    getBulb, getLamp, screwTogether, frayCord
  };

  Product lamp = productHome.create("LAMP01", "Custom Made Lamp",
                          routings);
  try {
    lamp.deleteRoutingInstruction(21);
```

```
        } catch (NoSuchRoutingInstruction nsri) {
          lamp.deleteRoutingInstruction(20);
        }
      }
    }
```

Let's now consider an exceptional case. Assume we have decided that our EJBs need to perform an action that is prohibited by the specification, and our current application server will support this behavior. If our application server enforces the restrictions of EJB, it will do this by using Java's security model. We may need to bypass the Java security limitations under which our bean executes, and which are intended to protect the server from insecure or potentially damaging operations. (This does not mean you are bypassing the access controls on EJBs, which is an entirely different system.) We will need to use a helper class to do this, along with a `doPrivileged()` call.

Java security is tied to the class loader. With most application servers, our EJBs will be loaded by one (or more) class loader(s), and the application server will have a different class loader that it uses for the classes on its classpath. To bypass security and perform the non-portable operation, we would put our helper class on the classpath and make the privileged call. Java security and its relationship to the class loader and the `doPrivileged()` call is a standard (if somewhat esoteric) Java language feature. Consult a language reference such as http://java.sun.com/j2se/1.3/docs/api/index.html if you need more information.

As a rule, unless you have a very good reason, don't do this. You will affect the portability of the components you write.

Implementation Helper Methods

Continuing with our implementation of `ManageOrdersEJB`, add this code to the previous code:

```
    // Implementation helpers
    private boolean orderExists(int salesDivision, int orderNumber) {

      try {
        OrderHome orderHome = getOrderHome();
        OrderPK orderPK = new OrderPK(salesDivision, orderNumber);
        Order order = orderHome.findByPrimaryKey(orderPK);
        return true;

      } catch (Exception e) {
        return false;
      }
    }

    private int getLeadTimeDays() throws NamingException {
      InitialContext initial = new InitialContext();
      Integer leadTimeDays =
              (Integer) initial.lookup("java:comp/env/lead_time");

      return leadTimeDays.intValue();
    }

    private int getMaxInventoryTimeDays() throws NamingException {
      InitialContext initial = new InitialContext();
      Integer inventoryTimeDays =
              (Integer) initial.lookup("java:comp/env/max_inventory_time");

      // A null pointer will roll back the transaction
      return inventoryTimeDays.intValue();
```

```
  }

  private ProductHome getProductHome() throws NamingException {
    InitialContext initial = new InitialContext();
    ProductHome home =
      (ProductHome) javax.rmi.PortableRemoteObject
        .narrow(initial.lookup("java:comp/env/ejb/Product"),
              ProductHome.class);
    return home;
  }

  private OrderHome getOrderHome() throws NamingException {
    InitialContext initial = new InitialContext();
    OrderHome home =
      (OrderHome) javax.rmi.PortableRemoteObject
        .narrow(initial.lookup("java:comp/env/ejb/Order"),
              OrderHome.class);
    return home;
  }
```

Notice that while business methods accessible through the remote interface must all be public, these implementation methods can be declared as `private`. The first method, `orderExists()`, was referenced above and is pretty self-explanatory. The order entity bean's home interface is used to try to find a pre-existing order with the same key. If one is found, `true` is returned, otherwise `false` is returned, indicated by an exception.

The next two implementation helper methods retrieve the lead-time (`getLeadTimeDays()`) and maximum-inventory-time (`getMaxInventoryTimeDays()`) parameters from the bean's JNDI environment. This read-only information is specified in the bean's deployment descriptor. This is less flexible than storing the information in the database, of course (which in a real manufacturing application is where it would be stored). To change this information, found in the deployment descriptor, we would need to redeploy the bean on our application server. However, storing the information in the deployment descriptor, as we do here, is more flexible than hard-coding values in code. To change the information in code, we would need to rebuild the bean *and* redeploy.

In general, the type of information that belongs in the bean's environment is customization information that is unlikely to be volatile for a particular deployment. Good candidates might be the company's name, SQL statements for direct database access, or an IP address of an ERP application's server. A very bad candidate would be the exchange rate between the Euro and the Dollar.

Environment entries can be any of the following types: `String`, `Boolean`, `Byte`, `Short`, `Integer`, `Long`, `Float`, and `Double`. These entries are typically specified using a tool provided by our application server vendor. The format in the XML deployment descriptor can be edited by hand, if you desire. The sample application's environment entries for the 'manage orders' bean looks like this:

```
<env-entry>
  <env-entry-name>lead_time</env-entry-name>
  <env-entry-type>java.lang.Integer</env-entry-type>
  <env-entry-value>3</env-entry-value>
</env-entry>

<env-entry>
  <env-entry-name>max_inventory_time</env-entry-name>
  <env-entry-type>java.lang.Integer</env-entry-type>
  <env-entry-value>10</env-entry-value>
</env-entry>
```

The names that we specify for our environment variables (with the `<env-entry-name>` element) will be available to our bean in the "`java:comp/env/`" context. See the code for an example of this mapping.

The next two implementation helper methods retrieve the home interfaces of the two entity EJBs that are referenced by this EJB (`Order` and `Product`). The bean developer declares the logical names of the beans that they reference in the deployment descriptor, as described above. Here are the declarations for the 'manage orders' EJB from the sample application:

```
<ejb-ref>
  <ejb-ref-name>ejb/Order</ejb-ref-name>
  <ejb-ref-type>Entity</ejb-ref-type>
  <home>factory.order.OrderHome</home>
  <remote>factory.order.Order</remote>
  <ejb-link>Orders</ejb-link>
</ejb-ref>

<ejb-ref>
  <ejb-ref-name>ejb/Product</ejb-ref-name>
  <ejb-ref-type>Entity</ejb-ref-type>
  <home>factory.product.ProductHome</home>
  <remote>factory.product.Product</remote>
  <ejb-link>Product</ejb-link>
</ejb-ref>
```

As mentioned above, the `ejb-link` entry is an optional entry that the bean developer can use to make sure that the deployer keeps the namespace consistent. In this case it says, "Whatever name you give to my `Product` or `Order` bean in the JNDI namespace, you need to use that same name to link to the `ejb/Product` or `ejb/Order` reference".

Lifecycle and Framework Methods

The lifecycle methods are all empty. For more information on their purpose, see the explanation earlier in this chapter:

```
// Framework & lifecycle methods

public void ejbCreate() {}

public void ejbActivate() {}

public void ejbPassivate() {}

public void ejbRemove() {}

public void setSessionContext(SessionContext ctx) {}
}
```

Stateful Session Bean Implementation

Our sample application's stateful session bean, `Manufacture`, has the main implementation class `factory.manufacture.ManufactureEJB`. This is the only class that we'll be creating in this section. There are two new ideas that we will look at in this code: **how to use database connections** and **how to retrieve environment variables**. Unlike the stateless session bean discussed earlier, the `Manufacture` bean maintains state:

```
package factory.manufacture;

import javax.ejb.*;
import javax.naming.*;
import java.rmi.RemoteException;
import java.sql.Connection;
import java.sql.SQLException;
import java.sql.PreparedStatement;
import javax.sql.DataSource;
import java.util.Arrays;
import java.util.List;
import java.util.Collections;
import java.util.Iterator;
import java.util.Date;

import factory.product.Product;
import factory.product.ProductHome;
import factory.order.Order;
import factory.order.OrderHome;
import factory.order.OrderPK;
import factory.order.StatusStrings;
import factory.manage_orders.OpenOrderView;
import factory.manage_orders.ManageOrders;
import factory.manage_orders.ManageOrdersHome;
import factory.manage_orders.NoSuchOrderException;
import factory.product.RoutingInstruction;

public class ManufactureEJB implements SessionBean {

  // Properties
  public String manufactureCellID;
  public List routingInstructions;
  public int currentPosition;
  public int lastPosition;

  public boolean orderSelected;
  public int selectedSalesDivision;
  public int selectedOrderNumber;
```

The manufactureCellID variable is set in the ejbCreate() call. Unlike the stateless session bean's ejbCreate() call, this has a one-to-one correspondence with a matching create() call by the client on the bean's home interface. Notice that we also use ejbCreate() like a constructor to initialize orderSelected. We'll look at this method next, along with the other (empty) lifecycle methods:

```
  // Framework & lifecycle methods
  public void ejbCreate(String manufactureCellID) {
    this.manufactureCellID = manufactureCellID;
    orderSelected = false;
  }

  public void ejbActivate() {}

  public void ejbPassivate() {}

  public void ejbRemove() {}

  public void setSessionContext(SessionContext ctx) {}
```

Next, the business methods:

```
// Business methods
public OpenOrderView[] getOpenOrders() {

  try {
    ManageOrdersHome homeManageOrders = getManageOrdersHome();
    ManageOrders manageOrders = homeManageOrders.create();
    return manageOrders.getSchedulableOrders();

  } catch (NamingException ne) {
    throw new EJBException(ne);
  } catch (RemoteException re) {
    throw new EJBException(re);
  } catch (CreateException ce) {
    throw new EJBException(ce);
  }
}
```

```
public void selectForManufacture(int salesDivision, int order_number)
        throws NoSuchOrderException, BadStatusException {

  try {
    OrderHome homeOrder = getOrderHome();
    OrderPK orderPK = new OrderPK(salesDivision, order_number);
    Order order = homeOrder.findByPrimaryKey(orderPK);
    String orderStatus = order.getStatus();
    if (!orderStatus.equals(StatusStrings.OPEN)) {
      throw new BadStatusException(orderStatus);
    }
    order.beginManufacture();
    Product product = order.getProductOrdered();
    RoutingInstruction[] productRouting =
                    product.getRoutingInstructions();
    routingInstructions = Arrays.asList(productRouting);
    Collections.sort(routingInstructions);
    currentPosition = 0;
    lastPosition = routingInstructions.size() - 1;
    selectedSalesDivision = salesDivision;
    selectedOrderNumber = order_number;
    orderSelected = true;

  } catch (NamingException ne) {
    ne.printStackTrace();
    throw new EJBException(ne);
  } catch (RemoteException re) {
    re.printStackTrace();
    throw new EJBException(re);
  } catch (FinderException fe) {
    fe.printStackTrace();
    if (fe instanceof ObjectNotFoundException) {
      throw new NoSuchOrderException();
    } else {
      throw new EJBException(fe);
    }
  }
}
```

```
public boolean hasNextRouting() throws NoSelectionException {
  if (!orderSelected) {
    throw new NoSelectionException();
  }
```

```
    return (currentPosition <= lastPosition);
}

public String getNextRouting() throws NoSelectionException {
  if (!orderSelected) {
    throw new NoSelectionException();
  }

  RoutingInstruction ri =
         (RoutingInstruction) routingInstructions.get(currentPosition++);
  return ri.instruction;
}

public void ship(String carrier, int loading_dock)
           throws NoSelectionException {

  // Sales division, order number, carrier,
  // loading dock, date completed, manufactured by

  if (!orderSelected) {
    throw new NoSelectionException();
  }
  Connection con = null;

  try {
    con = getConnection();
    PreparedStatement statement =
                   con.prepareStatement(getShipmentSQLString());
    statement.setInt(1, selectedSalesDivision);
    statement.setInt(2, selectedOrderNumber);
    statement.setString(3, carrier);
    statement.setInt(4, loading_dock);
    statement.setDate(5, new java.sql.Date((new Date()).getTime()));
    statement.setString(6, manufactureCellID);
    statement.executeUpdate();
    statement.close();
    con.close();
    orderSelected = false;

    OrderHome homeOrder = getOrderHome();
    OrderPK orderPK = new OrderPK(selectedSalesDivision,
                                  selectedOrderNumber);
    Order order = homeOrder.findByPrimaryKey(orderPK);
    order.completeManufacture();

  } catch (NamingException ne) {
    ne.printStackTrace();
    throw new EJBException(ne);
  } catch (SQLException sqle) {
    try {
      if (con != null) {
        con.close();
      }
    } catch (Exception e) {
    }
    sqle.printStackTrace();
    throw new EJBException(sqle);
  } catch (RemoteException re) {
    throw new EJBException(re);
  } catch (FinderException fe) {
    throw new EJBException(fe);
  }
```

```
    finally {
      try {
        if (null != con) {
          con.close();
        }
      } catch(Exception ignore) {}
    }
  }
```

The 'selected order' is indicated by two variables that represent the order's key,
selectedSalesDivision and selectedOrderNumber. They are set in the business method
selectForManufacture(). This business method performs the following additional steps:

❏   Verifies that the order exists and is eligible for manufacture

❏   Sets the status of the order so that other manufacturing cells will realize that the order is being built

❏   Retrieves the routing instructions for the ordered product, sorts them, and caches them in a variable

❏   Sets the orderSelected variable to true so that subsequent method calls in the workflow
    will be able to proceed

The first step in the workflow that the Manufacture bean embodies (even before selecting an order for
manufacture) is to get a list of open orders. The implementation of this business method is simple,
because it delegates all its work to the stateless session ManageOrders EJB discussed in the last section.
This is a simple example of a 'services layer' architecture. Notice that the stateful session bean calls the
stateless session bean – but not the other way around.

Following order selection, the next step in the workflow is to iterate through the product routings while we
are building the product. Again, this is quite simple. We iterate through the collection set up in the
selectForManufacture() method. Notice that we make sure the workflow has been followed, by
checking the orderSelected variable. If it hasn't been, we throw a business exception to the client to give
it the opportunity to correct the error. Notice also that we are iterating through stale data. The product design
could have changed during the manufacturing process, and it won't be reflected in the iteration. This is OK
with us, though: we don't want to change to a new routing list halfway through building the product.

The last business method, ship(), changes the order status to indicate that manufacturing is completed.
It does this using the Order entity bean, and also inserts a shipment record in the database. This is
included as an example of accessing a database directly from a session bean.

First, notice where the SQL text comes from: the bean's environment. The implementation helper
method getShipmentSQLString() (shown below) retrieves the SQL from the XML deployment
descriptor. This partially decouples the EJB from the specifics of the database. If we want to use the
same business logic with a different database structure, we can, without rewriting the bean. This is an
ideal case for storing information in the deployment descriptor:

```
private String getShipmentSQLString() throws NamingException {

  InitialContext initial = new InitialContext();
  String sql = (String) initial.lookup("java:comp/env/shipmentSQL");
  return sql;
}
```

The deployment descriptor environment entry looks as follows:

```
<env-entry>
  <env-entry-name>shipmentSQL</env-entry-name>
  <env-entry-type>java.lang.String</env-entry-type>
  <env-entry-value>insert into shipments (division, order_number, carrier,
                   loading_dock, date_completed, manufactured_by) values
                   (?, ?, ?, ?, ?, ?)
  </env-entry-value>
</env-entry>
```

On the database that we use for development, the table might be defined like this:

```
CREATE TABLE SHIPMENTS (DIVISION INTEGER NOT NULL,
                        ORDER_NUMBER INTEGER NOT NULL,
                        CARRIER CHAR(50),
                        LOADING_DOCK INTEGER,
                        DATE_COMPLETED DATE,
                        MANUFACTURED_BY CHAR(50),
                        PRIMARY KEY (DIVISION, ORDER_NUMBER));
```

The connection to the database must be retrieved under controlled circumstances. The bean programmer can't simply get one using JDBC's `DriverManager`. The EJB container needs to manage the process, to implement features such as transaction management and connection pooling. The programmer, therefore, must acquire a `DataSource` from the JNDI namespace (which is a "factory class" for JDBC connections), and use this to produce the connection. We can see an example of this in the `getConnection()` helper method below. Also, while an EJB is in a transaction, the bean programmer isn't allowed to interfere with the container by calling `commit()` or `rollback()` on the connection.

The bean programmer must declare in the XML deployment descriptor that they are going to use a resource such as a JDBC connection. (Other possible resources include JMS or JavaMail connections.) Note that this reference to a JDBC connection is a logical reference that will be mapped by the container into the JNDI namespace. An actual corresponding JDBC connection will be specified when the bean is deployed. The XML for our sample looks like this:

```
<resource-ref>
  <res-ref-name>jdbc/shipDB</res-ref-name>
  <res-type>javax.sql.DataSource</res-type>
  <res-auth>Container</res-auth>
</resource-ref>
```

The EJB can give a username and password itself, but hard-coding this in the bean code is usually a bad idea. In this sample, we depend on the container to authenticate the bean to the database. When we deploy the application, we can specify a username and password dynamically. (Exactly how to do this is specific to the application server, and the documentation that comes with it should help.)

Finally, here are the helper methods:

```
// Implementation helper
private OrderHome getOrderHome() throws NamingException {
  InitialContext initial = new InitialContext();
  OrderHome home =
    (OrderHome) javax.rmi.PortableRemoteObject
      .narrow(initial.lookup("java:comp/env/ejb/Order"),
              OrderHome.class);
  return home;
}
```

```
    private ManageOrdersHome getManageOrdersHome()
            throws NamingException {
    InitialContext initial = new InitialContext();
    ManageOrdersHome home =
        (ManageOrdersHome) javax.rmi.PortableRemoteObject
            .narrow(initial.lookup("java:comp/env/ejb/ManageOrders"),
                ManageOrdersHome.class);
    return home;
    }
```

```
    private Connection getConnection()
            throws SQLException, NamingException {
    Context initial = new InitialContext();
    DataSource dataSource =
        (DataSource) initial.lookup("java:comp/env/jdbc/shipDB");
    return dataSource.getConnection();
    }
```

```
    private String getShipmentSQLString() throws NamingException {
    InitialContext initial = new InitialContext();
    String sql = (String) initial.lookup("java:comp/env/shipmentSQL");
    return sql;
    }
}
```

The getConnection() helper method finds the connection factory class javax.sql.DataSource from the environment, in much the same way that we retrieve configuration parameters. From the connection factory, we retrieve and return a connection.

It's important to understand that this isn't an ordinary, database connection. The container will almost certainly have wrapped this connection in an enclosing class that also implements the Connection interface. We can use the wrapper just like we would the underlying connection, but when we close the connection, it doesn't really close. It sticks around, ready to complete this transaction or return to the connection pool.

Most programmers learn very quickly that connections to a database are expensive to open and close, and doing so should be avoided where possible. They learn to keep connections around, reusing them in their code. Programming with an application server turns that rule on its head. Opening and closing connections is cheap, because the connections don't really get opened or closed. With an application server, the expensive thing is to keep a connection around – because then it can't be pooled for use by multiple beans. It's possible to tuck a connection away in our bean to reuse in multiple transactions, but in general you shouldn't do this. Acquire a resource, use that resource, and let the resource go. It's worth repeating: acquire a resource, use that resource, and let the resource go:

```
con = getConnection();
PreparedStatement statement = con.prepareStatement(getShipmentSQLString());
statement.setInt(1, selectedSalesDivision);
statement.setInt(2, selectedOrderNumber);
statement.setString(3, carrier);
statement.setInt(4, loading_dock);
statement.setDate(5, new java.sql.Date((new Date()).getTime()));
statement.setString(6, manufactureCellID);
statement.executeUpdate();
statement.close();
con.close();
```

We close the connection here (`con.close()`), but it doesn't really close. The wrapper class intercepted this. We say 'close', but the application server hears 'reuse'.

Finally, here are a couple of exception classes that we need:

```
package factory.manufacture;

public class NoSelectionException extends Exception {

  public NoSelectionException() {}
}
```

```
package factory.manufacture;

public class BadStatusException extends Exception {
  private String status;

  public BadStatusException(String status) {
    this.status = status;
  }

  public String getStatus() {
    return status;
  }
}
```

At this point, we cannot deploy and run the sample application. We need to proceed to the next chapter, where we will add the entity beans.

Summary

This chapter discussed session beans in depth. Here is a review of some of the main points:

- ❑ Session beans represent a process, task, or workflow
- ❑ There are two types of session beans: stateful and stateless
- ❑ Stateful session beans may ease application development at the cost of scalability
- ❑ Stateless session beans can provide services to clients or to other beans
- ❑ The client view of server functionality should be through a session bean façade, thus hiding much of the complexity
- ❑ Environment entries and external resources can be declared in the deployment descriptor and accessed through the JNDI namespace

In the next chapter, we'll look at entity beans more closely. First, we'll show why session beans can't perform the same function in your application as entity beans. Then we'll consider some of the advantages of using entity beans, especially with regard to performance. Next, we'll look at two variations of entity beans: those with container-managed persistence and those with bean-managed persistence. We'll look at the advantages and disadvantages of each, while developing two versions of a single bean (much as we did in this chapter). We'll also look at the lifecycle and container callbacks of an entity bean, along with some entity-specific things like primary keys, finder methods, and caching. Finally, we'll complete and run our sample application.

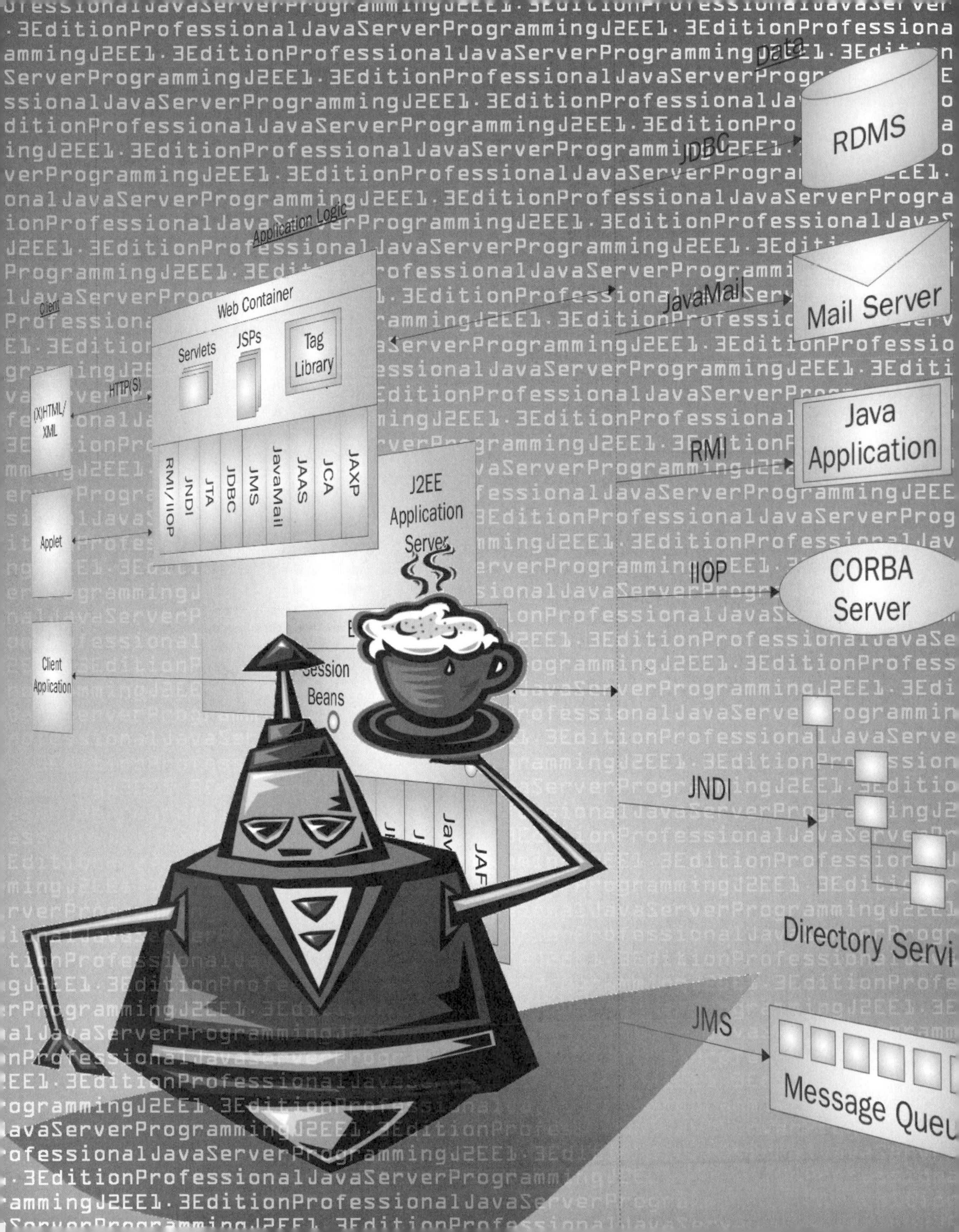

16

Entity Beans and Persistence

Entity Enterprise JavaBeans represent the entity objects in our analysis model. They can correspond to real-world concepts, such as customers or products, or they can correspond to abstractions, such as manufacturing processes, company policies, or customer purchases.

This notion of **representation** is important to understand. After all, a session bean can access any data that an entity bean can. Although a session bean can access data, it can't provide an object-oriented *representation* of that data. How does an entity bean differ? Why can't you have a 'customer' session bean or a 'product' session bean, like you can with entity beans?

The basic explanation is simple, even if the details are complicated. We've seen in the previous chapter that the state maintained by stateful session beans is private, in the sense that only the client that is currently using the session bean can manipulate this state. Entity beans are different because their state is stored in the database; several clients can therefore access their state simultaneously. So the fundamental problem in representing an object with a session bean is in how that state is made available to clients of that bean. An entity bean is (logically, anyway) a single point of access for that data: any client that accesses the data will go through that entity bean. A session bean, on the other hand, is only accessible to a single client. If there are multiple clients, there will be multiple session beans.

In this chapter we will:

- ❏ Compare and contrast the use of an entity bean with the use of session beans
- ❏ Compare and contrast entity beans whose persistence mechanism is container managed and those whose persistence mechanism is managed by the bean developer
- ❏ Learn how to develop entity beans (both container- and bean-managed persistent versions)
- ❏ Complete our manufacturing application from the last chapter

Why not use Session Beans?

To understand the difference between entity beans and session beans, let's consider how we might try to make session beans play the same role that entity beans do in representing an object such as a customer. We'll try to build an entity bean out of session bean parts, and then consider the limitations of what we have done.

Using a Stateful Session bean

First, let's try to use a stateful session bean. For a customer, we could write a bean class that looked something like this:

```
public class Customer implements SessionBean {
   private int customerID;
   private String customerName;
   private String customerAddr;
   private String city;
   private String state;
   private String postalCode;

   public void ejbCreate(String customerID) {
      this.customerID = customerID;
   }

   public void setCustomerName(String customerName) {
      this.customerName = customerName;
   }

   public String getCustomerName() {
      return customerName;
   }

   // ... Similar methods ...

   public void saveStateToDatabase() {

      // ... sql code ...
   }

   public void loadStateFromDatabase() {

      // ... sql code ...
   }

   // ... Lifecycle methods ...

}
```

This session bean's state is the customer data for a particular customer: name, address, and so on. The state is loaded from the database by one method (loadStateFromDatabase()), and saved to the database by another (saveStateToDatabase()). This bean is intended to provide an object-oriented representation of a particular customer; data is accessed as properties of the Customer object.

When do our methods to load and save the state to the database get called? You might be envisioning client code cluttered with calls to these methods, sitting around the business logic like a pair of bookends. This would be a disadvantage of session beans compared to entity beans, which have special callbacks that help the container manage their state automatically.

A session bean can, however, duplicate these special container-managed-state callbacks by implementing the `javax.ejb.SessionSynchronization` interface, which allows you to know when a transaction has begun, when it is about to complete, and when it has completed. This provides stateful session beans with optional callbacks that the container will use to notify the bean of when a transaction begins and when that transaction is about to end. Transaction boundaries are excellent points at which to synchronize object state with the database.

*A transaction is a set of operations that must be processed as a single unit. To be considered transactional, the set of operations composing this single unit of work must exhibit certain well-defined characteristics, often referred to by their mnemonic acronym ACID, which stands for **atomic, consistent, isolated,** and **durable**. For more information about transactions and their use in Enterprise JavaBeans technology, please see Chapter 17.*

When the bean is notified that the transaction has begun, it can call a `loadStateFromDatabase()` method or the equivalent. When the container notifies the bean that the transaction is about to end successfully, the session bean can save its data to the database at that time, by calling `saveStateToDatabase()`. Here is the pseudo-code we would need to add to the customer session bean to get it to synchronize on transaction boundaries:

```
public class Customer implements SessionBean, SessionSynchronization {

  // ...

  public void afterBegin() {
    loadStateFromDatabase();
  }

  public void afterCompletion(boolean commit) {

    /*
     * This could be used to restore the state
     * to what it was before the transaction began,
     * if commit were to be false (indicating a
     * rollback)
     */

    // Empty
  }

  public void beforeCompletion() {

    /*
     * this method will only be called
     * if the transaction has not been rolled back
     */
    ;
    saveStateToDatabase();
  }
}
```

It seems at first glance that we now have a perfectly adequate representation of a customer entity, using only a stateful session bean. Remember, though, that this session bean represents the state of the customer for a *single* client only. To understand the limitation of using private, conversational state to represent shared data, consider the case where we have two session beans within one transaction that need to access customer data.

Imagine that we're processing an order. As part of this order, we need to change the customer's ship-to address, and also change the customer's available credit. These activities are performed by the 'manage preferences' and 'manage accounts' stateless session beans, respectively. As part of their work, both of those session beans need to alter data managed by the `Customer` object. Each will create a stateful session bean to represent the customer, using the `create()` method to associate the customer ID with the bean. Each will then invoke the appropriate business method on their respective session bean. Let's say those methods are `setCustomerPreferences(CustomerPreferencesView preferences)` and `setAvailableCredit(double availableCredit)`.

As the business methods are invoked, each Customer bean (the one in 'manage preferences' and the one in 'manage accounts') is enlisted into the transaction. When this happens, `afterBegin()` is called on each bean, and the state data is loaded. Notice that we have two copies of the same state data. Each copy is accessible only by its client.

Now we face our first dilemma. The 'manage preferences' and 'manage accounts' session beans provide a service, but they do not maintain state associated with a particular client, transaction, or method. This would include any reference to the customer beans that they are using. What, then, do we do with the Customer beans? Remember, they have state and are consuming server resources.

We have two choices, one of them illegal and one of them bad:

❏ We could try to remove the bean, but this is illegal; a stateful session bean can't be removed while it is in the middle of a transaction. (Even if it could be removed, we'd have to call the `saveStateToDatabase()` method manually, because the bean wouldn't be around at the end of the transaction for it to be called automatically. But don't even think about calling `remove()` on the bean – the specification prohibits this and an exception will be thrown by the container.)

❏ Alternatively, we could let the beans time-out automatically and be removed by the application server. But this is messy, and can lead to performance problems. The EJB container will be managing our state, and references to the EJBs, even though they will never be accessed again.

Contrast this to the case of entity beans. They are shared objects, and the instantiation and destruction of the EJBs is managed directly by the container. In the example we are considering, the 'manage preferences' and 'manage accounts' session beans can use their entity bean references and forget about them. As the entity beans don't belong to any one client, the client isn't responsible for removing them from the container. Remember that the lifecycle methods for the creation and removal of session beans refer to the EJB in the container, but the lifecycle methods for creation and removal of entity beans refer to the underlying storage mechanism, such as a database.

This dilemma isn't the only one that we face in using this stateful session bean to represent a Customer object. We saw in the example above that there may be multiple copies of the same data, because a session bean represents private, conversational data, and not shared, transactional data. When there are multiple copies, those copies can become unsynchronized. In one or both of the copies, the data can be **stale**.

In our example, there are two copies of the customer stateful session bean participating in the transaction. One is owned by the 'manage preferences' bean, and has a new ship-to address; and one is owned by the 'manage accounts' bean, and has a new available-credit value. When the transaction is about to commit, the container will call `beforeCompletion()` sequentially on the two customer beans (in an undefined order). The first bean will update the information in the database when its `beforeCompletion()` method is called. When the second bean's `beforeCompletion()` method is called, it will write over the information in the database put there by the first bean. The data in the database will be left in an *inconsistent* state.

Contrast this to the case of entity beans. As they are shared objects, the changes from one client in a transaction (the 'manage preferences' bean) will be reflected in an access by a different client (the 'manage accounts' bean). As far as the clients are concerned, there is only one bean, which they both are accessing. The bean's data, because it is shared data, will be kept in a consistent state. (One way to think of this is that the entity bean is a proxy for the database data.)

Using a Stateless Session Bean

So we can't use state in a stateful session bean as a mechanism to represent an entity object. Let's consider how we might try to represent an entity object using a stateless session bean. There are two consequences to our lack of state:

❑   The stateless session bean being referenced by the client cannot be associated with an identity (with a primary key of a database row), because it could not remember that identity from method call to method call. (This is the same as the reason why a stateless session bean will never have a create() method with parameters.) So we'll have to pass the identity that represents the current session in to each method call.

❑   The stateless session bean cannot cache any information associated with the entity. This means that any information needed to process a business method must be read during that method, and any updates to information must be immediately written to the data store. Because of this, every method that accesses state is going to have some data-reading code at the start, and every method that modifies state is going to have some data-writing code at its close.

Our sample stateless Customer bean might look like this:

```
public class Customer implements SessionBean {

  public void setCustomerName(String customerID, String customerName) {
    Connection con = null;
    try {
      con = getConnection();
      PreparedStatement statement =
           con.prepareStatement("UPDATE Customer SET Name=? WHERE id=?");
      statement.setString(1, customerName);
      statement.setString(2, customerID);
      int updated = statement.executeUpdate();
      if (updated != 1) {
        throw new EJBException("Customer not found.");
      }
    } catch (SQLException sqle) {
      throw new EJBException(sqle);
    } finally {
      try {
        if (con != null) {
          con.close();
        }
      } catch (Exception e) {}
    }
  }

  public String getCustomerName(String customerID) {
    Connection con = null;
    try {
      con = getConnection();
      PreparedStatement statement =
           con.prepareStatement("SELECT Name FROM Customer WHERE id=?");
```

```
      statement.setString(1, customerID);
      ResultSet resultSet = statement.executeQuery();
      if (!resultSet.next()) {
         throw new EJBException("Customer not found.");
      }
      return resultSet.getString(1);
   } catch (SQLException sqle) {
      throw new EJBException(sqle);
   } finally {
      try {
         if (con != null) {
            con.close();
         }
      } catch (Exception e) {}
   }
}

// ...

}
```

This code suffers from none of the fatal flaws that were present in the stateful version of our customer session bean. First, the client need not worry about the removal of the session bean. Since each operation on a stateless session bean is atomic (changes in state will not be visible on subsequent calls), calling remove() on one during a transaction is not an error. Even if you don't call remove() at all, there probably will not be any negative consequences, because there are no server resources associated with this session bean's identity.

Second, there are no private caches of state that can become unsynchronized and inconsistent. All the state is kept in the database (or other data store), and any database that you use for enterprise data will be multi-user and transactional. This means that the database will manage concurrent accesses and ensure that your data remains consistent.

That doesn't mean that this approach renders entity beans obsolete. The first thing to notice about this code is that it will be somewhat painful to write, unless some kind of tool is used to generate data-access classes. Embedding SQL directly in your Java is a tedious and error-prone task, making future maintenance difficult. The second thing to notice is that the customer stateless session bean is not providing an object-oriented view of your data. Instead, it is providing a function library of the sort that is popular with C programming. There is nothing wrong with this approach from a code-correctness standpoint. The task we set ourselves, however, was to provide an object-oriented representation of a customer: functionality *plus* data. The stateless session 'customer' bean has only functionality; it does not have data, nor does it have identity.

As we mentioned in Chapter 16 on session beans, implementing your business model without entity beans might be a valid choice for a certain class of problems. For example, you might need very specific access to the database that is not well covered by the CMP model defined in the EJB 2.0 specification, such as the need to use SQL that is proprietary to your database. However, you will have to limit yourself to the 'function library' approach of direct-database access, rather than the more object-oriented approach allowed by entity beans. If you're only planning on reading the data (not writing), then there is no reason not to use stateless session beans; in fact, it's more efficient than using entity beans when we don't have to worry about writing to the database.

Benefits of Entity Beans

Entity beans provide benefits beyond simply allowing you to represent shared, transactional state in your object model (the data we access is retrieved in a transaction). In keeping with the general philosophy of Enterprise JavaBeans technology, the EJB container will provide the EJB developer with a number of system-level persistence services in order to free them to concentrate on business logic programming. Four major ones are:

❑ **Container callbacks that inform you about the progress of the current transaction**
These callbacks play the same role as our homemade `afterBegin()`, `loadStateFromDatabase()`, `beforeCompletion()`, and `saveStateToDatabase()` methods did when we tried to construct an entity bean from a stateful session bean.

❑ **Support for concurrent access**
The container has several strategies that it can employ to accomplish this. One is simply to defer concurrency control to the database, as we did with the customer stateless session bean in the above code. Another strategy, appropriate in certain circumstances, is to synchronize access to a single entity bean with a particular identity. EJB containers can also use a combination of these methods.

❑ **Maintaining a cache between transactions**
Depending on the application and the database access patterns, this can significantly improve performance.

❑ **Providing all the persistence management code**
Every EJB 2.0-compliant container will take care of saving your entity beans for you, if you choose, and this can be a tremendous productivity booster. Many developers would tell you that this is the main advantage of entity beans, if not Enterprise JavaBeans technology in general. Not only can container-managed persistence free the developer from writing data access code (usually JDBC and SQL), but it can also provide optimizations such as carefully tuned updates of only the relevant data

Container- vs. Bean-Managed Persistence

The EJB container can manage the process of saving and restoring the state of your entity beans; this is known as **container-managed persistence**, or **CMP**. Alternatively, bean developers can take control of the bean's persistence themselves; this is known as **bean-managed persistence**, or **BMP**.

One of the most important implementation decisions in any project that uses Enterprise JavaBeans technology is which form of persistence management the entity beans will use. There is no question that persistence is one of those system-level services that are not the appropriate domain of business-logic programmers. The most common manifestation of persistence code is SQL. Writing SQL code that moves the state of a Java object back-and-forth from a database is a tedious, time-consuming, error-prone process, especially if the data model exhibits any complexity. The Enterprise JavaBeans framework was written largely to move these system-level issues to the EJB container. For many projects, it will make sense to take advantage of the ability of the container to manage the persistence of your beans, as this leaves the task of synchronization to the container.

However, bean-managed persistence is an important choice in some circumstances. The basic problem is that, although every EJB 2.0-compliant container must provide support for container-managed persistence, the specification does not indicate *how* this support must be provided. In fact, a container need not necessarily provide any CMP support for mapping your entity bean's state to columns in a database. It could use Java serialization to write the whole bean to one column and still be compliant. This would rarely be adequate for a project, and might necessitate the use of bean-managed persistence if your EJB container used serialization.

On the other hand, this extreme case doesn't exist in real life. Every single application server with EJB support of which I am aware, including the open source ones, has some support for mapping your objects to the fields in a relational database.

The trick is determining whether your EJB container has the level of support for container-managed persistence that you require. If it does, take advantage of this support to free your business-logic programmers from writing persistence logic. The boost in productivity is potentially very large, and depending on the EJB container, the boost in application performance may be large, too.

EJB 2.0 introduces a CMP model that is a big improvement over 1.1. An EJB 2.0-compliant container will automatically take care of complex tasks such as maintaining relationships between your entity beans or generating complex SQL requests allowing you to navigate those relations.

The CMP model of EJB 2.0 also brings a lot of other, more discreet, benefits that you need to be aware of. For example, using bean-managed persistence, a finder query fetching several beans will usually be translated into two distinct calls to the database: one to query the primary keys and the other one to fetch the beans themselves. If you use CMP, the container can issue just one request to the database. This is not feasible with BMP due to the way the specification defines it. This is admittedly a subtle point but keep in mind that CMP 2.0 has a lot of similar hidden advantages, so you should definitely have excellent justifications if you decide to go the BMP route. If in doubt, go with CMP and consider switching to BMP when you are sure that you are seeing performance problems you could solve by writing the code yourself.

If your target data store is an ERP (Enterprise Resource Planning) system or some other existing application, you will probably need to use bean-managed persistence. Rather than writing SQL code you will probably be using vendor-specific protocols, which would not be supported by a generic EJB container. If your target data store is a relational database, and your EJB container does not have adequate CMP support for your project, you have four choices:

❑ **Find another EJB container**
This is not possible for everyone – perhaps you are writing components for resale, and don't want to limit your market, or perhaps you are an application developer constrained by the choice someone else made. However, there are capable application servers with sophisticated object/relational-mapping capabilities on the market. Due to the tremendous productivity advantages of using container-managed persistence, the capabilities of the application server in this regard should be considered when making a technology decision. As more EJB containers implement the EJB 2.0 specification, this will become less of an issue.

❑ **Use a third-party object/relational-mapping tool**
You can use a third-party object/relational-mapping tool either with entity beans and bean-managed persistence, or using session beans exclusively (such as TopLink or CocoBase). This is a good choice, although it has two major disadvantages: cost (many of these object/relational-mapping tools are expensive, although there is at least one major open source project to develop such a tool), and secondly you have tied your application to a proprietary third-party framework.

Some EJB containers are able to integrate third-party object/relational-mapping tools so that their functionality is accessible by beans using container-managed persistence. This makes entity beans easier to develop, keeps the developer from being tied to the product, and allows the third-party tool to take advantage of some additional optimizations.

❑ **Change your design**
You can change your design to reflect the limitations of your chosen tool, and use container-managed persistence. (Depending on what those limitations are, and what your needs are, this may not be possible.) For instance, your EJB container may not have support for mapping dependent objects into their own tables with a foreign-key relationship to the main table. If your container had better support for modeling relationships between entity beans, you could promote those dependent objects into first class entity beans to preserve a normalized database design. There are two disadvantages to this approach: performance (as in the dependent-object example, your new design may result in a heavier-weight object model implementation), and your altered design may be more difficult to implement, maintain, and understand.

❑ **Write your own data-access code**
It is a large commitment to decide to have your developers take responsibility for writing the persistence code that your application requires. If you do decide to do this, you should encapsulate the persistence code in data-access helper components of your entity beans. If you find that a significant portion of your development efforts are being spent on writing SQL statements inside of callback methods in entity beans, stop and reconsider. The expectation of the EJB specification writers was that most EJBs that used bean-managed persistence would be created using a tool. Section 12.1.1 of the EJB specification Proposed Final Draft 2 states:

"We expect that most enterprise beans with bean managed persistence will be created by application development tools which will encapsulate data access in components. These data access components will probably not be the same for all tools. Further, if the data access calls are encapsulated in data access components, the data access components may require deployment interfaces to allow adapting data access to different schemas or even to a different database type. This EJB specification does not define the architecture for data access objects, strategies for tailoring and deploying data access components or ensuring portability of these components for bean managed persistence..."

As the capabilities of EJB containers continue to improve in the face of the fierce competition that has developed between implementers of this API, and given the changes to the persistence model in the EJB 2.0 specification, sophisticated object/relational-mapping capabilities are bound to become ubiquitous – the application-server vendors will add these capabilities to their products, and because interfaces will develop to allow third party object/relational tools to be integrated with EJB containers. As time goes on, it will make no more sense for business logic programmers to be writing object/relational-mapping code than it would for them to be writing relational databases. That day has not quite arrived, but a careful evaluation of the requirements of the application and the capabilities of the tools is necessary before making a decision to write entity beans that manage their own persistence. (Chapter 23 considers some of the criteria you should consider in selecting an application server.)

New Features Introduced in EJB 2.0 for CMP

If you are already familiar with EJB 1.1 and are upgrading to EJB 2.0, this section will be of interest to you. The EJB 2.0 specification introduces some radical improvements, especially for container-managed persistence. The main additions are:

❑ Abstract accessors

❑ Local interfaces

❑ Relationships

❑ The EJB Query Language

These four features are made possible by the introduction of a new actor in the EJB model. Initially called the "Persistence Manager" in early drafts of the EJB 2.0 specification, this actor eventually lost its identity and became part of the container. Therefore, all the EJB 2.0 containers have to implement its services.

What this means for the container is that the tools you use to process your Enterprise JavaBeans (called ejbc in BEA WebLogic, for example) will generate more code in order to provide all those services. In particular, as you will see in the next three sections, the implementation of the above features is made through abstract methods that the container will implement in the generated code.

Abstract Accessors

A CMP entity bean is essentially defined by its CMP fields: Java fields that are mapped to tables in the database. The EJB 1.1 specification was very vague in how these fields were supposed to be represented on the bean class. The EJB 2.0 specification imposes that these CMP fields be defined by abstract accessors instead of Java fields. For example, a CMP field called nickName would be declared as follows in an EJB 2.0 entity bean:

```
public abstract String getNickName ();
public abstract void setNickName(String nickname);
```

Notice that in our database, we might not have a column named nickName; this is OK, since it is only in the deployment descriptor that we specify how to map CMP fields. We'll see this later.

This looks like an innocuous change but it has many consequences on the CMP model in general from a performance standpoint. The most important point is that the container now has total control on the access of fields. Since it will generate the code for each accessor, it is able to make all kinds of decisions and optimizations on how to retrieve the data. The EJB 2.0 specification doesn't mandate any particular implementation, but here are some benefits that EJB 2.0 containers typically provide thanks to this new design:

❑ **Lazy loading of beans**
Now that the container knows exactly when and what fields are being accessed, it no longer has to load the entire state of the bean on ejbLoad(). It can decide to do nothing when the bean is initially fetched and only decide to start loading the state on the first call of one of the getters. This can be especially important when your application starts and hundreds of beans are being fetched in memory on start-up. It is also a very important feature when it is coupled to "group loading" (see below).

❑ **Tuned updates**
A major flaw of the EJB 1.1 CMP model and how it failed to define access to CMP fields is that the container couldn't tell what fields had been modified during a transaction. Consequently, container vendors started providing proprietary extensions to the model in order to get this information. The most common one is the introduction of a method boolean isModified() which returned true if the bean had changed one of its fields during the transaction. This approach has two severe drawbacks:

  ❑ The bean provider must implement it, which involves keeping track of the fields that have been modified

  ❑ It is not fine grained: all the container knows is that the bean has been modified, but it doesn't know specifically what fields

The EJB 2.0 abstract accessors address all these shortcomings. The bean provider no longer has to track which fields were modified (after all, this is container-managed persistence, so we should rightfully expect the container to do all this work for us) but, most of all, it knows exactly what fields have been modified. Consequently, when the transaction commits, it is able to issue a "tuned update" to the database: a SQL request that will update only columns corresponding to fields modified during the transaction.

❑ **Group loading**

Another interesting feature that a container can provide is allowing you to define groups of fields. For example, suppose that your entity bean contains simple fields such as integers, strings, etc., but it also contains a large binary object (an image for example). If you code this naively and run a query that fetches your bean, the whole state is going to travel on the network, including the big image. This is a waste of bandwidth if the client that issued the request is not interested in the image.

To address this problem, WebLogic introduces the concept of "field groups". When a field is accessed, all the other fields that belong to the same group will also be fetched by the container, but not the others. In the example with the big image, you would put the image in one group, and all the other fields in a separate group. Therefore, as long as you are accessing a field that is not the image, the large binary object will never be fetched.

These are implementation-specific details but you can expect many EJB 2.0 containers to provide them as they clearly address real world concerns.

Local Interfaces

The EJB 2.0 specification introduces a new concept: local interfaces. In EJB 1.1, the only interfaces you needed in a bean were remote: remote home and remote object. One problem with remote interfaces is that since they use RMI as the remote access protocol, they have to abide by the RMI transport rules: parameters must be passed by value, methods must throw `RemoteException` in their signature, etc. Let's examine one of these constraints: pass by value.

This simple restriction has a deep performance impact on your beans: every method call suffers a big overhead since parameters have to be cloned to and from. While this restriction does make sense when caller and callee are effectively on different machine, why should we pay this price when both are in the same virtual machine? For example, a typical case is a bean invoking a method on another bean (a stateless session bean invoking an entity bean in the same container). In this particular case, the RMI restrictions are unnecessary and can make the calls needlessly expensive.

Therefore, the EJB expert group introduced local interfaces. A bean can now expose two kinds of interfaces: a remote and a local interface (it can expose both or just one of them). This duality has been extended to EJB objects, which can now be either remote or local. A local home interface will return local EJB objects. Method calls on local interfaces obey the standard Java call semantics: no copying of parameters is done, ensuring maximum performance.

The above scenario can now be rewritten as follows: the stateless session bean exposes a remote interface, which is the interface that remote clients will use to communicate. The stateless session bean itself will look up the entity bean's local home interface. From this interface, it will be able to create or look up local entity beans, and on these beans, invoke methods with standard "pass by reference" calling semantics.

Relationships

A Java program typically manipulates graphs of objects: objects that contain objects that contain more objects. Obviously, when we use entity beans, we want the persistent store to reflect these complex relationships, but the task is not very easy due to the fact that relational databases store tables (rows and columns). Therefore, a certain amount of work is needed in order to map a graph of Java objects to tables.

EJB 1.1 didn't specify anything in that area, so bean providers often resorted to bean-managed persistence to store their Java objects. EJB 2.0 introduces the concept of container-managed relationships, which addresses this problem.

Briefly, all the bean providers have to do now is define the relationship between their beans in their deployment descriptors and the EJB 2.0 container will generate all the Java code and SQL statements needed to persist and navigate the relations. Relationships can be either unidirectional (an order having line items, but the line items not having an order) or bi-directional (you can locate the order from the line item, as well as locating the line item from the order), and they can be of three sorts:

❑ One-to-One: Person and Social Security Number

❑ One-to-Many: Person and Shopping Order

❑ Many-to-Many: Person and Magazine Subscription

The container generates code that takes care of the following tasks:

❑ Maintaining referential integrity (if a person changes their social security number, the social security number bean should be destroyed as well)

❑ Handling addition and removal of beans from a many relationship, and persisting the new state

❑ Enabling navigation through relationships by generating SQL statements that select the right fields

EJB Query Language

One of the benefits of container-managed persistence is that it abstracts you from the underlying persistent store: you don't need to know how your beans are stored or what kind of database is being used. One consequence of this requirement is that you need a database-independent language to express queries. For example, you will want to have a query that performs, "Find all the employees whose last name is Beust".

Before EJB 2.0, there was no such standard language, so all the EJB container vendors designed their own. EJB 2.0 introduces **EJB QL**, the **EJB Query Language**. EJB QL is a language whose syntax resembles SQL (although it is different in several ways). Just like relationships, EJB QL statements are specified in your deployment descriptors and the container will generate the corresponding SQL statement (not that it has to be SQL) to perform your query. We will see some examples of EJB QL in the implementation of our example later in this chapter, but for now, let's take a look at some of EJB QL's characteristics.

The challenge that EJB QL is trying to address is to map two different worlds: Java objects and rows in databases. As of today, relational databases (RDBMS) are still prevalent, but this might change in the future as object-oriented databases (OODBMS) become more and more popular. EJB QL is trying to abstract you from this possible paradigm shift so that whatever underlying query language is used to fetch data from the database, your EJBs will still keep working.

The syntax of EJB QL is very similar to that of SQL, but do not be fooled: the underlying notions are very different, and you need to understand how Java objects and EJBs instances interact if you want to reap all the benefits that EJB QL brings.

Another thing about EJB QL is that once you understand how it works, you can use it to:

❑ Implement finders

❑ Implement select methods (`ejbSelect()` methods are new in EJB 2.0, they are basically "private finders": when you want to use EJB QL for your own benefit but you don't want to expose the method to remote client, as would be the case if you used a finder)

❑ Navigate relationships

An EJB QL query is a string that consists of the following three clauses (not all of them are mandatory depending on what the clause applies to):

❑ A SELECT clause, which determines the type of the objects or values to be selected

❑ A FROM clause, which provides declarations that designate the domain to which the expressions specified in the SELECT and WHERE clauses apply

❑ An optional WHERE clause which maybe be used to restrict the results returned by the query

Let's look at a simple query and try to understand it:

```
SELECT DISTINCT OBJECT(o)
FROM Order AS o, IN(o.lineItems) AS li
WHERE li.shipped = FALSE
```

Let's examine each line in turn.

The SELECT clause

Depending on the kind of method your query applies to, the SELECT clause can take different values:

❑ Finders (ejbFindByXXX()) are only allowed to return EJBs of the same type as those created by their home interface, therefore the type of the SELECT clause must match the **abstract schema** name of the EJB

❑ Select (ejbSelectXXX()) methods are different: they can return arbitrary EJB abstract schemas, so you are free to SELECT on any of the abstract schema names defined in the current deployment descriptor

Both these methods can be defined for either the local or remote interfaces, so the container guarantees that the type of the EJB objects returned by the query will match that of the home (EJBObject if defined on a remote home interface, EJBLocalObject otherwise).

The optional DISTINCT keyword allows you to eliminate duplicate values that might be returned by the query. This could happen if, for example, the WHERE clause is performed on something other than the primary key, or if it involves joining several tables.

The FROM clause

There are two parts to the FROM clause in this query. The first one declares a variable of type Order. This is not the name of the EJB. You are not allowed to use EJB names (as in <ejb-name> in ejb-jar.xml) in an EJB QL query, you have to specify an <abstract-schema-name> tag in your deployment descriptor and use that name in the query. Nothing prevents you from reusing the same name as the EJB's name, though. Here is the corresponding ejb-jar.xml section that would apply to the above query:

```
<!-- fragment of ejb-jar.xml -->
    <entity>
      <ejb-name>OrderEJB</ejb-name>
<!-- some elements skipped -->
      <abstract-schema-name>Order</abstract-schema-name>
```

Whenever you write an EJB QL query involving a specific EJB, that EJB needs to have an <abstract-schema-name> defined in its deployment descriptor.

The second part of this FROM clause defines a variable 'li' that will iterate over all the values of the CMP field lineItems of o. The keyword IN must be used if the CMP field you want to use is a Collection and not a single-value object.

Note that an unlimited number of statements can be cascaded this way: if you want the query to further reference CMP fields on li, you can add them, separated by a comma. Remember that the abstract schema name of li is that of lineItems (represented by the EJB LineItem), so only CMP fields on that EJB will be legal to use on li (as illustrated in the WHERE clause).

Another use for having multiple declarations in the FROM clause is when you need to make comparisons involving all beans in the current table. For example, the following will return all employees who have more vacation days left than employee Dave:

```
SELECT DISTINCT OBJECT(o1)
FROM Employee e1, Employee e2
WHERE e1.vacation_days > e2.vacation_days AND e2.first_name = 'Dave'
```

The WHERE clause

This clause contains Boolean expressions that can be used to limit the results of the query. The above query would be perfectly legal without this WHERE clause, but it would return all the orders, regardless of whether they shipped or not, hence the extra condition to make sure the Boolean CMP field shipped is false.

The conditional expression can be a mix of AND and OR clauses. It can also include the literals TRUE and FALSE. It also offers some powerful operators such as BETWEEN or IN, or pattern matching with the operator LIKE, with the underscore (_) representing any single character, and the percent sign (%) representing any string of characters. Equality is achieved with '=' and inequality with '<>'.

Here are some examples:

```
p.age BETWEEN 15 and 19 (is equivalent to p.age >= 15 AND p.age <= 19)

p.age NOT BETWEEN 15 and 19

o.color IN ('red', 'blue') (true for colors 'red' and 'blue')

person.first_name LIKE '_edric' (true for Cedric and Cedric)

person.phone_number like '415%' (true for any number starting with 415)

o.lineItems IS EMPTY (true if the Collection is empty)
```

One final word on expressions: you include the parameters passed to the finder/select method as question marks followed by the order in which they appear in the signature. For example, the following finder:

```
abstract public Person findByName(String firstName, String lastName);
```

would be implemented by the following query:

```
SELECT DISTINCT OBJECT(o)
FROM Person AS o
WHERE o.firstName = ?1 AND o.lastName = ?2
```

Now let's look at some examples to explain how entity beans work.

The SportBean Laboratory

The responsibility for implementing an entity bean's persistence services lies with:

❑ The developer for a bean with bean-managed persistence

❑ The EJB container for a bean with container-managed persistence

As we discuss the different aspects of an entity bean, we'll be building two different versions of a single entity bean that represents a sports team: one using bean-managed persistence, and one using container-managed persistence. You'll be able to compare the steps necessary to implement the two types of beans, to see the advantages, disadvantages, and differences of each.

There will be significant differences between the implementations of a CMP entity bean and a BMP entity bean, because of the differing responsibilities. Most of those differences will be in the container's persistence callbacks, the factory methods, and the primary key class, which we are going to examine as we code the two versions of these beans.

Our sample sports team bean is quite simple. A sports team is identified by a sport (like football or basketball) and a nickname (such as Packers or Knicks). In addition, it has an owner name and a single 'franchise player' who is the best player on that team. For our purposes, the business logic isn't relevant here; we've included some setter and getter methods for our testing. Business methods can be coded the same, regardless of the type of persistence.

Primary Keys

Every entity bean has a **primary key** that represents a unique identity. This primary key must be represented by a **primary key class**, which the bean developer defines or specifies. In other words, this class contains the information necessary to find that entity in the persistent store. It is used internally by the EJB container, and also by the client to find a particular instance of the entity. This class must follow certain rules.

For bean-managed persistence, the rules are very simple. The format of the class is pretty much left up to the bean developer, since it is they and not the EJB container who is will be using it:

❑ The primary key can be any legal value type in RMI-IIOP (which implies that it must be serializable; see Chapter 3 for more on RMI). Basically, you can use any Java object (as long as it is serializable) and also remote references. Types that do not make sense to be marshaled (such as Java interfaces) are not legal RMI-IIOP types.

❑ The EJB must also provide implementations of the hashCode() and equals() methods that respect the constraints explained in the documentation of java.util.Hashtable. For example, two identical objects must have a similar hash code, but two objects having the same hash code does not imply they are identical. For more details, please refer to the Hashtable (or Collections) API.

❑ The primary key must have a unique value within the set of all beans of a particular type.

These are the only formal rules. Obviously in practice, the primary key class will have state fields that correspond to the values of the entity bean's primary key. For instance, a Customer entity bean may have a primary key that has a customerID field of type int. Alternatively, the Customer entity in this example may use the type java.lang.Integer, which meets all the requirements.

There are a few extra rules for a bean with container-managed persistence. The basic problem is that the container is responsible for managing the entity's creation, finding, loading, saving, and deletion. To do all these things, the container needs to be able to create a primary key, so the key class must have a no-arguments public constructor.

The container also needs to be able to map the bean's state to the state of the primary key class, and vice versa. So there are a few rules that are designed to make this possible. The specification provides two different methods for providing key classes for beans using CMP. One is a general case, good for primary keys with any number of fields; the other is a special case, for convenience in dealing with a primary key with one field.

The general case accomplishes the mapping using a naming convention: the public fields in the primary key class correspond to the equivalent public fields in the bean class. For example, we will define a primary key class named SportTeamPK for our SportTeam entity bean that has two fields that form its primary key: sport and nickName. SportTeamPK would need corresponding fields of the same type and name. The class will look like this (change the package name, depending on whether you are typing in the CMP or BMP version:

```
package sportBean.cmp;

import java.io.Serializable;

// The primary key needs to be Serializable because it will
// be exchanged between clients and EJB's
public class SportTeamPK implements Serializable {
  // The specification imposes the fields to be public
  // It is good programming practice to provide getters and setters
  // for them anyway.
  public String sport;
  public String nickName;

  public SportTeamPK() {}

  public SportTeamPK(String sport, String nickName) {
    this.sport = sport;
    this.nickName = nickName;
  }

  public String getSport() {
    return sport;
  }

  public String getNickName() {
    return nickName;
  }

  public int hashCode() {

    // Assumes key cannot be null
    return (sport + nickName).hashCode();
  }

  public boolean equals(Object other) {
    if ((other == null) ||!(other instanceof SportTeamPK)) {
      return false;
    }

    SportTeamPK otherPK = (SportTeamPK) other;
    return sport.equals(otherPK.sport) && nickName.equals(otherPK.nickName);
  }
}
```

This same class can be used for the BMP and CMP versions of our sports team bean, though we could have more flexibility in the BMP version, if we wanted to use it. For instance, we could name the fields differently, or make them private and provide accessor methods. In this case, we'll use the same class to keep things simple.

Note that a primary key class must be immutable: once you have associated an entity bean with a primary key, you should not reuse the same primary key object. This constraint is the same for Java containers in the `java.util.Collection` package: reusing the key you used to store an object in a `HashMap` will result in undefined behavior. When you do this, you are really changing the identity of the object and the container has no way of knowing it. Hence the following rule:

> **Never provide setters in your primary key class. If you need a key with different values, create a new object.**

The fully qualified class of the primary key always has to be specified in the deployment descriptor for entity beans with bean-managed persistence. Here are some possible examples. The first example is for both versions (BMP and CMP, modified appropriately) of our sports team bean:

```
<prim-key-class>sportBean.cmp.SportTeamPK</prim-key-class>
```

The second case would be used if the identifying key for the sports team bean had only a single field as the key:

```
<prim-key-class>java.lang.String</prim-key-class>
```

In the case of an entity bean with container-managed persistence that uses a simple type as its primary key, the bean developer specifies in the deployment descriptor the container-managed field of the entity bean that contains the primary key. The field's type must be the same as the primary key type. Here are some possible examples:

```
<primkey-field>sportsTeamID<primkey-field>
```

or:

```
<primkey-field>socialSecurity<primkey-field>
```

The EJB developer may wish to use a synthetic key, such as an auto-incrementing key, as the primary key of their entity bean. There are two possible strategies. The first is to generate the key using a session bean. This session bean might retrieve a block of keys from the database, and distribute keys sequentially from this block to requesting entity beans. The second strategy is to depend on the database to automatically create the synthetic keys when the entity bean's state is inserted. If the entity bean uses container-managed persistence, the EJB container's object/relational-mapping tools must support this functionality for the target database.

The C.R.U.D. Callbacks

C.R.U.D. is an acronym that defines the four types of activities comprising persistence:

❑ Create

❑ Read

❑ Update

❑ Delete

There is one callback type defined for each of these activities in entity beans: the `ejbCreate()` and `ejbPostCreate()` methods; `ejbLoad()`; `ejbStore()`; and `ejbRemove()`, respectively. The signatures of these callback methods are the same whether container-managed or bean-managed persistence is used. However, the code that the bean programmer writes will be very different based on the type of persistence.

Create

When a client calls `create()` for an entity bean, state data is inserted into the corresponding data store (such as a relational database). This is transactional data that is accessible from multiple clients. In contrast, when a client calls `create()` for a stateful session bean, the EJB container creates a private, non-transactional store of data in the application server's temporary storage. This difference is important to understand.

> When you call **`create()`** on a session bean's home interface, you are creating an instance of that session bean, whereas when you call **`create()`** on an entity bean's home interface, you are actually inserting a record in the database.

The `create()` method defined in the entity bean's home interface may be overloaded to provide several versions, and these `create()` methods may take different parameters, which correspond to the bean's state at the time of creation. The parameters must have enough information to at least initialize the primary key of the entity and any fields that are mapped to columns specified as NOT NULL in the database. All the `create()` methods must return the bean's remote interface, so that when the client programmer calls `create()` on the home interface, they will have a reference to that bean on which business methods may be called.

All the `create()` methods must throw `java.rmi.RemoteException`, because they can be remote methods. (This actually applies to all the methods on the remote interface.) They must also throw `javax.ejb.CreateException`, which is used to indicate an application-level problem during the attempt at creation. (They may also throw user-defined exceptions.) An example of an application-level problem would be illegal parameters passed to `create()`.

The SportsTeam create() Methods, Home Interface

The `create()` methods for our sports team EJB (note that these are the same for the BMP version and the CMP version; just change the package name) are:

```
package sportBean.cmp;

import javax.ejb.*;
import java.rmi.RemoteException;
import java.util.Collection;

public interface SportTeamHome extends EJBHome {

  SportTeam create(String sport, String nickName) throws RemoteException,
                                                          CreateException;

  SportTeam create(String sport, String nickName, String ownerName,
                 String franchisePlayer)
        throws RemoteException, CreateException;
```

Each one of these overloaded instances of the `create()` method in the bean's home interface must have two matching methods in the bean's implementation class. So in our case, there will be four creation-related methods in our implementation class.

The two methods we write in the implementation class for each `create()` in the home interface must be named `ejbCreate()` and `ejbPostCreate()`, and must have the same parameters in the same order as the home `create()` method. The methods must be declared `public`, and must not be `final` or `static`. The return type of `ejbCreate()` is the primary-key class of the entity bean, and the return type of `ejbPostCreate()` is `void`. (We will finish the definition of this home interface when we add the finder methods, later.)

One point of confusion for many programmers is why an `ejbCreate()` and an `ejbPostCreate()` are both necessary. As a general rule, the bean programmer – for either bean-managed persistence or container-managed persistence – will do all their work in `ejbCreate()`, leaving `ejbPostCreate()` empty. The fundamental reason that the `ejbPostCreate()` method exists is because the programmer is never allowed to pass `this` as a parameter to a remote method; they must always use the remote interface instead. The remote interface for the bean is not, however, available until `ejbCreate()` returns. If they need the remote interface *during* the creation of the EJB component, there would be no way to proceed. Rather than leave this hole in the spec, an "after create" method was developed in which the remote interface would be available. This method is `ejbPostCreate()`.

The same situation exists with the primary key in container-managed persistence, because the container creates the key. If the primary key is needed for some reason, that work also needs to be done in `ejbPostCreate()`. Why would you need to pass the EJB's remote reference or primary key to another EJB during its creation? The only good reason I've seen is to set up relationships, for example when you create the employee you want the boss to have a reference.

In a container-managed bean, the parameters that are passed in by the client will be used to initialize the entity bean's state. Although the return type of the `ejbCreate()` method is the same as the primary key, the bean developer should just return `null`. The container will ignore the returned value, regardless. The reason why you should return `null` in the case of CMP is that the key will actually be created and initialized by the container based on the value of the fields you just initialized. You might wonder why `ejbCreate()` is returning a value at all. The reason is subtle: this way, you can create a BMP EJB class by extending a CMP EJB class. For this to work, the Java Language Specification says that methods that need to be overridden in the child class must have the same return type, hence this little trick.

In a bean-managed bean, the bean must insert its state into the underlying data store – for a relational database, this means that the developer will write an `INSERT` statement in SQL. The bean developer should use the data to initialize the state variables of the bean, except in the very unusual case that the BMP entity bean is storing its state directly in the database without using any instance variable intermediaries. (This would be like our stateless session bean implementation of customer, only with implicit identity.) Finally, the bean developer should construct an instance of its primary key and return it.

The CMP SportsTeam Implementation Class

Here is the CMP version of our sports team entity bean's creation callbacks (we'll be adding to this class as we discuss the various callbacks):

```
package sportBean.cmp;

import javax.ejb.*;
import javax.naming.*;
import java.rmi.RemoteException;
import java.sql.Connection;
import java.sql.SQLException;
import java.sql.PreparedStatement;
import java.sql.ResultSet;
import javax.sql.DataSource;
```

```
import java.util.*;

public abstract class SportTeamEJB implements EntityBean {

  public SportTeamPK ejbCreate(String sport,
                                  String nickName) throws CreateException {

    setSport(sport);
    setNickName(nickName);
    setOwnerName(null);
    setFranchisePlayer(null);
    return null;
  }

  // Could be used to log that an EJB has just been created, for example
  public void ejbPostCreate(String key, String relatedData) {}

  public SportTeamPK ejbCreate(String sport, String nickName,
                                  String ownerName, String franchisePlayer)
                                  throws CreateException {
    setSport(sport);
    setNickName(nickName);
    setOwnerName(ownerName);
    setFranchisePlayer(franchisePlayer);
    return null;
  }

  public void ejbPostCreate(String sport, String nickName,
                                  String ownerName, String franchisePlayer) {}
```

Also, we need to declare abstract accessors for all our CMP fields:

```
abstract public String getSport();
abstract public void setSport(String sport);

abstract public String getNickName();
abstract public void setNickName(String nickname);

abstract public String getOwnerName();
abstract public void setOwnerName(String ownerName);

abstract public String getFranchisePlayer();
abstract public void setFranchisePlayer(String franchisePlayer);
```

The BMP SportsTeam Implementation Class

Here is the same sports team entity bean with bean-managed persistence. (Again, we'll be adding to this class.) Notice that there are two basic differences:

❑ The ejbCreate() methods have JDBC and SQL code to insert a record into the database

❑ The method returns an instance of a primary key, rather than null

```
package sportBean.bmp;

import javax.ejb.*;
import javax.naming.*;
import java.rmi.RemoteException;
import java.sql.Connection;
```

```java
import java.sql.SQLException;
import java.sql.PreparedStatement;
import java.sql.ResultSet;
import javax.sql.DataSource;
import java.util.*;

public class SportTeamEJB implements EntityBean {

    public String sport;
    public String nickName;
    public String ownerName;
    public String franchisePlayer;

    EntityContext ctx;

    public SportTeamPK ejbCreate(String sport,
                                 String nickName) throws CreateException {
        this.sport = sport;
        this.nickName = nickName;
        ownerName = null;
        franchisePlayer = null;

        Connection con = null;
        try {
            con = getConnection();            // this method is discussed later
            PreparedStatement statement =
                con.prepareStatement ("INSERT INTO SPORTSTEAMS (SPORT, NICKNAME) " +
                                      "VALUES (?, ?)");
            statement.setString(1, sport);
            statement.setString(2, nickName);
            if (statement.executeUpdate() != 1) {
                throw new CreateException("Failed to create sports team.");
            }
        } catch (SQLException sqle) {
            throw new EJBException(sqle);
        } finally {
            try {
                if (con != null) {
                    con.close();
                }
            } catch (SQLException sqle) {}
        }

        return new SportTeamPK(sport, nickName);
    }

public void ejbPostCreate(String key, String relatedData) {}

    public SportTeamPK ejbCreate(String sport, String nickName,
                                 String ownerName,
                                 String franchisePlayer)
            throws javax.ejb.CreateException {
        this.sport = sport;
        this.nickName = nickName;
        this.ownerName = ownerName;
        this.franchisePlayer = franchisePlayer;

        Connection con = null;
        try {
            con = getConnection();
            PreparedStatement statement =
                con.prepareStatement("INSERT INTO SPORTSTEAMS (SPORT, NICKNAME, " +
```

```
                                  "OWNERNAME, FRANCHISEPLAYER ) VALUES " +
                                  "(?, ?, ?, ?)");
      statement.setString(1, sport);
      statement.setString(2, nickName);
      statement.setString(3, ownerName);
      statement.setString(4, franchisePlayer);
      if (statement.executeUpdate() != 1) {
        throw new CreateException("Failed to create sports team.");
      }
    } catch (SQLException sqle) {
      throw new EJBException(sqle);
    }
    finally {
      try {
        if (con != null) {
          con.close();
        }
      } catch (SQLException sqle) {}
    }

    return new SportTeamPK(sport, nickName);
  }

  public void ejbPostCreate(String sport, String nickName,
                      String ownerName, String franchisePlayer) {}
```

*We don't need to add the accessors for bean-managed persistence beans, so we won't add them here,
but it's a practice that I would recommend anyway for abstraction purposes, and also in case you
decide to migrate your bean to CMP in the future.*

It is possible and sometimes appropriate to have an entity bean with no `create()` methods. An entity
bean is just an object-oriented view on transactional, shared data. In an environment with non-EJB
applications, this data – and therefore, these entity beans – may exist without `create()` ever being
called. If this data should be created *only* by these non-EJB applications, then the entity beans can be
written without any `create()` methods. For instance, our sports team database records might be
created exclusively by someone with a Star Office spreadsheet linked to our database, with our EJB
application being used to keep the information about owners and franchise players up-to-date. No
`create()` methods would be required in this case.

Read

The `ejbLoad()` callback method corresponds roughly to the 'read' functionality of entity beans. A
simple way to look at it is that the entity will load the data from the database in correspondence to the
container's `ejbLoad()` call. With container-managed persistence, the EJB container will take care of
transferring the entity's state from the database to the entity's instance variables. In this case, the bean
programmer will often leave the `ejbLoad()` method blank, but may choose to do some post-processing
of the loaded data. With bean-managed persistence, the bean programmer will write their data-access
code (probably JDBC and SQL code) in `ejbLoad()` to transfer the entity's state to instance variables.

This description is a good way to understand the process, but it is not the whole story. Technically,
`ejbLoad()` doesn't tell the bean that it must actually load data: it just tells the bean that it must *re-
synchronize* its state with the underlying data store. This is a subtle but potentially important difference.

**The bean's persistence implementation may choose to defer loading the state until that
state is actually used.**

Let's consider an example. An Order entity bean may have an order number, a customer name, and a list of line items. When `ejbLoad()` is called for an entity bean that represents a particular order, the state of that order – the number, name, and line items – must be synchronized with the database. In this example, the persistence logic may choose to update the name and number immediately from the database. Retrieving the list of related line items, though, is a potentially expensive operation, so a 'dirty' flag is set instead. If the only method that is called on this order bean is `getCustomerName()`, the line items will never need to be loaded. Any method that must access the list, such as `totalLineItems()` for example, will need to check the dirty flag and load the list from the database if it is set.

Creating the Table

First, let's create the table that will contain our entity bean. The following SQL statement should be issued to your database:

```
CREATE TABLE SPORTSTEAMS (SPORT VARCHAR(25) NOT NULL,
                NICKNAME VARCHAR(25) NOT NULL,
                OWNERNAME VARCHAR(25),
                FRANCHISEPLAYER VARCHAR(25));
```

This is standard SQL, so it should work on pretty much any database. Consult your documentation if it doesn't.

CMP Entity Beans and ejbLoad()

The role of `ejbLoad()` in container-managed persistence is to process the data after it has been loaded from the database. Often, the data will not need processing at all, and your `ejbLoad()` method will be empty. Sometimes, however, changes will be necessary. A practical example is that you may store your `String` data in `char` database fields of a certain size, and the database may append blanks to your strings to pad them to the correct length. Although this may be more efficient than using a `varchar` data type, those trailing blanks can be annoying. You could use `ejbLoad()` to trim those trailing blanks. Since we used VARCHAR to create our table, `ejbLoad()` will be empty in our CMP example:

```
public void ejbLoad() {}
```

BMP Entity Beans and ejbLoad()

The role of `ejbLoad()` in bean-managed persistence is to notify the bean that it must invalidate the current cached state and prepare for business method invocations. In practical terms, this usually means replacing the state by loading it from the database.

To find the entity bean's data in the database, you will need the primary key. By the time that `ejbLoad()` is called, the primary key has been associated with the entity and is available from its context. This entity context is associated with the bean by a callback method, just as the session context is associated with a session bean. The `EntityContext` interface is:

```
package javax.ejb;

public interface EntityContext extends EJBContext {

    public abstract EJBLocalObject getEJBLocalObject()
        throws IllegalStateException;

    public abstract EJBObject getEJBObject()
        throws IllegalStateException;

    public abstract Object getPrimaryKey()
        throws IllegalStateException;
}
```

A bean that uses bean-managed persistence would need to use the entity context to retrieve its associated primary key in the implementation of `ejbLoad()`, using the `setEntityContext()` / `unsetEntityContext()` pair of callbacks when they are invoked by the container to save the entity context for use. Add the following methods to the bean-managed persistence version only of the sports team entity bean:

```
public void setEntityContext(EntityContext ctx) {
   this.ctx = ctx;
}

// The container will call this method. Any resources
// that you allocate in setEntityContext() should be freed here.
public void unsetEntityContext () {
   ctx = null;
}
```

The implementation for these methods may be empty for the container-managed persistence version:

```
public void setEntityContext(EntityContext ctx) {}

public void unsetEntityContext() {}
```

Here is the BMP version of `ejbLoad()` for the sports-team bean. Notice how we use the saved `EntityContext` to retrieve the primary key:

```
public void ejbLoad() {
   SportTeamPK primaryKey = (SportTeamPK) ctx.getPrimaryKey();

   Connection con = null;
   try {
     con = getConnection();
     PreparedStatement statement =
             con.prepareStatement("SELECT OWNERNAME, FRANCHISEPLAYER " +
                                  "FROM SPORTSTEAMS WHERE SPORT = ? " +
                                  "AND NICKNAME = ? ");
     statement.setString(1, primaryKey.getSport());
     statement.setString(2, primaryKey.getNickName());

     ResultSet resultSet = statement.executeQuery();
     if (!resultSet.next()) {
       throw new EJBException("Object not found.");
     }
     sport = primaryKey.getSport();
     nickName = primaryKey.getNickName();
     ownerName = resultSet.getString(1);
     franchisePlayer = resultSet.getString(2);
     resultSet.close();
     statement.close();
   } catch (SQLException sqle) {
     throw new EJBException(sqle);
   } finally {
     try {
       if (con != null) {
         con.close();
       }
     } catch (SQLException sqle) {}
   }
}
```

Update

The ejbStore() callback method corresponds roughly to the 'update' functionality of entity beans. Of course, the actual modification of the entity bean's cached state will be done through calls to business methods, such as setShipmentAddress() or calculateSalesTax(). The container will call the ejbStore() method to notify the bean that it must synchronize its state with the database.

For a bean with container-managed persistence, this method will be called directly before the container writes the altered bean state to the database, and the programmer of a CMP bean may use this opportunity to pre-process the bean's data to ensure that it is in an appropriate state for persistent storage. Typically, however, this method will be left empty.

For a bean with bean-managed persistence, the programmer is responsible for providing in this method the logic that will transfer the bean's state to the underlying data store. For a relational database, this will typically mean that the bean programmer will write JDBC code and SQL UPDATE statements.

> *With ejbLoad(), the bean had the option to defer the actual loading of state until it was used. There is no such option with ejbStore(). Any modifications to the object's state must be written to the data store immediately. The equivalent optimization is probably something called 'tuned updates'. In other words, only the modified state need be written to the data store; if something hasn't changed, you can leave it alone.*

CMP and the ejbStore() Method

As with ejbLoad(), the ejbStore() method for our CMP version of the SportTeam bean is empty:

```
public void ejbStore() {}
```

BMP and the ejbStore() Method

Here is ejbStore() for the sports team entity bean with bean managed persistence. Note that we do not need to retrieve the primary key from the entity context (although we could), because the information is available to us in the instance variables of this class:

```
public void ejbStore() {
  Connection con = null;
  try {
    con = getConnection();
    PreparedStatement statement =
            con.prepareStatement("UPDATE SPORTSTEAMS SET OWNERNAME=?, " +
                                 "FRANCHISEPLAYER=? WHERE SPORT = ? " +
                                 "AND NICKNAME = ? ");
    statement.setString(1, ownerName);
    statement.setString(2, franchisePlayer);
    statement.setString(3, sport);
    statement.setString(4, nickName);

    if (statement.executeUpdate() != 1) {
      throw new EJBException("Failed to save object state.");
    }
    statement.close();
  } catch (SQLException sqle) {
    throw new EJBException(sqle);
  } finally {
    try {
      if (con != null) {
```

```
            con.close();
        }
    } catch (SQLException sqle) {}
    }
}
```

Delete

When a client calls `remove()` on an entity bean, data is deleted from the corresponding data store. In contrast, when a client calls `remove()` for a stateful session bean, the EJB container discards the session bean instance in the application server's temporary storage. It is important to understand this difference. You should always call `remove()` when you are done using a stateful session bean; otherwise, the EJB container will waste resources managing this instance.

> **You should not call `remove()` on an entity bean unless you want to delete that record. The EJB container will manage the entity bean's instance in the container.**

CMP and the remove() Method

For an entity bean with container-managed persistence, the `ejbRemove()` method can usually be left empty, and the container will handle the deletion of the instance from the underlying data store. The programmer of an entity bean with container-managed persistence may use this method to implement any actions that must be done (such as updating related data or notifying other systems) before the entity object's representation is removed from the database. Here is the method for our sports-team bean with container-managed persistence:

```
public void ejbRemove() {}
```

BMP and the remove() Method

For an entity bean with bean-managed persistence, the programmer is responsible for providing the logic that will remove the object from the underlying resource. For a relational database, this will typically mean that the bean programmer will write JDBC code and SQL DELETE statements.

Note that, as with any business method, the data will be loaded by the container (by calling `ejbLoad()`) before `ejbRemove()` is called. This allows the programmer to perform validation of the remove request, and to update related data or systems, without loading the data independently of the EJB container callback.

Here is the version with bean-managed persistence:

```
public void ejbRemove() throws javax.ejb.RemoveException {
    Connection con = null;
    try {
        con = getConnection();
        PreparedStatement statement =
                con.prepareStatement("DELETE FROM SPORTSTEAMS " +
                                     "WHERE SPORT = ? AND NICKNAME = ? ");
        statement.setString(1, sport);
        statement.setString(2, nickName);

        if (statement.executeUpdate() != 1) {
            throw new EJBException("Failed to remove object.");
```

```
      }
      statement.close();
   } catch (SQLException sqle) {
      throw new EJBException(sqle);
   } finally {
      try {
         if (con != null) {
            con.close();
         }
      } catch (SQLException sqle) {}
   }
}
```

BMP Callbacks vs. CMP Callbacks

The signatures of the create, read, update, and delete callbacks are the same for bean-managed persistence and container-managed persistence. The implementations are very different, however:

- ❑   For entity beans with bean-managed persistence, these callbacks are responsible for solving the entire problem of synchronizing state with the underlying data store for creates, reads, updates, and deletes.

- ❑   For entity beans with container-managed persistence, these callbacks (with the exception of ejbCreate() methods) are just used for 'fine-tuning' the container's operations. All the operations related to storing and retrieving state from the database will be performed by the container, but you might want to perform other tasks yourself when this happens (such as logging, acquiring or releasing resources, etc.).

Just to make the difference clear, here is a typical implementation of these callbacks for a container-managed entity bean:

```
public String ejbCreate(String key, String relatedData) {
   this.key = key;
   this.relatedData = relatedData;
}

public void ejbPostCreate(String key, String relatedData) {}

public void ejbLoad() {}

public void ejbRemove() {}

public void ejbStore() {}
```

Notice that there is very little development cost, very little maintenance cost, and very little room for error in the implementation of any of these methods. That is part of what container-managed persistence buys you.

The Deployment Descriptor

In order to be fully specified, an Enterprise JavaBean must be accompanied by at least one deployment descriptor, called ejb-jar.xml (and stored in a directory META-INF in the JAR file). While the EJB 2.0 specification only mandates the existence of one deployment descriptor, it is not sufficient to actually provide enough information to the container in order to deploy the EJB.

The reason is that `ejb-jar.xml` is trying to remain as neutral as possible about what implementation means will be used to perform certain operations. For example, the following information is not part of `ejb-jar.xml`:

- ❑ JNDI name of the remote home interface
- ❑ JNDI names of the destinations used by message-driven beans (explained in Chapter 19)
- ❑ Names of the tables used by CMP entity beans
- ❑ Connection pools used by CMP entity beans
- ❑ What columns of the table map to what fields of CMP beans
- ❑ Other resources

This information must therefore be provided separately. Containers will typically expect you to enter this information in another deployment descriptor. For example, BEA's WebLogic will look for a deployment descriptor called `weblogic-ejb-jar.xml`. If your JAR file contains CMP entity beans, you will also be asked to provide an extra deployment descriptor that will contain exclusively CMP-related information. The name of this third deployment descriptor is up to you, but you need to reference it in `weblogic-ejb-jar.xml`. Note that you can actually have an arbitrary number of CMP deployment descriptors, but we will be using only one in this book for simplification.

To summarize, a legal (deployable) JAR file will contain the following deployment descriptors:

- ❑ One `ejb-jar.xml` (mandated by the EJB 2.0 specification)
- ❑ One `weblogic-ejb-jar.xml` (required by WebLogic)
- ❑ One or more CMP XML files (only needed if you have CMP entity beans, and the names of these files must be specified in `weblogic-ejb-jar.xml`)

The next sections will illustrate all these deployment descriptors.

Persistence in the Deployment Descriptors

The type of persistence – bean managed or container managed – is specified in the XML deployment descriptor for the EJB. The `<persistence-type>` element of the deployment descriptor will be one of the following:

```
<persistence-type>Bean</persistence-type>
```

or:

```
<persistence-type>Container</persistence-type>
```

If the bean's persistence is container-managed, the fields that are persisted must also be specified in the deployment descriptor. Each entry in the deployment descriptor has the name of the field in the class, and may also have a description. Here is an example of two fields from the CMP version of our sports-team entity bean (with an optional description thrown in):

```
<cmp-field>
  <field-name>sport</field-name>
  <description>Like basketball or cricket.</description>
</cmp-field>
<cmp-field>
  <field-name>nickName</field-name>
</cmp-field>
```

All the container-managed fields listed in the deployment descriptor must be declared in the bean class under the form of accessors, as shown previously. Both get and set methods must be provided and you must remember to capitalize the first letter of your field in the method name: thus, the CMP field nickName becomes getNickName()/setNickName() in your bean class.

Here is the almost complete ejb-jar.xml deployment descriptor for the CMP version of our bean:

```
<!DOCTYPE ejb-jar
    PUBLIC "-//Sun Microsystems, Inc.//DTD Enterprise JavaBeans 2.0//EN"
           "http://java.sun.com/dtd/ejb-jar_2_0.dtd">

<ejb-jar>
  <enterprise-beans>

    <entity>
      <ejb-name>CMPSportsBean</ejb-name>
      <home>sportBean.cmp.SportTeamHome</home>
      <remote>sportBean.cmp.SportTeam</remote>
      <ejb-class>sportBean.cmp.SportTeamEJB</ejb-class>
      <persistence-type>Container</persistence-type>
      <prim-key-class>sportBean.cmp.SportTeamPK</prim-key-class>
      <reentrant>False</reentrant>
      <cmp-version>2.x</cmp-version>
      <!-- Another element in here, we'll see this in the finder section -->
      <cmp-field><field-name>sport</field-name></cmp-field>
      <cmp-field><field-name>nickName</field-name></cmp-field>
      <cmp-field><field-name>ownerName</field-name></cmp-field>
      <cmp-field><field-name>franchisePlayer</field-name></cmp-field>
      <!-- More elements to be added here -->
    </entity>

  </enterprise-beans>


  <assembly-descriptor>

    <container-transaction>
      <method>
        <ejb-name>CMPSportsBean</cjb-name>
        <method-name>*</method-name>
      </method>
      <trans-attribute>Required</trans-attribute>
    </container-transaction>

  </assembly-descriptor>
</ejb-jar>
```

There's still a little to add to the CMP deployment descriptor, which we'll come to shortly. Next, we can add elements to represent the BMP bean to the same file.

Here is the portion of the ejb-jar.xml deployment descriptor for the version with bean-managed persistence. It doesn't have <cmp-field> elements, but does declare that we use a resource (the JDBC connection, declared in the <resource-ref> element):

```
<enterprise-beans>

  <entity>
    <ejb-name>CMPSportsBean</ejb-name>
    <!-- Rest of deployment descriptor for CMP not shown -->
  </entity>
```

```
    <entity>
      <ejb-name>BMPSportsBean</ejb-name>
      <home>sportBean.bmp.SportTeamHome</home>
      <remote>sportBean.bmp.SportTeam</remote>
      <ejb-class>sportBean.bmp.SportTeamEJB</ejb-class>
      <persistence-type>Bean</persistence-type>
      <prim-key-class>sportBean.bmp.SportTeamPK</prim-key-class>
      <reentrant>False</reentrant>
      <resource-ref>
        <res-ref-name>jdbc/sportsJDBC</res-ref-name>
        <res-type>javax.sql.DataSource</res-type>
        <res-auth>Container</res-auth>
      </resource-ref>
    </entity>

  </enterprise-beans>

  <assembly-descriptor>
    <!-- Rest of deployment descriptor for CMP not shown -->

    <container-transaction>
      <method>
        <ejb-name>BMPSportsBean</ejb-name>
        <method-name>*</method-name>
      </method>
      <trans-attribute>Required</trans-attribute>
    </container-transaction>

  </assembly-descriptor>
</ejb-jar>
```

Caching

A **cache** is a secondary copy of data that is typically made for reasons of performance or convenience. The instance variables in your entity bean that represent the object's persistent state are actually a cache of the data whose permanent storage location is in your database. For instance, in your Customer entity bean you may have three string variables for the customer's first name, middle name, and last name. These three variables might be secondary copies of the data from three columns in a relational database table named customer: fname, mname, and lname. Here is a simple table to make this example clearer:

Data	Primary Copy	Cached Copy
Customer's first name	Database column fname	Entity bean field fname
Customer's middle name	Database column mname	Entity bean field mname
Customer's last name	Database column lname	Entity bean field lname

The cache consisting of your entity bean instance variables will suffer from the same potential problem that any cache does: it may get out of synch with the primary copy of the data. To continue with our simple customer example, the record in the database may have an lname of 'Smith' after an update by a customer management system, but the corresponding entity bean field may still have the former name of 'Jones'. With both bean-managed persistence and container-managed persistence, it is the combined responsibility of the EJB container and the underlying data store to manage the synchronization of an entity's cache. The topic of caching is closely related to the C.R.U.D. callbacks and the transfer of an entity object's state to and from the persistent data store. The EJB container will call ejbLoad() and ejbStore() at the times that it feels is necessary to keep the local cache in synch with the primary copy of the data.

As a bean programmer, you do not need to concern yourself with exactly when the container will call `ejbLoad()` and `ejbStore()`. You must be prepared for either method call to happen at any time between business-logic methods. Still, it's nice to understand the common strategies that EJB containers will employ in various situations, so you can make informed decisions about application servers, deployment, and so on.

Let's say that a client wants to use a copy of our three-field customer bean. They want to call two methods on the bean: `setFirstName()` and `setMiddleName()`. There are two distinct cases we must consider, depending on whether or not these methods are called in the same transaction:

❑   In the first case, these two methods are called in the same transaction.

  Before the first business-logic method is called, the container or the bean (depending on CMP vs. BMP) will load the state from the database corresponding with a call to `ejbLoad()`. Now the `setFirstName()` business method is called. At this point, the container has the option of calling `ejbStore()` and `ejbLoad()` again, before calling `setMiddleName()`. It might do this if it was part of an application-server cluster, and it could not guarantee that the same entity bean instance would be used for both business methods. However, in the most common case, it will simply go ahead and call the `setMiddleName()` method right away. It can do this because both methods are part of the same transaction, and transactions are designed to ensure that modifications to a data store are isolated from other activities against that data. In other words, `ejbLoad()` and `ejbStore()` will be called for entity objects on transaction boundaries. (Note that this is not mandated by the specification; it is simply a common implementation strategy.)

❑   In the second case, these two methods are called in different transactions.

  Again, before the first business logic method is called, the container or the bean will load the state from the database corresponding with a call to `ejbLoad()`. Once `setFirstName()` has been called, the transaction completes and `ejbStore()` is called to update the datastore. Now `setMiddleName()` is called. In the general case, the EJB container will simply repeat the process, calling `ejbLoad()` and `ejbStore()` around the invocation of `setMiddleName()`. The cache must be resynchronized with `ejbLoad()` because, in between the two transactions, some other process or application could have modified the data.

There are, however, two special cases that may allow the EJB container to avoid calling `ejbLoad()` on the entity instance at the start of transactions subsequent to the first method call:

❑   The first is that all access to the data goes through the EJB container and that entity bean. If this were the case, then the container knows that the cache in the entity bean and the data in the persistent data store are in synch. Every change to the data will happen in the cache before it is reflected in the data store, if all access is through the bean. However, if any non-EJB technology is used to modify the data (an ERP system), then this approach cannot be used. This is because there is nothing to guarantee that the data won't change without the container and EJB knowing about it.

❑   The second case is when the particular application does not absolutely need the freshest data. Obviously this will not apply in the case of a banking system that must keep account information in synch. However, it will be the case for a surprising number of systems – an e-commerce system, perhaps. The cached data could be set to expire after a certain amount of time, and would be refreshed after that period. If the prices for products were changed by some non-EJB demand-management software, this change would not be reflected in the e-commerce application immediately. After the cached data expired, though (say in five minutes), it would be. The benefit might be far fewer database accesses, and much better application performance. The consequences – a five minute delay in changed prices – would probably be negligible.

If your application server provides this optimization of data caching between transactions, you would set this with an application server-specific configuration tool. Typically, the optimization is available if you indicate that the EJB container has 'exclusive access to the database', or similar (for example, WebLogic 6.1 offers a wide range of locking strategies, ranging from 'exclusive access to the database' to 'not performing any locking, deferring it to the database'

Although the EJB container can optimize away calls to `ejbLoad()` at the beginning of a transaction, it can never do this for `ejbStore()` at the completion of the transaction. The Enterprise JavaBeans 2.0 specification absolutely requires that `ejbStore()` be called when a transaction in which the entity bean is participating completes. This is because one of the ACID guarantees that a transactional system makes is that a transaction is *durable*. If the modified data is held in a temporary cache in the entity bean, and the entity bean is subsequently destroyed before it gets the chance to finally write its data to permanent storage, the 'durable' part of the transactional guarantee has been violated. This could happen because a subsequent call to the bean resulted in a non-application exception, or even because the application server crashed.

What about the case where no data has changed? In this case, since all field access goes through accessors that the EJB container generated, it knows that the entity bean is untouched and the `ejbStore()` operation will be an empty operation.

A bean that uses bean-managed persistence should implement a strategy to determine whether the data has changed. One possibility is to simply maintain a 'modified' flag, which is checked in the `ejbStore()` method to see if any action needs to be taken. Another possibility is to keep 'before' and 'after' copies of the data, and to compare them to build an UPDATE statement that affects only the data that has changed.

Finder Methods

Entity beans represent shared data. If this data is shared, there must be some mechanism for clients to get access to a particular entity bean. Notice that this problem doesn't come up for session beans; the client gets access to the bean when it is created, and no one else ever uses it. An entity bean, on the other hand, may be created by one client and used by any number of completely different clients (in this particular case, we will have different instances of the EJB but they manipulate the same data in the database). Each of these clients must be able to find the bean for which they are looking.

As a solution for this problem, the Enterprise JavaBeans specification defines a mechanism called **finder methods**. One or more of these finder methods are declared in the entity bean's home interface, one for each way of locating that entity object or a collection of that type of entity object. These finder methods follow a certain naming convention: they all start with the prefix **find**. Some examples are `findOpenAccounts()`, `findOrdersByDate()`, and `findManagerForEmployee()`. They can take any parameters that are necessary to specify the details of the search, as long as those parameters follow the normal rules for RMI/IIOP (the main rule, as mentioned before, is that they need to implement `java.io.Serializable`, be a primitive type, or be a remote interface).

Finder methods that will have at most one result will have a return type of the remote interface for that entity bean. For instance, the `findManagerForEmployee()` method defined on a `com.somecompany.personnel.ManagerHome` class might have a return type of `com.somecompany.personnel.Manager` (and, of course, a parameter of type `Employee`). (The `findByPrimaryKey()` method in any entity bean is an example of this type of finder.) Finder methods that can have zero or more results will have a return type of either `java.util.Enumeration` or `java.util.Collection`. (The `findByOwnerName()` method is an example from the `SportTeamHome` interface.) If compatibility with 1.1 JDKs is required, `Enumeration` must be chosen. Otherwise, it is probably better to return a `Collection`, which provides a more flexible interface to the results.

In addition to the `java.rmi.RemoteException` thrown by all remote methods, every finder method must also declare that it throws the `javax.ejb.FinderException`. If a finder of the type that has at most one result does not find any matching entity, the method will throw a subclass of the `FinderException` class: an instance of the `javax.ejb.ObjectNotFoundException`. If a finder of the type that has zero or more results does not find any matching entities, the method will simply return an empty collection or an enumeration with zero elements.

Every entity bean must declare a certain 'well known' finder named `findByPrimaryKey()`, that takes a single parameter of the same type as the entity's primary-key class. This finder will either return the instance of the entity bean with that primary key, or will throw an `ObjectNotFoundException`. Additional finders beyond `findByPrimaryKey()` are optional. Some entities will have no other finders; others may have several.

Implementing Finder Methods

The implementation of the finding logic will be provided by the EJB container for beans with container-managed persistence, and the bean developer need not write supporting Java code of any sort. There is, however, obviously not enough information in the finder method's signature for the container to figure out the finder's intent and implement the logic. How would a container know how to implement `findMostAppropriateWarehouse(Product product, Date dateNeeded)`? As we will see in the next sections, EJB QL performs this task.

For entity beans with bean-managed persistence, the EJB developer must provide a Java implementation of each finder's logic in the bean's implementation class. This method will have identical parameters, and will have a matching name of the following convention: if the finder method is `findXXX()`, the implementation of that finder method will be named `ejbFindXXX()`. The return type for a finder method that has at most one result will be an instance of the primary-key class for that entity, and the return type for a finder method implementation that has zero or more results will be either a concrete implementation of `Collection`, or an `Enumeration`, depending on the return type of the corresponding finder method in the home interface. The items contained in the `Collection` or returned by the `Enumeration` will be instances of the primary-key classes for the corresponding entities. Notice that the implementation of `findByPrimaryKey()` will take a primary key as a parameter, check to make sure the database record actually exists, and return that same primary key as the result if it does. Although the EJB container already has the primary key for this particular finder method, the EJB developer is asked to return it anyway so that its use is consistent with other finders that return at most one result.

You do not have any meaningful access to the state-related instance variables in the implementation of a finder method, nor any other identity-specific information. An entity bean that is used for a finder method will not be associated with a particular instance of state in the database. This is different from most other entity bean methods, such as the lifecycle methods and the business-logic methods. Although it must not be declared as static, you can think of it as having the same role as a static factory method might in a non-EJB Java class.

CMP and Finder Methods

Note that for the CMP version, you will need to provide EJB QL code to the container so that it can generate the finder methods for you. The following fragment of `ejb-jar.xml` does this (you don't have to provide `findByPrimaryKey()`, it will be automatically generated by the container):

```
<reentrant>False</reentrant>
<cmp-version>2.x</cmp-version>
<abstract-schema-name>SportEJB</abstract-schema-name>
<cmp-field><field-name>sport</field-name></cmp-field>
<!-- Other cmp-fields -->
```

```
<query>
  <query-method>
    <method-name>findByOwnerName</method-name>
    <method-params>
      <method-param>java.lang.String</method-param>
    </method-params>
  </query-method>
  <ejb-ql>
    <![CDATA[SELECT OBJECT(o) FROM SportEJB AS o
                          WHERE o.ownerName = ?1]]>
  </ejb-ql>
</query>

</entity>
```

Since this is the first real EJB QL clause we are using, let's examine it in detail.

❑   SELECT OBJECT(o) defines the type of the object we are returning. Since we are defining a finder, it has to return an EJB of the same type as those returned by the create() methods of the home (SportEJB in this case). OBJECT(o) doesn't have any particular meaning in EJB QL but it is standard in SQL and the EJB 2.0 committee did its best to have as much resemblance between the two languages as possible.

❑   One thing to note about the FROM argument (SportEJB) is that it is **not** the class of the EJB, nor is it its ejb-name; it is its **abstract schema**. You must provide an <abstract-schema-name> tag (as above, before the <cmp-field> tags) before you can write EJB QL queries. (On a personal note, I could never get a clear answer from the EJB 2.0 team why <abstract-schema-names> were introduced while all they do is map one-on-one to an EJB name. My guess is that it was introduced for possible future evolutions.)

❑   If the EJB QL clause stopped at this point, the finder would return all the EJBs contained in the table. Since this is obviously not what we want, we need to refine the request further, and that's what the WHERE clause does. It references the object o, one of its CMP fields (ownerName) and compares it with the first parameter (?1) that was passed to the Java method findByOwnerName() (which is a string, as specified a few lines above).

BMP and Finder Methods

Continuing with our sports team example, here is an example of a findByPrimaryKey() implementation for the version with bean-managed persistence (remember that there is no equivalent for the version with container-managed persistence; add these methods only to the BMP version of SportTeamEJB.java):

```
public SportTeamPK ejbFindByPrimaryKey(SportTeamPK primaryKey)
                  throws FinderException {
  Connection con = null;
  try {
    con = getConnection();
    PreparedStatement statement =
        con.prepareStatement("SELECT SPORT " +
                             "FROM SPORTSTEAMS WHERE SPORT = ? " +
                             "AND NICKNAME = ? ");
    statement.setString(1, primaryKey.getSport());
    statement.setString(2, primaryKey.getNickName());

    ResultSet resultSet = statement.executeQuery();
    if (!resultSet.next()) {
```

```
      throw new ObjectNotFoundException();
    }
    resultSet.close();
    statement.close();
    return primaryKey;
  } catch (SQLException sqle) {
    throw new EJBException(sqle);
  } finally {
    try {
      if (con != null) {
        con.close();
      }
    } catch (SQLException sqle) {}
  }
}
```

Here is an example of a finder implementation that has zero or more results and returns a collection:

```
public Collection ejbFindByOwnerName(String ownerName)
        throws FinderException {
  Connection con = null;
  try {
    con = getConnection();
    PreparedStatement statement =                    // Primary key info
            con.prepareStatement("SELECT SPORT, NICKNAME " +
                                 "FROM SPORTSTEAMS WHERE OWNERNAME = ? ");
    statement.setString(1, ownerName);
    ResultSet resultSet = statement.executeQuery();

    LinkedList queryMatches = new LinkedList();
    while (resultSet.next()) {
      SportTeamPK pk = new SportTeamPK(resultSet.getString(1),
                                       resultSet.getString(2));
      queryMatches.add(pk);
    }

    resultSet.close();
    statement.close();
    return queryMatches;
  } catch (SQLException sqle) {
    throw new EJBException(sqle);
  } finally {
    try {
      if (con != null) {
        con.close();
      }
    } catch (SQLException sqle) {}
  }
}
```

For both the CMP version and the BMP version of our sports-team bean, you should complete the home interface as follows:

```
SportTeam findByPrimaryKey(SportTeamPK sportTeam)
        throws RemoteException, FinderException;

Collection findByOwnerName(String ownerName)
        throws RemoteException, FinderException;
}
```

Activation and Passivation

Two of the callbacks for entity beans are ejbActivate() and ejbPassivate(). Session beans have these same callbacks, but they serve different purposes. Actually, for stateless session beans, they serve no purpose at all; they are there so that stateless and stateful session beans can implement the same interface. For stateful session beans, they indicate to the bean that it is about to be saved to or restored from secondary storage, to help the EJB container manage its working set. Entity beans have no need to be saved to secondary storage: by definition, they already exist in persistent storage. If the container isn't using an entity bean, it doesn't need to worry about preserving its state before freeing its resources.

For entity beans, ejbActivate() provides a notification that the entity bean instance has been associated with an identity (a primary key) and it is now ready for ejbLoad() to be called prior to business method invocation. A matching ejbPassivate() method will be called to notify the entity bean that it is being disassociated from a particular identity prior to reuse (with another identity or for finder methods), or perhaps prior to being de-referenced and made eligible for garbage collection.

The only case where the entity bean would care about the information provided by ejbActivate() and ejbPassivate() is if it were managing some resource that depended on a bean's identity. For example, you might need these callbacks to open and close database connections. Outside of this case, the implementation of these methods can be left empty. An example of where the entity bean might need a resource associated with a particular identity is if it had a remote reference to a non-Java object whose state needed to be synchronized with the state of the entity bean, such as a business object in a proprietary application server belonging to a vendor of ERP systems.

If the resource needs to be associated with a particular identity, you must actually provide for initialization of that resource in both ejbPostCreate() and ejbActivate(), because the entity can become associated with an identity through either of these paths. Note that you need ejbPostCreate() rather than ejbCreate(), because ejbPostCreate() is where the identity becomes available. Similarly, you must use both ejbPassivate() and ejbRemove() for resource release.

It's also possible that the resource doesn't need to be associated with a particular identity, but just needs to be generally available to any identity. For instance, you may have a connection to a legacy ERP system that you can use to synchronize data for any object. You can use the setEntityContext() and unsetEntityContext() callback methods to allocate and de-allocate the resource in this case.

Here are the methods for both versions of our sports bean implementation (these go in the SportTeamEJB files for BMP and CMP):

```
public void ejbActivate() {}

public void ejbPassivate() {}
```

With the addition of these methods, the CMP version of the implementation class is complete. There are a couple of methods left for the BMP bean.

The Complete Lifecycle

The following diagram summarizes the information about container callbacks for entity beans. In the **pooled state**, an entity instance is initialized but it is not associated with a particular identity. In other words, it doesn't have a particular primary key, nor does it represent the state of any particular row in the database. In this state, it can only be used for finder methods (which apply to entity beans in the aggregate) or for home business methods.

In the **ready state**, the instance is associated with a particular identity and can be used for business methods. The EJB container can create an instance of an entity bean and move it to the pooled or ready state at its discretion, calling `ejbLoad()` and `ejbStore()` according to the rules described earlier in this chapter. In practice, an EJB container will only move an entity to the ready state when a client wants to use it, and it will leave that entity in the ready state, move it to the pooled state, or destroy the bean depending on the caching strategy in place. Here is the diagram:

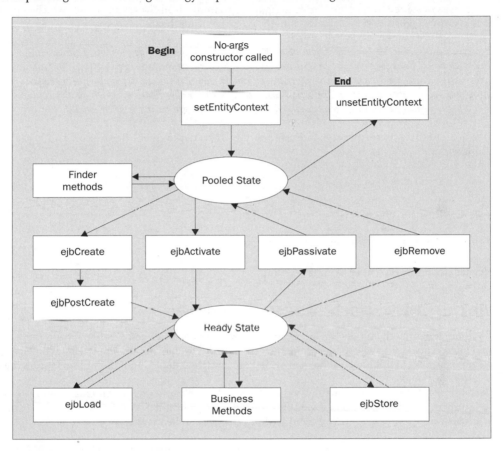

Reentrancy

Unlike session beans, which are never reentrant, an entity bean can be specified as reentrant or non-reentrant. A reentrant bean is one that allows a 'loopback' – for example, an Order entity bean calls a LineItem entity bean, which then calls the Order bean. The initial call to the LineItem 'looped back' to the Order. Another use for reentrant beans are recursive beans, that call themselves for whatever reason.

If the Order bean in this example were specified as reentrant, the call would be allowed. If the Order bean were specified as not being reentrant, the EJB container would disallow the call and throw a `java.rmi.RemoteException` (or `javax.ejb.EJBException` in the case of a local interface). Many programmers are used to a style of programming where child items (such as a line item) have a reference to their containing parent (such as an order). This is admittedly useful in a variety of situations, and is allowed. Making entity beans reentrant, however, is discouraged (not forbidden) by the specification. This is because it can prevent the container from catching a particular class of error (for example, the container might no longer be able to tell a loopback from a concurrent access by another client).

If a bean is coded as reentrant, the EJB container cannot prevent a multi-threaded client operating within a single transaction from making multiple calls to the entity bean. Although entity beans are designed to be single-threaded, this could lead to a situation where two (or more) threads of control were operating on a single instance of an entity bean simultaneously. This is the type of system error that Enterprise JavaBeans technology was designed to free the business-logic programmer from worrying about, which is partly why the specification suggests that bean programmers avoid reentrant beans.

> *Just as an aside, it seems to me that you would have to bend over backwards to create a situation where an entity bean was accessed by multiple threads of control in the same transaction. For instance, since session beans can't have multiple threads, you couldn't do it if you accessed your entity beans through a session bean façade. In any case, I won't contradict the specification, which advises caution if you write reentrant beans. In my experience, caution while programming is never wasted.*

Whether or not a bean is reentrant is indicated in the XML deployment descriptor, and looks like one of the following:

```
<reentrant>True</reentrant>
```

or:

```
<reentrant>False</reentrant>
```

Neither our CMP nor our BMP bean is reentrant.

Completing the Sports Team Example

In considering the differences between entity beans with container-managed persistence and those with bean-managed persistence, we have completed the home interface and much of the implementation class for the sports team example. In addition, we have provided the complete deployment descriptors for both examples.

In order to try out our two sports beans, we need to finish the implementation classes and provide a remote interface and a client. These examples were developed on the WebLogic Server 6.1 application server, so we'll also tell you what you need to do to deploy the beans there.

Let's start by looking at the remote interface. It is the same for both versions (CMP and BMP), except for the package name. The client need never care about the persistence mechanism used by the EJB:

```
package sportBean.bmp;

import javax.ejb.*;

public interface SportTeam extends EJBObject {

   public void setOwnerName(String ownerName)
           throws java.rmi.RemoteException;
```

```
    public String getOwnerName() throws java.rmi.RemoteException;

    public void setFranchisePlayer(String playerName)
          throws java.rmi.RemoteException;

    public String getFranchisePlayer() throws java.rmi.RemoteException;

}
```

Of course, we need to provide corresponding methods in our implementation class, `SportTeamEJB`. Note that we only provide these for the BMP version of our bean:

```
public void setOwnerName(String ownerName) {
  this.ownerName = ownerName;
}

public String getOwnerName() {
  return ownerName;
}

public void setFranchisePlayer(String playerName) {
  this.franchisePlayer = playerName;
}

public String getFranchisePlayer() {
  return franchisePlayer;
}
```

The BMP version uses a utility method to retrieve the connection:

```
private Connection getConnection() {
  try {
    Context initial = new InitialContext();
    DataSource dataSource =
      (DataSource) initial.lookup("java:comp/env/jdbc/sportsJDBC");
    return dataSource.getConnection();
  } catch (javax.naming.NamingException ne) {
    ne.printStackTrace();
    throw new EJBException(ne);
  } catch (java.sql.SQLException sqle) {
    sqle.printStackTrace();
    throw new EJBException(sqle);
  }
}
```

Now it, too, is complete. Finally, let's provide a simple client for testing our beans. The only differences in the clients will be the package names (of course even this isn't necessary), the properties for initializing the JNDI context, and the lookup of the home interface.

The CMP Client

Here is the version for CMP:

```
package sportBean.cmp;

import java.rmi.RemoteException;
import javax.ejb.*;
import javax.naming.*;
import javax.rmi.PortableRemoteObject;
import java.util.Properties;
```

```java
import java.util.Collection;
import java.util.Iterator;

public class TestClient {

  public static void main(String[] args) {
    try {
      Properties prop = new Properties();
      prop.setProperty(Context.INITIAL_CONTEXT_FACTORY,
                       "weblogic.jndi.WLInitialContextFactory");
      prop.setProperty(Context.PROVIDER_URL, "t3://localhost:7001");
      InitialContext initial = new InitialContext(prop);
      Object homeObject = initial.lookup("CMPSportsBean");

      SportTeamHome home =
        (SportTeamHome) PortableRemoteObject.narrow(homeObject,
            SportTeamHome.class);

      /*
       * Create a row in the database
       * (we will remove it at the end of this example)
       */
      System.out.println("Creating a row");
      home.create("basketball", "Kings", "Joe Maloof", "Jason Williams");

      System.out.println("Looking up by primary key...");
      SportTeam team = home.findByPrimaryKey(new SportTeamPK("basketball",
                                                    "Kings"));
      System.out.println("Current franchise player: ");
      System.out.println(team.getFranchisePlayer());

      System.out.println("Looking up by owner...");
      Collection collection = home.findByOwnerName("Joe Maloof");
      if (0 == collection.size()) {
        System.out.println("Found no such owner");
      } else {
        Iterator iter = collection.iterator();
        while (iter.hasNext()) {
          Object objRef2 = iter.next();
          SportTeam teamRef2 =
                  (SportTeam) PortableRemoteObject.narrow(objRef2,
                                                    SportTeam.class);

          System.out.println("Owner name: " + teamRef2.getOwnerName());
        }
      }

      // This will cause the team to be removed from the database
      team.remove();
    } catch (javax.ejb.RemoveException re) {
      re.printStackTrace();
    } catch (RemoteException re) {
      re.printStackTrace();
    } catch (NamingException ne) {
      ne.printStackTrace();
    } catch (CreateException ce) {
      ce.printStackTrace();
    } catch (javax.ejb.FinderException fe) {
      fe.printStackTrace();
    }
  }
}
```

The BMP Client

The version for BMP is quite similar:

```java
package sportBean.bmp;

import java.rmi.RemoteException;
import javax.ejb.*;
import javax.naming.*;
import javax.rmi.PortableRemoteObject;
import java.util.Properties;
import java.util.Collection;
import java.util.Iterator;

public class TestClient {

  public static void main(String[] args) {
    try {
      Properties prop = new Properties();
      prop.setProperty(Context.INITIAL_CONTEXT_FACTORY,
                       "weblogic.jndi.WLInitialContextFactory");
      prop.setProperty(Context.PROVIDER_URL, "t3://localhost:7001");

      InitialContext initial = new InitialContext(prop);

      Object homeObject = initial.lookup("BMPSportsBean");

      SportTeamHome home =
        (SportTeamHome) PortableRemoteObject.narrow(homeObject,
            SportTeamHome.class);

      SportTeam team = home.create("basketball", "Kings", "Joe Maloof",
                                   "Jason Williams");

      System.out.println("Current franchise player: " +
                         team.getFranchisePlayer());

      team.setFranchisePlayer("Cedric Beust");

      System.out.println("New franchise player: " +
                         team.getFranchisePlayer());

      Collection collection = home.findByOwnerName("Joe Maloof");
      Iterator iter = collection.iterator();
      if (!iter.hasNext()) {
        System.out.println("Found no such owner.");
      } else {
        Object objRef2 = iter.next();
        SportTeam teamRef2 =
                (SportTeam) PortableRemoteObject.narrow(objRef2,
                                                SportTeam.class);

        System.out.println("Owner name: " + teamRef2.getOwnerName());
      }

      team.remove();
    } catch (RemoteException re) {
      re.printStackTrace();
    } catch (NamingException ne) {
      ne.printStackTrace();
    } catch (CreateException ce) {
      ce.printStackTrace();
```

```
      } catch (javax.ejb.RemoveException re) {
        re.printStackTrace();
      } catch (javax.ejb.FinderException fe) {
        fe.printStackTrace();
      }
    }
  }
}
```

Since we are deploying our EJBs to WebLogic 6.1, we need to define two additional deployment descriptors: `weblogic-ejb-jar.xml` specifies some additional WebLogic-specific information, which you have already seen, and a new one, which can have an arbitrary file name (we'll call it `weblogic-cmp.xml` here). This deployment descriptor only makes sense if you have CMP entity beans. Its content is fairly self-explanatory, as you will see below: in this descriptor, you specify how the Java CMP fields are mapped to the database columns, what table you will be using, etc.

Here are the two deployment descriptors, starting with `weblogic-ejb-jar.xml` (note that this file must contain the name of the CMP deployment descriptor so that WebLogic knows what file to look for):

```xml
<!DOCTYPE weblogic-ejb-jar
       PUBLIC '-//BEA Systems, Inc.//DTD WebLogic 6.0.0 EJB//EN'
             'http://www.bea.com/servers/wls600/dtd/weblogic-ejb-jar.dtd'>

<weblogic-ejb-jar>
  <weblogic-enterprise-bean>
    <ejb-name>CMPSportsBean</ejb-name>
    <entity-descriptor>
      <persistence>
        <persistence-type>
          <type-identifier>WebLogic_CMP_RDBMS</type-identifier>
          <type-version>6.0</type-version>
          <type-storage>META-INF/weblogic-cmp.xml</type-storage>
        </persistence-type>
        <persistence-use>
          <type-identifier>WebLogic_CMP_RDBMS</type-identifier>
          <type-version>6.0</type-version>
        </persistence-use>
      </persistence>
    </entity-descriptor>

    <jndi-name>CMPSportsBean</jndi-name>
  </weblogic-enterprise-bean>

  <weblogic-enterprise-bean>
    <ejb-name>BMPSportsBean</ejb-name>

    <reference-descriptor>
      <resource-description>
        <res-ref-name>jdbc/sportsJDBC</res-ref-name>
        <jndi-name>jdbc/sportsJDBC</jndi-name>
      </resource-description>
    </reference-descriptor>

    <jndi-name>BMPSportsBean</jndi-name>
  </weblogic-enterprise-bean>
</weblogic-ejb-jar>
```

Note that the section corresponding to our CMP bean is more verbose than that of our BMP bean.

Here is `weblogic-cmp.xml` now:

```
<!DOCTYPE weblogic-rdbms-jar
    PUBLIC
        '-//BEA Systems, Inc.//DTD WebLogic 6.0.0 EJB RDBMS Persistence//EN'
        'http://www.bea.com/servers/wls600/dtd/
                                weblogic-rdbms20-persistence-600.dtd'>

<weblogic-rdbms-jar>
  <weblogic-rdbms-bean>
    <ejb-name>CMPSportsBean</ejb-name>
    <data-source-name>jdbc/sportsJDBC</data-source-name>
    <table-name>SPORTSTEAMS</table-name>

    <field-map>
      <cmp-field>sport</cmp-field>
      <dbms-column>SPORT</dbms-column>
    </field-map>
    <field-map>
      <cmp-field>nickName</cmp-field>
      <dbms-column>NICKNAME</dbms-column>
    </field-map>
    <field-map>
      <cmp-field>ownerName</cmp-field>
      <dbms-column>OWNERNAME</dbms-column>
    </field-map>
    <field-map>
      <cmp-field>franchisePlayer</cmp-field>
      <dbms-column>FRANCHISEPLAYER</dbms-column>
    </field-map>

  </weblogic-rdbms-bean>

</weblogic-rdbms-jar>
```

To review, the EJBs consist of the following files:

```
sportBean/
            cmp/
                SportTeam.class
                SportTeamEJB.class
                SportTeamHome.class
                SportTeamPK.class
            bmp/
                SportTeam.class
                SportTeamEJB.class
                SportTeamHome.class
                SportTeamPK.class
META-INF/
            ejb-jar.xml
            weblogic-ejb-jar.xml
            weblogic-cmp.xml
```

Configuring WebLogic 6.1 for our EJB's

The last step before we can deploy our EJBs is to configure the data sources in WebLogic 6.1. This is done in the file `config.xml`, which you can either edit through the WebLogic Console (easy to do), or by editing the file directly by hand (you'll find it in the `bea\wlserver6.1\config\mydomain` directory). The relevant `config.xml` fragment is:

```
   <JDBCDataSource
     Name="sportsJDBC"
     JNDIName="jdbc/sportsJDBC"
     PoolName="demoPool"
     Targets="myserver"
   />

  <JDBCConnectionPool
    Name="demoPool"
    Targets="myserver"
    URL="jdbc:weblogic:oracle"
    DriverName="weblogic.jdbc.oci.Driver"
    InitialCapacity="1"
    MaxCapacity="10"
    CapacityIncrement="1"
    Password="tiger"
    Properties="user=SCOTT;server=bay816"
  />
```

Note that you will have to adapt the properties of the connection pool to define what your database host is, what JDBC driver it should use, etc. Please refer to the server documentation for details on how to do that.

If you are adding the connection pools and data sources from the console, you don't have anything more to do: WebLogic Server will automatically create the resources. If you edited your config.xml by hand, you will need to stop and restart WebLogic Server in order for these changes to take effect.

To create your EJB, simply create a JAR file that contains the above hierarchy, then copy it to the applications/ directory of your WebLogic server.

Once the server is running, and the JAR file is deployed, you can then call both clients:

```
C:\WINDOWS\System32\cmd.exe                                        _ □ ×

C:\ProJavaServer\Ch16\SportBeanLab>java -classpath .;%WL_HOME%\lib\weblogic
.jar sportBean.cmp.TestClient
Creating a row
Looking up by primary key...
Current franchise player:
Jason Williams
Looking up by owner...
Owner name: Joe Maloof

C:\ProJavaServer\Ch16\SportBeanLab>_
```

```
C:\WINDOWS\System32\cmd.exe                                        _ □ ×

C:\ProJavaServer\Ch16\SportBeanLab>java -cp .;%WL_HOME%\lib\weblogic.jar sp
ortBean.bmp.TestClient
Current franchise player: Jason Williams
New franchise player: Cedric Beust
Looking up by owner...
Owner name: Joe Maloof

C:\ProJavaServer\Ch16\SportBeanLab>_
```

Relationships

One of the most common questions asked about entity beans is how to implement relationships between them. The good news is that relationships are an integral part of the EJB 2.0 specification, which means that all the low-level implementation details will be taken care of by the container. The bad news is that you need to become familiar with a few new notions before you can fully exploit them.

Creating Local Interfaces

The first thing you need to know is that beans can only be connected with a CMP relationship through their local interfaces. Therefore, you are going to need to create a Local interface for each of those beans (a corollary to this rule is that beans connected by a relationship need to be in the same deployment unit: same JAR or same EAR file). Creating a local interface to a bean is straightforward; it involves the following steps:

- ❑ Create a new interface that extends `javax.ejb.EJBLocalHome`. This class is similar to the remote home interface except that its methods are not allowed to throw `RemoteException`.

- ❑ Create a new interface that extends `javax.ejb.EJBLocalObjects`. This class is similar to the remote object interface except that its methods are not allowed to throw `RemoteException`.

- ❑ The local home interface can have the same methods as a remote home interface: create, finders, etc. The only difference is that the objects it returns are `EJBLocalObject`, not remote ones.

- ❑ Add `<local-home>` and `<local>` elements to your `ejb-jar.xml` deployment descriptor, in place of `<home>` and `<remote>`. They must refer to the above classes.

On top of these steps, you might have some additional deployment descriptors to modify depending on the application server you are using, such as giving a JNDI name to the local home interface, binding local references to EJBs, etc. The factory example detailed below explains the necessary steps for WebLogic 6.1.

Defining the Relationships

Now that you have local interfaces, your beans are allowed to participate in a relationship. Suppose you have two EJBs: Product and Order, and that an Order references a Product. First, we need to figure out some characteristics of this relationship:

- ❑ **Cardinality**
  A relationship can be one-one, one-many, or many-many. Let's arbitrarily go for one-one: an order is related to one product, and only one. Obviously, a more complicated example could allow an order to contain several products.

- ❑ **Direction**
  A relationship can be unidirectional or bi-directional. Then again, this is your decision. Obviously, when we have an order, we want to be able to reach the product. Do you want the reverse to be true? In that case, the relationship will be bi-directional, otherwise, it will be unidirectional. Let's opt for a unidirectional relationship.

- ❑ **CMR Fields**
  We need a field on the Order EJB that will reference the product. This field is called a CMR field, for container-managed relationship field. Let's call this field `productOrdered`. Since the relationship is unidirectional, we don't need another CMR field, but if such were the case, we would need to define a symmetric field on the Product EJB (which we could call `order`).

Now we have all the information we need to define the relationship in the `ejb-jar.xml` deployment descriptor. One last detail before we show you what it looks like: a relationship is defined by two roles, each role defining half of the relationship. In the example below, you will notice that the only difference between the roles is that the second one (Product to Order) doesn't have a CMR field, for the reason cited above.

Here is how we would define our relationship between `OrderEJB` and `ProductEJB`:

```
<relationships>
  <ejb-relation>
    <ejb-relation-name>Order-ProductOrdered</ejb-relation-name>
    <ejb-relationship-role>
      <ejb-relationship-role-name>
        Order-has-ProductOrdered
      </ejb-relationship-role-name>
      <multiplicity>one</multiplicity>
      <relationship-role-source>
        <ejb-name>Orders</ejb-name>
      </relationship-role-source>
      <cmr-field>
        <cmr-field-name>productOrdered</cmr-field-name>
      </cmr-field>
    </ejb-relationship-role>
    <ejb-relationship-role>
      <ejb-relationship-role-name>
        ProductOrdered-has-Order
      </ejb-relationship-role-name>
      <multiplicity>one</multiplicity>
      <relationship-role-source>
        <ejb-name>Product</ejb-name>
      </relationship-role-source>
    </ejb-relationship-role>
  </ejb-relation>
</relationships>
```

As far as Java code is concerned, a CMR field is no different from a CMP field: you need to declare abstract setters and the container will generate the implementation for you:

```
abstract public class OrderEJB implements EntityBean {
// ...

    // CMR field
    abstract public LocalProduct getProductOrdered();
    abstract public void setProductOrdered(LocalProduct p);
```

Note that the type of the CMR field is `LocalProduct`, not `Product`, as mandated by the specification.

Completing our Manufacturing Application

We began modeling a manufacturing facility in the last chapter. We referenced two entity beans in that chapter's code, while deferring a complete treatment of those two beans, `Order` and `Product`, until this chapter. As we chose container-managed persistence, the implementation of these two classes is quite simple.

Please note that the exact mapping of these classes to database tables will depend on the implementation of your EJB container's object/relational mapping for container-managed persistence. In the best case scenario, you will have great flexibility, enough to match your beans to pre-existing tables used for other systems. For an adequate container, the worst-case scenario is probably that the product's dependent objects get serialized into a single table column. (Most containers will handle the one-to-one relationship between order and product by storing the product's key in a column of the order table. This is the behavior you probably want.)

One optional feature that your container may have is to automatically create the tables that it will use for the CMP persistence of an entity bean. If you take advantage of this feature, you will automatically get a database structure appropriate for your container's capabilities. You will also save yourself the trouble of configuring the object/relational mapping. Of course, this feature would not be useful if you are working with an existing relational database design.

The Order Bean

Let's start with the interfaces for the Order bean.

The Order Bean Home Interface

The create() methods and the finder methods are declared in the home interface:

```
package factory.order;

import javax.ejb.*;
import java.rmi.RemoteException;
import factory.product.LocalProduct;
import java.util.Date;
import java.util.Collection;

public interface OrderHome extends EJBHome {

    Order create(int salesDivision, int orderNumber,
                LocalProduct productOrdered,
                Date dateDue) throws RemoteException, CreateException;

    Order create(int salesDivision, int orderNumber,
                String productOrdered,
                Date dateDue) throws RemoteException, CreateException;

    Order findByPrimaryKey(OrderPK order) throws RemoteException,
                                                FinderException;

    Collection findOpenOrders() throws RemoteException, FinderException;

    Collection findUncompletedOrders()throws RemoteException,
                                            FinderException;
}
```

The finder methods are specified in EJB QL. We have two here:

```
<query>
  <query-method>
    <method-name>findOpenOrders</method-name>
    <method-params>
    </method-params>
  </query-method>
  <ejb-ql>
    <![CDATA[SELECT OBJECT(o) FROM Orders AS o
                WHERE (o.internalStatus = 'o'
                OR o.internalStatus = 'm')]]>
  </ejb-ql>
</query>
<query>
  <query-method>
    <method-name>findUncompletedOrders</method-name>
```

```
                <method-params>
                </method-params>
            </query-method>
            <ejb-ql>
              <![CDATA[SELECT OBJECT(o) FROM Orders AS o
                             WHERE (o.internalStatus = 'o'
                             OR o.internalStatus = 'm')]]>
            </ejb-ql>
        </query>
```

The Order Bean Remote Interface

Here are the business methods for the order in the remote interface. They are pretty much self-explanatory:

```java
package factory.order;

import javax.ejb.*;
import java.rmi.RemoteException;
import java.util.Date;
import factory.product.Product;

public interface Order extends EJBObject {

    public int getSalesDivision() throws RemoteException;

    public int getOrderNumber() throws RemoteException;

    public Product getProductOrdered() throws RemoteException;

    public String getStatus() throws RemoteException;

    public void cancelOrder()throws RemoteException,
                                    OrderNotCancelableException;

    public void beginManufacture() throws RemoteException;

    public void completeManufacture() throws RemoteException;

    public Date getDateDue() throws RemoteException;
}
```

The Order Bean Implementation Class

The Order bean has five state properties. One of these is a reference to another entity bean (the product). This relationship is pretty intuitive: an order is for a product. Of course, in a real-world application, an order would probably have a list of line items; each of those line items would probably have a product and a quantity, as well as other information. But this is enough to get the idea:

```java
package factory.order;

import javax.ejb.*;
import javax.naming.*;
import java.rmi.RemoteException;
import factory.product.LocalProduct;
import factory.product.Product;
import factory.product.ProductLocalHome;
import factory.product.ProductHome;
import java.util.Date;
```

```
   public abstract class OrderEJB implements EntityBean {

   // Properties
   private static final String OPEN_STATUS = "o";
   private static final String DEFAULT_STATUS = OPEN_STATUS;
   private static final String CANCELED_STATUS = "c";
   private static final String IN_PROCESS_STATUS = "m";
   private static final String COMPLETED_STATUS = "f";


   abstract public int getOrderNumber();
   abstract public void setOrderNumber(int orderNumber);

   abstract public LocalProduct getProductOrdered();
   abstract public void setProductOrdered(LocalProduct p);

   abstract public int getSalesDivision();
   abstract public void setSalesDivision(int salesDivision);

   abstract public Date getDateDue();
   abstract public void setDateDue(Date date);

   abstract public String getInternalStatus();
   abstract public void setInternalStatus(String s);

   private String status;

   // class continues
```

Notice that we have defined five private static variables for use in the implementation. The specification allows static variables in EJBs, but they must be read-only. To enforce this, we declare them final. Also, note the pairs of accessors, one for each CMP field. As mandated by the EJB 2.0 specification, these are declared abstract and will be generated by the container.

The callback functions in OrderEJB are empty; we can leave everything to the container:

```
   public void ejbLoad() {}

   public void ejbStore() {}

   public void ejbActivate() {}

   public void ejbPassivate() {}

   public void ejbRemove() {}

   public void setEntityContext(EntityContext ctx) {}

   public void unsetEntityContext() {}
```

The Order bean provides two versions of its create() method. Although they take the same information, one version accepts the string name of a product and the other accepts a remote reference. The version that takes the string name uses a helper method to convert this into an actual product. If the name doesn't match to a product, a CreateException is thrown.

Note that in order to initialize our bean, we have to use the CMP setters (we don't have access to fields that represent CMP fields). We saw this part earlier. The only addition is that the product ordered is set in ejbPostCreate(), not ejbCreate().

841

The reason is that this field is not a container-managed persistent field, but a container-managed relationship field (CMR field). What makes it different is that the related bean might not have been created yet at the time of `ejbCreate()`, so it might not have a primary key yet. On the other hand, the container guarantees that it will be the case in `ejbPostCreate()`, so that the INSERT of its value in the database can happen:

```
  // Lifecycle and framework methods
  public OrderPK ejbCreate(int salesDivision, int orderNumber,
                           LocalProduct productOrdered,
                           Date dateDue) throws CreateException {
    setSalesDivision(salesDivision);
    setOrderNumber(orderNumber);
    setDateDue(dateDue);
    setInternalStatus(DEFAULT_STATUS);

    status = DEFAULT_STATUS;

    return null;   // for container-managed persistence
  }

  public void ejbPostCreate(int salesDivision, int orderNumber,
                            LocalProduct productOrdered, Date dateDue) {
    setProductOrdered(productOrdered);
  }

  public OrderPK ejbCreate(int salesDivision, int orderNumber,
                           String product,
                           Date dateDue) throws CreateException {
    setSalesDivision(salesDivision);
    setOrderNumber(orderNumber);
    setDateDue(dateDue);
    setInternalStatus(DEFAULT_STATUS);
    status = DEFAULT_STATUS;

    return null;   // for container-managed persistence
  }

  public void ejbPostCreate(int salesDivision, int orderNumber,
                            String product, Date dateDue) {

    // The product ordered must be set in ejbPostCreate since it's
    // part of a one-one relationships
    try {
      ProductLocalHome productHome = getProductHome();
      LocalProduct p = productHome.findByPrimaryKey(product);
      setProductOrdered(p);
    } catch (RemoteException re) {
      re.printStackTrace();
      throw new EJBException(re);
    } catch (FinderException fe) {
      fe.printStackTrace();
      throw new CreateException("Product does not exist");
    }
  }
  // Implementation helpers

  private ProductLocalHome getProductHome() {
    try {
      InitialContext initial = new InitialContext();
      ProductHome home =
```

```
            (ProductLocalHome) javax.rmi.PortableRemoteObject
                  .narrow(initial.lookup("java:comp/env/ejb/LocalProduct"),
                          ProductLocalHome.class);
        return home;
    } catch (NamingException ne) {
      ne.printStackTrace();
      throw new EJBException(ne);
    }
  }
}
```

`create()` methods must have at least enough information to specify the primary key of the new entity. In practice, they will usually have more. There are two possible patterns to initialize a new instance with a set of data:

❑   Call the `create()` method with that set of data

❑   Call a `create()` method, and then call update methods on the instance

> If the second method is used, you should make sure that the update method calls all take place in the same transaction as the call to `create()`. Otherwise, if something happens in between your `create()` call and the updates (such as your client crashing), your database might be left with a half-initialized entity lying around.

The Order Bean Primary-Key Class

The key for the order is a combination of the sales division and the order number, because every sales division has its own system for assigning order numbers, and the two systems would assign conflicting orders. Remember that every primary key must be unique. Here is the primary key for the Order bean:

```
package factory.order;

import java.io.Serializable;

public class OrderPK implements Serializable {

  public int salesDivision;
  public int orderNumber;

  // Mandatory empty constructor
  public OrderPK() {}

  // Convenience constructor
  public OrderPK(int salesDivision, int orderNumber) {
    this.salesDivision = salesDivision;
    this.orderNumber = orderNumber;
  }

  public int hashCode() {
    return (salesDivision << 8 ) + orderNumber;
  }

  public boolean equals(Object other) {
    if ((other == null) ||!(other instanceof OrderPK)) {
      return false;
```

```
        }
        OrderPK otherPK = (OrderPK) other;

        return (salesDivision == otherPK.salesDivision)
                && (orderNumber == otherPK.orderNumber);
    }
}
```

The public state fields (salesDivision and orderNumber) must be named exactly the same and have the same type as the corresponding fields in the bean.

One thing to note is that the order status is stored as a single letter in the database and in the cached state of the order bean. However, the client expects to get a human-readable string when it asks about the status. We have defined these strings in an outside class for simplicity, although the best approach is probably to load them from a resource (to support internationalization, for example):

```
package factory.order;

public class StatusStrings {
    public static final String OPEN = "open";
    public static final String CANCELED = "canceled";
    public static final String IN_PROCESS = "in process";
    public static final String COMPLETED = "completed";
}
```

The letter stored in the database is called internalStatus (and it has its own CMP field) but we expect our clients to use getStatus() to get the human-readable string. We translate the status when the client asks for it in the getStatus() method. We could have cached the status in human-readable form in a transient variable (and worked with it in the business logic in that form) by adding logic in ejbLoad() to translate it from its database format. Then in ejbStore() we could retranslate it into database form and save it in a container-managed non-transient field. This seemed like a lot of work for little value. In some other, more complicated, cases, this might be the way to go.

The OrderNotCancelableException

The OrderNotCancelableException thrown from the cancelOrder() method is an unremarkable class already discussed briefly in the last chapter. It is defined as follows:

```
package factory.order;

public class OrderNotCancelableException extends Exception {

    public OrderNotCancelableException() {}
}
```

The Product Bean

The Product bean has three state properties. Two are strings: product (which is the key) and name (which is the human-readable name of the product), and the third is a list of routing instructions. Routing instructions are the steps through which the product must pass in order to be created. A routing instruction is defined as follows:

```
package factory.product;

import java.io.Serializable;
```

```
public class RoutingInstruction implements Serializable, Comparable {
  public int sequence;
  public String instruction;

  public RoutingInstruction() {}

  public RoutingInstruction(int sequence, String instruction) {
    this.sequence = sequence;
    this.instruction = instruction;
  }

  public int compareTo(Object o) {
    RoutingInstruction ri = (RoutingInstruction) o;
    if (sequence < ri.sequence) {
      return -1;
    } else if (sequence == ri.sequence) {
      return 0;
    } else {
      return 1;
    }
  }
}
```

Note that this could have been modeled as a set of related entity beans. Why did we choose to make routing instructions an attribute?

❑   The lifecycle of a routing instruction is completely controlled by the product in which it is contained. A routing instruction is created for a particular product, and it should be deleted if the corresponding product is deleted.

❑   No entity other than a product will ever link to this routing instruction independently. If, hypothetically, some 'work station' needed to have a reference to all its associated routing steps, it might be worthwhile to make the routing a first class entity object to support this association.

❑   A routing is a lightweight object, and would suffer from the overhead of being a first class entity.

The Product Bean Home Interface

```
package factory.product;

import java.util.Collection;
import javax.ejb.*;
import java.rmi.RemoteException;

public interface ProductHome extends EJBHome {

  Product create(String product, String name,
             Collection routingInstructions) throws RemoteException,
                                                CreateException;

  ProductPK findByPrimaryKey(String product) throws RemoteException,
                                              FinderException;
}
```

The Product Bean Local Home Interface

```
package factory.product;

import java.util.Collection;
```

```
import javax.ejb.*;
import java.rmi.RemoteException;

public interface ProductLocalHome extends EJBLocalHome {

  LocalProduct create(String product, String name,
                     Collection routingInstructions) throws CreateException;

  LocalProduct findByPrimaryKey(String product) throws FinderException;
}
```

The Product Bean Remote Interface

The business methods of the product entity bean are defined as follows in the remote interface:

```
package factory.product;

import javax.ejb.*;
import java.rmi.RemoteException;

public interface Product extends EJBObject {
  public String getProduct() throws RemoteException;

  public String getName() throws RemoteException;

  public void setName(String name) throws RemoteException;

  // Business methods
  public void addRoutingInstruction(int sequence,
                        String instruction) throws RemoteException;

  public void deleteRoutingInstruction(int sequence)
         throws NoSuchRoutingException, RemoteException;

  public Collection getRoutingInstructions()
                              throws RemoteException;
  public void setRoutingInstructions(Collection c)
                     throws RemoteException;
  public void replaceRoutingInstructions(RoutingInstruction[]
                                   newRoutingInstructions)
                           throws RemoteException;
}
```

The Product Bean Implementation Class

Here is the state of our product entity bean:

```
package factory.product;

import javax.ejb.*;
import java.util.List;
import java.util.LinkedList;
import java.util.Arrays;
import java.util.Iterator;

public abstract class ProductEJB implements EntityBean {

  public abstract Collection getRI();
  public abstract void setRI(Collection c);
```

```
abstract public String getProduct();
abstract public void setProduct(String p);

abstract public String getName();
abstract public void setName(String name);
```

The implementation of the business methods are relatively simple: they are all getter and setter methods. The only interesting thing about them is their handling of the dependent routing instruction list:

```
// Business methods

public void setRoutingInstructions(Collection c) {
  setRI(c);
}

public Collection getRoutingInstructions() {
  return getRI();
}

public void addRoutingInstruction(int sequence, String instruction) {
  Collection c = getRI();
  c.add(new RoutingInstruction(sequence, instruction));
  setRI(c);
}

public void deleteRoutingInstruction(int sequence)
    throws NoSuchRoutingException {
  Collection instructions = getRoutingInstructions();
  Iterator iter = instructions.iterator();
  while (iter.hasNext()) {
    RoutingInstruction ri = (RoutingInstruction) iter.next();
    if (ri.sequence == sequence) {
      iter.remove();
      setRoutingInstructions(instructions);
      return;
    }
  }
  throw new NoSuchRoutingException();
}

public void replaceRoutingInstructions(RoutingInstruction[]
    newRoutingInstructions) throws RemoteException {
  LinkedList li = new LinkedList();
  for (int i = 0; i < newRoutingInstructions.length; i++) {
    li.add(newRoutingInstructions[i]);
  }
  setRoutingInstructions(li);
}
```

The callbacks are mostly empty, because the container provides most of the functionality for us. The create() method takes as parameters a complete description of the object's state: product, name, and routing instructions:

```
// Framework and lifecycle methods

public String ejbCreate(String product, String name,
                        Collection routingInstructions)
                        throws RemoteException {
  setProduct(product);
```

```
        setName(name);
        setRoutingInstructions(routingInstructions);
        return null;
    }

    public void ejbPostCreate(String product, String name,
                            Collection routingInstructions) {}


    public void ejbActivate() {}
    public void ejbLoad() {}
    public void ejbPassivate() {}
    public void ejbRemove() {}
    public void ejbStore() {}
    public void setEntityContext(EntityContext ctx) {}
    public void unsetEntityContext() {}
}
```

The NoSuchRoutingInstruction Exception Class

Once again, the exception class defined in this package (`NoSuchRoutingInstruction`) is rather unremarkable:

```
package factory.product;

public class NoSuchRoutingInstruction extends Exception {

    public NoSuchRoutingInstruction() {}
}
```

The implementations of the Product and Order entity beans are quite simple. Their focus is on business logic, and not system-level concerns such as persistence.

The Complete Deployment Descriptor

We've seen a few bits and pieces of the XML deployment descriptor for this example as we examined the Java code. Here is the completed deployment descriptor for all four beans (a stateless session bean for managing orders, a stateful session bean for manufacturing a product, an order entity, and a product entity):

```
<?xml version="1.0"?>
<!DOCTYPE ejb-jar
        PUBLIC '-//Sun Microsystems, Inc.//DTD Enterprise JavaBeans 2.0//EN'
                'http://java.sun.com/dtd/ejb-jar_2_0.dtd'>

<ejb-jar>
  <enterprise-beans>
```

Deployment information for the bean for managing orders (note that we declare local refs to Product):

```
    <session>
      <ejb-name>ManageOrders</ejb-name>
      <home>factory.manage_orders.ManageOrdersHome</home>
      <remote>factory.manage_orders.ManageOrders</remote>
      <ejb-class>factory.manage_orders.ManageOrdersEJB</ejb-class>
      <session-type>Stateless</session-type>
      <transaction-type>Container</transaction-type>
      <env-entry>
        <env-entry-name>lead_time</env-entry-name>
        <env-entry-type>java.lang.Integer</env-entry-type>
```

```
          <env-entry-value>3</env-entry-value>
        </env-entry>
        <env-entry>
          <env-entry-name>max_inventory_time</env-entry-name>
          <env-entry-type>java.lang.Integer</env-entry-type>
          <env-entry-value>10</env-entry-value>
        </env-entry>
        <ejb-ref>
          <ejb-ref-name>ejb/Order</ejb-ref-name>
          <ejb-ref-type>Entity</ejb-ref-type>
          <home>factory.order.OrderHome</home>
          <remote>factory.order.Order</remote>
          <ejb-link>Orders</ejb-link>
        </ejb-ref>
        <ejb-local-ref>
          <ejb-ref-name>ejb/LocalProduct</ejb-ref-name>
          <ejb-ref-type>Entity</ejb-ref-type>
          <local-home>factory.product.ProductLocalHome</local-home>
          <local>factory.product.LocalProduct</local>
          <ejb-link>Product</ejb-link>
        </ejb-local-ref>
      </session>
```

Deployment information for the bean for manufacturing products:

```
      <session>
        <ejb-name>Manufacture</ejb-name>
        <home>factory.manufacture.ManufactureHome</home>
        <remote>factory.manufacture.Manufacture</remote>
        <ejb-class>factory.manufacture.ManufactureEJB</ejb-class>
        <session-type>Stateful</session-type>
        <transaction type>Container</transaction-type>
        <env-entry>
          <env-entry-name>shipmentSQL</env-entry-name>
          <env-entry-type>java.lang.String</env-entry-type>
          <env-entry-value>INSERT INTO ch_shipments (division, order_number,
                         carrier, loading_dock, date_completed,
                         manufactured_by ) VALUES (?, ?, ?, ?, ?, ?)
          </env-entry-value>
        </env-entry>
        <ejb-ref>
          <ejb-ref-name>ejb/Order</ejb-ref-name>
          <ejb-ref-type>Entity</ejb-ref-type>
          <home>factory.order.OrderHome</home>
          <remote>factory.order.Order</remote>
          <ejb-link>Orders</ejb-link>
        </ejb-ref>
        <ejb-ref>
          <ejb-ref-name>ejb/ManageOrders</ejb-ref-name>
          <ejb-ref-type>Session</ejb-ref-type>
          <home>factory.manage_orders.ManageOrdersHome</home>
          <remote>factory.manage_orders.ManageOrders</remote>
          <ejb-link>ManageOrders</ejb-link>
        </ejb-ref>
        <resource-ref>
          <res-ref-name>jdbc/shipDB</res-ref-name>
          <res-type>javax.sql.DataSource</res-type>
          <res-auth>Container</res-auth>
        </resource-ref>
      </session>
```

Deployment information for the order entity bean:

```
<entity>
  <ejb-name>Orders</ejb-name>
  <home>factory.order.OrderHome</home>
  <remote>factory.order.Order</remote>
  <ejb-class>factory.order.OrderEJB</ejb-class>
  <persistence-type>Container</persistence-type>
  <prim-key-class>factory.order.OrderPK</prim-key-class>
  <reentrant>False</reentrant>
  <cmp-version>2.x</cmp-version>
  <abstract-schema-name>Orders</abstract-schema-name>
  <cmp-field><field-name>salesDivision</field-name></cmp-field>
  <cmp-field><field-name>orderNumber</field-name></cmp-field>
  <cmp-field><field-name>internalStatus</field-name></cmp-field>
  <cmp-field><field-name>dateDue</field-name></cmp-field>
  <ejb-local-ref>
    <ejb-ref-name>ejb/LocalProduct</ejb-ref-name>
    <ejb-ref-type>Entity</ejb-ref-type>
    <local-home>factory.product.ProductLocalHome</local-home>
    <local>factory.product.LocalProduct</local>
    <ejb-link>Product</ejb-link>
  </ejb-local-ref>
  <query>
    <query-method>
      <method-name>findOpenOrders</method-name>
      <method-params>
      </method-params>
    </query-method>
    <ejb-ql>
      <![CDATA[SELECT OBJECT(o) FROM Orders AS o
                   WHERE (o.internalStatus = 'o'
                   OR o.internalStatus = 'm')]]>
    </ejb-ql>
  </query>
  <query>
    <query-method>
      <method-name>findUncompletedOrders</method-name>
      <method-params>
      </method-params>
    </query-method>
    <ejb-ql>
      <![CDATA[SELECT OBJECT(o) FROM Orders AS o
                   WHERE (o.internalStatus = 'o'
                   OR o.internalStatus = 'm')]]>
    </ejb-ql>
  </query>
</entity>
```

Deployment information for the product entity bean:

```
<entity>
  <ejb-name>Product</ejb-name>
  <home>factory.product.ProductHome</home>
  <remote>factory.product.Product</remote>
  <local-home>factory.product.ProductLocalHome</local-home>
  <local>factory.product.LocalProduct</local>
  <ejb-class>factory.product.ProductEJB</ejb-class>
  <persistence-type>Container</persistence-type>
  <prim-key-class>java.lang.String</prim-key-class>
  <reentrant>False</reentrant>
```

```
        <cmp-version>2.x</cmp-version>
        <abstract-schema-name>Product</abstract-schema-name>
        <cmp-field><field-name>product</field-name></cmp-field>
        <cmp-field><field-name>name</field-name></cmp-field>
        <cmp-field><field-name>rI</field-name></cmp-field>
        <primkey-field>product</primkey-field>
    </entity>

  </enterprise-beans>
```

The relationship between `OrderEJB` and `productOrdered` is one-to-one and unidirectional (from an Order, we get the product ordered but not the other way around, we don't need it for this example). Consequently, we only need to specify one `<cmr-field>`. If we wanted the relationships to be directional, we would need to specify a CMR field on `ProductEJB` as well (we could call it `order` and we would have to declare abstract `getOrder()`/`setOrder()` on `ProductEJB`):

```
    <relationships>
      <ejb-relation>
        <ejb-relation-name>Order-ProductOrdered</ejb-relation-name>
        <ejb-relationship-role>
          <ejb-relationship-role-name>
            Order-has-ProductOrdered
          </ejb-relationship-role-name>
          <multiplicity>one</multiplicity>
          <relationship-role-source>
            <ejb-name>Orders</ejb-name>
          </relationship-role-source>
          <cmr-field>
            <cmr-field-name>productOrdered</cmr-field-name>
          </cmr-field>
        </ejb-relationship-role>
        <ejb-relationship-role>
          <ejb-relationship-role-name>
            ProductOrdered-has-Order
          </ejb-relationship-role-name>
          <multiplicity>one</multiplicity>
          <relationship-role-source>
            <ejb-name>Product</ejb-name>
          </relationship-role-source>
        </ejb-relationship-role>
      </ejb-relation>
    </relationships>
```

Assembly information for the application as a whole; specifically, declarative transactions:

```
<assembly-descriptor>
   <container-transaction>
     <method>
        <ejb-name>Orders</ejb-name>
        <method-name>*</method-name>
     </method>
     <trans-attribute>Required</trans-attribute>
   </container-transaction>
   <container-transaction>
     <method>
        <ejb-name>Product</ejb-name>
        <method-name>*</method-name>
     </method>
     <trans-attribute>Required</trans-attribute>
```

```
    </container-transaction>
    <container-transaction>
      <method>
         <ejb-name>ManageOrders</ejb-name>
         <method-name>*</method-name>
      </method>
      <trans-attribute>Required</trans-attribute>
    </container-transaction>
    <container-transaction>
      <method>
         <ejb-name>Manufacture</ejb-name>
         <method-name>*</method-name>
      </method>
      <trans-attribute>Required</trans-attribute>
    </container-transaction>
  </assembly-descriptor>
</ejb-jar>
```

Remarks on the deployment descriptor:

❑   The <env-entry> tags are new. They are a convenient way to pass information stored in the deployment descriptors to our EJBs. The EJB will have access to these values by looking them up in the java:comp/env namespace. An example of code to read the lead_time value would be:

```
InitialContext initial = new InitialContext();
Integer leadTimeDays =
         (Integer) initial.lookup("java:comp/env/lead_time");
```

❑   <ejb-link> offers a way to reference links across a deployment descriptor, or to reference EJBs that are defined in another JAR file (note that the linked EJBs must belong to the same EAR file.

We also need to declare some extra WebLogic-specific information in weblogic-ejb-jar.xml and weblogic-cmp.xml. Nothing remarkable in weblogic-ejb-jar.xml except that this time, we need to map some of the local references to Product that we declared in ejb-jar.xml. Here is the weblogic-ejb-jar.xml file:

```
<!DOCTYPE weblogic-ejb-jar
     PUBLIC '-//BEA Systems, Inc.//DTD WebLogic 6.0.0 EJB//EN'
            'http://www.bea.com/servers/wls600/dtd/weblogic-ejb-jar.dtd'>

<weblogic-ejb-jar>
  <weblogic-enterprise-bean>
    <ejb-name>ManageOrders</ejb-name>

    <reference-descriptor>
      <ejb-local-reference-description>
        <ejb-ref-name>ejb/LocalProduct</ejb-ref-name>
        <jndi-name>LocalProduct</jndi-name>
      </ejb-local-reference-description>
    </reference-descriptor>

    <jndi-name>ManageOrders</jndi-name>
  </weblogic-enterprise-bean>

  <weblogic-enterprise-bean>
    <ejb-name>Manufacture</ejb-name>
    <reference-descriptor>
      <resource-description>
```

```
          <res-ref-name>jdbc/shipDB</res-ref-name>
          <jndi-name>jdbc/sportsJDBC</jndi-name>
        </resource-description>
      </reference-descriptor>

      <jndi-name>Manufacture</jndi-name>
  </weblogic-enterprise-bean>

  <weblogic-enterprise-bean>
    <ejb-name>Orders</ejb-name>
    <entity-descriptor>
      <persistence>
        <persistence-type>
          <type-identifier>WebLogic_CMP_RDBMS</type-identifier>
          <type-version>6.0</type-version>
          <type-storage>META-INF/weblogic-cmp.xml</type-storage>
        </persistence-type>
        <persistence-use>
          <type-identifier>WebLogic_CMP_RDBMS</type-identifier>
          <type-version>6.0</type-version>
        </persistence-use>
      </persistence>
    </entity-descriptor>

    <reference-descriptor>
      <ejb-local-reference-description>
        <ejb-ref-name>ejb/LocalProduct</ejb-ref-name>
        <jndi-name>LocalProduct</jndi-name>
      </ejb-local-reference-description>
    </reference-descriptor>

    <jndi-name>Orders</jndi-name>

  </weblogic-enterprise-bean>

  <weblogic-enterprise-bean>
    <ejb-name>Product</ejb-name>
    <entity-descriptor>
      <persistence>
        <persistence-type>
          <type-identifier>WebLogic_CMP_RDBMS</type-identifier>
          <type-version>6.0</type-version>
          <type-storage>META-INF/weblogic-cmp.xml</type-storage>
        </persistence-type>
        <persistence-use>
          <type-identifier>WebLogic_CMP_RDBMS</type-identifier>
          <type-version>6.0</type-version>
        </persistence-use>
      </persistence>
    </entity-descriptor>
    <jndi-name>Product</jndi-name>
    <local-jndi-name>LocalProduct</local-jndi-name>
  </weblogic-enterprise-bean>

</weblogic-ejb-jar>
```

The `weblogic-cmp.xml` file is similar to the one you already saw at the beginning of this chapter except for one addition: the relationship specification. In `ejb-jar.xml`, we specified the nature of the relation but the container still needs some extra information in order to implement it. In this relationship, we are linking an Order to a Product, therefore, the container needs to know how to store the product inside the order. The container already knows that it must use the CMR field called `product` to do that, but it doesn't know what to store at this point. Relationships are maintained through the use of foreign keys. In this field, we are not going to store a full `Product` object, just its primary key. This information is sufficient for the container to materialize the other end of the relationship whenever it needs it.

Now that we understand the principle, we need to specify the mapping: we need to figure out what's needed in order to specify a product's primary key. A quick look at `ejb-jar.xml` tells us that `ProductEJB`'s primary key is a simple string, so that will be easy: let's create a column in the product table that will contain this string. Then we inform the container that `ProductEJB`'s primary key (stores in column 'product') will be mapped in `OrderEJB`'s column `product_ordered`.

Here is the complete `weblogic-cmp.xml` file:

```
<!DOCTYPE weblogic-rdbms-jar
    PUBLIC
        '-//BEA Systems, Inc.//DTD WebLogic 6.0.0 EJB RDBMS Persistence//EN'
        'http://www.bea.com/servers/wls600/dtd/
                                weblogic-rdbms20-persistence-600.dtd'>

<weblogic-rdbms-jar>
  <weblogic-rdbms-bean>
    <ejb-name>Product</ejb-name>
    <data-source-name>jdbc/shipJDBC</data-source-name>
    <table-name>cb_products</table-name>

    <field-map>
      <cmp-field>product</cmp-field>
      <dbms-column>product</dbms-column>
    </field-map>
    <field-map>
      <cmp-field>name</cmp-field>
      <dbms-column>name</dbms-column>
    </field-map>
    <field-map>
      <cmp-field>rI</cmp-field>
      <dbms-column>routingInstructions</dbms-column>
    </field-map>

  </weblogic-rdbms-bean>

  <weblogic-rdbms-bean>
    <ejb-name>Orders</ejb-name>
    <data-source-name>jdbc/shipJDBC</data-source-name>
    <table-name>cb_orders</table-name>

    <field-map>
      <cmp-field>salesDivision</cmp-field>
      <dbms-column>sales_division</dbms-column>
    </field-map>
    <field-map>
      <cmp-field>orderNumber</cmp-field>
      <dbms-column>order_number</dbms-column>
    </field-map>
    <field-map>
      <cmp-field>dateDue</cmp-field>
      <dbms-column>date_due</dbms-column>
```

```
        </field-map>
        <field-map>
          <cmp-field>internalStatus</cmp-field>
          <dbms-column>internal_status</dbms-column>
        </field-map>
    </weblogic-rdbms-bean>

    <weblogic-rdbms-relation>
      <relation-name>Order-ProductOrdered</relation-name>
        <weblogic-relationship-role>
          <relationship-role-name>
            Order-has-ProductOrdered
          </relationship-role-name>
          <column-map>
            <foreign-key-column>product_ordered</foreign-key-column>
            <key-column>product</key-column>
          </column-map>
        </weblogic-relationship-role>
    </weblogic-rdbms-relation>

</weblogic-rdbms-jar>
```

Notice that we're reusing the data source from the `SportTeam` example earlier in the chapter – this is to save a little time, although in a production environment we would want to use a different datasource.

What if the related bean happens to have a compound primary key? In this case, you simply extend the principle we just applied: figure out what columns constitute its primary key, create a corresponding column for each of them in your source EJB and then specify the mapping between them as above.

Running the Manufacturing Application

At this point, you have enough information to run the manufacturing sample application. You should have the following classes in your EJB JAR (or directory structure, if your EJB container supports this format):

```
factory/
        clients/
                BeginManufacture.class
                CompleteManufacture.class
                ContextPropertiesFactory.class
                CreateProducts.class
                ManageSampleOrders.class
                PlaceSampleOrders.class
        manage_orders/
                DuplicateOrderException.class
                ManageOrders.class
                ManageOrdersEJB.class
                ManageOrdersHome.class
                NoSuchOrderException.class
                NoSuchProductException.class
                OpenOrderView.class
                OverdueOrderView.class
                ProductCreationHelper.class
        manufacture/
                BadStatusException.class
                Manufacture.class
```

```
                    ManufactureEJB.class
                    ManufactureHome.class
                    NoSelectionException.class
            order/
                    Order.class
                    OrderEJB.class
                    OrderHome.class
                    OrderNotCancelableException.class
                    OrderPK.class
                    StatusStrings.class
            product/
                    NoSuchRoutingException.class
                    Product.class
                    ProductEJB.class
                    ProductHome.class
                    RoutingInstruction.class
    META-INF/
            ejb-jar.xml
            weblogic-ejb-jar.xml
            weblogic-cmp.xml
```

Note that the `clients`, `manage_orders`, and `manufacture` packages are from the previous chapter on session beans.

You also need to create the database table used by the manufacturing session bean for recording shipments. This was discussed in the previous chapter; as a refresher, here is the SQL to create this table:

```
CREATE TABLE cb_shipments (division INTEGER NOT NULL,
                    order_number INTEGER NOT NULL,
                    carrier VARCHAR(50),
                    loading_dock INTEGER,
                    date_completed DATE,
                    manufactured_by VARCHAR(50),
                    PRIMARY KEY (division, order_number));
```

We also need one for storing products:

```
CREATE TABLE cb_products (product VARCHAR(50),
                    name VARCHAR(50),
                    routingInstructions LONGVARBINARY,
                    PRIMARY KEY (product));
```

And finally one for storing orders:

```
CREATE TABLE cb_orders(order_number INTEGER,
                    sales_division INTEGER,
                    product_ordered VARCHAR(50),
                    date_due DATE,
                    internal_status VARCHAR(200),
                    PRIMARY KEY (sales_division, order_number));
```

Note that you'll need to be careful not to overwrite these tables if they already exist. Also, you'll want to create them in the database that the jdbc/SportsJDBC data source points to; if you don't, the application won't be able to store any data.

Now you should be able to run the clients that were described in Chapter 15. These clients just provide a simple test of the functionality provided by our EJBs:

❏   Run CreateProducts first to create some sample products.

❏   Next run PlaceSampleOrders. (Running either of these programs a second time without deleting the appropriate records from the database will result in harmless error messages.)

❏   Run ManageSampleOrders next; it will select an overdue order and cancel it:

```
C:\WINDOWS\System32\cmd.exe                                              _ □ X

C:\ProJavaServer\Ch16\Manufacturing>java -classpath .;%WL_HOME%\lib\weblogi
c.jar factory.clients.ManageSampleOrders
# overdue:2
Product Quality Plastic Chair is due on Wed Aug 08 00:00:00 GMT+01:00 2001.
 Its status is open.
Product Custom Made Lamp is due on Wed Aug 08 00:00:00 GMT+01:00 2001.  Its
 status is open.
About to cancel an order...
Canceled order for Quality Plastic Chair.
```

❏   Run BeginManufacture next; it will use a stateful session bean to select an appropriate order for manufacture and serialize a handle to that bean. (The handle will be stored in c:/current_product.ser. If this is not an appropriate name on your computer you should change it in BeginManufacture.java and CompleteManufacture.java.)

```
C:\WINDOWS\System32\cmd.exe                                              _ □ X

C:\ProJavaServer\Ch16\Manufacturing>java -classpath .;%WL_HOME%\lib\weblogi
c.jar factory.clients.BeginManufacture
Selecting from the following open orders:
Sales Division: 2; Order #: 2; Product: Compressed Wood DeskDate due: Mon A
ug 13 00:00:00 GMT+01:00 2001
Sales Division: 2; Order #: 3; Product: Custom Made LampDate due: Wed Aug 0
8 00:00:00 GMT+01:00 2001
Written object for next stage.
```

❏   Finally, run CompleteManufacture; it will deserialize the handle, print out the instructions for manufacture, and ship the product. (Note that in this case, the only reason we've broken up the manufacturing process into two sample applications is to demonstrate how to serialize the handle.)

If you are using Windows 2000 and the Sun JDK then you may get a JVM error when you try to call getEJBObject() on the serialized handle. This is a known bug with a workaround at:
http://developer.sun.java.com/developer/bugParade/bugs/4472743.html.

Summary

In this chapter we discussed entity beans in depth. The main points were:

- Entity beans represent the shared, transactional data in your application

- The persistence of entity beans can be managed by the bean programmer or by the container

- Container-managed persistence can boost productivity, but may not be capable enough for your needs, although EJB 2.0 should cover most of developers' needs

- Third party object/relational-mapping tools may provide capable persistence services, but are proprietary and potentially expensive

- Bean-managed persistence forces the bean programmer to assume the burden of transferring state from the object to the data store

- Caching data within a transaction is supported by the container and data store

- Caching data between transactions may provide a boost in performance if your application and environment allow this

- Finder methods allow a client to locate shared object state corresponding to a particular identity or particular criteria

- Relationships are automatically managed by the EJB 2.0 container; EJB QL is a powerful language that allows you to find beans or navigate relationships in a database-independent way

- Reentrant entity beans are allowed, but can prevent the container from catching a particular class of error and so are not recommended

In the next chapter, we examine four of the fundamental services that an EJB container can provide: declarative transactions, declarative security, support for remote communications, and an exception handling framework. Although every EJB container provides these services, you must have some understanding of each topic – and how it relates to EJB technology – to develop and deploy your EJB components effectively.

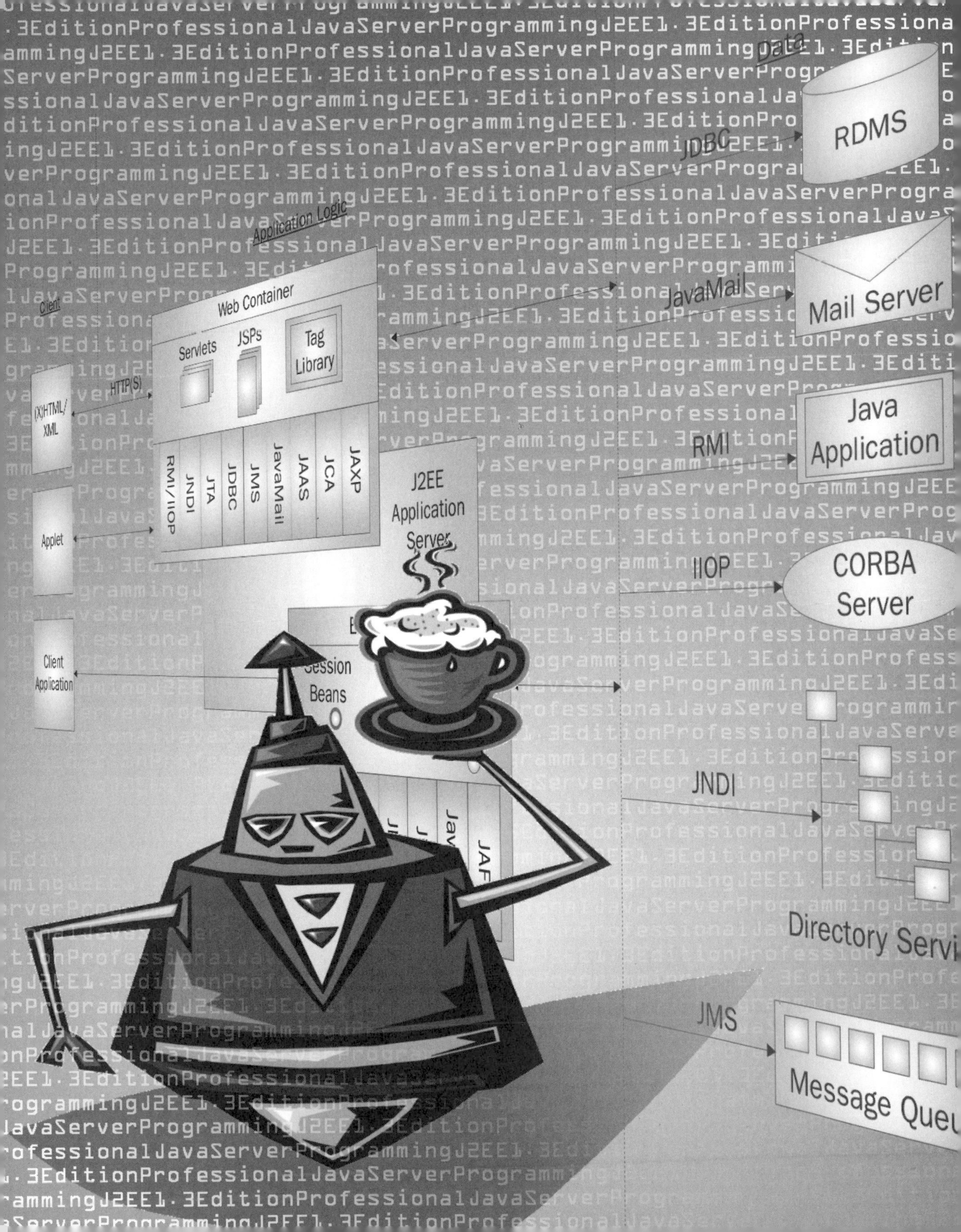

17

EJB Container Services

Although the intent of Enterprise JavaBeans technology is to free business-logic programmers from having to develop system-level services, it is still useful and important for developers to understand how these services work. Every significant enterprise application will need to provide support for transactions to protect the integrity of its data. Similarly, it will need to protect its resources against unauthorized access. An application will need to provide support for remote access to its data and business logic, and to handle exceptional conditions in a robust way.

All EJB specification-compliant containers provide support for transactions, security, communications, and exception handling. Although the actual implementation of these services will differ between EJB containers, the EJB specification is written so that an enterprise bean may take advantage of these services in a portable manner. This means that developers can write business logic to take advantage of these container services without sacrificing the ability to run their beans in multiple containers.

For the most part, an EJB programmer can take advantage of these services without writing any Java code at all, as one of the intentions of the EJB specification is to allow developers, where possible, to make a simple declaration of intent as to how services, such as transactions and security, should operate in a particular application. This allows an application to be deployed to any execution environment using only the tools provided by the application-server vendor, with no additional programming required.

This approach to using services is far easier, cheaper (as all the underlying technology costs money to develop), and more robust than programming the use of these services for each bean.

> **The presence of declarative container services does not absolve the bean developer (and deployer) from understanding how transactions, security, communications, and exception handling work in the context of EJB technology.**

The developers and deployer of an application need to understand the environment to which they are deploying, including the database, application server, and security system; although this is less true of the developer, who is insulated from the target deployment environment as much as possible.

In this chapter, we will examine the issues related to these declarative or automatic services. This means that we will be using our application server's deployment tools, rather than a code editor. As such, the examples that are code-oriented are designed to demonstrate techniques that are applicable in special cases (such as access to the security principal) or that are to be discouraged in general (such as use of the `javax.transaction.UserTransaction` interface).

We will want to see how each of these topics applies to specific application servers and EJB containers, and the best way to achieve this is to:

❑ Take the code samples from the last few chapters and configure the transactional attributes and security framework using the deployment tools that the vendor provides

❑ Study the vendor's documentation regarding the communication services that it provides

❑ Examine the logging that the EJB container performs when a system exception is thrown

❑ Take a look at any vendor-specific XML files that the container generates

The EJB technology attempts to separate system-level concerns from the domain of the business logic programmer, and to improve portability between different environments. As a result, it can make significant demands on the person who needs to configure an EJB application to fit a particular environment. At the end of this chapter, we will understand the basic services that the EJB container provides, and we will be in a position to make intelligent decisions during both application development and deployment.

As application servers and EJB containers vary so much, we must also read the documentation that comes with a particular tool. This is unavoidable because of the variety of implementations for EJB technology. The information in this chapter will apply to every EJB 2.0 container, and will help us to understand the generic options that they all present. Specifically, we will cover:

❑ **Transactions**
We will compare traditional programmatic transaction support and declarative transaction support. We will also look at specific declarative transaction situations and the existing options.

❑ **Security**
We will look at the enterprise-level security considerations and what part roles and permissions have to play. We will also look at the situations where programmatic access control is necessary.

❑ **Exception Handling**
We will examine our responsibility with regards to exceptions, both system and application-related, the consequences of these, and the resulting action by the containers in which our code resides.

❑ **Communication**
We will look at communication between heterogeneous application servers.

Transactions

A transaction is a set of operations that must be processed as a single unit. To be considered transactional, the set of operations composing this single unit of work must exhibit certain well-defined characteristics, referred to by the mnemonic acronym ACID – they must be **Atomic, Consistent, Isolated,** and **Durable**:

- ❑ **Atomic** means that the operations must succeed or fail as a group. If a bank account has money withdrawn and then credited into another account in a transaction, we must never have the situation where the debit failed and the credit succeeded, or vice versa. Either both must succeed and the money will be transferred, or both must fail and the accounting system must have neither stolen money from the customer, nor given money away.

- ❑ **Consistent** means that the database must be left in a state that does not violate the integrity of the database, regardless of the success or failure of any transaction. As a result, the business-logic programmer will not have to undo the effects of a failed transaction in their code. It also means that a database administrator won't need to clean up any orphaned records or mismatched data from operations that fail to complete.

- ❑ **Isolated** means that the business logic can proceed without consideration for the other activities of the system. For instance, while an EJB is checking to make sure that there is enough money in the account before transferring it, another process may be withdrawing money from this account to satisfy an ATM withdrawal. If the two processes aren't kept isolated from each other's effects, it's possible that the transfer and the withdrawal will both succeed – using the same money. Due to the isolation property (locking) of transactions, the business-logic programmer doesn't need to defend against this situation.

- ❑ **Durable** means that once a transaction has succeeded (has been committed), the results will be reflected in the persistent data store. As a result, the business logic programmer will not need to worry about a subsequent error of some kind causing their data to become inconsistent.

A transaction has a discrete starting point. After that starting point, changes made through any resource that is enlisted (participating) in the transaction – such as a database connection – will have the ACID properties that we just described. The transaction will also have a discrete endpoint. At the endpoint, the transaction can **commit** (make all its changes permanent) or **roll back** (undo all the changes that it has made in this transaction). There are two key points. First, these changes are all or nothing. Second, changes that other transactions are making won't interfere with these changes (subject to the isolation policy, described above).

Declarative transactions can simplify application development by freeing the business-logic programmer from writing code to deal with the system-level and complex issues of failure recovery and concurrent access from a multi-user system. An EJB container will provide support, managing these transactions without the application programmer needing to implement this logic in Java code.

Of course, transactions come at a cost in performance and scalability. Ensuring that these ACID properties are applied to a set of operations requires the coordination of the relevant resources (such as a database) and the application server. Therefore, some extra communication will take place between the participants and the transaction manager. More importantly, it may require that accesses to data be serialized, rather than being allowed to occur simultaneously. Applications may want some of their operation to occur outside of the control of a transaction for these reasons.

Additionally, some resources do not support transactions managed by an external transaction manager. A transaction manager is an entity external to our application that acts as the mediator when concurrent access to resources is requested. The EJB container cannot manage the transactions for beans that use such a resource. In such a case, the bean developer should use container-managed transactions and indicate that the bean's methods do not operate in a transaction.

The EJB programmer may choose between using a simple API to demarcate transaction boundaries, and providing information in the XML deployment descriptor to allow the container to manage the boundaries of the transaction. The first option is called **bean-managed transaction demarcation**, and the second **container-managed transaction demarcation**. Both options shield the programmer from the true complexity of the implementation of a transaction processing system, upholding the basic principle of deferring to the container where possible. It is much less likely that we will need to use bean-managed transactions than that we would need to use, say, bean-managed persistence. There are many hidden complexities to deal with if we decide to manage our own transactions. The real difficulties lie in handling errors and exceptions. Rolling back a transaction is a complex and costly operation that must be done very carefully. It is strongly recommend that we use the declarative semantics available with container-managed transactions, this will save us a lot of time.

> **Bean-managed transactions are only possible for session beans; entity beans using container-managed persistence must use container-managed transactions.**

The developer of a session bean must declare the type of transaction demarcation in the XML deployment descriptor. Typically, this information will be edited by the container provider; however, it can also be edited by hand. Here are example entries declaring each type of transaction demarcation:

```
<transaction-type>Bean</transaction-type>
```

or

```
<transaction-type>Container</transaction-type>
```

Transactions Without a Container

The EJB container takes responsibility for managing transactions, but of course it's possible to have transactions without EJBs. To help make the concept of a transaction clearer, let's look at transactions in a stand alone Java program. We'll examine an Account object that updates the database by a connection that is passed as a parameter. The `java.sql.Connection` class provides basic transaction management that we'll use in our simple example (but, we are not allowed to use it in an application server). We'll look at two clients: one that does not use transactions and one that does. We'll see how transactions are necessary for data integrity. The database table is defined with two integrity constraints, to provide a minimum and maximum value for an account:

```
CREATE TABLE ACCOUNT (ACCOUNTID VARCHAR(25) NOT NULL,
        CUSTOMERNAME VARCHAR(25),
        AMOUNT DOUBLE PRECISION,
        PRIMARY KEY (ACCOUNTID),
        CHECK (AMOUNT > 0),
        CHECK (AMOUNT < 15000)
);
```

Here is the definition of the Account object. It has getter and setter methods, and create, read, update, and delete lifecycle methods:

```
import java.sql.Connection;
import java.sql.PreparedStatement;
import java.sql.ResultSet;
import java.sql.SQLException;
```

```java
public class Account {
  private String accountID;
  private String customerName;
  private double amount;

  public String getAccountID() {
    return accountID;
  }

  public String getCustomerName() {
    return customerName;
  }

  public void setCustomerName(String customerName) {
    this.customerName = customerName;
  }

  public double getAmount() {
    return amount;
  }

  public void setAmount(double amount) {
    this.amount = amount;
  }

  public void create(String accountID, String customerName,
                     double amount,
                     Connection con) throws SQLException {
    this.accountID = accountID;
    this.customerName = customerName;
    this.amount = amount;

    PreparedStatement statement = null;

    try {
      statement =
        con.prepareStatement("INSERT INTO ACCOUNT (ACCOUNTID,
                              CUSTOMERNAME, AMOUNT ) "
                            + "VALUES ( ?, ?, ? )");
      statement.setString(1, accountID);
      statement.setString(2, customerName);
      statement.setDouble(3, amount);

      statement.executeUpdate();
    }
    finally {
      if (statement != null) {
        statement.close();
      }
    }
  }

  public void read(String accountID, Connection con)
          throws SQLException, RecordNotFoundException {
    PreparedStatement statement = null;

    try {
      statement =
        con.prepareStatement("SELECT CUSTOMERNAME, AMOUNT FROM ACCOUNT
                              WHERE ACCOUNTID = ?");
      statement.setString(1, accountID);
```

```
      ResultSet result = statement.executeQuery();
      if (result.next()) {
        this.accountID = accountID;
        this.customerName = result.getString(1);
        this.amount = result.getDouble(2);
      } else {
        throw new RecordNotFoundException();
      }
    }
    finally {
      if (statement != null) {
        statement.close();
      }
    }
  }

  public void update(Connection con) throws SQLException {
    PreparedStatement statement = null;

    try {
      statement =
        con.prepareStatement("UPDATE ACCOUNT SET CUSTOMERNAME=?,
                             AMOUNT=? WHERE ACCOUNTID = ?");
      statement.setString(1, customerName);
      statement.setDouble(2, amount);
      statement.setString(3, accountID);

      statement.executeUpdate();
    }
    finally {
      if (statement != null) {
        statement.close();
      }
    }
  }

  public void delete(Connection con) throws SQLException {
    PreparedStatement statement = null;

    try {
      statement =
        con.prepareStatement("DELETE FROM ACCOUNT WHERE ACCOUNTID = ?");
      statement.setString(1, accountID);

      statement.executeUpdate();
    }
    finally {
      if (statement != null) {
        statement.close();
      }
    }
  }
}
```

Here is the exception class that this account class uses:

```
public class RecordNotFoundException extends Exception  {
  public RecordNotFoundException() {}
}
```

The client will create two accounts, and transfer money between them. With the first set of values, the transfer will go smoothly. But if you comment out the first set of values, uncomment the second set of values, and run the client again, a constraint will be violated during the transfer. Unfortunately, the first account has been debited, but the second account can't be credited as the resulting account balance will equal more than the maximum allowable value. When the client exits, the bank will have stolen money from the customer. Here is that client (remember to include the `cloudscape.jar` file in your classpath when running this code):

```java
import java.sql.Connection;
import java.sql.DriverManager;

public class Client1 {
  private static final String ACCOUNT1 = "A32-116";
  private static final String NAME1 = "Lynne Older";
  private static final double AMOUNT1 = 10000.0;

  private static final String ACCOUNT2 = "A32-117";
  private static final String NAME2 = "Patricia Mahar";
  private static final double AMOUNT2 = 12000.0;

  private static final double TRANSFER_AMOUNT = 1000.0;

  /*
   * Mary has 14000 in her account, therefore a credit
   * of 2000 will fail to go through.
   * private static final String ACCOUNT1 = "B32-116";
   * private static final String NAME1 = "Christina Couglin";
   * private static final double AMOUNT1 = 10000.0;
   * private static final String ACCOUNT2 = "B32-117";
   * private static final String NAME2 = "Mary Klopot";
   * private static final double AMOUNT2 = 14000.0;
   * private static final double TRANSFER_AMOUNT = 2000.0;
   */

  static {
    try {
      Class.forName("COM.cloudscape.core.JDBCDriver");

    } catch (Exception e) {
      System.out.println(e);
    }
  }

  public static void main(String[] args) {
    createAccounts();
    transfer(ACCOUNT1, ACCOUNT2, TRANSFER_AMOUNT);
  }

  private static void createAccounts() {
    Connection con = null;

    try {
      con = DriverManager.getConnection(
          "jdbc:cloudscape:C:/ProJavaServer/Ch19/tx");

      Account account1 = new Account();
      account1.create(ACCOUNT1, NAME1, AMOUNT1, con);

      Account account2 = new Account();
      account2.create(ACCOUNT2, NAME2, AMOUNT2, con);
```

```
      System.out.println("Accounts created.");
    } catch (Exception e) {
      e.printStackTrace();
    }
    finally {
      try {
        if (con != null) {
          con.close();
        }
      } catch (Exception e) {}
    }
  }

  private static void transfer(String accountIDFrom,
                              String accountIDTo, double amount) {
    Connection con = null;

    try {
      con = DriverManager.getConnection(
          "jdbc:cloudscape:C:/ProJavaServer/Ch19/tx");

      Account accountFrom = new Account();
      accountFrom.read(accountIDFrom, con);

      Account accountTo = new Account();
      accountTo.read(accountIDTo, con);

      accountFrom.setAmount(accountFrom.getAmount() - amount);
      accountTo.setAmount(accountTo.getAmount() + amount);

      accountFrom.update(con);
      accountTo.update(con);

      System.out.println("Funds transferred.");

    } catch (Exception e) {
      e.printStackTrace();
    }
    finally {
      try {
        if (con != null) {
          con.close();
        }
      } catch (Exception e) {}
    }
  }
}
```

The code permanently records changes at each stage until it encounters an exception, whether driven by the business logic or by the system. At this point it will fast forward to the end of the file printing out any error message and bypassing all other operations. In this case, in the first example it should be fine, however, in the second there will be a loss of data integrity.

Here is an improved version of the client that uses transactions. When the database constraint is violated and the client exits, the first account will not have been debited (that is, the transaction will have been rolled back) and the bank's accounts will still balance:

```java
import java.sql.Connection;
import java.sql.DriverManager;

public class Client2 {
  private static final String ACCOUNT1 = "C32-116";
  private static final String NAME1 = "Lauren Mahar";
  private static final double AMOUNT1 = 10000.0;

  private static final String ACCOUNT2 = "C32-117";
  private static final String NAME2 = "Nick Older";
  private static final double AMOUNT2 = 14000.0;

  private static final double TRANSFER_AMOUNT = 2000.0;

  static {
    try {
      Class.forName("COM.cloudscape.core.JDBCDriver");
    } catch (Exception e) {
      System.out.println(e);
    }
  }

  public static void main(String[] args) {
    createAccounts();
    transfer(ACCOUNT1, ACCOUNT2, TRANSFER_AMOUNT);
  }

  private static void createAccounts() {
    Connection con = null;

    try {
      con = DriverManager.getConnection(
            "jdbc:cloudscape:C:/ProJavaServer/Ch19/tx");

      Account account1 = new Account();
      account1.create(ACCOUNT1, NAME1, AMOUNT1, con);

      Account account2 = new Account();
      account2.create(ACCOUNT2, NAME2, AMOUNT2, con);

      System.out.println("Accounts created.");
    } catch (Exception e) {
      e.printStackTrace();
    }
    finally {
      try {
        if (con != null) {
          con.close();
        }
      } catch (Exception e) {}
    }
  }

  private static void transfer(String accountIDFrom,
                               String accountIDTo, double amount) {
    Connection con = null;

    try {
      con = DriverManager.getConnection(
            "jdbc:cloudscape:C:/ProJavaServer/Ch19/tx");
```

```
        con.setAutoCommit(false);

    Account accountFrom = new Account();
    accountFrom.read(accountIDFrom, con);

    Account accountTo = new Account();
    accountTo.read(accountIDTo, con);

    accountFrom.setAmount(accountFrom.getAmount() - amount);
    accountTo.setAmount(accountTo.getAmount() + amount);

    accountFrom.update(con);
    accountTo.update(con);

    System.out.println("Funds transferred.");

        con.commit();

  } catch (Exception e) {
    try {
      con.rollback();
    } catch (Exception re) {}
    e.printStackTrace();
  }
  finally {
    try {
      if (con != null) {
        con.close();
      }
    } catch (Exception e) {}
  }
}
}
```

One value of allowing the EJB container to manage transactions for us is that we can develop components without worrying about when we should commit or roll back a transaction. In a sense, the EJB container acts as the client does in this example, by figuring out when the business logic begins and when it ends and managing transactions accordingly. It does this by examining the transactional attributes of the EJB methods that we declare in the deployment descriptor. Before and after each business method, it ensures that any necessary transaction is started, committed, or rolled back.

Of course, it's quite easy to add transaction management for this simple case. In a more complicated application, with many possible method sequences, application exceptions, and business object types, it's more difficult to keep all the balls in the air. It's not necessarily impossible, but certainly a lot more difficult.

That difficulty increases by orders of magnitude for a distributed transaction, that is, when there is more than one database being updated. If the account to be debited and the account to be credited are in different databases, it's no longer possible for the application programmer to use the `java.sql.Connection` class's simple transactional capabilities. Instead, we must manage a complicated process known as a 'two-phase commit'. As discussed in Chapter 4, a two-phase commit involves an XA-compliant transaction manager polling resources about their ability to commit changes, and then telling them to go ahead if every enlisted resource votes to commit. The implementation of this process is very complicated and error-prone, and the specific details are beyond the scope of this book.

Our EJB container may manage this complexity for us (some do not), although this is not required as part of the EJB specification. If it does not, and if we absolutely need this functionality, we must find a different application server, as there is really no workaround. A distributed transaction also needs the cooperation of the JDBC drivers.

A JDBC driver that participates in a distributed transaction must implement a special interface that the transaction manager will use to communicate with it during the transaction. This interface is an industry standard and is known as XA, the Java version of which is defined as part of the JDBC Optional Package. Note that XA actually refers to TransAction, although it's difficult to see why! Before we use a JDBC driver in a distributed transaction, we must ensure that it supports the XA interface. Currently all JDBC 2.0-compliant drivers provide XA compliance to manage distributed transactions. A list of JDBC drivers that support distributed transactions is available on Sun's web site at http://industry.java.sun.com/products/jdbc/drivers.

Declarative Semantics for Transactions

The bean developer must declare how a particular method in an EJB with container-managed transactions works with those transactions, by specifying a `<trans-attribute>` tag in the XML deployment descriptor. The EJB specification provides six options: `NotSupported`, `Supports`, `RequiresNew`, `Required`, `Mandatory`, and `Never`. Let's take a closer look at these transactional attribute options, in turn.

The NotSupported Transactional Attribute

The first option for a method's transactional attribute is `NotSupported`. When a method with a transaction attribute of `NotSupported` is called, it operates in an "unspecified transaction context". (A transaction context is simply the state that needs to be maintained so that the set of related operations can operate as a group.) The specification gives the EJB container wide latitude in how to access resources in the case of an unspecified transaction context. The possible ways that those resources may be accessed, as suggested (but not mandated) by the EJB 2.0 specification, are:

❑ The container may execute the method and access the underlying resource managers without a transaction context. Remember, 'resource manager' is the generic term for any Java driver class or store that interacts with an asset in the execution environment. For instance, a `java.sql.Connection` instance is a resource manager for a database. Another example of a resource manager is a JMS connection – `javax.jms.Connection`.

❑ The container may treat each call of an instance to a resource manager as a single transaction (for example, the container may set the auto-commit option on a JDBC API connection).

❑ The container may merge multiple calls of an instance to a resource manager into a single transaction.

❑ The container may merge multiple calls of an instance to multiple resource managers into a single transaction.

❑ If an instance invokes methods on other enterprise beans, and the invoked methods are also designated to run with an unspecified transaction context, the container may merge the resource manager calls from the multiple instances into a single transaction.

❑ Any combination of the above.

Whenever a business method is executed outside of an application-specified transaction, there is a danger that the resources accessed by that business method may become inconsistent. The variety of techniques that the EJB container can use in this case indicates even more strongly how much caution must be used, and how conservatively the bean developer must code.

If a method with an attribute of `NotSupported` is called by another method with a specified transactional context, the EJB container will suspend this transaction while the method with the `NotSupported` attribute is executed. No transaction context is ever passed to a client or a resource from a business method with the `NotSupported` attribute. However, once the method returns, any suspended transaction is restarted.

The RequiresNew Transactional Attribute

The `RequiresNew` transactional attribute for a method specifies that if a method with this attribute is called with an existing transaction context, the container will suspend that transaction and start a new one. This new transaction will be used for any resource access or other business method calls from that method. However, once the method completes, any suspended transaction will be resumed. If the method is called without an existing transaction, a new one will also be created. The transaction will commit when the method returns and the EJB container has completed its 'housekeeping' tasks (such as returning beans to the pools, freeing resources allocated during the operation, and so on.)

The Required Transactional Attribute

If a method's transactional attribute is `Required`, the EJB container will always invoke this method with a valid transaction context. If the method is called from a client (for example, another bean) with an existing transaction context, that context will be used. If the method is called without an existing transaction context, the EJB container will create a new one automatically. In this case, the transaction will commit after the method returns and the EJB container has completed its housekeeping, such as calling `ejbStore()`.

The Supports Transactional Attribute

If a method with the transactional attribute `Supports` is called by a client with a valid transaction context, the container acts the same as if the transactional attribute were `Required`. If this method is called without an existing transaction context, the container acts the same as if the transactional attribute were `NotSupported`. In other words, the EJB component developer must be prepared for either situation: transactional or non-transactional execution.

The Mandatory Transactional Attribute

If a method with the `Mandatory` transactional attribute is called with an existing transaction context, the container will use that context. If a method with this attribute is called without a valid existing transaction context, the container throws an exception (`javax.transaction.TransactionRequiredException`).

The Never Transactional Attribute

The final option for a method's transactional attribute is `Never`. If a client calls with an existing transaction context, the container throws an exception (`java.rmi.RemoteException`). The client must call without a transaction context, in which case the container behaves as in the case of `NotSupported`.

Specifying Transactional Attributes

The transactional attributes for a method are specified in the XML deployment descriptor. The deployment descriptor uses `<container-transaction>` elements to indicate which transaction attributes apply to the various methods. Each `<container-transaction>` element has two child elements: a method, and the transactional attribute. There are three legal ways to specify the method element.

The first way is to specify a default transaction attribute for all the methods in a particular bean. This default attribute would only apply if there were no more specific transaction attribute in the descriptor (specified by one of the next two methods). An example of this is:

```
<container-transaction>
  <method>
    <ejb-name>Product</ejb-name>
    <method-name>*</method-name>
  </method>
  <trans-attribute>Required</trans-attribute>
</container-transaction>
```

The `<ejb-name>` element refers to the name of one of the EJBs declared in that same deployment descriptor. The `*` in the `<method-name>` element is a 'wild card' that indicates the transaction attribute should apply to all the methods.

The second way is to specify a transaction attribute for methods in a particular bean, for example:

```
<container-transaction>
  <method>
    <ejb-name>Product</ejb-name>
    <method-name>getName</method-name>
  </method>
  <trans-attribute>Supports</trans-attribute>
</container-transaction>
```

If there are methods with the same name but different parameter lists, and they require different transaction attributes, this third method can be used that specifies the parameters:

```
<container-transaction>
  <method>
    <ejb-name>Product</ejb-name>
    <method-name>getTaxes</method-name>
    <method-params>
      <method-param>java.lang.String</method-param>
      <method-param>int</method-param>
    </method-params>
  </method>
  <trans-attribute>Supports</trans-attribute>
</container-transaction>
```

To set the transaction attribute for a method with no parameters, use a `<method-params>` element with no `<method-param>` child element. If there is an array passed as a parameter, it can be specified by the array elements' type, followed by one or more pairs of square brackets.

Choosing Transaction Attributes

Which of the available transaction attributes should we use? This will depend on the requirements of our business methods for the ACID properties (remember – atomic, consistent, isolated, and durable). It will also depend on the support for transactions provided by our persistent resources:

- ❑ If we have a method that modifies data in a relational database, we will almost certainly want it to participate in a transaction. However, we probably wouldn't have any special circumstances that required a new transaction. The best attribute would probably be `Required`.

- ❑ If we had a business method that retrieved a single piece of data, we wouldn't necessarily have circumstances that required us to manage a transaction, and could leave the determination up to the EJB container. However, if this data access took place in the context of some other operation that modified data, we would want to have a consistent view of the database. The attribute that would allow both these things is `Supports`.

- ❑ If the resource that our enterprise bean accesses does not support management by an external transaction coordinator, we should use the attribute `NotSupported` for all the methods of the bean.

The remaining transactional attributes are more obscure, but they give the container's declarative transaction service the ability to manage most situations.

An entity bean's persistence callback methods `ejbLoad()` and `ejbStore()` are called with the same transactional attributes as the business method that triggered the `ejbLoad()` or `ejbStore()`. This makes sense, because the transactional attributes of a business method primarily relate to the resources that the business method accesses, either directly (via SQL calls, for example) or indirectly, via the read and update logic of the bean or container associated with those callback methods. The `ejbStore()` method is also guaranteed to be called on the transaction's commit boundary.

However, the situation is more complicated in the cases where the business method is called without a transaction, which can happen with the transaction attributes of `NotSupported`, `Never`, or `Supports`. The EJB container's management of state caching works well only if the container can use transaction boundaries to drive the `ejbLoad()` and `ejbStore()` methods. There are only two guarantees that the specification makes about when these callback methods are called for a business method that operates outside of a transaction:

❑ The container calls `ejbLoad()` at least once between the time that the EJB is first associated with an object identity and the time that the business method is called. Note that this association with an identity is marked by the `ejbActivate()` callback.

❑ The container calls `ejbStore()` at least once between the time that the business method is called and the time that the EJB is disassociated from an object identity. Note that this disassociation from an identity is marked by the `ejbPassivate()` callback.

The guarantees given by the specification regarding when `ejbLoad()` and `ejbStore()` are called are not enough to support the correct caching of state. In between the time that `ejbLoad()` is called and the business method executes, the data in the persistent data store could have changed, and the EJB could potentially be operating on stale data. Of course, if the EJB has exclusive access to the database, or if the data does not have absolute requirements for freshness, this problem can be mitigated.

The more serious problem is that in between the time the business method executes and the `ejbStore()` method is called by the container, something could have happened to the EJB that caused the cached data to disappear without ever having been written to the database. For instance, a subsequent business method could cause an error in the EJB that forces the application server to eject that bean instance from the container. It's even possible that the EJB container could crash. The client would assume that its data changes had been made successfully, because the business method that it had called had returned without error. But in reality, the underlying resources would never be updated.

The easiest solution to this problem of non-transactional data access is to avoid using `ejbLoad()` and `ejbStore()` to control the caching of state in the EJB. Typically, the business method should access the state of the underlying resource directly (via SQL statements, for instance), and the callback methods `ejbLoad()` and `ejbStore()` should be left empty. However, if the bean's methods are read-only and it has exclusive access to the database or does not need totally fresh data, we can probably cache state in a non-transactional bean as we normally would. In other words, we may implement `ejbLoad()`, but `ejbStore()` should still be a no-op since our bean only reads the data and never modifies it.

To summarize, caching data with `ejbLoad()` is an appropriate solution in the following cases:

❑ To represent non-transactional data as an EJB entity

❑ To avoid repeated reads of this data

❑ If we do not need to update the data

❑ If we are not concerned about cached data getting out of sync with the persistent store

User-Controlled Transactions

It is possible for a session bean to control its own transaction demarcation, via the
`javax.transaction.UserTransaction` interface. The `UserTransaction` interface is defined as follows:

```
public interface UserTransaction {
  public void begin() throws NotSupportedException, SystemException;

  public void commit()
          throws RollbackException, HeuristicMixedException,
                 HeuristicRollbackException, SecurityException,
                 IllegalStateException, SystemException;

  public int getStatus() throws SystemException;

  public void rollback()
          throws IllegalStateException, SecurityException,
                 SystemException;

  public void setRollbackOnly()
          throws IllegalStateException, SystemException;

  public void setTransactionTimeout(int timeOut)
          throws SystemException;
}
```

Briefly, a client or session bean calls the `begin()` method to programmatically start a new transaction.
This transaction can be completed successfully by calling `commit()`, or unsuccessfully by calling
`rollback()`. Rather than simply rolling back a transaction, a business method can also mark the
transaction so that the only possible outcome is a rollback. This would make sense if subsequent
methods that should be part of this transaction might still be called. The `getStatus()` method can be
used to determine if the transaction has been marked for rollback.

A compliant EJB container or J2EE application server is not required to make the `UserTransaction` interface
available to all clients. It must, however, make it available to session beans, servlets, and JSPs, and can optionally
make it available to other types of clients – such as a stand alone Java client – and remain compliant.

A client that wants to use this interface should retrieve it from the JNDI namespace. An appropriate
implementation of the `UserTransaction` interface will be available under the name
`java:comp/UserTransaction`. It's worth noting that session beans can also use a legacy method of
retrieving the `UserTransaction` interface – the `SessionContext`.

To mark the start of a transaction, the client (a session bean, servlet, JSP page, or other) calls the
`begin()` method, and to mark the successful end of a transaction it calls `commit()`. Consider the case
where a servlet wants to call business methods in two different beans as part of the same transaction.
Assume the following session bean business methods:

```
public class SampleSessionA implements SessionBean {

  public void someBusinessMethod() {
    // some business logic
  }
  // ... callbacks, and so on
}
```

and:

```
public class SampleSessionB implements SessionBean {

  public void otherBusinessMethod() {
    // other business logic
  }
  // ... callbacks, and so on
}
```

Assuming we're using a J2EE application server, the servlet might have code that looks something like this:

```
try {
  InitialContext initial = new InitialContext();

  UserTransaction userTransaction =
    (UserTransaction)initial.lookup("java:comp/UserTransaction");

  SampleSessionAHome homeA =
    (SampleSessionAHome)javax.rmi.PortableRemoteObject.narrow(
    initial.lookup("java:comp/env/ejb/SampleA"), SampleSessionAHome.class);

  SampleSessionA sampleSessionA = homeA.create();

  SampleSessionBHome homeB =
    (SampleSessionBHome)javax.rmi.PortableRemoteObject.narrow(
    initial.lookup("java:comp/env/ejb/SampleB"), SampleSessionBHome.class);

  SampleSessionB sampleSessionB = homeB.create();

  try {
    userTransaction.begin();

    sampleSessionA.someBusinessMethod();
    sampleSessionB.otherBusinessMethod();

    userTransaction.commit();

  } catch (Exception e) {
    userTransaction.rollback();
  }
} catch (Exception e) {
  //...
}
```

One disadvantage of this approach is that the client is taking responsibility for managing the transaction, rather than leaving that to the EJB container. A second disadvantage is that changes to the transaction management strategy of the application must be made to Java code, rather than to an XML file using a tool.

Note that in the above example, the same effect could have been achieved by defining a new session-bean method with a transaction attribute of `Required`. The servlet could call the new session-bean method, and that new session-bean method could then call `someBusinessMethod()` and `otherBusinessMethod()`. Then `UserTransaction` interface need not be used at all.

Isolation Levels

Keeping one transaction isolated from the effects of other transactions against the same data can be an expensive operation. For many situations, less-than-perfect isolation is acceptable in terms of the business logic, and may yield a significant increase in performance and a decrease in the potential for deadlocks between conflicting transactions. Most multi-user databases offer some support for making tradeoffs in isolation *versus* performance, and JDBC provides a standard interface to control this functionality.

The EJB specification is not relational-database specific, however, it attempts to be a general-purpose technology that is useful for accessing many different resources, such as ERP systems, sales management systems, object databases, relational databases, and more. APIs for managing isolation levels are resource-specific, and so the EJB architecture does not define a general API for managing the isolation level of transactions. Regardless, such management may be important for a large-scale production system, or for a system with very strict data-correctness requirements.

EJBs that manage their own access to resources, such as session beans or entity beans with bean-managed persistence, can specify the isolation level of those resources programmatically. JDBC provides two methods in the `java.sql.Connection` interface to set and get the isolation level:

```
void setTransactionIsolation(int level) throws SQLException;
int getTransactionIsolation() throws SQLException;
```

It is likely that an EJB developer will know the target database or databases and be able to determine an appropriate isolation level by consulting the documentation for that database. However, it is also possible to programmatically discover whether or not a particular isolation level can be set for the data source referenced by a particular connection by calling the `getMetaData()` method of the `Connection` interface. This returns an object that implements the `DatabaseMetaData` interface. There are two relevant methods in this interface:

```
int getDefaultTransactionIsolation() throws SQLException;
boolean supportsTransactionIsolationLevel(int level) throws SQLException;
```

The first returns the default isolation level that the resource uses within a transaction, and the second indicates whether the resource supports an isolation level with particular characteristics.

EJBs that depend on the container to mediate access to their resources – or in other words, entity beans with container-managed persistence – do not manage isolation levels themselves. However, the EJB container may provide proprietary mechanisms to allow the deployer to adjust isolation levels when the application is deployed.

Regardless of whether the EJB or the container manages isolation levels, care must be taken that all accesses to a particular database or other resource within a single transaction use the same isolation level. In other words, bean A can't do a SELECT using one isolation level after bean B has done an UPDATE in the same transaction using a different isolation level. If an EJB accesses more than one resource within a transaction, each resource may use a different isolation level.

> *Technically, the requirement to use a consistent isolation level for a particular resource within a transaction is mandated by the resource, not the EJB spec. Most resources require that all accesses within a transaction be done using the same isolation levels. An attempt to change the isolation level in the middle of a transaction may cause undesirable behavior, such as an implicit commit of the changes done up to that point. The* `java.sql.Connection` *interface specifically forbids changing an isolation level in the middle of a transaction. If this does not apply to a particular resource you are using, by all means, take advantage of this if you can, and if the requirements of your application justify the additional complexity – which is rather unlikely.*

A resource such as a database can define arbitrary degrees of isolation with which a transaction can operate. However, the `java.sql.Connection` interface operates with four predefined isolation levels (these are integer constants defined in the `Connection` class):

❑ TRANSACTION_READ_UNCOMMITTED

❑ TRANSACTION_READ_COMMITTED

❑ TRANSACTION_REPEATABLE_READ

❑ TRANSACTION_SERIALIZABLE

These constants refer to specific levels of transaction isolation that deal with three well-defined problems of increasing difficulty – 'dirty reads', 'non-repeatable reads', and 'phantom reads'. Let's define these terms in more detail:

❑ A **dirty read** allows a row changed by one transaction to be read by another transaction before any changes in the row have been committed. Setting an isolation level that allows this much interference is pretty permissive, and while it may improve performance, it is often inappropriate from the standpoint of maintaining data integrity. Take an example of a simultaneous account balance transfer and ATM withdrawal. A user of our software tries to transfer funds from a savings account to a checking account. At the same time, the user's spouse tries to withdraw money from the ATM. Let's say that the transfer operation fails after it had incremented the checking account, so the operation will be undone by the database. However, if the current isolation level for the ATM withdrawal allows dirty reads, it may have read the uncommitted balance-transfer data and allowed the withdrawal to succeed – even if there was not really enough money in the account. Oops!

❑ A **non-repeatable read** is where one transaction reads a row, a second transaction alters or deletes the row, and the first transaction re-reads the row, getting different values the second time. Exactly how this is prevented depends on our database, and may influence our choice of isolation settings. It may be that updates to the relevant data are prevented by an isolation level that ensures repeatable reads, or it may be that updates to relevant data are hidden by this isolation level. The most point to note is that we should always understand the database to which we are deploying, if this is relevant to our application.

❑ A **phantom read** is where one transaction reads all rows that satisfy a WHERE condition, a second transaction inserts a row that satisfies that WHERE condition, and the first transaction re-reads for the same condition, retrieving the additional phantom row in the second read. Again, the exact influence that this isolation level has depends on how our database implements the isolation level, either by locking or by hiding changes (probably by making copies of the data). Once again, we must understand the database to which we are deploying.

Each isolation level prevents a different set of these problems. The most permissive isolation level, TRANSACTION_READ_UNCOMMITTED, actually prevents none of them. Caution should be used with this isolation level. It is appropriate in situations where absolute data integrity is a lower priority than performance. An example might be an e-commerce site that was providing recommendations to customers based on purchase patterns by other visitors to the site. It would be important to respond quickly, to avoid irritating or losing a customer, but it might not be important to have a precise set of recommendations.

The isolation level TRANSACTION_READ_COMMITTED prevents dirty reads, but allows non-repeatable and phantom reads. Although any decision about isolation levels must take into account application data-integrity requirements, the target database, and performance and scaling needs, a simple generic recommendation for many situations is to use this isolation level.

The isolation level TRANSACTION_REPEATABLE_READ prevents dirty reads and non-repeatable reads. Phantom reads are not prevented.

The isolation level TRANSACTION_SERIALIZABLE prevents dirty, non-repeatable, and phantom reads. This is a very restrictive isolation level, which, although it will probably affect performance, will guarantee correct results.

The table below summarizes the different isolation levels available through the JDBC API:

Isolation Level	Problems Prevented
TRANSACTION_READ_UNCOMMITTED	None
TRANSACTION_READ_COMMITTED	Dirty read
TRANSACTION_REPEATABLE_READ	Dirty read Non-repeatable read
TRANSACTION_SERIALIZABLE	Dirty read Non-repeatable read Phantom read

Long Transactions

EJB technology, along with the capabilities of a transactional resource, can ensure that our business logic operates with the advantages of a transaction. But maintaining a transaction is expensive, primarily because of the locking and/or copying that a data resource must do to ensure that the ACID qualities of a transaction apply. As a result, transactions should be kept short. That means that the data should be read, updated, and written in one logical operation.

Unfortunately, the reality of most applications is that the data will be read, presented to the user, edited, sent back to the server, and written to the database. In a perfect world with unlimited resources and no contention for data, this would all happen in one transaction. But the user may work on this data for an arbitrarily long period of time. Imagine a scenario where a user opens an application, begins editing some data, and leaves for a three-week vacation without committing their changes to the database. It is not usually appropriate to leave a transaction open through any user-interface action.

How would we even be able to leave a transaction open? Using container-managed transactions, it isn't possible. However, we can leave a transaction open across business method calls using the UserTransaction interface discussed earlier. For instance, during one business method, we could acquire the UserTransaction interface and begin the transaction. During a subsequent business method, we would reacquire the UserTransaction and automatically continue in that transaction. All further business methods on that session bean would occur in the same transaction until we called commit(). Note that this is possible only for stateful session beans. A stateless session bean must commit the transaction before the business method in which it was started returns. If it does not, the transaction is lost and will never be committed. Eventually, it will time out.

Here is how the code might look for a transaction that remained open between business methods:

```
class LongTransactionSessionBean implements SessionBean {
  public void method1() throws Exception {
    UserTransaction userTransaction =
```

```
        (UserTransaction) initial.lookup("java:comp/UserTransaction");
    userTransaction.begin();

    performBusinessLogic();
}

public void method2() throws Exception {
    performBusinessLogic2();
}

public void method3() throws Exception {
    performBusinessLogic3();

    UserTransaction userTransaction =
        (UserTransaction) initial.lookup("java.comp/UserTransaction");
    userTransaction.commit();
}

// ... callback methods, and so on
}
```

In general, don't take advantage of the ability to use a single transaction across multiple business method calls. Instead, we should use application-specific strategies that are more conservative of resources to achieve a similar effect to a transaction. The two main approaches are implementations of either **optimistic locking** or **pessimistic locking**.

Optimistic Locking

The optimistic locking strategy allows multiple clients to use the same data. However, when the data is sent back to the server in a business method call of an EJB, some checking is done to ensure that the state data of the EJB can be updated without conflict. For instance, the time of the last modification may be compared to what it was when the client first retrieved the data. If they match, the update is allowed to proceed. If they do not, the client is notified that it must refresh the data and redo the modifications. Some possible ways to implement this strategy are:

❑   Add a last-modified timestamp field to the database.

❑   Before sending the update query, compare the values we are about to modify with their value before the transaction was started. If they are equal, the update is safe. If they are different, the update will corrupt the database and the transaction should roll back.

Pessimistic Locking

The optimistic strategy is the most scalable, because multiple clients can read the data without interfering with an individual client that wants to update. However, if an update involves a lot of work, it may be inappropriate to tell a second client that it must discard this work because someone else was making a modification. In this case, a pessimistic locking approach can be used. A client that wants to make modifications must 'check out' the right to modify the data. While this token is checked out, no other client can modify the data. If another client has checked out the right to modify the data, an exception is thrown. A possible way to implement this strategy is to add a time-checked-out field to the database. If this field is null, the check out can succeed, whereas if the field has a checked-out time within a certain timeout period, the check-out fails. The period is adjustable, based on how long a client can keep the data checked-out before the lock expires.

Two-Phase Commit

As discussed earlier in this chapter (and in Chapter 4), a two-phase commit is a protocol that allows multiple transaction managers to participate in a single transaction. There are two scenarios where this will occur:

- ❑ Application logic accesses multiple resources (such as two databases) within a single transaction
- ❑ EJBs in multiple application servers participate in the same transaction

Either of these scenarios is quite likely in an enterprise with heterogeneous transactional computer systems. It's easy to imagine an application that needs to update a sales database and a manufacturing database being maintained on two different machines. It's also easy to imagine two application servers being run in different departments, with the need to use common business logic.

A business-logic programmer does not need to write special code to handle a scenario where a two-phase commit will occur: the burden of implementing transaction management is placed by the EJB specification on the EJB container and application server. However, because not all JDBC drivers and application servers support two-phase commits, the application architect needs to be aware of situations where this can occur, and the limitations of the technology. Note that in order to support two-phase commits, a driver needs to support the JDBC 2.0 Optional Package APIs – specifically, support for XA.

The EJB container/application server also needs to have support for distributed transactions, in the form of a transaction manager that can manage two-phase commits. Weblogic 6.1, which we've been using with the EJB examples in this book, supports two-phase commits and offers its own XA-compliant drivers.

Security

Most enterprises have a requirement to protect their data and processes from improper access, both from within and external to the enterprise. Protecting data and processes requires the following four services:

- ❑ **Identification**
  Every user of a secure system must be mapped onto an identifier. In Java security APIs, this identifier is known as a **principal**. An identifier is often expressed to the user as a 'user ID' during a log in process.

- ❑ **Authentication**
  When a user claims that they have a particular identity, they must be able to present credentials to prove it. Frequently, these credentials will be in the form of a password. However, there are numerous other possibilities for credentials, such as a swipe card, retinal scan, fingerprint, or digital certificate stored on the user's computer.

- ❑ **Access control**
  Every secure system must limit access to particular users. When a user attempts to access a resource, such as a database, an application, or even a particular function, a security service must validate the right of that user to that resource. The most common way to enforce access control is by maintaining lists of users with the privilege to access particular resources (known as **access control lists**).

- ❑ **Data confidentiality**
  This is actually a type of access control, but is different enough in practice that it deserves its own category. Confidentiality of data is maintained by encryption of some sort. It doesn't do any good to protect our data by enforcing authentication when a user logs onto a system, if others can read the password or other authentication information as it is transmitted across the network.

The EJB specification concerns itself exclusively with **access control**. Data confidentiality is outside its scope, although a common approach for secure communication is to use the secure sockets layer (SSL) protocol. Identification and authentication are also not currently part of the EJB specification. In fact, until recently, they weren't part of any Java API.

Java security is somewhat unusual, because at first its security concentrated on where code came from, rather than who was running it. For instance, code that ran from our hard drive typically had greater permission to perform various actions than code that came from the Web. This reflects its early use providing dynamic downloadable functionality in the form of applets.

As there hasn't been a standard Java method for determining 'who' is running code, application servers must resort to authenticating a user through proprietary means. For instance, some require a client application to provide a username parameter and a password parameter in the JNDI initial context, before looking up a home interface of an EJB. Others forward to the EJB container the identity provided by an implementation of the secure sockets layer protocol. Any technique that the application server chooses to use is legal; this issue is not addressed by EJB technology in any way.

The **Java Authentication and Authorization Service (JAAS)** API adds a standard for security, based on who is running the code, to supplement the security based on the code's origin. Part of this new API provides for pluggable authentication modules. A client using JAAS can be configured to use different login techniques, such as a simple username/password dialog or a smart card reader plugged into a computer's USB port; a server using JAAS can be configured to authenticate the user's identity (`LoginContext` authentication, in JAAS terminology) and credentials using different back-end security services. Any possible security technique could be used, as long as a pluggable module existed. It's likely that many application servers and application clients will standardize on this API in the future.

Authentication for a particular identity can be provided by a Netware server, an Oracle database, LDAP, Windows NT, a Unix server, or a simple application-server-specific XML file. All that is required is that the vendor's application server supports the method we choose. Once the application server validates the user's credentials against their claimed identity, it will map that identity onto a logical role that the EJB application developer or deployer defines.

> **This mapping of a user's actual security identity onto a logical security role is the key to understanding EJB security.**

We can develop our EJB application without consideration for the actual security systems, groups, identities, or credentials in use by our enterprise. When we determine the security requirements of our application, we are working in an ideal world, and we can specify security requirements at an abstract level. However, when the application is actually deployed into a container, the abstract security requirements must then be mapped onto real-world security identities in a manner specific to our application server and security implementation.

An application using EJBs can specify, in a standard, portable, and abstract way, who is allowed access to business methods. The EJB container is responsible for the following actions:

- ❑ Examining the identity of the caller of a business method

- ❑ Examine the EJB's deployment information to see if the identity is a member of a role that has been granted the right to call this business method

- ❑ Throwing a `java.rmi.RemoteException` if the access is illegal (or another more specific exception such as defined in JAAS, for example, `LoginException`)

❑ Making the identity and role information available to the EJB for additional fine-grained security checks

❑ Optionally logging any illegal accesses

Specifying the Security Requirements

There are only two types of information that the EJB developer needs to define in order to specify the security requirements for their application – **security roles** and **method permissions**.

Security Roles

A **security role** is the mechanism by which caller identities are mapped onto logical, abstract types that can be used in any security environment. The specification defines a security role as a "semantic grouping of permissions that a given type of users of the application must have in order to successfully use the application". In other words, similar types of activities – such as opening an account, closing an account, and increasing an account's overdraft allowance – may be grouped under a single name, such as 'Account Manager'.

The application server will provide deployment tools that map these abstract roles to users or groups of users that actually exist in the enterprise's security environment. For example, the account_manager role might be mapped to everyone who is a member of the NT security group 'Bank Manager'. In this example, whenever a member of the 'Bank Manager' group calls an EJB business method, they would have all the permissions available to the account_manager role.

The EJB-specific security roles are defined in the deployment descriptor. Each XML element to define a security role can have two child elements. The first, the name of the role, is mandatory, whereas the second, the role description, is optional. However, because it will be necessary at deployment time to map this role to groups or individuals in the run-time environment's security implementation, it is highly recommend that we provide a description.

For example, here are some roles that might be defined in a banking application:

```
<security-role>
  <description>
    This role includes every bank employee who
    is allowed to access the banking application.
    An employee in this role may make deposits
    and withdrawals on behalf of a third party.
    They may also make read-only inquiries for
    any information in the account.
  </description>
  <role-name>teller</role-name>
</security-role>
<security-role>
  <description>
    This role is allowed to open and close accounts,
    and increase an accounts overdraft allowance.
  </description>
  <role-name>account_manager</role-name>
</security-role>
<security-role>
  <description>
    A user in this role is allowed to close
    existing accounts, withdraw and deposit
    money, and make inquiries about their
```

```
        own account only.
      </description>
      <role-name>customer</role-name>
   </security-role>
   <security-role>
      <description>
        To protect the integrity of the data, a
        user in this role is allowed read-only
        access to accounts only.
      </description>
      <role-name>executive</role-name>
   </security-role>
```

Remember that these roles don't necessarily have exact equivalents in the enterprise's security environment. When the application is deployed, some mapping between existing security identities (either users or groups in most security schemes) and these EJB security roles must be made. This is done in an application server-specific manner, and independently of the development of the EJB application. The application developer need only define the exact roles that are required to secure the business logic in a consistent and appropriate manner.

There is a many-to-many relationship between the EJB-specific roles that are defined in the deployment descriptor and the roles that exist in the target environment's security system. For instance, there might be three groups and two other individuals that need to be mapped to the 'executive' role defined in the above example: 'Bank Manager', 'Vice President', 'Assistant VP', 'John Q. Smith', and 'Katherine Heigl'.

Method Permissions

A **method permission** is the granting to a particular security role of the right to call a business method. Once a security role has been defined, the activities that are allowed to that role must also be defined. Consider our account_manager example. That role is intended to represent permission to perform activities such as opening and closing an account. But the 'opening an account' and 'closing an account' activities need to be mapped to specific business methods, such as openAccount() or closeAccount(). This mapping is done using entries, known as method permissions, in the deployment descriptor.

There is a many-to-many relationship between roles and business method permissions. A single role may have permission to use many methods, and a single method may be accessible to many roles. The mapping between roles and business methods in the deployment descriptor is done using <method-permission> XML elements. Every <method-permission> element has one or more security role references, and one or more EJB business method references. Additionally, a <method-permission> element may include an optional <description> element.

The following diagram represents a possible mapping of security roles to business methods. These roles and methods will actually be implemented (along with others) in Chapter 18:

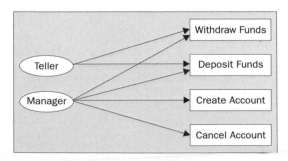

Business method references are specified for security using the same syntax as is used for transactions (see the section in this chapter on transactions for more information). We can specify that the roles in a particular method permission apply to all the methods in an EJB, just the methods with a particular name, or methods with a particular name and parameter list.

Here is an example of some method permissions that might be defined in our banking example. Notice that we only reference the logical roles that we have created in this same deployment descriptor, rather than actual entities in an actual security system implementation:

```
<method-permission>
  <role-name>teller</role-name>
  <role-name>account_manager</role-name>
  <method>
    <ejb-name>AccountManager</ejb-name>
    <method-name>findByPrimaryKey</method-name>
  </method>
  <method>
    <ejb-name>AccountManager</ejb-name>
    <method-name>deposit</method-name>
  </method>
  <method>
    <ejb-name>AccountManager</ejb-name>
    <method-name>withdraw</method-name>
  </method>
  <method>
    <ejb-name>AccountManager</ejb-name>
    <method-name>getAccountStatus</method-name>
  </method>
  <method>
    <ejb-name>AccountManager</ejb-name>
    <method-name>getRecentTransactions</method-name>
  </method>
</method-permission>

<method-permission>
  <role-name>account_manager</role-name>
  <method>
    <ejb-name>AccountManager</ejb-name>
    <method-name>create</method-name>
  </method>
  <method>
    <ejb-name>AccountManager</ejb-name>
    <method-name>closeAccount</method-name>
  </method>
  <method>
    <ejb-name>AccountManager</ejb-name>
    <method-name>extendOverdraftAllowance</method-name>
  </method>
</method-permission>
```

The combination of roles plus method permissions establishes the basic security framework for an application that depends on EJB technology. This framework can be mapped into any arbitrary combination of real-world users, groups, and authentication techniques, without changing the application at all. The EJB container will enforce the method access rules that are declared in the deployment descriptor without any further intervention on the part of the business logic programmer.

Programmatic Access Control

In some situations, the security policies of the application cannot be expressed using the method permissions in the deployment descriptor. Sometimes, whether or not an operation should be allowed depends on the data being manipulated, rather than on the operation being performed. For example, an account manager may be allowed to close the account of any individual, but not any corporation or governmental entity. Another case might be a division manager who can order raw material for their own division, but not for any other. The reality is that a large enterprise with significant operational and business-logic requirements will probably need this kind of data-driven access control.

In other situations, the business logic may need to know the actual identity of the caller of a method, rather than simply the role that the caller plays in the enterprise. This might be necessary for auditing financial transactions, or for limiting database access to only those records associated with the caller.

For these cases, there is a simple API that allows the business logic programmer to provide fine-grained security control below the business-method level. The `javax.ejb.EJBContext` interface, available as either the entity context or the session context, has the following two methods:

```
java.security.Principal getCallerPrincipal();
boolean isCallerInRole(String roleName);
```

The `getCallerPrincipal()` method is used to determine the actual identity of the caller. The `Principal` interface, which represents the underlying identity of that caller, is relatively opaque. Besides overriding `equals()`, `toString()`, and `hashCode()`, its only method is `getName()`. It is important to understand that the exact value of the principal depends on the operational environment. If the underlying security mechanism were changed, the name returned from `getName()` on the principal might also change. In other words, specifying a particular principal will make our application non-portable (not without a certain amount of conversion, anyway).

Furthermore, it may be necessary for the EJB container to translate from one principal to another before calling a business method. Although there is no API for a business-logic programmer to control the value of a principal, it is possible for an EJB 1.1-compliant container to provide proprietary tools to set up such translations at run time. An EJB 2.0-compliant container provides a deployment descriptor element (`<run-as-specified-identity>`) that can also be used in simple cases. This might be necessary in a diverse enterprise environment with multiple authentication systems. For instance, a telecommuter may be identified by a user and a password on the company's web site that would then be mapped to an identity in an Oracle database or an NT domain, before the application server could be accessed.

It is possible to use the principal returned from `getCallerPrincipal()` to provide additional access control to business logic. As a rule, this is a bad idea. By examining the principal directly in our code, we may be creating a dependency on a particular security implementation. Probably the most justifiable version of this is making sure that a particular user only alters their own information. If the underlying security system changed, only the database keys for individuals' records would need to change. The worst case scenario would be hard-coded values in the business logic like this:

```
if (principal.getName() == "SMITH_076") {
    // ...
}
```

The `isCallerInRole()` method is the best way to determine if the caller of a particular method has access to functionality based on the data they are trying to read or modify. We can use this method without introducing any dependencies whatsoever on the underlying security implementation. It works by programmatically applying additional screening criteria after the EJB container has allowed the function to be invoked.

Consider the case where an account manager or an executive can close an individual's account, but only an executive can close the account of a corporation. In the deployment descriptor, both would be given access to the `closeAccount()` method of the `AccountManager` bean, regardless of the type of account. There is no way to indicate to the EJB container that the `closeAccount()` method should be available to both roles for an individual, but only one of those roles for a corporation. However, in the business logic of the EJB, the programmer can write code that will check the type of account, and ensure that anyone trying to close a corporate account is authorized to do so. This is not complicated. The code would probably look something like this:

```
public class AccountManager implements SessionBean {
  private static final String CORPORATE_ACCOUNT_MANAGER =
                                  "corporate_account_manager";

  public void closeAccount(int customerNumber, int accountNumber) {

    Customer customer = getCustomer(customerNumber);
    if (customer.getType() == CustomerTypes.CORPORATE) {
      if (!isCallerInRole(CORPORATE_ACCOUNT_MANAGER)) {
        throw new java.lang.SecurityException(
          "Not authorized to close this account");
      }
    }
    CustomerAccount account = getCustomerAccount(accountNumber);
    account.close();
  }
  // ...
}
```

The application programmer may design an application to throw any exception in the event of an illegal access. One possibility is throwing `java.lang.SecurityException`, derived from `RuntimeException`. We could also throw JAAS exceptions such as `javax.security.auth.login.LoginException` or `FailedLoginException`. That means that any executing transaction will be rolled back, the instance will be discarded (probably overkill in this case), and the exception will be logged by the container. Some EJB containers can be configured to notify the system administrator when certain system exceptions, such as `SecurityException`, are thrown. If someone is trying to access the system inappropriately, it makes sense that the system administrator be notified immediately.

Just as we must declare the resources (such as database connections) and other EJBs that we reference in our code, we must also declare the roles that we reference in our code. The declaration of a role used in code is made in the deployment descriptor information relevant to that EJB. That role is then linked to a role defined as a `<security-role>` element in the deployment descriptor. This extra level of indirection allows the declarative security framework to change, without changing the code. Note that in the above sample code, we checked to see if the caller was in the role of `corporate_account_manager`, but this is not one of the roles that we have been using (`teller`, `account_manager`, `customer`, or `executive`). Our current policy is that only an executive may close a corporate account, so we would use the level of indirection in the security reference declaration to link `corporate_account_manager` to the `executive` role. The deployment descriptor information would probably look like this:

```
<security-role-ref>
  <description>
    The corporate account manager role is
    authorized to open, close, and change
    the terms and conditions of a corporate
    account.
```

```
        </description>
        <role-name>corporate_account_manager</role-name>
        <role-link>executive</role-link>
   </security-role-ref>
```

Note that the `<role-link>` element must be used even if the `role-name` is the same as the `security-role` element that was declared as part of the application's security framework.

Security and Application Design

As a rule, it's bad application design to enable user interface access to functionality that will be disallowed by the business logic. If an account manager logs into our system and opens up a record of a corporate customer, the Open Account, Close Account, and Change Terms of Account menu items should be inaccessible or disabled. On the other hand, if an executive logs into our system and opens up that same record, the menu items should be accessible and enabled.

As this is a book on server-side Java programming, you may wonder why we're mentioning this client-side design issue. Actually, this user-interface issue *is* a server-side Java programming issue as well, and not just if the user interface is a browser application using JSP. The problem is that deciding when to enable and disable user-interface access to a particular function requires business logic. For example, we may decide that a manager can close a corporate account if the corporation does less than $50,000/year banking with our bank; otherwise, only an executive can close the account. This is a business rule, and business logic is rightly the province of the server.

Consider the problem if we have distributed a Java Swing GUI to our 5,000 bank branches, and have hard-coded the menu items to be enabled or disabled based on the previously stated business rule. Now what happens if our policy changes, and a corporate account can only be closed by a manager if the corporation does less than $250,000/year banking with our bank? We need to reinstall all our client applications, perhaps at great trouble and expense.

If business logic in the application is limited to the server tiers, it can be changed quickly and easily. One possible solution is for the user interface code to query the server about the actions that are appropriate. The session bean that implements the analysis model's interface object for the application could have methods such as:

```
public boolean canOpenAccount(int customerNumber)
public boolean canCloseAccount(int customerNumber)
public boolean canChangeTerms(int customerNumber)
```

However, all these remote method calls would result in a lot of network traffic and sluggish performance. It's probably better to have a method that gets all the information at once, as long as some latency in the user interface is acceptable:

```
HashMap getCapabilities(int customerNumber, List whichActivities)
```

The business logic for the `getCapabilities()` method could combine the `isCallerInRole()` method with the customer data to determine a `boolean` value for each operation added to the query list of activities.

Exceptions

Although designing an application error-handling strategy is the responsibility of the business logic programmer, the EJB container provides a certain amount of support for the task. Specifically, there are two primary goals of the EJB specification regarding exception handling:

❑ An **application exception** thrown by the EJB or related code should be handled by business logic

❑ An **unexpected exception** or **system exception** thrown by the EJB or related code should be handled by the EJB container

Typical handling for an exception is a call to `commit()` or `rollback()` the relevant transaction. In addition, resources specific to that bean instance need to be kept consistent. The business logic is responsible for resource consistency with application exceptions, and the container is responsible for unexpected exceptions.

Application Exceptions

An application exception is any exception that is declared in the `throws` clause of a method in the home or remote interface of an EJB, except for `java.rmi.RemoteException`. An application exception must not be derived from `java.lang.RuntimeException` or `java.rmi.RemoteException` because these are defined as system exceptions and will be treated differently by the EJB container. Furthermore, since these exceptions are defined and thrown by the application, they must be sent back to the client, as opposed to `EJBExceptions`, which have a more severe impact at the container level (discarding instances of beans, and so on). An application exception can be derived from `java.lang.Exception`, or from other exception classes in an exception-handling hierarchy. Exactly how exceptions are used in an application is left to the architects of that application. There are, however, several application exceptions predefined in the EJB specification related to various container callbacks: `CreateException`, `DuplicateKeyException`, `FinderException`, `ObjectNotFoundException`, and `RemoveException`. These exceptions were mentioned in the previous two chapters, and are summarized at the end of this section.

To ensure that an application exception can be handled by EJB or client code, the specification requires that an application exception thrown by an EJB instance should be reported to the client precisely. In other words, the client gets exactly the same exception that the EJB threw. This may seem obvious: what other exception might it get? However, we will see that this rule does not hold for unexpected (non-application) exceptions. Remember that there is an interposition layer between the client and the EJB, and the EJB's code is never called directly. So it is possible for the EJB container to arbitrarily transform exceptions from one type to another. The specification makes this option illegal.

> *Note that this means that any application exception declared in the EJB implementation class must also be declared in the bean's remote interface. The reverse, however, is not true. Just because a bean's remote interface declares that it throws an exception does not mean that the implementation class must do likewise.*

An application exception thrown from a method participating in a transaction does not necessarily roll that transaction back. Again, this is to give the caller's business logic a chance to take steps to recover. If the developer of the code that throws the exception knows that recovery is impossible, they can mark the transaction so that it is rolled back.

Let's consider a concrete example. Take the case of a customer session bean that calls a debitAccount() method of another session bean in one transaction. Assume that the debit method throws an application exception called InsufficientFundsException if the account does not have enough money to cover the debit. Due to the rules of the Java programming language, the method must either catch the exception or declare that it throws it. Either might be appropriate, depending on the requirements of the application.

Let's first consider the case where the application might want to try to recover from the exception, by attempting a smaller debit:

```
private double attemptDebit(double amount, String customer) {
  AccountManager accountManager = getAccountManagerBean();
  try {
    accountManager.debitFunds( amount, customer );
  } catch (InsufficientFundsException insufficient) {
    try {
      amount /= 2;
      accountManager.debitFunds(amount, customer);
    } catch (Exception e) {
      throw new EJBException(e);
    }
  } catch (RemoteException re) {
    throw new EJBException(re);
  }
  return amount;
}
```

If an InsufficientFundsException is thrown by the AccountManager business method debitFunds(), we try a second debit at half the original amount. This new attempt may succeed, if there are sufficient funds in the account to cover the new request. The business logic in this method is not realistic, but it's easy to extrapolate to a real situation. Note the results – an exception is thrown, but the business logic handles the recovery. Assuming that sufficient funds existed to cover the new debit amount, the transaction can commit successfully at the end of processing.

If, however, sufficient funds don't exist to cover the new debit amount, an EJBException is thrown. This is a system exception, covered in the next section. This example is structured to show the full range of exception-handling options. In practice, a business method should usually rethrow the application exception if it can't recover, to give the calling function a chance to recover, as is demonstrated below.

Our business methods do not have to catch application exceptions if they're not sure how to handle them. We could simply declare this exception in our signature and let the caller take care of it. For example, in the following code, the method attemptDebit() performs an operation that might cause an InsufficientFundsException to be thrown. Since we have not specified exactly what the attemptDebit() method should do in this case (retry, notify the user, and so on), it will do nothing. The exception will be passed on to the caller, which will take appropriate action (or possibly pass the exception to its caller). The code would look like this:

```
private double attemptDebit(double amount, String customer)
                        throws InsufficientFundsException {
  AccountManager accountManager = getAccountManagerBean();

  try {
    accountManager.debitFunds(amount, customer);
  } catch (RemoteException re) {
    throw new EJBException(re);
  }
  return amount;
}
```

If the `amount` parameter is greater than the funds available, the `AccountManager` bean will throw the `InsufficientFundsException`. Rather than catching it, the `attemptDebit()` method declares in its signature that it throws that exception.

If this `attemptDebit()` method were called in the context of an existing transaction, it is the caller's responsibility to either recover from the exception or rethrow it. This is the same situation we saw with `debitFunds()` in the previous version of `attemptDebit()`. We could choose to attempt to recover from the exception or pass it up the call chain.

If the container started a new transaction directly before calling `attemptDebit()`, that transaction should complete when `attemptDebit()` returns. At this point, any necessary `ejbStore()` methods would be called and the changes would be committed to the persistent store. What happens in this case, when an exception is thrown by the business method for which the transaction was started? The EJB container will still attempt to commit all the changes to the database, and of course, the client will get the exception that was thrown.

This may be a little unintuitive, but it is an important point to understand. Even if we throw an application exception that isn't caught before being passed on to the client, the EJB container will still try to commit our transaction.

> **Throwing an exception does not equate to rolling back all your changes.**

It may be that under certain circumstances, the `debitFunds()` method has made changes to the database that make it mandatory for the transaction to be rolled back. In other words, it does not want the `attemptDebit()` business method or any other caller to be able to complete successfully.

Using the `EJBContext` interface (through either the `SessionContext` or `EntityContext` sub-interface), the bean throwing the application exception can mark the transaction for rollback, through the `setRollbackOnly()` method. The client code that catches the exception can determine if the transaction has been marked for rollback by calling the `EJBContext` method `getRollbackOnly()`. There are equivalent methods in the `UserTransaction` for beans with bean-managed transactions: `getStatus()` and `setRollbackOnly()`.

Let's imagine that before we attempt to debit the funds, we may impose a fee on the customer for account usage. We need to do this first, because if the fee is going to be imposed, there needs to be enough money in the account for both the debit and the fee. However, if the debit fails, we need to make sure that the transaction up to that point isn't committed, or else we'll be charging the fee for activity that never occurred. The business logic for the `debitFunds()` method might look like this:

```
public class AccountManagerEJB implements SessionBean {
  public SessionContext ctx;

  public void debitFunds(double amount, String customer)
          throws InsufficientFundsException {
    try {
      BankCustomer bankCustomer = getBankCustomer(customer);
      bankCustomer.imposeFeeForActivity();
      bankCustomer.withdrawFunds();
    } catch (InsufficientFundsException ife) {
      ctx.setRollbackOnly();
      throw ife;
    } catch (RemoteException e) {
```

```
      throw new EJBException(e);
    }
  }

  public void setSessionContext(SessionContext ctx) {
    this.ctx = ctx;
  }
  // ...
}
```

Even if the InsufficientFundsException is caught by a business method higher up on the call chain and an attempt at recovery is made, the transaction will never commit once setRollbackOnly() is called. As a result, the fee for activity in this example will never be applied, even though we've already called the imposeFeeForActivity() method. Of course, this makes any further processing in this transaction futile. If it is possible that a business method that throws an application exception may have marked a transaction for rollback, clients of that method (for example, other EJBs) in that same transaction should check via getRollbackOnly() to see if this is the case, before continuing with processing. Note that the methods getRollbackOnly() and setRollbackOnly() should only be used with CMP beans. BMP beans handle transactions themselves, so they can roll back their transactions directly.

Predefined Application Exceptions

There are five predefined application exceptions used in Enterprise JavaBeans technology:

- ❑ A CreateException or any subclass indicates that an application-level exception occurred during a create() operation on a home interface. This can be thrown by the EJB developer from ejbCreate() or (for entity beans) from ejbPostCreate(). In bean-managed persistence and container-managed persistence, the EJB can throw CreateException for beans. For an entity bean with container-managed persistence, or for a session bean, it may also be thrown by the container. A typical use for a CreateException might be if invalid parameters were supplied to the create() method. The usual rules for application exceptions apply to the CreateException: the transaction should be marked for rollback if data integrity is threatened, otherwise, client code should be given an opportunity to recover.

- ❑ The DuplicateKeyException is a subclass of the CreateException. It indicates that a data constraint such as a primary key or foreign key was violated. As the underlying database is typically protected from updates that violate a key constraint, there is usually no reason to mark the transaction for rollback.

- ❑ A FinderException or any subclass indicates that an application-level exception occurred during a findXXX() operation on a home interface. In the case of bean-managed persistence, this exception is thrown from the ejbFindXXX() methods of the implementation class. In the case of container-managed persistence, the exception will be thrown if necessary by the EJB container. As finder methods do not change any data, there is usually no reason to mark the transaction for rollback.

- ❑ The ObjectNotFoundException is a subclass of FinderException. It indicates that the entity requested by the find method does not exist. Note that finder methods that return a Collection or Enumeration should not use this exception, but should instead return an empty Collection or Enumeration. As finder methods do not change data, there is usually no reason to mark the transaction for rollback.

- ❑ The RemoveException indicates that an application-level exception occurred while trying to remove the bean. This can be thrown by the EJB developer from the ejbRemove() method, or by the container. The usual rules for application exceptions apply to the CreateException: the transaction should be marked for rollback if data integrity is threatened; otherwise, client code should be given an opportunity to recover.

System Exceptions

A system exception is one from which an application does not expect to recover. The EJB specification lists several examples of situations where this might be the case:

- Failure to obtain a database connection
- JNDI API exceptions
- Unexpected `RuntimeException` (such as a `NullPointerException`)
- JVM error
- Unexpected `RemoteException` from invocation of other EJBs

Although the business logic is free to have recovery code for any of these situations, it is quite likely that recovery is not possible. For instance, failing to obtain a database connection or getting an exception from the JNDI API most likely means that the application was misconfigured at deployment time. There is no portable way for an EJB to adjust its deployment in the EJB container, even if a strategy could be determined for a particular environment – which is unlikely anyway. Writing code to recover from an unexpected `RuntimeException` is often a wasteful approach, because such recovery code can usually be translated into precondition checking. Rather than throwing a `NullPointerException`, catching it, and figuring out what went wrong, we could instead simply check the parameters to the business logic to ensure that they are not null. If we still get an unexpected exception, something is wrong with the code and recovery is not appropriate.

Whenever a system exception is thrown, the EJB container must log the exception. This is because a system exception often indicates a problem that requires the attention of a system administrator. For instance, the failure to acquire a database connection may be because of a configuration error with the EJB container, a licensing problem with the database, an authentication problem for the connection, and so on. Only if the problem is recorded in some log can the system administrator deal with it effectively. Optionally, an application server can provide services such as e-mail or pager notification when certain system exceptions occur.

The EJB container provides two recovery services to help ensure that the application's state remains consistent in the face of a system exception.

Firstly, the current transaction is rolled back. This is different from an application exception, where the EJB container attempts to commit the transaction regardless of the exception handling. If a business method throws a system exception, no changes or database updates associated with that transaction are committed, regardless of client attempts at recovery.

The EJB container rolls back the current transaction when a system exception occurs so that the business-logic programmer doesn't need to surround every single business method with error recovery code. In the case of an application exception, the bean developer can indicate whether or not a transaction should be rolled back by setting `setRollbackOnly()`. To have the same ability for a system exception, every single business method would have to catch any exception derived from `java.lang.Throwable` and determine in the `catch` block whether or not to mark the transaction for rollback. To make matters worse, there would not necessarily be enough semantic information in the exception to decide whether or not recovery was possible by another business method. Did that `NullPointerException` happen before or after the database was updated? There's no way to tell, without adding even more exception handling code.

The second recovery service that the container provides to help ensure that the application's state remains consistent in the face of a system exception is to discard the EJB instance. In other words, once a bean throws a system exception, no other business or callback methods will be called on that Java class instance.

The benefit of having the container discard the instance is that the business-logic programmer does not need to ensure that the non-transactional state of that bean is consistent. For instance, imagine a stateless session bean that used a socket connection to do some work. Rather than create a new connection for every business method call, we instead might create a single reusable socket connection in each stateless session bean instance's ejbCreate() method. If an unexpected exception interrupted us in the middle of processing, that socket might be left with unread data from a previous request. If we were to reuse this instance for another business method call, that business method call might fail because the socket connection was out of sync. This is just an example, there are many ways in which the state of an EJB can become corrupted by an unexpected system exception. Since the EJB specification places great value on the virtues of reliability and stability, the safest course of action – discarding the instance – is made mandatory.

You may wonder what happens from the client's point of view after an instance is discarded. Can the client continue to use its remote reference to that bean? For an entity bean or a stateless session bean, the answer is yes. This behavior is mandated by the specification, and all compliant EJB containers will allow it. This is because for entity beans or stateless session beans, the container can simply delegate future calls to a different instance of the EJB. However, a stateful session bean whose business method throws a system exception will cease to exist from the client's point of view. Any subsequent invocations through the remote interface must result in a java.rmi.NoSuchObjectException. This can result in a significant amount of lost work, so a programmer using a stateful session bean should be particularly careful about the circumstances under which he or she will allow a system exception to be thrown.

We may also wonder what happens to the resources of the discarded bean, since the bean developer does not get a chance to call any cleanup code after a system exception is thrown. What happens to open sockets, database connections, and so on after a system exception is thrown? The EJB container should take responsibility and immediately close any resource that was obtained through a resource factory using the JNDI namespace. Unfortunately, the container probably cannot close any resources that we obtained using the JDK APIs, such as a TCP/IP connection. These resources will eventually be closed during the normal garbage-collection process.

A user-defined system exception must be derived from java.lang.RuntimeException or java.rmi.RemoteException. Additionally, exceptions derived from java.lang.Error are considered system exceptions, although java.lang.Error is not intended for application programmer use. Programmers should follow three basic rules to determine which system exception to throw:

❑ If the EJB encounters an exception derived from RuntimeException or Error, it should just propagate that exception or error to the container. In other words, the business-logic programmer shouldn't worry about catching these errors (unless they expect them and have a recovery strategy).

❑ If the EJB encounters a checked exception from which it cannot recover, it should wrap the original exception in the javax.ejb.EJBException class (by passing the original exception as a parameter to the constructor of EJBException). Since EJBException is derived from RuntimeException, it does not need to be declared in the throws clause of a business method. Remember that throwing EJBException, or any other class derived from RuntimeException, will cause the transaction to be rolled back and the bean instance to be garbage collected. If the EJB can recover by marking the transaction for rollback and throwing an application exception, this is the preferred strategy.

❑ If the EJB encounters any other error condition from which it cannot recover, it should simply throw an instance of javax.ejb.EJBException, which can wrap the original exception or error message.

Unlike application exceptions, a client does not receive a system exception as it was thrown by the EJB – the container translates every system exception into a `java.rmi.RemoteException` or a subclass. This greatly simplifies the error handling for the client. Rather than worrying about catching stray `IllegalArgumentExceptions` or `IndexOutOfBoundsExceptions` coming back from a call to the server, the client need only deal with one checked exception: `RemoteException`.

If the EJB that throws the exception is participating in a client's transaction, it will notify that client that further processing of that transaction is futile by throwing a subclass of `java.rmi.RemoteException` called `javax.transaction.TransactionRolledbackException`. If there is an unspecified transaction context, or if the container began the current transaction right before that business method was called, the container will throw a simple `RemoteException`.

To facilitate backwards compatibility with the 1.0 version of the EJB specification, an EJB may throw a `RemoteException` that will then be treated as a system exception. This is the only checked exception that is treated as a system exception. This practice is deprecated and we should therefore not do it. As a rule, we should never throw `RemoteException` from any method in our implementation class. That said, there are currently no consequences if we do.

Communication

The EJB spec enforces rules that are designed to support distributed access to EJB components. The most important rule is that the home and remote interfaces are defined as RMI interfaces. This makes it simple to use an implementation of RMI as a remote access protocol. Another rule is that method parameter and return types must be legal values for RMI-IIOP, which makes it possible to use an implementation of RMI over IIOP.

> *RMI-IIOP was included in the EJB specification mostly to provide interoperability with legacy CORBA systems. While this is indeed a requirement in some cases, this interaction is typically limited because RMI-IIOP fails to support advanced concepts that are traditionally offered in application servers, such as transactional support, clustering, failover, load balancing, and so on*

One of the more interesting features of the EJB 1.1 specification is that it does not mandate that RMI, or any other particular distributed communication interface or implementation, actually be used. One choice is to use the 'native' Java Remote Method Protocol (JRMP) version of RMI, although in the JDKs up to (and including) 1.3, this would impose limitations on the number of remote clients because of the way JRMP is implemented. Several EJB container vendors have implemented their own version of RMI. Other container vendors have chosen to use a version of RMI that runs over IIOP.

The EJB 2.0 specification requires that vendors provide support for RMI-IIOP. This is to ensure that EJB containers can interoperate at a basic level; however, EJB container vendors may offer other protocols as well.

Communication between Heterogeneous Servers

Communication between heterogeneous application servers is more difficult to achieve than it might seem at first glance. The problem is that there is *state* associated with every method call, such as the transaction context and the security identity of the caller. How to move this state from the client EJB to the server EJB isn't defined in the Enterprise JavaBeans 2.0 specification or the RMI specification. This lack of run-time compatibility between EJB containers is considered a weakness of the current situation.

The EJB 2.0 specification does specify RMI-IIOP as the solution to the interoperability problem. However, the 2.0 spec made transaction interoperability and certain aspects of security interoperability optional. In other words, the situation is still not completely resolved, although significant progress has been made.

> *One of the advantages of the RMI-IIOP protocol is that it can provide access to EJBs from non-Java clients. An excellent example of the non-Java client access that RMI-IIOP can facilitate is the Client Access Services COM. COM is Microsoft's **Component Object Model**, and this bridge lets developers create native MS-Windows clients that access EJBs directly. It provides a standard object model that serves as the basis for everything from Windows platform services such as drag and drop, to distributed communications, to transaction monitoring and load balancing. The bridge provides a set of COM objects that let Windows client applications establish a connection to an application server and find or create references to EJBs. The references to EJBs are themselves presented to the client as COM objects. Some other protocols are emerging to enable communication between heterogeneous systems, such as Simple Object Access Protocol (SOAP) or the Java Connector Architecture (JCA).*

There are four types of CORBA-EJB mappings implicit or explicit in the EJB 2.0 specification – **distribution**, **naming**, **transactions**, and **security**:

- ❑ The **distribution mapping** describes the CORBA IDL for the interfaces and classes. This mapping is implicit from the application programmer's point of view when a Java client is used.

- ❑ The **naming mapping** mandates that the OMG CosNaming service be used for publishing and resolving EJBHome objects. A typical Java client, including server-side Java components such as other EJBs, servlets, and JSP pages, would still use the standard Java JNDI interfaces to access that CosNamingService. The deployer of a client application would obtain the host address and port number of the server's CosNaming service and the CosNaming name of each referenced home interface, and configure the client container accordingly using application-server specific tools. The client programmer and EJB developer need do nothing to comply with the EJB-CORBA name mapping.

- ❑ The **transaction mapping** provides rules for an EJB runtime that wishes to use an implementation of the CORBA Object Transaction Service (OTS) version 1.1 for transaction support. Transaction propagation is defined completely in an OMG specification; the mapping only specifies the rules that allow transaction context propagation to occur for EJBs, based on the OTS. Transaction propagation between heterogeneous EJB containers is not mandatory in the EJB 2.0 specification. There are rules that EJB container vendors must follow if they choose not to provide transaction interoperability.

- ❑ The final mapping is the **security mapping**. Secure communications is provided through mandatory support for the SSL protocol. Interoperable propagation of the caller's identity is provided through RMI-IIOP according to the CORBA standard Common Secure Interoperability version 2 (CSIv2). However, support for the propagation of authentication data between heterogeneous containers is not mandatory. Instead, it is possible to set up 'trust relationships' between EJB or web containers that make further authentication unnecessary.

The bottom line is that CORBA does not provide perfect interoperability between different ORB-based application servers yet, and of course does not provide any help for interoperability with an EJB 1.1 non-ORB-based application server. It is likely that future versions of the specification will attempt to more completely specify the CORBA/EJB mapping to allow complete interoperability between all EJB containers. However, at present, the interoperability that is available for compliant EJB 2.0 containers may be enough to meet our needs.

In-VM Method Calls

If a method call from one EJB to another takes place within a single Java virtual machine, there is no need to use all the 'machinery' of remote communication, such as the marshaling of parameters and context state for network transport. As explained in the previous chapter, the EJB 2.0 specification addresses this problem by introducing local interfaces. Calls performed on local homes or local EJB objects are performed by reference, just like standard Java calls.

This impacts directly on how we should architect our J2EE applications. The EJB 2.0 specification states that only EJBs in the same deployment unit (an EAR file) can look up and invoke methods on local interfaces. Therefore, we should put EJB and JSP files (or servlets) in the same EAR file, thus ensuring that the application server will optimize calls between them. Chapter 24 looks in detail at packaging J2EE applications into EAR files.

Summary

In this chapter, we have examined four specific services that an EJB container will provide:

- ❑ Transactional support
- ❑ Security
- ❑ Exception handling
- ❑ Communications

Although the intent of Enterprise JavaBeans technology is to free the business logic programmer from having to develop system-level services, we must still understand how these services work in the context of EJB. The important services that we've covered are:

- ❑ The complete isolation of a transaction will often be traded off for an increase in performance.
- ❑ The behavior of business methods in a transaction can be controlled declaratively (the preferred method) or programmatically.
- ❑ Security is an important requirement for most enterprise applications, comprising identification, authentication, access control, and data confidentiality. The EJB specification concerns itself with access control.
- ❑ Security is specified declaratively in the deployment descriptor, using security roles and method permissions.
- ❑ Business logic code can access the identity of the caller of a business method, and can also determine if participates in a particular role.
- ❑ There are two types of exceptions: application exceptions and system exceptions.
- ❑ The business logic programmer is responsible for recovery from application exceptions. The current transaction will attempt to commit despite an application exception, unless the transaction is set for rollback only.
- ❑ The EJB container is responsible for recovery from system exceptions. Any current transaction will be rolled back and the bean instance will be discarded.
- ❑ The EJB specification provides rules that are designed to facilitate remote communication.
- ❑ The rules for communication between servers from different vendors are not adequately specified in this version of the EJB specification.

In the next chapter, we will look at the development process for EJBs. The EJB 2.0 specification defines various roles that are played in producing and using an application based on EJB components. Understanding these roles will help us to understand the reasons behind the design decisions of EJB technology, and will assist in our application development and use. We'll look at Sun's J2EE Reference Implementation server as a baseline for examining these various roles, as we develop a simple banking application. We'll also add a web interface to our manufacturing application as a way of exploring the full J2EE application development process.

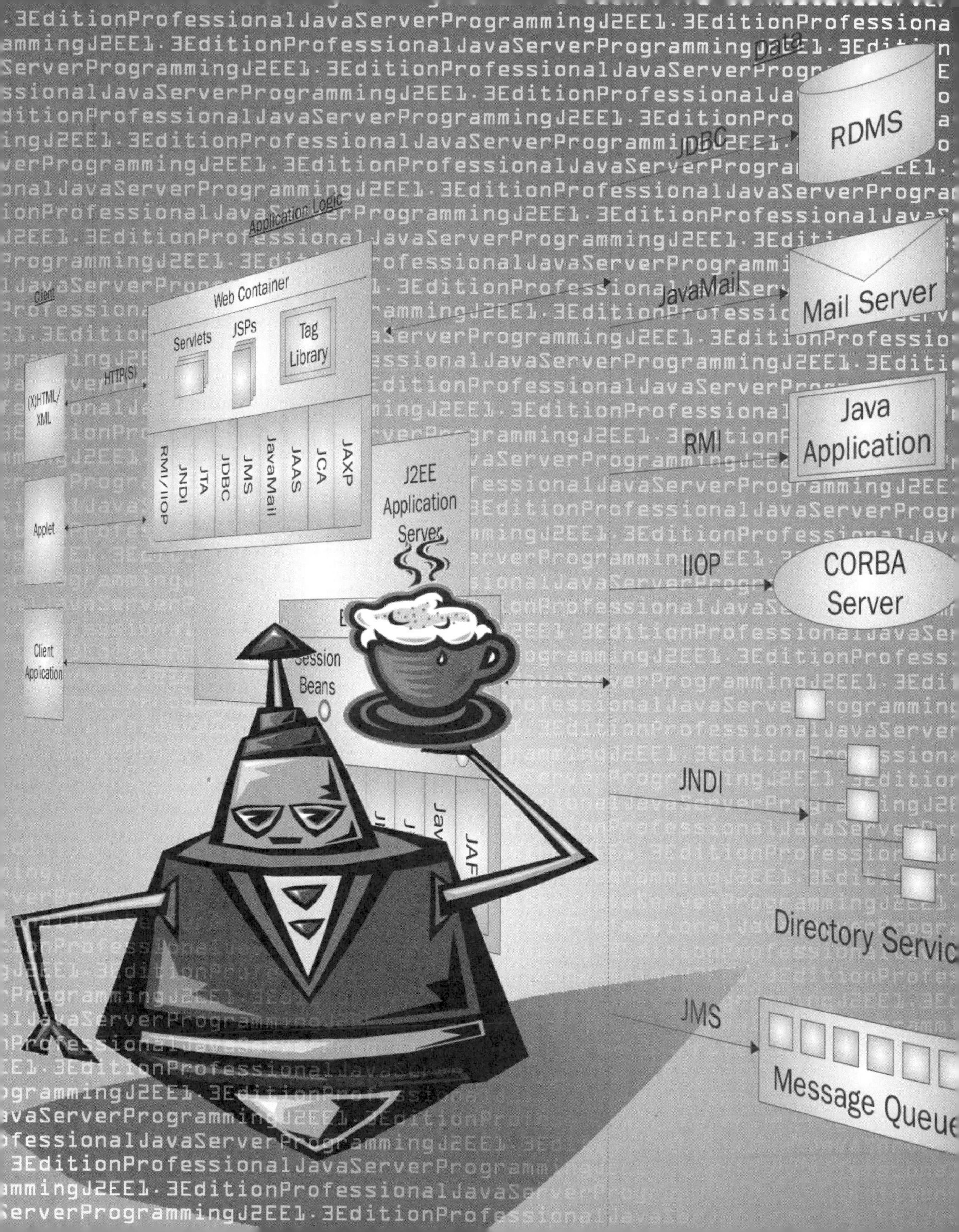

18

Development and Deployment Roles

Recent chapters have been heavily focused on EJB technology, so in this chapter, we will broaden the scope of our study and discuss some more general points about the development and deployment of EJBs. We'll also take some steps into using the presentation layer of J2EE with the EJBs we have created for our manufacturing application.

The Enterprise JavaBeans specification defines five distinct roles in the application development and deployment life cycle:

❑ **Enterprise bean provider** – develops EJB components

❑ **Application assembler** – combines EJB components with other software (for example, client programs or web components) in order to make a complete application

❑ **Deployer** – takes the application and installs it on an application server, resolving any references to existing resources in the target environment

❑ **Application server/EJB container vendor** – provides the application server on which the application is deployed

❑ **System administrator** – manages the application after it has been deployed into a target environment

This diagram illustrates the order in which the tasks should be executed:

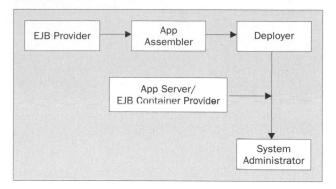

The EJB provider is a developer who implements EJBs. The assembler will take the EJBs (perhaps created by many different providers) and will package them into a J2EE archive. The assembler will usually create these archives using tools provided by the application server provider. The deployer will then take the archives and deploy them to the server. At this stage of the process, the EJBs are present in the server but are not yet running. Once a system administrator has performed any additional configuration, the application can be started.

> **These roles are abstract in nature and in a real development environment many people might be required for each role, or one person may perform multiple roles.**

These roles are not the product of a particular software engineering process or philosophy; instead, they grew naturally from the goals of Enterprise JavaBeans technology. Understanding the roles helps us to understand the technology and how it fits into an enterprise software process, whether there are hundreds of people working on a project or just one.

To demonstrate these concepts we will be further examining the banking application we introduced in Chapter 17. We'll look at it in terms of the division of labor among the various roles and make it less hypothetical in nature. Specifically, we'll look closely at two EJBs:

❑   An entity bean that represents an account

❑   A session bean that provides an interactive front to the Account bean

In order to provide a concrete example of the division of responsibilities defined in the Enterprise JavaBeans specification, we'll need to use an application server. We'll work through the steps required to create our application using the J2EE Reference Implementation (RI) from Sun. The RI is an important reference point for J2EE application servers, and it's in this capacity that we'll be using it.

As we progress through the example we'll explore each of the five roles, understanding how each role functions, and the activities it performs.

The Enterprise Bean Provider

The Enterprise JavaBeans specification provides a **component architecture**, which means that the data and business logic of an application is organized into discrete units (components). The enterprise bean provider is responsible for providing the EJB components. This 'provider' may be a single person, or it could be a team of people consisting of analysts, programmers, and quality assurance specialists – the provider could even be an outside vendor.

EJBs are software components and so they should be developed with as few dependencies on other EJBs, or other aspects of the application development process, as possible. The home and remote interfaces (together with their documentation) should provide a sufficient contract to allow the dependent parts of the application to be built. This means that components that are obtained from outside vendors can be treated as a black box.

The bean provider is usually an expert in the business logic that an enterprise requires, and is often referred to as an **application domain expert**. The EJBs the bean provider develops are usually reusable components that implement workflow, process, and business entities.

The enterprise bean provider produces a JAR file that contains files relating to one or more beans, including:

- ❑ The home interface(s)
- ❑ The remote and/or local interface(s)
- ❑ The implementation classes, and any supporting classes
- ❑ Any primary-key classes
- ❑ A (partially-complete) deployment descriptor

The classes are all placed in directories corresponding to their packages (which is standard procedure for Java JAR files). The deployment descriptor is placed in a directory named `META-INF`, and must have the name `ejb-jar.xml`. (See Chapter 14 for more information on how to package a JAR.)

The home interfaces, remote/local interfaces, implementation classes, and primary-key classes are not subject to change by the application assembler or deployer (and of course wouldn't be changed by the container vendor or the system administrator). On the other hand, the application assembler will change the XML deployment descriptor. (We will see exactly what the application assembler should change in the next section.)

Our development environment will include a tool (which could be anything from a command-line utility to an IDE) that we can use to build the parts of an EJB (with the possible exception of the deployment descriptor). Later on, we will use tools provided by a specific application-server vendor, although of course it's possible that an application server will include an IDE, or that an IDE will itself support multiple application servers.

However, in every application that uses EJBs, the business methods (the code that represents the whole point of an application) are portable. In addition to the portable Java classes and deployment descriptor an application server may also require mapping information, which is a set of instructions for how the application server should interact with our EJB. This mapping information is produced by the deployer and doesn't affect the code we write or the portability of our components.

Let's look at the remote and home interfaces in our example banking application.

Before we begin, create the following directory structure:

```
ISV\
    META-INF\
    src\
        wrox\
            some_isv\
```

We'll start with the remote interface for the entity bean; save this code in `src\wrox\some_isv\` as `Account.java`:

```
package wrox.some_isv;

import java.rmi.RemoteException;
import javax.ejb.*;

public interface Account extends EJBObject {
  void withdraw(double amount) throws InsufficientFundsException,
                                     RemoteException;

  void deposit(double amount) throws RemoteException;

  String getCustomerType() throws RemoteException;
}
```

This is the home interface for the entity bean; save it as `AccountHome.java` in `src\wrox\some_isv\`:

```
package wrox.some_isv;

import javax.ejb.*;
import java.rmi.RemoteException;

public interface AccountHome extends EJBHome {
  public Account create(int accountID, String customerName,
                        String customerType, double initialBalance)
            throws CreateException, RemoteException;

  public Account findByPrimaryKey(Integer accountID)
            throws FinderException, RemoteException;
}
```

This is the session bean's remote interface; save it as `AccountManager.java` in `src\wrox\some_isv\`:

```
package wrox.some_isv;

import javax.ejb.*;
import java.rmi.RemoteException;

public interface AccountManager extends EJBObject {
  void createAccount(int accountID, String customerName,
                     String customerType, double initialBalance)
        throws NoAccountCreatedException, RemoteException;

  void withdraw(int accountID, double amount)
        throws InsufficientFundsException, NoSuchAccountException,
               RemoteException;

  void deposit(int accountID, double amount)
        throws NoSuchAccountException, RemoteException;

  public void cancel(int accountID) throws RemoteException;
}
```

The home interface for the session bean looks like this; save it as `AccountMangagerHome.java` in `src\wrox\some_isv\`:

```
package wrox.some_isv;

import javax.ejb.*;
import java.rmi.RemoteException;

public interface AccountManagerHome extends EJBHome {
  AccountManager create() throws CreateException, RemoteException;
}
```

Finally, here are the exception classes we need; save them all in src\wrox\some_isv\ as InsufficientFundsException.java:

```
package wrox.some_isv;

public class InsufficientFundsException extends Exception {
  public InsufficientFundsException() {}
}
```

NoAccountCreatedException.java:

```
package wrox.some_isv;

public class NoAccountCreatedException extends Exception {
  public NoAccountCreatedException( String reason ) {
    super( reason );
  }

  public String getReason() {
    return getMessage();
  }
}
```

NoSuchAccountException.java:

```
package wrox.some_isv;

public class NoSuchAccountException extends Exception {
  public NoSuchAccountException() {}
}
```

For our component to be portable, it must avoid any dependencies on a particular implementation environment – such as using a proprietary security implementation. It's easy to keep a simple interface separate from an implementation environment, so it's no surprise that our home and remote interfaces don't introduce any particular dependencies. The implementation classes provide a sterner test. There are all sorts of opportunities to create dependencies on a particular security implementation, a particular database, or a particular set of requirements for transactional behavior. The rules that the Enterprise JavaBeans specification imposes on the bean developer are designed to reduce these dependencies.

To understand how this works, it's useful to consider the basics of what EJB technology does. One of the main benefits of using EJB technology is that it provides an abstract environment for business logic programming, free of concerns about system-level issues or the target environment. Accordingly the EJB container interposes on business method calls. That is, it intercepts the call, performs security checks, starts or resumes transactions as necessary, creates the environment, and then forwards the request to the actual business method.

Now for the last piece of the puzzle: the fundamental relationship between the EJB developer/application assembler roles and the finished, running product is **indirection**. Indirection is the use of a 'placeholder' in your Java code or deployment descriptor, rather than a reference to an actual entity in the implementation environment. If we understand these three things – abstraction, interposition, and indirection – the details will fall into place.

This indirection occurs at two levels: that of the EJB, and that of the application. To understand the difference, imagine that we have a banking account bean that uses an `isCallerInRole()` method to determine if the caller is using the permissions of an Automated Teller Machine (ATM). (We'll see an example of this shortly.) The bean may have a hard-coded role name of `ATM`, like in the following code:

```
if ((amount > 250) &&
     account.getCustomerType().equals(CustomerTypes.INDIVIDUAL)
     && ctx.isCallerInRole("ATM")) {
   throw new SecurityException();
}
```

However, this hard-coded role name may not be consistent with the security framework of other EJBs in our application. We may have purchased this account management bean from an independent software vendor, and want to mix it with other EJBs we wrote or purchased from other sources. As a result, the specification provides a level of indirection at the EJB level. We map this role reference in the EJB to a security role defined in the deployment descriptor. If our security framework defines a role named `UnmediatedAccess` that refers to access from the Web or an ATM, the mapping might look like this (the complete code for both this EJB and the deployment descriptor follows later):

```
<security-role>
  <description>
  This role is performed by any account access in which a bank employee
  is not involved, such as an Internet transaction or ATM
  withdrawal.
  </description>
  <role-name>UnmediatedAccess</role-name>
</security-role>
```

If we are writing all the EJBs ourselves, and combining them into an application for our own use, this constant indirection may seem unnecessary. We could just use the role-name `UnmediatedAccess` in our EJB and rid ourselves of this bean-specific `<security-role-ref>`. However, the system is designed to maximize the code portability and reuse of every EJB.

There are three types of reference that an EJB provider may code and which must be declared in the bean-specific part of the deployment descriptor:

❑   References to other EJBs

❑   References to resources (such as a JDBC connection)

❑   References to security roles

Whenever we use any of these references in our code, we should think of them as 'virtual' references. We can develop our EJB without worrying about the details of what should be referenced; for example, the specific data-source mapping we must use, the security roles that will exist in the assembled application, or the final JNDI deployment name of a particular EJB. We must, however, supply in the deployment descriptor a `<security-role-ref>`, a `<resource-ref>`, or an `<ejb-ref>`. We have encountered all of these reference types in the preceding chapters. Whenever we developed an EJB that used a database connection, another EJB, or a security role, we declared the use of that resource in the deployment descriptor.

<resource-ref>

A <resource-ref> element describes a resource reference used in the Java code of the EJB. It has an optional description sub-element, and three mandatory sub-elements: <res-ref-name>, <res-type>, and <res-auth>. The <res-ref-name> element contains the name that the Java implementation code uses to look up the resource in the EJBs JNDI context. The <res-type> element contains the Java type of the connection factory used to gain access to a resource connection. Standard types are:

- ❏ javax.sql.DataSource for JDBC connections

- ❏ javax.jms.QueueConnectionFactory and javax.jms.TopicConnectionFactory for JMS connections

- ❏ javax.mail.Session for JavaMail connections

- ❏ java.net.URL for URL connections

- ❏ javax.resource.cci.ConnectionFactory for Java Connectors to legacy systems

The <res-auth> element allows the EJB developer to indicate whether the container or the EJB developer provides a name and password for the connection. Valid values are Application or Container. This is an example of a <resource-ref> element in the deployment descriptor:

```
<resource-ref>
  <res-ref-name>jdbc/shipDB</res-ref-name>
  <res-type>javax.sql.DataSource</res-type>
</resource-ref>
```

This declares a DataSource called jdbc/shipDB. When the EJB is deployed, the container will make this resource available in the environment, allowing us to find it with the following code:

```
Context initialContext = new InitialContext();
DataSource dataSource = (DataSource)
initialContext.lookup("java:comp/env/jdbc/shipDB");
```

Note that this code is meant to work on the server (for example in the EJB class). If we want to perform the same kind of operation from a client, we will have to create a different initial context. For the WebLogic Server, the proper way to initialize a client context is:

```
Properties prop = new Properties();
prop.setProperty(Context.INITIAL_CONTEXT_FACTORY,
                "weblogic.jndi.WLInitialContextFactory");
prop.setProperty(Context.PROVIDER_URL,
                "t3://localhost:7001");
Context initialContext = new InitialContext(prop);
```

<ejb-ref>

An <ejb-ref> element describes a reference to another EJB used in the Java code of the EJB. It has an optional <description> sub-element, an optional <ejb-link> sub-element, and four mandatory sub-elements: <ejb-ref-name>, <ejb-ref-type>, <home>, and <remote>. The <ejb-ref-name> element contains the name that the Java implementation code uses to look up the EJB in its JNDI context. The <ejb-ref-type> element indicates the type of bean, of which valid values are Entity and Session.

Message-driven beans do not have home and remote interfaces, but instead receive asynchronous messages. To communicate with a message-driven bean, a resource reference would be used for a topic or queue.

The <home> element indicates the fully qualified class name of the home interface of the referenced EJB. The <remote> element indicates the fully qualified class name of the remote interface of the referenced EJB. The optional <ejb-link> reference can contain an EJB name, which indicates a particular EJB deployment to which this <ejb-ref> should refer.

The following fragment of a deployment descriptor illustrates how we can use <ejb-ref>. In this example, our EJB ManageOrders needs to access an EJB Orders. Therefore, we declare the following in the ManageOrders section of our deployment descriptor:

```
<ejb-ref>
  <ejb-ref-name>ejb/Order</ejb-ref-name>
  <ejb-ref-type>Entity</ejb-ref-type>
  <home>factory.order.OrderHome</home>
  <remote>factory.order.Order</home>
  <ejb-link>Orders</ejb-link>
</ejb-ref>
```

Our ManageOrders EJB can now reference the Orders EJB with the following code:

```
OrderHome home =
   (OrderHome) javax.rmi.PortableRemoteObject
      .narrow(initial.lookup("java:comp/env/ejb/Order"),
                       OrderHome.class);
```

<ejb-local-ref>

The <ejb-local-ref> element is used to reference an EJB that is accessed through its local home and local interfaces. Other than this difference, the semantics are similar to <ejb-ref>. The deployer creates a map between real resources (such as database connections) and the resource reference placeholders listed in the deployment descriptor. Of course, if it's obvious what a particular placeholder means, a smart application server can do this mapping without asking for any more information. For example, if there is only one database connection type available, all database resource references must map to that type.

Along with this EJB-level indirection, there is also application-level indirection. The security role that a particular EJB references with the isCallerInRole() method is linked to an application-level role declared in the deployment descriptor. But this application-level role is still an abstraction, not an actual real-world security system object.

In order to be independent of the underlying operating system, J2EE introduces the concept of a **principal**. A principal is a simple name that is used to determine the privileges of a user. Since this is a J2EE abstraction, there still needs to be a mapping of this principal to the name that is used in the underlying operating system to determine the level of security. This indirection will finally be resolved at deployment time. Consider the indirection for our ATM role that we referenced.

The ATM security role refers to the UnmediatedAccess security role, which at deployment time will be matched up to one or more real groups or principals in some security implementation. Neither the bean developer nor the application assembler needs to worry about the actual security implementation.

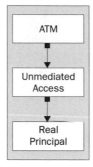

Another example of a similar indirection is an EJB that references a JDBC `Connection` object in code. The EJB could use an arbitrary name to refer to the JDBC connection, without consideration of the rest of the application, or deployment, environment. At deployment time, this arbitrary name would be linked to an actual `DataSource` connection factory that is bound into the namespace of the application server.

Here is our implementation class for the `AccountManager` session bean. It uses two references that must be declared: one to a security role, and one to the `Account` entity bean. For demonstration purposes, we're making full use of the indirection by using different names for both the role and the bean:

```
package wrox.some_isv;

import javax.ejb.*;
import javax.naming.*;
import java.rmi.RemoteException;

public class AccountManagerEJB implements SessionBean {
  public SessionContext ctx;

  public void createAccount(int accountID, String customerName,
                            String customerType, double initialBalance)
          throws NoAccountCreatedException {
    try {
      AccountHome accountHome = getAccountHome();
      accountHome.create(accountID, customerName, customerType,
                         initialBalance);
    } catch (CreateException ce) {
      throw new NoAccountCreatedException(ce.getMessage());
    } catch (RemoteException re) {
      throw new EJBException(re);
    }
  }

  public void withdraw(int accountID, double amount)
          throws InsufficientFundsException, NoSuchAccountException {
    try {
      Account account = getAccount(accountID);

      if ((amount > 250)
              && account.getCustomerType().equals(CustomerTypes.INDIVIDUAL)
              && ctx.isCallerInRole("ATM")) {
        throw new SecurityException();
      }
      account.withdraw(amount);
    } catch (RemoteException re) {
      throw new EJBException(re);
    }
```

```
    }

    public void deposit(int accountID, double amount)
                throws NoSuchAccountException {
      try {
        Account account = getAccount(accountID);
        account.deposit(amount);
      } catch (RemoteException re) {
        throw new EJBException(re);
      }
    }

    public void cancel(int accountID) {
      try {
        Account account = getAccount(accountID);
        account.remove();
      } catch (NoSuchAccountException nsae) {
        // Great, already done
      } catch (Exception e) {
        throw new EJBException(e);
      }
    }

    private Account getAccount(int accountID) throws NoSuchAccountException {
      try {
        AccountHome home = getAccountHome();
        return home.findByPrimaryKey(new Integer(accountID));
      } catch (RemoteException re) {
        throw new EJBException(re);
      } catch (FinderException fe) {
        throw new NoSuchAccountException();
      }
    }

    private AccountHome getAccountHome() {
      try {
        InitialContext initial = new InitialContext();
        AccountHome home =
                    (AccountHome) javax.rmi.PortableRemoteObject.narrow(
                            initial.lookup("java:comp/env/ejb/GenericAccount"),
                                    AccountHome.class);
        return home;
      } catch (NamingException ne) {
        throw new EJBException(ne);
      }
    }

    public void ejbCreate() {}
    public void ejbActivate() {}
    public void ejbPassivate() {}
    public void ejbRemove() {}
    public void setSessionContext(SessionContext ctx) {
      this.ctx = ctx;
    }
}
```

Here are the relevant resource declarations from the `ejb-jar.xml` deployment descriptor (complete versions of which follow) for the EJB development stage and the application assembly stage:

```xml
        <ejb-ref>
          <ejb-ref-name>ejb/GenericAccount</ejb-ref-name>
          <ejb-ref-type>Entity</ejb-ref-type>
          <home>wrox.some_isv.AccountHome</home>
          <remote>wrox.some_isv.Account</remote>
          <ejb-link>Account</ejb-link>
        </ejb-ref>
        <security-role-ref>
          <description>
          This role refers to automated customer withdrawals
          from the account; no bank intermediary is involved.
          </description>
          <role-name>ATM</role-name>
          <role-link>UnmediatedAccess</role-link>
        </security-role-ref>
```

An entity bean using container-managed persistence can automatically provide yet another type of indirection: the mapping of the bean's state data to fields in a persistent store. Our account bean has four such data fields: accountID, customerName, customerType, and accountBalance. These could be mapped to fields with any name in a table in any type of database, and (depending on the object/relational-mapping capabilities of our application server) they could also be mapped to fields in different tables. If our application server and JDBC driver support distributed two-phase commits, they could even be mapped to fields in different databases. This capability is especially important when EJB applications must co-exist with legacy data.

Here is the implementation class for the Account entity bean. Note that we're providing flexibility for our bean in the form of an environment parameter. In practice, this particular piece of information (the account minimum balance) probably belongs in a database where it can be changed without re-deploying the bean; the technique we are using is generally applicable to more stable information:

```java
package wrox.some_isv;

import javax.ejb.*;
import javax.naming.*;

public abstract class AccountEJB implements EntityBean {

  public abstract int getAccountID();
  public abstract void setAccountID(int accountID);

  public abstract String getCustomerName();
  public abstract void setCustomerName(String customerName);

  public abstract String getCustomerType();
  public abstract void setCustomerType(String customerType);

  public abstract double getAccountBalance();
  public abstract void setAccountBalance(double accountBalance);

  public void withdraw(double amount) throws InsufficientFundsException {
    if (getAccountBalance() - amount < 0) {
      throw new InsufficientFundsException();
    }
    setAccountBalance(getAccountBalance() -amount);
  }

  public void deposit(double amount) {
    setAccountBalance(getAccountBalance() + amount);
  }
```

```
    public Integer ejbCreate(int accountID, String customerName,
                             String customerType, double initialBalance)
              throws CreateException {
      if (!customerType.equals(CustomerTypes.CORPORATION)
              &&!customerType.equals(CustomerTypes.INDIVIDUAL)) {
        throw new CreateException("Unknown customer type.");
      }
      System.out.println("Account.ejbCreate() called");

      double minimumBalance = getMinimumBalance();
      if (initialBalance < minimumBalance) {
        throw new CreateException("Minimum balance required.");
      }
      setAccountID(accountID);
      setCustomerName(customerName);
      setCustomerType(customerType);
      setAccountBalance(initialBalance);
      return new Integer(getAccountID());
    }

    public void ejbPostCreate(int accountID, String customerName,
                              String customerType, double initialBalance)
              throws CreateException {}

    private double getMinimumBalance() {
      try {
        InitialContext initial = new InitialContext();
        Double minimumBalance =
          (Double) initial.lookup("java:comp/env/minimumBalance");
        return minimumBalance.doubleValue();
      } catch (NamingException ne) {
        throw new EJBException(ne);
      }
    }

    public void ejbActivate() {}
    public void ejbLoad() {}
    public void ejbPassivate() {}
    public void ejbRemove() {}
    public void ejbStore() {}
    public void setEntityContext(EntityContext ctx) {}
    public void unsetEntityContext() {}
}
```

The final implementation class is a simple interface that provides some string constants. (Ideally, we would put these constants in a package separate from our EJB so that several beans can use them.)

```
package wrox.some_isv;

public interface CustomerTypes {
  public static final String CORPORATION = "corporation";
  public static final String INDIVIDUAL = "individual";
}
```

A deployment descriptor is the repository of information about the EJBs in an application. The application server's tools will use this information to understand what instances of indirection need to be resolved at deployment time. We have examined small parts of the deployment descriptor in isolation while we discussed other features of EJB technology and it's time now to look at the deployment descriptor as a whole.

There are two types of information contained within a deployment descriptor:

❑ **Structural information related to particular EJBs**
This type of information relates to the Java code that the bean provider created, such as fully qualified class names, references used, and transaction demarcation type (container-managed or bean-managed).

❑ **Application Assembly Information**
This describes how the EJBs in a JAR are composed into a larger application deployment unit. Examples of such information could be the definition of security roles and method permissions, binding enterprise bean references to other beans, or the definition of transaction attributes on methods.

The root element of a deployment descriptor is `<ejb-jar>` and there are two elements underneath this:

❑ `<enterprise-beans>` contains structural information relevant to particular EJBs

❑ `<assembly-descriptor>` contains information about how the EJBs are composed into a larger application deployment unit

It's quite possible, even likely, that the same person or persons developing EJBs will also be responsible for assembling them into an application. In this case the division of responsibilities between the EJB developer and the application assembler may seem unimportant. However, with component reuse and resale by Independent Software Vendors (ISVs) in mind, the EJB specification clearly specifies who is responsible for which entries in the deployment descriptor, and even indicates which entries can be specified by the bean developer and which can be later changed by the application assembler. Generally, the bean developer is responsible for the entries that are children of the `<enterprise-beans>` element, and the application assembler is responsible for the entries that are children of the `<assembly-descriptor>` element, although there are exceptions to this.

According to the specification, the bean provider must ensure the deployment descriptor contains the following information for each bean:

❑ **EJB type: session or entity**
The `<session>` or `<entity>` element will be the immediate child of the `<enterprise-beans>` element.

❑ **EJB name**
This is just a way to identify the EJB. The name doesn't have any relationship to the JNDI name under which the EJB will be deployed or accessible to clients, nor does it relate to the name that other beans will use to find this bean. The bean provider specifies the name in the `<ejb-name>` element and this name must be unique throughout the same archive (JAR or EAR).

❑ **EJB implementation class**
The fully qualified Java class name of the enterprise bean's implementation class is specified using the `<ejb-class>` element.

❑ **EJB home and remote interfaces**
The bean provider must specify the fully qualified name of the enterprise bean's home and remote interfaces in the `<home>` element and `<remote>` elements.

❑ **Whether an entity bean is re-entrant or not**
The `<reentrant>` element is used, with a value of True or False. (Session beans are never re-entrant.)

❏ **Whether a session bean is stateful or stateless**
The <session-type> element is used, with a value of Stateful or Stateless.

❏ **Whether or not a session bean manages its own transactions**
The <transaction-type> element is used, with a value of Bean or Container.

❏ **Whether an entity bean uses BMP or CMP**
The <persistence-type> element is used with a value of Bean or Container.

❏ **Enterprise bean's primary-key class**
The fully qualified Java class name of an entity bean's primary-key class is specified using the <prim-key-class> element. Technically, this is only mandatory for an entity bean with bean-managed persistence. If your primary key maps to several fields, you will need to specify a Java class in this tag, and the class (which typically ends in "PK", for example, SportPK) will contain all the fields that are needed to uniquely identify your EJB.

❏ **Container-managed fields**
If the enterprise bean is an entity bean with container-managed persistence, the container-managed fields must be listed using <cmp-field> elements.

❏ **Abstract schema**
Again for beans using container-managed persistence, there should be an <abstract-schema> element for mappings such as EJB QL.

❏ **Environment entries**
Using the <env-entry> element.

❏ **Resource managers**
If there are any resource manager connection factory references in the Java code, such as a JDBC DataSource reference.

❏ **EJB references**
Any references in the code to other EJBs.

❏ **Security references**
Any references in the code to security roles.

Keep in mind that this information will typically be specified using a tool, but the deployment descriptor is simply an XML file that can be edited by hand if we wish. Here is the deployment descriptor produced by the bean developer. (Remember that this is not the completed product that we will deploy, as the application assembler will also edit it.)

```xml
<?xml version="1.0" encoding="UTF-8"?>

<!DOCTYPE ejb-jar PUBLIC '-//Sun Microsystems, Inc.//DTD Enterprise JavaBeans
2.0//EN' 'http://java.sun.com/dtd/ejb-jar_2_0.dtd'>

<ejb-jar>
  <display-name>ISVs</display-name>
  <enterprise-beans>
```

The name, state-management type, Java classes, and transaction type of the AccountManager bean:

```xml
    <session>
      <display-name>AccountManager</display-name>
      <ejb-name>AccountManager</ejb-name>
      <home>wrox.some_isv.AccountManagerHome</home>
```

```
        <remote>wrox.some_isv.AccountManager</remote>
        <ejb-class>wrox.some_isv.AccountManagerEJB</ejb-class>
        <session-type>Stateless</session-type>
        <transaction-type>Container</transaction-type>
```

Declaring our use of a reference to another EJB:

```
    <ejb-ref>
        <ejb-ref-name>ejb/GenericAccount</ejb-ref-name>
        <ejb-ref-type>Entity</ejb-ref-type>
        <home>wrox.some_isv.AccountHome</home>
        <remote>wrox.some_isv.Account</remote>
    </ejb-ref>
```

Declaring our use of a security role:

```
    <security-role-ref>
        <description>
        This role refers to automated customer withdrawals from the account.
        No bank intermediary is involved.
        </description>
        <role-name>ATM</role-name>
    </security-role-ref>
    <security-identity>
        <description></description>
        <use-caller-identity></use-caller-identity>
    </security-identity>
</session>
```

The name, persistence type, Java classes (including the primary-key class), and reentrancy of the Account bean:

```
<entity>
    <display-name>Account</display-name>
    <ejb-name>Account</ejb-name>
    <home>wrox.some_isv.AccountHome</home>
    <remote>wrox.some_isv.Account</remote>
    <ejb-class>wrox.some_isv.AccountEJB</ejb-class>
    <persistence-type>Container</persistence-type>
    <prim-key-class>java.lang.Integer</prim-key-class>
    <reentrant>False</reentrant>
```

The declaration of the fields for container-managed persistence:

```
    <cmp-version>2.x</cmp-version>
    <abstract-schema-name>AccountBean</abstract-schema-name>
    <cmp-field>
        <field-name>customerName</field-name>
    </cmp-field>
    <cmp-field>
        <field-name>customerType</field-name>
    </cmp-field>
    <cmp-field>
        <field-name>accountBalance</field-name>
    </cmp-field>
    <cmp-field>
        <field-name>accountID</field-name>
    </cmp-field>
    <primkey-field>accountID</primkey-field>
```

The declaration of an environment entry:

```
      <env-entry>
        <env-entry-name>minimumBalance</env-entry-name>
        <env-entry-type>java.lang.Double</env-entry-type>
        <env-entry-value>150.0</env-entry-value>
      </env-entry>
      <security-identity>
        <description></description>
        <use-caller-identity></use-caller-identity>
      </security-identity>
    </entity>
  </enterprise-beans>
</ejb-jar>
```

The Application Assembler

The application assembler combines one or more EJB JAR files (which are the output of the bean developer) into a deployable application. This means that the XML deployment descriptor must be edited so that application-level information (such as security roles and references between beans) can be added. The application assembler may, at this stage, also add other types of application components such as servlets, JSP pages, or client applications. The application assembler doesn't need to understand the implementation of the EJBs but they do need to understand the home and remote interfaces, and the business logic that the methods in the EJB represent.

In our banking application, the application assembler has two roles:

❑ To complete the editing of the deployment descriptor.

❑ To provide some client applications. These client applications will simply test the functionality of the server-side components (a real application would obviously need a real client interface to the business functionality that the server components provided).

According to the specification, the following information in the deployment descriptor is relevant to this stage of EJB development:

❑ The application assembler may use the <ejb-link> element to indicate which EJB in a JAR file should be mapped to an enterprise bean reference declared by an EJB in the <enterprise-beans> section

❑ The application assembler may define one or more security roles

❑ The application assembler may define method permissions

❑ The application assembler must link any security role references declared by an EJB to a security role that they have defined

❑ If the EJB uses container-managed transactions the application assembler must define the transactional properties of the business methods defined in the home and remote interfaces of the EJB

In addition, the following information that was provided by the EJB developer may be modified:

❑ The EJBs abstract schema name. This element is new in EJB 2.0, and we only need to mention it if we are going to use Enterprise JavaBean Query Language (EJB-QL) statements that reference this EJB.

❑   The values of the environment entries.

❑   The description field for any entry.

Here is the final version of our application's deployment descriptor:

```xml
<?xml version="1.0" encoding="UTF-8"?>

<!DOCTYPE ejb-jar PUBLIC '-//Sun Microsystems, Inc.//DTD Enterprise JavaBeans
2.0//EN' 'http://java.sun.com/dtd/ejb-jar_2_0.dtd'>

<ejb-jar>
  <display-name>ISVs</display-name>
  <enterprise-beans>
    <session>
      <display-name>AccountManager</display-name>
      <ejb-name>AccountManager</ejb-name>
      <home>wrox.some_isv.AccountManagerHome</home>
      <remote>wrox.some_isv.AccountManager</remote>
      <ejb-class>wrox.some_isv.AccountManagerEJB</ejb-class>
      <session-type>Stateless</session-type>
      <transaction-type>Container</transaction-type>
```

The `<ejb-ref>` element now links to the `Account` bean:

```xml
      <ejb-ref>
        <ejb-ref-name>ejb/GenericAccount</ejb-ref-name>
        <ejb-ref-type>Entity</ejb-ref-type>
        <home>wrox.some_isv.AccountHome</home>
        <remote>wrox.some_isv.Account</remote>
        <ejb-link>Account</ejb-link>
      </ejb-ref>
      <security-role-ref>
        <description>
        This role refers to automated customer withdrawals
        from the account; no bank intermediary is involved.
        </description>
        <role-name>ATM</role-name>
```

The role reference now links to a particular role defined in this deployment descriptor:

```xml
        <role-link>UnmediatedAccess</role-link>
      </security-role-ref>
    </session>

    <entity>
      <display-name>Account</display-name>
      <ejb-name>Account</ejb-name>
      <home>wrox.some_isv.AccountHome</home>
      <remote>wrox.some_isv.Account</remote>
      <ejb-class>wrox.some_isv.AccountEJB</ejb-class>
      <persistence-type>Container</persistence-type>
      <prim-key-class>java.lang.Integer</prim-key-class>
      <reentrant>False</reentrant>

      <cmp-version>2.x</cmp-version>
      <abstract-schema-name>AccountBean</abstract-schema-name>
      <cmp-field>
```

917

```
      <field-name>customerName</field-name>
   </cmp-field>
   <cmp-field>
      <field-name>customerType</field-name>
   </cmp-field>
   <cmp-field>
      <field-name>accountBalance</field-name>
   </cmp-field>
   <cmp-field>
      <field-name>accountID</field-name>
   </cmp-field>
   <primkey-field>accountID</primkey-field>
   <env-entry>
      <env-entry-name>env/minimumBalance</env-entry-name>
      <env-entry-type>java.lang.Double</env-entry-type>
      <env-entry-value>150.0</env-entry-value>
   </env-entry>
 </entity>

</enterprise-beans>
```

The assembly descriptor portion of the deployment descriptor may be omitted in the highly unlikely event that our application requires no security roles, method permissions, or transaction attributes:

```
<assembly-descriptor>
```

We declare that all methods, in both classes, require a new or existing transaction context:

```
<container-transaction>
  <method>
    <ejb-name>AccountManager</ejb-name>
    <method-intf>*</method-intf>
    <method-name>*</method-name>
  </method>
  <trans-attribute>Required</trans-attribute>
</container-transaction>
<container-transaction>
  <method>
    <ejb-name>Account</ejb-name>
    <method-intf>*</method-intf>
    <method-name>*</method-name>
  </method>
  <trans-attribute>Required</trans-attribute>
</container-transaction>
```

We define the security roles:

```
<security-role>
  <description>
  This role is performed by any customer-service
  representative who does not have account-manager status.
  They will be able to handle deposits and withdrawals, but
  not account management.
  </description>
  <role-name>Teller</role-name>
</security-role>
<security-role>
```

```
        <description>
        This role is performed by any account access
        in which a bank employee is not involved, such as an
        internet transaction or ATM withdrawal.</description>
        <role-name>UnmediatedAccess</role-name>
    </security-role>
    <security-role>
        <description>
        This role is performed by professionals who
        are allowed to manage an account (open, close).</description>
        <role-name>Manager</role-name>
    </security-role>
```

We define the methods that the Manager role has access to (all of them):

```
    <method-permission>
        <role-name>Manager</role-name>
        <method>
            <ejb-name>AccountManager</ejb-name>
            <method-name>*</method-name>
            <method-inft>*</method-inft>
        </method>
        <method>
            <role-name>Manager</role-name>
            <ejb-name>Account</ejb-name>
            <method-name>*</method-name>
            <method-inft>*</method-inft>
        </method>
    </method-permission>
```

We define the methods that the UnmediatedAccess role has access to:

```
    <method-permission>
        <role-name>UnmediatedAccess</role-name>
        <method>
            <ejb-name>AccountManager</ejb-name>
            <method-intf>Remote</method-intf>
            <method-name>deposit</method-name>
            <method-params>
                <method-param>int</method-param>
                <method-param>double</method-param>
            </method-params>
        </method>
        <method>
            <ejb-name>AccountManager</ejb-name>
            <method-intf>Remote</method-intf>
            <method-name>withdraw</method-name>
            <method-params>
                <method-param>int</method-param>
                <method-param>double</method-param>
            </method-params>
        </method>
        <method>
            <ejb-name>Account</ejb-name>
            <method-intf>Remote</method-intf>
            <method-name>deposit</method-name>
            <method-params>
                <method-param>double</method-param>
            </method-params>
```

```
    </method>
    <method>
      <ejb-name>Account</ejb-name>
      <method-intf>Remote</method-intf>
      <method-name>withdraw</method-name>
      <method-params>
        <method-param>double</method-param>
      </method-params>
    </method>
    <method>
      <ejb-name>Account</ejb-name>
      <method-intf>Remote</method-intf>
      <method-name>getCustomerType</method-name>
      <method-params />
    </method>
  </method-permission>
```

We define the methods that the `Teller` role has access to:

```
<method-permission>
  <role-name>Teller</role-name>
  <method>
    <ejb-name>AccountManager</ejb-name>
    <method-intf>Remote</method-intf>
    <method-name>deposit</method-name>
    <method-params>
      <method-param>int</method-param>
      <method-param>double</method-param>
    </method-params>
  </method>
  <method>
    <ejb-name>AccountManager</ejb-name>
    <method-intf>Remote</method-intf>
    <method-name>withdraw</method-name>
    <method-params>
      <method-param>int</method-param>
      <method-param>double</method-param>
    </method-params>
  </method>
  <method>
    <ejb-name>Account</ejb-name>
    <method-intf>Remote</method-intf>
    <method-name>withdraw</method-name>
    <method-params>
      <method-param>double</method-param>
    </method-params>
  </method>
  <method>
    <ejb-name>Account</ejb-name>
    <method-intf>Remote</method-intf>
    <method-name>deposit</method-name>
    <method-params>
      <method-param>double</method-param>
    </method-params>
  </method>
  <method>
    <ejb-name>Account</ejb-name>
    <method-intf>Remote</method-intf>
    <method-name>getCustomerType</method-name>
    <method-params />
  </method>
</method-permission>
```

Finally, we define the methods that anyone has access to:

```
<method-permission>
 <unchecked />
 <method>
   <ejb-name>AccountManager</ejb-name>
   <method-intf>Home</method-intf>
   <method-name>remove</method-name>
   <method-params>
     <method-param>java.lang.Object</method-param>
   </method-params>
 </method>
 <method>
   <ejb-name>AccountManager</ejb-name>
   <method-intf>Remote</method-intf>
   <method-name>cancel</method-name>
   <method-params>
     <method-param>int</method-param>
   </method-params>
 </method>
 <method>
   <ejb-name>AccountManager</ejb-name>
   <method-intf>Remote</method-intf>
   <method-name>getHandle</method-name>
   <method-params />
 </method>
 <method>
   <ejb-name>AccountManager</ejb-name>
   <method-intf>Home</method-intf>
   <method-name>remove</method-name>
   <method-params>
     <method-param>javax.ejb.Handle</method-param>
   </method-params>
 </method>
 <method>
   <ejb-name>AccountManager</ejb-name>
   <method-intf>Home</method-intf>
   <method-name>getHomeHandle</method-name>
   <method-params />
 </method>
 <method>
   <ejb-name>AccountManager</ejb-name>
   <method-intf>Remote</method-intf>
   <method-name>getPrimaryKey</method-name>
   <method-params />
 </method>
 <method>
   <ejb-name>AccountManager</ejb-name>
   <method-intf>Remote</method-intf>
   <method-name>remove</method-name>
   <method-params />
 </method>
 <method>
   <ejb-name>AccountManager</ejb-name>
   <method-intf>Home</method-intf>
   <method-name>getEJBMetaData</method-name>
   <method-params />
 </method>
 <method>
   <ejb-name>AccountManager</ejb-name>
   <method-intf>Home</method-intf>
   <method-name>create</method-name>
```

```
        <method-params />
    </method>
    <method>
      <ejb-name>AccountManager</ejb-name>
      <method-intf>Remote</method-intf>
      <method-name>isIdentical</method-name>
      <method-params>
        <method-param>javax.ejb.EJBObject</method-param>
      </method-params>
    </method>
    <method>
      <ejb-name>AccountManager</ejb-name>
      <method-intf>Remote</method-intf>
      <method-name>getEJBHome</method-name>
      <method-params />
    </method>
    <method>
      <ejb-name>Account</ejb-name>
      <method-intf>Home</method-intf>
      <method-name>remove</method-name>
      <method-params>
        <method-param>java.lang.Object</method-param>
      </method-params>
    </method>
    <method>
      <ejb-name>Account</ejb-name>
      <method-intf>Home</method-intf>
      <method-name>findByPrimaryKey</method-name>
      <method-params>
        <method-param>java.lang.Integer</method-param>
      </method-params>
    </method>
    <method>
      <ejb-name>Account</ejb-name>
      <method-intf>Remote</method-intf>
      <method-name>getHandle</method-name>
      <method-params />
    </method>
    <method>
      <ejb-name>Account</ejb-name>
      <method-intf>Home</method-intf>
      <method-name>create</method-name>
      <method-params>
        <method-param>int</method-param>
        <method-param>java.lang.String</method-param>
        <method-param>java.lang.String</method-param>
        <method-param>double</method-param>
      </method-params>
    </method>
    <method>
      <ejb-name>Account</ejb-name>
      <method-intf>Home</method-intf>
      <method-name>remove</method-name>
      <method-params>
        <method-param>javax.ejb.Handle</method-param>
      </method-params>
    </method>
    <method>
      <ejb-name>Account</ejb-name>
      <method-intf>Home</method-intf>
      <method-name>getHomeHandle</method-name>
      <method-params />
    </method>
```

```
            <method>
              <ejb-name>Account</ejb-name>
              <method-intf>Remote</method-intf>
              <method-name>getPrimaryKey</method-name>
              <method-params />
            </method>
            <method>
              <ejb-name>Account</ejb-name>
              <method-intf>Home</method-intf>
              <method-name>getEJBMetaData</method-name>
              <method-params />
            </method>
            <method>
              <ejb-name>Account</ejb-name>
              <method-intf>Remote</method-intf>
              <method-name>remove</method-name>
              <method-params />
            </method>
            <method>
              <ejb-name>Account</ejb-name>
              <method-intf>Remote</method-intf>
              <method-name>isIdentical</method-name>
              <method-params>
                <method-param>javax.ejb.EJBObject</method-param>
              </method-params>
            </method>
            <method>
              <ejb-name>Account</ejb-name>
              <method-intf>Remote</method-intf>
              <method-name>getEJBHome</method-name>
              <method-params />
            </method>
          </method-permission>
        </assembly-descriptor>
      </ejb-jar>
```

As the application assembler, we added everything that is a child of the `<assembly-descriptor>` element. For the container-managed transactions, we specified that all methods must execute in a transactional context. For any business method call, if there is no current transaction the container will create one. For security, we defined three roles: `UnmediatedAccess`, `Teller`, and `Manager`. The manager has access to all the methods; the teller and 'unmediated access' (that is, the Web or an ATM) can only deposit and withdraw funds.

In addition, we added two things to the children of the `<enterprise-beans>` element:

❑ A `<role-link>` element to the security role reference in the session bean. Remember that the code (perhaps obtained from an independent software vendor) referred to a security role of `ATM`. Our application wants to be more general, and so we use the role `UnmediatedAccess`. The indirection of a reference allows us to do this; the `<role-link>` element closes the loop.

❑ A similar resolution of a reference, in this case to another bean. In our code, the `AccountManager` bean refers to the account bean as `ejb/GenericAccount`. However, the actual name of the bean is simply `Account`. The two are linked together by the `<ejb-link>` element.

We have now linked our EJBs together to form a single, deployable application unit. Our duty as application assembler stops here. Although we still need to implement the clients they are obviously not a part of the application unit.

923

We provide three clients: the first one will be run with the security identity of a manager and will create a couple of accounts and make a deposit and then a withdrawal:

```java
package wrox.some_isv;

import java.rmi.RemoteException;
import javax.ejb.*;
import javax.naming.*;
import javax.rmi.PortableRemoteObject;

public class TestClient {

  public static void main(String[] args) {

    try {
      InitialContext initial = new InitialContext();
      Object objref = initial.lookup("java:comp/env/ejb/AccountAccess");

      AccountManagerHome home =
        (AccountManagerHome) PortableRemoteObject.narrow(objref,
            AccountManagerHome.class);

      AccountManager accountManager = home.create();

      System.out.println("create individual account");
      accountManager.createAccount(1, "Dan OConnor",
                          CustomerTypes.INDIVIDUAL, 1500.0);

      System.out.println("deposit");
      accountManager.deposit(1, 550.0);

      System.out.println("withdraw");
      accountManager.withdraw(1, 75.0);

      System.out.println("create corporate account");
      accountManager.createAccount(2, "Wrox Press",
                          CustomerTypes.CORPORATION, 150000.0);
    } catch (Exception e) {
      e.printStackTrace();
    }
  }
}
```

The second client will be run with the security identity of either an ATM machine or a web client. It will not succeed in its attempt to create an account, because the EJB container will prevent access to the method based on our declarative security permissions in the deployment descriptor. The following code looks up our AccountManager and tries to create an Account. Since the security credentials of this client are insufficient for this kind of operation, the request will fail:

```java
package wrox.some_isv;

import java.rmi.RemoteException;
import javax.ejb.*;
import javax.naming.*;
import javax.rmi.PortableRemoteObject;

public class TestClient2 {
  public static void main(String[] args) {
    try {
```

```
            InitialContext initial = new InitialContext();
            Object objref = initial.lookup("java:comp/env/ejb/AccountAccess");

            AccountManagerHome home =
              (AccountManagerHome) PortableRemoteObject.narrow(objref,
                  AccountManagerHome.class);

            AccountManager accountManager = home.create();

            System.out.println("create");
            accountManager.createAccount(3, "John Smith",
                                    CustomerTypes.INDIVIDUAL, 500.0);
          } catch (Exception e) {
          e.printStackTrace();
          }
      }
  }
```

The third client will be run with the security identity of either an ATM machine or a web client. It will succeed in withdrawing a small amount of money from the individual account and a large amount of money from the corporate account. However, because of the security check we wrote, the attempt to withdraw a large amount of money from an individual account will fail:

```
package wrox.some_isv;

import java.rmi.RemoteException;
import javax.ejb.*;
import javax.naming.*;
import javax.rmi.PortableRemoteObject;

public class TestClient3 {
  public static void main(String[] args) {
    try {
      InitialContext initial = new InitialContext();
      Object objref = initial.lookup("java:comp/env/ejb/AccountAccess");

      AccountManagerHome home =
        (AccountManagerHome) PortableRemoteObject.narrow(objref,
            AccountManagerHome.class);

      AccountManager accountManager = home.create();

      System.out
        .println("withdrawing small amount from individual account");
      accountManager.withdraw(1, 100.0);

      System.out.println("withdrawing large amount from corporate account");
      accountManager.withdraw(2, 1000.0);

      System.out
        .println("withdrawing large amount from individual account");
      accountManager.withdraw(1, 1000.0);

      System.out.println("done");

    } catch (Exception e) {
    e.printStackTrace();
    }
  }
}
```

Remember that there is no standard procedure for the authentication of the client in the Enterprise JavaBeans specification. However, as well as a standalone client, the J2EE specification provides for the concept of a client executing in a container. This container provides system-level services, just as an EJB or a servlet that executes in a container that provides system-level services.

> *Although authentication techniques are not specified for the client container, some sort of authentication is mandatory. The RI provides such authentication automatically for clients that are executing in its 'client container'. (A client container is just a standard application that 'wraps' your application. We call it, passing our application name as a parameter, and it will call our application's* main() *method for us.)*

Although there is no authentication code in these three examples, when they are executed, a window will still appear asking for a user name and password:

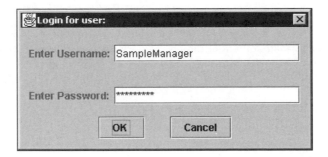

At the end of the application assembly stage, we will have a completed application ready for deployment into an application server. As we have with other examples, we should package our EJB components into a JAR file.

Let's compile these classes by running the following command:

```
javac -d . -classpath .;%J2EE_HOME%\lib\j2ee.jar src\wrox\some_isv\*.java
```

We should now have the following files and directories:

```
ISV\
    META-INF\
    wrox\
        some_isv\
                Account.class
                AccountEJB.class
                AccountHome.class
                AccountManager.class
                AccountManagerEJB.class
                AccountManagerHome.class
                CustomerTypes.class
                InsufficientFundsException.class
                NoAccountCreatedException.class
                NoSuchAccountException.class
                TestClient.class
                TestClient2.class
```

We can create the JAR file by running the following command:

```
jar cvf account.jar META-INF/ wrox/some_isv/
```

The TestClient classes do not need to be in our JAR file, however we will need to have the JAR file in our classpath when we run the clients.

The Deployer

Once the application is completed, it must be inserted into the target environment. Remember that the business-logic programmer does not need to worry about the target database, security system, how to find other referenced components, or how clients will find the EJB. But these issues need to be considered eventually and the logical references that the bean provider uses must be mapped onto actual resources or identities. How this is done is specific to an application server vendor and responsibility for doing it rests with the deployer. A deployer does not need to be a domain expert (that is, an expert in the business); a person in this role must instead be an expert in the environment in which the application will execute (that is, an expert in the company's database, security system, application server, operating systems, and network).

Let's consider what we need to do to deploy our application to the J2EE reference application server. To deploy the application into our configured environment, we'll use the RI- tool, deploytool.

Once deploytool has started up, create a new application called Wrox, then select File | Add to Application | EJB JAR...:

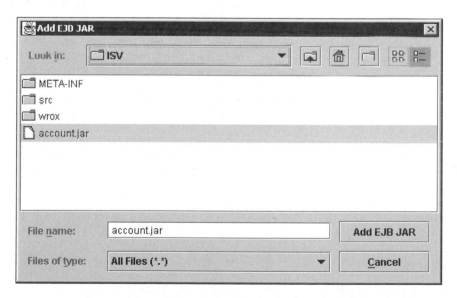

Select our account.jar and click Add EJB JAR. We can see that we have successfully added two EJBs to our application, AccountManager and Account:

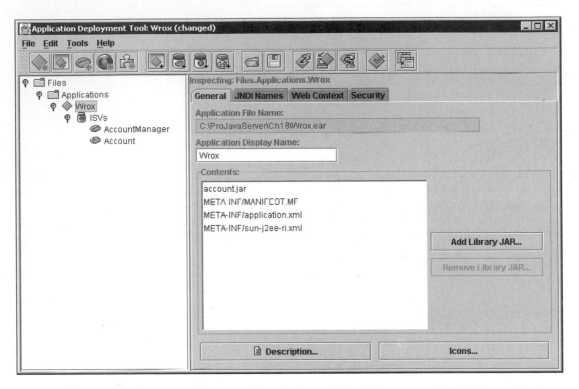

Next, we need to map the logical security roles, which we defined when we assembled the application, to actual users and groups in the underlying security system. We will use the simple security system that comes with the reference application server as a demonstration. Note that although this security system is included with the Reference Implementation, it is in no way part of the J2EE platform. The only requirement that applies to a J2EE server or EJB container is that they map to some security system – the Reference Implementation includes this simple security system in order to fulfill this requirement. (Actually, there are two security systems that come with the J2EE platform; along with the simple security system we will use, the other is a certificate-based system for browser clients using the HTTPS protocol.)

Select the Security tab for our application. This tab is used for mapping logical roles (such as UnmediatedAccess, Manager, and Teller) to the actual users and groups of the security system (such as WebGroup and ATMGroup):

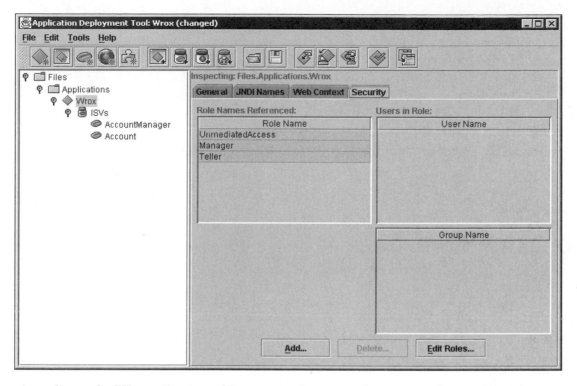

According to the EJB specification, adding users and groups to the operational environment is a system administrator's task. However, to allow the deployer to select some from a list, we'll put on our system administrator's hat and briefly look at how they are added using the RI.

The J2EE server allows us to add and subtract users and groups using a command-line tool called `realmtool`. We will add four groups: `TellerGroup`, `ATMGroup`, `ManagerGroup`, and `WebGroup`. Each group has one user: `SampleTeller`, `SampleATMUser`, `SampleManager`, and `SampleWebUser` respectively. These are the 'real' security groups that we map to the abstract roles in the banking application.

To create the required groups and users we run the following command, using the `realmtool` utility located in the `%J2EE_HOME%\bin` directory:

```
realmtool -addGroup TellerGroup
realmtool -addGroup ATMGroup
realmtool -addGroup ManagerGroup
realmtool -addGroup WebGroup
realmtool -add SampleTeller password1 TellerGroup
realmtool -add SampleATMUser password2 ATMGroup
realmtool -add SampleManager password3 ManagerGroup
realmtool -add SampleWebUser password4 WebGroup
```

Restart the J2EE server so these changes can take effect. Now we can put our deployer hats back on and connect the deployment tool to the J2EE server and return to the Security tab of our application. To map a user or group to a role, we can just select it from the available options using the Add... button. To map an actual user or group to a logical role in the J2EE reference implementation, we select the role and then click the Add... button:

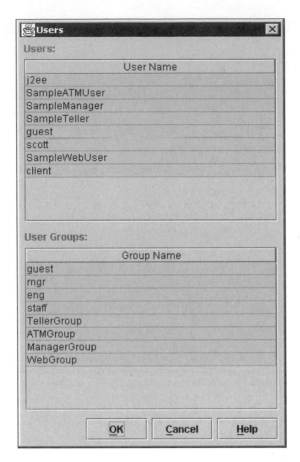

We can now select the groups and user names we just created with the `realmtool`. Add `SampleATMUser`, `SampleWebUser`, `WebGroup`, and `ATMGroup` to the `UnmediatedAccess` role; `SampleManager` and `ManagerGroup` to the `Manager` role, and `SampleTeller` and `TellerGroup` to the `Teller` role:

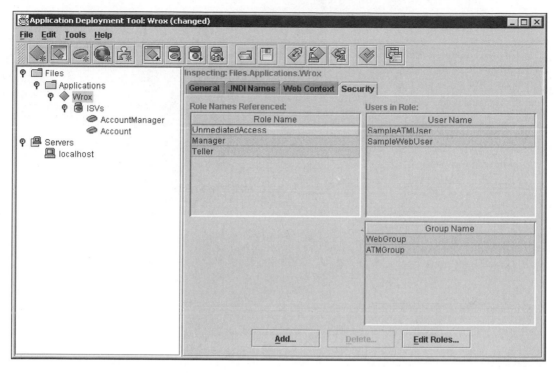

Now we need to map our logical database access to an actual database. We've only set up one database in our environment, the default Cloudscape database that comes with the J2EE RI, and which is bound to the JNDI name jdbc/Cloudscape.

In addition, we will need to map the properties of our Account entity beans' container managed persistence to actual fields in the database. We will accept a default mapping and allow the application server to create our database table when we deploy our bean. (Although this probably wouldn't be possible in a production environment it's a great convenience when we are experimenting with the platform.)

Select the Account bean, then select the Entity tag, and finally choose Deployment Settings. This screen allows us to map our entity's state to a particular database bound into the global JNDI namespace; it also allows us to specify mappings to a particular table or columns. Click Database Settings, enter jdbc/Cloudscape for the Database JNDI Name and click OK:

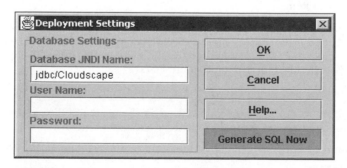

Then select Container Methods and then click Generate Default SQL:

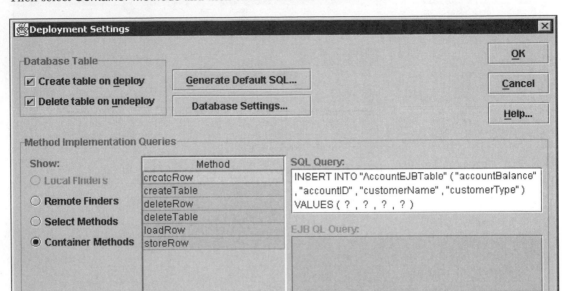

A commercial application server (or an open source server) would usually provide more sophisticated object/relational-mapping capabilities. The current limitations of the reference server in this regard are quite severe. The following information is taken from Sun's release notes:

- ❏ The entity bean class may be mapped to only one table in the database.

- ❏ A container-managed field may be mapped to only one column in the table.

- ❏ When the container loads the container-managed fields from the underlying database, it loads all of them. If there is a large amount of data loaded, this approach may be inefficient because a business method may not need all of the container-managed fields.

- ❏ If the container-managed field of multiple entity beans maps to the same data item in a database, and if these beans are invoked in the same transaction, they may see an inconsistent view of the data item.

- ❏ The deployment tool generates SQL statements for the ejbCreate(), ejbRemove(), ejbLoad(), and ejbStore() methods. We may modify only the table and column names of these SQL statements. We may not modify the number and order of the question marks, which are placeholders for the input parameters.

- ❏ We cannot call stored procedures in the generated SQL statements.

- ❏ In the CREATE TABLE SQL statement, we may change the SQL type of a table column, provided the SQL type is compatible with its corresponding instance variable.

- ❏ The table and column names in all of the SQL statements must be consistent.

- ❏ The generated SQL statements have been tested with Cloudscape, Oracle, and Microsoft SQL Server. You may need to edit the generated SQL statements to satisfy the requirements of other databases.

Finally, we need to map all the beans and references into the JNDI namespace. Note that the deployment tool will respect any links between beans that the application assembler declared using the `<ejb-link>` element.

In this example, the `AccountManager` bean is bound to the global namespace under the name `AccountManager`. The `Account` bean is bound to the global namespace under the name `Account`. It's convenient to use the same name for the bean and the namespace, but it isn't required at all. A client that isn't executing in a 'client container' will use this JNDI name to find the bean from the JNDI initial context. The `ejb/GenericAccount` reference that the `AccountManager` bean uses is automatically mapped to `Account`, because the `<ejb-link>` forces them to be the same. The three clients we have defined as J2EE application clients (that will execute in a client container) use the same sort of link that an EJB reference would. In their code, they look up `ejb/AccountAccess` from the initial context, which is bound here to the `AccountManager` bean:

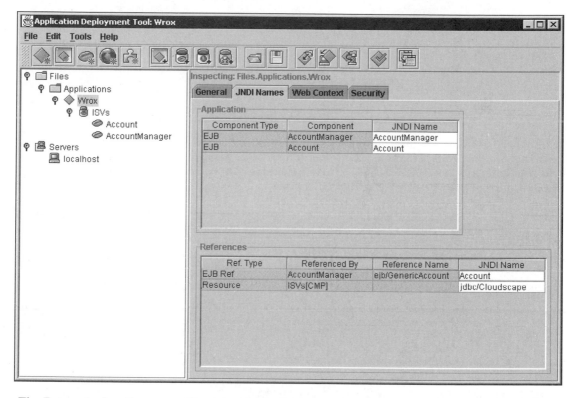

The Enterprise JavaBeans specification requires that an application server provide tools with which to do this mapping. It does not require that these tools have a GUI – they may simply be XML files that are edited by hand.

Now we can add the test clients to our application. For each client in turn, select File | New | Application Client and add the relevant class to the application:

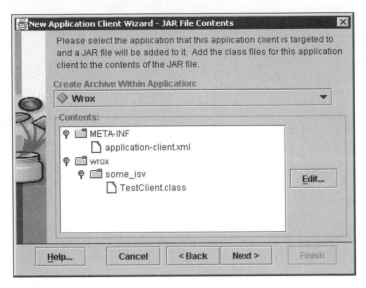

Click Next until we reach the Enterprise Beans References screen. Click Add and then enter ejb/AccountAccess as the value for Coded Name, wrox.some_isv.AccountManagerHome for Home Interface, and wrox.some_isv.AccountManager for Local/Remote Interface. Then select JNDI Name and enter AccountManager as the value:

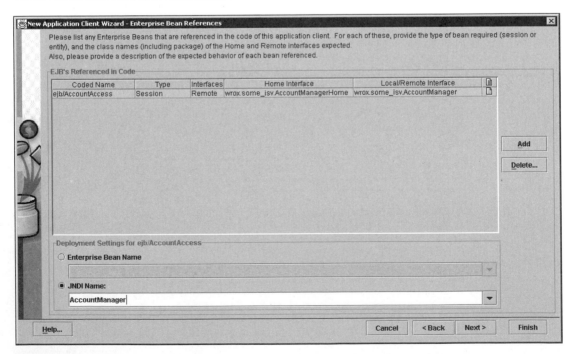

Click Finish, and repeat for all three clients. When we've finished our main screen looks like:

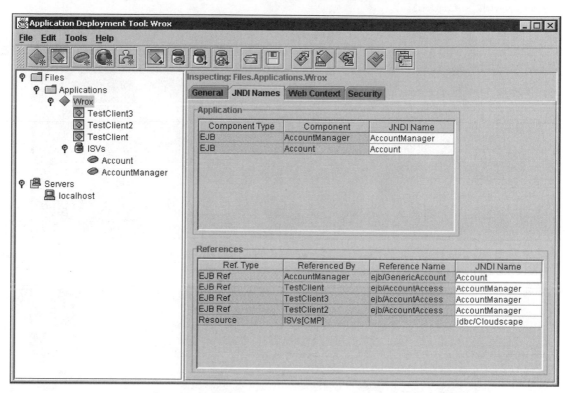

We have completed the configuration for this application so now is a good chance to deploy the application and run the clients. Make sure that the J2EE server is running and select Tools | Deploy, accept the defaults, and deploy the Wrox application to the server.

To run the clients we need to set the APPCPATH environment variable to reference account.jar, and then run the following commands from the directory in which we have stored Wrox.ear:

```
runclient -client Wrox.ear -name TestClient
runclient -client Wrox.ear -name TestClient2
runclient -client Wrox.ear -name TestClient3
```

We are prompted for a user name and password (if the -textauth flag is used with runclient we can enter the login information at the command prompt):

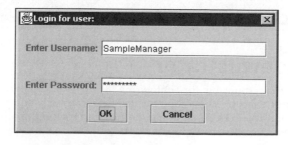

For `TestClient` we can use the user name of `SampleManager` and the password of `password3` that we set up with `realmtool`:

```
Command Prompt                                                    _ □ ×
Microsoft Windows 2000 [Version 5.00.2195]
(C) Copyright 1985-2000 Microsoft Corp.

C:\ProJavaServer\Ch18>set APPCPATH=C:\ProJavaServer\Ch18\ISV\account.jar

C:\ProJavaServer\Ch18>runclient -client Wrox.ear -name TestClient -textauth

Initiating login ...
Enter Username:SampleManager
Enter Password:password3
Binding name:`java:comp/env/ejb/AccountAccess`
create individual account
deposit
withdraw
create corporate account
Unbinding name:`java:comp/env/ejb/AccountAccess`
C:\ProJavaServer\Ch18>
```

Try using `SampleATMUser` with `TestClient2` and you'll find that the client doesn't execute correctly because the user doesn't have the correct security permissions. Try running it again, but this time as `SampleManager`:

```
Command Prompt                                                    _ □ ×
C:\ProJavaServer\Ch18>runclient -client Wrox.ear -name TestClient2 -textauth

Initiating login ...
Enter Username:SampleManager
Enter Password:password3
Binding name:`java:comp/env/ejb/AccountAccess`
create
Unbinding name:`java:comp/env/ejb/AccountAccess`
C:\ProJavaServer\Ch18>
```

Try running `TestClient3` as `SampleATMUser` and you'll find that although you can succeed in withdrawing a small amount of money, the application will not allow a large withdrawal. Again, if `TestClient3` is run as `SampleManager`, it executes successfully:

```
Command Prompt                                                    _ □ ×
C:\ProJavaServer\Ch18>runclient -client Wrox.ear -name TestClient3 -textauth

Initiating login ...
Enter Username:SampleManager
Enter Password:password3
Binding name:`java:comp/env/ejb/AccountAccess`
withdrawing small amount from individual account
withdrawing large amount from corporate account
withdrawing large amount from individual account
done
Unbinding name:`java:comp/env/ejb/AccountAccess`
C:\ProJavaServer\Ch18>
```

The System Administrator

The system administrator is responsible for configuring the application server, EJB container, and the environment in which they execute – including the database, network, and security systems. The system administrator is also responsible making sure that the EJB performs optimally depending on the resources the environment provides, including memory and network bandwidth.

The system administrator configures the application server environment. The RI, (although not intended to be a commercial system) provides a certain opportunity for configuration. In particular, the following items can be configured by manually editing configuration files that reside in the `config` directory (they are documented in `%J2EE_HOME%\doc\release\ConfigGuide.html`):

- ❑   JDBC Drivers
- ❑   Transactions
- ❑   Port Numbers
- ❑   Log Files
- ❑   Security
- ❑   Memory Threshold for Passivation
- ❑   HTTP Document Root

The JDBC driver we choose will depend on the database we use. For some databases, more than one JDBC driver may be available. We can also configure the user ID and password for the database connections (unless we obtain and authenticate a connection in code). A JDBC driver is added by configuring the `default.properties` property file and by adding the driver to the classpath of the server.

Distributed transactions can be configured to recover, or to not be recovered, in the event of a server crash. For EJBs with container-managed transactions, the period for transaction time-outs can be set in `default.properties`.

The J2EE Reference Implementation uses four TCP/IP ports:

- ❑   The EJB service uses one to download stub classes to the client
- ❑   The HTTP service uses one to service requests
- ❑   The HTTPS service uses another to service requests
- ❑   Finally, the Object Request Broker (ORB) underlying the JNDI name server uses a port

The port numbers used for downloading EJB stub classes can be set in `ejb.properties`. The other ports can be set in `web.properties`. The J2EE server also produces several log files and we can change the default directory or name for these files in `default.properties`.

We can configure several security options. The `keystore` password by default is "changeit". We can change this by editing the `keystore.password` entries in the `web.properties` file. When an authenticated web client makes a method call on an EJB, it gets a principal of a generic user. We can modify the name of the unauthenticated user by editing `auth.properties`. In the reference edition's deployment tool, methods are assigned a default role named ANYONE, which represents the set of all users and groups. We can change the name of this default role in `auth.properties`.

Passivation was discussed in Chapter 15 on session beans. By default, the server will passivate session beans when memory usage exceeds 128 megabytes. We can change this threshold in `default.properties`.

The J2EE specification includes servlets and JSP pages, and the reference implementation contains a web server with a default document root of `public_html`; we can change this in `web.properties`.

These configurations are specific to the J2EE reference implementation, and other application servers will have a different set of configurations. This configuration may be done in a property file, as with the reference implementation, or using a GUI tool. Regardless, you will always need to configure your chosen application server to fit your particular environment.

The system administrator must also monitor the execution environment using application-server-specific tools. The only tool that is mandated by the EJB specification is a log in which a record of system exceptions can be made. Logs are, in fact, the only monitoring tools provided by the reference implementation.

There is a new Java specification for application and network management called the Java Management Extensions (JMX, http://java.sun.com/products/JavaManagement/). This is a comprehensive framework that includes monitoring of properties, dynamic management services, support for various management protocols such as Simple Network Management Protocol (SNMP), and the ability to manage these via the Web. At least one of the open source EJB containers, JBoss, is being designed completely around JMX and it is quite likely that most Java-based application servers will standardize around these management extensions in the future. This will allow an EJB developer to make their application manageable in a standard and portable way. It will not, however, remove management tools from the arena of competition among application vendors and this will continue to be an area where vendors can differentiate themselves.

Container/Application-Server Vendor

This is the final role defined by the EJB specification. Although this book is not addressed to the provider of an application server, we still need to choose an application server/EJB container and because that EJB container will be responsible for all our system-level services, this choice will be very important to the success of our project. There are more than 35 products supporting EJB on the market, with varying capabilities and price, and choosing between them can be quite difficult.

Most vendors will provide an evaluation copy of their application server for a certain amount of time. We can develop a product on a free or inexpensive implementation and then deploy on a commercial product that meets our run-time needs. The reference implementation, the three opensource J2EE projects, and the Orion application server (which is free for development) are all possible choices for low-cost development. Of course, if you already know your target application server, you may want to develop on this platform to gain experience with it and to receive early warning about things that might not work.

There's no substitute for evaluating a product in your environment but this can be carried too far. It is unlikely that it would be worthwhile spending the time and money it would take to evaluate a dozen different products that support EJBs in a quest to find the perfect one for a particular situation.

We should understand what our requirements are before making a choice, and the following criteria will likely be important considerations:

❑ Do we need an ORB-based product to communicate with non-Java clients or for vendor interoperability?

❑ What object/relational-mapping capabilities do we require? Do we need (and does the vendor support) mapping an entity to multiple tables? What are the performance characteristics of a vendor's solution?

❑ If we aren't happy with a vendor's object/relational-mapping capabilities, is there a third-party product that will integrate with the application server?

❑ What kind of development and deployment tools does a vendor's application server support? Some products come from a background of providing productive toolsets.

- ❑ What are the performance characteristics of a particular product? Does it support clustering for performance and high availability?

- ❑ What version of the Enterprise JavaBeans specification does the application server support? Some well-known, and popular, products can lag behind.

- ❑ What platform(s) does the application server run on?

- ❑ How much does the product you are considering cost?

- ❑ What kind of support for the product is available?

In general, it's best to start experimenting with EJBs with a free container. The problem with free servers is that while they are good at providing technologies, they usually stop short when it comes down to delivering a true product (for example, none of them currently support clustering). After becoming familiar with EJBs, you should look into the commercial servers and try their (usually free) evaluation version. It is also important to note how advanced the server we are using is regarding the EJB version; any server that already offers an EJB 2.0 is likely to have a robust 1.1 implementation.

Chapter 23 takes a closer look at the questions and parameters to bear in mind when selecting a J2EE-compatible application server.

A Web Interface for the Manufacturing App

As a further example of how EJB components can be used to create a complete J2EE application, we're going to provide a web interface for the manufacturing application that we developed in Chapters 14 to 16. (Like most sample applications, it will be light on error handling and robust behavior, in order to keep things simple and clear.) The web application will present a menu of choices to the user that allows them to create a sample product, place a sample order, manage orders, or manufacture a product for an order. The menu screen will look like this:

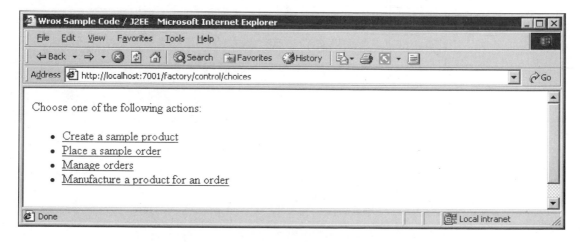

In Chapter 14, we discussed the model-view-controller architecture and how it applies to web applications. Recall the diagram that represented a possible model-view-controller design:

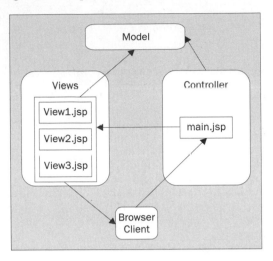

Our factory application will implement this design. The model will be our existing EJB façades (the ManageOrders and Manufacture session beans), plus a JavaBean class called ModelManager that will act as a proxy to the EJBs. The controller will be a JSP page, called main.jsp, which will forward processing to a JavaBean called RequestProcessor. RequestProcessor will update the model and then return the appropriate view to main.jsp. The main.jsp JSP will forward processing to the view that the RequestProcessor returned, which will also be a JSP component. Here is a diagram of the implementation:

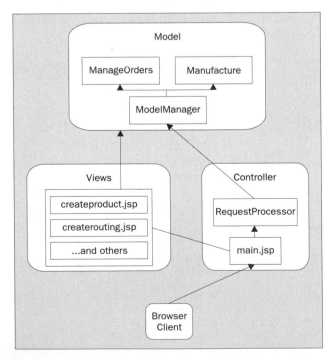

Let's look at the source code for these classes. (One thing to note is that we're not using `tablibs` in our JSP pages. Although they are more maintainable than large amounts of script, they involve some up-front work that would distract from the focus of this chapter.) First, `main.jsp`, in which the model and request processor are at `session` scope:

```jsp
<jsp:useBean
    id="modelManager"
    class="factory.ModelManager"
    scope="session" >
  <%
    modelManager.init(config.getServletContext(), session);
  %>
</jsp:useBean>

<jsp:useBean
    id="rp"
    class="factory.RequestProcessor"
    scope="session"
  >
  <%
    rp.init(config.getServletContext(), session);
  %>
</jsp:useBean>
```

We forward the request to the `RequestProcessor` class, which updates the model and returns the next view in the application sequence:

```jsp
<%
    String targetView = rp.processRequest(request);
```

Now we dispatch the request to the appropriate view:

```jsp
    getServletConfig().getServletContext().
      getRequestDispatcher(targetView).forward(request, response);
%>
```

Here is the code for the `RequestProcessor` class. For each request, it updates the model and decides on the next view in the sequence:

```java
package factory;

import java.text.DateFormat;
import java.util.Date;
import javax.servlet.ServletContext;
import javax.servlet.http.HttpServletRequest;
import javax.servlet.http.HttpServletResponse;
import javax.servlet.http.HttpSession;
import factory.manage_orders.NoSuchOrderException;
import factory.manage_orders.NoSuchProductException;
import factory.manage_orders.DuplicateOrderException;
import factory.manufacture.BadStatusException;
import factory.order.OrderNotCancelableException;

public class RequestProcessor {
  private ModelManager mm;
  private HttpSession session;
```

```
private ServletContext context;
private String stackURL;

private DateFormat dateFormat =
                 DateFormat.getDateInstance(DateFormat.SHORT);
```

In the `init()` method, we get a copy of the model proxy:

```
public void init(ServletContext context, HttpSession session) {
  this.session = session;
  this.context = context;
  mm = (ModelManager)session.getAttribute("modelManager");
}
```

The rest of the class is dedicated to processing the request. This may involve getting parameters from the request and updating the model accordingly, or setting attributes in the request that a subsequent view may examine. The screen flow is implicit in the code. A more complex application would need a more elegant mechanism; perhaps a generic finite state machine processor, with the state transitions defined in the database.

Although a bit intimidating, the following piece of code is a simple dispatcher process: it parses the URL that is being requested and returns a code corresponding to the action the user desires.

```
public String processRequest(HttpServletRequest req) {
  String selectedURL = req.getPathInfo();

  if ((selectedURL == null) || selectedURL.equals(ScreenNames.CHOICES)) {
    return ScreenNames.CHOICES_URL;
  } else if (selectedURL.equals(ScreenNames.CHOOSE_FOR_MANUFACTURE)) {
    String cellName = mm.getCurrentCell();
    if (cellName == null) {
      // requires "log on"
      stackURL = ScreenNames.CHOOSE_FOR_MANUFACTURE_URL;
      return ScreenNames.CHOOSE_CELL_URL;
    }
    return ScreenNames.CHOOSE_FOR_MANUFACTURE_URL;

  } else if (selectedURL.equals(ScreenNames.ORDER_CHOSEN)) {
    try {
      String salesDiv =
                   req.getParameter(ScreenNames.SALES_DIVISION_PARAM);
      String orderID = req.getParameter(ScreenNames.ORDER_NUMBER_PARAM);
      mm.selectForManufacture(Integer.parseInt(salesDiv),
        Integer.parseInt(orderID));
      if (mm.hasNextRouting()) {
        return ScreenNames.ROUTE_FOR_MANUFACTURE_URL;
      } else {
        return ScreenNames.SHIP_URL;
      }
    } catch (NoSuchOrderException nsoe) {
      req.setAttribute(ScreenNames.MESSAGE_ATTRIB,
        "The order does not exist in the system.");
      return ScreenNames.MESSAGE_URL;
    } catch (BadStatusException bse) {
      req.setAttribute(ScreenNames.MESSAGE_ATTRIB,
        "The order is not eligible for manufacture.");
      return ScreenNames.MESSAGE_URL;
    }
```

```
    } else if (selectedURL.equals(ScreenNames.CREATE_PRODUCT)) {
      return ScreenNames.CREATE_PRODUCT_URL;

    } else if (selectedURL.equals(ScreenNames.CELL_CHOSEN)) {
      String cellName = req.getParameter(ScreenNames.CELL_PARAM);
      mm.setCurrentCell(cellName);
      return stackURL;

    } else if (selectedURL.equals(ScreenNames.PRODUCT_CREATED)) {
      String prodID = req.getParameter(ScreenNames.PRODUCT_ID_PARAM);
      String prodName = req.getParameter(ScreenNames.PRODUCT_NAME_PARAM);
      mm.createProduct(prodID, prodName);
      return ScreenNames.CREATE_ROUTING_URL;

    } else if (selectedURL.equals(ScreenNames.CREATE_ROUTING)) {
      return ScreenNames.CREATE_ROUTING_URL;

    } else if (selectedURL.equals(ScreenNames.ROUTING_CREATED)) {
      String sequence =
              req.getParameter(ScreenNames.ROUTING_SEQUENCE_PARAM);
      String action =
              req.getParameter(ScreenNames.ROUTING_ACTION_STEP_PARAM);
      mm.addRouting(Integer.parseInt(sequence), action);
      return ScreenNames.CREATE_ROUTING_URL;

    } else if (selectedURL.equals(ScreenNames.CANCEL_ORDER)) {
      String salesDivision =
        req.getParameter(ScreenNames.SALES_DIVISION_PARAM);
      String orderNumber =
        req.getParameter(ScreenNames.ORDER_NUMBER_PARAM);
      String orderType = (req.getParameter(ScreenNames.ORDER_TYPE_PARAM));
      try {
        mm.cancelOrder(Integer.parseInt(salesDivision),
          Integer.parseInt(orderNumber));
        prepareManageOrdersRequest(orderType, req);
        return ScreenNames.MANAGE_ORDERS_URL;
      } catch (OrderNotCancelableException once) {
        req.setAttribute(ScreenNames.MESSAGE_ATTRIB,
          "This order is not cancelable.");
        return ScreenNames.MESSAGE_URL;
      } catch (NoSuchOrderException nsoe) {
        req.setAttribute(ScreenNames.MESSAGE_ATTRIB,
          "This order does not exist.");
        return ScreenNames.MESSAGE_URL;
      }

    } else if (selectedURL.equals(ScreenNames.MANAGE_ORDERS)) {
      String orderType = (req.getParameter(ScreenNames.ORDER_TYPE_PARAM));
      prepareManageOrdersRequest(orderType, req);
      return ScreenNames.MANAGE_ORDERS_URL;

    } else if (selectedURL.equals(ScreenNames.PLACE_ORDER)) {
      return ScreenNames.PLACE_ORDER_URL;

    } else if (selectedURL.equals(ScreenNames.ORDER_PLACED)) {
      try {
        String salesDiv =
        req.getParameter(ScreenNames.ORDER_SALES_DIV_PARAM);
        String orderNum = req.getParameter(ScreenNames.ORDER_NUM_PARAM);
        String productID = req.getParameter(ScreenNames.ORDER_PROD_PARAM);
```

```
            String dateDueString =
                       req.getParameter(ScreenNames.ORDER_DUE_DATE_PARAM);

            Date dateDue = dateFormat.parse(dateDueString);

            mm.placeOrder(Integer.parseInt(salesDiv),
                        Integer.parseInt(orderNum),
                        productID, dateDue);

            req.setAttribute(ScreenNames.MESSAGE_ATTRIB,
                        "Thank you for placing this order.");

        } catch (NoSuchProductException nspe) {
          req.setAttribute(ScreenNames.MESSAGE_ATTRIB,
            "There is no such product.");
        } catch (DuplicateOrderException doe) {
          req.setAttribute(ScreenNames.MESSAGE_ATTRIB,
            "There is already an order in that sales division
            with that number.");
        } catch (java.text.ParseException pe) {
          req.setAttribute(ScreenNames.MESSAGE_ATTRIB,
            "That is not a valid date.");
        }
        return ScreenNames.MESSAGE_URL;

    } else if (selectedURL.equals(ScreenNames.ROUTE_FOR_MANUFACTURE)) {
      if (mm.hasNextRouting())
        return ScreenNames.ROUTE_FOR_MANUFACTURE_URL;
      else
        return ScreenNames.SHIP_URL;

    } else if (selectedURL.equals(ScreenNames.SHIP_PRODUCT)) {
      String loadingDock =
                req.getParameter(ScreenNames.SHIP_LOADING_DOCK_PARAM);
      String carrier = req.getParameter(ScreenNames.SHIP_METHOD_PARAM);
      mm.shipProduct(carrier, Integer.parseInt(loadingDock));
      return ScreenNames.CHOICES_URL;

    } else {
      return ScreenNames.CHOICES_URL;
    }
}
```

The `prepareManageOrdersRequest()` method is just a helper method to abstract out some functionality that was used twice:

```
private void prepareManageOrdersRequest(String orderType,
                                        HttpServletRequest req) {
  if (orderType.equals(ScreenNames.ORDER_TYPE_OVERDUE)) {
    req.setAttribute(ScreenNames.ORDER_URL_ATTRIB,
      ScreenNames.ORDER_TYPE_OVERDUE);
    req.setAttribute(ScreenNames.ORDER_ALT_URL_ATTRIB,
      ScreenNames.ORDER_TYPE_OPEN);
    req.setAttribute(ScreenNames.ORDER_ALT_VIEW_ATTRIB,
      ScreenNames.ORDER_TYPE_OPEN_TEXT);
    req.setAttribute(ScreenNames.ORDER_VIEW_ATTRIB,
      ScreenNames.ORDER_TYPE_OVERDUE_TEXT);
```

```
      } else // orderType  is ScreenNames.ORDER_TYPE_OPEN {
        req.setAttribute(ScreenNames.ORDER_URL_ATTRIB,
          ScreenNames.ORDER_TYPE_OPEN);
        req.setAttribute(ScreenNames.ORDER_ALT_URL_ATTRIB,
          ScreenNames.ORDER_TYPE_OVERDUE);
        req.setAttribute(ScreenNames.ORDER_ALT_VIEW_ATTRIB,
          ScreenNames.ORDER_TYPE_OVERDUE_TEXT);
        req.setAttribute(ScreenNames.ORDER_VIEW_ATTRIB,
          ScreenNames.ORDER_TYPE_OPEN_TEXT);
      }
    }
  }
}
```

The constants that the application uses are defined in the ScreenNames interface:

```
package factory;

public interface ScreenNames {
  // paths
  public static final String CHOICES = "/choices";
  public static final String CREATE_PRODUCT = "/createproduct";
  public static final String CREATE_ROUTING = "/createrouting";
  public static final String MANAGE_ORDERS = "/manageorders";
  public static final String CHOOSE_FOR_MANUFACTURE = "/manufacturechoose";
  public static final String ROUTE_FOR_MANUFACTURE = "/manufactureroute";
  public static final String PLACE_ORDER = "/placeorder";
  public static final String ORDER_PLACED = "/order_placed";
  public static final String PRODUCT_CREATED = "/product_created";
  public static final String ROUTING_CREATED = "/routing_created";
  public static final String ORDER_CHOSEN = "/order_chosen";
  public static final String CANCEL_ORDER = "/cancelorder";
  public static final String CELL_CHOSEN = "/cell_chosen";
  public static final String SHIP_PRODUCT = "/ship_product";

  // jsps
  public static final String CHOICES_URL = "/choices.jsp";
  public static final String CREATE_PRODUCT_URL = "/createproduct.jsp";
  public static final String CREATE_ROUTING_URL = "/createrouting.jsp";
  public static final String MANAGE_ORDERS_URL = "/manageorders.jsp";
  public static final String CHOOSE_FOR_MANUFACTURE_URL =
                                      "/manufacturechoose.jsp";
  public static final String ROUTE_FOR_MANUFACTURE_URL =
                                      "/manufactureroute.jsp";
  public static final String PLACE_ORDER_URL = "/placeorder.jsp";
  public static final String MESSAGE_URL = "/message.jsp";
  public static final String CHOOSE_CELL_URL = "/cellid.jsp";
  public static final String SHIP_URL = "/ship.jsp";

  // parameters
  public static final String ORDER_TYPE_PARAM = "ordertype";
  public static final String ORDER_VIEW_ATTRIB = "order_view";
  public static final String ORDER_ALT_VIEW_ATTRIB = "order_alt_view";
  public static final String ORDER_ALT_URL_ATTRIB = "order_alt_url";
  public static final String ORDER_URL_ATTRIB = "order_url";
  public static final String ORDER_TYPE_OPEN = "openorders";
  public static final String ORDER_TYPE_OVERDUE = "overdueorders";
  public static final String ORDER_TYPE_OPEN_TEXT = "open orders";
```

```
    public static final String ORDER_TYPE_OVERDUE_TEXT = "overdue orders";

    public static final String SALES_DIVISION_PARAM = "salesdivision";
    public static final String ORDER_NUMBER_PARAM = "ordernumber";

    public static final String MESSAGE_ATTRIB = "message";

    public static final String PRODUCT_ID_PARAM = "product_id";
    public static final String PRODUCT_NAME_PARAM = "product_name";

    public static final String ROUTING_SEQUENCE_PARAM = "sequence";
    public static final String ROUTING_ACTION_STEP_PARAM = "routing";

    public static final String ORDER_SALES_DIV_PARAM = "sales_div";
    public static final String ORDER_NUM_PARAM = "order_num";
    public static final String ORDER_PROD_PARAM = "prod";
    public static final String ORDER_DUE_DATE_PARAM = "due_date";

    public static final String CELL_PARAM = "cell";

    public static final String SHIP_METHOD_PARAM = "shipping_company";
    public static final String SHIP_LOADING_DOCK_PARAM = "loading_dock";

}
```

The `ModelManager` class is the web-tier proxy for the EJB-tier model:

```
package factory;

import javax.ejb.EJBException;
import javax.naming.InitialContext;
import javax.naming.NamingException;
import javax.rmi.PortableRemoteObject;
import javax.servlet.http.HttpSession;
import javax.servlet.ServletContext;

import java.util.Date;
import java.util.Iterator;
import java.util.LinkedList;

import factory.manage_orders.DuplicateOrderException;
import factory.manage_orders.OpenOrderView;
import factory.manage_orders.OverdueOrderView;
import factory.manage_orders.ManageOrders;
import factory.manage_orders.ManageOrdersHome;
import factory.manage_orders.NoSuchOrderException;
import factory.manage_orders.NoSuchProductException;
import factory.manufacture.BadStatusException;
import factory.manufacture.Manufacture;
import factory.manufacture.ManufactureHome;

import factory.order.OrderNotCancelableException;

public class ModelManager {
  private ServletContext context;
  private HttpSession session;
```

The model manager maintains references to the two session bean façade objects in our application. Obviously we need to save a persistent Manufacture reference, because it is a stateful session bean. We could reacquire the ManageOrders interface every time we use it, which might add some overhead, but might also allow the EJB container to perform load balancing more effectively:

```java
private ManageOrders manageOrders;
private Manufacture manufacture;

private String currentCellID;
private String currentProductID;

public void init(ServletContext context, HttpSession session) {
  this.session = session;
  this.context = context;
  manageOrders = getManageOrdersEJB();
}

public void createProduct(String productID, String productName) {
  try {
    manageOrders.createProduct(productID, productName);
    currentProductID = productID;
  } catch (java.rmi.RemoteException re) {
    throw new EJBException(re);
  }
}

public String getCurrentCell() {
  return currentCellID;
}

public void setCurrentCell(String currentCell) {
  currentCellID = currentCell;
}

public String getCurrentProductID() {
  return currentProductID;
}

public void addRouting(int sequence, String action) {
  try {
    manageOrders.addRoutingInstruction(currentProductID,
                                       sequence, action);
  } catch (java.rmi.RemoteException re) {
    throw new EJBException(re);
  }
}

public void placeOrder(int salesDivision, int orderNumber,
                   String product, Date dateDue)
        throws NoSuchProductException, DuplicateOrderException {
  try {
    manageOrders.placeOrder(salesDivision, orderNumber, product, dateDue);
  } catch (java.rmi.RemoteException re) {
    throw new EJBException(re);
  }
}

public void cancelOrder(int salesDivision, int orderNumber)
  throws NoSuchOrderException, OrderNotCancelableException {
  try {
    manageOrders.cancelOrder(salesDivision, orderNumber);
```

```
      } catch (java.rmi.RemoteException re) {
        throw new EJBException(re);
      }
    }

    public synchronized Iterator getOrdersToManufacture() {
      try {
        LinkedList list = new LinkedList();
        manufacture = getManufactureEJB();
        OpenOrderView[] openOrders = manufacture.getOpenOrders();
        for (int iter=0; iter<openOrders.length; iter++) {
          list.add(new OrderView(openOrders[iter]));
        }
        return list.iterator();
      } catch (java.rmi.RemoteException re) {
        throw new EJBException(re);
      }
    }

    public synchronized void selectForManufacture(int salesDiv, int orderNum)
                            throws NoSuchOrderException, BadStatusException {
      try {
        manufacture.selectForManufacture(salesDiv, orderNum);
      } catch (java.rmi.RemoteException re) {
        throw new EJBException(re);
      }
    }

    public synchronized boolean hasNextRouting() {
      try {
        return manufacture.hasNextRouting();
      } catch (factory.manufacture.NoSelectionException nse) {
        throw new EJBException(nse);
      } catch (java.rmi.RemoteException re) {
        throw new EJBException(re);
      }
    }

    public synchronized String getNextRouting() {
      try {
        return manufacture.getNextRouting();
      } catch (factory.manufacture.NoSelectionException nse) {
        throw new EJBException(nse);
      } catch (java.rmi.RemoteException re) {
        throw new EJBException(re);
      }
    }

    public synchronized void shipProduct(String carrier, int loadingDock) {
      try {
        manufacture.ship(carrier, loadingDock);
      } catch (factory.manufacture.NoSelectionException nse) {
        throw new EJBException(nse);
      } catch (java.rmi.RemoteException re) {
        throw new EJBException(re);
      }
    }

    public Iterator getOrders(String type) {
      try {
        LinkedList list = new LinkedList();
```

```
        if (type.equals(ScreenNames.ORDER_TYPE_OPEN_TEXT)) {
          OpenOrderView[] openOrders = manageOrders.getSchedulableOrders();
          for (int iter=0; iter<openOrders.length; iter++) {
            list.add(new OrderView(openOrders[iter]));
          }
        } else if (type.equals(ScreenNames.ORDER_TYPE_OVERDUE_TEXT)) {
          OverdueOrderView[] overdueOrders = manageOrders.getOverdueOrders();
          for (int iter=0; iter<overdueOrders.length; iter++) {
            list.add(new OrderView(overdueOrders[iter]));
          }
        } else throw new IllegalStateException();
        return list.iterator();
      } catch (java.rmi.RemoteException re) {
        throw new EJBException(re);
      }
    }
```

Finally, we have some helper methods:

```
    private ManageOrders getManageOrdersEJB() {
      try {
        InitialContext initial = new InitialContext();
        Object objref = initial.lookup("java:comp/env/ejb/ManageOrders");
        ManageOrdersHome home =
                    (ManageOrdersHome) PortableRemoteObject.narrow(objref,
                                          ManageOrdersHome.class);
        return home.create();
      } catch (NamingException ne) {
        throw new EJBException(ne);
      } catch (java.rmi.RemoteException re) {
        throw new EJBException(re);
      } catch (javax.ejb.CreateException ce) {
        throw new EJBException(ce);
      }
    }

    private Manufacture getManufactureEJB() {
      try {
        InitialContext initial = new InitialContext();
        Object objref = initial.lookup("java:comp/env/ejb/Manufacture");
        ManufactureHome home = (ManufactureHome) PortableRemoteObject.narrow(
          objref, ManufactureHome.class);
        return home.create(currentCellID);
      } catch (NamingException ne) {
        throw new EJBException(ne);
      } catch (java.rmi.RemoteException re) {
        throw new EJBException(re);
      } catch (javax.ejb.CreateException ce) {
        throw new EJBException(ce);
      }
    }
  }
```

We use a view class to return information from the model to the various JSP views. The view is basically just a container for the information:

```
package factory;

import java.util.Date;
import factory.manage_orders.OpenOrderView;
```

```
import factory.manage_orders.OverdueOrderView;

public class OrderView {
  private int salesDivision;
  private int orderNumber;
  private String product;
  private String status;
  private Date dateDue;

  public OrderView(int salesDivision, int orderNumber,
                   String product, String status, Date dateDue) {
    this.salesDivision = salesDivision;
    this.orderNumber = orderNumber;
    this.product = product;
    this.status = status;
    this.dateDue = dateDue;
  }

  public OrderView(OpenOrderView view) {
    this(view.salesDivision, view.orderNumber, view.product,
         "open", view.dateDue);
  }

  public OrderView(OverdueOrderView view) {
    this(view.salesDivision, view.orderNumber, view.product,
      view.status, view.dateDue);
  }

  public OrderView() {}

  public int getSalesDivision() {
    return salesDivision;
  }

  public int getOrderNumber() {
    return orderNumber;
  }

  public String getProduct() {
    return product;
  }

  public String getStatus() {
    return status;
  }

  public Date getDateDue() {
    return dateDue;
  }
}
```

The 'main menu' view is provided by choices.jsp:

```
<html>
  <head>
    <title>Wrox Sample Code / J2EE</title>
    <meta http-equiv="Content-Type" content="text/html; charset=iso-8859-1">
  </head>

  <body bgcolor="#FFFFFF">
    <p>Choose one of the following actions:</p>
```

```
   <ul>
     <li><a href="createproduct">Create a sample product</a></li>
     <li><a href="placeorder">Place a sample order</a></li>
     <li><a href="manageorders?ordertype=openorders">Manage orders</a></li>
     <li><a href="manufacturechoose">
           Manufacture a product for an order
       </a></li>
   </ul>
   <p> </p>
 </body>
</html>
```

The 'create a product' view looks like this:

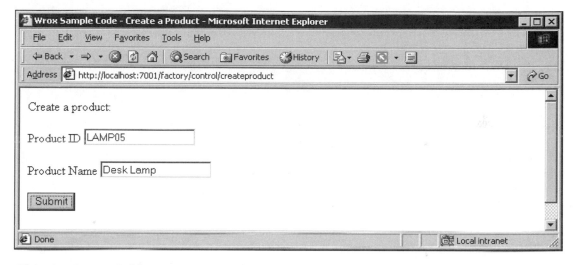

This view is provided by `createproduct.jsp`:

```
<html>
  <head>
    <title>Wrox Sample Code - Create a Product</title>
    <meta http-equiv="Content-Type" content="text/html; charset=iso-8859-1">
  </head>

  <body bgcolor="#FFFFFF">
    <p>Create a product:</p>
    <form method="post" action="product_created">
      <p>Product ID
        <input type="text" name="product_id">
      </p>
      <p>Product Name
        <input type="text" name="product_name">
      </p>
      <p>
        <input type="submit" name="Submit" value="Submit">
      </p>
    </form>
    <p>  </p>
  </body>
</html>
```

After adding a product we can add routing steps:

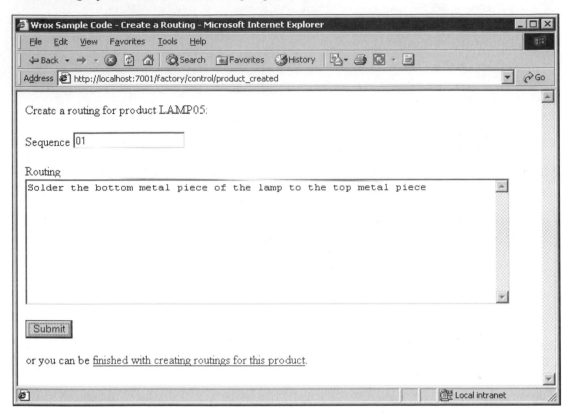

This view for adding the routing steps is provided by `createrouting.jsp`:

```jsp
<jsp:useBean
   id="modelManager"
   class="factory.ModelManager"
   scope="session"
 />

<html>
  <head>
     <title>Wrox Sample Code - Create a Routing</title>
     <meta http-equiv="Content-Type"
           content="text/html; charset=iso-8859-1">
  </head>

  <body bgcolor="#FFFFFF">
    <p>Create a routing for product
      <%=modelManager.getCurrentProductID()%>:
    </p>
    <form method="post" action="routing_created">
      <p>Sequence
        <input type="text" name="sequence">
      </p>
      <p>Routing
        <textarea name="routing" cols="75" rows="10"></textarea>
```

```
        </p>
        <p>
          <input type="submit" name="Submit" value="Submit">
        </p>
      </form>
      <p>or you can be <a href="choices">finished with creating
    routings for this product</a>.</p>
  </body>
</html>
```

You can place an order:

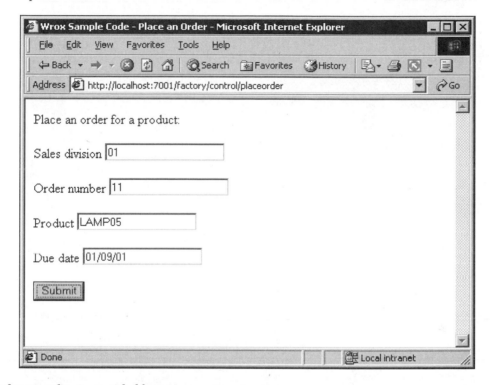

This functionality is provided by `placeorder.jsp`:

```
<html>
  <head>
    <title>Wrox Sample Code - Place an Order</title>
    <meta http-equiv="Content-Type" content="text/html; charset=iso-8859-1">
  </head>

  <body bgcolor="#FFFFFF">
    <p>Place an order for a product:</p>
      <form method="post" action="order_placed" name="PlaceOrder">
      <p>Sales division
        <input type="text" name="sales_div">
      </p>
      <p>Order number
        <input type="text" name="order_num">
```

```
    </p>
    <p>Product
      <input type="text" name="prod">
    </p>
    <p>Due date
      <input type="text" name="due_date">
    </p>
    <p>
      <input type="submit" name="Submit" value="Submit">
  </p>
    </form>
    <p> </p>
  </body>
</html>
```

After the order has been placed, a thank-you message is shown, provided by `message.jsp`

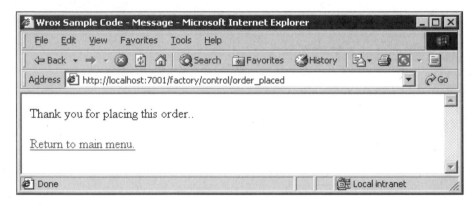

```
<html>
  <head>
    <title>Wrox Sample Code - Message</title>
    <meta http-equiv="Content-Type" content="text/html; charset=iso-8859-1">
  </head>

  <body bgcolor="#FFFFFF">
    <p>
      <%= request.getAttribute("message")%>.
    </p>

    <p><a href="choices">Return to main menu.</a></p>
  </body>
</html>
```

There are two versions of the order-management view, one for open orders and one for overdue orders. Any listed order can be canceled by clicking on a hyperlink. Here is the open order view:

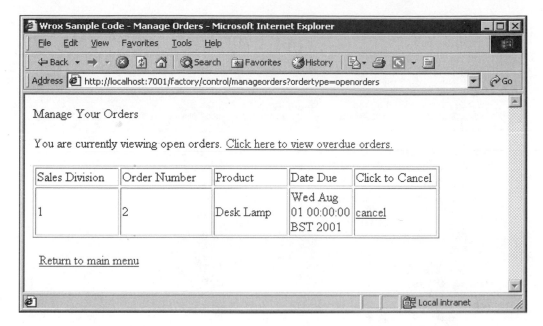

Here is the overdue order view:

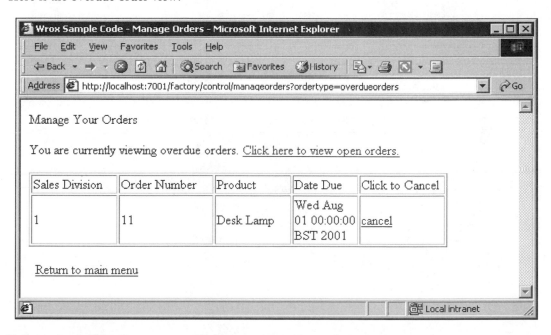

Both versions of the view are provided by manageorders.jsp:

```
<jsp:useBean
    id="modelManager"
    class="factory.ModelManager"
    scope="session"
```

```
    />
<%@ page import="java.util.Iterator" %>
<%@ page import="factory.OrderView" %>

<html>
  <head>
    <title>Wrox Sample Code - Manage Orders</title>
    <meta http-equiv="Content-Type" content="text/html; charset=iso-8859-1">
  </head>

  <body bgcolor="#FFFFFF">
    <p>Manage Your Orders</p>

    <p>You are currently viewing
      <%= request.getAttribute("order_view")%>.
      <a href="manageorders?ordertype=<%=
      request.getAttribute("order_alt_url")%>">
        Click here to view <%= request.getAttribute("order_alt_view") %>.
      </a>
    </p>

    <table width="87%" border="1">
      <tr>
        <td width="21%">Sales Division</td>
        <td width="23%">Order Number</td>
        <td width="19%">Product</td>
        <td width="16%">Date Due</td>
        <td width="21%">Click to Cancel</td>
      </tr>
      <%
        String orderView = (String) request.getAttribute("order_view");
        Iterator iter = modelManager.getOrders(orderView);
        while (iter.hasNext()) {
        OrderView view = (OrderView) iter.next();
      %>
      <tr>
        <td width="21%"><%=view.getSalesDivision()%></td>
        <td width="23%"><%=view.getOrderNumber()%></td>
        <td width="19%"><%=view.getProduct()%></td>
        <td width="16%"><%=view.getDateDue()%></td>
        <td width="21%"><a href="cancelorder?salesdivision=<%=view.
        getSalesDivision()%>&ordernumber=<%=view.getOrderNumber()
        %>&ordertype=<%=request.getAttribute("order_url")%>">cancel</a></td>
      </tr>
      <%}%>
    </table>
    <p>  <a href="choices">Return to main menu</a></p>
  </body>
</html>
```

An order can be chosen for manufacture in the following view:

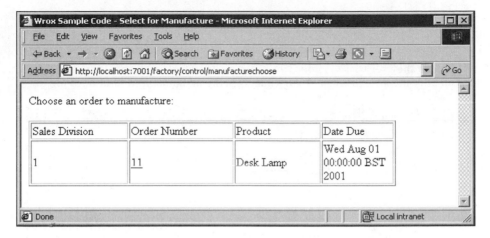

This view is provided by `manufacturechoose.jsp`:

```jsp
<jsp:useBean
   id="modelManager"
   class="factory.ModelManager"
   scope="session"
 />

<%@ page import="java.util.Iterator" %>
<%@ page import="factory.OrderView" %>

<html>
  <head>
    <title>Wrox Sample Code - Select for Manufacture</title>
    <meta http-equiv="Content-Type" content="text/html; charset=iso-8859-1">
  </head>

  <body bgcolor="#FFFFFF">
    <p>Choose an order to manufacture:</p>
    <table width="87%" border="1">
      <tr>
        <td width="21%">Sales Division</td>
        <td width="23%">Order Number</td>
        <td width="19%">Product</td>
        <td width="16%">Date Due</td>
      </tr>
      <%
        Iterator iter = modelManager.getOrdersToManufacture();
        while (iter.hasNext()) {
          OrderView view = (OrderView) iter.next();
      %>
      <tr>
        <td width="21%"><%=view.getSalesDivision()%></td>
        <td width="23%"><a href="order_chosen?salesdivision=
        <%=view.getSalesDivision()%>&ordernumber=<%=view.getOrderNumber()
        %>">
        <%=view.getOrderNumber()%></a></td>
        <td width="19%"><%=view.getProduct()%></td>
        <td width="16%"><%=view.getDateDue()%></td>
```

```
      </tr>
      <% }%>
    </table>
  </body>
</html>
```

The first time that the user tries to choose an order for manufacture, they will be asked to enter a cell ID number to identify the area in which the product is being manufactured (that is, to log in):

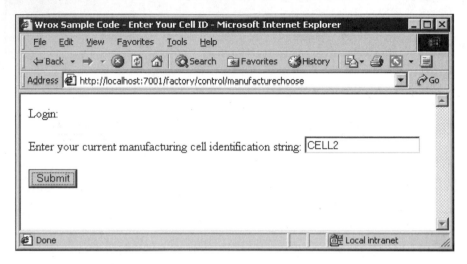

The following JSP page is used to identify the user. The user types in the name of their cell and when the form is submitted they are taken to the main servlets:

```
<html>
  <head>
    <title>Wrox Sample Code - Enter Your Cell ID</title>
    <meta http-equiv="Content-Type" content="text/html; charset=iso-8859-1">
  </head>

  <body bgcolor="#FFFFFF">
    <p>Login:</p>
    <form method="post" action="cell_chosen">
      <p>Enter your current manufacturing cell identification string:
        <input type="text" name="cell">
      </p>
      <p>
        <input type="submit" name="Submit" value="Submit">
      </p>
    </form>
    <p>  </p>
  </body>
</html>
```

Once an order has been chosen for manufacture, the routing steps are displayed one at a time:

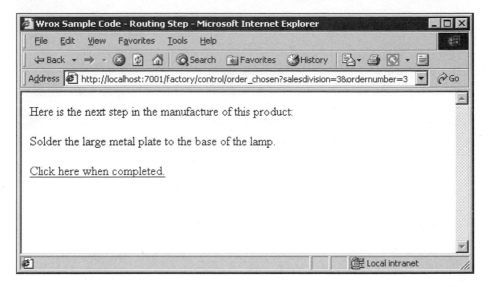

The view is provided by `manufactureroute.jsp`:

```
<jsp:useBean
    id="modelManager"
    class="factory.ModelManager"
    scope="session"
/>

<html>
  <head>
    <title>Wrox Sample Code - Routing Step</title>
    <meta http-equiv="Content-Type" content="text/html; charset=iso-8859-1">
  </head>

  <body bgcolor="#FFFFFF">
    <p>Here is the next step in the manufacture of this product:</p>
    <p><jsp:getProperty name="modelManager" property="nextRouting"/></p>
    <p><a href="manufactureroute">Click here when completed.</a></p>
    <p>  </p>
    <p>  </p>
  </body>
</html>
```

Finally, after all the routing steps have been displayed, the shipping information is entered:

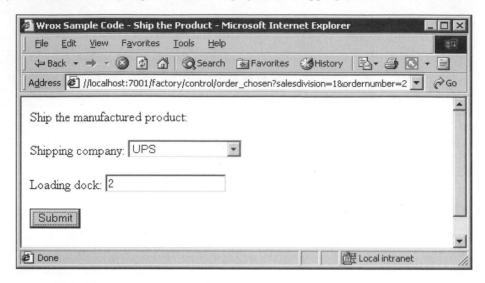

The view is provided by `ship.jsp`:

```html
<html>
  <head>
    <title>Wrox Sample Code - Ship the Product</title>
    <meta http-equiv="Content-Type" content="text/html; charset=iso-8859-1">
  </head>

  <body bgcolor="#FFFFFF">
    <p>Ship the manufactured product:</p>
    <form method="post" action="ship_product">
      <p>Shipping company:
        <select name="shipping_company">
          <option>UPS</option>
          <option>Federal Express</option>
          <option>US Postal Service</option>
          <option>Private Carrier</option>
        </select>
      </p>
      <p>Loading dock:
        <input type="text" name="loading_dock">
      </p>
      <p>
        <input type="submit" name="Submit" value="Submit">
      </p>
    </form>
    <p>  </p>
  </body>
</html>
```

We provide an HTML file that can be used as the welcome file for this application, called `index.html`:

```html
<html>
  <head>
    <title>Wrox Sample Code - Manufacturing Application</title>
  </head>
```

```
    <body text="#000000" bgcolor="#FFFFFF"
      link="#0000EE" vlink="#551A8B" alink="#FF0000">
      <center>
        <h1>Factory Demo for JSPs and EJBs</h1>
      </center>
      <center><hr width="100%"></center>

      <p>This web site provides a simple interface to the manufacturing
         example that we developed for the chapters on Enterprise JavaBeans
         in the Wrox Server Side Java book.</p>

      <p><a href="control/choices">See the demo...</a>

    </body>
  </html>
```

The welcome screen looks like this:

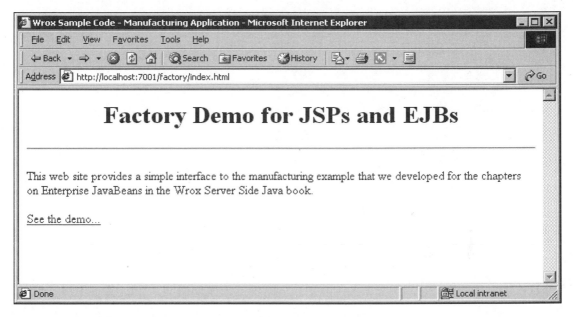

The web components are collected into a WAR. This web archive has a web.xml deployment descriptor, located in the WEB-INF directory, that specifies the welcome file, the servlet(s), the mapping of URLs to servlets, and the references to Enterprise JavaBeans. Here is the web.xml file:

```
<?xml version="1.0" encoding="UTF-8"?>

<!DOCTYPE web-app PUBLIC "-//Sun Microsystems, Inc.//DTD Web Application 2.3//EN"
                 "http://java.sun.com/dtd/application_1_3.dtd">

<web-app>
  <display-name>factoryWeb</display-name>
  <description>no description</description>
  <servlet>
    <servlet-name>entryPoint</servlet-name>
    <display-name>centralJsp</display-name>
    <description>no description</description>
```

```
      <jsp-file>main.jsp</jsp-file>
   </servlet>
   <servlet-mapping>
     <servlet-name>entryPoint</servlet-name>
     <url-pattern>/control/*</url-pattern>
   </servlet-mapping>
   <welcome-file-list>
     <welcome-file>/index.html</welcome-file>
   </welcome-file-list>

   <ejb ref>
      <ejb-ref-name>ejb/ManageOrders</ejb-ref-name>
      <ejb-ref-type>Session</ejb-ref-type>
      <home>factory.manage_orders.ManageOrdersHome</home>
      <remote>factory.manage_orders.ManageOrders</remote>
   </ejb-ref>

   <ejb-ref>
      <ejb-ref-name>ejb/Manufacture</ejb-ref-name>
      <ejb-ref-type>Session</ejb-ref-type>
      <home>factory.manufacture.ManufactureHome</home>
      <remote>factory.manfacture.Manufacture</remote>
   </ejb-ref>

</web-app>
```

To deploy this on WebLogic we also need a `weblogic.xml` file in the `WEB-INF` directory:

```
<!DOCTYPE weblogic-web-app PUBLIC "-//BEA
Systems, Inc.//DTD Web Application 6.0//EN"
"http://www.bea.com/servers/wls610/dtd/
weblogic-web-jar.dtd">

<weblogic-web-app>

<reference-descriptor>

  <ejb-reference-description>
    <ejb-ref-name>ejb/ManageOrders</ejb-ref-name>
    <jndi-name>ManageOrders</jndi-name>
  </ejb-reference-description>
  <ejb-reference-description>
    <ejb-ref-name>ejb/Manufacture</ejb-ref-name>
    <jndi-name>Manufacture</jndi-name>
  </ejb-reference-description>

</reference-descriptor>

</weblogic-web-app>
```

The directory structure of the web archive (`jsps.war`) is as follows:

```
cellid.jsp
choices.jsp
createproduct.jsp
createrouting.jsp
index.html
main.jsp
manageorders.jsp
```

```
manufacturechoose.jsp
manufactureroute.jsp
message.jsp
placeorder.jsp
ship.jsp
WEB-INF/
        web.xml
        weblogic.xml
        classes/
                factory/
                        ModelManager.class
                        OrderView.class
                        RequestProcessor.class
                        ScreenNames.class
```

This web archive is added to an EAR at the same level as the EJB archive. We must add references to both in the J2EE-standard file `application.xml`. Assuming that the EJB JAR (or directory, if your application server supports this format) is named `ejbs.jar`, and the web archive (or directory) is named `jsps.war` (note that these names are arbitrary), the `application.xml` file will look like this:

```
<?xml version="1.0" encoding="UTF-8"?>
<!DOCTYPE application PUBLIC '-//Sun Microsystems, Inc.//DTD J2EE Application
1.2//EN' 'http://java.sun.com/j2ee/dtds/application_1_2.dtd'>
<application>
  <display-name></display-name>
  <module>
    <ejb>ejbs.jar</ejb>
  </module>
  <module>
    <web>
      <web-uri>jsps.war</web-uri>
      <context-root>factory</context-root>
    </web>
  </module>
</application>
```

Once the EAR has been deployed, we can test it by navigating to
http://localhost:7001/factory/index.html.

Troubleshooting Tips

Writing enterprise software is a difficult process, regardless of the tools and techniques used. Sooner or later, we'll come across an application server we can't get to work, an EJB that won't deploy, or an application that just doesn't work as intended. Often it will take hours or even days to fix the problem. Here a few tips on how to approach some of the more common problems:

❑   Whether we are writing a complex application or a just single EJB component, we will need to repeatedly perform the **develop-assemble-deploy-test** cycle. This process can be slow and infuriating so it is best to automate it as far as possible. This automation can be achieved by using a good IDE or a tool such as Ant. Ant is the all-Java build system from the Jakarta Project (available from http://jakarta.apache.org/ant/index.html).

❑   Always read the documentation that comes with an application server. Although this might seem obvious, it's important to remember that application servers can have their own little quirks and bugs. A thorough read of the documentation can alert you to potential problems early on.

❑ Try running the application server in debug mode. Most application servers will have such a mode and if yours doesn't you can always run the application in one that does.

❑ However, it's good practice no to immediately turn to the debugger when we run into a problem. By attempting to work out the problem through inspection of the code, we can improve our overall understanding of the application and its code, which may well help to solve future problems more quickly.

❑ We should also bear in mind that debugging EJB components can be difficult with an application debugger. Stepping through the code can change the behavior of our components: from 'fixing' timing bugs, to causing a transaction to time out. Writing information to a log is often a less-invasive way to see what's happening.

❑ Some application servers provide proprietary optimizations, such as checking an isModified() method before synchronizing the state of an entity bean with the database. Try turning these optimizations off to see if you have made a mistake in their use.

❑ The log file of the application server can be a rich source of information. A clear error message or obvious stack trace can often point to the cause of a problem.

❑ As a rule, when we catch an unexpected exception, it is useful to print a stack trace before re-throwing the exception. This will cause an entry to be made in the application server's logs, which may prove useful in solving the problem.

❑ If an EJB JAR fails to deploy, we should take comfort as this type of issue is often much easier to solve than a run-time error. The application server should provide us with a useful error message that helps to identify the source of the problem. Some solutions to a few of the more common problem are to make sure our callback methods and CMP entity data are declared as public, and to make sure the deployment descriptor is in the META-INF directory.

❑ If all else fails, it's worth deploying the JAR on a different application server. Maybe the problem is the fault of the application server, rather than the code.

Summary

We saw in this chapter that there are five roles defined in the Enterprise JavaBeans specification, corresponding to activities that must be performed for the successful development, deployment, and maintenance of an EJB-based application:

❑ The bean developer provides the EJB components for an application. The application server provides many services and so the bean developer doesn't need to write code to support transactions, concurrency, security, communication, error handling beyond an application exception framework, load balancing, fail-over, or even persistence. In fact, the bean developer doesn't even need to be an expert in the target operational environment.

❑ The application assembler combines EJBs (from one or more bean developers) into a deployable application. The deployment descriptor that the bean developer provided is has application-level information added. At this stage, the application assembler may also add other types of application components, such as servlets, JSP pages, or client applications. The application assembler doesn't need to understand the implementation of the EJBs. They do however need to understand the contract that the home and remote interfaces represent, as well as the business logic that the EJB executes.

❑ Once the application is completed, it is deployed into the target environment by the deployer. The logical references used by the bean developer must be mapped to actual resources or identities. This step is specific to a particular application server. A deployer doesn't need to be a domain expert, but rather an expert in the environment in which the application will execute.

❑ The system administrator is responsible for configuring the application server and EJB container, as well as the environment in which they execute. The system administrator is also responsible for monitoring logs for any system or security problems.

❑ A third-party vendor will provide the application server/EJB container. The selection of an appropriate application server for development and deployment is important to the success of the application and must take into account various factors such as cost, support, and specification compliance, as well as any optional features that may be provided.

Remember that these roles are abstract concepts, and the personnel who perform them in a real application development team may perform multiple roles; or multiple people may be needed to perform a single role.

We also developed a complete J2EE application, finishing the manufacturing application we have been building since Chapter 14. We used two of the most important enterprise technologies (EJB and servlets) as well as some auxiliary ones as well (JSP, JNDI, and security).

In the next chapter we will be introduced to a new type of Enterprise JavaBean, the message-driven bean. As we learn how to create and use these new beans, we will also learn about the Java Messaging Service and how to create applications to use it.

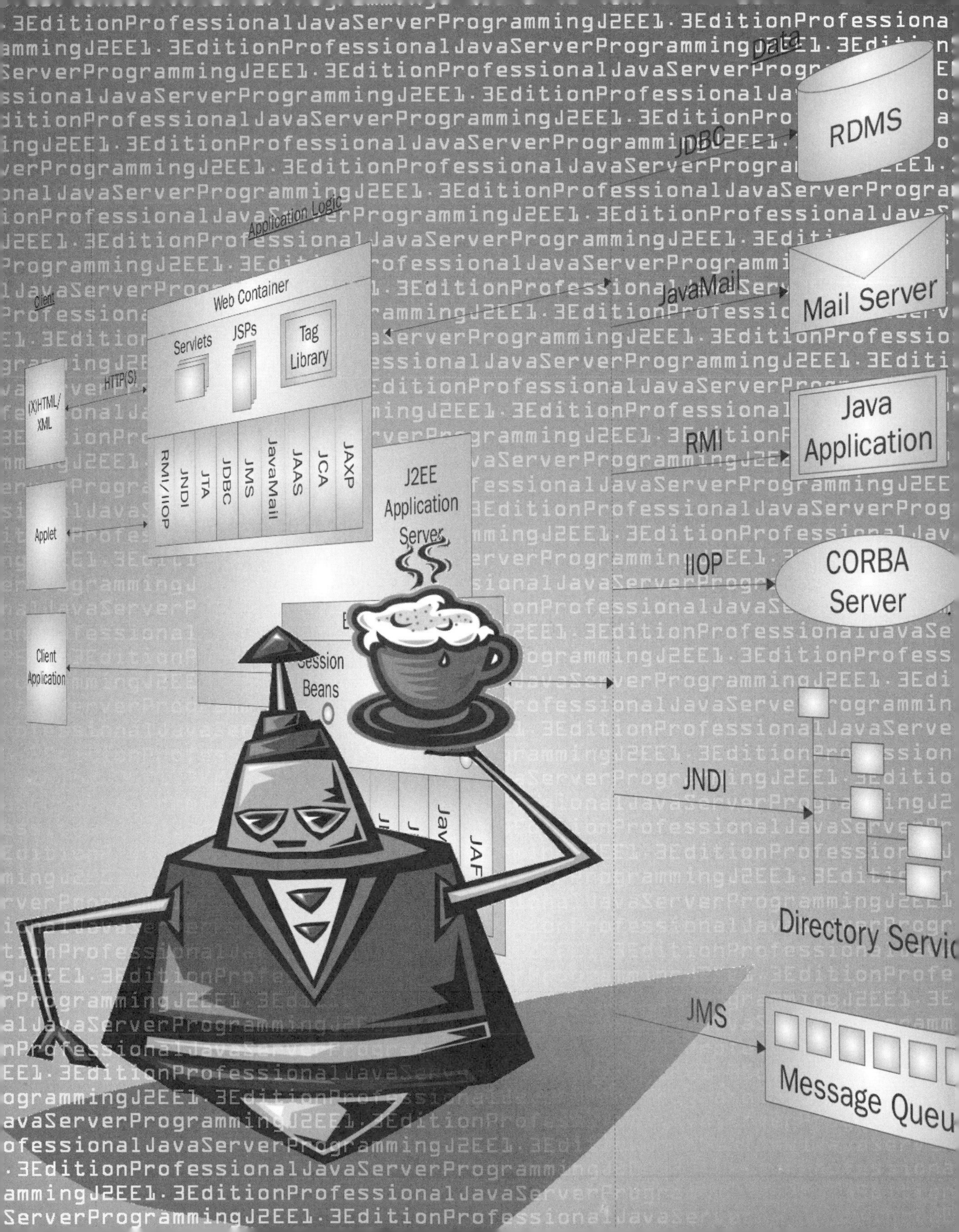

JMS and Message-Driven Beans

In this chapter, we'll be looking at the **Java Message Service (JMS)** and **Message-Driven Enterprise JavaBeans (MDB)**. JMS combines Java technology with enterprise messaging to form a robust tool for solving distributed enterprise computing problems and is accelerating the use of Java in new areas; much as the introduction of JDBC did in the early days of the language.

We'll begin by reviewing how messaging technology and **Message-Oriented Middleware (MOM)** has been used in the past, and how it is used today. This will allow us to see that, far from replacing these older messaging technologies, JMS will instead *increase* their use, as it becomes the industry standard for messaging APIs. We will then go on to look at how JMS can handle asynchronous calls between distributed applications.

After looking at several JMS examples, we will study message-driven beans, newly introduced in the EJB 2.0 specification. We will learn how to construct such a bean and understand how they can participate in transactions by using the **Java Transaction API (JTA)**.

The examples in this chapter were developed and tested with the J2EE Reference Implementation, version 1.3. However, they should work with the majority of standalone JMS implementations with little or no change to the code. Any functionality unique to the reference implementation will be indicated. Message-driven beans require a J2EE 1.3 implementation, as does JMS integration with the JTA.

In addition to the reference implementation, the JMS example code will work with little change on the following JMS implementations:

❑ **SwiftMQ** available from http://www.swiftmq.com/

❑ **SpiritWAVE** available from http://www.spirit-soft.com/

❑ **SonicMQ** available from http://www.sonicsoftware.com/

If possible, it is best to use the reference implementation from Sun, as you will be able to run the example code unchanged.

As developers, we have a large choice of JMS providers – there are well over a dozen industrial-strength implementations. We'll use independent and standalone implementations, rather than using JMS packaged as part of an Application Server. This excludes the likes of IBM, Oracle, SilverStream, Allaire, and BEA's JMS, but they are by no means lesser versions.

A Brief History of Messaging

Computers that are connected over a network have interfaces so that they can communicate with each other. Creating these interfaces involves many issues, including:

❑   How can we ensure a reliable connection between the sender and receiver?

❑   How do we package the message?

❑   What happens if the network fails?

Three of the early methods that were used to connect computers are:

❑   **RS232**
A standard serial connector, still used today to talk to modems. This was a very common way of providing message-based communication between any two systems in the 1970s. Most protocols using RS232 are synchronous; the receiver had to be actively receiving at the same time as the sender sent the message. This is obviously rather limiting, and leads to the communicating applications being **tightly-coupled**.

❑   **File Transfer Protocol (FTP)**
This simple protocol does not provide a means of synchronizing machine-based file transfers; the receiver never knows if or when the sender had finished sending. FTP was designed to transfer files, although there is no restriction as to the content of the files.

❑   **E-mail**
Like FTP, it is better suited to human interaction rather than machine-based message transfer, as there is no standard defined for acknowledging the receipt of an e-mail, so there is no standard way of knowing whether an e-mail has arrived. **Post Office Protocol (POP)** provides asynchronous messaging by separating the requirement that both machines need to be active during message transfer. This form of messaging is defined as **loosely-coupled**.

An application that required messaging technology could use different purchased protocol and messaging packages, each of which had their benefits and disadvantages. Often, a development team within a company would elect to implement a company-wide enterprise solution rather than purchase these technologies. More recently, the advent of **Message-Oriented Middleware (MOM)** technologies (such as IBM's MQSeries and TIBCO's Rendezvous) have allowed organizations to implement a secure, guaranteed message transport layer, on top of which, enterprise-wide system-integration strategies can be more easily based.

MQSeries and Rendezvous are the most commonly used technologies, allowing almost any system to connect and reliably communicate with virtually any other. Several others exist, often fitting into specific verticals and providing more features where needed.

Using these transport layer technologies as a foundation, many companies have produced so-called 'message broker' middleware systems (based on MOM), that provide a combination of data transformation and delivery services built on top of the lower-level messaging components. New Era of Networks (NEON), Mercator (formerly TSI), Vitria, SeeBeyond, BEA, and Candle are all involved in what has become a very crowded market.

Most organizations are now aware of the tremendous value of **Enterprise Application Integration (EAI)**, and in conjunction with the exponential growth in e-business, this has extended the fundamental importance of messaging technology beyond the boundaries of the enterprise, and out onto the Web.

> **Enterprise Application Integration (EAI) is the practice of connecting disparate distributed applications.**

Driven by this growth, many companies have moved into Java-based technologies. Although their products often keep their C or C++ based cores, Java has been adopted as the preferred language to create the messaging tools and libraries.

As part of the **Java Community Process (JCP)**, and in cooperation with the leading enterprise messaging vendors, Sun set out to provide a Java-based message API that could wrap up the generic message delivery semantics provided by the established MOM providers. The result was the Java Message Service API. First published in August 1998, it provides a framework that enables the development of portable message-based applications in Java. These applications, which are generally distributed, communicate asynchronously through messages.

Many companies are playing a role in the future development of the JMS API. An up-to-date list of licensed JMS vendors can be found at http://java.sun.com/products/jms/licensees.html. A similar list of (non-licensed) JMS vendors can be found at http://java.sun.com/products/jms/nonlicensedvendors.html.

The Java Message Service

> **The Java Message Service is a Java API that provides interfaces for applications to create, send, receive, and read messages using any implementation conforming to the API.**

This is possible as the management and low-level packaging of the messages is up to the implementation, which restricts interoperability to cooperating implementations only. The JMS API (like the JNDI and JDBC APIs) prescribes only interfaces. It is left to third parties to provide actual implementations.

The intention behind this approach was to provide a minimal API, which would maximize portability but still provide a powerful set of messaging features. Such an approach reduces the dependency on a specific implementation and lowers the learning curve needed to provide basic functionality.

As a direct side effect, this approach to the design of the JSM API tends to increase the competition between vendors to provide support, scalability, and performance rather than API or features – an advantage all round.

JMS enables a loosely-coupled communication framework that is **asynchronous** and **reliable**:

❑ **Asynchronous** means that the receiver does not have to actively request a message in order to receive it. This is comparable to how we don't go to FedEx every morning to check for packages; instead we just provide an address for delivery.

❑ **Reliable** means that we can be assured of a once, and once only, delivery of messages; this is essential in modern systems. If a non-reliable messaging system was used to order the weekly shopping and the Internet connection was lost during the order, we might assume the order didn't go through. If we placed the order a second time we might very well get two weeks worth of shopping.

Messaging systems can be divided into two general domains: **point-to-point** and **publish/subscribe**. Although JMS supports both domains, a standalone provider (that is, one that is not part of a J2EE application server) only has to implement one of them. However, most providers will support both domains. A J2EE provider must implement both domains in order to fulfill the J2EE specification.

Point-to-Point

Point-to-point (PTP) defines a messaging domain, based fundamentally on **queues**.

> **Queues are persistent (but sometimes in-memory) stores located at the JMS destination.**

Queues obey the **First In First Out (FIFO)** rule; that is, the messages leave the queue in the same order that they were sent. All messages are sent to a specific queue, where they remain until they expire or are consumed by a receiver. The sender does not need to have knowledge of the receiver, and the receiver does not need to know where the message was produced. However, due to the precise nature of point-to-point messaging it is common for both parties to be known in the application. This means that the message queue is always the common point of exchange.

The following figure illustrates the processes involved with sending messages between the producer and consumer via the message queue:

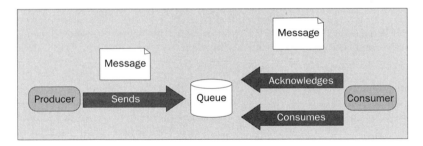

There are three parts here: the producer, queue, and consumer. Each can reside on a different machine or on the same machine. The queue itself runs as part of the JMS and could be implemented in Java, C, C++ or any other language.

There are three important points to keep in mind when thinking about point-to-point messaging in the JMS:

❑ Each message has a **single consumer**. There can be several consumers attached to a queue but one and only one consumer will consume an individual message. Several producers can send to the same queue, and there is no reason why a consumer cannot also consume messages from many queues.

❑ Sending and receiving messages is **not time dependent**. A producer can send a message at any time; the queued message can then be consumed at any later time before it expires. The only thing that must be running, for either side to work, is the message queue (which can be a 24/7 process). JMS clients (the producer and consumer) need not be running at the same time and the consumer does not have to have registered with a queue before the message is sent. Both producer and consumer do, however, need to agree upon a common queue.

❑ The consumer must **acknowledge receipt** of the message. This can either be hidden from the application and done automatically, be done manually after processing, or be done as part of a transaction. Once the consumer has acknowledged receipt, the message is removed from the queue.

Given a queue of messages, we can use several consumers (on different machines if we wish) to pick off messages from the queue. This is a simple form of load balancing, not at the JMS level but rather by using JMS for load balancing at the application level. Each new message will be consumed by one (and only one) of the consumers. If that consumer is busy processing a message, another consumer will take the next message, spreading the load across the machines.

Point-to-point messaging is typically used when each and every message results in an action that must be processed once, and only once. Examples include financial applications, ordering systems, and applications transmitting control orders (for example, sending a "shutdown" command).

Publish/Subscribe

A **publish/subscribe (pub/sub)** domain can have multiple recipients per message. This is not possible in a point-to-point domain and is the main difference between the two domains. There are no queues in the pub/sub domain, instead messages are **published** and sent to **topics**. Topics are similar to queues except that multiple consumers can share a single message. Like queues, topics are FIFO once the consumer has subscribed and, just as in the point-to-point domain, several producers may publish messages to a single topic. Topics retain messages as long as it takes to distribute them to consumers. Subscribers in a pub/sub domain are usually, but not strictly, anonymous. That is, they are unknown to the publisher:

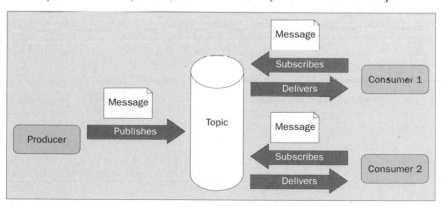

The important points to keep in mind about publish/subscribe domain are that:

❑ Each message can have multiple (zero, one, or more) consumers.

❑ Subscribers can only consume messages that are published after their subscription. This time dependency is unlike messages sent point-to-point. If in the above case for example, the producer publishes a new message both consumers 1 and 2 (assuming they have subscribed) will receive the message. If however consumer 3 comes along later and subscribes to the same topic it will not receive the message.

❏ Subscribers must, in general, remain active in order to consume messages. (The exception to this is with **durable** subscriptions, which provide the asynchronous flexibility of queues while retaining multiple consumers. We will look at these in more detail later on.)

A typical scenario for using a publish/subscribe domain is a client-server system where the server publishes data for subscribing clients. This means that the server can publish information to topics that clients can optionally subscribe to. The server application doesn't have to manage which clients want what information; everything is taken care of by the JMS. Essentially it is a distributed event-handling mechanism to which we subscribe rather than add ourselves as event listeners.

The JMS Architecture

There are six principal building blocks in the JMS architecture. They are used one-by-one to build the JMS application:

❏ **Administered Objects**
Objects that are normally maintained outside the program, often through some type of administration tool. These are generally factory objects that are unique to the JMS implementation. If the JMS API implementation is part of a J2EE implementation (as per the J2EE specifications) it is managed by using JNDI. Sun's J2EE 1.3 Reference Implementation provides an admin tool (`j2eeadmin`) that can be used to administer JMS.

❏ **Connections**
A generic term for the connections to the JMS provider's server, often a socket connection between the client and JMS server. Connections are obtained from a `ConnectionFactory` and can be used to create one or more sessions. There are two types of connection, the `QueueConnection` and the `TopicConnection`. As with all the JMS classes, these connections are in fact interfaces.

Once a connection has been made, it is started using the `start()` method. The service can also be stopped and restarted without losing the connection. Stopping a connection means that messages cannot be consumed, but it does not end the ability to handle produced messages. Connections use system resources and so they should be closed after use.

There is normally little reason to have more than one connection; however in certain cases a second may be required. For example, gateways can make a connection to one JMS server to consume messages and a make a second connection to produce messages to a different JMS server, providing a link between the two.

❏ **Sessions**
Provide the transactional context for grouping a set of messages. The `Session` object is used to create the message producers, consumers, and the messages themselves. Just as with the connections, sessions come in two flavors: `TopicSession` and `QueueSession`.

❏ **Message producers**
Message producers are created by the session. They send messages to the destination(s). Once again there are two types: the `QueueSender` for point-to-point and `TopicSender` for publish/subscribe. These senders each have a sender method: `send()` in the case of `QueueSender` and `publish()` in the case of `TopicSender`.

❏ **Message consumers**
These are at the other end of the JMS topic/queue from the producers and they receive the messages sent to a destination. Once again there are two versions: `QueueReceiver` and the `TopicSubscriber`. Message consumers start to receive messages as soon as the connection has been started (after `start()` has been called). Messages can be either consumed synchronously using `receive()` or asynchronously using the `onMessage()` method of `MessageListener`. Messages can also be selectively consumed using message `selectors`.

❑ **Messages**

These wrap the data, sent from the producers, that is to be received by consumers. Messages are made up of three parts; the **header** contains details like the destination, reply-to destination, expiration, priority and timestamp: the **properties** are an extension of the header and contain optional header fields as well as a set of application-specific name-value pairs accessible from the Message object; and the **message body** itself, which can be one of several sub-types:

❑ BytesMessage – raw bytes, most commonly used to talk to non-Java message consumers and producers.

❑ MapMessage – rather like a HashMap of key-value pairs. The key is a String object and the value can be any Java object.

❑ Message – an empty body, just the header and properties.

❑ ObjectMessage – serializable Java objects.

❑ StreamMessage – a sequential stream of Java primitives.

❑ TextMessage – a String message (often used to send XML messages).

Messages are created from the Session object and the type of message is defined in the creation method.

This figure summarizes the dependencies and relationships between the JMS building blocks:

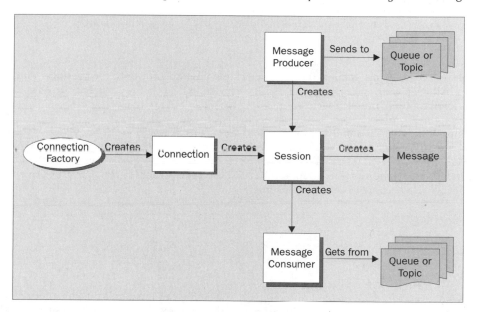

Point-to-Point Queue Example

It's about time we looked at some code. First we are going to look at point-to-point messaging, creating a message and then sending it. Then we can reuse much of the code, making only a few changes so that we can receive the message that we've sent.

Producing a Message

The class below, `WroxQueueSender`, simply follows the steps we discussed to send a simple message. Additionally, we'll add a `StringProperty` to the message to make the example more realistic:

```java
import javax.jms.*;
import javax.naming.*;

public class WroxQueueSender {
  public static void main(String[] args) {
    Queue queue = null;
    QueueConnectionFactory queueConnectionFactory = null;
    QueueConnection queueConnection = null;
```

We use the administered objects to get the connection factory. In this case we are using JNDI to get a reference to the JMS `QueueConnectionFactory`. The queue itself is also obtained from the naming service; so if the hard-coded queue does not exist an exception will be thrown:

```java
try {
  Context jndiContext = new InitialContext();
  queueConnectionFactory =(QueueConnectionFactory)jndiContext.lookup(
                          "QueueConnectionFactory");
  queue = (Queue) jndiContext.lookup("WroxOrders");
} catch (NamingException nEx) {
  System.out.println(nEx.toString()+"\nDoes the queue exist?");
  System.exit(1);
}
```

The code we have seen up to this point will be virtually identical for both the producer and the consumer. All we have done is to ask the naming service for the `QueueConnectionFactory`. (A JMS administration tool will usually set this.)

Next, we use the `QueueConnectionFactory` to create a `QueueConnection`, which is then used to create the session. The first parameter allows us to turn on transaction mode; if this is set to, `true` then `Session` methods like `commit()` and `rollback()` can be used to group messages into a transaction. The second parameter, `Session.AUTO_ACKNOWLEDGE` is irrelevant for the producer but will assume importance when we come to create a consumer:

```java
try {
  queueConnection = queueConnectionFactory.createQueueConnection();
  QueueSession queueSession = queueConnection.createQueueSession(
                              false,
                              Session.AUTO_ACKNOWLEDGE);
```

From this point on there are marked differences between the producer and the consumer classes. We now use the `QueueSession` to create the producer, the `QueueSender`, and the message itself (in this case a `TextMessage`):

```java
QueueSender queueSender = queueSession.createSender(queue);
TextMessage message = queueSession.createTextMessage();
```

The `Message` object (or in this case the `TextMessage` object) has a number of setter and getter methods. The majority of these methods can be ignored in this simple example but we use two in order to demonstrate the basics:

```
message.setText("Please send me the new J2EE book on my account");
message.setStringProperty("Client","Rachel Davies");
```

We then call the `send()` method to send the message to the queue we defined:

```
queueSender.send(message);
System.out.println("Your book has been ordered");
```

We catch any exceptions that might be thrown:

```
} catch (JMSException jmsEx) {
System.out.print("Something went wrong with your book order, ");
System.out.println("please try again...");
System.out.println("Exception: " + jmsEx.toString());
```

Finally, we close down the `QueueConnection` to release the resources:

```
} finally {
if (queueConnection != null) {
  try {
    queueConnection.close();
  } catch (Exception any) {}
 }
}
}
}
```

Now, to get this code working there are two things that need to be done. The order in which these are done will depend on the JMS implementation being used. We need to:

❑ Create the queue, which in the our example is called `WroxOrders`

❑ Start up the JMS services

❑ Run `WroxQueueSender`

We'll walk through how to do this using the J2EE Reference Implementation (version 1.3). Sun provides an administration tool called `j2eeadmin` (which is well documented in the accompanying Javadoc). This is a command-line tool that can be used to add, remove, or list drivers, and JMS destinations and factories. To add the JMS queue `WroxOrders` for use in the example above, execute the following command:

```
j2eeadmin -addjmsDestination WroxOrders queue
```

To check that it's been created use the `-listjmsDestination` command option by executing the following command:

```
j2eeadmin -listjmsDestination
```

You will see the following output, confirming that our queue has been created:

```
Command Prompt                                                              _ □ ×
C:\ProJavaServer\Ch19>j2eeadmin -addjmsDestination WroxOrders queue
C:\ProJavaServer\Ch19>j2eeadmin -listjmsDestination
jmsDestination
─────────────────
< JMS Destination : jms/Topic , javax.jms.Topic >
< JMS Destination : jms/Queue , javax.jms.Queue >
< JMS Destination : WroxOrders , javax.jms.Queue >
C:\ProJavaServer\Ch19>
```

We are now ready to start the J2EE server. So we can follow what is going on, we should use the
-verbose option. Execute the following command:

```
j2ee -verbose
```

You should notice that WroxOrders is included as a JMS destination:

```
Command Prompt - j2ee -verbose                                              _ □ ×
Starting JMS service ... Initialization complete - waiting for client requests
Binding : < JMS Destination : WroxOrders , javax.jms.Queue >
Binding : < JMS Destination : jms/Topic , javax.jms.Topic >
Binding : < JMS Destination : jms/Queue , javax.jms.Queue >
Binding : < JMS Cnx Factory : jms/QueueConnectionFactory , Queue , No properties
>
Binding : < JMS Cnx Factory : TopicConnectionFactory , Topic , No properties >
Binding : < JMS Cnx Factory : QueueConnectionFactory , Queue , No properties >
Binding : < JMS Cnx Factory : jms/TopicConnectionFactory , Topic , No properties
>
```

At this point we are almost ready to compile and run the WroxQueueSender. There is one further step
before we can do this, and that is to provide the J2EE server with a few parameters before it starts up the
JMS. These parameters could be configured in our program but to keep the code as portable as possible
they should be configured at run time. There are a few ways to do this but the simplest is to set the
jms.properties property on the command line. The default properties file for the J2EE Reference
Implementation can be found at %J2EE_HOME%\config\jms_client.properties and contains:

```
#comments jms properties file
com.sun.jms.internal.java.naming.factory.initial=com.sun.enterprise.naming.SerialI
nitContextFactory
com.sun.jms.internal.java.naming.provider.url=

com.sun.jms.client.transport_preference=IIOP

#Possible values are SEVERE,WARNING,INFO, FINE, FINER, FINEST.
com.sun.jms.default.loglevel=WARNING
```

Now, compile WroxQueueSender (don't forget to include j2ee.jar in the classpath):

```
javac -classpath .;%J2EE_HOME%\lib\j2ee.jar WroxQueueSender.java
```

Then run the program, setting the `jms.properties` property on the command line:

```
java -Djms.properties=%J2EE_HOME%\config\jms_client.properties
     -cp .;%J2EE_HOME%\lib\j2ee.jar; WroxQueueSender
```

You should see something like:

So, the book has been ordered but where has the message gone? Our message has been lost! At this point, we can stop the J2EE while we learn how to receive a message.

Consuming a Message Synchronously

We need to import `java.util.Date` but much of the code for our `WroxQueueReceiver` will be the same as for `WroxQueueSender`:

```java
import java.util.Date;
import javax.jms.*;
import javax.naming.*;
```

```java
public class WroxQueueReceiver {
    public static void main(String[] args) {
        Queue queue = null;
        QueueConnectionFactory queueConnectionFactory = null;
        QueueConnection queueConnection = null;
        try {
            Context jndiContext = new InitialContext();
            queueConnectionFactory =(QueueConnectionFactory)jndiContext.lookup(
                            "QueueConnectionFactory");
            queue = (Queue) jndiContext.lookup("WroxOrders");
        } catch (NamingException nEx) {
            System.out.println(nEx.toString()+"\nDoes the queue exist?");
            System.exit(1);
        }
```

We only need to discuss the `try` section that differs from the sender class. We will again use the `QueueConnectionFactory` to create the `QueueConnection`. The `QueueConnection` is then used to create a `QueueSession`. This time, `Session.AUTO_ACKNOWLEDGE` is used to configure the `QueueSession` to automatically send acknowledgements to consumed messages:

```java
        try {
            queueConnection = queueConnectionFactory.createQueueConnection();
            QueueSession queueSession = queueConnection.createQueueSession(
```

```
                                                false,
                                                Session.AUTO_ACKNOWLEDGE);
        QueueReceiver queueReceiver = queueSession.createReceiver(queue);
        queueConnection.start();
```

To consume or receive the message, all we have to do is to call the `receive()` method, which is overloaded. The version with no parameters blocks until a message is available. The other method, `receive(long)`, takes a timeout argument in milliseconds and returns `null` if the timeout expires or if the `QueueConnection` has not been started; it is this we will use. (There is also a `receiveNoWait()` method.)

If a message is received we read the `JMSTimestamp` and the `Client` property, which should have been set by the producer. The `JMSTimestamp` is a predefined field in the message header, and is set by the sender.

```
        TextMessage message = (TextMessage) queueReceiver.receive(1);

        if (message != null) {
          Date timeStamp = new Date(message.getJMSTimestamp());
          String client = message.getStringProperty("Client");
          System.out.println("New order from "+client+" at "+timeStamp);
          System.out.println("--> "+message.getText());
        } else {
          System.out.println("No new orders...");
        }
      } catch (JMSException jmsEx) {
        System.out.print("Something went wrong with your book order, ");
        System.out.println("please try again...");
        System.out.println("Exception: " + jmsEx.toString());
      } finally {
        if (queueConnection != null) {
          try {
            queueConnection.close();
          } catch (Exception any) {}
        }
      }
    }
  }
```

Follow these steps to run the example. Execute the following command to compile `WroxQueueReceiver`:

```
javac -classpath .;%J2EE_HOME%\lib\j2ee.jar WroxQueueReceiver.java
```

Restart the J2EE server:

```
j2ee -verbose
```

Then, run `WroxQueueReceiver`, including the same properties file as before:

```
java -Djms.properties=%J2EE_HOME%\config\jms_client.properties
     -cp .;%J2EE_HOME%\lib\j2ee.jar; WroxQueueReceiver
```

You should see something like:

```
Command Prompt                                                        _ □ ×
Microsoft Windows 2000 [Version 5.00.2195]
(C) Copyright 1985-2000 Microsoft Corp.

C:\ProJavaServer\Ch19>java -Djms.properties=%J2EE_HOME%\config\jms_client.proper
ties -cp .;%J2EE_HOME%\lib\j2ee.jar; WroxQueueReceiver
Java(TM) Message Service 1.0.2 Reference Implementation (build b13)
New order from Rachel Davies at Sun Aug 12 16:01:04 BST 2001
--> Please send me the new J2EE book on my account

C:\ProJavaServer\Ch19>
```

Even though we stopped the J2EE server the message was still available (it would even have been there if your computer had been rebooted). This shows that the J2EE destination queue is **persistent**. This is not always the case; the producer in our example used the default parameters when sending the message. To be portable, these parameters really need to be explicitly defined in the more thorough version of the send() method.

If we replace:

```
queueSender.send(message);
```

In WroxQueueSender with:

```
queueSender.send(message,
                 DeliveryMode.PERSISTENT,
                 Message.DEFAULT_PRIORITY,
                 60*1000L);
```

The same message will be sent but it will only last for a minute.

Consuming a Message Asynchronously

So far we have sent (or produced) a message, and then received (or consumed) it. We have covered ways in which we can use the receiver() method, but we would need to continually poll (loop), in order to consume messages as they come in. In an environment like JFC, asynchronous events like mouse movements and keyboard clicks are handled by **listeners**. The same is true if we want to asynchronously receive JMS messages; we need to use a MessageListener. Using a MessageListener means that the application can get on with other things while leaving the listener to handle incoming messages.

Let's create a new class WroxQueueReceiverA that can consume messages asynchronously. Much of the code will be the same as for WroxQueueReceiver:

```
import java.util.Date;
import javax.jms.*;
import javax.naming.*;

public class WroxQueueReceiverA {
    public static void main(String[] args) {
        Queue queue = null;
        QueueConnectionFactory queueConnectionFactory = null;
```

```
QueueConnection queueConnection = null;
try {
  Context jndiContext = new InitialContext();
  queueConnectionFactory =(QueueConnectionFactory)jndiContext.lookup(
                                 "QueueConnectionFactory");
  queue = (Queue) jndiContext.lookup("WroxOrders");
} catch (NamingException nEx) {
  System.out.println(nEx.toString()+"\nDoes the queue exist?");
  System.exit(1);
}
try {
  queueConnection = queueConnectionFactory.createQueueConnection();
  QueueSession queueSession = queueConnection.createQueueSession(
                                       false,
                                       Session.AUTO_ACKNOWLEDGE);
  QueueReceiver queueReceiver = queueSession.createReceiver(queue);
```

So far everything is the same, but now we need to set up the `MessageListener` before we start the `QueueConnection`. The reason for this is that as soon as the `QueueConnection` is started, the `MessageListener` could be called at any time:

```
WroxListener wroxListener = new WroxListener();
queueReceiver.setMessageListener(wroxListener);
queueConnection.start();
```

Now we can get on and do whatever we need to do in the application without worrying about the messages. For example, we could start displaying some message statistics, process the messages but assume that the `MessageListener` is writing them to a database or sorting the messages and re-sending them to other queues or topics.

The `MessageListener` could be some form of 'safe store', a term often used in MOM systems that require messages to be stored to disk. Safe stores are most commonly used in financial applications as, once on disk, the messages are safe from MOM crashes. Another frequent use is to insert the message into a database for later retrieval.

We're not going to do anything as complicated as this, instead we are just going to wait for about a minute to see if there are any further messages:

```
      System.out.println("Waiting 1 minute for messages...");
      for(int i = 60; i > 0; i--) {
        System.out.print("Count down... "+i+" \r");
        Thread.sleep(1000L);
      }
    } catch (JMSException jmsEx) {
      System.out.println("JMSException: " + jmsEx.toString());
    } catch(InterruptedException intEx ) {
      System.out.println("InterruptedException: " + intEx.toString());
    } finally {
      if (queueConnection != null) {
        try {
          queueConnection.close();
        } catch (Exception any) {}
      }
    }
  }
}
```

We need to catch any instance of `InterruptedException` that might be thrown because of our use of `Thread.sleep()`. Now let's look at our `MessageListener` class. This is the main message handling part of the application. In this example our `MessageListener` is called `WroxListener`. It implements the `MessageListener` interface, which requires us to provide an implementation for the method `onMessage()`:

```
import java.util.Date;
import javax.jms.*;

public class WroxListener implements MessageListener {

  public void onMessage(Message message) {
    try {
      if (message instanceof TextMessage ) {
        TextMessage textMessage = (TextMessage) message;
        Date timeStamp = new Date(textMessage.getJMSTimestamp());
        String client = textMessage.getStringProperty("Client");
        System.out.println("\nNew order from "+client+" at "+timeStamp);
        System.out.println("--> "+textMessage.getText());
```

We can also handle other message types if we have them:

```
      } else if (message instanceof ObjectMessage) {
        ObjectMessage objectMessage = (ObjectMessage) message;
      }
    } catch (JMSException jmsEx) {
      System.out.println("JMSException in onMessage(): " +
                          jmsEx.toString());
    } catch(Exception e) {
      System.out.println("Exception: " + e.toString());
    }
  }
}
```

It's that simple! This method is now called every time a message arrives at the `Queue` destination. Execute the following command to compile `WroxQueueReceiverA` and `WroxListener`:

```
javac -classpath .;%J2EE_HOME%\lib\j2ee.jar WroxQueueReceiverA.java
    WroxListener.java
```

Remember to start up the J2EE server, and then execute the following command to run the example (remembering to pass the properties file on the Java command line):

```
java -Djms.properties=%J2EE_HOME%\config\jms_client.properties -cp
    .;%J2EE_HOME%\lib\j2ee.jar; WroxQueueReceiverA
```

While this is running, you should run `WroxQueueSender` a few times to send some new messages. You should see something like:

```
Command Prompt                                                         _ □ ×
Microsoft Windows 2000 [Version 5.00.2195]
(C) Copyright 1985-2000 Microsoft Corp.

C:\ProJavaServer\Ch19>java -Djms.properties=%J2EE_HOME%\config\jms_client.proper
ties -cp .;%J2EE_HOME%\lib\j2ee.jar; WroxQueueReceiverA
Java(TM) Message Service 1.0.2 Reference Implementation (build b13)
Waiting 1 minute for messages...
Count down... 55
New order from Rachel Davies at Sun Aug 12 17:10:28 BST 2001
--> Please send me the new J2EE book on my account
Count down... 36
New order from Rachel Davies at Sun Aug 12 17:10:50 BST 2001
--> Please send me the new J2EE book on my account
Count down... 6
New order from Rachel Davies at Sun Aug 12 17:11:20 BST 2001
--> Please send me the new J2EE book on my account
Count down... 1
C:\ProJavaServer\Ch19>
```

You can see from this screenshot that WroxQueueReceiverA received three messages.

It is worth pointing out the ExceptionListener interface. This can be used to build exception handlers. Since we have essentially decoupled the receiver in the above example we have no way of handling exceptions; this can be achieved by implementing the ExceptionListener and providing an implementation for the onException(JMSException) method. A simple example would be to call printStackTrace() on the exception parameter.

Publish/Subscribe Topic Example

A program that uses topics and publish/subscribe is just as easy to implement as a program that uses queues and point-to-point. However there are more features available in this domain.

To create a program that uses topics and publish/subscribe, we can literally take the WroxQueueSender code above and replace "queue" with "topic", "sender" with "publisher", and "send" with "publish", rename the file, and compile it!

However, to make it a little more interesting, we'll add three messages rather than just one. Our application will announce its new books to subscribers; for example, wholesale buyers or individuals who have registered an interest in particular types of books. We'll assume the following books have just been published:

❑   Professional J2EE Java Server Programming

❑   Java XML Programmers Reference

❑   Professional ASP.NET

Each book could have properties such as subject coverage, languages, authors, ISBN number, and price but only some of these properties have been implemented in our example code. The code for this class, WroxTopicPublisher, is very similar to that for WroxQueueSender. As usual, the new code is highlighted:

```
import javax.jms.*;
import javax.naming.*;

public class WroxTopicPublisher {
  public static void main(String[] args) {
    Topic topic = null;
```

```
      TopicConnectionFactory topicConnectionFactory = null;
      TopicConnection topicConnection = null;

    try {
      Context jndiContext = new InitialContext();
      topicConnectionFactory = (TopicConnectionFactory)
          jndiContext.lookup("TopicConnectionFactory");
      topic = (Topic) jndiContext.lookup("WroxPublications");
    } catch (NamingException nEx) {
      System.out.println(nEx.toString()+"\nDoes the topic exist?");
      System.exit(1);
    }
    try {
      topicConnection = topicConnectionFactory.createTopicConnection();
      TopicSession topicSession = topicConnection.createTopicSession(
                                        false,
                                        Session.AUTO_ACKNOWLEDGE);
      TopicPublisher topicPublisher = topicSession.createPublisher(topic);

      TextMessage message1 = topicSession.createTextMessage();
      TextMessage message2 = topicSession.createTextMessage();
      TextMessage message3 = topicSession.createTextMessage();

      message1.setText("The new Pro J2EE book is now out");
      message1.setStringProperty("MetaData","Java,J2EE,EJB,JMS");
      message1.setStringProperty("Languages","English");

      message2.setText("The new Java XML book is now out");
      message2.setStringProperty("MetaData","Java,XML");
      message2.setStringProperty("Languages","English");

      message3.setText("The new Pro ASP.NET book is out");
      message3.setStringProperty("MetaData","Microsoft,.NET,ASP");
      message3.setStringProperty("Languages","English,Deutsche,Alsacien");
```

The four parameters in the publish() method below are, the message, the delivery mode (either PERSISTENT or NON_PERSISTENT), the priority, and finally the length of time the message should live (in milliseconds):

```
      topicPublisher.publish(message1, DeliveryMode.PERSISTENT,
          Message.DEFAULT_PRIORITY, 7*24*3600*1000L);
      topicPublisher.publish(message2, DeliveryMode.PERSISTENT,
          Message.DEFAULT_PRIORITY, 7*24*3600*1000L);
      topicPublisher.publish(message3, DeliveryMode.PERSISTENT,
          Message.DEFAULT_PRIORITY, 365*24*3600*1000L);

      System.out.println("3 books have been published today.");
    } catch (JMSException jmsEx) {
      System.out.println("Sorry, something went wrong with publishing...");
      System.out.println("Exception: " + jmsEx.toString());
    } finally {
      if (topicConnection != null) {
        try {
          topicConnection.close();
        } catch (JMSException any) {}
      }
    }
  }
}
```

We need to create the topic in the J2EE, using the following command:

```
j2eeadmin -addjmsDestination WroxPublications topic
```

Then compile `WroxTopicPublisher` by executing the following command:

```
javac -classpath .;%J2EE_HOME%\lib\j2ee.jar WroxTopicPublisher.java
```

Finally, start up the J2EE server, and execute the following command to run `WroxTopicPublisher`:

```
java -Djms.properties=%J2EE_HOME%\config\jms_client.properties
    -cp .;%J2EE_HOME%\lib\j2ee.jar; WroxTopicPublisher
```

You should see something like:

```
Command Prompt                                                    _ □ X
Microsoft Windows 2000 [Version 5.00.2195]
(C) Copyright 1985-2000 Microsoft Corp.

C:\ProJavaServer\Ch19>java -Djms.properties=%J2EE_HOME%\config\jms_client.proper
ties -cp .;%J2EE_HOME%\lib\j2ee.jar; WroxTopicPublisher
Java(TM) Message Service 1.0.2 Reference Implementation (build b13)
3 books have been published today.

C:\ProJavaServer\Ch19>
```

Once again the three messages we've created and sent to the `WroxPublications` topic have disappeared into thin air because there is nothing actually subscribing to the topic (until, of course, we create and run `WroxTopicSubscriber`).

Although we specified `DeliveryMode.PERSISTENT`:

```
topicPublisher.publish(message1, DeliveryMode.PERSISTENT,
    Message.DEFAULT_PRIORITY, 7*24*3600*1000L);
topicPublisher.publish(message2, DeliveryMode.PERSISTENT,
    Message.DEFAULT_PRIORITY, 7*24*3600*1000L);
topicPublisher.publish(message3, DeliveryMode.PERSISTENT,
    Message.DEFAULT_PRIORITY, 365*24*3600*1000L);
```

the publish/subscribe mechanism will only persist or retain messages that have subscribers, so even messages that do not expire will disappear if sent to a topic with no subscribers.

The code to implement our topic subscriber is similar to that for `WroxQueueReceiverA`. Once again, we'll add a few more features, this time in order to demonstrate message selectors and durable subscriptions:

```
import java.util.*;
import javax.jms.*;
import javax.naming.*;

public class WroxTopicSubscriber {
  public static void main(String[] args) {
```

```
Topic topic = null;
TopicConnectionFactory topicConnectionFactory = null;
TopicConnection topicConnection = null;

try {
  Context jndiContext = new InitialContext();
  topicConnectionFactory = (TopicConnectionFactory)
      jndiContext.lookup("TopicConnectionFactory");
  topic = (Topic) jndiContext.lookup("WroxPublications");
} catch (NamingException nEx) {
  System.out.println(nEx.toString()+"\nDoes the topic exist?");
  System.exit(1);
}

try {
  topicConnection = topicConnectionFactory.createTopicConnection();
  TopicSession topicSession =
      topicConnection.createTopicSession(false,
                               Session.AUTO_ACKNOWLEDGE);
```

Everything until now has been the same, barring of course the topic/queue replacements. Next, we create four `TopicSubscribers`; the first is a **durable subscriber** (more about this later) that will listen for messages where the `MetaData` property contains the word J2EE. The second `TopicSubscriber` is set up to listen for books published in "Alsacien" (a German dialect spoken in eastern France). The third listens for any book with "Java" in it, and the last just listens for everything (the default):

```
TopicSubscriber topicSubscriberDurableJ2EE =
    topicSession.createDurableSubscriber(topic,
                                "Wrox",
                                "MetaData LIKE '%J2EE%'",
                                false);

TopicSubscriber topicSubscriberAlsacien =
    topicSession.createSubscriber(topic,
                                "Languages LIKE '%Alsacien%'",
                                false);

TopicSubscriber topicSubscriberJava =
    topicSession.createSubscriber(topic,
                                "MetaData LIKE '%Java%'",
                                false);

TopicSubscriber topicSubscriberAll =
    topicSession.createSubscriber(topic);
```

In case you are wondering what the last parameter is, the "noLocal" parameter allows messages from the local (its own) connection to be accepted or blocked, in this case `false` means that local messages are permitted.

Now we need to set up four separate listeners. The constructor of the listener class takes a `name` parameter to enable identification of a particular instance:

```
topicSubscriberDurableJ2EE.setMessageListener(
    new WroxTopicListener("Durable, J2EE" ));
topicSubscriberAlsacien.setMessageListener(
    new WroxTopicListener("alsacien"));
topicSubscriberJava.setMessageListener(new WroxTopicListener("Java"));
topicSubscriberAll.setMessageListener(new WroxTopicListener("All"));
```

```
        topicConnection.start();

        System.out.println("Waiting 1 minute for messages...");
        for (int i = 60; i > 0; i--) {
          System.out.print("Count down... "+i+" \r");
          Thread.sleep(1000L);
        }
      } catch (JMSException jmsEx) {
        System.out.println("Exception: " + jmsEx.toString());
      } catch(Exception lazy) {
        System.out.println("Exception: " + lazy.toString());
      } finally {
        if (topicConnection != null) {
          try {
            topicConnection.close();
          } catch (JMSException e) {}
        }
      }
    }
  }
}
```

We need to create our new listener, WroxTopicListener. The changes from WroxListener are highlighted:

```
import java.util.Date;
import javax.jms.*;

public class WroxTopicListener implements MessageListener {

  private String name;

  public WroxTopicListener(String name) {
    this.name = name;
    System.out.println(name+" MessageListener created");
  }

  public void onMessage(Message message) {
    try {
      TextMessage textMessage = (TextMessage) message;
      System.out.println(name + " --> " + textMessage.getText());
    } catch (JMSException jmsEx) {
      System.out.println("JMSException in onMessage(): " +
                          jmsEx.toString());
    } catch(Exception e) {
      System.out.println("Exception: " + e.toString());
    }
  }
}
```

There is one more thing we have to do before we can run this example. Durable subscribers need to have a **client ID** to identify them. The client ID is the subscriber's context across different sessions; remember that we might come back to a subscription we set up some time ago in a totally different session or application. We will look into durable subscriptions in more detail in a moment, but for now the clientId can be set programmatically by using:

```
javax.jms.Connection.setClientID("Wrox")
```

However, there are a number of conditions that make this programmatic approach prone to throwing exceptions. Generally, the most reliable way to do this is to use the `j2eeadmin` tool:

```
j2eeadmin -addjmsFactory TopicConnectionFactory topic -props clientId=Wrox
```

Run this command to set a `clientId` property to `Wrox`. This is set as a property of the `ConnectionFactory`. We are now ready to compile and run the consumer `WroxTopicSubscriber`. Execute the following command to compile both `WroxTopicSubscriber` and `WroxTopicListener`:

```
javac -classpath .;%J2EE_HOME%\lib\j2ee.jar WroxTopicSubscriber.java
        WroxTopicListener.java
```

Make sure the J2EE server is running and then run `WroxTopicSubscriber`:

```
java -Djms.properties=%J2EE_HOME%\config\jms_client.properties
        -cp .;%J2EE_HOME%\lib\j2ee.jar; WroxTopicSubscriber
```

You should see something like:

Nothing is received because the topic `WroxPublications`, has no subscribers at present. But if we re-run `WroxTopicPublisher`:

```
java -Djms.properties=%J2EE_HOME%\config\jms_client.properties
        -cp .;%J2EE_HOME%\lib\j2ee.jar; WroxTopicPublisher
```

and then run `WroxTopicSubscriber` again:

```
java -Djms.properties=%J2EE_HOME%\config\jms_client.properties
        -cp .;%J2EE_HOME%\lib\j2ee.jar; WroxTopicSubscriber
```

You should see something like:

```
Command Prompt - java -Djms.properties=C:\j2sdkee1.3\config\jms_client.properties -cp .;C:\j2sdke...
Microsoft Windows 2000 [Version 5.00.2195]
(C) Copyright 1985-2000 Microsoft Corp.

C:\ProJavaServer\Ch19>java -Djms.properties=%J2EE_HOME%\config\jms_client.proper
ties -cp .;%J2EE_HOME%\lib\j2ee.jar; WroxTopicSubscriber
Java(TM) Message Service 1.0.2 Reference Implementation (build b13)
Durable, J2EE MessageListener created
alsacien MessageListener created
Java MessageListener created
All MessageListener created
Waiting 1 minute for messages...
Durable, J2EE --> The new Pro J2EE book is now out
Count down... 37
```

The first time WroxTopicSubscriber was run, it subscribed to the WroxPublications topic indefinitely. What the durable subscriber does is set up a connection that remains in effect until we explicitly call the unsubscribe() method. This means that the JMS provider is responsible for storing and later forwarding missed and un-expired messages when the subscriber, identified by the same clientId, renews its connection.

As its functionality suggests, this is known as **store and forward** messaging, and, functionality-wise it is similar to the way queues work. Store and forward messaging is a vital part of today's messaging solutions, as the fact that messages get through regardless of connection durability provides a perfect basis for reliable B2B connectivity.

To unsubscribe from the durable connection we would have to first close the subscriber, like this:

```
topicSubscriberDurableJ2EE.close();
topicSession.unsubscribe("Wrox");
```

If we run the WroxTopicSubscriber and then WroxTopicPublisher we get the following results:

```
Command Prompt - java -Djms.properties=C:\j2sdkee1.3\config\jms_client.properties -cp .;C:\j2sdke...
C:\ProJavaServer\Ch19>java -Djms.properties=%J2EE_HOME%\config\jms_client.proper
ties -cp .;%J2EE_HOME%\lib\j2ee.jar; WroxTopicSubscriber
Java(TM) Message Service 1.0.2 Reference Implementation (build b13)
Durable, J2EE MessageListener created
alsacien MessageListener created
Java MessageListener created
All MessageListener created
Waiting 1 minute for messages...
Durable, J2EE --> The new Pro J2EE book is now out
Java --> The new Pro J2EE book is now out
All --> The new Pro J2EE book is now out
Java --> The new Java XML book is now out
All --> The new Java XML book is now out
alsacien --> The new Pro ASP.NET book is out
All --> The new Pro ASP.NET book is out
Count down... 41
```

The message order will be random because the messages are received asynchronously. We can see that, with the exception of the "All" WroxTopicListener, each listener received the messages they selectively subscribed to. It is clear that more than one WroxTopicListener subscriber received the messages.

To achieve the selectivity we used a **message selector**. These can be set up during the createSubscriber() method. Message selectors are extremely powerful and provide virtually limitless possibilities for selecting messages. The syntax is based on a subset of SQL-92. Essentially it uses everything that you would normally find after the "WHERE" statement in normal SQL-92. There are a few examples below:

```
Price < 50
Price BETWEEN 15 AND 50
Price < 50 OR (Price < 80 AND MetaData LIKE '%Java%')
Currency IN ('CAD', 'GBP', 'AUD', 'NZD', 'INR')
JMSPriority=9
Title NOT NULL
```

Not only can the user properties be used for selection, but some of the fixed properties of the message like the Priority can also be used. Others that can be used include: JMSDeliveryMode, JMSPriority, JMSMessageID, JMSTimestamp, JMSCorrelationID, and JMSType. Some of these can return null, so if we want to have reliable selection criteria we should use the IS NULL or NOT NULL operators.

Full details can be found in the Javadoc of the Message interface and section 3.8.1.1 of the JMS specification (see http://java.sun.com/products/jms/docs.html).

The JMS API

The JMS interfaces are part of the javax.jms package. Here, we present some of the more complex, unusual, or comprehensive methods of the interfaces. The majority of missing interfaces, and some of the missing methods, are the XA (transactional) ones. These are generally XA versions of the standard (non-XA) interfaces or methods and they are used when including JMS transactions in a Java Transaction Service (JTS) transaction. The JMS provider exposes its JTS support using a JMS XAConnectionFactory, which is used by an application server uses to create an XASession.

Interface	Description
BytesMessage	Used to send a message containing a stream of uninterpreted bytes.
Connection	A client's active connection to its JMS provider; it includes the following methods: void setClientID(String clientID), sets the client ID for the connection. The preferred way of setting the client ID is to configure the ConnectionFactory using the JMS administration tools provided. If the client ID was set by the administration tool then calling this will throw an IllegalStateException. void start(), start or restart the connection's delivery of messages. void stop(), temporarily stop the connection's message delivery; however, blocks until receives and/or message listeners in progress have completed. Stopping a session has no affect on its ability to send messages and calling start() again will restart it.

Table continued on following page

Interface	Description
Connection Factory	Encapsulates a set of connection configuration parameters that has been defined by an administrator.
Connection MetaData	Provides information describing the `Connection`.
DeliveryMode	Delivery modes supported by JMS, quite simply `PERSISTENT` and `NON_PERSISTENT`. The delivery mode only covers the transport of the message to its destination.
Destination	Encapsulates provider-specific addresses since JMS does not define a standard address syntax, Although a standard address syntax was considered, it was decided that the differences in address semantics between existing MOM products were too wide to bridge with a single syntax.
Exception Listener	If a JMS provider detects a serious problem with a `Connection` it will inform the `Connection`'s `ExceptionListener`, if one has been registered.
MapMessage	Used to send a set of name-value pairs where names are strings and values are Java primitive types. The name-value entries can be accessed sequentially by enumerator or by name.
Message	The root interface of all JMS messages. `void setJMSCorrelationID(String correlationID)` sets the ID that could have been set by the JMS provider (if it supports message IDs) or by the JMS client using the set method. This is often used to correlate messages from application to application. You might use this to identify a response message to a previous request the request ID would be used in the response. The response could arrive some time after the request and the correlationID is a good way to tie them together. Application-specified values must not start with the `"ID:"` prefix; this is reserved for provider-generated message ID values.
Message Consumer	A client uses a message consumer to receive messages from a `Destination`; a message consumer is synchronous and provides methods like `receive()` and `receiveNoWait()`.
Message Listener	Used to receive asynchronously delivered messages, there is only one method defined by this interface, `onMessage()`.

Interface	Description
Message Producer	A client uses a message producer to send messages to a `Destination`. `void setDeliveryMode(int deliveryMode)` sets the delivery mode. Valid options are `DeliveryMode.NON_PERSISTENT` and `DeliveryMode.PERSISTENT`. `void setDisableMessageID(boolean value)` is for turning on/off the message IDs. It can be used to reduce the message size and sometimes increase performance. `void setDisableMessageTimestamp(boolean value)`, for turning on/off the message time stamps. It can be used to reduce the message size and sometimes increase performance. `void setPriority(int defaultPriority)` sets the default message priority. 0 is the lowest, 0-4 are gradients of 'normal' priority, 5-9 are considered 'expedited' priority. For normal priority use `Message.DEFAULT_PRIORITY`. `void setTimeToLive(long timeToLive)` sets the default time to live in milliseconds. Setting the time to live to zero (the default value) effectively means 'unlimited'
ObjectMessage	Used to send a message that contains a serializable Java object. If a collection of Java objects is needed we may use a Java collection class.
Queue	Encapsulates a provider-specific queue name.
QueueBrowser	A client uses a `QueueBrowser` to look at messages on a queue without removing them.
QueueConnection	An active connection to a JMS point-to-point provider.

QueueConnection Factory	A client uses a `QueueConnectionFactory` to create `QueueConnections` with a JMS PTP provider with the following methods:
	
	`QueueConnection createQueueConnection()`
	
	`QueueConnection createQueueConnection(String userName, String password)`

QueueReceiver	A client uses a `QueueReceiver` for receiving messages that have been delivered to a queue.
QueueSender	A client uses a `QueueSender` to send messages to a queue. `void send(Queue queue, Message message, int deliveryMode, int priority, long timeToLive)` sends a message to a queue for an unidentified message producer, specifying delivery mode, priority, and time to live.

Table continued on following page

Interface	Description
QueueSession	Provides methods for creating QueueReceivers, QueueSenders, QueueBrowsers, and TemporaryQueues.
	QueueBrowser createBrowser(Queue queue, String messageSelector) creates a QueueBrowser to browse, but not consume, messages in a queue with a specific message selector.
	Queue createQueue(String queueName) this is provided for rare cases where clients need to dynamically manipulate queue identity. Its use is not portable.
	TemporaryQueue createTemporaryQueue() creates a temporary queue whose lifetime is no longer than the QueueConnection.
Session	A single threaded context for producing and consuming messages.
	void recover(), stops message delivery in this session, and restarts sending messages with the oldest unacknowledged message.
	void setMessageListener(MessageListener listener); infrequently used, more often used by app servers.
StreamMessage	Used to send a stream of Java primitives.
TemporaryQueue	A unique Queue object created for the duration of a QueueConnection.
TemporaryTopic	A unique Topic object created for the duration of a TopicConnection.
TextMessage	Used to send a message containing a String.
Topic	Encapsulates a provider-specific topic name.
TopicConnection	An active connection to a JMS pub/sub provider.
TopicConnection Factory	A client uses a TopicConnectionFactory to create TopicConnections with a JMS pub/sub provider.
TopicPublisher	A client uses a TopicPublisher for publishing messages on a topic.
	void send(Topic topic, Message message, int deliveryMode, int priority, long timeToLive) sends a message to a topic for an unidentified message producer, specifying delivery mode, priority, and time to live.
TopicSession	Provides methods for creating TopicPublishers, TopicSubscribers, and TemporaryTopics.
	TopicSubscriber createSubscriber (Topic topic, String messageSelector, boolean noLocal) creates a TopicSubscriber for the specified topic using message selectors. The noLocal parameter allows messages from the local (its own) connection to be accepted or blocked.
	TopicSubscriber createDurableSubscriber (Topic topic, String name, String messageSelector, boolean noLocal) creates a durable TopicSubscriber for the specified topic. The supplied name must match the client ID of the connection (see example above). The noLocal parameter allows messages from the local (its own) connection to be accepted or blocked.

Interface	Description
Topic Subscriber	A client uses a `TopicSubscriber` for receiving messages that have been published to a topic.

Using Transactions with JMS

The simplest way of using the JMS with transactions is to use a transacted JMS session. This however restricts us to the JMS only. That is, we can group messages together and either commit them or roll them back. This is rather limiting. For example, we could not consume a message and then write it to the database in a single transaction; to do this requires the use of the Java Transaction Service (JTS).

Creating a transacted JMS session is quite simple; the first parameter in the `createXXXSession()` method can be used to set up a transacted session:

```
QueueSession queueSession = connection.createQueueSession(
                                    true
                                    Session.AUTO_ACKNOWLEDGE );

TopicSession topicSession = connection.createTopicSession(
                                    true,
                                    Session.AUTO_ACKNOWLEDGE );
```

Messages sent, or received, using this session are now automatically grouped in a transaction. It is important to note that there is no `begin()` method:

```
TextMessage textMessage1 = queueSession.createTextMessage();
TextMessage textMessage2 = queueSession.createTextMessage();
TextMessage textMessage3 = queueSession.createTextMessage();

textMessage1.setText("Send J2EE book to client 45827");
textMessage2.setText("Reduce J2EE book stock by 1"),
textMessage3.setText("Add $49.95 client 45827's bill");

queueSender.send(textMessage1);
queueSender.send(textMessage2);
queueSender.send(textMessage3);
```

These three messages above can now either be committed using `commit()`:

```
queueSender.commit();
```

or rolled back with `rollback()`:

```
queueSender.rollback();
```

`TextMessage1`, `TextMessage2`, and `TextMessage3` are now either sent (or received) as a single group.

We are not restricted to just sending or receiving. We can combine both and tie up receive and send actions in a single transaction. This is useful when we are forwarding messages in a gateway. Another use is to link queues with topics. For example, news comes in on the queue and is then 'broadcast' to the subscribers of a particular topic in a single transaction. If something were to go wrong with the publishing, the message would not be read from the queue (assuming the call to `rollback()` occurred).

Three Industrial-Strength JMS Implementations

There are well over a dozen good JMS implementations to choose from. Our choice of provider will depend largely on usage: some are free, some open source, some designed for performance and/or reliability, and some are sold as part of larger applications or application servers.

The three below are easy to download and get started (although SonicMQ and SpiritWAVE both require license keys in order to use them, which are provided quickly and hassle-free). They are all professional implementations, and all Java-based.

For any given scenario there is probably one JMS that is slightly faster, more reliable, or scales better than all the others. These are a few of the questions we need ask when choosing a JMS:

❑ Can the destination server be clustered?

❑ How does the clustering scale?

❑ What operating system does the provider recommend?

❑ Do you really need all the nice but non-standard features?

❑ If we are looking for speed, do we need point-to-point or pub/sub messaging?

❑ What happens to the performance when you start adding message selectors? What happens when you add a durable subscriber?

❑ If the loss of a message or delivery of a duplicate will cost you money, does the provider focus on reliability rather than speed?

> **It is important to test any JMS implementation in a real environment with conditions as close as possible to the intended solution.**

Let's now take a closer look at three of these JMS implementations.

SwiftMQ

SwiftMQ (http://www.swiftmq.com), in contrast to its competitors, is totally free. Not just free to develop with, but also free to deploy. The license reads as follows:

> *"SwiftMQ Binary Code License Agreement. SwiftMQ is completly (sic) FREE for private and commercial use as well as for deployment and for bundling with your commercial product or open source application server."*

The latest version, 2.01, fully implements point-to-point and pub/sub messaging to the JMS version 1.0.2 spec and comes with a very rich set of utilities, all easily configurable via properties files, a command-line interface (CLI), and the GUI using the SwiftMQ Explorer. The documentation, in Javadoc format, is easy to follow and very complete.

Also downloadable from the same site is the SMTP Mailer Extension, which provides an SMTP bridge that allows e-mails to be sent from JMS clients. For example:

```
QueueSender sender = session.createSender(mailQueue);
TextMessage msg = session.createTextMessage();
msg.setStringProperty("from","reader@work.com");
msg.setStringProperty("to","John@C24Solutions.com");
```

```
msg.setStringProperty("replyto","reader@home.com");
msg.setStringProperty("cc","Wayne.Meikle@C24Solutions.com");
msg.setStringProperty("subject","JMS");
msg.setText("This JMS API is great stuff! ");
sender.send(msg);
```

There is also a JMS bridge extension that provides bridging functionality between SwiftMQ and any foreign JMS 1.0.2-compliant systems.

SwiftMQ comes pre-configured with two queues, one topic, and a whole set of examples to get started with. From download, it can be up and running minutes after installation. Modifying the examples and supplied queues is the easiest way to get started from there. Most importantly, it's completely free!

SpiritWave

SpiritWave from SpiritSoft (http://www.spirit-soft.com) is one of the most fully featured implementations in terms of core implementation and extended features.

Fully JMS (1.0.2)-compliant, SpiritWAVE extends XA support, HTTP/Firewall tunneling and SSL support, hot failover, fault tolerance, and clustering. Another key feature is support for plug-and-play drivers and transformations for legacy messaging with, for example, Tibco Rendezvous 5.x, 6.x and ETX, IBM MQ Series, MSMQ, Talarian SmartSockets, and WebMethods ActiveWorks. It also integrates with several application servers and, interestingly, it has SpiritWave JMS adapters for Microsoft COM applications.

There are several extensions for the selector capabilities of the JMS. For example, you can make advanced selections based on the XML content in the message body. These powerful features allow, for example, message routing based on XML content, but this comes at the cost of portability across JMS implementations.

SpiritWave comes with an extensive set of examples, and the documentation is supplied in PDF format.

SonicMQ

SonicMQ from Sonic Software (http://www.sonicsoftware.com) is probably the best-known JMS implementation.

SonicMQ is also a full implementation of the JMS 1.0.2 spec with XA support. It has excellent documentation (in PDF format), and it also includes some instructive sample code. SonicMQ boasts built-in XML messaging, dynamic routing architecture (DRA), clustering, and full SSL and PKI support. SonicMQ can also be integrated with bridges, such as IBM MQ Series, and FTP and SMTP e-mail services.

Message-Driven Beans

After taking a look at some of the message-driven bean (MDB) API, we'll examine the lifecycle of an MDB and look at a simple example that demonstrates its use with EJB transactions.

Message-driven beans were introduced to the EJB specification in version 2.0; the aim was to provide a mechanism for handling asynchronous messaging in EJBs. This complements the existing Session and Entity beans available in EJB 1.0, 1.1, and 2.0.

> **The message-driven bean is essentially a message listener that can consume messages from a queue or a durable subscription through the J2EE container; the container invokes the bean as a result of the arrival of a JMS message.**

The client views the message-driven bean as a JMS consumer that implements business logic but can only communicate with the bean by sending it a message through the JMS. Message-driven beans can communicate with both session and entity beans to extend business logic or to provide some form of application persistence.

> **Message-driven beans are anonymous, have no conversational state with the client, and can be pooled like stateless session beans. Unlike the other types of EJB, message-driven beans have no home or remote interfaces. Because they lack these client-side interfaces, clients cannot interact with them; the bean is invoked by the arrival of a message.**

The EJB container performs the functions of resource pooling, security, and transaction management, and maintains the lifecycle of the message-driven beans. Message-driven beans are not ideal in situations that require multiple queues or topics to be serviced by a single JMS consumer. In this case, a better option would be to use several message-driven beans for each queue or to simply use 'standard' JMS consumers.

MDBs are also rather restricted in that the queue or topic is defined in the deployment descriptor at deployment time rather than at run time. Worse still, the message selectors are also defined in the deployment descriptor. This is one of the most powerful features of the JMS and it's a shame that it has to be set in stone in the deployment descriptor. There are ways around this in most application servers but if we use these options we are deviating from the J2EE/EJB specification and risk tying our application to a specific implementation.

Message-driven beans must implement `javax.jms.MessageListener` and `javax.ejb.MessageDrivenBean`. The body of the receiver is implemented in the `onMessage()` method of `MessageListener`. This must not throw JMS or application exceptions; instead they must be caught, and preferably handled. At the very least they must be re-thrown as an `EJBException`. A well-behaved MDB (like other EJBs) should not throw a `RuntimeException`.

`MessageDrivenBean` specifies just two methods:

- ❑   `void ejbRemove()` is invoked by the container just before the bean is removed

- ❑   `void setMessageDrivenContext(MessageDrivenContext ctx)` sets the context for the bean

Finally, the create and remove methods need to be defined. The relevant signatures are:

- ❑   `public void ejbCreate()`
  Where you should create the JMS connections if you intend to send messages from this bean

- ❑   `public void ejbRemove()`
  Where you should close any connections made in the `ejbCreate()` method

There are no other business methods in the MDB. Other methods can be defined to provide business functionality but they would normally only be called from `onMessage()` as this message is the only way to communicate with the bean.

Message-Driven Bean Lifecycle

The message-driven EJB starts with the invocation of the following methods:

1. `newInstance()`

2. `setMessageDrivenContext(MessageDrivenContext mdc)`

3. `ejbCreate()`

At this point there is a MDB instance in the container's method-ready pool, ready to handle messages from its destination. The container invokes `ejbRemove()` when it's finished with the EJB:

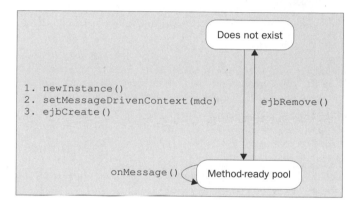

Transactions in Message-Driven Beans

There are two types of transaction management for message-driven beans:

- ❏ Bean-managed
- ❏ Container-managed

These affect the transactional attributes of the `onMessage()` method and the handling of the guaranteed message delivery.

Bean-Managed Transactions

Transactional boundaries should be defined in the `onMessage()` method and either committed or rolled back before it returns. Message delivery is not guaranteed because the process of de-queuing is outside the transactional boundaries, unless `javax.transaction.UserTransaction` is used. If `javax.transaction.UserTransaction` is used a client application can explicitly demarcate the transaction boundaries.

Container-Managed Transactions

This guarantees the delivery of the message. Only two transactional attributes are allowed here: `NotSupported` and `Required`. Message-driven beans do not propagate distributed transactions. In the case of `NotSupported`, the bean is executed without a transaction. If `Required` is set, the bean is executed in a new transaction.

A Message-Driven Bean Example

All that is being done in this very simple example is to print the type of message and, in most cases, the message content to System.out. If you are wondering where all the connection factories and connections are, they are set up in the bean deployment phase, discussed shortly. Here's the code for our MessageDrivenWroxBean example:

```
import javax.ejb.*;
import javax.jms.*;
import javax.naming.*;

public class MessageDrivenWroxBean
            implements MessageDrivenBean, MessageListener {
  private MessageDrivenContext ctx;

  public void setMessageDrivenContext(MessageDrivenContext ctx) {
    this.ctx = ctx;
  }

  public void ejbCreate () throws CreateException {
    System.out.println("Message-Driven bean created");
  }

  public void onMessage(Message msg) {
    System.out.println("Message received: ");

    try {
      if(msg instanceof TextMessage) {
        System.out.println("TextMessage: "+((TextMessage)msg).getText());
      } else if(msg instanceof ObjectMessage) {
        System.out.println("ObjectMessage: " +
                            ((ObjectMessage)msg).getObject());
      } else if (msg instanceof StreamMessage) {
        System.out.println("StreamMessage: " +
                            ((StreamMessage)msg).readString());
      } else if (msg instanceof BytesMessage) {
        System.out.println("BytesMessage: "+((BytesMessage)msg).readUTF());
      } else if (msg instanceof MapMessage) {
        System.out.println("MapMessage: " +
                            ((MapMessage)msg).getString("msg"));
      }
    } catch(Exception any) {
      System.out.println("Exception: "+any.getMessage());
    }
  }
  public void ejbRemove() {}
}
```

Deploying the Message-Driven Bean

As with any type of EJB, writing it is only half the work; the rest is in the deployment. Compile your bean with the following command:

```
javac -classpath .;%J2EE_HOME%\lib\j2ee.jar MessageDrivenWroxBean.java
```

Then start the application server's deployment tool; this is done in the J2EE reference implementation with the deploytool command from the %J2EE_HOME%\bin directory.

Make sure at this point that you are working with an EJB 2.0-compliant app server, otherwise you will not see the "message-driven bean" options. Some third-party JMS providers offer MDB features that complement application services; as time goes on though there are more and more 'real' MDB -compliant application servers.

The following instructions relate specifically to the J2EE Reference Implementation; other application servers will differ in their deployment techniques, and the relevant documentation should be referred to.

Once the deployment tool has loaded, select File | New | Application, and enter WroxApp, then select File | New | Enterprise Bean. This will take you through a series of dialogs:

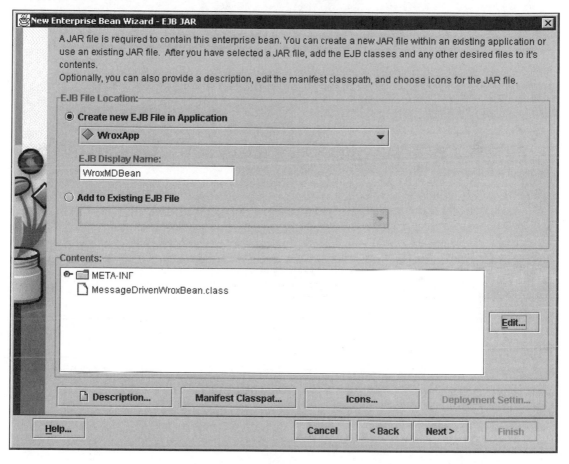

Select your new application and enter WroxMDBean as the bean name. Click on Edit and add your MessageDrivenWroxBean class (the class file not the Java source), then click on Next.

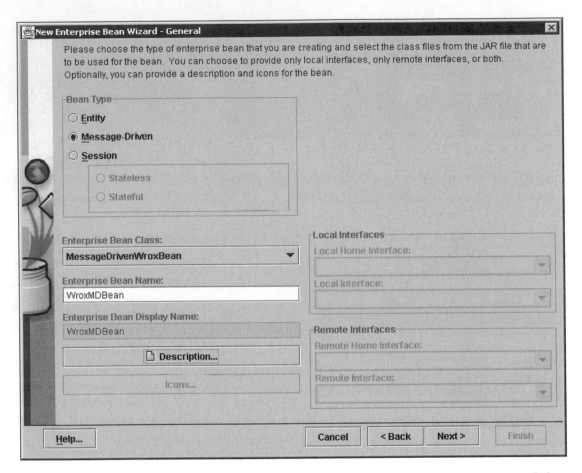

Select the **Message-Driven** bean type, the bean class itself, and enter the name again. Again, click on
Next to continue:

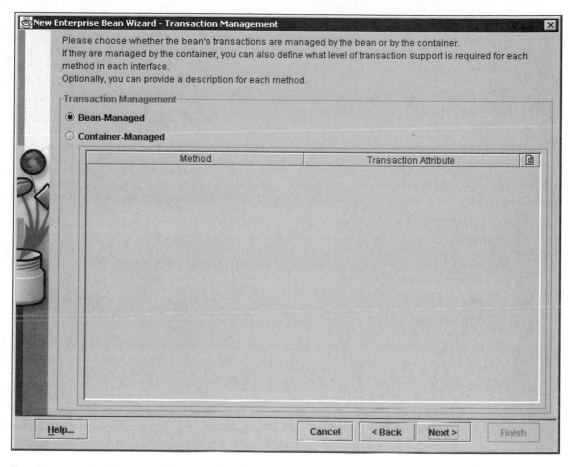

For the purposes of our simple example, select Bean-Managed, and click on Next:

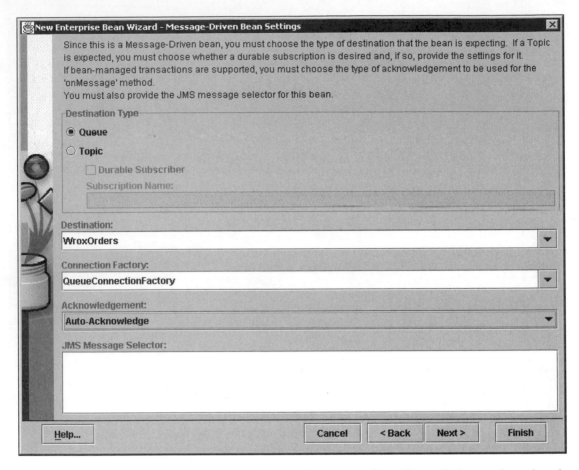

Now select the queue or topic you want to consume the message from. You will also need to select the `ConnectionFactory` and the acknowledgement method (for this example choose Auto-Acknowledge). We're almost there and you can click on Finish at this point.

What you have now is a message-driven bean that is created but not yet deployed. Remember to start, and connect to, the J2EE server and, in the deployment tool, select the new MDB. Then select Tools | Deploy:

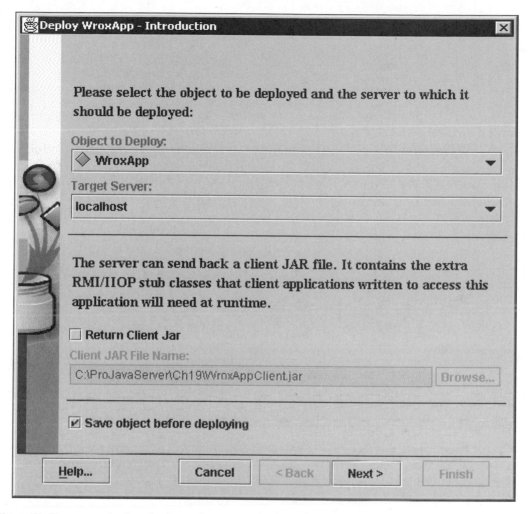

This will allow us to deploy the bean into the J2EE container; pick the application to deploy and the server to deploy it on (probably `localhost`). As usual, click on Next, confirm that the JNDI name is correct, then click Finish to deploy your message-driven bean:

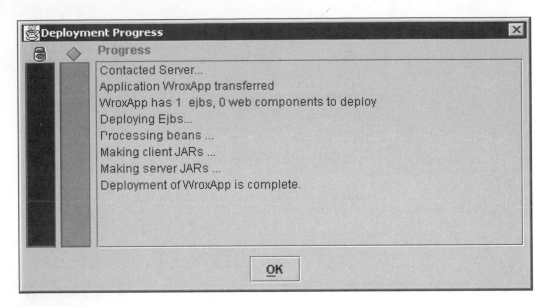

To prove that our message-driven bean is indeed working, we should see a message like the following in the command window from which the J2EE server was started:

If we run the `WroxQueueSender` we used earlier in this chapter with the following command:

```
java -Djms.properties=%J2EE_HOME%\config\jms_client.properties
    -cp .;%J2EE_HOME%\lib\j2ee.jar; WroxQueueSender
```

We should see the J2EE Server print out the following:

```
Command Prompt - j2ee -verbose

No code generation required...
C:\j2sdkee1.3\repository\SARAHWOOD1\applications\WroxApp997641900622Server.jar
Deploying message driven bean WroxMDBean, consuming from WroxOrders
Application WroxApp deployed.

Message-Driven bean created
Message received:
TextMessage: Please send me the new J2EE book on my account
```

> If you leave this deployed in the J2EE server, then every time you run the server this MDB will also run. If you then go back to the earlier examples you will not see your messages because this MDB will consume them for you.

Let's take a quick look at the deployment descriptor. This is an XML file that contains the setup information for the bean and was created by deployment tool:

```xml
<ejb-jar>
  <display-name>WroxMDBean</display-name>
  <enterprise-beans>
    <message-driven>
      <description>This is the Wrox description</description>
      <display-name>WroxMDBean</display-name>
      <ejb-name>WroxMDBean</ejb-name>
      <ejb-class>MessageDrivenWroxBean</ejb-class>
      <transaction-type>Bean</transaction-type>
      <message-selector>Client NOT NULL</message-selector>
      <acknowledge-mode>Auto-acknowledge</acknowledge-mode>
      <message-driven-destination>
        <destination-type>javax.jms.Queue</destination-type>
      </message-driven-destination>
      <security-identity>
        <description></description>
        <run-as>
          <description></description>
          <role-name></role-name>
        </run-as>
      </security-identity>
    </message-driven>
  </enterprise-beans>
</ejb-jar>
```

We can see that all the parameters we set up while deploying the MDB have been written into the deployment descriptor.

Summary

In this chapter we looked at the early days of messaging, before going on to look at how the JMS has become the first (and only) MOM standard that covers point-to-point and publish/subscribe domains.

Using simple examples, we experienced first-hand how simple it is to create a JMS session, and to produce and consume messages. We also looked at the flexibility of consuming methods, both synchronous and asynchronous, and the very powerful message selectors. In particular, we looked at:

- ❑ The differences between point-to-point and publish/subscribe domains
- ❑ The building blocks of the JMS architecture: administered objects, connections, sessions, message producers, message consumers, and messages
- ❑ How to handle messages asynchronously (using a message listener) and how to use message selectors
- ❑ How to use transactions with JMS.

Finally, we covered the latest addition to the EJB family, message-driven beans:

- ❑ We examined the lifecycle of MDBs
- ❑ We saw how to create, and deploy, a simple MDB using the J2EE Reference Implementation

JMS is becoming one of the most powerful and important features of J2EE, and it will certainly be an important technology for a long time to come.

In the next chapter, we'll look at another new feature in J2EE 1.3, the Connector Architecture that provides another means of integrating J2EE application with legacy systems.

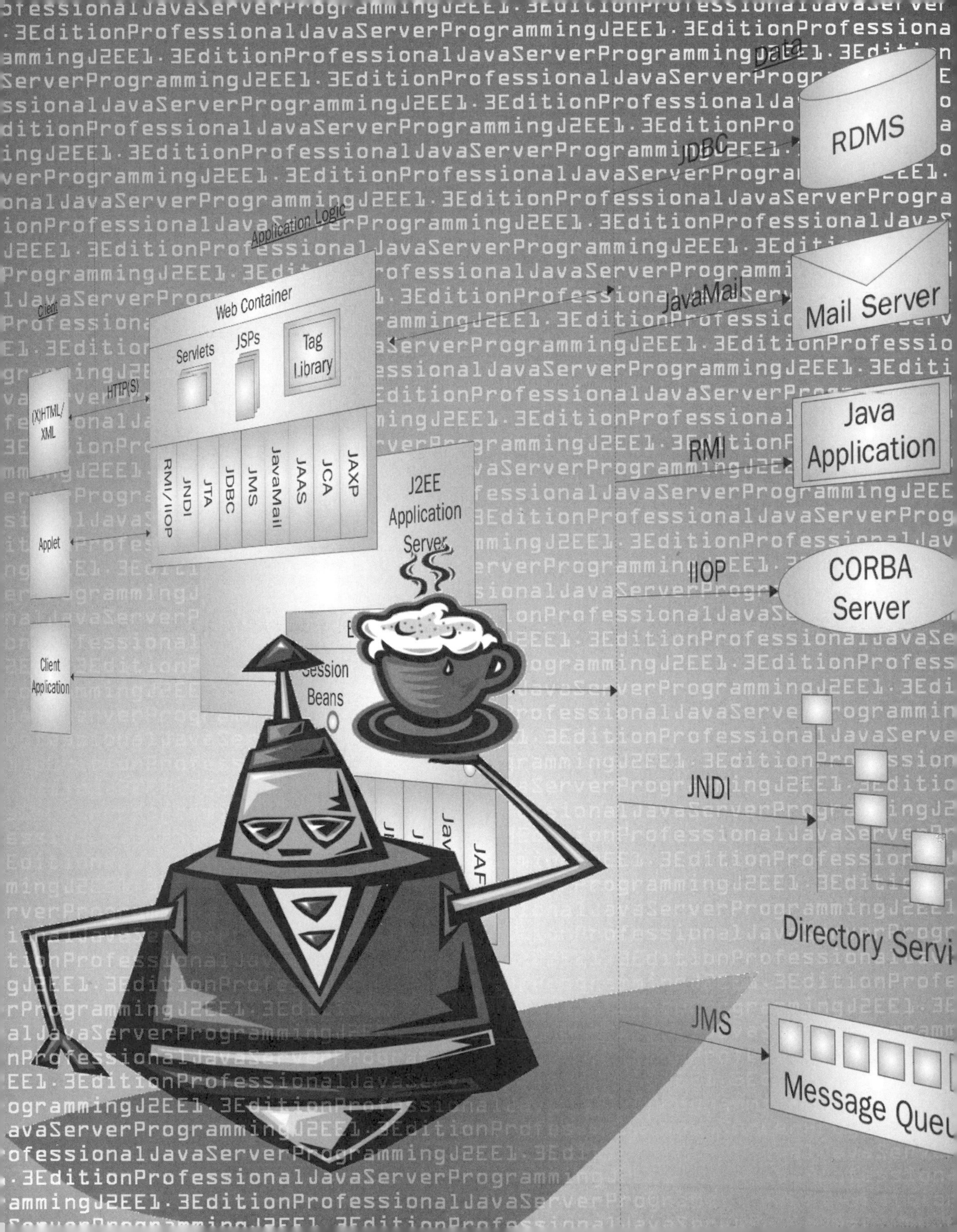

20

The J2EE Connector Architecture

This chapter presents an introduction to the **J2EE Connector Architecture (JCA),** a significant new addition to the J2EE platform in version 1.3. JCA is an enterprise application integration initiative providing a standardized architecture to enable J2EE components to have "plug-and-play" access to heterogeneous **Enterprise Information Systems (EIS),** which include ERP, transaction processing, and legacy database systems.

Over the course of this chapter we'll study the J2EE Connector Architecture and develop J2EE Connector components to allow J2EE applications to integrate and interact with backend EIS resources. In particular, we will be focusing on the following:

- ❑ EIS integration issues and the role of JCA
- ❑ JCA architecture, services, and API
- ❑ How JCA works within a J2EE framework
- ❑ Programming with the Common Client Interface (CCI)
- ❑ Building a JCA component
- ❑ The rules that a JCA developer must follow
- ❑ How to deploy and test JCA components
- ❑ Potential benefits of using JCA
- ❑ Current limitations of JCA 1.0

The current Connector Architecture specification is available at Sun's Java site at http://java.sun.com/j2ee/connector/. Additionally, there is a list of J2EE vendors supporting the specification available at http://java.sun.com/j2ee/connector/products.html, but at this time only the J2EE 1.3 Reference Implementation and couple of J2EE vendors have made their beta implementations available. Also available is a list of EIS vendors supporting this architecture to provide their EIS-specific resource-adapters. However, at the time of writing, no EIS vendors have made their beta EIS resource-adapters available.

EIS Integration and the Role of JCA

In this age of e-business, Internet-enabling business applications and integrating businesses across the Internet has become fundamental for their competitive advantages. However, prior to the Internet economy, many companies and businesses had already invested heavily in business and management information application systems, such as:

❑ Enterprise Resource Planning (ERP) applications, like SAP R/3 and BAAN.

❑ Customer Relationship Management (CRM) applications, such as Siebel and Clarify.

❑ Database applications, such as DB2 and Sybase.

❑ Mainframe transaction processing applications, such as CICS.

❑ Legacy Database systems, such as IBM's IMS

These systems are generally referred to as **Enterprise Information Systems (EIS)**.

> An Enterprise Information System (EIS) provides the information infrastructure and services for an enterprise. This information may be in the form of a set of records in a database, business objects in an ERP, a workflow object in a customer relationship management (CRM) system, or a transaction program in a transaction processing application.

Leveraging these complex business applications into a multi-tiered application framework is quite challenging, and implementing them for a high-availability web application is a mammoth project.

Before the Connector Architecture, some application server vendors provided or supported a variety of custom adapters for integrating EIS systems. These adapters basically provided custom native interfaces, which were complex to understand and were limited in that they attempted to support a standard architecture. More specifically, some of these limitations were as follows:

❑ Application programming for EIS is proprietary in nature, and the sheer variety of application systems meant there was no generic interface mechanism for integration with open architectures.

❑ Large-scale web applications require high-availability and scalability in respect of the number of clients, connection management, etc. Traditionally, the number of clients and their active connections are expensive in an EIS and custom adapters lack support for connection management mechanisms provided by application servers.

❑ Managing security and distributed transactions with multiple backend applications is extremely complex and lacks reliable mechanisms. This meant there was no standard infrastructure solution available to provide a vendor-neutral security mechanism and generic transaction-management support to multiple EIS resource managers. This can pose huge problems with the implementation of EAI.

Addressing the above challenges, Sun Microsystems has released the J2EE Connector Architecture 1.0 to provide a standard architecture for integration of J2EE servers with heterogeneous EIS resources. Its primary goal is to simplify the development process for integration by defining a common API and a common set of services within a consistent J2EE environment.

> **The J2EE Connector Architecture (JCA) provides an easy approach for developers to seamlessly integrate Enterprise Information Systems (EIS) with J2EE platform components.**

The following diagram shows the new face of a J2EE 1.3 application server with JCA components and examples of potential Enterprise Information Systems:

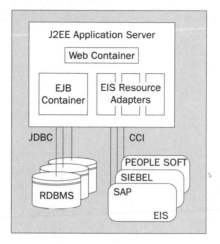

So, if we need to integrate a J2EE-based application with an existing EIS, all we need to do is install the appropriate EIS connector (a JCA-compliant **Resource-adapter**) into our application server. With the adapter installed, we can develop J2EE components to interface with the EIS using the **Common Client Interface (CCI)** API, in the same manner that we can use JDBC to interface with relational databases. In other words, development is simplified by having no EIS-specific programming, and a configuration completely independent of the backend EIS.

The idea is that all application server vendors will eventually implement JCA services and the EIS vendors will implement JCA-compliant EIS resource-adapters. By supporting the J2EE Connector Architecture, all J2EE compliant application servers are assured of handling multiple and heterogeneous EIS resources.

Thus, JCA boosts J2EE application developer's productivity in parallel with reducing development costs and protecting the existing investment in EIS systems by providing a scalable integration solution through J2EE.

J2EE Connector Architecture and its Elements

JCA is implemented in a J2EE 1.3-compliant application server, with a JCA-compliant resource-adapter provided by an EIS vendor. This resource-adapter is an EIS-specific, pluggable J2EE component in the application server, which provides an interface for communicating with the underlying EIS system.

Basically JCA defines the following list of elements and service:

❑ **System-level contracts and services** – define the standard interface between the J2EE components, the application server provider and the EIS system. These contracts and services are implemented in the application server by the J2EE server provider and also in the resource-adapter by the EIS vendor. The implementation of contacts and services defines a logical separation (not physical) between the application server and the resource-adapter in terms of system-level roles and responsibilities. This allows the J2EE server and the resource-adapter to co-ordinate with each other (for example, connection pooling, security, and transactions). Furthermore, it enables a JCA-compliant resource-adapter to be pluggable into any J2EE server.

❑ The JCA **Common Client Interface (CCI)** – defines a client API that J2EE components (like JSPs, EJBs, etc.) can use to connect to and interact with EIS systems. In addition to J2EE client components, it also allows non-managed applications (like Java applets and application clients) to integrate with an EIS using a JCA-compliant resource-adapter.

❑ **Packaging and deployment interfaces** – allow various EIS resource adapters to plug into J2EE applications.

The following diagram illustrates the J2EE connector architecture and components accessing EIS resources:

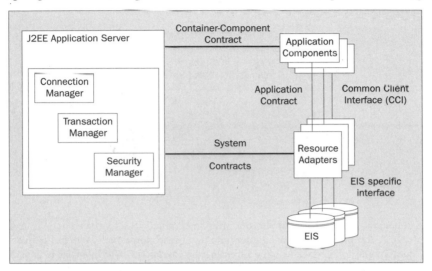

The resource-adapter can clearly be seen as the fundamental component of the JCA, as it serves as the central connector between the J2EE components, the application server, and the EIS system.

In a J2EE application framework using JCA, EIS vendors provide JCA-compliant resource-adapters with CCI as a part of their implementation. J2EE server vendors provide application servers supporting JCA system-level contracts that enable these resource-adapters to plug into the application servers and provide connectivity with underlying EIS resources. This allows the J2EE application developers to develop integration components using CCI. They are therefore able to stay away from the connection, security, and transaction mechanisms meant for connectivity with an EIS or multiple EIS resources.

The JCA specification supports two types of environments, based on which type of client application uses the resource-adapter:

❑ **Managed Environment**
Defines a multi-tier, web-enabled, J2EE-based application that accesses EIS(s). The application may contain one or more application components (for example, EJBs, JSP pages, servlets), which are deployed on their respective containers. In the context of JCA, these applications are referred as managed applications.

❑ **Non-managed Environment**
The connector architecture supports access to EIS(s) from clients like applets or Java client applications. Typically it is in a two-tier architecture where an application client directly uses a resource-adapter library. In this case the resource-adapter provides low-level transactions and security to its clients. In a JCA context, these applications are referred as non-managed applications.

We'll look at connecting with both of these environments later in this chapter.

Comparing JCA with JDBC

In general, JCA and JDBC are similar technologies with identical mechanisms with respect to connection and transaction management.

> Resource-adapters for EIS systems are analogous to JDBC drivers for relational databases.

The following table presents a comparison between JCA and JDBC, and demonstrates the similarities (and differences) between the two:

	JDBC 2.0	JCA 1.0
Definition	Provides a generic interface to interact with relational databases	Provides a standard architecture for J2EE and Java applications to integrate and interact with EIS resources
API	Defines a standard Java API for accessing relational databases	Uses Common Client Interface (CCI) to provide an EIS-independent API
Connection	Uses JDBC drivers specific to a RDBMS	Uses an EIS-Resource-adapter to interact with an EIS
Server implementation	J2EE servers implement JDBC connection pool mechanisms to create connections to a database	J2EE servers implement JCA service-contracts to establish a connection factory and manage connections with an EIS.
Support for non-managed applications	Supports non-managed applications (two-tier applications), which use JDBC	Supports non-managed applications (two-tier application), which uses CCI
Service Provider Interface (SPI) support	Provides support (since JDBC 3.0) for and relationship with JCA SPI	JCA defines SPI for integrating application server services, like transactions, connection, and security
Transaction support	Supports both XA and Non-XA transactions with underlying XA data sources	Supports both XA and Non-XA transactions with underlying EIS resources
JTA support	Provides an interface to support JTA and JTS	Supports JTA with a contract between the J2EE transaction manager and EIS resource manager

So, after the comparison, the difference between the two technologies is clear – JDBC provides drivers and a client API for connection and integration with relational database applications, whereas the JCA provides resource-adapters and a client API (CCI) to enable seamless integration to EIS resources.

The Resource-adapter and its Contracts

The resource-adapter contains an EIS-specific library (which can be written in Java or with native interface components) that provides the connectivity to the EIS it represents. In the J2EE application server, the resource-adapter runs in the application server's address space and manages the connectivity to the underlying EIS.

JCA requires that all JCA-compliant EIS resource-adapters and the J2EE application servers support the system-level contracts. JCA also recommends (but does not mandate) that all resource-adapters support CCI as their client API. This provides a J2EE-based solution for application development integrating multiple EISs, and enables that 'pluggability' of EIS resource-adapters into an application server, in collaboration with all system-level mechanisms.

As per the JCA specification, resource-adapters generally implement two main types of contracts. These are discussed in the following sections.

> **In general, a contract in this context is simply a statement of responsibilities between layers of the application that implements a standard interface between those layers.**

Application Contracts

Application contracts define the Common Client Interface (CCI) API through which a J2EE client component (an EJB or servlet, for example) or a non-managed client communicates with the underlying EIS resources.

System-Level Contracts

System-level contracts define a set of system contracts, which enable the resource-adapter to link with the application server services to manage the connections, transactions, and security. The JCA specification defines a number of system-level contracts for the resource-adapter and the J2EE application server to implement. These are discussed in depth in the following sub-sections.

Connection Management

Connection management is represented by a service contract that enables an application server to offer its own services to create and manage connection pools with the underlying EIS resource. This provides a scalable connection-management facility to support a large number of clients.

The connection-management contract is intended to do the following:

❑ Establish a consistent application programming practice to provide connection acquisition for both managed (J2EE application) and non-managed (two-tier) applications.

❑ Enable an EIS resource-adapter to provide a connection factory and connection interfaces based on the CCI specific to the type of resource-adapter and EIS.

❑ Provide a generic mechanism for the J2EE managed components by which a J2EE application server can provide services like transactions, security, advanced pooling, error tracing/logging, etc.

❑ Provide support for connection pooling.

Transaction Management

This contract extends the applications server's transactional capability to the underlying EIS resource managers. In the context of JCA, an EIS resource manager manages a set of shared EIS resources to participate in transactions. A resource manager can manage two types of transaction, as follows:

- **XA Transaction**

  These transactions are controlled and coordinated by external transaction managers. They support a JTA XAResource transaction management contract with a JCA-compliant resource-adapter and its underlying EIS resource manager. This also means that the participating EIS resource also supports JTA-based XA transactions by implementing an XAResource through its resource-adapter.

  The JTA XAResource interface enables two resource managers to participate in transactions coordinated by an external transaction manager. This allows the transaction to be managed by a transaction manager external to the resource adapter.

  When a J2EE application component demarcates an EIS connection request as part of a transaction, the application server is responsible for enlisting the XA resource with the transaction manager. When the client closes that connection, the application server un-lists the XA resource from the transaction manager and once the transaction is completed it cleans up the EIS connection. This allows the business component to participate in two-phase commit scenarios.

- **Local Transaction**

  These are transactions managed internally, which involves no external transaction managers In this case the transactions are demarcated by the J2EE server container (container-managed) or by the J2EE component (component-managed). This allows the application server to manage resources local to the application and its resource-adapter. In component-managed transactions, the J2EE components use JTA UserTransaction interface or a transaction API specific to the EIS.

  When an application component requests an EIS connection, the application server starts a local transaction using the currently available transaction context. When the application component closes that connection, the application server commits (or rolls back, if necessary) on the local transaction and cleans up the EIS connection.

These two transaction types enable the transaction manager provided within the application server to manage transactions across multiple EIS resource managers.

Security Management

This service enables the developer to define the security between the application server and the EIS resource. There are a variety of mechanisms used to protect an EIS against unauthorized access and other security threats, which include:

- User identification, authentication, and authorization

- Secure communication between the application server and the EIS resource, using open network communication security protocols like Kerberos, which provide end-to-end security with authentication and confidentiality services

- Enabling an EIS-specific security mechanism

Basically the security contract between the J2EE server and the EIS resource-adapter extends the connection-management contract along with security. This security contract provides an EIS **sign-on** mechanism as follows:

- Passing the connection request from the resource-adapter to the J2EE application server and enabling the server with its authentication and authorization services

- Propagating the security context with security credentials from the application server to the resource-adapter

EIS Sign-On

In a new connection to EIS, creating an EIS connection usually creates a sign-on process. This is based on the security context, which creates an authentication and authorization process for a user to obtain the access rules. In any case, if the security context changes it requires re-authentication for the connection.

An EIS sign-on requires one or more of the following steps:

❑ Determine the resource principal (identity of the initiating caller) under whose security context a new connection to an EIS will be established.

❑ Authenticate the resource principal if the connection is not already authenticated.

❑ Establish a secure association between the application server and the EIS. Additional mechanisms like SSL or Kerberos can also be deployed.

❑ Control access to EIS resources.

Once a secure association is established, the connection is associated with the security context of the initiating user. Subsequently, all application-level invocations to the EIS instance using the connection happen under the security context of that user.

JCA recommends that the J2EE server vendors provide and support container-managed sign-on for J2EE managed applications and application-managed sign-on for non-managed applications. Let's define these two sign-on techniques:

❑ **Application-managed sign-on**
The client component provides the security credentials (typically username and password) while obtaining a connection to an EIS.

❑ **Container-managed sign-on**
The J2EE client component does not present any security credentials, and it is the responsibility of the J2EE container to find the necessary sign-on credentials and provide them to the resource-adapter while requesting a connection to an EIS. In this scenario, the container must find the **resource principal** (identity of the initiating caller) and provide information about this resource principal to the resource-adapter in the form of a Java Authentication and Authorization Service (JAAS) subject.

Packaging and Deploying a Resource-adapter

The JCA defines packaging and deployment interfaces, so that various resource-adapters can easily plug into a compliant J2EE application server in a modular and portable manner. This is known as the Resource-adapter module (.rar) and is similar to a J2EE application module (.ear), which can include web and EJB components.

The following diagram illustrates the steps involved in the packaging and deployment process of a resource-adapter module intended to connect a J2EE application with an EIS resource. Typically this process is very similar to how we deploy EJBs and web components in a J2EE container.

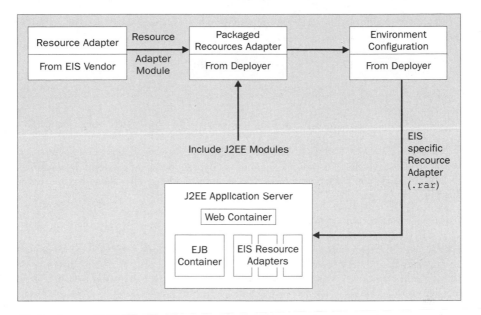

Thus, the packaging and deployment process of a resource module is as follows:

❑ The EIS resource-adapter provider (usually the EIS vendor) develops a set of Java interfaces and utility classes as part of the resource-adapter implementation. These Java classes implement the JCA contracts and EIS-specific functionality provided by the resource-adapter.

❑ The Java classes and the native libraries (if available) provided by the resource-adapter provider are packaged, together with a deployment descriptor, to build a **resource-adapter module (RAR file)**. Similar to other J2EE component deployment descriptors, the deployment descriptor of the **resource-adapter** module defines the service contract attributes between the resource-adapter provider and a deployer for the deployment of a resource-adapter.

❑ During deployment, the application deployer installs a resource-adapter module on an application server and then configures it with the J2EE applications server and the target underlying EIS environment.

As mentioned earlier, the packaging and deployment process of a resource-adapter module for an application is similar to other J2EE packaging and deployment process, especially for web and EJB components. However, the roles and responsibilities involved in packaging and deploying resource-adapter are slightly different when compared to other J2EE components.

Packaging a Resource-adapter

An EIS resource-adapter is a J2EE server component contained in a RAR archive. You can stage one or more resource-adapters in a directory and package them as .rar files.

The following task list indicates the typical sequence involved with packaging a resource-adapter:

1. Create a temporary staging directory.

2. Compile or copy the resource-adapter Java classes into the staging directory.

3. Create a `.jar` file to store the resource-adapter Java classes, and add this `.jar` file to the top level of the staging directory.

4. Create a `META-INF` subdirectory in the staging directory.

5. Create a `ra.xml` deployment descriptor file in the `META-INF` subdirectory, and add entries for the resource-adapter.

6. Create a J2EE vendor-specific deployment descriptor in the `META-INF` subdirectory and add entries for the resource-adapter.

7. When all of the resource-adapter classes and deployment descriptors are made available in the staging directory, you can create the resource-adapter module `.rar` file with a `jar` command, like this:

```
jar cvf wroxResourceAdapter.rar -C staging-dir .
```

Finally, we can deploy this `.rar` file on any JCA-compliant J2EE server, or package it within an application `.jar` file. Note that the `-C` *staging-dir* option defines the `jar` command to change to the `staging-dir` directory so that the directory paths defined in the `rar` file are relative to the directory where you staged the resource-adapters.

A packaged resource-adapter module defines the contract between an EIS resource-adapter provider and deployer, and includes the following elements:

❑ Java classes and interfaces that are required for the implementation of both the connector architecture contracts and the functionality of the resource-adapter

❑ Utility Java classes for the resource-adapter

❑ Platform-dependent native libraries required by the resource-adapter

❑ Help files and documentation

❑ Descriptive meta-information that ties the above elements together

The deployment process begins with the `.rar` file or a deployment directory, both of which contain the compiled resource-adapter interfaces and implementation classes provided by the EIS resource-adapter provider. Resource-adapters in a J2EE environment use a common directory format. A resource-adapter is structured in a directory as shown in the following example:

```
\J2EEserverHome
\config
\wroxdomain
\applications
\wroxResourceAdapter
\images
        \ra.jpg
\readme.html
\eis.jar
\utilities.jar
\windos.dll
\solaris.so
\META-INF
        \ra.xml
        \XYZServerProvider-ra.xml
```

This same format can be used when a resource-adapter is packaged as a `.rar` file. After creating a `.rar` file, your J2EE server installation looks like this:

```
\J2EEserverHome
\config
\wroxdomain
\applications
            \wroxResourceAdapter.rar
```

In the above structure, `ra.xml` is the deployment descriptor for the resource-adapter. `XYZServerProvider-ra.xml` is the J2EE vendor deployment descriptor, which defines the operational parameters unique to the server provider. We'll look at the deployment descriptor in greater detail in the next section. The `eis.jar` and `utilities.jar` contain Java interfaces and implementation classes of the EIS resource-adapter. The `windos.dll` and `solaris.so` files are examples of native libraries.

The Resource-adapter Deployment Descriptor (`ra.xml`)

Similar to other J2EE Applications, EIS resource-adapters also use descriptors to define the contract between an EIS resource adapter provider and a deployer of that environment. This provides the attributes intended for the deployer to enable the deployment of an EIS resource-adapter in its environment. The J2EE vendor also requires an additional deployment descriptor, which defines the operational parameters unique to the server provider.

A resource-adapter module also includes the deployment requirements specified by the resource-adapter provider in the deployment descriptor. That is, the `ra.xml` file contains the deployment attributes of a resource-adapter. To set the necessary deployment properties for the resource-adapter, it is necessary to edit the `ra.xml` file packaged with a resource-adapter. The XML document type definition of the deployment descriptor for a resource-adapter module is available at http://java.sun.com/dtd/connector_1_0.dtd.

The resource-adapter provider is responsible for providing the deployment descriptor for an EIS-specific resource-adapter. As per JCA 1.0, the following information is available from a resource-adapter deployment descriptor provided by an EIS resource-adapter provider:

- ❑ General information about a resource-adapter. As seen in the following code extract, this can include details like the name of the resource-adapter, name of the vendor who provides the resource-adapter, type of EIS system supported, version of the JCA supported, and so on. For example:

```
<display-name>BlackBoxNoTx</display-name>
<vendor-name>Java Software</vendor-name>
<spec-version>1.0</spec-version>
<eis-type>JDBC Database</eis-type>
<version>1.0</version>
```

- ❑ `ManagedConnectionFactory` class – the resource-adapter provider specifies the fully-qualified name of the Java class that implements the `javax.resource.spi.ManagedConnectionFactory` interface. For example:

```
<managedconnectionfactoryclass>
com.sun.connector.blackbox.NoTxManagedConnectionFactory
</managedconnectionfactory-class>
```

- ❑ `ConnectionFactory` interface and implementation class – the resource-adapter provider specifies the fully qualified name of the Java interface and implementation class for the connection factory. For example:

```
<connectionfactory-interface>
    javax.sql.DataSource
</connectionfactory-interface>
<connectionfactory-impl-class>
com.sun.connector.blackbox.JdbcDataSource
</connectionfactory-impl-class>
```

❑ Connection implementation class – the resource-adapter provider specifies the fully-qualified name of the Java interface and implementation class for the connection interface:

```
<connection-impl-class>
com.sun.connector.blackbox.JdbcConnection
</connection-impl-class>
```

❑ Transactional support – the resource-adapter provider specifies the level of transaction support provided by the resource-adapter implementation. The level of transaction support is usually one of the following: NoTransaction, LocalTransaction, or XATransaction. For example:

```
<transaction-support>NoTransaction</transaction-support>
```

❑ Configurable properties of the ManagedConnectionFactory instance – the resource-adapter provider defines name, type, description, and an optional default values for the properties that have to be configured for each ManagedConnectionFactory instance (note that we are using the default Cloudscape database – CloudscapeDB – in this example):

```
<config-property>
    <config-property-name>ConnectionURL</config-property-name>
    <config-property-type>java.lang.String</config-property-type>
    <config-property-value>
        jdbc:cloudscape:rmi:CloudscapeDB;create=true
    </config-property-value>
</config-property>
```

❑ Authentication mechanism – the resource-adapter provider specifies all the authentication mechanisms supported by the resource-adapter. This includes the support provided by the resource-adapter implementation but not by the underlying EIS instance. The standard values are BasicPassword and Kerbv5, for example:

```
<authentication-mechanism>
    <authentication-mechanism-type>
        BasicPassword
    </authentication-mechanism-type>
    <credential-interface>
        javax.resource.security.PasswordCredential
    </credential-interface>
</authentication-mechanism>
```

❑ Re-authentication support – the resource-adapter provider specifies whether its resource-adapter supports re-authentication of an existing connection:

```
<reauthentication-support>false</reauthentication-support>
```

The following example illustrates a complete deployment descriptor for a black-box resource-adapter – with no transaction support (included in .rar file):

```xml
<?xml version="1.0" encoding="UTF-8"?>
<!DOCTYPE connector PUBLIC '-//Sun Microsystems, Inc.//DTD Connector 1.0//EN'
'http://java.sun.com/j2ee/dtds/connector_1_0.dtd'>

<connector>

    <display-name>BlackBoxNoTx</display-name>
    <vendor-name>Java Software</vendor-name>
    <spec-version>1.0</spec-version>
    <eis-type>JDBC Database</eis-type>
    <version>1.0</version>

    <resourceadapter>
        <managedconnectionfactoryclass>
            com.sun.connector.blackbox.NoTxManagedConnectionFactory
        </managedconnectionfactory-class>
        <connectionfactory-interface>
            javax.sql.DataSource</connectionfactory-interface>
        <connectionfactory-impl-class>
            com.sun.connector.blackbox.JdbcDataSource
        </connectionfactory-impl-class>
        <connection-interface>java.sql.Connection</connection-interface>
        <connection-impl-class>
            com.sun.connector.blackbox.JdbcConnection
        </connection-impl-class>
        <transaction-support>NoTransaction</transaction-support>
        <config-property>
            <config-property-name>ConnectionURL</config-property-name>
            <config-property-type>java.lang.String</config-property-type>
            <config-property-value>
                jdbc:cloudscape:rmi:CloudscapeDB;create=true
            </config-property-value>
        </config-property>
        <authentication-mechanism>
            <authentication-mechanism-type>
                BasicPassword
            </authentication-mechanism-type>
            <credential-interface>
                javax.resource.security.PasswordCredential
            </credential-interface>
        </authentication-mechanism>
            <reauthentication-support>false</reauthentication-support>
    </resourceadapter>

</connector>
```

Roles and Responsibilities in Deployment

The roles and responsibilities specific to the deployment are as follows.

Resource-adapter Provider

The resource-adapter provider, as the name suggests, is responsible providing a resource-adapter for an EIS. An EIS vendor or its third-party vendor typically provides the resource-adapter and its application deployment tools system. It is also responsible for specifying the deployment descriptor for its resource-adapter, which includes:

❑ General information – general details of the resource-adapter (name, description, vendor name, licensing, EIS supported, version, etc.).

❑ ManagedConnectionFactory class – specifies the fully-qualified name of the Java class that implements the javax.resource.spi.ManagedConnectionFactory interface.

❑   ConnectionFactory interface and implementation class – specifies the fully qualified name of the Java interface and implementation class for the connection factory.

❑   Transactional support – specifies the level of transaction support provided by the resource-adapter implementation (NoTransaction, LocalTransaction or XATransaction).

❑   Authentication mechanism – specifies authentication mechanisms supported by the resource-adapter. This includes the support for BasicAuthentication and Kerberos v5.

Application Server Vendor

The application server vendor provides the JCA implementation in its J2EE application server, which supports JCA component-based applications. Also referred to as the container-provider, it insulates the J2EE application components from the underlying system-level services.

Application Component Provider

The application component provider develops the J2EE application component that interacts with EISs to provide the application functionality. The provider develops programs using the CCI, but does not specifically program the transactions, security, concurrency, and distribution. Instead, it uses the J2EE server to provide these services.

Deployer

The deployer is responsible for configuring a resource-adapter in the target J2EE environment. The configuration of a resource-adapter is based on the attributes defined in the deployment descriptor as part of the resource-adapter module which include the following tasks:

❑   Configuring the property set per ManagedConnectionFactory for creating connections to various underlying EIS instances.

❑   Configuring the application server for the transaction management based on the level of transaction support specified by the resource-adapter.

❑   Configuring security in the operational environment based on the security requirements specified by the resource-adapter in its deployment descriptor.

Deployment Options

Deploying a resource-adapter is possible in the following ways in a J2EE Reference Implementation:

❑   Dynamically, by either using the deploytool command line (or the deploytool UI console), for example:

```
deploytool -deployConnector %J2EE_HOME%\lib\connector\blackbox-tx.rar
localhost
```

❑   As part of a J2EE Enterprise Application, deploying as an archive file called an .ear. We'll take a closer look at this option in the next section.

Deploying a Resource-adapter as a J2EE Application

As we have seen, JCA also specifies the possibility of including a resource-adapter archive (.rar) file inside an enterprise application archive (.ear), and then deploying the application in a J2EE server.

The following tasks are involved in deploying a J2EE application that contains a resource-adapter archive:

❑   Including the .rar file inside the .ear archive just as you would include a .war (web component) or .jar (EJB component).

❑ Creating a valid `application.xml` and place it in the `META-INF` directory of the `.ear` archive. While creating an `application.xml`, make sure that the application deployment descriptor contains a new `<connector>` element to identify the resource-adapter archive within the `.ear` archive. For example:

```
<connector>wroxBlackBoxNoTx.rar</connector>
```

So far we have discussed resource-adapters, resource-adapter contracts, and the packaging and deployment procedures of a resource-adapter. Now let's demonstrate the configuration and deployment of resource-adapters using the black-box resource-adapters provided by the Sun J2EE 1.3 reference implementation.

At the time of publishing this book, EIS resource-adapters were hardly available even as a beta implementation. So in our examples we are using the black-box resource-adapters provided in the J2EE Reference Implementation, which are meant for testing the packaging and deployment process and also testing CCI. Black-box adapters are not meant for production applications.

Black-Box Resource-adapters

Black-box adapters are the same as EIS resource-adapters but they use a relational database as an underlying EIS and are intended for testing purposes only. They are, however, ideal for the purpose of our simple demonstrations.

Black-box resource-adapters are primarily used for testing end-to-end connectivity with a JCA-compliant J2EE application server and its J2EE compatibility as per the JCA 1.0 specification. In this section, we'll discuss using the black-box resource-adapters that are bundled with Sun's J2EE 1.3 Reference Implementation. These black-boxes use JDBC calls to interact with a DBMS.

> **Black-box resource-adapters are not intended to replace JDBC, they merely provide a simple mock environment for testing purposes only.**

The examples that will be discussed in this chapter use the J2EE 1.3 Reference Implementation server and use Cloudscape as the database.

Using a Black-Box Adapter – The DemoConnector Example

`DemoConnector` is an example that demonstrates a black-box resource-adapter accessing a Cloudscape database using JDBC. The example is an entity EJB that performs transactions using the black-box adapter configured with a database and displays the output.

We'll discuss the `DemoConnector` example in the following order:

❑ Selecting a black-box adapter and the transaction level from the J2EE 1.3 Reference Implementation

❑ Configuring and deploying the black-box adapter

❑ Testing the black-box adapter within a transaction using an entity bean

1023

Selecting a Black-box Adapter

Let's take a look at the black-box adapters available in the J2EE 1.3 Reference Implementation. First, we should make sure that our installation includes the black-box resource-adapters. Usually they are located in the %J2EE_HOME%\lib\connector\ directory. We should have five black-box resource-adapters (identified by their .rar extension) to support different transaction levels, as we discussed earlier, in the section on resource-adapter transaction management. These adapters are described in the following table:

Black-box Resource-adapter	Description
blackbox-notx.rar	To support NO_TRANSACTION
blackbox-tx.rar	To support LOCAL_TRANSACTION
blackbox-xa.rar	To support XA_TRANSACTION
cciblackbox-tx.rar	Implemented with CCI to support LOCAL_TRANSACTION
cciblackbox-xa.rar	Implemented with CCI to support XA_TRANSACTION

In our example, we'll be using the blackbox-tx.rar resource-adapter to demonstrate the use of local transactions.

XA and Non-XA Transactions Using a Black-box Adapter

All the black-box resource-adapters require an URL to create connection factories with underlying EIS. These black-box resource-adapters generally use JDBC drivers to connect with the database. For non-XA transactional resources this requires us to configure the ConnectionURL property, whereas for XA-supported resources you need to configure the XADataSource property.

This example, we'll use the Cloudscape database-server provided in the J2EE Reference Implementation, the default values provided in the deployment descriptor of a black-box adapter are as follows:

❑ For non-XA black-box adapters (using non-XA transaction levels):

```
ConnectionURL = jdbc:cloudscape:rmi:CloudscapeDB;create=true
```

❑ For XA black-box adapters (using XA transaction levels):

```
XADataSource = jdbc/XACloudscape_xa
```

Deploying the Black-box Resource-adapter

To configure and deploy a black-box resource-adapter, we need to perform the following:

❑ Configure your database and JDBC drivers, and create your application specific tables

❑ Deploy your packaged black-box resource-adapter module

Configuring the Database and Demoaccount Table

To deploy and test this black-box resource-adapter example, blackbox-tx.rar requires a database table. As mentioned above, we'll be using the Cloudscape database provided with the J2EE 1.3 Reference Implementation. To create the table, start the Cloudscape engine (using the cloudscape -start command from the %J2EE_HOME%\bin directory), and then run the following SQL:

```
CREATE TABLE demoaccount    (accountid VARCHAR(3)
                                    CONSTRAINT Demoaccount_pk PRIMARY KEY,
                             firstname VARCHAR(25),
                             lastname VARCHAR(25),
                             balance DECIMAL(12,2)
                             );
```

You can either run this SQL using Cloudview or save the SQL into a text file and run it from the command prompt with cloudscape -isql create_demoaccount_table.sql

Now we are all set with the database configuration.

Deploying the Resource-adapter

First we need to start the J2EE server, using j2ee -verbose, as you're no doubt familiar with by now. Once the server is up and running, we can deploy the black-box adapter using the deployment tool. First we'll create a new application for our example, called Blackbox:

Then select Add to Application | Resource-adapter RAR from the File menu:

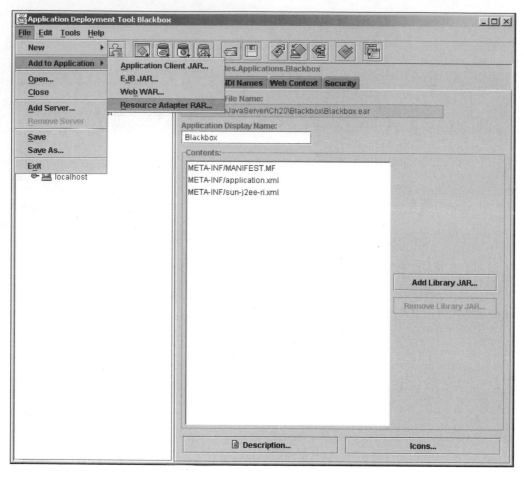

From the resulting open dialog, browse to where the RAR files are located
(%J2EE_HOMe%\lib\connector) and select the blackbox-tx.rar file, and add it to the application:

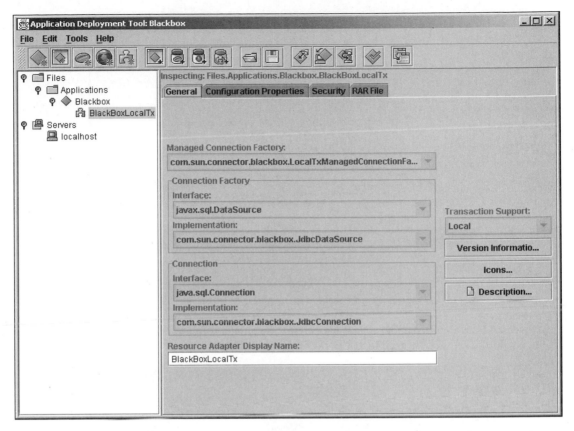

You can see from the General dialog that the connection factory for this resource-adapter is in fact simply a javax.sql.DataSource.

To deploy the adapter, select the Blackbox application and use Deploy from the Tools menu:

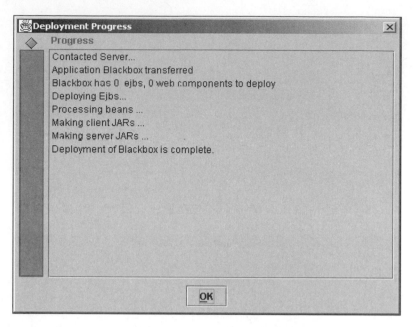

Now expand the **Servers** node so that you can see the attached Reference Implementation server and select it. In the right-hand pane switch to the **Resource-adapters** tab:

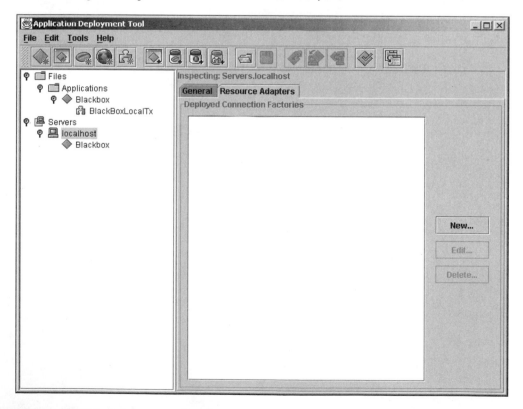

Hit the New button to add a new connection factory. You'll see that the blackbox-tx.rar adapter is already selected, so all we need to add is the JNDI Name (eis/WroxEIS in this case):

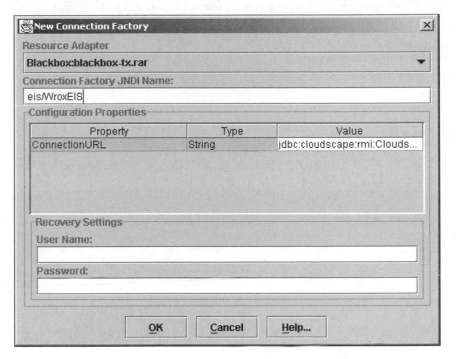

Note that the ConnectionURL property is pointing to a Cloudscape database. Obviously, the value of this property would need to be altered if you are using a different database.

Hit the OK button and, if everything worked out, you'll get a confirmation prompt:

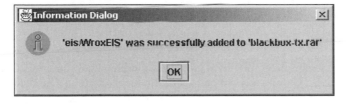

The Resource-adapters tab should now look like this:

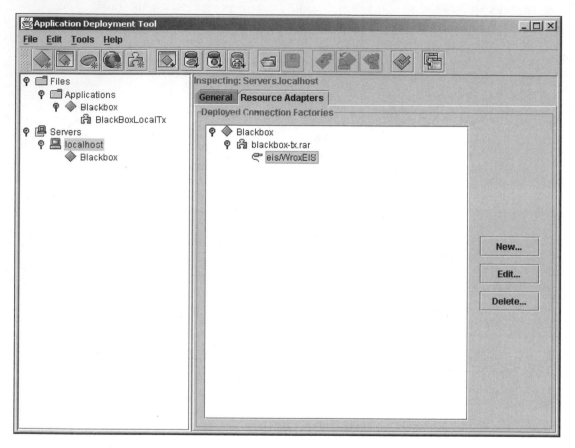

We are now ready to create the entity bean to test this adapter.

Testing the Black-box Resource-adapter

The DemoConnector example is an entity bean and a simple client that uses the black-box resource-adapter to transact with a Cloudscape database. We'll now present the sourcecode for the EJB.

> *Note that all of the source code for the examples shown in this chapter (and all the other examples in this book) is available for download from http://www.wrox.com/*

The Home Interface

```
import java.util.Collection;
import java.rmi.RemoteException;
import javax.ejb.*;

public interface DemoAccountHome extends EJBHome {

    public DemoAccount create(String accountid, String firstName,
                              String lastName, double balance)
```

```
        throws RemoteException, CreateException;

    public DemoAccount findByPrimaryKey(String accountid)
        throws FinderException, RemoteException;

    public Collection findByLastName(String lastName)
        throws FinderException, RemoteException;

    public Collection findInRange(double low, double high)
        throws FinderException, RemoteException;
}
```

The Remote Interface

```
import javax.ejb.EJBObject;
import java.rmi.RemoteException;

public interface DemoAccount extends EJBObject {

    public void debit(double amount) throws ProcessingException,
        RemoteException;
    public void credit(double amount) throws RemoteException;
    public String getFirstName() throws RemoteException;
    public String getLastName() throws RemoteException;
    public double getBalance() throws RemoteException;
}
```

The Bean Implementation Class

```
import java.sql.*;
import javax.sql.*;
import java.util.*;
import javax.ejb.*;
import javax.naming.*;

public class DemoAccountBean implements EntityBean {

    private String accountid;
    private String firstName;
    private String lastName;
    private double balance;
    private EntityContext context;
    private Connection con;
    private String eisName = "java:comp/env/eis/WroxEIS";

    public void debit(double amount)  throws ProcessingException {
        if (balance - amount < 0) {
            throw new ProcessingException();
        }
        balance -= amount;
    }

    public void credit(double amount) {
        balance += amount;
    }

    public String getFirstName() {
        return firstName;
    }
```

```java
public String getLastName() {
  return lastName;
}

public double getBalance() {
  return balance;
}

public String ejbCreate(String accountid, String firstName,
                        String lastName, double balance)
    throws CreateException {
  if (balance < 0.00) {
    throw new CreateException("Negative balance not permitted.");
  }
  try {
    insertRow(accountid, firstName, lastName, balance);
  } catch (Exception ex) {
    throw new EJBException("ejbCreate: " + ex.getMessage());
  }
  this.accountid = accountid;
  this.firstName = firstName;
  this.lastName = lastName;
  this.balance = balance;

  return accountid;
}

public String ejbFindByPrimaryKey(String primaryKey) throws
    FinderException {
  boolean result;
  try {
    result = selectByPrimaryKey(primaryKey);
  } catch (Exception ex) {
    throw new EJBException("ejbFindByPrimaryKey: " + ex.getMessage());
  }
  if (result) {
    return primaryKey;
  } else {
    throw new ObjectNotFoundException("Account Id " + primaryKey +
                                      " not found.");
  }
}

public Collection ejbFindByLastName(String lastName)
    throws FinderException {
  Collection result;
  try {
    result = selectByLastName(lastName);
  } catch (Exception ex) {
    throw new EJBException("ejbFindByLastName " + ex.getMessage());
  }
  return result;
}

public Collection ejbFindInRange(double low, double high)
    throws FinderException {
  Collection result;
  try {
    result = selectInRange(low, high);
  } catch (Exception ex) {
    throw new EJBException("ejbFindInRange: " + ex.getMessage());
  }
```

```
      return result;
   }

public void ejbRemove() {
   try {
      deleteRow(accountid);
   } catch (Exception ex) {
      throw new EJBException("ejbRemove: " +  ex.getMessage());
   }
}

public void setEntityContext(EntityContext context) {
   this.context = context;
   try {
      makeConnection();
   } catch (Exception ex) {
      throw new EJBException("database failure " + ex.getMessage());
   }
}

public void unsetEntityContext() {

   try {
      con.close();
   } catch (SQLException ex) {
      throw new EJBException("unsetEntityContext: " + ex.getMessage());
   }
}

public void ejbActivate() {
   accountid = (String)context.getPrimaryKey();
}

public void ejbPassivate() {
   accountid = null;
}

public void ejbLoad() {
   try {
      loadRow();
   } catch (Exception ex) {
         throw new EJBException("ejbLoad: " +
            ex.getMessage());
      }
}

public void ejbStore() {

      try {
         storeRow();
      } catch (Exception ex) {
         throw new EJBException("ejbStore: " +
            ex.getMessage());
      }
}

public void ejbPostCreate(String accountid, String firstName,
   String lastName, double balance) { }

private void makeConnection() throws NamingException, SQLException {
```

```
        InitialContext ic = new InitialContext();
        DataSource ds = (DataSource) ic.lookup(eisName);
        con =  ds.getConnection();
    }

    private void insertRow (String accountid, String firstName,
                            String lastName, double balance)
        throws SQLException {

            String insertStatement =
                "INSERT INTO demoaccount VALUES ( ? , ? , ? , ? )";
            PreparedStatement prepStmt =
                con.prepareStatement(insertStatement);

            prepStmt.setString(1, accountid);
            prepStmt.setString(2, firstName);
            prepStmt.setString(3, lastName);
            prepStmt.setDouble(4, balance);

            prepStmt.executeUpdate();
            prepStmt.close();
    }

    private void deleteRow(String accountid) throws SQLException {

        String deleteStatement =
            "DELETE FROM demoaccount WHERE accountid = ? ";
        PreparedStatement prepStmt =
            con.prepareStatement(deleteStatement);

        prepStmt.setString(1, accountid);
        prepStmt.executeUpdate();
        prepStmt.close();
    }

    private boolean selectByPrimaryKey(String primaryKey)
        throws SQLException {

        String selectStatement =
            "SELECT accountid " +
            "FROM demoaccount WHERE accountid = ? ";
        PreparedStatement prepStmt =
            con.prepareStatement(selectStatement);
        prepStmt.setString(1, primaryKey);

        ResultSet rs = prepStmt.executeQuery();
        boolean result = rs.next();
        prepStmt.close();
        return result;
    }

    private Collection selectByLastName(String lastName)
        throws SQLException {

        String selectStatement =
            "SELECT accountid " +
            "FROM demoaccount WHERE lastname = ? ";
        PreparedStatement prepStmt =
            con.prepareStatement(selectStatement);

        prepStmt.setString(1, lastName);
        ResultSet rs = prepStmt.executeQuery();
```

```java
        ArrayList al = new ArrayList();

    while (rs.next()) {
        String accountid = rs.getString(1);
        al.add(accountid);
    }

    prepStmt.close();
    return al;
}

private Collection selectInRange(double low, double high)
    throws SQLException {

    String selectStatement =
            "SELECT accountid FROM demoaccount " +
            "WHERE balance BETWEEN  ? and ?";
    PreparedStatement prepStmt =
            con.prepareStatement(selectStatement);

    prepStmt.setDouble(1, low);
    prepStmt.setDouble(2, high);
    ResultSet rs = prepStmt.executeQuery();
    ArrayList al = new ArrayList();

    while (rs.next()) {
        String accountid = rs.getString(1);
        al.add(accountid);
    }

    prepStmt.close();
    return al;
}

private void loadRow() throws SQLException {

    String selectStatement =
            "SELECT firstname, lastname, balance " +
            "FROM demoaccount WHERE accountid = ? ";
    PreparedStatement prepStmt =
            con.prepareStatement(selectStatement);

    prepStmt.setString(1, this.accountid);

    ResultSet rs = prepStmt.executeQuery();

    if (rs.next()) {
        this.firstName = rs.getString(1);
        this.lastName = rs.getString(2);
        this.balance = rs.getDouble(3);
        prepStmt.close();
    }
    else {
        prepStmt.close();
        throw new NoSuchEntityException("Account " + accountid +
            " not found");
    }
}

private void storeRow() throws SQLException {
```

```
        String updateStatement =
            "UPDATE demoaccount SET firstname =  ? ," +
            "lastname = ? , balance = ? " +
            "WHERE accountid = ?";
        PreparedStatement prepStmt =
            con.prepareStatement(updateStatement);

        prepStmt.setString(1, firstName);
        prepStmt.setString(2, lastName);
        prepStmt.setDouble(3, balance);
        prepStmt.setString(4, accountid);
        int rowCount = prepStmt.executeUpdate();
        prepStmt.close();

        if (rowCount == 0) {
            throw new EJBException("Account update" + accountid + " failed.");
        }
    }
```

The ProcessingException Class

```java
public class ProcessingException extends Exception {

  public ProcessingException() { }

  public ProcessingException(String msg) {
     super(msg);
  }
}
```

The EJB Deployment Descriptor

```xml
<?xml version="1.0" encoding="UTF-8"?>

<!DOCTYPE ejb-jar PUBLIC '-//Sun Microsystems, Inc.//DTD Enterprise JavaBeans
2.0//EN' 'http://java.sun.com/dtd/ejb-jar_2_0.dtd'>

<ejb-jar>
  <display-name>DemoAccount</display-name>
  <enterprise-beans>
    <entity>
      <display-name>DemoAccount</display-name>
      <ejb-name>DemoAccount</ejb-name>
      <home>DemoAccountHome</home>
      <remote>DemoAccount</remote>
      <ejb-class>DemoAccountBean</ejb-class>
      <persistence-type>Bean</persistence-type>
      <prim-key-class>java.lang.String</prim-key-class>
      <reentrant>False</reentrant>
      <security-identity>
        <description></description>
        <use-caller-identity></use-caller-identity>
      </security-identity>
      <resource-ref>
        <res-ref-name>eis/WroxEIS</res-ref-name>
        <res-type>javax.sql.DataSource</res-type>
        <res-auth>Container</res-auth>
        <res-sharing-scope>Shareable</res-sharing-scope>
```

```
        </resource-ref>
      </entity>
    </enterprise-beans>
  </ejb-jar>
```

Deploying the Bean

Compile the various `java` files and create the EJB JAR file, as directed in Chapters 14-19. Then, with our `Blackbox` application selected in the deployment tool, add the newly created JAR file to the application:

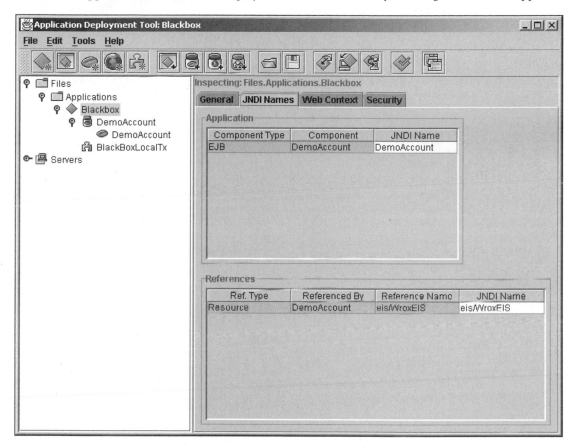

Next, we need to provide the application with the JNDI names shown above, and finally deploy the `Blackbox` application into the running server, remembering to create the client JAR file.

The Client

Here is the client code:

```
import java.util.*;
import javax.naming.Context;
import javax.naming.InitialContext;
import javax.rmi.PortableRemoteObject;
```

```java
public class DemoAccountClient {

  public static void main(String[] args) {

    try {
        Context initial = new InitialContext();
        Object objref = initial.lookup("DemoAccount");

        DemoAccountHome home =
            (DemoAccountHome)PortableRemoteObject.narrow(objref,
            DemoAccountHome.class);

        DemoAccount ramesh = home.create("100", "Ramesh", "Roger", 0.00);
        ramesh.credit(50.00);
        ramesh.debit(10.15);
        double balance = ramesh.getBalance();
        System.out.println("Account Balance = " + String.valueOf(balance));
        ramesh.remove();

        DemoAccount craig = home.create("200", "Craig", "Berry", 0.00);
        craig.credit(100.59);

        DemoAccount nikki = home.findByPrimaryKey("200");
        nikki.debit(2.00);
        balance = nikki.getBalance();

        System.out.println("Account Balance = " + String.valueOf(balance));
        DemoAccount bill = home.create("300", "Bill", "Clinton", 0.00);
        bill.credit(2000.00);

        DemoAccount bob = home.create("400", "Bob", "Clinton", 0.00);
        bob.credit(1000.00);

        DemoAccount jim = home.create("500", "Jimmy", "Clinton", 0.00);
        jim.credit(1000.00);

        Collection c = home.findByLastName("Clinton");
        Iterator i=c.iterator();

        while (i.hasNext()) {
          DemoAccount account = (DemoAccount)i.next();
          String accountid = (String)account.getPrimaryKey();
          double amount = account.getBalance();
          System.out.println(accountid + ": " + String.valueOf(amount));
        }

        c = home.findInRange(20.00, 99.00);
        i = c.iterator();

        while (i.hasNext()) {
          DemoAccount account = (DemoAccount)i.next();
          String accountid = (String)account.getPrimaryKey();
          double amount = account.getBalance();
          System.out.println(accountid + ": " + String.valueOf(amount));
        }

        System.exit(0);

    } catch (ProcessingException ex) {
        System.err.println("Caught an ProcessingException: "
                            + ex.getMessage());
```

```
      } catch (Exception ex) {
        System.err.println("Caught an exception." );
        ex.printStackTrace();
    }
  }
}
```

Finally, run the `DemoAccountClient`, from a command window, remembering to include the `BlackboxClient.jar file in your classpath`. The client should display the following results in your command window:

```
C:\WINNT\System32\cmd.exe                                                    _ □ ×
C:\Wrox\ProJavaServer\Ch20\Blackbox\ejb>java -classpath %j2ee_home%\lib\j2ee.jar;..\BlackboxClient.jar;. DemoAccountClie
nt
Account Balance = 39.85
Account Balance = 98.59
300: 2000.0
400: 1000.0
500: 1000.0
200: 98.59
C:\Wrox\ProJavaServer\Ch20\Blackbox\ejb>
```

The Common Client Interface (CCI)

The **Common Client Interface** provides a simple approach to the problem of writing a more complex Java interface to an underlying EIS resource. Until the emergence of CCI, this problem has been an issue between the Java developers and EIS vendors commonly known as 'integration chaos'. By implementing CCI in resource-adapters, EIS vendors can provide a Java interface to their EIS products that will run on any J2EE 1.3 compliant application server.

The CCI defines an EIS-independent client API for J2EE application components that enables such components to integrate and interact across heterogeneous EIS resources. It defines the remote function call interfaces for executing queries and transactions with an EIS and also to obtain the results.

> Basically, CCI provides function call APIs for J2EE application servers and their
> components via a JCA resource-adapter to create and manage connections with an
> EIS resource, to execute an operation with an EIS resource, and to manage data
> objects/records as input, output, or return values.

The JCA specification recommends that the CCI should form the basis for richer functionality and an extensible programming model provided by the EIS resource-adapter vendors, rather than being the API used by most application developers.

Although the CCI is independent of a specific EIS (for example, data types specific to an EIS), the CCI is capable of being driven by EIS-specific meta data from a repository. The CCI is also designed to use the JavaBeans architecture and Java the `Collections` framework. For example, a resource-adapter can implement the `ManagedConnectionFactory` interface as a JavaBean, which would improve the ability of the JavaBeans framework tools to manage the configuration of `ManagedConnectionFactory` instances.

The JCA 1.0 specification recommends (but does not mandate) that all EIS resource-adapters implement CCI as their client API, while it also requires that these resource-adapters provide the system contracts with a J2EE application server. It is worth noting that a resource-adapter may also choose to have an additional client API different from the CCI, similar to the vendor-provided client API available in JDBC implementations.

1039

The results of using CCI are greater developer productivity, reduced cost of integration, portable code, scalable application frameworks, and maintainability.

CCI Interfaces and Classes

JCA defines the CCI Interfaces and classes representing the following parts:

❑   **Connection interfaces** – represent the connection factory and an application-level connection:

```
javax.resource.cci.ConnectionFactory
javax.resource.cci.Connection
javax.resource.cci.ConnectionSpec
javax.resource.cci.LocalTransaction
```

❑   **Interaction interfaces** – provide a component to drive an interaction (specified using an InteractionSpec) with an EIS instance:

```
javax.resource.cci.Interaction
javax.resource.cci.InteractionSpec
```

❑   **Data representation interfaces** – used to represent data structures involved in an interaction with an EIS instance:

```
javax.resource.cci.Record
javax.resource.cci.MappedRecord
javax.resource.cci.IndexedRecord

javax.resource.cci.RecordFactory
javax.resource.cci.Streamable
javax.resource.cci.ResultSet
java.sql.ResultSetMetaData
```

❑   **Meta data interfaces** – provide basic meta data information about a resource-adapter implementation and an EIS-specific connection:

```
javax.resource.cci.ConnectionMetaData
javax.resource.cci.ResourceAdapterMetaData
javax.resource.cci.ResultSetInfo
```

❑   **Exception and Warning classes** – provide exception handling and resource warning during interaction with an EIS resource:

```
javax.resource.ResourceException
javax.resource.cci.ResourceWarning
```

The following is a list of most important Java interfaces/classes/methods in the CCI API that are worth remembering:

❑   `javax.resource.cci.ConnectionFactory` – a public interface that enables connections to an EIS instance via the resource-adapter. An EIS resource-adapter usually provides this interface. An application looks up a ConnectionFactory instance from the JNDI namespace and uses it to obtain EIS connections, as shown in the following code snippet:

```
public interface javax.resource.cci.ConnectionFactory
        extends java.io.Serializable, javax.resource.Referenceable {

  public RecordFactory getRecordFactory() throws ResourceException;

  public Connection getConnection() throws ResourceException;
```

```
    public Connection getConnection(javax.resource.cci.ConnectionSpec
                                    properties) throws ResourceException;
    public ResourceAdapterMetaData getMetaData() throws ResourceException;
}
```

❑   getConnection() – creates a Connection instance. Using the getConnection() method
    with the javax.resource.cci.ConnectionSpec parameter requires security information
    and connection parameters.

❑   getRecordFactory() – creates a RecordFactory instance.

❑   javax.resource.cci.ConnectionSpec – provides the connection request-specific
    information and properties like username, password, and other parameters to the
    ConnectionFactory while making a connection to an EIS.

❑   javax.resource.cci.Connection – represents a connection to an EIS resource and it is
    used for subsequent operations with an underlying EIS.

❑   createInteraction() – creates an Interaction object to perform EIS-specific operations.

❑   javax.resource.cci.Interaction – creates an interaction with a connected EIS with
    specific operations, as shown in the code extract below:

```
public interface javax.resource.cci.Interaction {

    public Connection getConnection();

    public void close() throws ResourceException;

    public boolean execute(InteractionSpec ispec, Record input, Record output)
        throws ResourceException;

    public Record execute(InteractionSpec ispec, Record input)
        throws ResourceException;

    // ...
}
```

❑   InteractionSpec – defines the interaction providing the EIS- specific object properties (for
    example: data types, schema, etc.) associated with an EIS.

❑   A Record is the Java representation of a data structure used as input or output to an EIS function.

❑   RecordFactory – creates a Record objects (IndexedRecord, ResultSet or
    MappedRecord).

❑   LocalTransaction – creates a transaction context to perform, obviously, a local transaction
    (similar to UserTransaction) and manages its own transaction and persistence. The
    javax.resource.cci.LocalTransaction defines a transaction demarcation interface for
    resource manager local transactions, as shown below:

```
public interface javax.resource.cci.LocalTransaction {

    public void begin() throws ResourceException;

    public void commit() throws ResourceException;

    public void rollback() throws ResourceException;

}
```

To establish a connection to an EIS resource and to perform interactions such as querying and transactions, the developer need to adhere to the standard approach defined by the JCA 1.0 specification. The specification explains two scenarios for obtaining a connection to an EIS, which include discussions about connection to a managed application (J2EE application) and connection to a non-managed application (applets or two-tier Java applications).

In the following sections we'll discuss these two scenarios and the steps involved for connecting and interacting with each.

Connection with a Managed-Application (J2EE)

In this scenario, the application obtains a connection provided by the connection factory, which is configured during the deployment of a resource-adapter module in the J2EE server. This connection factory is usually defined in the deployment descriptor of the resource-adapter.

The UML sequence diagram below shows the steps involved when a managed-application obtains a connection to an EIS instance from a connection factory and then interacts with an EIS:

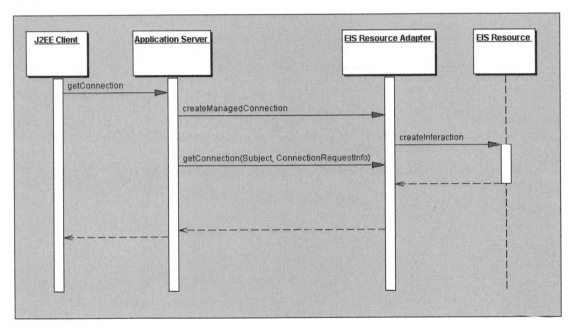

Let's take a closer look at the steps involved:

1. The application assembler specifies the connection factory requirements for a J2EE application component using its deployment descriptor (that is, either web.xml or ejb-jar.xml). This connection factory reference is part of the <resource-ref> element of the deployment descriptor for EJB or web components (rather than the resource-adapter). Thus, an EJB assembler specifies the following elements in the deployment descriptor for a connection factory reference:

    ❑ <res-ref-name>eis/WroxEIS</res-ref-name>
    ❑ <res-type>javax.resource.cci.ConnectionFactory</res-type>
    ❑ <res-auth>Container</res-auth> or <res-auth>Container</res-auth>

2. The J2EE application server uses the configured resource-adapter to create connections to the underlying EIS resource.

3. The J2EE component looks up a connection factory instance in the environment using JNDI services. More specifically:

```
//Obtain initial Naming context
Context initctx = new InitialContext();

// JNDI lookup to obtain the connection factory
javax.resource.cci.ConnectionFactory cf =
                    (javax.resource.cci.ConnectionFactory)
                        initctx.lookup("java:comp/env/eis/wroxEIS");
```

The JNDI lookup results in a connection factory instance of type `java.resource.cci.ConnectionFactory` as specified in the application's deployment descriptor. We should also note that, although not discussed, another type of connection factory exists for the Service Provider Interface (SPI).

4. The application invokes the `getConnection()` method on the connection factory to obtain an EIS connection. It returns a `Connection` instance, which represents a physical handle to an EIS. Also note that the application component can obtain multiple connections by calling the `getConnection()` on the connection factory as required:

```
javax.resource.cci.Connection cx =
    (javax.resource.cci.Connection)cf.getConnection();
```

5. Then the application uses the `Connection` object's `createInteraction()` method to create an `Interaction` instance. The `javax.resource.cci.Interaction` enables a component to execute EIS functions.

6. The application component creates `Record` instances using `RecordFactory` create methods (methods available include `createIndexedRecord()`, `createMappedRecord()`, or `createResultSet()`).

7. The application componrnt uses `LocalTransaction` by defining a transaction context to perform operations with an EIS. The `javax.resource.cci.LocalTransaction` defines a transaction demarcation interface for resource manager local transactions. The J2EE application component uses `LocalTransaction` interface to demarcate local transactions.

8. Once the J2EE application finishes with the connection, it closes the connection using the `cx.close()` method on the `Connection` interface. If the application fails to close an allocated connection after its use, the connection is considered as unused and the application server takes care of the clean up of unused connections.

Connection with a Non-Managed Application (Two-tier)

In a non-managed application connection scenario, which involves an applet or a two-tier Java application, it is the application developer's responsibility to create a connectivity model by using the low-level APIs exposed by the resource-adapter equivalent to that of a configured managed application in a J2EE environment. Typically a non-managed application involves lookup of a connection factory instance, obtaining an EIS connection, using the connection for EIS operations and closing the connection. This model is similar to the way a two-tier JDBC application client accesses a database system in a non-managed environment.

The following sequence diagram shows the steps involved when a non-managed application obtains a connection to an EIS instance from a connection factory and then interacts with an EIS:

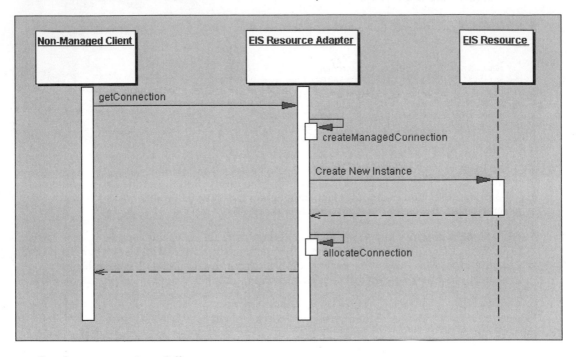

So, the sequence is as follows:

1. The non-managed application component calls a method on the `javax.resource.cci.ConnectionFactory` instance (returned from the JNDI lookup) to get a connection to the underlying EIS resource.

2. The `ConnectionFactory` instance delegates the connection request from the non-managed application to the default `ConnectionManager` instance provided by the resource-adapter. As per the JCA 1.0 specification, the EIS resource-adapter provides the `ConnectionManager` implementation as equivalent to the J2EE server.

3. Then the `ConnectionManager` instance creates a new connection to the EIS resource by calling the `ManagedConnectionFactory.createManagedConnection()` method.

4. The `ManagedConnectionFactory` instance handles the `createManagedConnection()` method by creating a new connection to the underlying EIS resource represented by a `ManagedConnection` instance. The `ManagedConnectionFactory` uses the `ConnectionRequestInfo`, and its configured set of properties (like port number, server name, etc.) to create a new `ManagedConnection` instance.

5. The `ConnectionManager` instance calls the `ManagedConnection.getConnection()` method to get an application-level connection handle. This actually provides a temporary handle for the non-managed application client to access the underlying `ManagedConnection` instance.

6. Then the `ConnectionManager` instance returns the connection handle to the `ConnectionFactory` instance, which then returns the `Connection` to the non-managed application client that initiates a connection request.

7. The application then uses the `Connection` object's `createInteraction()` method to create an `Interaction` instance. The `javax.resource.cci.Interaction` enables a component to execute EIS functions.

8. The application component creates `Record` instances using the `RecordFactory` create methods (which include `createIndexedRecord()`, `createMappedRecord()`, and `createResultSet()`).

9. The application component uses `LocalTransaction` by defining a transaction context to perform operations with an EIS.

10. Finally, once the non-managed application finishes with the connection, it must close the connection using the `cx.close()` method on the `Connection` interface.

At the time of publishing this book, EIS resource-adapters with CCI support were hardly available, even as a beta implementation. As such, we've been using the CCI black-box resource-adapters provided in the J2EE reference implementation in our examples. Note that these resource-adapters were actually meant for testing the packaging and deployment process, and also testing CCI.

In the next section, we'll illustrate an example of using a CCI black-box resource-adapters and how to write J2EE application clients to invoke CCI API methods available from the resource-adapter. We'll also discuss how to use the different interfaces and classes defined by the CCI to access a resource-adapter for a database or EIS.

Using a CCI Black-box Adapter

The example is a fictitious bookstore application to add new books and to get the total quantity available from a database. In this example, we'll implement a stateful session bean, which uses a CCI black-box adapter to run SQL stored procedures for querying and executing transactions with a RDBMS. It is quite similar to a JDBC application but instead of using JDBC calls, the CCI API is used to pass parameters and execute the SQL stored procedures on the an underlying database.

The steps involved in implementing the `BookStore` example using CCI black-box adapter are as follows:

❑ Session bean implementation using CCI

❑ Deployment of the CCI black-box adapter

❑ Deployment of the session bean

❑ Testing the CCI black-box adapter

Developing a Session Bean with CCI

In this `BookStore` example, a stateful session bean is used to maintain a record of the number of books in the book store. Our bean will invoke CCI calls on a CCI black-box adapter to execute stored procedures in a database. As usual, our session EJB contains a home interface (`BookStoreHome`), a remote interface (`BookStore`), and a bean implementation class (`BookStoreBean`).

Let's now see how this session bean implementation uses CCI calls, by taking a closer look at the `BookStore` bean interfaces and classes.

The Home Interface

BookStoreHome simply defines a `create()` method to return a reference to the Book remote interface:

```
import javax.ejb.*;
import java.rmi.RemoteException;

public interface BookStoreHome extends EJBHome {
  BooksStore create() throws RemoteException, CreateException;
}
```

The Remote Interface

BookStore contains the definition for two business methods as follows:

```
import javax.ejb.EJBObject;
import java.rmi.RemoteException;

public interface BookStore extends EJBObject {
  public void insertBooks(String name, int quantity) throws RemoteException;
  public int getBooksCount() throws RemoteException;
}
```

The Bean Implementation Class

BookStoreBean is the bean implementation class, which uses CCI. BookStoreBean imports the CCI interfaces (that is, `javax.resource.cci.*`), and also the interface classes (`com.sun.connector.cciblackbox.*`) specific to the black-box adapter, along with `javax.resource.ResourceException`:

```
import java.math.*;
import java.util.*;
import javax.ejb.*;
import javax.resource.cci.*;
import javax.resource.ResourceException;
import javax.naming.*;
import com.sun.connector.cciblackbox.*;

public class BookStoreBean implements SessionBean {
```

In the `setSessionContext()` method, the bean uses environmental variables for the username and password to instantiate a `ConnectionFactory` for the CCI black-box adapter:

```
private SessionContext sc;
private String user;
private String password;
private ConnectionFactory cf;

public void ejbRemove() {}
public void ejbActivate() {}
public void ejbPassivate() {}
public void ejbCreate() throws CreateException {}

public void setSessionContext(SessionContext sc) {
  try {
    this.sc = sc;
    // Establish a JNDI initial context
    Context ic = new InitialContext();
```

```
        // Use the JNDI IntialContext.lookup method to fetch
        // the user and password values.
        user = (String) ic.lookup("java:comp/env/user");
        password = (String) ic.lookup("java:comp/env/password");
        // Use the lookup method to locate the ConnectionFactory and
        // obtain a reference to it.
        cf = (ConnectionFactory) ic.lookup("java:comp/env/eis/wroxCCIEIS");
    } catch (NamingException ex) {
        ex.printStackTrace();
    }
}
```

The bean uses its private method getCCIConnection() to establish a connection with the database using the black-box adapter. Prior to getCCIConnection(), it instantiates a new CciConnectionSpec object, which represents the implementation of the ConnectionSpec interface, with the user and password values obtained from the bean's context and then calls the getConnection() method to obtain the connection. This creates a connection handle to the underlying EIS resource:

```
private Connection getCCIConnection() {
  Connection con = null;
  try {
    // Instantiate a new CciConnectionSpec object with the
    // user and password values

    ConnectionSpec spec = new CciConnectionSpec(user, password);

    // Use the CCIConnectionSpec to provide the required connection
    // specific parameters to the ConnectionFactory and
    // use the ConnectionFactory's getConnection method to obtain
    // the connection to the database.

    con = cf.getConnection(spec);
  } catch (ResourceException ex) {
    ex.printStackTrace();
  }
  return con;
}
```

The bean also contains a private method closeCCIConnection() to close a connection with the resource manager. The session bean uses this method internally to invoke a Connection object's close() method.

As we have learned previously, if the application fails to close an allocated connection after its use, the connection is considered as unused and the application server takes care of the clean up of unused connections (this applies to managed-application connections only). This terminates a connection with the underlying EIS resource:

```
private void closeCCIConnection(Connection con) {
  try {
    con.close();
  } catch (ResourceException ex) {
    ex.printStackTrace();
  }
}
```

Now that we have defined the methods that allow our bean to interact with the underlying resource using CCI, let's create the methods to perform operations with the resource, in this case – a database.

The BookStore session bean implements an insertBooks() method, which executes a local transaction to insert new records into the Book database table. This method invokes the database-stored procedure INSERTBOOKS that adds a new record with two values as arguments. Typical of a JDBC method call, the insertBooks() method first establishes a connection to the database (via the black-box adapter) using getCCIConnection(), then creates a new Interaction instance. Then the bean instantiates a new CciInteractionSpec object to define the database interaction properties required to communicate with a database (like setting the stored procedure name and its parameters):

```java
public void insertBooks(String name, int qty) {
  try {
    // Establish a connection
    Connection con = getCCIConnection();

    // Create an Interaction
    Interaction ix = con.createInteraction();

    // Instantiate a CciInteractionSpec Object
    CciInteractionSpec iSpec = new CciInteractionSpec();

    // Set the Interaction properties
    // (note that 'null' sets the default catalog).
    iSpec.setFunctionName("INSERTBOOKS");
    iSpec.setSchema(user);
    iSpec.setCatalog(null);

    // Uses the ConnectionFactory to obtain RecordFactory
    RecordFactory rf = cf.getRecordFactory();

    // Invoke the createIndexedRecord method
    IndexedRecord iRec = rf.createIndexedRecord("InputRecord");
    // Set the values
    boolean flag = iRec.add(name);
    flag = iRec.add(new Integer(qty));
    // Executes the interaction
    ix.execute(iSpec, iRec);
  }
  finally {
  // Closes the Connection
  closeCCIConnection(con);
  System.out.println("Closed connection");
  }
}
```

The getBooksCount() method, using CCI, reads records from an underlying database table by running the stored procedure COUNTBOOKS. The method uses an IndexedRecord (the only Record currently supported by the CCI black-box adapter), which holds its elements in an indexed collection based on java.util.List:

```java
public int getBooksCount() {
  int count = -1;
  try {

    // Obtain a Connection
    Connection con = getCCIConnection();

    // Create a new Interaction instance
    Interaction ix = con.createInteraction();

    // Instantiate an CciInteractionSpec object
    CciInteractionSpec iSpec = new CciInteractionSpec();
```

```
            // Set the parameters for the Interaction
            iSpec.setSchema(user);
            iSpec.setCatalog(null);
            iSpec.setFunctionName("COUNTBOOKS");

            // Use ConnectionFactory to obtain RecordFactory
            RecordFactory rf = cf.getRecordFactory();

            // Use createIndexedRecord method
            IndexedRecord iRec = rf.createIndexedRecord("InputRecord");

            // Execute the Interaction
            Record oRec = ix.execute(iSpec, iRec);

            // Use Iterator to retrieve elements
            Iterator iterator = ((IndexedRecord)oRec).iterator();
            while(iterator.hasNext()) {
              // Extract the element as a Java object
              Object obj = iterator.next();
              if(obj instanceof Integer) {
                count = ((Integer)obj).intValue();
              } else if(obj instanceof BigDecimal) {
                count = ((BigDecimal)obj).intValue();
              }
            }
          }
      finally {
        // Close the connection
        closeCCIConnection(con);
        System.out.println("Closed Connection");
      }
      return count;
    }
```

The EJB Deployment Descriptor

In the deployment descriptor this time, note that the `<resource-ref>` element (highlighted in bold) is of type `javax.resource.cci.ConnectionFactory`:

```xml
<?xml version="1.0" encoding="UTF-8"?>

<!DOCTYPE ejb-jar PUBLIC '-//Sun Microsystems, Inc.//DTD Enterprise JavaBeans
2.0//EN' 'http://java.sun.com/dtd/ejb-jar_2_0.dtd'>

<ejb-jar>
  <display-name>BookStore</display-name>
  <enterprise-beans>
    <session>
      <display-name>BookStore</display-name>
      <ejb-name>BookStore</ejb-name>
      <home>BookStoreHome</home>
      <remote>BookStore</remote>
      <ejb-class>BookStoreBean</ejb-class>
      <session-type>Stateful</session-type>
      <transaction-type>Bean</transaction-type>
      <env-entry>
        <env-entry-name>user</env-entry-name>
        <env-entry-type>java.lang.String</env-entry-type>
      </env-entry>
      <env-entry>
        <env-entry-name>password</env-entry-name>
```

```
        <env-entry-type>java.lang.String</env-entry-type>
      </env-entry>
      <security-identity>
        <description></description>
        <use-caller-identity></use-caller-identity>
      </security-identity>
      <resource-ref>
        <res-ref-name>eis/WroxCCIEIS</res-ref-name>
        <res-type>javax.resource.cci.ConnectionFactory</res-type>
        <res-auth>Container</res-auth>
        <res-sharing-scope>Shareable</res-sharing-scope>
      </resource-ref>
    </session>
  </enterprise-beans>
</ejb-jar>
```

The Client

The client invokes the `getBooksCount()` and `insertBooks()` methods on the session bean to test the CCI black-box adapter:

```java
import java.util.*;
import javax.naming.Context;
import javax.naming.InitialContext;
import javax.rmi.PortableRemoteObject;

public class BookStoreClient {

  public static void main(String[] args) {
    try {
      Context initial = new InitialContext();
      Object objref = initial.lookup("BookStore");

      BookStoreHome home =
        (BookStoreHome)PortableRemoteObject.narrow(objref,
                                          BookStoreHome.class);
      BookStore book = home.create();

      int count = book.getBooksCount();
      System.err.println("Current Book count = " + count);

      System.err.println("Inserting 2 new books...");
      book.insertBooks("USA Tour guide", 100);
      book.insertBooks("Europe Tour guide", 20);

      count = book.getBooksCount();
      System.err.println("Current Book count = " + count);
    } catch (Exception ex) {
      System.err.println("Caught an unexpected exception!");
      ex.printStackTrace();
    }
  }
}
```

Deploying the CCI Black-box Resource-adapter

As with our `DemoAccount` example earlier, this is a two-stage process. First, we need to configure the database to create the table and add the stored procedures, and secondly we need to deploy the adapter itself.

Configuring the Database

This is a slightly more complex process than in the previous example because, as well as creating the `Books` table, we also need to create the two stored procedures. We'll be using Cloudscape again, however, this database has a rather unusual method of handling stored procedures. We'll explain the method for this is in just a moment, but first let's create the `Books` table.

Use the following SQL to create the very simple `Books` table:

```
CREATE TABLE Books (name VARCHAR(32), qty INTEGER);
```

Now let's get back to those stored procedures. In order to use them with Cloudscape we need to write a Java class that provides the implementation of the procedure using basic JDBC. Then within in the database, we create an `ALIAS` for the stored procedures that points to this class. So, for our `COUNTBOOKS` stored procedure, we'll add a method to our class that looks like this:

```
import java.lang.Integer;
import java.sql.*;
import java.io.*;

public class BookProcs implements Serializable {

  public static int countBooks() {
     int count = 0;
     try {
        Connection con =
        DriverManager.getConnection("jdbc:cloudscape:;current=true");
        PreparedStatement ptstmt =
        con.prepareStatement("SELECT COUNT(*) FROM BOOKS");
        ResultSet rs = ptstmt.executeQuery();
        while (rs.next()) {
          count = rs.getInt(1);
        }
        ptstmt.close();
     } catch (Exception ex) {
        ex.printStackTrace();
     }
     return count;
  }
}
```

Then to the Cloudscape database we add the following `ALIAS`:

```
CREATE METHOD ALIAS COUNTBOOKS FOR BookProcs.countBooks;
```

Remember, you can run SQL either by using Cloudview directly or from a command line using the `cloudscape -isql` prompt from `%J2EE_HOME%\bin`.

> Note that in order for this to work, we need to make sure that the `BookProcs` class is in the classpath of the database. The easiest way to do this is to modify the `%J2EE_CLASSPATH%` variable (set in the `userconfig.bat` file).

For the `INSERTBOOKS` stored procedure, add another method to `BookProcs`:

```
public static void insertBooks(String name, int qty) {
   try {
      Connection con =
      DriverManager.getConnection("jdbc:cloudscape:;current=true");
      PreparedStatement ptstmt =
```

```
        con.prepareStatement("INSERT INTO BOOKS VALUES (?,?)");
        ptstmt.setString(1, name);
        ptstmt.setInt(2, qty);
        ptstmt.executeUpdate();
        ptstmt.close();
    } catch(Exception ex){
        ex.printStackTrace();
    }
  }
```

And use the following `ALIAS`:

```
CREATE METHOD ALIAS INSERTBOOKS FOR BookProcs.insertBooks;
```

Deploying the Adapter

We'll use a similar method to before, except this time of course we'll be deploying the `cciblackbox-tx.rar` file.

With the J2EE 1.3 Reference Implementation server running, open the deployment tool and create a new application called `CCIAdapter`:

Then add an existing resource-adapter `.rar` file as before but this time select the `%J2EE_HOME%\lib\connector\cciblackbox-tx.rar` file before deploying the enterprise application.

Expand the server's node until you can see your running server (most likely `localhost`) and select the server in the left-hand pane. On the right-hand pane, switch to the **Resource-adapters** tab, and hit the **New** button. On the **New Connection Factory** dialog, select the `CCIAdapter:cciblackbox-tx.rar` as the **Resource-adapter** and give it a JNDI Name of `eis/WroxCCIEIS`, as shown opposite:

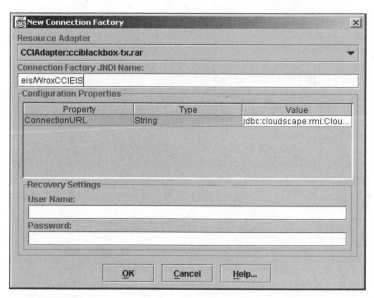

Make sure that the ConnectionURL property is pointing to the correct database (CloudscapeDB in our case) and hit OK to add the adapter:

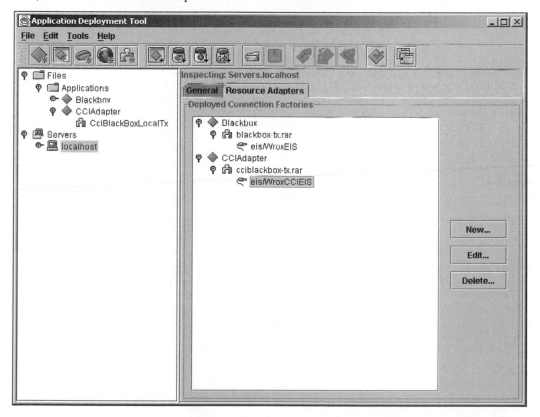

Now that we've deployed the CCI black-box resource-adapter module with a connection factory into the J2EE 1.3 Reference Implementation server and created the database tables and stored procedures, we're ready to deploy the session bean and run the client.

Deploying and Testing the CCI Application

Compile the EJB java files, remembering to add the cciblackbox-tx.jar file (found within the cciblackbox-tx.rar archive) to your classpath, and then add them to the deployment tool either using the EJB creation wizard or generate your own EJB JAR file:

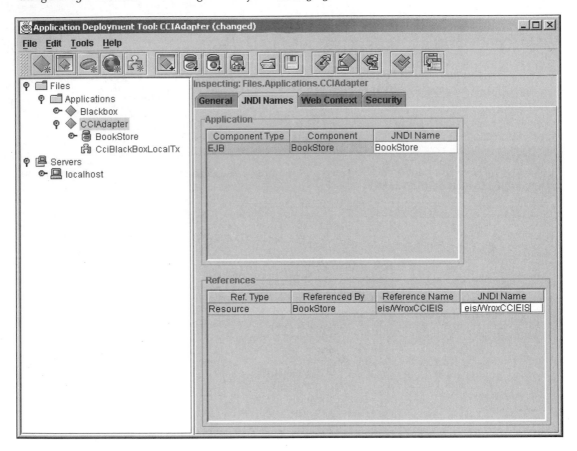

Add the relevant JNDI names and deploy the application again, remembering to create the client JAR file this time.

Finally, run the client using a command line as shown below. If everything works successfully, you will get the following thrilling output:

This concludes our `BookStore` example using the CCI black-box resource-adapter to interact with a Cloudscape database.

Benefits of the J2EE Connector Architecture

With the success of J2EE in web-based enterprise applications, it is strongly anticipated that JCA will emerge as the primary integration mechanism to interact with backend EIS resources. A couple of important benefits worth remembering are:

❑ JCA enables organizations to leverage the advantages of both their existing EIS systems and J2EE.

❑ JCA allows developers to write (or rewrite) new applications using J2EE, encapsulating functional parts of existing applications in EJB or web components.

Let's briefly discuss some scenarios in which JCA offers a potential solution, focusing on the obvious benefits.

Enterprise Application Integration (EAI) with JCA

Managing and integrating diverse EIS applications to share data and processes usually adds challenges to the development, transactions, security, and scalability of an application. As EIS resources are uniquely built with their own proprietary API and transaction and security mechanisms, it becomes extremely complex to build an EAI framework using multiple proprietary APIs and adapting native mechanisms.

Though a strategic EAI strategy demands a checklist of requirements, with a mix and match of different adapter technologies, in most case it ends up with limitations and issues related to the scalability of the framework due to either a proprietary API or non-standard mechanisms. Sometimes it can end up more like enterprise application *spaghetti* than integration!

JCA provides a standard architecture that fixes those shortfalls of common EAI solutions. With a long list of EIS vendors standing behind JCA by providing EIS-specific resource-adapters, JCA features seamless integration characteristics with its application-independent CCI API, supporting distributed transactions and also supporting both generic and application-specific security mechanisms.

Web-Enabled Enterprise Portals with JCA

Enterprise portals usually fulfill the need to provide a single corporate "desktop" that unifies all information, services, applications, and processes for the members of an enterprise, such as the employees, partners, and customers. Integrating the content and applications using a generic infrastructure adds complexity if it involves integration with heterogeneous backend applications and legacy systems with proprietary architectures and security mechanisms.

Portals generally require a global sign-on requiring centralized authentication and authorization support to heterogeneous applications and distributed transactions with multiple enterprise information systems. Generally, portals are mission-critical applications that demand high-availability and central manageability.

Being a part of J2EE family, JCA is ideal for building enterprise portals. With the success of J2EE-based portals, JCA leverages non-Java EIS resources by enabling them to become part of a J2EE-based enterprise portal. Relevant strengths include:

- Application-independent CCI API
- EIS sign-on mechanisms that support generic and application-specific authentication mechanisms
- J2EE component-based distributed transactions with XA support

Thus, JCA clearly presents a perfect solution for leveraging EIS applications to an enterprise portal.

Business-to-Business Integration with JCA

Business-to-Business (B2B) integration leverages end-to-end process automation and allows application interaction within an enterprise and across partners through the Internet. To truly support external trading-partner interactions, the backend internal business systems need to be seamlessly integrated into the same process. Without this, end-to-end process integration cannot be achieved. Though XML over HTTP provides B2B client integration within an enterprise and across the Internet, it has its own limitations with regard to application-to-application integration, security, and transactions.

JCA solves the B2B puzzle by specifically providing integration with backend EIS resources and demonstrates genuine end-to-end process integration. JCA can be deployed to query and transact data with backend EIS resources, and the data can be subsequently converted to XML using the Java XML APIs for B2B interaction with partners.

With the strength of CCI and its application-independent API developers, we could handle any application-level security mechanisms and distributed transactions with multiple EIS resources. Having J2EE platform-based enterprise server applications to use JCA enables highly scalable B2B applications without compromising the value and the functionality of EIS resources.

It is clear that JCA offers countless benefits to the users by reducing the cost to build complex EAI solutions, enhancing developer productivity, investment protection of standard architectures, and the extension of custom applications.

Missing Elements in JCA 1.0

In the previous sections, we looked at the features and the most promising factors of the J2EE Connector Architecture 1.0, now let's close by briefly discussing what's missing from this version of the specification.

The two key missing elements of the J2EE Connector Architecture 1.0 specification are:

- The current specification does not support asynchronous communication, and it supports only the synchronous request/reply communication model. This could be a limiting problem to connect with message queues.
- There is no built-in XML support mechanism available to retrieve XML data although CCI can be used to support XML.

These limitations will be resolved in the next version of the specification (JCA 1.1). For further details, take a look at http://java.sun.com/j2ee/connector/.

Summary

In this chapter, we have taken a tour of the J2EE Connector Architecture 1.0, demonstrating with examples using the black-box resource-adapters provided with the J2EE 1.3 Reference Implementation. We have discussed how J2EE connector architecture addresses its solutions to solve application-integration issues faced by the industry today. This chapter also explained and demonstrated the steps involved to integrate and interact with an EIS using the Common Client Interface API.

We have looked at:

- ❑ The role of J2EE Connector Architecture
- ❑ J2EE Connector Architecture and its elements
- ❑ Resource-adapters
- ❑ Deploying and testing a resource-adapter
- ❑ Programming with the Common Client Interface (CCI)
- ❑ Deploying and testing a JCA-based application
- ❑ Potential benefits of JCA
- ❑ Current status of the specification and missing elements

In the next chapter, we'll be examining some important design considerations that should be taken into account when developing our J2EE applications. With the help of some UML diagrams, we'll take a look at a variety of J2EE-specific patterns that can be applied to solve some common design issues.

Data
RDMS
JDBC
Application Logic
Client
Web Container
Servlets
JSPs
Tag Library
HTTP(S)
(X)HTML/ XML
RMI/IIOP
JNDI
JTA
JDBC
JMS
JavaMail
JAAS
JCA
JAXP
J2EE Application Server
Applet
Client Application
Session Beans
JAF
JavaMail
Mail Server
RMI
Java Application
IIOP
CORBA Server
JNDI
Directory Servi
JMS
Message Queu

21

Design Considerations for J2EE Applications

The Java 2 Platform, Enterprise Edition (J2EE) delivers a whole range of useful technologies. So far, we have spent a great deal of time in this book covering what these technologies are and how they should be applied.

> The key to creating usable, flexible, and maintainable applications is to apply technologies that are appropriate to the *context* of the problem being solved.

In this chapter we will look at some common ways of applying J2EE technologies to solve design issues in particular contexts.

We will look at:

- ❑   What we mean by design and architecture
- ❑   The relationship between design and the context in which it occurs
- ❑   The forces at work when designing a typical e-commerce application for the J2EE platform
- ❑   A variety of J2EE-specific patterns that solve many common design issues encountered when designing J2EE-based business systems
- ❑   The advantages and disadvantages of various J2EE technologies when applied in certain design contexts

The World is Still Changing

When software vendors – who are usually at war – agree on something, is it a good omen or a bad one? Consider the enterprise application platforms promoted by Sun and Microsoft. Viewed from a high level, the Java 2 Platform Enterprise Edition (J2EE) and the .NET Framework (previously incarnated as Windows Distributed InterNet Architecture, or DNA) look frighteningly similar. Both combine multiple tiers, thin or thick clients, distributed object protocols, standard data access APIs, messaging services, middle-tier component environments, and transactions.

The arrival of e-commerce and Internet timescales has changed the way that most business applications are defined and developed. The requirements are more demanding than before and the timescales shorter. There is an increasing need for solutions to become adaptable since tomorrow's business requirements will almost certainly not be the same as today's. To design and develop applications under these conditions, we need serious (some would say 'professional') help.

This help usually takes two forms:

❑ A **standardized framework** on which applications can be built and deployed. The framework should provide appropriate levels of functionality and should also help to automate the creation of standard 'plumbing' to plug the application into itself.

❑ A set of **best practices** for using that framework. Software developers do not have an infinite amount of time to spend on contemplating the philosophy of design or learning the most efficient ways of using certain APIs. What they need are guidelines to help them write good applications using the framework.

> In Java terms, the framework for development of distributed business applications is J2EE. The features and functionality of the platform allow the creation of scalable, distributed, flexible, and component-based applications.

The buzzwords listed above are just a few of those regularly applied to J2EE in the average marketing 'blurb'. They are very easy to promise but far more difficult to deliver. When creating applications or application components, requirements such as the level of scalability must be specified and designed. The underlying application architecture is a key element in determining whether or not such requirements are achievable. J2EE provides the foundations on which the architecture of modern, Java-based enterprise and e-commerce applications can be built.

Now, with the 1.3 version, the J2EE platform delivers further refinements in the use of Enterprise JavaBeans (EJB), native XML support, improved security, and a generic resource connector framework. Although this brings with it a few more tools and strategies, it does not change the fundamental way that J2EE is applied. Design strategies remain pretty much the same. Indeed, it is the nature of design that the best application of tools and technologies is discovered only after they have been used for a time. The discussion of patterns throughout this chapter is a good reflection of this.

The move from J2EE version 1.2 to version 1.3 has indeed added more functionality, but is this a benefit or a bane? Recently, even the vendors have come to understand that developers need help in exploiting the ocean of functionality that has already been delivered. Sun Microsystems has built the Sun Blueprints Design Guidelines for J2EE (hereafter referred to as the 'J2EE Blueprints') and the associated Java Pet Store to provide illustration of the best practices for the J2EE platform. The J2EE Blueprints can be found at http://java.sun.com/j2ee/blueprints/.

There is no easy way of obtaining the knowledge required for effective application design on an enterprise platform. The J2EE Blueprints version 1.0 runs to around 350 pages. In addition, there are also a multitude of other resources, such as books, e-mail/newsgroups, newsletters, and articles that provide insights, discussion, advice, and sometimes controversial opinions on the creation of enterprise applications. A sample of these resources are listed below:

- *Software Architecture in Practice*, Bass, Clements, and Kazman, ISBN 0-201-19930-0
- *Client/Server Programming with Java and CORBA*, Orfali and Harkey, ISBN 0-471-24578-X
- *Enterprise JavaBeans, Second Edition*, Monson-Haefel, ISBN 1-565-92869-5
- *The Java 2 Enterprise Edition Developer's Guide* (referenced in the J2EE documentation and available at http://java.sun.com/j2ee/docs.html)
- *J2EE Patterns* discussion e-mail list at Sun, sign up at http://developer.java.sun.com/developer/technicalArticles/J2EE/patterns/WhatsNext.html
- J2EE design discussions at http://www.theserverside.com/discussion/index.jsp

The combined thoughts and opinions found in these sources (and many more besides) cannot all be condensed into one chapter. Therefore the rest of this chapter examines some of the main issues in enterprise development and the types of solution that apply in a J2EE environment.

Architecture and Design

The use of the terms 'architect' and 'architecture' in the world of software development is the subject of some debate. In building terms, the role of an architect is reasonably well understood. In software terms, it is regularly used interchangeably with the term "design". The architecture of an application can define some or all of the following:

- The components that perform the business tasks of the application
- The type of interaction between those components
- The services used by those components
- The underlying platform that delivers or supports those services
- Other characteristics or capabilities (such as scalability) that address the non-functional requirements of the application

Overall, the architecture of an application provides a framework within which individual, detailed design decisions can be made. The idea that an application fits into a particular type of architecture can help to clarify its overall structure.

> When considering these topics we will use the term architecture in its general meaning of the structure or form of an application.

Architectural Styles

People will refer to service-based architectures and layered or tiered architectures. However, it is not a case of making a straight choice between them. Many systems use aspects of multiple architectural styles in order to solve different parts of their overall problem.

Layered and tiered architectures have much in common. In many senses, tiered architectures can be viewed as a particular form of layered architecture. The main aim is to abstract some elements of a system in order to simplify the overall structure. A layer represents a cluster of functionality or components that have similar characteristics, for example, type of function or physical location. Each layer provides functionality to the layers around it.

When discussing layered architectures, many people will think of top-to-bottom layers, such as those seen in a network stack. In the OSI model of a network stack, for example, the transport layer makes use of functionality provided by the network layer, which in turn uses the functionality of the data-link layer. Such layering provides abstraction of the underlying layers to allow for substitution. In terms of our application, the J2EE platform provides multiple layers – hardware, operating system, J2EE, and the application itself – as shown in this diagram:

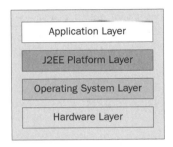

Since the application sits on top of the J2EE platform, the underlying hardware or operating system can be changed to provide better characteristics (faster, cheaper, more stable, for example) without needing to re-write parts of the application.

Tiered architectures are a specific type of layered architecture based on a user-focused view of the system. This leads to a front-to-back partitioning with the user at the front and the underlying data (and so on) at the back. A typical 3-tiered architecture consists of:

- ❑ A user interface tier that presents application data to the user and through which the user interacts with the application.

- ❑ A business tier that encapsulates the business logic of the application, for example the steps involved in submitting an insurance claim.

- ❑ A data tier that provides access to underlying data sources, such as databases, Enterprise Resource Planning (ERP) applications, or mainframes. This tier is also sometimes called the Enterprise Information Services (EIS) tier.

The tiers reflect some form of physical partitioning, such that the three sets of components will exist in different processes and typically on different machines. Communication will flow between the various tiers as the application goes about its work.

The use of tiers makes the separation of concerns easier to judge. One of the key motivations for layered architectures is that they reduce coupling between components in different layers. Highly coupled components have intimate knowledge of the other components they interact with. This means that they are more difficult to replace or re-locate individually. By defining the overall roles performed by the components in each tier, it becomes easier to create fixed interfaces between the tiers and hence to reduce the coupling between components in those tiers. The separation of the user interface, business logic, and data access allow us to substitute better products or techniques at each tier without disturbing the others. This leads to a more flexible application.

An application can also use a tiered architecture for scalability reasons. The decoupling between the tiers allows us to add more capability at each tier as the system scales. An example would be adding more web servers at the user interface tier to service more clients. This would not automatically require more database servers on the data tier (although it might!).

A web-based 3-tier architecture can be seen below:

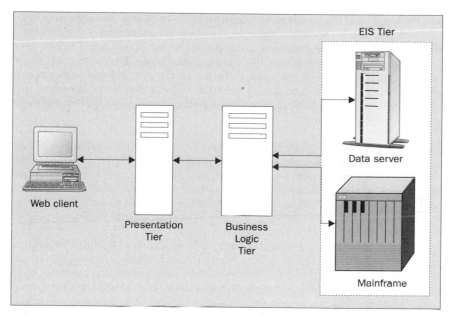

A service-based architecture views the components of a system in terms of black box services. An example from the system level would be a transaction service, such as the Java Transaction API (JTA) provided by J2EE. In this case, the user of the service is solely concerned with the interface to and characteristics of the service, not its implementation. Service-based architectures can be viewed as a larger form of component architectures since applications will be created by creating programs or scripts that call upon various services to perform their required tasks. The concept of a service starts to get away from the concept of fixed clients and servers since services might call other services to perform their tasks. There is no implicit requirement for calls to flow in a particular direction.

Services can be vertical or horizontal – vertical services reflect functional requirements, such as an approval service for purchase orders, whereas horizontal services provide underlying mechanisms, such as authentication or persistence.

Design Context

Software is developed to solve a problem. That problem may be of a business nature, such as how to reduce the amount of time it takes an organization to process a customer's order, or it may be more technical, such as ensuring that a satellite control system responds correctly when instructed to change course. In either case, you cannot make an absolute judgment of the quality of the proposed solution. You can only judge the solution in the context of the problem to be solved.

Consider the design for an airplane. Conventional wisdom would say that stability is a very important factor for an airplane design. However, many modern fighter aircraft are intentionally designed to be unstable since this improves their maneuverability. This is a good design decision for a fighter plane since a slight improvement in maneuverability can mean the difference between success or failure of a mission. Also, the organizations that use such planes are willing to pay for the extensive computer systems that help turn the unstable machine into something that can be controlled by a human pilot.

If you change the context of the problem, for example by looking at a passenger aircraft, safety considerations are paramount. Suddenly stability becomes very important – much more so than maneuverability. For such a plane, the extra maneuverability is not worth the risk to safety or the cost of the extra computer systems to control an inherently unstable plane. Hence, the correct design decision in one context can, in a slightly different context, be the wrong one. No design decision is inherently good or bad, it all depends on the context and the internal and external factors acting on the design (often called forces). This applies both to the modeling of the proposed solution and the mapping of the model onto the underlying platform.

So, at what level does this chapter cover design issues? Essentially, it is a reflection of some considerations, tradeoffs, best practices, and rules of thumb commonly encountered when mapping some form of higher-level model onto the J2EE platform. This, then, is the design that sits between analysis and implementation. Some of this design can be independent of implementation technology. As a UML model is refined, some of those refinements work well across all potential architectures. Other refinements must be influenced by the platform onto which they will be deployed.

When discussing specific aspects of design, it is useful to have a context in which to judge decisions. With this in mind, we will provide the context in this chapter through the use of a simple e-commerce case study. More specifically, the design and development of a typical purchasing application, and its associated requirements will be referred to throughout this chapter. Moreover, we will examine good J2EE design practices by exploring the design issues surrounding a system for submitting and processing purchase orders. This provides one context in which to judge the pros and cons of particular design decisions.

The Business Requirements

Our fictional company, Acme Multinational Plc., wishes to automate its purchasing systems that handle the creation, submission, and processing of purchase orders.

The Existing System

Currently, an employee must look up the products they require in printed catalogs from multiple suppliers. These catalogs are of varying age and accuracy. The employee must then fill out a paper-based purchase order listing the items they require. They must supply additional information, such as their location and department code. The completed form is then sent via the internal post to the appropriate manager for approval.

The manager will first judge whether the items are relevant to the role of the employee, and then consult their financial spreadsheets, or phone the accounts department, to check if sufficient departmental budget remains to fund the purchase. There may also be a personal limit that must be checked for that employee. If the items are inappropriate, or there are insufficient funds, the manager will reject the purchase order and send it back to the individual. This can be anything up to 2 weeks after the initial order submission.

If the purchase order is approved, it is forwarded to the purchasing department who will separate out the items that come from different suppliers. At this stage, they may discover that items specified have come from old catalogs and are no longer supplied or that the price has changed. They may have changed supplier for a particular type of item, meaning that the specification has changed. In all of these cases, the original requester must be informed of the changes and the purchase order may potentially require re-submission through the whole process again.

The Desired System

The intention is that all of the existing system will be automated. The overall objective is to save costs by reducing the number of human interactions required to process the purchase order and consequently reducing the possibility of error. The system should also improve employee morale by speeding up the processing of purchase orders and removing the need to re-submit.

The overall functional requirements include the following:

❑ All catalog information will be provided online. This ensures that all information is up to date and reduces the number of resubmissions required. It also provides the potential to limit the items offered to the employee based on their role and individual purchasing budget.

❑ The employee will fill out the purchase order online. Items can only be added by selection from the online catalog (that is, they are not typed in by the employee). This should be provided in a shopping cart style that is familiar to web users. Standard information about that employee, such as location and department code, will be automatically inserted into the document based on their authenticated identity. This will reduce errors due to incorrect completion of product codes and department codes.

❑ The employee will submit the purchase order online. An employee's individual budget can be checked on submission and the order rejected immediately if they exceed their budget. The manager to whom the order is to be sent will be determined from the employee's identity, or from the contents of the order (that is, an order for a computer may go to the IT manager rather than the employee's line manager). The document will be delivered electronically to the manager.

❑ The manager can view any purchase orders submitted to them online. The same system should give them access to up-to-the-minute departmental budget figures and also any purchasing rules that apply to their department. Any purchase orders that are received when the manager is not available should be queued for examination later.

❑ The manager can approve or reject the purchase online. Any rejection will be sent back to the employee electronically. Approval will result in the purchase order being forwarded to the purchasing system, once it has been automatically checked that this purchase will not exceed the departmental budget.

❑ The purchasing system will take care of splitting up the purchase order, and will batch together items from different purchase orders required from the same supplier. This can serve to gain bulk discounts from some suppliers by submitting all items in one go. All submission to suppliers will be electronic – ideally over the Web, but it may mean sending an automated fax. The purchase order information will be logged so that it is available to the goods receiving clerks who will forward the received items to the requesting employee. All of this saves a large amount of time in processing, filing, and retrieving purchase orders.

As well as the actual processing of purchase orders, the business places other requirements on the system.

The Business Context

There are also key requirements of the system that are not related directly to the processing of purchase orders:

- **Scalable** – the system must scale to be able to service all of Acme's 75,000 staff. Up to 8,000 of these users may be online at any one time, although not all of them will necessarily be using the purchase order system.

- **Distributed** – the system must be accessible from all of Acme's sites. Since Acme already has a company-wide intranet, a web-based system is strongly favored.

- **Flexible** – it must be possible to easily add new functionality as required by changes in business practice.

- **Component-based** – the system must conform to a component framework so that it is possible to buy common off-the-shelf components to form part of the system instead of building everything from scratch. This saves development time and cost.

In addition, one of the most common non-functional requirements for systems is "short time to market". Systems are required 'yesterday' but with higher functionality, scalability and so on, than ever before. It would be impossible to build everything required in the timeframe from simple, low-level APIs. What is required is an environment that provides a common framework to host bought or built components around which the application can be constructed. The environment should also provide a large amount of the functionality "out of the box" and present the developer with high-level abstractions that make it easier to use.

In the past, the application was king to the extent that it relied only on the basic functionality of its underlying operating system or environment. This could be seen from the efforts to port applications between different platforms. Environments such as J2EE help to raise the bar in this respect. Much of the functionality that was previously part of the application can now be delegated elsewhere – to horizontal layers or vertical services. This gives rise to the "tear off application" since the application code itself forms only a small part of the overall functionality. Since there is a lower investment in the application it can be re-written more often and thrown away more easily when it becomes outdated. E-Commerce applications are typical of this sort of application (or should be). This transition is shown in the following diagram:

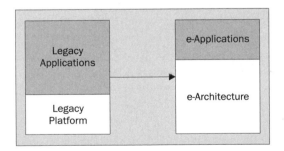

The short development times expected for e-commerce applications have also changed the way that systems are developed. In one report on e-commerce, Gartner states that the transition to e-commerce is "a programme, not a project". This reflects the realities in a world of rapidly changing business requirements. In such an environment, a commercial application cannot remain largely the same for two or three years after delivery. The changes required of the application in that timeframe will be significant – not simply bug fixes and usability improvements. In order to avoid becoming a legacy application, it must constantly evolve to meet changing demands.

Elaborating the Requirements

Once the functional requirements have been defined, a model can be built that encapsulates the business process and the main business entities in it. UML can be used to capture the main elements of the system as described by the functional requirements. This will create a model of the "problem domain", that is, the actual business system to be implemented.

Building the Model

A first-pass model for the system of our example is shown below:

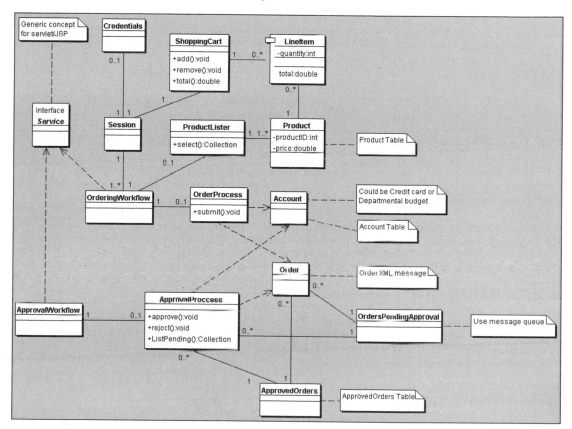

This is by no means the finished article, but provides a basis around which design decisions can be discussed. Indeed, some of the design decisions will affect how the model evolves. The initial stages of analysis and design involve the creation of a model that maps the problem to be solved. The inputs for the creation of this model are the use cases or user stories that describe the desired system functionality. In fact, our list of business requirements noted in the earlier section on *The Desired System* could form the beginnings of a set of use cases.

These inputs can be crystallized in UML notation such as class diagrams and sequence diagrams. This initial problem-domain model, which reflects 'real' things (people, documents, and so on), is then used as the basis on which to create a model of the proposed solution (the classes, components, and interactions that will make up the software system). This solution will be shaped to a degree by the environment into which it will be deployed. Although this is not necessarily defined at this point, the comments do indicate that J2EE is the target environment, as will be discussed later.

The model of the system is reasonably simplistic and there are no doubt many aspects of the model that we might elaborate on, or where we may organize things somewhat differently. Remember, however, that all solutions reflect the context of their design, and one of the main forces in this case is that the model should be simple enough to be readily understood. The intention at this early stage is to capture the essence of the system and not necessarily the detail. This is sufficient to discuss the move from model to system architecture. We do not need to build a complete working model and hence become bogged down in the domain detail of purchasing systems. You can see a more involved (or, in fact, evolved) solution for an n-tier e-commerce system in the Java Pet Store provided as part of the J2EE Blueprints.

Exploring the Model

A quick look at the model of the system reveals that the building of a purchase order revolves around the Product class. Products can be listed on some basis (product code, category) and presented to the user. The products selected by the user will be stored in a ShoppingCart represented by a series of LineItems. The interaction with the user will be governed by the OrderingWorkflow, which encapsulates the user interface logic for displaying products, selecting products, and submitting a purchase order. As part of the ordering process, the purchase order must be sent to the appropriate manager. This will require some form of identification of the user and also of the manager. Credentials can be gathered from the user for this purpose. When the purchase order is submitted, it will be checked against departmental limits of various sorts, including how much money is left in the departmental budget.

The purchase order produced will be stored somewhere, pending retrieval by the manager. The manager will progress through the ApprovalWorkflow user-interface logic to view and approve or reject purchase orders that have been submitted.

This, in essence, is the application to be implemented. However, there are many more decisions that must be taken to evolve this model into an implementation using J2EE technologies.

Elaborating the Context

Once the problem-domain model has been built, a solution-domain model must be evolved from it. This model will be subject to the "real-world" forces of application development such as the capabilities of the tools and environments applied, the topology of the infrastructure on which the application is to be deployed, and the skills available for development.

Fitting the Terrain

Consider a 'real' architect designing a house. The architect is given a set of requirements stating that the house must contain four bedrooms, a bathroom, living room, garage, and so on. If the house is to be built on the side of a hill, the design will differ from a house designed for a flat piece of land. The design of the former may make use of the slope of the ground to site the garage underneath the rest of the house, or it may build parts of the house into the hillside to improve its thermodynamic efficiency.

Similarly in software, the solution that evolves from a basic model will differ depending on the "terrain" onto which it will be deployed. A pattern that is prevalent in this environment may suggest a convenient solution to a particular problem (such as the ground-floor garage described above). In this way, the environment will shape the model in the same way that the initial requirements do.

The evolved model can give us useful information about the system such as the relationships between the different classes. This information is very useful when deciding deployment issues like componentization and packaging. Again, if there is a known constraint relating to the deployment of different parts of the system (for example, one component must live on a particular database server) then this may mean that two related components cannot be packaged together. This in turn affects the relationship between the classes involved and hence affects the shape of the model. In this case, the interface of one or more of the classes involved may need to be altered to allow for the effects of distribution or a proxy class may be introduced.

In our case, the terrain is J2EE. This choice may be made for many reasons:

- ❑ The organization may have a lot of skills in Java development

- ❑ Java or J2EE-based application servers may be part of a standard platform mandated for application development

- ❑ A J2EE-based application server may offer superior performance or functionality compared to other alternatives

Whatever the reasons, the designers of the application will be able to take advantage of the component-based framework provided by a J2EE application server.

Distributed Design

Distribution lies at the heart of J2EE applications and, as such, forms a major part of the J2EE landscape. Distributing functionality provides much of the flexibility in the J2EE platform. However, analysis and high-level design frequently does not consider distribution, seeking first to create the correct business components. In this ideal world, all access between clients and servers would be transparent, as if the services were located on the same machine. Distribution also introduces complexity in the form of additional method calls and different programming paradigms. This much should have become clear from reading the early chapters of this book, particularly from topics like *JNDI* (see Chapter 2) and *RMI* (Chapter 3). In a distributed environment, method calls are no longer deterministic like they are in local processing. For example:

- ❑ A call may fail due to a network-related error.

- ❑ Partial failure of a networked operation can cause problems. This must be detected and corrected by the application.

- ❑ Timing and sequencing issues arise. There is no guarantee of the order in which a sequence of calls from multiple processes will be received.

Other factors must also be considered:

- ❑ The time taken to make a method call across a network will be many orders of magnitude greater than for a local method call.

- ❑ The potential for communication to dominate computation.

- ❑ Implicit concurrency in the system.

- ❑ The need to repeatedly locate remote components as they migrate between servers over time.

- ❑ The levels of unpredictability, which make it difficult or impossible to guarantee the consistency of all the data in the system at any one time.

These and other issues must be considered when designing solutions for distributed environments. A good, if slightly dated, discussion of the issues with distribution can be found in the paper *A Note on Distributed Computing* by S. C. Kendall, et al., 1994, available from http://www.sun.com/research/techrep/1994/abstract-29.html.

The design of interfaces between distributed components is an art in itself. The interfaces of distributed components should conform to the usual good practices for any interfaces. The methods in an interface should form a cohesive set rather than a disparate collection. The methods themselves should be meaningful operations, not just a set of property accessors. As with all good design, minimalism is a good principle so long as it does not create too much extra work for the user of the interface (a certain amount of de-normalization is allowed!). An example of this could be where there is a single method that takes many parameters. If you can identify a set of common tasks for which there are various default values, you could create a method for each of these tasks. From a purist point of view, these extra methods may seem wasteful, but from a practical point of view it can save much unnecessary client code for creating or specifying empty or standard parameters.

When creating distributed systems, such as J2EE applications, you must design the interfaces between components to take the distribution into account. Care must be taken when deciding whether to pass objects by reference or by value. Passing by reference is flexible but can lead to increased overhead through remote calls. Passing by value makes for local interaction at the client but it is not always the solution since it can cause problems for non-Java clients. If only a small part of the data is required, passing an object by value can lead to greater overhead than a handful of distributed calls. In addition, passing by value is not appropriate for fast-changing data.

In the context of our purchase order system, we must ensure that we take the following steps:

❑   Partition the system well, so that components that communicate frequently and in bulk are co-located on the same machine where possible. Since communication over a network is comparatively slow and complex we should seek to remove it where possible.

In the purchase order system, it would not make sense for the `ShoppingCart` to be on a different machine from the `OrderingWorkflow`. This would unnecessarily increase the complexity of the interaction between these components.

❑   Where communication over a network is unavoidable, the interactions and method calls must be designed in a network-friendly way.

If our system is large, it is almost certain that the `OrderingWorkflow` will be on a different machine from the `ProductLister`. There are common design patterns in the area of distributed computing that can help the designer when approaching this type of problem. At a practical level, these can be realized as the use of batched methods between components or of serialized JavaBeans to hold data snapshots. Some J2EE-specific patterns for distribution are discussed later in this chapter.

Designing distributed systems is difficult. It is important to have a good understanding of what is going on under the covers of the system and what sorts of compromises are being made. This knowledge will enable you to make informed design decisions to keep the system decoupled and efficient. However, to gain this knowledge, you do not have to write every line of code yourself. The type of distributed middleware typified by J2EE helps the designer and developer by providing much of the infrastructure and "glue code" required when developing distributed systems. The benefits of these contracts and services, and the use of interposition were discussed in Chapter 14

The need to deliver performance, scalability, and data integrity in distributed systems underlies much of the functionality delivered in J2EE. Some examples of these features are:

❑ Containers that can control concurrency and optimize performance while maintaining isolation

❑ Distributed transactions for data integrity

❑ Message passing to improve performance, scalability, and address varying levels of availability

❑ A naming service that provides location-independence

Choosing and Refining an Architecture

The need to distribute components is just one of the typical real-world factors that starts to evolve the idealized domain model into a concrete design that can be implemented on a particular set of machines using a particular language and runtime environment. This evolution will first involve the selection of an overall architecture that fits the requirements. Once the overall architecture is known, a series of design decisions can be made that will map that architecture successfully onto the underlying systems, platforms, and frameworks.

Architecture for the Purchase Order System

So far we have stressed the need to judge architecture and design in context. The requirements that different types of application make on their application architecture will vary, for example:

❑ **E-Commerce apps**
Many clients, lots of reading, less updating, low contention for key resources, a large working set of data that encourages caching

❑ **Banks and ATMs**
Many clients, low levels of concurrent access, high isolation level, no working set of data to be cached

The requirements will have a large influence on the decisions you make about your architecture. The most common application types give rise to architectural templates. The purchase order systems fits into a common application type – namely web-based e-commerce applications. Therefore, it will use a standard architecture for this type of application – namely a 3-tier architecture using a thin (web browser) client. Other architectural templates exist for different types of applications.

Within this architecture, various design decisions must be made. Design can be considered as the solution to a given problem in a given context. The context will consist of a series of forces that must be understood and balanced by the designer. There will be various forces at work constraining enterprise architecture, such as:

❑ The business problem being modeled.

❑ Required technologies including legacy systems.

❑ Desired system qualities – scalability, availability, and so on.

❑ Reach of the application (that is, the number of users to whom the application is available). This is usually embodied as thick (application) versus thin (web browser) clients since web-based applications are more easily made available to a wider audience – hence they have longer 'reach'.

All of these forces, and many more, will impact on the specific shape of the eventual system and the architecture that best suits it. The suitability of a design depends entirely on its context, that is, on the problems addressed and the forces at work in the system. When defining the requirements for the purchase order system earlier, various forces were specified such as the need to process purchase orders asynchronously and the desire to implement the system on top of J2EE.

Iteration and Feedback

The forces on the evolution of the system can be functional or non-functional and can vary from high-to low-level. As this implies, design must occur at many levels and stages:

- ❑ The solution model (although it may be called an 'elaboration' of the problem model)
- ❑ The broad system architecture
- ❑ Interfaces of system components
- ❑ Interactions between system components
- ❑ Internals of individual system components

Does this imply that architecture is an output of design? Hopefully, the answer to this is 'yes'. However, architecture can also evolve as well as being designed, but designing an architecture implies intent.

The effects of high-level architectural decisions cascade down through the design. If the need for scalability is translated into the use of a stateless model (see the discussion of state with reference to our example in the section *Going Shopping*, later in this chapter), then this in itself may affect lower-level design decisions, such as the use of stateless session EJBs and the style of their interfaces. Semi-functional requirements such as extensibility may have a wide-ranging impact on design decisions throughout the system. Taking the example of extensibility, if a system currently uses two possible data exchange mechanisms but it is anticipated that more will be required, an extra layer could be created to accommodate the required extensions.

Similarly, other decisions will be made further down in the application hierarchy for reasons of efficiency or suitability to the underlying platform. These decisions can then feed back up the chain and require changes to higher-level parts of the architecture. Hence feedback loops will form. Most mainstream formal development processes, such as the Rational Unified Process (http://www.rational.com/products/rup/) and eXtreme Programming (XP) (http://www.armaties.com/extreme.htm), encompass an idea of iteration and feedback between the phases of a software development. Implementation issues or changing technologies may generate valid feedback into the higher-level design or analysis.

Remember that most problems have multiple solutions. If the feedback changes the forces in operation at a certain point, a different decision may well be more appropriate. For example, it may be found that the need for a `LineItem` to refer to a `Product` in order to retrieve the item price leads to inefficiencies that slow the system down. It may be decided to replicate this price information in the `LineItem` itself in order to reduce these inefficiencies. This will slightly change the model of the purchase order system shown previously, but the overall functionality is unchanged.

So what does this mean for design? It means that we should approach design as an ongoing process, not as a once-only event. Approaching it as such can actually reduce the cost and impacts of incorrect design decisions. Over the life of any application, the technological landscape will change. This landscape is part of the context in which design decisions are made. Decisions made on the basis of previous technology landscapes may look stupid in a new one. Hence, what is needed is an acceptance that change will occur and that it must be factored into the application lifecycle.

The acceptance of change leads to projects where functionality is handed off in stages, where the design evolves as the project progresses and where refactoring is a part of everyday life (see *Refactoring: Improving the Design of Existing Code*, ISBN 0-201-48567-2). Changes in technology and implementation issues should feed back up the chain so that their implications can be taken into account in the mapping of the problem model onto the solution model (Frank Buschmann uses a yo-yo as an analogy for this effect).

Although an open and flexible architecture is a good asset, care should be taken that too much time is not spent turning simple classes into libraries or frameworks that may never be exploited. It is useful to bear in mind the eXtreme Programming principle of YAGNI, or "You Ain't Gonna Need It", when considering such exercises.

Applying Patterns

Many practicing software developers will not have time to keep track of informed debate about the nature of design and architecture. Even if they do, their hope is to extract something of concrete use which will help them make better or more informed choices next time they sit down to design a system. Patterns are a very good source of architectural and design information for practicing software designers.

What are Patterns?

One key principle in many professional disciplines is not to re-invent the wheel. Civil engineers and architects know a lot about designing buildings. When creating most buildings, no new ideas are required, just the application of common design mechanisms that have been used many times before. Largely, software engineering has not yet achieved this level of maturity, so there is still a tendency to approach every project with a blank canvas. Picasso is reported to have said that "Good artists copy, great artists steal". Although it has some negative connotations, it does reflect the reality of design in that it largely consists of a synthesis of many ideas from elsewhere applied to the desired context. No software designer will have a completely new set of ideas on how to create software systems; the key, as in other disciplines, is to pool knowledge so that the whole body of software designers can create better systems. Another comment, this time from Sun's Bill Joy reflected the fact that not all good ideas will come from inside Sun, hence people must be open to ideas from elsewhere. Thankfully, software developers tend to be keen on sharing thoughts and ideas and, in the case of the Open Source community, code. This tendency to co-operate and pool ideas has led to the development of catalogs of software design **patterns** that are publicly available and can assist in the design of a variety of software systems.

> A pattern is a proven solution to a problem in a given context. The broader the context, the more widely applicable a pattern is. In software terms, patterns are essentially the distillation of the 'wisdom' gained by practitioners of what works well when specifying, designing, and implementing software.

The software patterns movement was initially popularized by the book *Design Patterns – Elements of Reusable Object-Oriented Software* by Gamma et al., Addison-Wesley, ISBN 0-201-63361-2. However, patterns are not solely applied in the realms of micro-architecture as described in that book.

Patterns can be found in many areas of software and systems. At a high level, patterns can be found when performing analysis in specific domains. The entities and relationships discovered during such analysis will be repeated across a business sector. This repetition leads to the discovery of such patterns. If you are working in a specific domain, such as finance or telecommunications, it would be worthwhile investigating the existence of domain-specific patterns to save time and effort.

Patterns can also be specific to a particular technology or language (sometimes described as "idioms" when they become more specific). Java-specific patterns exist at a variety of levels all the way down to language idioms.

J2EE Patterns

Of most interest in this book are patterns that apply specifically to J2EE. Probably the most visible incarnation of this interest is the work done by some of the Java architects from the Sun Java Center. They have created a set of J2EE-specific patterns based on several years' worth of practical implementation of J2EE-based systems by Sun's Professional Services arm. The set of patterns are hosted online at the Java Developer Connection and are being evolved and refined through discussion on the J2EE Patterns e-mail list (j2eepatterns-interest@java.sun.com).

The Sun Java Center's J2EE patterns are targeted firmly at n-tier business systems and are categorized based on the tier in which they reside, namely Presentation, Business, and Integration. The table below introduces some of the more common example patterns from the catalog.

Tier	Pattern	Description
Presentation	Front Controller	Introduce a central controller (servlet or JSP) that controls the management of system services and navigation as used by a typical web-based workflow.
Presentation	Composite View	Provide flexibility in the display of information by building the overall web page view from a set of sub-components.
Business	Session Façade	Reduce coupling and network traffic by using an EJB session bean to implement common, related use cases on the serverside.
Business	Service Locator	Aid decoupling of business components from the underlying implementation by hiding the EJB-specific lookup and creation required when using them.
Business	Value Object	Reduce the network traffic associated with the retrieval of related values from an EJB by passing a serialized Java object containing a snapshot of those values.
Business	Business Delegate	Reduce coupling between presentation and business tiers by introducing a presentation-tier proxy to hide the details of the interaction with the business tier.
Integration	Data Access Object	Provide pluggable access to different data sources, by creating an interface for data access that is independent of the underlying data source. This interface can then be implemented by various objects that provide access to specific data sources without requiring changes to the code that uses the data.

This list provided is only part of the list of the J2EE patterns identified by the Sun Java Center. J2EE patterns are also identified as part of the J2EE Blueprints (http://java.sun.com/j2ee/blueprints/design_patterns/catalog.html). Many of these are the same as those identified by the Sun Java Center, but there are others that are not, such as the Fast-Lane Reader (described later in this chapter) aimed at accelerating the read-only access to data by bypassing EJB-based access. At the time of writing, efforts are ongoing at merging the Blueprints patterns with the Java Center patterns. There are also other online sources that contain J2EE-based patterns, such as The Server Side (http://theserverside.com/patterns/) and O'Reilly's onJava web site (http://www.onjava.com/design/).

> The provision of instances of patterns that are proven to work on the J2EE platform is a great bonus to the designer. We can learn from the experience of others and see how they implemented the pattern for their situation. Often, code samples are also provided that are specific to the J2EE environment. However, beware! We cannot just use J2EE-specific patterns, or any patterns for that matter, as you would a set of jigsaw pieces, simply copying and pasting the code to snap together your own solution without altering any code. An experienced designer will use a pattern as an overall guide, but will adapt it to fit the particular context.

All application contexts have some degree of uniqueness, hence the pattern implementations must be adapted to fit our specific requirements. Also, the set of patterns will certainly not cover the entirety of our application's requirements. We should think of the patterns as we would a set of "design time" components that can be customized and then glued together with custom logic (which in itself can be sizeable) to make the final product.

As we discuss the options for the design of a new system, the purchase order application in our case, various patterns will present themselves as suitable solutions for some of the problems that we will encounter. As such, it will be useful to first take a look at the motivation and structure of these patterns before applying them directly to the context of our example.

In the following sub-sections, we'll define all the design patterns that are relevant to our example. Note, however, that these descriptions are rather simplified introductions. For more information regarding design patterns in general, the following are useful resources:

- Sun Java Center Patterns Catalog at
  http://developer.java.sun.com/developer/technicalArticles/J2EE/patterns/
- Sun J2EE Blueprints at http://java.sun.com/j2ee/blueprints/design_patterns/catalog.html
- *Core J2EE Patterns: Best Practises and Design Strategies* by D. Alur, et al., Prentice Hall, ISBN 0-13-064884-1

Front Controller Pattern

The views that generate the display for the user should contain minimal business code so that such code can be shared among multiple views and also so that it can be changed independently of the view. These principles also apply to code that provides common services for views and to the code that provides workflow and navigation between views. Common services, such as security and state management, should not be replicated in multiple views, since this leads to maintainability problems and consistency issues. The workflow associated with part of an application, such as the sequence of steps leading up to an online purchase, is more difficult to alter when the code to control the associated navigation is split among multiple views.

The Front Controller pattern introduces a component that intercepts the client request and does one or more of the following:

- Applies common services such as authentication and access control
- Determines the appropriate view to handle the request
- Builds up state for the request by processing user tokens and accessing data sources

The diagram below shows how a front controller can mediate between a client and multiple views. This mediation may be part of a workflow within the application or may be a choice based on language or other factors:

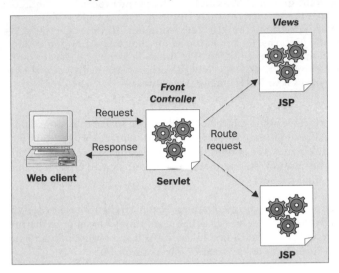

A Front Controller may interact with other components or helpers to provide the required service. It is common for a Front Controller to use a separate dispatcher component that implements any required workflow. It will also use helpers (as in the View Helper pattern, described shortly) to perform business-specific processing or to pass state to views. The sequence diagram below shows the interaction between these components:

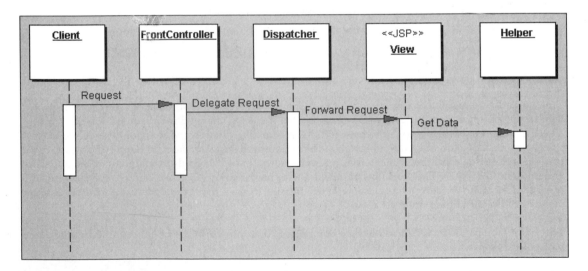

Composite View Pattern

Most web-based systems consist of many different pages or views. Each view will consist of some specific functionality, such as a partial list of products that can be selected at this time, together with common navigational, informational, or functional elements. If the code and formatting for each of these elements is duplicated in each view that uses it, the system becomes very hard to update and maintain since any fixes and changes must be applied wherever that code and formatting appears.

As a solution, the Composite View pattern defines various strategies for effectively partitioning a user interface into multiple sub-views that can be re-combined to create the overall view required. Each sub-view forms an individual component that can be maintained, updated, and enhanced separately from other sub-views. An example of a web page conforming to the composite view pattern is shown below. In this case, we see a Header View along the top of the screen, Navigation views running both below the header and down the left-hand side of the page, and, of course, the centralized Main Body view:

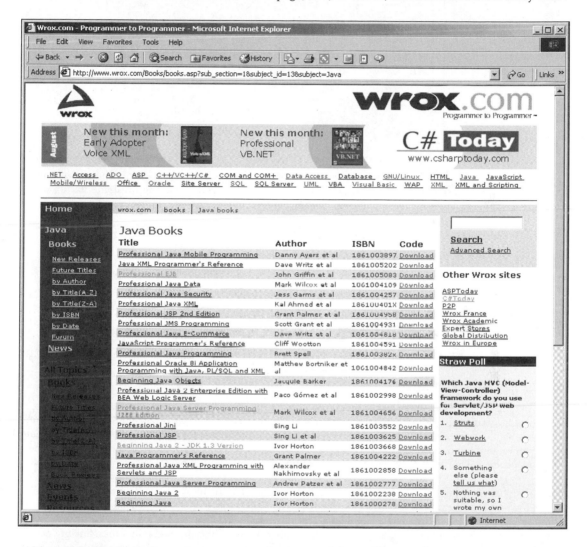

Although the example shown is not necessarily generated from JSP pages (as we are suggesting for our purchase order application), the principle remains the same. The overall composite view might use the other views as shown in the sequence diagram overleaf:

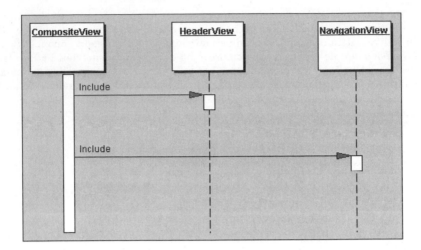

A view manager can be included between the Composite View and the sub-views. The use of a view manager is optional, but is useful if conditional inclusion is required. A simple implementation of a composite view implemented as a JSP page without a view manager is shown below:

```
<table border="0" valign="top" width="100%">
  <tr>
    <td><jsp:include page="templates/header.jsp" /></td>
  </tr>
  <tr>
    <td><jsp:include page="templates/navigation.jsp" /></td>
  </tr>
  <tr>
    <td><jsp:include page="content/java_book_list.jsp" /></td>
  </tr>
</table>
```

Session Façade Pattern

If EJBs are used simply as repositories for business data and simple business services, then most of the business logic will still reside on the client that makes use of such EJBs. This is detrimental for two reasons. Firstly, it will lead once more to excessive network access (also discussed in the Value Object pattern, later) as the client requests fine-grained business services and data. It will also bind the client very strongly to the business process. This leads to unnecessary distribution and repetition of business code between clients.

The solution is a variation on the Façade pattern as documented in the book *Design Patterns – Elements of Reusable Object-Oriented Software* by Gamma et. al., Addison-Wesley, ISBN 0-201-63361-2. A Façade is an object or component introduced between the client and a complex subsystem. The Façade exposes only those services required by the client and aggregates services so that they become coarse-grained rather than fine-grained. In J2EE pattern terms, a Session Façade performs this role for business logic and services encapsulated by multiple EJBs. The Session Façade, as its name suggests, takes the form of a session EJB. The client communicates with the Session Façade ,which provides business services based on other EJBs such as entity beans.

The following diagram shows how a Session Façade could control access to multiple entity beans and provide a uniform interface to a client. Although commonly used as a shield for underlying entity EJBs, a Session Façade can access services and data from other session EJBs as well as Data Access Objects. The relationship between the classes is shown below:

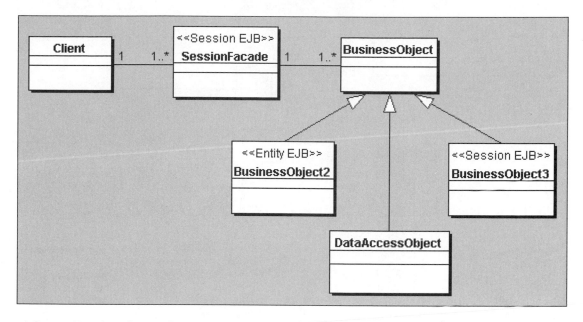

A Session Façade will typically encapsulate the functionality for one or more business use cases. Multiple business operations can be achieved through one call to the façade (this is sometimes referred to as the Batch Method distributed pattern/idiom). Rather than a session bean returning a set of Value Objects to be operated on by the client, the operation that the client wishes to perform can be migrated into the Session Façade. The iteration through the data then takes place on the server with only the results being passed back to the client. This reduces network traffic, albeit at the cost of some server-processing overhead.

Service Locator Pattern

In code terms, the overhead of using the methods on an EJB's business interface is relatively small – simply the handling of remote exceptions. However, the creation of EJBs requires specific, JNDI-based code to discover the home interface and create the required EJB. This forces the client to include JNDI code dealing with context creation, lookups, and narrowing of references. Again, any additional sophistication, such as caching of home interface references, must be duplicated by every client.

The Service Locator pattern defines how a single object can perform the lookup and creation tasks associated with multiple EJBs for multiple clients. The client simply finds the Service Locator and asks for a reference to the required EJB. All interaction with JNDI and EJB home interfaces is delegated to the Service Locator. The sequence diagram overleaf shows the interaction between the client, the Service Locator, and the EJB home and business implementations:

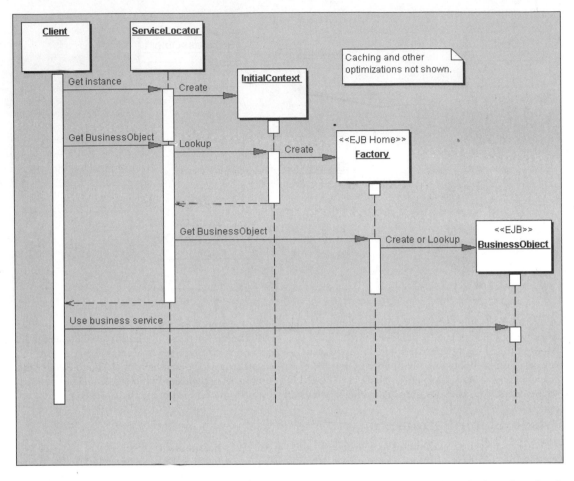

Note that the Service Locator is typically implemented as a singleton in order to share the benefits of caching.

Value Object Pattern

Simple data objects will commonly expose their data as properties. A client will access those properties using getter or setter methods as and when required. The relatively low overhead associated with in-process method calls has made this common practice, particularly in "draggy-droppy-pointy-clicky" environments such as Integrated Development Environments (IDEs) for creating user interfaces based around JavaBeans. However, once a network is introduced between the client and the data object, such property-based programming leads to an ugly 'sawtooth' effect as data is constantly passed back and forth across the network. When this happens, communication dominates computation, most of the time required to access data is spent waiting for network calls to return, and network performance degrades due to the large amount of data passed.

This issue can be seen when accessing data or data-centric services exposed by EJBs. The effect is amplified if the required data is spread across multiple EJBs, since each must be individually accessed across the network.

Another consideration here is that most data access is for reading rather than for writing.

These problems can be solved by the creation of a Value Object. The Value Object encapsulates business data in the form of a plain Java object rather than a heavyweight distributed object such as an EJB. Rather than making multiple requests, each for one property of the EJB, a single request is issued that returns the Value Object. The Value Object will be passed back to the client, typically through Java serialization. The client then accesses the properties of the Value Object in its local address space, thus saving many network roundtrips. The relationship between the EJB and its Value Object is shown below:

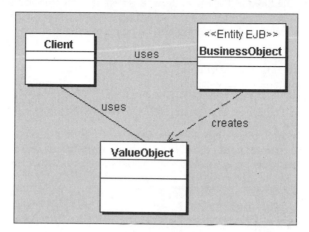

The interaction between the client, the EJB, and the Value Object are shown below:

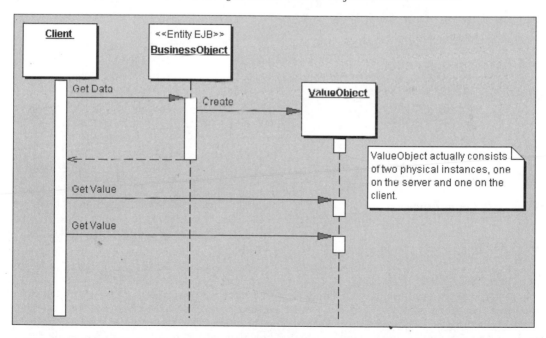

There are different variations that can be used depending on the requirements of the application. The Value Object can encapsulate only part of the business data represented by the EJB, it could be updatable with changes propagated back to its parent EJB, or the Value Object could take the form of an XML document if non-Java interoperability is required.

Value objects can be used with entity EJBs, session EJBs, and Data Access Objects (see below) where appropriate.

Business Delegate Pattern

It is not a good idea for clients to interact directly with business services. This exposes them to potential changes in implementation. It is possible to encapsulate some of the interaction with business services into a single EJB by applying the Session Façade pattern. Even so, the client is still left to deal with the lookup, instantiation, and remote error handling required to manipulate an EJB. Any increased sophistication in dealing with the business layer, such as caching and batching of calls is also left to the client.

As a solution, a Business Delegate acts as a client-side abstraction of a business service. It can potentially work directly with individual business components or it can act as the client-side gateway to a Session Façade. The Business Delegate will take care of all the EJB-specific interaction and provides a local interface for the client. This interface can provide methods that serve to encapsulate multiple server interactions. The Business Delegate can also map remote exceptions to meaningful application exceptions.

The Business Delegate is the logical place to perform client-side caching of business information, such as Value Objects, or for retrying of failed calls and failover to different servers. The relationship between the client, the Business Delegate and the business object is shown below:

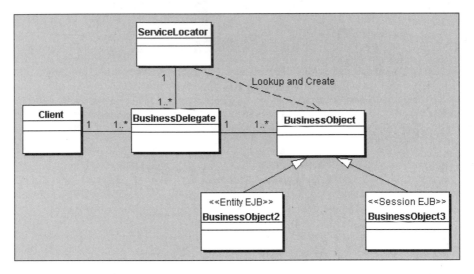

The Service Locator shown in the class diagram is another pattern that can be used on its own or in conjunction with a Business Delegate. Again, the intention is to hide away the complexities of dealing with naming services and provide a convenient location to add caching and optimizations to the retrieval of references to business objects and their factories.

Data Access Object Pattern

Almost every application uses data of some form. This data can be stored in a variety of places, such as databases, mainframe systems, flat files, or other external services. The business and user interface code of the application will require access to the data in order to perform tasks for the user. The tasks performed on the data are usually independent of how that data is stored. Including specific data access code in the business and display logic ties that code to a specific data source. This reduces the flexibility of the solution since the code will require changing whenever the datasource changes. Changes to the underlying data source may include a change of database (SQL Server to Oracle for example) or changes to the overall model such as migrating from JDBC-based data access to access via entity EJBs.

The solution is to provide a Data Access Object (DAO) to abstract access to the data. The DAO will encapsulate the code required to locate and access the data source. All business or presentation logic will use the DAO to retrieve and store data as shown below:

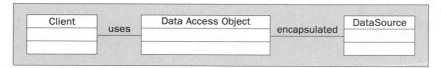

The interface of the DAO defines the relationship between the business or presentation logic and the data. If the underlying location and storage mechanism used to access the data changes, a new DAO can be created to access it. Since the DAO has a fixed interface for its clients, this will not require any changes to the business or presentation logic as shown below:

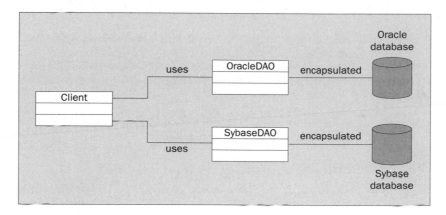

The actual implementation of the DAO will vary depending on context. If the client is a JSP, the DAO may be a plain Java class, a servlet, or an EJB. If the client is itself an EJB, then the DAO is likely to be a plain Java class or possibly another EJB.

View Helper Pattern

Poor partitioning between presentation mechanisms and business logic leads to inflexible systems and increased maintenance costs. The use of JSP pages for web-based user interfaces is a prime example, since it is easy to include too much Java code in the JSP. If this code takes the form of business logic, then this serves to increase the coupling between presentation and business logic, which is bad for flexibility. Whether the code is business or presentation logic, the inclusion of large quantities of Java code in a JSP means that it cannot be maintained and adapted solely by web designers. It also potentially leads to the repetition of code across many JSP pages.

Using the View Helper pattern, Java code is encapsulated in helper classes, such as JavaBeans or custom tags. The view delegates the business or presentation processing to the helper object. In the case of a JSP, this removes the Java code from the JSP and allows web designers to interact with it through the use of standard or custom JSP tags. A typical sequence of interaction is shown below:

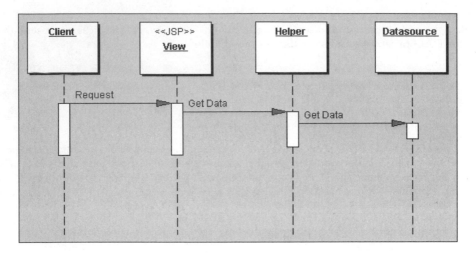

Notice how, in this case, the view simply instantiates the helper and gets data from it. If the helper is implemented as a JavaBean, a JSP can access the required functionality through the standard useBean and getProperty tags.

In this case, the helper accesses business functionality, however View Helpers can also be used to encapsulate complex presentation processing or temporary state.

Dispatcher View Pattern

This pattern suggests a way to combine the Front Controller and View Helper patterns in order to create an integrated solution to the problems they address. These problems include repeated and scattered business logic, the need to separate workflow from presentation and the need to impose common services such as authentication.

The Dispatcher View pattern is a combination of a Front Controller and multiple views and View Helpers. Unlike the Service to Worker pattern (discussed next), in Dispatcher View the Front Controller and dispatcher do not instantiate View Helpers and use their data to help determine the target view. Any such selection of view will be done based on information in the user request. When the request is propagated to the view, the appropriate View Helpers will be instantiated and will access the data required by the view. The relationship between the different classes is shown below:

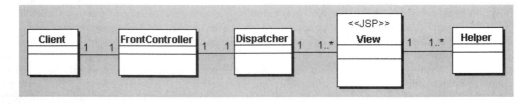

As you can see, in this model all external data access occurs only once the view is accessed.

Service to Worker Pattern

This pattern suggests a way to combine the Front Controller and View Helper patterns in order to create an integrated solution to the problems they address. These problems include repeated and scattered business logic, the need to separate workflow from presentation and the need to impose common services such as authentication.

The Service to Worker pattern is based around a Front Controller. The Front Controller delegates data access to View Helpers, which are created and populated before the view is accessed. A dispatcher, which forms part of the Front Controller, decides which view to display to the client and propagates the request together with the View Helpers. The relationship between the different classes is shown below:

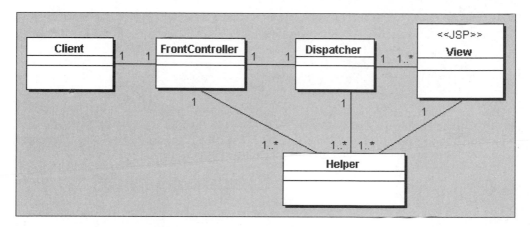

The main difference between this pattern and the Dispatcher View is that Service to Worker is more appropriate where more processing is required up front. The Front Controller and dispatcher interact with the View Helpers before forwarding the request to the view. For example, in Service to Worker, some of the data retrieved may actually govern the view to which the request is dispatched.

Value List Handler Pattern (Page-by-Page Iterator)

When accessing large amounts of data, the client should try to avoid repeated network requests to access each data object in turn. Such simple use of remote objects that encapsulate data, like entity EJBs for instance, can be highly inefficient in terms of network and server resource usage.

The Value List Handler is commonly implemented as a stateful session bean that queries underlying data sources to obtain the data required. The data source could be a database, a set of entity EJBs or any other source of data encapsulated as a Data Access Object. The data will be cached and then supplied to the client as requested. The relationship between a web client, a Value List Handler, and a set of underlying entity EJBs is shown overleaf:

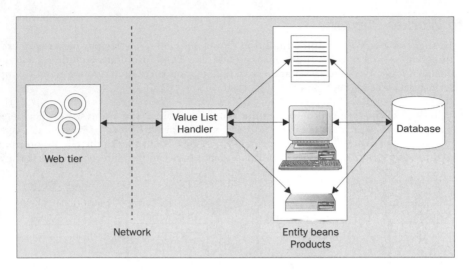

The Value List Handler pattern will generate Value Objects to represent the underlying data. These Value Objects will then be cached and provided back to the client as requested. The client can control the number of Value Objects returned at one time through the iterator interface. The relationships between the classes involved are shown in the class diagram below:

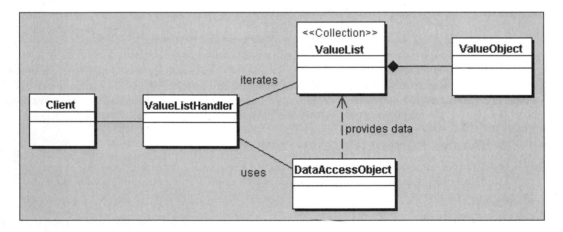

The sequence diagram looks like this:

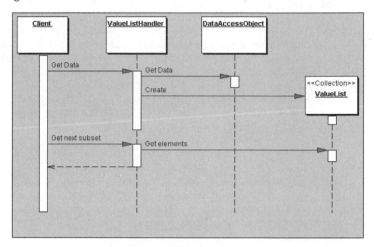

Note that this pattern is referred to as Value List Handler in the Sun Java Center J2EE Patterns catalog but as the Page-by-Page Iterator in the Sun J2EE Blueprints.

Fast Lane Reader Pattern

Although entity EJBs are a powerful mechanism for concurrent data access and persistence, they are rather heavyweight for listing large amounts of data. Taking the example of listing data in a catalog, the usual requirement is to obtain read-only data for browsing. Also, the underlying data will change infrequently and it is not vital that any snapshot of the data reflects the absolute latest state of the data. Accessing such data through EJB finder methods will result in many EJBs being created for little useful work. This is a large overhead in a situation where speed is usually a key factor in application usability.

The solution is to bypass the entity EJBs associated with the data and to access the data more directly through a Data Access Object. Such a DAO will usually encapsulate database access, so effectively the data comes direct from the database. This will lead to improved performance without destabilizing the application.

The Fast Lane Reader can be implemented as a DAO or a session EJB acting as a Session Façade for DAOs. The relationship between the client and the Fast Lane Reader is shown below:

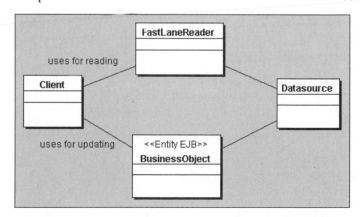

Now, armed with the background details of these design patterns, we can confidently begin the analysis of our purchase-order application beginning, naturally, with a list of products.

Start at the Beginning

We must start the examination of the system somewhere, so let us start with the first thing the user needs: the listed products. Since the purchase order system is to be used as part of an intranet, we will need to provide an HTML interface for it. To generate the required HTML, the user interface, such as the product listing functionality, could be implemented as a set of JavaServer Pages (JSP pages) or servlets. Of the two technologies, JSP pages are best suited to the generation of HTML, so the user interface for the Ordering Workflow and Approval Workflow in the purchase order system (refer to our original UML diagram, earlier in the chapter) will consist largely of a set of JSP pages. However, servlets will also have an important part to play in the provision of common services and control of workflow for these parts of the system.

Note that the following is not a discussion of the way that servlets and JSP pages actually work, since this was given sufficient coverage in Chapters 5 to 12. Instead, some aspects of these technologies will be revisited from a design viewpoint.

Displaying Product Data to the User

We can explore some of the main JSP and servlet design issues by considering how certain parts of the Ordering Workflow could be implemented. When listing products for the user to select, use of one or more JSP pages would work well. The product data could be obtained directly from the database via JDBC. This simple architecture is shown below:

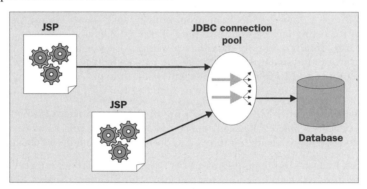

Even at this simple stage, design choices can be made to create a more flexible and maintainable system. One aspect is the use of database connection pools to aid scalability by more effectively sharing the database connections between the JSP pages or servlets that use them. The issue of scalability and resource recycling is discussed later in the chapter.

The access to the product data will most likely be required from within JSP pages. JSP pages make it relatively easy to combine visual user interface design with the Java code required to extract the product data from the database.

Stepping back for a moment, we can define some guiding principles that can benefit even this simple design:

❑ Abstract the data access

❑ Separate out functionality from presentation

❑ Partition the control of user interaction from presentation and data handling

Let us examine each of these points in turn.

Abstracting Data Access

From previous discussions on J2EE design patterns, we have learned that in cases where a component retrieves data, benefits can be gained by using a Data Access Object (DAO) to abstract the underlying data source. If we do not know whether the underlying data source will change over time, a DAO brings a lot of flexibility. For example, in the case of the purchase order system, the initial implementation of the catalog may involve direct access to the data source via JDBC. As the system evolves, the use of third-party data sources may require the use of EJBs or web-service-based access. If multiple supplier catalogs must be incorporated, the associated business and presentation code can quickly become a mess of switch statements. Using a DAO allows new sources of data to be added relatively painlessly.

The downsides of using a DAO come in two forms:

❑ Almost any form of abstraction involves extra steps and handling of the data. This means that performance can suffer.

❑ More design effort and coding is required initially to implement the DAO.

As with any design decision, a tradeoff is involved here. You will have to decide if the flexibility and maintainability benefits of a DAO outweigh the amount of extra initial effort required and potential performance reduction. Since the purchase order system will encompass multiple suppliers, this sort of up-front investment would almost certainly be worth doing.

Separating Functionality from Presentation

The main design imperative for JSP pages is to remove as much of the code as possible from the page. This separation of the presentation and the code has many benefits, such as:

❑ Common code can be shared by multiple pages, providing common services and reducing maintenance effort

❑ Reduced or eliminated Java code will make life easier for the non-coding web page designer

❑ Most changes to the workings of the code will not require the pages that use that code to be edited

This guarantees that any use of JSP pages beyond the most simplistic will involve such partitioning of HTML and Java code. The partitioning can take various forms, including:

❑ The code for the page can be encapsulated in some form of Java component following the View Helper pattern

❑ Web pages that share common functionality, information, or navigational elements can be built from a set of common components following the Composite View pattern

Use of the View Helper pattern will reduce the amount of code required in the JSP pages that will provide the presentation for the Ordering Workflow and Approval Workflow in our purchase-order system. Whether the helpers are JavaBeans or custom tags will depend on the specific context in which a helper is needed. It may be decided that one style of helper, such as JavaBeans, is used consistently throughout to aid maintainability or back-compatibility.

It is worth noting that patterns will build on and use other patterns. For example, given the earlier decision to use DAOs in the purchase order system, whenever the code in the View Helper implementation needs to access data, they will use the appropriate DAO. This type of relationship is typical of a pattern language, rather than just a list of patterns. The patterns in a pattern language have strong relationships. Each pattern solves particular problems within the framework and delegates functionality to implementations of other patterns as and where appropriate. Again, it is not just a case of making a solution from a jigsaw of patterns, but certain patterns work well together and are commonly found performing similar roles in similar systems.

The user interface of the Ordering Workflow and Approval Workflow will consist of HTML pages, or views, containing product listings and forms that the user must fill out. The usability of a system containing multiple views is greatly enhanced by providing a degree of consistency in style and content (for example, consistent positioning and content of a navigation bar). In such a user interface there will be certain consistent parts of the user's screen as the rest changes based on context, such as going from the detailed product view to the overall purchase order view.

This style of user interface can be achieved by applying the Composite View pattern to break out common sub-views, such as headers and navigation, and re-combine them with view-specific content. As well as providing consistency for the user, the Composite View makes it easier to maintain and evolve the system. As an example, the navigation on all existing views can be updated by simply updating the shared navigation sub-view. Equally, the creation of a new view is simplified since large parts of it can be templated.

One variation to note here is that some parts of the Approval Workflow may be intended only for managers (such as figures on current levels of departmental budget). In this case, the Composite View provides strategies involving view managers that can act as filters on the content displayed. Hence, a manager may see different content on an order tracking page from a less privileged user.

Partitioning User Interaction, Presentation, and Data

Strategies such as View Helper provide a convenient way of separating business logic from presentation logic. However, some application logic works best when processed before the view is accessed. As their names suggest, the Ordering Workflow and Approval Workflow both require a sequence of steps to be enforced in order to guide the user through the ordering and approval processes. If a step is missed, vital information may be lost, leading to an incorrect order.

The sequencing of such steps could be built into the views. Each view would have links back and forth to the next and previous views in the workflow. However, this leads to a very brittle workflow that cannot be easily altered. The solution is to separate out the workflow from the view, keeping each view independent of its place in the workflow and adding the potential for view reuse. We could look at View Helper as a way of separating the workflow, but the key issue here is that such workflow decisions need to be taken before the view is accessed. What is needed is a mechanism to intercept the user request, determine where the user is in the current workflow and then dispatch them to the appropriate view.

To perform this type of pre-processing, we can introduce a servlet to act as a Front Controller, as defined in the Front Controller pattern, discussed previously. The Front Controller is typically a servlet whose sole task in life is to process user input (sometimes called user gestures). The servlet contains no code to generate output for the user; instead it captures data from the user, processes it, and decides which view should be displayed to the user.

In terms of the purchase order application, the Front Controller is the ideal place to house common processing such as authentication. Authentication is particularly important since both the submission and approval of purchase orders depend strongly on authenticating the identity of the user. As mentioned earlier, some of the Composite Views in the Approval Workflow may only display certain information to managers. It is therefore vital that authentication is always performed before views are accessed (note that this does not mean that the user has to log in before every page view, simply that credentials for some forms are checked – this may take the form of an authentication cookie passed from the user's browser). The Front Controller is the ideal place to add such common services.

> **A system may have multiple Front Controllers. In the case of our purchase order system, there will be at least two – one for the Ordering Workflow and one for the Approval Workflow. These Front Controllers will provide the presentational workflow through the creation and approval of purchase orders. In order to ensure that the authentication code (and any other common services) are shared between the Front Controllers and are not re-implemented every time, the Front Controller may delegate the application of such services to other objects or components.**

The Front Controller may also perform additional processing that builds up state, used by the view to which the request is forwarded. Such state is passed as helper objects. A Front Controller that uses helper objects is part of the way towards the classic Model-View-Controller (MVC) architecture popularized by Smalltalk and used in a modified form in the Java Foundation Classes (JFC). The Front Controller contains the knowledge of what should happen at a particular point in time in response to a user gesture. The View reflects the state of this part of the system to the user. The final part of the equation is the Model. This is the data part of the system. The view refers to the model to retrieve the data that it should display to the user. The controller will alter the state and contents of the model appropriately based on user input.

The figure below shows how JSP pages, servlets, and JavaBeans can be used to create a model that splits up responsibilities in the same way as MVC:

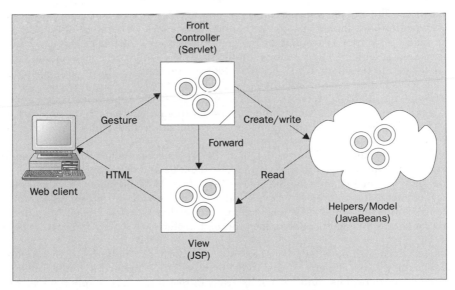

The View Helper classes that make up the model may be simple representations of data retrieved by the Front Controller. Alternatively, these classes may encapsulate the data access for this part of the system. The data represented could be garnered from the client request or retrieved from a data source on the server. The precise balance of responsibilities between the Front Controller, the View Helpers, and the views will vary depending on the amount of data retrieval needed and whether the request can be routed without any other data being retrieved. Two 'macro-patterns' that are described in the Sun Java Center's J2EE Pattern catalog, Service to Worker and Dispatcher View, discuss how such responsibilities may be shared. Although these patterns were introduced earlier in this chapter, it is worth examining their full documentation for a more in-depth exploration.

There is much discussion about the suitability of the MVC paradigm as a metaphor for web-based systems. A lot of this revolves around the inability to update the user's view directly in response to changes in the model, since there is no way to 'push' it down to the browser. However, it does serve a suitable purpose when discussing the separation of roles. For other opinions, check out the archives of the J2EE Patterns mailing list (j2eepatterns-interest@java.sun.com)

The Java Pet Store that comes with the J2EE Blueprints provides an interesting slant here. It allows presentation-tier components, such as business delegates, to register their interest in particular data models with an instance of a local class called the `ModelManager`. *The models themselves live on the EJB tier. Rather than setting up a distributed event system, each logical action submitted to the workflow on the EJB tier will return a list of the models that it has updated. The* `ModelManager` *instance will then inform the appropriate listeners in the presentation tier of these changes and this ensures that the business delegates in the presentation tier are up to date the next time the view is refreshed.*

Evolution of the System

Whatever the balance in the implementation, an architecture based around the Front Controller, View Helper, and Data Access Object patterns gives us some worthwhile advantages. Changes to the workflow would not necessarily require changes to the view or model. Similarly, changes to the data access mechanism can be made transparent to the view and controller. This three-way separation gives a large number of options, should changes be required in the style or location of the user interface. Since the resultant separation of responsibilities conforms largely to the MVC model, if the client had to be re-implemented as a Swing UI, the model (in the shape of JavaBeans) could remain the same and simply be re-located to the client. If the workflow logic of the controller were implemented as a separate class from the servlet, then this too would be re-locatable quite easily. Alternatively, a proxy could be created for use on the client that would map the Swing input to the appropriate user gestures expected by the JSP/servlet controller. The view could then be substituted with one that generated XML instead of HTML. The proxy on the client could then use this output to update its local model.

There is, of course, one slight problem with one of the suggested strategies above. Moving the model to the client is not quite the simple task that some tools would have you believe. If our model is accessing the database via JDBC or EJB, moving this functionality from server to client has some serious performance, connectivity, and security issues. Indeed, even moving it from server to server may cause such problems. This is just one issue when examining a JavaBeans-based model. If we were creating an application that had to be highly scalable, then this architecture will generally prove to be sub-optimal.

Holding state on the server on behalf of a client is a tricky business. In this case, the model will contain data, which occupies physical memory, and (potentially) a JDBC connection to the underlying database through which it can refresh its contents. For a variety of reasons, this is simply not scalable. Consider the following issues associated with this scenario:

❑ To solve the memory problems, it may be possible to keep adding more memory. As the physical memory limit of the hardware is reached, another server can be added to handle some of the clients. The immediate problem here is that we then get lock-in between clients and servers. A particular server will hold the model for a particular client. This can potentially work against any load-balancing strategies used by the system.

❑ Physical memory is only one of the resources used by an application. In the case of the model, it also requires a database connection to access its underlying data. While memory may be relatively cheap, database licenses tend not to be. If each model holds one of these resources, they will be exhausted fairly quickly. If it must create one every time it needs to refresh or update its data, performance will be impaired. The use of pooled resources, such as JDBC connection pools, can help to alleviate some of the problems here, as can an appropriate approach to state management as discussed later in the chapter.

If you have read the earlier chapters on EJBs (Chapters 14 to 19), you will probably know where this is leading. To achieve serious scalability for most J2EE applications you should introduce EJBs into the architecture as shown below:

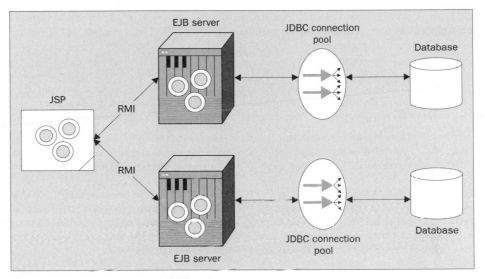

The J2EE Blueprints acknowledge that some applications will begin from a simple base HTML/JSP and then evolve as the requirements on the system change. In fact, they provide what might be thought of as a maturity model for web-based J2EE applications, as shown in the following table:

Application Type	Technologics	Complexity	Functionality	Robustness
HTML Pages	HTML pages	Very low	Very low	High
Basic JSP Pages and Servlets	HTML pages, JSP pages, servlets	Low	Low	Low
JSP Pages with Modular Components	HTML pages, JSP pages, servlets, JavaBeans components, custom tags	Medium	Medium	Medium

Table continued on following page

Application Type	Technologies	Complexity	Functionality	Robustness
JSP Pages with Modular Components and Enterprise JavaBeans	HTML pages, JSP pages, servlets, JavaBeans components, Custom tags, templates, Enterprise JavaBeans	High	High	High

This model acts as a good rule of thumb when considering which technologies will be required to implement a particular application. However, be aware that it will have its exceptions. Some very scalable applications can be built simply with servlets as long as you use the right server products.

Adding the Middle-Tier

Returning to the running theme of our example, we see that our system has expanded somewhat because the state it uses now resides on the middle tier in an EJB. This presents us with several new design issues that must be addressed:

❑   What type of EJB should we use to provide the data access? Should we model the database as an entity EJB or should we use a session EJB and fire SQL queries at the database from there? The pros and cons of the different types of EJB themselves were discussed in Chapters 14 to 16. What we need to do now is consider how they might best be applied in the context of our application.

❑   How will the presentation tier components interact with the EJB? This is particularly important if the data is modeled as an entity. Although we are gaining scalability and flexibility when using EJBs, we are potentially incurring a considerable communication overhead.

Think back to the application being used as the context for this design consideration. As a first pass, we might want to model our Product data as entity EJBs. This would mean that we could take advantage of Container-Managed Persistence (CMP) to save us writing some JDBC code and allow the container to optimize data access. Our presentation-tier components would then use the entity's home interface to search for appropriate Products to display based on the user's preference.

The immediate danger here is that this will degenerate into a frenzy of network-unfriendly property-based programming. To overcome this, the Value Object pattern can be applied where multiple properties are obtained together. Hence, rather than have the JSP interact with the Product EJB to obtain each property individually, the JSP can make a single call to the EJB to obtain the ProductValueObject, which would contain all the information required by the JSP to display that product information to the client. This pattern can also be found under the name Combined Attributes in some places.

Applying the Value Object to create a ProductValueObject would provide us a certain amount of optimization. However, the 'sawtooth' effect that we noted earlier will quickly reappear if the web tier must repeatedly access multiple Product entity EJBs asking each for its ProductValueObject. There is a need here to ask for multiple value objects at one time. A Collection of Value Objects can then be returned in a single response, reducing network overhead. The Value List Handler pattern defines strategies for returning collections of Value Objects to clients. The ProductLister in the purchase order system can apply this pattern to deliver collections of ProductValueObjects to the JSP pages that make up the Ordering Workflow. The web client can tune the number of Value Objects returned to the HTML page size.

The product data in the purchase order system is typical of catalog data in that it is mostly read-only and slow to change. In cases such as this, the use of entity EJBs for access may impose undue overhead on searching functionality. We can apply the Fast Lane Reader pattern to speed up access to bulk data by using a separate object to provide read-only access to the data source directly – bypassing the entity EJB layer. This would make catalog access faster in most cases with some additional development cost and a small increase in application complexity. However, the decision to apply the Fast Lane Reader pattern depends on whether the performance you get from a caching Value List Handler is sufficient for your needs. Essentially, this is a speed vs. simplicity tradeoff.

Another thing to bear in mind when using a Value Object is that of interoperability. In the Java-to-Java scenario, it is easy to pass such serialized objects through an RMI interface. However, if any of your clients are potentially CORBA clients, then this interface is potentially off-limits to them. Even if the client Object Request Broker (ORB) implements the objects-by-value functionality required by CORBA 3, it still implies that more work needs to be done when unmarshaling the bean on the client. In this case, it may be better to use an XML-based representation for the value object to make it cross-platform.

The `ProductValueObject` need not contain the whole of the data in the `Product`. As a general rule, the data in such beans should be read-only. Since it represents a snapshot of the data, there may be limited value in including volatile data in the Value Object. If, for example, the `Product` EJB contained the current stock level for that product, this may not be relevant to include in the `ProductValueObject` since such information may be out of date by the time it is used. Such information should be retrieved 'fresh' from the `Product` when needed.

That last statement suggests another issue. It is considered bad practice for clients (either application clients or servlets/JSP pages) to access entity EJBs directly. As we have seen, this tends to lead to very fine-grained access to the EJB's properties and couples the client more closely to the implementation of the business logic and data. What we need to do is to decouple the client from the detail of the business layer implementation. This can be achieved by applying the Session Façade pattern. The session bean will serve to abstract the structure of the Product EJB by only providing access to functionality required by the client. In the case of the EJB Product, the primary focus of such a façade is to hide the data structure of the Product EJB itself. A Session Façade can in fact be used to hide a whole business subsystem and present a simplified interface to the client.

The final question relating to the `Product` is whether it should actually be modeled as an entity at all. In the current scenario, clients are using a Value List Handler (or Fast Lane Reader) and a Session Façade to access the entity's data. Would we not be better off accessing the database directly from these session beans (as we would be doing anyway if we chose the Fast Lane Reader) and forgetting about using an entity bean? In fact, the use of collections of Value Objects could be avoided by passing back the `RowSets` received from database queries. `RowSets` were introduced in JDBC 2.0 as a handy way of representing tabular data. A `RowSet` appears as a JavaBean and can be used while disconnected from the database. It is also `Serializable` so that it can be passed in an RMI method call.

While it can be very useful in certain circumstances, passing a `RowSet` is not compatible with creating typesafe methods. If a method takes or returns a `RowSet`, this really represents an opaque data type – there is no indication of what form the data should take. Any `RowSet` retrieved from any table could be passed to such a method. This could cause untold errors when the `RowSet` is processed. Similarly, a field in a `RowSet` is potentially more open to incorrect interpretation than a property of a JavaBean, or an element or attribute in XML. Passing data in `RowSets` mirrors the popular use of `RecordSet` in ActiveX Data Objects (ADO) in Microsoft Windows applications. In both cases, it tends to lock the architecture into one technology and create brittle dependencies between the data format and the programmatic users of the data. This seriously affects the flexibility of the application in the face of change.

There are no absolute right and wrong answers regarding either the use of entities versus data access objects or the use of **RowSets** versus specific data types. I personally would vote for abstraction over direct access, unless there are serious speed issues with the application. Judicious use of abstraction will add to the flexibility and maintainability of the application. Traditionally, a large amount of the cost and developer heartache associated with an application comes after the initial development, so anything that makes an application simpler to maintain should be welcomed.

Having said that, much will depend on the origin of the data, the efficiency of the database, the efficiency of the EJB container, whether the entity's data is used by multiple beans on the EJB-tier, and the amount of communication overhead between the EJB container and the database. Two big deciding factors here are whether a Product has associated functionality as well as data and whether it needs transactions. If a Product is simply the mapping of a single database row, you should ask whether it is really sufficiently coarse-grained to be an entity bean. Again, unfortunately, there is no fixed answer here. Simple data entities work well in some situations and not in others. In terms of transactions, entity beans will provide transaction control over the data in a database-independent way. However, if the data in our Product bean cannot be updated, then there is no need for transaction support. So, for example, the decision about whether to include the stock level in the Product class in our UML model would be very relevant here.

Going Shopping

Now that we can list the products, we need to actually do something useful, like allowing a user to order some. Creating a purchase order has a particular workflow associated with it:

- ❑ Identify the user
- ❑ Show list of products to the user
- ❑ Allow the user to select one or more products from the list
- ❑ Forward the completed purchase order to the appropriate manager

This will have iterations and other conditions but, again, this captures the essence of what we are trying to do. This workflow is encapsulated by OrderingWorkflow on our original purchase order system UML class diagram.

Encapsulating the Ordering Workflow

The Ordering Workflow, that is, the actual interaction with the business objects, could be implemented either on the web tier or the business tier. Implementing the workflow on the web tier means that the business logic is very coupled to the user interface code. If the same business logic were required by another part of the system then it would have to be re-implemented. If the workflow is implemented in a session EJB, this decouples the business logic from the presentation tier and makes it reusable and replaceable. For a large system, such as our Acme system, another advantage of using a stateless session EJB rather than a servlet is the improved scalability when using this type of component.

Hence, the Ordering Workflow becomes a session EJB that hides the implementation of the business logic behind it. It may interact with other session EJBs, entity EJBs, and Data Access Objects. If this sounds familiar it is because it is acting as a Session Façade. The Session Façade for the Ordering Workflow is more sophisticated than that hiding the Product entity EJB. It will provide a set of methods, such as `addLineItemToPurchaseOrder`, for example, that encapsulate a logical business operation for the client. The client does not care how many databases or other objects are used to perform this task in the business tier.

Encapsulating the Ordering Workflow in a session EJB removes complexity from the client. However, the client must still contain code to look up and instantiate the EJB. Calling methods on the EJB may raise `RemoteExceptions`, and the client must perform any catching or retrying required. It would be better to bundle all of this functionality in one place so that handling interaction with the business tier became the responsibility of one class. The Business Delegate pattern offers a strategy for doing this. The Business Delegate can hide the use of Value Objects and cache them to reduce network traffic. All of this would benefit our distributed application in terms of performance and increased simplicity of the client code.

As mentioned, one benefit of using a Business Delegate is the ability to map remote exceptions to exceptions that are meaningful to the client. A general principle when designing object and component interfaces is that they should throw meaningful exceptions (for example `BudgetLimitExceeded`, `ProductNotFound`) rather than just propagating lower-level ones (`RemoteException`, `ArrayIndexOutOfBoundException`). The Business Delegate can perform a useful role in this layering of exceptions such that they either catch and handle an exception from the server or generate an exception that makes sense to their clients as shown below:

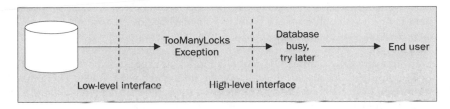

Given that a Session Façade exists for the Ordering Workflow, we may decide that a Business Delegate is not required. Again, there is a tradeoff between the amount of work required to implement and the benefits. In this case, the primary argument for using a Business Delegate would be to remove the EJB lookup and creation code from the client. As such, the Service Locator pattern could be applied to deliver this abstraction without forcing all access through the Business Delegate.

The key thing to note here is that the Business Delegate and the Session Façade deal with the business workflow – the sequence of logical steps to perform a business task. From the user-interface perspective, the dispatcher in the Front Controller controls the steps performed in the user interface to enter information and make choices related to the overall business task. The dispatcher governs which view is shown next. It is important to distinguish between these two flows. The user gestures captured by the Front Controller may match one-to-one with the business tasks and each may be translated into an associated logical event and passed to the Session Façade. Alternatively, it may take multiple user interface interactions before a business method is called. It is important to distinguish between these two workflows.

Examination of the overall UML class diagram will show that the `OrderingWorkflow` class uses a `Session` class to hold the client's state, such as the contents of the shopping cart. Anyone who has worked with JSP pages or servlets will immediately recognize this concept from the in built session object provided by the servlet API as described in Chapter 8. However, caution should be exercised here. The class represents the concept of a session and does not necessarily map onto a servlet session implementation. When previously discussing the holding of state on the server, several issues were highlighted about storing state in this client-specific way. The management of memory, recycling of resources, and avoidance of server lock-in are trickier in the web container than in the EJB container. Since the EJB container has a defined recycling and persistence mechanism for component state, resources used for a the shopping cart will be managed more efficiently in the EJB tier than in the web tier. Using a session EJB for the shopping cart functionality is also more flexible in that it can be used by both thick and thin clients.

Stateful vs. Stateless Models

Given that we are now potentially working with several session beans, it is worth quickly digressing into considerations of stateful versus stateless models. Under the stateful model, a server-side component instance is dedicated to one particular client and holds its data in temporary storage for ease of access. Under the stateless model, there is no dedicated server-side component instance for the client and all data must be retrieved from persistent storage. The choice between stateless and stateful server-side components is the subject of many debates and arguments. Although the stateless model is unarguably scalable, it does bring in overheads related to the storage and retrieval of state for every client access. The stateful model has no such overheads but its scalability is entirely dependent on effective pooling and activation/passivation algorithms being provided by the EJB container. Stateful EJBs also present a challenge in the face of failure. A stateless EJB can fail-over to another container instance with only a small amount of potential data loss. If a stateful session EJB has been holding the conversational state and this is lost, the user may have to start their transaction again.

As well as requiring more data transfer, the stateless model also requires more work on the part of the designer and client application, since it must always be told which state to use. This impacts on our choice of session bean to implement the functionality in the `OrderingWorkflow` and `ProductLister` classes. As it stands, the work of the `ProductLister` is entirely stateless – it is presented with a category and it lists the product within it. In accordance with good practice, the results would be returned as a collection of Value Objects leaving no state on the server. Hence, this would suggest that the `ProductLister` would work well as a stateless session bean. However, in order to gain the benefits of caching and efficiency from the Value List Handler pattern being used, a stateful session bean may be more appropriate. Refer to the original description of the Value List Handler pattern in the Sun Java Center patterns for more detailed discussion of this.

The `OrderingWorkflow` must have some concept of state to understand where the client currently is in the ordering process. This opens up a key design question over where the state should be stored – with the client, in the EJB, or in a database:

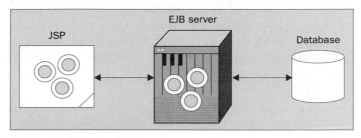

Each of these has benefits and issues:

❑ **State at the client**
The client must pass the state to each method call that needs it. This allows for stateless EJBs and so delivers scalability for all EJB containers. However, it puts more of a load on the client and the network and can cause a security risk if done through cookies for thin clients. In some cases, client-site security policy will disable the use of cookies, requiring the use of URL re-writing or hidden fields. None of these mechanisms is really suitable to hold any large amount of state. Any form of client-held state also serves to complicate the design of the EJB's remote interface.

❑ **State in the EJB**
By using a stateful session EJB, the required state can be loaded or acquired over time. This simplifies the design of the EJB's remote interface and lightens the load on the client and network. However, it does reduce the ability of the EJB server to reuse beans and can also lead to the client being locked into one server, defeating server load-balancing.

If the system is to support thin clients, then some method of associating the client with the appropriate EJB must be provided. The client is then issued with a cookie that identifies the EJB containing its state. This mapping must be handled by one of the components on the presentation tier.

❑ **State in a database**
The state for a stateless EJB can be stored in a database. The client is then issued with a cookie or identifier that identifies the state (usually the primary key of the record containing that state in the database). This has less of an impact in interface design than holding the state at the client but has a small impact on the network load and client complexity. It does, however, retain the guaranteed scalability of a stateless implementation at the cost of more time spent looking up and retrieving the data from the database. Remember, however, that using the database cache or modeling the state as an entity bean could reduce this significantly. The term 'database' here really refers to any server-side repository, ideally a transactional one. However, if the state is not intended to be persistent then alternative storage, such as a JNDI-compliant directory service would work well.

Scalability and performance requirements will have a large role to play in the decision about where state is held. Once the state location is determined, it will have an impact on the design of the remote interface for the session EJB.

Submitting the Order

Once the user has progressed through the workflow for product selection, they will be ready to submit their completed purchase order for approval. The OrderProcess class (again, refer to the UML diagram) would have various responsibilities for checking the order. In addition to checking the validity of the order itself, it may also check to see whether the department has sufficient budget left for such an order or it may check to see if that particular user is allowed to raise purchase orders of that value. The OrderProcess class could be implemented either as a stateless session bean that performs a one-time business process on state passed to it, or it could become part of an implementation of the ordering workflow if implemented as a stateful session bean. Once the OrderProcess is satisfied with the order, it must forward it for approval.

At this point, a major issue in distributed design appears. The user's manager must approve the order, but it is not possible to include the manager in the system. At this point the system becomes **asynchronous** since there is no manager to whom the purchasing process can deliver a synchronous approval request. Instead, the purchase order must be captured and stored, waiting until the manager can examine and approve it.

Choosing an Asynchronous Mechanism

All of the interactions we have dealt with so far (RMI and HTTP) have been synchronous in nature. The architecture for this asynchronous requirement will have to use a different technology or approach. The mechanism used will depend on the tightness of the coupling between the ordering system and the approval system. Three possibilities would suggest themselves:

❑ **E-mail**
The application could use the JavaMail API to send an e-mail containing the purchase order to the manager. This would be very flexible for the manager since they could even approve it from their web-based e-mail account while away from the office. However, it does present more issues around the processing of the approval or rejection. Firstly, the application must be able to monitor the reply to the e-mail and process it when it arrives. The purchase order information must have been presented to the manager in human-readable form. To recover the original order information, the application must either parse the e-mail message for all the order information or at least to recover some form of order identifier. An order identifier would refer to the original order data stored in a database somewhere. To provide authentication, the manager would have to use a digital certificate to sign the e-mail reply.

This solution gives good reach (that is, it only requires the manager to have an e-mail client to perform the approval) and is very loosely coupled. However, it is somewhat unwieldy and potentially insecure.

❑ **Database**
The order could be stored in a database within the system. The manager would then have to access some form of application that queried the database for orders awaiting that manager's approval. The manager would then interact with that application to approve or reject the orders. Since all of the information is stored in a database, there would be no issue with handling a return value as with e-mail. However, some way would be required of indicating that the order had been approved or rejected, such as a flag in the database or by moving it to another table. Security would be provided by authenticating the manager before they use the application.

This solution has less reach since it ties the two parts of the application to a common database (although this may be required anyway to access product and budgetary information). This puts more responsibility on the manager, since they will have to go and access the data in the database, even if they are notified by e-mail of its arrival. It is also tightly coupled to the order representation. However, it is all performed within a common security domain and means that the developer does not have to explicitly deal with some of the negative issues of asynchronous communications (discussed later).

❑ **Messaging System**
The Java Message Service (JMS) could be used to send an asynchronous message to the manager via a dedicated messaging system. This message would wait on an appropriate queue until it could be delivered to (or is retrieved by) the approval application. Since the message is not intended to be human-readable, it could be encoded in a convenient form such as XML or a serialized JavaBean. The serialized bean would be more convenient to use for completely Java solutions, but XML is more flexible and aids integration as described in Chapter 25.

The arrival of the XML Data Binding (JAXB) functionality should make XML an even better choice here, as shown schematically in the following diagram:

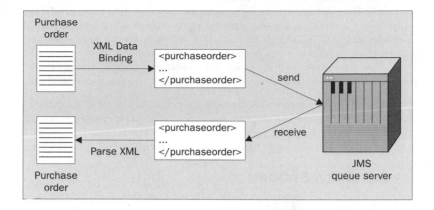

Once the order is approved or rejected, it could be moved to a specific 'approved' or 'rejected' queue. The design choice here is between the status of the purchase order being signified by its location (that is, which queue it is in) or by providing a flag in the message itself. Transacted queues should be used in order to guarantee that no message is left in limbo should the operation fail for whatever reason. These make the removal of the message from one queue and its storage on another part of a transaction. Once on the appropriate queue, the purchase order would be available for further processing, which could involve it being passed to another application, such as that of an external supplier.

This solution has a reasonable reach since messages can potentially cross boundaries between organizations. The flexible message format provides low coupling between the applications, and security is included as part of the messaging system. One downside is that while most J2EE developers are familiar with the use of EJB, servlets, and RMI, fewer are familiar with JMS and so they would take time to learn a new API and paradigm for programming.

The Java APIs for XML Messaging (JAXM) also promise to make this form of interaction between applications easier by passing SOAP-based messages, potentially removing the need to directly access queues.

An XML payload can also be used with an e-mail message to provide an Internet-friendly messaging system when used with application-oriented message stores. In this case, an application would have to retrieve the message from the store and present its contents to the manager, probably in the guise of a servlet providing a web-based interface. This removes the immediacy of sending the message directly to the manager, but it makes it far more workable.

Again, the precise requirement of the application would govern the forces on these decisions. Since the purchase-order system will potentially be distributed around the globe, it is likely that the JMS-based messaging solution with XML-encoded messages would be more efficient. This balances ease of processing, integration characteristics, and potentially global reach for Acme Corporation's remote sites.

Scalability and Availability through Asynchronicity

As we have seen, the timeframe between the submission of the purchase order and its approval or rejection by the manager can be very long (a matter of weeks if they are on vacation). While this is potentially acceptable for the purchase order system, it would be unacceptable for an e-commerce storefront. Indeed, for the typical transactional e-commerce system, a delay in the order of minutes or even tens of seconds during the processing of a user order can lead to backlogs and 'system busy' screens.

For this reason, even some things that might intuitively be thought of as synchronous may be performed asynchronously. Take online credit card processing as an example. Since the credit card must be checked and approved by a credit card processor (typically a third-party company), this approval call can be queued for later delivery. Calls can be made in a batch or when the system has spare capacity. On the positive side, this can improve the performance and scalability of the system immensely since no waiting is involved. The only real downside is for any credit card holder whose verification fails. In this case, they must be informed later (typically via e-mail) that their transaction could not proceed.

Messaging is also a useful tool at times when the target server is not available, either by accident (server crash), design (maintenance), or overuse through too many users. The client can still deliver messages to the queue and they can sit there until the server returns. In this way, it brings a level of robustness to the application that is difficult to achieve when using exclusively synchronous mechanisms.

Issues with Asynchronous Systems

As we have seen, there are some advantages to using asynchronous operation and messaging systems. There are, however, several downsides. The first one is that there is no return value from an asynchronous operation. If an output is needed, the sender and receiver must agree that the result will be posted on a particular queue. They must also agree to an identifier for the particular message to which it is a response. Finally, the sender of the original message must listen for message deliveries or poll the queue to await the arrival of their response. Another issue is that transactions need special management when they reach asynchronous boundaries. The synchronous transaction cannot propagate with the message, so some form of transaction state storage is required. While this makes a lot of sense (synchronous transactions must complete as quickly as possible), it does mean that handling failure becomes more complex and other mechanisms are required for reporting failure to the user of the system. In the credit card case, the order must be canceled and an e-mail message sent to the user. Both of these actions take place outside of the scope of the synchronous transaction within which the user ordered their goods.

It is also more difficult to obtain a return value from the asynchronous processing. Although most messaging systems provide a way of obtaining an acknowledgement that the message has been delivered, messages are very much a one-way mechanism. If a return value is required, a separate route back (that is, another queue) is required between server and client.

Interfacing between messaging systems and EJBs has traditionally been a problem. However, in J2EE 1.3 and beyond, a message-driven EJB can be used as the direct recipient for a message queue or topic. Messages received can be processed or forwarded on to normal entity or session EJBs with the message-driven EJB performing the role of an adapter. Prior to J2EE 1.3, an adapter object that implements the JMS `MessageListener` interface had to be registered as a recipient of the messages. This adapter then forwards the messages to the appropriate EJB using the normal synchronous interface calls. Although not covered here, the delivery of messages to pre-J2EE 1.3 EJBs, and also the use of message-driven EJBs as adapters, is discussed in detail in the original documentation for the Service Activator pattern from the Sun Java Center J2EE Patterns catalog.

Approving the Order

Returning to our purchase-order system, `ApprovalWorkflow` and `ApprovalProcess` are analogous to `OrderingWorkflow` and `OrderProcess`. They are subject to many of the same forces on their design and hence would be implemented in generally the same way, such as the `ApprovalWorkflow` being a Session Façade. One major difference is that there is only one type of data being handled (`Orders`). All of the data being worked on is to be processed by this part of the application. There is no static data such as the product catalog. Another difference is that the workflow associated with accepting or rejecting an order is very linear. There is no separate iteration phase as there is when loading the shopping cart followed by submission. Because of these factors, the functionality of `ApprovalProcess` includes the control of the data used during approval. To facilitate this, it has a method to list the purchase orders currently awaiting the manager's approval. This simplifies the overall shape of this part of the system.

The Account class used in the approval process would check any requests against departmental limits and rules to ensure that the manager conformed to, say, their maximum debit. The Account would be modeled as an entity EJB. This is justifiable since Account contains business logic as well as data. The debit of funds from the department's account would be coupled with the approval of the order. In a more closely coupled system, the approval process may also decrement the stock level of each product held in a database. In both cases, Account will form part of a transaction since the debit must only happen if the order is successfully approved (that is, moved onto the 'approved' queue).

The need for a transaction by the approval process could usually be discovered from the associated use case when modeling the system:

1. Manager logs on to approval system

2. Manager is shown the list of purchase orders awaiting their approval

3. Manager selects a purchase order and views detail

4. Manager approves purchase order

5. System debits the departmental account by the amount on the purchase order

6. System forwards purchase order for fulfillment

Alternatives here would be for the user to reject the purchase order, for the debit to fail, or for the forwarding of the purchase order to fail. Steps 5 and 6 suggest a transactional relationship between them, hence when they are mapped to the solution domain they would be noted as requiring a transaction. Putting this in class terms, the approve() method of ApprovalProcess would need to be marked as requiring a transaction and the Account's debit() method would also need to be transactional. Use of transactional message queues would ensure that the move of the purchase order between the 'pending' and 'approved' queues formed an atomic operation with the debit.

The key to transactions is to keep them as short as possible. There is no need for all of the processing performed by ApprovalWorkflow or ApprovalProcess to be transactional. Indeed, this would have the effect of slowing down the system unnecessarily. The primary goal of transactions is to maintain data integrity. This requires that changes are isolated from each other and is essentially achieved by locking some of the underlying data. The more data that is locked, the more likely it is that another transaction will have to wait until that lock is released.

> Although you can play many games with isolation levels, the bottom line is that the more transactions you use, the more contention you have for resources. Down this road lie timeouts and unhappy users. The only real solution to this is to keep transactions as short as possible. Hence, you should only use transactions where required and ensure that transactional methods do not perform lots of unnecessary processing. Short transactions and rapid resource recycling are the two major factors in middle-tier scalability.

It is worth pursuing the issue of resource recycling for a moment. This is an important concept in all tiers. If you have an infinite amount of resource, then it does not matter how long a component holds on to a particular resource instance since other components can retrieve another one out of the infinite pool. As the number of resource instances drops, the amount of time a component holds the resource becomes more critical. This relationship can be represented by the following diagram:

1103

Most applications contend for more than one resource, but it is still important to recycle resources as quickly as possible to aid scalability. The J2EE model for EJBs is designed to aid scalability by passivating EJBs when they are not needed and returning them to the object pool. As they are passivated, they can release the resources they hold and these then become available to other instances serving other clients.

However, the question arises of when an object will be passivated. Consider a stateful session EJB that is written so that it obtains and holds a database connection. If there are 10 connections available under the database license and there are 20 of these stateful session beans in the object pool, what happens when the 11th concurrent client appears? Since stateless session beans are passivated after each method, they should not have any problems with holding resources. However, if a developer programmed it badly and obtained their resources in the object constructor this could still cause problems.

The reason that stateless session beans do not usually have problems with resource management is because developers conform to a lifecycle that is good for such recycling. However, such good recycling practices work in all forms of EJB and also in servlets, JSP pages, and any other form of Java object. The principle that underpins good resource recycling (and hence good scalability) is to acquire and release resources when we need them throughout our component code. We should acquire a resource just before we need it and release it as soon as possible afterwards. It may even be possible that another component we call could reuse a resource we have released earlier in the method. Many developers tend to avoid this policy since they consider resource creation and allocation to be expensive and so they do it once at initialization time. The key is to use resources from resource pools since these are pre-built and can be allocated quickly. This means that we do not have to "take the hit" of resource acquisition when we need one.

In the business tier, there is a tendency to be less concerned about resource recycling since it is presumed that the container will handle all of this for you. However, the principle of releasing resources as quickly as possible still applies.

Beyond the Purchase Order System

Design always occurs within a context. The context we have used so far has been the electronic purchase order system for our fictional company. However, there are many mechanisms and patterns that are useful in the design of J2EE systems that are not required or not used in this scenario. In this section, we will look briefly at some of these and the contexts in which they may apply.

EJB Interface Design

When writing an EJB, it is a bad idea for the bean to implement its remote (business) interface. This would allow a reference to the bean itself to be accidentally passed back to a client rather than passing the associated `EJBObject`. However, implementing the remote interface is tempting since it allows you to pick up any incorrect method signatures on the bean before the container's introspector does.

We can achieve the same end, by defining a non-remote version of our business interface that can be implemented by the bean. We can then create our bean's remote interface by inheriting from both the non-remote business interface and from `EJBObject`. The diagram below shows the inheritance hierarchy of the interfaces. Note that the methods on our non-remote business interface will still have to be declared to throw `RemoteException` in order to work correctly in the remote version:

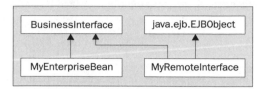

Unlike Microsoft's COM or the CORBA Components environment, Enterprise JavaBeans have only a single business interface. This means that there are issues with the design of EJBs that must be worked around. If the design of the bean suggests that it should implement two separate interfaces then this requirement can be addressed by using inheritance.

The next figure shows a potential inheritance hierarchy for two account interfaces, `CurrentAccount` and `SavingsAccount`. Both will have some common administrative operations but may well differ in the rest of their operations. Rather than just grafting a list of administrative methods into each interface and risking them getting out of sync, each interface can inherit from two others – the `AccountAdmin` interface containing the common methods and an interface containing the account-specific methods, for example, `CurrentOperations`. This would allow a client to narrow a `CurrentAccount` reference to either type `AccountAdmin` or `CurrentOperations`. The rest of the client code could then be written as if these were separate interfaces and so type safety could be assured:

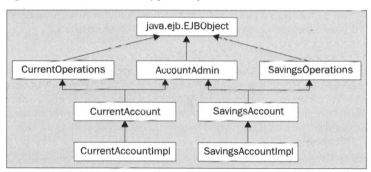

Note that this can only be done for the remote interfaces of EJBs. Home interfaces will need to return different types from their methods and hence cannot be used in this way.

Another consideration for EJB interfaces is the consequence of using role-based discovery of interfaces. The identification of a role during analysis will often lead to the discovery of a role-specific interface containing methods specific to that role. An example of such an interface is the `AccountAdmin` interface in the figure above that should be restricted to an administrator role. There are two possible routes here.

❑   First, you could implement the interface on an entirely separate bean. However, this would not be desirable if the methods on `AccountAdmin` and `CurrentOperations` acted on the same underlying data.

❑   The second route is to implement the type of inheritance hierarchy shown above and use the security attributes in the deployment descriptor to apply the correct security to this virtual interface. Although this is slightly unwieldy, it is the only safe alternative in the absence of multiple interfaces.

EJB 2.0 introduced the concept of local interfaces for entity beans that have dependent relationships and use container-managed persistence. The dependent EJB exposes a local interface to the containing EJB since they are both guaranteed to be running in the same container. In this case, the usual rules for local Java interaction apply (pass by value semantics for object references) and interface design is not so critical. However, you should ensure that there will never be a need to split these two EJBs in the future by using bean-managed persistence, before making the interface less network-friendly.

Distributed Events

As discussed previously, efficient operation is achieved by splitting most state between the presentation and business tiers. A Value Object can act as a read-only representative of the data in the associated EJB. One consideration here is what to do when the data represented changes. When data is manipulated locally (in the same JVM), the delegation event model works fine for this. The model can fire some form of change event at the view. The view would implement the appropriate listener interface for that event. The Swing API uses this form of event mechanism as part of its MVC implementation.

An issue arises when the data model is not local to the view. If the view is in the web (or client) tier and the model is in the EJB tier, there is no pre-supplied Java distributed event mechanism. However, there is enough of a framework to create your own. RMI allows you to set up callbacks from server to client. These can be used as the basis for a distributed version of the delegation event model. The server can implement a registration interface and the client (or view) can add itself as a listener. When its data changes, the server can inform all of its listeners of the change and the views can update themselves based on this new data. If you wish to implement this type of framework, the Jini Distributed Event Specification, available from Sun's web site, provides some food for thought.

Another alternative for a distributed event system is to use asynchronous messages. These can be integrated with EJB-based business logic as outlined earlier in the chapter.

JMS itself can be used to implement various message-based or event-based patterns. The functionality of interest will depend very much on the forces at work on the particular sub-system you are trying to design. A message queue can be used to pass messages from a producer to one or more consumers. Using point-to-point messages ensures a one-to-one relationship between the producer and consumer (although the behavior in the case where multiple consumers are silly enough to register for messages from the same queue is somewhat vague). Point-to-point would be good to use where the producer is creating items of work that must be processed by the consumer. Alternatively, when dealing with the distribution of information, such as the ubiquitous stock quotes, a publish-and-subscribe model can be used. In this case, multiple clients will receive the same information by registering for messages on a specific topic.

Messages can be made persistent if the application would have problems should they be lost in transit. Similarly, consumers can request that a server retain a copy of any publish-and-subscribe messages that have arrived for them when they were disconnected. These will be delivered when the consumer reappears. All of this helps the robustness of an application.

Designing for Databases

There are many clever things you can do with databases that are beyond the scope of this chapter. If you are seriously interested in Java and database interaction you should find Chapters 4 interesting, or refer to a more specific title, like *Database Magic with Ken North*, Prentice Hall PTR, ISBN 0-13-647199-4. However, from an overall design standpoint there are one or two principles to consider.

Firstly, don't be a Java snob. EJBs are great and they do a fine job of providing scalable data and business workflow. However, if performance is a high priority, why not let the database do as much work as possible? It is more efficient to run code inside the database than it is to extract the data, work on it and then put it back. Although embedding a stored procedure in your database and calling it to perform the work may not be as flexible, portable, or even as 'cool' as using an entity EJB, you may find that it works many times faster and so could be a better fit for the forces on your application. If you must code everything in Java, try to ensure that you have a database server that allows you to run your Java code within the database to get the best of both worlds.

If you are using entity EJBs, try to avoid fighting the database. If you find you are querying many tables to build your entity's state then you may have a serious impedance mismatch between your bean and database. You might want to consider denormalizing your database somewhat to ease the fit with your entity. Alternatively, you could split one entity up into a set of dependent entities that communicate using local interfaces (from J2EE 1.3 onwards). Again, although it is not covered in this chapter, there is a good discussion on the use of entities as dependent objects in the Composite Entity pattern from the Sun Java Center J2EE Patterns catalog.

In general, it is worth spending a lot of time on your data design. The data design tends to move a lot more slowly than the middle tier or client tier. If you get it wrong it can require serious rework of the other tiers.

Lessons Learned

We could potentially have followed the purchase-order system application through to the delivery of the order to the supplier system and so on. However, this would not really bring in any major new design issues. At this point, we can take stock of the main lessons to be learned from the example and expand on these where appropriate.

Separate Concerns Where Possible

The separation of concerns leads to improved flexibility and maintainability in a system. We have seen various example of this throughout the purchase order system:

❑   The use of (pseudo-)MVC to split the user interface handling into display (view), behavior (controller), and data (model)

❑   Using the View Helper pattern in JSP pages splits out the Java coding from the presentation of data

❑   The client can use the functionality of an EJB without worrying about EJB-specific lifecycle and exceptions if it is hidden behind a Business Delegate

❑   Elements of user interface functionality can be addressed separately by building a Composite View

This principle runs through the patterns and other design decisions encountered in this chapter

Minimize Network Traffic

Excessive network calls lead to performance bottlenecks as networks fill up with data and components spend time waiting for those calls to complete. Any reduction in the number of network calls, the amount of data passed, and the ratio of network overhead to data passed is useful. Again, this principle can be seen at work in:

❏ The use of Value Objects to avoid property-based programming across the network. Value Objects representing a partial data set can also reduce data-transfer levels.

❏ Value List Handlers passing collections of Value Objects to pass more data in a single call. Value List Handlers also allow the client to stop retrieving data once enough has been received.

❏ Use of a Session Façade reduces the number of calls from the client to the business tier.

❏ A Business Delegate can cache data and batch method calls from the client perspective, reducing network traffic.

It is important to consider the effects of distribution when designing component interfaces.

Use Abstraction to Aid Flexibility

Forcing a client to become too intimately involved in an underlying implementation leads to excessive coupling and a lack of flexibility in an application. By abstracting the service to be provided to the client, the actual details of the interaction can be hidden, and hence changed as and when necessary. This can be seen in:

❏ The use of the Business Delegate and Service Locator patterns to hide underlying details of interaction with remote EJBs.

❏ Application of the Data Access Object pattern to provide a common client interface to multiple data sources.

Measured use of abstraction can make an application far more intuitive and so far easier to maintain and extend.

Use Common Patterns

The set of patterns identified that are specific to J2EE form the beginnings of a pattern language. In such a language, the patterns inter-relate in common ways. By understanding both the patterns themselves and any common combinations of them, a designer can make best use of the patterns available as seen in:

❏ The Service to Worker and Dispatcher View macro-patterns that present common alternative ways of using a Front Controller with View Helpers.

❏ All of the J2EE-specific patterns presented in this chapter. Just knowing that there are patterns in these areas can save a lot of time and guesswork on the part of the designer.

Patterns should be part of the toolkit of any J2EE designer or architect.

Reduce Coupling with Asynchronous Mechanisms

In many applications, certain operations will take a long time to complete. For the application to move on, the operation must be made asynchronous. This can help to address issues of scalability and availability.

Asynchronous working can be implemented in different ways:

❏ Specific messaging services built on message-oriented middleware with multiple architectures such as point-to-point and publish-and-subscribe

❏ Ad hoc message systems built on e-mail or other simple transports

❏ The use of a persistent store to provide the rendezvous point for the producer and consumer of the messages

Asynchronous exchanges are a good way of reducing coupling between components.

Plan Transactions

Systems should only use transactions as required. Transactions can be discovered from use cases and designed in as appropriate. The time spent in transactions should be minimized as far as possible to avoid resource contention. Failure to plan transactional requirements can lead to buggy or slow systems.

Summary

For many years I have been involved in the evaluation of new technologies. At the beginning, I tended to focus on the technology itself and the various "bells and whistles" it provided. Over time, it dawned on me that 90% of the developers in the world would never use all of these bells and whistles. What they want to do is to use the technology to solve their business problems. In order to do that, they need to understand the technology and apply it in their own particular context. The key is to ensure that developers use the core features of the particular technology appropriate to their context. The technology itself is of little use unless it is correctly applied. I hope that you have found some familiar context in this chapter and will be able to apply some of the principles described.

In this chapter we have examined aspects of J2EE design, specifically:

- ❑   The relationship between design and architecture.

- ❑   How the context provided by a particular type of application can affect the design decisions made.

- ❑   Some of the issues typically found when designing a common J2EE-based application.

- ❑   A variety of J2EE-specific patterns that solve many common design issues encountered when designing J2EE-based business systems.

- ❑   How different J2EE technologies may be applied to solve different design problems.

In the next chapter we'll turn our attention to the interesting and rapidly growing topic of Web Services.

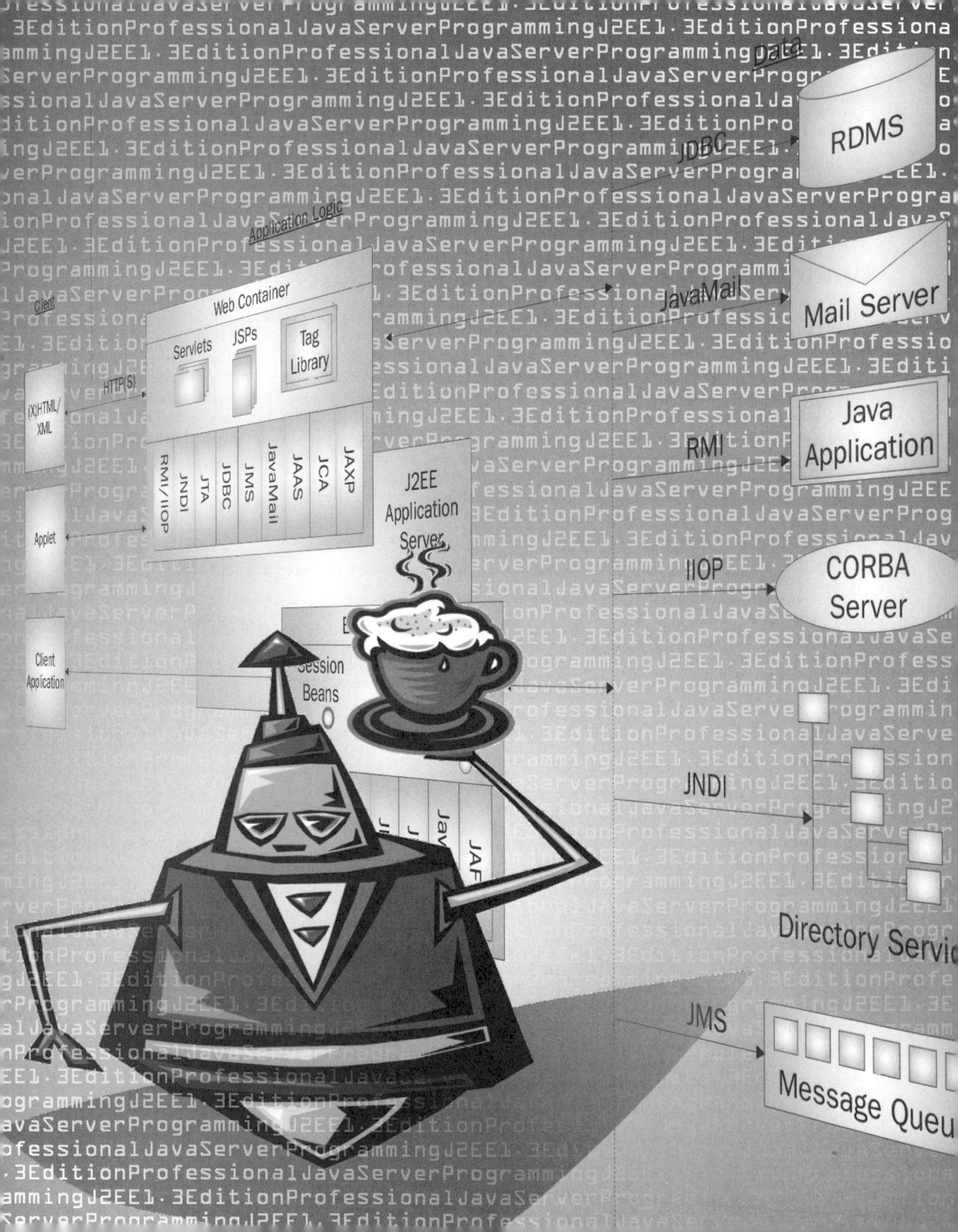

22

J2EE and Web Services

With the widespread use of the Internet, the way we use computers has changed radically. In the early days, computers used to run monolithic applications and the application user had to learn from scratch each and every application that they wanted to use. Thus, as technology kept on changing, users were forced to learn new applications on a continuous basis. Rather than technology adapting to human needs, we human beings were forced to adapt to the ever-changing technology.

With the Internet, the focus is shifting towards services-based software. People use computers to read e-mail, get current stock prices, pay their utility bills, or simply to locate the best Chinese restaurant. The software required to service such user requirements shouldn't be a traditional monolithic application. Also, the user of such a service may access the service using a wide variety of devices such as PDAs, mobile phones, desktop computers, and so on. Thus, traditional software should be converted into service-based software that is easily accessible over a wide variety of client devices. This has given rise to a new breed of software development that is service-oriented.

Service-oriented software development is possible using many known techniques such as COM, CORBA, RMI, Jini, RPC, and so on. Some of these techniques are capable of delivering the services over the Web and some are not. Most of these use proprietary protocols for communication and with no standardization. This makes it difficult for two different services to interoperate with each other. Ideally, not only should such services interoperate with each other, but also we should be able to integrate and compose micro-level services into a single larger service. However, if different application programmers use different technologies to create such services, the integration may not be always an easy task. This concept of creating services that can be accessed over the Web gave rise to a new term called **web service**.In this chapter, we will be looking at this new software paradigm, and in particular how it can be applied to the J2EE platform. Although web services are not specified as part of the J2EE 1.3 specification, a lot of the technology that we need to implement them is already there.

More specifically we will look at:

- ❑ Types of web services
- ❑ Web service technologies
- ❑ Java technologies for developing web services
- ❑ Smart web services

But before we go any further let's understand exactly what we mean by the term web service.

What are Web Services?

A web service may be defined as:

> **An application component accessible via standard web protocols.**

A web service is a like a unit of application logic. It provides services and data to remote clients and other applications.

Remote clients and applications access web services via ubiquitous Internet protocols. They use XML for data transport, and **SOAP (Simple Object Access Protocol)** for using services. Due to the use of XML and SOAP, accessing the service is independent of the implementation. Thus, a web service is like a component architecture for the Web.

As with a component development model, a web service must have the following two characteristics:

- ❑ Registration with a lookup service
- ❑ A public interface for the client to invoke the service

Each web service must register itself with a central repository so that the clients can look up the registry for a desired service. Once a service is located, the client obtains a reference to the service. The client then uses the service by invoking various methods implemented in the service with the help of a published public interface. Thus, each service must publish its interface for clients to use.

In addition to the above essential characteristics, a web service should also possess the following characteristics:

- ❑ Its should use standard web protocols for communication
- ❑ It should be accessible over the Web
- ❑ It should support loose coupling between uncoupled distributed systems so that the systems running on different platforms and based on different technologies can cooperate with each other to form a distributed system

Web services receive information from clients as messages, containing instructions about what the client wants, similar to method calls with parameters. These messages, which are also delivered by a web service to the client upon completion of the service, are encoded using XML, and the public interfaces are also described in XML. XML provides a platform-neutral data transport. Thus, XML-enabled web services can theoretically interoperate with other XML-enabled web services provided the two services agree on a common protocol for communication. The protocols used by web services for communication are being standardized and we will discuss this in the following sections.

Smart Services

In these days, the mere introduction of web services is not enough. The users of a web service want the service to be smart enough to understand the context under which the service is invoked and act accordingly. For example, if you are using a web service to look up a restaurant, the service should be intelligent enough to look up your personal preferences, your history over the last few days as to where have you been eating, and come up with appropriate suggestions.

Alternatively, consider that you are using a web service to make a travel reservation. Your company's policy may allow you to travel in executive class, while you may travel by coach class on your personal trips. The service should automatically detect the context and accordingly come up with the suggestions for your travel reservations. Such services are called **smart services** and can provide contents using personalization techniques. Smart services are discussed in depth later in this chapter.

Having seen what web services are, we will now look into what technologies are required in the development of such web services.

Web Service Technologies

A wide variety of technologies support web services. The following technologies are available for the creation of web services. These are vendor-neutral technologies. We shall briefly discuss these technologies before moving on to what Java has to offer us in the way of web services:

❑   SOAP

❑   SOAP Messages with attachments

❑   WSDL

❑   UDDI

❑   ebXML

SOAP

SOAP (**Simple Object Access Protocol**, see http://www.w3.org/TR/SOAP/ for more details) is a lightweight and simple XML-based protocol. SOAP enables the exchange of structured and typed information on the Web, by describing a messaging format for machine-to-machine communication. SOAP enables the creation of web services based on an open infrastructure.

SOAP consists of three parts:

❑ **SOAP Envelope**
Defines what is in a message, who the message recipient is, and whether the message is optional or mandatory

❑ **SOAP Encoding Rules**
Defines a set of rules for exchanging instances of application-defined data types.

❑ **SOAP RPC Representation**
Defines a convention for representing remote procedure calls and responses

SOAP can be used in combination with a variety of existing Internet protocols and formats including HTTP, SMTP, and MIME and can support a wide range of applications from messaging systems to RPC. However, at the time of writing, only HTTP binding is supported.

A typical SOAP message is shown below:

```
<IVORY:Envelope xmlns:IVORY="http://schemas.xmlsoap.org/soap/envelope/"
        IVORY:encodingStyle="http://schemas.xmlsoap.org/soap/encoding/">

  <IVORY:Body>
    <m:GetLastTradePrice xmlns:m="Some-URI">
      <symbol>DIS</symbol>
    </m:GetLastTradePrice>
  </IVORY:Body>
</IVORY:Envelope>
```

As seen from this example, a SOAP message is encoded using XML. SOAP defines two standard namespaces, one for the envelope (http://schemas.xmlsoap.org/soap/envelope/) and the other for encoding rules (http://schemas.xmlsoap.org/soap/encoding/). A SOAP message must not contain a DTD (Document Type Definition) and must not contain any processing instructions. The above SOAP message defines a method called GetLastTradePrice that takes a stock symbol as parameter.

The consumer of the web service creates a SOAP message as above, embeds it in an HTTP POST request, and sends it to the web service for processing:

```
POST /StockQuote HTTP/1.1
Host: www.stockquoteserver.com
Content-Type: text/xml;
charset="utf-8"
Content-Length: nnnn
SOAPAction: "Some-URI"
  ...
  SOAP Message
  ...
```

The web service processes the message, executes the requested operation, and returns the result to the client as another SOAP message. The message now contains the requested stock price. A typical returned SOAP message may look like the following:

```
<SOAP-ENV:Envelope
      xmlns:SOAP-ENV="http://schemas.xmlsoap.org/soap/envelope/"
      SOAP-ENV:encodingStyle="http://schemas.xmlsoap.org/soap/encoding/"/>
```

```
<SOAP-ENV:Body>
  <m:GetLastTradePriceResponse xmlns:m="Some-URI">
    <Price>34.5</Price>
  </m:GetLastTradePriceResponse>
</SOAP-ENV:Body>
</SOAP-ENV:Envelope>
```

The message may be returned to the client as an HTTP response and will contain the proper HTTP header at the top of the message. As you can probably see, in this message we are telling the client that the response from its call to `GetLastTradePrice` is `34.5`; if the client had made requests to more methods, the response would contain more return values.

Interoperability

The major goal in the design of SOAP was to allow for an easy creation of interoperable distributed web services (through providing easy access to objects). Since the services can be described in XML, it is lot easier to describe services than in RMI, CORBA, or EJB architectures. Since a few details of SOAP specifications are open for interpretation, however, the implementation across vendors does differ. Thus, the messages created by different applications differ in their conformance-level resulting in non-interoperable applications.

Note that a valid XML document may not necessarily be a valid SOAP message and similarly a valid SOAP message may not be a conformant SOAP message. What this means is that a SOAP message, though it is a conformant XML message, may not strictly follow the SOAP specification. To test for the conformance, third-party tools may be used. One such tool called SOAP Message Validator is developed by Microsoft and is available at http://www.soaptoolkit.com/soapvalidator/. Using the validator, you can test any SOAP code for conformance to the SOAP 1.1 specification.

Implementations

SOAP technology was developed by DevelopMentor, IBM, Lotus, Microsoft, and Userland. More than 50 vendors have currently implemented SOAP. The most popular implementations are by Apache, which is an open source Java-based implementation, and by Microsoft, within their .NET platform. The two implementations have a few discrepancies that make applications developed using the two technologies non-interoperable. The SOAP specification has been submitted to W3C (World Wide Web Consortium), which is now working on new specifications called XMLP (XML Protocol) that are based on SOAP version 1.1.

SOAP Messages with Attachments (SwA)

You may need to send a SOAP message with an attachment consisting of another document or an image, and so on. On the Internet, the GIF and JPEG data formats are treated as de facto standards for image transmission. In general, the attachments may be in text or in binary formats. The second iteration of the SOAP specification (SOAP 1.1) allowed for attachments to be combined with a SOAP message by using a multipart MIME structure. This multipart structure is called a **SOAP Message Package**. This new specification was developed by HP and Microsoft and has been submitted to W3C. A sample SOAP message containing an attachment (`myimmage.tiff`) is shown here:

```
MIME-Version: 1.0
Content-Type: Multipart/Related; boundary=MIME_boundary; type=text/xml;
       start="<myimagedoc.xml@mysite.com>"
Content-Description: This is the optional message description.
```

```
--MIME_boundary
Content-Type: text/xml; charset=UTF-8
Content-Transfer-Encoding: 8bit
Content-ID: <myimagedoc.xml@mysite.com>

<?xml version='1.0' ?>
<SOAP-ENV:Envelope
xmlns:SOAP-ENV="http://schemas.xmlsoap.org/soap/envelope/">
<SOAP-ENV:Body>
..
<theSignedForm href="cid:myimage.tiff@mysite.com"/>
..
</SOAP-ENV:Body>
</SOAP-ENV:Envelope>

--MIME_boundary
Content-Type: image/tiff
Content-Transfer-Encoding: binary
Content-ID: <myimage.tiff@mysite.com>

...binary TIFF image...
--MIME_boundary--
```

WSDL

The **Web Services Description Language** (**WSDL**) is an XML format for describing a web service interface. A WSDL file defines the set of operations permitted on the server and the format that the client must follow while requesting the service. The WSDL file acts like a contract between the client and the service for the effective communication between the two parties. The client has to request the service by sending a well formed and conformant SOAP request.

As an example, if we were creating a web service that offered the latest stock quotes, we would need to create a WSDL file on the server that describes the service. The client would first obtain a copy of this file, understand the contract, create a SOAP request based on the contract and dispatch the request to the server using say an HTTP Post. The server validates the request and, if found valid, executes the request. The result, which is the latest stock price for the requested symbol, is then returned to the client as a SOAP response.

WSDL Document

A WSDL document is an XML document that consists of a set of definitions. First, we declare the namespaces required by the schema definition:

```
<schema xmlns="http://www.w3.org/2000/10/XMLSchema"
        xmlns:wsdl="http://schemas.xmlsoap.org/wsdl/"
        targetNamespace="http://schemas.xmlsoap.org/wsdl/"
        elementFormDefault="qualified">
```

The root element is definitions as shown here:

```
<wsdl:definitions name="nmtoken"? targetNamespace="uri"?>
    <import namespace="uri" location="uri"/>*
    <wsdl:documentation .... /> ?
  ...
</wsdl:definitions>
```

The name attribute is optional and can serve as a lightweight form of documentation. The nmtoken represents name tokens that are qualified strings similar to CDATA, but the character usage is limited to letters, digits, underscores, colons, periods, and dashes. Optionally, a targetNamespace may be specified by providing a uri. The import tag may be used to associate a namespace with a document location. Thus, the definitions may contain the target namespace, which is then associated with the document location in a subsequent import statement. The following code segment shows how the declared namespace is associated later with a document location specified in the import statement:

```
<definitions name="StockQuote"

targetNamespace="http://example.com/stockquote/definitions"
        xmlns:tns="http://example.com/stockquote/definitions"
        xmlns:xsd1="http://example.com/stockquote/schemas"
        xmlns:soap="http://schemas.xmlsoap.org/wsdl/soap/"
        xmlns="http://schemas.xmlsoap.org/wsdl/">

    <import namespace="http://example.com/stockquote/schemas"
            location="http://example.com/stockquote/stockquote.xsd"/>
```

Finally, the optional wsdl:documentation element is used for declaring human readable documentation. The element may contain any arbitrary text.

Within the definitions, you will add other elements. There are six major elements in the document structure that describe the service. These are listed below:

- ❑   types
- ❑   message
- ❑   portType
- ❑   binding
- ❑   port
- ❑   service

The types Element

The types element provides definitions for datatypes used to describe how the messages will exchange data. The syntax for the types element is as follows:

```
<wsdl:types> ?
    <wsdl:documentation .... />?
    <xsd:schema .... />*
    <-- extensibility element --> *
</wsdl:types>
```

The wsdl:documentation tag is optional as in the case of definitions. The xsd type system may be used to define types in a message. As it may not be possible to have a single type system grammar to describe all abstract types, WSDL allows type systems to be added via the extensibility element.

A typical example of a <types> section is shown overleaf. Here an element called StockQuoteService is defined. The service will require an input parameter of a string type, with the name tickerSymbol:

```
<types>
    <schema targetNamespace="http://example.com/stockquote.xsd"
            xmlns="http://www.w3.org/2000/10/XMLSchema">
        <element name=" StockQuoteService ">
            <complexType>
                <all>
                    <element name="tickerSymbol" type="String"/>
                </all>
            </complexType>
        </element>
    </schema>
</types>
```

The message Element

A message element represents an abstract definition of the data being transmitted. The syntax for the message element follows:

```
<wsdl:message name="nmtoken"> *
    <wsdl:documentation .... />?
    <part name="nmtoken" element="qname"? type="qname"?/> *
</wsdl:message>
```

The message name attribute is used for defining a unique name for the message within the document scope. As in earlier cases, wsdl:documentation is optional and may be used for declaring human-readable documentation. The message consists of one or more logical parts. part describes the logical abstract content of a message. Each part consists of a name and an optional element and type attributes. The element and its type may be declared earlier in the types section.

An example of a typical message is shown below. The name of the message is StockQuoteService. The StockQuotes should be defined in the namespace in the definitions section:

```
<message name="StockQuoteService">
    <part name="body" element="xsd1:StockQuotes"/>
</message>
```

The portType Element

The portType defines the set of abstract operations. An operation consists of both input and output messages. As shown in the syntax below, the operation tag defines the name of the operation, the input defines the input for the operation and the output defines the output format for the result. The fault element is used for describing the contents of the SOAP fault-details element. The fault-detail element specifies the abstract message format for the error messages that may be output as a result of the operation:

```
<wsdl:portType name="nmtoken">*
    <wsdl:documentation .... />?
    <wsdl:operation name="nmtoken">*
        <wsdl:documentation .... /> ?
        <wsdl:input name="nmtoken"? message="qname">?
            <wsdl:documentation .... /> ?
        </wsdl:input>
        <wsdl:output name="nmtoken"? message="qname">?
```

```
            <wsdl:documentation .... /> ?
        </wsdl:output>
        <wsdl:fault name="nmtoken" message="qname"> *
            <wsdl:documentation .... /> ?
        </wsdl:fault>
    </wsdl:operation>
</wsdl:portType>
```

The binding Element

The binding element defines the protocol to be used and specifies the data format for the operations and messages defined by a particular portType. The full syntax for binding is given below:

```
<wsdl:binding name="nmtoken" type="qname">*
    <wsdl:documentation .... />?
    <-- extensibility element --> *
    <wsdl:operation name="nmtoken">*
        <wsdl:documentation .... /> ?
        <-- extensibility element --> *
        <wsdl:input> ?
            <wsdl:documentation .... /> ?
            <-- extensibility element -->
        </wsdl:input>
        <wsdl:output> ?
            <wsdl:documentation .... /> ?
            <-- extensibility element --> *
        </wsdl:output>
        <wsdl:fault name="nmtoken"> *
            <wsdl:documentation .... /> ?
            <-- extensibility element --> *
        </wsdl:fault>
    </wsdl:operation>
</wsdl:binding>
```

The operations in the WSDL file can be "document" oriented or "remote procedure call (RPC)" oriented. The style attribute of the <soap:binding> element defines the type of operation.

If the operation is document-oriented, the input and output messages will consist of XML documents. For example, you may send an order for a stock purchase to the StockQuote web service as an XML document. In return, you will receive an XML document that confirms the order execution on the stock exchange. Such XML documents may be processed using any available XML parsers.

If the operation is RPC-oriented, then the input message contains the operation's input parameters and the output message contains the results of the operation. The web service may define an RPC-oriented operation such as multiplying two matrices. In this case, the input parameters will be the two matrices and the output will consist of the resultant matrix returned by the server.

The port Element

A port defines an individual endpoint by specifying a single address for a binding:

```
<wsdl:port name="nmtoken" binding="qname"> *
    <-- extensibility element (1) -->
</wsdl:port>
```

The `name` attribute defines a unique name for the port within the current WSDL document. The `binding` attribute refers to the binding and the extensibility element is used to specify the address information for the port.

The service Element

The `service` element aggregates a set of related ports. Each `port` specifies an address for a binding:

```
<wsdl:service name="nmtoken"> *
    <wsdl:documentation .... />?
    <wsdl:port name="nmtoken" binding="qname"> *
        <wsdl:documentation .... /> ?
    <-- extensibility element -->
    </wsdl:port>
    <-- extensibility element -->
</wsdl:service>
```

UDDI

Having created web services, you will need to publish them so that your customers and business partners can locate the services offered by you. Thus, what is required is a common registry where you would register your web service for clients to find it.

For this purpose, an industry consortium lead by Accenture, Ariba, Commerce One, Compaq, Edifecs, Fujitsu, HP, I2, IBM, Intel, Microsoft, Oracle, SAP, Sun Microsystems, and Verisign was formed. They founded the **Universal Description, Discovery, and Integration (UDDI)** project. Today more than 250 companies have joined the UDDI project. The main task of the project is to develop specifications for a web-based business registry. The registry should be able to describe a web service and allow others to discover the registered web services. A sample implementation of the specification, along with other resources, is currently available at http://www.uddi.org.

The UDDI registry allows any organization to publish information about its web services. The framework defines a standard for businesses to share information, describe their services and their business, and to decide what information is made public and what information is kept private. The specification also defines an interface for a programmer to interact with the registry. The interface is based on XML and SOAP and uses HTTP to interact with the registry.

The registry itself holds information about a business such as company name, contacts, and so on., and also holds both the descriptive and technical information about the web service provided by the business. Such information consists of the URL for the web service and pointers to service contracts, and the technical specifications of the service.

The UDDI registry provides search facilities that allow you to search specific industry segments and/or geographic locations. The search also allows you to locate partners having compatible software so that you can share documents created using this software.

Implementation

As mentioned above, the implementation of the current specifications is available at the http://www.uddi.org/ site. This is a global, public registry called UDDI business registry. It is possible for individuals to set up up private UDDI registries. The implementations for creating private registries are available from IBM, Idoox, jUDDI.org, and the Mind Electric.

Microsoft has developed a UDDI SDK that allows a Visual Basic programmer to write program code to interact with UDDI registry. The UDDI SDK may be downloaded from the MSDN site (http://msdn.microsoft.com). The use of this SDK greatly simplifies the interaction with the registry and shields the programmer from local-level details of XML and SOAP.

ebXML

Like the above specifications, **ebXML** (**electronic business XML**) is a set of specifications that allow businesses to collaborate (http://www.ebxml.org/). ebXML enables a global electronic marketplace where business can meet and transact with the help of XML-based messages. The businesses may be geographically located anywhere in the world and could be of any size to participate in the global marketplace. The ebXML initiative is jointly sponsored by the United Nations Centre for Trade Facilitation and Electronic Business (UN/CEFACT, http://www.unece.org/cefact/) and the Organization for the Advancement of Structured Information Standards (OASIS, http://www.oasis-open.org/). The current membership includes representation from more than 2000 businesses, governments, institutions, standard bodies, and individuals.

The framework defines specifications for the sharing of web-based business services. It includes specifications for a message service, collaborative partner agreements, core components, a business process methodology, a registry, and a repository.

ebXML defines a registry and a repository where businesses can register themselves by providing their contact information, address, and so on. through a standard document format. Such information is called the core component. Once the business submits core components, it can next supply the information about its products and services.

After a business has registered with the ebXML registry, other partners (say, buyers of services) can look up the registry to locate that business. Once a business partner (say, a seller of services) is located, the core components of the located business are downloaded. The buyer may then download the technical specifications for the service. Once the buyer is satisfied with the fact that the seller service can meet its requirements, it negotiates a contract with the seller. Such collaborative partner agreements are defined in ebXML. Once both the parties agree on contract terms, they sign the agreements and do a collaborative business transaction by exchanging their private documents.

The ebXML provides a marketplace and defines several XML-based documents for business to join and transact in such a marketplace.

J2EE Technologies for Web Services

Having seen several technologies for creating web services, we will now look at what J2EE has to offer. The J2EE platform provides a **JAX pack** (**Java APIs** for **XML**, http://java.sun.com/xml/jaxpack.html) containing several further packages for XML technologies that help in creation of a web service. JAX provides APIs for SAX, DOM, XSLT, SOAP, UDDI, WSDL, and ebXML, making all these technologies accessible through a common programming language (Java), thus, allowing an easy interoperability between applications created using these technologies. With Java being platform-neutral, and XML being vendor-neutral, these APIs will help businesses to create applications and web services that are platform- and vendor-neutral, allowing for the easy sharing of documents and services.

The JAX pack is still emerging and all the APIs are not yet in final release. In fact, only a few of these APIs have a reference implementation available, and some only through Sun's early access program. Sun has promised frequent updates to JAX to ensure that the latest Java XML technology is available to developers of web services.

The JAX pack includes the following technologies:

- ❑ **JAXP** – Java API for XML Processing
- ❑ **JAXB** – Java Architecture for XML Binding
- ❑ **JAXM** – Java API for XML Messaging
- ❑ **JAX-RPC** – Java API for XML-based RPC
- ❑ **JAXR** – Java API for XML Registries

We'll now briefly discuss each one of these technologies.

For more information on any of these APIs, look at either Professional Java XML *(ISBN 1-861004-01-X) or the* Java XML Programmer's Reference *(ISBN 1-861005-20-2).*

JAXP

The JAXP API supports processing of XML documents using either **SAX** (**Simple API** for **XML** processing) or **DOM** (**Document Object Model**). It also serves as an API for XML transformations (**XSLT, Extensible Stylesheet Language Transformations**). The API provides a further abstraction to XML processors and allows the developer to plugin any XML processor depending on the need of the time. Some of XML processors may provide high performance at the cost of resources consumed while other processors may conserve the use of resources. The developer has the flexibility to swap between these processors. This high-level abstraction allows developers to XML-enable their current Java applications and convert them into web-based applications.

The JAXP package provides a reference implementation that includes a parser for both SAX and DOM and a transformation engine supporting XSLT. The latest release (version 1.1) supports both SAX 2.0 and DOM level 2. The 1.1 API also includes an XSLT framework based on **Transformation API** for **XML** (**TrAX**).

JAXB

By using the above described JAXP, you can plugin an XML parser of your choice into your program code. Parsers are useful if you wish to parse the entire document, however, there are situations where you may need to access partial data in an XML document. For example, if your program wants to read the value of the purchase quantity from an XML-based order document, it is lot easier to use a method such as getQuantity() rather than parsing the whole document using SAX or DOM parsers. Similarly, while placing the order, to set the quantity a method like setQuantity() would be more efficient. Thus, an application developer needs an easy way for accessing and manipulating the data contained in an XML document; something as simple as get and set methods.

The XML data-binding technique is based on this idea. The technique requires the use of **XML Schemas**. We will briefly discuss XML Schemas before proceeding with the explanation of the XML data-binding technique.

XML Schema

The most common way of describing the structure of an XML document is by way of creating a Document Type Definition (DTD). XML Schema is a new standard for describing the document structure and data type for its contents.

A portion of a typical XML Schema is shown here:

```
<?xml version="1.0"?>
<schema targetNamespace="http://www.abcom.com"
        xmlns="http://www.w3.org/1999/XMLSchema"
        xmlns:abcom="http://www.abcom.com"
>
  <ElementType name="Catalog">
    <attribute name="bookName" type="string" />
    <attribute name="edition" type="float" />
  </ElementType>
```

XML Schema not only describes the structure for the XML document, but also allows type checking for the element data. Thus, it is easy to write a Java program that validates the XML document against its schema for the structure, and the type of each element. For example, it is very easy to validate if a given element contains a numeric or a non-numeric value against its definition in the schema. The program can easily trap such errors and throw exceptions if the data types do not match against those defined in the schema. To summarize, XML Schemas offer the following benefits:

❑   Defines structure of XML document like DTD

❑   Allows type checking for element data

❑   Allows easy validation for both structure and data type

Thus, the use of XML Schemas was preferred over DTDs while designing XML data binding.

XML Data Binding

The XML data-binding technique is the result of a Sun project code named Adelard and now known as JAXB. The project had the following goals while designing these APIs:

❑   Easy to use – developers need not be XML experts

❑   Customizable – XML Schema standard is still evolving so the new API should reflect the changes made in the schema specifications

❑   Fast – should be able to handle large documents efficiently

❑   Small – the generated code should be small enough to fit in small devices

❑   Support DTDs – though XML Schema is used in the current project, the future release should support DTDs as these are still in wide use

> **The data-binding technique maps XML Schema into Java classes, which can be used by your program code.**

Each element of the schema may be mapped to a unique Java class that contains several get/set methods to operate on the element attributes. The generated classes should meet the following goals:

- ❑ Based on standard API conventions
- ❑ Represent schema conceptually
- ❑ No need for parsing, no SAX, no DOM
- ❑ Allow subclassing for customization
- ❑ Objects serializable
- ❑ Allow validation of document instances without marshaling

To map the XML Schema into Java classes a schema compiler was developed in the reference implementation. The compiler converts the given schema into a set of Java classes that can be directly used in your program code:

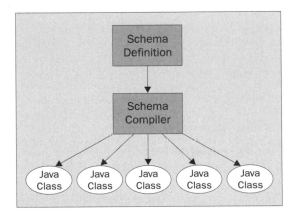

The generated code includes both structure validation and data content validation as defined in the schema. This relieves the programmer from implementing validation rules in the program code.

The generated Java classes are compiled into Java bytecode and thus give better performance compared to any dynamic validation implemented in SAX or DOM-based programs. Also, if the schema changes, the Java classes can be quickly and automatically re-created by using the schema compiler. This reduces the code maintenance to a great extent. As the compiler automatically generates the required Java code along with the specified validations, this greatly reduces the application development time. An application using the data-binding technique can run as fast as a SAX-based application. At the same time, it also gives the benefits of an in-memory structure of the XML document similar to the DOM-based parser.

To summarize, the data-binding technique uses an XML Schema compiler to map the schema into a set of Java classes that can be directly used by a Java application. Such Java classes provide both structure and content validation and greatly reduce the development time and maintenance cost. The generated classes also provide a mechanism for conversion between XML document and Java objects. The use of the data-binding technique can greatly simplify the development of web services that require XML for data interchange.

JAXM

The **Java API for XML Messaging** (**JAXM**) allows applications to send and receive document-oriented XML messages using a Java API. It supports the SOAP 1.1 specification, and SOAP with attachments. The conceptual model showing the relationship between JAXM and other elements in a B2B messaging scenario is shown below:

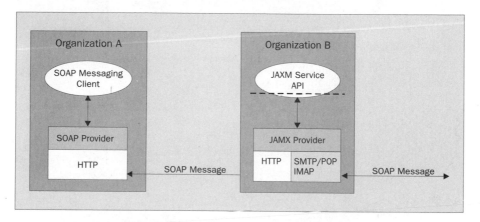

The server in Organization B implements the JAXM API. The JAXM provider is responsible for transmission and reception of SOAP messages. The client uses JAXM to communicate with the server. The message is always document-centric and may be delivered synchronously or asynchronously. In case of synchronous message delivery, the client waits until the message has been completely processed by the server and will wait for the server acknowledgement before proceeding further. In case of asynchronous delivery, the client does not wait for the server acknowledgement and would continue with its work.

JAXM providers should support HTTP; additionally, they may support other protocols such as FTP and SMTP in their implementations.

The SOAP packaging model used by JAXM is depicted in the following diagram:

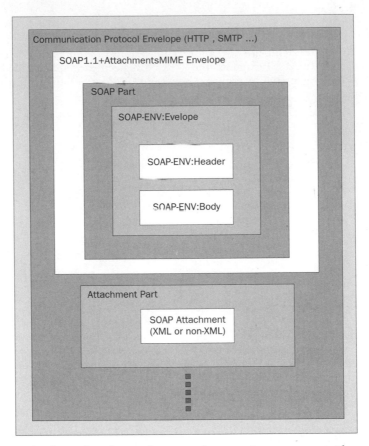

JAXM defines a standard interface for producing and consuming messages with or without attachments. JAXM uses the **JavaBeans Activation Framework** (**JAF**) to handle attachments based on MIME type.

In addition to SOAP and SOAP with attachment messages, the JAXM specification supports the higher-level standards-based messaging protocols. Such higher-level protocols generally provide additional functionality beyond that provided by SOAP-based messaging. An example of such a higher-level standard is ebXML. This feature is called **messaging profiles** and allows developers to have a pluggable XML messaging capability in their application programs. This results in scalable, robust, and secured messaging-based applications.

JAX-RPC

This API provides a transport-independent API for standard XML-based RPC (Remote Procedure Calls) protocols. The API is still under development under the Java Community Process (JCP) and no reference implementation is available at the time of writing. This API uses XML for transmitting Remote Procedure Calls.

In JAXB, we saw the mapping provided between an XML Schema and a Java class. Similarly, JAX-RPC defines a mapping for XML-based RPC calls to Java interfaces, classes, and methods. This will allow the RPC calls defined in other languages to be mapped into Java. The API also defines the reverse mapping that allows the existing Java-based program code to be mapped into XML-based RPCs. Such reverse mapping is also provided in Java IDL (RMI-IIOP) to convert the existing RMI based applications to IDL. The expert group working on this project is studying the existing mappings used in CORBA and RMI-IIOP to align the new mappings with the existing ones.

In addition to these mappings, the API should support marshaling and unmarshaling of method arguments. The API will be independent of specific protocols and data formats allowing the creation of "pluggable" applications as described in JAXP API described above. W3C is developing a new standard XML protocol called XP that supports XML-based RPC calls. The proposed JAX-RPC API will primarily provide support for XP.

This API will be useful in writing Java clients that use remote web services based on remote procedure calls. SOAP, however, provides a more generalized way of accessing a web service.

JAXR

JAXR is a new API that is under development under the Java Community Process (JCP) and the first public draft of the specifications was released on August 10, 2001. Currently, there are several business registries available in the market. To list a few, these are UDDI, ebXML, ISO11179, OASIS, and eCo Framework. The APIs for accessing these registries vary considerably and thus make it difficult to write portable client programs. The JAXR specification tries to unify access to these registries and probably the future registries by defining a new Java API.

Architecture

The following diagram illustrates the general architecture. The service provider implements the interface to a registry. A Java-based client then uses the JAXR API to access the registry using a standard Java interface:

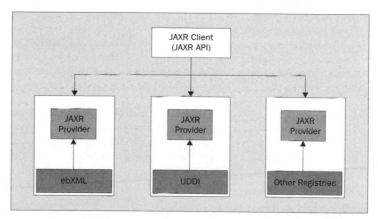

The JAXR service provider may use other XML related APIs such as JAXP, JAXB, or JAXM to provide XML support to the existing registries. The JAXR provider is responsible for implementing the JAXR specification. This will be generally be implemented as a façade around the existing registry provider.

A JAXR client is a Java program that uses the JAXR API to access the services provided by the JAXR provider.

Design Goals

As mentioned earlier, the JAXR specification is still under public draft. While designing this API, the following goals are sought:

❏ Define a general-purpose standardized Java API that allows Java clients to access a wide variety of business registries in use via the JAXR provider

❏ Define a pluggable JAXR provider architecture to support a variety of registries

❏ Provide support for the best features of all dominant registries rather than defining a least common denominator of such features

❏ Ensure support for the two most dominant registries, ebXML and UDDI, while making it sufficiently general to support others

❏ Follow the Java specifications standards

Thus, the JAXR, as and when it becomes available, will be helpful in creating collaborative web services that require access to diversified registries through Java code.

Developing Web Services

Having seen the various technologies involved in the creation of web services and what Java offers, it is now time to apply what we have learned so far to the creation of web services.

As we have seen, a web service must be web accessible and must expose an XML interface through a WSDL document. The service should be accessible using a standard protocol, such as HTTP, and should provide input and output in XML format. We should be able to register the service with a local or global XML-based registry so that the clients can look up the registry for the desired service.

In its simplest form, creating a web service with the J2EE platform is not too difficult. Looking at the requirements for creating a web service, it is sufficient to say that most of the infrastructure for creating a web service is already available. To create a simple web service, we can write a servlet that parses a SOAP message, processes the message, executes the requested operation on the server, and returns the result in XML format to the client.

Web Service Architecture

The general architecture for developing a web service on a J2EE platform is shown in the following diagram:

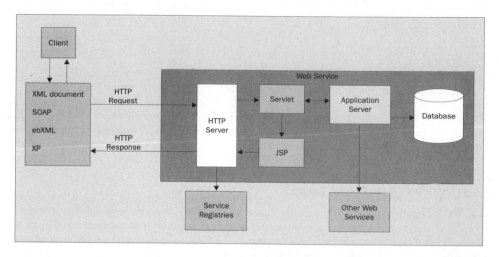

A web service consists of a web service interface that communicates with the client using XML messages, and one or more components (implemented in servlets, JSP pages, EJBs) that implement the business logic. The components use external resources such as databases, other web services, and backend systems to achieve the desired functionality of the business logic. The service itself should be registered with a web service registry.

The consumer of a web service uses the service by first contacting the web address (URL) at which the service is provided. Thus, the web interface must be running on a web server. The interface is designed using servlets or JSP pages, which run on an HTTP server. The consumer uses HTTP to communicate with the web server.

Locating Web Services

The first task for the consumer is to locate a desired web service. For this purpose, a consumer may contact a global registry or a private registry maintained at a specified URL. The interface to the service registry may be implemented in a servlet or a JSP page.

The client gets access to the registry by first contacting the web server that has deployed the servlet or JSP page and uses JAXR (yet to come) to interact with the registry. Currently, one can use the UDDI implementations provided by different vendors to interface with the registry.

Once the service is located, the client obtains the contract for using the service. The contract describes the web interface by specifying the methods provided, the parameters required by each method, and the returned value, which the client can use to build the SOAP request.

The Web Service Interface

The web interface itself is implemented in a servlet or a JSP page. The client creates a service request in a SOAP message and sends the message to the web server that acts as a front-end to the web service. Once the server receives the SOAP message from the client, it processes the received SOAP-based XML document. We may use any of the earlier discussed XML processing technologies to implement the XML messaging. The technologies that could be used are:

❏   SOAP

❏   SOAP with attachments

❏   ebXML

❏   XMLP (XML Protocol)

Typically, the XML document is extracted from the received message by using SOAP or ebXML APIs. It is possible to use JAXM or JAX-RPC to process an incoming XML message. However, these technologies are still under development; as and when they become available, we could use them instead of the aforementioned APIs.

Implementing the Business Logic

Once the XML document received from the client is processed, the web service can provide the desired service to the client by invoking an appropriate method implemented somewhere in the business logic. The location of the business logic depends largely on how much traffic is expected. For sites not expecting any heavy traffic, servlets would be fine for implementing business logic; while sites with anticipated heavy traffic would need to use EJBs for better scalability. The front-end servlet takes the responsibility of session management.

Integrating Other Resources

The business logic will probably need to use other resources for carrying out the desired business functionality. For example, you may need to access a backend database or a legacy system to fetch in the data required by a particular business operation. You could use JDBC to communicate with an underlying database engine. You can use J2EE connectors to talk to a legacy system, and JMS for asynchronous communication with other messaging-enabled applications. The messages themselves may be constructed using the SOAP, SwA, and ebXML APIs discussed earlier. In future, you may use JAXM or JAX-RPC for messaging.

Returning Results to Clients

Once the business logic processes the request and generates the desired data, it passes on this information to the front-end servlet or JSP component. The front-end component can now format the result for the client by embedding it in a SOAP message. Once again, you may use DOM (through JAXP) to create an XML document, or in future you could use Java Data Binding (JAXB) to create such a document. The packaged XML message will be returned to the client.

A Simple Web Service

In this section, we develop a simple web service, using the IBM web services toolkit. The evaluation copy of the toolkit may be downloaded from IBM AlphaWorks site at http://www.alphaworks.ibm.com/tech/webservicestoolkit.

The web service that we are going to develop, will supply the stock quotes to the remote client. We'll call this service **StockQuoteService**. The development starts with writing the Java file that implements the desired functionality of providing the stock quotes for the requested stock symbol. The service exposes its functionality with the help of public methods. In the current situation, we will define one public method called `getStockPrice()` that receives a string argument containing the requested stock symbol and returns the latest stock price, from a database, as a string to the client.

Developing the StockQuote Java File

The source program for the stock quote service is given below:

```java
import java.sql.*;

public class StockQuote {

  // Load the database driver
  static {
    try {
      Class.forName("COM.cloudscape.core.JDBCDriver").newInstance();
    } catch (Exception e) {
      e.printStackTrace();
    }
  }

  // This method is exposed as a web service.
  public String getStockPrice(String symbol) {
    Connection con = null;
    boolean result= false;

    String url = "jdbc:cloudscape:c:/j2sdk1.3/cloudscape/CloudscapeDB";
    String price="";

    try {
      con = DriverManager.getConnection(url);

      // Retrieve data from the database
      Statement stmt = con.createStatement();
      String sql = "SELECT * FROM stockdetails WHERE (stocksymbol='" +
                 symbol + "')";
      ResultSet rs = stmt.executeQuery(sql);

      // Display the result set
      while (rs.next()) {
        price = rs.getString(2);
        result= true;
        break;
      }

      rs.close();
      stmt.close();
    } catch(Exception e) {
      e.printStackTrace();
    }

    if(result) {
      return price;
    } else {
      return "Enter a valid Stock Symbol";
    }
  }
}
```

Before you run this code, you will need to create a table called `stockdetails` in your database and add a few records to it. Here is the SQL to create the table:

```
CREATE TABLE stockdetails (stocksymbol VARCHAR(10) NOT NULL,
                           stockprice VARCHAR(10))
```

Creating the JAR

Next step in the development is to compile and JAR the created class file. Use the following command to create a JAR file called `stock.jar`:

```
jar cvf stock.jar StockQuote.class
```

Generating WSDL Files

Next, we will generate the WSDL file that exposes the `getStockPrice()` method of our Java class as a web service. This could mean writing the whole lot of XML code. Fortunately, the IBM toolkit provides a tool for generating the WSDL file. Start the tool by running the `wsdlgen.bat` file provided in the `\bin` folder of the IBM web-service toolkit. This opens the window shown below:

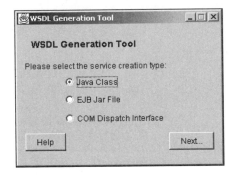

The tool allows you to create a web service description from any of the shown interfaces. We will use the Java Class option to generate description for our web service. Click Next to move to the next screen of the wizard:

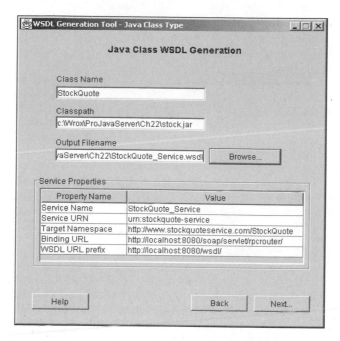

In the **Class Name** field type `StockQuote` and in the **Classpath** give the full path of the `stock.jar` file. Accept the default output file name, but make sure to output it to the same directory as where you created the class file. The service properties are displayed in the table as shown in the screenshot.

Click **Next** to move to the next screen. On this screen, you will see the list of methods discovered by the tool:

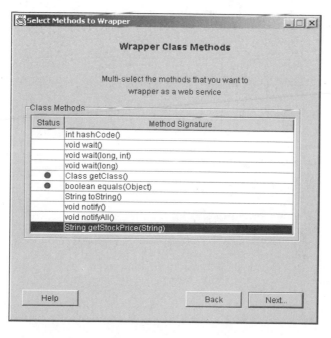

Scroll down the list of methods to find the getStockPrice() method. Select this method and click Next. The next screen gives you an opportunity to confirm your choices before the WSDL file is generated by the tool:

Click Finish to generate the WSDL file. On successful creation of the file, a message pops up on the screen to indicate the success:

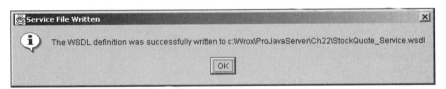

As part of the WSDL generation process, the following files will be created in the current folder:

❑ StockQuote_Service.wsdl

❑ StockQuote_Service-interface.wsdl

The StockQuote_Service.wsdl File

The generated StockQuote_Service.wsdl file is shown below:

```xml
<?xml version="1.0" encoding="UTF-8"?>
<definitions name="StockQuote_Service"
  targetNamespace="http://www.stockquoteservice.com/StockQuote"
  xmlns="http://schemas.xmlsoap.org/wsdl/"
  xmlns:soap="http://schemas.xmlsoap.org/wsdl/soap/"
  xmlns:tns="http://www.stockquoteservice.com/StockQuote"
```

```
            xmlns:xsd="http://www.w3.org/1999/XMLSchema">

    <import
        location="http://localhost:8080/wsdl/StockQuote_Service-interface.wsdl"
        namespace="http://www.stockquoteservice.com/StockQuote-interface">
    </import>

    <service
      name="StockQuote_Service">
      <documentation>
          IBM WSTK 2.0 generated service definition file
      </documentation>
      <port
          binding="StockQuote_ServiceBinding"
          name="StockQuote_ServicePort">
        <soap:address location="http://localhost:8080/soap/servlet/rpcrouter"/>
      </port>
    </service>

    </definitions>
```

As can be seen from the above listing, the WSDL file declares a service called StockQuote_Service. It also declares the location of the rpcrouter servlet that is used for routing the service requests to the appropriate Java class. You will need to modify this WSDL file to set the location for the interface file to the current folder. Modify the import tag's location attribute to the following:

```
    location="StockQuote_Service-interface.wsdl"
```

We will now look at the generated interface file.

The StockQuote_Service-interface.wsdl File

The wsdlgen tool generates the service interface file that is listed below:

```
<?xml version="1.0" encoding="UTF-8"?>
<definitions name="StockQuote_Service"
    targetNamespace="http://www.stockquoteservice.com/StockQuote-interface"
    xmlns="http://schemas.xmlsoap.org/wsdl/"
    xmlns:soap="http://schemas.xmlsoap.org/wsdl/soap/"
    xmlns:tns="http://www.stockquoteservice.com/StockQuote"
      xmlns:xsd="http://www.w3.org/1999/XMLSchema">

<message
        name="IngetStockPriceRequest">
    <part name="meth1_inType1"
          type="xsd:string"/>
</message>

<message
        name="OutgetStockPriceResponse">
    <part name="meth1_outType"
          type="xsd:string"/>
</message>
```

```
<portType
    name="StockQuote_Service">
  <operation
      name="getStockPrice">
    <input
        message="IngetStockPriceRequest"/>
    <output
    message="OutgetStockPriceResponse"/>
  </operation>
</portType>

<binding
    name="StockQuote_ServiceBinding"
      type="StockQuote_Service">
  <soap:binding style="rpc"
      transport="http://schemas.xmlsoap.org/soap/http"/>
  <operation
      name="getStockPrice">
    <soap:operation
        soapAction="urn:stockquote-service"/>
    <input>
      <soap:body
          encodingStyle="http://schemas.xmlsoap.org/soap/encoding/"
          namespace="urn:stockquote-service"
          use="encoded"/>
    </input>
    <output>
      <soap:body
          encodingStyle="http://schemas.xmlsoap.org/soap/encoding/"
          namespace="urn:stockquote-service" use="encoded"/>
    </output>
  </operation>
</binding>

</definitions>
```

As seen from the above listing, the input parameters are listed first. The type of the input parameter is a string:

```
name="IngetStockPriceRequest">
<part name="meth1_inType1"
      type="xsd:string"/>
```

Then, the return type of the method is declared as below:

```
name="OutgetStockPriceResponse">
<part name="meth1_outType"
      type="xsd:string"/>
```

Next, the operation is declared as follows, the name of the operation is getStockPrice. Note that this is the method of our Java class that we wish to expose as a web service. The method requires one input parameter as defined by the name IngetStockPriceRequest and returns an output as defined by the name OutgetStockPriceResponse:

```
<operation
    name="getStockPrice">
  <input
      message="IngetStockPriceRequest"/>
  <output
  message="OutgetStockPriceResponse"/>
</operation>
```

Finally, the `binding` tag defines the style using the following statement. The indicated style is a remote procedure call and uses HTTP for transport:

```
<soap:binding style="rpc"
    transport="http://schemas.xmlsoap.org/soap/http"/>
```

The `binding` tag next lists the operations. In our case, we have only one operation exposed. The encoding style for input and output parameters is declared here.

Next, we will generate the proxy class for the use of our client application.

Generating the Proxy Class

The IBM toolkit again comes to our rescue here by providing a utility for generating a proxy class for our web service. Run the `proxygen.bat` file to invoke the proxy generation utility:

```
%WSTK_HOME%\bin\proxygen StockQuote_Service.wsdl
```

```
C:\ProJavaServer\Ch22>%WSTK_HOME%\bin\proxygen StockQuote_Service.wsdl
>> Importing StockQuote_Service-interface.wsdl ..
>> Transforming WSDL to NASSL ..
>> Generating proxy ..
Created file C:\Wrox\ProJavaServer\Ch22\StockQuote_ServiceProxy.java
Compiled file C:\Wrox\ProJavaServer\Ch22\StockQuote_ServiceProxy.java
Done.

C:\ProJavaServer\Ch22>
```

The batch file generates a file called `StockQuote_ServiceProxy.java` and also compiles it. In the next step, we need to deploy the service onto the web server.

Registering the Service with the Web Server

We'll use the embedded WebSphere server that comes along with the WSTK toolkit for testing our web service. Before you start the server, make sure to add the `stock.jar` file and your database driver to your classpath. Start the web server with the following command:

```
%WSTK_HOME%\bin\websphere run
```

Next, open the browser and type in the following URL:

http://localhost:8080/soap/admin/

This starts the administration utility for managing your web services:

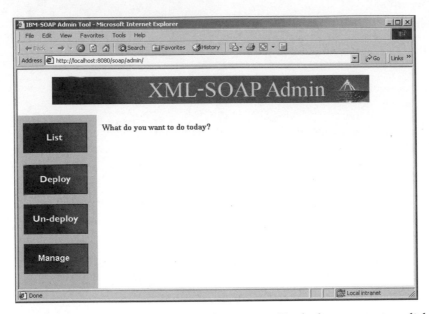

The admin utility allows you to manage and list the services. To deploy our service, click on the Deploy button. It opens the screen as shown below:

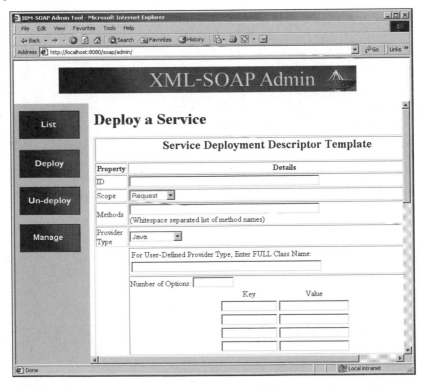

You will need to set few parameters as listed below on this screen:

- ❑ Set ID to `urn:stockquote-service`
- ❑ Set Scope to Application
- ❑ Set Methods to `getStockPrice`
- ❑ Set Provider Type to Java (this is the default)
- ❑ Set Java Provider – Provider Class to `StockQuote`

For the rest of the fields, accept the defaults. Scroll down to the bottom of the screen and click on the Deploy button. On successful deployment, a message is displayed as shown below:

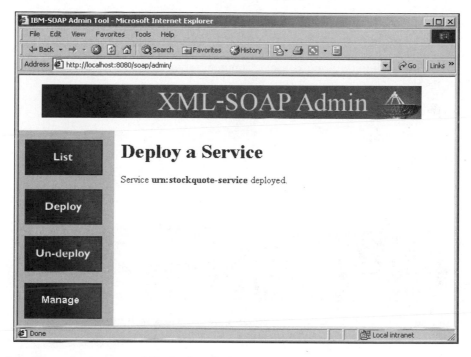

Once, the web service is successfully deployed, the next step is to write a client program to test the web service.

Developing a Client

Writing the client for our web service is very simple. The client program uses the generated proxy class to obtain a reference to the remote service object and invokes the desired method on it. The client code is shown below:

```
import StockQuote_ServiceProxy;

public class StockClient {

  public static void main(String[] args) {
```

```
      try {
          // Create an instance of proxy class
          StockQuote_ServiceProxy proxy = new StockQuote_ServiceProxy();
          // Invoke the remote web service method using proxy object
          String Price = proxy.getStockPrice(args[0]);
          // Print the returned value
          System.out.println("Current Stock Price: " + Price);
      } catch(Exception e) {
          System.out.println(e);
      }
    }
  }
```

The client program is a Java console-based application. The main() method creates an instance of the proxy object that represents the remote web service. The remote service method is then invoked on the created proxy object. The method runs on the remote machine and returns a result to the client. The program prints the result to the user's console. Communication between the client and the server takes place using SOAP.

To run the application you will need the following in your classpath:

❑ The SOAP JAR file

❑ The Xerces JAR file

❑ The JavaMail JAR file

❑ The Activation JAR file

From this simple example, you can see that creating web services with the help of proper tools is not as difficult as it sounds in its theoretical discussions.

Making Services Smarter

As web services are created using vendor-neutral technologies, with XML as a data transport, it is easily possible to integrate smaller (micro-level) services into a large (macro-level) service. When such a macro-level service is created, other questions such as security, authentication, transaction-control, and so on., crop up. Not only that, but as far the consumer is concerned, such services should be available transparently (just like we aim to do now with more standard applications).

Just imagine a situation whereby we are using a macro-level service that in turn uses several micro-level services provided by a number of third parties. As we keep traversing the various sites while using this macro service, if we were asked to logon to each site with our user name and password, the experience of using this service could be very frustrating. In the worst case, if we had created a different user name and password for each site, it could be even more frustrating trying to remember all those user names and passwords and using them at the right place every time.

This problem could be solved if the login context was saved somewhere and shared by every site that we visited. Besides the login context, the sites may require the use of session contexts to provide you with a rich experience while surfing. With this comes a new concept called **shared context**.

Shared Context

A web service needs to remember a few things about the consumer to provide a personalized experience. This is known as **context**. Such context may include user's identity, location, language choice, personal information, and so on. While creating a macro-level service, such context information may be shared with other concerned parties involved in providing the service; of course, with the proper permissions obtained from the consumer.

There are no standards currently available for creating shared context. Microsoft has announced 'a user-centric architecture and set of XML web services, codenamed "HailStorm "' (see http://www.microsoft.com/net/hailstorm.asp for more details), where an individual may store personal information with this service. Such information can be shared by other applications complying with HailStorm. However, it will be tightly integrated to the Microsoft platform.

The specifications for creating shared context should not come from a single vendor, and such a service should not be proprietary. If the solution is open, it will help in creating interoperable web services. Thus, individuals who allow their contexts to be shared should be assured of the security and privacy of the input information. Such a standard is yet to come.

Smart Web Services

A **smart web service** is one that understands the context of a requesting client, and shares that context with other services. A smart web service can obtain and use information about several situational circumstances. For example, it may obtain contexts for the following situations:

- ❑ Identity of the service consumer
- ❑ Consumer role
- ❑ Individual preferences, if any
- ❑ Consumer security policy
- ❑ Consumer privacy policy
- ❑ Business policy associated with consumer
- ❑ Consumer's location
- ❑ Client device used by consumer
- ❑ Past history
- ❑ Any agreements between the consumer and the current web service provider

The smart web service, after obtaining such context information, will provide a richly personalized service to the consumer and may share such information with collaborating web services. Many web sites today provide personalization; such sites maintain the context information in proprietary formats. There is no standard for sharing the context information with others.

The Sun ONE Initiative

In February 2001, Sun Microsystems announced its architecture for creating interoperable, smart web services. The architecture is called **The Sun Open Net Environment** (**Sun ONE**) and addresses many important issues relating to privacy, security, and identity. It defines practices and conventions to create interoperable smart web services. It can support a wide variety of client devices right from PDAs and WAP-enabled devices to large web farms. More details can be found at http://www.sun.com/sunone/.

The Sun ONE architecture is based on XML and Java technologies and other core infrastructure standards. Such technologies and standards include DOM, ebXML, HTTP, JAXM, JDBC, JSP, LDAP, SOAP, SSL, WML, WSDL, XHTML, XML Parsers, XML Schemas, XPATH, XSLT, and several others mentioned earlier in the chapter.

Functional Architecture Overview

The proposed Sun ONE functional architecture is depicted in the following diagram:

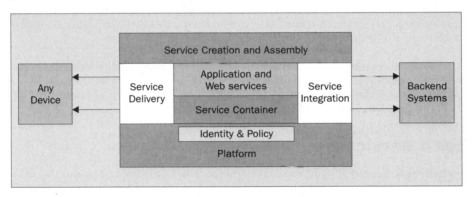

This is a high-level functional overview of the architecture. The **Service Creation and Assembly** component refers to the process of creating micro-level services and aggregating them into a composite macro-level service. The micro-level services are created using integrated development environments, context-sensitive editors, and the core technologies and APIs discussed in the earlier section. The assembler of the service uses many such micro services to create a macro-level service. The assembler also defines the security policies, context-sensitive policies and other run-time parameters for the service. The security policies are set in the **Identity and Policy** block.

The **Application and Web Services** block illustrates the deployed web services. The web services may be deployed on any platform and any device, ranging from a palmtop to a high-end multiprocessor server. The service itself may be composed of many micro services.

The **Service Container** block indicates a container in which the services are deployed. The container can be a simple servlet engine, or a more complex application server that deploys EJB components as well. Such containers will provide many services to the web service such as transaction management, security, concurrency, and so on. The **Platform** designates the OS or the virtual machine on which the container runs. The container obtains the OS-level services from this block.

The **Service Delivery** block indicates a communication link to the client and is responsible for all interactions with the client. This block will parse the XML requests from the client and format the XML output for the client. This block may interface with clients such as a palmtop, WAP-enabled device, another web service, and so on.

Lastly, the **Service Integration** block indicates the connection to the backend resources such as databases, legacy systems with J2EE connectors, and so on.

Smart Web Services Architecture

The proposed architecture for providing smart web services is depicted in the following diagram:

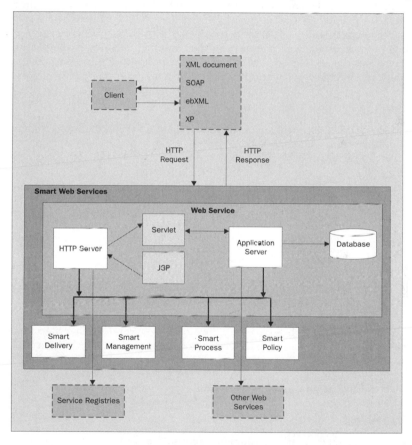

As seen from the diagram, smart web services will be implemented by adding several blocks to the architecture that capture and use context-sensitive information. These are summarized below

- ❏ Smart Delivery
- ❏ Smart Management
- ❏ Smart Process
- ❏ Smart Policy

1143

Smart Delivery

The smart delivery module facilitates the aggregation of micro-services into a macro-level service. It also provides customization and personalization for the client. The module obtains the context information from the delivery channel, customizes the response to the client and delivers it through the delivery channel. It supports a wide variety of client devices and presentation formats that include HTML, XHTML, WML (Wireless Markup Language), and VoiceXML. It is also responsible for content transformations and uses XSLT for such transformations.

Smart Management

The smart management facility is responsible for the overall management of the web service and ensures privacy of the shared data to the consumer of the service. It also provides security, and controls access using the access rights defined for the consumer. Besides these, this module is also responsible for the proper registration and availability of the service through the use of a service registry. It also ensures the proper execution of the subscription agreement for the consumer and assures the consumer a minimum quality of service as per the service agreement between the two parties. It obtains the management and run-time policies from the smart policy module and ensures the proper implementation of the same.

Smart Process

This module is responsible for process management and allows the alteration of sequences in a web service based on the current user context.

Smart Policy

This module obtains the latest user and policy information from a registry, possibly using LDAP. It uses the authentication service provided by the PKI (Public Key Infrastructure) service provider and accordingly authorizes the use of service to the client. As the information is obtained at run time, the security policies can change depending on the current context of the user. This module is responsible for dynamically adapting the service based on the current context.

Vendor Support for Web Services

With the gaining popularity of web services, application-server vendors have started giving support for creation of web services in their products. Such vendors include BEA, IBM (naturally), SilverStream, and CapeClear.

BEA classifies web services into two categories, simple and complex.

Simple Web Service

A simple web service provides merely a request/response type of functionality and does not support transactions or provide sophisticated security. These services have following characteristics:

❑ **Point-to-Point**
    The client invokes the service on a remote server and the server returns the response to the client.

❑ **RPC and messaging-based**
    The service involves calling a remote procedure and uses XML messaging for both request and response.

❑ **Non-transactional**

As such services involve a simple request followed by a response to the client, the service by its very nature becomes non-transactional. A transactional service would require participation of other resources and/or web services.

❑ **Web security**

The service uses only the basic security provided by the web server, such as authentication.

Complex Web Service

A complex web service, on the other hand, provides the framework for businesses-to-business collaboration and business process management. These services have the following characteristics:

❑ **Multi-party**

A complex web service involves multiple business partners. For example, if the store inventory falls below a certain threshold, a request for quote (RFQ) may be sent to the multiple suppliers.

❑ **Collaboration and workflow**

All the involved parties in the service will collaborate and assist in the control of the workflow defined in the web service.

❑ **Transactional**

As the complex web service involves multiple partners and aggregation of many micro-level services, it must run under transaction control spanning several servers.

❑ **Sophisticated security**

The complex web service uses digital signatures for authentication, access control, implementation of security policies, and non-repudiation so that no party can refuse a completed business transaction.

❑ **Conversation state**

A complex service maintains the conversation state with the client, obtains the context, and may share this with collaborating partner services.

❑ **Based on agreements**

The complex service is based on the agreements between the two parties. This is similar to smart services discussed earlier.

Summary

In this chapter, we looked at the emerging technology known as web services. The creation and use of web services has caught the minds of many developers and vendors. Web services can be created using several different technologies. We saw that the following technologies are instrumental in the creation of web services:

❑ SOAP

❑ SOAP with Attachments (SwA)

❑ WSDL

❑ UDDI

All the above technologies are XML-based and help in the creation of vendor-neutral services that can interoperate with other services.

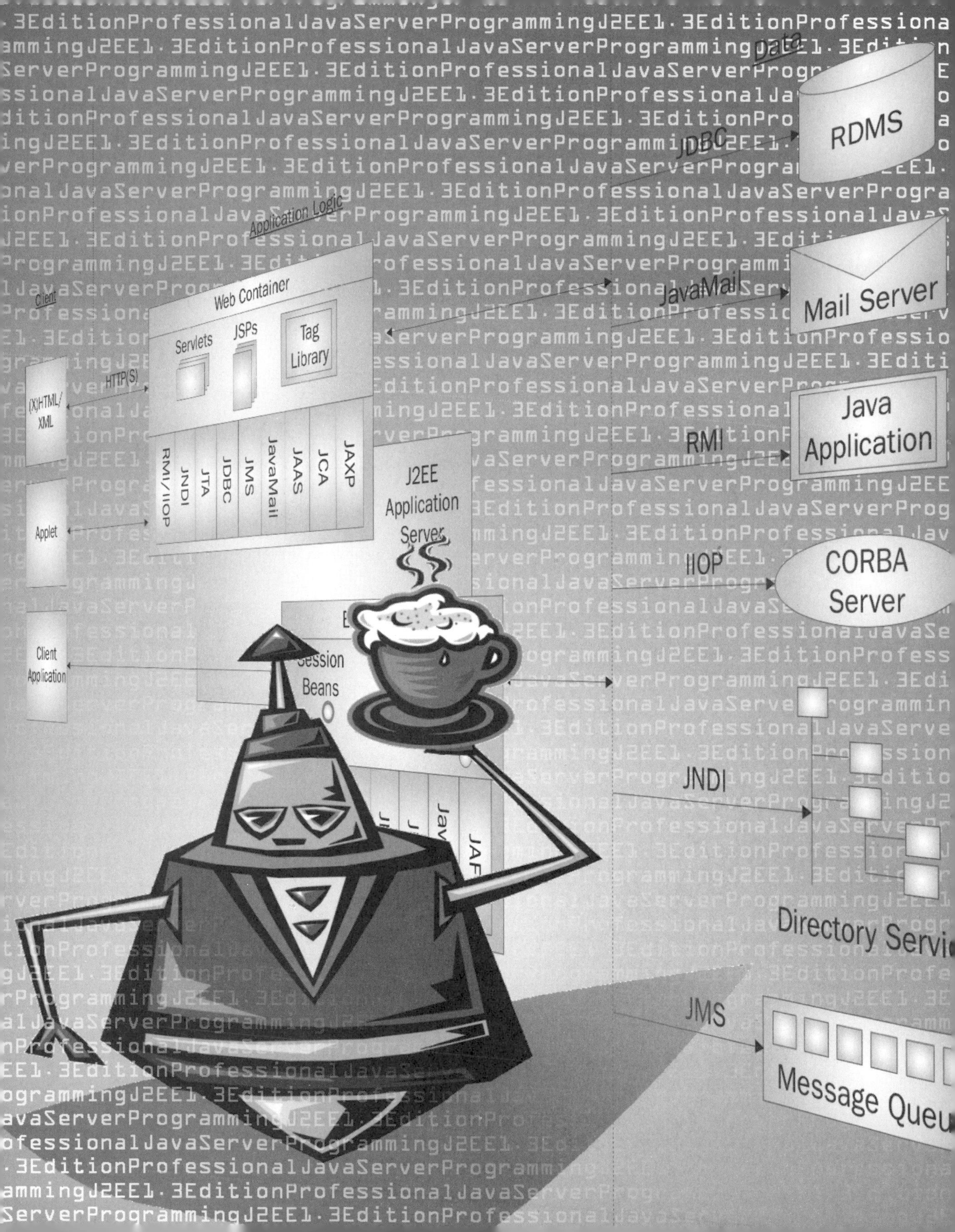

23

Choosing a J2EE Implementation

In this chapter we will take a look at what is at the core of a J2EE implementation, and how vendors go about implementing the J2EE standards. By noting any additional value-added functionality, we'll examine the competition between various vendors. Also, we will take a look at some key comparison items that one should take into consideration before making a technology or buying decision, and review the learning curve associated with using a J2EE implementation.

It is important to note that the J2EE standards do not define how the elements of a J2EE implementation should be implemented. In fact, vendors are free to create products as they see a need in the market. The most common implementation choices found in the market today are **servlet engines** and **application servers**. Depending on the project, one or both maybe needed. Application servers are expected to have both a servlet engine in the web container and an Enterprise JavaBeans (EJB) container. Vendors are inclined to create a separation between the web container and the EJB container in order to enforce the separation between the presentation layer and the business-logic layer.

Application Servers

The J2EE platform represents a single standard for implementing and deploying enterprise applications. It has been designed through an open process, engaging a range of enterprise computing vendors to ensure it meets the widest possible range of enterprise application requirements. The J2EE platform is designed to provide server-side and client-side support for developing enterprise applications. Such applications are typically configured as a client tier to provide the user interface, one or more middle-tier modules that provide client services and business logic for an application, and the backend enterprise information systems providing data management.

The middle-tier components usually run inside an application server, which can handles all system-level services, so that developers can concentrate on building business-logic components. The middle tier supports client services through a layer called the web container in the web tier.

> Containers are frameworks that provide a standardized run-time environment for servlets, components, and so forth, thereby providing the services that these objects offer and relieving the programmer of the tedious and complex task of connecting applets to the Internet.

The web tier is the most appropriate area for the presentation logic to reside. The middle tier also supports business-logic components services through EJBs and containers in the EJB tier. Vendors have created products that encompass both the web container and the EJB container. These types of products are known as application servers. In theory, components can expect these services to be available on any J2EE platform from any vendor.

Containers have automated support for transaction and lifecycle management for EJB components, as well as bean lookup and other services. Containers also provide standardized access to enterprise information systems, and database access via JDBC. Furthermore, they should provide a mechanism for selecting application behaviors at assembly and deployment time. This is done with the use of deployment descriptors using well defined XML tags.

Deployment descriptors are actually one of the areas where different vendors have small differences between products. For example, the additional deployment descriptor (as opposed to the J2EE-defined one) from an IBM application server will be slightly different from one from BEA application server. Some of the features that can be configured during deployment time include security checks, transaction controls, and other management responsibilities. Depending on the product and the vendor, the amount of RAM in your system can be configured for system processes and user processes.

The term application server as we know it today is assigned to a product that implements the J2EE standard and offers a web container and EJB container, as a minimum, packaged as server software. This product must comply with a version of the J2EE standards, preferably the latest, and be able to provide:

❑ **Web and EJB containers**
An environment for component-based applications to map easily to the functionality desired from the application.

❑ **Component behavior**
To enable assembly and deploy-time behaviors. Components can expect the availability of services in the run-time environment, and can be connected to other components providing a set of well-defined interfaces. As a result, components can be configured for a certain type of behavior at application assembly or deployment time without any recoding required.

❑ **Scalability**
J2EE containers must provide a mechanism that supports simplified scaling of distributed applications, without requiring any effort on the part of the application development team. Clustering is one of the features used to fulfill this standard requirement.

❑ **Integration with existing enterprise systems**
This can be done with a number of standard APIs that have to be supported in a J2EE implementation:

❑ JDBC APIs for accessing relational data from Java.

❑ Java Transaction API (JTA) for managing and coordinating transactions across heterogeneous enterprise information systems. A good example could be to connect transactions taking place over a CORBA-based system with a J2EE systems connected to a web site.

❑ Java Naming and Directory Interface (JNDI) API for accessing information in enterprise name and directory services.

❑ Java Messaging Service (JMS) API for sending and receiving messages via enterprise messaging systems like IBM MQ Series, or TIBCO Rendezvous.

❑ JavaMail API for sending and receiving e-mails.

❑ Java IDL APIs for calling CORBA services.

❑ Security services like the Java Authentication and Authorization Service (JAAS).

While the J2EE specification defines the component containers that must be supported and the APIs that should be available, it does not try to specify or restrict the configuration of these containers, and the layout of the services. Thus, both container types can run either on a single platform or on a distributed environment.

Both BEA WebLogic and IBM WebSphere, for example, have a web container and an EJB container in their application server product. Other vendors have a similar approach. The diagram below shows the typical layout for an application server product:

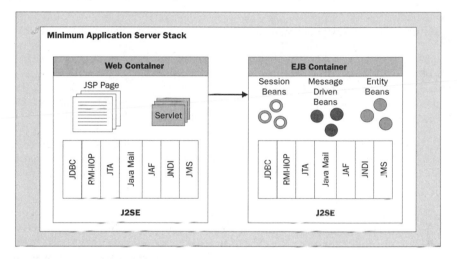

It is important to realize that an application server is made up of a collection of services, containers, and also the J2SE implementation in addition to the J2EE-related items. Together they make up the set of services to support the J2EE specifications.

This is by no means the only way, or even the very best method; however, it is the most widely used approach in the market. As we will see, once the minimum requirements are met in terms of implementation, vendors use other services to make their products more attractive. Also keep in mind that your 'full-blown' application server may not be needed to complete a project; you may not need the whole suite of functionality present in application servers.

Sometimes the web container alone can provide the services you need, for example, a servlet engine to render JSP pages. BEA WebLogic Express is a commercial-grade product that includes a servlet engine in addition to other features. However, it does not include the EJB container, making the product more suitable for front-end work in web architecture.

In the next section we'll turn our attention to how the J2EE specification is actually implemented.

Implementing the J2EE Specifications

The J2EE specification is created and reviewed under the Java Community Process (http://www.jcp.org/) by a set of industry experts with representation from companies such as BEA, Bluestone Software, Borland, Bull S.A., Exoffice, Fujitsu Limited, GemStone Systems, IBM, Inline Software, IONA Technologies, IPlanet, jGuru.com, Orion Application Server, Persistence, POET Software, SilverStream, Sun, and Sybase.

The J2EE standard is defined through a set of related specifications:

❑   EJB specification – defines the responsibilities of both the component developers and the EJB server and container vendors

❑   Servlet specification   provides web developers with a simple, consistent mechanism for extending the functionality of a web server and for accessing existing business systems

❑   JavaServer Pages (JSP) specification – allows web developers and designers to rapidly develop and easily maintain, information-rich, dynamic web pages that leverage existing business systems

Together, these specifications define the key architectur components required in a J2EE implementation. In addition to the specifications, several other offerings are available to support the J2EE standard, including the **J2EE Compatibility Test Suite (CTS)** and the J2EE SDK. The latest news about compatibility is available online from Sun at http://java.sun.com/j2ee/compatibility.html and at http://developer.java.sun.com/developer/technicalArticles/J2EE/build/.

The J2EE CTS helps maximize the portability of applications by validating the specification compliance of a J2EE platform product. CTS tests conform to the Java standard extension APIs that are not covered by the **Java Conformance Kit (JCK)**. In addition, it tests a J2EE platform's ability to run standard end-to-end applications.

The J2EE SDK is intended to achieve several goals. First, it provides an operational definition of the J2EE platform, used by vendors as the "gold standard" to determine what their product must do under a particular set of application circumstances. It can be used by developers to verify the general portability of an application (as well as the portability across application servers), and it is used as the standard platform for running the J2EE CTS.

Another important role for the J2EE SDK is to provide the developer community with a freely available implementation of the J2EE platform to help expedite adoption of the J2EE standard. Although it is not a commercial product and its licensing terms prohibit its commercial use, the J2EE SDK is freely available to download, in binary or source code form, to use in developing application demos and prototypes. For further details, go to http://java.sun.com/j2ee/download.html.

The J2EE specification doesn't require that a J2EE product be implemented by a single program, a single server, or even a single machine. In general, the specifications do not describe the partitioning of services or functions between machines, servers, or processes. As long as the requirements in the specifications are met, J2EE product vendors can partition the functionality in many different ways for a particular application or tool. A J2EE product must be able to deploy application components that execute with semantics described by the specification. IBM and BEA implement the functionality in different ways, but they both follow the J2EE specifications very closely.

A very simple J2EE product might be provided as a single Java Virtual Machine that supports web components and enterprise beans in one container. A typical low end J2EE product will support applets in one of the popular browsers, application clients in their own Java Virtual Machine, and will provide a single server that supports both web components and enterprise beans.

The J2EE specification describes a minimum set of facilities that all J2EE products must provide. Most J2EE products will provide facilities beyond the minimum required by this specification. This specification includes a few limits to the ability of a product to provide extensions. In particular, it includes the same restrictions as J2SE on extensions of Java APIs. A J2EE product may not add classes to the Java programming language packages included in this specification, and it may not add methods or otherwise alter signatures of the specified classes. This step guarantees that an EJB that is developed for a project under a specific requirement, such as full transaction support during a particular logic operation, can run on different J2EE vendor implementations without recoding.

However, many other extensions are allowed. A J2EE product may provide additional Java APIs, either other Java optional packages (JavaHelp, Java 3D, Java MediaFramework, etc.) or other packages (this includes some early-access packages like Java Management). A J2EE product may include support for additional protocols or services not specified in the standards. A J2EE product may support applications written in languages other than Java, or may support connectivity to other platform applications.

This provides room for strong competition in various aspects of quality of services. Products will provide different levels of performance, scalability, ease of use, availability, and security. In some cases the J2EE specifications requires minimum levels of services. Future versions of the specification may allow applications to describe the requirements in these areas.

Sun has made available (in both source and binary format) a J2EE reference web application, the Java Pet Store Application. Any implementation of the J2EE standard from some of the well know companies like BEA, IBM, HP, Oracle, and others should be able to install and run the Pet Store. This reference web application can be downloaded from http://java.sun.com/j2ee/download.html#blueprints and run on any certified application server that is 100% J2EE-compliant. The Pet Store was recently updated to be compliant with and take advantage of the J2EE 1.3 standard. Other good examples can be found online at http://www-106.ibm.com/developerworks/ and at http://developer.java.sun.com/developer/.

Competition in the Application Server Market

Several companies are competing in the J2EE space with their application server products. There are several levels of competition. In the top tier BEA WebLogic competes directly with IBM's WebSphere and more recently with the Sun-Netscape Alliance's iPlanet server families and the new Oracle IAS. To a lesser degree, IBM and BEA, compete with Bluestone/Hewlett-Packard's Sapphire/Web, SilverStream's SilverStream Application Server, Gemstone Systems' GemStone/J, Progress's Apptivity, and Sybase's Enterprise Application Server. Below is a list of links for more information:

❏ ATG Dynamo, http://www.atg.com/en/products/das.jhtml

❏ BEA WebLogic, http://www.bea.com/

❏ Hewlett-Packard Bluestone, http://www.bluestone.com/

❏ Borland AppServer, http://www.inprise.com/appserver/

❏ Gemstone Systems' GemStone/J, http://www.gemstone.com/

❑ IBM WebSphere, http://www-4.ibm.com/software/webservers/appserv/

❑ Oracle IAS, http://www.oracle.com/ip/deploy/ias/

❑ Progress Apptivity, http://www.progress.com/apptivity/

❑ SilverStream Application Server, http://www.silverstream.com/

❑ Sun-Netscape Alliance's iPlanet, http://www.iplanet.com/products/iplanet_application/

❑ Sybase's Application Server, http://www.sybase.com/products/easerver/

The question is which vendor has the best product for the target project. Also, which product best matches the skill set of the development team and system administrators. In the past two to three years, the application server market has been a race between two companies, BEA and IBM. However, the race now includes Oracle, Sun, and Hewlett Packard among others. The majority of the space today is divided between BEA and IBM, although there are as many as 14 companies working on Application Server type products, and this does not even include open source offerings.

Open source is the term applied to a software that is usually available free of charge and that has its source code also available. This type of software usually follows the licensing model from http://www.gnu.org/ or http://www.opensource.org/. Basically, what this means is that you are getting free software with source code without commercial support behind it. Some other restrictions may apply. The code may be just as good as or better than a commercial alternative, but thereisn't a support line to call in case of a problem. Apache is a great example of an open source software package. It is one of the best web servers available. You can get both the binaries and the source code from http://www.apache.org/.

In the application server space and the servlet engine space there are some alternatives. If all you need is a Servlet engine, one of the most popular open source options is Tomcat. It is free and supports up to JDK 1.3. JonAS is another option that goes beyond the servlet engine. It supports EJB 1.1 and some functionality found in EJB 2.0. JonAS is compatible with the latest JDK 1.3. Another good option to explore is JBoss; it also goes beyond a servlet engine to support EJB 1.2 and some 2.0 capabilities. Enhydra is another J2EE implementation that follows the open source approach, but its authors seem to be slow to post new versions out. Last time I checked they were still working on a commercial version for one of their sponsors. Below is a list of links for more information on open source application servers:

❑ Enhydra http://enhydra.enhydra.org/

❑ JonAS http://www.evidian.com/jonas/index.htm

❑ JBoss http://www.jboss.org/

❑ Tomcat http://jakarta.apache.org/tomcat/

J2EE Implementations

The main areas in the implementation can change from one vendor to another, but there is some consistency with the areas of functionality listed below:

❑ **Presentation Services**
Usually application servers deliver content to the user interface and maintain state over a stateless protocol. The presentation services are hosted in the web container. Some vendors have simple implementations just for the presentation services such as the BEA WebLogic light edition.

❑ **Distributed Object Services**
At the core of Java servers is the ability to help components communicate with each other. Modules of functionally related code make up a component. Java standards lay out how the components (EJBs) should communicate.

❑ **Transaction Services**
Many events generate multiple transactions. For example, a typical order to a supplier company has to decrement inventory, generate an invoice, make a receivables entry, mark the order as fulfilled, and generate an advanced ship notice. Typically there are multiple steps and transactions related to a single event, which are communicated in batch across disparate applications that deal with each of these functions. The time delay and lack of two-phase commit introduces inconsistencies across applications. Moreover, the delay in reflecting these transactions detracts from the currency and reliability of the information for decision support applications. Transaction services coordinate these related transactions across multiple systems and can update them in near real time simultaneously.

❑ **Security Services**
Distributed security is essential in order to authenticate and grant access to requests from users and applications of a distributed nature.

❑ **Availability Service**
Application servers take radically different approaches to ensuring reliability through failover, load balancing, and clustering features. The trade off is performance. The higher the quality of the services built into an application, the more that application taps into features that create redundancies for backup insurance and affects performance in the process.

❑ **Directory Services**
These services are used by components to find other components. Java Naming Directory Interface (which sits on top of LDAP) and Active Directory are the dominant standards.

❑ **Database Connection Pooling**
An application server connects to a database and pools the connections so that multiple users can efficiently share fewer connections.

If we take a step deeper and look at what must be supported by J2EE vendors, we will find a set of J2EE platform contracts that must be fulfilled by the J2EE product provider. There are four platform contracts that must be in place in any application server:

❑ **J2EE APIs**
Define the contract between the J2EE specification components and the J2EE platform. The contract specifies both the runtime and deployment interfaces. The J2EE product provider must implement the J2EE APIs in a way that supports the semantics and policies described in the specifications. The application component provider supplies components that conform to these APIs and policies.

❑ **Service Provider Interfaces (SPIs)**
SPIs define the contract between the J2EE platform and service providers that may be plugged into a J2EE product. The Connector APIs define service-provider interfaces for integrating resource adapters with J2EE application servers. Resource adapters are J2EE components that implement the J2EE Connector technology for a specific enterprise information system. The J2EE product provider must implement the J2EE SPIs in a way that supports the semantics and policies described in these specifications. A supplier of service-provider components should make sure their components conform to these SPIs and policies.

❏ **Network Protocols**
This specification defines the mapping of application components to industry-standard network protocols. The mapping allows client access to the application components from systems that have not installed J2EE product technology. This allows for better inter-operability.

❏ **Deployment Descriptors**
As we have seen throughout this book, these are used to communicate the needs of application components to the deployer. The deployment descriptor is a contract between the application component provider or assembler and the deployer. The application component provider is required to specify the application component's external resource requirements, security requirements, environment parameters, and so forth in the component deployment descriptor. The J2EE product provider is required to provide a deployment tool that interprets the J2EE deployment descriptor and allows the deployer to map the application component's requirements to the capabilities of a specific J2EE product and environment.

The main areas of implementation and the four platform contracts are present in any J2EE-certified application-server product. The market, however, does not focus on a predefined set of services and platform contracts alone. J2EE vendors add many new services and improvements to their products to better compete in the market.

Once all the J2EE specification is implemented, and the code is optimized, vendors take different approaches to add more value to their product. They can try to differentiate their offerings by adding more features that are not necessarily required by the J2EE standard. They can also take a look ahead to possible technologies that may become part of the standard.

Value-Added Features

Besides implementing the full J2EE standards, vendors can extend the application server functionality to complete the most complex tasks and to allow their products to be part of highly heterogeneous systems. Choosing an application server for a project is almost like choosing an operating system. Once you are committed and the work is in progress, it is difficult to change directions and start again with a new product. Be sure to include a systems engineer and one of your senior software architects in the decision making process.

> Developers should aim to use standard features and server-independent extensions so that their code is not tied down to a specific product. If an EJB is written with features that are only available to a particular vendor that code will not be able to run under a different product.

Some of the areas that we will look at below are with regard to possible integration paths with other heterogeneous systems like COM and .NET implementations; integration with development tools; improvements in high availability options; support for application management; support for different languages; support for different operating systems; integration of additional application functionality like personalization. Also, there are implementations of future standards.

The areas of expansion that vendors are exploring are mainly the connectivity to CORBA, COM, and .Net systems. In some products, developers can wrap COM/COM+ objects as Java classes for use with the application server, or wrap Java objects and EJBs with COM+ bindings for invocation by Microsoft applications like Microsoft Internet Information Server, IIS, or other services in the .NET framework. This can be very desirable when building a system that must work with existing systems written for a Microsoft environment. It is also beneficial if integrated transactions are needed between the two systems via extended transaction capabilities. Connectivity with CORBA makes it easier to integrate legacy systems into an application.

For developers, the integration of J2EE with different Integrated Development Environments (IDEs) is critical. Several Java development environments, like WebGain Studio – a Java toolset based on Visual Café – IBM's VisualAge, Borland JBuilder, and Forte for Java from Sun have integration support into application servers.

Clustering can be extended beyond the EJB container to provide clustering of JSP pages and the user session can be stored and replicated across a web farm, which is a set of web server machines responding to browser requests. J2EE application server vendors define a cluster as a group of machines working together to transparently provide enterprise services. They leave the definition vague because each vendor implements clustering differently. This is a desirable capability especially for very large web sites that involve hundreds of thousands of transactions per second. We can cluster web pages and components across multiple servers, as well as cluster multiple servers running on different hardware and operating systems into a single network entity. Clustered servers must all be located on the same LAN. Clustering lets a server replicate different parts of an application across multiple machines, providing failover, load balancing, and scalability. Both IBM and BEA offer clustering at multiple levels within an application, as well as clustering of the server platform itself. What makes the WebLogic product line unique, however, is its support for web page and EJB component clustering. Web page clustering allows WebLogic to replicate the application logic that creates responses for web clients, while component clustering makes it possible to fully recover stateful session and entity EJBs.

Additional areas of competition can include features like full Simple Network Management Protocol (SNMP) support, Wireless Markup Language (WML) and XML handling, improved caching of pages, object and user session replication, new auditing and logging interfaces, and connection filtering.

Load balancing implemented via IIOP handlers, transaction clustering, and server load analysis can use object factories (processes that create object references) to influence where to locate individual objects.

Implementing Future Standards Today

Another popular type of competition is by implementing future standards before they become a standard. This has some risks associated with it, to both the vendor and the developer. However, large vendors usually have short follow up releases to make standards compatible with newly approved standards when they actually become available. The last update to the J2EE standards also makes note of a set of possible future directions that could be added to later versions of the J2EE standards, such as:

❑ **Web Services**
This is a very hot topic that is likely to be part of the next J2EE standards. A number of contributions will aid the definition of web services, including Java APIs for XML Messaging (JAXM), Java API for XML Registries (JAXR), Java APIs for XML-RCP, (JAX-RPC), and definitions for implementing web services.

❑ **XML Data-Binding APIs**
As XML becomes more important in the industry, more and more enterprise applications will need to make use of XML. This specification requires basic XML SAX and DOM support through the JAXP API, but many applications will benefit from the easier-to-use XML data binding technology.

❑ **Java Network Launching Protocol (JNLP)**
Also known as Java WebStart. The Java Network Launching Protocol defines the mechanism for deploying Java applications on a server and launching them from a client. Future versions of this specification may require J2EE products to be able to deploy application clients in a way that allows them to be launched by a JNLP client, and that application client containers be able to launch application clients deployed using the JNLP.

❑ **J2EE SPI**
Many of the APIs that make up the J2EE platform include an SPI layer that allows service providers or other system-level components to be plugged in. This specification does not describe the execution environment for all such service providers, or the packaging and deployment requirements for all service providers. The J2EE Connector architecture defines the requirements for certain types of service providers called resource adapters. Future versions of this specification will more fully define the J2EE SPIs.

❑ **JDBC RowSet**
This provides a standard way to send tabular data between the remote components of a distributed enterprise application.

❑ **Security APIs**
The goal of the J2EE platform is to separate security from business logic, providing declarative security controls for application components. Some applications, however, need more control over security than can be provided by this approach. Future versions of this specification may include additional APIs.

❑ **Deployment APIs**
Deployment tools may follow the Deployment API standard to allow work with all J2EE products.

❑ **Management APIs**
J2EE applications and J2EE products must be manageable. Future versions of this specification will include APIs to support management functions. A simple example is the notion of a centralized management console to start and stop all your related J2EE services.

❑ **SQLJ Part 0**
This supports embedding of SQL statements in programs written in the Java programming language. A compiler translates the program into another program that uses a SQLJ runtime. The SQLJ run-time classes can be packaged with a J2EE application that uses SQLJ, allowing that application to run on any J2EE platform.

The latest and most comprehensive developments in terms of future direction for J2EE standards can be found at http://java.sun.com/j2ee/.

Potential Future Avenues for Value-Added Features

Over time application servers are moving upwards in the software food chain, adding more and more functionality (previously only found in specialized applications and services). Some other possible areas of footprint expansion from the application server vendors are listed below:

❑ **Portal Capabilities**
A consolidated view on web pages that are customized for a particular user class (for example, customer, employee, supplier, partner portals). Portals are becoming very popular as a way to connect to all the systems in an enterprise, offering as they do a diverse range of topics on one site; often topics and services taken from other sites. Some of the large vendors are already offering portal capabilities with their products like IBM Portal Server, BEA Portal Server, and IPlanet Portal Server. There is not a real set of portal specifications, but you can find what are called Portlet APIs being developed by the Apache group. This is a low-level approach to develop APIs to support the most common portal-like functionality.

❑ **Workflow**
All the functions to address a complete business process in a large enterprise are rarely contained in a single application or system. Consequently, customers need a way to automate process flow, including manual interaction with users, across multiple application areas. For example, an order on the web might get handed off to the Enterprise Resource Planning (ERP) order entry system, and, in turn, some components of that order might get passed on to a supplier or partner. This can also take place in parallel with multiple steps between departments and companies.

❑ **Personalization**
Site usage and profiles are tracked for individual users and content presented that is customized for their interest.

❑ **Content Management**
Stores tags; indexes, manages, secures, and retrieves content like documents and images to be displayed on web pages. There is also the need to manage all sorts of content, both in the file system and in the database. Anything from an image, row of data, general file, to a Java file, or stream media, can be classified as content to be managed.

❑ **Integration**
An integration platform for applications, which over EAI (Enterprise Application Integration) functions. The Java Connector Architecture (JCA) is slowly becoming popular in the market. Enterprise information system vendors can follow the JCA specifications and provide standard resource adapters for their products. These adapters can plug into an application server and provide integration and connectivity between the EIS and the application server. You can, for example, integrate an Oracle system with Siebel and several other products. For a full list of connectors available in the market, visit http://java.sun.com/j2ee/connector/products.html. This list is constantly updated.

❑ **Caching**
Performance enhancing techniques that rely on replicated copies of content, data, and applications to remove performance bottlenecks around the network. Caching can work in different levels from file systems and RDBMS systems, all the way to object instantiation, web server activities, authentication activities, and network traffic.

❑ **Provisioning for user entitlements and administration services**
Not only do we have to create and deploy J2EE applications, we have to manage them over time and expand and improve their existing functionality. The need for easy-to-use tools for system management and control is a key area of future J2EE standards.

Competition in the market space can help bring better products and lower prices, but it also can create some level of confusion. As such, in the next section, we'll review the set of parameters that we should consider when choosing a J2EE implementation.

Evaluation Parameters

The Java platform provides a very open environment for vendors to compete in. The set of J2EE products available in the market has grown to a large number, and many people see this number continuing to grow. Several vendors already implement the full set of J2EE specifications and other extended sets of functionality. Making a final decision can become an exercise of comparison between functionality, level of fidelity in the specifications, latest implementation of specifications, price, support, and enterprise adoption.

In the following table we list some items to compare while choosing your Application server. Examples are given using the three main vendors on the market today: BEA, IBM, and Oracle. Some of these numbers may change by the time you see this list, but you can probably use this as a reference for areas in which to compare J2EE vendors:

> **Do not attempt to use the data in this table to compare these products, it is merely provided as guide for you to complete yourself.**

Vendors	BEA WebLogic	IBM WebSphere	Oracle IAS
Average Price per Processor	$10K	$8K	$10K
Enterprise product	$17K	$35K	$20K
Caching	Yes	No	Yes
Clustering	Yes	Yes	Yes
Connection Pooling	Yes	Yes	Yes
EJB Support	2.0	1.2	2.0
Failover	Yes	Yes	Yes
JSP Support	1.2	1.1	1.1
LDAP Support	Yes	Yes	Yes
Load Balancing	Yes	Yes	Yes
Portal Services	Yes	Yes	No
Servlet Support	2.3	2.2	2.3
XML SAX	2.0	1.0	1.0

If you're interested in the most up to date figures for this table, consult the vendor web sites for these products.

It is very important to know what is supported and what is not supported in a J2EE implementation. A vendor may include some features of the latest J2EE specifications in one area of its product, and sell that product until the other areas get upgraded. Yes, this really happens! There are often times when vendors will label the product to be J2EE 1.x compliant and have a road map indicating when all components will actually all be at the same J2EE level. Depending on the project ahead, we may be able to use a product that has different levels of support for different services. This can sometimes become an issue during installation and configuration time, and it can also create an issue with regard to JDK requirements for your systems.

Below is a quick reference table for the two latest J2EE releases. This table can help you during the analysis phase before it is time to commit to a particular vendor. This can also help during the review of your existing systems to make sure your application server is the best possible match:

J2EE Standard	J2EE 1.3	J2EE 1.2/1.2.1
XML	❑ JAXP 1.1 XML parser	❑ No required XML parser
	❑ XML view of JSP editable	❑ Cannot edit XML view of a JSP
	❑ JSP pages can generate XML output	❑ JSP pages can generate XML output
	❑ Servlet filters useful for XML output	❑ No filters available
	❑ Servlets can generate XML output	❑ Servlets can generate XML output
	❑ EJB descriptors in XML	❑ EJB descriptors in XML
JMS (Java Message Service)	❑ JMS 1.0 implementation required	❑ JMS implementation optional
JCA (Java Connector Architecture)	❑ J2EE Connector 1.0	❑ J2EE Connectors not available
Enterprise JavaBeans 2.0	❑ Message-driven beans	❑ No EJB model for asynchronous communication
	❑ Required interoperability	
	❑ Improved container-managed persistence	❑ First release with container-managed persistence
	❑ EJB Query Language (EJB QL)	❑ No query language for container managed data
	❑ Local interfaces	
RMI-IIOP	❑ Interoperability required	❑ No interoperability required
	❑ Updated OMG specification requirements	❑ IIOP requirements not specifically aligned with OMG
Java Mail	❑ JavaMail 1.2	❑ JavaMail 1.1
JAF (JavaBeans Activation Framework)	❑ No change in JAF requirements	❑ JavaBeans Activation Framework 1.0 (JAF)

Table continued on following page

J2EE Standard	J2EE 1.3	J2EE 1.2/1.2.1
JTA (Java Transaction API)	❑ No change in JTA requirements	❑ JTA 1.0
JDBC	❑ No change in JDBC requirements	❑ JDBC Optional Package 2.0
J2SE	❑ J2SE 1.3 or later	❑ J2SE 1.2 or later
Servlet	❑ Servlet 2.3	❑ Servlet 2.2
	❑ Filters (new type of web component)	
	❑ Application events (main use is for application lifecycle management and communicating global application state to sessions)	
	❑ Support for migrating application sessions in clustered or distributed server configurations	
	❑ Install-time validation of library dependencies	
	❑ 'Run-as' roles to enable Servlets to use EJBs that require authentication	
	❑ Improved control over character encoding for localization of application output	
JSP (JavaServer Pages)	❑ JSP 1.2	❑ JSP 1.1
	❑ XML view of JSP page	
	❑ Developer-defined translation-time validators for JSP pages	
	❑ Incremental changes to simplify development	
	❑ Improve performance	
	❑ Deliver better portability	

At present, there is a trend in which J2EE vendors are bundling their products with operating systems. Sun will bundle the iPlanet Application Server with Solaris. Sun could be a one-stop shop providing both hardware and software products. Sun's future bundling strategy is evident today – the vendor already includes a free evaluation copy of its iPlanet app server with Solaris.

HP will bundle Bluestone with HP-UX. HP bought the application server vendor Bluestone last year for more than half a billion dollars when it was already reselling BEA WebLogic. HP competes on hardware margins with IBM and Sun, so it clearly needed its own application server tuned to run on HP-UX.

For these infrastructure vendors, preloading their application servers on their hardware with the operating system is the right thing to do. The application server is a logical extension of the operating system. It provides a set of services like load balancing, messaging, and fault tolerance that let developers focus on application development. Companies that get their application server and operating system from a single vendor will benefit from easier deployment and administration.

Installing an application server and deploying applications well requires experienced consultants, skilled developers, knowledgeable IT staff, and vendor support. In simple terms, it takes talent, time, and money! These factors represent a learning curve that organizations need to overcome. A new programming style and new IT skill set is required. Next we will review some of the changing aspects when J2EE technology arrives in organizations that are new to it.

Development Community

It is worth taking a look at the different development communities that are formed around certain J2EE vendors. If the project is going to require a long development cycle there could be several unknowns due to the nature of the project and the target deployment environment. The presence of a strong development community is very important. A company may not have premium support available for its engineering and IT staff. This could mean reduced levels of support from the vendor beyond the traditional options. Some vendors provide online resources for developers as a starting point. These communities can expand beyond the vendor's initial effort. Below are some developer focused web sites from different vendors and open source groups:

- ❑ BEA http://developer.bea.com/index.jsp
- ❑ IBM http://www-106.ibm.com/developerworks/
- ❑ iPlanet http://developer.iplanet.com/
- ❑ JBoss http://www.jboss.org/lists.jsp
- ❑ Oracle http://otn.oracle.com/index.html
- ❑ Sybase http://www.sybase.com/developer/
- ❑ Tomcat http://jakarta.apache.org/site/getinvolved.html

Electronic news groups are also an excellent resource for developers to get more information and support on different products. For a comprehensive list of news groups you can search http://groups.google.com/.

Summary

J2EE is a living standard that is going to be updated in the future to provide more functionality and better services for Java-based enterprise applications. Application servers are the main product representation for J2EE specifications; they provide both the web and EJB containers that are key to any J2EE application.

There are several commercial products available in the market today, as well as some very good open source alternatives. Depending on what the project or tasks are, one will have to do some research to find the best match for the work ahead. Application server vendors do not implement the J2EE specifications alone; they usually take a step further and provide additional value-added features to differentiate their offerings. This means there is a learning curve associated with using application servers. Learning options and a good development community are key for a successful project. Keep this in mind during any technology decision process.

Finally, hardware and systems architecture are also important in deciding which application server is best for a project.

In the next chapter, we'll take a look at packaging and deploying our J2EE applications.

24

J2EE Packaging and Deployment

As you know, the J2EE specification comprises a number of functional sub-specifications. However, it is not always obvious how these should be put together to form a complete J2EE application. The J2EE specification provides guidelines for the structuring and the creation of J2EE applications and one of the major ones is related to **packaging**. Individual specifications provide guidelines for the packaging of individual components such as EJBs, JSP pages, and servlets. The J2EE specification then dictates how these heterogeneous components are themselves to be packaged together.

This chapter provides a thorough analysis of the J2EE packaging mechanism. We will not cover how to build EJB, web application, or resource adapter archive files. These aspects of J2EE are discussed in earlier chapters of their own. Instead, we will focus on the relationships that these components have within an EAR file, and the process involved in building EAR files.

Some of the questions we will ask are:

❑ What are the rules for using J2EE packaging as opposed to component packaging?

❑ What can be placed into a J2EE package?

❑ Is J2EE packaging necessary and are there behavioral changes that occur as a result of using J2EE packaging?

In answering these questions we will learn:

❑ How J2EE class loading schemes work

❑ How to create Enterprise Archive (EAR) files

❑ How to deal with dependency and utility classes

J2EE Packaging Overview

A J2EE application is composed of:

❑ One or more J2EE components

❑ A J2EE application deployment descriptor

When one or more heterogeneous J2EE components need to use one another, a **J2EE application** must be created. There are many considerations that must be taken into account when building a J2EE application, including:

❑ The types of J2EE components that can be packaged into a J2EE application

❑ The roles that people play when creating J2EE packages

❑ The current limitations of J2EE packaging

❑ The class loading approaches that different vendors use to meet the needs of J2EE component interactions

What can be Packaged?

The J2EE specification differentiates between resources that run within a container and resources that can be packaged into a J2EE **Enterprise Application ARchive (EAR)** file.

> **An EAR file is used to package one or more J2EE modules into a single module so that they can have aligned classloading and deployment into a server.**

J2EE clarifies the difference between run time containers and deployment modules. Run time containers are request-level interceptors that provide infrastructure services around components of the system. A deployment module is a packaging structure for components that will ultimately execute in a run time container. Recall how J2EE containers are structured:

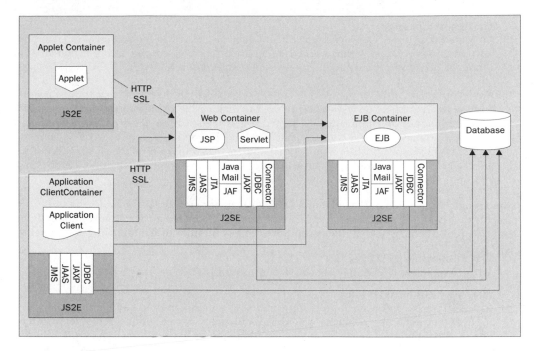

❑ **The EJB Container**
The EJB container provides containment and request-level interception for business logic. The EJB container allows EJBs to have access to JMS, JAAS, JTA, JavaMail (which uses JAF), JAXP, JDBC, and the Connector architecture.

❑ **The Web Container**
The web container provides interception for requests sent over HTTP, FTP, SMTP, and other protocols. Most web containers only provide support for HTTP(S), but could support a broader range of protocols if they so chose. The web application container allows JSP pages and servlets to have access to the same resources as the EJB container provides.

❑ **The Application Client Container**
An application client container provides request-level interception for standalone Java applications. These applications run remotely, in a different JVM from that in which the web container and EJB container operate.

A program running in an application client container is very similar to a Java program with a main() method. However, instead of the application being controlled by a JVM, a wrapper controls the program. This wrapper is the application client container. Application client containers are a new concept in the J2EE specification and should be provided by your application server provider.

An application client container can optimize access to a web container and EJB container through direct authentication, performing load balancing, allowing fail-over routines, providing access to server-side environment variables, and properly propagating transaction contexts.

Programs that run within an application client container have access to JAXP, JDBC, JMS, and JAAS resources on a remote application server.

❑ **The Applet Container**
An applet container is a special type of container that provides request-level interception for Java programs running within a browser. An important point to remember is that an applet container does not provide access to any additional resources such as JDBC or JMS.

Applets running within an applet container are expected to make requests for resources directly to an application server (as opposed to making the request to the container and letting the container ask the application server). The EJB specification doesn't make any regulations as to how an applet should communicate with an EJB container, but the J2EE specification does. The J2EE specification requires that applets that want to directly use an EJB must use the HTTP(S) protocol and tunnel RMI invocations. Many application server vendors support a form of HTTP tunneling to allow for this.

The components that can be packaged into a J2EE EAR file do not directly correlate to those components that contain containers. There are no basic requirements for what must minimally be included into an EAR file. An EAR file is composed of any number of the following components:

❑ **EJB Application JAR Files**
An EJB application JAR file contains one or more EJBs.

❑ **Web Application WAR Files**
A WAR file contains a single web application. As an EAR file can contain multiple web applications, each web application in an EAR file must have a unique deployment context. The deployment mechanism for EAR files allows just such a specification of different contexts.

❑ **Application Client JAR Files**
The application client JAR file contains a single, standalone Java application that is intended to run within an application client container. The application client JAR file contains a specialized deployment descriptor and is composed similarly to the way an EJB JAR file is composed.

The JAR file contains the classes required to run the stand alone client, in addition to any client libraries needed to access JDBC, JMS, JAXP, JAAS, or an EJB client.

❑ **Resource Adapter RAR Files**
The resource adapter RAR file contains Java classes and native libraries required to implement a Java Connector Architecture (JCA) resource adapter to an enterprise information system.

Resource adapters do not execute within a container. Rather, they are designed to execute as a bridge between an application server and an external enterprise information system.

Each of these components are developed and packaged individually apart from the J2EE EAR file and own deployment descriptor. A J2EE EAR file is a combination of one or more of these components into a unified package with a custom deployment descriptor.

Packaging Roles

During the building, deployment, and use of an EJB, web application, or other component, different people will play different roles. The J2EE specification defines broad **platform roles** that developers play during the creation of an enterprise application. Even though there are many roles that individuals assume during the development and deployment process, these roles are nothing more than just logical constructs that allow an application to be better planned and executed. It is likely (and expected) that a single individual or organization will perform multiple roles. The common roles involved in building, deploying, or using an EAR file include:

❏ **J2EE Product Provider**
The J2EE product provider provides an implementation of the J2EE platform including all appropriate J2EE APIs and other features defined in the specification. The J2EE product provider is typically an application-server, web-server, or database-system vendor who provides an appropriate implementation by mapping the specifications and components to network protocols.

❏ **Application Component Provider**
The application component provider provides a J2EE component, for example an EJB application or a web application.

There are also many roles within the J2EE specification that can be characterized as an application component provider. These include document developers, JSP authors, enterprise bean developers, and resource-adapter developers.

❏ **Application Assembler**
The application assembler is responsible-combining one or more J2EE components into an EAR file to create a J2EE application. The application assembler is also responsible for creating the J2EE application deployment descriptor and identifying any external resources that the application may depend upon. These can include class libraries, security roles, and naming environments. The application assembler will commonly use tools provided by the J2EE product provider and the tool provider.

❏ **Tool Provider**
A tool provider provides utilities to automate the creation, packaging, and deployment of a J2EE application. A tool provider can provide tools that automate the generation of deployment descriptors for an EAR file, the creation of an EAR file, and the deployment of an EAR file into an application server. Utilities provided by a tool provider can be either platform-independent (work with all EAR files irrespective of the environment) or be platform-dependent (working with the native capabilities of a particular environment).

❏ **Deployer**
The deployer is responsible for deploying web applications and EJB applications into the server environment. The deployer is not responsible for deploying a resource-adapter archive or an application-client archive, but may be responsible for additional configuration of these components. These components, even though they are packaged as part of a J2EE EAR file, are not considered when the enterprise application is deployed. They are part of the J2EE application, but don't group through a run time "activation" process that web application and EJB containers go through during deployment. Resource adapter archives are simply libraries that are dropped into a valid JCA implementation. Although they are packaged as part of a J2EE EAR file they do not operate within the context of a J2EE container. Therefore, since resource-adapter archives do not have a J2EE container, the do not need to have a J2EE deployer involved with their activation.

Application client programs do operate within the context of a J2EE container, but they are not deployed into an application server. Application client programs run standalone, and the deployer is not responsible for configuring the container environment for these programs.

The deployer produces container-ready web applications, EJB applications, applets, and application clients that have been customized for the target environment of the application server.

❏ **System Administrator**
The system administrator is responsible for configuring the networking and operational environment that application servers and J2EE applications execute within. The system administrator is also responsible for the monitoring and maintenance of J2EE applications.

In this chapter, during the discussion of the creation of EAR files and resolution of conflicts, we will be acting in the roles of application assembler and deployer.

The Limitations of Packaging

EAR files meet the basic requirements for packaging an application as most web-based J2EE applications are composed solely of web and EJB applications. However, EAR files lack the capability of packaging complicated J2EE applications. For example, the following components cannot be declared in an EAR file, but are often used in a J2EE application:

❏ JDBC `DataSource` objects.

❏ JMS `ConnectionFactory` and `Destination` objects.

❏ JMX `MBeans`.

❏ Some JMS consumers that run within an application server such as a `MessageConsumer` that runs as part of a `ServerSession`.

❏ Classes that are triggered when an application is deployed or un-deployed. (These classes are proprietary extensions provided by vendors not defined in the J2EE specification. However, all vendors generally supply them.)

At present, these components have to be manually configured and deployed via an administration interface provided by the implementation vendor and are the responsibility of the system administrator. Over time, the usage of these items will increase and consequently it will become important for EAR files to support the packaging of these components so that application portability is possible.

Understanding Class Loading Schemes

At runtime, when a class is referenced, it needs to be loaded by the Java Virtual Machine. The JVM uses a standard class loading structure for loading classes into memory. A class loader is a Java class that is responsible for loading Java classes from a source. Java classes can be loaded from disk, socket, or some other media; they can reside anywhere. Class loaders are hierarchical in the sense that they can be chained together in a parent-child relationship. Classes loaded by a child class loader have visibility (can use) classes loaded by any of the parent class loaders. Classes loaded by a parent class loader do not have visibility to classes loaded by any of its children's class loaders. Class loaders and EAR files are important since application server vendors can deploy application modules using common or different class loaders.

If, within an application, a web application needs to access an EJB, the web application will need to be able to load those classes it requires. Because of this implied dependency between different modules, application server vendors must consider different approaches for structuring EAR classloaders so that these dependencies are resolved.

A standalone application is deployed in its own class loader. This means that if you deploy a web application archive and an EJB application archive separately, the respective classes for each application will be loaded in different class loaders that are siblings of one another. The classes in the web application class loader will not be visible to the classes loaded by other class loaders. This creates a problem for web applications that want to use EJBs that have been deployed separately.

Before the advent of EAR files, many developers would deploy an EJB and then repackage the same EJB JAR file as part of the WEB-INF\lib directory of the web application. The same class files would exist in two different places so that the overall application could work correctly, a situation to be avoided. EAR applications were introduced to solve this problem. EAR files are not only a convenient packaging format; they also provide a special class loading scheme that allows applications within the EAR file to access the classes of other applications.

The J2EE 1.3 specification makes no specific requirements as to how an EAR class loader should work. This allows application server vendors flexibility in deciding how classes should be loaded. Before implementing an EAR class loader, a vendor needs to decide:

❑   Will all classes in all applications in the EAR file be loaded by a single class loader, or will separate files be loaded by different class loaders?

❑   Should there be any parent-child class loader relationships between different applications in the EAR file? For example, if two EJB applications depend upon log4j.jar, should appropriate visibility be maintained by loading log4j.jar in a parent class loader and loading the EJB applications in a child class loader so that?

❑   If a hierarchy of class loaders is created, to what depth will the hierarchy be allowed to extend?

❑   EJBs have inherent relationships with one another but web applications do not. So, will EJB applications be loaded differently from web applications so that web application integrity can be maintained?

The Pre-EJB 2.0 Option

Prior to the EJB 2.0 Public Final Draft 2, vendors had a lot of flexibility in choosing how to set up a class loading scheme. JSP pages and servlets that needed to make use of an EJB only needed to be able to load the home interface, remote interface, common classes, and stub classes of the EJB. The common classes such as exceptions and parameters should be placed into a dependency JAR file and loaded as a dependency package. This configuration requires vendors to determine a way for a web application that depends upon an EJB to load the home interface, remote interface, and stubs.

A vendor could implement this simple class loading scheme:

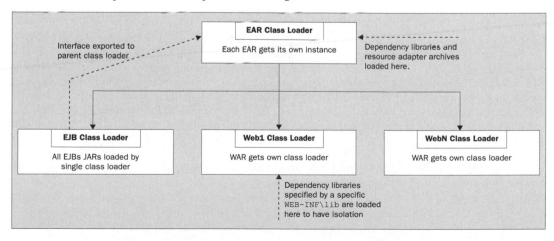

Client application class loading is not included in this model since a client application will execute within another virtual machine and will be isolated from all other components.

In this model, each EAR application would be loaded by a custom EAR class loader instance. EJB applications and web applications would each be loaded by custom class loaders that are children of the EAR class loader. Any class file that is to be shared by more than one application in the EAR will be loaded by the EAR class loader. (This includes any common dependency libraries and resource adapter archives.) Any files loaded at the EAR class loader level are automatically visible to all classes loaded by child class loaders.

All EJB applications are loaded by a single EJB class loader that is a child of the EAR class loader. Even if you have different EJB JAR files, they will all be loaded by the same class loader. This is done to facilitate EJB-to-EJB calls in different applications that are hosted on the same JVM.

Each web application is loaded in a different class loader to maintain class isolation. For example, if every web application contains a file called index.jsp, that servlet created from the JSP page could have the same class name as the equivalent servlets in other web applications. Each web application needs to be able to load its own version of that servlet, so each web application must be isolated in its own class loader.

In order for web applications to make use of the EJBs deployed in the same EAR file, the web applications need to have visibility to the external interfaces and stub implementation classes of those EJBs. Since the EJB and web application class loaders are siblings, the web applications do not have direct visibility to the right class files. The web application class loader and the EJB application class loader do have the same parent class loader, however. To allow the web application to be able to use the class files of the EJB, the EJB class loader can take all of the public interfaces of each of the EJBs and their stub implementation files and 'export' them to the EAR class loader in which they will be visible to all applications in the EAR. The public interfaces and stub implementation files are the classes needed by a client to make use of an EJB. The web applications will then be able to load the classes required to use any EJB.

Dependency utility libraries can be loaded in different places depending on where the library is specified. If a single web application lists a dependency library in its WEB-INF\lib directory, then that library is unique to that web application. There is no need for other applications to access the contents of that library and so the EAR class loader should not load that library. In this situation, the web application class loader will load the utility JAR file. Other web applications should include the same dependency in their own WEB-INF\lib to maintain this isolation.

Dependency utility libraries that must be shared between EJB and web applications need to be loaded at the EAR class-loader level. It turns out that an EAR class loader will load any library specified as a dependency of an EJB in order to give the right visibility to those dependency classes. This allows an EJB developer to package any common exception classes, custom input parameter classes that are visible to a web application, and the EJB into a dependency library. This library is commonly called common.jar but does not have to be named that. In addition to the public interfaces and stub implementation classes, the common utility library will also be loaded at the EAR level, which allows a web application visibility to all of the classes used by the EJB.

Resource-adapter archives that are packaged within the EAR file along with EJBs and web applications are automatically loaded at the EAR class-loader level.

The Post-EJB 2.0 Option

The EJB 2.0 Public Final Draft 2 introduced the concept of local interfaces and placed an interesting twist on the EAR class loading problem. Local interfaces allow co-located clients and EJBs to be accessed using pass-by-reference semantics instead of pass-by-value semantics.

Having visibility to the public interfaces and stub implementation classes of an EJB is not sufficient for a client of an EJB to perform pass-by-reference invocations. The client needs to have a direct reference to the implementation classes of the EJB's container. With local interfaces, clients of EJBs need access to much more than before. This restriction means that the class loading scheme used pre-EJB 2.0 will not work. To solve this problem the class loaders of any applications that act as clients to an EJB must be loaded as children of the EJB class loader:

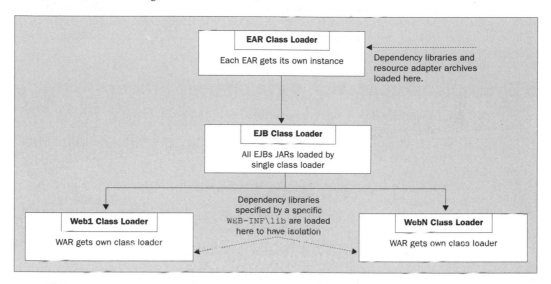

In this model, web application class loaders are children of the EJB class loader. This allows all web applications to have visibility to the files they need to allow them to behave as clients of the EJBs. Each web application is still loaded in a custom class loader to achieve isolation, though. The overall structure of this implementation is simpler to understand, as it does not require the EJB class loader to export any files to the EAR class loader.

An Ambiguity in the J2EE Specification

An ambiguity in the J2EE specification has been exposed by certain implementations. It arises because the J2EE specification is ambiguous as to how dependency libraries of a web application should be loaded. It is very clear that a utility library specified by WEB-INF\lib should remain isolated and be loaded by the class loader of the web application only. However, if a utility library is specified as a dependency library of the web application, it is not stated whether the library should be loaded by the web application's class loader or exported to the EAR class loader. This can have a behavioral impact. If it is known that a dependency utility library will only be loaded once for all web applications, the web applications can take advantage of knowing that a singleton class will only create a single object that can be shared among all web applications. However, if each web application's class loader isolated the utility library, a singleton class, which is a class that is intended to only create a single instance in the virtual machine, would create a single object in each web application.

Currently, Silverstream's application server and the J2EE Reference Implementation load utility libraries specified as a dependency library of a web application at the EAR class-loader level. WebLogic Server 6.0 loaded these libraries as part of the web application class loader. However, WebLogic Server 6.1 modified this approach to support the loading of web application dependency libraries at the EAR level. This makes sense since web application isolation can always be achieved by placing utility libraries in the `WEB-INF\lib` directory. This provides the best of both worlds: a dependency library loaded at the EAR class-loader level or a dependency library loaded at the web application class-loader level.

Configuring J2EE Packages

Now that we have a basic understanding of how the J2EE architecture is implemented, specifically the different roles and the behavior of class loaders, we are ready to configure and deploy enterprise applications. To do this we need to understand the process of EAR file creation, and the contents of the deployment descriptors that describe their contents.

The Enterprise Application Development Process

The overall process that is used to build an enterprise application is:

1. Developers build individual components; these can be EJBs, JSP pages, servlets, and resource adapters.

2. Some number of components are packaged into a JAR file along with a deployment descriptor to a J2EE module. A J2EE module is a collection of one or more J2EE components of the same component type, so an EJB module can comprise more than one EJB; a web application module can comprise multiple JSP pages and servlets; a resource adapter archive can comprise multiple resource adapters.

3. One or more J2EE modules are combined into an EAR file along with an enterprise application deployment descriptor to create a J2EE application. The simplest J2EE application is composed of a single J2EE module. More complicated J2EE applications are composed of multiple J2EE modules. A complex J2EE application comprise multiple J2EE modules, and dependency libraries that are used by the classes contained within the modules. A J2EE application may also contain help files and other documents to aid the deployer.

4. The J2EE application is deployed into a J2EE product. The J2EE application is installed on the J2EE platform and then integrated with any infrastructure that exists on an application server. As part of the J2EE application deployment process, each J2EE module is individually deployed according to the guidelines specified for deployment of that respective type. Each component must be deployed into the correct container that matches the type of the component.

    For example, if you have a `my.ear` with a `my.jar` and a `my.war` contained within the EAR file, when the application is deployed, the application server's deployment tool will copy the `my.ear` file into the application server. Next, the application server's deployment mechanism will extract the `my.jar` and `my.war` modules and deploy them separately following the class loading guidelines of that platform. If each of the modules deploys successfully, then the J2EE application is considered to have deployed successfully.

The J2EE enterprise application development and deployment process might work like this:

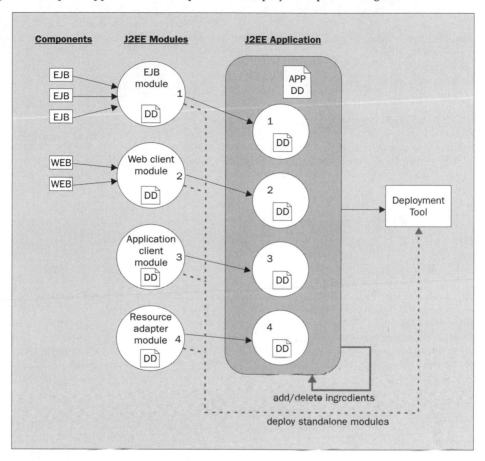

Components are built and packaged into a J2EE module with a deployment descriptor; a deployment tool can be used to create these J2EE modules. The deployment tool can also be used to deploy and undeploy standalone J2EE modules; to take one or more J2EE modules and package them into a J2EE application with another deployment descriptor; to add or remove items from the J2EE application; or to deploy the entire application to an application server.

The Structure of a J2EE Package

The structure of a J2EE enterprise application package is straightforward; it is composed of one or more J2EE modules and a deployment descriptor named `application.xml` in a directory named `META-INF\`. The files are packaged using the JAR file format and stored in a file with an `.ear` extension. Optionally, you can include dependency libraries within the EAR file. The general structure of an EAR file is:

```
EJB .jar Files
Web Application .war Files
Resource Adapter .rar Files
Application Client .jar Files
Dependency Library .jar Files
```

```
META-INF\
          application.xml
```

An example EAR file that has an EJB module and a web application module with no dependency libraries might look like:

```
FirstEJB.jar
FirstWeb.war
META-INF\
          application.xml
```

J2EE modules that are stored in the EAR file do not necessarily have to be in the root directory of the structure. For example, the contents of an EAR file that has an EJB module and a resource adapter archive stored in subdirectories might look like:

```
ejbs\
      SecondEJB.jar
resources\
          LegacyAdapter.rar
META-INF\
          application.xml
```

Finally, an EAR file that has many components and dependency libraries may look like:

```
ejbs\
      ThirdEJB.jar
      FourthEJB.jar
resources\
          LegacyAdapter.rar
web\
      WebApp1.war
      WebApp2.war
lib\
      xmlx.jar
      common.jar
META-INF\
          application.xml
```

The EAR file is created using a deployment tool provided by a tool provider or alternatively by using the `jar` tool provided with the JDK. The creation steps are:

- ❑ Create a staging directory that will contain the contents of the EAR file
- ❑ Place all of the J2EE modules into the staging directory and create the `META-INF\` directory
- ❑ Create the `application.xml` deployment descriptor and place it into the `META-INF\` directory
- ❑ After you have built up the staging directory, go to the root of the directory and run the `jar` utility to create the EAR file

An example execution of the `jar` utility for the complex example discussed earlier might be:

```
jar cvf Application.ear ejbs resources web lib META-INF
```

Once the EAR file has been created, you are free to deploy the J2EE application into the application server.

Working with the EAR Deployment Descriptor

Ideally, a graphical deployment tool would be used to build the `application.xml` files. However, there may be many situations where you need to construct or maintain `application.xml` manually, and so it is important to understand the tags that are used.

The `application.xml` deployment descriptor is straightforward. A valid descriptor doesn't require many tags. The possible tags contained within the DTD of the deployment descriptor are:

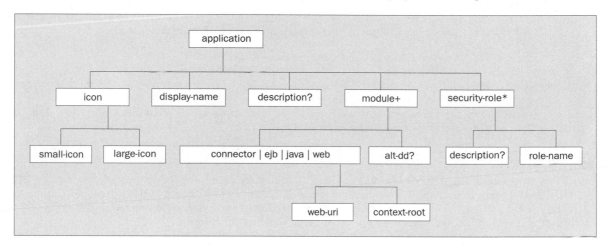

All valid J2EE application deployment descriptors must contain the following DOCTYPE declaration:

```
<!DOCTYPE application PUBLIC "-//Sun Microsystems, Inc.//DTD J2EE Application
1.3//EN" "http://java.sun.com/dtd/application_1_3.dtd">
```

Configuring a simple `application.xml` deployment descriptor takes only a few steps:

1. The `<application>` tag is used to declare an enterprise application. The `<application>` tag can contain an `<icon>`, `<display-name>`, and `<description>` for use by a deployment tool to provide descriptive information about the application. The content of these tags is the same as the content for the same tags in EJB, web application, and resource adapter deployment descriptors.

2. Each J2EE module included in the enterprise application must have an equivalent `<module>` tag describing the module. EJBs are described using the `<ejb>` tag, web applications are described using the `<web>` tag, resource adapters are described using the `<connector>` tag, and application client programs are described using the `<java>` tag. With the exception of the `<web>` tag, the content of the other tags is a relative URI naming the file that contains the J2EE module within the EAR file. The URI must be relative to the root of the EAR file.

1177

3. If your enterprise application contains a web application J2EE module, you need to provide a `<web-uri>` and a `<context-root>`. The `<web-uri>` tag is a relative URI naming the file that contains the J2EE module within the EAR file. This is the same type of URI that is specified for the `<ejb>`, `<connector>`, and `<java>` tags. The `<context-root>` specifies the name of the context under which the web application will run. Subsequently, all requests for JSP pages and servlets for that web application must be preceded by this web context. For example, if you deploy a web application with:

```
<context-root>web1</context-root>
```

all HTTP requests for JSP pages and servlets will always be preceded with:

```
http://host:port/web1/<AsSpecifiedInServletSpec>
```

Each web application packaged within the EAR file must have a unique `<context-root>` value. Two web applications packaged in the same EAR file cannot have identical `<context-root>` values. If there is only one web application in the EAR file, the value of `<context-root>` may be an empty string.

Example

The most common use of EAR files will be the scenario where an enterprise application has a single EJB module and a single web application module that makes use of the EJB components deployed in the EJB module. In this example, the EJBs and web applications do not depend upon any dependency libraries. This section describes the steps involved in building this example.

Packaging the Components

This example has a servlet invoke an `invoke()` method on the remote interface of a stateless session EJB. The servlet and EJB print out statements to the console to indicate that they are successfully executing. If the console receives any exceptions, it is likely to be an indication that the packaging of the components was not done correctly. All of the EJB source files for this example are in the `wrox` package. The servlet is in the unnamed package. The Java files used to implement this example include:

❑ `EnterpriseServlet.java`
The servlet implementation class that invokes the EJB

❑ `Enterprise.java`
The remote interface of the EJB

❑ `EnterpriseHome.java`
The home interface of the EJB

❑ `EnterpriseBean.java`
The implementation class of the EJB

For complete information on how to author servlets and EJBs, please reference the appropriate chapters in this book. This section will only list the relevant code snippets to allow the reader to follow the example. Authoring EJB and web application deployment descriptors, creating JAR files, and creating web application WAR files are not demonstrated here and discussed in Chapters 7 to 21.

The sourcecode for the `EnterpriseBean.java` bean implementation class is:

```
package wrox;

import javax.ejb.*;

public class EnterpriseBean implements SessionBean {

private InitialContext ctx;

public void ejbCreate() {}
public void ejbRemove() {}
public void ejbActivate() {}
public void ejbPassivate() {}
public void setSessionContext(SessionContext c) {}

public void invoke() {
System.out.println("Executing in EJB.");
}
}
```

The sourcecode for the EnterpriseServlet.java servlet class is:

```
import javax.servlet.*;
import javax.servlet.http.*;
import java.io.*;
import javax.naming.*;

public class EnterpriseServlet extends HttpServlet {

  public void service(HttpServletRequest req, HttpServletResponse res)
              throws IOException{
    res.setContentType("text/html");
    PrintWriter out = res.getWriter();

    try {
      System.out.println("Servlet Executing in Server");
      InitialContext ctx = new InitialContext();

      wrox.EnterpriseHome eHome = (wrox.EnterpriseHome)
                               ctx.lookup("EnterpriseEJB");
      wrox.Enterprise e = eHome.create();
      e.invoke();

    } catch(Exception e) {
      out.println("Exception: " + e);
      System.out.println("Exception: " + e);
    }

    out.println("<html><head><title>Title</title></head>");
    out.println("<body>");
    out.println("<h1>See console to ensure EJB was invoked.</h1>");
    out.println("</body></html>");
  }
}
```

After the development of the EJB code and the relevant deployment descriptors (not listed here), the EJB should be packaged into a file named `EnterpriseBean.jar`. The EJB is configured to bind itself to `EnterpriseEJB` in the JNDI namespace.

After the development of the servlet code and the relevant deployment descriptors (also not listed here), the servlet should be packaged into a file named `WebApp.war`. The servlet class is registered to execute with the `/enterpriseservlet/` mapping.

Application Assembly

After completing the component build process, the enterprise application deployment descriptor must be developed. We need to register the EJB and web application as modules of the enterprise application. We also want the web application's components to execute under the `/web/` context root. The `application.xml` file for this example becomes:

```xml
<?xml version="1.0"  encoding="UTF-8"?>

<!DOCTYPE application PUBLIC '-//Sun Microsystems, Inc.//DTD J2EE Application
1.3//EN' 'http://java.sun.com/dtd/application_1_3.dtd'>

<application>
  <display-name>Enterprise Application</display-name>
  <module>
    <ejb>EnterpriseBean.jar</ejb>
  </module>
  <module>
    <web>
      <web-uri>WebApp.war</web-uri>
      <context-root>web</context-root>
    </web>
  </module>
</application>
```

After creating the `application.xml` deployment descriptor, the enterprise application build directory should resemble:

```
EnterpriseBean.jar
WebApp.war
META-INF\
          application.xml
```

To create an EAR file named `Enterprise.ear` using the `jar` utility, the following command should be entered on the console:

```
jar cvf Enterprise.ear EnterpriseBean.jar WebApp.war META-INF
```

> *What's interesting about the `deploytool` that is provided with the J2EE Reference Implementation is that developers are never expected to author `ejb-jar.xml`, `web.xml`, or `application.xml` deployment descriptors. These files are always automatically generated for you. In the case of this enterprise application, the `application.xml` that is placed into the EAR file is generated automatically for the developer.*

Application Deployment

After the EAR file has been built, it needs to be deployed. Keep in mind that deployment is vendor specific and each vendor provides custom tools to allow this. The J2EE `deploytool` utility has an option to deploy an enterprise application to the Reference Implementation.

Running the Application

After the enterprise application has been successfully deployed, executing the client involves invoking the servlet that was deployed in the web application. Since the context root of the enterprise application is `/web`, the servlet is invoked as part of that. For example, to invoke the servlet, you would enter the following in a browser's window:

http://<server_name>:<server_port>/web/enterpriseservlet/

You should see the following appear in the browser after the servlet executes:

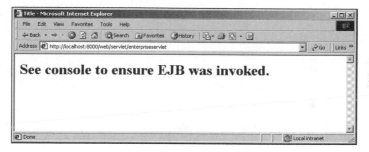

Optional Deployment Descriptor Tags

Two optional deployment descriptor tags can be used in certain scenarios. They are `<alt-dd>` and `<security-role>`.

`<alt-dd>` is a sub-tag of `<module>`. The value of this tag is a URI that would point to another deployment descriptor file for the module referenced from the root of the EAR file. The file does not have to be named the same as it is named inside the J2EE module. For example, all EJB module deployment descriptors must be named `ejb-jar.xml`. The value of this tag can be a file named other than `ejb-jar.xml` if it is referencing an alternative deployment descriptor for an EJB module.

The deployment descriptor file would override the one contained within the J2EE module. This is a type of post-assembly deployment descriptor. This tag can be used to reference an external version of the deployment descriptor that should be used if a deployer wants to use a deployment descriptor that is different from the one contained within an EJB, a web application, a resource adapter, or an application client module. If this value is not specified, then the deployment tool must use the values specified within the JAR, WAR, or RAR files provided in the EAR file. For example, to specify a web application with an external, alternative deployment descriptor that is located at the root of the EAR file, you would write:

```
<module>
  <web>
    <web-uri>web.war</web-uri>
    <context-root>web</context-root>
  </web>
```

```
    <alt-dd>external-web.xml</alt-dd>
  </module>
```

`<security-role>` allows the deployer to specify application-level security roles that should be used for all J2EE modules contained within the EAR file. If an EAR file contains multiple EJB modules and/or multiple web application modules, each of those modules may have its own security roles defined within. One of the deployer's responsibilities is to ensure that the names of all security roles contained within all J2EE modules are unique and have meaning for the application as a whole. Security roles can be 'pulled up' from the J2EE module level to the enterprise application level and included in this tag. If there is a duplicate security role value in one of the J2EE modules, that value can be removed if the value is provided at the enterprise application level.

This tag requires a `<role-name>` sub tag to actually provide the symbolic name of the security role. An example of configuring a `<security-role>` tag is:

```
<security-role>
  <description>
    This is administrator's security role
  </description>
  <role-name>Administrator</role-name>
</security-role>
```

Issues with the Ordering of Modules

The J2EE specification doesn't make any specifications for how J2EE modules contained within an EAR file should be deployed. In particular, the order in which modules must be deployed is not explicitly outlined in the specification. This can be an issue if a component in one module needs to make use of another component in another module that has yet to be deployed.

Most application servers will deploy EAR files using the same approach:

1. All resource adapters contained within the EAR file will be deployed into the connector infrastructure. If multiple resource adapters are configured, they will be deployed in the order that they are listed in the `application.xml` deployment descriptor.

2. All EJB modules will be deployed. EJBs are deployed after resource adapters since EJBs may make use of a particular resource adapter during their initialization stage. If multiple EJB modules are configured, they will be deployed in the order that they are listed in the `application.xml` deployment descriptor.

3. All web application modules will be deployed. Web applications are deployed after EJBs and resource adapters since web applications may make use of these resources during their initialization stage. If multiple web application modules are configured, they will be deployed in the order that they are listed in the `application.xml` deployment descriptor.

Issues with Dependency Packages

The most frequent question raised about J2EE packaging is about utility and support classes. When packaging a web application or an EJB application, where should these libraries be placed? If you place these classes into the standard classpath of your application server, they will likely lose any unloading ability that web and EJB applications have that are driven by the class loaders used to load them at deployment. If your web/EJB applications need to change the version of the libraries that they use, then the dependent library will need to be re-deployed when the web/EJB application is re-deployed. In this scenario, storing utility classes on the standard classpath is not a feasible option since the entire application server would have to be restarted for each deployment of a web/EJB application, which is clearly not ideal.

Given the standard definition of J2EE, where are dependency libraries supposed to be placed so that they can be re-deployed with an application at run time? There are two creative, yet ultimately undesirable, solutions:

❑ Dependency libraries that are packaged as JAR files can be placed in the WEB-INF\lib directory of a web application. Generally, the WEB-INF\lib directory should primarily be used for the storage of servlet classes, but servlets and JSP pages will look for classes in this directory when loading new ones. If the utility library that you are using is only needed by your servlets and JSP pages then this solution will be sufficient. However, if the same libraries are also needed by EJBs, JMS consumers, or startup and shutdown classes, then this option will not work as the WEB-INF\lib directory is not visible to these items.

❑ A complete copy of all of the utility libraries is placed in each EJB JAR file in addition to the WEB-INF\lib directory. When an EJB is deployed, an EJB class loader will only look within its own JAR file for any utility classes that are referenced. It will not look within the JAR files of other EJB applications that have been deployed or in the WEB-INF\lib directory. If all of your EJB applications require the use of the same library, then placing a copy of that library's classes in each JAR file will meet your needs. The utility classes will be re-deployable along with the EJB.

Although the second scenario achieves redeploy ability of dependency libraries, it is incredibly inefficient. The purpose of having multiple JAR files for packaging is to promote modularity of applications and placing the same class in multiple JAR files destroys this. In addition, having multiple copies of the same classes unnecessarily bloats your applications. Finally, there is an added step in the build process, as every JAR file will have to be rebuilt if you want to change even a single library.

Solutions

One of the possible solutions to this problem is to eliminate the need for multiple JARs in J2EE applications by converging all EJBs and their utility classes into a single, unified package. The EJB 2.0 specification is driving some projects to do this. This version of the specification mandates that entity EJBs participating in a relationship do so using local interfaces and so requires both of the EJBs in the relationship to be packaged into the same JAR file. Earlier drafts of EJB 2.0 allowed EJBs in different JAR files to participate in relationships, promoting greater modularity of the system, but ultimately limited the persistence optimizations available for CMP entity beans in a relationship.

Public Final Draft 2 eliminated remote relationships; so many vendors are thinking about providing tools that perform EJB JAR convergence. These tools will take as input two valid EJB JAR files and merge their classes and deployment descriptors into a single, unified package. You could potentially use one of these convergence tools to re-package your existing JAR applications to reduce redundancy of dependency libraries among EJB JAR files. At the time of writing, these convergence utilities were still being developed. Check with your application server provider to see if they have a convergence utility available for you to use.

Keep in mind that even if all of the EJBs are converged into a single JAR application, you will have eliminated copies of your dependency library among the EJBs, but a copy will still need to exist in a `WEB-INF\lib` library if a web application depends upon it. Additionally, the need for modularity of EJB applications still exists since many companies desire to re-deploy EJBs on an individual basis. Since every EJB in a JAR will be re-deployed when that JAR file is re-deployed, an unnecessary amount of deployment processing could occur if your only desire is to re-deploy a single EJB.

A Better Solution

With the release of JDK 1.3, Sun Microsystems redefined the "extension mechanism" which is the functionality necessary to support optional packages. The extension mechanism is designed to support two things:

- ❑ JAR files can declare their dependency upon other JAR files allowing an application to consist of multiple modules

- ❑ Class loaders are modified to search optional packages and application paths for classes

Additionally, the J2EE 1.3 specification mandates that application servers must support the extension mechanism as defined for JAR files. This requires any deployment tool that references a JAR file be capable of loading any optional libraries defined through the extension mechanism. It also implies that if an application server or deployment tool supports run time un-deployment and re-deployment of EJB applications that use libraries via the extension mechanism, then that tool or application server must also support un-deployment and re-deployment of any dependent libraries.

Support for the extension mechanism does not exist for EAR or resource adapter applications as defined in the J2EE specification, since these applications are not directly loaded by an instance of `ClassLoader`. Web applications have the freedom of using the extension mechanism or the `WEB-INF\lib` directory when specifying a dependency library. As we discussed earlier, how a dependency library is loaded can vary depending upon whether the library is specified using the extension mechanism or the `WEB-INF\lib` directory.

Enterprise applications need to re-package any libraries that are needed by the web application or EJB application as part of the EAR file. Once packaged, the extension mechanism provides a standard way for web application WAR files and EJB application JAR files to specify which dependency libraries that exist in the enterprise application EAR file are needed.

Understanding the Manifest Classpath

How does the extension mechanism work with EJB applications? A JAR file can reference a dependent JAR file by adding a `Class-Path:` attribute to the manifest file that is contained in every JAR file. The `jar` utility automatically creates a manifest file to place in a JAR file and names it `manifest.mf` by default. This file can be *edited* to include a `Class-Path:` attribute entry in addition to the other entries that already exist in the file. In fact, many EJB packaging tools that are being released by vendors are taking dependency packages into account as part of the packaging process and will automatically create an appropriate `manifest.mf` file that contains a correct `Class-Path:` attribute entry.

For example, if you create an EJB JAR file and modify the `manifest.mf` to include a `Class-Path:` attribute, the container generation utility provided by your application server vendor *must* preserve this entry when it generates a new EJB application file. With WebLogic Server 6.1, if you provide an EJB JAR utility that already contains a `Class-Path:` entry in the `manifest.mf` file, the `weblogic.ejbc` utility will preserve this entry when it generates a new EJB application with the container files. At the time of printing of this book, a tool that creates and inserts the `Class-Path:` entry into a `manifest.mf` file does not yet exist. Unfortunately, this task has to still be done by hand by editing the `manifest.mf` file of a JAR file.

The `Class-Path:` manifest attribute lists the relative URLs to search for utility libraries. The relative URL is always from the component that contains the `Class-Path:` entry (not the root of the EAR file). Multiple URLs can be specified in a single `Class-Path:` entry and a single manifest file can contain multiple `Class-Path:` entries. The general format for a `Class-Path:` entry is:

```
Class-Path: list-of-jar-files-separated-by-spaces
```

For example, a JAR file might have:

```
Class-Path: log4j.jar xmlx.jar foo/bar/util.jar
```

If you use the extension mechanism in a J2SE application, the `Class-Path:` manifest entry can reference directories too. However, for J2EE applications that are wholly contained within JAR files, the `Class-Path:` manifest entry can only reference other JAR files. Additionally, the `Class-Path:` entry must reside on a separate line apart from other attribute entries in the same manifest file.

The extension mechanism is a nice capability especially since it is designed to handle circular redundancies by creating a unified classpath containing all dependencies in first-parsed-based ordering. For example, if the first EJB application parsed is `EJB1.jar` and it references:

```
Class-Path: jaxp.jar EJB2.jar ..\xmlx.jar
```

a class loader will then parse `EJB2.jar` that references:

```
Class-Path: jaxp.jar EJB1.jar
```

The resulting "application" classpath that a class loader would ultimately use would be:

```
Class-Path: jaxp.jar EJB2.jar ..\xmlx.jar EJB1.jar
```

Dependency Example

This example is designed to demonstrate every possible loading configuration for an enterprise application. It demonstrates multiple EJB modules, multiple web applications, and dependency libraries that are unique and shared between these applications. Deploying and executing this example allows us to see how an application server loads different classes from different applications.

By printing out the `ClassLoader` hierarchy for different classes as they are executed we can see if all classes loaded in a single class loader, or different class loaders, and if so, what the hierarchy of the class loaders is.

Our example consists of two EJB modules, two web application modules, and seven dependency libraries that are used in different scenarios. The structure of the EAR file is:

```
Depend1-container.jar
Depend2-container.jar
WebApp1.war
WebApp2.war
Util1.jar
Util2.jar
Util3.jar
Util4.jar
Util5.jar
Util6.jar
Util7.jar
META-INF\
        application.xml
```

There is a single EJB in each of the Depend JAR files. There is also a servlet, TestServlet, which exists in each web application. Each of the dependency libraries contains a single class with a single method that prints out the ClassLoader hierarchy. This example causes different scenarios to occur to see how classes are loaded in the context of an EAR file. In particular, the following scenarios are tested:

❏ How is a dependency library loaded when used by an EJB and referenced in that EJB's manifest classpath?

❏ How is a dependency library loaded that is shared between EJBs in different EJB modules? The dependency library is specified in the manifest classpath of both EJBs.

❏ How is a dependency library loaded when it is referenced by a web application and stored in the manifest classpath of the web application module?

❏ How is a dependency library loaded when it is referenced by a web application and stored in the WEB-INF\lib directory of the web application module?

❏ How is a dependency library loaded when an EJB module and a web application module reference it in both of their manifest classpath?

To execute this example, deploy the Depend.ear file (available from http://www.wrox.com) and then run the TestServlet that is deployed in each of the web applications. The TestServlet will invoke the appropriate EJB methods that, in turn, invoke the methods on the classes in the dependency library. For example, to execute both servlets, you would use the following URIs in a browser:

http://<server_name>:<port_number>/web1/testservlet
http://<server_name>:<port_number>/web2/testservlet

You should see something like this appear in the server window:

```
C:\WINNT\System32\cmd.exe                                                    _ □ ×
***UTIL1 --> EJB1 manifest.mf
***UTIL2 --> EJB2 manifest.mf
***UTIL3 --> EJB1&2 manifest.mf
***UTIL4 --> WebApp1&2 manifest.mf
***UTIL5 --> WebApp1&2 WEB-INF/lib
***UTIL6 --> WebApp1&EJB1 manifest.mf
***TestServlet1 --> WebApp1 --> /web/testservlet/
***TestServlet2 --> WebApp2 --> /web2/testservlet/

== TestServlet1 Class Information.
== Execute Depend1.test() --> Util1 & Util3
========================================================
CLASSLOADER INFO:
TestServlet ==> weblogic.utils.classloaders.ChangeAwareClassLoader ==> 7481256
TestServlet ==> weblogic.utils.classloaders.GenericClassLoader ==> 7436915
TestServlet ==> sun.misc.Launcher$AppClassLoader ==> 7435051
TestServlet ==> sun.misc.Launcher$ExtClassLoader ==> 8379614
CLASSLOADER INFO:
test1.Depend1Bean_wi9aew_Impl ==> weblogic.utils.classloaders.GenericClassLoader ==> 7436915
test1.Depend1Bean_wi9aew_Impl ==> sun.misc.Launcher$AppClassLoader ==> 7435051
test1.Depend1Bean_wi9aew_Impl ==> sun.misc.Launcher$ExtClassLoader ==> 8379614
CLASSLOADER INFO:
common.Util1 ==> weblogic.utils.classloaders.GenericClassLoader ==> 7436915
common.Util1 ==> sun.misc.Launcher$AppClassLoader ==> 7435051
common.Util1 ==> sun.misc.Launcher$ExtClassLoader ==> 8379614
CLASSLOADER INFO:
common.Util3 ==> weblogic.utils.classloaders.GenericClassLoader ==> 7436915
common.Util3 ==> sun.misc.Launcher$AppClassLoader ==> 7435051
common.Util3 ==> sun.misc.Launcher$ExtClassLoader ==> 8379614
========================================================
== Depend2.test() --> Util2 & Util3
========================================================
CLASSLOADER INFO:
test2.Depend2Bean_wi9xef_Impl ==> weblogic.utils.classloaders.GenericClassLoader ==> 7436915
test2.Depend2Bean_wi9xef_Impl ==> sun.misc.Launcher$AppClassLoader ==> 7435051
test2.Depend2Bean_wi9xef_Impl ==> sun.misc.Launcher$ExtClassLoader ==> 8379614
CLASSLOADER INFO:
common.Util2 ==> weblogic.utils.classloaders.GenericClassLoader ==> 7436915
common.Util2 ==> sun.misc.Launcher$AppClassLoader ==> 7435051
common.Util2 ==> sun.misc.Launcher$ExtClassLoader ==> 8379614
CLASSLOADER INFO:
common.Util3 ==> weblogic.utils.classloaders.GenericClassLoader ==> 7436915
common.Util3 ==> sun.misc.Launcher$AppClassLoader ==> 7435051
common.Util3 ==> sun.misc.Launcher$ExtClassLoader ==> 8379614
========================================================
== WebApp1 uses Util4
========================================================
CLASSLOADER INFO:
common.Util4 ==> weblogic.utils.classloaders.ChangeAwareClassLoader ==> 7481256
common.Util4 ==> weblogic.utils.classloaders.GenericClassLoader ==> 7436915
common.Util4 ==> sun.misc.Launcher$AppClassLoader ==> 7435051
common.Util4 ==> sun.misc.Launcher$ExtClassLoader ==> 8379614
========================================================
== WebApp1 uses Util5
========================================================
```

The `application.xml` deployment descriptor is:

```xml
<?xml version="1.0"  encoding="UTF-8"?>

<!DOCTYPE application PUBLIC "-//Sun Microsystems, Inc.//DTD J2EE Application
1.3//EN" "http://java.sun.com/dtd/application_1_3.dtd">

<application>
  <display-name>Pretty Name</display-name>
  <module>
    <ejb>Depend1-container.jar</ejb>
  </module>
  <module>
    <ejb>Depend2-container.jar</ejb>
  </module>
  <module>
    <web>
      <web-uri>WebApp1.war</web-uri>
      <context-root>web1</context-root>
    </web>
```

```
      </module>
      <module>
        <web>
          <web-uri>WebApp2.war</web-uri>
          <context-root>web2</context-root>
        </web>
      </module>
    </application>
```

The manifest classpath for the first EJB module is:

```
    Class-Path: Util1.jar Util3.jar Util6.jar Util7.jar
```

The manifest classpath entries for the other EJB module and the web application modules vary and have different combinations of the seven dependency libraries contained in the EAR file. The servlets contained within each web application are fully documented outlining the thread of execution and which test case is being demonstrated for each dependency library.

The Impact of Dependency Libraries

The manifest classpath will definitely spur better modularity of J2EE packages in the future. Using this model, developers can employ a simple scheme for determining which EJBs should be packaged into a single JAR file and those that should be packaged in separate JAR files:

❑   Identify an entity EJB that participates in a CMR relationship. Identify all entity EJBs that are reachable via CMR relationships from the source entity EJB. This graph of entity EJBs must be packaged into a single EJB JAR application. This process should be repeated for each unique graph of entity EJB relationships.

❑   Package all remaining EJBs into separate JAR files.

❑   Analyze your business and technical requirements and "converge" multiple JAR files if it makes sense. Convergence of multiple EJBs into a single JAR file should occur if a scenario where re-deploying all of the EJBs when only a single one has been modified is acceptable.

❑   Each EJB JAR file should list its dependencies using the manifest Class-Path: attribute as described above. An intelligent class loader will resolve any circular or repeating dependencies. For example, in the dependency example provided, both EJB applications referenced the third library as a dependency. Despite this double referencing, the EAR class loader was still intelligent enough to load the library only once.

The only limitation that developers are now faced with is locating an application server that fully supports this packaging capability. Developers will need to look for application servers that run in a 1.3 JDK and fully support the J2EE 1.3 specification. This has the consequence that any J2EE 1.3-certified application server must only run in a 1.3 JRE environment.

Summary

This chapter covered J2EE applications in depth, including:

- How the J2EE packaging mechanism is ideal for providing better interoperability between multiple J2EE modules
- J2EE applications, modules, and EAR files
- The process of J2EE application development
- Application assembly and deployment
- An example application

We've now seen the entire range of J2EE technologies, from the basic building blocks of RMI, JDBC, JNDI, and JAXP, through the servlet and JSP web content APIs and Enterprise JavaBeans, to complete J2EE applications. We hope this book has inspired you to get stuck into creating your own J2EE applications – enjoy!

Data

RDMS

JDBC

Application Logic

JavaMail

Mail Server

Web Container

Servlets   JSPs   Tag Library

Client

HTTP(S)

(X)HTML/ XML

RMI

Java Application

RMI/IIOP   JNDI   JTA   JDBC   JMS   JavaMail   JAAS   JCA   JAXP

J2EE Application Server

Applet

IIOP

CORBA Server

Client Application

Session Beans

JNDI

Directory Servi

JMS

Message Queu

Index

A Guide to the Index

The index is arranged alphabetically, word by word, with symbols preceding the letter A. Angle-brackets and hyphens have been ignored in the sorting process (thus loadClass() method will be found before <load-on-startup> element). Acronyms used in the text - rather than their expansions - have been preferred as main entries, on the grounds that unfamiliar acronyms are easier to construct than to expand. Unmodified entries denote the main coverage of a topic, with sub-headings indicating a more partial treatment.

Inevitably, indexes to Java books are as swollen about the letter 'J' as Scottish telephone directories are about 'M'. Readers should be aware that plural forms of main entries may be found at some distance from compound phrases and camel-and Pascal-cased derivatives beginning with the singular form (e.g servlet context, ServletContext interface and servlets).

Symbols

T

p2p.wrox.com
The programmer's resource centre

A unique free service from Wrox Press
with the aim of helping programmers to help each other

Wrox Press aims to provide timely and practical information to today's programmer. P2P is a list server offering a host of targeted mailing lists where you can share knowledge with your fellow programmers and find solutions to your problems. Whatever the level of your programming knowledge, and whatever technology you use, P2P can provide you with the information you need.

ASP Support for beginners and professionals, including a resource page with hundreds of links, and a popular ASP+ mailing list.

DATABASES For database programmers, offering support on SQL Server, mySQL, and Oracle.

MOBILE Software development for the mobile market is growing rapidly. We provide lists for the several current standards, including WAP, WindowsCE, and Symbian.

JAVA A complete set of Java lists, covering beginners, professionals,and server-side programmers (including JSP, servlets and EJBs)

.NET Microsoft's new OS platform, covering topics such as ASP+, C#, and general .Net discussion.

VISUAL BASIC Covers all aspects of VB programming, from programming Office macros to creating components for the .Net platform.

WEB DESIGN As web page requirements become more complex, programmer sare taking a more important role in creating web sites. For these programmers, we offer lists covering technologies such as Flash, Coldfusion, and JavaScript.

XML Covering all aspects of XML, including XSLT and schemas.

OPEN SOURCE Many Open Source topics covered including PHP, Apache, Perl, Linux, Python and more.

FOREIGN LANGUAGE Several lists dedicated to Spanish and German speaking programmers, categories include .Net, Java, XML, PHP and XML.

How To Subscribe

Simply visit the P2P site, at **http://p2p.wrox.com/**

Select the 'FAQ' option on the side menu bar for more information about the subscription process and our service.

Programmer to Programmer™